COMPARATIVE COMPANY LAW

CW00551289

It can be difficult for students of comparative company law both to understand the internationally relative nature of a legal system and to grasp it in practical detail. This book is designed to address that problem. Each chapter begins with a discursive analysis of the laws in Germany, the UK and the USA, framed by a comparative presentation. Chapters also contain edited judicial decisions from at least two of the jurisdictions, which allow readers to perform their own comparisons in more detail and leaves room for original analysis and discussion.

ANDREAS CAHN is a professor of law and Director of the Institute for Law and Finance at Goethe-University in Frankfurt.

DAVID C. DONALD is a professor in the Faculty of Law, The Chinese University of Hong Kong. He has previously worked in securities and banking law practices in Frankfurt, corporate law practices in Milan and Rome, and an international trade law practice in Washington, DC.

COMPARATIVE COMPANY LAW

Text and Cases on the Laws Governing
Corporations in Germany, the UK and the USA

ANDREAS CAHN

AND

DAVID C. DONALD

CAMBRIDGE
UNIVERSITY PRESS

CAMBRIDGE
UNIVERSITY PRESS

University Printing House, Cambridge CB2 8BS, United Kingdom

Cambridge University Press is part of the University of Cambridge.

It furthers the University's mission by disseminating knowledge in the pursuit of education, learning and research at the highest international levels of excellence.

www.cambridge.org
Information on this title: www.cambridge.org/9780521143790

© Andreas Cahn and David C. Donald 2010

First published 2010
Reprinted 2011

A catalogue record for this publication is available from the British Library

Library of Congress Cataloguing in Publication data
Cahn, Andreas.
Comparative company law : text and cases on the laws governing corporations in Germany, the UK and the USA / Andreas Cahn, David C. Donald.
p. cm.
Includes bibliographical references and index.
ISBN 978-0-521-76873-3 – ISBN 978-0-521-14379-0 (pbk.)
1. Corporation law. 2. Business enterprises–Law and legislation.
I. Donald, David C., 1958– II. Title.
K1315.C34 2010
346´.065–dc22
2010014637

ISBN 978-0-521-76873-3 Hardback
ISBN 978-0-521-14379-0 Paperback

CONTENTS

FIGURES

TABLES

PREFACE AND ACKNOWLEDGMENTS

The groundwork for this text began in 2002 as materials for a course in "National and International Company Law" at the Institute for Law and Finance (ILF) in Frankfurt. Students were asked to read cases, statutory provisions and supervisory authority rules from the three jurisdictions, and then the comparisons were drawn in the lectures and class discussions. It was very much three courses packed into a single set of credit hours. We must thank those students of the first few years who voluntarily agreed to triple reading for a single course. Summary "notes" were then drafted to accompany the cases, following a classic US model for case books. As the synthesis and comparative analyses of the US, UK and German law gradually developed and took shape, the notes were extended into chapters, approaching their current form.

The text you see now aims: (i) to present the essentials of the company laws of all three jurisdictions on the topics covered; (ii) to guide the student through a comparative analysis by highlighting some of the techniques (such as understanding functions in context and the complementarities between individual sets of rules) and conclusions (company law as a set of default rules to address agency costs) advocated in the corporate and comparative law scholarship; and (iii) to allow students to conduct their own comparative study by giving them lengthy excerpts from cases in all three jurisdictions, references to the key statutory provisions and regulatory rules in each chapter, and questions for thought and discussion. We hope the text enables the reader to see both the forest of overarching comparative relationships and the trees of the individual legal systems.

We are grateful to the Incorporated Council of Law Reporting for England and Wales and to Reed Elsevier (UK) Limited for their permission to reproduce edited versions of the judicial opinions in this text for which either the Incorporated Council or LexisNexis Butterworths holds the copyright. Without their kind generosity, it would not have been possible to offer this text in its present form.

Many people gave us their time and support to make this text possible. First of all, there were the classes of students at the ILF and later also at the Chinese University of Hong Kong (CUHK), who studied and commented on earlier drafts of the manuscript, pointing out what was clear for them and what tended toward the opaque. Geoff Miller, Michael Lower, Terence Grady, Frank Gevurtz, Paul Davies, Jim Cox, Xi Chao, Annie Carver, Theodor Baums and John Armour gave us great encouragement and helpful comments on the text at various points in its rather long genesis. The citation-checking work of CUHK PhD candidates, Zhang Zhang, Zhang Yihong, Frank Meng and Tan Fugui, was extraordinarily diligent. ILF graduate Arzoo Ismail proved invaluable in preparing the list of references, and ILF Dr jur. candidate Henny Müchler was of great assistance in collating the judicial decisions and seeking approvals to reprint them. Derek Savelle of Bowne Financial Printers provided handsome prospectus-like volumes of early drafts for use in our classes. The editorial team of Cambridge University Press, in particular Kim Hughes and Richard Woodham, have been kind, supportive and encouraging from the outset.

Without the kind encouragement, insightful comments and diligent assistance of these people, this text might well have been dropped before reaching press. Thank you.

GLOSSARY

Germany	United States	United Kingdom
ad hoc Mitteilungen	current disclosure	disclosure of significant events
Aktiengesellschaft	stock corporation	company limited by shares
Aktiengesetz	Stock Corporation Act	Companies Act
angemessen	appropriate, suitable	appropriate, proper
Aufsichtsrat	(supervisory board)	(supervisory board)
Betriebsverfassungsgesetz	Works Constitution Act	Works Constitution Act
Bezugsrecht	stock option	share option
Bezugsrechte	preemptive rights	preemption rights
Börse	securities exchange	stock exchange
Börseneinführung	listing	quotation, listing
Börsengesetz	(Exchange Act)	(Exchange Act)
Bundesgesetzblatt (BGBl, Federal Law Reporter)	(Federal Law Reporter)	
D&O insurance	directors & officers (or D&O) insurance	directors & officers (or D&O) insurance
due diligence	due diligence	due diligence
Freiverkehr	over-the-counter market	
Gattung	class	class
Gesetz betreffend die Gesellschaften mit beschränkter Haftung	(Close Corporation Act)	(Private Limited Company Act)
Gesellschaft mit beschränkter Haftung	closely held corporation	private limited company
gleichgestellt	pari passu	pari passu
Haftung	liability	liability
Handelsgesetzbuch	(Commercial Code)	(Commercial Code)
Handelsregister	commercial register	companies registry
Insiderhandel	insider trading	insider dealing
Kodex	code	code

Germany	United States	United Kingdom
Mitbestimmung	co-determination	co-determination
Mitbestimmungsgesetz	(Co-Determination Act)	(Co-Determination Act)
öffentliches Angebot	public offer, offering	public offer, offering
Prokurist	attorney-in-fact	(attorney-in-fact)
Sorgfaltspflicht	duty of care	duty of care
Stammaktien	common stock	ordinary shares
Treuepflicht	duty of loyalty	duty of loyalty
Treuhänder	trustee	trustee
treuhänderische Pflicht	fiduciary duty	fiduciary duty
Umwandlung	reorganization	(transformation)
Umwandlungsgesetz	(Reorganization Act)	(Transformation Act)
Unternehmensinteresse, Wohl der Gesellschaft	interest of the corporation	interest of the company
unverzüglich	promptly	as soon as possible
Vergütung	compensation	remuneration
Vollmacht	proxy	proxy
Vorstand	(management board)	(management board)
Vorzugsaktien	preferred stock	preference shares
Wertpapierbörse	securities exchange	stock exchange
Wertpapiererwerbs- und Übernahmegesetz	(Tender Offer Act)	(Takeover Act)
Wertpapierhandelsgesetz	(Securities Trading Act)	(Securities Trading Act)
Wertpapierprospekt	securities prospectus	listing (non-listing) prospectus
Wertpapierprospektgesetz	(Securities Prospectus Act)	(Securities Prospectus Act)

ABBREVIATIONS

AG	*Aktiengesellschaft* (stock corporation)
AktG	*Aktiengesetz* (Stock Corporation Act)
ARUG	*Gesetz zur Umsetzung der Aktionärsrechterichtlinie* (Act for the Implementation of the Shareholder Rights Directive)
BaFin	*Bundesanstalt für Finanzdienstleistungsaufsicht* (German Securities Supervisory Authority)
BERR	Department for Business, Enterprise and Regulatory Reform
BetrVG 1952	*Betriebsverfassungsgesetz* 1952 (Labor Management Relations Act 1952)
BGB	*Bürgerliches Gesetzbuch* (Civil Code)
BGBl I/III	*Bundesgesetzblatt Teil* I/III (Federal Law Reporter), Part I/III
BGHSt	*Entscheidungen des Bundesgerichtshofs in Strafsachen* (German Federal Law Reporter on Criminal Cases)
BGHZ	*Entscheidungen des Bundesgerichtshofs in Zivilsachen* (German Federal Law Reporter on Civil Cases)
BilMoG	*Gesetz zur Modernisierung des Bilanzrechts* (Act for the Modernization of Accounting Law)
BIS	Department for Business, Innovation and Skills
BörsG	*Börsengesetz* (Stock Exchange Act)
BörsO FWB	*Börsenordnung der Frankfurter Wertpapierbörse* (Exchange Regulation for the Frankfurt Stock Exchange)
BVerfG	*Bundesverfassungsgericht* (Federal Constitutional Court)
BVerfGE	*Entscheidungen des Bundesverfassungsgerichts* (Federal Constitutional Court Reporter)
CA 1985	Companies Act 1985
CA 2006	Companies Act 2006
CEO	Chief Executive Officer
CESR	Committee of European Securities Regulators
CFO	Chief Financial Officer
CFR	Code of Federal Regulations
Del. Ch.	Delaware Court of Chancery
Del. Supr.	Supreme Court of Delaware
DGCL	Delaware General Corporation Law

xiii

DrittelbG	*Gesetz über die Drittelbeteiligung der Arbeitnehmer im Aufsichtsrat* (Law providing for One-Third Representation of the Employees on the Supervisory Board)
DTI	Department of Trade and Industry
DTR	Disclosure and Transparency Rules
EC	European Community
ECJ	European Court of Justice
EEA	European Economic Area
EU	European Union
FS	*Festschrift* (essays in honor of)
FSA	Financial Services Authority
FSMA	Financial Services and Markets Act 2000
GAAP	Generally Accepted Accounting Principles
GbR	*Gesellschaft bürgerlichen Rechts* (civil law partnership)
GewO	*Gewerbeordnung* (Business Practice Act)
GG	*Grundgesetz* (Federal Constitution)
GmbH	*Gesellschaft mit beschränkter Haftung*
GmbHG	*Gesetz über Gesellschaften mit beschränkter Haftung* (Limited Liability Company Act/Close Corporation Act)
HGB	*Handelsgesetzbuch* (Commercial Code)
InsO	*Insolvenzordnung* (Insolvency Act)
IOSCO	International Organization of Securities Commissions
KgaA	*Kommanditgesellschaft auf Aktien* (partnership limited by shares)
KonTraG	*Gesetz zur Kontrolle und Transparenz im Unternehmensbereich* (Law for Monitoring and Transparency in Business Undertakings)
LBO	leveraged buy-out
LPA 1907	Limited Partnership Act 1907
LR	Listing Rules
MAPC	Model Articles for Public Companies (SI 2009 No. 3229)
MBO	management buy-out
MitbestG	*Mitbestimmungsgesetz* (Co-Determination Act)
MMC	Monopolies and Mergers Commission
mn.	margin note
MoMiG	*Gesetz zur Modernisierung des Aktienrechts und zur Verhinderung von Missbräuchen* (Act for the Modernization of the Limited Liability Company Law and the Prevention of Abuse)
Nasdaq	National Association of Securities Dealers Automated Quotations
NYSE	New York Stock Exchange
OFT	Office of Fair Trading
OJ	*Official Journal of the European Communities*
PA 1890	Partnership Act 1890
PartG	professional partnership (Partnerschaftsgesellschaft)

RUPA	Revised Uniform Partnership Act
SEC	Securities and Exchange Commission
TFEU	Treaty on the Functioning of the European Union
ULPA 2001	Revised Uniform Limited Partnerships Act 2001
UmwG	*Umwandlungsgesetz* (Reorganization Act)
VorG	*Vorgesellschaft* (corporation in formation)
VorstAG	*Gesetz zur Angemessenheit der Vorstandsvergütung* (Act on the Adequacy of Executive Compensation)
WpHG	*Wertpapierhandelsgesetz* (Securities Trading Act)
WpPG	*Wertpapierprospektgesetz* (Securities Prospectus Act)
WpÜG	*Wertpapiererwerbs- und Übernahmegesetz* (Securities Acquisition and Takeover Act)

TABLE OF CASES

Cases with names in bold are reprinted in edited form in this text.

Germany

European Union

United Kingdom

UK Takeover Panel

United States

European Union legislation

Directives

Company law

Capital markets

Regulations

Communications, Recommendations and Notices

German legislation

Statutes

Regulations

United Kingdom legislation

Statutes

Statutory instruments, regulations and other authoritative texts

United States legislation

Federal statutes

State statutes and model laws

Federal rules and regulation

PART I

The essential qualities of the corporation

Approaching comparative company law*

Required reading

EU: First Company Law Directive, art. 1
D: AktG, § 1
UK: CA 2006, secs. 1, 3, 4
US: DGCL, § 101(b); Model Act, §§ 1.40(4), 3.01(a)

Approaching comparative company law

I.   *The approach coordinates*

The disciplines of "comparative law" in general and "comparative company law" in particular are natural companions to the globalization of social, political and economic activity. The course of economic and political developments in recent decades has thus increased the amount of comparative law taking place at every level, whether it be that of fact-oriented practitioners, result-seeking legislators and development agencies, or theory-focused academics. Each of these activities has its own interests, priorities and goals. Nevertheless, there are certain "approach coordinates" that mark the path for all their comparative studies. This introductory chapter will outline some important approach coordinates for the comparison of the laws that govern public companies in the United States, the United Kingdom and Germany.

Just as the merchants who engaged in the earliest forms of international trade developed a commercial law that was trans-jurisdictional,[1]

---

* The text of this chapter is adapted from an article of the same title, first published in *Fordham Journal of Corporate and Financial Law* (2008) 14: 83. We are grateful to the *Fordham Journal of Corporate and Financial Law* for permission to use the text in the context of this larger project.

[1] See e.g. Merryman and Pérez-Perdomo (2007: 13); Horn (1995: Intro. VI mn. 3 *et seq.*); Glenn (2005: 114–116).

so today merchants and their counsel are often at the forefront of comparative legal activity. When a transaction spans international borders, the persons responsible for structuring it must of necessity become comparatists. As Professor Klaus Hopt has observed, lawyers and legal counsel "are the real experts in both conflict of company laws and of foreign company laws ... Working out the best company and tax law structures for international mergers, and forming and doing legal work for groups and tax haven operations, is a high, creative art."[2] Legal counsel's repeated choices of a given structure or law can gradually crystallize into a "best practice," which independently or under the auspices of professional associations[3] can lead to many jurisdictions adopting the practice and converging toward a perceived optimal rule. In this way, the practical choices of lawyers eventually collect into recognized legal norms. Comparative scholars like Professor Philip R. Wood, whose numerous books focus on the practical details of the financial laws and instruments in many countries,[4] give internationally active lawyers the information they need to approach transnational problems. His is a comparative law that focuses on providing detailed and accurate information about disparate legal systems rather than either reflecting on the policy goals of legislation or seeking the overall coherence of a given system's solution to a specific problem.[5]

Comparative activity with great practical impact also occurs at venues quite removed from commercial transactions. The unprecedented level of international cooperation occurring on the regulatory side of contemporary globalization creates systematic comparative studies that have dramatically accelerated legal understanding and convergence. Any project to harmonize national laws or draft a convention to govern an area of law among nations will likewise of necessity compare laws to find the best, or at least the most mutually acceptable, solution. Institutions such as the

---

[2] Hopt (2006: 1169).

[3] Such "associations" can range from the International Chamber of Commerce and their "Incoterms" for international sales transactions, to the International Bar Association and their numerous practice guides, to the voluntarily adopted master framework agreements created by organizations like the International Swaps and Derivatives Association, Inc.

[4] See e.g. Wood (2007); Wood (1995).

[5] The method used, as is appropriate for the goal of the comparative study, centers around the practitioner's desire to use the law: "There are three broad steps in this type of measurement: (1) the legal rules; (2) the weighting of the importance of the legal rules in practice; and (3) actual implementation or compliance by the jurisdiction concerned." Wood (2007: 16).

European Union,[6] the United Nations,[7] the International Institute for the Unification of Private Law (UNIDROIT)[8] and the Hague Conference on Private International Law[9] engage in comparative law on a grand scale in order to produce their directives, regulations and conventions. This activity falls under the rubric of "legislative comparative law" in the descriptive schema offered by Professors Konrad Zweigert and Hein Kötz, and has historically been one of comparative law's most solid domains.[10] If legislative efforts seek to achieve a specific result,[11] like economic prosperity, stable government or investor protection, then a second-level problem arises: the legislator must correctly ascertain a real, causal connection between the chosen law or legal system and the desired social or economic effect. The latter type of project falls squarely within the mission of institutions such as the World Bank, which seeks to "help developing countries and their people ... [by] building the climate for investment, jobs and sustainable growth."[12] In addition to the studies prepared by their own staffs and experts, much of the academic comparative law produced in universities also supports the activities of legislators and development agencies.

The increasingly high stakes for the success of commercial transactions of correctly understanding foreign law and of comparing, choosing and

---

6   As it developed from an initial six to its current twenty-seven member states over a fifty-year period, the European Economic Community (now the European Union) harmonized a core of minimum standards in many areas and followed this up with mutual recognition of member state law while introducing a parallel movement toward European standardization. See Craig and de Búrca (2008: 620–627). This combination of legislative strategies allowed mandatory harmonization to implement an initial uniformity, which made home rule and voluntary convergence acceptable and then led to greater harmonization becoming unproblematic, so that the laws of individual member states – particularly the later entrants, which were forced to adopt packages of introductory laws – became ever more tightly matched.

7   This activity is performed, in particular, by the United Nations Commission on International Trade Law (UNCITRAL) and the Office of Legal Affairs, Codification Division's Codification of International Law. See www.un.org/law/.

8   UNIDROIT "is an independent intergovernmental organisation ... [whose] purpose is to study needs and methods for modernising, harmonising and co-ordinating private and, in particular, commercial law as between States and groups of States." See www.unidroit.org.

9   "Since 1893, the Hague Conference on Private International Law, a melting pot of different legal traditions, develops and services Conventions which respond to global needs." See www.hcch.net.

10   Zweigert and Kötz (1998: 51). Also see Donahue (2006: 3).

11   Zweigert and Kötz call this "applied comparative law" (1998: 11).

12   See the "Challenge" of the World Bank, at www.worldbank.org.

implementing laws have naturally drawn an increasing amount of academic attention to comparative law. Although the steady growth actually began in the nineteenth century, with the major codifications in continental Europe,[13] the increase was dramatic as efforts to develop the economies of the former Soviet Union, Eastern Europe and China took off in the 1990s. This activity has been particularly intense in the area of comparative company law, specifically addressing questions of "comparative corporate governance," comparative "shareholder rights"[14] and, within the European Union itself, comparative methods of "creditor protection."[15] Major events in this "academic comparative law" were the publication in 2006 of a collection of theoretical essays on the activity of comparative law in the *Oxford Handbook to Comparative Law*,[16] and, with particular regard to comparative company law, the teaming up of seven leading corporate law scholars from different jurisdictions to produce in 2004 a high-level comparison of the company law of the United States, Europe and Japan, which is now in its second edition.[17]

Comparative company law is thus expanding quickly at various levels of abstraction and practice. Each level has its own focus and its own tasks. While practical comparatists might concern themselves with the type of document filed or lodged in order to perfect a security interest, the legislative comparatists could focus on whether a specific regime for collateral could stimulate desired commercial activity, and the theoretically oriented academic comparatists might well be occupied with whether a practical comparatist's understanding of both "filings" and "creditor possession" as two forms of "publicity"[18] is a tenable functional analysis or displays unacceptable levels of an Aristotelian teleological essentialism.[19] All three levels of activity occur separately but are closely related, and many works, like that of Wood, tend to cross the line from practice to theory and back again. Like any other theoretical activity, academic comparative law examines the steps taken in the practical activity of comparison in an attempt to make its methods more transparent and conscious and its results more objective and accurate. This includes, at a minimum, scrutiny of the perspective from which foreign legal systems

---

[13] Zweigert and Kötz (1998: 51).   [14] Siems (2008).

[15] See e.g. the special issues of the *European Business Organization Law Review* (2006) on creditor protection and the *European Company And Financial Law Review* (2006) on legal capital in Europe.

[16] Reimann and Zimmermann (2006).

[17] Kraakman, Armour, Davies, Hansmann, Hertig, Hopt, Kanda, Enriques and Rock (2009).

[18] Wood (2007: 140 *et seq.*).   [19] Michaels (2006: 345–347).

are investigated and understood, the scope and content of such investigation, the conceptual tools that are used to compare and evaluate laws, and the basis on which causal links between law and a desired social or economic result are posited.[20]

One of the best methodological analyses of comparative law, that of Zweigert and Kötz, proposes a flexible, inductive process of preliminary hypotheses, investigation of functional values, checking of preliminary results, and a reformulation of the hypotheses.[21] This method moves back and forth between functional parts understood as parts of a hypothetical whole, and adjustments to the initial understanding of that whole based on new information gained from an analysis of the parts. Although the type of caution a comparatist should exercise when using this circular method of assuming a whole to determine the functions of the parts and then employing a deepened understanding of the parts' complementary functions to reformulate the idea of the whole cannot be reduced to a simple checklist, it would include at least the following approach coordinates to reduce the risk of committing certain, predictable mistakes.

At the most basic level, it is important that accurate information about the respective legal systems be procured and only comparable items indeed be compared, so as to avoid creating useless or misleading comparisons. Next, it must be remembered that, unlike discrete objects (e.g. apples and oranges), legal rights, duties and forms cannot be accurately compared in isolation. Even if a problem is universal to humanity, the rights and duties selected to address this problem within a given legal system present only one possible configuration of solution, which serves a relative (not a transcendently essential) function within the chosen framework.[22] The functions of a given right, duty or organizational form might also complement other functions within the same system, so that the functions create an almost organic network of interdependence within the legal system. In order better to understand what is strictly considered "law," comparatists must also remember that legal systems exist within societies, and both receive and exercise influence *vis-à-vis* such societies.[23] Further, societies and their legal systems exist in history. They evolve in reaction to historical events, and such evolution is restricted by paths earlier taken,[24] which

---

[20] Zweigert and Kötz (1998 34–47).   [21] Zweigert and Kötz (1998: 46).

[22] Michaels (2006: 358–359). Such contingency would not affect the debate on natural law, for the same principle or norm argued to have universally prescriptive force could be protected by various, differing, functionally equivalent rights and duties.

[23] Luhmann (2004: 142–147).

[24] Roe (1996b: 641); Bebchuk and Roe (1999: 139–142).

means that the comparatist should be aware of the historical position of the legal system being studied. Finally, since at least one leg of a legal comparison will include a law or legal system of a foreign state or country or from a distant time, accurate comparison will require an acute awareness of the distorting tendencies of one's own perspective in time, nation and culture. The foregoing indicates that comparatists should exercise caution with regard to at least the following points of approach:

1. They should obtain accurate information (particularly texts and translations) and compare only comparable items.
2. They should examine the functional values of rights, duties, procedures and forms as system components within the context also of society as a whole.
3. They should consider history's impact on the legal system.
4. They should be aware of the natural distorting tendencies of one's own perspective.

In drafting this text, we have tried to respect these approach coordinates. Each of the legal systems examined in this volume has first been studied from within, relying on the best available understanding offered by experts on their own domestic law, followed by a comparative analysis that attempts to take into account the differences in perspective when a national legal system is seen from the vantage point of each of the other two systems. We hope that an intrinsic analysis of each legal system, combined with a view from each to the other, can help us overcome the circus phenomenon sometimes found in comparative law, in which local institutions (e.g. German co-determination, UK voting by show of hands and US contingent fees) are trotted out as exotic oddities that are interesting primarily as curious deviations from our familiar domestic norm. Society and history must be drawn into the analysis of the object of study, but to the extent possible excluded from the perspective of the studying subject.

An essential prerequisite for the first point listed above is to define the object of our study, to know exactly what we are attempting to compare. We must therefore draw a boundary with some specificity around the concept of "company law." To this end, the following subsection will examine the content of company law in Germany, as expressed primarily in the Stock Corporation Act (*Aktiengesetz* or AktG),[25] in the United Kingdom, as expressed primarily in the Companies Act 2006 (Companies Act 2006

[25] Law of September 6, 1965, as amended most recently on January 5, 2007, BGBl I, p. 20.

or CA 2006),[26] and in the United States, as expressed primarily in a state corporate law, represented here by the Delaware General Corporation Law (DGCL or Title 8, Del. Code)[27] and the Model Business Corporation Act (the Model Act).[28]

II. Defining company law functionally

"Company law" or "corporate law"[29] in all jurisdictions is generally understood as a body of law enabling the creation of an entity with "five core structural characteristics": "(1) legal personality, (2) limited liability, (3) transferable shares, (4) centralized management under a board structure, and (5) shared ownership by contributors of capital."[30] If a law other than a "company" law were to regulate one of these "core characteristics"

---

[26] CA 2006, Chapter 46, 8 November 2006.

[27] Delaware Code Annotated, Title 8.

[28] The Model Act is drafted by the Section on Business Law of the American Bar Association. It was originally published in 1950, was revised substantially in 1984, and has been revised on a regular basis since. The Model Act has been adopted in substance in thirty of the fifty US states. See Chapter 3, Section V.A, below.

[29] This text uses the terms "company" law and "corporate" law indistinguishably. "Corporate law" is a US term and "company" law is the preferred term in the UK, as well as in the English-language versions of EU legislation. From a German perspective, the term "corporate" law might be more accurate for this text, as the object of this study is stock corporations that may well be large enough to be listed on a stock exchange, an area of study that German scholars might call the "law of capital collecting companies" (*Kapitalgesellschaftsrecht*), as opposed to "company law" (*Gesellschaftsrecht*), which would likely include various forms of partnerships and limited liability companies (*Gesellschaften mit beschränkter Haftung*) as well as stock corporations (*Aktiengesellschaften*). The German understanding of the term "company law" might be rendered as "corporations and other business organizations." Here, both "company law" and "corporate law" will refer to the law governing entities with the five characteristics listed below.

[30] Armour, Hansmann and Kraakman (2009a: 5). These characteristics are by no means a recent invention. For similar lists of core characteristics, at least with respect to US law, see Clark (1986: 2); and Ballantine (1946: 1). For historical discussions of the development of these characteristics, see Cheffins (2009) (focusing on the power of shareholders to control management), Harris (2005) (discussing the early stock corporation as a device to allow impersonal cooperation among investors), Gevurtz (2004: 89) (focusing on central management under a board) and Mahoney (2000) (focusing on legal personality and limited liability). Although limited liability is considered to be one of the most valuable characteristics of a corporation, it should be noted that both German and UK law offer companies with unlimited liability: the German limited partnership by shares (*Kommanditgesellschaft auf Aktien* or KGaA) and the English "unlimited company" both offer the possibility of an entity that issues shares to investors but leaves at least one of their owners with unlimited liability. Moreover, UK law also provides for limited companies in which a guarantee replaces capital as the financial core of the company.

of the corporate entity, it would require treatment in a study of company law. This is unproblematic when another law is expressly linked to the company law. Labor co-determination in Germany provides a good example. The sections of the *Aktiengesetz* that refer to the number, qualifications and appointment of members of the supervisory board expressly refer to the provisions of the various laws providing for co-determination in Germany.[31] The inclusion of co-determination laws in any study of German company law is thus beyond question.

Difficulties arise, however, when a law's function closely complements the corporation law in the jurisdiction in question, but the law is not expressly linked to the company law. If such laws are excluded from treatment, any picture of the jurisdiction's "company law" will be incomplete. If different mixes of topical laws govern the same area in different jurisdictions, a comparison that does not take this difference into account could be distorted. For example, if we compared the German company law rule requiring disclosure of an interest in a stock corporation that exceeds 25 percent of its capital, expressed in § 20(1) of the *Aktiengesetz*, exclusively with the DGCL and the case law related to that statute, which states no such requirement, we would have to conclude that German company law creates greater transparency. However, if we add to the mix a US federal law, the Securities Exchange Act of 1934 (the Exchange Act), particularly § 13(d) thereof and the rules issued under it requiring disclosure of any holding exceeding 5 percent of a class of shares "registered" under the Exchange Act,[32] we tend to reach the opposite conclusion, and German law appears less extensive. Yet when the requirements of § 21 of the German Securities Trading Act (*Wertpapierhandelsgesetz* or WpHG), which applies to listed companies, are also added to the comparison,[33] we see that the obligations of Delaware and German listed companies are quite similar in this respect. Because the rules governing companies

---

[31] §§ 95–104 AktG. See Chapter 10.

[32] 17 CFR § 240.13d-1(a). Securities must be registered under § 12 of the Exchange Act if either (i) they are listed on a national securities exchange or (ii) the issuer of the securities has more than 500 shareholders and total assets exceeding $10 million (see § 12(g) of the Exchange Act, in connection with Exchange Act Rule 12g-1, 17 CFR § 240.12g-1). In addition to securities registered under § 12 of the Exchange Act, Rule 13d-1 also applies to "any equity security of any insurance company which would have been required to be so registered except for the exemption contained in section 12(g)(2)(G) of the Act, or any equity security issued by a closed-end investment company registered under the Investment Company Act of 1940." 17 CFR § 240.13d-1(i).

[33] Securities Trading Act (*Wertpapierhandelsgesetz*) published on September 9, 1998, BGBl vol. I, p. 2708, as most recently amended by art. 4 of the Law of July 31, 2009, BGBl vol. I, p. 2512.

are often differently distributed among the companies laws and various other relevant laws in different countries, knowledge of the applicable relevant laws, including their nature and the range of their application, is necessary.

Moreover, each of the five "core" characteristics of a corporation may be closely tied to other areas of law. Bankruptcy (or insolvency) law presents a good example. One purpose of legal personality and limited liability is to demarcate the assets against which creditors may have recourse to recover the debts of the corporation,[34] and such recourse is often taken in insolvency proceedings over the company's assets. The inclusion of bankruptcy law in the study of company law is, however, still debated. In choosing not to address most aspects of bankruptcy law in a 2004 study of corporate law, Professors Henry Hansmann and Reinier R. Kraakman argued that "bodies of law *designed to serve* objectives that are largely unrelated to the core characteristics of the corporate form ... do not fall within the scope of corporate law."[35] Following this view, the lawmaker's legislative purpose would determine whether a given piece of legislation should be included within a study of corporate law. However, as discussed above, the functional method of comparative law should not limit itself to intention, but rather to the systemic role played by the given law within the legal system and the society. The intention behind a topical law would then not be the best criterion for deciding whether to include it in a study of company law. For example, German labor laws express a legislative *intention* to have employees treated fairly by corporations, but as one means to this end the law serves the *function* of specifying the composition of the supervisory board. US securities laws have the express legislative intention to protect investors regardless of who or what is selling the relevant securities, but as one means to this end such laws have the *function* of, *inter alia*, regulating the information a registered corporation must disclose. The fiduciary principles and rules of agency law that are central to corporate governance were also in no way devised with the intention of regulating the centralized management of a corporation. It would seem that a test based on legislative intent would not be the best way to separate company law from related but extraneous norms.

In a different context, Professor John Armour asked in 2005 whether EU member states could successfully use their bankruptcy laws to

---

[34] Armour, Hansmann and Kraakman (2009a: 9–10); Hansmann and Kraakman (2000: 393 *et seq.*).

[35] Hansmann and Kraakman (2004: 17) (emphasis added).

compete for charters in the free space opened by the decisions of the European Court of Justice (ECJ) preventing member states from imposing burdens on the establishment of companies from other EU states within their borders.[36] He argued convincingly that "[c]orporate insolvency law supplies rules which govern companies experiencing financial distress, and so it is appropriate to consider it as being within the scope of a functional account of 'company law'. In particular, there may be complementarities between insolvency law and other aspects of a country's corporate governance regime."[37] Viewed from this perspective, which is that of a corporate promoter or incorporator, complementarities would exist between a corporate statute and an insolvency law if the latter had a material impact on the choice of jurisdiction in which to incorporate due to its effect on a core corporate characteristic. Such an "effects" test is essentially a functionality test seen from a practical rather than a theoretical vantage point. It would demand that provisions of other laws be considered together with the jurisdiction's company law – regardless of whether the legislative purpose of such law is to regulate corporations – if it affects or functionally complements the corporate law statute with respect to a core corporate characteristic. Pursuant to this test, all rules, laws and organizational forms that have the function of regulating the corporation, its activities, or the rights of persons *vis-à-vis* the corporation in respect of a core characteristic should be seriously considered for inclusion in an analysis of company law. Hansmann, Kraakman and Armour seemed to have reached a consensus position approaching such an effects test when, in 2009, they wrote: "There are many constraints imposed on companies by bodies of law designed to serve objectives that are, in general, independent of the form taken by the organizations they effect ... [W]e will ... discuss them where they are specifically tailored for the corporate form in ways that have important effects on corporate structure and conduct."[38]

Along these lines, tax law, which is one of the most important considerations when planning the incorporation of a company or the establishment of a subsidiary, would not come within a study of company law because it does not have a close relation to a core characteristic of companies. Tax treatment of income in a given structure is often an economic incentive to adopt one business form or another, but the effect of linking tax and company law here is purely economic. For example, if tort

---

[36] See Chapter 3, below.   [37] Armour (2005: 39).
[38] Armour, Hansmann and Kraakman (2009a: 19).

awards were extravagant in a given jurisdiction, encouraging a flight to limited liability, this does not mean that tort law is part of company law. Similarly, under this "effects test," rules on secured debt can be removed from our treatment of company law as they are not essentially linked to any of the five core characteristics of the corporation. From a purely functional point of view, rules allowing a lender to earmark an asset as security for the repayment of a debt could apply in similar form to physical persons, as is evidenced by mortgages and by the law on security interests in the US and Germany.[39] The historical choice of the UK expressly to regulate fixed and floating charges in the Companies Act 2006[40] and its predecessors would not seem to contradict this. On the other hand, rules on fraudulent conveyances would be part of "company law," as they serve a capital maintenance function (closely related to the limited liability and investor ownership characteristics of corporations) in the United States, whilst the same function is served by the legal capital rules of German and UK company law. As this example makes clear, it can reasonably be assumed that the topical laws seen as having corporate law functions and thus included in a functional definition of company law will not be identical in each jurisdiction. The core characteristics of a stock corporation and some topical laws that are closely enough related to these characteristics to be studied with company law can be graphically represented as shown in Figure 1.1.

A.   Germany

In Germany, the *Aktiengesetz* provides a comprehensive regulation of stock corporations that is mandatory unless provided otherwise.[41] Tracking the core characteristics of the stock corporation listed above, the *Aktiengesetz* provides for the creation of an entity with legal personality, limited liability and transferable shares,[42] having a centralized management under a two-tier board structure[43] that is subject in certain respects

---

[39] See e.g. art. 9 of the Uniform Commercial Code and the treatment of *Sicherungsübereignungen*, in Weber (1997).

[40] See CA 2006, Part 25.

[41] § 23(5) AktG, discussed in detail in Section 1.III.A.

[42] §§ 1–53a AktG.

[43] §§ 76–116 AktG. Under the *Aktiengesetz*, a stock corporation has a two-tier board. The two levels are the supervisory board (*Aufsichtsrat*), provided for in §§ 95–116 AktG, and the management board (*Vorstand*), provided for in §§ 76–94 AktG. The shareholders elect all or some (if co-determination applies) of the supervisory directors (§ 101(1) AktG), and the supervisory board in turn appoints the managing directors (§ 84(1) AktG), who have direct responsibility for managing the company (§ 76(1) AktG). For discussions of this structure, see Baums (2002) and Hopt (1997: 3).

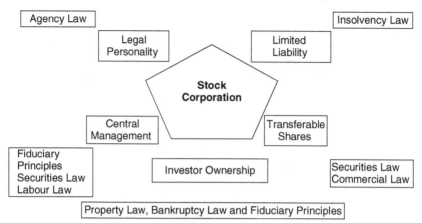

Figure 1.1   The five characteristics of a corporation and related topical laws

to the shareholders.[44] The *Aktiengesetz* also incorporates by reference provisions of the Commercial Code (*Handelsgesetzbuch* or HGB) on the preparation of the annual financial statements, including the specification of reserves and distributable profits,[45] provides shareholders with a right to demand a special audit,[46] and requires the financial statements to be made available to the shareholders for their approval.[47] Going beyond the range of coverage that would be expected by a US lawyer, the *Aktiengesetz* contains provisions on the disclosure of equity holdings,[48] and on the solicitation of proxies by banks holding shares in custody,[49] incorporates the Co-Determination Act to place labor representatives on the supervisory board,[50] specifies the rights, duties and financial statements required of companies operating in corporate groups,[51] and requires listed companies to adopt a governance code on a "comply or explain" basis.[52] One exception to the inclusionary tendency of the *Aktiengesetz* is the hiving off of rules on mergers between stock corporations in a special law, the Reorganization Act (*Umwandlungsgesetz* or UmwG).[53] Like Delaware law, but unlike the UK Companies Act 2006, the *Aktiengesetz* does not contain extensive provisions on accounting, which were moved to the Commercial Code in 1985.[54] As will be discussed in Chapter 3 below, the

---

[44] §§ 118–147.   [45] § 150 AktG.   [46] §§ 142–146 AktG.   [47] § 175 AktG.
[48] § 20 AktG.   [49] § 128 AktG.   [50] § 101 AktG.
[51] §§ 291–328 AktG.   [52] § 161 AktG.
[53] *Umwandlungsgesetz* (UmwG) of October 28, 1994, as most recently amended by the Law of April 19, 2007, BGBl vol. I, p. 542.
[54] This was done in the context of implementing three EC directives on individual and group accounts. See the Law of December 19, 1985, BGBl vol. I, p. 2355.

Aktiengesetz has been shaped over the years through the implementation of many EU directives. The resulting law is broad, comprehensive and mandatory.

In the area of company law, German courts clearly break the mould of robotic obedience to the law's letter that uninformed commentators on contemporary Civil Law would impose. At all levels, these courts have created doctrines going beyond statutory law through a significant body of decisions on topics such as pre-incorporation liability, the equitable subordination of loans made by shareholders to the company and the fiduciary duties of management.[55] Indeed, as will be seen in the next chapter, the German High Federal Court went further than any US court has dared to tread in reading an entity theory of partnership into the Civil Code because of the impracticality of continuing to follow an aggregate theory. Some leading company law decisions were handed down with reference to the Limited Liability Companies Act (*Gesetz betreffend die Gesellschaften mit beschränkter Haftung* or GmbHG) rather than the *Aktiengesetz* and then applied to stock corporations by analogy. In the *Holzmüller* and *Gelatine* decisions, reprinted in part in Chapter 23 below, the High Federal Court extended the governance rights of the shareholders of a parent corporation to management decisions regarding the corporate group's structure as well as to certain shareholder decisions in the subsidiaries.

This manner of developing the law through judicial decisions, in particular the interaction between the courts, legal scholarship and legal practice, is referred to as *Rechtsfortbildung*. The High Federal Court's former president, Robert Fischer, once gave a classic warning that courts should exercise judicial restraint to remain within the acceptable boundaries of judicial activism:

> The judiciary is well advised to exercise self restraint and to focus on the particular facts of the individual case and to refrain from general, systematizing statements. It should rather leave the systematic classification of its cases to the critical assessment by legal scholars and analyze the compatibility of its decisions on the basis of such assessment. On the basis of an individual case, courts are frequently unable to foresee the impact their decision will have on the further development of the law. On the other hand, once the consequences of a line of cases have become clear, courts must strive to bring the extension of the law to a close. In doing that they should be aware that for the sake of transparency and legal certainty they will be bound by their own decisions.[56]

---

[55] See e.g. the High Federal Court's creation of a German business judgment rule in the *ARAG v. Garmenbeck*, reprinted in part in Chapter 13.

[56] Fischer (1969: 97).

Although the *Aktiengesetz* itself includes provisions that other jurisdictions might attribute to areas outside corporate law proper – such as on the disclosure of holdings and the behavior of custodian banks in the proxy solicitation process – most studies of German company law would also include, in addition to the Co-Determination Act and the Reorganization Act, a number of rules from the Securities Trading Act (*Wertpapierhandelsgesetz* or WpHG)[57] and the Takeover Act (*Wertpapiererwerbs- und Übernahmegesetz* or WpÜG)[58] in any comprehensive treatment of company law proper, especially when discussing listed companies. As the converse of the principle of *lex specialis derogat legi generali*, a German court will also look to the more general rules on company forms contained in the Limited Liability Companies Act, the Commercial Code and the Civil Code (*Bürgerliches Gesetzbuch* or BGB) if a given situation is not expressly governed in the specifically applicable *Aktiengesetz*.[59] This would be a direct consultation of the law, quite different from the situation referred to in the preceding paragraph in which decisions regarding a GmbH are applied analogically to an AG. Companies listed on the Frankfurt Stock Exchange are also governed by the exchange's rules, and therefore these rules should also be taken into account. The Frankfurt rules are less extensive than their counterparts in London or New York both because the *Aktiengesetz* already includes rules on a number of matters – such as the requirement for a separate body of independent directors – which might otherwise be provided in listing rules, and because listed companies should follow the German Corporate Governance Code (*Deutscher Corporate Governance Kodex*)[60] (listed companies must state in the notes to their financial statements whether they have adopted the Code, or, if they have not adopted the Code, explain their reasons for that non-adoption).[61]

Thus, the complete picture of what we understand as "company law" in Germany is rather broad, but easily defined. It includes a central, detailed statute and a number of laws specifically incorporated by reference to cover accounting, mergers and co-determination, the laws and rules on

---

[57] Habersack, in *MünchKommAktG* (2008: Intro. mn. 190 *et seq.*); Schmidt (2002: 32).

[58] Kübler and Assmann (2006: 506 *et seq.*).

[59] For example, most of the rules on pre-incorporation liability for an AG are derived from cases regarding GmbHs, which in turn may depend on general principles of company membership found in the BGB's provisions on civil law companies (partnerships). See Kübler and Assmann (2006: 376 *et seq.*).

[60] The *Kodex* in its currently updated form is available at www.corporate-governance-code.de.

[61] § 161 AktG.

takeovers and securities regulation, as well as applicable exchange rules and a corporate governance code.

B.   United States

In the United States, corporate law statutes are state law. The statute of the state in which a company is incorporated governs its existence and its "internal affairs,"[62] and US states generally allow corporations incorporated in other states to do business in their state as "foreign" corporations subject to minimal requirements, such as designating an agent for service of process.[63] Today, most major US corporations, including over 60 percent of the so-called Fortune 500, are incorporated under the law of the State of Delaware.[64] Some of the other states, such as Oklahoma, follow the DGCL. Although the Model Act is used in some form in the great majority of US states, the companies employing it are more likely to be small and unlisted, and thus Delaware remains the most important corporate law in the United States for public companies. The Model Act is highly significant, however, because novel ideas on the preferred shape of company law have often been channeled through the efforts of the American Bar Association's Section on Business Law in order to update and improve the Model Act. For example, one of the first statutory provisions to articulate the duty of care of company directors was in the Model Act, and a provision of this type, albeit with different content, was introduced into the UK Companies Act 2006. We will thus point to the Model Act where it presents interesting, alternative solutions to those found in the DGCL.

The DGCL governs each of the five core characteristics of the business corporation. It provides for the creation of an entity with legal personality,[65] limited liability,[66] management by a centralized board[67] and transferable shares.[68] The aspect of shared ownership by investors is implicit in the company's existence as an entity that must issue stock,[69]

---

[62] Scoles, Hay, Borchers and Symeonides (2000: § 23.2). See Chapter 3, Section V.A, for a detailed definition of "internal affairs."

[63] Gevurtz (2000: 36). Although states do not require local incorporation as a prerequisite for doing business, the US Supreme Court has held that such a request would not impermissibly burden the interstate commerce whose regulation lies solely within the jurisdiction of the federal government. See *Railway Express Agency, Inc.* v. *Virginia*, 282 US 440 (1931).

[64] According to the State of Delaware's Division of Corporations, consulted in June 2009, 850,000 legal entities have been established in the state, including 63 percent of Fortune 500 companies and over half of all US publicly traded companies.

[65] § 106 DGCL.   [66] § 102(b)(6) DGCL.

[67] § 141 DGCL.   [68] §§ 201–202 DGCL.   [69] § 102(a)(4) DGCL.

which must be paid for,[70] and which represents a property interest in the corporation in the form of a "chose in action."[71] Although shareholders rarely use this power, § 141 DGCL also gives shareholders the right to eliminate centralized management by vesting executive control in a body other than the board of directors, such as a council including all shareholders. The greatest difference between the DGCL and the *Aktiengesetz* is that the Delaware law is almost completely composed of optional, default terms that shareholders may modify, supplement or eliminate in the company's certificate of incorporation.[72] On this point it resembles the UK Companies Act 2006, which allows many aspects to be regulated by the articles of association.[73] Delaware corporate law also comprises a very large body of decisions handed down by the Delaware Supreme Court and Court of Chancery on all aspects of corporate law, and particularly on such matters as fiduciary duties, which are not provided for in the statute.[74] The regulation of corporate groups, for example, which the *Aktiengesetz* expressly governs, is left to judicially crafted fiduciary duties imposed on majority shareholders.[75]

The Delaware statute contains no provisions on disclosure, accounting or audits, but does have rules to govern mergers[76] and takeovers.[77] Given the thin and relatively optional character of the DGCL, it is not surprising that corporate law is generally considered to include substantial elements of securities regulation.[78] As will be discussed in more detail in Chapter 3, including "securities regulation" in company law means looking to the requirements of some or all of the federal laws grouped under Title 15 of the US Code, which includes not only the Exchange Act, but also the

---

[70] § 152 DGCL.   [71] *Equitable Trust Co. v. Gallagher*, 67 A 2d 50, 54 (Del. Ch. 1949).
[72] Pistor (2005: 9).   [73] See Section C below.
[74] For the two years, 1999 and 2000, Professors Robert B. Thompson and Randall Thomas found that approximately 78 percent of Delaware Chancery Court cases addressed fiduciary duty issues. See Thompson and Thomas (2004: 167). It should also be noted that the use of cases as weighty authority is one area in which common law and civil law are certainly on a convergence path in many European countries. In conversations and experience during the period between 1992 and 2008, the authors have repeatedly received confirmation that case precedent is the soundest authority used in Italy and Germany on the meaning of a given statutory provision.
[75] Chapter 19 below.   [76] §§ 251–266 DGCL.   [77] § 203 DGCL.
[78] See e.g. Ballantine (1946: 858–886); Clark (1986: 293–240 and 719–749); and Gevurtz (2000: 537–529). Gevurtz notes at p. 39 that "federal securities laws have become a significant component of corporation law." It should be remembered that the US securities laws apply not only to companies whose securities (including debt securities) are listed on a stock exchange, but also to large companies with more than 500 shareholders.

Securities Act of 1933 (the Securities Act)[79] and the Trust Indenture Act of 1939 (the Trust Indenture Act),[80] among others. Beyond these laws and the extensive body of rules that the Securities and Exchange Commission (SEC) has issued under their authority, a listed company would also have to comply with the rules of the relevant exchange, which can be quite extensive. It is also common to include basic principles of revocable or fraudulent transfers from bankruptcy law in studies of US corporate law.[81] The latter serve to supplement the relatively permissive capital maintenance rules found in the DGCL, the Model Act and other similar statutes.

The enabling nature of the DGCL, which is composed mostly of non-mandatory "default" rules, would allow a company, in its certificate of incorporation, to comprehensively govern most rights, duties and circumstances, which leaves a rather limited ambit for the binding range of "company law." However, once the company is large enough to trigger application of the securities laws, such laws begin to regulate annual meetings, accounting practices, and directors' dealings in shares, among other things. When the company is listed, both the securities laws and the relevant set of exchange rules would impose yet another layer of mandatory regulation, governing the composition of the board of directors and the type of securities that may be issued. The composition of US "company law" thus changes significantly with the proximity of a corporation to the capital markets.

C.   United Kingdom

As a jurisdiction with a Common Law system that has significantly influenced US law, and as a member state of the European Union that, like Germany, must implement EU directives and obey EU regulations and ECJ decisions, the company law of the United Kingdom takes a middle position between the US and Germany. The UK, which had some of the oldest rules on corporations, dating back to the seventeenth century, now has the newest company law of the three jurisdictions examined. Both the core statute and many of the outlying rules serving a corporate law function were substantially amended in 2006. The Companies Act 2006 revised the 1985 version of that law and restated rules developed by over a century of case law on fiduciary duties and the duty of care owed by

---

[79] Securities Act of 1933, 15 USCA §§ 77a-77aa (2000).
[80] Trust Indenture Act of 1939, 15 USCA §§ 77aaa–77bbbb (2000).
[81] Eisenberg (2005: 858 *et seq.*); Clark (1986: 40–52). Dean Clark also includes bankruptcy provisions on equitable subordination of creditor claims in his treatment of corporate law. Clark (1986: 52–71).

company directors,[82] thus codifying rules that Delaware and German law express primarily through judicial decisions.[83] The Companies Act 2006 provides for the creation of all types of companies (public or private limited by shares or by guarantee, as well as unlimited)[84] and provides rules for a corporate entity with the five core characteristics discussed in our functional definition of "company law." A company limited by shares is a "body corporate,"[85] with limited liability,[86] transferable shares,[87] centralized management under a board,[88] and shared ownership by contributors of capital.[89]

The Companies Act 2006 removed a number of rules, such as those regarding the mandatory disclosure of significant shareholdings[90] and share dealings by directors,[91] from the Companies Act and placed them instead in newly issued rules of the UK Financial Services Authority (FSA). This resembles earlier decisions to hive off rules from the Act, such as when insolvency rules were removed from a pre-1985 version of the Act and placed in the Insolvency Act 1986.[92] As mentioned, other matters, such as detailed rules on directors' duties, were added to the Act, and it remains the most extensive and most detailed of the three laws being examined here. Like the *Aktiengesetz*, the Companies Act provides strict rules on the constitution and maintenance of capital[93] and requirements for annual mandatory disclosure[94] (both from EU law), but, like the DGCL, the Companies Act is flexible, and allows such matters as the method of appointing directors[95] and the operation of the board[96] to be freely shaped in the company's articles. In contrast to the other

---

[82] See generally Chapter 2 of the CA 2006. Sec. 170(3) CA 2006 provides that: "The general duties are based on certain common law rules and equitable principles as they apply in relation to directors and have effect in place of those rules and principles as regards the duties owed to a company by a director."

[83] The *Aktiengesetz* does provide a standard of care for managing and supervisory directors (§§ 93 and 116 AktG), prohibits managing directors from competing with the company (§ 88 AktG), and imposes a duty of confidentiality on all directors (§§ 93 and 116 AktG), but the detailed parameters of the duty of loyalty (*Treupflicht*) have been worked out by the courts in a manner one would expect from a traditional Common Law jurisdiction. The Model Act provides statutory standards of conduct for directors somewhat less extensive than those of the CA 2006 but rather more detailed than those found in the *Aktiengesetz*.

[84] Secs. 3 *et seq.* CA 2006.   [85] Sec. 16(2) CA 2006.

[86] Sec. 9(2)(c) CA 2006.   [87] Secs. 10 and 544 CA 2006.

[88] Sec. 154(2) CA 2006.   [89] Sec. 8(1)(b) CA 2006.

[90] Previously secs. 198 *et seq.* CA 1985.   [91] Previously secs. 323 *et seq.* CA 1985.

[92] Davies (2008: 57).   [93] See e.g. Parts 17 and 18 CA 2006.

[94] See e.g. secs. 414 *et seq.* CA 2006.   [95] Reg. 17, SI 2008 No. 3229.

[96] Regs. 6 *et seq.*, SI 2008 No. 3229.

laws, the Companies Act 2006 provides extensive and detailed rules on accounting,[97] and is accompanied by model articles that govern a significant part of a company's internal management affairs. The model articles are prescribed by the Secretary of State,[98] and drafted by the Department for Business, Enterprise and Regulatory Reform (BERR), which replaced the Department of Trade and Industry (DTI) in 2007. It must also be noted that the BERR was short-lived, and, in 2009, was replaced by the Department for Business, Innovation and Skills (BIS). This new acronym is doubly confusing because, since 1930, the acronym has referred to the Bank for International Settlements, the highest-level regulator for international banking regulation, particularly capital requirements. The UK BIS has taken on the tasks previously performed by the DTI and the BERR in connection with drafting the statutory instruments as necessary under the Companies Act.

Beyond the Companies Act and its related statutory instruments, company law in the UK contains basically the same capital market elements as in Germany, given that they both derive from EU directives, plus the insider dealing provisions of the Criminal Justice Act 1993.[99] The fact that rules on company insolvency, directors' dealings and shareholder disclosures were originally located in the Companies Act argues for including such laws and rules under the rubric "company law." The FSA's Disclosure and Transparency Rules thus constitute a central element of UK company law.[100] The FSA's Listing Rules also contain important rules of company law for listed corporations, such as requirements that shareholders approve significant transactions and mandatory restrictions on directors' dealings in their company's securities.[101] Unlike either the US or Germany, takeovers involving listed companies in the UK are regulated by a code adopted by a private panel endowed with regulatory authority.[102] In addition to the 2006 Act, the UK has the Insolvency Act 1986 containing a doctrine of "wrongful trading,"[103] which can serve as an additional tool for capital maintenance,[104] and is an important part of company law. Like Delaware, the UK has an extensive body of case law addressing every

---

[97] See e.g. Part 15 CA 2006.   [98] Sec. 19(1) CA 2006.
[99] Part V of the Criminal Justice Act 1993.
[100] See FSA, Disclosure and Transparency Rules.
[101] See FSA Listing Rules, Rule 9 (Model Code, Nos. 3 *et seq.*), FSA Listing Rules, Rule 10.
[102] Secs. 942 *et seq.* CA 2006 and Takeover Code. See also Armour and Skeel (2007: 1744 *et seq.*).
[103] Chapter X of the Insolvency Act 1986; Davis (2008: 77).
[104] Armour (2005: 44).

Table 1.1 *Functional components of company law*

	Germany	United Kingdom	United States
Main statute	*Aktiengesetz*	Companies Act 2006	State Corporations Acts
Linked statute	Co-Determination Act		
Linked statute	Reorganization Act		
Upper-level regulations	Applicable EU regulations	Applicable EU regulations	Exchange Act and Rules (federal)
Related area	Takeover Act and Regulation	Takeover Code (linked rules)	(as above)
Related area	Securities Trading Act and Rules	FSA Disclosure and Transparency Rules under FSMA	(as above)
Individual rules		Criminal Justice Act 1993	
Individual rules		Insolvency Act 1986	Fraudulent Conveyance Rules (state) Bankruptcy Rules (federal)
Related area	Listing Rules	Listing Rules	Listing Rules
Related area	EU Regulations and Advice	EU Regulations and Advice	

aspect of corporate law, with particular focus on the duties of directors and the rights of the minority shareholders to relief, which, despite the broad coverage of statutory and administrative rules, remains central to any study of UK company law.

Leaving aside the very significant area of accounting rules (which are in the text of the Companies Act 2006 and incorporated by reference into the *Aktiengesetz*), we submit that the laws falling under the rubric "company law" in Germany, the UK and the US should be those set out in Table1.1.

2

The partnership as a form of business organization

Required reading

D: HGB, §§ 114–116, 125, 126, 128–130, 159, 160, 161–177a; Income Tax Act (*Einkommensteuergesetz*), § 15(1), no. (2)

UK: Scan for main concepts such as the nature of a partnership, the liability of partners, management by partners, representation, and the transferability of shares: Partnership Act 1890 and Limited Partnership Act 1907

US: Revised Uniform Partnership Act, table of contents, and §§ 201–202 (and Comment), 401, 404 (and Comment), 301–303 (and Comment), 306, 503, 703 (and Comment); US Internal Revenue Code, § 701

Partnerships in Germany, the UK and the US

I.   Partnerships and corporations

In the preceding chapter, we looked at the essential characteristics of the stock corporation. Before moving on to study these characteristics in detail, let us pause briefly to examine the characteristics of an alternative organizational form: the partnership. Both partnerships and corporations are organizational forms that allow a number of people to join together to pursue a common (commercial) purpose. Both are freely established by contract among the members, in both cases the organization serves as a vehicle to pursue an end, and, for both, the members are obliged to contribute something of value that enables the association to operate. As will be highlighted below, there are clear differences between a corporation and what one might call the "central" or "traditional" concept of the partnership, but law has developed in accommodation to business needs over the years so as to blur the distinction between the two forms. In the United States, some refer to this as "entity proliferation" and call for a countervailing "entity rationalization."[1] Aside from the broader policy question of the "proliferation" of organizational forms, it is important for a student of corporate law to clearly understand (i) the differences between a corporation and a (general) partnership and (ii) that the flexible laws of some jurisdictions or even just creative lawyering will allow organizations to be crafted combining corporate and partnership characteristics.

Traditionally, the main difference between corporations and partnerships is to be found in the nature of the relationship between the association and its members: *corporations are legal persons* distinct from their members.[2] Therefore, the rights and obligations of the corporation are distinct from those of its members, and *vice versa*. This is the essence of what is referred to as "limited liability": a shareholder is not liable for the company's debts beyond her investment in the company. The corporation can continue in time regardless of the exit of old and the entrance of new members, which also allows shares in the corporation to be *freely transferable*. The corporate entity has its own management, and shareholders may not act on behalf of the corporation without authority from this entity.

In contrast, a partnership emphasizes the interpersonal mingling of the talents and assets of the partners: a group of people who pool their assets and act as mutual agents and principals to pursue a common goal. Indeed, partnership law developed from the law of agency, and *each partner* is understood *as an agent* for the other partners. There is no structural separation of ownership and control. This origin is still visible in today's partnership statutes, such as in § 714 of the *Bürgerliches Gesetzbuch*, which provides that partners with management authority are presumed to have authority to act as an agent for the other partners, section 5 of the UK Partnership Act 1890, which states that "[e]very partner is an agent of the firm and his other partners," and § 301 of the US Revised Uniform Partnership Act (RUPA), which similarly provides that "[e]ach partner is an agent of the partnership for the purposes of its business." It follows from this power that obligations of the partnership are obligations of the partners.[3] However, as Hansmann, Kraakman and Squire have shown, because the personal obligations of the partner have in most times and

---

[1] See Ribstein (2003).

[2] On German law, see § 1(1) AktG and § 13 GmbHG. On English law, see e.g. *Salomon* v. *Salomon* [1897] AC 22, 51 (HL). On US law, see e.g. *Bank of the United States* v. *Dandridge*, 12 Wheat 64 (1827); *Buechner* v. *Farbenfabriken Bayer Aktiengesellschaft*, 154 A 2d 684 (Del. 1949).

[3] See e.g. § 714 BGB; sec. 9 PA 1890; § 306 RUPA.

jurisdictions not been enforceable against the partnership, this form also provides vital asset partitioning that allows its business to function despite the personal finances of its partners.[4]

As the obligations are those of *a given group of partners*, the entry and exit of partners to this group must dissolve the existing partnership or otherwise be carefully regulated. Thus, the basic concept of a partnership is that of an agreement between the partners governing the *joint management* of assets *jointly owned* by the partners, in which partners are *jointly liable* for obligations incurred. The distinction between the traditional concepts of corporation and partnership is thus that a corporation is a legal entity, a juridical person, with rights and duties of its own, but the rights and obligations of a partnership are nothing more than the aggregate of the rights held and the obligations incurred by the partners under a common name. This has led to one of the major economic advantages of using the partnership form in most jurisdictions, namely, that partnership income is taxed just once, in the hands of the partners, while the income of a corporation is taxed once as its own and again as income of the shareholders if distributed to them in the form of a dividend. The interpersonal characteristic of a partnership is also evidenced by the fact that, unlike a corporation, a partnership cannot exist with just one partner, and this fact is provided for in German,[5] UK[6] and US[7] law.

II.   Types of partnerships

In each of our three jurisdictions (Germany, the United Kingdom and the United States), there are both partnership forms with unlimited liability and those with limited liability. The former are divided in Germany between commercial partnerships, professional partnerships and partnerships for other purposes, and the latter are divided in the United Kingdom and the United States between partnerships in which the liability of some partners is limited and those in which the liability of all partners is limited. The following describes each of these organizational forms.

A.   Germany

The law of Germany provides for five types of partnerships: the "civil law partnership," the "commercial partnership," the "professional

---

[4] Hansmann, Kraakman and Squire (2006: 1337).
[5] § 705 BGB.   [6] Sec. 1(1) PA 1890.   [7] § 202 RUPA.

partnership," the "limited partnership" and the "partnership limited by shares."

1.   Civil law partnership   The basic partnership type under German law is the civil law partnership (*Gesellschaft bürgerlichen Rechts* or GbR) under §§ 705–740 BGB. A GbR can be established by implied or express oral or written agreement for any common purpose, and could be something as small as two people jointly renting an automobile for a weekend trip, to a large firm of lawyers or a syndicate of banks jointly underwriting a multi-billion euro securities offering.[8] The GbR arises with the agreement of the partners to jointly pursue a common goal and the contribution of each partner to the partnership.[9] There is no register in which its existence must or can be inscribed. It characteristically presents itself to the world as an aggregate of persons rather than under a unified trade name.

The operative management of a partnership includes two, distinct legal steps in dealings with third parties. The first is the (internal) process of making decisions for the partnership (management authority), and the second is the process of carrying out these decisions *vis-à-vis* third parties (authority to represent). In a GbR, unless otherwise provided in the partnership agreement, all partnership decisions must be made unanimously by the partners, and all partners are presumed to have authority to bind the partnership *vis-à-vis* third parties.[10] Each partner owes the others a duty of loyalty.[11] All partners have a claim to a portion of the assets upon liquidation of the partnership, and all are liable without limit for the debts of the partnership.[12] Partners entering a GbR are immediately liable for all the debts of the partnership, and partners exiting the GbR remain liable for a period of five years from the date their exit is made known to the

---

[8] § 705 BGB. Syndicated underwriting is not deemed a commercial activity within the meaning of the HGB because only business ventures with substantial durations and which entail a large number of transactions constitute commercial activities within the HGB's definition. If a placement of securities is to be concluded within a few weeks, the partnership between the banks would be governed by the BGB rather than the HGB, even though all members of the partnership themselves unquestionably carry out commercial activities.

[9] § 705 BGB. The partners must merely agree on a common purpose and to make some kind of contribution (which can consist of rendering services) toward the pursuit of that purpose. There is no need either to establish joint property or for all partners to share in the partnership's profits. Ulmer, in *MünchKommBGB* (2009: § 705 mn. 150, 282).

[10] §§ 709, 714 BGB.

[11] § 713 BGB.

[12] BGHZ 142, 315; 154, 88.

respective creditor for those debts incurred up to the point of their exit from the GbR.[13]

Individual partners can trigger the dissolution of the partnership.[14] Depending on the partnership agreement, the entrance of a new partner may require the unanimous or majority approval of the other partners, and the exit or death of a partner may cause either the partnership to dissolve or the continuing partners' shares to expand with appropriate compensation for the deceased's heirs.[15] As discussed later in this chapter, over 100 years after the GbR form came into existence through statutory enactment, the German High Federal Court decided in *ARGE Weißes Ross* that it should be considered a legal entity for the purposes of exercising rights and acting as a party in court, but internally, between the partners, as an aggregate of related individuals.[16] This decision directly contradicts the classical understanding of Civil Law judges rigidly applying the letter of the law, in contrast to innovative Common Law judges adapting the law to a changing society: here, the Civil Law court replaced the highly impractical and troublesome "aggregate" characteristic, which Common Law courts in the US were unwilling to do without statutory action from the lawmaker.

2. Professional partnership Because German law does not consider the "liberal" professions (e.g. lawyers, physicians, architects and accountants) to be commercial activities, professionals cannot use the commercial partnership form discussed below. As an alternative to the GbR, Germany enacted legislation in 1994 to allow for a professional partnership (*Partnerschaftsgesellschaft* or PartG) as an association of professionals. The PartG is intended to provide an equivalent to the general commercial partnership; accordingly, the rules governing the PartG are fashioned to a great extent on those of the commercial partnership, and in part on those for the GbR. Given its purpose, a PartG may have only natural persons as partners.[17]

---

[13] § 736(2) BGB, in connection with § 160(1) HGB, and BGHZ 117, 168, at 178 *et seq.*

[14] § 723 BGB.   [15] § 727 BGB.

[16] The dominant view has traditionally been that a partnership is not a legal entity. However, for practical purposes § 124 HGB achieves the same result for commercial partnerships, as discussed below. The BGB partnership provisions do not contain a provision like § 124 HGB. Therefore, the GbR was conceived merely as a label for the aggregate of the partners. The view on this issue has been reversed by several recent decisions of the Federal Supreme Court, including *ARGE Weißes Ross*.

[17] § 1 PartGG.

The main benefit of the PartG form is that its liability structure is tailored to the nature of professional activity. Beyond her contribution to partnership assets, an individual partner will be liable only for her own malpractice, and the partners who were not actually involved in providing the faulty services have no obligation to contribute their personal assets toward satisfying the claim.[18] In effect, she forfeits the right to receive contributions from other partners to cover liability from her own malpractice in exchange for being relieved of the obligation to contribute to the similar liability of other partners in cases where partnership assets are insufficient to cover damages. Beyond this limitation in the organizational structure, if a statute regulating the relevant profession so provides, liability may be limited to a fixed amount provided that the PartG takes out malpractice insurance.[19]

3. Commercial partnership   Commercial businesses conducted in partnership form may use the general commercial partnership (*offene Handelsgesellschaft* or OHG) provided for in §§ 105–160 HGB. Although an OHG resembles a GbR by requiring a common agreement among partners to pursue a purpose, the purpose of an OHG must be commercial. Unlike a GbR, an OHG acquires its existence through registration in the commercial register,[20] and must operate under a registered trade name,[21] although its status as an OHG may begin if a GbR's activity takes a direction and dimension sufficient to call it a commercial enterprise.[22]

In an OHG, which is designed for commercial agility, the default rule is that all partners can both make management decisions for the partnership and represent it for "ordinary business" (*gewöhnlicher Geschäftsbetrieb*)[23] *vis-à-vis* third parties, unless the partnership agreement specifies otherwise.[24] If the power of representation is delegated only to certain partners, this must be specified in the commercial

---

[18] § 8 PartGG.   [19] § 8(3) PartGG.

[20] § 123 HGB. An alternative means of bringing an OHG into existence is to begin commercial trade with the unanimous approval of the partners, which does not however eliminate the duty to register.

[21] § 105 I HGB.   [22] § 123(2) HGB.   [23] § 116 HGB.

[24] § 114 HGB. According to § 126(1) HGB, a partner's authority to represent the partnership extends to all transactions and disputes even if outside the usual course of business. Partnerships will be bound by representations of partners even for transactions unrelated to the partnership business. Under § 126(2) HGB, this agency power may not be limited as against third parties. Although a partner may incur liability to the other partners for unauthorized acts of representation, they remain binding on the partnership.

register so that third parties have notice.[25] "Extraordinary" matters may not be decided by a single managing partner, but require a resolution by all partners including the non-managing partners.[26] A vote is taken by a head count, not by share of capital invested, unless otherwise provided in the partnership agreement,[27] which can lend power to "minority" partners with smaller capital positions. A third category of decisions not expressly mentioned in the law is matters outside the scope of the partnership's business, such as amendments to the partnership agreement and the admission of new partners. These require a resolution by all parties to the agreement.[28]

Partners owe a duty of loyalty to each other and to the partnership and may not compete with the partnership.[29] Each partner has a claim to receive an annual payout and a portion of the profits[30] from the partnership, as well as a share of the assets upon liquidation.[31] Every partner also has to bear an appropriate portion of the losses.[32] The partners of an OHG are jointly and severally liable for the debts of the partnership on primary recourse: i.e. a creditor need not first fail to receive satisfaction from the partnership before suing the individual partner for the full amount of the

---

[25] §§ 106–107 HGB. Pursuant to § 125(3) HGB, any such limit on a partner's power of representation must be registered with the commercial register, and § 15(2) HGB allows such a restriction to be asserted against a third party after publication in the *Bundesanzeiger* (*Federal Gazette*), regardless of actual knowledge. This makes it difficult for a third party to plead good faith reliance on apparent authority.

[26] § 116(2) HGB. The definition of "extraordinary matters" has been developed by the courts as matters whose object, purpose or risk place them beyond the ordinary course of that OHG's business. See BGHZ 76, 160, 162; Schilling, in Staub (1983–: § 164 mn. 5). For example, courts have found "extraordinary" in individual cases: acts granting loans unrelated to the OHG's business, the closing down of plants, a change of business policy, a purchase or sale of real estate, a grant of general power of attorney, and the sale of parts of the business. See Schilling, in Staub (1983–: § 164 mn. 5).

[27] § 119(2) HGB.

[28] §§ 105(3) HGB; §§ 717–719 BGB. German Law permits free assignment of economic rights to receive profit and payouts, but not of management-related membership rights. The purpose of this is to protect the existing partners against unwanted accession of new partners. Assignments are restricted to the claims of the partner against the partnership for sums certain.

[29] § 112 HGB.

[30] Pursuant to §§ 168(1), 121(1) HGB, every partner is entitled to an initial share in the annual profit in the amount of 4 percent of his capital share, and, under § 168(2), every partner is entitled to an appropriate share of the remaining profit.

[31] §§ 120, 121, 155 HGB.

[32] § 168(2) HGB. A portion of losses is deducted from each partner's capital share (§§ 161(2), 120(2) HGB).

partnership obligation.[33] Partners entering the OHG are jointly and severally liable for all existing debts, and partners exiting the OHG remain liable for five years for all debts existing at the time of exit.[34] The nature of the OHG as a commercial entity is exemplified by the fact that, unless the partnership agreement provides otherwise, the death or exit of a partner *does not* dissolve the partnership; rather, both events only pass the share on to the heirs or to the other partners.[35]

4. Limited partnership   The limited partnership (*Kommanditgesellschaft* or KG), which is provided for in §§ 161–177a HGB, traces its roots back to the medieval transactional structure known as the *commenda*, in which a silent partner would contribute funds to an active partner (usually a ship's captain) to undertake a trading voyage.[36] The KG takes a significant step toward the corporate form by creating a class of non-managing investors whose liability is limited to their stake in the company. In the KG, there are two types of partner: general partners (*Komplementäre*) with management functions and unlimited liability, and limited partners (*Kommanditisten*) who are expressly excluded from management and are liable for the KG's debts only up to the amount of their contributions.[37] Like an OHG, a KG must conduct a commercial activity and takes its existence as a KG through registration in the commercial register.[38] The registration must indicate which partners are limited partners and the amount up to which they are liable.[39] If the partnership commences its operations prior to registration, all partners who have agreed to the commencement are liable as general partners; their liability becomes limited only for obligations incurred after registration of the KG and of their status as limited partners.[40] Since an early twentieth-century decision of the

---

[33] See § 128 HGB. This section draws no distinction between contractual and other (i.e. tort) claims against the partnership. The partners are jointly and severally liable for all debts and obligations of the partnership irrespective of their basis.

[34] §§ 130, 160 HGB. In order to inform the public about the change in the list of partners, the transfer has to be registered pursuant to §§ 107 and 143(2) HGB. Until the registration is effected and published in the *Bundesanzeiger* and another paper (see §§ 10, 11 HGB), the transfer cannot be asserted against a third party without actual knowledge. § 15(1) HGB. Although the exiting partner remains liable, since the validity of the share transfer does not depend on its registration, the incoming partner also bears liability.

[35] §§ 138–142.

[36] Horn (1995: Intro. VI mn. 10), and, on the *commenda* generally, see Harris (2008: 8 *et seq.*); Hansmann, Kraakman and Squire (2006: 1372).

[37] § 161 HGB.   [38] § 161 HGB.   [39] § 162 HGB.   [40] § 176 HGB.

High Court of Bavaria, it has generally been accepted in Germany that corporations can be the sole general partner of a limited partnership, the typical case being that of a limited liability company (*Gesellschaft mit beschränkter Haftung* or GmbH) acting as sole general partner, referred to as a GmbH & Co. KG.[41] Moreover, as the decision of the German High Federal Court in *W. J. v. S. Sch.*[42] makes clear, the limitation of liability will not be waived even when the KG has been used as a device to allow the actual economic owner and director of the partnership business to shield his personal assets.

German law makes generous use of the converse to *lex specialis derogat legi generali* when filling gaps in the specific regulation of the KG by looking to the OHG, and, for the latter, looking to the GbR provisions.[43] This is necessary in particular with respect to the rights and duties of general partners, whose status thus resembles that of partners in an OHG. Unless provided otherwise in the partnership agreement, all general partners are assumed to have power to manage and represent the partnership, and may not compete with it.[44] With the exception of extraordinary transactions, limited partners are expressly deprived of management power and, without exception, representative authority.[45] However, they have a right to receive a copy of the annual accounts and to inspect books and records.[46] As in an OHG, a limited partner has a claim to a portion of profits and of the assets at dissolution, but may not demand payment of profit so long as his contribution to capital is reduced by losses to less than the agreed amount.[47] If, through withdrawal of her capital share, a limited partner's contribution is reduced below the agreed amount, she will not enjoy limited liability until the deficit is eliminated.[48] A limited partner who enters a KG is liable for existing debts,[49] but only up to the amount of his partnership share.[50]

---

[41] Today, the legality of a GmbH & Co. KG can be inferred from § 19(2) HGB and § 15a(1) InsO.

[42] For reasons of privacy protection, the decisions of German courts do not bear the memorable names of their parties like those of the US and the UK.

[43] §§ 161(2), 105(3) HGB.

[44] §§ 114 *et seq.*, 125 *et seq.*, 112 HGB.

[45] §§ 164, 170. However, German courts have not held that management power triggers unlimited liability, and thus participation in management will not make a limited partner a general partner. See BGHZ 45, 204 (the *Rektor* decision). Such authority is achieved in practice by granting a limited partner a general proxy (*Prokura*) under § 48 HGB, just as could be done with any other person.

[46] § 166 HGB.   [47] § 169 HGB.   [48] § 172 HGB.   [49] § 173 HGB.

[50] § 171 HGB.

Limited partners have neither management nor fiduciary duties. They may compete with the partnership.[51] Because entrance or exit of limited partners has very little impact on the KG, the shares of a limited partner may be freely transferred unless provided otherwise in the partnership agreement.[52]

5. Partnership limited by shares German law also provides a form of partnership that even more closely approximates the characteristics of a stock corporation: the partnership limited by shares (*Kommanditgesellschaft auf Aktien* or KGaA). The KGaA is regulated by §§ 278–290 of the *Aktiengesetz*. It is a hybrid between a limited partnership and a stock corporation. Like a stock corporation, it is a legal person distinct from its members.[53] Like a KG, it has two types of members. There must be at least one general partner, who need not make a contribution to the corporation's capital but is in any case personally liable for the corporation's debts, and at least one shareholder, who has a status similar to that of a shareholder in a regular stock corporation, i.e. one who does not participate in management and whose obligation is limited to payment of consideration for the shares held.[54] The KGaA is managed similarly to a stock corporation.[55]

Table 2.1 summarizes the salient features of the partnership forms discussed above.

B.   England

UK law provides for three types of partnerships: the "partnership," the "limited partnership" and the "limited liability partnership."

1. Partnership The "partnership," which existed traditionally under both law and equity in the English courts,[56] is now governed by the provisions of the Partnership Act 1890 (PA 1890) together with case law. As the PA 1890 was not designed to work changes in the existing law, UK partnership law resembles that developed in the courts and remains very close to the basis used in the US (prior to recent amendments that will be discussed in the next section).

---

[51] § 165 HGB.
[52] However, § 162(3) HGB provides that changes in the membership shares must be registered in the commercial register. The assignment of partnership shares must also be registered.
[53] § 278 AktG.   [54] § 278 AktG.   [55] §§ 283, 285 AktG.
[56] Morse (2006: 28 *et seq.*); Banks (2002: 3).

Table 2.1 *Partnership forms and characteristics, Germany*

Name	Activity	Registration	Representation	Liability	Entity
BGB partnership	Not commercial	No	All	Unlimited	Yes
Professional partnership	Liberal professions	Yes	Each	Mixed	Yes
OHG (commercial partnership)	Commercial	Yes	Each	Unlimited	Yes
KG (limited partnership)	Commercial	Yes	General partner	Mixed	Yes
KGaA (partnership limited by shares)	Any	Yes	General partner	General partner	Legal person

Pursuant to section 1(1) PA 1890, a partnership is "the relation which subsists between persons carrying on a business in common with a view of profit." The limitation of this form to businesses is not as restrictive as it may seem because, in contrast to German law, the Act defines "business" to include both the professions,[57] and "one-off" trading ventures. Thus, both the activities of lawyers and physicians and those of an underwriting syndicate could qualify as "carrying on a business" for purposes of forming a partnership. The latter's being a partnership is also facilitated by the word "person" including limited companies.[58] There are neither formal requirements for the partnership agreement nor a register in which the existence of a partnership can be entered. English and Welsh – as opposed to Scots – law does not recognize the partnership as an entity separate from the aggregate of the partners.[59] Although there are some exceptions, such as its capacity to bring

---

[57] Sec. 45 PA 1890.   [58] Banks (2002: 10).

[59] See e.g. Banks (2002: 35), citing *Green* v. *Hertzog* [1954] 1 WLR 1309; *Meyer & Co. v. Farber (No. 2)* [1923] 2 Ch 421; *Ex parte Gliddon* (1884) 13 QBD 43. Scots law does recognize the partnership as a separate legal entity. See sec. 4(2) PA 1890. In 2003, the Law Commission and the Scottish Law Commission recommended that the law be changed to classify the partnership as a legal entity separate from the aggregate of its partners. No change is currently predicted in this regard for English law.

judicial actions in its own name,[60] the law considers the partnership a mere aggregate of its partners at any one time. The nature of "partnership property" displays the delicate balance involved in the partnership existing as a "firm" without separate legal existence. The partnership property belongs to the partners, but the Act requires them to use property originally brought into or later acquired on account of the partnership "exclusively for the purposes of the partnership."[61]

The partnership form does not separate ownership and control. Subject to contrary provision in the partnership agreement, all partners have equal rights in the management of the partnership business.[62] The lineage of partnership law, which finds some of its origin in the law of agency, is visible in the default rule that every partner is an agent of the firm and his other partners for the purpose of the business of the partnership, and his acts connected with usual business bind the firm.[63] It is permissible for partners to agree that one or more of them will have only limited or no authority to bind the firm, but this will have effect against a third party only if this is actually known by the third party.[64] Notice that is given to a partner who is active in management with respect to a partnership matter will be attributed to all partners in the firm.[65]

The management structure shows similarities to and differences from the corporate form. Ordinary matters connected with the partnership business are determined by the decision of a majority of the partners.[66] Absent the now very common delegation by agreement to certain partners,[67] decisions on day-to-day business would be decided collegially by majority rule.[68] The Act does not provide for decisions on extraordinary matters except for expressly providing that "no change may be made in the nature of the partnership business without the consent of all existing partners."[69] The line between "ordinary" matters and those that change the firm's nature has been for the courts to regulate, and, for example, a decision to expand a partnership from a travel agency to a tour operator was found to fall into the latter category, demanding unanimous approval.[70]

---

[60] Banks (2002: 35).   [61] Sec. 20(1) PA 1890.   [62] Sec. 24(5) PA 1890.

[63] Sec. 5 PA 1890.   [64] Sec. 8 PA 1890.   [65] Sec. 16 PA 1890.

[66] Sec. 24(8) PA 1890.   [67] Banks (2002: 464).

[68] However, it is unclear, for example, whether a decision to change business premises (see *Clements* v. *Norris* (1878) 8 ChD 129) and whether a decision to restrict a partner's authority without placing a similar restriction on all partners is an ordinary matter connected with the partnership business.

[69] Sec. 24(8) PA 1890.

[70] See *Bissel* v. *Cole* (1997) LTL, December 5, 1991 (CA), discussed in Morse (2006: 182).

The pre-1890 English law recognized that partners owed each other a duty of "utmost" good faith "tried by the highest standard of honour,"[71] and the rules of equity and of Common Law deriving from such cases continue in force under the Act.[72] They are reinforced by an express duty to render true accounts and full information concerning all things affecting the partnership,[73] and to account to the firm for any benefit derived from a transaction concerning the partnership or use of its property, name or business connections without the consent of the other partners.[74] Further, a partner may not compete with the firm absent consent of her co-partners.[75]

Unless otherwise agreed, all partners share the profits and the losses of the firm equally.[76] Partners are also jointly liable for the debts and obligations of the firm.[77] Thus, one partner can be sued and found liable for the whole debt, with a right to recover a proportionate contribution from the other liable partners. Moreover, if one partner commits a wrongful act or omission "in the ordinary course of the business of the firm," the firm (and thus each partner) is liable for any injury.[78] The situations that courts have found to be covered by this principle range from negligent driving by coachmen[79] to solicitors drafting contracts designed to violate the law.[80]

Unlike shares of a corporation, partnership shares are not freely transferable: no person can be introduced into an existing partnership without the consent of all the partners.[81] As the partnership is not a legal person, its financial standing can change with a change of partners.[82] However, UK (like German and US) law makes a distinction between economic rights and control rights that we will also see in corporate law. A transfer of a partnership share without the required approval gives the assignee only rights to the share of profits to which the assigning partner was entitled, but not to participate in management.[83] A person who is admitted as a partner into an existing firm assumes joint liability for new obligations

---

[71] *Blisset* v. *Daniel* (1853) 10 Hare 493. With respect to one partner trying to squeeze another out through a buyout, see *Chandler* v. *Dorsett* (1679) Finch 431. Also see Banks (2002: 469 *et seq.*); Morse (2006: 162 *et seq.*).

[72] Sec. 46 PA 1890.   [73] Sec. 28 PA 1890.   [74] Sec. 29 PA 1890.

[75] Sec. 30 PA 1890.   [76] Sec. 24(1) PA 1890.   [77] Sec. 9 PA 1890.

[78] Sec. 10 PA 1890.

[79] See the discussions in Banks (2002: 335 *et seq.*); Morse (2006: 130 *et seq.*).

[80] See *Dubai Aluminium Co. Ltd* v. *Salaam* [2002] UKHL 48.

[81] Sec. 24(7) PA 1890.

[82] That a change in shareholders does not change the financial standing of a corporation strengthens the transferability of its shares. Easterbrook and Fischel (1985: 95).

[83] Sec. 31(1) PA 1890.

but is not liable to the creditors of the firm for anything done before her entrance.[84] A partner who retires from a firm does not cease to be liable for partnership debts or obligations incurred before his retirement,[85] unless otherwise agreed with the firm and the respective creditor,[86] and such retirement does not become effective until the exiting partner has given notice of her retirement.[87]

Subject to any contrary agreement among the partners, a single partner may file to dissolve the partnership if the partnership was entered into for an indefinite time.[88] Subject to contrary provisions in the partnership agreement, the death or bankruptcy of a partner may also dissolve the partnership.[89] This derives primarily from understanding the partnership as the aggregate of its members rather than as an entity distinct from them. The entrance or exit of a partner brings with it a new aggregate.

2.   Limited liability partnership   The "limited liability partnership" (LLP) resembles the German PartG in form and purpose. It was introduced into UK law by the Limited Liability Partnerships Act 2000 (LLPA), and responded to the needs of large firms of professionals facing increasing, vicarious liability for the acts of their co-partners.[90] The primary characteristics of an LLP are that such vicarious liability is limited, and it does not create two classes of partners so that – in contrast to a limited partnership – all partners may enjoy a shield of limited liability even if actively involved in management.

Although it may only be used for commercial purposes, an LLP is not restricted to professionals, and even corporations may be members.[91] An LLP takes on existence through the filing of "incorporation" documents with the registrar of companies.[92] The LLP is a body corporate with legal personality separate from that of its members,[93] to which the law of partnerships does not apply except as expressly provided for in the LLPA.[94]

---

[84] Sec. 17 (1) PA 1890.   [85] Sec. 17(2) PA 1890.
[86] Sec. 17(3) PA 1890; and Banks (2002: 417).
[87] Sec. 36(1) PA 1890 with regard to notice.
[88] Secs. 32(c), 26 PA 1890.   [89] Sec. 33(1) PA 1890.
[90] Morse (2006: 293).
[91] Limited Liability Partnerships Regulations 2001, Schedule 2, Part I, Note to s. 288 CA 1985. These regulations were adopted on March 19, 2001, SI 2001 No. 1090.
[92] Secs. 2, 3 LLPA.
[93] Sec. 1(2) LLPA. Under UK legal doctrine, the LLP is thus not a "partnership" but rather a "private limited company." See Morse (2006: 295).
[94] Sec. 1(5) LLPA.

The LLP's hybrid status is evidenced by the fact that many provisions of the Companies Act 2006 apply to it *mutatis mutandis.*

The registration of the LLP must specify "designated" members who are responsible for performing a number of management functions related to governance, such as appointing auditors, signing accounts and making filings with the registrar.[95] Most relationships among the partners of an LLP are governed by the partnership agreement, or, absent such an agreement, by the Limited Liability Partnerships Regulations 2001.[96] The law provides that every member of an LLP is an agent of the partnership unless agreed otherwise.[97] The regulations ascribe every partner a right to take part in the management of the LLP, drawn from the tasks assigned to corporate directors by the Companies Act 2006,[98] and every partner has an equal claim to receive profits and capital,[99] which are for tax purposes directly attributed to the members, despite the fact that the LLP has separate legal identity.[100] Specific regulations apply Companies Act 2006 accounting and reporting rules to LLPs.[101]

As noted, the primary impetus for the Act was to allow professionals to avoid prohibitively high vicarious liability. Similarly to the German *Gesetz über Partnerschaftsgesellschaften Angehöriger Freier Berufe (Partnerschaftsgesellschaftsgesetz* or PartGG), the Act provides that any liability in tort incurred personally by a partner in the course of the LLP's business is deemed equally an obligation of the LLP,[102] and the LLP – not the partners individually – must indemnify any partner for such tort liability incurred "in the ordinary and proper conduct of the business" of the LLP.[103] Thus, a professional must cover her own malpractice with available partnership assets and her private assets. As a default position, the Regulations also ascribe fiduciary duties to members: they must disgorge profits from any competition with the LLP and any private benefit taken from the LLP, as well as render a full, transparent accounting of their activities to the LLP.[104] Subject

---

[95] Secs. 2(2)(f), 8 LLPA. The tasks to be performed by "designated" members are taken from tasks delegated to the board of directors of a limited company under the Companies Act. See Schedule 1, SI 2001 No. 1090.

[96] SI 2001 No. 1090.   [97] Sec. 6(1) LLPA.

[98] Sec. 7(3), SI 2001 No. 1090.

[99] Sec. 7(1), SI 2001 No. 1090.

[100] Sec. 10 LLPA; HM Revenue and Customs, ITTOIA05/S863.

[101] Limited Liability Partnerships (Accounts and Audit) (Application of Companies Act 2006) Regulations 2008, SI 2008 No. 1911.

[102] Sec. 6(4) LLPA.   [103] Sec. 7(2), SI 2001 No. 1090.

[104] Sec. 7(8)–(10), SI 2001 No. 1090.

to contrary provision in the partnership agreement, no partner may assign his partnership share and no new partner may be introduced into the LLP without the unanimous approval of the other partners.[105] Any change in membership must be registered within fourteen days of its occurrence.[106]

3. Limited partnership The "limited partnership" (LP) is governed by the Limited Partnerships Act 1907 (LPA 1907). An overlapping structure of legislation in England resembles that used in German law: the rules on general partnerships apply to fill any gaps left by the specific law on LPs.[107] BERR proposed in 2008 to eliminate the LPA 1907 completely, and instead regulate LPs through special provisions inserted into the PA 1890, as well as to introduce a number of changes to the status of limited partners (resembling changes that have been adopted in the US).[108] The proposal was not accepted by the government.[109]

As under German law, an English LP consists of two classes of partners: general partners and limited partners. General partners are liable for the debts and obligations of the partnership without any limitation, and limited partners are not liable beyond the amount of a contribution stated in the partnership agreement.[110] As a result, the LP must also have at least two partners.[111] Corporate entities may serve as partners, both limited and general.[112] General partners manage the firm and have authority to bind it, whilst limited partners do not.[113] An LP is established through registration, and will be deemed a general partnership until such registration occurs.[114] Registration requires delivery of a statement containing particulars regarding the firm and its partners to the registrar of companies at the Companies Registration Office.[115] Registration is complete as soon as the statement has reached the registrar. Each limited partner must be described in the registration,[116] and her potential liability is limited to the

---

[105] Sec. 7(5), SI 2001 No. 1090.
[106] Sec. 9(1) LLPA; and Morse (2006: 303).
[107] Sec. 7 LPA 1907 and § 161 III HGB.
[108] Department for Business, Innovation and Skills (BIS) (2008).
[109] Department for Business, Innovation and Skills (BIS) (2009).
[110] Sec. 4(2) LPA 1907.   [111] Banks (2002: 848).
[112] Sec. 4(4) LPA 1907; and Banks (2002: 849).   [113] Sec. 6(1) LPA 1907.
[114] Sec. 5 LPA 1907. BERR is in the process of attempting to clarify this. See Department for Business, Innovation and Skills (BIS) (2008; 2009) and www.berr.gov.uk, under "Reform of Limited Partnership Law."
[115] Sec. 8 LPA 1907.   [116] Sec. 8(f) LPA 1907.

amount of her contribution to the firm, which must be made in cash or property, i.e. not a promise to render services.[117]

Although they may not draw down their capital contribution to the firm,[118] limited partners can and normally do receive a share of the profits. The provisions on distribution of profits and losses in the LPA refer to the PA 1890, which, as discussed above, provides a default position of equal shares of profits and losses for all partners.[119] A limited partner may be expressly authorized to act on behalf of the firm,[120] but, if the partner acts in such a way constituting "taking part in management," this would trigger treatment as a general partner and unlimited liability.[121] Limited partners in all cases have a statutory right to inspect the partnership books as well as examine the state and prospects of the business and advise the general partners on those matters.[122] The consent of the limited partners is needed for any change to the nature of the business or the partnership agreement,[123] but limited partners have no say on the admission of new partners to the firm.[124]

Limited partners may assign their shares with the consent of the general partners.[125] The assignee becomes a limited partner with all the rights of the assignor. The assignment must be registered and notice given in the *Official Gazette*. Until the assignment has been registered and published, the assignment is deemed to be of no effect.[126]

Table 2.2 presents the partnership forms available under UK law and some of their key characteristics.

C.   United States

1.   General partnership   In this text, we will often see the laws of Germany and the US at two opposite poles, with England located somewhere in the middle because England is a Common Law country whose law formed the basis for its former North American colony and the UK is also a member of the EU and must implement the same EU law as Germany. In the case of partnership law – which is not harmonized by EU directives except for the unpopular "European Economic Interest Grouping"[127]

---

[117] Sec. 4(2) LPA 1907.   [118] Sec. 4(3) LPA 1907.
[119] Sec. 7 LPA 1907 and sec. 24(1) PA 1890.
[120] Banks (2002: 861).
[121] Sec. 6(1) LPA 1907; see Banks (2002: 863 *et seq.*).
[122] Sec. 6(1) LPA 1907.
[123] Sec. 7 LPA 1907, in connection with secs. 19 and 24(8) PA 1890.
[124] Sec. 6(5)(d) LPA 1907.   [125] Sec. 6(5)(b) LPA 1907.
[126] Secs. 9(1)(d), 10 LPA 1907.

Table 2.2 *Partnership forms and characteristics, UK*

Name	Activity	Registration	Representation	Liability	Entity
Partnership	Business	No	All	Unlimited	No
Limited liability partnership	Business	Yes	All	Limited	Yes
Limited partnership	Business	Yes	General	Mixed	Yes

and which existed under Common Law long before being codified – the US appears to play the middle position. US partnership law is state law. Because the US law of partnerships evolved from Common Law, it closely tracks English law in its general structure. However, it was codified in 1914 in a piece of model legislation called the Uniform Partnership Act (UPA), as part of a codification movement that had existed since the seventeenth century and had been newly inspired by the Code Napoleon and the German Commercial and Civil Codes.[128] The UPA was drafted by the National Conference of Commissioners on Uniform State Law (NCCUSL), which still produces model legislation based on what it believes to be the best available doctrine and case law at the time of drafting. It proposes its model laws to the individual states for voluntary adoption as state legislation. The UPA was revised in 1992 and 1997. Here we will discuss the most recent revision, the 1997 RUPA (Revised UPA), which has been adopted in every US state except Louisiana.[129] Just like UK law, US law provides for partnerships, limited partnerships and limited liability partnerships.

The definition of a partnership in § 101(6) RUPA is almost identical to that found in the UK 1890 Act: "an association of two or more persons to carry on as co-owners a business for profit," and, as in the UK Act, "business" includes a profession.[130] As we see in the *Salmon* decision later in

[127] Council Regulation 2137/85 of 25 July 1985 on the European Economic Interest Grouping (EEIG), 1985 OJ L199/1.

[128] On the popularity of codes in the North American colonies and the US, see Friedman (2005: 50 *et seq.* and 302 *et seq.*).

[129] The NCCUSL keeps updated information on the latest texts and implementation of all of its uniform and model laws. See www.nccusl.org. It should be remembered, however, that adoption of a uniform act is not the same as implementation of a directive. The state is completely free to change and adapt the text of the act as it sees fit. It is expected that every state will have some (albeit small) deviations from the model text.

[130] § 101(1) RUPA.

this chapter, joint ventures have been classified as partnerships, and this is still the case. There is no requirement that the agreement to form a partnership be registered or even written, and it is not even necessary that the partners intend to form a "partnership," as long as they intend to associate to carry on a business for profit as co-owners.[131]

Unlike under English law, the US joins Germany in considering the partnership an entity distinct from its partners,[132] and this switch from the "aggregate" to the "entity" theory of partnership was introduced statutorily through the RUPA. Compare *Fairway Development*, in which a Common Law court throws up its hands and accepts the arbitrary injustice of a statute, with *ISM GmbH* v. *ARGE Wua*, in which a Civil Law court actively introduces the entity theory into German law because it serves justice to do so. Do these cases correspond to our traditional understanding of differences between Common Law and Civil Law? The RUPA expressly provides that "property acquired by a partnership is property of the partnership and not of the partners individually,"[133] which goes further than the position under German law. This still leaves unanswered the important question whether such property belongs to the partners as a collective, even if not individually. It is useful to note that, as long as the practical aspects of liability and claims to profits and payouts are separately regulated, the US scholarship pays less attention to the exact legal nature of the arrangement.[134]

Unless the partnership agreement provides otherwise, each partner has equal rights in the management and conduct of the partnership business,[135] and each partner is an agent of the partnership for the purpose of the partnership business.[136] Matters in the ordinary course of business of the partnership are decided by a majority of the partners, and both matters outside the ordinary course and amendments to the partnership agreement are decided only with the consent of all of the partners.[137] A partnership may file a statement with a central state office (usually called

---

[131] § 202 RUPA.   [132] § 201(a) RUPA.   [133] § 203 RUPA.

[134] Although it works in practice, this setup presents a conceptual problem. A partnership requires that the partners be "co-owners" (§ 202(a) RUPA), but the property belongs to the partnership entity, not the partners (§ 203 RUPA), yet the "entity" is not a "legal person" that the partners could co-own, as shareholders do a corporation. Thus, the mixture of *ad hoc* rules (e.g. unlimited liability and shared profits as in an aggregate) and conceptual, blanket solutions (the partnership is an entity, so it does not dissolve each time a change of partnership occurs) creates a legal gap. Perhaps it would be better just to follow the English rule, and add the *ad hoc* rule that the aggregate of partners does not dissolve each time a change of partnership occurs.

[135] § 401(f) RUPA.   [136] § 301(1) RUPA.   [137] § 401(j) RUPA.

"the secretary of state") expressing either a limitation on or confirmation of a given partner's authority.[138] A limitation that prevents a partner from transferring real property is effective against third parties if filed in the office where transfers of real property are registered,[139] but other limitations are not effective unless the third party has knowledge of them.[140]

As in Germany and the UK, partners have certain fiduciary duties, but the RUPA focuses them on the partnership itself rather than on the other partners. US law moves away from the broad duty presented in the classic case of *Meinhard* v. *Salmon*, and specifies the exact contents of the duty of loyalty. Partners must (i) hold partnership property, profits and benefits derived from the partnership as a trustee for the partnership; (ii) refrain from acting adversely to partnership interests; and (iii) refrain from competing with the partnership.[141] These duties may not be eliminated in the partnership agreement, although it may specify activities that will not be deemed to violate the duty of loyalty, provided they are not "manifestly unreasonable."[142] The RUPA also sets the "duty of care" for partners at the level of gross negligence and recklessness,[143] which the partnership agreement may adjust, but not "unreasonably reduce."[144]

Just as in German and UK law, partners are entitled to an equal share of the partnership profits and are chargeable with a corresponding share of the partnership losses.[145] They are also jointly and severally liable for the debts and obligations of the partnership.[146] However, a judgment against a US partnership may not be satisfied from a partner's assets unless there is also a judgment against the partnership,[147] and the RUPA allows only *secondary recourse* against the individual assets of a partner by requiring a judgment creditor to exhaust the partnership's assets before enforcing against the separate assets of a partner.[148] A partner who leaves a firm remains liable for obligations incurred before the exit for the duration of the statute of limitations of such obligations,[149] although the other partners may guarantee indemnification to smooth retirement.[150] In a gesture toward protecting third parties, the RUPA addresses the danger of a retired partner holding herself out and attempting to bind the partnership for a period of two years following retirement.[151] A third person is deemed to have notice that a partner has retired

---

[138] § 303(a) RUPA.   [139] § 303(d)(2) RUPA.   [140] § 303(f) RUPA.
[141] § 404(b) RUPA.   [142] § 103(b) RUPA.   [143] § 404(c) RUPA.
[144] § 103(b)(4) RUPA.
[145] § 401(b) RUPA. Again, the proportions of profit and loss sharing can be customized in the partnership agreement.
[146] § 306(a) RUPA.   [147] § 307(c) RUPA.   [148] § 307(d) RUPA.
[149] § 703(a) RUPA.   [150] § 701(d) RUPA.   [151] §§ 702(a), 703(b) RUPA.

ninety days after her statement of dissociation is filed with the secretary of state.[152] An incoming partner's joint and several liability does not include partnership obligations incurred before his admission.[153]

Without the consent of the other partners, a partner may only transfer his interest in the profits and losses of the partnership and the right to receive distributions.[154] The transferor retains the rights and duties of a partner other than the interest in distributions transferred, including joint and several liability for partnership debts.[155] A single partner may file to dissolve the partnership if the partnership was entered into for an undefined time (a partnership "at will"), unless the partnership agreement provides otherwise.[156] The primary reason for the RUPA "entity approach" was to prevent the changing of partners from affecting the existence of the partnership and its contractual relations, with the consequences that one sees in the *Fairway Development* case in this chapter. Under the entity introduced by the RUPA, a partnership may still be dissolved and wound up on the death or dissociation of a partner, but only if, within ninety days after the death or dissociation, a majority of the partners affirmatively vote for winding up.[157]

2. Limited liability partnership US law provides rules for limited liability partnerships (LLPs) within the legal framework for general partnerships established by RUPA. This is the model that BERR has proposed for regulation of limited partnerships in the UK. In the case of an LLP, regulation through special provisions of a general partnership law highlights a structure very similar to the latter, but with a liability-limiting function that applies to all partners, rather than just to "limited partners." A partnership can be transformed into an LLP by a partnership vote equivalent to that necessary to amend the partnership agreement, namely, unless the agreement provides otherwise, unanimity.[158] The transformation would then be completed by filing a statement of qualification with the secretary of state,[159] which provides information (name, address) on the partnership but not on the partners. Like a corporation, an LLP must indicate through an appropriate appellation that it is an LLP.[160] Under penalty of forfeiting its qualification as an LLP, the partnership must then file an annual report, updating the information in the original filing.[161]

---

[152] § 704(c) RUPA.   [153] § 306(b) RUPA.   [154] § 502 RUPA.
[155] § 503(d) RUPA.   [156] § 801(1) RUPA.   [157] § 801(2)(i) RUPA.
[158] § 1001(b) RUPA.   [159] § 1001(c) RUPA.   [160] § 1002 RUPA.
[161] § 1003 RUPA.

The limitation of liability resulting from LLP status arises from two basic rules. First, any obligation of a partnership incurred, whether arising in contract or in tort, is solely the obligation of the partnership.[162] Secondly, a partner remains liable for personal misconduct,[163] but retains a right to indemnification from the partnership.[164] As a result, if a given partner in an LLP commits a tort (such as legal malpractice) in the ordinary course of the LLP's business, she may be indemnified out of the LLP's assets, but then have to pay any remaining sum with her personal assets. The other partners have no liability to contribute their personal assets to satisfy the obligation.

3.   Limited partnership   The US followed the UK by drafting in 1916 express statutory rules for limited partnerships, but in the US this took the form of a model act drafted by the NCCUSL. Forty-nine US states have adopted the Revised Uniform Limited Partnerships Act (RULPA) and fifteen, including California, have adopted a 2001 revision of the RULPA referred to as "ULPA 2001."[165] The new Act is a "stand alone" law that copies certain provisions from the RUPA, but does not need to make cross-reference to it. Thus, unlike German and English law, US law for LPs does not use general partnership rules to fill gaps. This legislative scheme is diametrically opposed to the model recently proposed by BERR to revoke the LPA 1907 and incorporate new terms in the PA 1890. Under the ULPA 2001, the partnership agreement can freely alter most of the default terms given in the law, with the exception that it cannot remove fiduciary duties and protective rights, such as the right to receive information or bring suit.[166] An LP may be formed for "any lawful purpose," and is not limited to business use.[167]

The ULPA 2001 defines a limited partnership as "an entity, having one or more general partners and one or more limited partners ... formed under this Act."[168] Both types of partners may be physical persons or legal persons, including corporations, joint ventures, government subdivisions and trusts."[169] The ULPA 2001 expressly provides that the same person may be both a general and a limited partner.[170] An LP is formed by filing a certificate of limited partnership with the secretary of state.[171] As the

---

[162] §§ 305(a), 306(c) RUPA.   [163] § 306(a) RUPA.
[164] § 401(c) RUPA.   [165] See www.nccusl.org.
[166] § 110(b) ULPA 2001.   [167] § 104(b) ULPA 2001.
[168] § 102(11) ULPA 2001.   [169] §§ 102(8), (10), (14) ULPA 2001.
[170] § 113 ULPA 2001.   [171] § 201(a) ULPA 2001.

certificate need not provide details regarding limited partners and their contributions, the filing is less detailed than that required for a limited partnership under either German or English law.

Like the rules in our other two jurisdictions, a general partner participates in the management of the LP,[172] is an agent of the LP,[173] is jointly and severally liable for the LP's obligations,[174] and owes duties of care and loyalty to the partnership comparable to that of a partner in a general partnership.[175] A limited partner has no power to represent or bind the LP,[176] and the law expressly declares that an "obligation of a limited partnership, whether arising in contract, tort, or otherwise, is not the obligation of a limited partner."[177] Previous US law, like current English law, provided that, if a limited partner took part in the management or control of the LP, she would lose the shield of limited liability. The ULPA 2001 reverses this by providing a limit of liability "even if the limited partner participates in the management and control of the limited partnership."[178] In all cases, a limited partner may for "purposes reasonably related to his interest as a limited partner" obtain and copy "full information regarding the state of the activities and financial condition" and "other information regarding the activities" of the LP.[179] Subject to the partnership agreement, distributions are allocated to all partners in proportion to the value of their respective contribution.[180] The ULPA 2001 does not provide default rules on the allocation of losses.[181]

Although limited partnership shares are often traded in securities markets,[182] such transferability would be provided for in the partnership agreement, as under the ULPA 2001 limited partners have no right to dissociate from the LP,[183] although they do have a right freely to transfer their rights to receive distributions.[184] Of course, a limited partner entering an LP would not be liable for any debts of the LP either before or after the entrance, except the price of the partner's contribution. A general partner who enters an LP is liable only for obligations arising after his entrance

---

[172] § 406(a) ULPA 2001.   [173] § 402(a) ULPA 2001.
[174] § 404(a) ULPA 2001.   [175] § 408 ULPA 2001.
[176] § 302 ULPA 2001.   [177] § 303 ULPA 2001.
[178] § 303 ULPA 2001.   [179] § 304(b) ULPA 2001.
[180] § 503 ULPA 2001.
[181] The Official Comment to § 503 ULPA 2001 states: "Nearly all limited partnerships will choose to allocate profits and losses in order to comply with applicable tax, accounting and other regulatory requirements. Those requirements, rather than this Act, are the proper source of guidance for that profit and loss allocation."
[182] Slater (1984).   [183] § 601(a) ULPA 2001.
[184] § 701 ULPA 2001.

into the LP.[185] A general partner may exit the LP as provided for in the partnership agreement or for one of the reasons listed in ULPA 2001, which include after providing due notice and expulsion by unanimous consent of the other partners.[186] An exiting general partner is liable for obligations incurred before her dissociation up to the statute of limitations of such obligations.[187]

4. Limited liability company   As we will turn to the stock corporation in the next chapter, and dwell there for the remainder of this text, it will be useful here to consider another, hybrid business form, which supplies a clean link between partnership and corporation. In 1977, the previously (in this context) insignificant state of Wyoming entered the market of regulatory competition by launching America's first limited liability company (LLC). This form combines limited liability, pass-through taxation and the possibility of central management. Following US Internal Revenue Service approval of the LLC for pass-through taxation, many more of the fifty US states adopted LLC statutes, and the NCCUSL then drafted a uniform act. Section 201 of the Revised Uniform Limited Liability Company Act (RULLCA) provides that, like a corporation, an LLC is a "legal entity distinct from its members." Like a corporation, an LLC is established by the LLC's members drafting and approving a "certificate of organization" and by the secretary of state filing (i.e. registering) such articles.[188] Members have no inherent authority to manage the LLC, and thus, if any member is to have authority to represent the LLC, she must have a power of attorney.[189] Pursuant to § 301.7701–1 *et seq.* of the US Internal Revenue Code, an LLC may choose to be taxed as a partnership, thus avoiding a second tax on distributions to members. The LLC presents a good example of how the essential characteristics of partnerships and corporations can be mixed to create hybrid entities designed to meet investors' needs.

Table 2.3 summarizes the main features of the partnership forms discussed above.

---

[185] § 404(b) ULPA 2001.   [186] § 603 ULPA 2001.
[187] § 605(b) ULPA 2001.   [188] § 201 RULLCA.
[189] § 301 RULLCA. This moves beyond the two options of "member-managed" (like a partnership) or "manager-managed" (like a corporation) that first-generation LLC statutes commonly offered.

Table 2.3 *Partnership forms and characteristics, US*

Name	Activity	Registration	Representation	Liability	Entity
Partnership	Business	No	All	Unlimited	Yes
Limited liability partnership	Open	Yes	All	Limited	Yes
Limited partnership	Any	Yes	General partner	Mixed	Yes
Limited liability company	Any	Yes	Possible	No	Yes

III.   *The basic characteristics of partnerships*

Partnerships, like corporations, are vehicles for individuals to associate with each other to pursue a common business purpose. We have seen that certain types of partnerships – especially those with limitations on liability and a distinct class of managing members – have corporate characteristics. This section sums up the general characteristics of a general partnership in order to present a clear foil to the corporate model that will be studied in depth in this text.

A.   Informal establishment

Although partnerships are established by agreement, they require neither a written deed nor a public registration to come into existence. This is why in some jurisdictions, when entrepreneurs hope to establish a type of entity that requires registration, and fail to meet the requirements, they might be found to operate *de facto* as a partnership. Registration is in part a state-sponsored form of publication; without having notice of limited liability, it would be unfair to subject third parties to such limit when dealing with entrepreneurs. Informal establishment accelerates venture taking, but can increase transaction costs. What is the correct balance?

B.   Management and capital tied to partners

The partners actively control the partnership. Subject to the partnership agreement, they have the power to manage and to represent the firm in dealings with third parties. It also appears arguable that, even if the partnership assets are ascribed to the firm as an entity, they could still – as between the firm and the partners themselves – be considered to be co-owned by these partners because the "entity" is nothing more than the group of partners at any given time, and does not fully constitute a legal person. Partnership creditors may take recourse against both partnership assets and the personal assets of the partners to satisfy their claims, and, while this added source of financial backing increases the credit standing of the firm, it also means that the acts of a partner significantly affect all co-partners, and thus the entrance or exit of a partner has a substantial impact on the partnership.

C.   Duties of partners to each other

As the partners are co-owners and co-obligors, they can significantly affect the assets of their fellow partners, and thus it is necessary that they have a duty of utmost good faith and loyalty to the partnership and to each other. No reasonable person would place his fate in the hands of another without at least such a duty as protection. Moreover, partnership agreements are usually entered into as a long-term relationship, and the duty of loyalty serves as a basis for addressing conflicts that cannot be foreseen when drafting the partnership agreement. The duty of loyalty is the safeguard that everyone would ask for prior to joining one's interests with those of others in a partnership.

D.   Restrictions on the transfer of partnership shares

As noted above, the exit or entrance of a partner has a significant impact on a partnership. This explains why they are not freely transferable. We have seen that the attempt to transfer a partnership share may result in a transfer of only the financial rights of such share, or require approval through a majority or unanimous decision of the continuing partners, or even lead to the dissolution of the partnership. When the management rights and personal liability tied to such shares are removed, as in the case of a limited partner's share, its transferability is be substantially facilitated.

Questions for discussion

1. What are the sources of partnership law in Germany, the United Kingdom and the United States?
2. How are ownership and control allocated in a partnership?
3. Who is liable for partnership liabilities?
4. Why do some partnerships require registration to be formed?
5. Is a partnership an entity or merely an aggregate of the partners' property?

6. What kinds of rights and duties do partners owe each other?
7. What issues arise if partners can freely transfer their shares in the partnership?
8. What are the advantages of a limited partnership?
9. Why have limited liability partnerships been created?
10. If a corporation has five essential characteristics, what are those of the partnership?

Cases

Fairway Development Co. v. Title Insurance Company of Minnesota
US District Court, ND Ohio, Eastern Division
621 F Supp 120 (1985)

DOWD, District Judge

... Plaintiff [Fairway Development Co.] filed this action against the defendant [Title Insurance Company of Minnesota] alleging breach of contract under a title guarantee insurance policy. Plaintiff avers that under that policy, "defendant agreed to insure plaintiff against any loss sustained by it by reason of any defects, liens or encumbrances in the title of the insured to [the real property in question]." Plaintiff avers that defendant failed to reference on the exception sheet to the title policy issued by the defendant an easement granted in favor of The East Ohio Gas Company for the purpose of maintaining a gas line over the property in question. Plaintiff claims that the easement "is a defect and encumbrance in plaintiff's title to the Property." Plaintiff avers that it gave notice to the defendant of the existence of the defect and encumbrance in the title to the property, and made a demand upon the defendant for payment of damages which it sustained as a result thereof ...

Defendant has filed an answer in response to plaintiff's complaint, admitting that it issued the title guarantee in question and that it received a letter from plaintiff's counsel regarding the alleged existence of a high pressure East Ohio gas line. Defendant denies the remainder of plaintiff's allegations ...

[Text omitted]

Defendant seeks summary judgment on plaintiff's complaint on two grounds. First, defendant asserts that it is liable under the title guaranty policy in question only to the named party guaranteed. Defendant asserts that it originally guaranteed a general partnership, which it refers to as Fairway Development I, consisting of three partners: Thomas M. Bernabei, James V. Serra, Jr., and Howard J. Wenger ... Defendant argues that Fairway Development I commenced on October 15, 1979 and terminated on May 20, 1981, when two partners in Fairway Development I, Bernabei and Serra, sold and transferred their respective undivided one-third interests in the partnership to the remaining partner, Wenger, and a third-party purchaser, James E. Valentine. Defendant argues that a new partnership resulted from this sale, called Fairway Development II. Defendant concludes that it cannot be held liable to the plaintiff since it is not in privity with the plaintiff as the named party guaranteed. Defendant argues that the named party guaranteed was Fairway Development I, a partnership which dissolved in 1981 upon formation of Fairway Development II, and that its liability does not extend to Fairway Development II.

[Text omitted]

In response to defendant's argument that the plaintiff is not the party guaranteed under the title guaranty issued by the defendant, the plaintiff argues that under Ohio Rev. Code § 1775.26(A), the transfer of Bernabei and Serra of their partnership interests was not in itself sufficient to dissolve the partnership. Plaintiff states that in the instant case, the facts are clear that there was an intent between the partners of what defendant calls Fairway Development I and II to continue the operation of the Fairway Development Company … without dissolving the partnership …

Discussion and law

It is a fundamental principle of law that any change in the personnel of a partnership will result in its dissolution … The Court must thus determine whether the general rule has been modified by statute.

The resolution of this case is governed by the law of the forum state, Ohio. Ohio has adopted the Uniform Partnership Law, modeled after the Uniform Partnership Act enacted by the National Conference of Commissioners on Uniform State Laws in 1914. Ohio follows the Common Law aggregate theory of partnership, under which a partnership is regarded as the sum of the persons who comprise the partnership, versus the legal entity theory of partnership, under which the corporation, like a partnership, is regarded as an entity in itself … Three sections of the Ohio Uniform Partnership Law are particularly applicable to this case, and are set out in relevant part, as follows:

§ 1775.26 Effect of conveyance of interest of a partner

(A) A conveyance by a partner of his interest in the partnership does not of itself dissolve the partnership, nor, as against the other partners in the absence of agreement, entitle the assignee, during the continuance of the partnership, to interfere in the management or administration of the partnership business or affairs …

§ 1777.03 New certificate on change in membership

On every change of the members of a partnership transacting business in this state under a fictitious name or under a designation that does not show the names of the persons interested as partners in the business … a new certificate shall be filed for record with the county recorder …

§ 1775.28 Dissolution distinguished from winding up of affairs

The dissolution of a partnership is the change in the relation of the partners caused by any partner's ceasing to be associated in the carrying on as distinguished from the winding up of the business.

... The Court's review of the applicable statutory law supports a finding that the Common Law rule that "a dissolution occurs and a new partnership is formed whenever a partner retires or a new partner is admitted" ... survives the enactment of the Ohio Uniform Partnership Law.

[*Text omitted*]

The terms of Ohio Rev. Code § 1775.26 permit a partner to assign his interest to another and allow the assignee to receive the assigning partner's interest in the partnership upon dissolution, but limit the assignee from taking part in the management of partnership affairs. However, under Ohio Rev. Code § 1775.23, a partner's property rights consist of "his rights in specific partnership property, his interest in the partnership, and his right to participate in the management." A "partner's interest" is defined in Ohio Rev. Code § 1775.25 as "his share of the profits and surplus, and the same is personal property." A partner's interest is thus a subset of a partner's entire partnership rights.

[*Text omitted*]

Ohio Rev. Code § 1775.26 is thus not dispositive of the instant case where not one but two partners have transferred not just their interest in the partnership, i.e. their respective shares of profits and surplus, but their entire respective bundles of partnership rights ... The Court's conclusion accords with the aggregate theory of partnership, which, applied to this case, recognizes Fairway Development I not as an entity in itself, but as a partnership made up of three members, Bernabei, Serra, and Wenger. That partnership ceased when the membership of the partnership changed.

[*Text omitted*]

The Court finds that the law as applicable to the facts of this case supports a finding that the named party guaranteed in the contract in question is not the plaintiff, and that the plaintiff is a new partnership which followed the termination of Fairway Development I ...

[*Text omitted*]

ISM GmbH, Plaintiff v. ARGE Wua
High Federal Court, Second Civil Division
BGHZ 146, 341 (2001)
[*Unofficial, partial translation of official opinion text*]

Official head note

a) A civil law partnership that engages in outward dealings with third parties ((*Außen-*)*Gesellschaft*) has legal capacity to the extent that it engages in such dealings to establish rights and duties in its own name.

b) To this extent, such a partnership also has the capacity to sue and be sued in civil litigation.

c) As far as a partner of a civil law partnership is personally liable for the obligations of the partnership, the relationship between the obligations of the partnership and the liability of the partner corresponds to the relationship of secondary liability (*Akzessorietät*) found in a commercial partnership (*Offene Handelsgesellschaft*). This further develops the holding in BGHZ 142, 315.

Facts

The Plaintiff sues in proceedings on a bill of exchange for payment of the face amount of DM 90,000.00 plus additional charges against Defendant 1 [hereinafter, the "Partnership"], a labor syndicate (*Arbeitsgemeinschaft* – ARGE) active in the construction industry and organized in the legal form of a general partnership (*Gesellschaft bürgerlichen Rechts*), as acceptor of the bill, and Defendants 2 and 3, as partners. The Plaintiff bases its claim for liability on the bill of exchange against Defendant 4 on a theory that he held himself out to be party to the bill of exchange. The Regional Court condemned the Defendants to joint and several liability for full payment as requested in the Complaint. The Regional Court of Appeals dismissed the claims against the Partnership and Defendant 4 on their appeals. In the appeal to this Court, the Plaintiff seeks to have the judgments against such Defendants reinstated.

Discussion

A.

The Court of Appeals found the claim against the Partnership inadmissible because this Defendant is a civil law partnership without capacity to act as a party in court. That finding must be reversed in this appeal. In light of the cases decided to date, the Civil Division finds it advisable to treat a civil law partnership that engages in outward dealings with third parties ((*Außen-)Gesellschaft*) as having legal capacity to sue and be sued (§ 50 ZPO) to the extent that it may enter into commercial dealings in its own name and contract rights and duties.

    I. Pursuant to the more recent decisions of the Federal High Court, a civil law partnership may – as the joint ownership community of the partners – generally assume every legal position in dealings with third parties unless special considerations speak to the contrary (BGHZ 116, 86, 88; 136, 254, 257; this principle was expressed earlier in BGHZ 79, 374, 378 *et seq.*). To the extent that the partnership establishes its own rights and duties in this context, it has legal capacity (without constituting a legal entity) (see § 14(2) BGB).

    1. The law does not offer comprehensive and conclusive rules regarding the legal nature of the civil law partnership. In the first draft of the German Civil Code (*Bürgerliches Gesetzbuch* – BGB), this partnership was modeled after Roman law as an exclusively contractual relationship among the partners, and could not own assets separate from those of its partners (see Mot. II 591 = Mugdan II 330). The Second Commission changed this and constituted partnership assets as a joint

ownership community (see the current version of §§ 718, 719 BGB) without, however, regulating the specifics that arise in connection with this principle of joint ownership. Rather, the partnership relationships remained essentially contractual relationships, over which joint ownership was "tossed" in an incomplete gesture (Flume, General Part of the Civil Code, vol. I/1 1977, pp. 3 *et seq.*; also see Ulmer, FS Robert Fischer 1979, S. 785, 788 *et seq.*). With regard to the meaning of the joint ownership principle, the legislative history only states that opinions "diverged on the theoretical meaning of the joint ownership community of rights and what should be understood as its characteristic qualities" (Prot. II 429 = Mugdan II 990). "The Commission believed that it did not have to take a position in the scholarly debate regarding the essence of joint property, but only to decide which provisions presented actual advantages" (Prot. II 430 = Mugdan II 990).

2. The incompleteness of the law's wording and the discernable attempt by the turn of the century legislator to avoid a concrete commitment leave room for a decision on the legal nature of the civil law partnership that is oriented to the practical needs of applying the principle of joint ownership. Such a practical orientation favours the conception of the civil law partnership as having limited legal capacity in dealings with third parties. This conception finds its roots in the nineteenth-century German scholarship on joint ownership (see Otto Gierke, German Private Law, vol. 1 1895, pp. 663 *et seq.*, 682). This conception was introduced into modern discussion primarily by Flume (see supra at 50 *et seq.*; ZHR 136 [1972], 177 *et seq.*) and has been widely accepted in the newer literature (see above all the Munich Commentary to the Civil Code/Ulmer, 3rd ed. § 705 no. 130 *et seq.* with further references in footnote 373; the same author in AcP 198 [1998], 113 *et seq.*; likewise K. Schmidt, *Gesellschaftsrecht* 3rd ed. § 8 III, pp. 203 *et seq.*; Wiedemann, WM 1994 Sonderbeilage 4, pp. 6 *et seq.*; Huber, FS Lutter 2000, 107, 122 *et seq.*; Hüffer, Gesellschaftsrecht 5th ed. pp. 47 *et seq.*; Dauner-Lieb, Die BGB-Gesellschaft im System der Personengesellschaften, in: Die Reform des Handelsstandes und der Personengesellschaften [Schriftenreihe der Bayer-Stiftung für deutsches und internationales Arbeits- und Wirtschaftsrecht] 1999, pp. 95, 99 *et seq.*; Reiff, ZIP 1999, 517, 518; Mülbert, AcP 1999, pp. 39, 43 *et seq.*; Wertenbruch, *Die Haftung von Gesellschaften und Gesellschaftsanteilen in der Zwangsvollstreckung* 2000, pp. 211 *et seq.*).

a) This understanding of the legal nature of the joint ownership community under company law offers a practical and largely consistent model for the law's attempt to separate company assets from personal assets (§§ 718–720 BGB). When compared to this understanding, the "traditional view" that understood the individual partners as the exclusive subjects to which the rights and duties concerning the partnership could be attributed (see Zöllner, FS Gernhuber 1993, pp. 563 *et seq.*; the same author, in FS Kraft 1998, pp. 701 *et seq.*; Hueck, FS Zöllner 1998, pp. 275 *et seq.*) displays conceptual weaknesses. If the obligations of the partnership are viewed solely as the common obligations of the partners pursuant to § 427 BGB, the principle of joint ownership is contradicted. Pursuant to § 719 BGB, an individual partner cannot alone pay out as joint obligor an asset that is part of the partnership assets. This fact forces even the defenders of the traditional view to differentiate between obligations of the partnership and obligations of the partners. Obligations incurred for the "partnership" are thus "unitary obligations with dual effects" referring to the assets in joint ownership, on the one hand, and to the personal assets of the partners on the other (see Hueck, FS Zöllner, p. 293; Zöllner, FS Gernhuber, p. 573). However, this blurs the boundary between obligation and liability, for an obligation must always refer to a subject, not to the assets in an estate (Aderhold, The Obligation Model of the Civil Law Partnership 1981, pp. 110 *et seq.*; Dauner-Lieb cited supra, at 100 *et seq.*).

b) An important practical advantage that results from a civil law partnership having an enduring legal capacity in dealings with third parties, as described above, is that a change of partners will not affect the continued existence of contracts with the partnership (see Senat, BGHZ 79, 374, 378 *et seq.*). Strict application of the traditional view required that contracts with the "partnership" be newly concluded or confirmed each time there was a change of partners. If the partnership only presented an obligatory relationship to third parties, the obligations existing with two different sets of partners would not be identical. However, there is no logical reason why continuing contracts should be newly concluded upon every change of partners; this would significantly impair the ability of the partnership to take part in commercial dealings. The traditional view also fails to provide a satisfactory explanation for why the partnership assets contributed by a new partner must be used to answer for pre-existing debts of the partnership. The usual explanation is that every new partner enters through a type of universal succession "into all existing legal and contractual relationships" (Zöllner, FS Kraft, p. 715); this is fundamentally inconsistent with the view of the partnership as a purely contractual relationship among the partners (on this point also see Ulmer, AcP 198 [1998], 113, 142).

c) The conception of the partnership presented in this opinion also more readily accounts for a civil law partnership's retention of legal identity when it is transformed into or out of another organizational form. If a civil law partnership operates a business, it will – by operation of law and without any formal notice – transform into an entity identical to a commercial partnership (offene Handelsgesellschaft – OHG) in structure and partnership attributes the moment it begins to need a business operation whose type and size is that normally used by a merchant (§ 105(1) in connection with § 1 HGB). Since the OHG as referred to above has the legal capacity to acquire rights (see § 124(1) HGB), a consistent application of the traditional view would mean that the property rights in the assets belonging to the partnership estate would have to change upon transformation into an OHG. This would create difficult problems in practice (see Reiff, ZIP 1999, 517, 518 *et seq.*) because the exact point in time at which the need (for a "business operation whose type and size" is that of a merchant) appears in the civil law partnership, triggering its transformation into an OHG, is almost impossible to discern. Another problem arises in connection with the new law on organizational transformations (§§ 190 *et seq.*, 226 *et seq.* Transformation Act / Umwandlungsgesetz – UmwG), which allows corporations to transform into partnerships, including civil law partnerships, while preserving their identity (see § 191(2)(1) UmwG). Such transformations can be understood easily under the view presented in this opinion, but if the traditional view allows such explanation at all, it does so only with difficulty (on this point, see Wiedemann, ZGR 1996, 286, 289 *et seq.*; Mülbert, AcP 199 [1999], 38, 60 *et seq.*; Timm, NJW 1995, 3209 *et seq.*; Hueck, FS Zöllner, p. 280 *et seq.*; Zöllner, FS Claussen 1997, 423, 429 ff.).

d) Finally, the assumption that a civil law partnership has legal capacity is also supported by the fact that the legislator has recently given such partnerships the capacity to enter bankruptcy (§ 11(2)(1) Insolvency Code / *Insolvenzordnung* – "InsO" and also § 1(1) GesO) and to be the legal owner of the bankruptcy estate.

3. The letter of the law, in particular the wording of § 714 BGB, offers no argument against the view here adopted. It is true that the provision of a power to represent the partners, but not the "partnership," does indicate that when this provision was written, there was no self-evident understanding that the civil law partnership was an entity capable of incurring obligations (Senat, BGHZ 142, 315, 319 f.). However, when we understand that this provision was essentially carried unchanged into the BGB from § 640(1) of the first draft, and that such first draft (printed in Mugdan II CVI) did not yet recognize the joint ownership principle, the wording of the provision adds nothing to an understanding of the legal nature of the civil law partnership. This Court thus need not decide whether the legislator at the turn of the century viewed the nineteenth-century German scholarship on joint ownership as implicitly attributing legal capacity to the civil law partnership (see Wertenbruch, cited supra, at 34 *et seq.*). What is important is that there was no intention to exclude such view.

4. The recognition of the partnership's legal capacity is not contradicted by §§ 21, 22 and 54 BGB, in which legal capacity apparently means the capability of the entity to hold rights and incur obligations because of its own legal personality and thus "for itself," rather than for the aggregate of its joint owner partners. As is shown in § 14(2) BGB, the law assumes that partnerships may also have legal capacity. For example, it is practically beyond argument that commercial partnerships (OHGs) and limited partnerships (*Kommanditgesellschaften* – KGs) can hold rights and incur obligations, and thus – albeit joint ownership communities – posses legal capacity without taking on the status of a legal person. Such understanding has been consistently supported by our decisions (BGHZ 80, 129, 132; 117, 323, 326) regarding the pre-incorporation entities of corporations.

II. If the capacity of civil law partnerships to hold rights and incur obligations is recognized, its capacity to sue and be sued in civil litigation pursuant to § 50 ZPO, which is equivalent to legal capacity, cannot be denied.

[Text omitted]

B.

The claim against the Partnership may be admitted. In particular, the Partnership is capable of being the originator of a bill of exchange. The reasons that the High Federal Court has given for the capacity of a civil law partnership to originate cheques (BGHZ 136, 254, 257 *et seq.*) have the same weight in supporting its capacity to originate a bill of exchange (also see Flume, General Part, cited supra, pp. 108 *et seq.*; Baumbach/Hefermehl, Wechselgesetz und Scheckgesetz, 21st ed. Einl. WG no. 20a).

On this point, the decision of the Regional Court was correct with regard to its judgment against the Partnership and Defendants 2 and 3. However, a reading of that opinion reveals that true joint liability did not exist between the claims against the Partnership, on the one hand, and those against Defendants 2 and 3 on the other, even though the Partnership stands jointly liable with its partners (who are all jointly and severally liable among themselves). In our opinion of September 27, 1999 (BGHZ 142, 315, 318 *et seq.*), we left the question of the legal ranking of liability among partners open. At this time, as a consequence of the recognition that civil law partnerships have limited legal capacity, we find that a partner is secondarily (*akzessorisch*) liable for the obligations of the partnership. As far as a partner has such personal liability for the obligations of the partnership (BGHZ 142, 315, 318), the relevant amount of the partnership's debt thus also determines the measure of this personal liability. In this respect, the relationship between the liability of the partnership and the partners thus corresponds to the legal treatment of secondary (*akzessorisch*) liability in a commercial partnership (OHG) pursuant to §§ 128 *et seq.* HGB. Here, it is not possible to directly apply §§ 420 *et seq.* BGB because no true joint and several liability exists; we must however examine whether an analysis of the various interests of the parties concerned could lead to the direct application of §§ 420 *et seq.* BGB in individual cases (BGHZ 39, 319, 329; 44, 229, 233; 47, 376, 378 *et seq.*; 104, 76, 78). It would generally be fitting for the partnership – as the bearer of primary liability – to employ the rules for joint and several liability mutatis mutandis against the partners. If, for example, the partners had individual defenses within the meaning of § 425 BGB claims on their personal liability, it would be unfair if they were able to raise such defenses also against the partnership.

C.

… Defendant 4 could be held liable on the Partnership's bill of exchange under the theory that he held himself out as a partner only if he reasonably gave the Plaintiff the impression that he was himself a partner of the ARGE and thus a personally liable partner (see BGHZ 17, 13, 15) … In particular, it was not sufficient grounds for such a conclusion that Defendant 4 appeared [as construction foreman] on the letterhead used by the ARGE in its relations with the Plaintiff, who worked as a sub-contractor for the ARGE.

Meinhard v. Salmon et al.
Court of Appeals of New York
164 NE 545 (1928)

CARDOZO, CJ

On April 10, 1902, Louisa M. Gerry leased to the defendant Walter J. Salmon the premises known as the Hotel Bristol at the northwest corner of Forty-Second street and Fifth avenue in the city of New York. The lease was for a term of 20 years, commencing May 1, 1902, and ending April 30, 1922. The lessee undertook to change the hotel building for use as shops and offices at a cost of $200,000. Alterations and additions were to be accretions to the land.

Salmon, while in course of treaty with the lessor as to the execution of the lease, was in course of treaty with Meinhard, the plaintiff, for the necessary funds. The result was a joint venture with terms embodied in a writing. Meinhard was to pay to Salmon half of the moneys requisite to reconstruct, alter, manage, and operate the property. Salmon was to pay to Meinhard 40 percent of the net profits for the first five years of the lease and 50 percent for the years thereafter. If there were losses, each party was to bear them equally. Salmon, however, was to have sole power to 'manage, lease, underlet and operate' the building. There were to be certain pre-emption rights for each in the contingency of death.

They were coadventures, subject to fiduciary duties akin to those of partners … As to this we are all agreed. The heavier weight of duty rested, however, upon Salmon. He was a coadventurer with Meinhard, but he was manager as well. During the early years of the enterprise, the building, reconstructed, was operated at a loss. If the relation had then ended, Meinhard as well as Salmon would have carried a heavy burden. Later the profits became large with the result that for each of the investors there came a rich return. For each the venture had its phases of fair weather and of foul. The two were in it jointly, for better or for worse.

When the lease was near its end, Elbridge T. Gerry had become the owner of the reversion. He owned much other property in the neighborhood, one lot adjoining the Bristol building on Fifth avenue and four lots on Forty-Second street. He had a plan to lease the entire tract for a long term to some one who would destroy the buildings then existing and put up another in their place … Then, in January, 1922, with less than four months of the lease to run, he approached the defendant Salmon. The result was a new lease to the Midpoint Realty Company, which is owned and controlled by Salmon, a lease covering the whole tract, and involving a huge outlay. The term is to be 20 years, but successive covenants for renewal will extend it to a maximum of 80 years at the will of either party. The existing buildings may remain unchanged for seven years. They are then to be torn down, and a new building to cost $3,000,000 is to be placed upon the site. The rental, which under the Bristol lease was only $55,000, is to be from $350,000 to $475,000 for the properties so combined. Salmon personally guaranteed the performance by the lessee of the covenants of the new lease until such time as the new building had been completed and fully paid for.

The lease between Gerry and the Midpoint Realty Company was signed and delivered on January 25, 1922. Salmon had not told Meinhard anything about it. Whatever his motive may have been, he had kept the negotiations to himself. Meinhard was not informed even of the bare existence of a project. The first that he knew of it was in February, when the lease was an accomplished fact. He then made demand on the defendants that the lease be held in trust as an asset of the venture, making offer upon the trial to share the personal obligations incidental to the guaranty. The demand was followed by refusal, and later by this suit. A referee gave judgment for the plaintiff, limiting the plaintiff's interest in the lease, however, to 25 percent. The limitation was on the theory that the plaintiff's equity was to be restricted to one-half of so much of the value of the lease as was contributed or represented by the occupation of the Bristol site. Upon cross-appeals to the Appellate Division, the judgment was modified so as to enlarge the equitable interest to one-half of the whole lease. With this enlargement of plaintiff's interest, there went, of course, a corresponding enlargement of his attendant obligations. The case is now here on an appeal by the defendants.

Joint adventurers, like copartners, owe to one another, while the enterprise continues, the duty of the finest loyalty. Many forms of conduct permissible in a workaday world for those acting at arm's length, are forbidden to those bound by fiduciary ties. A trustee is held to something stricter than the morals of the market place. Not honesty alone, but the punctilio of an honor the most sensitive, is then the standard of behavior. As to this there has developed a tradition that is unbending and inveterate. Uncompromising rigidity has been the attitude of courts of equity when petitioned to undermine the rule of undivided loyalty by the 'disintegrating erosion' of particular exceptions ...

The owner of the reversion, Mr. Gerry, had ... turned to the defendant Salmon in possession of the Bristol, the keystone of the project ... To the eye of an observer, Salmon held the lease as owner in his own right, for himself and no one else. In fact he held it as a fiduciary, for himself and another, sharers in a common venture ... The pre-emption privilege, or, better, the pre-emption opportunity, that was thus an incident of the enterprise, Salmon appropriate [sic] to himself in secrecy and silence ... The trouble about his conduct is that he excluded his coadventurer from any chance to compete, from any chance to enjoy the opportunity for benefit that had come to him alone by virtue of his agency. This chance, if nothing more, he was under a duty to concede. The price of its denial is an extension of the trust at the option and for the benefit of the one whom he excluded.

No answer is it to say that the chance would have been of little value even if seasonably offered. Such a calculus of probabilities is beyond the science of the chancery. Salmon, the real estate operator, might have been preferred to Meinhard, the woolen merchant. On the other hand, Meinhard might have offered better terms, or reinforced his offer by alliance with the wealth of others ... The very fact that

Salmon was in control with exclusive powers of direction charged him the more obviously with the duty of disclosure, since only through disclosure could opportunity be equalized ... He might steal a march on his comrade under cover of the darkness, and then hold the captured ground. Loyalty and comradeship are not so easily abjured.

Little profit will come from a dissection of the precedents. None precisely similar is cited in the briefs of counsel. What is similar in many, or so it seems to us, is the animating principle. Authority is, of course, abundant that one partner may not appropriate to his own use a renewal of a lease, though its term is to begin at the expiration of the partnership ... The lease at hand with its many changes is not strictly a renewal. Even so, the standard of loyalty for those in trust relations is without the fixed divisions of a graduated scale.

[Text omitted]

Equity refuses to confine within the bounds of classified transactions its precept of a loyalty that is undivided and unselfish. Certain at least it is that a 'man obtaining his *locus standi*, and his opportunity for making such arrangements, by the position he occupies as a partner, is bound by his obligation to his copartners in such dealings not to separate his interest from theirs, but, if he acquires any benefit, to communicate it to them.' ... Certain it is also that there may be no abuse of special opportunities growing out of a special trust as manager or agent ...

[Text omitted]

We have no thought to hold that Salmon was guilty of a conscious purpose to defraud. Very likely he assumed in all good faith that with the approaching end of the venture he might ignore his coadventurer and take the extension for himself. He had given to the enterprise time and labor as well as money. He had made it a success. Meinhard, who had given money, but neither time nor labor, had already been richly paid. There might seem to be something grasping in his insistence upon more ... A different question would be here if there were lacking any nexus of relation between the business conducted by the manager and the opportunity brought to him as an incident of management ... For this problem, as for most, there are distinctions of degree. If Salmon had received from Gerry a proposition to lease a building at a location far removed, he might have held for himself the privilege thus acquired, or so we shall assume. Here the subject-matter of the new lease was an extension and enlargement of the subject-matter of the old one. A managing coadventurer appropriating the benefit of such a lease without warning to his partner might fairly expect to be reproached with conduct that was underhand, or lacking, to say the least, in reasonable candor, if the partner were to surprise him in the act of signing the new instrument. Conduct subject to that reproach does not receive from equity a healing benediction.

A question remains as to the form and extent of the equitable interest to be allotted to the plaintiff. The trust as declared has been held to attach to the lease which was in the name of the defendant corporation. We think it ought to attach at the option of the defendant Salmon to the shares of stock which were owned by him or were under his control. The difference may be important if the lessee shall wish to execute an assignment of the lease, as it ought to be free to do with the consent of the lessor. On the other hand, an equal division of the shares might lead to other hardships. It might take away from Salmon the power of control and management which under the plan of the joint venture he was to have from first to last. The number of shares to be allotted to the plaintiff should, therefore, be reduced to such an extent as may be necessary to preserve to the defendant Salmon the expected measure of dominion. To that end an extra share should be added to his half.

[Text omitted]

W. J. (Plaintiff) v. S. Sch. (Defendant)
High Federal Court, 2nd Civil Division
March 17, 1966; BGHZ 45, 204
[Unofficial, partial translation]
In 1957, the Defendant established a limited partnership together with Mrs. E, who was a destitute, untrained fabric cutter and whose husband had filed a declaration of bankruptcy. The Defendant sought a way to profitably invest his money. He could not directly conduct commercial activity because of his position as a school principal, so he became a limited partner with a capital contribution of DM 10,000. Mrs. E became the general partner. She gave her labor as her contribution to the partnership, and her husband was to work for the partnership as a knitter. The partnership leased a textile production facility and purchased the necessary machinery. The Defendant immediately paid in his contribution and made other, sizeable contributions to the partnership; indeed, before the collapse of the partnership in 1960, he made at least DM 83,000 in capital contributions. In addition, he purchased a plot of land for DM 5,000 on which he constructed a building for the partnership's operations.

The Plaintiff began providing the partnership with yarn in May or June of 1958. In July 1958, the Plaintiff and the partnership had discussions, in which the Defendant participated, regarding credit. In connection with such discussions, the Plaintiff granted the partnership a credit of up to DM 5,000.

The Plaintiff commenced the underlying action to collect the DM 5,032.76 plus interest that the partnership still owes the Plaintiff. The Plaintiff asserts that the Defendant may not take recourse to the limit defined by his capital contribution because he only used the partnership to conduct his own business and Mrs. E. is destitute. The Plaintiff also alleges that the Defendant more than once offered to guarantee the debts of the partnership.

The trial court found for the Plaintiff.

The appeals court reversed.

Reasons for the decision

I. The conclusion of the appeals court is correct that a limited partner will not be subjected to unlimited liability in all cases when, from an economic point of view, he is the sole owner of the commercial partnership and the general partner is destitute.

1. The provisions of law that apply optionally or in default to partnerships and silent partnerships generally provide that management power is internally and directly linked to unlimited liability. That is manifest in the various kinds of company structures that the law gives to commercial partnerships (*Handelsgesellschaften*), limited partnerships (*Kommanditgesellschaften*) and silent partnerships (*stille Gesellschaften*). The nature of these legal rules do not, however, support the conclusion that they present a mandatory, fundamental principle of commercial law that is present in these company forms despite the fact that a different arrangement of managerial power may be achieved through the partnership agreement ... The link between managerial power and liability displayed in the optional and default provisions of law for the types of partnerships referred to above cannot alone support a conclusion that a limited partner who holds the managerial powers of a general partner pursuant to the partnership agreement must be liable without limit ... It is evident from the text of the law that the relevant provisions are not mandatory; therefore, they do not present a mandatory principle of law that would also have to apply to every contractual arrangement that sought a different company structure. The models provided for by law for the forms of partnership referred to above leave the parties a good measure of room for free discretion, and allow the partnership agreement to eliminate – to a greater or lesser extent – the optional, underlying link between managerial authority and liability. If another intention was present in the law, the law should have made the provisions regarding managerial power and liability mandatory, as it did in the case of close corporations (*Gesellschaften mit beschränkter Haftung*) and to a greater degree in the case of stock corporations (*Aktiengesellschaften*). It certainly may not be assumed that the law expresses an intention to, on the one hand, allow the management structure of partnerships and silent partnerships to be freely set by contract and, on the other hand, fix a degree of liability that applies irrespective of the company structure selected. That would lead to an undesirable amount of legal uncertainty given the great number of possible structures that could be created from mixing the company types provided. One could never say with certainty how liability would apply to a given partnership type in an individual case; in particular, the allegedly mandatory fundamental principal of commercial law that links management authority to liability would have to be applied to a partner in a general commercial partnership who was excluded from managerial or representative powers and was limited to something like the supervisory rights provided by law for a limited partner ...

2. Nor can support for the opposing position be found in an assertion that our conclusion could lead to the undesirable or even impermissible result of a commercial partnership being operated with complete limited liability. In this regard, the development of the law over the last 50 to 60 years has taught us that our legal system can no longer do without the possibility of managing a commercial partnership by one or more natural persons with limited liability. One need only think of closed corporations with a single shareholder or limited partnerships in which the general partner is a corporation.

3. Finally, in this regard, it will be argued that there is an abuse of the legal form of the limited partnership when a person is a limited partner but in reality runs the business and presents a destitute person as the general partner; thus, such a limited partner must certainly be liable without limit regardless of the registration [as a limited partner] … This position can, however, not be so simply accepted.

There can simply be no question of an abuse of the law in this case because the limited partner is availing himself of a structural combination that the law itself makes available. An essential characteristic of an abuse of the law is that such abuse remains within the formal framework or possibilities offered by the law. However, an abuse of the law by abusive employment of a legally provided form is present only when the use in question pursues goals and purposes that are not intended for the relevant form, or when the use produces the effect of misleading persons who generally come into commercial contact with the business or specific persons. In a case like the one at hand, it may not be generally asserted that the prerequisites for a finding of an abuse of the legal form of a limited partnership are present. As already discussed, no legally grounded objection may be raised when the actual owner of a business takes recourse in this way to the possibility of creating a limitation of liability with respect to the debts of the business. Also, contrary to the position held by Weipert, no violation may be concluded from the fact that the actual owner of the business does not make his limited liability publicly known through the choice of a corresponding business form. Current law contains no principle attributing such a duty; rather, a partner fulfills his legal obligation of disclosure to the public when he declares whether his liability for the debts of the business is unlimited or limited, and in this case, the extent of the liability. Moreover, there is also no ground to forbid the use of the form of limited liability in this case because it generally creates or could create deceit on good faith in commercial dealings. It creates no such deceit. The true situation, in particular, the degree of liability of individual partners, was in this case accurately disclosed. Thus, in similar company structures, the question whether the legitimate interests of third parties have been adversely affected will be answered on the basis of the facts of an individual case, depending on whether the occurrence of specific circumstances have given third parties a false impression or misleading representation of the degree of liability or the assets of the general partner.

Thus, it can be held that the Defendant may not be found to be liable without limit for the obligations of the partnership simply because, in the opinion of the trial court, he was the sole economic owner of the commercial partnership and set up a destitute person as the general partner.

II. The trial court was of the opinion that this case presents special circumstances justifying a finding that the Defendant abused the legal form of the limited partnership and should thus be prevented from invoking a limitation of liability against the Plaintiff. The court finds such special circumstances in the fact that, in the context of the negotiations in 1958, the Defendant made reference to his good credit standing and his position as a school principal, as well as to his good name and reputation, and presented himself as the real owner of the partnership, thereby inducing the Plaintiff to increase the amount of the credit granted. In reaching this conclusion, the trial court left the question open whether such representations could be understood to constitute a contract of guaranty or suretyship.

The trial court's reasoning in this regard is incorrect. It is to be assumed that the Plaintiff was aware of the essential aspects of the limited partnership structure. (Omission).

It is irrelevant whether the Plaintiff knew that the Defendant had ultimate management authority in the partnership. It is not essential for a creditor of a partnership to know the nature of the internal restraints to which a general partner is subject; the important thing for the creditor is to know who is liable for the partnership's debts and the extent of such liability. Regardless of the foregoing, in light of the optional nature of § 164 Commercial Code and the great variety of legal forms that are created by contract in contemporary business practice, a creditor of the partnership must assume that the general partner will be subject to some form of internal restraint from the limited partners.

Thus the Plaintiff did not suffer from any form of misrepresentation or deception regarding the essential facts at the time of making a decision to grant credit to the limited partnership. Under the circumstances, the Plaintiff should have made provision to receive an appropriate amount of security for the credit. If the representations that the trial court found the Defendant to have made were mere general, factual statements without any legally binding effect, this would be to the Plaintiff's detriment. The Plaintiff could not then assert the position that it assumed the Defendant intended to be liable to the Plaintiff without limit as actual owner of the business.

III. Whether the Plaintiff may collect from the Defendant thus depends upon whether the Defendant – in the credit negotiations in 1958 or later when entering into the credit agreement – provided an assurance of guaranty or suretyship.

3

Corporations in a global market: the law applicable to corporations

Required reading

EU: EC Treaty, arts. 43, 46, 48
UK: CA 2006, secs. 1046, 1049, 1052
US: DGCL, §§ 371, 383; California Corporations Code, § 2115

The dynamics of regulatory competition

I. *The whole and its parts*

The term "regulatory competition" refers to a competition that may arise between the laws or other rules (such as stock exchange rules) in different jurisdictions because of differences between the legal requirements for companies. Not all jurisdictions can compete with each other. Some are simply superior to and trump others (such as when the laws of a federal jurisdiction are superior to those of a state jurisdiction). In order to understand how "regulatory competition" has affected the three jurisdictions we address in this text, we must first understand what these jurisdictions are and the nature of their composition. Each is a sub-unit of a larger jurisdiction.

Germany and the UK belong to the EU, and all US states belong to the US.[1] Because both the upper- and the lower-tier jurisdictions enact legislation that is or functions as company law, it is necessary to understand the nature of the rules coming from each jurisdiction and their respective standing *vis-à-vis* each other. The rule-giving bodies[2] affecting the

---

[1] Although Germany itself is a federation of states and the UK unites England, Wales, Scotland and Northern Ireland, this aspect is much less important because with very few exceptions company law is uniform at the national level.

[2] The word "jurisdiction" would be used here very loosely, as it would also include securities exchanges. The agreement between an issuer and the securities exchange on which its shares are listed is a contract, and the exchange has "regulatory" power only over a very narrow group of persons, particularly its members and participants and its listed companies.

governance of public companies in each of our jurisdictions are found at the primary, nation or state level (i.e. Germany or Delaware), at an upper, supranational or national level (i.e. the EU or the US), and at the level of a private or quasi-public organization (e.g. the New York Stock Exchange or the UK Takeover Panel). There is also a growing number of cooperative plans between the securities regulators of the EU and the US, such as on the recognition of accounting principles[3] and the regulation of derivatives,[4] which could eventually lead to treaty or treaty-like obligations creating yet another layer of jurisdictional interaction. This subsection will restrict itself to defining the legal relationships of the relevant jurisdictions to each other and analyzing the specific content of the rules issued by each.

II.   *The European Union and its member states*

A.   Pursuant to the Treaty on the Functioning of the European Union

Germany was a founding member of the European Economic Community (EEC) in 1957,[5] and the UK joined the EEC in 1973.[6] Through the Treaty on European Union signed in Maastricht in 1992, the EEC and the other European communities were transformed into the European Union (EU).[7] As from December 1, 2009, the Treaty of Lisbon,[8] consisting of the Treaty on European Union[9] and the Treaty on the Functioning of the European Union (TFEU),[10] replaced the previous treaty framework.[11] The Union's legal relationship to the member states varies depending on the area in question. Within areas where the Union has been delegated competence that is not concurrent, the ECJ

---

[3] See Press Release, "Developing Cross-Atlantic Financial Markets: CESR and the SEC Launch a Work Plan Focused on Financial Reporting" (August 2, 2006).

[4] CESR–CFTC Common Work Program to Facilitate Transatlantic Derivatives Business (June 28, 2005), available at www.cesr.eu.

[5] Judt (2005: 303).   [6] Judt (2005: 308).

[7] Craig and de Búrca (2008: 15).

[8] Treaty of Lisbon amending the Treaty on European Union and the Treaty establishing the European Community, December 17, 2007, OJ 2007 C306/1.

[9] See the consolidated version of the Treaty on European Union, May 5, 2008, OJ 2008 C115/3.

[10] See the consolidated version of the Treaty on the Functioning of the European Union, May 5, 2008, OJ 2008 C115/47.

[11] See art. 1(3) Treaty on European Union.

has interpreted the relevant provisions under the former EC Treaty, which have not in substance been altered in the new framework, to mean that EU law is supreme over that of the Member States.[12] The German Constitutional Court (*Bundesverfassungsgericht*) has, however, expressly reserved national, sovereign power, which it has nevertheless pledged not to exercise so long as the Community remains within its delegated powers and does not violate basic rights guaranteed in the German Constitution.[13] Within those areas where the European Community has not been given exclusive competence, the relationship between the Community and the member states is governed by the relationship of "subsidiarity" provided for in article 5 of the EC Treaty, which includes the imperative that "the Community shall take action ... only if and in so far as the objectives of the proposed action cannot be sufficiently achieved by the Member States and can therefore, by reason of the scale or effects of the proposed action, be better achieved by the Community."[14] In articles 49–54 TFEU,[15] the Community is given the express duty to guarantee the freedom of a citizen or company from one member state to establish him-, her- or itself in any other member state, but the promulgation of company law beyond a certain level of safeguarding harmonization is not an express Community function. The company law area should therefore be thought of as one of "concurrent jurisdiction,"[16] to which the principle of subsidiarity could apply. Article 50(2)(g) TFEU[17] expressly instructs the European Council to adopt directives to coordinate "[only] to the necessary extent the safeguards ... required by Member States of companies ... with a view to making such safeguards equivalent throughout the Community."[18] This express, yet limited, delegation of authority means that the Community's exercise of power is evaluated primarily

---

[12] Case 6/64, *Costa* v. *ENEL* [1964] ECR 585. For a good discussion in German, see Zuleeg, in von der Groeben and Schwarze (2003: Art. 1 EG mn. 23–27).

[13] See most recently the decision of the Constitutional Court of June 7, 2000, 2 BvL 1/97, BVerfGE 102, 147, available at the website of the German Constitutional Court at www. bverfg.de, under "*Entscheidungen*." An older decision (reprinted in English) expressing a similar line of reasoning on sovereignty is *Brunner* v. *European Union Treaty* [1994] 1 CMLR 57.

[14] Art. 5 EC Treaty. Judt wryly calls the difficult concept of "subsidiarity" "a sort of Occam's razor for eurocrats." Judt (2005: 715).

[15] Formerly arts. 43–48 EC Treaty.

[16] Zuleeg, in von der Groeben and Schwarze (2003: Art. 1 EG mn. 11–13).

[17] Formerly art. 44(2)(g) EC Treaty.

[18] Grundmann and Möslein (2007: 53 *et seq.*); Edwards (1999: 3–14).

for any abuse of such delegation rather than by application of the principle of subsidiarity, which would add little to the analysis.[19]

A "directive," as referred to in article 50 TFEU[20] and defined in article 288(3) TFEU,[21] is binding as to the result to be achieved, and member states must carry its substance into their national law, but it leaves them free to choose the form and method of implementation.[22] Once a directive has been adopted, however, it works to preempt conflicting national legislation. The ECJ made this point clear in its *Inspire Art* decision,[23] where it concluded that the Eleventh Company Law Directive's list of required and optional disclosures for branches established in other member states is "exhaustive," and that any disclosure requirements imposed by a member state (in that case, the Netherlands) are preempted.[24] The harmonization program under article 50 TFEU[25] goes hand in hand with the regulatory competition discussed in the next subsection, and harmonization of company law was originally seen as a *quid pro quo* for allowing companies from other member states to operate in the host country. ECJ Justice Timmerman has observed that the harmonization program conducted on the basis of former article 44 EC Treaty[26] was thus seen as "an entrance fee Member States accepted to pay for market integration."[27]

B.   The company law directives

Ten of the company law directives adopted since 1968 have harmonized company law on many key aspects of forming and operating *public* companies,[28] with only minor attention given to private companies. The

---

[19] Grundmann and Möslein (2007: 55), with further citations, and the discussion of art. 44 EC Treaty by Troberg and Tiedje, in von der Groeben and Schwarze (2003: Art. 44 EG mn. 24 *et seq.*).

[20] Formerly art. 44(2)(g) EC Treaty.

[21] Formerly art. 249(3) EC Treaty.

[22] A "directive" is an instrument proposed by the European Commission and issued by the European Council after consultation with, approval of, or notification to, the European Parliament, and is defined as an instrument that is "binding, as to the result to be achieved, upon each Member State to which it is addressed, but shall leave to the national authorities the choice of form and methods." Art. 249 EC Treaty. See Craig and de Búrca (2008: 85 *et seq.*). EU company law has been harmonized almost exclusively through directives enacted under art. 44(2)(g) EC Treaty. See Grundmann and Möslein (2007: 58 *et seq.*); and Edwards (1999: 3 *et seq.*).

[23] *Kamer van Koophandel en Fabrieken voor Amsterdam and Inspire Art Ltd* [2003] ECR I-10155.

[24] See *Inspire Art* [2003] ECR I-10155, paras. 65–71.

[25] Formerly art. 44 EC Treaty.

[26] Now art. 50 TFEU.   [27]   Timmermans (2003: 628).

[28] Grundmann and Möslein (2007: 59 *et seq.*); Edwards (1999: 1 *et seq.*).

First Company Law Directive, adopted in 1968, imposed a harmonized system of register disclosure for companies to publish facts regarding their incorporation, legal capital and financial results, as well as to specify those persons authorized to represent the company in dealings with third parties. The Second Company Law Directive, adopted in 1976, provided harmonized rules for the incorporation of public companies and the maintenance of their capital, including a procedure for auditing the value of in-kind contributions to capital, restrictions on dividend distributions and share repurchases, a prohibition of "financial assistance," mandatory preemption rights, and a mandatory shareholder vote for certain changes in the company's capital. Even considered alone and taking into account that the Second Company Law Directive was somewhat pared down through 2006 amendments, it is obvious that these two directives regulate core corporate characteristics. They provide rules on the creation and actual representation of the corporation as a legal person, the capital maintenance requirements that are by many considered a *quid pro quo* for its limited liability, the nature of certain rights attaching to its shares, and the rights of shareholders with respect to changes in the company capital. The remaining company law directives adopted through the 1980s harmonize accounting,[29] or address specific company actions or topics, such as mergers and divisions,[30] the establishment of branches in other member states,[31] or the guarantee that the existence of a single-shareholder company will be respected throughout the Union.[32] Following long and difficult negotiations among the member states, the EU finally adopted long-standing proposals for a directive regulating takeovers[33] and a regulation/directive package enabling the creation of a "European company" (*Societas Europaea* or SE), which is a porous framework of EU law filled in by the national company law of its member state of incorporation and seat.[34] The company law directives and regulations outlined above prescribe mandatory minimum rules, but the SE Regulation introduces a certain amount of flexibility into national law. The Regulation allows shareholders to choose either a single-tier or a two-tier management board

---

[29] Accounting measures include: the Fourth Company Law Directive, the Seventh Company Law Directive, the Eighth Company Law Directive, as well as the more recent IFRS Regulation. For a thorough discussion of these measures, see Grundmann and Möslein (2007: §§ 15–18); Edwards (1999: Chs. V–VII).

[30] Third Company Law Directive and the Sixth Company Law Directive.

[31] Eleventh Company Law Directive. This Directive is discussed at length in the European Court of Justice's decision in *Inspire Art* [2003] ECR I-10155.

[32] Twelfth Company Law Directive.   [33] Takeover Directive.

[34] SE Regulation and the SE Directive.

structure in setting up a *Societas Europaea*,[35] and to specify a percentage of less than 10 percent of the shareholders to call a shareholders' meeting.[36] Germany and the UK have implemented all of the EU directives into their company law, and the SE Regulation is both directly binding as law and tied into national law with special, national legislation directing how the gaps in the loose, supranational framework are to be filled in.[37] More recent company law directives facilitate cross-border mergers[38] and harmonize a number of shareholder rights with respect to receiving notice of an annual meeting, casting votes at the meeting, and granting a proxy for such votes.[39] Although no directive has directly set out to harmonize directors' duties of care and loyalty, the many *ex ante* rules in the directives referred to above, such as those restricting distributions to shareholders, prescribing procedural conduct for mergers, and limiting defenses against takeovers, as well as delineating how accounts should be prepared and signed, place significant restrictions on management behavior. Such rules should be factored in when comparing the development of fiduciary duties in the US states and EU member states. A growing body of ECJ decisions, which will be discussed in Section IV below, also has had an extremely important impact on company law.

EU law regulates every aspect of the capital markets through general framework directives, directly applicable regulations and detailed "interpretive" directives. The areas covered include public offerings of securities,[40] the disclosures that listed companies and their major shareholders must make to the market,[41] insider trading and market manipulation,[42] as well as the activities of brokers and trading facilities[43] and the operation of investment funds.[44] The shape of these capital market rules has also often been influenced by the International Organization of Securities Commissions (IOSCO) or another

---

[35] Art. 38(b) SE Regulation.   [36] Art. 55(1) SE Regulation.

[37] For Germany, see the European Company Implementation Act (*Gesetz zur Einführung der Europäischen Gesellschaft*), BGBl I, p. 3675 (December 22, 2004). Although national law will fill in gaps in the Regulation, it is important to remember that many of the gaps have been left in areas already harmonized by earlier EU directives.

[38] Cross Border Merger Directive.   [39] Shareholder Rights Directive.

[40] Prospectus Directive.   [41] Transparency Directive.   [42] Market Abuse Directive.

[43] Markets in Financial Instruments Directive (MiFID). The content of this directive clearly falls outside what is usefully considered as "company law" and will not be discussed in this paper.

[44] At the time of this writing, the EU framework for the regulation of undertakings for collective investment in transferable securities (UCITS) is undergoing substantial modification. See the White Paper and other documents available at http://ec.europa.eu/internal_market/investment/index_en.htm.

international body, and thus they greatly resemble similar rules adopted in the US. One important element of securities regulation that has not been harmonized at the EU level is the standard for civil liability in cases of securities fraud.[45]

C. EU implementing regulations

The detailed EU rules implementing general directives are adopted pursuant to a four-level approach devised in 2001 by an expert committee under the direction of Baron Alexandre Lamfalussy in its "Final Report of the Committee of Wise Men on the Regulation of European Securities Markets."[46] This report set out "four levels," namely:

- Level 1: general principles, directives that member states implement;
- Level 2: detailed, implementing legislation adopted by the European Commission, in consultation with the Committee of European Securities Regulators (CESR);
- Level 3: interpretive regulations developed by CESR; and
- Level 4: Commission policies for compliance.

Pursuant to this procedure, the Insider Dealing and Market Manipulation Directive, for example, has been fleshed out both by detailed implementing legislation[47] and by CESR advice on further implementing measures.[48] Similarly, the Prospectus Directive has been supplemented with a very detailed Prospectus Regulation,[49] which operates something like the instructions the SEC issued on the information to be provided in disclosure documents under the name of "Regulation S-K."[50] This capillary web of upper-level rules obviates national guidance on the content of prospectuses. In fact, the German Securities Prospectus Act defines the required minimum content of a prospectus under German law with a brief reference to the EU Prospectus Regulation.[51] The FSA's disclosure and transparency rules for listed companies are to a great extent taken without alteration from this EU legislation.

---

[45] Enriques and Tröger (2007: 12 *et seq.*); Enriques and Gatti (2007: 194 *et seq.*).
[46] The text of the report is available at http://europa.eu.int. For a detailed analysis of this four-level procedure, see Ferran (2004: 61–126).
[47] See the Level 2 Market Abuse Directive, the Buy-back Regulation and the Level 2 Market Abuse Directive on Broker Advice.
[48] See CESR, CESR/03–212c.   [49] Prospectus Regulation.
[50] 17 CFR Part 229.   [51] § 7 WpPG.

D.   The Europeanization of national law

The growth of EU activity in the area of securities regulation has transferred much of the legislative volume of rules in this area from the member states to the supranational entity. The hierarchical relationship between the EU and its member states and the density of the EU measures in the areas of company law and capital markets also mean that member state law has, to a very significant extent, been shaped by EU law. For a US observer, the "marbling" of national law with supranational elements clearly contrasts with the two-tiered federal/state structure that prevails in the US. As will be discussed in more detail below, the ECJ also reviews national law that has not already been harmonized or supplanted for compliance with rights and guarantees expressed in the EC Treaty, thus effecting an additional supranational influence on local law.

An awareness of the pervasive presence of EU law in both the German and the UK legal systems should lend caution to those who would argue a strong form of legal origin influence in Europe. The respective bodies of company law have both been "Europeanized" and exist alongside a large body of EU securities law. Although EU law has not yet focused on private limited companies – and thus ECJ decisions have addressed conflicts in national law regarding this business form – the *Aktiengesetz* and the Companies Act 2006 contain a very large number of substantially identical provisions that implement EU law. In public companies, the appointment of directors and their management of the company has largely been left to national law, and thus in this important area of the law divergences do exist and continue to arise, although economic reason and the influence of institutional investors seeking the adoption of international best practices have led convergence toward significant uniformity in this area as well.

III.   *Jurisdictions within Germany and the United Kingdom*

Although company law is national law in both Germany and the UK, each of these countries contains sub-jurisdictions and regulatory bodies to which power must be delegated or with which jurisdiction must be shared. Thus the Companies Act 2006 makes special allowances for divergence in the case of the law of Scotland and Northern Ireland, and the adoption of rules for the Frankfurt Stock Exchange occurs partly in cooperation with the state (*Land*) of Hesse, where the city of Frankfurt am Main is located.

A. Germany

Germany is a federation, but the states (*Länder*) do not adopt company or securities laws of their own, and thus there is no competition for charters within Germany. The *Aktiengesetz* is also quite inflexible, and leaves little room for individualized company structures. Section 23(5) AktG provides that the company charter may deviate from the provisions of the law only where expressly provided for in the law, and such express grants are not generously provided. As Professor Karsten Schmidt notes, pursuant to German corporate law, "*the constitution-like, prescribed structure of the stock corporation* may be altered only slightly by the articles of incorporation, given that – contrary to limited liability companies and partnerships – the stock corporation is governed by *the principle that the form of constitutional documents is strictly prescribed.*"[52] Indeed, Professor Hans-Joachim Mertens quipped in an essay written shortly after German reunification that a future economic historian would have great difficulty in discerning whether the *Aktiengesetz*, with its strictly prescribed structure, originated in the capitalist or in the communist half of Germany.[53] In addition, unlike either US or UK companies, the size, composition and procedure for electing the board is mostly predetermined for larger AGs by the Co-Determination Act.[54]

As mentioned above, Germany's largest securities exchange, the Frankfurt Stock Exchange, is in the *Land* of Hesse. Securities exchanges also exist in other German *Länder*, and in each case their rules are adopted in a semi-public manner in connection with the *Land*. Pursuant to § 32 of the German Exchange Act, the federal government has issued an exchange admission regulation providing guidelines on the procedure to be used and requirements to be met when admitting securities to listing on a German exchange.[55] The governing body of each exchange, the "exchange council" (*Börsenrat*), on which representatives of listed companies and market participants are seated, is responsible for drafting the exchange rules.[56] These rules must be approved by the supervisory authority of the *Land*, which in Hesse is the Commerce Ministry.[57] As the Exchange Rules are issued pursuant to the German Exchange Act and

---

[52] Schmidt (2002: 771) (emphasis in original) (author's translation). For an interesting discussion of mandatory corporate law in continental Europe, see Cools (2005).

[53] Mertens (1994: 426).   [54] §§ 6 *et seq.* MitbestG.

[55] *Börsenzulassungs-Verordnung.*   [56] §§ 9 and 13 BörsG.

[57] § 13(5) BörsG. For a discussion of the approval process, see Foelsch (2007: mn. 7/171, 7/183).

under the supervision of the local state authority, they take on the character of a public law charter (*öffentlich-rechtliche Satzung*).[58] This gives listed companies additional options to challenge disputed exchange actions, such as the delisting of a company under circumstances not expressly provided for in the exchange admission regulation.[59]

Although German exchange rules are drafted by private parties who can expect the sympathetic cooperation of the commerce ministry in their local *Land*, they coexist with an extensive body of EU securities regulation and the *Aktiengesetz*, which, as we have seen, comprehensively regulates the governance structure of corporations. As a result, a local institution like the Frankfurt Stock Exchange has little room to shape its listing rules. The Frankfurt rules do contain some requirements on disclosure and accounting that make certain exchange segments somewhat stricter than required by law. For example, on the "prime standard" market segment, a company must publish reports, including financial statements, on a quarterly, rather than merely a semi-annual basis, as required by the Securities Trading Act (*Wertpapierhandelsgesetz*)[60] and EU law. The density of the listing requirements is thin compared to their UK and US counterparts. Some minor, additional provisions on the composition of company boards are added by the Corporate Governance Code, which is modeled on the UK Combined Code,[61] and compliance with which must be declared (or non-compliance disclosed and explained) in the notes to a listed company's financial statements.[62] The Code recommends requirements comparable to the corporate governance standards found in the Combined Code and in the NYSE's *Listed Company Manual*, such as the creation within the supervisory board of a committee to focus on company accounts, referred to as an "audit committee," with a chair who is an accounting expert and not a former manager.[63] The Code also disapproves of the general practice of managing directors migrating into the supervisory board,[64] recommends that supervising directors of public corporations sit on the boards of no more than five companies (the *Aktiengesetz* sets the limit at ten),[65] promotes a general policy of one share/one vote,[66]

---

[58] Foelsch (2007: mn. 7/182).

[59] Wolf (2001), for an excellent analysis of the contract law problems arising in the unilateral amendment of this type of quasi-contract.

[60] Rules of the Frankfurt Stock Exchange, §§ 62 and 63 (available at www.deutsche-boerse.com) and § 37w WpHG.

[61] FSA Listing Rules, Rule 9.8.6.   [62] § 161 AktG.

[63] Para. 5.3.2 *Kodex*.   [64] Para. 5.4.4 *Kodex*.

[65] See para. 5.4.5 *Kodex* and § 100(2)(1) AktG for the statutory rule.

[66] Para. 2.1.2 *Kodex*.

Figure 3.1   The jurisdictional breakdown of rules governing German corporations

and advocates a shareholder-friendly calling and holding of the annual meeting.[67]

Particularly with regard to takeovers and securities trading, German law also delegates authority to the German Financial Services Supervisory Agency (*Bundesanstalt für Finanzdienstleistungsaufsicht* or BaFin) to adopt regulations. However, as the EU and CESR have issued increasingly detailed rules and guidance, the added value of national regulations has decreased. Given that the Frankfurt listing rules are comparatively light and that the Governance Code – aside from the few items mentioned above – offers only a slight variation on the *Aktiengesetz* requirements, there is little or no jurisdictional interaction within Germany. Nearly all company law is national law. Figure 3.1 shows the main jurisdictional relationships affecting German law.

B.   The United Kingdom

Although the UK is composed of England, Wales, Scotland and Northern Ireland – with each having a certain degree of autonomy and slight differences in laws that affect companies – there is no regulatory competition between the component "states" of the UK. This contrasts with one distinctly

---

[67] Para. 2.3 *Kodex.*

competing difference that we saw in the last chapter, namely, that a partnership in Scotland is considered an entity, whilst in England and Wales it is considered a mere aggregate of members. The Companies Act 2006 applies equally to each state, with only slight differences between the laws of the various states, such as with respect to variations in the requirements for registering charges against the company, which are closely linked to principles of local property law,[68] or the requirements for entering into contracts that bind the company, which are closely linked to principles of local contract law.[69] The Financial Services and Markets Act 2000 (FSMA) makes fewer, but similar, adjustments as a result of differences in such areas as criminal law and related authorities, which display differences in the various UK states.[70] The most significant "jurisdictional" interaction in the area of company law occurs as between the UK Parliament and the bodies, primarily the Secretary of State, the FSA and the Panel on Takeovers and Mergers (the Takeover Panel), to which the UK Parliament delegates specific powers.

The Secretary of State has significant delegated authority under the Act, particularly in connection with the constitution of companies, such as prescribing model articles of association,[71] and is granted the power to issue other statutory instruments affecting a number of different rights.[72] Through the Companies Act 2006, the Takeover Panel is granted powers to issue rules for the regulation of takeovers in accordance with the EU Takeover Directive,[73] to enjoin persons from acting in violation of the rules,[74] to order the production of documents,[75] and to conduct hearings on the alleged violation of its rules.[76] The historical position of the Takeover Panel as a body composed of representatives of the financial services industry meant that the type of person who was able to shape the UK takeover rules (e.g. institutional investors in the City of London) has been quite different from the type of person (predominately non-financial corporations) who could lobby the US Congress to shape the US takeover rules.[77] Because different rule-giving bodies represent different constituencies and have different

---

[68] Part 25 CA 2006.

[69] Secs. 43–51 CA 2006. See Explanatory Notes to the Companies Act 2006, Introduction, for other such differences within the UK.

[70] See e.g. sec. 176 FSMA 2000 regarding the issuance of warrants.

[71] Sec. 19 CA 2006.

[72] See e.g. sec. 71 CA 2006, giving the Secretary of State the power to issue rules regulating challenges to company names.

[73] Sec. 943 CA 2006.   [74] Sec. 946 CA 2006.

[75] Sec. 947 CA 2006.   [76] Sec. 951 CA 2006.

[77] See the very instructive discussion in Armour and Skeel (2007). The analysis found there shows how the nature of a rule-making body can channel certain types of constituency

procedures for drafting and issuing their rules, the constituencies that can exercise influence on those bodies are different. Thus, an understanding of the relevant jurisdictions, their powers and the manner in which their rules are formulated and promulgated lends insight into the type of forces acting to cause legal historical development. Section IV of this chapter attempts to sketch certain key elements in this dynamic. As the Takeover Panel has recently been brought formally under the law through the Companies Act 2006, it will be interesting to see whether its rules and decisions move at all in the direction of the more industry-friendly US counterparts.

The FSMA both created the FSA and delegated power to it, including the power to authorize applicants to pursue a regulated financial activity.[78] FSA rules address matters ranging from the disclosure of inside information and of shareholdings,[79] to the listing standards for UK securities exchanges[80] (the London Stock Exchange or LSE). The LSE's own rules regulate primarily its members rather than listed companies. Unlike in Germany, local government is not involved in the exchange's rulemaking process. The FSA Listing Rules (LRs) provide an extensive set of initial and continuing obligations for listed companies that not only specify financial criteria and regulate disclosure, but also provide guidelines on how specific types of transactions are to be approved,[81] and the manner in which company directors may buy and sell the company's stock.[82] Thus, similarly to the regulatory composition in the US, the shift from a non-listed to a listed UK company brings with it a substantial increase in regulation. Unlike the US, however, because the bulk of the listing rules come from the FSA rather than the exchange, it would be next to impossible for another UK exchange to compete for listing applicants by offering less regulation, although a "race-to-the-top" strategy based on stricter standards should be possible. Moreover, as discussed below, the EU Transparency Directive's applicable law provisions allow competition between the shares of issuers from different home member states on the same exchange, altering the traditional rule according to which the marketplace controls applicable regulation.

---

influences into its rules. It builds on ideas found in Romano (2004), which focuses on the rule-maker's state of mind in accepting or rejecting solutions offered by various constituencies.

[78] Sec. 20 FSMA 2000.

[79] FSA Disclosure and Transparency Rules, Rules 2 and 5.

[80] The FSA is the "competent authority" under EU law for supervising and regulating securities exchanges. See sec. 72 FSMA 2000.

[81] FSA Listing Rules, Rule 9.5.

[82] Transactions requiring shareholder approval include stock and stock option plans for management. See FSA Disclosure and Transparency Rules, Rule 3.

IV. Regulatory competition in Europe

A. Centros and its progeny

We have seen that European directives have shaped the company laws of the member states since 1968. This program has substantially harmonized the laws governing public companies and created a system of securities laws that is nearly identical across the Union. About the time that this drive to harmonization was beginning to wane, a new preference for home country rule and subsidiarity came upon Europe,[83] partly from the judicial initiative of the ECJ,[84] and partly in connection with the politics of introducing majority rule through the Single European Act.[85] The harmonization process stopped. However, a series of ECJ decisions beginning about a decade later in 1999 and decided on the basis of the right of establishment guaranteed to companies in articles 43 and 48 of the EC Treaty[86] made deep inroads into the national company laws of the member states, including Germany. As the substance of *public* companies, particularly the creation and maintenance of their capital, has been harmonized, the relevant cases arose in respect of *private* companies.

In *Centros Ltd* v. *Erhvervs- og Selskabsstyrelsen*,[87] the ECJ decided that Denmark must allow a UK private limited company freely to establish itself in its territory, even if the UK company was created for the sole purpose of evading Denmark's stricter laws on capital adequacy and conducted none of the company's business in the UK.[88] *Überseering BV* v. *Nordic Construction Company Baumanagement GmbH*,[89] reprinted in part in this chapter, followed *Centros*. Unlike the US, which applies the

---

[83] Timmermans (2003: 626–629).

[84] A major breakthrough in the philosophy of home country rule came in the famous *Cassis de Dijon* import (movement of goods) case, Case 120/78, *Rewe-Zentrale AG* v. *Bundesmonopolverwaltung für Branntwein* [1979] ECR 649.

[85] The "Single European Act" was a political commitment signed in 1986 to create a single, integrated European market ("an area without internal frontiers in which the free movement of goods, persons, services and capital is ensured") by 1992. Among other things, it introduced voting by qualified majority on a number of matters that had required unanimity and were consequently deadlocked, addressed increased cooperation as a monetary union, and gave more power to the European Parliament. See Craig and de Búrca (2008: 12–14).

[86] Now arts. 49 and 54 TFEU.

[87] Case C-212/97, *Centros Ltd* v. *Erhvervs- og Selskabsstyrelsen* [1999] ECR I-1459.

[88] *Centros* [1999] ECR I-01459, para. 39.

[89] Case C-208/00, *Überseering BV* v. *Nordic Construction Company Baumanagement GmbH* [2002] ECR I-09919.

"incorporation theory,"[90] meaning that the internal affairs of a corporation are governed by the laws of its state of incorporation, Germany has traditionally applied the "real seat" (or *siège réel*) theory, meaning that the internal affairs of a corporation are governed by the laws of the state where it has its central administration.[91] When reading *Überseering*, note how application of the real seat theory to a Dutch company whose shares came to be owned by Germans and which operated in Germany affected the decision of the German courts. How did the ECJ react to Germany's argument that application of its own company law to pseudo-foreign corporations was justified because it enhanced legal certainty and the protection of creditors and minority shareholders? In its next, major decision in this area, *Kamer van Koophandel en Fabrieken voor Amsterdam and Inspire Art Ltd*,[92] which is also reprinted in part in this chapter, the ECJ reviewed a Dutch outreach statute against "pseudo-foreign" corporations. The statute required the branches of companies incorporated abroad to make disclosures beyond those provided for in the Eleventh Company Law Directive, and imposed unlimited liability as a penalty for a failure to comply with these and other requirements, such as a minimum capital requirement.[93] How does the ECJ's reasoning compare to the US notion of preemption discussed in section VI of this chapter? How do the rights of companies from one EU member state to operate in another, as expressed in *Überseering* and *Inspire Art*, compare to that of Delaware companies to operate in California under Delaware law as described in the *Vantagepoint Venture Partners* decision, which is also set out in this chapter? Under the ECJ decisions in *Überseering* and *Inspire Art*, what test must a member state law meet if it burdens the free establishment of a company formed under the laws of another member state?[94]

The vertical impact of these decisions is to apply a clear principle of supremacy of EU law over member state national company law, and the horizontal impact is to create standards that a member state may use in assessing the permissibility of the impact its company law and related legislation

---

[90] Scoles, Hay, Borchers and Symeonides (2000: § 23.2).

[91] Roth (2003: 180–181) (the "center of administration" as understood in Germany is "the location where the internal management decisions are transformed into the day-to-day activities of a company"), citing the decision of the German High Federal Court reported in BGHZ 97, 269, at 272. Also see Scoles, Hay, Borchers and Symeonides (2000: § 23.1).

[92] *Inspire Art* [2003] ECR I-10155.

[93] *Inspire Art* [2003] ECR I-10155, para. 143.

[94] See *Inspire Art* [2003] ECR I-10155, para. 133; and *Gebhard* v. *Consiglio dell'Ordine degli Avvocati e Procuratori di Milano* [1995] ECR I-4165, para. 37.

may have on companies formed under the law of another member state. One clear rule from the decisions is that, although member states may protect themselves from fraudulent actions by foreign companies, the deliberate use of a system of company law that relies on disclosure, especially one found in the First and Eleventh Company Law Directives, rather than legal capital, to protect creditors does not constitute such fraudulent action.[95]

B.   A curious twist for EU securities law

Especially from a comparative point of view, EU securities law currently offers an interesting chance for observation. A securities exchange is essentially an organized market with specific rules for entry, and these rules apply only to persons participating in or listed on the market. This "market-oriented" logic is the foundation for the theory on the "bonding" function of dual listing[96] and has traditionally governed rules for applying securities law.[97] The applicability of a nation's securities laws is usually determined by a trader's or a vendor's entrance into that nation's territory or market. The US Regulation S,[98] for example, takes the rational step to remove sales of securities from US supervision if no offers or sales are made to persons in the United States and the US market is not conditioned for sales of the securities through "directed selling efforts" in the US.[99] Unlike the rules governing a corporation's "internal affairs" – which under the incorporation theory are derived from the state of incorporation and travel with the corporation wherever it goes – the rules applicable to the *sale* of securities had been derived from the place of sale. However, in an interesting twist that locks securities law and company law together, the EU Transparency Directive has turned this traditional rule around with respect at least to disclosure rules. Under the title "Integration of securities markets," article 3 of that Directive provides:

1. The home Member State may make an issuer subject to requirements more stringent than those laid down in this Directive. The home Member State may also make a holder of shares … subject to requirements more stringent than those laid down in this Directive.

---

[95] Timmermans (2003: 633).

[96] For classic discussions of the bonding function, see Karolyi (1998); Coffee (2002: 1779 *et seq.*); and Doidge, Karolyi and Stulz (2004); for a more critical view of the bonding hypothesis, see Frésard and Salva (2007).

[97] See e.g. the Market Abuse Directive, art. 10.

[98] 17 CFR §§ 230.901 *et seq.*   [99] Fox (1998: 708 *et seq.*).

2. A host Member State may not … as regards the admission of securities to a regulated market in its territory, impose disclosure requirements more stringent than those laid down in this Directive or in Article 6 of [the Market Abuse Directive].[100]

For EU issuers of equity securities, the "home member state" is the state of its registered office,[101] which would be the state of incorporation. As a result, EU issuers will carry any disclosure obligations exceeding the EU floor with them regardless of the market on which their securities are traded. This reverses the traditional choice-of-law rule for securities regulation, advances the need to consider a venue for listing to the time of incorporating the company, and adds an element that will be taken into consideration in regulatory competition between member states. As Professor Eilís Ferran has observed, this regime removes competition with respect to home state issuers because they will be locked into any higher standard of disclosure, but could in a race-to-the-top climate cause a flight to re-incorporate in states where securities regulators have the strongest reputations.[102] If member states' private remedies for securities fraud remain expressed in their traditional remedies for tortious misrepresentation, they may retain meaningful differences (such as who are the potential plaintiffs or defendants, the standards used to determine culpability, and matters of proof and causation) that could reinforce or counteract this migratory pressure. Following a detailed survey of EU securities legislation in connection with provisions on applicable law, Professors Luca Enriques and Tobias H. Tröger conclude that considerable latitude for regulatory arbitrage exists in Europe "with regard to the regime of private liability for false statements in disclosure documents, the public administration and enforcement of securities laws in general, and less densely harmonized takeover law."[103] Regulatory competition in European securities law could thus contribute more to future competition for company charters than the differences in corporate law statutes.

---

[100] Transparency Directive, art. 3. The law applicable under art. 10 of the Market Abuse Directive retains the traditional market-orientation approach and is that of the member state in which the securities are listed on a regulated market. Also see Enriques and Tröger (2007: 22).

[101] Transparency Directive, art. 3.   [102] Ferran (2004: 153–155).

[103] Enriques and Tröger (2007: 58).

C.   A future for regulatory competition of corporate law in Europe?

By rolling back the member state regulation of foreign corporations affecting freedom of establishment, the ECJ opened the gates for regulatory competition of company law. Indeed, as discussed above, scholarly speculation in recent years has focused only on whether the motivational and legal conditions for regulatory competition exist in Europe,[104] not on the legality of the competition itself. Disclosure and securities fraud regimes could provide such a motive. For the private companies addressed by the recent ECJ decisions, however, as Professor Theodor Baums has observed, even though the Commission is moving away from harmonized regulation,[105] the proposed creation of a European Private Company (EPC) "could well take the form of a regulation so as to create a true organizational form that can be used in all member states."[106] The existence of such an entity under EU law, if well designed, would greatly reduce incentives for incorporators to respond to state competition for private company charters. For public companies, a European task force set out in 2007 to create a "European Model Company Law Act" comparable to the US Model Business Corporation Act.[107] Such a model act would offer member states a chance voluntarily to harmonize that part of company law which has not already been shaped by directives and the decisions of the ECJ. Especially for the newer and smaller member states, this type of *prêt-à-porter* company law statute could present an economically attractive route to high-quality legislation.[108] Given the currently foreseeable range of technical possibilities in company law, the pressure of internationally active investors to seek ever-increasing uniformity in securities regulation, the possible introduction of an EPC and the creation of a European Model Company Law Act, the space for competitive signaling in the future will likely become even smaller than it is now. However, as in the past, competition might well arise from unforeseen innovations.

V.   *The United States and its states*

The bodies with power to issue rules governing public companies in the US are the states (e.g. the State of Delaware), the federal government

---

[104] See e.g. Armour (2005); Enriques and Tröger (2007).
[105] Baums (2007: 9 *et seq.*).   [106] Baums (2007: 16).
[107] Baums and Andersen (2008).   [108] Baums and Andersen (2008: 8).

(which enacted, for example, the Exchange Act and the Securities Act) and the securities exchange on which a given company's shares are listed (e.g. the New York Stock Exchange).[109] The rules issued by these bodies tend to overlap and supplement each other.

A.   The constitutional position of the federal government

Federal law focuses on disclosure in the contexts of securities offerings,[110] takeovers,[111] annual and quarterly reporting,[112] and the solicitation of proxies[113] for the annual meetings of shareholders, as well as combating fraud in connection with such activities.[114] In the area of company law proper, the federal government could constitutionally supplant state law, but has traditionally chosen not to do so.

Pursuant to article VI, clause 2, of the US Constitution, known as the "Supremacy Clause," the laws of the federal government preempt the laws of a state.[115] Preemption is not uniformly present in all cases. The federal preemption power runs on a sliding scale, beginning with those cases where exclusive powers of the federal government are specified in the Constitution, and gradually decreasing through cases in which the Supreme Court has found that there is a presumption in favor of pre-emption, to where the legal position is neutral, to cases where it has been held that there is a presumption against preemption, and finishing with those cases in which the states have a constitutional immunity from preemption.[116] Because the Constitution, in a provision known as the "Commerce Clause,"[117] vests the federal Congress with the power to regulate commerce among the states, interstate commercial activity is a field where the argument for preemption is at its strongest.[118] Congress

---

[109]   The initial and continued listing standards of the NYSE are set out in the NYSE *Listed Company Manual* (LCM), which is available in a continuously updated form at www.nyse.com. The initial and continued listing standards of the Nasdaq Stock Market are set out in the Nasdaq Marketplace Rules (Rules 4000–7100), which are available in a continuously updated form at www.nasdaq.com.

[110]   15 USC § 77e(a) (2000).   [111]   15 USC § 78n(d) (2000).

[112]   15 USC § 78m(a)–(b) (2000).   [113]   15 USC § 78n(a) (2000).

[114]   15 USC §§ 77j(b), 78j(b) (2000).

[115]   US Constitution, art. VI, cl. 2. For an informative historical analysis of the US federalist structure, see McConnell (1987).

[116]   This sliding scale analysis is borrowed from Professor Mark V. Tushnet, who uses it in a discussion of the foreign policy area, with the caveat that the five-point scale is "sufficient" for "the present purposes," which of course indicates that finer distinctions might be appropriate in different circumstances. See Tushnet (2000: 19).

[117]   US Constitution, art. VI, § 8, cl. 3.

[118]   See Tushnet's discussion of *Gibbons* v. *Ogden*, 22 US (9 Wheat) 1 (1824), in Tushnet (2000: 19–20).

based its enactment of the various securities laws discussed above on the Commerce Clause,[119] and there is little doubt that Congress could replace state corporate laws with a federal statute.[120] For example, although most US states have some form of law providing for disclosures in connection with the sale of securities (often referred to as "blue sky laws"), Congress in 1996 provided that these laws will not apply to any securities listed on a national exchange.[121] The preempted state law was simply displaced. The same result could be achieved through the adoption of a federal company law, although this has not been seriously considered since the beginning of the 1920s,[122] and in the meantime a "tradition" has developed according to which corporations are understood as "creatures of state law,"[123] and corporate law is understood as an area in which there is a "longstanding prevalence of state regulation."[124] Thus, "except where federal law expressly requires certain responsibilities of directors with respect to stock holders, state law will govern the internal affairs of the corporation,"[125] as states are understood to have "broad latitude" in regulating such "internal affairs."[126] As explained in the *Vantagepoint Venture Partners* decision in this chapter, internal affairs generally include the formation and governance of a corporation and the rights and duties of its owners and managers. For the reasons outlined, the federal government avoids encroaching on this area.

1. Federal laws   The bulk of the federal securities laws and rules affecting companies that are not registered market participants (such as brokers) focus on requiring registration of securities and disclosure

---

[119]   Loss, Seligman and Parades (2004: 98 *et seq.*).

[120]   See e.g. Seligman (2005: 1169); Roe (2003: 597).

[121]   See the National Securities Markets Improvement Act. The "blue sky" laws have become progressively less important as federal law has either expressly or tacitly preempted their application. Along these lines, the Securities Litigation Uniform Standards Act of 1998 also removed a significant amount of activity from the state jurisdictions by preempting state class actions for specified types of securities fraud. See Loss, Seligman and Parades (2004: 28 *et seq.* and 1189 *et seq.*).

[122]   Bratton and McCahery (2006: 653).

[123]   *Santa Fe Industries, Inc.* v. *Green*, 430 US 462, 479 (1977) (refusing to apply the federal securities laws to matters of internal corporate management), citing *Cort* v. *Ash*, 422 US 66, 84 (1975).

[124]   *CTS Corp.* v. *Dynamics Corp. of America*, 481 US 69, 70 (1987).

[125]   *Cort* v. *Ash*, 422 US 66, 84 (1975).

[126]   *CTS Corp.* v. *Dynamics Corp. of America*, 481 US 69, 78 (1987), citing the Appeal Court's decision in the same case, *Dynamics Corp. of America* v. *CTS Corp.*, 794 F 2d 250, 264 (7th Cir. 1986).

of financial and other information about the company and management while making only minimal incursions into internal affairs.[127] Controversies arise, however, in connection with borderline areas where there is uncertainty as to whether the field has been preempted by federal law,[128] or when a federal remedy could be applied to an action taken under state corporate law. For example, when a shareholder raised a federal challenge against a "short-form" merger under Delaware law, which did not require shareholder approval, arguing that the transaction amounted to securities fraud, the Supreme Court denied the existence of a federal claim, pointing out that the matter was "internal" and did not exhibit the characteristics, such as misrepresentation, that the federal rules against securities fraud were enacted to combat.[129] Federal/state conflicts also arise when the SEC oversteps its authority under the Exchange Act in regulating an "internal" matter (such as the type of voting rights embodied in shares), which is usually provided for in state corporate statutes.[130] No *legal* controversy arises, however, when the federal government expressly enters internal corporate affairs, as it did with §§ 301 and 402 of the Sarbanes–Oxley Act of 2002,[131] which respectively regulated (i) board composition by requiring independent audit committees and (ii) internal procedures by prohibiting most loans to directors. Thus, by tradition, but not by law, the states control most of the internal affairs of corporations.

[127] In the original Exchange Act, incursions into the management of the corporation were limited to such requirements as disclosure of the shareholdings of managers and 10 percent stockholders, and the disgorgement of profits that such insiders made through short-term dealings (within a period of six months) in the company's shares. See 15 USCA §§ 78p(b) (2000). An exception to the limitation to disclosure rules was found in the Investment Company Act, which included a requirement that a specified percentage of independent or unaffiliated directors be seated on the board. See 15 USC § 80a-10 (2000).

[128] *Edgar* v. *MITE Corp.*, 457 US 624 (1982) (invalidating a state statute that imposed a waiting period of the consummation of takeover offers that was deemed to frustrate the balance achieved in the § 14 of the Exchange Act). On the question of "field preemption" as applied to corporate and securities law, see Karmel (2003: 500–507).

[129] *Santa Fe Industries, Inc.* v. *Green*, 430 US 462 (1977) (the court found that, absent an allegation of misrepresentation or fraud – which are the key elements of Rule 10b-5 under the Exchange Act – the federal rule could not be used to invalidate a merger effected properly under state law). For an excellent discussion of this case, see Langevoort (2001).

[130] See *Business Roundtable* v. *Securities and Exchange Commission*, 905 F 2d 406 (1990) (finding that the SEC's attempt to guarantee that all listed stock carried proportional voting rights exceeded the agency's authority under § 14 of the Exchange Act).

[131] See the Sarbanes–Oxley Act.

An important difference between US and EU company law arises because the US Congress may not – unlike the EU – command the states to implement specified policies.[132] As a result, laws like the DGCL are essentially different from their counterparts in Germany and the UK because they are not marbled with elements of federal law; rather, state law and federal law occupy separate realms. For example, section 441 of the Companies Act 2006 requires companies to deliver their annual accounts for each financial year to the companies registrar. This requirement is found in UK law because the First Company Law Directive required it.[133] The same EU law requirement is found in German law[134] and will be found in a substantially similar form in the various company laws of all twenty-seven EU member states because national legislatures must comply with an obligation to implement the supranational directive. Because the US federal government cannot issue instructions to a state legislature, US federal laws, such as the Exchange Act, operate on a plane separate from that occupied by state company law and blue sky statutes. These two parallel systems maneuver around each other, and at times leave gaps or collide. The closest thing to an instruction to implement as used in the EU is found in legislative orders via the SEC to the national securities exchanges to issue specific listing rules, as discussed below, and explains why listing rules serve a harmonizing function that is not found in state company law with the exception, perhaps, of the regulatory harmonization sought through the Model Act.

The Model Act might be thought of as a voluntary form of European-style harmonization. Since the 1950s, the American Bar Association's (ABA's) Section on Business Law has continuously updated and improved the Model Act, and it regularly publishes drafts for discussion in the ABA publication, *The Business Lawyer*. State legislatures are free to adopt the provisions with or without change. In 2008, the ABA reported that thirty

---

[132] In 1997, the US Supreme Court reaffirmed that, "[t]he Federal Government may neither issue directives requiring the States to address particular problems, nor command the States' officers, or those of their political subdivisions, to administer or enforce a federal regulatory program." *Printz v. United States*, 521 US 898, 935 (1997).

[133] Arts. 2(1)(f), 3(1), (2) of the First Company Law Directive.

[134] Germany implemented the First Company Law Directive in 1969. See BGBl vol. I, p. 1146 (1969). The required filing was previously specified in §§ 177 and 178 AktG, but has since been moved for housekeeping purposes into §§ 325–329 of the HGB, which apply to all stock corporations. The Commercial Code also provides for the creation of the register in which the filing must be made. Hüffer (2006: §§ 177, 178 mn. 1); Henn (2002: 589).

states had substantially adopted the Model Act, and others had adopted many of its provisions.[135] The existence of thirty states with almost identical law also multiplies the precedent decisions that a court in any one state may consult when addressing a particular set of facts. This generates a body of precedents for which there is no *stare decisis*, but only persuasive authority, much as in a Civil Law jurisdiction. The resulting map of corporate law in the US is essentially divided into three areas: the majority of the states follow the Model Act, a few states, such as Oklahoma, follow the DGCL, and some large states like California and New York choose to draft their law without closely following either Delaware or the Model Act.[136] Federal law has not been directly implemented into any of these corporate statutes.

Because US corporate law statutes offer creditors few safeguards against shareholders paying out the corporate capital to themselves, US company law reaches out in various directions to cobble together creditor rights. Some protections are found in federal law and others in harmonized, model laws. Federal law bankruptcy provisions on both fraudulent conveyances and equitable subordination are used to address cases in which shareholders unfairly vote themselves preferential treatment.[137] Rules on fraudulent conveyances are also used to limit such payouts.[138] The NCCUSL has drafted such rules and offered them to the states for voluntary adoption.[139] This process has significantly harmonized the shape of fraudulent conveyance rules in the US.[140]

2. **Exchange rules**   The initial and continued listing requirements of national securities exchanges are merely contractual in nature,[141] and would be invalid if they violated either state or federal law.[142] Pursuant to the Exchange Act, national securities exchanges are "self-regulatory

---

[135] A BA Section of Business Law (2008: v).

[136] See Macey (2002) for a discussion of the states that have followed a specific provision of the DGCL or the Model Act.

[137] Skeel and Krause-Vilmar (2006).

[138] See e.g. *Moody* v. *Security Pacific Credit Business, Inc.* 971 F 2d 1056 (1992), reprinted in part in Chapter 26; *US* v. *Tabor Court Realty*, 803 F 2d 1288 (1986).

[139] The Uniform Fraudulent Transfer Act, which was drafted by NCCUSL in 1984, revised a Uniform Fraudulent Conveyance Act that had existed since 1918.

[140] The NCCUSL website shows 44 states that adopted the Uniform Fraudulent Transfer Act as at June 2009.

[141] *Merrill Lynch, Pierce, Fenner & Smith* v. *Ware*, 414 US 117, 131 (1973).

[142] Restatement (Second) of Contracts § 178 (2005); Calamari and Perillo (1998: 495). Aside from the invalidity under contract law, § 19(b)(3)(C) Exchange Act provides that a "rule change of a self-regulatory organization which has taken effect … may be enforced by

organizations" (SROs), and their rules, including the listing standards, are subject to the approval of the SEC,[143] which supervises their adoption according to a procedure provided for in the Exchange Act.[144] The SEC not only supervises all significant rule changes, but may instruct the exchanges to adopt specific rules. Because the SEC operates under power delegated to it through the Exchange Act, it may not instruct a securities exchange to adopt a rule in an area not covered by such delegated power. The Court of Appeals for the Federal Circuit found in 1990 that an SEC rule that would have required exchanges to maintain a one share/ one vote policy was beyond the agency's statutory authority because, in the court's opinion, voting rights were part of internal corporate governance and beyond the disclosure focus of the Exchange Act.[145] This decision, although certainly binding, is generally not considered to demarcate the limits of the SEC's delegated power with great authority, and, as Professor Joel Seligman has observed, the court's decision is inconsistent with the SEC's plenary power under the Exchange Act to change or abrogate exchange rules.[146] It fails to explain how, if exchanges are free to adopt rules that go well beyond disclosure, and the SEC is to have unlimited power to supervise this process, the SEC's competence can be limited to disclosure rules.[147] The expansion of the Exchange Act into "internal" matters through the Sarbanes–Oxley Act may lead future courts to reach different conclusions regarding the scope of the SEC's power in such matters. Figure 3.2 roughly sketches the relationship of the jurisdictions within the US.

B.   Within Delaware

In accordance with the jurisdictional rules discussed above, if a company is listed, the composition and behavior of its board will to a certain extent

---

such organization to the extent it is not inconsistent with the provisions of this title, the rules and regulations thereunder, and applicable Federal and State law."

[143] § 19(b) Exchange Act and Loss, Seligman and Parades (2004: 776).

[144] According to § 19(b) Exchange Act, a national securities exchange must file copies of any proposed rule change with the SEC, stating its basis and purpose. The SEC then publishes a notice which allows interested persons to comment. The SEC will then order the rule change or institute proceedings to determine whether the proposal should be disapproved. Under certain circumstances rules may enter into effect immediately without waiting for the comment period. No rule proposal can become effective without SEC approval. See Loss, Seligman and Parades (2004: 776 *et seq.*).

[145] *Business Roundtable*, 905 F 2d at 411–413.

[146] 15 USC § 19(b)(3)(C) Exchange Act.

[147] Loss, Seligman and Parades (2004: 778 *et seq.*).

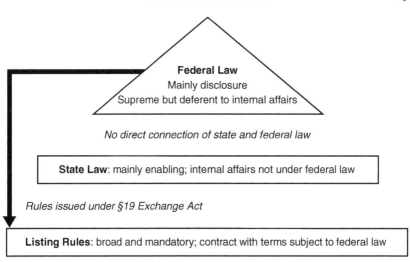

Figure 3.2   The jurisdictional breakdown of rules governing US corporations

be governed by listing requirements and federal rules, and, even if it is not listed but must register with the SEC, the conduct of its general meetings and the disclosure required from directors and major shareholders will be governed by the same federal rules. Because the DGCL offers a flexible set of default terms, what remains mandatory within Delaware law are the constitution of the company and certain matters falling under the rubric "internal affairs," particularly the duties of care and loyalty owed by directors and controlling shareholders to the company and the minority shareholders. Professor Jeffrey Gordon has aptly described laws like the DGCL as containing "four sorts of mandatory rules ... : procedural, power allocating, economic transformative, and fiduciary standards setting."[148] These categories would include such matters as (*procedural*) establishing a mandatory procedure for calling shareholder meetings, (*allocating*) giving shareholders the right to elect and remove directors, (*transformative*) requiring a shareholder vote on transactions that would change the nature of the corporation, and (*fiduciary*) duties of care and loyalty applied by courts to "to restrain insiders in exercising their discretionary power over the corporation and its shareholders in contingencies not specifically foreseeable and thus over which the parties could not contract."[149] The elaboration of this last category, fiduciary duties, has been the most important contribution of the Delaware courts, particularly

[148]   Gordon (1989: 1591).   [149]   Gordon (1989: 1593).

through decisions handed down during the second half of twentieth century.[150] Allocation of power and the opportunity to vote on major decisions that would affect the nature of the company are provided for in the DGCL, but may be shaped significantly in the certificate of incorporation. The way in which a matter is put up for a vote will be governed by federal proxy rules if the company is registered with the SEC or by a combination of minimalist rules and fiduciary standards under Delaware law if it is not.

There is no interaction between Delaware and a lower, local body or a securities exchange. As explained above, national securities exchanges adopt their rules in coordination with the SEC. Although the DGCL and other state laws following the Model Act do refer to a "secretary of state," this office is a document depository that has neither the authority to issue statutory instruments nor any significant role in checking the substance of a company's incorporation documents. Fraudulent conveyance rules, if applied, would be taken from the law of the State of Delaware or another state, depending on the law applicable to the transaction, or from federal bankruptcy law.

VI.   Regulatory competition in the United States

A.   Systemic balance of state and federal law

It is a simple fact of the dynamics of any jurisdictional system that the more topically comprehensive the law enacted by an authority with power over the entire territory (here, the federal government), the less matters the territorial sub-units (here, the states) will have on which they can distinguish themselves and compete. An increase in the amount of corporate law found at the federal level thus leads to a decrease in competition among laws at the state level. As discussed above, the US federal government has largely avoided regulating corporate "internal affairs." Congress has historically entered the field of company law only after economic and political shocks convinced a significant portion of the national population

---

[150] In the case of Delaware, it is thought that the courts' introduction of stricter fiduciary duties was a reaction to the critical stance taken by former SEC Chairman William Cary in 1974, when he accused the state of leading a "race to the bottom." See Cary (1974); Seligman (1993: 61–63). In a landmark decision of 1977, *Singer v. Magnavox Co.*, 380 A 2d 969 (Del. 1977) following Cary's call for national legislation, the Delaware Supreme Court placated its critics by imposing strict fiduciary duties on the management of a parent company in a cash out merger with a subsidiary. See Bratton and McCahery (2006: 680).

that state law had failed to prevent insiders from deceiving outside investors. Thus, intervention of the federal government has not eliminated the "equilibrium" of regulatory competition between the states because it has restrained itself from straying too far from mere disclosure rules, and reacted only when its hand was forced by events.[151]

Between the turn of the nineteenth century and the completion of the New Deal, various US presidents seriously considered replacing the state corporate statutes with federal law, "[b]ut the state charter system was too deeply entrenched, and had strong support from business; nothing came of these attempts at national legislation,"[152] to supplant state law directly. Instead, individual industries like railroads were directly regulated through administrative acts such as the Interstate Commerce Act,[153] and, eventually, a regime of securities regulation was created to foster disclosure and punish fraud.[154] Thus, after the stock market crash of 1929 and the severe economic depression that followed, the federal government entered the securities field in force with the Securities Act, the Exchange Act (which created the SEC), the Public Utility Holding Company Act of 1935,[155] the Trust Indenture Act of 1939, the Investment Company Act and the Investment Advisers Act of 1940.[156] The SEC's creation of the antifraud Rule 10b-5 in 1942 was another step that would have considerable impact on the shape of US company law.[157] In 2002, following the revelation of serious accounting misrepresentations by major corporations such as Enron and WorldCom, and the collapse of the stock markets, the federal government enacted the Sarbanes–Oxley Act. This Act sought to reinforce the existing system of disclosure by decreasing conflicts of interest, increasing accountability, and adding new types of disclosure. Conflicts of interest were reduced by strictly controlling the services that auditors could provide to the companies they audit,[158] by inserting an audit committee composed of independent directors into the boards of listed companies,[159] and by flatly outlawing company loans to directors.[160] The Sarbanes–Oxley Act contained clear incursions into the internal affairs of regulated companies, but these were incursions related to the overall disclosure system. Disclosures were improved by imposing internal checks

---

[151] Bratton and McCahery (2006: 619 *et seq.*).
[152] Friedman (2002: 51).   [153] Friedman (2002: 53).
[154] See Seligman (2003: 42–72); Roe (2003: 602–607); Chandler (1990: 78–79).
[155] 15 USCA §§ 79–79z-6 (2000).   [156] 15 USCA §§ 80b-1–80b-21 (2000).
[157] Loss, Seligman and Parades (2004: 936 *et seq.*).
[158] §§ 201–202 Sarbanes–Oxley Act.
[159] § 301 Sarbanes–Oxley Act.   [160] § 402 Sarbanes–Oxley Act.

on the creation of disclosure documents (i.e. accounts) and the persons who were responsible for their preparation. Accountability was increased by requiring chief operating officers and chief financial officers to personally sign required disclosures and attest to the accuracy and completeness of their contents subject to civil and criminal liability.[161]

With regard to the federal element in the regulatory competition system, it will be remembered that bankruptcy law, certain provisions of which serve capital maintenance functions, is federal law,[162] and fraudulent conveyances are regulated by a state law usually modeled on the NCCUSL's Uniform Fraudulent Transfer Act. Nevertheless, even when one takes into account the federal elements discussed above, the degree of freedom left to the states to shape their corporate statutes is still significantly higher than what is left to EU member states. Regardless of this leeway, for listed companies, the extensive, mandatory listing requirements are likely to bring the respective amounts of harmonized regulation more or less into alignment.

The initial and continued listing requirements of US securities exchanges are indeed quite extensive, and, before the 1930s, they attempted to serve the investor protection function later performed by the securities laws and federal rules.[163] They cover a broad range of matters, from the "internal" composition of a company's board[164] and transactions that must be put to the shareholders for approval,[165] to the "external" provision of information to the public,[166] to minimum requirements for total assets and the required public dispersion of the company's shares.[167] These requirements are contractual conditions to a company's listing on a given exchange, and a serious violation of these conditions can lead to a company being expelled from the market through involuntary de-listing.[168] These requirements thus tend to be pervasive and mandatory, and thus further reduce the range of possible competition between the laws of individual states.

B.   Outreach statutes and foreign corporations

The relationships among the US states in the area of company law offer interesting opportunities for comparison with similar relationships in the EU. Unlike EU member states, US states have significant power to

---

[161] §§ 302 and 906 Sarbanes–Oxley Act.   [162] 11 USC §§ 101–1330 (2000).
[163] Coffee (2001: 34 *et seq.*); Thompson (2003: 972).
[164] Paras. 303A.01 *et seq.* NYSE LCM.   [165] Para. 312.03 NYSE LCM.
[166] Paras. 202.00 *et seq.* NYSE LCM.
[167] Para. 101.00 NYSE LCM. For an analysis of the NYSE listing process and requirements, see Gruson, Jánszky and Weld (2005).
[168] Para. 8 NYSE LCM.

dampen the competitive force of foreign law when companies formed under such law operate primarily within their territory. Because US state law in this area exists in the shadow of federal power to regulate interstate commerce, the states in their dealings with each other may not enter an area preempted by federal law or unduly impede interstate activity.[169] A state's treatment of "foreign" and "pseudo-foreign" corporations should be seen as a balance between its traditional powers to police business within its borders and its obligations under the federal Constitution. The term "foreign corporation" is used to denote a company established and existing under the laws of a jurisdiction, whether a foreign country or another US state, other than the state in which it is doing business.[170] Although the term "pseudo-foreign" corporation is not found in statutes, the legal literature uses it to designate a corporation that, although incorporated elsewhere, has most of its shareholders and business activity in the host state. Most states require merely that a foreign corporation register with the state and provide an in-state agent who can be served with process papers if a judicial action is filed against the foreign corporation.[171] Some states, however, apply significant parts of their own corporate statutes to pseudo-foreign corporations. For example, California applies rules regarding the election of directors (including by cumulative voting), their duties, and the participation of shareholders in the company to any corporation that is not listed on a national stock exchange if over half of its shareholders of record have California addresses and the company's payroll is mainly paid in the state.[172] New York requires the same type of foreign corporations (i.e. unlisted companies with significant operations in the state) to provide information to shareholders and applies New York law to actions against and liability of company directors.[173]

The power that states have to impose such requirements on corporations formed under the law of another state has not been clearly defined,[174] but is considered to be extensive. A state may completely ban foreign corporations from operating within state territory,[175] but may not deprive

---

[169] *Edgar* v. *MITE Corp.*, 457 US 624 (1982); and *Pike* v. *Bruce Church, Inc.*, 397 US 137 (1970).

[170] See e.g. § 371(a) DGCL; and § 1.40(10) Model Act.

[171] See e.g. § 371(b) DGCL; and § 15.03(a) Model Act.

[172] § 2115 California Corporations Code.

[173] §§ 1315–1320 New York Business Corporation Law.

[174] See the remarks of Coffee in Coffee (1999a: 103); Klein (2004).

[175] Fletcher (2005: § 8386); 36 Am. Jur. 2d, *Foreign Corporations*, § 182 (2001), as well as *Railway Express Agency, Inc.* v. *Virginia*, 282 US 440 (1931); and *Eli Lilly & Co.* v. *Sav-On-Drugs, Inc.*, 366 US 276, 279 (1961).

such corporations of their constitutional rights or interfere with inter-state commerce (thus foreign corporations retain the right to do business *through* state territory).[176] There is no authoritative federal court decision on whether a state may regulate the internal affairs of a corporation in the manner done by the laws of California and New York, although there has been considerable speculation on the matter.[177] Aside from a finding that such statutes interfere with interstate commerce or are preempted by an expanding federal regulation of corporations,[178] there is little con-stitutional basis for challenging the statutes. First, a principal constitu-tional tool for guaranteeing the citizens of one state legal freedoms and rights in another state, the "privileges and immunities clause" of the US Constitution,[179] has been held not to apply to corporations.[180] Secondly, no federal decision has authoritatively applied another potentially applicable constitutional provision, the "full faith and credit clause,"[181] to guarantee that the structure of internal affairs governance of a corporation created in one state be respected in such form in another state.[182] It is import-ant for this question that pseudo-foreign corporation laws of the type used in California have already existed without significant challenge for about fifty years, making it unlikely that they would be struck down on any ground other than federal preemption – if federal rules on internal affairs continue to expand as they have in the Sarbanes–Oxley Act and in the very unlikely event that they would apply to *unlisted* companies. Read *Vantagepoint Venture Partners* in this chapter. Are the Delaware court's arguments convincing? Given that state courts do not have ultimate authority in matters of federal constitutional law, are you convinced by the Delaware Court's presentation of the US Supreme Court's decisions?

---

[176] See e.g. *Phillips Petroleum Co.* v. *Jenkins*, 297 US 629 (1936); *Furst* v. *Brewster*, 282 US 493 (1931); *Cudahy Packing Co.* v. *Hinkle*, 278 US 460 (1929); Fletcher (2005: § 8388); and 36 Am. Jur. 2d, *Foreign Corporations*, § 192 (2001).

[177] Buxbaum (1987); Reese and Kaufman (1958); Langevoort (1987); Klein (2004: 360 *et seq.*).

[178] On this question, see Langevoort (1987: 110 *et seq.*).

[179] US Constitution, art. IV, § 2 ("The Citizens of each State shall be entitled to all Privileges and Immunities of Citizens in the several States.").

[180] *Bank of Augusta* v. *Earle*, 38 US 519 (1839), discussed in Gevurtz (2000: 37–38); *Pembina Consolidated Silver Mining & Milling Co.* v. *Pennsylvania*, 125 US 181 (1888).

[181] US Constitution, art. IV, § 1 ("Full Faith and Credit shall be given in each State to the public Acts, Records, and judicial Proceedings of every other State.").

[182] For a thorough, recent discussion (in German), see Klein (2004: 383 *et seq.*); for older treatment by US scholars, see Buxbaum (1987: 43 *et seq.*); and Reese and Kaufman (1958).

Therefore, although cases addressing possible conflicts between *federal* and state law have stressed that, because corporations are "creatures of the states," state law should be given considerable deference in questions of internal affairs,[183] it remains unsettled whether this requires deference in equal degree when there is a conflict between two *states* with regard to "foreign" corporations that base their operations in the host state. In any case, it will be clear from the discussion of EU law in the preceding section that US states have a considerably freer hand than their EU member state counterparts under the decisions of the ECJ in regulating the presence of "foreign" corporations doing business on their soil.

C.   A foreseeable future of stable development

In the US, the comparatist can look back on a 200-year history of company law that has not been significantly interrupted by war or tumultuous ideological turnarounds. The long-term trends have been for statutes to evolve along with the organizational needs of business and for authority to gradually pass from the states to the federal government. States, originally held back by various cultural, economic and political forces, entered the fray to compete for franchise revenues by loosening their grip on companies until abuses and market breakdowns provoked federal action, such as the "trust busting" at the turn of the twentieth century, the enactment of the securities laws in the 1930s, the various amendments and rules added to the latter over the decades, and most recently the Sarbanes–Oxley Act of 2002. Professors William W. Bratton and Joseph A. McCahery see "no political incentives that might encourage federal micromanagement of the charter market." They observe: "Failing that, corporate federalism remains robust, so long as the federal government and stock exchanges continue to refrain from allocating to themselves so much subject matter as to cause Delaware's customers to question the efficacy of their rent payments."[184] Along these lines, the future shape of US company law will likely be decided by a combination of the stability of the securities markets and the popular weight of the respective arguments for and against state chartering. Those arguments may well be led in person or by the intellectual successors of Professor Lucien A. Bebchuk in one corner and Professor Roberta Romano in the other. Romano has convincingly argued that market forces lead the way to higher quality law:

---

[183]   *CTS Corp.* v. *Dynamics Corp. of America*, 481 US 69, 86 (1987); and *Santa Fe Industries, Inc.* v. *Green*, 430 US 462, 479 (1977).

[184]   Bratton and McCahery (2006: 696).

> [T]he diffusion of corporate law reform initiatives across the states [leads to] ... experimental variation regarding the statutory form thought to be best suited for handling a particular problem, followed by a majority of states eventually setting upon one format ... The dynamic production of corporation laws exemplifies how federalism's delegation of a body of law to the states can create an effective laboratory for experimentation and innovation ... Innovation enhances revenues from charter fees and the local corporate bar's income from servicing local clients.[185]

Nevertheless, Bebchuk has countered that such market forces are driven by the interests of the constituencies in control of corporations, not by the general good:

> [There is a] divergence between the interests of managers and controlling shareholders and the interests of public shareholders ... [M]anagers may well seek, and states in turn may well provide, rules that ... serve the private interests of managers and controlling shareholders ... [S]tates seeking to attract incorporations have an incentive to focus on the interests of shareholders and managers, they will tend to ignore the interests of other parties. As a result, state competition may well produce undesirable rules whenever significant externalities are present.[186]

This argument is unlikely to be settled in the near future. The comparative view from Europe, however, is relatively clear. It is safe to say that the manner in which the US states and federal government have engaged in and reacted to diversity in company law among the individual states and the need to develop uniform rules has been and will continue to be markedly different from the process in Europe.

Questions for discussion

1. What is the difference between the "real seat" theory and the "place of incorporation" theory for determining the law applicable to corporate affairs?
2. Which theory is preferable, "real seat" or "place of incorporation"?
3. What is the distinction between the "internal" and "external" affairs of a corporation?
4. What is meant by "regulatory competition"?
5. Under *Überseering* and *Inspire Art*, what would justify a host member state's regulation of a corporation in a way that restricts its freedom of establishment?
6. Will *Centros*, *Überseering* and *Inspire Art* lead to a "race to the bottom" in Europe?

---

[185] Romano (2006: 246–247).   [186] Bebchuk (1992: 1509).

7. Pursuant to *Vantagepoint Venture Partners*, what is the relationship between US states as to companies incorporated in one state and operating in another?

8. How does the US position compare to that expressed by the ECJ in *Überseering* and *Inspire Art*?

9. Should company laws be allowed to "compete" through the mobility of corporations?

10. Are market forces proper determinants of the shape of company law?

Cases

Überseering BV v. Nordic Construction Company Baumanagement GmbH (NCC)
European Court of Justice
November 5, 2002, [2002] ECR I-09919
[*Text omitted*]
© European Communities

THE COURT,
    in answer to the questions referred to it by the Bundesgerichtshof by order of 30 March 2000, hereby rules:

    1. Where a company formed in accordance with the law of a Member State ('A') in which it has its registered office is deemed, under the law of another Member State ('B'), to have moved its actual centre of administration to Member State B, Articles 43 EC and 48 EC preclude Member State B from denying the company legal capacity and, consequently, the capacity to bring legal proceedings before its national courts for the purpose of enforcing rights under a contract with a company established in Member State B.

    2. Where a company formed in accordance with the law of a Member State ('A') in which it has its registered office exercises its freedom of establishment in another Member State ('B'), Articles 43 EC and 48 EC require Member State B to recognise the legal capacity and, consequently, the capacity to be a party to legal proceedings which the company enjoys under the law of its State of incorporation ('A').
[*Text omitted*]

Judgment

1. By order of 30 March 2000, received at the Court Registry on 25 May 2000, the Bundesgerichtshof (Federal Court of Justice) referred to the Court for a preliminary ruling under Article 234 EC two questions on the interpretation of Articles 43 EC and 48 EC.

    2. Those questions were raised in proceedings between (i) Überseering BV ('Überseering'), a company incorporated under Netherlands law and registered

on 22 August 1990 in the register of companies of Amsterdam and Haarlem, and (ii) Nordic Construction Company Baumanagement GmbH ('NCC'), a company established in the Federal Republic of Germany, concerning damages for defective work carried out in Germany by NCC on behalf of Überseering.

National law

3. The *Zivilprozessordnung* (German Code of Civil Procedure) provides that an action brought by a party which does not have the capacity to bring legal proceedings must be dismissed as inadmissible. Under Paragraph 50(1) of the Zivilprozessordnung any person, including a company, having legal capacity has the capacity to be a party to legal proceedings: legal capacity is defined as the capacity to enjoy rights and to be the subject of obligations.

4. According to the settled case-law of the Bundesgerichtshof, which is approved by most German legal commentators, a company's legal capacity is determined by reference to the law applicable in the place where its actual centre of administration is established (Sitztheorie or company seat principle), as opposed to the Grundungstheorie or incorporation principle, by virtue of which legal capacity is determined in accordance with the law of the State in which the company was incorporated. That rule also applies where a company has been validly incorporated in another State and has subsequently transferred its actual centre of administration to Germany.

5. Since a company's legal capacity is determined by reference to German law, it cannot enjoy rights or be the subject of obligations or be a party to legal proceedings unless it has been reincorporated in Germany in such a way as to acquire legal capacity under German law.

The main proceedings

6. In October 1990, Überseering acquired a piece of land in Düsseldorf (Germany), which it used for business purposes. By a project-management contract dated 27 November 1992, Überseering engaged NCC to refurbish a garage and a motel on the site. The contractual obligations were performed but Überseering claimed that the paint work was defective.

7. In December 1994 two German nationals residing in Düsseldorf acquired all the shares in Überseering.

8. Überseering unsuccessfully sought compensation from NCC for the defective work and in 1996 it brought an action before the Landgericht (Regional Court), Düsseldorf, on the basis of its project-management contract with NCC. It claimed the sum of DEM 1 163 657.77, plus interest, in respect of the costs incurred in remedying the alleged defects and consequential damage.

9. The Landgericht dismissed the action. The Oberlandesgericht (Higher Regional Court), Düsseldorf, upheld the decision to dismiss the action. It found that Überseering had transferred its actual centre of administration to Düsseldorf

once its shares had been acquired by two German nationals. The Oberlandesgericht found that, as a company incorporated under Netherlands law, Überseering did not have legal capacity in Germany and, consequently, could not bring legal proceedings there.

10. Therefore, the Oberlandesgericht held that Überseering's action was inadmissible.

11. Überseering appealed to the Bundesgerichtshof against the judgment of the Oberlandesgericht.

12. It also appears from Überseering's observations that, in parallel with the proceedings currently pending before the Bundesgerichtshof, an action was brought against Überseering before another German court based on certain unspecified provisions of German law. As a result, it was ordered by the Landgericht Düsseldorf to pay architects' fees, apparently because it was entered on 11 September 1991 in the Düsseldorf land registry as owner of the land on which the garage and the motel refurbished by NCC were built.

The questions referred for a preliminary ruling

...

14. First, it is appropriate to discount any solution which entails (through taking account of different connecting factors) assessing a company's legal situation by reference to several legal systems. According to the Bundesgerichtshof, such a solution leads to legal uncertainty, since it is impossible to segregate clearly the areas of law to be governed by the various legal orders.

15. Second, where the connecting factor is taken to be the place of incorporation, the company's founding members are placed at an advantage, since they are able, when choosing the place of incorporation, to choose the legal system which suits them best. Therein lies the fundamental weakness of the incorporation principle, which fails to take account of the fact that a company's incorporation and activities also affect the interests of third parties and of the State in which the company has its actual centre of administration, where that is located in a State other than the one in which the company was incorporated.

16. Third, and by contrast, where the connecting factor is taken to be the actual centre of administration, that prevents the provisions of company law in the State in which the actual centre of administration is situated, which are intended to protect certain vital interests, from being circumvented by incorporating the company abroad. In the present case, the interests which German law is seeking to safeguard are notably those of the company's creditors: the legislation relating to Gesellschaften mit beschrankter Haftung ('GmbH') (limited liability companies under German law) provides such protection by detailed rules on the initial contribution and maintenance of share capital. In the case of related companies, dependent companies and their minority shareholders also need protection. In Germany such protection is provided by rules governing groups of

companies or rules providing for financial compensation and indemnification of shareholders who have been put at a disadvantage by agreements whereby one company agrees to manage another or agrees to pay its profits to another company. Finally, the rules on joint management protect the company's employees. The Bundesgerichtshof points out that not all the Member States have comparable rules.

17. The Bundesgerichtshof nevertheless wonders whether, on the basis that the company's actual centre of administration has been transferred to another country, the freedom of establishment guaranteed by Articles 43 EC and 48 EC does not preclude connecting the company's legal position with the law of the Member State in which its actual centre of administration is located. The answer to that question cannot, according to the Bundesgerichtshof, be clearly deduced from the case-law of the Court of Justice.

18. It points out, in that regard, that in Case 81/87 The Queen v. Treasury and Commissioners of Inland Revenue, ex parte Daily Mail and General Trust 1988 ECR 5483 the Court, having stated that companies could exercise their right of establishment by setting up agencies, branches and subsidiaries, or by transferring all their shares to a new company in another Member State, held that, unlike natural persons, companies exist only by virtue of the national legal system which governs their incorporation and operation. It is also apparent from that judgment that the EC Treaty has taken account of the differences in national rules on the conflict of laws and has reserved resolution of the problems associated therewith to future legislation.

19. In Case C-212/97 Centros 1999 ECR I-1459, the Court took exception to a Danish authority's refusal to register a branch of a company validly incorporated in the United Kingdom. However, the Bundesgerichtshof points out that the company had not transferred its seat, since, from its incorporation, its registered office had been in the United Kingdom, whilst its actual centre of administration had been in Denmark.

20. The Bundesgerichtshof wonders whether, in view of Centros, the Treaty provisions on freedom of establishment preclude, in a situation such as that in point in the main proceedings, application of the rules on conflict of laws in force in the Member State in which the actual centre of administration of a company validly incorporated in another Member State is situated when the consequence of those rules is the refusal to recognise the company's legal capacity and, therefore, its capacity to bring legal proceedings in the first Member State to enforce rights under a contract.

21. In those circumstances, the Bundesgerichtshof decided to stay proceedings and to refer the following questions to the Court for a preliminary ruling:

1. Are Articles 43 EC and 48 EC to be interpreted as meaning that the freedom of establishment of companies precludes the legal capacity, and capacity to be a party to legal proceedings, of a company validly incorporated under the law of one Member State from being determined according to the law of

another State to which the company has moved its actual centre of administration, where, under the law of that second State, the company may no
longer bring legal proceedings there in respect of claims under a contract?

2. If the Court's answer to that question is affirmative: Does the freedom of establishment of companies (Articles 43 EC and 48 EC) require that a company's
legal capacity and capacity to be a party to legal proceedings is to be determined according to the law of the State where the company is incorporated?'

The first question

22. By its first question, the national court is, essentially, asking whether, where a
company formed in accordance with the legislation of a Member State ('A') in which
it has its registered office is deemed, under the law of another Member State ('B'), to
have moved its actual centre of administration to Member State B, Articles 43 EC
and 48 EC preclude Member State B from denying the company legal capacity, and
therefore the capacity to bring legal proceedings before its national courts in order
to enforce rights under a contract with a company established in Member State B.

[Text omitted]

Findings of the Court

As to whether the Treaty provisions on freedom of establishment apply

52. In limine and contrary to the submissions of both NCC and the German,
Spanish and Italian Governments, the Court must make clear that where a company which is validly incorporated in one Member State ('A') in which it has its
registered office is deemed, under the law of a second Member State ('B'), to have
moved its actual centre of administration to Member State B following the transfer
of all its shares to nationals of that State residing there, the rules which Member
State B applies to that company do not, as Community law now stands, fall outside
the scope of the Community provisions on freedom of establishment.

53. In that regard, it is appropriate to begin by rejecting the arguments based
on Article 293 EC, which were put forward by NCC and the German, Spanish and
Italian Governments.

54. As the Advocate General maintained at point 42 of his Opinion, Article 293
EC does not constitute a reserve of legislative competence vested in the Member
States. Although Article 293 EC gives Member States the opportunity to enter into
negotiations with a view, inter alia, to facilitating the resolution of problems arising
from the discrepancies between the various laws relating to the mutual recognition
of companies and the retention of legal personality in the event of the transfer of
their seat from one country to another, it does so solely so far as is necessary, that is
to say if the provisions of the Treaty do not enable its objectives to be attained.

55. More specifically, it is important to point out that, although the conventions
which may be entered into pursuant to Article 293 EC may, like the harmonising

directives provided for in Article 44 EC, facilitate the attainment of freedom of establishment, the exercise of that freedom can none the less not be dependent upon the adoption of such conventions.

56. In that regard, it must be borne in mind that, as the Court has already had occasion to point out, the freedom of establishment, conferred by Article 43 EC on Community nationals, includes the right for them to take up and pursue activities as self-employed persons and to set up and manage undertakings under the same conditions as are laid down by the law of the Member State of establishment for its own nationals. Furthermore, according to the actual wording of Article 48 EC, companies or firms formed in accordance with the law of a Member State and having their registered office, central administration or principal place of business within the Community shall, for the purposes of the provisions of the Treaty concerning the right of establishment, be treated in the same way as natural persons who are nationals of Member States.

57. The immediate consequence of this is that those companies or firms are entitled to carry on their business in another Member State. The location of their registered office, central administration or principal place of business constitutes the connecting factor with the legal system of a particular Member State in the same way as does nationality in the case of a natural person.

58. The Court's reasoning in Centros was founded on those premisses (paragraphs 19 and 20).

59. A necessary precondition for the exercise of the freedom of establishment is the recognition of those companies by any Member State in which they wish to establish themselves.

60. Accordingly, it is not necessary for the Member States to adopt a convention on the mutual recognition of companies in order for companies meeting the conditions set out in Article 48 EC to exercise the freedom of establishment conferred on them by Articles 43 EC and 48 EC, which have been directly applicable since the transitional period came to an end. It follows that no argument that might justify limiting the full effect of those articles can be derived from the fact that no convention on the mutual recognition of companies has as yet been adopted on the basis of Article 293 EC.

61. Second, it is important to consider the argument based on the decision in Daily Mail and General Trust, which was central to the arguments put to the Court. It was cited in order, in some way, to assimilate the situation in Daily Mail and General Trust to the situation which under German law entails the loss of legal capacity and of the capacity to be a party to legal proceedings by a company incorporated under the law of another Member State.

62. It must be stressed that, unlike Daily Mail and General Trust, which concerned relations between a company and the Member State under whose laws it had been incorporated in a situation where the company wished to transfer its actual centre of administration to another Member State whilst retaining its legal

personality in the State of incorporation, the present case concerns the recognition by one Member State of a company incorporated under the law of another Member State, such a company being denied all legal capacity in the host Member State where it takes the view that the company has moved its actual centre of administration to its territory, irrespective of whether in that regard the company actually intended to transfer its seat.

63. As the Netherlands and United Kingdom Governments and the Commission and the EFTA Surveillance Authority have pointed out, Überseering never gave any indication that it intended to transfer its seat to Germany. Its legal existence was never called in question under the law of the State where it was incorporated as a result of all its shares being transferred to persons resident in Germany. In particular, the company was not subject to any winding-up measures under Netherlands law. Under Netherlands law, it did not cease to be validly incorporated.

64. Moreover, even if the dispute before the national court is seen as concerning a transfer of the actual centre of administration from one country to another, the interpretation of Daily Mail and General Trust put forward by NCC and the German, Spanish and Italian Governments is incorrect.

65. In that case, Daily Mail and General Trust Plc, a company formed in accordance with the law of the United Kingdom and having both its registered office and actual centre of administration there, wished to transfer its centre of administration to another Member State without losing its legal personality or ceasing to be a company incorporated under English law. This required the consent of the competent United Kingdom authorities, which they refused to give. The company initiated proceedings against the authorities before the High Court of Justice, Queen's Bench Division, seeking an order that Articles 52 and 58 of the EEC Treaty gave it the right to transfer its actual centre of administration to another Member State without prior consent and without loss of its legal personality.

66. Thus, unlike the case before the national court in this instance, Daily Mail and General Trust did not concern the way in which one Member State treats a company which is validly incorporated in another Member State and which is exercising its freedom of establishment in the first Member State.

67. Asked by the High Court of Justice whether the Treaty provisions on freedom of establishment conferred on a company the right to transfer its centre of management to another Member State, the Court observed, at paragraph 19 of Daily Mail and General Trust, that a company, which is a creature of national law, exists only by virtue of the national legislation which determines its incorporation and functioning.

68. At paragraph 20 of that judgment, the Court pointed out that the legislation of the Member States varies widely in regard both to the factor providing a connection to the national territory required for the incorporation of a company and to the question whether a company incorporated under the legislation of a Member State may subsequently modify that connecting factor.

69. The Court concluded, at paragraph 23 of the judgment, that the Treaty regarded those differences as problems which were not resolved by the Treaty rules concerning freedom of establishment but would have to be dealt with by legislation or conventions, which the Court found had not yet been done.

70. In so doing, the Court confined itself to holding that the question whether a company formed in accordance with the legislation of one Member State could transfer its registered office or its actual centre of administration to another Member State without losing its legal personality under the law of the Member State of incorporation and, in certain circumstances, the rules relating to that transfer were determined by the national law in accordance with which the company had been incorporated. It concluded that a Member State was able, in the case of a company incorporated under its law, to make the company's right to retain its legal personality under the law of that State subject to restrictions on the transfer of the company's actual centre of administration to a foreign country.

71. By contrast, the Court did not rule on the question whether where, as here, a company incorporated under the law of a Member State ('A') is found, under the law of another Member State ('B'), to have moved its actual centre of administration to Member State B, that State is entitled to refuse to recognise the legal personality which the company enjoys under the law of its State of incorporation ('A').

72. Thus, despite the general terms in which paragraph 23 of Daily Mail and General Trust is cast, the Court did not intend to recognise a Member State as having the power, *vis-à-vis* companies validly incorporated in other Member States and found by it to have transferred their seat to its territory, to subject those companies' effective exercise in its territory of the freedom of establishment to compliance with its domestic company law.

73. There are, therefore, no grounds for concluding from Daily Mail and General Trust that, where a company formed in accordance with the law of one Member State and with legal personality in that State exercises its freedom of establishment in another Member State, the question of recognition of its legal capacity and its capacity to be a party to legal proceedings in the Member State of establishment falls outside the scope of the Treaty provisions on freedom of establishment, even when the company is found, under the law of the Member State of establishment, to have moved its actual centre of administration to that State.

74. Third, the Court rejects the Spanish Government's argument that, in a situation such as that in point before the national court, Title I of the General Programme subordinates the benefit of the freedom of establishment guaranteed by the Treaty to the requirement that there be a real and continuous link with the economy of a Member State.

75. It is apparent from the wording of the General Programme that it requires a real and continuous link solely in a case in which the company has nothing but its registered office within the Community. That is unquestionably not the position in the case of Überseering whose registered office and actual centre of administration

are within the Community. As regards the situation just described, the Court found, at paragraph 19 of Centros, that under Article 58 of the Treaty companies formed in accordance with the law of a Member State and having their registered office, central administration or principal place of business within the Community are to be treated in the same way as natural persons who are nationals of Member States.

76. It follows from the foregoing considerations that Überseering is entitled to rely on the principle of freedom of establishment in order to contest the refusal of German law to regard it as a legal person with the capacity to be a party to legal proceedings.

77. Furthermore, it must be borne in mind that as a general rule the acquisition by one or more natural persons residing in a Member State of shares in a company incorporated and established in another Member State is covered by the Treaty provisions on the free movement of capital, provided that the shareholding does not confer on those natural persons definite influence over the company's decisions and does not allow them to determine its activities. By contrast, where the acquisition involves all the shares in a company having its registered office in another Member State and the shareholding confers a definite influence over the company's decisions and allows the shareholders to determine its activities, it is the Treaty provisions on freedom of establishment which apply (see, to that effect, Case C-251/98 Baars 2000 ECR I-2787, paragraphs 21 and 22).

As to whether there is a restriction on freedom of establishment

78. The Court must next consider whether the refusal by the German courts to recognise the legal capacity and capacity to be a party to legal proceedings of a company validly incorporated under the law of another Member State constitutes a restriction on freedom of establishment.

79. In that regard, in a situation such as that in point in the main proceedings, a company validly incorporated under the law of, and having its registered office in, a Member State other than the Federal Republic of Germany has under German law no alternative to reincorporation in Germany if it wishes to enforce before a German court its rights under a contract entered into with a company incorporated under German law.

80. Überseering, which is validly incorporated in the Netherlands and has its registered office there, is entitled under Articles 43 EC and 48 EC to exercise its freedom of establishment in Germany as a company incorporated under Netherlands law. It is of little significance in that regard that, after the company was formed, all its shares were acquired by German nationals residing in Germany, since that has not caused Überseering to cease to be a legal person under Netherlands law.

81. Indeed, its very existence is inseparable from its status as a company incorporated under Netherlands law since, as the Court has observed, a company exists only by virtue of the national legislation which determines its incorporation and functioning (see, to that effect, Daily Mail and General Trust, paragraph 19). The

requirement of reincorporation of the same company in Germany is therefore tantamount to outright negation of freedom of establishment.

82. In those circumstances, the refusal by a host Member State ('B') to recognise the legal capacity of a company formed in accordance with the law of another Member State ('A') in which it has its registered office on the ground, in particular, that the company moved its actual centre of administration to Member State B following the acquisition of all its shares by nationals of that State residing there, with the result that the company cannot, in Member State B, bring legal proceedings to defend rights under a contract unless it is reincorporated under the law of Member State B, constitutes a restriction on freedom of establishment which is, in principle, incompatible with Articles 43 EC and 48 EC.

As to whether the restriction on freedom of establishment is justified

83. Finally, it is appropriate to determine whether such a restriction on freedom of establishment can be justified on the grounds advanced by the national court and by the German Government.

84. The German Government has argued in the alternative, should the Court find that application of the company seat principle entails a restriction on freedom of establishment, that the restriction applies without discrimination, is justified by overriding requirements relating to the general interest and is proportionate to the objectives pursued.

85. In the German Government's submission, the lack of discrimination arises from the fact that the rules of law proceeding from the company seat principle apply not only to any foreign company which establishes itself in Germany by moving its actual centre of administration there but also to companies incorporated under German law which transfer their actual centre of administration out of Germany.

86. As regards the overriding requirements relating to the general interest put forward in order to justify the alleged restriction, the German Government maintains, first, that in other spheres, secondary Community law assumes that the administrative head office and the registered office are identical. Community law has thus recognised the merits, in principle, of a single registered and administrative office.

87. In the German Government's submission, the German rules of private international company law enhance legal certainty and creditor protection. There is no harmonisation at Community level of the rules for protecting the share capital of limited liability companies and such companies are subject in Member States other than the Federal Republic of Germany to requirements which are in some respects much less strict. The company seat principle as applied by German law ensures that a company whose principal place of business is in Germany has a fixed minimum share capital, something which is instrumental in protecting parties with whom it enters into contracts and its creditors. That also prevents distortions of competition since all companies whose principal place of business is in Germany are subject to the same legal requirements.

88. The German Government submits that further justification is provided by the protection of minority shareholders. In the absence of a Community standard for the protection of minority-shareholders, a Member State must be able to apply to any company whose principal place of business is within its territory the same legal requirements for the protection of minority shareholders.

89. Application of the company seat principle is also justified by employee protection through the joint management of undertakings on conditions determined by law. The German Government argues that the transfer to Germany of the actual centre of administration of a company incorporated under the law of another Member State could, if the company continued to be a company incorporated under that law, involve a risk of circumvention of the German provisions on joint management, which allow the employees, in certain circumstances, to be represented on the company's supervisory board. Companies in other Member States do not always have such a body.

90. Finally, any restriction resulting from the application of the company seat principle can be justified on fiscal grounds. The incorporation principle, to a greater extent than the company seat principle, enables companies to be created which have two places of residence and which are, as a result, subject to taxation without limits in at least two Member States. There is a risk that such companies might claim and be granted tax advantages simultaneously in several Member States. By way of example, the German Government mentions the cross-border offsetting of losses against profits between undertakings within the same group.

91. The Netherlands and United Kingdom Governments, the Commission and the EFTA Surveillance Authority submit that the restriction in question is not justified. They point out in particular that the aim of protecting creditors was also invoked by the Danish authorities in Centros to justify the refusal to register in Denmark a branch of a company which had been validly incorporated in the United Kingdom and all of whose business was to be carried on in Denmark but which did not meet the requirements of Danish law regarding the provision and paying-up of a minimum amount of share capital. They add that it is not certain that requirements associated with a minimum amount of share capital are an effective way of protecting creditors.

92. It is not inconceivable that overriding requirements relating to the general interest, such as the protection of the interests of creditors, minority shareholders, employees and even the taxation authorities, may, in certain circumstances and subject to certain conditions, justify restrictions on freedom of establishment.

93. Such objectives cannot, however, justify denying the legal capacity and, consequently, the capacity to be a party to legal proceedings of a company properly incorporated in another Member State in which it has its registered office. Such a measure is tantamount to an outright negation of the freedom of establishment conferred on companies by Articles 43 EC and 48 EC.

94. Accordingly, the answer to the first question must be that, where a company formed in accordance with the law of a Member State (A') in which it has its registered office is deemed, under the law of another Member State (B'), to have moved its actual centre of administration to Member State B, Articles 43 EC and 48 EC preclude Member State B from denying the company legal capacity and, consequently, the capacity to bring legal proceedings before its national courts for the purpose of enforcing rights under a contract with a company established in Member State B.

The second question referred to the Court

95. It follows from the answer to the first question referred to the Court for a preliminary ruling that, where a company formed in accordance with the law of a Member State (A') in which it has its registered office exercises its freedom of establishment in another Member State (B'), Articles 43 EC and 48 EC require Member State B to recognise the legal capacity and, consequently, the capacity to be a party to legal proceedings which the company enjoys under the law of its State of incorporation (A') ...

Kamer van Koophandel en Fabrieken voor Amsterdam and Inspire Art Ltd
European Court of Justice
September 30, 2003, [2003] ECR I-10155
[*Text edited*]
© European Communities

[*Text omitted*]

I – The legal framework

The relevant provisions of Community law

3. The first paragraph of Article 43 EC provides:

> Within the framework of the provisions set out below, restrictions on the freedom of establishment of nationals of a Member State in the territory of another Member State shall be prohibited. Such prohibition shall also apply to restrictions on the setting-up of agencies, branches or subsidiaries by nationals of any Member State established in the territory of any Member State.

4. Article 48 EC extends entitlement to freedom of establishment, subject to the same conditions as those laid down for individuals who are nationals of the Member States, to companies or firms formed in accordance with the law of a Member State and having their registered office, central administration or principal place of business within the Community.

5. Article 46 EC permits the Member States to restrict the freedom of establishment of foreign nationals by adopting provisions laid down by law, regulation or administrative action, in so far as such provisions are justified on grounds of public policy, public security or public health.

6. Article 44(2)(g) EC empowers the Council of the European Union, for the purpose of giving effect to freedom of establishment, to coordinate to the necessary extent the safeguards which, for the protection of the interests of members and others, are required by Member States of companies or firms within the meaning of the second paragraph of Article 48 of the EC Treaty with a view to making such safeguards equivalent throughout the Community.

7. Various directives have in that manner been adopted by the Council on that basis ('company-law directives') and, in particular, the following directives referred to in the dispute in the main proceedings.

[Text omitted]

The relevant provisions of national law

22. Article 1 of the WFBV defines a 'formally foreign company' as a 'capital company formed under laws other than those of the Netherlands and having legal personality, which carries on its activities entirely or almost entirely in the Netherlands and also does not have any real connection with the State within which the law under which the company was formed applies ... '.

23. Articles 2 to 5 of the WFBV impose on formally foreign companies various obligations concerning the company's registration in the commercial register, an indication of that status in all the documents produced by it, the minimum share capital and the drawing-up, production and publication of the annual documents. The WFBV also provides for penalties in case of non-compliance with those provisions.

24. In particular, Article 2 of the WFBV requires a company falling within the definition of a formally foreign company to be registered as such in the commercial register of the host State. An authentic copy in Dutch, French, German or English, or a copy certified by a director, of the instrument constituting the company must also be filed in the commercial register of the host State, and a copy of the memorandum and articles of association if they are contained in a separate instrument. The date of the first registration of that company, the national register in which and the number under which it is registered must also appear in the commercial register and, in the case of companies with a single member, certain information concerning that sole shareholder.

25. Article 4(4) provides for directors to be jointly and severally liable with the company for legal acts carried out in the name of the company during their directorship until the requirement of registration in the commercial register has been fulfilled.

26. Pursuant to Article 3 of the WFBV, all documents and notices in which a formally foreign company appears or which it produces, except telegrams and advertisements, must state the company's full name, legal form, registered office and chief place of business, and the registration number, the date of first registration and the register in which it is required to be registered under the legislation applicable to it. That article also requires it to be indicated that the company is formally foreign and

prohibits the making of statements in documents or publications which give the false impression that the undertaking belongs to a Netherlands legal person.

27. Pursuant to Article 4(1) of the WFBV, the subscribed capital of a formally foreign company must be at least equal to the minimum amount required of Netherlands limited companies by Article 2:178 of the Burgerlijke Wetboek (Netherlands Civil Code, the 'BW'), which was EUR 18 000 on 1 September 2000 (Staatsblad 2000, N 322). The paid-up share capital must be at least equal to the minimum capital (Article 4(2) of the WFBV, referring back to Article 2:178 of the BW). In order to ensure that formally foreign companies fulfil those conditions, an auditor's certificate must be filed in the commercial register (Article 4(3) of the WFBV).

28. Until the conditions relating to capital and paid-up share capital have been satisfied, the directors are jointly and severally liable with the company for all legal acts carried out during their directorship which are binding on the company. The directors of a formally foreign company are likewise jointly and severally responsible for the company's acts if the capital subscribed and paid up falls below the minimum required, having originally satisfied the minimum capital requirement. The directors' joint and several liability lasts only so long as the company's status is that of a formally foreign company (Article 4(4) of the WFBV).

29. Nevertheless, Article 4(5) of the WFBV states that the minimum capital provisions do not apply to a company governed by the law of a Member State or of a Member State of the European Economic Area ('the EEA') to which the Second Directive is applicable.

30. Article 5(1) and (2) of the WFBV requires the directors of formally foreign companies to keep accounts and hold them for seven years. Directors must produce annual accounts and an annual report. Those documents must be published by being lodged in the commercial register and must satisfy the conditions laid down in Title 9 of Book 2 of the BW, which makes it possible to be sure that they are consistent with the annual documents produced by Netherlands companies.

31. Directors are additionally bound to lodge in the commercial register before 1 April each year proof of registration in the register determined by the law applicable to the company (Article 5(4) of the WFBV). For the application of the WFBV persons responsible for the day-to-day management of the company are treated in the same way as directors, in accordance with Article 7 of that law.

32. Articles 2:249 and 2:260 of the BW are applicable by analogy to formally foreign companies. Those articles provide for the joint and several liability of directors and auditors for damage caused to others by the publication of misleading annual documents or interim figures.

33. Article 5(3) of the WFBV provides, however, that the obligations under Article 5(1) and (2) of the WFBV relating to accounts and annual documents are not to apply to companies governed by the law of a Member State or by the law of a Member State of the EEA and falling within the ambit of the Fourth and/or the Seventh Directive.

II – The dispute in the main proceedings and the questions referred for a preliminary ruling

34. Inspire Art was formed on 28 July 2000 in the legal form of a private company limited by shares under the law of England and Wales and it has its registered office at Folkestone (United Kingdom). Its sole director, whose domicile is in The Hague (Netherlands), is authorised to act alone and independently in the name of the company. The company, which carries on activity under the business name 'Inspire Art Ltd' in the sphere of dealing in objets d'art, began trading on 17 August 2000 and has a branch in Amsterdam.

35. Inspire Art is registered in the commercial register of the Chamber of Commerce without any indication of the fact that it is a formally foreign company within the meaning of Article 1 of the WFBV.

36. Taking the view that that indication was mandatory on the ground that Inspire Art traded exclusively in the Netherlands, the Chamber of Commerce applied to the Kantongerecht te Amsterdam on 30 October 2000 for an order that there should be added to that company's registration in the commercial register the statement that it is a formally foreign company, in accordance with Article 1 of the WFBV, which would entail other obligations laid down by law, set out in paragraphs 22 to 33 above.

37. Inspire Art denies that its registration is incomplete, primarily because the company does not meet the conditions set out in Article 1 of the WFBV. As a secondary point, if the Kantongerecht were to decide that it met those conditions, it maintained that the WFBV was contrary to Community law, and to Articles 43 EC and 48 EC in particular.

38. In its order of 5 February 2001 the Kantongerecht held that Inspire Art was a formally foreign company within the meaning of Article 1 of the WFBV.

39. As regards the compatibility of the WFBV with Community law, it decided to stay proceedings and refer the following questions to the Court of Justice for a preliminary ruling:

1. Are Articles 43 EC and 48 EC to be interpreted as precluding the Netherlands, pursuant to the Wet op de formeel buitenlandse vennootschappen of 17 December 1997, from attaching additional conditions, such as those laid down in Articles 2 to 5 of that law, to the establishment in the Netherlands of a branch of a company which has been set up in the United Kingdom with the sole aim of securing the advantages which that offers compared to incorporation under Netherlands law, given that Netherlands law imposes stricter rules than those applying in the United Kingdom with regard to the setting-up of companies and payment for shares, and given that the Netherlands law infers that aim from the fact that the company carries on its activities entirely or almost entirely in the Netherlands and, furthermore, does not have any real connection with the State in which the law under which it was formed applies?

2. If, on a proper construction of those articles, it is held that the provisions of the Wet op de formeel buitenlandse vennootschappen are incompatible with them, must Article 46 EC be interpreted as meaning that the said Articles 43 EC and 48 EC do not affect the applicability of the Netherlands rules laid down in that law, on the ground that the provisions in question are justified for the reasons stated by the Netherlands legislature?

III – Preliminary observations

[Text omitted]

Consideration of the questions referred

52. By those questions, which may appropriately be considered together, the national court seeks in substance to ascertain:

- whether Articles 43 EC and 48 EC must be interpreted as precluding legislation of a Member State, such as the WFBV, which attaches additional conditions, such as those laid down in Articles 2 to 5 of that law, to the establishment in that Member State of a company formed under the law of another Member State with the sole aim of securing certain advantages compared with companies formed under the law of the Member State of establishment which imposes stricter rules than those imposed by the law of the Member State of formation with regard to the setting-up of companies and paying-up of shares;
- whether the fact that the law of the Member State of establishment infers that aim from the circumstance of that company's carrying on its activities entirely or almost entirely in that latter Member State and of its having no genuine connection with the State in accordance with the law of which it was formed makes any difference to the Court's analysis of that question;
- and whether, if an affirmative answer is given to one or other of those questions, a national law such as the WFBV may be justified under Article 46 EC or by overriding reasons relating to the public interest.

53. In the first place, Article 5(1) and (2) of the WFBV, mentioned in the questions referred for a preliminary ruling, concerns the keeping and filing of the annual accounts of formally foreign companies. Article 5(3) of the WFBV provides, however, that the obligations laid down in those subparagraphs are not to apply to companies governed by the law of another Member State and to which the Fourth Directive, inter alia, applies. Inspire Art is covered by that exception, since it is governed by the law of England and Wales and since it falls within the scope ratione personae of the Fourth Directive.

54. There is therefore no longer any need for the Court to consider whether a provision such as Article 5 of the WFBV is compatible with Community law.

55. Secondly, several of the provisions of the WFBV fall within the scope of the Eleventh Directive, since that concerns disclosure requirements in respect of branches opened in a Member State by companies covered by the First Directive and governed by the law of another Member State.

56. In that connection, first, as the Commission observes, some of the obligations imposed by the WFBV concern the implementation in domestic law of the disclosure requirements laid down by the Eleventh Directive.

57. Those are, more specifically, the provisions requiring: an entry in the business register of the host Member State showing registration in a foreign business register, and the number under which the company is registered in that register (Article 2(1) of the WFBV and Article 2(1)(c) of the Eleventh Directive), filing in the Netherlands business register of a certified copy of the document creating the company and of its memorandum and articles of association in Dutch, French, English or German (Article 2(1) of the WFBV and Articles 2(2)(b) and 4 of the Eleventh Directive), and the filing every year in that business register of a certificate of registration in the foreign business register (Article 5(4) of the WFBV and Article 2(2)(c) of the Eleventh Directive).

58. Those provisions, the compatibility of which with the Eleventh Directive has not been called into question, cannot be regarded as constituting any impediment to freedom of establishment.

59. Nevertheless, even if the various disclosure measures referred to at paragraph 57 above are compatible with Community law, that does not automatically mean that the sanctions attached by the WFBV to non-compliance with those disclosure measures must also be compatible with Community law.

60. Article 4(4) of the WFBV provides for directors to be jointly and severally liable with the company for legal acts adopted in the name of the company during their directorship for so long as the requirements concerning disclosure in the business register have not been met.

61. It is true that Article 12 of the Eleventh Directive requires the Member States to provide for appropriate penalties where branches of companies fail to make the required disclosures in the host Member State.

62. The Court has consistently held that where a Community regulation does not specifically provide any penalty for an infringement or refers for that purpose to national laws, regulations and administrative provisions, Article 10 EC requires the Member States to take all measures necessary to guarantee the application and effectiveness of Community law. For that purpose, while the choice of penalties remains within their discretion, they must ensure in particular that infringements of Community law are penalised in conditions, both procedural and substantive, which are analogous to those applicable to infringements of national law of a

similar nature and importance and which, in any event, make the penalty effective, proportionate and dissuasive ...

63. It is for the national court, which alone has jurisdiction to interpret domestic law, to establish whether the penalty provided for by Article 4(4) of the WFBV satisfies those conditions and, in particular, whether it does not put formally foreign companies at a disadvantage in comparison with Netherlands companies where there is an infringement of the disclosure requirements referred to in paragraph 56 above.

64. If the national court reaches the conclusion that Article 4(4) of the WFBV treats formally foreign companies differently from national companies, it must be concluded that that provision is contrary to Community law.

65. On the other hand, the list set out in Article 2 of the Eleventh Directive does not include the other disclosure obligations provided for by the WFBV, namely, recording in the commercial register the fact that the company is formally foreign (Articles 1 and 2(1) of the WFBV), recording in the business register of the host Member State the date of first registration in the foreign business register and information relating to sole members (Article 2(1) of the WFBV), and the compulsory filing of an auditor's certificate to the effect that the company satisfies the conditions as to minimum capital, subscribed capital and paid-up share capital (Article 4(3) of the WFBV). Similarly, mention of the company's status of a formally foreign company on all documents it produces (Article 3 of the WFBV) is not included in Article 6 of the Eleventh Directive.

66. It is therefore necessary to consider, with regard to those obligations, whether the harmonisation brought about by the Eleventh Directive, and more particularly Articles 2 and 6 thereof, is exhaustive.

67. The Eleventh Directive was adopted on the basis of Article 54(3)(g) of the EC Treaty (now, after amendment, Article 44(2)(g) EC) which provides that the Council and Commission are to carry out the duties devolving on them under that article by coordinating to the necessary extent the safeguards which, for the protection of the interests of members and others, are required by Member States of companies or firms within the meaning of the second paragraph of Article 58 with a view to making such safeguards equivalent throughout the Community.

68. Furthermore, it follows from the fourth and fifth recitals in the preamble to the Directive that the differences in respect of branches between the laws of the Member States, especially as regards disclosure, may interfere with the exercise of the right of establishment and must therefore be eliminated.

69. It follows that, without affecting the information obligations imposed on branches under social or tax law, or in the field of statistics, harmonisation of the disclosure to be made by branches, as brought about by the Eleventh Directive, is exhaustive, for only in that case can it attain the objective it pursues.

70. It must likewise be pointed out that Article 2(1) of the Eleventh Directive is exhaustive in formulation. Moreover, Article 2(2) contains a list of optional measures imposing disclosure requirements on branches, a measure which can have no

raison d'etre unless the Member States are unable to provide for disclosure measures for branches other than those laid down in the text of that directive.

71. In consequence, the various disclosure measures provided for by the WFBV and referred to in paragraph 65 above are contrary to the Eleventh Directive.

72. It must therefore be concluded on this point that it is contrary to Article 2 of the Eleventh Directive for national legislation such as the WFBV to impose on the branch of a company formed in accordance with the laws of another Member State disclosure obligations not provided for by that directive.

73. Thirdly, several of the provisions of the WFBV do not fall within the scope of the Eleventh Directive. Those are the rules relating to the minimum capital required, both at the time of registration and for so long as a formally foreign company exists, and those relating to the penalty attaching to non-compliance with the obligations laid down by the WFBV, namely, the joint and several liability of the directors with the company (Article 4(1) and (2) of the WFBV). Those provisions must therefore be considered in the light of Articles 43 EC and 48 EC.

The existence of an impediment to freedom of establishment

[*Text omitted*]

The Court's answer

95. The Court has held that it is immaterial, having regard to the application of the rules on freedom of establishment, that the company was formed in one Member State only for the purpose of establishing itself in a second Member State, where its main, or indeed entire, business is to be conducted … The reasons for which a company chooses to be formed in a particular Member State are, save in the case of fraud, irrelevant with regard to application of the rules on freedom of establishment (Centros, paragraph 18).

96. The Court has also held that the fact that the company was formed in a particular Member State for the sole purpose of enjoying the benefit of more favourable legislation does not constitute abuse even if that company conducts its activities entirely or mainly in that second State …

97. It follows that those companies are entitled to carry on their business in another Member State through a branch, and that the location of their registered office, central administration or principal place of business serves as the connecting factor with the legal system of a particular Member State in the same way as does nationality in the case of a natural person …

98. Thus, in the main proceedings, the fact that Inspire Art was formed in the United Kingdom for the purpose of circumventing Netherlands company law which lays down stricter rules with regard in particular to minimum capital and the paying-up of shares does not mean that that company's establishment of a branch in the Netherlands is not covered by freedom of establishment as provided for by Articles 43 EC and 48 EC. As the Court held in Centros (paragraph 18), the question

of the application of those articles is different from the question whether or not a Member State may adopt measures in order to prevent attempts by certain of its nationals improperly to evade domestic legislation by having recourse to the possibilities offered by the Treaty.

99. The argument that freedom of establishment is not in any way infringed by the WFBV inasmuch as foreign companies are fully recognised in the Netherlands and are not refused registration in that Member State's business register, that law having the effect simply of laying down a number of additional obligations classified as 'administrative', cannot be accepted.

100. The effect of the WFBV is, in fact, that the Netherlands company-law rules on minimum capital and directors' liability are applied mandatorily to foreign companies such as Inspire Art when they carry on their activities exclusively, or almost exclusively, in the Netherlands.

101. Creation of a branch in the Netherlands by companies of that kind is therefore subject to certain rules provided for by that State in respect of the formation of a limited-liability company. The legislation at issue in the case in the main proceedings, which requires the branch of such a company formed in accordance with the legislation of a Member State to comply with the rules of the State of establishment on share capital and directors' liability, has the effect of impeding the exercise by those companies of the freedom of establishment conferred by the Treaty.

102. The last issue for consideration concerns the arguments based on the judgment in Daily Mail and General Trust, namely, that the Member States remain free to determine the law applicable to a company since the rules relating to freedom of establishment have not led to harmonisation of the provisions of the private international law of the Member States. In this respect it is argued that the Member States retain the right to take action against 'brass-plate companies', that classification being in the circumstances of the case inferred from the lack of any real connection with the State of formation.

103. It must be stressed that, unlike the case at issue in the main proceedings, Daily Mail and General Trust concerned relations between a company and the Member State under the laws of which it had been incorporated in a situation where the company wished to transfer its actual centre of administration to another Member State whilst retaining its legal personality in the State of incorporation. In the main proceedings the national court has asked the Court of Justice whether the legislation of the State where a company actually carries on its activities applies to that company when it was formed under the law of another Member State ...

104. It follows from the foregoing that the provisions of the WFBV relating to minimum capital (both at the time of formation and during the life of the company) and to directors' liability constitute restrictions on freedom of establishment as guaranteed by Articles 43 EC and 48 EC.

105. It must therefore be concluded that Articles 43 EC and 48 EC preclude national legislation such as the WFBV which imposes on the exercise of freedom of secondary

establishment in that State by a company formed in accordance with the law of another Member State certain conditions provided for in domestic law in respect of company formation relating to minimum capital and directors' liability. The reasons for which the company was formed in that other Member State, and the fact that it carries on its activities exclusively or almost exclusively in the Member State of establishment, do not deprive it of the right to invoke the freedom of establishment guaranteed by the Treaty, save where abuse is established on a case-by-case basis.

Whether there is any justification

106. As a preliminary point, there can be no justification for the disclosure provisions of the WFBV, which have been found to be contrary to the Eleventh Directive (see paragraphs 71 and 72 above). As a result, only the arguments concerning the provisions of the WFBV relating to minimum capital and directors' liability will be considered below.

107. Given that those rules constitute an impediment to freedom of establishment, it must be considered whether they can be justified on one of the grounds set out in Article 46 EC or, failing that, by an overriding reason relating to the public interest.

[Text omitted]

The Court's answer

131. It must first of all be stated that none of the arguments put forward by the Netherlands Government with a view to justifying the legislation at issue in the main proceedings falls within the ambit of Article 46 EC.

132. The justifications put forward by the Netherlands Government, namely, the aims of protecting creditors, combating improper recourse to freedom of establishment, and protecting both effective tax inspections and fairness in business dealings, fall therefore to be evaluated by reference to overriding reasons related to the public interest.

133. It must be borne in mind that, according to the Court's case-law, national measures liable to hinder or make less attractive the exercise of fundamental freedoms guaranteed by the Treaty must, if they are to be justified, fulfil four conditions: they must be applied in a non-discriminatory manner; they must be justified by imperative requirements in the public interest; they must be suitable for securing the attainment of the objective which they pursue, and they must not go beyond what is necessary in order to attain it …

134. In consequence, it is necessary to consider whether those conditions are fulfilled by provisions relating to minimum capital such as those at issue in the main proceedings.

135. First, with regard to protection of creditors, and there being no need for the Court to consider whether the rules on minimum share capital constitute in

themselves an appropriate protection measure, it is clear that Inspire Art holds itself out as a company governed by the law of England and Wales and not as a Netherlands company. Its potential creditors are put on sufficient notice that it is covered by legislation other than that regulating the formation in the Netherlands of limited liability companies and, in particular, laying down rules in respect of minimum capital and directors' liability. They can also refer, as the Court pointed out in Centros, paragraph 36, to certain rules of Community law which protect them, such as the Fourth and Eleventh Directives.

136. Second, with regard to combating improper recourse to freedom of establishment, it must be borne in mind that a Member State is entitled to take measures designed to prevent certain of its nationals from attempting, under cover of the rights created by the Treaty, improperly to circumvent their national legislation or to prevent individuals from improperly or fraudulently taking advantage of provisions of Community law ...

137. However, while in this case Inspire Art was formed under the company law of a Member State, in the case in point the United Kingdom, for the purpose in particular of evading the application of Netherlands company law, which was considered to be more severe, the fact remains that the provisions of the Treaty on freedom of establishment are intended specifically to enable companies formed in accordance with the law of a Member State and having their registered office, central administration or principal place of business within the Community to pursue activities in other Member States through an agency, branch or subsidiary ...

138. That being so, as the Court confirmed in paragraph 27 of Centros, the fact that a national of a Member State who wishes to set up a company can choose to do so in the Member State the company-law rules of which seem to him the least restrictive and then set up branches in other Member States is inherent in the exercise, in a single market, of the freedom of establishment guaranteed by the Treaty.

139. In addition, it is clear from settled case-law ... that the fact that a company does not conduct any business in the Member State in which it has its registered office and pursues its activities only or principally in the Member State where its branch is established is not sufficient to prove the existence of abuse or fraudulent conduct which would entitle the latter Member State to deny that company the benefit of the provisions of Community law relating to the right of establishment.

140. Last, as regards possible justification of the WFBV on grounds of protection of fairness in business dealings and the efficiency of tax inspections, it is clear that neither the Chamber of Commerce nor the Netherlands Government has adduced any evidence to prove that the measure in question satisfies the criteria of efficacy, proportionality and non-discrimination mentioned in paragraph 132 above.

141. To the extent that the provisions concerning minium capital are incompatible with freedom of establishment, as guaranteed by the Treaty, the same must necessarily be true of the penalties attached to non-compliance with those obligations, that is to say, the personal joint and several liability of directors where the

amount of capital does not reach the minimum provided for by the national legislation or where during the company's activities it falls below that amount.

142. The answer to be given to the second question referred by the national court must therefore be that the impediment to the freedom of establishment guaranteed by the Treaty constituted by provisions of national law, such as those at issue, relating to minimum capital and the personal joint and several liability of directors cannot be justified under Article 46 EC, or on grounds of protecting creditors, or combating improper recourse to freedom of establishment or safeguarding fairness in business dealings or the efficiency of tax inspections.

143. In light of all the foregoing considerations, the answers to be given to the questions referred for a preliminary ruling must be:

- It is contrary to Article 2 of the Eleventh Directive for national legislation such as the WFBV to impose on the branch of a company formed in accordance with the laws of another Member State disclosure obligations not provided for by that directive.
- It is contrary to Articles 43 EC and 48 EC for national legislation such as the WFBV to impose on the exercise of freedom of secondary establishment in that State by a company formed in accordance with the law of another Member State certain conditions provided for in domestic company law in respect of company formation relating to minimum capital and directors' liability. The reasons for which the company was formed in that other Member State, and the fact that it carries on its activities exclusively or almost exclusively in the Member State of establishment, do not deprive it of the right to invoke the freedom of establishment guaranteed by the EC Treaty, save where the existence of an abuse is established on a case-by-case basis.

[Text omitted]

Vantagepoint Venture Partners 1996 v. Examen, Inc.
Supreme Court of Delaware
871 A 2d 1108 (2005)
[Text omitted; most footnotes omitted]

HOLLAND, Justice

This is an expedited appeal from the Court of Chancery following the entry of a final judgment on the pleadings. We have concluded that the judgment must be affirmed.

Delaware action

On March 3, 2005, the plaintiff-appellant, Examen, Inc. ("Examen"), filed a Complaint in the Court of Chancery against VantagePoint Venture Partners, Inc. ("VantagePoint"), a Delaware Limited Partnership and an Examen Series A Preferred shareholder, seeking a judicial declaration that pursuant to the controlling

Delaware law and under the Company's Certificate of Designations of Series A Preferred Stock ("Certificate of Designations"), VantagePoint was not entitled to a class vote of the Series A Preferred Stock on the proposed merger between Examen and a Delaware subsidiary of Reed Elsevier Inc.

California action

On March 8, 2005, VantagePoint filed an action in the California Superior Court seeking: (1) a declaration that Examen was required to identify whether it was a "quasi-California corporation" under section 2115 of the California Corporations Code [Note 1]; (2) a declaration that Examen was a quasi-California corporation pursuant to California Corporations Code section 2115 and therefore subject to California Corporations Code section 1201(a), and that, as a Series A Preferred shareholder, VantagePoint was entitled to vote its shares as a separate class in connection with the proposed merger; (3) injunctive relief; and (4) damages incurred as the result of alleged violations of California Corporations Code sections 2111(a) (2)(F) and 1201.

[Note 1] Section 2115 of the California Corporations Code purportedly applies to corporations that have contacts with the State of California, but are incorporated in other states ... [It] provides that, irrespective of the state of incorporation, *foreign corporations' articles of incorporation are deemed amended* to comply with California law and are subject to the laws of California if certain criteria are met ... (emphasis added). To qualify under the statute: (1) the average of the property factor, the payroll factor and the sales factor as defined in the California Revenue and Taxation Code must be more than 50 percent during its last full income year; and (2) more than one-half of its outstanding voting securities must be held by persons having addresses in California. *Id.* If a corporation qualifies under this provision, California corporate laws apply "to the exclusion of the law" of the jurisdiction where [the company] is incorporated." *Id.* Included among the California corporate law provisions that would govern is California Corporations Code section 1201, which states that the principal terms of a reorganization shall be approved by the outstanding shares of each class of each corporation the approval of whose board is required ...

Delaware action decided

On March 10, 2005, the Court of Chancery granted Examen's request for an expedited hearing on its motion for judgment on the pleadings. On March 21, 2005, the California Superior Court stayed its action pending the ruling of the Court of Chancery. On March 29, 2005, the Court of Chancery ruled that the case was governed by the internal affairs doctrine as explicated by this Court in *McDermott v. Lewis* ... In applying that doctrine, the Court of Chancery held that Delaware law governed the vote that was required to approve a merger between two Delaware corporate entities.

On April 1, 2005, VantagePoint filed a notice of appeal with this Court. On April 4, 2005, VantagePoint sought to enjoin the merger from closing pending its appeal. On April 5, 2005, this Court denied VantagePoint's request to enjoin the merger from closing, but granted its request for an expedited appeal.

Merger without mootness

Following this Court's ruling on April 5, 2005, Examen and the Delaware subsidiary of Reed Elsevier consummated the merger that same day. This Court directed the parties to address the issue of mootness, simultaneously with the expedited briefing that was completed on April 13, 2005. VantagePoint argues that if we agree with its position "that a class vote was required, then VantagePoint could pursue remedies for loss of this right, including rescission of the Merger, rescissory damages or monetary damages." Examen submits that "the need for final resolution of the validity of the merger vote remains important to the parties and to the public interest" because a decision from this Court will conclusively determine the parties' rights with regard to the law that applies to the merger vote. We have concluded that this appeal is not moot.

Facts

Examen was a Delaware corporation engaged in the business of providing web-based legal expense management solutions to a growing list of Fortune 1000 customers throughout the United States. Following consummation of the merger on April 5, 2005, LexisNexis Examen, also a Delaware corporation, became the surviving entity. VantagePoint is a Delaware Limited Partnership organized and existing under the laws of Delaware. VantagePoint, a major venture capital firm that purchased Examen Series A Preferred Stock in a negotiated transaction, owned eighty-three percent of Examen's outstanding Series A Preferred Stock (909,091 shares) and no shares of Common Stock.

On February 17, 2005, Examen and Reed Elsevier executed the Merger Agreement, which was set to expire on April 15, 2005, if the merger had not closed by that date. Under the Delaware General Corporation Law and Examen's Certificate of Incorporation, including the Certificate of Designations for the Series A Preferred Stock, adoption of the Merger Agreement required the affirmative vote of the holders of a majority of the issued and outstanding shares of the Common Stock and Series A Preferred Stock, *voting together as a single class*. Holders of Series A Preferred Stock had the number of votes equal to the number of shares of Common Stock they would have held if their Preferred Stock was converted. Thus, VantagePoint, which owned 909,091 shares of Series A Preferred Stock and no shares of Common Stock, was entitled to vote based on a converted number of 1,392,727 shares of stock.

There were 9,717,415 total outstanding shares of the Company's capital stock (8,626,826 shares of Common Stock and 1,090,589 shares of Series A Preferred Stock), representing 10,297,608 votes on an as-converted basis. An affirmative vote of at least 5,148,805 shares, constituting a majority of the outstanding voting power on an as-converted basis, was required to approve the merger. If the stockholders were to vote by class, VantagePoint would have controlled 83.4 percent of the Series A Preferred Stock, which would have permitted VantagePoint to block the merger. VantagePoint acknowledges that, if Delaware law applied, it would not have a class vote.

Chancery Court decision

The Court of Chancery determined that the question of whether VantagePoint, as a holder of Examen's Series A Preferred Stock, was entitled to a separate class vote on the merger with a Delaware subsidiary of Reed Elsevier, was governed by the internal affairs doctrine because the issue implicated "the relationship between a corporation and its stockholders." The Court of Chancery rejected VantagePoint's argument that section 2115 of the California Corporation Code did not conflict with Delaware law and operated only in addition to rights granted under Delaware corporate law. In doing so, the Court of Chancery noted that section 2115 "expressly states that it operates 'to the exclusion of the law of the jurisdiction in which [the company] is incorporated.'"

Specifically, the Court of Chancery determined that section 2115's requirement that stockholders vote as a separate class conflicts with Delaware law, which, together with Examen's Certificate of Incorporation, mandates that the merger be authorized by a majority of all Examen stockholders voting together as a single class. The Court of Chancery concluded that it could not enforce both Delaware and California law. Consequently, the Court of Chancery decided that the issue presented was solely one of choice-of-law, and that it need not determine the constitutionality of section 2115.

Vantage Point's argument

According to VantagePoint, "the issue presented by this case is not a choice of law question, but rather the constitutional issue of whether California may promulgate a narrowly tailored exception to the internal affairs doctrine that is designed to protect important state interests." VantagePoint submits that "Section 2115 was designed to provide an additional layer of investor protection by mandating that California's heightened voting requirements apply to those few foreign corporations that have chosen to conduct a majority of their business in California and meet the other factual prerequisite of Section 2115." Therefore, VantagePoint argues that "Delaware either must apply the statute if California can validly enact it, or hold the statute unconstitutional if California cannot." We note, however, that when an issue or claim is properly before a tribunal, "the court is not limited to the particular legal theories advanced by the parties, but rather retains the independent power to identify and apply the proper construction of governing law."

Standard of review

In granting Examen's Motion for Judgment on the Pleadings, the Court of Chancery held that, as a matter of law, the rights of stockholders to vote on the proposed merger were governed by the law of Delaware – Examen's state of incorporation – and that an application of Delaware law resulted in the Class A Preferred shareholders having no right to a separate class vote. The issue of whether VantagePoint was entitled to a separate class vote of the Series A Preferred Stock on the merger is a question of law that this Court reviews *de novo*.

Internal affairs doctrine

In *CTS Corp.* v. *Dynamics Corp. of Am.*, the United States Supreme Court stated that it is "an accepted part of the business landscape in this country for States to create corporations, to prescribe their powers, and to define the rights that are acquired by purchasing their shares." In *CTS*, it was also recognized that "[a] State has an interest in promoting stable relationships among parties involved in the corporations it charters, as well as in ensuring that investors in such corporations have an effective voice in corporate affairs." The internal affairs doctrine is a long-standing choice of law principle which recognizes that only one state should have the authority to regulate a corporation's internal affairs – the state of incorporation.

The internal affairs doctrine developed on the premise that, in order to prevent corporations from being subjected to inconsistent legal standards, the authority to regulate a corporation's internal affairs should not rest with multiple jurisdictions. It is now well established that only the law of the state of incorporation governs and determines issues relating to a corporation's internal affairs. By providing certainty and predictability, the internal affairs doctrine protects the justified expectations of the parties with interests in the corporation.

The internal affairs doctrine applies to those matters that pertain to the relationships among or between the corporation and its officers, directors, and shareholders. The *Restatement (Second) of Conflict of Laws* § 301 provides: "application of the local law of the state of incorporation will usually be supported by those choice-of-law factors favoring the need of the interstate and international systems, certainty, predictability and uniformity of result, protection of the justified expectations of the parties and ease in the application of the law to be applied." Accordingly, the conflicts practice of both state and federal courts has consistently been to apply the law of the state of incorporation to "the entire gamut of internal corporate affairs."

The internal affairs doctrine is not, however, only a conflicts of law principle. Pursuant to the Fourteenth Amendment Due Process Clause, directors and officers of corporations "have a significant right ... to know what law will be applied to their actions" and "stockholders ... have a right to know by what standards of accountability they may hold those managing the corporation's business and affairs." Under the Commerce Clause, a state "has no interest in regulating the internal affairs of foreign corporations." Therefore, this Court has held that an "application of the internal affairs doctrine is mandated by constitutional principles, except in the 'rarest situations,'" e.g. when "the law of the state of incorporation is inconsistent with a national policy on foreign or interstate commerce."

California section 2115

VantagePoint contends that section 2115 of the California Corporations Code is a limited exception to the internal affairs doctrine. Section 2115 is characterized as an outreach statute because it requires certain foreign corporations to conform to a broad range of internal affairs provisions. Section 2115 defines the foreign corporations for which the California statute has an outreach effect as those foreign corporations, half of whose voting securities are held of record by persons with California addresses, that also conduct half of their business in California as measured by a formula weighing assets, sales and payroll factors.

VantagePoint argues that section 2115 "mandates application of certain enumerated provisions of California's corporation law to the internal affairs of 'foreign' corporations if certain narrow factual prerequisites [set out in section 2115] are met." Under the California statute, if more than one half of a foreign corporation's outstanding voting securities are held of record by persons having addresses in California (as disclosed on the books of the corporation) on the record date, *and* the property, payroll and sales factor tests are satisfied, then on the first day of the income year, one hundred and thirty five days after the above tests are satisfied, *the foreign corporation's articles of incorporation are deemed amended to the exclusion of the law of the state of incorporation*. If the factual conditions precedent for triggering section 2115 are established, many aspects of a corporation's internal affairs are purportedly governed by California corporate law to the exclusion of the law of the state of incorporation. [Note 22]

[Note 22] If Section 2115 applies, California law is deemed to control the following: the annual election of directors; removal of directors without cause; removal of directors by court proceedings; the filing of director vacancies where less than a majority in office are elected by shareholders; the director's standard of care; the liability of directors for unlawful distributions; indemnification of directors, officers, and others; limitations on corporate distributions in cash or property; the liability of shareholders who receive unlawful distributions; the requirement for annual shareholders' meetings and remedies for the same if not timely held; shareholder's entitlement to cumulative voting; the conditions when a supermajority vote is required; limitations on the sale of assets; limitations on mergers; limitations on conversions; requirements on conversions; the limitations and conditions for reorganization (including the requirement for class voting); dissenter's rights; records and reports; actions by the Attorney General and inspection rights ...

In her comprehensive analysis of the internal affairs doctrine, Professor Deborah A. DeMott examined section 2115. As she astutely points out:

> In contrast to the certainty with which the state of incorporation may be determined, the criteria upon which the applicability of section 2115 hinges are not constants. For example, whether half of a corporation's business is derived from California and whether half of its voting securities have record holders with California addresses may well vary from year to year (and indeed throughout any given year). Thus, a corporation might be subject to section 2115 one year but not the next, depending on its situation at the time of filing the annual statement required by section 2108.

Internal affairs require uniformity

In *McDermott*, this Court noted that application of local internal affairs law (here California's section 2115) to a foreign corporation (here Delaware) is "apt to produce inequalities, intolerable confusion, and uncertainty, and intrude into the domain of other states that have a superior claim to regulate the same subject matter ... " Professor DeMott's review of the differences and conflicts between the Delaware and California corporate statutes with regard to internal affairs, illustrates why it is imperative that only the law of the state of incorporation regulate the relationships among a corporation and its officers, directors, and shareholders. To require a factual determination to decide which of two conflicting state laws governs the internal affairs of a corporation at any point in time, completely contravenes the importance of stability within inter-corporate relationships that the United States Supreme Court recognized in *CTS*.

In *Kamen v. Kemper Fin. Serv.*, the United States Supreme Court reaffirmed its commitment to the need for stability that is afforded by the internal affairs doctrine. In *Kamen*, the issue was whether the federal courts could superimpose a universal-demand rule upon the corporate doctrine of all states. The United States Supreme Court held that a federal court universal-demand rule would cause disruption to the *internal affairs* of corporations and that its holding in [*Burks* v. *Lasker*] had counseled "against establishing competing federal – and state – law principles on the allocation of managerial prerogatives within [a] corporation." In *Kamen* v. *Kemper*, the Restatement (Second) of Conflict of Laws was cited for the proposition that "uniform treatment of directors, officers and shareholders is an important objective which can only be attained by having the rights and liabilities of those persons with respect to the corporation governed by a single law." If a universal-demand rule in federal courts would be disruptive because the demand rule in a state court would be different, *a fortiori*, it would be disruptive for section 2115's panoply of different internal affairs rules to operate intermittently within corporate relationships under either the law of California or the law of the state of incorporation – dependent upon the vissitudes of the ever-changing facts.

State law of incorporation governs internal affairs

[Text omitted]

Examen is a Delaware corporation. The legal issue in this case – whether a preferred shareholder of a Delaware corporation had the right, under the corporation's Certificate of Designations, to a Series A Preferred Stock class vote on a merger – clearly involves the relationship among a corporation and its shareholders. As the United States Supreme Court held in *CTS*, "no principle of corporation law and practice is more firmly established than a *State's authority* to regulate domestic corporations, including the authority to *define the voting rights of shareholders*."

... In *CTS*, the Supreme Court concluded that "so long as each State regulates voting rights *only in the corporations it has created*, each corporation will be subject to the law of only one State." Accordingly, we hold Delaware's well-established choice of law rules and the federal constitution mandated that Examen's internal affairs, and in particular, VantagePoint's voting rights, be adjudicated exclusively in accordance with the law of its state of incorporation, in this case, the law of Delaware.

Any forum – internal affairs – same law

... If the statutory prerequisites were found to be factually satisfied, VantagePoint submits that the California Superior Court would have applied the internal affairs law reflected in section 2115, "to the exclusion" of the law of Delaware – the state where Examen is incorporated.

In support of those assertions, VantagePoint relies primarily upon a 1982 decision by the California Court of Appeals in *Wilson* v. *Louisiana-Pacific Resources, Inc.* ... [in which] a panel of the California Court of Appeals held that section 2115 did not violate the federal constitution by applying the California Code's mandatory cumulative voting provision to a Utah corporation that had not provided for cumulative voting but instead had elected the straight voting structure set out in the Utah corporation statute ...

Wilson was decided before the United States Supreme Court's decision in *CTS* and before this Court's decision in *McDermott*. Ten years after *Wilson*, the California Supreme Court cited with approval this Court's analysis of the internal affairs doctrine in *McDermott*, in particular, our holding that corporate voting rights disputes are governed by the law of the state of incorporation. Two years ago, in *State Farm* v. *Superior Court*, a different panel of the California Court of Appeals questioned the validity of the holding in *Wilson* following the broad acceptance of the internal affairs doctrine over the two decades after *Wilson* was decided. In *State Farm*, the court cited with approval the United States Supreme Court decision in *CTS Corp.* v. *Dynamics* and our decision in *McDermott*. In *State Farm*, the court also quoted at length that portion of our decision in *McDermott* relating to the constitutional imperatives of the internal affairs doctrine.

... [We have] no doubt that after the *Kamen* and *CTS* holdings by the United States Supreme Court, the California courts would "apply Delaware [demand] law [to the internal affairs of a Delaware corporation], given the vitality and constitutional underpinnings of the internal affairs doctrine." We adhere to that view in this case.

[*Text omitted*]

PART II

The corporation and its capital

4

Incorporating the company

Required reading

EU: First Company Law Directive, arts. 11, 12
D: AktG, §§ 23–41; GmbHG, §§ 1–11
UK: CA 2006, secs. 7–20
US: DGCL, §§ 101–108, 124; Model Act, § 2.04

Incorporation procedures and liability for transactions

The procedures for setting up a corporation and the liability incurred by persons purporting to represent it before the incorporation process is complete are substantially similar in the UK, Germany and the US, but do still display interesting differences. Differences arise from the types of documents that must be filed and the contents of such documents. Where, as in the UK, the composition of the board and the mode of appointing directors are determined solely by the constitutional documents, the drafting of these documents takes on more importance than in Germany, where such important matters are determined without exception by the *Aktiengesetz*.[1] Differences also arise where one jurisdiction has mandatory prerequisites not found in the law of the other. Where, as in the EU, strict procedures are prescribed for the constitution of a mandatory amount of minimum capital, the process of incorporation can become much more formal and time-consuming.[2] These aspects can in turn affect the court's determination of fairness when incorporators enter into contracts before the body corporate has come into existence. Incorporation procedures thus exemplify the workings of corporate law models ranging from the most formalistic to the most informal, as well as how courts may react differently to problems thrown out by different statutory configurations.

---

[1] See the discussion in Davies (2008: 62–64).
[2] The procedures for constituting capital will be discussed in Chapter 5.

The following section will present the incorporation procedures for each of our jurisdictions. Section II will discuss liability for pre-incorporation transactions.

I.   Incorporation procedures

A.   Germany: the Aktiengesellschaft

The formation process for the *Aktiengesellschaft* (AG) is tightly and exhaustively regulated in §§ 23–53 AktG, which provide detailed rules for checking the value of assets that the original shareholders contribute in exchange for their stock. The first step is for one or more incorporators to draft articles of incorporation (*Satzung*), which must be memorialized in the form of a notarized deed. The articles must contain the items listed in § 23(3)–(5) AktG, which include:

- the name[3] and the domicile of the corporation;
- the object of the corporation;
- the amount of the share capital (which must be at least €50,000);
- a sub-division of the share capital into one or more class of either par value shares or shares without par value. In the case of par value shares, the *Satzung* must specify the nominal value and the number of shares of each nominal value. In the case of no-par shares, it must specify their number;
- the number of members of the *Vorstand* or the rules for determining such number;
- rules on how the company will make its official announcements;
- details of any special benefits, compensation or remuneration for incorporators, any in-kind shareholder contributions, and whether the company will acquire assets upon incorporation;
- the articles may deviate from the form provided for in the AktG only if expressly permitted by law pursuant to § 23(5) AktG.

Once the *Satzung* is complete and notarized, the incorporators must subscribe to all the shares in order to "establish" (*errichten*)[4] the company, at which point it gains the status of a "corporation in formation" (*Vorgesellschaft* or VorG) which is important for the liability of the incorporators, as discussed below. The shares are usually subscribed together with the notarization of the *Satzung* on a separate, notarized deed that

---

[3] § 4 AktG; and §§ 17 *et seq.* HGB.   [4] § 29 AktG.

includes the names of the incorporators, information on the shares, and the amount of the share capital paid in. A third, notarized deed must appoint the first supervisory board and the auditors for the first fiscal year.[5] The first supervisory board then appoints the first management board.[6]

As will be discussed in more detail in Chapter 5, an AG may issue shares with a "par" or "nominal" value (*Nennbetragsaktien*) or without such fixed value (*Stückaktien*), the latter shares each representing an equal portion of legal capital. German rules on payments for shares follow the Second Company Law Directive. Cash payments for shares must be at least one-quarter of their lowest issue price,[7] which would be their par value (if there is one), plus the whole share premium (if any),[8] and any in-kind contributions (i.e. non-cash assets) must be for the full price, but a promise to transfer an asset to the corporation is valid payment if performed within five years.[9] The incorporators must prepare a written report on the formation process pursuant to § 32 AktG. If in-kind contributions are made or the corporation acquires assets, the report must include detailed information on the assets and their value, on the contracts related to the transfer of the assets, and on the historical costs connected with the acquisition or creation of the assets.[10] The members of the management and supervisory boards must examine and report on the formation process.[11] If shares are allotted against an in-kind contribution, a board member is also an incorporator, or an indirect subscriber receives a material benefit from the incorporation, an independent auditor must audit the formation process.[12] This will be discussed in more detail in Chapter 5.

Once all contributions have been made, the incorporators must apply to the court to have the AG registered in the commercial register (*Handelsregister*).[13] The application must be made by all the incorporators and all members of the management and supervisory boards.[14] The court will review the *Satzung* to ascertain that it contains all elements required by law and does not conflict with mandatory provisions of law, and check any report on in-kind contributions for plausibility.[15] If the court accepts the application for registration, it will enter the company's name, registered office, object, capital and managing directors in the commercial register,[16] and publish the registration in the *Bundesanzeiger* (*Federal*

---

[5] § 30 AktG. [6] § 30(4) AktG. [7] § 9(1) AktG. [8] § 36a(1) AktG.
[9] § 36a(2) AktG. The nature of contributions will be addressed in detail in Chapter 5.
[10] § 32(2) AktG. [11] § 33(1) AktG. [12] § 33(2) AktG. [13] § 36 AktG.
[14] § 36 AktG. [15] § 38 AktG. [16] § 39 AktG.

Gazette) and at least one newspaper.[17] Upon registration, the company acquires legal existence.[18]

B.   United Kingdom: the public limited company

The formation process for a public limited company (plc) is more flexible than for an AG. However, it follows the same, basic steps of drafting constitutional documents and filing them with an official register, as well as EU requirements regarding in-kind contributions. The 2006 Act changed the traditional practice of requiring two separate documents – a "memorandum of association" and "articles of association" – for incorporating a company,[19] by reducing the "constitution" to the articles and any supplementing resolutions.[20] Although the 2006 Act does continue to refer separately to both "articles" and "memorandum," the latter is a bare undertaking, signed by each subscriber of the company's shares, that they:

- wish to form a company under the Companies Act, and
- agree to become members of the company and, in the case of a company that is to have a share capital, to take at least one share each.[21]

In connection with this transformation of the memorandum into a declaration of intent to incorporate, the 2006 Act converts the more "constitutive" memorandum provisions (such as the name, object and capital) of preexisting companies into provisions of the articles.[22] The 2006 Act also removes the requirement of a mandatory corporate object. The Second Company Law Directive requires the "statutes or the instrument of incorporation" to state "the objects of the company,"[23] but the UK government, in transposing the directive, interpreted this to mean that a company must state its objects if it has any, "but not as requiring the company to have objects."[24] As a result, the requirement that the memorandum

---

[17] § 40 AktG; and § 10(1) HGB.   [18] § 41(1) AktG.

[19] This practice was likely an historical product of the royally chartered companies, for which the unchanging charter was supplemented by a more flexible "byelaws." See Davies (2003: 57).

[20] Sec. 17 CA 2006. Also see Davies (2008: 65).

[21] Sec. 8 CA 2006. This minimal content will eliminate the need to amend the memorandum at a later date, and thus, unlike its predecessor (see secs. 4(1) and 378(1) CA 1985), the 2006 Act makes no provision for such amendment.

[22] Sec. 28 CA 2006.   [23] Art. 2(b) Second Company Law Directive.

[24] Davies (2008: 154, note 12). As Davies points out, removing the objects clause is a more radical way of eliminating the old and troublesome doctrine of *ultra vires*, a goal that clearly conforms to EU law. See art. 9 First Company Law Directive.

specify an "object" or "purpose" for a company has been dropped. The Act now provides that "[u]nless a company's articles specifically restrict the objects of the company, its objects are unrestricted."[25] Because the memorandum now contains almost no information about the company, it must now be accompanied, in the filing with the companies registry, by an application for registration, which – pursuant to sections 9, 10, 12 and 13 of the Companies Act 2006 – contains:

- the company's proposed name;
- the sub-jurisdiction within the UK in which it is to be registered (i.e. England, Wales, Scotland or Northern Ireland);
- the company's intended, registered address;
- whether the liability of members is to be limited, and, if so, by shares or by guarantee;
- whether the company is to be private or public;
- a statement of share capital and initial shareholdings;
- a statement containing the name of its proposed officers;
- a copy of its articles, unless it intends to use the default articles;[26] and
- a statement of compliance.

As mentioned above, the articles of a UK company are extremely important, for they supplement the Companies Act by providing rules governing the internal affairs of the company. Incorporators may either draft articles or use the "default"[27] set of model articles issued by the Secretary of State,[28] which were drafted by BERR (now BIS). Model articles for both private and public companies under the Companies Act 1985 were appended to that Act as Table A,[29] and BERR has issued a new set of articles for the 2006 Act.[30] The incorporators must register the articles with the Companies Registry and indicate whether the model articles will be excluded in whole or in part; the model articles will apply to the extent that they are not excluded.[31]

   The procedure followed at the companies registry is, for public companies, divided into two steps. First, if the filed memorandum and the

---

[25] Sec. 31(1) CA 2006.

[26] The default articles prepared by BERR can be found in SI 2008 No. 3229.

[27] The word "default" in this context has a meaning completely different than in the debtor/creditor context. Here, it means provisions than apply unless the parties contract otherwise. The term is used frequently in discussing Anglo-American law because often large parts of the law may be overridden by contract and thus are mere "default" provisions.

[28] Sec. 19 CA 2006.   [29] SI 1985 No. 805.   [30] SI 2008 No. 3229.

[31] Sec. 20(1) CA 2006.

other necessary information and documents meet the requirements of law, the registrar will issue a "certificate of incorporation," which constitutes "conclusive evidence" that the requirements of the Companies Act on registration have been met and the company is "duly registered" under that Act.[32] The effect of this registration is that the company becomes a "body corporate" "capable of exercising all the functions of an incorporated company."[33] This is subject to an additional certificate as to the amount of share capital.[34] The second step is then to comply with requirements similar to those under German law regarding proof of paid-in capital before it may commence trading.[35] The requirements of EU law[36] as implemented in the UK require that the nominal share capital be at least the "authorised minimum" of £50,000,[37] and that the allotted shares are paid up in cash[38] at least to one-quarter of their nominal value.[39] The detailed rules on how such payments must be made, particularly with regard to in-kind contributions, are discussed in Chapter 5. The filing with the registrar must also specify at least an estimated amount of the company's preliminary expenses, any benefit paid or intended to be paid to any promoter of the company, and the consideration for the payment or benefit.[40] If the Registry is satisfied, it will issue a "trading certificate," which is "conclusive evidence" that the company is entitled to do business and exercise any borrowing powers.[41] Directors are jointly and severally liable to indemnify other parties for damages from transactions entered into before such certificate is issued.[42]

C.   United States: the stock corporation

As we have seen in earlier chapters, US corporate law is state law. Although the law of the states differ, no US state requires formalities for incorporation that in any way approach those of Germany. Like all other states, the law of Delaware requires the filing of a certificate of incorporation with a state office (referred to as the "secretary of state") in order to establish a stock

---

[32] Sec. 15 CA 2006.   [33] Sec. 16 CA 2006.   [34] Sec. 10 CA 2006.
[35] Sec. 761(1) CA 2006.
[36] The requirements originate in the Second Company Law Directive.
[37] Secs. 762(1), 763(1) CA 2006.   [38] Secs. 584, 583 CA 2006.
[39] Sec. 586(1) CA 2006.   [40] Sec. 762(1) CA 2006.   [41] Sec. 761(4) CA 2006.
[42] Sec. 767 CA 2006. It should be noted that this provision gives the directors twenty-one days to correct the situation, presumably by obtaining the certificate, before the liability is triggered. Liability for transactions entered into before incorporation or when incorporation is defective or null is discussed in sections III and IV below.

corporation.[43] This certificate need not be notarized and must contain only the names and addresses of the incorporators, the company's name and address, the corporate purpose (it is sufficient to declare the corporate purpose as "to engage in any lawful act or activity"), the classes of stock authorized, including the number of shares and their par value or a statement that they are no par, as well as the rights of each class, and, if the powers of the incorporators are to terminate upon incorporation, the names and addresses of the initial directors.[44]

There are few *mandatory* requirements for the certificate. However, because most of the Delaware statute can be overridden by the certificate, the certificate *can* regulate almost every aspect of the company – from making shareholders liable without limit for debts and giving bondholders voting rights to taking away the board's powers and placing them in a shareholder council.[45] Procedural rules and powers of a subsidiary nature will then be expressed in by-laws that need be neither filed nor publicly disclosed. The required threshold for US incorporation is thus extremely low, but the work to be done to ensure the desired governance and financial structures for the company can be significant. Although lawyers and other advisors would be able to provide standard certificates and by-laws that companies can quickly adapt to their needs, the state does not get involved in this process, unlike the process employed in the UK.

The incorporators or initial directors (if named) must sign the certificate, file it with the secretary of state and pay all incorporation taxes.[46] Although the secretary will review the document for obvious errors, there is no substantive analysis of the document required or permitted by law. The corporation comes into existence at the moment that the certificate is duly filed with the secretary.[47] If, despite a good faith effort by the incorporators, the company does not legally come into existence because a formal requirement has not been fulfilled, some US states apply a doctrine of *de facto* corporation to limit the liability of incorporators. This is discussed in more detail in section III of this chapter.

---

[43] § 103(a)(1) DGCL.

[44] § 102(a) DGCL.

[45] See e.g. § 102(b)(6) (permitting unlimited liability for shareholders), § 221 (permitting debt instruments to be treated functionally like shares) and § 141(a) DGCL (permitting the board's management authority to be transferred to other persons). Much of the internal affairs of the company will be regulated not by the certificate of incorporation, but through the "by-laws." See § 109 DGCL.

[46] § 103(c) DGCL.   [47] § 106 DGCL.

II.   Liability of promoters before incorporation is complete

A.   Germany

As discussed above, once a *Satzung* is complete and notarized and the incorporators have subscribed for all the shares, the corporation is considered "established" (*errichtet*), although it does not yet have legal personality.[48] The law expressly provides that the persons acting in the name of a stock corporation before its entry in the commercial register are liable for all obligations, and, if more than one person acts, then they are jointly liable.[49] This follows clearly from the imperative of article 7 of the First Company Law Directive.[50] Before the company is "established" (*errichtet*), it is considered a "pre-incorporation company" (*Vorgründungsgesellschaft*), which for dealings with third parties is understood to have the characteristics of a general partnership, with joint liability of the persons acting in concert, as provided in the statute. German (Civil Law!) judges have filled this gap between the laws on partnership and corporations by creating a more detailed set of rules for the corporate limbo between *Errichtung* and registration, and calling the result a "pre-company" (*Vorgesellschaft* or VorG). Courts have applied the VorG doctrine not only to the *Aktiengesellschaft*, but also to the GmbH. In fact, the leading decisions on the VorG arose from cases regarding similar problems in GmbHs, and courts then extended the doctrine by analogy to the AG. Such activity should make the comparative lawyer wary of characterizing the Civil Law court as a place of robotic application of codified rules.

The decisions of the High Federal Court make it clear that promoters may deal on behalf of the company before its entry in the commercial register, and that, when it is registered, the obligations that the promoters incur on the company's behalf within their delegated authority will automatically become obligations of the company.[51] Thus, before the company is registered, promoters and "active" shareholders are jointly and severally liable for obligations incurred in the name of the company in formation, but, once the company is registered, this liability ends and the company assumes all such obligations. "Active" shareholders in this context are

---

[48] § 29 AktG.   [49] § 41(1) AktG.

[50] "If, before a company being formed has acquired legal personality, action has been carried out in its name and the company does not assume the obligations arising from such action, the persons who acted shall, without limit, be jointly and severally liable therefor, unless otherwise agreed." First Company Law Directive, art. 7.

[51] BGHZ 80, 129, at 140 (1981).

understood to be those who have instructed the promoters or other agents to enter into transactions on behalf of the company.[52] Shareholders who merely contribute capital, but remain passive with respect to company activities, do not share this liability.

If, when the company is registered, its initial capital is insufficient to cover the debts of the VorG (i.e. the sum of liabilities plus equity exceeds assets), the promoters and active shareholders will be jointly liable to pay the shortfall.[53] Thus, no direct action for liability exists against these natural persons. It is necessary for creditors to act first against the company, and the existence of a shortfall will trigger the contribution liability of its promoters and active shareholders. Shareholders are liable to cover this shortfall in proportion to their shareholding, not severally for the whole amount.[54] However, the persons found liable will have an obligation to cover – again on a *pro rata* basis – amounts that others in the group of liable persons fail to pay. Unlike the situation of pre-incorporation liability, the absence of a specific instruction from shareholders to directors is not a relevant criterion for triggering post-incorporation liability. It is sufficient in this context that a shareholder has given his general consent to commence business operations prior to registration. Thus, even a passive investor can be caught by this liability.

B.   United Kingdom

Pursuant to Common Law, a company has no legal existence before it is incorporated. It is incapable of entering into a contract itself and equally incapable of acting through an agent.[55] As the case of *Kelner* v. *Baxter* in this chapter explains, it is impossible for a person to pretend to act as an agent for a principal that does not exist. A similar logic applies to attempted ratification. The Companies Act, like German law, follows article 7 of the First Company Law Directive. The UK provision[56] implementing the relevant article of that Directive is discussed in the *Phonogram* decision, reprinted in part in this chapter.

Moreover, there would be no reason for the contract to become binding on the company if the company is subsequently established, and the company may not "ratify" a contract purported to be made on its behalf before it

---

[52] The majority position is that an "active" shareholder who incurs liability for such transactions is one who exercises active influence on the decision to enter into the transaction (see BGHZ 47, 25, 27; BGHZ 65, 378, 380 *et seq.*).

[53] BGHZ 105, 300, at 303 (1988).   [54] BGHZ 80, 129, at 141 (1981).

[55] Pennington (2001: 100).

[56] Sec. 51(1) CA 2006, and, in the 1985 Act, sec. 36C.

was incorporated,[57] although it would be free expressly to assume the contract like any other obligation. The latter could be a fresh contract that either inserts the company as an additional obligor or a "novation" that replaces the promoter with the company as sole obligor, in which case the company alone would acquire the rights and duties of the promoter on the contract.[58] Thus pre-incorporation contracts are binding on the persons concluding them. This includes not only the promoters, but also their counterparties; the agreement is effective in this manner even if all the persons who negotiate the contract are aware that the company has not yet been incorporated. The persons who purport to represent the company can enforce the contract against the other party by suing for damages or specific performance.

C.   United States

The corporate statutes of the US states continue the Common Law position that a corporation does not exist before it is incorporated. Corporate existence arises upon due filing of the certificate of incorporation with the appropriate secretary of state.[59] Pursuant to general principles of agency law in the United States, if a person purports to conclude an agreement acting as agent for a non-existent principal, she herself is bound by the agreement.[60] As a result, a third party who enters into a contract with a promoter when the company is in formation creates one of four situations:

- a revocable offer to the non-existent corporation, which the latter can accept when formed;
- an irrevocable offer, which the corporation can accept (within a limited time) when formed;
- an agreement with the promoter, whose duties the corporation may assume when formed; or
- an agreement with the promoter, who will remain liable even if the corporation assumes the obligations from the agreement.[61]

The intentions of the parties will determine which of the above options are applied to a contract between a promoter and the third party.[62] For example,

---

[57] *Natal Land and Colonization Company Ltd* v. *Pauline Colliery and Development Syndicate Ltd* [1904] AC 120, 126.
[58] Pennington (2001: 101).
[59] § 106 DGCL; and § 2.03(a) Revised Model Business Corporation Act.
[60] Restatement of Agency 2d, § 326.
[61] Restatement of Agency 2d, § 326, Comment (b).
[62] See e.g. *Company Stores Development Corp.* v. *Pottery Warehouse, Inc.*, 733 SW 2d 886 (Tenn. App. 1987).

if the contract calls for performance even before the company is established, this would tend to indicate a contract with the promoter. If the intention of the parties cannot be clearly determined, courts will usually hold that the promoter must perform the contract.. Thus, a contract solely with the promoter is the standard, default position unless the parties prove otherwise. If the corporation begins to perform the contract after formation, this could lead to a novation, depending on the circumstances. The *Jacobson* decision, reprinted in part in this chapter, discusses the kinds of facts that might lead to the state of affairs referred to in the third and fourth bullet points above.

III. Liability of shareholders when attempt at incorporation is defective

A. Germany

To cater for the unlikely event that a *Satzung* has been drafted, the company has been registered, but the company is neither validly incorporated nor merits a declaration of nullity, German scholars and courts have developed the doctrine of "defective corporation" (*fehlerhafte Gesellschaft*). This area, like that of the VorG, is governed by decisions primarily concerning entities other than the AG; the court has issued decisions primarily regarding commercial partnerships (OHGs) and silent partnerships (*stille Gesellschaften*). In comparison to the US and UK, the court which registers an AG focuses on the *Satzung* to a somewhat greater degree, making it unlikely that a defective stock corporation can arise if there is no cause for a declaration of nullity.

Under the "defective corporation" doctrine, it would be necessary that a *Satzung* in fact be drafted and that there be dealings with third parties on behalf of the company. The primary thrust of the doctrine is that the company may not be wound up from its point of establishment (*ex tunc*), but only from the moment that the defect is proven (*ex nunc*), which creates significant stability for the contractual rights and obligations of both third parties and shareholders incurred during the life of the company.[63] This doctrine does not alter the statutory rule enacted to implement the liability requirement of the First Company Law Directive, as discussed above.

B. United Kingdom

For the same reasons mentioned in regard to Germany, the chance of a defective incorporation (one that factually occurs but legally is invalid) is

---

[63] BGHZ 55, 5, at 8 (1970).

slight in the United Kingdom. If the company has not been formed, pre-incorporation liability would apply, and, if the company has been formed, it will rarely be open to challenge. Pursuant to the Companies Act 2006, the companies registrar, who acts in a quasi-judicial capacity, must examine the incorporation documents filed and register the company only after becoming "satisfied that the requirements of [the Companies Act] as to registration are complied with."[64] As a result, the certificate of incorporation that the registrar issues is "conclusive evidence that the requirements" of the Act have been met.[65] As such, an allegation of a "defective" incorporation cannot stand against the "conclusive evidence" of the certificate. There are, however, cases where assertions of nullity may arise, as discussed below.

C. United States

US law is obviously not subject to article 7 of the First Company Law Directive, and it also has a less rigorous registration process. However, like the policy evidenced in the German doctrines of the VorG and defective corporations, US courts are very interested in creating an environment of trust and fairness for the conduct of business. Under US principles of agency law, if persons hold themselves out to be directors or officers of a corporation while entering into a transaction with a third party, and the corporation turns out not to have been properly incorporated or is later incorporated and then goes bankrupt without making payment on the contract, the third party may look to the individuals associated with the defective entity for performance. These persons have two defenses at their disposal: (1) although a *de jure* corporation did not arise, there was a *de facto* corporation that should be understood to have adopted the contract for performance; and (2) the third party should be estopped from asserting a claim against the promoter because she intended to contract with the corporation and the liability of the individual promoter, director or shareholder would be an element for which she did not bargain and thus she should not be able to recover from them.

The idea behind the status of the *de facto* corporation is that trust in the market should not suffer because of the imperfect fulfillment of technicalities or because of formal errors in the incorporation process, and normal business dealings should not be burdened with the high costs of investigating the valid corporate existence of every contractual counterparty. Delaware recognizes *de facto* corporations, while the Model Act does not.

---

[64] Sec. 14 CA 2006.   [65] Sec. 15(4) CA 1985.

The prerequisites for achieving the status of a *de facto* corporation are discussed in *North Delaware A-OK Campground*, reprinted in part in this chapter. Note how the court has recourse to legal scholarship in reaching its decision. The use of authoritative scholarship is supposed to be a trait of Civil Law courts, but not of courts in Common Law jurisdictions. Why does the Delaware court turn to legal treatises? What sort of issue are they addressing? The *Timberline Equipment Company* decision, also in this chapter, presents the position under the Model Act, which has statutorily eliminated the theory of *de facto* incorporation. How do the laws and the approaches to the law differ in these two cases? Under Delaware law, *de facto* incorporation is available when there is a good faith effort to incorporate, and, under the Model Act, a "knowing" failure to incorporate disallows a finding of incorporation. Do these two sets of law differ in substance?

The defense of estoppel presents a completely different theory. It rests neither on the presence of good faith nor on the nature of the error in the incorporation process, but on the parties' expectations when contracting. If the third party knew and accepted the corporation as his counter-party, why should he be given the un-bargained-for advantage of holding the promoter, director or shareholder liable for performance?[66] This doctrine is discussed in the *Timberline* decision.

IV. *Declaring a corporation null and void*

In many jurisdictions, a material and incurable error in obtaining a formal deed, permission or other act will render the content of the formal act null and void *ab initio*. This can also apply to corporations, which would entail substantial disruption of commercial dealings, as all rights and obligations of third parties and shareholders *vis-à-vis* the corporation would cease to exist. The First Company Law Directive seeks to contain such risks by restricting judicial declarations of nullity to an exclusive set of grounds:

- the failure to execute a constitutive document or comply with legal formalities;
- a company's objects are unlawful or contrary to public policy;
- the constitutive document omits the name of the company, the amount of the capital subscriptions, the total capital subscribed or the objects of the company; or
- the failure to comply with minimum capital requirements.[67]

---

[66] On this point, see Gevurtz (2000: 63).

Because, as mentioned, a declaration of nullity of the company *ex tunc* would also nullify the rights and obligations received and incurred by a company since it came into existence, thereby creating possible hardships for shareholders and third parties, the Directive subjects the company to orderly insolvency proceedings in the event it is declared null. Thus, nullity entails the winding up of the company (i.e. orderly dissolution) with preservation of commitments entered into by or with the company, and the holders of shares in the capital remain obliged to pay up any outstanding capital subscribed.[68] This relatively obscure provision on nullity became standard reading for every student of EU law through the ECJ's *Marleasing* decision, reprinted in part in this chapter. In *Marleasing*, the Court explained that a national court must interpret national law so as to give effect to the provisions of an EU directive (here, the First Company Law Directive's exclusive list of grounds for nullity), thus declaring that EU law has "direct" application in the member states.[69]

A.   Germany

Germany has implemented the First Company Law Directive in the *Aktiengesetz*. An exclusive list of the grounds for nullity are provided,[70] a declaration of nullity can only be sought through the courts, and only within three years after the registration of the company.[71] The effect of such a declaration is forward-looking, not retroactive.[72] German law also provides a company with an opportunity to cure the offending defect before declaring it null.[73]

B.   United Kingdom

The First Company Law Directive states that "Member States may not provide for the nullity of companies otherwise than" for those grounds it lists.[74] Given this wording, it appears that UK law does not violate the Directive by failing to provide for nullity at all in the Companies Act. However, one scholar, R. R. Drury, has pointed out that UK courts will in fact declare companies null and void if they are either formed to pursue an object that is illegal or pursue the activity of a trade union (which may

---

[67]   Art. 11(2) First Company Law Directive.
[68]   Art. 12(5) First Company Law Directive.
[69]   See Case C-106/89, *Marleasing SA* v. *La Comercial Internacional de Alimentacion SA* [1990] ECR I-4135, paras. 7–12.
[70]   § 275(1) AktG.   [71]   § 275(3) AktG.   [72]   § 277 AktG.
[73]   § 276 AktG.   [74]   Art. 11(2) First Company Law Directive.

not be organized in corporate form).[75] As Drury points out, there is no provision for a preservation of previous transactions or an orderly winding up of the company as required by EU law. The registrar's examination of the memorandum, the conclusiveness of the certificate of incorporation, and the politically sensitive matter of declaring a labor union null and void have probably led to the fact that no UK case has appeared on this question before the ECJ.

C.   United States

Pursuant to Delaware law, the Delaware Court of Chancery has broad jurisdiction to take action having the same impact as a declaration of nullity. It may "revoke or forfeit the charter of any corporation for abuse, misuse or nonuse of its corporate powers, privileges or franchises."[76] The Model Act gives similar power to the secretary of state in circumstances where the corporation fails to comply with its obligations under the Model Act.[77] In a situation comparable to the UK case of a labor union illegally being formed as a corporation, the Delaware court has revoked the charter of a non-profit corporation whose activities in fact contradicted its declared status as non-profit.[78] Delaware courts may also "administer and wind up the affairs of any corporation whose charter shall be revoked or forfeited."[79] Since a corporation may only be established for "any lawful business,"[80] the Delaware Court of Chancery has also used its power to revoke the charter of a corporation engaged in a sustained course of fraud, immorality or violation of statutory law.[81]

Question for discussion

A and B want to sell used cars. In February, they agree to establish a GmbH with a share capital of €25,000, which they each are to subscribe 50 percent. The articles of incorporation are notarized in April. Pursuant to these articles, A is appointed as the managing director of "A and B Used Cars GmbH." In April, A and B pay €6,250 each into an account set up for the company. On 25 April, A files for registration of the company. Registration procedures usually take several months, and the company is registered on 31 August. A and B are eager to get "their" business started

[75] Drury (1985: 649 *et seq.*); Davies (2008: 95–97).
[76] § 284(a) DGCL.   [77] § 14.20 Model Act.
[78] *Southerland, ex rel. Snider* v. *Decimo Club, Inc.*, 142 A 786 (Del. Ch. 1928).
[79] § 284(b) DGCL.   [80] § 101(b) DGCL.
[81] *Young* v. *National Association for Advancement of White People*, 109 A 2d 29 (Del. Ch. 1954).

immediately. They agree that A will commence business activities prior to the registration of the company.

In May, A, acting as director of "A and B Used Cars GmbH i.G." (i.e. "in formation"), purchases a piece of land for the company's car lot from S for €200,000. In June, A buys a used Mercedes from G for €25,000.

1. In September, S wants to know who is liable for payment of the purchase price for the real estate.
2. In June, G asks you from whom he may demand payment of the €25,000 for the Mercedes.

Cases

Marleasing SA v. La Comercial Internacional de Alimentacion SA
European Union, Court of Justice
[1990] ECR I-04135
© ELLIS Publications
© European Communities
[*Text edited*]

[*Text omitted*]

Grounds

1. By order of 13 March 1989 … the Juzgado de Primera Instancia e Instruccion No 1, Oviedo, referred a question to the Court pursuant to Article 177 of the EEC Treaty for a preliminary ruling on the interpretation of Article 11 of Council Directive 68/151/EEC of 9 March 1968 on coordination of safeguards which, for the protection of the interests of members and others, are required by Member States of companies within the meaning of the second paragraph of Article 58 of the Treaty, with a view to making such safeguards equivalent throughout the Community.

2. Those questions arose in a dispute between Marleasing SA, the plaintiff in the main proceedings, and a number of defendants including La Comercial Internacional de Alimentacion SA (hereinafter referred to as 'La Comercial'). The latter was established in the form of a public limited company by three persons, including Barviesa SA, which contributed its own assets.

3. It is apparent from the grounds set out in the order for reference that Marleasing's primary claim, based on Articles 1261 and 1275 of the Spanish Civil Code, according to which contracts without cause or whose cause is unlawful have no legal effect, is for a declaration that the founders' contract establishing La Comercial is void on the ground that the establishment of the company lacked cause, was a sham transaction and was carried out in order to defraud the creditors of Barviesa SA, a co-founder of the defendant company. La Comercial contended

that the action should be dismissed in its entirety on the ground, in particular, that Article 11 of Directive 68/151, which lists exhaustively the cases in which the nullity of a company may be ordered, does not include lack of cause amongst them.

4. The national court observed that in accordance with Article 395 of the Act concerning the Conditions of Accession of Spain and the Portuguese Republic to the European Communities (Official Journal 1985 L 302, p. 23) the Kingdom of Spain was under an obligation to bring the directive into effect as from the date of accession, but that that had still not been done at the date of the order for reference. Taking the view, therefore, that the dispute raised a problem concerning the interpretation of Community law, the national court referred the following question to the Court:

> 'Is Article 11 of Council Directive 68/151/EEC of 9 March 1968, which has not been implemented in national law, directly applicable so as to preclude a declaration of nullity of a public limited company on a ground other than those set out in the said article?'

[Text omitted]

6. With regard to the question whether an individual may rely on the directive against a national law, it should be observed that, as the Court has consistently held, a directive may not of itself impose obligations on an individual and, consequently, a provision of a directive may not be relied upon as such against such a person …

7. However, it is apparent from the documents before the Court that the national court seeks in substance to ascertain whether a national court hearing a case which falls within the scope of Directive 68/151 is required to interpret its national law in the light of the wording and the purpose of that directive in order to preclude a declaration of nullity of a public limited company on a ground other than those listed in Article 11 of the directive.

8. In order to reply to that question, it should be observed that … the Member States' obligation arising from a directive to achieve the result envisaged by the directive and their duty under Article 5 of the Treaty to take all appropriate measures, whether general or particular, to ensure the fulfilment of that obligation, is binding on all the authorities of Member States including, for matters within their jurisdiction, the courts. It follows that, in applying national law, whether the provisions in question were adopted before or after the directive, the national court called upon to interpret it is required to do so, as far as possible, in the light of the wording and the purpose of the directive in order to achieve the result pursued by the latter and thereby comply with the third paragraph of Article 189 of the Treaty.

9. It follows that the requirement that national law must be interpreted in conformity with Article 11 of Directive 68/151 precludes the interpretation of provisions of national law relating to public limited companies in such a manner that the nullity of a public limited company may be ordered on grounds other than those exhaustively listed in Article 11 of the directive in question.

10. With regard to the interpretation to be given to Article 11 of the directive, in particular Article 11(2)(b), it should be observed that that provision prohibits the

laws of the Member States from providing for a judicial declaration of nullity on grounds other than those exhaustively listed in the directive, amongst which is the ground that the objects of the company are unlawful or contrary to public policy.

11. According to the Commission, the expression 'objects of the company' must be interpreted as referring exclusively to the objects of the company as described in the instrument of incorporation or the articles of association. It follows, in the Commission's view, that a declaration of nullity of a company cannot be made on the basis of the activity actually pursued by it, for instance defrauding the founders' creditors.

12. That argument must be upheld. As is clear from the preamble to Directive 68/151, its purpose was to limit the cases in which nullity can arise and the retroactive effect of a declaration of nullity in order to ensure 'certainty in the law as regards relations between the company and third parties, and also between members' (sixth recital). Furthermore, the protection of third parties 'must be ensured by provisions which restrict to the greatest possible extent the grounds on which obligations entered into in the name of the company are not valid'. It follows, therefore, that each ground of nullity provided for in Article 11 of the directive must be interpreted strictly. In those circumstances the words 'objects of the company' must be understood as referring to the objects of the company as described in the instrument of incorporation or the articles of association.

13. The answer to the question submitted must therefore be that a national court hearing a case which falls within the scope of Directive 68/151 is required to interpret its national law in the light of the wording and the purpose of that directive in order to preclude a declaration of nullity of a public limited company on a ground other than those listed in Article 11 of the directive.

[*Text omitted*]

Kelly A. Cleary v. North Delaware A-OK Campground, Inc., et al.
Superior Court of Delaware
CA No. 85C-OC-70, 1987 Del. Super. LEXIS 1374
[*Text edited; footnotes omitted*]

VINCENT A. BIFFERATO, Judge

... Plaintiff Kelly A. Cleary claims she was injured when the saddle of a horse she was riding at Double J Riding Stables in Bear, Delaware, came loose. She was a paying customer at the riding stable, and believes she was injured because of negligence.

Ms. Cleary sued North Delaware A-OK Campground, Inc. ("A-OK"); Cedrick D. Justis, Chairman of the Board of A-OK and landlord of the property on which Double J Riding Stables is located; and Thomas and Betty Hutchens, as owners and operators of Double J Riding Stables, or as agents or joint venturers of A-OK and Mr. Justis.

Defendants respond by saying Ms. Cleary has sued the wrong parties. The Hutchens claim to have never done business as Double J Riding Stables. Rather, a separate corporation, "Double Jay, Inc." does business as Double J Riding Stables.

Betty Hutchens is the wife of Dewey G. Hutchens (50 percent shareholder of Double Jay, Inc.) and mother of Thomas D. Hutchens (25 percent shareholder of Double Jay, Inc.). Mrs. Hutchens claims she has never been a stockholder, officer or director of Double J, Inc., and that she has never been employed by the corporation.

Affidavits support the contention that Thomas D. Hutchens' interest in Double Jay, Inc. is purely financial, as a 25 percent stockholder. He claims not to be an officer, director, or employee.

A-OK is a corporation which operates a picnic ground and campground in the general vicinity of Double J Riding Stables. Defendants claim there is absolutely no connection between A-OK and Double Jay, Inc. and/or Double J Riding Stables. The corporation's stockholders are completely different. Plaintiff argues that A-OK is vicariously liable for the acts of its alleged joint venturer or agent, Double J Riding Stables.

Cedrick D. Justis, a defendant, and his brother, Robert Justis, own the land upon which the campground and riding stables are located. Mr. Justis is also a stockholder and chairman of the Board of A-OK. He leases the ground to Double Jay, Inc., pursuant to an oral lease.

Double J Riding Stables began operating on or about April 21, 1983. The principals immediately took steps to have the business incorporated. Apparently, due to the unavailability of the corporate name, "Double J, Inc.," the business' accountant failed to file the Certificate of Incorporation with the Secretary of State until December 16, 1983, approximately two months after Ms. Cleary was injured. Still, defendants claim a de facto corporation existed at the time of the accident, insulating defendant Thomas Hutchens from personal liability.

In summary, defendants suggest that each defendant should be dismissed because none of them owned or operated Double J Riding Stables, and that summary judgment should be granted.

Plaintiff opposes the motion for summary judgment. She claims that there is a question of fact regarding the relationship between A-OK and Double J Riding Stables. She provides information showing A-OK advertised that it had horseback riding at its facility. Apparently, these ads referred to the services of Double J Riding Stables.

As to Cedrick D. Justis, Ms. Cleary presents two advertising pamphlets which state that "the Justis Family" is the "host" at the campground.

Ms. Cleary also directs the Court to the April 12, 1984 edition of the local newspaper in which the author states "[Betty Ann] Hutchens ... also works with her husband, their son and two of their three daughters in the family business, Double J Riding Stables, Bear." Plaintiff's Exhibit J. She believes this indicates the existence of a mere partnership, not an insulating de facto corporation.

[Text omitted]

The Court agrees with defendants here. The fact that A-OK advertises the availability of the nearby riding stables does not make it an owner or operator. A-OK also advertises, under "59 Fun Things to See and Do While at North Del A-OK," in the brochure marked "Plaintiff's Exhibit C," visits to Longwood Gardens and

Winterthur Museum. To claim that A-OK owns or operates these facilities because it takes advantage of their physical proximity is absurd ...

Next, Mrs. Cleary emphasizes that two of the pamphlets state that "the Justis Family" are the "hosts" of the campground ...

While Mr. Justis, as owner of the land upon which the campground is located, and a stockholder of the corporation which operates the campground, is a "host" of the campers, he is no more than a landlord as to the riding stables' property. The brochures merely speak to his status as "host" of the campground, not the riding stables. Since the plaintiff was allegedly injured by negligent actions of employees of the riding stables, and not due to any dangerous condition on the land, Mr. Justis, as landlord, has no legal vulnerability ... Ms. Cleary then argues that an April 12, 1984 Wilmington News Journal newspaper article creates a material question of fact regarding Betty Ann Hutchens' status. Without discussing the article's admissibility, the Court notes first that the article does not state that Mrs. Hutchens owns or operates the business. It merely states that she "works with her husband, their son and two of their three daughters in the family business, Double J Riding Stables, Bear." At most, according to the article, she is an employee. She cannot be liable, as an agent, for the torts of her principal unless she participated in them ...

Ms. Cleary also claims the article raises a material question of fact as to Thomas Hutchens. Thomas Hutchens was sued as "Thomas Hutchens, doing business as Double J Riding Stables." The article only alludes to the fact that he was an employee, not an owner or operator, or one "doing business as Double J Riding Stables." Plaintiff does not allege that he was the negligent employee, but instead seems to attack him in his status as a 25 percent shareholder of Double J, Inc. Therefore, the article does not give rise to a material issue of fact as to Thomas Hutchens.

Mrs. Cleary goes on to stress that Thomas Hutchens may be liable in his individual capacity as a "partner" of Double Jay, Inc. Defendants respond by noting that there was no partnership but, instead, a "de facto" corporation in existence at the time of the accident. Defendants claim Thomas Hutchens is insulated by the corporate veil.

So, the Court must determine if Double J, Inc. was a de facto corporation on or about October 16, 1983, the date of the accident.

A de jure corporation exists when there is substantial compliance with all mandatory conditions precedent to incorporation. H. Henn and J. Alexander, *Law of Corporations* 329 (3rd ed. 1983). In Delaware, a corporation does not come into existence until the Certificate of Incorporation is duly filed with the Secretary of State. 8 Del. C. § 106 (1983). There is no question here that despite the principals' efforts to incorporate on April 21, 1983, the Certificate of Incorporation for Double Jay, Inc. was not actually filed until December 16, 1983. Therefore, there was no de jure corporate existence on October 16, 1983, the date of the accident.

However, a corporation which fails to qualify as de jure may still assume "de facto" corporate status. Henn and Alexander at 329; R. Stevens, *Handbook on the Law of Corporations*, §§ 26–27 (2nd edn., 1949); Comment, *Defective Incorporation: De facto Corporations by Estoppel*, and § 21–2054, 5 8 Neb.Law Review 763 (1979); Note, *The De facto Doctrine in Montana*, 39 Mont. Law Review 305 (1978).

In Delaware, a business organization seeking de facto status must meet three general requirements: there must be "a general law under which a corporation may lawfully exist; a bona fide attempt to organize under the law and colorable compliance with the statutory requirements; and actual use or exercise of corporate powers in pursuance of such laws." …

Delaware has a general law under which a corporation may lawfully exist … There was a good faith attempt to incorporate here, and colorable compliance with the statutory requirements. Double Jay made a bona fide attempt to incorporate on April 21, 1983 under the name Double J Inc. After a two-month delay, the parties were informed that the name was unavailable, and the accountant filed for a corrected name. Another delay regarding filing fees, which was apparently not the principal's fault, occurred. The Certificate of Incorporation was not filed until December 16, 1983.

The business did exercise its corporate power here, as of April 21, 1983. As of that date, it took several steps which indicated its use of corporate powers. It began operations as a business. It obtained an IRS corporate identification number. It made an election for Subchapter S status.

The factors for de facto status have been satisfied.

Generally, a stockholder cannot be held personally liable for tortious acts of the corporation unless he has participated or aided in the commission of the acts. See generally, Henn and Alexander at 546; 18A Am.Jur. 2d, Corporations § 851. Innocent stockholders of a de facto corporation have the same rights and are entitled to the same protection as stockholders of a corporation de jure. 18 CJS. Corporations § 96. Therefore, Thomas Hutchens cannot be held personally liable for the alleged torts of the de facto corporation.

[Text omitted]

Timberline Equipment Co., Inc. v. Davenport
Supreme Court of Oregon (*en banc*)
514 P 2d 1109 (1973)
[Text edited; some footnotes omitted]

DENECKE, Justice

Plaintiff brought this action for equipment rentals against the defendant Dr. Bennett and two others. In addition to making a general denial, Dr. Bennett alleged as a defense that the rentals were to a de facto corporation, Aero-Fabb Corp., of which Dr. Bennett was an incorporator, director and shareholder. He also alleged plaintiff was estopped from denying the corporate character of the organization to whom plaintiff rented the equipment. The trial court held for plaintiff. Dr. Bennett, only, appeals.

On January 22, 1970, Dr. Bennett signed articles of incorporation for Aero-Fabb Co. The original articles were not in accord with the statutes and, therefore, no certificate of incorporation was issued for the corporation until June 12, 1970, after new articles were filed. The leases were entered into and rentals earned during the period between January 22nd and June 12th ...

ORS 57.321 of the Oregon Business Corporation Act ... is virtually identical to s 56 of the Model Act [now § 2.03]. The Comment to the Model, prepared as a research project by the American Bar Foundation and edited by the American Bar Association Committee on Corporate Laws, states:

> 'Under the Model Act, de jure incorporation is complete upon the issuance of the certificate of incorporation, except as against the state in certain proceedings challenging the corporate existence ...'
> 'Under the unequivocal provisions of the Model Act, any steps short of securing a certificate of incorporation would not constitute apparent compliance. Therefore a de facto corporation cannot exist under the Model Act.'

[Text omitted]

ORS 57.793 provides:

> 'All persons who assume to act as a corporation without the authority of a certificate of incorporation issued by the Corporation Commissioner, shall be jointly and severally liable for all debts and liabilities incurred or arising as a result thereof.'

This is merely an elaboration of s 146 of the Model Act [now § 2.04]. The Comment states:

> 'This section is designed to prohibit the application of any theory of de facto incorporation. The only authority to act as a corporation under the Model Act arises from completion of the procedures prescribed ... No other means being authorized, the effect of section 146 is to negate the possibility of a de facto corporation.'
> 'Abolition of the concept of de facto incorporation, which at best was fuzzy, is a sound result. No reason exists for its continuance under general corporate laws, where the process of acquiring de jure incorporation is both simple and clear. The vestigial appendage should be removed.' 2 Model Business Corporation Act Annotated s 146 ...

In *Robertson* v. *Levy* ... the court held the president of a defectively organized corporation personally liable to a creditor of the 'corporation.' The applicable legislation was similar to Oregon's. The court held the legislation ended the common-law doctrine of de facto corporation.

The Alaska court upheld the cancellation ground that the applicant had not yet been issued its certificate of incorporation at the time the permit was issued. *Swindel* v. *Kelly* ... Alaska has a statute similar to Oregon's. The court commented: 'The concept of de facto corporations has been increasingly disfavored, and Alaska is among the states whose corporation statutes are designed to eliminate the concept.' ...

[Text omitted]

We hold the principle of de facto corporation no longer exists in Oregon.

The defendant also contends that the plaintiff is estopped to deny that it contracted with a corporation.

The doctrine of 'corporation by estoppel' has been recognized by this court but never fully dissected ... Corporation by estoppel is a difficult concept to grasp and courts and writers have 'gone all over the lot' in attempting to define and apply the doctrine. One of the better explanations of the problem and the varied solutions is contained in Ballantine, *Manual of Corporation Law and Practice* ss 28–30 (1930):

> 'The so-called estoppel that arises to deny corporate capacity does not depend on the presence of the technical elements of equitable estoppel, viz., misrepresentations and change of position in reliance thereon, but on the nature of the relations contemplated, that one who has recognized the organization as a corporation in business dealings should not be allowed to quibble or raise immaterial issues on matters which do not concern him in the slightest degree or affect his substantial rights.' Ballantine, supra, at 92.

As several writers have pointed out, in order to apply the doctrine correctly, the cases must be classified according to who is being charged with estoppel. Ballantine, supra, at 91; 1 Hornstein, *Corporation Law and Practice* s 30, p. 31, n. 6 (1959).

When a defendant seeks to escape liability to a corporation plaintiff by contending that the plaintiff is not a lawful corporate entity, courts readily apply the doctrine of corporation by estoppel. *Thompson Optical Institute* v. *Thompson* ... well illustrates the equity of the doctrine in this class of cases R. A. Thompson carried on an optical business for years. He then organized a corporation to buy his optical business and subscribed to most of the stock in this corporation. He chaired the first meeting at which the Board resolved to purchase the business from him. The corporation and Thompson entered into a contract for the sale of the business which included a covenant by Thompson not to compete. Thereafter, Thompson sold all of his stock to another individual. Some years later Thompson re-entered the optical business in violation of the covenant not to compete. The corporation brought suit to restrain Thompson from competing. Thompson defended upon the ground that the corporation had not been legally organized. We held, 'The defendant cannot be heard to challenge the validity of the contract or the proper organization of the corporation.' ...

The fairness of estopping a defendant such as Thompson from denying the corporate existence of his creation is apparent.

On the other hand, when individuals such as the defendants in this case seek to escape liability by contending that the debtor is a corporation, Aero-Fabb Co., rather than the individual who purported to act as a corporation, the courts are more reluctant to estop the plaintiff from attacking the legality of the alleged debtor corporation. Ballantine, supra, at 96; 8 Fletcher, *Cyclopedia of the Law of Private Corporations* (perm. ed.) s 3914, p. 228.

The most appealing explanation of why the plaintiff may be estopped is based upon the intention of the parties. The creditor-plaintiff contracted believing it could look for payment only to the corporate entity. The associates, whatever their relationship to the supposed corporate entity, believed their only potential liability was the loss of their investment in the supposed corporate entity and that they were not personally liable ...

From the plaintiff-creditor's viewpoint, such reasoning is somewhat tenuous. The creditor did nothing to create the appearance that the debtor was a legal corporate entity. The creditor formed its intention to contract with a debtor corporate entity because someone associated with the debtor represented, expressly or impliedly, that the debtor was a legal corporate entity.

[Text omitted]

The trial court found, and its findings are supported by the evidence, that all the defendants were partners prior to January 1970 and did business under the name 'Aero-Fabb Co.' Not until June 1970 were the interests in this partnership assigned to the corporation 'Aero-Fabb Co.' and about the same time the assumed business name 'Aero-Fabb Co.' was cancelled.

The trial court found, and the evidence supported the finding, that two of the leases entered into by plaintiff were with 'Kenneth L. Davenport, dba Aero-Fabb Co.' The other was with 'Kenneth L. Davenport, dba Aero-Fabb Corp.' 'Aero-Fabb Corp.' was never the corporate name; the name of the corporation for which a certificate was finally issued was 'Aero-Fabb Co.' The correspondence and records of plaintiff sometimes referred to the debtor as 'Aero-Fabb Co.' and others as 'Aero-Fabb Corp.'

... [P]laintiff's salesman said Mr. Davenport, speaking for the organization, stated several times that he was in a partnership with Drs. Gorman and Bennett. The salesman was dubious and checked the title to the land on which the debtors' operation was being conducted and found it was in the name of the three defendants as individuals.

A final question remains: Can the plaintiff recover against Dr. Bennett individually?

In the first third of this century the liability of persons associated with defectively organized corporations was a controversial and well-documented legal issue. The orthodox view was that if an organization had not achieved de facto status and the plaintiff was not estopped to attack the validity of the corporate status of the corporation, all shareholders were liable as partners. This court, however, rejected the orthodox rule. In *Rutherford* v. *Hill* ... we held that a person could not be held liable as a partner merely because he signed the articles of incorporation though the corporation was so defectively formed as to fall short of de facto status. The court stated that under this rule a mere passive stockholder would not be held liable as a partner. We went on to observe, however, that if the party actively participated in the business he might be held liable as a partner ...

The Model Act and the Oregon Business Corporation Act, ORS 57.793, solve the problem as follows:

'All persons who assume to act as a corporation without the authority of a certificate of incorporation issued by the Corporation Commissioner, shall be jointly and severally liable for all debts and liabilities incurred or arising as a result thereof.'

We have found no decisions, comments to the Model Act, or literature attempting to explain the intent of this section.

We find the language ambiguous. Liability is imposed on '(a)ll persons who assume to act as a corporation.' Such persons shall be liable 'for all debts and liabilities incurred or arising as a result thereof.'

We conclude that the category of 'persons who assume to act as a corporation' does not include those whose only connection with the organization is as an investor. On the other hand, the restriction of liability to those who personally incurred the obligation sued upon cannot be based upon logic or the realities of business practice. When several people carry on the activities of a defectively organized corporation, chance frequently will dictate which of the several active principals directly incurs a certain obligation or whether an employee, rather than an active principal, personally incurs the obligation.

We are of the opinion that the phrase, 'persons who assume to act as a corporation' should be interpreted to include those persons who have an investment in the organization and who actively participate in the policy and operational decisions of the organization. Liability should not necessarily be restricted to the person who personally incurred the obligation.

[Text omitted]

There is evidence from which the trial court could have found that while Drs. Bennett and Gorman, another defendant, entrusted the details of management to Davenport, they endeavored to and did retain some control over his management. All checks required one of their signatures. Dr. Bennett frequently visited the site and observed the activity and the presence of the equipment rented by plaintiff. He met with the organization's employees to discuss the operation of the business. Shortly after the equipment was rented and before most of the rent had accrued, Dr. Bennett was informed of the rentals and given an opinion that they were unnecessary and ill-advised. Drs. Bennett and Gorman thought they had Davenport and his management 'under control.'

This evidence all supports the finding that Dr. Bennett was a person who assumed to act for the organization and the conclusion of the trial court that Dr. Bennett is personally liable.

Affirmed.

Kelner v. Baxter
Court of Common Pleas
(1866–67) LR 2 CP 174
Reproduced with permission of the Incorporated Council of Law Reporting for England and Wales
[Text edited; headnotes and footnotes omitted]

[Text omitted]

[Kelner sold wine for a livelihood. He dealt with Baxter for a sale of wine. Baxter purported to act for a company named "The Gravesend Royal Alexandra Hotel Company, Limited" (directors: Baxter, Edmands, Dales, Macdonald, Hulse, Calisher), but this company was not yet formed when the transaction was concluded. The contract was concluded with the exchange of correspondence reprinted immediately below this summary. The wine was delivered, consumed, but not paid for. When the company was formed, it formally ratified the contract. However, it became insolvent and never paid Kelner. The latter sued Baxter and the other persons who signed the sales contract. They claimed that the company, not the signatories personally, were liable for performance on the contract.]

"To John Dacier Baxter, Nathan Jacob Calisher, and John Dales, on behalf of the proposed Gravesend Royal Alexandra Hotel Company, Limited.

"Gentlemen, – I hereby propose to sell the extra stock now at the Assembly Rooms, Gravesend, as per schedule hereto, for the sum of 900£, payable on the 28th of Feb.ruary, 1866.

(Signed) "John Kelner."

Then followed a schedule of the stock of wines, &c., to be purchased, and at the end was written as follows:

"To Mr. John Kelner.

"Sir, We have received your offer to sell the extra stock as above, and hereby agree to and accept the terms proposed.

(Signed) "J. D. Baxter,
"N. J. Calisher,
"J. Dales,

"On behalf of the Gravesend Royal Alexandra Hotel Company, Limited."

[Text omitted]

ERLE, CJ

I am of opinion that this rule should be discharged. The action is for the price of goods sold and delivered: and the question is whether the goods were delivered to the defendants under a contract of sale. The alleged contract is in writing, and commences with a proposal addressed to the defendants, in these words: – "I hereby propose to sell the extra stock now at the Assembly Rooms, Gravesend, as per schedule hereto, for the sum of 900£., payable on the 28th of February, 1866." Nothing can be more distinct than this as a vendor proposing to sell. It is signed by the plaintiff, and is followed by a schedule of the stock to be purchased. Then comes the other part of the agreement, signed by the defendants, in these words, – "Sir, We have received your offer to sell the extra stock as above, and hereby agree to and accept the terms proposed." If it had rested there, no one could doubt that there was a distinct proposal by the vendor to sell, accepted by the purchasers. A difficulty has arisen because the plaintiff has at the head of the paper addressed it to the plaintiffs, "on behalf of the proposed Gravesend Royal Alexandra Hotel Company, Limited," and the defendants have repeated those words after their signatures to the document; and the question is, whether this constitutes any ambiguity on the face of the agreement, or prevents the defendants from being bound by it. I agree that if the Gravesend Royal Alexandra Hotel Company had been an existing company at this time, the persons who signed the agreement would have signed as agents of the company. But, as there was no company in existence at the time, the agreement would be wholly inoperative unless it were held to be binding on the defendants personally. The cases referred to in the course of the argument fully bear out the proposition that, where a contract is signed by one who professes to be signing "as agent," but who has no principal existing at the time, and the contract would be altogether inoperative unless binding upon the person who signed it, he is bound thereby: and a stranger cannot by a subsequent ratification relieve him from that responsibility. When the company came afterwards into existence it was a totally new creature, having rights and obligations from that time, but no rights or obligations by reason of anything which might have been done before. It was once, indeed, thought that an inchoate liability might be incurred on behalf of a proposed company, which would become binding on it when subsequently formed: but that notion was manifestly contrary to the principles upon which the law of contract is founded. There must be two parties to a contract; and the rights and obligations which it creates cannot be transferred by one of them to a third person who was not in a condition to be bound by it at the time it was made. The history of this company makes this construction to my mind perfectly clear. It was no doubt the notion of all the parties that success was certain: but the plaintiff parted with his stock upon the faith of the defendants' engagement that the price agreed on should be paid on the day named. It cannot be supposed that he for a moment contemplated that the payment was to be contingent on the formation of the company by the 28th of February. The paper expresses in terms a contract to buy. And it is a cardinal rule that no oral evidence shall be admitted to shew an intention different from that which appears on the face of the writing. I come, therefore, to the conclusion that the defendants, having no principal who was bound originally, or who could become so by a subsequent ratification, were themselves bound, and that the oral evidence offered is not admissible to contradict the written contract.

WILLES, J

I am of the same opinion. Evidence was clearly inadmissible to shew that the parties contemplated that the liability on this contract should rest upon the company and not upon the persons contracting on behalf of the proposed company. The utmost it could amount to is, that both parties were satisfied at the time that all would go smoothly, and consequently that no liability would ensue to the defendants. The contract is, in substance, this, – "I, the plaintiff, agree to sell to you, the defendants, on behalf of the Gravesend Royal Alexandra Hotel Company, my stock of wines;" and, "We, the defendants, have received your offer, and agree to and accept the terms proposed; and you shall be paid on the 28th of February next." Who is to pay? The company, if it should be formed. But, if the company should not be formed, who is to pay? That is tested by the fact of the immediate delivery of the subject of sale. If payment was not made by the company, it must, if by anybody, be by the defendants. That brings one to consider whether the company could be legally liable. I apprehend the company could only become liable upon a new contract. It would require the assent of the plaintiff to discharge the defendants. Could the company become liable by a mere ratification? Clearly not. Ratification can only be by a person ascertained at the time of the act done, – by a person in existence either actually or in contemplation of law; as in the case of assignees of bankrupts and administrators, whose title, for the protection of the estate, vests by relation ... I would refer to Gunn v. London and Lancashire Fire Insurance Company, where this Court, upon the authority of Payne v. New South Wales Coal and International Steam Navigation Company, held that a contract made between the projector and the directors of a joint-stock company provisionally registered, but not in terms made conditional on the completion of the company, was not binding upon the subsequent completely registered company, although ratified and confirmed by the deed of settlement: and Williams, J, said, that, "to make a contract valid, there must be parties existing at the time who are capable of contracting." That is an authority of extreme importance upon this point; and, if ever there could be a ratification, it was in that case. Both upon principle and upon authority, therefore, it seems to me that the company never could be liable upon this contract ... Putting in the words "on behalf of the Gravesend Royal Alexandra Hotel Company," would operate no more than if a person should contract for a quantity of corn "on behalf of my horses." ...

[Text omitted]

Phonogram Ltd v. Lane
Court of Appeal
[1982] QB 938
Reproduced with permission of the Incorporated Council of Law Reporting for England and Wales
[Text edited; headnotes and footnotes omitted]

LORD DENNING MR

In 1973 there was a group of "pop" artists. They included two gentlemen called Brian Chatton and John McBurnie. The suggestion was that they should perform under the name "Cheap Mean and Nasty." A company was going to be formed to run the group. It was to be called "Fragile Management Ltd."

Before the company was formed, negotiations took place for the financing of the group. It was to be financed by one of the subsidiaries of a big organisation called the Hemdale Group. It was eventually arranged that money should be provided by Phonogram Ltd. The agreed amount was £12,000, and the first instalment was to be £6,000. The first instalment of £6,000 was paid.

But the new company was never formed. The group never performed under it. And the £6,000 was due to be repaid. But it was never repaid. Phonogram Ltd then tried to discover who was liable to repay the money. Mr. Roland Rennie was the man who had negotiated on behalf of Phonogram. Mr. Brian Lane was the man who had negotiated on behalf of the new company which was to be formed. I will read the letter from Mr. Rennie to Mr. Lane of July 4, 1973. It is the subject matter of this action:

> "Brian Lane, Esq.,
> Fragile Ltd,
> 39 South Street,
> London, W1.
>
> "Dear Brian,
> "In regard to the contract now being completed between Phonogram Ltd and Fragile Management Ltd concerning recordings of a group consisting of Brian Chatton, John McBurnie and one other with a provisional title of 'Cheap Mean and Nasty' and further to our conversation this morning, I send you herewith our cheque for £6,000 in anticipation of the contract signing, this being the initial payment for the initial LP called for in the contract. In the unlikely event that we fail to complete within, say, one month you will undertake to repay us the £6,000. As per our telephone conversation the cheque has been made payable to Jelly Music Ltd. For good orders sake, Brian, I should be appreciative if you could sign the attached copy of this letter and return it to me so that I can keep our accounts people informed of what is happening.
>
> > "Yours sincerely,
> > "Roland G. Rennie
> > "Signed by ... for and on behalf of Fragile Management Ltd."

That was signed by Mr. Lane. So there is the written contract embodying the agreement between those concerned. An invoice was sent by Phonogram Ltd ...

The money was paid over. According to the accounts, it went into the account of Jelly Music Ltd, which was one of the subsidiaries of the Hemdale Group of which Mr. Lane, with others, was a director.

The first question is whether, on the true construction of the contract, Mr. Lane made himself personally liable. As I read the words of the contract – "I send you herewith our cheque for £6,000" and "In the unlikely event that we fail to complete within, say, one month you will undertake to repay us the £6,000" – the word "you" referred to Mr. Lane personally. The cheque was made out in favour of Jelly Music Ltd only as a matter of administrative convenience (as the judge found). It did not affect the fact that the agreement to repay was made by Brian Lane: especially when it is realised that it was known to all concerned that Fragile Management Ltd had not been formed. So I would have construed the contract, without recourse to any other aids, as making Mr. Lane personally liable.

But Phillips J construed the contract differently. He had heard a lot of evidence. He said in his judgment: "But I am quite satisfied that the events of July 4 did not of themselves involve a contract with Mr. Lane personally."

I will accept for the moment that the judge was correct in so holding. Even so Phonogram Ltd say that the law of England has been much altered by section 9 (2) of the European Communities Act 1972. It says:

> "Where a contract purports to be made by a company, or by a person as agent for a company, at a time when the company has not been formed, then subject to any agreement to the contrary the contract shall have effect as a contract entered into by the person purporting to act for the company or as agent for it, and he shall be personally liable on the contract accordingly."

That seems to me to cover this very case. The contract purports to be made on behalf of Fragile Management Ltd, at a time when the company had not been formed. It purports to be made by Mr. Lane on behalf of the company. So he is to be personally liable for it.

Mr. Thompson, on behalf of Mr. Lane, argued very skilfully that section 9(2) did not apply. First, he said: "Look at the directive under the European Community law which led to this section being introduced." It is Council Directive of March 9, 1968 (68/151/EEC). In 1968 English was not one of the official languages of the European Community. So Mr. Thompson referred us to the French text of article 7 of the Directive:

> "Si des actes ont été accomplis au nom d'une société en formation, avant l'acquisition par celle-ci de la personnalité morale, et si la société ne reprend pas les engagements résultant de ces actes, les personnes qui les ont accompli en sont solidairement et indéfiniment responsables, sauf convention contraire."

Mr. Thompson says that, according to the French text, that Directive is limited to companies which are "en formation," that is companies which have already started to be formed.

Mr. Thompson's submission is reinforced by passages from a French textbook – *Ripert, Traité Elémentaire de Droit Commercial*, 7th ed. (1972). As I read the passage at pp. 601 and 604 of that treatise – interpreting the French as best I can – in the case of a French company or société there may be, recognised by law, a period of time while a company is in the course of formation when people have put their signatures to what I may call "the articles of association." That period is called the period when the société is "en formation." At p. 604 a parallel is drawn with a baby at the time of gestation – between the time of conception and the time of birth – and a company when it is "en formation."

I reject Mr. Thompson's submission. I do not think we should go by the French text of the Directive. It was drafted with regard to a different system of company law from that in this country. We should go by section 9(2) of our own statute, the European Communities Act 1972. Under article 189 of the EEC Treaty, directives are to be binding only in so far as the spirit and intent are concerned. Article 189 says:

> " ... A directive shall be binding, as to the result to be achieved, upon each member state to which it is addressed, but shall leave to the national authorities the choice of form and methods."

Section 9(2) is in accordance with the spirit and intent of the Directive. We should go by our own statute, and not by the Directive (68/151/EEC).

That brings me to the second point. What does "purports" mean in this context? Mr. Thompson suggests that there must be a representation that the company is already in existence. I do not agree. A contract can purport to be made on behalf of a company, or by a company, even though that company is known by both parties not to be formed and that it is only about to be formed.

The third point made by Mr. Thompson was that a company can be "a person" within the second line of section 9 (2). Mr. Thompson says that Jelly Music Ltd was "a person" which was purporting to contract on behalf of Fragile Management Ltd. I do not agree. Jelly Music Ltd were not entering into a contract. Mr. Lane was purporting to do so.

So all three of Mr. Thompson's points fail.

But I would not leave the matter there. This is the first time the section has come before us. It will have much impact on the common law. I am afraid that before 1972 the common law had adopted some fine distinctions. As I understand *Kelner* v. *Baxter* (1866) LR 2 CP 174 it decided that, if a person contracted on behalf of a company which was nonexistent, he himself would be liable on the contract. Just as, if a man signs a contract for and on behalf "of his horses," he is personally liable. But, since that case was decided, a number of distinctions have been introduced by Hollman v. Pullin (1884) Cab. & Ell. 254; *Newborne* v. *Sensolid* (Great Britain) Ltd [1954] 1 QB 45 and *Black* v. *Smallwood* (1965) 117 CLR 52 in the High Court of Australia. Those three cases seem to suggest that there is a distinction to be drawn according to the way in which an agent signs a contract. If he signs it as "agent for 'X' company" – or "for and on behalf of 'X' company" – and there is no such body as "X" company, then he himself can be sued upon it. On the other hand, if he signs it as "X" company per pro himself the managing director, then the position may be different: because he is not contracting personally as an agent. It is the company which is contracting.

That distinction was disliked by Windeyer J in *Black* v. *Smallwood*. It has been criticised by Professor Treitel in *The Law of Contract*, 5th ed. (1979), p. 559. In my opinion, the distinction has been obliterated by section 9(2) of the European Communities Act 1972. We now have the clear words, "Where a contract purports to be made by a company, or by a person as agent for a company, at a time when the company has not been formed ... " That applies whatever formula is adopted. The person who purports to contract for the company is personally liable.

[Text omitted]

... The words "subject to any agreement to the contrary" mean – as Shaw LJ suggested in the course of the argument – "unless otherwise agreed." If there was an express agreement that the man who was signing was not to be liable, the section would not apply. But, unless there is a clear exclusion of personal liability, section 9(2) should be given its full effect. It means that in all cases such as the present, where a person purports to contract on behalf of a company not yet formed, then however he expresses his signature he himself is personally liable on the contract.

[Text omitted]

Jacobson v. Stern

Supreme Court of Nevada
605 P 2d 198 (1980)
[Text edited; footnotes omitted]

[Text omitted]

In January, 1969, Jacobson contacted Stern and asked him to draw plans for Jacobson's new hotel/casino [the "Kings Castle"] at Lake Tahoe. Stern immediately began preliminary work on the project and contacted soil engineers and surveyors in this regard. At this time Stern dealt directly with Jacobson, who referred to the project as "my hotel," and with Taylor of Nevada which was to be the general contractor.

On February 18, 1969, Stern wrote to Jacobson detailing, among other things, the architect's services and the fee. Stern's plans were subsequently discussed by the two men and Stern's fee was agreed to be $250,000. Stern was told by Jacobson to proceed, and he completed the preliminary plans by March ... highrise foundation ... on May 1, 1969 ... Stern testified at trial that by May 6, 1969, at least 60% of the architectural services were complete ... A letter from Jacobson to Stern, written March 10, 1970, acknowledges that the parties entered into a contract in April, 1969, but no written contract was ever admitted into evidence despite Jacobson's testimony that such a document was executed.

At the same time ... Jacobson was negotiating financing and setting up business structures to own and manage the property. On May 1, 1969, Jacobson acquired all of the stock of ALW, Inc., a corporation which had previously operated a casino on this site, and which was to operate the Kings Castle. Levin-Townsend Computer Corporation subsequently purchased 20% of the ALW, Inc. stock for $300,000. On May 9, 1969, a business structure for ownership of Kings Castle was set up and a number of documents were executed. The business structure included the formation of Lake Enterprises, a corporation of which Jacobson was the sole stockholder and president. Kings Castle, Limited Partnership was formed with Lake Enterprises, Inc. as the general partner and Jacobson and others as limited partners. Jacobson was the most substantial investor in Kings Castle, Limited Partnership, with investments in excess of $3 million.

After May 9, 1969, ALW, Inc. operated the hotel and casino and Kings Castle, Limited Partnership, leased the land. All monies were subsequently paid and received through these two entities. Stern billed Jacobson beginning in June of 1969. Some of the billings were disputed, but Stern was in fact paid $30,000 on June 13, 1969; $30,000 on August 11, 1969; $58,000 on September 12, 1969, and $32,000 on October 17, 1969. All of the checks were drawn on the account of ALW, Inc.; only one of the checks was signed by Jacobson.

The Kings Castle opened in July 1970. On February 3, 1972, ALW, Inc., as owner of Kings Castle and Casino, filed its petition for arrangements under Chapter XI of the Bankruptcy Act. Stern did not file a claim in that proceeding. [In separate proceedings, a court awarded Stern $132,590.37 plus interest against Jacobson personally.]

[Text omitted]

In this appeal Jacobson contends: (1) that there was insufficient evidence presented at trial to support the judgment of his personal liability; (2) that the obligations of Jacobson were adopted by ALW, Inc., and that such adoption constituted a novation; and, (3) that it was improper for the court to assess costs against Jacobson for a continuance of the trial.

1. Appellant contends there is no evidence to support the district court's findings that Stern was not dealing with any of the existing corporate entitles; Levin-Townsend Computer Corporation; Bonanza No. 2; J. J. Enterprises; Jacobson as agent for any of these; or with Jacobson as agent for Kings Castle or any other principal.

The evidence shows that Jacobson was, in the early months of 1969, President of J. J. Enterprises, which wholly owned Bonanza No. 2, and Chairman of the Board of Caesar's Palace. There is no evidence, however, that at that time Jacobson was acting on behalf of any of these entities in contracting for the building of Kings Castle Casino, and this is born out by the fact that none of these entities subsequently became involved with the Kings Castle Casino. Although Stern may have known of Jacobson's affiliations, and known that many of the same people who owned and managed the Bonanza were involved in the Kings Castle project, there is little evidence, if any, that he contracted with Jacobson in any capacity connected with those existing corporations. There is no evidence the Levin-Townsend Computer Corporation had anything more than a 20% ownership interest in ALW, Inc. The record is also devoid of evidence that they were involved with Stern directly, or that Jacobson ever represented them in negotiations with Stern.

Kings Castle, Limited Partnership, and Lake Enterprises, Inc., did not exist until May 9, 1969. ALW, Inc. existed from 1965, but Jacobson had no connection with it at all until he purchased the stock on May 1, 1969. The contract for architectural services, which was certainly for the benefit of ALW, Inc. and Kings Castle, Limited Partnership, was made before May 1, 1969. Stern maintains that he had a contract with Jacobson from February 18, 1969, and Jacobson admits a contract as of April 1969, but in any event the contract was in existence before Kings Castle, Limited Partnership, and Lake Enterprises, Inc., and before Jacobson's involvement with ALW, Inc. Thus, none of these corporations could contract, or have Jacobson contract for them because they were not yet organized.

Appellant, citing *Gillig & Co.* v. *Lake Bigler Road Co.* ... further argues that a course of conduct between the parties created a presumption that Jacobson was acting as agent of J. J. Enterprises, as owner of the Bonanza. The record supports the determination that there was no course of dealing or custom and practice between these parties which would tend to establish Jacobson's agency for J. J. Enterprises in his relationship with Stern in the Kings Castle.

In the absence of any evidence to the contrary, and in the presence of testimony by Stern that he thought he was dealing with Jacobson as an individual, the district court concluded that the contract was made between Jacobson, as promoter of the Kings Castle project, and Stern. A contract with the promoter is not one with the corporation absent some subsequent corporate act or agreement ... Thus, the district court properly found Jacobson, as promoter, liable on the contract.

2. Under Nevada law, if a pre-incorporation contract made by a promoter is within the corporate powers, the corporation may, when organized, expressly or impliedly ratify the contract and, thus, make it a valid obligation of the corporation. If the corporation accepts the benefits of the contract, it will be required to perform the contractual obligations ... The evidence supports a finding that the ALW corporation accepted the benefits of the contract for architectural services, and in fact adopted the contractual obligations and made partial payments on the obligation. However, liability of the corporation by adoption does not, absent a novation, end the liability of the promoter to the third party.

Appellant argues that there was, in fact, a novation by ALW, Inc. in its adoption of all agreements as its corporate liabilities. Where there is a valid express or implied novation, the corporation is substituted for the promoter as a party to the contract in all respects, and the promoter is divested of his rights and released of his liabilities. In order to constitute a valid novation, however, the creditor must assent to the substitution of a new obligor, but this assent may be inferred from his acceptance of part performance by the new obligor, if the performance is made with the understanding that a complete novation is proposed.

Appellant contends that, because the evidence shows that after May 1, 1969, Stern probably knew, or should have known, that he was performing for the benefit of ALW, Inc., and was paid by ALW, Inc., he impliedly consented to a novation. There is no evidence, however, showing that Stern agreed to the substitution of ALW, Inc. for Jacobson in the contract, or that he performed with the knowledge or understanding that a novation was proposed ... In fact he maintained throughout that he had contracted with Jacobson and felt that Jacobson was personally liable on the contract. The intent of the parties to cause a novation must be clear. The trial court found there was no novation and that Stern never agreed to release Jacobson from his obligations. We agree with this finding.

[*Text omitted*]

5

Constituting the company's share capital

Required reading

EU: Second Company Law Directive, arts. 1(1), 2c, 3, 6–11
D: AktG, §§ 6–10, 23(2) nos. 2 and 3, (3) nos. 3–5, 26, 27, 29, 31–38, 46–54, 63–66(1), 150–152; GmbHG, §§ 3(1) nos. 3 and 4, §§ 5, 7(2) and (3), 8(1) and (2), 9–9c, 19(2) and (5); HGB, §§ 266(3)(A), 272
UK: CA 2006, secs. 542, 580–587, 593–598, 610–615
US: Scan for comparison: DGCL, §§ 102(a)(4), 152–154, 156, 162–164, and Model Act, § 6.21 (including nos. 1 and 2 of the Official Comment); DGCL, §§ 101–108, 124; Model Act § 2.04

The function of share capital and rules governing its constitution

I. Introduction

A. The "par" or "nominal" value of shares

It is an essential characteristic of a stock corporation that the company is owned by investors who receive transferable shares of stock certificating their rights as members and owners: this is exemplified by referring to such persons as "shareholders" (*Aktionäre*). If – as might be the case at the outset – the only assets of a stock corporation were the contributions of cash and assets made by its shareholders in exchange for their shares, the company's "capital" would equal the sum of such contributions for shares: it would be "share capital." In Chapter 3, we saw that differences in capital requirements led to regulatory competition among charters for private companies in Europe in the late 1990s, and, in Chapter 4, we discussed how, in connection with the incorporation of a company, incorporators must specify the initial share capital. In Germany and the United Kingdom, a minimum capital of €50,000 (*Grundkapital*)[1] and £50,000

---

[1] § 7 AktG.

(allotted share capital),[2] respectively, must be subscribed to for a public company to be incorporated (Germany) or commence trading (United Kingdom). It was never common in the US to require a minimum capital for companies other than those performing regulated activities such as banking or insurance.[3]

As the corporation comes into existence, it will issue shares to its first members, and it must be paid at least in part for such shares. Because, as we will see often in future chapters, shareholders holding the same class of shares must be treated equally, and because the "incorporating" or majority shareholders of a company will often have informational advantages and disproportionate power in a firm, it is reasonable to be concerned about insiders giving themselves special advantages with respect to the price at which and conditions on which they purchase their shares. In each of our jurisdictions, one common way of ensuring equal treatment was originally to assign a "par" or "nominal" value to each share and to require that each shareholder subscribe for shares with a promise to pay at least the par value when purchasing shares. The product of the par value times the number of shares issued and allotted would then equal the "share capital." The amount of this "share capital" might reflect the book value of the company at the moment of incorporation, but, once the real value of the company changes, it has no relation to such real value or the market price of the company's shares. Par or nominal value is thus purely an accounting convention. If a company were to issue 100 shares at a par value of 50 to its initial shareholders, its "share capital" would simply be the product of these two numbers, that is, 5,000:

$$\text{Share capital} = \text{par or nominal value of each share} \times \text{number of shares}$$
$$= 50 \times 100$$
$$= 5,000$$

As par or nominal value would be static, a way to account for actual value would be to have the investor pay a "premium" beyond par when purchasing the shares. This "premium" could change the figure understood as "share capital" only if considered a part of that item:

$$\text{Share capital} = (\text{par or nominal value of each share} + \text{premium}) \times \text{number of shares}$$
$$= (50 + 10) \times 100$$
$$= 6,000$$

---

[2] Sec. 763(1) CA 2006.   [3] Manning (1981: 17).

Otherwise, the premium could be placed in a reserve, which may or may not be distributable to shareholders, depending on what the law requires. The allocation of paid-in sums to share capital or to a reserve and the classification of such reserve as distributable or not is thus an arbitrary accounting norm, and varies among our jurisdictions.

Share capital = par or nominal value of each share × number of shares
$$= 50 \times 100$$
$$= 5{,}000$$

Reserve = premium × number of shares
$$= 10 \times 100$$
$$= 1{,}000$$

As we can see, the amount of the "par" or "nominal" value of a share is a figure fixed at the time a company is incorporated and may – but need not – have some relation to the original value of the company; this renders the amount of the "share capital" just as arbitrary. Especially after a company commences operations, however, as it begins to generate a positive cash flow or record losses, the arbitrary nature of these figures and conventions become very evident. As Dean Bayless Manning has observed:

> [T]he concept of par as a standard for shareholder investment did not work badly in the prototypical model of the corporate enterprise since par was nearly always the subscription price and since everyone agreed that a subscriber-shareholder should as a matter of contract be held to do what he had agreed to do. The system may not have helped the creditor very much, but at least it had a plausibility to it and could be made to work. But as the enterprise moved from the stage of initial financing to that of an ongoing enterprise, the system lost both plausibility and workability.[4]

Manning underlines the main problem with par or nominal value. When the corporation is a mere shell holding assets that have been contributed but not yet applied to business operations, a share issue price derived by dividing the book value of the company's assets by the number of shares is reasonable. However, when a company becomes a going concern, its share price will include many other factors, such as goodwill and certain growth expectations. The par value and the requirement that shares be sold at par or above then becomes rather arbitrary. Both Delaware and Germany now allow shares to be issued without par value. German law

---

[4] Manning (1981: 22).

is, however, more restrictive, for no par shares must have a "notional" or accounting value of at least €1,[5] while Delaware law places no restrictions on value or denomination. One might thus argue whether Germany has actually eliminated the nominal value requirement. In Delaware, the board of directors is entrusted to state that a specific sum[6] is "legal" or "stated" capital (which is the US equivalent to the term "share" capital) and in Germany a notional accounting value exceeding €1 is calculated by dividing the amount of share capital by the number of shares issued.[7] The initial par value of a share can become even more unrelated to the actual, capital needs of a business corporation when the law requires that a specific amount of share capital be constituted upon incorporation or commencement of trading and maintained throughout the life of the company.

B.   Minimum "legal" or "share" capital

As explained above, when the allocated number of shares of par, nominal, assigned or notional value stock are multiplied by their respective values, one has what is referred to in the United Kingdom as "share capital," in the United States as "legal" or "stated" capital, and in Germany as *Grundkapital*. A minimum capital is required in public companies by article 6 of the Second Company Law Directive and is therefore found in the legislation of all EU member states. The primary reason for minimum capital is to protect creditors against a decision by the shareholders to distribute the assets securing company debts[8] to themselves. This capital is protected by the rules on distributions discussed in detail in Chapters 7 and 8. By requiring every public company to constitute and maintain such capital, European company law intends to reduce the transaction costs that third parties might otherwise incur when entering into credit relationships with them. Legal capital can also be considered as dues that are paid for receiving the privilege of limited liability, which is certainly the view expressed in the nineteenth-century *Ooregum Gold Mining Company* case,[9] or a barrier against the frivolous incorporation of a stock corporation.[10] The efficacy of legal capital to serve such ends has, however, been strongly challenged in the legal scholarship.

---

[5] § 8(3) AktG.   [6] § 154 DGCL.   [7] § 8(3) AktG.

[8] The Second Company Law Directive expresses the position that share capital "constitutes the creditors' security." Preamble, 4th Consideration.

[9] *Ooregum Gold Mining Company of India Ltd* v. *Roper* [1892] AC 125 (HL).

[10] Santella and Turrini (2008: 434).

First, it is argued that the requirement of legal capital deceives potential creditors. This is because the capital rules protect only against distributions to *shareholders*, but not use of the capital in other ways, such as to pay for the operating expenses of the company.[11] As such, "as soon as a firm starts to operate, it can use its capital to purchase assets that decline in value,"[12] yet the capital will still appear on the corporation's financial statements as if it were a source available to cover debts. Secondly, a uniform minimum capital both deters the launching of startup companies necessary for economic prosperity and is in most cases completely insufficient to cover the exposure of creditors to established companies.[13] At least one study shows "a negative correlation between size of minimum capital requirements (scaled for GDP) and self-employment – a common proxy for entrepreneurship – in European countries."[14] Thirdly, sophisticated voluntary creditors (referred to as "adjusting"), such as banks, and both unsophisticated voluntary creditors such as employees and involuntary creditors such as tort victims (referred to as "non-adjusting")[15] are better protected in other ways. As they are aware that the initial, mandatory capital offers little or no protection, sophisticated lenders adjust existing protections by negotiating for the provision of collateral, guarantees or covenants restricting new debt or distributions.[16] Given that involuntary tort victims would rank as unsecured creditors in any insolvency proceedings of the malefactor and probably fail to collect anything of value,[17] they are best protected from dangerous activity by insurance requirements for such activities.[18] Fourthly, as will be seen below and in the following chapters, the labyrinth of procedures used to ensure that the minimum capital has actually been paid in and is not distributed, is complex and expensive.[19] These rules have spawned a world of their own populated by tricky evasions and regulatory responses – complex machinations devised by lawyers and accountants on both sides – that increase transaction costs to the point that they far outweigh the marginal utility of the underlying principle. These objections were known when the Second Company Law Directive was amended in 2006, and some changes – as discussed below – were made.

---

[11] Ferran (1999: 47).   [12] Macey and Enriques (2001: 1186).
[13] Mülbert (2006: 386).   [14] Armour (2006: 18).   [15] Armour (2006: 11).
[16] Armour (2006: 18 *et seq.*).   [17] Santella and Turrini (2008: 434).
[18] Armour (2006 : 18–19).
[19] Macey and Enriques (2001: 1195); Mülbert (2006: 384 *et seq.*) with further references.

C.   Preventing "watered" stock

The first page in the book of tricks on how to evade the capital rules is to underpay for stock. A company's share capital is paid in (at least in part) by shareholders, and, if such payments are not made or are underpaid, then the rules on capital would be useless. One popular term used to describe underpayment for shares is "watered stock." The word "stock" has a number of meanings in English, including the inventory of items a merchant keeps on hand for sale and the animals a rancher raises to sell on the market. In the latter case, as animals such as bulls are sold by weight, a traditional type of fraud in the livestock business was to lead the "stock" to drink before bringing them to the scales, thus artificially increasing their weight with water, so as to inflate the price. As it is common to use colorful metaphors in company law (from "white knights" and "poison pills" to "Chinese walls"), so, when shares of stock are sold for less than they are worth, the expression "watering stock" is used. The rules that regulate capital contributions to fight stock "watering" take a number of forms:

- par value stock may not be sold for less than par;
- payment of a certain percentage of the issue price must be made before shares can be issued;
- if payment is made with assets other than cash, the value of these assets must be reliably ascertained; and
- the set of non-cash assets that are eligible for payment are restricted.

Below, we will address each type of rule for each of our three jurisdictions.

II.   Paying for the initial shares

A.   The German rules

1. Cash payments Germany faithfully implements the Second Company Law Directive[20] by making it illegal to issue shares for less than their par or notional accounting value.[21] *Cash* payment for shares must cover at least one-quarter of the nominal value and the full premium above that figure, if any.[22] The shareholder remains liable for the remainder, and

---

[20] Art. 8(1) Second Company Law Directive.   [21] § 9(1) AktG.
[22] §§ 188(2), 36a(1) AktG.

must make full payment when the directors call such payment in – which must happen within a maximum period of ten years – or if the company enters insolvency proceedings.[23] In Germany, the word "cash" means just that, and is limited to euros in hand or a transfer of euros duly confirmed by a bank.[24] As will be seen, this definition is significantly more restrictive than under UK law. The *Vorstand* and *Aufsichtsrat* will have to examine all payments for shares at the time of incorporation, and if, as is often the case, a board member is also an incorporator, or an indirect subscriber, or one of these persons receives a material benefit from the incorporation, then the formation process must be audited by one or more independent auditors.[25] In the case of shares with a nominal, rather than a par, value, any payments exceeding such value will be treated as a share premium and placed in a restricted reserve pursuant to the *Aktiengesetz*.[26]

An issue that is much litigated in Germany arises when a shareholder pays cash to a company for an issue of shares and the company at an earlier or later point in time purchases an asset from the shareholder. If this is considered a valid cash payment, the shareholder's contribution falls under the simpler rules for cash payments for the shares and the asset purchase will not be subjected to the extensive scrutiny required for in-kind contributions that is discussed in the next subsection. The cost of the approval procedure in time and money is significant, and creates a powerful incentive for companies and shareholders to circumvent it. One popular technique has been for the investor to pay cash for her shares with the express or tacit understanding that the company will at a later date use the cash to purchase an asset from that same shareholder. The German rules designed to catch such transactions are divided into two categories. The first is an *ex ante* statutory norm deriving from the Second Directive,[27] which triggers a requirement for audit, disclosure and shareholder approval of the transaction; the second is an *ex post* judicial examination that can result in rescinding the transaction.

A bright line, statutory rule provides that, if within two years of being established, the company contracts with an incorporator or a shareholder whose stake in the company exceeds 10 percent of the company's capital to purchase an asset with a purchase price exceeding 10 percent of the

---

[23] § 54(4) AktG.   [24] § 54(2) AktG.   [25] § 33 AktG.

[26] Share premiums are transferred to a capital reserve, § 272(2) No. 1 HGB. This reserve is available only for limited purposes pursuant to § 150 AktG, depending on whether the capital reserve, together with a statutory reserve under § 150(1), (2) AktG, exceeds 10 percent of the nominal capital (§ 150(4) AktG) or not (§ 150(3) AktG).

[27] Art. 11 Second Company Law Directive.

same capital, this purchase will be viewed as a continuation of the incorporation process, a "post-incorporation" transaction (*Nachgründung*), and
require both shareholder approval and the disclosure and audit process for
in-kind contributions discussed below in the following subsection.[28] The
audit of the asset's value, disclosure of the details to all shareholders and
the requirement that the transaction be approved by three-quarters of the
capital represented at the meeting (with an additional requirement that
at least one-quarter of the total capital approve if the transaction occurs
within one year of incorporation),[29] uses disclosure to shareholders and
approval by a supermajority to screen for and check possible abuses per-
petrated by an insider.

Judges react with flexibility to violations not caught by the statute.
German courts have developed a doctrine in conjunction with scholarly literature to supplement the reach of the statutory law. This doctrine
looks to the substance, rather than to the form, of a transaction to catch
"disguised in-kind contributions" (*verdeckte Sacheinlage*). Like "post-
incorporation" transactions, a disguised in-kind contribution will typically consist of a cash payment for shares coupled with the company
previously or subsequently purchasing assets from the same shareholder
or a related person. The court will attempt to discern whether such combination of transactions is designed to evade the rules on asset contributions. The doctrine is limited neither to specific persons nor to a specific
time after incorporation and could be applied to cases not caught by the
"post-incorporation" criteria discussed immediately above. For a disguised in-kind contribution to be found, it will always be necessary that
there be an agreement about the sale of an asset to the company in connection with the allotment of the relevant shares. However, since express
agreement may not exist, courts look to the circumstances surrounding
the two transactions for evidence of a disguised in-kind contribution. The
cases provide that a rebuttable presumption of such contributions will
arise where:

- the issue of the shares and the purchase of the asset occur within six
  months of each other; and
- the shares issued and the asset purchased have comparable values.[30]

A short turnaround time for the company's sale and purchase would
reduce the need for a clear agreement and indisputable evidence of an
agreement would likely overcome even a significant interval between the

---

[28] § 52 AktG.   [29] § 52(5) AktG.   [30] Kübler and Assmann (2006: 191–192).

transaction's first and second leg.[31] If a court finds that a transaction was used to disguise a contribution otherwise falling under the rules on in-kind contributions, the transaction will be declared without effect, which triggers a statutory liability for the shareholder to make a cash payment to the company for the shares.[32] Although the shareholder would then have a claim for return of the asset sold to the corporation, if the latter were to be bankrupt, the shareholder would not receive her asset back and would have paid twice for the shares. Kübler and Assmann find that this penalty is punitive in nature and thus technically invalid because couched in the civil, rather than the criminal, law, where punitive measure should be found.[33] In 2008, the GmbHG was amended to reduce these harsh consequences in connection with private companies,[34] and the amendments were extended to the AG in 2009.[35] Under the new rules, a transaction that is qualified as a disguised in-kind contribution is not denied effect; instead, the value of the asset at the time of its contribution is counted toward the shareholder's liability for payment of a cash contribution. Thus, the shareholder will be liable only for a shortfall in value of his in-kind contribution. Despite this relaxation of the law, the risk connected with disguised in-kind contributions is still significant. Since the shareholder bears the burden of proving the value of the asset at the time of its contribution, and since it may be difficult, if not impossible, to determine the value of the asset at a specific point in the past without having gone through the evaluation process prescribed for in-kind contributions, the shareholder may still end up having to pay the entire contribution in cash.

2. **In-kind payments**   The rules governing in-kind contributions for share issues drive companies and shareholders to construct the complex structures discussed above in the hope of escaping their strictures. As one commentator has put it, "this laborious, time-consuming, and costly arrangement for in-kind contributions has in practice created the temptation to evade the procedure mandated by law."[36] For stock corporations, disadvantaging in-kind payments is unwise, as most public companies are incorporated with assets contributed in connection with

---

[31] Pentz, in *MünchKommAktG* (2008: § 27 mn. 96).   [32] § 27 AktG.
[33] Kübler and Assmann (2006: 192).
[34] See § 19(4) GmbHG, as amended by art. 1 no. 17(c) MoMiG.
[35] See § 27(3) AktG, as amended by art. 1 no. 1 ARUG.
[36] Pentz, in *MünchKommAktG* (2008: § 27 mn. 84).

transforming a growing partnership or private limited company.[37] This means that the rules on in-kind contributions negatively affect the principal route to forming an AG. The procedure was originally mandated by the 1977 version of the Second Company Law Directive, and was somewhat relaxed in the 2006 amendments to that Directive to allow listed securities (which are valued by the market) and items that have been recently appraised professionally to be contributed without a new audit – provided a number of conditions are met and certain details are published.[38] Whilst Germany recently amended its law to implement these changes,[39] the United Kingdom has left its rules on in-kind contributions unchanged. In fact, when drafting the Companies Act 2006, the UK government noted that the "relaxations were so minor and so hedged about with qualifications that it was not worth taking them up."[40]

In accordance with article 7 of the Second Directive, a promise to perform services may not serve as an in-kind contribution.[41] If shares are purchased with an in-kind contribution, the asset must cover the entire purchase price and any premium (issue price), but a commitment to transfer an asset may remain outstanding for up to five years.[42] Germany applies the rules on in-kind contributions both to straight contributions of assets in payment for shares (*Sacheinlage*) and to transactions resembling those discussed in subsection 1 above, in which the company agrees to purchase an asset (*Sachübernahme*). Both types of transaction must be audited by an expert (usually an accountant),[43] in order to ascertain whether the facts provided regarding the transaction and the asserted value of the asset are correct.[44] On the basis of this audit, the incorporators must prepare a report on the incorporation process, dwelling in detail on the asset, its value and valuation, and specifying the shares purchased by board members and any advantages or commissions received by the same.[45] The *Satzung* must include reference to the asset contributed, its value, the contributor, and the shares issued in return for its contribution.[46] If the non-cash asset is contributed in connection with the incorporation of the company, the contracts for the transfer, the audit report and the management report must be submitted to the court with the request for incorporation.[47]

---

[37] Kübler and Assmann (2006: 187).
[38] Arts. 10a and 10b Second Company Law Directive.
[39] See § 33a AktG, as implemented by art. 1 no. 1(a) ARUG.
[40] Davies (2008: 274, note 85).   [41] § 27(2) AktG.   [42] § 36a(2) AktG.
[43] § 33(2) no. 4 AktG.   [44] § 34(1) no. 4 AktG.   [45] § 32 AktG.
[46] § 27(1) AktG.   [47] § 37(4) AktG.

B.   The UK rules

1.   Cash payments   As the Second Directive closely regulates payments for the allocation of shares, the UK rules closely resemble those found in Germany. The UK position, at least since the Companies Act of 1867,[48] has been that shares may not be allotted at a discount, and this rule is found both in the Second Directive and in the Companies Act 2006.[49] Following article 9 of the Directive, consideration for shares must cover at least one-quarter of the nominal value and the full premium above that figure, if any.[50] Somewhat less strict than Germany, this one-quarter payment applies to both in-kind and cash consideration.[51] Moreover, "cash" includes some cash equivalents that are readily accepted in commercial practice, such as promises to pay and releases of liability toward the company,[52] provided that any such undertaking will be performed within five years.[53] This facilitates debt-for-equity swaps in troubled companies where creditors release their claims in exchange for shares.[54] UK law is also more generous than German law with regard to the denomination of a company's capital and to the currency in which payments of cash contributions may be made.[55]

As it derives from article 11 of the Second Directive, UK law – like the *Aktiengesetz* – also contains rules for a "post-incorporation" transaction. The Companies Act 2006 requires an expert evaluation and shareholder approval before the company may acquire from an incorporator any asset for a price reaching 10 percent of its issued share capital.[56] This is somewhat narrower than the German rule, in that it applies only to purchases from incorporators.[57] UK courts have not ventured beyond the clear text of the statute to develop a doctrine comparable to the German "disguised contribution in kind."

Comparable to the *Aktiengesetz*, UK law specially provides for the semi-capitalization of premiums paid in addition to the nominal value of shares. Any such premiums must be placed in an account called "the share premium account."[58] This account is treated as part of the share capital and may be used, in addition to funding ordinary operations, only for a specified number of purposes, such as to pay commissions in

---

[48] See *Ooregum Gold Mining* [1892] AC 125 (HL).
[49] Sec. 580 CA 2006.   [50] Sec. 586 CA 2006.
[51] Sec. 586 CA 2006, which does not make a distinction in the type of consideration used.
[52] Sec. 583(3) CA 2006.   [53] Sec. 587(1) CA 2006.   [54] Davies (2008: 276).
[55] Secs. 763, 765 CA 2006; and *In Re Scandinavian Bank Group plc* [1987] 2 WLR 752.
[56] Sec. 598 CA 2006.   [57] Sec. 598(1)(a) CA 2006.   [58] Sec. 610(1) CA 2006.

connection with the issue of shares or to issue bonus shares.[59] However, the Companies Act does provide for special treatment of share premiums (referred to as "merger relief") when they are paid in connection with certain mergers. This treatment applies if:

- the issuing company acquires at least a 90 percent holding in the target company;
- this holding is acquired in exchange for an allotment of the issuing company's shares; and
- the target transfers its shares to the acquiring company or cancels its shares not already held by the acquiring company as part of the exchange agreement.[60]

Merger relief is particularly advantageous for the acquiring company and its shareholders when the target company has pre-acquisition profits that are available for distribution.[61] As will be discussed in more detail in Chapter 7, "share" or "legal" capital is used to demarcate those company assets that may not be distributed to shareholders. Whether or not a share premium is treated like share capital is therefore of great significance to the shareholders of an issuing company. For example, if in the course of a merger the value of a target share were £10 and the acquirer issues one of its own shares – each perhaps having a market value of £10, but a nominal value of £1 – for each target share, the acquiring company would record on the liabilities side of its balance sheet under share capital a nominal value of £1 and in a related reserve a share premium of £9 for each of the shares it allots. On the assets side of its balance sheet, the acquiring company will show each target share with a value of £10.

If the target were to make a dividend payment to the acquirer, this would increase the acquiring company's cash account. Whether the acquiring company can treat this amount as a realized profit that it can pass on to its own shareholders through a declaration of dividends depends on the effect that the target's dividend payment has on the acquiring company's financial statements. Since a dividend payment would take value out of the target company, the value of the acquirer's investment in the target would be reduced. This reduction would be reflected in a write-down of the value entered for the target shares. This write-down would have the effect of canceling out the increase in the acquirer's cash account caused by

---

[59] Sec. 610(2) CA 2006; and Ferran (2008: 116–120).
[60] Sec. 612(1) CA 2006; and Ferran (2008: 120–123).
[61] Ferran (2008: 122).

the dividend payment. In this way, the additional profits that the acquirer could pass on to its shareholders in the form of a dividend would be eliminated; the target's profits would be locked within the corporate group. Merger relief allows non-application of the rules on share premiums,[62] and thus permits the acquiring company to record its investment in the target at nominal value (i.e. the nominal value of the acquirer shares issued in exchange for the target shares). Consequently, it would not be necessary to write down the target shares if the target pays a dividend to the acquiring company, and the acquiring company could treat these dividend payments as realized profits, which it could pass on to its own shareholders.

2. In-kind payments   The relatively expansive definition of "cash" reduces the set of assets to which the UK rules on in-kind consideration apply. Further exclusions of the rules on in-kind consideration for transfers of shares in connection with reorganizations (where the shareholders of the disappearing company yield up their shares in exchange for shares of the new company) and mergers[63] substantially reduce the inconvenience of the in-kind consideration rules, and facilitate the transition from a private to a public company without engaging an auditor for an appraisal. This could also have contributed to the UK Parliament's decision not to revisit its rules on in-kind contributions following the 2006 amendments to the Second Directive.

Other in-kind payments for the shares of a public company must be officially appraised, reported and filed with the registrar.[64] The filing with the registrar must also specify at least an estimated amount of the company's preliminary expenses, any benefit paid or intended to be paid to any promoter of the company, and the consideration for the payment or benefit.[65] If the registry is satisfied, it will issue a "trading certificate," which is "conclusive evidence" that the company is entitled to do business and exercise any borrowing powers.[66]

C.   The US rules

1. Cash payments   Neither the DGCL nor the Model Act requires a minimum capital, and only very lightly regulates contributions to capital. The laws allow corporations to issue partly paid shares and place no numerical restriction – such as one-half or one-quarter – on the amount

---

[62] § 612(2) CA 2006.   [63] Secs. 594, 595 CA 2006.
[64] Sec. 593 CA 2006.   [65] Sec. 762(1) CA 2006.   [66] Sec. 761(4) CA 2006.

that must be paid in at issue.[67] Par value shares may not be sold for less than par, but this has little effect, as a Delaware corporation may issue no-par shares,[68] and the Model Act no longer contains the concept of par value.

2. In-kind payments Neither the DGCL nor the Model Act places restrictions on the form of consideration that may be used to pay for a company's shares;[69] they also provide no formal procedure through which in-kind contributions are to be appraised. In Delaware, the law simply declares that the board's judgment "as to the value of such consideration shall be conclusive" "in the absence of actual fraud in the transaction,"[70] and the Model Act provides that the "determination by the board of directors is conclusive."[71]

As this text will extensively evidence, the regulatory tool of choice in the US is the board of directors and the fiduciary duties to which they are subject. Directors control not only the valuation of asset contributions, but also whether a derivative action will go to court, the decision to distribute dividends, and defenses against oppressive takeovers – matters that Germany and the UK regulate with rules that either give power to shareholders or judges, or *ex ante* protections (such as a mandatory bid rule). Thus, under Delaware law, the overvaluation of an asset used to pay for shares to the detriment of the other shareholders would not be caught by an *ex ante* audit, but rather by an *ex post* court review of the type seen in the *Lewis* v. *Scotten Dillon* case in this chapter. Do you think that questions of assessing capital contributions can be left to the board and policed by this type of shareholder action?

Questions for discussion

1. What is the purpose of requiring a stated share capital?
2. Does the required minimum capital successfully achieve this purpose?
3. Consider the statutory requirements for the amount of share capital and the amount attributable to each share: What does "fixed nominal value" (section 542 of the Companies Act 2006) mean? Must the stated capital and the

---

[67] § 156 DGCL.   [68] § 153 DGCL.

[69] A restriction in art. IX, § 3, of the Constitution of the State of Delaware of 1897 which placed certain restrictions on the forms of acceptable consideration for shares was repealed in 2004. See House Bill 399 of the 142nd General Assembly of Delaware. As to the Model Act, see § 6.21(b).

[70] § 152 DGCL.   [71] § 6.21(c) Model Act.

value of shares be expressed in national currency? In what currency must contributions to capital be paid?

4. What are the minimum par values of shares of a UK company and of a German corporation?

5. While section 542(1) of the Companies Act 2006 mandates that the share capital must be divided into shares of a fixed nominal value, § 8 I AktG allows for the creation of no par shares. Is § 8 I AktG compatible with articles 1 and 6(1) of the Second Company Law Directive, pursuant to which a stock corporation must have a stated minimum capital? Is there a difference between the no par shares issued by a German stock corporation and those issued by a Delaware corporation pursuant to §§ 102(4), 152, 153 DGCL?

6. Pursuant to the Second Company Law Directive and UK and German company law, shares of a corporation can be paid up in cash or in kind. How are contributions in cash and in kind distinguished? What assets other than cash may be contributed as consideration, and what assets may not? Why is the distinction between cash and in-kind consideration important in terms of policy and in terms of the law applicable to shareholder contributions?

7. Pursuant to the Second Company Law Directive and UK and German company law, services cannot be contributed toward a corporation's capital. What is the reason for this rule? Difficulties in enforcing the claim? Difficulties in assessing the value of services? Does the rule prohibit the contribution of a claim for compensation for services that have already been rendered?

8. What does the "no-discount rule" mean? What is the statutory basis of that rule in EC, UK and German law? Does such a rule exist under the DGCL? What are the consequences of the no-discount rule for the holders of convertible securities (i.e. securities that can be exchanged for shares at the option of the holder)? Does § 194 I no. 2 AktG provide an answer?

9. Work out the following hypothetical. In March 2007 A, B, C and D established X-Co, a German AG, the object of which is to sell kitchen appliances. Each one of the incorporators subscribed to 100,000 common shares with a par value of €1 per share. The issue price for each share was set at €2. In July 2007, X-Co wants to purchase two delivery trucks from C for a total of €60,000. Advise X-Co and C on how they should structure the purchase.

10(a). In the above hypothetical, how must X-Co account for the €1 per share that has been paid in excess of the par value if X-Co were:
   (i) a German AG?
   (ii) an English public company? For what purposes could X-Co use the funds in the account to which the €1 per share surplus of the consideration has been credited?

10(b). Can you explain the purpose of the merger relief provisions of the UK Companies Act 2006?

11. Compare sections 582, 583 and 585 of the Companies Act 2006 with §§ 27(2), (3), 54(1) and 66(1) AktG.

Cases

IBH/Lemmerz
High Federal Court, Second Civil Division
November 25, 2002 / BGHZ 110, 47
[Partial, unofficial translation of official opinion text]

Official head note

a) Pursuant to the corporate law principles on "disguised in-kind contributions," the rules on preventative maintenance of contributions to capital may not be evaded, including in the context of a capital increase. The provisions on post-formation acquisitions (§§ 52 *et seq.* AktG) and the rules of § 27(1), sentence 2 AktG, do not exclude application of these principles. A finding of evasion does not require an intention to evade. No decision is reached on whether the existence of proximity in time and subject matter with a payment into company capital is sufficient or if, in spite of the general rule that evasion is determined by objective circumstances, there must be an agreement between the contributor of cash and the board having the economic result of evading the norm in question.

b) The protection of current and future shareholders, as well as potential creditors, advises that these provisions generally be applied also to the contribution of a claim against the company for repayment of a loan.

c) The maturity of the duty to make a cash contribution presupposes a demand for payment within the meaning of § 63(1) AktG. Arrears measures are triggered for a contribution not made in accordance with the timing of the demand for payment only if such demand specifies a payment date, notice is provided to the shareholders pursuant to a provision of the Satzung, and it is actually delivered.

d) The Second Directive of the Council of the European Communities of 13 December 1976 (OJ 1977, L26/1) does not exclude the continued existence of national law containing stricter requirements as long as the provisions of the Directive do not set a ceiling. The doctrine of "disguised in-kind contributions" is from this perspective compatible with the relevant provisions of the Directive. The High Federal Court need not submit this legal question to the European Court of Justice for an advance ruling pursuant to art. 177(3) of the EC Treaty.

e) Pursuant to § 55(1) no. 1 of the Bankruptcy Code, bankruptcy creditors may not set off against a claim for interest a claim for cash contribution to the extent that the claim for interest arose after the commencement of the bankruptcy proceedings.

Facts

Since the opening of insolvency proceedings on December 13, 1983, the Plaintiff is the bankruptcy administrator of the assets of I-Holding AG (hereinafter the "Joint

Debtor" [or IBH]) ... To the extent still relevant, Plaintiff claims from Defendant a contribution for a capital increase (of DM 5 million) and damages for untimely payment of the contribution (inter alia capitalized compounded interest of DM 761,622.47 DM). The complaint is based on the following facts: Pursuant to a December 16/21 1979 contract, L-Werke KGaA (hereinafter [Lemmerz]) provided the Joint Debtor with DM 5 million sales financing to be repaid in nine equal installments. When the Joint Debtor did not pay the installment due on January 20, 1982, [Lemmerz] negotiated with the Joint Debtor about terminating the credit agreement, including the connected supply agreement of December 16/21 1979. During negotiations, the Joint Debtor proposed that [Lemmerz] take a holding in its capital, and explained that if [Lemmerz] took a DM 5 million shareholding, [IBH] would tie it to the loan. [Lemmerz] agreed under these conditions to take the proposed shareholding. It incorporated the Defendant and entered into a domination and transfer of profit agreement (*Beherrschungs- und Gewinnabführungsvertrag*), as well as a trust agreement. Essentially, this obliged the Defendant to subscribe to shares of the Joint Debtor with a nominal value of DM 1,562,500 in exchange for paying DM 5 million in cash, as well as to hold them in trust for [Lemmerz] as the trust settlor, whilst [Lemmerz] agreed to indemnify the Defendant as trustee from all liability and reimburse it for all costs incurred in performing the contract.

On July 27, 1982 the Defendant subscribed to the shares of the Joint Debtor for the amount referred to above in connection with a capital increase out of authorized capital, which was entered in the commercial register on August 6, 1982. On August 2, 1982 the Defendant paid ... DM 5 million by crediting the Joint Debtor's capital increase account kept at SMH-Bank. On August 9, 1982, the Joint Debtor transferred [Lemmerz] a check for DM 5 million to settle the sales financing, and this check was paid out of the business account of the Joint Debtor on August 13, 1982. The amount was paid out of the account by a transfer from the capital increase account on August 16, 1982. The Defendant's credit at the SMH-Bank was reduced to zero between 11 and 13 August 1982 by the transfer to [Lemmerz].

The parties ... disagree on whether the Defendant fulfilled its obligation to pay a cash contribution and on whether the Joint Debtor effectively paid off the financing from [Lemmerz] or in the alternative the rules on disguised in-kind contributions apply to the payment transactions and underlying agreements, with the result that such transactions and agreements are without effect against the Joint Debtor.

[*Text omitted*]

Discussion

A.

The Defendant's appeal is without merit. The appellate court found correctly that the Defendant did not pay its contribution obligation of DM 5 million for the subscription of the Joint Debtor's shares. The court thus correctly awarded the Plaintiff

... DM 4,909,209.74 and declared the main issue of the case settled to the extent that the Plaintiff ... set off the claim for contribution against the Defendant's claim for reimbursement of DM 90,790.26.

I.

According to the appellate court's findings, the Defendant as trustee for [Lemmerz] ... subscribed to 31,250 shares of the Joint Debtor with a par value of DM 1,562,500 for a cash price of DM 5 million ... According to the pleadings of the Defendant and the findings of the trial court ... the Defendant was willing to subscribe to the capital of the Joint Debtor because [it] ... offered [Lemmerz] repayment of a loan in connection with the assumption of the shareholding. The understandings of the parties regarding the Defendant's holding and the Joint Debtor's repayment of [Lemmerz's] loan ... were seen as being a single economic unity. They were divided into two transactions and payment processes only in appearance. That allows these transactions to be seen as the Defendant's agreement to and actual surrender of [Lemmerz's] loan claim as payment for the shares. As the contribution of a claim against the issuer is a type of contribution in kind, the Defendant and the Joint Debtor agreed to and carried out an in-kind contribution as understood pursuant to the rules on "disguised in-kind contributions." However, the *Vorstand*'s resolution makes no reference to an in-kind contribution ... even though the shareholder resolution on the capital increase delegated power for both a cash and an in-kind contribution. The applications to and entries in the commercial register also referred to a cash rather than an in-kind contribution. Under these circumstances, the subscription agreement concluded in connection with the obligation to make an in-kind contribution is without effect, and following the entry of the capital increase in the commercial register, the Defendant must pay the contribution amount in cash, uncoupled from the Joint Debtor settling the loan obligation.

II.

[Text omitted]

1. The Appellant argues that the provisions on post-formation acquisitions (§§ 52 *et seq.* AktG) are the exclusive rules for evasions of the provisions on capital contributions in connection with the incorporation of a stock corporation and increases of capital, so that the [judicially crafted – editors' note] doctrine of "disguised in-kind contributions" has no place in corporate law. This Division does not accept that argument.

a) The legislative history of the law does not demand the conclusion that the provisions on post-formation present exclusive rules against evasions of the provisions on protecting capital contributions in the context of a capital increase ... The above mentioned argument only proves that the legislator in 1897 did not think itself able to shape specific rules for capital increases in the interest of the stock corporation like those rules for post-formation. This does not mean, however, that an individual case of evading the protective provisions must also go unsanctioned. That conclusion cannot be deduced from the legislative history of the law. The law's development alone allows us to assume there is a legislative gap, which can be filled with the doctrine of disguised in-kind contributions.

b) Today, protection against evasion is even more important, given that capital increases through in-kind contributions have become an even more meaningful and indispensible manner of financing the stock corporation in a modern economy, following the general economic and business strategy trends seen in conditional capital (§§ 192 *et seq.* AktG), authorized capital (§§ 202 *et seq.* AktG) and capital increases from surplus (§§ 207 *et seq.* AktG). These developments have been reflected in the adoption of a series of supplements to protective measures, in particular the increase in disclosure obligations and the introduction of a capital increases audit (see §§ 183–185,188 AktG), which have led to similarity to the rules for incorporation using in-kind contributions (see e.g. §§ 27, 32–38 AktG), particularly after the implementation of the [Second Company Law Amendment]. The precautionary regulation of the constitution of capital resulting from this under current economic conditions protects not only shareholders, particularly minority shareholders, but also protects current and future creditors and other vulnerable stakeholders in the economy, as well as workers (see Wiedemann, *Gesellschaftsrecht* I, 1980, § 1.V.2 (p. 86 *et seq.*); Lutter/Hommelhoff/Timm BB 1980, p. 737) …

c) The Appellant argues that the scope of this protective doctrine must be restricted to the letter of the statutory rules. Such wording covers only in-kind contributions and the exceptional cases that are treated as such, like when a claim for payment from an allotment is credited to the contribution (§ 183(1), sentence 1, § 205(1), § 27(1) AktG). In view of the above arguments this contention is not convincing. The Appellant's position also contradicts the real capital contribution requirement, which is served by the provisions discussed above. If persons in a position to make a contribution in kind, after reaching an agreement with the *Vorstand* of the company, instead of following the prescribed procedure, were free to sell the company the object that should have been contributed as an in-kind contribution and take the holding in exchange for cash payment, it would have the same effect as taking the holding in exchange for an in-kind contribution, but it would be necessary neither for the shareholder nor the company to comply with the protective disclosure and audit requirements. If such a procedure were permitted, it would be reasonable to assume that the procedure for in-kind contributions would fall into disuse, the protective rules would be avoided, and it would be progressively harder to achieve an effective protection of minority shareholders and creditors because of the disregard for the rules …

The Appellant does correctly observe that the language of § 27(1), sentence 1 AktG does not include the making and settlement of a loan agreement, as the company does not "receive an asset." However, we may not hinge our decision solely on the wording of this provision. Rather it is decisive that this provision flows from the principle that real value must be given for a capital increase, which it serves to secure ...

d) Contrary to the position of the Appellant, the rule in § 27(1), sentence 2 AktG never presented an exceptional case applied to this factual setting. It corresponds to the partial regulation of receipt of a holding through set off ... in § 279(1) HGB in the version of May 10, 1897 ... This rule was introduced into current law by the Law of December 13, 1978 (BGBl I, 1959) for the purpose of extending the provision on notification of in-kind contributions to the commercial register ... to the case where an asset is assumed ...

2. The Appellant is of the opinion that the law does not prohibit the repayment of the company's obligation from a loan incurred before the capital increase with cash received from the lender. The regulatory purpose of the protective provisions on in-kind contribution transactions does not foresee treating loan claims as in-kind contributions ... Also on this point must we disagree with the Appellant.

It is generally understood that a loan claim held by a shareholder against the company may be transferred as an in-kind contribution to the company. The object contributed is the claim. The obligation to make the in-kind contribution is satisfied either by transferring the claim to the company, so that it is extinguished by unity of obligor and obligee, or by release (see e.g. Eckardt in Geßler/Hefermehl/Eckhardt/ Kropff, AktG, 1984 § 27 mn. 10; Lutter, *Kapital, Sicherung der Kapitalaufbringung und Kapitalerhaltung in den Aktien- und GmbH-Rechten der EWG*, 1964, p. 239 *et seq.*, Fn. 90; Priester DB 1976,1801 with further references; Flume DB 1964,21) ...

[*Text omitted*]

III.

The appellant accepts the arguments in this Division's judgment of April 19, 1982 (II ZR 55/81, WM 1982, 660, 662 = ZIP 1982, 689, 692, Holzmann ...), according to which it is a violation of the rules on in-kind contributions in §§ 183,184 AktG if the resolution amending the Satzung provides for a cash increase in capital, but the company intends to receive assets other than cash in exchange for an allotment of new shares, and this economically unified transaction is split into a purchase transaction and an allotment for cash. This further entails that the principle would apply if the bifurcated transaction hid the contribution of a loan claim against the company. The appellant errs, however, in assuming that this principle formulated in the Holzmann judgment does not apply to the case at hand ...

[*Text omitted*]

IV.

The Appellant further errs in arguing that the appellate court did not sufficiently consider that the loan creditor and the Defendant as shareholder were separate payment of [Lemmerz's] loan claim – which was equal to the claim for capital contribution and had a term of performance temporally proximate to it – as a disguised in-kind contribution. It is recognized that disguised in-kind contributions are present not only when the funds paid are by agreement used to pay the shareholder's claim, but also when a person related to the entering shareholder is involved in such a transaction (BGHZ 96, 231, 240) …

V.

[Text omitted]

Contrary to the position of the Appellant, this Division has no obligation in the present case to seek a preliminary ruling from the European Court of Justice …

The doctrine of disguised in-kind contributions, which was already recognized in the decisions of the Reichsgericht and in the literature published regarding the *Aktiengesetz* of January 30, 1937 (RGBl I, 107), and which the High Federal Court and the literature published regarding the *Aktiengesetz* of September 6, 1965 followed (see the references in Lutter/Gehling, supra, p. 1446 Fn. 10–14), was not affected by the provisions of the Second Directive …

[Text omitted]

The court of appeals thus correctly ordered the Defendant to pay the contribution, to the extent that the Plaintiff's set off is not found binding by the main issue decided in this litigation.

[Text omitted]

Lewis v. Scotten Dillon Co.
Court of Chancery of Delaware
306 A 2d 755 (1973)
[Text edited; footnotes omitted]

OPINION BY: DUFFY

[Text omitted]

A.

Under date of May 15, 1970 the respective boards of Iroquois Industries, Inc. and Scotten Dillon Company, both Delaware corporations, approved an agreement providing for the acquisition by Iroquois of all assets of Scotten Dillon in exchange for 450,000 shares of Iroquois common stock. The exchange was related to all outstanding stock of Scotten Dillon and, in effect, involved a 1.5 ratio of Iroquois shares to Scotten Dillon (that is, 450,000 to 300,000). On July 6, 1970 plaintiff, an Iroquois stockholder, filed this action to enjoin the proposed transaction on the ground that it would be a waste of Iroquois assets. Seventeen days after the complaint was filed and before action by the stockholders, the plan was abandoned. [The plaintiff asked for attorney's fees, and the Court found that in order to receive such fees, his claim must be "meritorious." The following discussion goes to the merit of his challenge to the board's valuation of consideration for shares.]

[*Text omitted*]

C.

Iroquois argues that the complaint is not and cannot be regarded as meritorious because at bottom it is based on a disagreement about the value of the Scotten Dillon assets to be acquired. Relying on 8 Del. C. § 152, defendant says that actual fraud has not been shown and hence the statute makes the judgment of the directors conclusive on the valuation issue.

Actual fraud may, of course, be shown directly but it may also be inferred from the attendant circumstances, *West* v. *Sirian Lamp Co.*, 28 Del. Ch. 398, 44 A 2d 658 (1945); and inadequacy of consideration is a part of such circumstances, *Diamond State Brewery* v. *De La Rigaudiere*, 25 Del. Ch. 257, 17 A 2d 313 (1941). However, excessive valuation, standing alone, is not enough unless it is so gross as to lead the Court to conclude that it was due, not to an honest error of judgment but to bad faith or a reckless indifference to the rights of others. *Fidanque* v. *American Maracaibo Co.*, 33 Del. Ch. 262, 92 A 2d 311 (1952).

In applying these rules to this case, I assume that all Iroquois directors, other than Fox, were independent in all necessary aspects. Indeed that is more than an assumption because there is nothing in the record to show that they are not. But the position of Fox is quite different.

Certainly Fox was the central figure in the transaction. He was president and board chairman of Iroquois. He negotiated the terms of the acquisition with Scotten Dillon. He presented the proposal to the Iroquois Board. Compare *Fidanque* v. *American Maracaibo Co.*, *supra*. At the time of negotiation and at the time of presentation Fox owned (or at least had a substantial claim to ownership of) $1,500,000 in value of convertible debentures of Scotten Dillon. How much of this he revealed to the Iroquois Board is not clear from the record. But it is clear that he did not disclose to the Board that he had pledged the debentures to secure three bank loans totaling $475,000. I need not determine what inference should be drawn from these facts. I need note only that one inference which may be drawn is that Fox had a significant personal interest in consummation of the transaction which required the fullest disclosure on his part; and it was not made. By the terms of the contract which he negotiated and recommended Iroquois would have assumed, apparently, the obligation to convert his debentures into its stock at the 1.5 to 1 ratio. I need not decide that Fox would have had an enforceable legal right to conversion at that ratio but certainly he would have been in position to strongly argue a right to do so and that is enough for present purposes.

| | Market Price/Share | | Total Market Value | | |
Date	Iroquois	Scotten Dillon	Iroquois	Scotten Dillon	Excess
5/1/70	9 5/8	8 1/4	$4,331,250	$2,475,000	$1,856,250
5/6/70	Purchase approved by the Iroquois Board of Directors				
5/14/70	8 1/4	9 1/8	3,712,500	2,737,500	975,000
7/6/70	6 3/4	6 1/8	3,037,500	1,837,500	1,200,000
7/23/70	7 3/4	6 1/2	3,487,500	1,950,000	1,537,500
10/29/71	22 1/2	9	10,125,000	2,700,000	7,425,000
10/11/72	14 1/8	8 7/8	6,356,250	2,662,500	3,693,750

In terms of market price Iroquois would have been required to pay a substantial premium for Scotten Dillon, as shown by the following comparison between market value of 450,000 Iroquois shares and 300,000 Scotten Dillon shares:

Iroquois argues that the "control" which would accompany its acquisition of all Scotten Dillon assets is a value factor to be weighed. And so it is. And I agree that market price is not necessarily conclusive in these matters, particularly under the statute and because assets, not shares, were to be acquired. But I am unable to find from the record facts which eliminate all reasonable hope of success for plaintiff. *Chrysler Corporation* v. *Dann, supra.*

Iroquois argues that in *Puma* v. *Marriott*, Del. Ch., 283 A 2d 693 (1971) this Court applied the business judgment test to the decision of independent directors who approved a stock-for-stock transaction. There the case went to final hearing and the Court found that the plaintiff had not shown fraud. And that points up the critical difference between *Puma* and this case: plaintiff is not obliged to prove fraud at this time in this case. Under *Chrysler* his burden is not "absolute assurance" but only "reasonable hope" of ultimate success. *Puma* is not controlling.

We have, then, a situation in which the chief executive of and negotiator for Iroquois (Fox) apparently stood to gain significantly through his investments in the *other* company, if the deal were consummated. And on the face of things, the difference in market value of the respective shares is significant. Under these circumstances I conclude that § 152 does not cut off inquiry as a matter of law. In short, plaintiff has demonstrated a triable issue on fraud under § 152. Given the significant difference in "value" on the respective sides (as shown by the market prices for shares), the key position of Fox in the negotiation and his failure to disclose his special interest, I conclude that plaintiff has shown such reasonable hope of ultimate success ...

[*Text omitted*]

6

Increasing the company's capital

Required reading

EU: Second Company Law Directive, arts. 25–29
D: AktG, §§ 182–220
UK: CA 2006, secs. 549–554, 560–573
US: DGCL, §§ 102(a)(4), 152–154, 156, 162–166

Choosing a capital structure and increasing the share capital

I.   Introduction

We have seen that all of our jurisdictions require the creation of a share capital as a prerequisite to establishing a stock corporation. In Chapter 4, we briefly examined the constitution of such initial share capital in the context of the incorporation process, and, in Chapter 5, we discussed how members contribute assets to the company in exchange for their shares. Here we will examine a company's options when approaching an increase of the capital assets it uses to fund its activities, the factors it would consider when making a decision about the composition of its capital structure,[1] and the rules governing capital increases in our three jurisdictions.

II.   The determinants of capital structure

A.   Sources of financing

Two basic sources of corporate finance present themselves to a company. First, it can retain earnings to increase capital surplus (internal financing)

---

[1] "Capital structure" in the sense we use it here should be thought of as the sum of "financial capital" (reflected as claims of creditors against the company) and "share capital" (reflected as the equity investments of the members in the company).

that can be used to fund operations. The decision to use internal financing is made in connection with a company's payout policy,[2] as the distributable profits that the company does not pay out to shareholders as dividends or use to repurchase shares can be applied to the finance of ongoing operations. Absent sufficient expansion of profits, an increase in internal financing means a decrease in the amount of dividends distributed. A second financing option is for the company to obtain new funds from persons outside it (external financing). External financing can be obtained by incurring debt or selling equity stakes. "Equity" financing basically means selling ownership shares – for a stock corporation these are certificated in shares of stock – in the company to either existing or prospective shareholders.[3] Stock can be divided into various classes with differing rights, a topic that will be discussed in detail in Chapter 9. Debt financing can take two, basic forms: any person (including a shareholder, but more usually a bank or banking syndicate) can be asked to lend the company money pursuant to an agreement to pay interest on the principal amount under a negotiated loan contract, or the company can sell negotiable instruments (debentures or bonds – in German, literally "a writing evidencing part of a debt," or *Teilschuldverschreibung* – and short-term notes) on the capital markets.[4] The legal and financial characteristics of such bonds, debentures and notes are largely contractual, and

[2] See the discussion in Myers (1984: 581 *et seq.*).
[3] The word "equity" is used in two ways in the company law context. On the one hand, it refers (as it does here) to an ownership interest, and, on the other (with regard to the duties of directors and controlling shareholders not to abuse their power), it refers to fairness and evenhanded dealing. The term "equity" derives from an informal system of justice administered in the Middle Ages in England by the King's Chancellor as a flexible alternative to the complex, formalistic and often unfair system of "writ" pleadings characteristic of English Common Law. Equity's focus on fair determinations through informal procedures, which was likely influenced by Canon Law (see Glenn (2005: 113)), eventually developed into the UK High Court of Chancery. The Court of Chancery of the US State of Delaware, many of whose decisions are reprinted in this text, is a "court of equity" in this tradition. English courts of equity developed the property arrangement of a "trust," in which ownership of property is divided for various reasons between an "equitable" owner who has ultimate control and a "legal" owner who has actual managerial control. This type of property interest is what we are referring to here with the word "equity" share. On the development of trusts through equity, see e.g. Martin (2008: 8–14). For a succinct and authoritative definition of equity share, see sec. 548 CA 2006.
[4] The terminology used for such debt instruments can be a little confusing. For example, in the US, the word "bond" is more likely to be used to refer to a secured instrument than the word "debenture." Klein and Coffee (2007: 251). In the UK, "bond" is a generic term, and types of bonds might be referred to as "debentures" if secured or as "loan stock" if not secured. Ferran (1999: 50).

such provisions are limited only by the boundaries of law and the imagination of the company, its bankers and its lawyers. Thus, interest payable on the instruments can be fixed, floating, or replaced by a discounted purchase price, the term, allocation and frequency of payments can be creatively structured, and other options – such as a right to vote on certain decisions – can also be incorporated into the instrument where law permits.[5] The ranking of and any collateral securing payment on a debt instrument can also be structured in many different ways. Moreover, the external financing methods listed above can be combined and connected in a number of ways, such as by selling bonds that can be converted into shares (convertible bonds) or packaging bank loans into a pool to fund payments on bonds (securitization).

B.   Does capital structure affect a firm's value?

If a company can obtain an important input into its production process such as "energy" from various sources (e.g. oil, coal or wind) for different prices, the cost of energy resulting from the source the company chooses as its main supplier will have an impact on the company's net profits and ultimately on its value. The same is true for its cost of capital. A company's choice of the best source for raising capital should hypothetically be able to increase its value. What determines this choice? Is there a capital structure that is consistently better than others?

These very important, basic questions have been the subject of extensive investigation by scholars, particularly financial economists, for more than half a century. Although the findings are by no means in perfect agreement, they do present certain basic principles and causal determinants regarding capital structure. Causal determinants arise both from straight legal rules and from the relationship between the nature of a specific kind of firm and specific types of investors. The effect of law on capital structure has become a central topic of study in comparative company law, for legislatures seek to create a legal environment that is most conducive to economic prosperity, and look to foster the use of capital structures that are considered most financially beneficial for businesses to thrive.

One of the most observed phenomena of capital structure is the effect of altering the ratio between debt and equity. The fact that shares of stock give the holder an ownership claim in the company that includes

---

[5] For general discussions of debt instruments in Germany, the UK and the US, see Habersack, Mülbert, and Schlitt (2008: §§ 10 et seq.); Ferran (2008: 319–341, 511–524); and Klein and Coffee (2007: 251–286), respectively.

no economic guarantee other than that the holder will share in the company's profits and losses (with the downside being limited to the investment), whilst a loan or bond gives the holder a contractual right to receive repayment and a specific amount of interest on the principal, creates the possibility of "leverage" or "gearing" a capital structure by increasing the debt/equity ratio. Take a look at the simplified financial statements of two companies presented in the following table. Company E (for equity) has been financed solely by issuing 100 shares with a par value of 1 each, while Company L (for leverage) has been financed by issuing 50 shares with a par value of 1 each and 50 bonds with a principal amount of 1 each.[6]

	Company E		Company L	
	Assets = 100	Equity = 100	Assets = 100	Equity = 50 Debt = 50 at 8 percent
	bad year	*good year*	*bad year*	*good year*
Profit	2	20	2	20
Interest	0	0	4	4
Net return on equity	2 percent	20 percent	−2 percent	32 percent

In this simplified example, all of Company E's capital comes from its shareholders and all of its profits go to those shareholders. Thus, the shareholders' net return on equity (net profit divided by equity) rises and falls in a 1:1 ratio to the firm's profits. Company L's capital, on the other hand, comes 50 percent from its shareholders and 50 percent from its bondholders, and, because the bondholders have a contractual right to receive an 8 percent per annum return on their investment, only the residual amount of net profit beyond this interest payment will constitute a net return on equity. The negative aspect of this arrangement is that there will always be an obligation to pay interest regardless of the company's performance; the positive aspect is that this obligation does not increase in good years, and for any profit exceeding interest obligations, the return on equity rises in

---

[6] See the discussions of leverage in Klein and Coffee (2007: 8–11); Ferran (2008: 62–65); and the somewhat more detailed treatment in Brealey, Myers and Allen (2006: 445–461).

a 2:1 ratio to net profits. Put differently, debt increases the assets available to generate profit, but has only a limited claim to share in such profit; anything beyond that limit goes to the claim of the equity owners, which is open-ended. In good years, leverage improves the owner's return on investment in the company and in bad years it reduces it. Moreover, if in a bad year the company were unable to pay interest when due, it could be driven into insolvency, and thus a higher debt/equity ratio will increase the risk of insolvency. A target ratio might be found at the point where the benefits of leverage still outweigh rising insolvency risk.[7]

This significant effect of capital structure on the risk and profit profiles for investing in a given firm would seem to affect the firm's value. However, in 1958, Professors Franco Modigliani and Merton H. Miller put forward the extremely influential proposition that a firm's total value is independent of the nature (i.e. debt or equity) of the claims against it.[8] As an example of how Modigliani and Miller's proposition works, take our discussion of Company E and Company L, and the latter's use of "leveraging" or "gearing." If Company L can reasonably expect good profits in coming years, its leveraged structure clearly offers shareholders the better investment. However, rather than purchasing shares in Company L, an investor could simply leverage the investment herself by borrowing half of the money needed to purchase shares in Company E. The leveraged result would be the same as investing in Company L: total assets invested would be 50 percent debt, and, after the interest on the debt was paid, all profits generated by the invested loan proceeds would go to the investor.[9] Given the possibility of a leveraged investment, the value of leverage at the firm level is reduced.

This argument of course assumes a world in which there are no market distortions, such as taxes, and no risk of bankruptcy. Under the laws of many countries, interest paid on debt may be deducted from taxable income. Debt increases insolvency risk because, as mentioned above, interest payments – unlike dividends – must be made even when the firm is not generating profits, and a failure to do so can trigger involuntary insolvency proceedings. The Modigliani and Miller proposition has therefore been supplemented by a number of theories that take market distortions caused by law and other factors into account. The two leading hypotheses in this regard for over twenty years have been the "pecking

---

[7] Finding this point is the goal of management according to the tradeoff model, discussed below. Also see Ferran (2008: 63).

[8] Modigliani and Miller (1958: 295–296); Brealey, Myers and Allen (2006: 448).

[9] Brealey, Myers and Allen (2006: 447–448).

order hypothesis" and the "tradeoff model."[10] The tradeoff model sees companies working to set an optimal target ratio of debt and equity, and the pecking order framework assumes an order of preferences among sources of financing.

C.   Legal and economic determinants of capital structure

In an early paper on capital structure determinants, Professor Stewart Myers explained that the tradeoff model seeks "a tradeoff of the costs and benefits of borrowing," which "is portrayed as balancing the value of interest tax shields against various costs of bankruptcy or financial embarrassment."[11] Any use of debt will mean an immediate tax savings (for a profitable company) from the deduction of interest payments, but as the amount of debt and interest obligations increases, the chance of missing interest payments in an unprofitable year grows, and a point is reached where the costs and benefits of using debt financing trade off.[12] According to the pecking order hypothesis, "internally generated financing is preferred first, followed by debt (safe and then risky), and lastly outside equity."[13] Myers, in his 1984 paper, argued that the main reason why firms would follow the pecking order framework with a preference for internal financing is "asymmetric" information, because management knows what projects it intends to undertake with the funds, and can better assess the expected rate of return on the investment used to fund this project than can outside investors who have no information regarding the internal plans to undertake the project.[14] In a 2008 article, Professor Veikko Vahtera has added to this, that, in Europe, where controlling shareholders are common, internal or debt financing would also be preferred, for the different reason that a majority shareholder would not want to dilute his controlling share.[15] If the law of a given country protected the rights of bondholders more fully than those of shareholders, one would also expect to see capital structures with significant leverage. Thus company law rules such as provisions on mandatory disclosure and corporate governance will have an impact on the capital structure of a company.

Company law can affect capital structure at a number of levels. At the most basic level, law may require a company to issue a certain kind of security, such as the requirement in US and German law that at least one

---

[10] See e.g. Myers (1984); Vahtera (2008); Seifert and Gonenc (2008).
[11] Myers (1984: 577).   [12] Myers (1984: 577–581).
[13] Seifert and Gonenc (2008: 245).   [14] Myers (1984: 582–585).
[15] Vahtera (2008: 73).

class of voting shares be issued and remain outstanding.[16] At another
level, as we have seen, the financing decisions a company makes will be
influenced by the legal characteristics of a given security. For example,
while debt creates specific, contractual rights in favor of creditors (such
as to be paid in the event of liquidation before the shareholders), equity
lends shareholders specially tailored property interests in the corporation
that grants not only a participation in profits but also a number of control
rights. As will be discussed in detail in Chapter 16, shareholders have a
right directly or indirectly to appoint the company's management and to
approve or veto major structural changes, such as mergers. The characteristics of the different instruments will line up with investors' different
appetites for risk and control. Normal investment practices can mean that
a younger company with high growth potential will offer equity, while
older companies with significant fixed assets can profitably offer high-
quality debt at relatively low interest rates. Yet another level can come
from the transaction costs occasioned by the legal system, which may
facilitate the management incurring debt or issuing equity, depending on
the nature of the applicable law.

One must be careful, however, in formulating conclusions on the basis
of presumed effects of company law rules in jurisdictions whose legal system one does not fully understand. A failure clearly to understand the
nature and function of sometimes quickly changing and often functionally interrelated company law rules can lead to distorted results. In this
text, you will look at much of German, UK and Delaware law from the
bottom up, and come to understand some of the fine details and functional interrelations that are often misunderstood by scholars who quickly
compare a basket of foreign countries, regarding whose law they may have
only summary information, to construct an index of governance ratings.
For an example of what we mean, take a look at the otherwise insightful
2008 paper by Professors Bruce Seifert and Halit Gonenc, which bases
itself on previously performed ratings of German corporate governance
by other financial economists.[17] Seifert and Gonenc draw conclusions on
differences between US and German capital structure relying in part on a
2006 paper rating German and US securities law, a study that apparently
failed to take EU law (which dominates the securities law area in Europe)
into account.[18] For example, with respect to the disclosure of information
in prospectuses in connection with the offering of securities – which in

[16] § 151(b) DGCL; § 12 I AktG.   [17] Seifert and Gonenc (2008).
[18] La Porta, Lopez-de-Silanes and Shleifer (2006: 6 *et seq.*).

the European Union is minutely governed by a framework directive and a very detailed regulation[19] – the authors of the study rated the UK disclosure rules at 0.83/1 and the Austrian rules at 0.25/1,[20] although the two countries apply the same EU regulation on prospectuses and have implemented the same EU directive on disclosure. Indeed, the EU Prospectus Regulation closely tracks Regulation S-K,[21] which has been issued by the US, the country used in the study as the control with a perfect "1." The present text aims to allow students to develop the tools that will enable them to find the correct law and understand its content in the US, Germany and the UK through reference to the statutes, reading of cases, and discussion of the law, so as to avoid drawing false conclusions from inaccurate facts.

As noted, Seifert and Gonenc rely only in part on this analysis of disclosure rules for securities offerings. From the broader analysis they perform, they find that, between 1980 and 2004, capital structure leverage averaged about 46.5 percent for US companies, 52 percent for UK companies, and 62.7 percent for German companies.[22] This would seem to indicate that German creditor protection is the strongest, or that German investors prefer the risk profile of debt over equity, or that German companies tend to be controlled by large shareholders who avoid diluting their controlling stakes by avoiding the issue of additional equity – all of which are substantiated by repeated study. It would also indicate that US creditor protection is relatively weaker, or US investors have a greater appetite for risk, or that the shares of US companies are dispersed between smaller shareholders who do not enjoy the benefits of control – which also are generally accepted characterizations of the US market.

III.   Increasing corporate capital

A.   Main legal issues

Once a company has decided on a source of financing, it must carry forward the transaction in compliance with the applicable company and capital markets law. In this respect, it is important to remember the distinction between the term "capital" in the legal sense, as it applies to the product of the nominal or par value of each outstanding share multiplied

---

[19] See the Prospectus Directive and the Prospectus Regulation. As discussed in Chapter 1, a regulation is *directly applicable* in every member state, and thus member state laws may not differ in areas covered by the Regulation.

[20] La Porta, Lopez-de-Silanes and Shleifer (2006: 15, Table II). Germany is rated at 0.42/1.

[21] See 17 CFR § 229.   [22] Seifert and Gonenc (2008: 253, Table 2, Panel A).

by their total number ("legal" or "share" capital) plus any premium for amounts paid over par, and "capital" in the economic sense, which includes both share capital and sums received from lenders (financial capital). The increase of share capital, in particular, triggers extensive procedural requirements.

As we saw in section II above, financing can be "internal" or "external," and the latter can be divided into borrowing, on the one hand, and selling equity stakes, on the other. The only restriction on internal financing (retaining earnings) in our three jurisdictions is the desire and legal right of shareholders to receive distributions of the company's earnings rather than allowing them to be retained as reserves. As will be discussed in more detail in later chapters, the division of power between shareholders and directors regarding the decision to declare dividends differs significantly in our three jurisdictions: it ranges from Delaware,[23] where management has sole discretion whether to declare dividends, subject only to the threat of not being re-elected, to Germany, where shareholders control the distribution of dividends by resolution,[24] subject only to the figure for distributable profits, which is usually determined by directors.[25]

It will usually be possible in each of the three jurisdictions for directors acting alone without shareholder approval to tap external financing by causing the company to borrow funds. Such borrowing will, however, trigger different requirements depending on whether a loan is contracted or represented by debt securities. In both cases, any covenants in the debt instrument(s) limiting the actions of the company – such as promises not to incur further indebtedness or to limit payouts to shareholders – will again be limited by the scope of the powers granted to management by company law. Thus, as mentioned above, because German shareholders control the payout of dividends, a condition in a loan contract or bond under which the board commits the company not to pay out dividends cannot bind the shareholders and would be without effect. An issue of bonds, debentures or notes on the open market will in many cases be a "public offering of securities" on the primary market, and will subject the issuer to various requirements under capital markets law, such as the preparation and distribution of a prospectus. Regardless of whether bonds are sold on the open market, however, the laws of our European jurisdictions require shareholder approval of bond issues when the instruments resemble, or can be converted into, shares.[26]

---

[23] § 170(a) DGCL.   [24] § 174(1) AktG.   [25] § 172 AktG.

[26] Art. 25(4) Second Company Law Directive; sec. 990 CA 2006 applies all rules on share allotment to debentures carrying voting rights. § 221 AktG requires that the same

Here we will focus on the third type of financing: an increase of corporate capital through the issue and sale of common stock. Such capital increases raise three main questions. How must the issue of new shares be approved? How may the shares be paid for? Do existing shareholders have a right to purchase the new shares in an amount necessary to protect their current economic stake and influence in the company ("preemption rights")? These questions will be answered below for each of the three jurisdictions we examine.

B.   German rules on increasing share capital

1. **Approving the capital increase**   From a financial point of view, capital increases can be either "effective" or "nominal," with the former being an actual payment of funds to the company in exchange for the issue of shares, and the latter being a use of reserves to pay for stock that is issued as "bonus" shares to shareholders. A nominal capital increase is thus a form of internal financing that capitalizes reserves, and would increase the "share capital" without changing the capital assets available for funding. The *Aktiengesetz* restricts the sources available for such increases to the capital reserves and profit reserves.[27] A nominal capital increase requires shareholder approval under German law in the form of a resolution approved by at least three-quarters of the capital[28] and a simple majority of the votes[29] represented at the meeting. The increase becomes effective when the approving resolution is entered in the commercial register,[30] and the shares deriving from it must be distributed to the current members in proportion to their holdings.[31]

An "effective" capital increase brings fresh funds into the company, and thus the primary difference from a nominal increase is that the company must receive payment for the new shares. Just as for a nominal increase, an effective increase must be approved by at least three-quarters of the capital represented at the meeting,[32] as well as a simple majority of the votes.[33] In addition, because the share capital must be stated in the *Satzung*, any increase will require a charter amendment, which also requires approval by a vote of at least three-quarters of the capital

---

requirements as for the issue of shares be met for the issue of *Genussrechte* (rights to participate in the profits) and convertible bonds. See § 221 AktG.

[27] § 207(1) AktG.   [28] §§ 207(2) AktG, referring to § 182(1) AktG.

[29] § 133 AktG and Volhard, in *MünchKommAktG* (2005: § 207 mn. 14).

[30] § 211 AktG.   [31] § 216(1) AktG.

[32] § 182(1) AktG. The company's *Satzung* may provide for a higher majority.

[33] § 133 AktG and Veil, in Schmidt and Lutter (2008: § 182 mn. 27).

represented at the meeting.[34] In practice, the two points would be put to the shareholders simultaneously. As will be discussed in Chapter 9, where a company has issued more than one class of shares, any capital increase that might affect the rights of a certain class cannot be approved without a separate class vote. The resolution on an effective capital increase must state the amount of shares and their characteristics and may specify an issue price, which must in all cases at least equal the nominal value of the shares but may be higher, or empower the *Vorstand* to set the price at a later date.[35] In the latter case, at least when preemption rights have been waived as discussed below, the *Vorstand* must set a price for the shares that is "appropriate" (*angemessen*).[36] German law requires that both the resolution approving the capital increase and the declaration that the increase has been made and the shares have been purchased be registered in the commercial register,[37] and the increase becomes effective only when both registrations have been made.

Two types of advance vote on increases of capital are also available under German law. First, shareholders may authorize management in advance to increase capital and issue shares according to their own discretion excluding the shareholders' preemption right pursuant to the delegation of authority during a future period, which can have a maximum term of five years (*genehmigtes Kapital*).[38] Secondly, shareholders may create a conditional increase of capital that may be used only for specific purposes listed in the *Aktiengesetz* (*bedingte Kapitalerhöhung*),[39] such as to cover convertible bonds being exchanged for shares. Just as for a regular capital increase, both such increases would require approval by the majorities of three-quarters of the capital represented at the meeting and a simple majority of the votes cast.[40] Authorized capital has the advantages that it allows management to offer shares to the market quickly at a later date when conditions seem most favorable, and that any litigation to prevent the creation of the shares by blocking entry of

---

[34] § 179(1) AktG.   [35] Veil, in Schmidt and Lutter (2008: § 182 mn. 14 *et seq.*).

[36] Veil, in Schmidt and Lutter (2008: § 182 mn. 23). § 255 AktG provides the shareholders with a specific cause of action for challenging this price in court.

[37] §§ 184 and 188 AktG.

[38] §§ 202–206 AktG. The five-year period derives from art. 25(2) of the Second Company Law Directive, and is thus also found in UK law.

[39] §§ 192–201 AktG.

[40] §§ 193(1), 202(1) AktG. The resolution creating conditional capital would note the capital in the company's *Satzung*, thus requiring the three-quarters majority as specified for an amendment in § 179 AktG.

the approving resolution in the commercial register[41] would be fought well before the crucial date on which the company intends to sell the shares.[42] It has the disadvantages that it is both limited (to 50 percent of the existing corporate capital),[43] and can increase shareholders' monitoring costs. Conditional capital, by contrast, gives shareholders the flexibility of approving an increase in advance, while limiting it to the extent actually needed because of a future event, thus avoiding the monitoring costs that arise when management is given a blank check to issue shares at their discretion. Once the conditional increase has been registered, capital is increased without further registration as each new share is issued.[44] However, conditional capital increases may be undertaken only for three purposes, which are listed in the *Aktiengesetz*: to satisfy the conversion rights of convertible bonds, to pay for mergers, and to fund stock option plans.[45]

An authorized capital that management can issue at its discretion will be expressed in the *Satzung*, and must specify the amount of the increase, the nominal value of the shares, the term of the authorization (with a maximum of five years), whether preemption rights have been waived, and whether the *Vorstand* is authorized to accept in-kind payment for the shares.[46] The resolution creating conditional capital must specify the purpose of the capital, the persons eligible to receive the shares, the issue price or the criteria for determining it, and the terms of the relevant employee stock option plan, where applicable.[47]

---

[41] §§ 181, 184, 189 AktG.

[42] Generally, authorized capital resolutions are only challenged when the shareholders' preemption right is excluded. Since the *Siemens/Nold* decision (BGHZ 136, 133), however, the chances of contesting a resolution authorizing a capital increase and the exclusion of the shareholders' preemption rights are almost zero. Prior to that decision, the board was required to disclose its plans for the use of the additional capital to the shareholders meeting resolving on the authorization (see *Holzmann*, BGHZ 83, 319). Frequently, the board either had no concrete plans or a disclosure of plans would have been self-defeating (e.g. if the shares were to be used as consideration for an acquisition). Since management was reluctant to give away information, shareholders challenged the authorization for the capital increase on the grounds that they did not receive sufficient information to make an informed decision. Such suits were so frequently successful that the possibility of an authorization for a capital increase combined with the authorization to exclude the preemption right was very low. In the *Siemens/Nold* decision, the BGH substantially relaxed the standard for shareholder information. Now, management does not have to disclose concrete plans for the use of the shares; it is sufficient if it states in very general terms one or more purposes for which the shares might be used.

[43] § 202(3) AktG.   [44] § 200 AktG.   [45] § 192(2) AktG.   [46] §§ 202, 203, 205 AktG.

[47] § 193(2) AktG.

2. Paying for shares   Payment for shares in an effective capital increase is governed by the rules on initial contributions to capital discussed in Chapter 5. Cash payment for shares must cover at least one-quarter of the nominal value and the full premium above that figure, if any.[48] "Cash" literally means euros or a funds transfer in euros,[49] and thus the term is significantly narrower than under UK law. In-kind contributions in payment for shares must be officially appraised, and must cover the entire nominal value and premium.[50] Promises to render services cannot serve as consideration for shares.[51] As the German High Federal Court stated in its *IBH/Lemmerz* decision, reprinted in part in the preceding chapter, the rules and penalties for disguised in-kind contributions apply equally to capital increases.

If existing shareholders will subscribe to the shares, they must tender the necessary capital contributions to the company, but it is common for underwriting banks to subscribe to the shares for further distribution to the shareholders and any other buyers. The *Aktiengesetz* expressly provides that such sales to banks in the context of firm commitment underwriting will not be considered to prejudice the shareholders' preemption rights which, as discussed below, must be waived if the shares are to be sold to persons other than the existing shareholders.

3. Preemption rights   With a rule somewhat stricter than that of the Second Company Law Directive, which requires preemption rights when shares are issued for cash payment,[52] all shares of an AG carry preemption rights whether the new issue is paid for in cash or in-kind assets.[53] A "preemptive" (US)[54] or "preemption" (UK) right (*Bezugsrecht*, literally "subscription right") is a right to purchase any new shares the company issues in proportion to the member's current shareholding on the same or more favorable terms than the shares are offered to third parties.[55] Preemption rights both allow a shareholder to maintain his current voting power in

---

[48] §§ 188(2), 36a(1) AktG.   [49] § 54(2) AktG.   [50] §§ 188(2), 36a(2) AktG.

[51] See § 27(2) AktG.

[52] See art. 29 Second Company Law Directive ("Whenever the capital is increased by consideration in cash, the shares must be offered on a preemption basis to shareholders in proportion to the capital represented by their shares.").

[53] § 186(1) AktG.

[54] "Preemp*tive*" is the American term, used in the DGCL and the Model Act, whereas "preemp*tion*" is the UK term. As these rights play a much greater role in UK law under the Second Company Law Directive than in US law, we have chosen to use the UK term throughout the text.

[55] See e.g. § 186(1) AktG. See also sec. 561(1) CA 2006 for a good definition in English.

the company and prevent his position from becoming "watered" through a proportional increase in the amount of the company's stock held by others. Preemption rights do not oblige a shareholder to purchase the stock offered, and he may sell the right itself to a third party. Such rights thus contain significant advantages for shareholders, as discussed below in the context of the United Kingdom, but also pose obstacles for a company's access to the capital markets. During the period that shareholders are allowed to exercise or trade their preemption right,[56] the price of the stock can substantially fluctuate. This presents a problem for the pricing of an issue. Since investors will not subscribe to shares if their issue price exceeds the market price at the time of issue, the existence of preemption rights causes issuers to set issue prices at a substantial discount (up to 25 percent) as compared to the (derived or actual market) price at the time of the offering. As will be discussed below, Delaware law no longer includes a mandatory preemption right.

In the context of an effective capital increase or the creation of authorized capital, as discussed above, each shareholder will have the right to be offered the new shares preemptively in proportion to her current holding. In the case of a nominal capital increase, such rights will not exist because the new shares will in any case go only to shareholders in the same manner as would a dividend, and, in the case of conditional capital, as the resolution approving the increase specifies the persons entitled to the shares (e.g. employees participating in a stock bonus program). Preemption rights are not foreseen in the statute.

Thus, unless the new shares resulting from an effective or authorized capital increase will be purchased by the existing shareholders, the latter must waive their preemption rights either in a resolution to that effect or (for authorized capital) by empowering the *Vorstand* to exclude preemption rights from the shares when issued. In each case, the *Vorstand* must prepare a written report setting out the "objective reasons in the company's interest"[57] for waiving the preemption rights and submit it to the shareholders with the relevant resolution, which must be approved by an affirmative vote of three-quarters of the capital represented at the meeting,[58] usually the same meeting that approves the capital increase. In addition to these procedural prerequisites, German courts also require management to show that the corporation has a valid business interest in

[56] The minimum period prescribed by art. 29(3) of the Second Company Law Directive and implemented by § 186(1) AktG is fourteen days.

[57] See the German High Federal Court's *Kali und Salz* decision, BGHZ 71, 40, 46.

[58] § 186(3), (4) AktG.

a waiver of the preemption right that is sufficient to outweigh the share-holders' interest in preemptive subscription. The *Aktiengesetz*, however, was amended in the 1990s to make an exception to the business purpose requirement. A waiver should not be found to violate shareholder rights if (i) the company is listed, (ii) the capital increase is paid in cash and does not exceed 10 percent of the current share capital, and (iii) the issue price is not substantially lower than the market price at the time of the issue.[59] In addition, a sale of shares to a financial institution for offer to the share-holders serves a simple underwriting function and will not be understood as a waiver of preemption rights.[60]

C.   UK rules on increasing share capital

1.   Approving a capital increase   UK law also addresses capital increases within the framework of the Second Company Law Directive, and thus its rules closely resemble those in Germany. The model articles allow directors to undertake *nominal* increases of share capital by capital-izing company profits if so authorized by an "ordinary" resolution, which equals the majority of voting rights present, eligible and used, if the vote is taken on a poll,[61] and to use such sums in paying up new shares.[62] The company may then on the board's proposal distribute such shares as a non-cash distribution to the members.[63] An *effective* capital increase with an issue (allotment) of shares must be approved by the company's articles or by the general meeting through an ordinary resolution.[64] The board may be given *advance authorization* for up to five years by the articles or a like resolution to allot shares.[65] The empowering resolution must state the maximum amount of shares that may be allotted, any conditions for exer-cising the authority, and the date on which authorization will expire.[66] The Companies Act also gives management the power to allot shares where the allotment takes place "in pursuance of an employees' share scheme" or pursuant to "a right ... to convert any security into" shares,[67] provided shareholder authorization was given to allot the rights of conversion,[68] which would have to have followed the same procedure as for shares.[69] This reflects the situations available under the Second Directive and for

---

[59] § 186(3) AktG.   [60] § 186(5) AktG.

[61] See Chapter 16 of this text for the definitions of required majorities. The relevant section of the CA 2006 is sec. 282.

[62] Reg. 78 of the Model Articles for Public Companies (SI 2009 No. 3229) (MAPC).

[63] Reg. 76 MAPC.   [64] Sec. 551(1) CA 2006.   [65] Sec. 551(3) CA 2006.

[66] Sec. 551(3) CA 2006.   [67] Sec. 549(2) CA 2006.   [68] Sec. 549(3) CA 2006.

[69] Sec. 549(1)(b) CA 2006.

bedingtes Kapital under German law. The primary difference between UK and German law is thus that the former provides for a nominally lower "simple" majority of the eligible votes cast for approval.

An allotment of shares must be registered with the companies registry within two months.[70]

2. **Paying for shares**   Payment for shares in public companies follows the rules on initial allotments discussed in Chapter 5. Following article 8 of the Second Directive, no shares may be allotted at a discount,[71] and, following article 9 of that Directive, consideration for shares must cover at least one-quarter of the nominal value and the full premium above that figure, if any.[72] This is somewhat more permissive than German law, where in-kind contributions must cover the entire price. Moreover, the division between cash, in-kind consideration, and disallowed consideration are also more permissive than under German law. "Cash" includes promises to pay and releases of liability toward the company,[73] provided that any such undertaking will be performed within five years.[74] This facilitates debt-for-equity swaps in troubled companies where creditors release their claims in exchange for shares.[75]

The relatively expansive definition of "cash" reduces the set of objects to which the rules on in-kind consideration apply. As discussed in Chapter 5, except in the context of a merger with another company, any in-kind payment for shares must be officially appraised.[76] The only asset that UK law expressly excludes from the consideration that is permissible for an allotment of shares is a promise to do work or perform services for the company.[77]

3. **Preemption rights**   UK law cleaves closely to the Second Directive by granting preemption rights only when the relevant new shares are issued against a payment in cash,[78] but is somewhat more shareholder friendly than both the Directive and German law by granting preemption rights to shares in both public and private limited companies.[79] The limitation of preemption rights to cash payments could well give management an

---

[70] Sec. 554(1) CA 2006.   [71] Sec. 580 CA 2006.   [72] Sec. 586(1) CA 2006.
[73] Sec. 583(3) CA 2006.   [74] Sec. 587(1) CA 2006.   [75] Davies (2008: 276).
[76] Sec. 593 *et seq.* CA 2006.   [77] Sec. 585 CA 2006.
[78] Sec. 565 CA 2006.
[79] However, it should be noted that the power the Companies Act 2006 gives to private companies to exclude preemptive rights (such as in their articles, see sec. 567) or by delegating authority to directors to disapply them (see sec. 569) is broader than that given to public companies.

incentive to structure transactions as exchanges of assets for shares so that they would have a free hand in allotting shares, but this would then trigger the cumbersome evaluation procedures referred to above with respect to in-kind contributions. Davies points out that the definition of preemption rights under the Companies Act also fails to distinguish between different classes of ordinary shares, with the result that a capital increase of one such class would have to be offered to the holders of all classes.[80] The Act includes a formal offering procedure, according to which the right of preemption must be communicated to the current members in hard copy or electronic form and made irrevocable for a period of at least twenty-one days.[81] As in Germany, no preemption rights attach to bonus shares,[82] for these shares are distributed only to existing members in proportion to their holdings, or to securities allotted pursuant to an employee's share scheme,[83] for the scheme itself specifies the persons who will receive the shares.

The procedures for waiving preemption rights track those under German law, although they employ a somewhat more complex terminology. The rights may be either "excluded" by shareholder action or the directors may be given authority to "disapply" them to a given issue. Private companies may completely exclude preemption rights in their articles,[84] or those with only one class of shares may give directors open-ended power to disapply them.[85] Public companies may exclude the application of the *statutory* rules on preemption rights on issues of all "ordinary shares" by incorporating a preemption scheme in their articles that grants rights allocated to each, individual class of shares.[86] "Disapplication" may be authorized by a "special" resolution – requiring 75 percent of the eligible votes cast[87] – which directors must recommend to shareholders together with a statement sent to them and presenting the reasons for disapplication, the amount of money to be paid to the company for the shares and a justification of that amount.[88] `A director who knowingly or recklessly allows inclusion of false or misleading information in such a statement may be imprisoned or fined.[89] Members may give authorization for disapplication only when they have authorized the directors to allot shares – as discussed above – and the term of the authorization is limited to the term of the authorization given for the allotment.[90]

---

[80] Davies (2008: 839), commenting on sec. 561(1) CA 2006.
[81] Sec. 562 CA 2006.   [82] Sec. 564 CA 2006.   [83] Sec. 566 CA 2006.
[84] Sec. 567 CA 2006.   [85] Sec. 569 CA 2006.   [86] Sec. 568 CA 2006.
[87] This figure refers to voting on a "poll." See Chapter 16 of this text for the definitions of voting techniques and required majorities. The relevant section of the CA 2006 is sec. 283(5).
[88] Sec. 571 CA 2006.   [89] Sec. 572 CA 2006.   [90] Sec. 570 CA 2006.

The presence of perhaps the world's strongest institutional investor lobby in London has produced guidelines for such investors that forcefully argue against the waiver of preemption rights.[91] Davies succinctly summarizes the corporate governance argument expressed in this policy against waiving preemption rights: "This doctrine makes it difficult for a management, which has failed its existing shareholders, to obtain financing from a new group of investors, letting them into the company cheaply (and at the expense of the existing investors) as part of an implicit bargain to back the existing management against the complaints of the first group of investors."[92]

D. Increasing share capital in Delaware

1. Approving a capital increase   As discussed in earlier chapters, the certificate of incorporation of a Delaware corporation must specify one or more classes of shares, stating the number of shares that the company is authorized to issue.[93] This "authorized stock" may be increased through an amendment to the certificate,[94] which requires a majority vote of the outstanding stock entitled to vote on the issue.[95] The law places no limit on the amount of or the maximum term of validity for authorized capital. Within the limits of the authorized stock, the board of directors is free to issue stock on its own authority until all the authorized stock has been issued.[96] Delaware law thus places considerably more power in the hands of the board than either Germany or the United Kingdom.

2. Paying for shares   As discussed in Chapter 5, the Delaware statute allows corporations to issue "partly paid shares" and places no numerical restriction – such as one-half or one-quarter – on the amount that must be paid in at issue.[97] Par value shares may not be sold for less than par, but a corporation may also issue no-par shares.[98] Further, Delaware places no restrictions on the form of consideration that may be used to pay for a company's shares,[99] and states that the board's judgment "as to the value of such consideration shall be conclusive" "in the absence of actual fraud in the transaction."[100] In this way, Delaware replaces the various *ex ante* rules on payment for shares found in European law with

---

[91]   See the 2006 Statement of Principles of the Pre-Emption Group, available at www.pre-emptiongroup.org.uk/principles/index.htm.
[92]   Davies (2008: 844).   [93]   § 102(a)(4) DGCL.   [94]   § 242(a)(3) DGCL.
[95]   § 242(b)(1) DGCL.   [96]   § 161 DGCL.   [97]   § 156 DGCL.   [98]   § 153 DGCL.
[99]   A restriction in art. IX, § 3, of the Constitution of the State of Delaware of 1897 which placed certain restrictions on the forms of acceptable consideration for shares was repealed in 2004. See House Bill 399 of the 142nd General Assembly of Delaware.
[100]   § 152 DGCL.

the *ex post* control of the fiduciary duties of directors, which will be discussed at length in Chapters 11 and 12.

3.   Preemption rights   The Delaware General Corporation Law provides that: "No stockholder shall have any preemptive right to subscribe to an additional issue of stock or to any security convertible into such stock unless, and except to the extent that, such right is expressly granted to such stockholder in the certificate of incorporation."[101] This default position under which preemption rights are not granted unless expressly provided for was introduced in 1967 amendments to the statute, which replaced a scheme comparable to the current European framework under the Second Company Law Directive.

Questions for discussion

1. What is leverage?
2. What distinguishes debt from equity?
3. Does a firm's capital structure change its value? How?
4. What are the major differences of the capital increase procedures in our jurisdictions?
5. What are the purposes of preemptive rights? Are preemptive rights necessary for the protection of shareholders?
6. How can preemptive rights be waived under UK and German law?

Cases

Benihana of Tokyo, Inc. v. Benihana, Inc.
Court of Chancery of Delaware
891 A 2d 150 (2005)
[*Text of opinion edited; footnotes omitted*]
© 2008 Thomson Reuters/West

PARSONS, Vice Chancellor

Plaintiff, Benihana of Tokyo, Inc. ("BOT"), seeks rescission of an agreement between Defendants Benihana Inc. ("Benihana" or the "Company") and BFC Financial Corporation ("BFC") to issue $20 million of Benihana preferred stock to BFC (the "BFC Transaction" or "Transaction") …
[*Text omitted*]

---

[101] § 102(b)(3) DGCL.

I. Facts

A. *The parties*

Rocky Aoki founded BOT in 1963 as a New York corporation. BOT owns and operates Benihana restaurants outside the continental United States ... Rocky Aoki also founded nominal Defendant Benihana ... a Delaware corporation with its principal place of business in Florida; it operates and franchises Benihana restaurants within the continental United States. BOT has been a controlling stockholder of Benihana since its incorporation.

Initially, Rocky Aoki owned 100% of BOT and thereby indirectly controlled Benihana. In 1998, after he pled guilty to insider trading charges unrelated to Benihana, Rocky Aoki put his 100% ownership interest of BOT into the Benihana Protective Trust (the "Trust") to avoid regulatory problems regarding Benihana's liquor licenses ... Defendant Dornbush, a trusted friend and the family attorney, advised Rocky Aoki in that matter. The trustees of the Trust are Rocky Aoki's three children, Kana Aoki Nootenboom ("Kana Aoki"), Kyle Aoki and Kevin Aoki, and, until recently, Defendant Dornbush. The directors of BOT are Kana Aoki, Defendant Dornbush, and until recently, Kevin Aoki and Defendant Yoshimoto. Kevin Aoki also serves as a vice president of marketing and a director of Benihana.

Benihana has two classes of common stock outstanding, common stock ("Common Stock") and Class A common stock. Benihana has 3,018,979 shares of Common Stock issued and outstanding. Each share of Common Stock entitles its holder to one vote. Additionally, Benihana has 6,134,225 shares of Class A common stock issued and outstanding, with each share having 1/10 vote. The holders of Class A common stock have the right to elect 25% of the Benihana Board of Directors, rounded up to the nearest whole director. The holders of the Common Stock elect the remaining directors.

BOT owns 50.9%, or 1,535,668 shares, of Benihana's Common Stock and 2%, or 116,754 shares, of Benihana's Class A common stock. Before the BFC Transaction, BOT also had 50.9% of the Common Stock voting power. The Transaction caused a decrease in BOT's voting power in two steps: first to 42.5% and then to 36.5%.

Since June 2003, Benihana has had a nine member board of directors (the "Benihana Board" or "Board"). Defendants Abdo, Becker, Dornbush, Pine, Sano, Schwartz, Sturges and Yoshimoto are all directors of Benihana. The Benihana Board is classified; the holders of Class A common stock elect three directors, and the holders of Common Stock elect six directors. Each year the stockholders elect one third of the directors for three year terms, including one director elected by Class A common stockholders.

Defendant BFC is a publicly traded Florida corporation with its principal place of business in Florida. BFC is a holding company for various investments, including a 55% controlling ownership interest in Levitt Corporation, which in turn has a 37% ownership interest in Bluegreen Corporation. BFC invests in companies they like and can understand and that have managements that BFC admires as having a high degree of integrity and character. BFC does not get involved in the management of the companies they invest in or frequently change boards of directors or management. Abdo's job at BFC is to identify opportunities for investments in companies that are run by people BFC would admire.

At all times material to this case, Abdo was a director and the vice chairman of BFC and owned approximately 30% of its stock. He and BFC Chairman, Alan Levan, together control BFC. Abdo also serves as president of Levitt Corporation and vice chairman of the boards of directors of both Levitt and Bluegreen.

Abdo has long had an interest in Benihana. He was appointed to the Board in 1991 as an independent director. On the day he was nominated to the Board he purchased 10,000 shares of Benihana stock. He subsequently purchased more Benihana stock. After it was announced that Rocky Aoki would resign from the board due to an insider trading conviction Abdo told Dornbush that if Rocky sold any of his stock he would have an interest in purchasing it. That is the only situation Abdo recalled where he initiated a conversation in which he expressed an interest in purchasing stock from Rocky Aoki or BOT.

Defendant Dornbush is a director and corporate secretary of Benihana and, in effect, acts as its general counsel. He served as counsel to Benihana in the BFC Transaction. Together with Abdo, Dornbush also serves as a director on Levitt's board.

Defendant Schwartz is a director of Benihana as well as its president and chief executive officer. Thus, Schwartz receives a significant portion of his income from his salary, bonuses and options in Benihana. In addition, Schwartz is a partner in the Dorsan Group, a financial consulting firm whose other partners include Defendants Dornbush and Sano.

Defendant Yoshimoto works for Benihana as Executive Vice President of Restaurant Operations. His position is subordinate to Dornbush and Schwartz.

Both Yoshimoto and Schwartz have multi-year employment contracts that guarantee their annual salaries and require the Company to pay all salary remaining under the contract within 20 days of any termination without cause. Yoshimoto's contract expires in 2006, Schwartz's in 2009.

In addition to being a director of Benihana, Defendant Becker is a director of Bluegreen Corporation along with Abdo.

B.   Concern regarding future control of BOT

In early 2003, Rocky Aoki became displeased with the actions of his trusted advisors and members of his family to whom he had ceded control of BOT (and indirect control of Benihana). Around this time period, Rocky Aoki first retained counsel other than Dornbush to advise him with regard to the Trust. Rocky even suggested that Dornbush and Yoshimoto resign as directors of Benihana. In or around August 2003, Rocky Aoki also prepared a codicil to his will that provided for distribution of all of BOT's stock to his new wife, Keiko Aoki, 25% passing to her in fee simple and 75% passing to her in the form of a life estate with the remainder to his children. Thus, upon Rocky Aoki's death, complete control of BOT and indirect control of Benihana would pass to Keiko Aoki and not to his children. This development created varying degrees of concern among not only Kevin and Kana Aoki, two of Rocky Aoki's children who served as trustees of the Trust, but also some members of the Benihana Board.

According to Schwartz, Benihana frequently received comments from investors and Wall Street about changing from two classes of common stock to one, because it would improve the liquidity of Benihana. Due to the two tiered structure of Benihana's stock Schwartz always asked Dornbush "whether [he] thought the trust would be interested in selling any of their BOT shares." Dornbush always responded to these inquiries by saying that BOT would not sell their shares during Rocky's lifetime.

The Certificate of Incorporation provides that if the number of shares of Common Stock falls below a specified threshold (12 1/2%) of the total number of shares of Class A and Common Stock, then the Class A stock not only votes separately for 25% of the directors, but also votes with the Common Stock for the remaining 75% of the directors. In all cases, however, the Class A stock would have only a 1/10 vote.

In late August 2003, Dornbush and Schwartz examined different means by which they could trigger the provision of the certificate which would cause the Common Stock and Class A stock to vote together for the directors previously elected by the Common Stock alone. In one scenario, Schwartz determined that Benihana would have to issue 16.5 million Class A shares to meet the threshold in the Certificate. Such a stock issuance would have reduced BOT's percentage of the vote to approximately 29%. Schwartz asked Dornbush whether that scenario was feasible. Dornbush responded that it would not be and suggested that there would not be a legitimate business purpose for issuing that number of shares.

1.   The proposal of an option to purchase BOT's interest in Benihana
On September 10, 2003, shortly after learning of the change to his father's will, Kevin Aoki had dinner with Abdo and discussed the growing tension among the Aoki family. Kevin told Abdo that the amount of control their father's new wife exerted over their father disturbed the Aoki children ...

In the second half of 2003 and into 2004, the Aoki children who served as trustees experienced many pressures and concerns as a result of their father's changed behavior ... their relationship had deteriorated to the point where Rocky Aoki, through counsel, informed them that he would not meet with them outside of Keiko's presence.

... The Aoki children sought a solution to protect themselves against their father's threats and pressures. Additionally, they wanted to protect Benihana, as well as Kevin and Kyle's jobs at Benihana, from Keiko's control and find a way to pay the insurance premiums. At [a] March 2004 meeting, Dornbush suggested issuing an option to purchase BOT's interest in Benihana. This effectively would have shielded

Benihana, and Kyle and Kevin's jobs, from Keiko's control and provided cash to BOT so the children could pay Rocky's life insurance premiums. The Aoki children, however, felt uncomfortable selling BOT's interest in Benihana during their father's lifetime, so they suggested that the option would be exercisable only upon Rocky's deathbed. The Aoki children also wanted to "[k]eep [the] door open for dad," i.e. provide a mechanism through which they could cancel the option if they reconciled with their father. Dornbush expressed skepticism about finding a buyer willing to accept a transaction with such a cancellation feature. In fact, Dornbush "identified as the only person [he knew] who would entertain buying" such an option. Abdo knew of the pressure Rocky Aoki had placed on Kevin Aoki, and Dornbush felt that Abdo "was truly supportive" of Kevin.

After the meeting Dornbush had with Kyle, Kevin and Kana Aoki, Dornbush and Kevin met with Abdo for lunch in March 2004 ...

... Kevin Aoki approached Abdo at the ... meeting about purchasing an option for the BOT shares.

... [Abdo] had no need, financial or otherwise, to keep his director position at Benihana. Though he may have found an opportunity to acquire BOT's Benihana Common Stock attractive, the cancellation feature of the option offered by the Aoki children made the proposed investment much less enticing ...

C.　The state of Benihana's businesses

In 2003, Benihana realized that it needed to renovate many of its restaurant facilities because they were aging and quickly becoming outmoded ... Implementation of the Construction and Renovation Plan would require capital. In 2003, Benihana had an existing line of credit with Wachovia. Mark Burris, Benihana's CFO, approached Wachovia to determine their ability to finance Benihana's Construction and Renovation Plan ... Burris concluded that, "the need for additional financing is clear if we are to continue capex [capital expenditures] at our projected rate." At trial, Burris explained that he felt uncomfortable relying solely upon the Wachovia proposal to satisfy Benihana's financing needs because it contained a provision limiting the amount Benihana could borrow to 1.5 times earnings before interest, taxes, depreciation, and amortization ("EBITDA"). This restriction on the financing plan, which spanned five years, threatened to limit substantially Benihana's ability to borrow funds.

[Text omitted]

1.　Financing alternatives explored

Given the less than satisfactory financing option offered by Wachovia, Benihana retained the investment banking firm Morgan Joseph & Co., Inc. ("Morgan Joseph") to determine what other financing options the Company might use to carry out its five year Construction and Renovation Plan ...

[Text omitted]

3.   January 29 meeting of the Benihana board

... Morgan Joseph decided to recommend convertible preferred stock as an appropriate financing vehicle for Benihana and created a board book that analyzed the recommended stock issuance and set out the anticipated terms for it. Morgan Joseph presented the board book to the Benihana Board at a January 29, 2004 meeting. Once again, they reviewed the financing alternatives of bank debt, high yield notes, convertible debt or preferred stock, traditional equity financing and sale/leaseback options, and the Board discussed them. Morgan Joseph recommended that Benihana obtain equity financing first to gain flexibility, then use the equity financing as leverage to negotiate better terms on their existing line of credit with Wachovia. According to Joseph, "the oldest rule in our business is you raise equity when you can, not when you need it. And Benihana's stock had been doing okay. The markets were okay. We thought we could do an equity placement." Morgan Joseph recommended a convertible preferred stock specifically because it felt "that adding the additional long-term capital match[ed] the company's long term needs [for capital expenditures,] ... provide[d] the flexibility for the company to grow internally and pursue the other opportunities [i.e. acquisitions] ... [a]nd reduce[d][the] company's dependence on bank debt." The Benihana directors were told to take the board books home to study and deliberate.

4.   February 17 meeting of the Benihana board

On February 17, 2004, the Benihana Board met again to discuss the terms of the recommended convertible preferred stock issuance. Morgan Joseph discussed the feasibility of obtaining certain terms the Company wanted ... the Board understood that, while Morgan Joseph would endeavor to negotiate the best deal for Benihana, several of the terms they had discussed were more akin to a "wish list."

At the conclusion of the ... meeting, the Benihana Board decided to pursue convertible preferred stock as an additional means of financing. Abdo attended both the January 29 and February 17 meetings. At the February 17 meeting Morgan Joseph proposed that the convertible preferred stock should have immediate voting rights as though they had been converted ...

The convertible preferred stock discussed at the February 17 meeting differed in certain respects from the three classes of preferred stock (Series A, A-1 and A-2) Benihana previously had authorized. None of those classes carries with it the right to a directorship, voting rights or preemptive rights.

[*Text omitted*]

D.   *Abdo approaches Morgan Joseph on behalf of BFC*

Shortly after the February 17 Board meeting Abdo talked to his partner Alan Levan about having BFC attempt to purchase the preferred stock Benihana planned to issue to finance the Construction and Renovation Plan. Levan responded that he thought it was a good deal ...

... Morgan Joseph sent its private placement memorandum to BFC and negotiations began ... the parties agreed not to shop the issuance to anyone else for a short period to foster more productive negotiations with BFC ...

1.   Negotiation of the convertible preferred stock issuance

Negotiations between BFC (Abdo) and Benihana (Morgan Joseph) continued through the end of April 2004. The ultimate terms of the BFC Transaction are reflected in a stock purchase agreement (the "Stock Purchase Agreement" or "SPA"). Those terms include the issuance of 800,000 shares of convertible preferred stock for $20 million in two separate tranches of $10 million apiece. The second tranche would issue within one to three years after the first.

BFC negotiated to obtain the following terms: (1) the right to require Benihana to draw down the second tranche of convertible preferred stock; (2) BFC's right to one director seat on the Benihana Board and an additional seat if Benihana missed its dividend for two consecutive quarters; (3) BFC's preemptive right to purchase a proportional amount of any new voting securities issued by Benihana; (4) BFC's right to require Benihana to redeem the full $20 million of convertible preferred stock at any time after 10 years; (5) anti-dilution and liquidation provisions; (6) BFC's right to a standby fee; and (7) BFC's right to immediately vote on all matters, including elections of directors, with the voting power associated with the amount of Common Stock into which their preferred stock was convertible, even if such stock has not yet been converted.

For its part, Morgan Joseph negotiated several terms that they considered beneficial to Benihana. Those terms included: (1) no performance criteria could be placed on Benihana as a condition of executing the second tranche; (2) a coupon rate, or dividend, of five percent; and (3) a conversion price of 115% of the original volume based on a 10 day average *before* the announcement of the Transaction ...

Schwartz sent the negotiated term sheet to the Board on April 30, 2004, but did not indicate that BFC was the other party to the negotiations. Schwartz, however, informally told Becker, Sturges, Sano, and possibly Pine of BFC's role as the counterparty before the May 6, 2004 Board meeting.

E.   *The May 6 Benihana board meeting*

On May 6, 2004, the Benihana Board met again to consider the convertible preferred stock issuance. At this meeting, the entire Board formally was informed of BFC's negotiations with Benihana. Abdo made a presentation on behalf of BFC ... He then excused himself from the remainder of the meeting. Morgan Joseph ... reviewed the new terms with the Board and pointed out the changes in the net debt figures. In addition, the Board specifically discussed changes that had been made with regard to the conversion price and preemptive rights.

[Text omitted]

... the Board voted to approve the BFC Transaction subject to receipt of a fairness opinion. Dornbush and Kevin Aoki attended the meeting and participated in the discussions but abstained from voting. All six remaining directors voted in favor of the Transaction.

F.   Closing of the BFC transaction

On May 20, 2004, the Benihana Board met again to consider the BFC Transaction, which now was supported by a favorable fairness opinion from Morgan Joseph. The Board then approved the transaction. On June 8, 2004, Schwartz executed the Stock Purchase Agreement on behalf of Benihana, and Abdo executed it on behalf of BFC.

1.   BOT's concern over the dilutive effect of the BFC transaction

After the May 6 Board meeting, Kevin Aoki approached Schwartz, Abdo and Dornbush to inquire if either his father or BOT could finance the second tranche of the BFC Transaction in order to avoid dilution of BOT's interest in Benihana. The proposals Kevin Aoki made, however, were not realistic ... management did not view Rocky as a viable funding source ...

... The trustees of the Trust objected to the dilutive effect of the Transaction ... Thereafter, representatives of the Trust and Rocky Aoki communicated their objections regarding the BFC Transaction to the Benihana Board and recommended alternative financing offers for Benihana's consideration.

[Text omitted]

3.   Filing of the certificate of designations

Benihana's Certificate of Incorporation gives the Benihana Board the power to issue "blank check" preferred stock. Accordingly, and as required by § 4(l) of the Stock Purchase Agreement, Benihana filed a Certificate of Designations, Preferences and Rights of Series B Convertible Preferred Stock of Benihana ("Certificate of Designations") with the Delaware Secretary of State on June 29, 2004. This action immediately reduced BOT's voting interest from 50.9% to 42.5%, and then further reduced it to 36.5% in or around August 2005, when BFC took down the second tranche. Likewise, BFC acquired a 16.5% voting interest in Benihana when the Certificate of Designations was filed, which increased to 28.3% upon issuance of the second tranche.

[Text omitted]

II.   Analysis

BOT challenges the BFC Transaction on several grounds. First, BOT contends that the transaction is void because it violated 8 Del. C. § 151 and the applicable provisions of Benihana's Certificate of Incorporation.

BOT also claims that the BFC Transaction is invalid because the Board adopted it for an improper primary purpose of diluting BOT's interest in Benihana and entrenching certain Director Defendants and that the Director Defendants breached their fiduciary duties of loyalty and care in approving the Transaction.

The issues raised by BOT's legal argument under 8 Del. C. § 151 are distinct from the entrenchment and breach of fiduciary duty claims. Therefore, the Court begins its analysis with the § 151 claim.

A.   *The validity of the BFC transaction under 8 Del. C. § 151(a)*

Benihana's Certificate of Incorporation states that: "No stockholder shall have any preemptive right to subscribe to or purchase any issue of stock or other securities of the Corporation or any treasury stock or other security." In connection with the sale of preferred stock to BFC, Benihana granted BFC preemptive rights to purchase Benihana stock ... BFC has the right to purchase at the same price up to the number of offered shares necessary for BFC to maintain the percentage ownership in the Company it had immediately before such issuance based on its purchase of preferred shares.

... Benihana argues that the Court should interpret the language in its Certificate of Incorporation as not prohibiting Benihana from granting preemptive rights by contract ...

[Text omitted]

Section 151 of the DGCL allows corporations to issue one or more classes of stock or one or more series of stock within a class, including stock with redemption rights, conversion features and other special rights. The powers, preferences, rights and other characteristics of such shares, however, "shall be stated and expressed in the Certificate of Incorporation or of any amendment thereto, or in the resolution or resolutions providing for the issue of such stock adopted by the board of directors pursuant to authority expressly vested in it by the provisions of its certificate of incorporation." In addition, 8 Del. C. § 151(g) provides ... "When any corporation desires to issue any shares of stock of any class or of any series of any class ... not ... set out in the certificate of incorporation ... but ... provided for in a resolution or resolutions adopted by the board of directors *pursuant to authority expressly vested in it by the certificate of incorporation or any amendment thereto,* a certificate of designations setting forth a copy of such resolution ... shall be ... filed, recorded and shall become effective ...

Therefore, the Court also must consider the terms of Benihana's charter.

... Benihana's Certificate of Incorporation ... vests the Board with authority to "issue from time to time the Preferred stock of any series and to state in the resolution or resolutions providing for the issuance of shares of any series the voting powers, if any, designations, preferences and relative, participating, optional or other special rights" – i.e. a blank check authorization ...

[Text omitted]

... Before the 1967 amendments, § 102(b)(3) [DGCL] provided that a certificate of incorporation may contain provisions "limiting or denying to the stockholders the preemptive rights to subscribe to any or all additional issues of stock of the corporation." As a result, a common law rule developed that shareholders possess preemptive rights unless the certificate of incorporation provides otherwise. In 1967, the Delaware Legislature reversed this presumption. Section 102(b)(3) was amended to provide in pertinent part: "No stockholder shall have any preemptive right to subscribe to an additional issue of stock or to any security convertible into such stock unless, and except to the extent that, such right is expressly granted to him in the certificate of incorporation."

Thereafter, companies began including boilerplate language in their charters to clarify that no shareholder possessed preemptive rights under common law. Consistent with that practice Benihana's Certificate of Incorporation states that "[n]o stockholder shall have any preemptive right to subscribe to or purchase any issue of stock or other securities of the Corporation, or any treasury stock or other treasury securities." I conclude that this type of boilerplate language concerning preemptive rights applies only to common law preemptive rights and not to contractually granted preemptive rights …

The blank check provision in Benihana's Certificate of Incorporation suggests that the certificate was never intended to limit Benihana's ability to issue preemptive rights by contract to purchasers of preferred stock … Hence, I conclude that the Board did have the authority to issue the preferred stock with preemptive rights that is the subject of the BFC Transaction under Benihana's Certificate of Incorporation and the applicable provisions of the DGCL.

B.   The applicable standard of review for the BFC transaction

[*Text omitted*]

[Here the court stated the standard of review for the challenged decisions of directors when they are alleged to have an interest in a transaction on which they decide. This standard of review will be discussed in detail in Chapter 12.]

[*Text omitted*]

Because BOT also contends that the Director Defendants breached their fiduciary duties of loyalty and care, my analysis does not end with the "safe harbor" provisions of § 144(a).

C.   Improper primary purpose

Plaintiff contends that the Board approved the BFC Transaction for the improper purpose of entrenching the Board members in office. Defendants argue that BOT has not met their burden on this issue because: (1) BOT has not shown that any of the directors subjectively had entrenchment as the sole or primary purpose of their actions; (2) the BFC Transaction had a *de minimis* entrenchment effect, if any, given Benihana's preexisting corporate governance structure; and (3) a majority of the directors voting on the BFC Transaction did not have an entrenchment purpose and their assent to the transaction was not the result of fraud or manipulation by their fellow-directors.

Corporate fiduciaries may not utilize corporate machinery for the purpose of perpetuating themselves in office ...

A successful claim of entrenchment requires plaintiffs to prove that the defendant directors engaged in action which had the effect of protecting their tenure and that the action was motivated *primarily or solely* for the purpose of achieving that effect.

Where a board's actions are shown to have been taken for the purpose of entrenchment, they may not be permitted to stand.

The fact that a plan has an entrenchment effect, however, does not mean that the board's primary or sole purpose was entrenchment. Conversely, where the objective sought in the issuance of stock is not merely the pursuit of a business purpose but also to retain control, a court will not accept the argument that the control effect of an agreement is merely incidental to its primary business objective.

Plaintiff asserts that Dornbush and Schwartz pursued the BFC Transaction in order to entrench themselves in office. BOT further asserts that Dornbush and Schwartz subsequently misled the Board when they convinced them that debt financing did not represent the best mechanism to fund the renovation project ... Dornbush further testified that he "shared" a "concern" that, upon obtaining control of Benihana, Keiko Aoki, would "remove all of the people who were there for 20 years of service." ...

Although ... Keiko may be "hostile to management," it still would take her several years to exert meaningful control over Benihana. Further, although Keiko's potential hostility may have given the directors a reason to entrench themselves that does not mean *ipso facto* that the directors approved the BFC transaction primarily or solely for that purpose. The law requires more than just a motivation to entrench.

... Dornbush is 75 ... and no longer a profit sharing partner in his law firm. Dornbush separately received $5,000 a month from Benihana for consulting services ... I find that Dornbush did not facilitate the BFC Transaction primarily or solely for the purpose of protecting his tenure or that of any other director.

Although Schwartz had no significant source of income other than the compensation he received from Benihana, he has an employment agreement with Benihana that prevents his termination as CEO, without cause, until 2009 ... Moreover, although BFC generally invests for the long term and does not frequently change management, there is no evidence of any special relationship between BFC or Abdo on the one hand and Schwartz and Dornbush on the other. BFC presumably will expect good performance from Benihana and its managers. Hence, it is reasonable to infer that BFC would not hesitate to remove Schwartz from his positions if grounds for a termination for cause existed.

[*Text omitted*]

... I find that Schwartz's concern did not infect his own or the Board's decisionmaking process in connection with the BFC Transaction. I likewise conclude that neither Dornbush nor a majority of the members of the Benihana Board had entrenchment or dilution of BOT as their sole or primary purpose in approving the BFC Transaction. Instead, I find that the directors who approved the BFC transaction did so on an informed basis, acting in good faith, and believing they were acting in the best interests of Benihana.

Plaintiff cites three cases in which the court found a motive to entrench because the Board could have addressed the asserted need by alternative nondilutive means and failed to give an adequate explanation as to why the directors chose a dilutive financing scheme ...

In *Canada Southern Oils* v. *Manabi Exploration Co.*, the board approved a dilutive issuance which caused the majority shareholder to lose control of the company. The board claimed it needed to issue the shares to raise funds to solve their financial crisis. The court, however, did not believe the company had a major financial crisis ...

Further, the court found persuasive several facts not present in this case. First, the directors never offered the controlling shareholder the option to purchase the shares, choosing instead to blindly assume they would not help. In this case BOT had the opportunity to help fund the construction and Renovation Plan, but failed to make any proposal demonstrating that they had the necessary funds. Second, the notice for the directors' meeting made no reference to the possibility of selling shares of the company. In contrast, the Benihana directors met several times to discuss their funding options and knew each time they would discuss the funding issue ...

[*Text omitted*]

That is not the case here. The Benihana Board had valid reasons to use equity as opposed to debt financing. Everyone, including Kevin Aoki, agreed that the Company needed to proceed with its Construction and Renovation Plan ... Morgan Joseph concluded that debt financing was not the best option because they feared it might reduce the flexibility Benihana needed to take advantage of attractive acquisition opportunities that might present themselves. For example, the Wachovia financing offer contained a provision limiting the amount Benihana could borrow to 1.5 times EBITDA. This restriction, which spanned five years, could have substantially limited Benihana's ability to borrow funds.

[*Text omitted*]

Plaintiff relies on *Packer* v. *Yampol* for the proposition that "[a]n inequitable purpose can be inferred where the directors' conduct has the effect of being unnecessary under the circumstances, of thwarting shareholder opposition, and of perpetuating management in office." The situation in *Packer* v. *Yampol*, however, was far more egregious than here. In *Packer* the board approved the issuance of stock in the midst of a proxy fight. The issuance included "supervoting" features, conferring upon the holders 44% of the corporation's total voting power. This allowed defendants to "virtually assur[e] the outcome of the election of directors."

[*Text omitted*]

Condec Corp. v. *Lunkenheimer Co.* is equally distinguishable. There the transaction at issue was a share exchange that brought in no new capital to the Company and had no corporate purpose other than to reduce plaintiff's stock holdings. The court also noted the "haste with which the basic ... transaction was hammered out." Such extreme circumstances do not exist in this case.

[*Text omitted*]

D.   Director defendants' alleged breaches of the duty of loyalty

BOT contends that Schwartz, Dornbush and Abdo, with the help of Morgan Joseph, manipulated the board process that led to the approval of the BFC Transaction, thereby breaching their fiduciary duties. Further, Plaintiff asserts that each of the directors breached their duty of loyalty by approving the BFC Transaction in order to protect their own incumbency.

[*Text omitted*]

In my opinion, Schwartz, Dornbush and Abdo, did not manipulate the Board to approve the BFC Transaction, either individually or in concert with one another or Morgan Joseph. As discussed above, the directors did not act out of a motivation to entrench themselves or any other self-interest or as a result of domination or control by an interested director. In addition, because the Board is staggered, it would have taken Keiko Aoki two or three years after Rocky Aoki's death to remove the directors from their positions, even if the BFC Transaction had not occurred.

Having already found that a majority of disinterested and independent directors approved the BFC Transaction and that the Transaction was not entered into for an improper purpose, I find no grounds to believe that the directors breached their fiduciary duty of loyalty. BOT has the burden of proving their contrary allegation by a preponderance of the evidence. They have not met their burden. Therefore, I conclude that none of the Director Defendants breached their fiduciary duty of loyalty.

E.   Director defendants' alleged breaches of the duty of care

Plaintiff contends that the directors violated their fiduciary duty of care by failing to inform themselves of basic information about the BFC Transaction ...

[*Text omitted*]

[For a discussion of judicial review of the standard of care, see Chapter 12.]

... I found that the directors acted with a good faith belief that equity financing represented the best method to finance Benihana's Construction and Renovation Plan and that the directors believed equity financing best served the interests of the Company. Finally, after reviewing the process through which the directors approved the Transaction I have found that the directors reached their decision with due care. Consequently, the Board validly exercised their business judgment in approving the BFC Transaction. This Court will not disturb that decision.

[*Text omitted*]

7

Distribution of dividends and maintenance of share capital

Required reading

EU: Second Company Law Directive, arts. 15, 16
D: AktG, §§ 57–62, 66, 119(1) no. 2, 150, 158, 174, 254; HGB, § 272; GmbHG, § 30; BGB, §§ 134, 985
UK: CA 2006, secs. 829–831, 836–846; SI 2008 No. 3229, Regs. 70–77
US: DGCL, §§ 154, 170, 173, 174, 244; Uniform Fraudulent Transfers Act, §§ 1–5

Maintaining the share capital

In the preceding chapters, we examined the rules designed to constitute the company's share capital and ensure that the funds paid or assets contributed for this purpose have the promised value. Here we will discuss capital maintenance rules that seek to protect unsecured creditors by preventing shareholders from paying those corporate assets to which such creditors look to for repayment out to themselves. Legal limits on dividends go to the heart of a company's value. Although in theory the payment of dividends should not have a significant impact on share price because capital gains serve to compensate for an absence of such distributions, in practice dividend payments are indeed crucial to share price.[1] This is particularly true for corporate shareholders, which some jurisdictions tax more favorably for dividend than for capital gain income.[2] Thus, shareholders have a strong interest in the distribution of dividends and creditors have an equally strong interest in not having the corporate capital of their debtor excessively depleted by such distributions. If some shareholders draw a salary from the company and control the use of its assets, differences may also arise between the shareholders in control and

---

[1] Ferran (1999: 409–410).   [2] Barclay, Holderness and Sheehan (2003).

the "outside" shareholders, as the *Sam Weller* case, reprinted in part in this chapter, makes quite clear.

The rules limiting distributions in our two European jurisdictions are more restrictive than those in the US, and, because the provisions found in both the *Aktiengesetz* and the Companies Act 2006 derive from a common EU directive, they also display significant similarities, at least at the level of the public company. Capital maintenance in stock corporations (in the UK, public companies) is regulated by the provisions of the Second Company Law Directive. This chapter will review the general legal problems connected with capital maintenance, then look at the Second Directive, followed by a discussion of the current rules in Germany and the UK. The US presents both an odd case and a potential future for Europe, in that during the last fifty years US statutes have gradually replaced minimum capital requirements and restrictions on distributions with the tandem scheme of a disclosure-oriented system that provides creditors with a view of the company's financial condition and bankruptcy rules that restrict distributions when the company is approaching insolvency. We will look at the US rules at the close of this chapter.

I.   *Protecting creditors through capital maintenance*

A capital maintenance regime has two obvious components: first, the law prescribes a certain minimum capital as a prerequisite for incorporating an entity with limited liability; and, secondly, it requires that this capital be maintained. We looked at the rules addressing the first component of this protection, including the mandatory amounts of minimum capital, the nominal value of shares, and procedures for evaluating in-kind contributions, in Chapters 5 and 6. Here we will address the maintenance of this capital through restrictions on distributions to shareholders. In Chapter 8, we will look at the most significant non-cash transaction affected by these rules, share buy-backs, and, in Chapter 26, we will discuss the regulation of a technique that could be considered an indirect share buy-back: a company's providing credit or other financial assistance to a buyer of its shares.

The most significant historical development in capital maintenance rules has been the shift away from a specific amount of protected capital toward a disclosure-based system. As mentioned above, this shift has been completed in the US, and was most forcefully advocated by Manning, whose argument was that the creation and protection of a legal capital never effectively protected creditors. Instead, a reasonable creditor sought complete, accurate information on the company's assets and financial condition, then demanded assurances that the company would not deplete the assets or worsen the financial condition without prior approval of the creditor, and statutory capital maintenance requirements distracted from the need to demand such real protections.[3] Similar arguments are currently being debated in Europe, but the 2006 amendments to the Second Directive, which left the rules on dividends essentially untouched, indicate that capital maintenance in Europe will not in the near future follow the US model.

In connection with the disclosure argument, it is very important to distinguish between creditors who are able to negotiate security for their credit and other creditors. The most prominent group of "other" creditors is tort victims ("involuntary" creditors). Unlike a bank lending to the corporation, someone who is hit and injured by a corporation's truck, damaged by using a corporation's defective product, or afflicted with illness from a corporation's emission of toxic substances has no advance opportunity to negotiate security for the payment of such obligation in tort.[4] For such creditors, the guarantee of a certain minimum capitalization is not only useful, but one of the only ways – together with requiring corporations to carry liability insurance for such cases – that victims can be assured of available funds to compensate their damages. Employees and suppliers who do not have bargaining power sufficient to negotiate security arrangements for the payment of their credit toward the corporation would also benefit from a legal requirement that companies maintain a certain minimum capital. The argument for eliminating capital requirements therefore has rough edges when applied to involuntary creditors or creditors who are not in a position to negotiate security for their credits. Only mandatory schemes providing alternative sources for such compensation serve as adequate replacements.

II.   Capital maintenance under the Second Directive

As discussed in Chapters 5 and 6, the Second Directive includes mandatory rules on minimum capital, contributions to capital and the valuation of in-kind contributions, and it was in regard to this last element that the 2006 amendments to the Directive were most far-reaching. The restrictions on distributions of amounts exceeding capital and legal reserves were not changed by the amendments. They have two components, a

---

[3] Manning (1990).   [4] Hansmann and Kraakman (1991).

measure by the balance sheet and a measure by the profit and loss statement, both of which must be met. First, article 15(a) of the Directive prohibits distributions to shareholders if they result in net assets (as shown in the most recent annual accounts) being less than the sum of subscribed capital and required reserves. Secondly, article 15(c) provides that a distribution may not exceed the profits for the last financial year (plus profits brought forward, less losses brought forward) and sums drawn from or placed in reserves. Shareholders must return any distributions in violation of this requirement unless under the circumstances they could not have been aware that the distribution was prohibited.[5] If a "serious loss" of subscribed capital – which a member state may not set higher than one-half of capital – occurs, a general meeting must be called to take corrective measures (such as replenishing capital) or to dissolve the company.[6] It is important to remember that, while in the vast majority of cases "distribution" means a cash dividend or a bonus share, it could potentially include any valuable asset belonging to the corporation.

III.   Capital maintenance in the European jurisdictions

A.   Germany

Because the board may place no more than one-half of distributable profits in reserves and the shareholders vote on dividends, the shareholders of an AG have more control than their counterparts in the US and the UK over the amount they will receive as dividends.[7] Since the *Aktiengesetz* is mandatory in this respect, it also leaves little room for creditors to control corporate action through restrictive covenants in loan agreements. The law compensates for this shareholder freedom by limiting the potential volume of distributions to shareholders through a rigorous regime of capital maintenance rules under the Second Directive. First, the law provides as a basic principle that shareholders may not be refunded their capital contributions.[8] This provision is not limited to the euro amount of the actual contribution, but actually covers all company assets other than those expressly permitted to be distributed – the distributable

---

[5] Art. 16 Second Company Law Directive.
[6] Art. 17 Second Company Law Directive.
[7] See §§ 58(1), 174(1) AktG. It should be noted, however, that shareholder action in this regard is bound by the amount of distributable profits determined by the *Aufsichtsrat* and the *Vorstand* (unless the latter decides to allow the general meeting to make such determination).
[8] § 57(1) AktG.

profits as calculated pursuant to law (literally, the "balance sheet profit," *Bilanzgewinn*) calculated as the result of adding and subtracting the first four items in § 158 I AktG.[9] The limitation of distributions applies to all assets irrespective of whether they are or can be recorded on the company's balance sheet, as well as to reserves not shown on the balance sheet (sale of an asset to a shareholder for its book value but for less than its actual market value) and to services rendered by the company. Shareholders must return any payments received in violation of this rule, or, where a return in kind is not possible, reimburse the company.[10] All reserves that are not available for distribution are subtracted from the balance sheet surplus and profits eligible for distribution.[11] In all cases, reserves that are created for a specific purpose designated in the statute or the *Satzung* may be used only for such purpose.

As a result, the company's accounting items to which the capital maintenance restrictions refer consist of three interlocking elements: capital, profit and required reserves. In order for distributable profits to exist, the balance sheet value of the company's assets must first exceed its liabilities, the shareholder equity and the mandatory reserves, creating a *Jahresüberschuss*.[12] Secondly, distributable profit is calculated on the basis of the profit (or loss) for the financial year preceding that in which the distribution is to be made, and such profits will only exist when they exceed any losses carried forward and amounts that must be placed in undistributable reserves.[13] Although other reserves may potentially be distributed, any distribution must be made pursuant to the procedure specified by law, which creates both a substantive and a procedural check on distributions.

In Germany, there is some debate whether the capital maintenance rules are to be understood as an extension of the capital contribution rules, and thus be interpreted strictly without regard to the intention or position of the parties, or as a means of preventing shareholders in their capacities as members from using their power to the detriment of creditors. In the latter case, a technical violation of the capital maintenance rules not involving knowledge reasonably attributable to the board that the receiving party was a shareholder would likely not result in sanction.

---

[9] § 57(3) AktG with regard to distributions upon dissolution; and § 174(1) AktG with regard to dividends.

[10] § 62(1) AktG.   [11] §§ 150, 158, 172 AktG; and § 275 HGB.

[12] For example, it is generally agreed that undeclared (*stille*) reserves may not be freely distributed.

[13] § 158 AktG.

The majority opinion, however, is that the rules are to be understood objectively, and thus, if a diligent and prudent director under similar circumstances would have understood the transaction to be in violation of the rules, the distribution will not stand, regardless of whether it included a special shareholder advantage. Because the company will, as a matter of law, continue to own the assets that are transferred illegally, and it will have an enforceable claim against the shareholder for their restitution.

In what is referred to as its 2003 "November" judgment[14] the High Federal Court held that, for capital maintenance purposes, loans to shareholders were to be assessed as if the company did not have a claim for repayment, thus treating loans like gifts. The court based its holding on the arguments that (a) deferred claims for repayment were not as valuable for the corporation's creditors as liquid assets and that (b) with respect to the loan the corporation's creditors lost their priority over the shareholder's creditors. This disregard of a valuable claim constituted a departure from the balance sheet approach to capital maintenance and presented a major obstacle to corporate finance techniques such as cash pooling. In 2008, the legislature reversed the November judgment by adding a new provision to the capital maintenance rules of the AktG and GmbHG. Under new § 57(1) AktG and § 30(1) GmbHG,[15] a loan to shareholders is not an illegal distribution if the claim for repayment is unimpaired (*vollwertig*). In a December 2008 judgment, the High Federal Court acknowledged the return to the traditional balance sheet approach and suggested that the relevant test is whether the claim for repayment is impaired by a concrete probability of default (*konkrete Ausfallwahrscheinlichkeit*). In a recent judgment concerning the responsibility of a subsidiary's management pursuant to §§ 311 and 318 AktG, the court expressly abandoned the principles developed in its November judgment and adopted the view expressed in the new statutory rules.[16] Since neither the statute nor the new judgment explains the circumstances under which a "concrete probability of default" is to be presumed, the new rules have introduced legal uncertainty for managers making decisions to approve company loans to shareholders.[17] In light of the EU-wide freedom of establishment discussed in Chapter 3, this state of affairs provides yet another reason for the flight to other member states with less cumbersome capital maintenance regimes.

---

[14] BGH, *Der Konzern*, 2004, 196 (MPS).
[15] These provisions were added by art. 1 no. 20 and art. 5 no. 5 MoMiG.
[16] BGH, *Der Konzern* 2009, 49.   [17] See Cahn (2009b: 67, 69 *et seq.*).

The determination of distributable profits of course depends heavily upon the way company assets and liabilities are processed through accounting principles. The higher the values assigned to assets and the lower the values assigned to liabilities, the greater will be the distributable profits. The conservative nature of German accounting principles under the HGB works to minimize the available profits. The HGB includes a principle of conservative valuation,[18] and a realization principle and lowest value principle for assets,[19] which, together with the principle of highest value for liabilities, work to decrease assets and increase liabilities in comparison to the results achieved through accounting principles designed to present a true and fair view. Thus, if a German company employs IFRS rather than HGB, this would likely increase the amount available for distribution. As pursuant to the IFRS Regulation all companies listed in the EU must use IFRS for their financial reporting, a difference between the constitution of the accounts of listed and unlisted German companies therefore currently exists.

Traditional capital maintenance seeks to preserve a cushion of assets above and beyond those corresponding to the company's liabilities, and to disallow their distribution to shareholders. In recent years, critics of this approach to creditor protection have raised a number of objections. At the core of these objections is the concern that using the balance sheet as a measure does not provide adequate and meaningful creditor protection: accounts are not an appropriate tool to determine the amount of assets a company may distribute since the relevant accounting rules serve a number of purposes other than creditor protection. Moreover, the balance sheet value of a company's assets does not necessarily mean that these funds will be available to pay company debts as and when they fall due. German legislation has responded to these concerns by adding new solvency restrictions on distributions as part of the 2008 MoMiG reform. Pursuant to the new § 92(2) sentence 3 AktG and § 64 sentence 3 GmbHG, directors of an AG or a GmbH are liable for payments to shareholders if these payments render the company insolvent, unless a prudent and diligent director was unable to foresee the company's insolvency. Unlike the capital maintenance provisions, the solvency restrictions are not concerned with maintaining the value of the company's assets in the face of possible distributions to shareholders, but only with preserving the company's ability to pay its debts as they fall due. Even transactions with shareholders that offer adequate consideration to the company may

---

[18] § 252(1) no. 4 HGB.   [19] § 253(1), (5), 280(1) HGB.

still violate the solvency restrictions if the consideration received by the company is less liquid than the asset transferred to the shareholder. The relevant test is whether the company will be rendered insolvent because the claim for repayment matures only after the point in time at which the company requires the money to pay its debts.[20]

B.   United Kingdom

The full procedure for determining and declaring dividends is not set out in the Companies Act, and the model articles currently give authority over the process to both members and directors: first, the directors will recommend that a specific portion of distributable profits be paid out as dividends,[21] and then the shareholders will declare the dividend by ordinary resolution.[22] The restriction on such distributions in the Companies Act resembles German law, as it also implements article 15 of the Second Company Law Directive. A *public* company – those to which the Directive applies – may only make a distribution if its net assets are not less than the aggregate of its share capital and undistributable reserves, and the distribution does not reduce the assets below such aggregate.[23] The general rule for all companies tracks article 15(c) of the Directive, and focuses on income rather than net assets: a company may only make a distribution out of its "accumulated, realised profits" not already distributed or capitalized, less "accumulated, realised losses" not already written off.[24] A public company must meet both of these tests. If, at the time of the distribution, a member knows or has reasonable grounds to believe that the distribution violated these rules, she will be liable to repay it (or the value of an in-kind distribution) to the company.[25]

As discussed above for German law, the determination of the size of the distribution will hinge to a great extent on how the assets, liabilities and "undistributable" reserves are determined. The Companies Act contains specific provisions on accounting related to distributions,[26] and, as

---

[20] See Cahn (2009a: 7, 13)
[21] Sec. 416(3) CA 2006; Reg. 70(2) MAPC. Unlike under German law, the amount the board may recommend to allocate to reserves is not restricted.
[22] Reg. 70(1) MAPC; also see Ferran (2008: 237–238).
[23] Sec. 831(1) CA 2006. The Act defines "undistributable reserves" to be its share premium account, its capital redemption reserve, the amount by which its accumulated, unrealized profits (so far as not previously utilized by capitalization) exceed its accumulated, unrealized losses (so far as not previously written off in a reduction or reorganization of capital duly made), and any other reserve that the company is prohibited from distributing by its articles. Sec. 831(4) CA 2006.
[24] Sec. 830 CA 2006.   [25] Sec. 847 CA 2006.   [26] Secs. 841–853 CA 2006.

a general matter, UK accounting principles aim to present a "true and fair view" rather than to serve the goal of creditor protection.[27] They will likely yield a higher figure for distributable profits than would the HGB in a company having a like financial condition. In any case, under the IFRS Regulation, a UK listed company will employ the same accounting principles as a German listed company.

IV.   Creditor protection in the United States

As mentioned above, US state laws have moved away from capital maintenance laws over the last fifty years. No leading corporate law statute in the US requires a minimum capital for the establishment of a corporation, and the Model Act has removed the concepts of "par value" and "legal capital" from the law.[28] In statutes such as the DGCL, the protective value of legal capital has been rendered empty through the power of corporations to issue shares having extremely low par or without any par value. Pursuant to US company law statutes, directors have complete control over the distribution of dividends,[29] which from a strict balance of power perspective means that directors stand between shareholders and the company's creditors. This allows directors to make significant commitments in loan covenants, making such covenants a particularly effective means of protecting negotiating (i.e. not tort) creditors under US law.

Delaware law uses a "capital impairment" test and a "net profits" test to determine the fund from which distributions may be paid. First, distributions may be made from capital surplus.[30] "Surplus" is defined to mean the amount by which assets exceed liabilities and the "stated" or "legal" capital.[31] The stated or legal capital is equal either to par times the number of shares outstanding, or, if no par shares are issued, to an amount specified by the board of directors.[32] Capital surplus may be created at any time by reducing par value or the amount designated to serve as stated capital.[33] Although directors may set aside reserves, the statute does not require that any reserves be excluded from the fund out of which dividends may be paid.[34] Dividends may also be paid out of net profits for the fiscal year in which the dividend is declared,[35] and even

---

[27] Sec. 939 CA 2006.   [28] See § 6.40 Model Act, Official Comment.

[29] § 170(a)(1) DGCL; and § 6.40(a) Model Act. Pursuant to each of these provisions, the articles of incorporation may alter this power of the directors.

[30] § 170(a)(1) DGCL.   [31] § 154 DGCL.   [32] § 154 DGCL.

[33] § 244(a)(4) DGCL.   [34] § 171 DGCL.   [35] § 170(a)(2) DGCL.

if there are no net profits for the current year, dividends may be paid out of net profits for the preceding fiscal year (referred to as "nimble dividends").[36] This test was applied by the court in a share repurchase case, *Klang* v. *Smith's Food & Drug Centers*, reprinted in part in the next chapter. If an illegal distribution is made, directors are held liable, although they are also subrogated into the rights of the corporation to collect the sums paid out from any shareholder who received them in knowing violation of law.[37]

Given that directors may change stated capital to create surplus and pay dividends (out of past profits) even if the company incurs losses during the current year, the Delaware rules cannot really be compared to the "capital maintenance" rules enacted under the Second Directive. Does this mean that US creditors remain unprotected? As said above, the power of the board to control distributions means that the same board can, in a loan covenant, promise a lender to restrict distributions. This contractual freedom is not available for German directors and in most cases is also not held by UK directors. The effectiveness of this contractual approach depends on the terms of the covenant, but would of course not apply to a tort victim or to the company's non-union employees who have no opportunity to bargain for protection. So far, the general culture in the US has accepted this situation.

The trend of US judicial decisions restricting distributions is to prevent companies from paying dividends if this would render the company insolvent. This is the statutory rule used in the Model Act,[38] and the common law rule employed in cases such as *Desert View Building Supplies* (in this chapter), both of which invalidate distributions to shareholders in a bankruptcy situation.[39]

Questions for discussion

1. What are the advantages and disadvantages of distributing and retaining profit?
2. How do the interests of shareholders and creditors differ with respect to distributions?
3. What forms can distributions take in practice?
4. Is the holding of the High Federal Court in *EM.TV* (below) compatible with article 15 of the Second Company Law Directive?

---

[36] § 170(a)(2) DGCL.   [37] § 174 DGCL.   [38] § 6.40(c)(1) Model Act.
[39] Baird (2006).

5. Who can declare dividends? How does this differ in our three jurisdictions?
6. What is the effect of covenants in loan agreements that restrict dividend payments?
7. How do European law on the one hand and US law on the other restrict the distribution of dividends?
8. What are the consequences of unlawful distributions?
9. Should distributions be limited by a company law capital maintenance regime, as in Europe, or primarily by contract or in the context of bankruptcy, as in the US?

Cases

In Re EM.TV
German High Federal Court, 2nd Civil Division
May 9, 2005; Doc. No. II ZR 287/02
[*Text of opinion edited and translated from German*]

Official head note

a) In a case in which the members of a stock corporation's management board incur personal liability pursuant to § 826 Civil Code for false ad hoc reports, the measure of damages is not restricted to the difference between the price paid for shares and the price that would have existed if all disclosures had been dutifully made (investor's differential damages); rather, an investor may demand restitution [*Naturalrestitution*] in the form of a reimbursement of the purchase price paid, in return for the purchased shares, or – if they have been sold in the mean time – by setting off the sales price received against such restitution amount (see 2nd Civil Div. decision of July 19, 2004 – II ZR 402/02, ZIP 2004, 1593; 1597 – to be published in BGHZ 160, 149).

b) By analogical application of § 31 Civil Code, a corporation is also jointly and severally liable to make restitution for illegal [*sittenwidrige*], intentional [*vorsätzliche*] damage inflicted by its management board through false ad hoc reports. Restitution as a form of compensation for damages is neither excluded nor limited by the special, corporate law creditor protection rules prohibiting a return of corporate contributions (§ 57 AktG) or prohibiting the repurchase of own shares (§ 71 AktG).

Facts

The Plaintiffs ... purchased shares of EM.TV AG (Defendant 1) between early March and December 1, 2000. Defendant 2 was the corporation's Management Board Chairman and Defendant 3 was the corporation's Management Board member for financial matters. On October 30, 1997, the day they were listed on the stock exchange, the shares of EM.TV were priced at €18.15 and climbed to approximately €116 by February 2000. However, they fell – with a few, temporary peaks along the way – to about €20.00 by November 2000, before falling to €10.00 on December 1, 2000 following EM.TV's release of a warning regarding its earnings. Plaintiffs seek damages from the Defendants under the theory that they purchased and refrained from selling EM.TV shares because of ad hoc reports and other information regarding the corporation's business operations that Defendants 2 and 3 released to the public knowing that it was false ...

[Text omitted]

We find merit in the arguments of those Plaintiffs we have permitted to appeal, and we hereby reverse the decisions below and remand the matter to the Court of Appeals for further proceedings consistent with this judgment.

Discussion of reasons

[Text omitted]

Based on the Court of Appeals' assumption that Plaintiffs were induced to purchase their shares by intentionally wrong and misleading ad hoc reports, the Plaintiffs' claims for damages pursuant to § 826 BG are not restricted to the difference between the price as inflated by the false disclosure and an appropriate, hypothetical price that would have existed if the disclosure had not been made; rather, as this court has decided after the Court of Appeals' judgment in the present case, the investors can demand restitution of the purchase price against return of the purchased shares or, if the shares have been sold in the mean time, such price offset by the lower sale price they received for their shares.

[Text omitted]

2. a) Joint and several liability for restitution also includes EM.TV. As a legal entity represented pursuant to its charter by a management board, when such board commits illegal, intentional damage (§ 826 Civil Code) and an intentional violation of a protective law (§ 823(2) Civil Code, § 400 AktG) through false ad hoc current reports, the corporation is vicariously liable by analogical application of § 31 Civil Code.

[Text omitted]

b) The restitution due under § 249 Civil Code as a senior claim for the compensation of damages is neither excluded nor limited by the special, corporate law creditor protection rules prohibiting a return of corporate contributions (§ 57 AktG) or prohibiting the repurchase of own shares (§ 71 AktG).

aa) However, in its earlier decisions, the Imperial Court at first found that stock corporations were not liable under §§ 823 *et seq.*, 31 Civil Code in cases in which its management board induced investors to purchase the company's shares through misrepresentation. The Court supported its holding with the argument that the principle of capital maintenance for the protection of third-party creditors of the company ranked higher than the general liability norms of the Civil Code (see RGZ

(Imperial Court Reporter) 54, 128, 132; RGZ 62, 29, 31; also see RGZ 72, 290, 293). Even so, in its is later decisions, the Court differentiated between various types of share purchases: both the general liability of an issuer under the Civil Code and prospectus liability pursuant to the Exchange Act were excluded only for those shareholders who purchased their shares either through subscription or by exercising a (primary) pre-emption right. A company remained liable under these norms in the case that the securities were purchased in a normal (derivative) sale and the shareholder's relationship to the company resembled that of an outside creditor (RGZ 71, 97 *et seq.*; 88, 271, 272). It is questionable whether the distinction employed – until today both in appellate court decisions (Frankfurt Court of Appeals, ZIP 1999, 1005, 1007 f.) and in leading scholarship (see Henze in GroßkommAktG 4th ed. § 57 mn. 18 *et seq.*; also in: NZG 2005, 115, with further references) – can still be applied to resolve the problematic competition between liability under capital market (prospectus) rules and the corporate law principle of capital maintenance (§ 57 AktG). This is particularly true in light of the unambiguous statements of the legislature that a corporation's capital market liability should be without limit (see regarding the secondary market: Parliamentary Doc. 12/7918 p. 102 – on § 15(6), sentence 2 of the Securities Trading Act, and also more recently §§ 37b, 37c Securities Trading Act; regarding the primary market: Par. Doc. on Draft Leg. 13/8933 p. 78, and §§ 44 *et seq.*, 47(2) Exchange Act). On the basis of this longstanding, majority position, the capital maintenance idea under § 57 AktG must, to the disadvantage of EM.TV, take second place, at least in the case at hand of an illegal, intentional damage pursuant to § 826 Civil Code and an intentional violation of § 400 AktG as a law meant to protect investors within the meaning of § 823(2) Civil Code. Because of the intentionally false ad hoc reports released by EM.TV's management board, the Plaintiffs acquired EM.TV shares through derivative transactions on the secondary market, and the acquisitions were in no way directly from EM.TV, but rather from a third-party market participant. The Plaintiffs' claim for compensation against the corporation for damages suffered because a violation of law does not primarily rest on their special legal status as shareholders, which first arose because of the illegal actions of the management board, but rather on their status as third-party creditors. The corporation's tort liability arises from a violation of legal disclosure requirements (§ 15 Securities Trading Act) that were imposed on it for the primary purpose of protecting the operation of the (secondary) capital market (see Steinhauer, *Insiderhandelsverbot und Ad-hoc- Publizität* 1999, p. 141 *et seq.*, and Schwark/Zimmer, KMRK 3rd ed. § 37b, § 37c WpHG mn. 12 with further citations). The corporate capital will be no more impaired by this type of liability for damages than it would be in the case of any other tort claim by an unrelated third party. Therefore, when the management board illegally induces investors to act in a certain way, principles of capital maintenance do not provide a reason to free the corporation of its obligation to compensate for damages or even to reduce such obligation to the limit of "free assets," i.e. assets exceeding legal capital and required reserves (see Schwark/Zimmer, cited supra, mn. 14 with further references, and Henze, NZG 2005, 109, 120 *et seq.*).

bb) It is also an invalid argument against restitution damages to say that in some cases this will lead to the corporation formally violating § 71 AktG by "acquiring" its own shares from the damaged Plaintiffs in return for restitution of their purchase price. Here as well, there is an overriding interest in placing investors – who have been injured by illegal or punishable action of a management board that is attributable to the company – as near as possible to a state in which damages are completely repaired (§ 249(1) Civil Code). This interest overrides the prohibition of share repurchases (see § 71(2), sentence 2 AktG), which serves the end of capital maintenance under § 57 AktG. The fact that the recommended form of compensation for damages may lead to a corporation acquiring its own shares is merely a peculiarity of restitution pursuant to capital markets law that companies must accept. Although the use of corporate capital arises because of the duty to return the investor's payment, the duty of the damaged party to return shares held against reimbursement by the responsible party, who took no part in the original purchase, rests above all on the principle that the damaged party should not gain an advantage from the damages (prohibition of enrichment). If the investors have already (re)sold the shares, the same reasoning leads to setting off the amount received from the purchase price when settling the damages. Considerations of valuation would also fail to justify a distinction between these two cases – because of § 71 AktG, damages would be awarded if the shares had been resold and they would not when the shares were still held. We so hold because, first, the "acquisition of own shares" arising only in the second variant is more or less accidental, and second, misled investors could at any time avoid such result by simply selling their shares. The same would apply if investors restricted their claims – as is permissible – to the alternative of differential damages. This is another reason why the principle of restitution of damages, to the extent that it may conflict with formal aspects of the prohibition against share repurchases (§ 71 AktG) must – in the context of damage settlements – take priority.

[*Text omitted*]

In Re Sam Weller & Sons Ltd
Chancery Division
[1990] Ch 682
Reproduced with permission of the Incorporated Council of Law Reporting for England and Wales

[*Text omitted*]

PETER GIBSON J

... This is an application to strike out a petition presented under section 459 of the Companies Act 1985.[40] It raises a question of some importance on the construction and scope of the section. The petitioners are James Weller and his sister Rosemary

---

[40] *Editors' note:* now sec. 994 CA 2006 ("Protection of members against unfair prejudice").

Sheppey, who are the registered owners of 2,450 and 450 shares respectively in the company. The applicants are some of the respondents to the petition, namely the company, Mr. Sam Weller and his sons Christopher and Anthony. Mr. Sam Weller is the uncle of the petitioners. He is the sole director of the company, holding 1,800 shares. Christopher and Anthony are employees of the company, each holding 1,350 shares.

There are four further holdings in the company. Mr. Sam Weller's sister, Miss E. H. Weller, who died on 24 May 1985, held 4,900 shares; a Mr. Green is the sole executor of her will. Each of the petitioners has become absolutely entitled to 1,225 of the shares in her estate. The trustees of the will of another deceased sister of Mr. Sam Weller, Mrs. Keighley, hold 2,900 shares; under the trusts of that will, upon the death of Miss E. H. Weller each of the petitioners became absolutely entitled to 725 of such shares. 2,700 shares are held by the trustees ("the Weller trustees") of the will of the late Sam Weller, the father of Mr. Sam Weller and the founder of the company. Upon the death of Miss E. H. Weller, under the trusts of that will, each of the petitioners has become absolutely entitled to 450 shares. Accordingly, the petitioners say that they hold or are beneficially interested in 7,700 of the 18,000 shares in the company.

The company was incorporated in 1947. Its principal business is the manufacture of textile cloths from cotton and synthetic yarns and the merchanting of jute and cotton textiles. The company's certified accounts for the calendar year 1985 show net assets of nearly £500,000 including £216,969 cash, and undistributed revenue profits of £464,623. The company's net profits for 1985 were £36,330, on which a dividend of 14 pence per share was paid, absorbing £2,520. In other words, the dividend was covered more than 14 times. The same dividend has been paid for at least 37 years.

The petition was presented on 21 January 1987. In it, the petitioners plead that in 1985 the company purchased at a cost of £22,400 a seaside flat at Abersoch in North Wales but that the company has no commercial interest requiring such a purchase, which was made to provide a holiday home for Anthony and Christopher. The petitioners further plead that by a letter dated 11 July 1986 Mr. Sam Weller's solicitors stated that registration would be declined if transfers of shares out of the estate of Miss E. H. Weller, or by Mrs. Keighley's trustees, or by the Weller trustees, in favour of either of the petitioners were to be presented for registration. But it is pleaded that there are no grounds on which Mr. Sam Weller, as the sole director of the company, could properly decline such registration. It is pleaded that in the same letter it was stated that, having regard to fluctuations in the textile trade, the uncertain future and the circumstances that the company faced, the sole director and management were not prepared to recommend any increase in dividend, but that it was also stated that capital expenditure of approximately £130,000 would be required during the then current year and the company could face difficult and uncertain trading conditions. It is also pleaded that on 8 October 1986 the petitioners' solicitors wrote to Mr. Sam Weller asking him to justify the capital expenditure in view of the company's uncertain future, and repeated an earlier request for a statement of the total emoluments of Mr. Sam Weller and Anthony and Christopher for 1985; but no such justification or statement has been supplied.

Paragraphs 18 and 19 of the petition are in this form:

> "18. The interests of the petitioners as members of the company and as beneficially entitled to part of the shares registered in the names of Miss E. H. Weller, Mrs. Keighley's trustees and the Weller trustees, have been and are unfairly prejudiced (a) by the payment on the insistence of Mr. Sam Weller of the same derisory dividend for many years past on the share capital of the company and his refusal to approve larger dividends; (b) by the purchase at the expense of the company of the said flat at Abersoch without commercial justification; (c) by the proposed capital expenditure by the company of £130,000 without any evidence that it will prove profitable; and (d) by the refusal of Mr. Sam Weller to register transfers of the shares of the company to which the petitioners are entitled in equity, or to disclose the emoluments of himself, Anthony and Christopher.
>
> "19. As sole director of the company Mr. Sam Weller is conducting its affairs for the exclusive benefit of himself, Anthony and Christopher and in breach of his duty to the other shareholders including the petitioners."

The relief the petitioners seek is the purchase by Mr. Weller, or some other purchaser to be procured by him, of the 7,700 shares of the petitioners at a value representing the appropriate proportion of the value of the whole of the issued share capital.

[Text omitted]

Mr. Spalding for the applicants accepted that the pleaded complaints in paragraph 18(b) and (d) should not be struck out, sub-paragraph (b) because the petition contained the allegation that the purchase of a holiday flat was to provide a holiday home for Anthony and Christopher and so, if that allegation is proved, that might be conduct unfairly prejudicial to the interests of the other shareholders, and sub-paragraph (d) because, in relation to the shares which Miss E. H. Weller owned at her death, the applicants relied on a provision in the articles of association of the company relating to shares held by an officer of the company, and there is a dispute of fact as to whether she was an officer of the company immediately before her death. Although there are references to other trust holdings in sub-paragraph (d), Mr. Spalding has not sought to dissect the various parts of that sub-paragraph and I say no more about it. But he submitted that the pleaded complaints in paragraph 18(a) and (c) were demurrable, primarily on the ground that they affected all members equally and so could not be conduct unfairly prejudicial to the interests of some part of the members, including at least the petitioners.

For that, Mr. Spalding relied on the recent decision of Harman J in In Re A Company (No. 00370 of 1987), Ex parte Glossop [1988] 1 WLR 1068, where a majority shareholder of a company which had very substantial accumulated profits sought to allege, by way of a proposed amendment to a section 459 petition, that the directors of the company had failed to give any, or any adequate consideration to the question of what proportion of the profits of the company should be distributed by way of dividend. It was accepted by the company that the payment of dividends was a part of the conduct of the affairs of a company and that it could be unfairly prejudicial to a member not to receive adequate dividends. But the company's arguments, to which Harman J acceded, were that since dividends are paid to all members holding shares an inadequate dividend could never be unfairly prejudicial only to some part of the members of a company, and that so far as the company is concerned, the declaration of a dividend must affect all members equally ...

[Text omitted]

The crucial question is whether conduct by a company which prima facie affects all the members equally, such as the payment of a dividend, can never be conduct unfairly prejudicial to the interests of some part of the members. Harman J recognised that some conduct, although affecting all members equally in one sense, could nevertheless be unfairly prejudicial to some members' interests. In In Re A Company (No. 002612 of 1984) [1985] BCLC 80, he held that a rights issue to all shareholders pari passu was capable of being unfairly prejudicial if it was known that some of the shareholders were unable to take up their rights; accordingly he refused to strike out a petition under section 459 of the Act. At the hearing of that petition, Vinelott J found as a fact that the rights issue was part of a scheme to reduce the petitioner's shareholding and that that was unfairly prejudicial to the interests of the petitioner ... On appeal, the Court of Appeal held that, on the facts as found, the proposed rights issue was clearly unfairly prejudicial to the petitioner's interests ... In the light of those decisions Harman J formulated his test that a section 459 petition could not be based on conduct which had an equal effect on all the shareholders and was not intended to be discriminatory between shareholders.

For my part, I doubt if any paraphrase of the test of section 459(1) adds to its clarity; and a paraphrase may well distort the natural meaning of the language of the subsection. With very great respect to Harman J, his test puts a gloss on the statutory wording whilst omitting reference to the important words "the interests of" in relation to "some part of the members," as well as "unfairly" in relation to "prejudicial." The word "interests" is wider than a term such as "rights," and its presence as part of the test of section 459(1) to my mind suggests that Parliament recognised that members may have different interests, even if their rights as members are the same. Further, the adverb "unfairly" introduces the wide concept of fairness in relation to the prejudice to the interests of some part of the members that must be established. Again, that reinforces the notion that it is possible that even if all the members are prejudiced by the conduct complained of, the interests of only some may be unfairly prejudiced.

Harman J's test is open to question in two other respects. First, by his reference to intentional discrimination, he appears to suggest that a subjective test of intention is applicable. To my mind, the wording of the section imports an objective test.

One simply looks to see whether the manner in which the affairs of the company have been conducted can be described as "unfairly prejudicial to the interests of some part of the members." That, as Mr. Instone submitted, requires an objective assessment of the quality of the conduct. Thus, conduct which is "unfairly prejudicial" to the petitioner's interests, even if not intended to be so, may nevertheless come within the section. That is supported by the remarks of Slade J in In Re Bovey Hotel Ventures Ltd ...:

> "The test of unfairness must, I think, be an objective, not a subjective, one. In other words it is not necessary for the petitioner to show that the persons who have had de facto control of the company have acted as they did in the conscious knowledge that this was unfair to the petitioner or that they were acting in bad faith; the test, I think, is whether a reasonable bystander observing the consequences of their conduct, would regard it as having unfairly prejudiced the petitioner's interests."

[Text omitted]

... the circumstances necessary for a section 459 petition under the Act of 1985, the section is not concerned with the consequences to the interests of those responsible for the unfairly prejudicial conduct but with the consequences to the interests of those who complain of the unfairly prejudicial conduct, and the question posed by the section, viz., are the affairs of the company being conducted in a manner unfairly prejudicial to the interests of some part of the members, including the petitioner, can be answered in the affirmative even if, qua members of the company, those responsible for the conduct complained of have suffered the same or even a greater prejudice.

[Text omitted]

To return to the facts alleged in the present case, here it is asserted by the petitioners that the sole director is conducting the affairs of the company for the exclusive benefit of himself and his family, and that while he and his sons are taking an income from the company, he is causing the company to pay inadequate dividends to the shareholders. The facts are striking because of the absence of any increase in the dividend for so many years and because of the amount of accumulated profits and the amount of cash in hand. I ask myself why the payment of low dividends in such circumstances is incapable of amounting to conduct unfairly prejudicial to the interests of those members, like the petitioners, who do not receive directors' fees or remuneration from the company. I am unable to see any sufficient reason. It may be in the interests of Mr. Sam Weller and his sons that larger dividends should not be paid out and that the major part of the profits of the company should be retained in order to enhance the capital value of their holdings. Their interests are not necessarily identical with those of other shareholders. It may well be in the interests of the other shareholders, including the petitioners, that a more immediate benefit should accrue to them in the form of larger dividends. As their only income from the company is by way of dividend, their interests may be not only prejudiced by the policy of low dividend payments, but unfairly prejudiced.

I do not intend to suggest that a shareholder who does not receive an income from the company except by way of dividend is always entitled to complain whenever the company is controlled by persons who do derive an income from the company and when profits are not fully distributed by way of dividend. I have no doubt that the court will view with great caution allegations of unfair prejudice on this ground. Nevertheless, concerned as I am with an application to strike out, I must be satisfied, if I am to accede to the application, that the allegations in the petition relating to the payment of dividends are incapable of amounting to unfair prejudice to the interests of some part of the members, including the petitioners. For the reasons that I have given, I cannot be so satisfied.

I confess that I am the happier to reach this conclusion when the only alternative is to petition on the same facts for the winding up of the company. It would seem to me deplorable if the only relief which the court could give, were the alleged facts proved, and were such relief sought on the petition, was the drastic remedy of a winding up order …

Finally, I turn to the allegation in paragraph 18(c) of the petition relating to the proposed capital expenditure of £130,000. Mr. Instone submitted that this allegation was linked to the allegation relating to dividends because such expenditure reduced the company's liquid resources which would have been available for the payment of dividends. Mr. [Spalding] … submitted that in any event this type of allegation could not found a section 459 petition, as otherwise the managerial decisions of a company could always be the subject of such a petition. I see the force of the latter point and I have no doubt that the court will ordinarily be very reluctant to accept that decisions of this kind could amount to unfairly prejudicial conduct. But because of the link between this allegation and the allegation relating to the payment of dividends, with some hesitation I have concluded that I should not strike it out.

It follows that I must dismiss this application.

Wells Fargo Bank v. Desert View Building Supplies, Inc.

US District Court for the District of Nevada
475 F Supp 693 (1978)
[*Text edited; footnotes omitted*]

FOLEY

This action centers around a transaction entered into between Prosher Corporation (Prosher), Desert View Building Supplies, Inc. (Desert View), the herein bankrupt, and Wells Fargo Bank (Wells Fargo). This case is presently before this Court on Wells Fargo's appeal from a decision of the bankruptcy court which found that the transaction was fraudulent as to the unsecured creditors of Desert View …

The findings of the bankruptcy court must be sustained unless found to be clearly erroneous …

In 1969, a Mr. Irving Waller owned all or substantially all of the corporate stock of Desert View. In that year, Waller sold his Desert View stock to Prosher in return for Prosher stock, thus making Desert View a wholly owned subsidiary of Prosher. At some point in time prior to November 13, 1975, the Desert View stock, as owned by Prosher, was pledged to Wells Fargo as collateral for a loan from Wells Fargo to Prosher. Subsequently, Prosher defaulted on its loan from Wells Fargo and, as part of a refinancing agreement, the Desert View stock, held as collateral by Wells Fargo, was returned to Prosher in exchange for an agreement by Desert View to take out a secured loan in the amount of $250,000. The proceeds of that loan went, first, to Prosher in the form of a dividend and, then, to Wells Fargo as partial payment of Prosher's debt. This entire transaction occurred on November 13, 1975. In connection with the refinancing agreement, Prosher transferred 100,000 shares of its stock to Wells Fargo.

The unaudited financial statement of Desert View as of December 31, 1974, indicated that Desert View had retained earnings of $280,000 and a total stockholders' equity of $386,000. Included as an asset of the December 31, 1974, statement was a $44,000 note receivable from Howard Homes which had been due or owing since 1972 or 1973 and concerning which payments had not been received since 1973. Also included on the December 31, 1974, statement was a $15,000 account receivable from Coronado Construction Company on which there had been no payment since mid-1974. All accounts were delinquent as of December 31, 1974.

As a result of the refinancing agreement between Prosher and Wells Fargo, Prosher's debt was reduced substantially, while Desert View's total liabilities were nearly doubled. The unaudited financial statement issued on December 31, 1975, reveals that Desert View was then running a retained earnings deficit of $47,929.00 with total stockholders' equity listed at $57,804 above solvency. This statement again counted as assets the Howard Homes note receivable and the Coronado Construction Company account receivable even though no payment had been received for over 18 months.

In February 1976, Waller regained ownership of Desert View. By mid-1976, total stockholder equity stood at $32,058. The company was undergoing serious cash flow problems with some $1,100 in cash on hand. The cash flow problems began in February 1976.On October 18, 1976, Desert View was clearly insolvent. A financial statement of that date revealed an equity deficit of Desert View in the amount of $212,029. The Howard Homes note and the Coronado Construction Company accounts receivable were not considered as assets on this statement.

On November 29, 1976, Wells Fargo issued a notice of acceleration pursuant to a provision contained in the loan agreement. On December 6, 1976, Desert View filed an original petition under Chapter XI of the Bankruptcy Act.

The bankruptcy court held the November 13, 1975, loan agreement was made without fair consideration to Desert View and as a result thereof Desert View was left with an unreasonably small capital after the transaction, all in violation of NRS

112.060, a provision of the Fraudulent Conveyance Act. NRS 112.060, which is incorporated into the Bankruptcy Act by Bankruptcy Act § 70(e), provides:

> "Every conveyance made without fair consideration when the person making it is engaged or is about to engage in a business or transaction for which the property remaining in his hands after the conveyance Is an unreasonably small capital is fraudulent as to creditors and as to other persons who become creditors during the continuance of such business or transaction without regard to his actual intent."

The primary intent of this statute is to prevent an under-capitalized company from being thrust into the market place to attract unwary creditors to inevitable loss while one or more preferred creditors are provided relative safety of a security interest in the company's assets.

The bankruptcy court did not err in finding that the $250,000 loan transaction was made without fair consideration ... In holding that the primary benefit of the loan transaction went to parties other than Desert View, the bankruptcy court stated:

> "However much Prosher might have been strengthened by the transaction, it is apparent that Desert View did not receive any concomitant benefit. Just the opposite, it was immediately released on its own with a debt which had taken it to the brink of insolvency without the superior assets of the parent company to aid it in sustaining the added economic burden brought about by that debt ...
> "Also, with regard to the fairness of consideration, there appears to be a question of a lack of good faith on the part of Wells Fargo Bank as the transferee. "Good faith,' in the fraudulent conveyance context, has generally been defined as carrying with it "the earmarks of an arms-length bargain.' (cases omitted) While there has been no conclusive showing of an actual intent to defraud other creditors, it is apparent that Wells Fargo Bank did use its influence with Desert View through Prosher to attain an enhanced position as a secured creditor. The lack of adequate consideration to Desert View, coupled with this undue influence, does constitute a failure by Wells Fargo Bank to operate in good faith toward the Debtor and its other creditors." (Bankruptcy court opinion, page 13.)

... Desert View was pushed toward bankruptcy by the added Wells Fargo liability.

The bankruptcy court did not err in finding that the $250,000 loan transaction left Desert View with an unreasonably small capital with which to operate its business.

The degree of corporate undercapitalization is a question of fact that must be ascertained on a case by case basis. The bankruptcy court found that Desert View was left with an unreasonably small capital with which to operate its business, relying on an analysis presented in *US v. 58th Street Plaza Theatre, Inc.*, 287 F Supp 475 (SDNY 1968). In Plaza Theatre, the Court looked to the probability, as of the date of transfer, that certain tax claims, then being judicially determined, would turn out to be valid, and thus voided a transfer which would have left the debtor with insufficient funds to pay those claims if they were approved.

Wells Fargo contends that Desert View was not inadequately capitalized because it was able to continue the operations of its business at the same yearly gross. Wells Fargo argues that Desert View did not incur difficulty in obtaining merchandise at a fair price, or of obtaining credit from its trade creditors. In rejecting these contentions, the bankruptcy court relied on the testimonies of a Mr. Robert Estee, a loan officer of Wells Fargo, and Irving Waller to the effect that the amount of cash which Desert View had on hand was "low" or "extremely low" for a business of its size. In examining the impact which the loan agreement had on Desert View's ability to operate its business, the bankruptcy court correctly noted the loan agreement took a company which, though marginal in its net income, had accumulated some $280,000 in retained earnings as of December 31, 1974, and placed it in a situation where it had little working capital at a time when it needed to expand its sales in order to repay a loan from which it derived little or no benefit.

As such, the decision of the bankruptcy court shall be affirmed.

8

Repurchases of shares

Required reading

EU: Second Company Law Directive, arts. 18–22, 24, 24a, 39; Buy-back Regulation, arts. 2–6
D: AktG, §§ 16, 17, 56, 57(1) no. 2, 71, 71b–71e, 291(3); GmbHG, § 33; HGB, § 272(1) nos. 4–6, (4)
UK: CA 2006, secs. 690–732; FSA Listing Rules, Rule 12
US: DGCL, § 160; Exchange Act § 9(a)(2); SEC Rule 10b-18

Rules on share repurchases

I. Introduction

This chapter builds on many of the issues discussed in our analysis of dividends and capital maintenance. When a company repurchases its shares, it transfers company assets (the purchase price) to the members from whom the shares are purchased. Thus, from a capital maintenance perspective, share repurchases are merely an alternative to the payment of dividends and should be subject to the same limitations. Creditor protection and capital maintenance are not, however, the only issues involved in share repurchases. Because shares, when accumulated in sufficient quantities, lend the capacity to control the company, the ability to purchase them is also the power to deal in corporate control. Also, because one of the ways that shares can be repurchased is "redemption," i.e. the repurchase of securities at the option of the holder or the issuer, as contractually agreed in advance between these parties, repurchase can sometimes be achieved without the voluntary consent of the seller. Thus, if the law did not regulate the repurchase of shares, a company's management could under some circumstances use share repurchases to usurp power for itself. That is why all of our jurisdictions regulate the corporate governance problems entailed in share repurchases even if they are unequal on the capital maintenance aspects. Beyond creditor protection and corporate governance, a company might repurchase its shares on the open markets to inflate (manipulate) its share price or exploit non-public information. Thus, both the EU and the US also have rules that restrict buy-back activity to those purchases unlikely to involve insider abuse or otherwise distort market prices. When looking at share repurchases, we thus address issues of capital maintenance, corporate governance and market regulation.

Below, we will first review the possible advantages and dangers of repurchases. We will then turn to the Second Company Law Directive's capital maintenance rules and the Market Abuse Directive's capital market rules. Next we will look at the German and UK laws and rules in light of this European framework. The US will be treated separately. Its corporate law rules on repurchases are essentially those applicable to other distributions, as the Delaware court observed in *Klang* v. *Smith's Food & Drug Centers*, reprinted in part in this chapter. The US rules against market manipulation are found in the Exchange Act and SEC rules and display marked similarities with the EU framework. To refresh your memory on "redeemable" shares, you may want to review the relevant discussion in Chapter 9.

II. The benefits and dangers of share repurchases

A. Advantages[1]

Like the payment of dividends, share repurchases transfer company assets to shareholders. They reduce the number of outstanding shares, and can thus improve both the earnings per share and the P/E ratios of the company, with resulting positive effects on the price of the company's shares. This can have especially positive effects on the share price in periods of significant fluctuation caused by short selling or negative media coverage. Option holders generally prefer declarations of repurchases rather than those of dividends for these reasons. For shareholders with lower tax rates on capital gains than on dividend income, repurchases also offer tax savings. In unlisted companies, repurchases offer a source of liquidity for shareholders otherwise unable to cash out of their holding. Similarly, in a merger, judicially monitored repurchases of the dissenting minority's shares (referred to as "appraisal rights" in the US) can both facilitate

---

[1] Ferran (2008: 203–208) presents a good summary of these policy arguments. For a detailed discussion of this issue in German, see Cahn (2007a: 767 *et seq.*).

execution of the transaction and provide the minority with a fairly priced exit.

B. Dangers

Like other distributions to shareholders, repurchases present dangers for the company's unsecured creditors because the company's assets available for repayment of debts are reduced. In contrast to dividends, however, repurchases can also reduce the number of available shareholders who could potentially be held liable for unpaid debts if the "corporate veil" were to be "pierced."[2]

As noted above, repurchases can also present governance dangers. If directors have authority to repurchase company shares through a delegation from the shareholders, a provision in the constitutional documents or even the law itself, they can use this power to entrench themselves against shareholders seeking to replace them.[3] If shares have a right of redemption exercisable at the option of the company, management can simply buy out the members holding those shares when it finds this convenient for economic or strategic reasons. Repurchases can also be used to compete with an unfriendly takeover offer (referred to as a "self-tender" in the US), which employs company assets to defeat an opportunity that could bring a premium to all shareholders. In addition, management can use selective repurchases to reward cooperative shareholders by repurchasing their shares.

A third danger of repurchases is, as mentioned above, that a company's management could conduct repurchases on the basis of inside information or use them to inflate the company's share price.

III. Repurchases of own shares under European law

A. Corporate law rules

The Second Company Law Directive as amended in 2006 allows a member state to completely forbid issuer repurchases, and subjects the disbursement of funds for the purchase to the same limits as those for other distributions, as discussed in Chapter 7.[4] It also requires that, where the shares are included among the assets shown in the balance sheet, a reserve of

---

[2] On the extraordinary decision to look beyond a limited company for payment of the latter's debts, see Chapter 23.

[3] See the technique management employed in the *Unocal* decision, reprinted in part in Chapter 13.

[4] That is, pursuant to art. 15 of the Directive, the purchase may not result in net assets being lower than the sum of subscribed capital and required reserves.

equal amount that is unavailable for distribution must be included among the liabilities.[5] In this way, the repurchase will not reduce the capital of the company available to secure its liabilities. Where a member state does permit repurchases, the directive provides that only fully paid-up shares may be purchased,[6] and that the required authorization of the general meeting must specify a maximum and minimum price and cannot have a duration exceeding five years.[7] The directive also provides that member states may impose a nominal value limit for the purchase of no less than 10 percent of the subscribed capital,[8] and may require that the acquisition not "prejudice the satisfaction of creditors' claims."[9]

These rules are significantly more favorable for repurchases than those found in the 1977 version of the Second Directive. Professor Eddy Wymeersch sums up the shift in attitude as follows: "When the directive was enacted buy-backs were frowned upon: they were analysed as a partial dissolution of the company ... [Now] share buy-backs belong to the standard paraphernalia of corporate finance, consisting of distributing excess cash to shareholders."[10] Thanks to the legislative power of the European Community, this change was commanded simultaneously in all twenty-seven EU member states rather than spreading out gradually from the individual jurisdictions more attuned to newer trends of corporate finance. The shift has not, however, altered the dangers of buy-backs for corporate governance; thus all voting rights attaching to repurchased shares remain suspended,[11] and companies must provide the reasons for and the details of repurchases in their annual reports.[12] The amended article 19 also expressly restates the principle that all shareholders must be treated equally and that the provisions of the Market Abuse Directive apply.

B.   Capital market rules

We discuss the insider trading rules of the Market Abuse Directive in Chapter 15. When an issuer repurchases its own shares, there is a high risk that nonpublic information is involved, and, because a company can neither vote nor receive dividends on its own shares, a primary motive

---

[5] Art. 22(1)(b) Second Company Law Directive.
[6] Art. 19(1)(c) Second Company Law Directive.
[7] Art. 19(1)(a) Second Company Law Directive.
[8] Art. 19(1)(c)(i) Second Company Law Directive. This limit includes "shares previously acquired by the company and held by it, and shares acquired by a person acting in his own name but on the company's behalf." See art. 19(1)(b) Second Company Law Directive.
[9] Art. 19(1)(c)(v) Second Company Law Directive.
[10] Wymeersch (2006).   [11] Art. 22(1)(a) Second Company Law Directive.
[12] Art. 22(2) Second Company Law Directive.

for the purchases could be to manipulate their market price. In order to avoid catching all such purchases under its prohibitions, article 8 of the Market Abuse Directive provides for a "safe harbor" to be created in a second-level regulation (the Buy-back Regulation was enacted in 2003) that should outline permitted "buy-back programs" and "stabilization" activities.[13]

The Buy-back Regulation restricts the permissible goals of buy-back programs to reducing capital or meeting obligations from employee stock option programs or outstanding convertible debt instruments.[14] Before beginning a buy-back program, a company must publish details of the shareholder approval of the program, the program's objective, the maximum consideration for the shares, the maximum number of shares to be acquired and the duration of the period for which authorization for the program has been given; it must also similarly publish the details of any subsequent changes to the program.[15] During the life of the program, the issuer must report all trades effected within it to the supervisory authorities,[16] and publicly disclose the same trades within seven days thereafter.[17]

The price, volume and timing of the buy-backs are also regulated. The price must not be higher than the "last independent trade and the highest current independent bid" for the securities,[18] and the volume must not – with some exceptions for inactive markets – exceed 25 percent of the average daily trading volume in the securities on the relevant, regulated market.[19] Unless the issuer is an investment firm with adequate confidentiality barriers in place, it may trade neither during a "closed period" designated by a member state (such as immediately before financial statements are released) nor when it is in the possession of inside information that it has decided not to disclose (such as negotiations whose disclosure could damage the value of a transaction for the company), and the issuer may never sell shares during an active program.[20] This prohibition can be overcome by eliminating the discretionary action that could be informed by such information, and thus "time-scheduled" programs – i.e. those

---

[13] Although an issuer may attempt to stabilize the price of its own securities through repurchases, the Regulation defines permitted "stabilization" as purchases or offers in the securities or associated derivative instruments undertaken by *investment firms or credit institutions* in the context of a public distribution, and thus does not address repurchases of securities." See art. 2(7) Buy-back Regulation.

[14] Art. 3 Buy-back Regulation.   [15] Art. 4(2) Buy-back Regulation.
[16] Art. 4(3) Buy-back Regulation.   [17] Art. 4(4) Buy-back Regulation.
[18] Art. 5(1) Buy-back Regulation.   [19] Art. 5(2), (3) Buy-back Regulation.
[20] Art. 6 Buy-back Regulation.

in which dates and quantities are set out and disclosed in advance, and programs run by financial institutions, independently of the issuer – are permitted even during closed periods and periods when the company has undisclosed inside information.[21]

IV.   Repurchases in our European jurisdictions

A.   Germany

An AG's direct and indirect repurchases of its own shares are regulated by §§ 71–71e of the *Aktiengesetz*. These provisions closely track the rules in the Second Directive before the 2006 amendments by specifying an exclusive list of circumstances in which repurchases are permitted. Article 19(1) (a) and (b) of the Directive are reflected in the possibility to conduct repurchases on the basis of an authorization (maximum duration five years) from the general meeting, with the maximum and minimum price being specified, and the requirement that shares purchased under the authorization not exceed 10 percent of capital – even if the actual holdings were to be less than that because of cancellation or resale of shares.[22] Since article 19(1) of the Directive provides an exhaustive list of conditions that may be imposed for an authorization to repurchase, and since quantitative limits are not part of that list, the 10 percent purchase limit of § 71(1) no. 8 AktG is probably in violation of the Directive and, therefore, void.[23] In addition to this 10 percent *purchase* limit, there is a 10 percent *holding* limit that applies for shares purchased pursuant to such an authorization.[24] This holding limit also applies to repurchases under the exceptions not requiring express shareholder authorization,[25] such as to prevent serious and imminent harm to the company,[26] for distribution to that company's employees, and to the employees of an associate company,[27] and to buy out minority shareholders through "appraisal rights."[28] As the latter limit applies to holdings, space in the cap for future transactions may be created by canceling or reselling shares.

Other permissible grounds taken directly from the Directive are reductions of capital[29] and universal transfers of assets.[30] Any repurchase must treat all shareholders equally, and the authorization must be given with a

---

[21] Art. 6(3) Buy-back Regulation.   [22] § 71(1) no. 8 AktG.

[23] Cahn (2007b: 385, 392 *et seq*.).   [24] § 71(2) AktG.   [25] § 71(2) AktG.

[26] § 71(1) no. 1 AktG. See Article 19(2) of the 1977 version of the Directive.

[27] § 71(1) no. 2 AktG. See art. 19(3) of the 1977 version of the Directive.

[28] § 71(1) no. 3 AktG. See art. 20(1)(d) of both the 1977 and the 2006 versions of the Directive.

[29] § 71(1) no. 6 AktG.   [30] § 71(1) no. 5 AktG.

simple majority of votes at the meeting.[31] Both purchases effected for the company through a third party[32] and the company's accepting pledges of its own securities[33] will be treated as repurchases and subjected to the applicable approval requirements. In any case, the company may repurchase only fully paid-up shares, which prevents the company from becoming its own creditor for outstanding contributions.[34] Shares acquired contrary to law must be disposed of within one year.[35] The *Aktiengesetz* is stricter than the Directive as it provides that *all rights* (i.e. not just voting rights) of the acquired shares are suspended.[36]

Prior to the 2009 amendments to the AktG and the HGB by the BilMoG, repurchased shares had to be shown as an asset on the corporation's balance sheet at their repurchase price and neutralized for accounting purposes by a restricted reserve of the same amount;[37] otherwise, the distributable profits would not be reduced by payment of the purchase price and the amount paid as a purchase price could be distributed a second time as a dividend. This accounting treatment has been fundamentally amended by the BilMoG: Under the new law, the nominal value of repurchased shares is deducted from the corporation's nominal capital and any excess of the purchase price reduces the reserves available for distributions; however, the company may not purchase shares for a purchase price exceeding these reserves. Upon a sale of the shares, this accounting treatment is reversed. The nominal capital is, again, increased by the nominal value of the shares. An excess of the proceeds over the nominal share value is used to replenish the distributable reserves by an amount equal to their reduction upon the purchase, while any remaining part of the proceeds is added to the capital reserve.[38] The somewhat surprising effect of these new rules is that by a combination of share repurchases and dividends an AG can distribute more to its shareholders than by either measure alone.[39]

---

[31] § 71(1) no. 8 AktG. See Cahn in Spindler and Stilz (2010: § 71 mn. 110).

[32] § 71d AktG.

[33] § 71e AktG. An exception allows credit institutions to receive their own securities as collateral in the ordinary course of business.

[34] § 71(2) AktG, implementing art. 19(1)(d) of the Directive.

[35] § 71e(1) AktG, following art. 21 Second Company Law Directive.

[36] § 71b AktG; compare art. 22(1)(a) Second Company Law Directive.

[37] § 72(2) AktG; § 272(4) HGB, implementing art. 22(1)(b) of the Directive.

[38] § 72(2) AktG; § 272(1)(a), (b) HGB.

[39] Think, for example, of an AG with free reserves of 20. By repurchasing shares with a nominal value of 10 for a purchase price of 20, it has made full use of statutory authorization,

B.   United Kingdom

The Companies Act 2006 has assembled all of the issues connected to a limited company purchasing its own shares in Part 18 of the Act, and these statutory rules have been amended by a statutory instrument to comply with the 2006 amendments to the Second Directive.[40] Further prohibitions or restrictions may be included in a company's articles.[41] As a general matter, a limited company may purchase its own shares only out of distributable profits or the proceeds of a fresh issue of shares made for this purpose,[42] and public companies must create a restricted reserve for any purchased shares shown on the balance sheet as an asset.[43] Any lien or charge of a public company on its own shares is void, except – as in Germany – when the company is a financial institution that receives the lien or charge in the ordinary course of business.[44] As required by the Directive, only fully paid-up shares may be repurchased.[45]

Authorization requirements for the purchases are bifurcated into market purchases and off-market purchases. A market purchase requires that an ordinary resolution grant a general or limited authority for the purchase of shares of a particular class, specifying the maximum number of shares that may be acquired and a maximum and minimum price for the acquisition.[46] The authority for an off-market purchase is somewhat stricter, requiring that shareholders be able to inspect and then approve the actual purchase contract by a special resolution (75 percent of votes cast, excluding those from the shares to be purchased), with the names of the shareholders whose shares will be purchased specifically disclosed.[47] The Companies Act 2006 sets the maximum term of the authorization for either type of purchase at eighteen months,[48] but this was extended

---

since the total purchase price may not exceed its reserves available for distribution. However, only half of the purchase price (10) is in fact deducted from these reserves while the other half is directly deducted from the corporation's capital. Thus, the corporation still has distributable reserves of 10 which it can subsequently pay to its shareholders as a dividend. Even though the company had only 20 that it could have paid as a dividend, it ends up distributing a total of 30 to its shareholders.

[40] See the Companies (Share Capital and Acquisition by Company of its Own Shares) Regulations 2009, SI 2009 No. 2022.

[41] Sec. 690(1) CA 2006.

[42] Sec. 692(2) CA 2006. Any premium on the purchase must be paid only out of distributable profits.

[43] Sec. 669(1) CA 2006.   [44] Sec. 670 CA 2006.

[45] Secs. 686(1), 691(1) CA 2006.   [46] Sec. 701 CA 2006.

[47] Secs. 694–696 CA 2006.   [48] Secs. 694(5), 701(5) CA 2006.

in 2009 to five years.[49] The right of a company to enter into an authorized transaction may not be assigned.[50] The Companies Act 2006 set the maximum volume of repurchased shares at 10 percent of the nominal value of the issued share capital of the shares of that class,[51] but this limit was repealed in 2009.[52] Companies must make detailed disclosures regarding repurchases to the companies registrar.[53]

A significant change in the Companies Act 2006 is a statutory allowance for "treasury shares," which were not previously permitted under UK law.[54] Under earlier law, reacquired shares had to be canceled. Now, shares that are traded on a regulated market may be held in treasury and resold,[55] which provides the company with significant flexibility, given that the resale of treasury shares is not an "allotment" requiring the relevant approval.[56] As discussed below, the FSA Listing Rules do, however, subject such sales to certain requirements. As in Germany, all rights attached to shares held by the company are suspended while they are in the company's treasury,[57] with the exception of the right to receive bonus shares if issued.[58]

For companies with a primary listing in the UK, Chapter 12 of the FSA Listing Rules addresses the capital market issues raised by repurchases, and follows the requirements of EC Regulation No. 2273/2003. However, the disclosure provisions of the FSA Listing Rules go beyond the Regulation by requiring publication of any proposal to the shareholders to request authorization to repurchase shares[59] – which means publication is required even before authorization is granted. The Rules also provide for disclosure on a graduated scale, requiring publication of the fact that repurchases have reached the 10 percent mark of any class of listed equity securities, and of every 5 percent increase thereafter.[60] Like US law (discussed below), the Rules make provision for the case that repurchasing activity crosses the line to become a self-tender for the company's securities, and provide that any purchase of 15 percent or more of any class of equity securities must be by way of a tender offer.[61] The

---

[49] Para. 4, Companies (Share Capital and Acquisition by Company of its Own Shares) Regulations 2009, SI 2009 No. 2022.

[50] Sec. 704 CA 2006.   [51] Sec. 725(2) CA 2006.

[52] Para. 5, Companies (Share Capital and Acquisition by Company of its Own Shares) Regulations 2009, SI 2009 No. 2022.

[53] Sec. 707 CA 2006.   [54] Davies (2008: 330).   [55] Sec. 727 CA 2006.

[56] See Davies (2008: 331–332); Ferran (2008: 220).

[57] Sec. 726(2) CA 2006.   [58] Sec. 726(4) CA 2006; Ferran (2008: 220).

[59] FSA Listing Rules, Rule 12.4.4(1).   [60] FSA Listing Rules, Rule 12.5.2.

[61] FSA Listing Rules, Rule 12.4.2.

Rules also prohibit sales of treasury shares within specified periods before the publication of accounts,[62] and require disclosure of any sale.[63] Thus, although the EU Regulation requires no implementation, the FSA Rules supplement the latter and provide detailed regulation of particular issues raised by national law.

V.   Repurchases in the United States

The US state laws do not provide any detailed set of requirements for the repurchase of own shares. Delaware law provides that "[e]very corporation may purchase, redeem, receive, take or otherwise acquire, own and hold, sell, lend, exchange, transfer or otherwise dispose of, pledge, use and otherwise deal in and with its own shares," provided the transaction does not impair capital pursuant to the test used for other distributions.[64] For an example of how the courts apply the capital impairment rules to repurchases, see *Klang* v. *Smith's Food & Drug Centers*, in this chapter. Shares that the company repurchases and holds (also referred to in Delaware as "treasury" shares)[65] are no longer considered "outstanding,"[66] and may be neither voted nor counted for quorum purposes.[67] The board – or the general meeting if the certificate of incorporation so provides – may resell treasury shares at a price they are free to decide.[68]

The federal securities law rules that apply to companies registered with the SEC are more detailed. First, an offer by the issuer to repurchase its shares is treated like an offer by a third party to do the same (i.e. a "tender offer"). The Exchange Act thus provides that it is unlawful for a registered issuer "to purchase any equity security issued by it if such purchase is in contravention of" SEC rules.[69] The applicable rules distinguish three types of transaction: self-tender offers,[70] which are subject to all the safeguards of ordinary tender offers; defensive purchases, in which the company buys its own shares responding to a third party tender offer;[71] and "going private transactions," in which the company repurchases its shares with the result of drastically reducing the number of shareholders or

---

[62] FSA Listing Rules, Rule 12.6.1.   [63] FSA Listing Rules, Rule 12.6.4.

[64] § 160(a) DGCL.

[65] The Model Act has eliminated the concept of "treasury shares," and now refers to own shares held by the company as authorized but unissued shares. See § 721(b) Model Act and accompanying Comment.

[66] § 160(d) DGCL.   [67] § 160(c) DGCL.   [68] § 153(c) DGCL.

[69] 15 USC § 78m(e)(1).   [70] 17 CFR § 240.13e-4.   [71] 17 CFR § 240.13e-1.

ending its listing on an exchange.[72] Very generally speaking, these rules require extensive disclosure to the SEC and the parties involved, punish any misrepresentations or omissions in such disclosures, and require equal treatment of shareholders. The US rules applicable to tender offers will be discussed in some detail in Chapters 24 and 25.

A second set of federal rules address the possibility of market manipulation, and resemble the rules of the EU Buy-back Regulation. Section 9 of the Exchange Act contains a general prohibition of trade-based market manipulation, i.e. trading in a security for the purpose of raising or depressing its price or inducing others to trade in it.[73] In other chapters of this text, we will see that Rule 10b-5 can be used to punish a large array of possible fraudulent actions. Similarly to the Buy-back Regulation, Rule 10b-18 under the Exchange Act provides a "safe harbor" to issuers who plan to repurchase their securities, so that compliance will ensure that they will not be found to have engaged in market manipulation or fraudulent behavior. The safe harbor, which the SEC moved to clarify and modernize in 2010,[74] requires that purchases must:

- be conducted through a single broker-dealer on a given day (this prevents hidden trades);
- not be at times when the market is sensitive (opening or closing) to price manipulation;
- not exceed the highest independent bid (this prevents leading prices upwards or downwards); and
- not exceed a volume of 25 percent of the average daily trading volume in the security.[75]

It might be said that the US rules on repurchases focus on protecting equity investors and neglect creditor protection. Thin capital maintenance rules address repurchases from the corporate law side and capital market rules focus on protecting market investors rather than creditors. On the other hand, as we discussed in the preceding chapter, it has been argued that the rules on creditor protection are evolving from a static "security deposit" paradigm toward an interactive "disclosure and negotiated protection" model. Comparing the overall balance of the EU and US frameworks, which do you think presents the most successful regulatory regime?

---

[72] 17 CFR § 240.13e-3.   [73] 15 USC § 78i(a)(2).

[74] See Proposed Rule: Purchases of Certain Equity Securities by the Issuer and Others, SEC Release No. 34–61414, 75 *Federal Register* 4713 (January 29, 2010). The fate of this proposed rule had not been determined when this manuscript went to press.

[75] 17 CFR § 240.10b-18(b).

Cases

Review *Re EM.TV* (in Chapter 7).

Klang v. Smith's Food & Drug Centers, Inc.
Supreme Court of Delaware
702 A 2d 150 (1997)
  [*Text edited, footnotes omitted*]

VEASEY, Chief Justice

[*Text omitted*]

Facts

Smith's Food & Drug Centers, Inc. ("SFD") is a Delaware corporation that owns and operates a chain of supermarkets in the Southwestern United States. Slightly more than three years ago, Jeffrey P. Smith, SFD's Chief Executive Officer, began to entertain suitors with an interest in acquiring SFD. At the time, and until the transactions at issue, Mr. Smith and his family held common and preferred stock constituting 62.1% voting control of SFD. Plaintiff and the class he purports to represent are holders of common stock in SFD.

On January 29, 1996, SFD entered into an agreement with The Yucaipa Companies ("Yucaipa"), a California partnership also active in the supermarket industry. Under the agreement, the following would take place:

(1) Smitty's Supermarkets, Inc. ("Smitty's"), a wholly owned subsidiary of Yucaipa that operated a supermarket chain in Arizona, was to merge into Cactus Acquisition, Inc. ("Cactus"), a subsidiary of SFD, in exchange for which SFD would deliver to Yucaipa slightly over 3 million newly issued shares of SFD common stock;

(2) SFD was to undertake a recapitalization, in the course of which SFD would assume a sizable amount of new debt, retire old debt, and offer to repurchase up to fifty percent of its outstanding shares (other than those issued to Yucaipa) for $36 per share; and

(3) SFD was to repurchase 3 million shares of preferred stock from Jeffrey Smith and his family.

SFD hired the investment firm of Houlihan Lokey Howard & Zukin ("Houlihan") to examine the transactions and render a solvency opinion. Houlihan eventually issued a report to the SFD Board replete with assurances that the transactions would not endanger SFD's solvency, and would not impair SFD's capital in violation of 8 Del. C. § 160. On May 17, 1996, in reliance on the Houlihan opinion, SFD's Board determined that there existed sufficient surplus to consummate the transactions, and enacted a resolution proclaiming as much. On May 23, 1996, SFD's stockholders voted to approve the transactions, which closed on that day. The self-tender offer was over-subscribed, so SFD repurchased fully fifty percent of its shares at the offering price of $36 per share.

[*Text omitted*]

Plaintiff's capital-impairment claim

A corporation may not repurchase its shares if, in so doing, it would cause an impairment of capital, unless expressly authorized by Section 160. A repurchase impairs capital if the funds used in the repurchase exceed the amount of the corporation's "surplus," defined by 8 Del. C. § 154 to mean the excess of net assets over the par value of the corporation's issued stock.

Plaintiff asked the Court of Chancery to rescind the transactions in question as violative of Section 160. As we understand it, plaintiff's position breaks down into two analytically distinct arguments. First, he contends that SFD's balance sheets constitute conclusive evidence of capital impairment. He argues that the negative net worth that appeared on SFD's books following the repurchase compels us to find a violation of Section 160. Second, he suggests that even allowing the Board to "go behind the balance sheet" to calculate surplus does not save the transactions from violating Section 160. In connection with this claim, he attacks the SFD Board's off-balance-sheet method of calculating surplus on the theory that it does not adequately take into account all of SFD's assets and liabilities. Moreover, he argues that the May 17, 1996 resolution of the SFD Board conclusively refutes the Board's claim that revaluing the corporation's assets gives rise to the required surplus. We hold that each of these claims is without merit.

SFD's balance sheets do not establish a violation of 8 Del. C. § 160

In an April 25, 1996 proxy statement, the SFD Board released a pro forma balance sheet showing that the merger and self-tender offer would result in a deficit to surplus on SFD's books of more than $100 million. A balance sheet the SFD Board issued shortly after the transactions confirmed this result. Plaintiff asks us to adopt an interpretation of 8 Del. C. § 160 whereby balance-sheet net worth is controlling for purposes of determining compliance with the statute. Defendants do not dispute that SFD's books showed a negative net worth in the wake of its transactions with Yucaipa, but argue that corporations should have the presumptive right to revalue assets and liabilities to comply with Section 160.

Plaintiff advances an erroneous interpretation of Section 160. We understand that the books of a corporation do not necessarily reflect the current values of its assets and liabilities. Among other factors, unrealized appreciation or depreciation can render book numbers inaccurate. It is unrealistic to hold that a corporation is bound by its balance sheets for purposes of determining compliance with Section 160 ...

It is helpful to recall the purpose behind Section 160. The General Assembly enacted the statute to prevent boards from draining corporations of assets to the detriment of creditors and the long-term health of the corporation. That a corporation has not yet realized or reflected on its balance sheet the appreciation of assets is irrelevant to this concern. Regardless of what a balance sheet that has not been updated may show, an actual, though unrealized, appreciation reflects real economic value that the corporation may borrow against or that creditors may claim or levy upon. Allowing corporations to revalue assets and liabilities to reflect current realities complies with the statute and serves well the policies behind this statute.

The SFD Board appropriately revalued corporate assets to comply with 8 Del. C. § 160.

Plaintiff contends that SFD's repurchase of shares violated Section 160 even without regard to the corporation's balance sheets. Plaintiff claims that the SFD Board was not entitled to rely on the solvency opinion of Houlihan, which showed that the transactions would not impair SFD's capital given a revaluation of corporate assets. The argument is that the methods that underlay the solvency opinion were inappropriate as a matter of law because they failed to take into account all of SFD's assets and liabilities. In addition, plaintiff suggests that the SFD Board's resolution of May 17, 1996 itself shows that the transactions impaired SFD's capital, and that therefore we must find a violation of 8 Del. C. § 160. We disagree, and hold that the SFD Board revalued the corporate assets under appropriate methods. Therefore the self-tender offer complied with Section 160, notwithstanding errors that took place in the drafting of the resolution.

On May 17, 1996, Houlihan released its solvency opinion to the SFD Board, expressing its judgment that the merger and self-tender offer would not impair SFD's capital. Houlihan reached this conclusion by comparing SFD's "Total Invested Capital" of $1.8 billion – a figure Houlihan arrived at by valuing SFD's assets under the "market multiple" approach – with SFD's long-term debt of $1.46 billion. This comparison yielded an approximation of SFD's "concluded equity value" equal to $346 million, a figure clearly in excess of the outstanding par value of SFD's stock. Thus, Houlihan concluded, the transactions would not violate 8 Del. C. § 160.

Plaintiff contends that Houlihan's analysis relied on inappropriate methods to mask a violation of Section 160. Noting that 8 Del. C. § 154 defines "net assets" as "the amount by which total assets exceed total liabilities," plaintiff argues that Houlihan's analysis is erroneous as a matter of law because of its failure to calculate "total assets" and "total liabilities" as separate variables. In a related argument, plaintiff claims that the analysis failed to take into account all of SFD's liabilities, i.e. that Houlihan neglected to consider current liabilities in its comparison of SFD's "Total Invested Capital" and long-term debt. Plaintiff contends that the SFD Board's resolution proves that adding current liabilities into the mix shows a violation of Section 160. The resolution declared the value of SFD's assets to be $1.8 billion, and stated that its "total liabilities" would not exceed $1.46 billion after the transactions with Yucaipa. As noted, the $1.46 billion figure described only the value of SFD's long-term debt. Adding in SFD's $372 million in current liabilities, plaintiff argues, shows that the transactions impaired SFD's capital.

We believe that plaintiff reads too much into Section 154. The statute simply defines "net assets" in the course of defining "surplus." It does not mandate a "facts and figures balancing of assets and liabilities" to determine by what amount, if any, total assets exceed total liabilities. The statute is merely definitional. It does not require any particular method of calculating surplus, but simply prescribes factors that any such calculation must include. Although courts may not determine compliance with Section 160 except by methods that fully take into account the assets and liabilities of the corporation, Houlihan's methods were not erroneous as a matter of law simply because they used Total Invested Capital and long-term debt as analytical categories rather than "total assets" and "total liabilities."

We are satisfied that the Houlihan opinion adequately took into account all of SFD's assets and liabilities. Plaintiff points out that the $1.46 billion figure that approximated SFD's long-term debt failed to include $372 million in current liabilities, and argues that including the latter in the calculations dissipates the surplus. In fact, plaintiff has misunderstood Houlihan's methods. The record shows that Houlihan's calculation of SFD's Total Invested Capital is already net of current liabilities. Thus, subtracting long-term debt from Total Invested Capital does, in fact, yield an accurate measure of a corporation's net assets.

The record contains, in the form of the Houlihan opinion, substantial evidence that the transactions complied with Section 160. Plaintiff has provided no reason to distrust Houlihan's analysis. In cases alleging impairment of capital under Section 160, the trial court may defer to the board's measurement of surplus unless a plaintiff can show that the directors "failed to fulfill their duty to evaluate the assets on the basis of acceptable data and by standards which they are entitled to believe reasonably reflect present values." In the absence of bad faith or fraud on the part of the board, courts will not "substitute [our] concepts of wisdom for that of the directors." Here, plaintiff does not argue that the SFD Board acted in bad faith. Nor has he met his burden of showing that the methods and data that underlay the board's analysis are unreliable or that its determination of surplus is so far off the mark as to constitute actual or constructive fraud. Therefore, we defer to the board's determination of surplus, and hold that SFD's self-tender offer did not violate 8 Del. C. § 160.

On a final note, we hold that the SFD Board's resolution of May 17, 1996 has no bearing on whether the transactions conformed to Section 160. The record shows that the SFD Board committed a serious error in drafting the resolution: the resolution states that, following the transactions, SFD's "total liabilities" would be no more than $1.46 billion. In fact, that figure reflects only the value of SFD's long-term debt. Although the SFD Board was guilty of sloppy work, and did not follow good corporate practices, it does not follow that Section 160 was violated. The statute requires only that there exist a surplus after a repurchase, not that the board memorialize the surplus in a resolution. The statute carves out a class of transactions that directors have no authority to execute, but does not, in fact, require *any* affirmative act on the part of the board. The SFD repurchase would be valid in the absence of any board resolution. A mistake in documenting the surplus will not negate the substance of the action, which complies with the statutory scheme.

Plaintiff's disclosure claims

When seeking stockholder action, directors must disclose all material reasonably available facts. A material fact is one that a reasonable stockholder would find relevant in deciding how to vote. It is not necessary that a fact would change how a stockholder would vote. It is necessary only that it "would have been viewed by the reasonable investor as having significantly altered the 'total mix' of information available." Directors must also disclose facts that, standing alone, may not be material if their omission in light of other facts disclosed would cause stockholders to be misled.

Plaintiff advances four nondisclosure claims against the SFD Board. He argues that the SFD directors violated their fiduciary duty of candor by failing to disclose: (1) "equity valuations" that Houlihan used in rendering its solvency opinion, (2) the amount of SFD's pre- and post-transaction surplus, (3) the decision of the SFD Board to alter the financing of the merger and self-tender by eliminating $75 million in newly issued preferred stock and providing for an additional $75 million in debt, and (4) the manner in which defendants arrived at the $36 per share self-tender price.

Whether a board's disclosures to stockholders are adequate is a mixed question of law and fact, "requiring an assessment of the inferences a reasonable shareholder would draw and the significance of those inferences to the individual shareholders." If the trial court's findings "are sufficiently supported by the record and are the product of an orderly and logical deductive process ... we will accept them, even though independently we might have reached opposite conclusions."

Houlihan's equity valuations were not material

An "equity valuation" is an accounting, rather than a legal or economic, concept. Houlihan derived equity valuations of SFD in the course of rendering its solvency opinion. Plaintiff contends that the SFD Board should have disclosed the equity valuations prior to obtaining stockholder approval of the merger and self-tender offer. Plaintiff claims that Houlihan's equity valuations were material as indicators of SFD's "economic" or "intrinsic" value. At the same time, plaintiff acknowledges that Houlihan did not intend its equity valuations to serve as predictors of the market price of SFD shares, and that defendants neither accepted them as such, nor used the equity valuations to derive the price for the self-tender offer.

In *Barkan* and again in *Citron* v. *Fairchild Camera & Instrument*, we expressed our reluctance to force disclosure of data generated solely for accounting purposes. In *Barkan*, we held that an estimate of a corporation's "liquidation value" prepared as part of a capital-impairment test was not material. Similarly, in *Citron* we held that valuation estimates "prepared primarily for accounting purposes rather than for establishing the fair market value of [the corporation's] share" were immaterial. The holding in both cases was premised upon the sentiment that figures generated for purely accounting purposes are useless predictors of market value, and are at least as likely to mislead stockholders as to enlighten them. In light of *Barkan* and *Citron*, we defer to the finding of the Court of Chancery that Houlihan's equity valuations would not alter the "total mix" of information available to SFD's stockholders.

The amount of pre- and post-transaction surplus was not material

For similar reasons, we hold that the SFD Board was not obliged to disclose the amount of pre- and post-transaction surplus. Surplus is a statutory construct that bears no necessary relation to the financial health of a corporation. And as in *Barkan* and *Citron*, we are skeptical that the exact amount of surplus would have been relevant to the average SFD stockholder in deciding how to vote on the merger and self-tender offer.

... A corporation should not have to disclose that its transactions are not in violation of 8 Del. C. § 160. Most reasonable stockholders would assume that corporations do not knowingly violate the Delaware General Corporation Law. Thus, it would add nothing to the total mix of information for a corporation to proclaim, "what we are doing right now is legal."

Accordingly, we hold that calculating surplus prior to executing a repurchase triggers no disclosure obligations on the part of the board.

The substitution of $75 million of debt for $75 million of preferred stock was not material.

SFD's proxy statement of April 25, 1996 stated that the SFD Board "anticipated" financing a $575 million portion of the transactions with Yucaipa by issuing $500 million in notes and $75 million in preferred stock. This method of financing changed prior to the vote of SFD stockholders. The change eliminated the $75 million in preferred stock and tacked on an additional $75 million in debt. Plaintiff argues the SFD Board should have disclosed this change prior to the stockholder vote.

The importance of this change in financing is subject to varying interpretations. The record shows that the adjustment of the financial package resulted in a mere 0.2% increase in SFD's total liabilities. On the other hand, plaintiff is able to massage the numbers to present a somewhat different picture. The additional debt load, plaintiff points out, amounts to a full $5 per share. Meanwhile, long-term debt and interest expense climb 6% and 7%, respectively, as a result of the change in financing. In light of this conflicting evidence on materiality, we defer to the finding of the Court of Chancery that the alteration of the financing package was not material.

The SFD board adequately disclosed the source of the self-tender offer

The SFD proxy statement stated that Yucaipa proposed the $36 per-share price used in the self-tender offer. Plaintiff argues that this constituted inadequate disclosure of how the board arrived at the price, in light of evidence suggesting alternative sources. For instance, the record contains the testimony of one of SFD's outside directors that the tender-offer price derived from a Goldman, Sachs valuation of SFD, rather than simply from Yucaipa's suggestion. On the other hand, the record is replete with testimony that the price was Yucaipa's and not Goldman's.

The Court of Chancery made a judgment that the SFD Board made adequate disclosure. We have deferred to the trial court's finding that the tender-offer price was proposed by Yucaipa and not SFD's investment bankers. Accordingly, we affirm the Court of Chancery's dismissal of this claim, as plaintiff has offered no evidence that the SFD Board's disclosure of that fact is inadequate.

[Text omitted]

9

The nature of shares and classes of shares

Required reading

D: AktG, §§ 11, 23(2), 139–141, 179(3), 182(2), 202(2), 221 sentence 4, 222(2)
UK: CA 2006, secs. 629–640
US: DGCL, §§ 102(b)(3), 151, 221; Model Act, §§ 1.40(13A), (22), 6.01, 6.02, 6.30

The types of rights embodied in shares

Investor ownership is an essential characteristic of the stock corporation. The investing members own the corporation through securities called "shares" (*Aktien*). As we see from the topics covered in this text, much of company law has to do with the exercise of rights embodied in these "shares." In this chapter, we will take a closer look at shares and the rights they embody, but, instead of focusing on the exercise and protection of these rights under company law, we will look at their origin in the share of stock and how the rights can be arranged differently in different classes of shares. The type of interest embodied in shares is a property interest, so we will begin with the basic nature of this interest in relation to the company and its assets.

I. Shareholders own the corporation, not its assets

Nobel laureate Milton Friedman was once chided for referring to shareholders as the "owners" of corporations, and his critic explained: "A lawyer would know that the shareholders do not, in fact, own the corporation. Rather, they own a type of corporate security commonly called 'stock.' As owners of stock, shareholders' rights are quite limited. For example, stockholders do not have the right to exercise control over the corporation's assets."[1] This critique equates owning a corporation with owning

---

[1] Stout (2002: 1191).

its assets, which would disregard the separate corporate personality, an essential characteristic of the stock corporation. The mistake is made often. Here is another example:

> A share of stock does not confer ownership of the *underlying assets owned by the corporation* ... Shareholders have no more claim to intrinsic ownership and control of the *corporation's assets* than do other stakeholders ... The rights we choose to confer on shareholders ... cannot be justified on the basis of their intrinsic right as the "owners" to control the corporation.[2]

To avoid the confusion expressed in the above quotations, one must remember that the separate corporate entity has its own assets and liabilities. The shareholders are separate persons and, from their status as shareholders, have no relationship to the company's property and debts; instead, they own the corporate entity itself. Davies expresses this very well in a reference to Farwell J's classic definition of a share of stock in *Borland's Trustee* v. *Steel Brothers & Co.*:[3]

> The company itself is treated not merely as a person, the subject of rights and duties, but also as a *res*, the object of rights and duties. It is the fact that the shareholder has rights in the company as well as against it, which, in legal theory, distinguishes the member from the debenture-holder whose rights are also defined by contract ... but are rights against the company and, if the debenture is secured, in its property, but never in the company itself.[4]

To keep the property interests straight, one should remember that there are three levels of proprietary interests: (1) a person owns a share and in this way becomes a share-*holder*; (2) the share is a negotiable instrument that embodies certain property rights in the company; and (3) the company owns the corporate assets. It is also useful to focus on the legal relationships rather than be distracted by the picture of thousands of shareholders buying and selling these negotiable shares on a daily basis, for this picture conflicts with our notion of what the property owner should be. The following observation exemplifies this: "[T]he ownership of a share of stock in a public company is simply not analogous to the ownership of a car or a building ... A share of stock is a financial instrument, more akin to a bond than to a car or a building ... The owner of the building ... is an individual ... in a position to have full knowledge ... [and who] generally views the property or business as a complete entity ... In contrast, the

---

[2] Lipton and Rosenblum (2003: 72–73) (emphasis added).
[3] [1901] 1 Ch 279, 288.   [4] Davies (2008: 817).

shareholder of the large public corporation is one of a far-flung, diverse, and ever-changing group."[5] Shareholders are indeed a collective, a mass in continuous change, with their property interests expressed by negotiable instruments that are readily transferable. From the perspective of commercial law, shares of stock are doubtless "akin" to bonds.[6] It is also quite certain that shareholders do not own a company in the same way that someone owns a car or a building. How, then, do shareholders own companies?

II.   *The nature of a shareholder's property interest*[7]

Shareholders have statutory rights specified in the applicable corporate law statute. Shareholders also have contract rights against the company and each other as expressed in the articles of association, *Satzung*, articles of incorporation, by-laws or other constitutional document.[8] Beyond these statutory and contract rights, and sometimes overlapping with them, shareholders have property rights in the company.

As this point is less than clear for many, a few words on property will be helpful. What we call "property" can be understood as various types of "bundles" of different kinds of rights, with variations in the bundle constituting different kinds of interests.[9] The property rights we have in a patent, which are shaped by policies aiming to promote technological development, differ from the property rights we have in a house pet, which are shaped by other concerns. Ownership can be absolute, restricted in time, joint or common, among other constellations. In the list assembled by A. M. Honoré, property rights include not only the more intuitively appealing rights to "use," "manage" and "exclude," but also "the right to the income of the thing, the right to the capital, the right to security ... the rights or incidents of transmissibility and absence of term ... and the incident of residuarity."[10] The incident of "residuarity" is perhaps the best known of the bundle in contemporary corporate law: "Equity investors are paid last, after debt investors, employees, and other investors with

---

[5] Lipton and Rosenblum (2003: 72–73).
[6] For the UK, see Goode (2004: 477); for Germany, see Hueck and Canaris (1986: 20); for the US, see Guttman (2007: § 1:1).
[7] Material in this section is adapted from "Shareholder Voice and Its Opponents," *Journal of Corporate Law Studies* (2005) 5: 305–361. We are grateful to Hart Publishing for permission to use this material.
[8] See e.g. Davies (2008: 65–76); Ferran (2008: 158–161).
[9] Bell and Parchomovsky (2005a: 587–588). Also see Merrill (2000: 899). For discussion of problems with and challenges to the "bundle" theory, see Mossoff (2003: 372–376).
[10] Honoré (1961: 107, 113); also see Bell and Parchomovsky (2005a: 545).

(relatively) 'fixed' claims. These equity investors have the 'residual' claim in the sense that they get only what is left over – but they get all of what is left over."[11] Indeed, shares of stock embody a *pro rata* right to the residual assets of a corporation upon dissolution.[12] However, "residuarity" has more than a temporal (i.e. last in line) meaning: it can also mean that which remains in reserve behind the expressly defined rights, such as the subterranean mineral rights to a summer cottage rental that would remain with the owner if not mentioned in the lease. As Armour and the late Professor Michael Whincop note: "'Residual' implies that the rights to control over all states of the world which are not specified by law or contract *ex ante*. Residuarity matters because it is still possible to allocate *residual* rights even if specific directions about what should (not) be done in particular circumstances cannot be written or enforced."[13] This type of residual remains with the shareholder in a stock corporation in addition to those set out in the statute and in case law.

The types of property interests embodied in shares fit the nature of the stock corporation. If the terms of issue or constitutional documents do not provide otherwise, shares in a stock corporation are without term. US corporate statutes provide shareholders with (rarely used) residual control over a corporation that can in some jurisdictions be near absolute, as management may be taken away from the board of directors in the corporate charter.[14] Through their control over the articles, UK shareholders have extensive control over the shape of the company's management. In each of Germany, the US and the UK, shareholders have control through the right to elect or remove directors,[15] as well as the right to veto a merger[16] or the sale of corporate assets to a third party.[17] In addition to the right to receive capital as a residual claimant at dissolution, shareholders also have a statutorily recognized right to receive income in the form of dividends,[18] and such distributions cannot be invalidated by creditors if they comply with the statutory capital maintenance rules. Shareholders also have the right to exclude directors, third parties, and other shareholders from their property through various types of judicial remedies under

[11] Easterbrook and Fischel (1996: 11); also see Goode (2004: 477).
[12] See e.g. §§ 275 and 281 DGCL; § 14.01(5) Model Act; Ferran (2008: 53).
[13] Armour and Whincop (2005: 6).   [14] § 141(a) DGCL; § 7.32(a) Model Act.
[15] §§ 211(b), 141(k) DGCL; and §§ 8.03(c), 8.08(a) Model Act.
[16] § 251(c) DGCL; § 11.04(b) Model Act.
[17] See e.g. § 271(a) DGCL; § 12.02 Model Act.
[18] See e.g. §§ 170, 154 DGCL; § 6.40 Model Act; Ferran (2008: 149–150); § 119(1) no. 2 AktG.

corporate law statutes, such as actions against management for breach of statutory or common law fiduciary duties, including self-dealing, waste of corporate assets, dilution of their *pro rata* interest through the issuance of stock below par value, or a failure of any stockholder to pay the subscription price.[19] Unlike a contract right, ownership will "run with the assets," which is a primary characteristic that separates a property from a contract right.[20] This can be seen, for example, in a shareholder's action for recovery of a corporation's property at liquidation if such assets are improperly transferred to a third party, including the holders of a different class of shares.[21]

In spite of shares evidencing the property rights listed in the above paragraph, the nature of shares as property interests are still disputed by some. Perhaps the intangible nature of the share of stock adds to the confusion about its nature, as does the further confusion between a share of stock and the certificate that will evidence it if the share is "certificated." In the US and UK, shares are a type of interest referred to as a "chose in action."[22] A "chose in action is a known legal expression used to describe all personal rights of property which can only be claimed or enforced by action and not by taking physical possession."[23] The Delaware Court of Chancery has explained that "[a] certificate of stock is evidence of ownership, in the nature of a chose in action."[24] The stock certificate is *evidence* of the share of ownership, which itself is not tangible, and thus the share, quota or portion of the corporation owned by the shareholder cannot be taken into possession the way the certificate that evidences it can be. Thus, it has the name "chose" (thing) in "action," as opposed to thing in possession. Thus, to understand the share of stock, we should focus on the incorporeal thing, and be distracted neither by the certificate nor by the fact that the certificate might be held through a broker or other financial institution. The latter only affects how the rights in the share can be exercised, not the rights themselves.

---

[19] See e.g. sec. 580 CA 2006; § 327 DGCL; § 7.40 Model Act; § 9 AktG.
[20] "For our purposes, the attribute that distinguishes a property right from a contract right is that a property right is enforceable, not just against the original grantor of the right, but also against other persons to whom possession of the asset, or other rights in the asset, are subsequently transferred. In the parlance of property law, the burden of a property right "runs with the asset." Hansmann and Kraakman (2002: 378–379).
[21] See e.g. *Mohawk Carpet Mills, Inc. v. Delaware Rayon Co.*, 110 A 2d 305 (Del. Ch. 1954).
[22] Morse (2003: 2.006).
[23] Vaines (1962: 221), citing Channel J in *Torkington* v. *Magee* [1902] 2 KB 247, 430.
[24] *Equitable Trust Co.* v. *Gallagher*, 67 A 2d 50, 54 (Del. Ch. 1949).

The *shared* and *limited* nature of the interests embodied in shares also make the property interests seem less like our intuitive picture of the owner. However, this *pro rata* and *cooperative* nature of the rights does not decrease their proprietary aspect, but allows the rights to function in a way that adds value to the asset owned – the company. The cooperative and limited aspect of a shareholder's interest is essential to the corporate form, and history has shown that property interests are constructed and evolve to meet the particular legal and economic purposes they are meant to serve.[25] We will see in Chapter 18 that shareholder rights are exercised cooperatively by majority rule, and in Chapter 10 that certain powers are delegated to management. The rights as to control and management are mainly voting rights that may be exercised in various circumstances.[26] The proprietary rights are primarily rights to share *pro rata* in dividend payments,[27] and payouts upon liquidation of the corporation.[28] The remedial and ancillary rights include the right to bring a derivative suit[29] and the right to inspect corporate books and records.[30] Without such limitations on the ownership rights of each shareholder, the corporation would not be able to function effectively.

III.   *The economic and governance functions of share classes*

We have seen that shares embody a number of types of rights, including economic rights to receive dividends on a regular basis, if declared, and to receive a residual, *pro rata* payout of assets upon liquidation of the company; they also embody control rights, such as the power to elect directors or approve important changes in the company, such as mergers.[31] Within certain limits that vary from jurisdiction to jurisdiction, these rights can be attributed to different shares in differing degrees to create a customized mix of rights that caters to the needs of each type of investor. Although each of our three jurisdictions has its own definition of what constitutes a

---

[25] Mahoney (2000: 877–878).

[26] §§ 212, 211(b), 242(b), 251(c), 271, 275(c) DGCL; §§ 7.21(a), 7.28, 8.08, 9.21, 9.52, 10.03, 10.20, 11.04, 12.02, 14.02 Model Act.

[27] See e.g. § 151(c) DGCL; § 6.01(c)(3) Model Act.

[28] § 151(d) DGCL; § 6.01(b)(2) Model Act.   [29] § 327 DGCL; § 7.01 Model Act.

[30] § 220 DGCL; §§ 16.02, 16.04, 16.20 Model Act.

[31] Supporting rights, such as the right to inspect the books and records of the company or to derivatively request that a court take action to protect a company against the disloyal actions of its management are generally not specifically included or excluded in or from classes of shares, and it is unlikely that such rights could be excluded, given their nature.

"class" of shares, the term basically means a set of shares having a certain mix of rights uniform within the class. Although the various combinations of possible rights are nearly infinite, in practice two classes of shares are the most widely used in our three jurisdictions: "common" (US) or "ordinary" (UK) shares on the one hand, and "preferred" (US) or "preference" (UK) shares on the other.[32] Other rights commonly attributed only to specific sets of shares are the right for the shares to be redeemed (called) by the issuer or the shareholder (put), and the right to convert a security – whether share, bond or warrant – into another security.

Typical common shares might carry one vote per share and an equal, *pro rata* claim to distributions upon a declaration of dividends and upon liquidation after satisfaction of creditors and preferred stockholders. Typical preferred shares might carry a right to receive dividends and/or liquidation distributions of a certain amount or percentage of nominal value before like distributions are made to the common shareholders. In addition, preferred shares might also have the right to "participate" equally in the distributions made to the common shareholders (referred to as *participating preferred*). However, because preferred shares usually have lower or no voting rights, it would be possible for the common shareholders to simply use their power – within the limits of the law – to prevent the declaration of dividends. Thus, if the preferred shareholders were to have a right to €5 per share whenever dividends are declared, and the common shareholders were to cause dividends to be declared only every five years, the preferred shareholders would receive during the five year period only one-fifth of the dividends they thought they were bargaining for. This problem can be addressed in two ways. First, the right to dividends can be made "cumulative," so that, upon the declaration in year five, the company would owe the preferred stockholders all back dividends, here €25 (referred to as *cumulative preferred*). Secondly, control rights can be used to protect economic rights. A failure to declare dividends could trigger a right of the preferred stockholders to replace all or a part of the board of directors, or in a jurisdiction in which the shareholders control dividends directly, cast the majority of votes at the general meeting on the dividend issue.

The creation of such customized securities to address the particular needs of investors is one of the more interesting aspects of practicing corporate law. For example, if a company were formed by an entrepreneur and a venture capital (VC) investor injecting cash, with the former

---

[32] The corresponding German terms are *Stammaktien* and *Vorzugsaktien*.

contributing a promise to manage the company full-time and the latter contributing €400,000 in cash, and the company were to issue 100 shares with each party receiving 50 shares having equal rights, a liquidation of the company one week later would look like this: after satisfying creditors, the company's residual assets would be divided equally between the two shareholders. If the €400,000 cash contribution were still intact, the two would each have an equal claim to €200,000, which would be an immediate transfer of €200,000 from the VC investor to the entrepreneur. If the VC investor were given shares of a different class having a right to receive the first €400,000 of the company's assets upon liquidation, this would not guarantee full protection against loss (as a security interest or charge might), but it would prevent an undeserved windfall to the entrepreneur. An investor might also want to invest primarily in a particular segment of a company, such as a new technology. To this end, some jurisdictions allow what is referred to as *tracking stock*. Comparable to the isolating effect that securitization structures achieve for debt secured by specific assets of a company, tracking stock provides its holders with an interest linked to a specific business division of the corporation.[33]

If the VC investor referred to above also backed competitors, the entrepreneur might be hesitant to give it equal control rights, as the VC investor could attempt to use control of one company to serve its interests in another. If the entrepreneur took shares of a different class, with control rights sufficient to outvote the VC investor, or do so in important transactions, this might sufficiently address the control concerns. A similar adjustment of control rights lies at the heart of so-called *golden shares*. Such shares were often used in the context of privatizing previously state-owned companies, and give exceptional control rights to the privatizing government as a stabilizing factor for the privatization.[34] Thus, within the limits of the law, the various rights attached to shares can be bundled in various ways to meet the needs of specific investors.

Customizing share classes can also serve the specific needs of an issuer. For an issuer, preferred shares stand somewhere between common shares and debt financing, as they commit to a relatively stable outflow of funds, but give up only limited control rights. They have the

---

[33] Instead of isolating the target assets in a special purpose vehicle, a tracking stock structure will provide that the target division of the corporation be treated *as if* it were a stand-alone company when determining the availability and amount of dividends. Hass (1996: 2096–2099).

[34] Such multiple-vote shares also distort the market for corporate control, and thus are addressed in takeover legislation such as the EU Takeover Directive.

advantage that they do not use up borrowing limits promised in loan covenants or otherwise, and a failure to pay dividends will not trigger an event of default (as might a failure to pay interest on a bond) that could push the issuer into bankruptcy. Disadvantages of preferred shares are that dividend payments might not be deductible under the relevant tax laws, while interest payments on bonds could be, and that the equity capital contributed for the shares might well be subject to stricter capital maintenance requirements than a sum received as credit. An issuer can use a right of *redemption* to take preferred shares off the market if it decides that, for example, debt financing would be cheaper than paying preferred dividends. In a market downturn, an issuer might take the reverse tack of issuing *convertible bonds* that a holder could change into shares when the profits of the company begin to look more attractive than interest payments. *Warrants* (certificated options issued by the company), subscription rights and convertible bonds can also be used in the US as a *poison pill* to protect a company against hostile bidders, as discussed in Chapter 25.

IV. Specific rules on classes of shares in the three jurisdictions

A. Germany

1. What is a "class"? Pursuant to § 11 of the *Aktiengesetz*, "shares having the same rights constitute a class." German courts and legal scholars have added the corollary that shares having the same *duties* also constitute a class.[35] Thus, under German law, shares with the same rights and duties constitute a class of shares. A class can contain just a single shareholder.[36] As we have seen, the rights embodied in shares include the rights to receive dividends and a portion of the assets upon liquidation, as well as the right to vote on matters specified in the law and the constitutional documents. According to German legal scholars, characteristics that only affect the *quantity* of rights held, such as the nominal value of a share, are not "rights" that would serve to distinguish individual classes.[37] The same applies to characteristics that have no essential relation to the rights in shares, such as whether the share is sold for one issue price or another, is partially or fully paid up, is certificated or uncertificated, has a par value

---

[35] Heider, in *MünchKommAktG* (2008: § 11 mn. 28), citing Regional Court of Hamburg, DB 1994 (1968).
[36] Heider, in *MünchKommAktG* (2008: § 11 mn. 29).
[37] Heider, in *MünchKommAktG* (2008: § 11 mn. 31).

or is no-par, or takes the form of a bearer or registered share.[38] In addition, if the law specifies a shareholding threshold to trigger a statutory right, such as the right of shareholders with 5 percent of the corporate capital to call a general meeting,[39] the shares composing that 5 percent do not constitute a separate class of shares, as the right does not attach to the shares themselves, but only to an accidental accumulation.[40] From the above it follows that a class of shares considered as such under German law must be evidenced by positive rights or duties attributed to the specific shares in the *Satzung*, and the latter must, in fact, specify "the classes of shares and the number of shares in each class."[41] Whether a given security belongs to a discrete class is extremely important from a legal point of view because, as discussed in subsection 3 below, any change of the rights of such class – including through the issue of new securities – can trigger special rules for approval of the measure by a qualified majority of the affected class.

2. How can rights be bundled?   Although the *Aktiengesetz* indicates complete freedom to create classes by stating that shares can carry "various rights,"[42] the way that rights may actually be bundled in shares is closely regulated by the same law. For example, three sections of the statute lay out rules for the rights to be bundled under the term *Vorzugsaktien* (preferred shares): shares with a preferred claim to dividend distributions are the only type of shares that may be issued without voting rights,[43] and even these shares are expressly stated to have all the other rights of common stock.[44] The statute makes the claim to dividends cumulative and, if a sum of dividends due from the preceding year is not paid, together with the full preference dividend for the current year, the statute gives the preferred shares full voting rights until the arrears payment is made.[45] Such preferred shares may only be issued for up to one-half of the corporate capital.[46]

Special rules also apply if a company desires to cause the voting rights of non-preferred shares to deviate from the one share-one vote principle. First, the creation of new, multiple voting rights shares has been outlawed

---

[38] The distinction between bearer and registered shares creates differences in the transfer of shares, the manner in which notice is given to shareholders, and the manner in which shareholders are certified as eligible to receive shareholder rights (i.e. entry in the register or tender of the certificate), and thus some German scholars find these sufficient to constitute separate classes. See Brändel, in *GroßKommAktG* (1992: § 11 mn. 37).

[39] § 122(2) AktG.   [40] Heider, in *MünchKommAktG* (2008: § 11 mn. 33).

[41] § 23(3) no. 4 AktG.   [42] § 11 AktG.   [43] § 139(1) AktG.   [44] § 140(1) AktG.

[45] § 140(2) AktG.   [46] § 139(2) AktG.

since 1998.[47] The same law provided that all previously existing multiple voting rights would lapse on June 1, 2003 unless approved by a majority of three-quarters of the shares present at a general meeting – excluding the holders of the multiple voting rights up for approval.[48] Reduced voting rights are, however, possible. If a company's shares are not listed on a securities exchange, it may insert a provision in its *Satzung* that limits the number of votes any single shareholder can exercise.[49] Since such limitation would apply to the maximum votes of *a given shareholder*, however, it is not a restriction that would make the shares held by that person a class under German law.[50] From the above, it is clear that the shares of an *Aktiengesellschaft* listed on a securities exchange would each have one vote unless they are non-voting preferred shares.

3.   How can rights be changed?   Attempts to change legal obligations when the environment surrounding the initial commitment to such obligations changes (e.g. exiting a long-term supply contract entered into before the price of a commodity drastically changes) make up much of commercial litigation. The problem of durable rights in changing circumstances is a real one, and thus the *Aktiengesetz* contains detailed rules on how the creation of a new class of shares or the modification of the rights in an existing class of shares must be approved. As a basic rule, it is assumed that the creation of any class of shares that has rights superior or *equal to* an existing class of shares will alter the proportionate value of the preexisting rights, and thus must be specially approved by the affected persons.

The creation of a new class of shares would always require an amendment to the *Satzung* and usually require an increase in capital and a waiver of preemption rights. If the new class has rights that are inferior to the existing classes of shares, the normal rules for charter amendments and capital increases apply – an affirmative vote of three-quarters of the shareholders of each class,[51] plus compliance with the procedure for waiving preemption rights as discussed in Chapter 6. If the amendment changes the existing ratio among classes, it must be approved by the affirmative vote of three-quarters of the *affected* shareholders casting

---

[47]   See § 12(2) AktG; and Heider, in *MünchKommAktG* (2008: § 12 mn. 10).
[48]   See art. 11(1) KonTraG.   [49]   § 134(1) AktG.
[50]   Heider, in *MünchKommAktG* (2008: § 12 mn. 35).
[51]   § 179(2), 182 (approving capital increase), § 193 (approving conditional capital), § 202 (approving authorized capital) AktG; Heider, in *MünchKommAktG* (2008: § 11 mn. 41).

votes at the meeting.[52] If the new class ranks higher or *pari passu* to one or more existing classes, the majority of legal scholars find that such a dilution in the membership rights would require a unanimous decision of the disadvantaged shareholders.[53] Special provisions regulate acts affecting the holders of preferred shares. Any decision to limit or eliminate the preferential rights or introduce another class of preferred shares with superior or equal rights must be approved by three-quarters of the affected class of preferred shares meeting alone.[54]

Although this would not technically create a new class of shares under German law, it should nonetheless be noted that a *Satzung* provision limiting the number of votes any single shareholder can exercise may be introduced with a three-quarters affirmative vote of the votes cast by shares affected by the limitation.[55]

B.   United Kingdom

1.   What is a "class"?   The Companies Act 2006 defines shares as "of one class if the rights attached to them are in all respects uniform."[56] Thus, as discussed in relation to German law, shares that have special rights to dividends, liquidation, voting, redemption or conversion would in most cases constitute a distinct class of shares.[57] Prior to the 2006 Act, the courts had extended the definition of class rights to include rights granted by the articles to a particular person in his capacity as shareholder. In *Cumbrian Newspapers Group Ltd* v. *Cumberland & Westmorland Herald Newspaper & Printing Co. Ltd*,[58] the articles of association of a company were altered to the benefit of an investor who brought a much needed injection of capital. The articles granted preemption rights to the investor both in the case of a capital increase and in that of a sale of shares by an existing member and also provided that so long as the investor held at least 10 percent of the ordinary share capital it could appoint a director. Two decades after the rescue and the writing of the provisions, the board proposed to remove these provisions from the articles and the investor claimed they were class rights subject to the rules on variation of class rights. With reference to

---

[52] § 179(2), (3) AktG.
[53] Heider, in *MünchKommAktG* (2008: § 11 mn. 43).
[54] § 141 AktG; Heider, in *MünchKommAktG* (2008: § 11 mn. 48).
[55] Heider, in *MünchKommAktG* (2008: § 12 mn. 36).   [56] Sec. 629(1) CA 2006.
[57] However, the rights of shares are not regarded as different from those of other shares if the only difference is that "they do not carry the same rights to dividends in the twelve months immediately following their allotment." See sec. 629(2) CA 2006.
[58] [1986] 3 WLR 26.

the language of the 1985 Act ("the rights of any class of members"), Scott J found that the rights were indeed class rights, as they referred to the person *qua* shareholder.[59] Davies and Ferran both observe that the elimination of the cited language from the 2006 Act might well mean that *Cumbrian* no longer enjoys an extremely firm standing.[60] This would leave the UK definition of class rights quite close to the express provisions required under German and US state law. Would an express provision stating a difference in nominal value – all other rights remaining equal – constitute a separate class? Take a look at the *dicta* of Lord Green in *Greenhalgh* v. *Arderne Cinemas Ltd* in this chapter with regard to the distinction between 2p and 10p shares.

2.   How can rights be bundled?   UK law contains assumptions regarding the rights that will be bundled in "ordinary" and "preference" shares. For *ordinary shares*, unless otherwise provided in the articles, any distributable surplus during the life or at the dissolution of a company is assumed to be distributable equally among the shareholders in proportion to the nominal value of their shares,[61] and each member has an equal vote for an equal shareholding.[62] For *preference shares*, the relevant priority (to dividends, liquidation or voting) must be expressly specified,[63] and rights not expressly provided will not be presumed to exist.[64] One exception to this rule is that an express provision of preferential liquidation rights will be assumed to imply a like preference in the analogical circumstance of a reduction of capital leading to a distribution.[65] Also, if preferred dividends are provided for, a court will assume that such dividends are cumulative over years when no dividends are paid.[66] A provision giving preference shareholders a right to vote only if their dividends fall into arrears will be presumed to be triggered even if a company has no profits in the years it fails to make distributions.[67]

---

[59] [1986] 3 WLR 26, 42.   [60] Davies (2008: 673); Ferran (2008: 165).
[61] *Birch* v. *Cropper* (1889) 14 App Cas 525 (HL); and Ferran (2008: 149).
[62] Depending on the type of vote taken (written, show of hands or poll), the voting power of a member will be one vote per member or one vote per every £10 held. See sec. 284 CA 2006.
[63] *Re London India Rubber Co.* (1869) LR 5 Eq 519; and Ferran (2008: 152).
[64] *Scottish Insurance Corporation* v. *Wilson & Clyde Coal Co. Ltd* [1949] AC 462 (HL); and Ferran (2008: 152).
[65] *Re Saltdean Estate Co. Ltd* [1968] 1 WLR 1844; see Ferran (2008: 153).
[66] *Bond* v. *Barrow Haematite Steel Co.* [1902] 1 Ch 353, 362.
[67] *Re Bradford Investments plc* [1990] BCC 740, 746.

UK issuers may issue *redeemable shares* provided that some non-redeemable shares are outstanding and that only fully paid shares may be redeemed.[68] Redeemable shares may be either ordinary or preference shares, and, as with other classes of shares, the terms and conditions of redeemable shares must be specified in the articles. The Companies Act provides detailed rules on the financing of redemption,[69] which has been addressed in the chapter on distributions and capital maintenance.

3. How can rights be changed? The Companies Act 2006 sets out rules for the variation of class rights in section 630.[70] The procedure applicable will depend on whether rules for the variation are specified in the articles of association. The simplest scenario is where the articles do contain such rules, in which case, the rights may be changed by following the rules.[71] The model articles issued by BERR in 2008 do not contain rules for this circumstance. When no procedure is set out in the articles, a variation will require either the written consent of three-quarters (measured in nominal value) of the class or an extraordinary resolution of the affected class.[72] In addition, a change to the articles themselves requires a special resolution of the voting members.[73] Similarly to the past practice of placing provisions in the memorandum of association before the 2006 Act changed that document's status, incorporators or all the members may now specify that, for certain provisions of the articles, the requirements for amendment will be stricter than those specified in the Act.[74] If such a "provision for entrenchment" specifies class rights, the rights may only be altered according to the procedure specified in the articles. In any case, the holders of at least 15 percent of the issued shares of a given class whose rights are varied without their consent may apply to the court to have the variation canceled.[75]

UK law is thus quite clear on how class rights may be changed. A difficulty occasionally arises, however, in deciding *whether* class rights have been changed. For example, if two classes of shares were to have equal voting rights, and one class was to be changed so as to augment its voting

---

[68] Sec. 684 CA 2006.   [69] Sec. 687 CA 2006.

[70] Class rights can also be significantly affected by a merger or other change in the company's structure or capital structure. Thus, sec. 907 CA 2006 also provides rules for a class vote on mergers. For a detailed discussion of mergers under UK law, see Chapter 22.

[71] Sec. 630(2)(a) CA 2006.

[72] Sec. 630(4) CA 2006. Sec. 334 provides special rules for the calling and holding of shareholders' meetings for the variation of class rights.

[73] Sec. 21(1) CA 2006.   [74] Sec. 22 CA 2006.   [75] Sec. 633 CA 2006.

power fivefold, the real voting power of the other class would proportionately decrease. Does such an action change the voting rights of the weakened class or only the ability to *enjoy* such rights? See *Greenhalgh* v. *Arderne Cinemas Ltd*, in this chapter. UK courts have found that the issue of a second class of shares ranking *pari passu* with an existing class does not constitute a variation of the first class, and this applies to both existing ordinary shares to which ordinary shares are added[76] and to existing preference shares to which preference shares are added.[77]

C.   United States

1.   What is a "class"?   A "class" of securities under the corporate statute of a US state must be specified either in the company's constitutional document, naming the "preferences and relative, participating, optional or other special rights, and qualifications, or restrictions thereof,"[78] or in a resolution of the board of directors with respect to the class, provided the constitutional document gives the directors such power.[79] Only those rights named in the certificate (articles) of incorporation or resolution will belong to the shares.[80] As in UK law, a specific par value will act as a distinguishing feature of a set of shares, but, because US law recognizes sub-classes (called "series"), if the rights and preferences of the shares are equal, different par values will then likely create a different *series* within a single *class* of shares.[81] Neither issue price nor the amount paid up on a share will create a separate class of shares. A significant difference from both German and UK law is that the certificate (articles) of incorporation may authorize directors to create series or classes of shares and specify their rights without a further shareholder action.[82] This allows directors to respond quickly to financial needs and market conditions, as well as to create classes of securities designed to protect the company against a hostile takeover (*poison pills*). Particularly as the shares of US companies generally do not carry preemption rights, this puts significant power over the shareholding structure in the hands of the board.

2.   How can rights be bundled?   The types of rights that may be attributed to shares in full or modified measure are unlimited, and the Model

---

[76]   *Re Schweppes Ltd* [1914] 1 Ch 322 (CA); and see Ferran (2008: 169).

[77]   *Underwood* v. *London Music Hall Ltd* [1901] 2 Ch 309; and see Ferran (2008: 169).

[78]   § 151(a) DGCL; § 6.01(a) Model Act.   [79]   § 151(a) DGCL; § 6.02 Model Act.

[80]   Balotti and Finkelstein (2008: § 5.4).

[81]   § 151(a) DGCL; Balotti and Finkelstein (2008: § 5.3); § 6.02(a) Model Act.

[82]   § 151(a) DGCL; § 6.02 Model Act.

Act even states that the "description of the designations, preferences, limitations, and relative rights of share classes in [the Act] is not exhaustive."[83] The only unalterable rule is that there must be at least one share outstanding at all times with unlimited voting rights and – under the Model Act – unlimited residual rights to the assets upon dissolution.[84]

Because US corporate statutes are generally a loose set of default rules when compared to either the German or the UK acts, the range of options open to companies when structuring class rights is very broad. As pre-emption rights do not exist unless so specified in the certificate (articles) of incorporation,[85] the presence of such rights does not limit the distribution of new shares. As capital maintenance rules are very flexible,[86] the consideration given in purchasing and redeeming shares is also open to flexibility. The law places no limitation on the manner in which shareholder rights may be amended and combined in a given class. Specific shares may be given rights to elect a specific number of directors.[87] Rights may be made contingent upon outside triggering "facts," which can include a decision by the board of directors.[88] Shares may be made redeemable by either their holder or the corporation for "cash, property or rights, including securities of the same or another corporation."[89] Debt instruments may be given voting rights and treated *mutatis mutandis* as shares.[90] Indeed, in Delaware, a class of shares could even be given the right to eliminate the board of directors and place management power in the hands of some other body or group.[91]

All special rights must be expressly set out in the certificate of incorporation or in an approved resolution of the board of directors, and no rights – such as the right of preferred shares to be cumulative or participating – will be inferred by presumption.[92] The single exception is that, if no provision for voting rights is made, all shares will have the right to vote equally on corporate matters as provided for by law.[93] Thus, the bulk of the legal work on classes of shares under US law is strategic rather than compliance oriented.[94] For example, if a shareholder were to obtain a right

---

[83] § 6.01(d) Model Act.   [84] § 151(b) DGCL; § 6.01(b) Model Act.

[85] § 102(b)(3) DGCL; § 6.30 Model Act.   [86] See Chapters 7 and 8 of this text.

[87] § 141(d) DGCL; § 8.04 Model Act. The similar prerogative available under German law does not qualify as a class under German law. See § 101(2) AktG; Habersack, in *MünchKommAktG* (2008: § 101 mn. 39).

[88] § 151(a) DGCL; § 6.01(d) Model Act.   [89] § 151(b) DGCL.   [90] § 221 DGCL.

[91] § 141(a) DGCL, in connection with § 151(a).

[92] *Elliott Associates, LP* v. *Avatex Corp.*, 715 A 2d 843, 852 (Del. 1998).

[93] Balotti and Finkelstein (2008: § 5.6).

[94] For an excellent discussion of the strategic bundling of rights in classes of shares, see Booth (2002: § 2A).

to high dividend payments with cumulative preferred stock, the company might attempt to reduce its value by reserving a right of redemption at its option (to eliminate the preferred when cheaper financing becomes available) or by denying liquidation preference in event of voluntary dissolution (to reorganize the company and eliminate the preferred stock). Because preferred dividends can be paid in kind (payment-in-kind or PIK preferred), it would be important to specify exactly what kind of consideration is allowed in light of the company's financial prospects and the state of the market.

3. How can rights be changed? Although neither the DGCL nor the Model Act contain a special provision on variation of class rights, as in German and UK law, the basic rule is that the rights of a class may not be changed without the consent of the holders of such class of shares. The primary instruments used to achieve this end are that (1) class rights are specified in the certificate of incorporation, and (2) any amendment to the certificate changing such rights must be specially approved by a majority vote of the class voting as a separate body.[95] Under the DGCL, as under the Companies Act 2006, the creation of a class of shares that alters the *relative position* of another, existing class of shares does not trigger a class vote unless the result is found to be inequitable.[96] Under the Model Act, the creation or increase of the rights of such a class, if it has "rights or preferences with respect to distributions or to dissolution that are prior or superior to the shares of the class" will trigger a class vote.[97] The recent amendment to this provision to remove the words "or substantially equal to" – which allowed a class vote for the introduction of another class with *pari passu* rights[98] – shows an evolution away from the position we see in Germany toward that found in Delaware and the UK.

US law also offers two *post hoc* remedies for a vote to alter class rights: appraisal rights, or the right to sell one's shares at a fair price,[99] and an appeal to the court under the theory that the approval of the alteration was achieved through unfair means. For an example of the latter type of challenge, see *Lacos Land Company* v. *Arden Group, Inc.* in this chapter.

---

[95] § 242(b)(2) DGCL; § 10.04 Model Act. The required majority is a "simple" majority calculated on the basis of shares present, not in absolute terms.

[96] *Hartford Accident & Indemnity Co.* v. *W. S. Dickey Clay Manufacturing Co.*, 24 A 2d 315, 318–319 (Del. 1942).

[97] § 10.04(a)(5), (6) Model Act.   [98] § 10.04(a) and Official Comment, Model Act.

[99] § 262(c) DGCL (appraisal rights exist for changes in class rights only if provided for in the certificate of incorporation); § 13.02(a) Model Act (for certain forced share exchanges, reduction of shares to fractional interests, or as provided for in the articles of incorporation).

4. Listing requirements supplement the corporate statutes The rather loose US rules should be read in conjunction with the stock exchange listing requirements that would apply to any US public company. For example, the New York Stock Exchange (NYSE) permits the listing of all types of securities, including non-voting securities and securities with preferred rights to dividends and assets upon liquidation, but includes certain shareholder protections that go beyond those found in the corporate statutes. The rules provide that the voting rights of common stock that is *already* listed "cannot be disparately reduced or restricted through any corporate action or issuance" such as "the adoption of time phased voting plans, the adoption of capped voting rights plans, the issuance of super voting stock, or the issuance of stock with voting rights less than the per share voting rights of the existing common stock through an exchange offer."[100] They also state that the rights of "non-voting common stock should, except for voting rights, be substantially the same as those of the holders of the company's voting common stock."[101] Preferred stock "should have the right to elect a minimum of two directors upon default of the equivalent of six quarterly dividends … [and this right] should remain in effect until cumulative dividends have been paid in full or until non-cumulative dividends have been paid regularly for at least a year."[102] Protection against the introduction of another class of stock with *pari passu* rights, which is omitted by the DGCL and the Model Act, is included in the NYSE's *Listed Company Manual*: "the creation of a *pari passu* issue should be approved by a majority of the holders of the outstanding shares of the class or classes to be affected."[103] Also, the *Listed Company Manual* increases the state rule of majority approval for a change in class rights to a mandatory vote of two-thirds of the outstanding shares of the class.[104] The combination of loose state law and strict listing requirements thus leads to an overall body of regulation that is not significantly different from that found in Germany and the UK.

Questions for discussion

1. According to the court in *Borland's Trustee* v. *Steel* [1901] 1 Ch 279, 288:

   A share is the measure of a shareholder in the company measured by a sum of money, for the purposes of liability in the first place, and of interest in the second,

---

[100] § 313.000(A) NYSE LCM.   [101] § 313.000(B)(1) NYSE LCM.
[102] § 313.000(C) NYSE LCM.   [103] § 313.000(C) NYSE LCM.
[104] § 313.000(C) NYSE LCM.

but also consisting of a series of mutual covenants entered into by all the share-holders *inter se*. The contract contained in the articles is one of the original incidents of the share. A share is not a sum of money … but is an interest measured by a sum of money and made up of the various rights contained in the contract.

(a) What rights does a share confer on its holder with respect to the corporation's assets?

(b) Is it true that a par value share is not a claim for a sum of money?

(c) Is the contention that shares represent an interest in the company measured by a sum of money true for shares without par value?

(d) The definition expressed in Borland's Trustee refers to "mutual covenants entered into by all shareholders *inter se*." Do these promises (covenants) arise from the contract contained in the articles or from the property interest embodied in the shares?

(e) If the rights contained in shares arise from the articles as a contract, who are the parties to the contract? Do the rules of contract law fully explain how the rights embodied in shares function?

(f) How would you describe the status of a shareholder? If a joint owner of an enterprise, why can't she take her piece of the enterprise and go? If a member of an association, why doesn't the membership carry any duties to participate in meetings? If a passive investor supplying a certain type of capital to the management's business, why can the investors appoint the management or have a say in important decisions?

2. Work out the following hypothetical problem. Assume that a corporation has issued one million ordinary shares with a par value of €1 per share and one million ordinary shares with a par value of €10 per share. The issue price for the shares is set at 400 percent of the nominal value for the €1 par shares (i.e. €4 per share) and 300 percent of the nominal value for the €10 shares (i.e. €30 per share).

(a) How are profits to be distributed among the shareholders pursuant to the Companies Act 2006 and to the German AktG if all shareholders have made their contributions in full?

(b) How would profits be distributed if some of the shareholders had made their contribution in full while others had only paid in part?

(c) What types of preferences with respect to corporate distributions are possible under the DGCL, the Companies Act 2006 and the AktG? Are preferences cumulative or non-cumulative? May voting rights be attached to preference shares?

3. What are the rules on voting rights – including non-voting shares and multiple-vote shares – attached to shares under UK law, US law and the German AktG?

4. Why is it important to identify shares as belonging to different classes?

5. What constitutes a class of shares?

6. With respect to variations of class rights, *Greenalgh* distinguishes between interference with a right attaching to a share and the mere variation of the enjoyment

of a right. Does that distinction make sense? Would it be an issue under German stock corporation law?

Cases

Lacos Land Company v. Arden Group, Inc., et al.
Court of Chancery of Delaware
517 A 2d 271 (1986)
[*Text edited; some footnotes omitted*]

ALLEN, Chancellor

This action constitutes a multi-pronged attack upon a proposed recapitalization of defendant Arden Group, Inc., authorized by a vote of Arden's shareholders at their June 10, 1986 annual meeting. The recapitalization, if effectuated, will create a new Class B Common Stock possessing ten votes per share and entitled, as a class, to elect seventy-five percent of the members of Arden's board of directors. This new stock is, pursuant to the terms of a presently pending exchange offer, available on a share-for-share basis to all holders of Arden's Class A Common Stock. It is, however, acknowledged by defendants that the new Class B Common Stock has been deliberately fashioned to be attractive mainly to defendant Briskin – Arden's principal shareholder and chief executive officer. Thus, the recapitalization is not itself a device to raise capital but rather is a technique to transfer stockholder control of the enterprise to Mr. Briskin.

Plaintiff is an Arden stockholder owning approximately 4.5% of Arden's Class A Common Stock; an additional stockholder owning approximately 4.6% of that stock has moved to intervene in this action as a plaintiff. Defendants are the members of Arden's board of directors. Pending is an application to preliminarily enjoin the issuance of Class B Common Stock which was originally scheduled to occur on July 18, 1986, but which has been voluntarily delayed by defendants.

The legal theories proffered to support the relief now sought fall into three categories. First, plaintiff claims that the June 10, 1986 shareholder vote approving the charter amendment that authorized the new Class B stock was fatally defective by reason of material misrepresentations and omissions in the Company's proxy statement. Second, it claims that the pending exchange offer constitutes an impermissible entrenchment scheme designed principally to thwart all possible changes in corporate control not personally agreeable to Mr. Briskin and to perpetuate him in office. Third, in a series of technical corporation law arguments plaintiff asserts that the charter amendments authorizing the issuance of the supervoting stock are inconsistent with certain provisions of the Delaware General Corporation Law and were not adopted by a supermajority vote as purportedly required by Arden's restated certificate of incorporation.

I find it unnecessary to address plaintiff's claims of impermissible motivation or its technical corporation law arguments. I conclude for two independent reasons that the stockholder vote amending the certificate so as to permit the issuance of the supervoting Class B stock is likely to be found on final hearing to be fatally flawed and the amendments it approved voidable …

I.

[*Text omitted*]

… [W]ith respect to voting rights, the recent charter amendment provides that "on every matter submitted to a vote or consent of the stockholder, every holder of Class A Common Stock shall be entitled to one vote … for each share … and every holder of Class B Common Stock shall be entitled to 10 votes … for each share …"

As to the election of directors, the restated certificate provides that Class A shares, together with the Company's preferred stock, voting as a class shall "be entitled to elect 25% of the total number of directors to be elected" rounded up to the nearest whole number. The Class B shares are entitled to vote as a separate class and to elect the remaining 75% of directors to be elected.

With respect to dividend rights, Class A Common Stock will, following the initial issuance of Class B shares, have the right to receive a one-time dividend of $.30 per share; Class B shares are to have no right to participate to any extent in that cash dividend. Excepting this one-time $.30 dividend, each share of Class B stock is to be entitled to participate in all dividends declared and paid with respect to a share of Class A stock but only to the extent of 90% of such dividend.

Class B shares may be transferred only to a Permitted Transferee, [Note 2] but under certain circumstances may be converted on a share-for-share basis into Class A stock. A transfer of Class B to a person other than a Permitted Transferee at a time when conversion to Class A would be permitted would convert the transferred stock into Class A stock. Generally, Class B stock may, at the option of the holder, be converted to Class A stock on a share-for-share basis at the earlier of (i) the third anniversary of its issuance or (ii) the death of the holder.

[Note 2] For a natural person Permitted Transferees include (1) the holder's spouse or any lineal descendant of a grandparent of the holder or the holder's spouse, (2) the trustee of any trust for the benefit of the holder or a Permitted Transferee, (3) charitable organizations, (4) a corporation or partnership under majority control of the holder or a Permitted Transferee and (5) the holder's estate.

Defendant Briskin owns or controls 16.9% of Arden's Class A Common Stock (21.1% were he to exercise certain presently exercisable stock options). The proxy statement states (at p. 20):

> Based on Mr. Briskin's expressed intention to exchange all of the Briskin Shares for Class B Common Stock, the Briskin Shares would represent approximately 67.7% of the combined voting power of the capital stock of the Company if no

shares of Class A Common Stock other than the Briskin Shares were exchanged for Class B Common Stock.

...

In view of the lack of transferability and reduced dividend rights of the Class B Common Stock, the Board of Directors does not anticipate that any significant number of holders of Class A Common Stock other than Mr. Briskin will accept the Exchange Offer.

II.

The creation of a dual common stock structure with one class exercising effective control of the company is, of course, not a novel idea, although it is one that, thanks to its potential as an anti-takeover device, has recently emerged from the reaches of the corporation law chorus to strut its moment upon center stage where corporate drama is acted out. In this instance, the notion of employing this dual common stock structure apparently originated with defendant Briskin.

Mr. Briskin became Arden chief executive officer in 1976 at a time when the Company was apparently in a desperate condition. Its stock was then trading between $1 and $2 per share. Briskin's stewardship has apparently been active and effective. While Arden has paid no dividends since 1970, during Briskin's tenure Arden's stock price has risen steadily; currently Arden common stock is publicly trading at around $25 per share, a price somewhat higher than the range of prices at which its stock traded in the weeks prior to the announcement of the plan that is the subject matter of this litigation.

In instigating the dual common stock voting structure, Mr. Briskin was apparently not responding to any specific threat to existing policies or practices of Arden posed by a specific takeover threat. Rather, he apparently was motivated to protect his power to control Arden's business future. Such a motivation, while it may be suspect – since it may reflect not a desire to protect business policies and capabilities for the benefit of the corporation and its shareholders but rather a wish simply to retain the benefits of office – does not itself constitute a wrong ...

In this instance, Briskin initially took his idea to the board of directors at its November 22, 1985 meeting. The Board established a three member committee of non-officer directors to consider the matter. Prior to the committee's first meeting, its chairman sent the other two committee members the proxy statement of another company that had adopted a dual class common stock structure, together with materials on other companies that had adopted supervoting plans and some materials relating to a report written by Professor Fischel on "Organized Exchanges and the Regulation of Dual Class Common Stock." The special committee retained neither independent counsel nor an independent financial advisor. At its first meeting, held on April 7, 1986, the chairman of this group distributed to the committee a draft report that he had previously prepared which gave approval to a supervoting stock plan. The committee reviewed this draft and suggested changes. The chairman noted the suggested changes and prepared a final three page report which was signed four days later at the committee's second, and final, meeting.

The committee's report was presented to the board at its April 22 meeting at which time the board approved the supervoting stock plan.

At that meeting the board fixed the date of the Company's annual meeting for June 10, 1986. Management of the Company prepared a proxy statement describing the proposed charter amendments authorizing the new supervoting Class B Common Stock, describing the Exchange Offer by which it was proposed that such new stock be distributed and setting out the background of, and the reasons for, this proposal.

At the June 10 annual meeting the Arden stockholders approved the proposed certificate amendments. Of 2,303,170 shares outstanding, 1,463,155 voted in favor (64%) and 325,004 (14%) voted to reject the proposal. Of the affirmative votes, 427,347 were voted by Briskin or his family and 388,493 were voted by a trustee as directed by Arden's management. As to the preferred stock, 74.4% of the 136,359 shares outstanding voted in favor of the proposal, more than half of which were voted by a trustee as directed by Arden's management.

As a consequence of the stockholders' approval of the proposal, the Company, on June 18, 1986, distributed to all holders of its Class A Common Stock an Offering Circular offering to exchange for each share of such common stock one share of Class B Common Stock with the rights, preferences, etc. described above.

III.

Our corporation law provides great flexibility to shareholders in creating the capital structure of their firm ... Differing classes of stock with differing voting rights are permissible under our law ... restriction on transfers are possible ... and charter provisions requiring the filling of certain directorates by a class of stock are, if otherwise properly adopted, valid ... Thus, each of the significant characteristics of the Class B Common Stock is in principle a valid power or limitation of common stock. The primary inquiry therefore is whether the Arden shareholders have effectively exercised their will to amend the Company's restated certificate of incorporation so as to authorize the implementation of the dual class common stock structure. The charge is that they have not done so – despite the report of the judge of elections that the proposed amendments carried – in part because the proxy statement upon which the vote was solicited was materially misleading and in part because the entire plan to put in place the Class B stock constitutes a breach of duty on the part of a dominated board.

For the reasons that follow I conclude that plaintiff has demonstrated a reasonable probability that on final hearing it will be demonstrated that the June 10, 1986 vote of the Arden shareholders has been fundamentally and fatally flawed and that, therefore, the amendments to Arden's restated certificate of incorporation purportedly authorized by that vote are voidable. In summary, the basis for this conclusion is two-fold. First, I conclude provisionally on the basis of the record now available, that the June 10 vote was inappropriately affected by an explicit threat of Mr. Briskin that unless the proposed amendments were approved, he would use his power (and not simply his power qua shareholder) to block transactions that may be in the best interests of the Company, if those transactions would dilute his ownership interest in Arden. I use the word threat because such a position entails, in my opinion, the potential for a breach of Mr. Briskin's duty, as the principal officer of Arden and as a member of its board of directors, to exercise corporate power unselfishly, with a view to fostering the interests of the corporation and all of its shareholders. Second, I conclude provisionally, that the proxy statement presents a substantial risk of misleading shareholders on a material point concerning Mr. Briskin's status as a "Restricted Person" under Article Twelfth of the Company's certificate of incorporation.

IV.

[Text omitted]

To a shareholder who wondered why his board of directors was recommending a plan expected to place all effective shareholder power in a single shareholder, the proxy statement gives a clear answer: Mr. Briskin is demanding it; it's not such a big deal anyway since, as a practical matter, he has great power already; and if he doesn't get these amendments, he may exercise his power to thwart corporate transactions that may be in the Company's best interests. Thus, in order for the board to be "permitted to consider" (proxy p. 20) certain transactions that might threaten to reduce Mr. Briskin's control, the board approved the proposal. This story is disclosed more or less straight forwardly in the proxy solicitation materials.

As to Mr. Briskin's position, the proxy statement states (emphasis added throughout):

> Purpose and effects of the proposal
>   1. **Purpose**. Mr. Briskin, the Company's largest single stockholder who beneficially owns in the aggregate approximately 21.1% of the outstanding Common Stock, has informed the Company of his concern that certain transactions *which could be determined by the Board of Directors to be in the best interests of all of the stockholders*, such as the issuance of additional voting securities in connection with financings or mergers or acquisitions by the Company, might make the Company vulnerable to an unsolicited or hostile takeover attempt or to an attempt at "greenmail," and that *he would not give his support to any such transactions for which his approval might be required unless steps were taken to secure his voting position in the Company.*

As to the asserted fact that Mr. Briskin already really has, as a practical matter, the power to control the Company, the proxy statement says (immediately following the foregoing quoted matter):

> *As a practical matter*, given the present stock ownership of Mr. Briskin and certain supermajority vote requirements and other provisions of the existing Certificate

(see "Possible Adverse Consequences"), *explicit or implicit approval of Mr. Briskin would be required for every such major transaction* the Company might choose to engage in (whether or not a vote of stockholders is actually required). Similarly, *it is unlikely that the Company would engage in transactions to which Mr. Briskin is opposed. Such transactions, including the issuance of additional capital stock, although dilutive of Mr. Briskin's stock ownership, could be in the best interests of stockholders other than Mr. Briskin.*

Accordingly, the purpose of the proposal – stated at page 20 as "to allow the Company to engage in [a broad range of] ... activities ... without diluting the power of Mr. Briskin ... " – is restated more completely on the same page as follows:

> The Special Committee and the Board of Directors of the Company approved the proposed amendments to the Certificate and the proposed Exchange Offer based, in part, *on their judgment that the Company can enjoy superior long-term performance if permitted to consider* the desirability of *transactions which would significantly dilute Mr. Briskin's voting power* in the Company or which might otherwise subject the Company to some risk of an unsolicited or hostile takeover attempt and which might therefore be opposed by Mr. Briskin. The Board of Directors believes that *if the Proposal is approved and Mr. Briskin's voting power is increased* as described herein under "Effects on Relative Voting Power," *Mr. Briskin will be more inclined not to oppose such transactions* and *that the Proposal is therefore in the best interests of the Company* and all of its stockholders. See "Action by Board of Directors."

... Using the term in the vague way which we ordinarily do, a vote in such circumstances as these could be said to be "coerced." But that label itself supplies no basis to conclude that the legal effect of the vote is impaired in any way. As stated in *Katz v. Oak Industries, Inc.* ...:

> ... [F]or purposes of legal analysis, the term "coercion" itself – covering a multitude of situations – is not very meaningful. For the word to have much meaning for purposes of legal analysis, it is necessary in each case that a normative judgment be attached to the concept ("inappropriately coercive" or "wrongfully coercive," etc.). But, it is then readily seen that what is legally relevant is not the conclusory term "coercion" itself but rather the norm that leads to the adverb modifying it.

The determination of whether it was inappropriate for Mr. Briskin to structure the choice of Arden's shareholders (and its directors), as was done here, requires, first, a determination of which of his hats – shareholder, officer or director – Mr. Briskin was wearing when he stated his position concerning the possible withholding of his "support" for future transactions unless steps were taken "to secure his voting position." If he spoke only as a shareholder, and should have been so understood, an evaluation of the propriety of his position might be markedly different ... than if the "support" referred to could be or should be interpreted as involving the exercise of his power as either an officer or director of Arden.

... [I]n taking this position, Mr. Briskin did not limit, and could not be understood to have limited, himself to exercising only stockholder power. Defendants have emphasized that Briskin's "practical" power derives in part from his notable success as a chief executive officer ... Moreover, the proxy statement made clear that the approval that Briskin threatened to withhold included approval of transactions that did not require a vote of stockholders ...

As a director and as an officer, of course, Mr. Briskin has a duty to act with complete loyalty to the interests of the corporation and its shareholders ... His position as stated to the shareholders in the Company proxy statement seems inconsistent with that obligation. In form at least, the statement by a director and officer that he will not give his support to a corporate transaction unless steps are taken to confer a personal power or benefit, suggests an evident disregard of duty ...

Two alternative motivations suggest themselves. Mr. Briskin may have been motivated, as plaintiff warmly contends is the fact, by a selfish desire to protect his salary and the perquisites of his office from the threat to them that a hostile takeover of Arden would represent ...

On the other hand, Briskin may have been motivated selflessly to put in place the most powerful of anti-takeover devices so that he could be assured the opportunity to reject (for all the shareholders) any offer for Arden that he – who presumably knows more about the Company than anyone else – regards as less than optimum achievable value. Accordingly, while I regard the form of the Briskin position ("I, as fiduciary will not support ... unless a personal benefit is conferred") as superficially shocking, I recognize that Mr. Briskin's position as stated in the proxy statement is logically consistent with and may indeed in fact be driven by a benevolent motivation.

Mr. Briskin's motivation in fact, however, need not be determined in order to conclude that the stockholder vote of June 10, 1986 was fatally flawed by the implied (indeed, the expressed) threats ... Shareholders who respect Mr. Briskin's ability and performance – and who are legally entitled to his undivided loyalty – were inappropriately placed in a position in which they were told that if they refused to vote affirmatively, Mr. Briskin would not support future possible transactions that might be beneficial to the corporation. A vote of shareholders under such circumstances cannot, in the face of a timely challenge by one of the corporation's shareholders, be said, in my opinion, to satisfy the mandate of Section 242(b) of our corporation law requiring shareholder consent to charter amendments.

V.

I turn now to the alternative basis for my finding of a probability of ultimate success. It also relates to the integrity of the stockholder vote approving the amendments; in this case, however, it relates to the quality of the disclosure.

[*Text omitted*]

... [I]n assessing whether defendants have met their duty of candor with respect to the May 12, 1986 proxy statement, the Court must determine whether "there is a material likelihood that a reasonable shareholder would consider [an omitted fact] important in deciding how to vote ... [...] Put another way, there must be a substantial likelihood that the disclosure of the omitted fact would have been viewed by the reasonable investor as having significantly altered the 'total mix' of information made available." ...

... I conclude that the proxy statement's implication that Mr. Briskin would be a "Restricted Person" under Article Twelfth of Arden's restated certificate of incorporation is misleading in a way that was material in the circumstances ...

A.

Article Twelfth requires that a merger or other business combination with an entity controlled by a "Restricted Person" be authorized by a supermajority vote of shareholders. Specifically, it states that "the prior affirmative vote or written consent of the holders of 70% of the outstanding shares of the common stock of the corporation, voting separately as a class" is required in order to authorize any "Business Combination" with a "Restricted Person" or his "Affiliate." In order to "amend, alter or repeal, directly or indirectly" any part of Article Twelfth, there is required, "notwithstanding any other provision of this Certificate of Incorporation," "the affirmative vote of the holders of 70% of the issued and outstanding shares of common stock ... excluding all voting securities owned directly or indirectly by any Restricted Person ..."

Finally, a Restricted Person is defined, generally, as any person who has, during any period of twelve consecutive months, acquired 5% or more of the outstanding shares of any class of the Company's voting securities. However, in making the calculation of percentage ownership "shares shall not be counted ... if the transaction in which such shares were acquired was approved in advance" by two-thirds of the members of Arden's board of directors. The vote required by Article Twelfth is a special and distinct vote, under Arden's certificate, "in addition to the vote ... otherwise required by law ..."

The amendments to Arden's certificate approved on June 10, did not amend the language of Article Twelfth. Therefore, a "Business Combination" with a "Restricted Person" still requires the "affirmative vote ... of the holders of 70% of the outstanding shares." Article Fourth now, however, provides that:

> On every matter submitted to a vote ... of stockholders ... every holder of Class B Common Stock shall be entitled to 10 votes ... for each share of Class B Common Stock standing in the holder's name ...

What is not immediately or obviously apparent is how Article Twelfth and amended Article Fourth relate to each other. That is, does the "affirmative vote ... of the holders of 70% of the stock" mean, after Article Fourth has been amended, that in the distinct vote required by Article Twelfth each holder of Class B stock will have 10 votes for each such share or does the literal meaning of the words "holders of 70% of the stock" require a different result? ...

B.

In seeking shareholder approval of the proposed certificate amendments, the proxy statement reviewed the protections that Article Twelfth afforded ... The proxy statement did not state a view as to how those protections would, either legally or as a practical matter, be affected by the issuance of the proposed Class B stock. Nor did the proxy statement expressly state that Mr. Briskin (if, as it stated was expected to occur, he obtained most or all of the new Class B stock) would be a Restricted Person under Article Twelfth – but that is the clear implication that arises from the proxy statement's description of a Restricted Person and its statement that Briskin was expected to exchange all of his Class A stock for Class B if the amendments were approved ...

This implication is incorrect; Mr. Briskin will not be a Restricted Person under Article Twelfth since he would acquire his shares in a transaction approved by two-thirds of the members of Arden's board.

Would such an incorrect implication be material, as above defined, to a shareholder asked to approve a proposal that he or she is told will have the likely consequence of delivering 67% of the voting power to Mr. Briskin? It could hardly be thought to be material if in voting affirmatively on the proposal a shareholder believed that Mr. Briskin would be able to cast his 67% vote in order to satisfy Article Twelfth's requirement ("the holders of 70% of the stock"). In that circumstance, it could not be considered important whether Briskin was or was not a Restricted Person.

But having read the proxy statement several times, I conclude that it is more likely than not that a reasonably attentive shareholder would – in the absence of a specific discussion of the inter-relationship between amended Article Fourth and Article Twelfth – rely upon the literal meaning of the words used to describe Article Twelfth and its effect, to conclude incorrectly that Mr. Briskin (whom he was lead to believe would be a Restricted Person) would not be able, if the proposal was approved, to satisfy the voting requirements of Article Twelfth essentially single-handedly. I also conclude that there is a material likelihood that such a conclusion would, considering the importance and character of the proposal ... and the entirety of the disclosure, be important to a reasonable shareholder deciding how to vote on this matter.

VI.

Finally, I have considered the harm that may befall the Company, Mr. Briskin and the other shareholders if the closing of the Exchange Offer is preliminarily enjoined and, on a fuller record, that injunction is determined to have been improvidently granted. In the circumstances, I conclude that the balance of the equities favors plaintiff. I will, of course, not enjoin the declaration and payment of the $.30 per share dividend. That is a matter for the board to decide upon.

For the foregoing reasons, plaintiff's motion shall be granted. Plaintiff shall submit a form of implementing order on notice.

Greenhalgh v. Arderne Cinemas Ltd
Court of Appeal
[1946] 1 All ER 512
Reproduced by permission of Reed Elsevier (UK) Limited, trading as LexisNexis Butterworths
[*Text edited; headnotes and footnotes omitted*]

LORD GREENE, MR

… In the present case [the appellant] is endeavouring to maintain a certain voting power which he acquired when he first became associated with the defendant company, and he contends that on one or other of two grounds he is entitled to conserve the position of comparative safety in the company which he originally obtained in that respect. However, in my opinion, he fails on both grounds. He could, no doubt, in one way or another at the outset have secured for himself that measure of control which he now says he is entitled to keep. If it had been the intention of the parties that his position should be secured in a manner which would be effective in law, there were various devices by which that result could have been achieved, but those methods were not incorporated in the bargain which the parties made …

The object of these proceedings is to attack the validity of a resolution of the company which subdivided certain 10s. ordinary shares, part of the issued capital of the company, into five 2s. ordinary shares. That is the first resolution that was attacked. The second resolution that was attacked was a resolution for increasing the capital of the company by the issue of further ordinary shares. As a result of those two resolutions, if they are valid, the voting power of the appellant, which previously gave him a satisfactory measure of voting control, is liable to be completely swamped by the votes of the other ordinary shareholders …

The appellant's case is put on two grounds: First, it is said that in the original agreement which was signed when the appellant first became associated with the company, a term is to be implied as a result of which the company would be precluded from acting in any way which would interfere with the voting control which he acquired as a result of that agreement. The agreement, to which (it is now admitted) the company must be treated as being a party, is set out in the statement of claim, and there are only two paragraphs that I need read. The appellant was putting a considerable amount of money into the company, which at the time was in a bad financial position, and it would not be unreasonable to expect that he would insist upon a very stringent measure of security. However, he has, I am afraid, failed to get it. The clauses of the agreement to which attention may be called are, first, cl. 2:

> That the company subdivide the whole of the present unissued ordinary shares of 10s. each into ordinary shares of 2s. each ranking pari passu with the other ordinary shares for voting and dividend …

Then cl. 3 provides that to carry out the provisions of that clause an extraordinary general meeting was to be called for the purpose of passing a resolution for the sub-division of the shares in accordance with cl. 2 and for authorising their allotment in various proportions. The great bulk of them were to be allotted to the appellant, and, by later provisions, he was to become the chairman of the company. The effect of that transaction, the subdivision and issuing of those unissued ordinary shares, was to put the appellant in a position in which, by force of his own voting power alone, he could prevent the passing of a special resolution. He obtained control of a further measure of voting power by means of a collateral agreement with the other principal shareholders under which they agreed to use their votes in support of him in the future. The effect of that collateral agreement would have been, as I say, to give the appellant a substantially greater measure of voting control. That agreement, however, was side-tracked by a manoeuvre executed by the other parties under which they disposed of the greater part of their shares; and in previous litigation it was held – and this court affirmed it [Greenhalgh v. Mallard (1)] – that neither could they be prevented from parting with their shares nor would the transferees of the shares be bound by the collateral agreement. In the result, the appellant lost the benefit of that agreement. He was, therefore, driven back on to his own share-holding as his safeguard against the passing of special resolutions or extraordinary resolutions which might be contrary to his wishes. It was that remaining measure of control which was attacked and sought to be destroyed by the next manoeuvre, which was the passing of the resolution now in question under which the issued 10s. shares were split, with the consequence that the holders of each of those shares acquired five times as many votes as they originally had.

At the request of the court, counsel for the appellant formulated what he said was the undertaking which must be implied in this agreement in order to give it effect, and this is what he said:

> That the company will not alter the measure of voting control of Mr. Greenhalgh resulting from the alteration in and the issue of capital hereinbefore agreed to either by the creation of new capital or by the alteration of the rights of the existing capital without the consent of Mr. Greenhalgh.

To imply into this contract such a term would, I think, be a very serious operation. It is a very far-reaching clause and gives to Greenhalgh, among other things, the power to veto the creation of any new capital in the company. I do not propose to examine in detail the nature of this clause or to examine the law which deals with the implication of terms in contracts. I may, however, say this: for a court to imply, in a complicated business agreement, a farreaching term is a very ser-ious matter. There is the pronouncement of SCRUTTON LJ [see Reigate v. Union Manufacturing Co. (Ramsbottom)] which is very frequently referred to, that the clause must be such that an impartial onlooker, who asked whether the parties intended it, would in effect be met with the answer, "of course we did." For the court to say that such an answer would be given, without the assistance of knowing all the circumstances, is in any case a very serious responsibility. For example, I cannot myself see that evidence would be admissible to prove that the parties had in effect considered such a term and had rejected it, since the question is fundamentally one of construction; and in the absence of any such evidence as that, it is putting upon the court the responsibility of saying, merely by looking at the agreement and with-out knowing all the circumstances, that the parties must have meant it. I am not saying that implied terms cannot be read into contracts; of course they can. There is abundant authority to that effect. But the case must be very exceptional and abso-lutely clear, and the court must remember that there may be many things of which it must necessarily be ignorant. In the present case, I cannot by any effort bring myself to think that the parties, if they had been asked whether this particular clause was one which they must have intended to put in, would have answered, "Yes." Both par-ties must answer; it is not sufficient for one to answer, "Yes." I can only say that I am quite unable to be convinced that any such clause can be implied.

The other argument is of a more technical nature. It is to this effect. The articles of association of the company incorporate certain of the provisions of Table A, and among others they incorporate art. 3 of Table A, which is in the following terms:

> If at any time the share capital is divided into different classes of shares, the rights attached to any class (unless otherwise provided by the terms of issue of the shares of that class) may be varied with the consent in writing of the holders of three-fourths of the issued shares of that class, or with the sanction of an extraordinary resolution passed at a separate general meeting of the holders of the shares of the class.

The rest of the article merely deals with procedure. It is said that the 2s. shares which came into existence through the subdivision of the unissued 10s. shares under the agreement between Greenhalgh and the company form a class of shares within the meaning of that article. VAISEY J was inclined to think that that was so, although he did not find it necessary to decide it. We also do not find it necessary to decide it, and I, like VAISEY J, am inclined to think that these shares form a class of shares within the meaning of the article, but it is not necessary to give a final answer to that question.

It is then said that the effect of the resolution which is now impugned is to vary the rights attached to those 2s. shares, and, as neither the consent in writing of the holders of three-fourths of those shares nor the sanction of an extraordinary reso-lution had been obtained, the resolution of the company which purported to sub-divide the issue of the 10s. shares was not effective.

The first thing to ascertain is: What are the rights attached to those original 2s. shares? In order to find that out one must look at the articles and the resolutions. I may say that we are not concerned with any rights except the voting rights. No ques-tion arises as to the dividend right or any other right. The voting powers attached to the shares of the company are to be found first in art. 21 of the company's articles. In para. (a) of that article the preference shareholders' voting rights are restricted by certain conditions, and then by para. (b), subject to those provisions as to the preference shares, arts. 54–62 of Table A are to apply. Art. 54 of Table A is as follows:

> On a show of hands every member present in person shall have one vote. On a poll every member shall have one vote for each share of which he is the holder.

Now I turn to the provisions relating to the subdivision of shares which are to be found in sect. 50 of the Act itself. Sect. 50 (1) provides:

> A company limited by shares or a company limited by guarantee and having a share capital, if so authorised by its articles, may alter the conditions of its memorandum as follows … it may … (b) consolidate and divide all or any of its share capital into shares of larger amount that its existing shares … (d) sub-divide its shares, or any of them, into shares of smaller amount than is fixed by the memorandum …

Then there is a provision:

> … that in the subdivision the proportion between the amount paid and the amount, if any, unpaid on each reduced share shall be the same as it was in the case of the share from which the reduced share is derived.

The necessary sanction in the articles is to be found by referring to art. 14 of the company's articles, which incorporates art. 37 of Table A. Art. 37 of Table A says:

> The company may by ordinary resolution … (b) subdivide its existing shares, or any of them, into shares of smaller amount than is fixed by the memorandum of association subject, nevertheless, to the provisions of sect. 50 (1) (d) of the Act.

The resolution passed at an extraordinary general meeting of the company held on Apr. 16, 1941, was to this effect:

> That the 4,705 ordinary shares of 10s. each be subdivided into 23,525 ordinary shares of 2s. each, ranking for dividend, voting and winding-up pari passu with the other ordinary shares for the time being issued.

The effect of what I have referred to is this: Each of those split 2s. shares was given one vote per share, and in that respect they rank pari passu with the 10s. ordinary shares for voting. Each 10s. share had one vote and each 2s. share had one vote, and that right was attached unquestionably to the 2s. shares. The resolution which is attacked is the resolution of Mar. 12, 1943, which is to this effect:

> That subject to the necessary consent in writing (in accordance with the articles of association of the company) of the holders of the present 10s. shares, the 26,295 issued ordinary shares of 10s. each to be subdivided into 131,475 ordinary shares of 2s. each ranking so as to form one class of shares with the existing 23,525 ordinary shares of 2s. each, and ranking for dividend, voting and winding-up pari passu with the said existing 2s. shares.

The 10s. shares so split into 2s. shares were those which throughout the relevant history were held, or the greater part of which were held, by the parties in the company who were opposing Greenhalgh. The 23,525 ordinary shares of 2s. each referred to in that resolution were the 2s. shares which resulted from the subdivision and issue in pursuance of the original agreement.

Looking at the position of the original 2s. ordinary shares, one asks oneself: What are the rights in respect of voting attached to that class within the meaning of art. 3 of Table A which are to be unalterable save with the necessary consents of the holders? The only right of voting which is attached in terms to the shares of that class is the right to have one vote per share pari passu with the other ordinary shares of the company for the time being issued. That right has not been taken away. Of course, if it had been attempted to reduce that voting right, e.g. by providing or attempting to provide that there should be one vote for every five of such shares, that would have been an interference with the voting rights attached to that class of shares. But nothing of the kind has been done; the right to have one vote per share is left undisturbed. In order, therefore, to make good the argument that what was done was an interference with the voting rights of that class of shares, it had to be argued, in effect, that those shares had attached to them a right within the meaning of art. 3 to object to the other ordinary shares being split so as to increase their voting power: in other vords [sic], that it was a right attached to these 2s. shares that they could object to any increase in the voting power attached to the 10s. shares resulting from a subdivision of those shares. If an attempt had been made, without subdividing the 10s. shares, to give them five votes per share, it may very well be that the rights attached to the original 2s. shares would have been varied, because one of the rights attached to that class of shares was that they should have voting powers pari passu with the other ordinary shares of the company and that right might well have been affected if in the result you had two kinds of ordinary shares, one a 10s. share carrying five votes and the other a 2s. share carrying one vote. But that is not what was done. The present position under the resolution which is attacked is that the ordinary shares are now all 2s. ordinary shares and each of them has one vote per share, and accordingly the voting power of the original 2s. shares is in fact entirely pari passu with the other ordinary shares. It only shows that these things are of a technical nature; but I cannot myself see how it can be said that there is attached to the original 2s. shares a right to object to the other ordinary shares having more than one vote, provided that is done, as I say, by the method of subdivision, which was the method employed here.

I now come to a point which to my mind, throws a good deal of light on the validity of the argument. It was conceded by counsel for the appellant that if the company had created a number of new ordinary shares of 2s. each and had issued them, each share carrying one vote, that would not have been an interference with the rights of the original 2s. shares. Had that been done, of course, it would have been just as possible to swamp the appellant's voting rights as it has turned out to be by the passing of these resolutions. I do not find anything in the answers of counsel which satisfactorily explains why it would be an interference with the 2s.

shares in the one case and not in the other case, because, if the 2s. shares had the right to prevent the voting equilibrium being upset in the way in which it has been upset, I cannot see why they could not object to the creation of new shares which would have the same result. However, it was said that the right claimed was limited to a right to veto the conferring on the existing 10s. shareholders, by the method of subdivision, an aggregate voting power greater than that which they had possessed in the past. It will be seen, as I have pointed out, that any such right could only arise by implication; it was not expressly conferred by the articles, or by the resolution, or by anything in the Act, or the general law, and I myself cannot find any justification for reading into the provisions of art. 3 of Table A any implied right of that kind. It is important, I think, in considering this matter, to remember that art. 3 is merely one clause in the constitution of this company. The constitution of the company is to be found in various documents; part of it is in the Act, part of it is in the articles, part of it is in Table A incorporated in the articles, and part of it is to be found in the relevant resolution. Art. 3 of Table A is merely one clause in the constitution of this company, and it must be construed in relation to the constitution as a whole. In the constitution as a whole, there is the power to subdivide the shares, and it is necessary for the appellant's argument to read that power to subdivide the shares as cut down by the suggested implied right in art. 3. As a matter of construction, I cannot do that. A person who took one of the original 2s. shares did so on the footing that the company by its constitution had power to subdivide its 10s. shares.

Several authorities have been cited, but the only one, I think, which throws any light on the matter is *Re Mackenzie & Co.* (2), a decision of ASTBURY J which I do find, up to a point, helpful. It was a case of a petition for reduction of capital, and under the memorandum and articles the only right of the preference shareholders was to have a fixed cumulative preferential dividend of a certain amount. A rateable reduction of all the shares, preference and ordinary, was proposed to be carried out, subject to the sanction of the court. All the shares, preference and ordinary, suffered the rateable reduction, and the result of that was that the dividend rights of the preference shareholders were substantially affected because, by reducing their capital, as they were only entitled to a fixed cumulative preferential dividend on the nominal amount of their capital for the time being paid up, it reduced the dividend accordingly, although the dividend still remained at 4 percent. That reduction operated in a certain way to the benefit of the ordinary shareholders, who were entitled to what is commonly called the equity. The agrument [*sic*] for the preference shareholders was this: "The reduction decreases our fixed dividend. The bargain was that we should have a fixed dividend notwithstanding reduction from loss of capital." ASTBURY J pointed out that the only dividend right was a right to 4 percent, per annum on the nominal amount of the capital from time to time paid up or credited as paid up, and that, under the articles, the company had power to reduce its capital. He then said ... :

> The result of the memorandum and articles shortly is this. Subject to the right of the company to reduce its capital by the votes of the ordinary shareholders in any manner sanctioned by statute these preference shares are to be of the denomination of £20 each, and the only special right, privilege, or advantage attached to those shares is a cumulative 4 percent preferential dividend on the nominal amount of capital from time to time paid up or credited as paid up thereon.

There, I think, the judge was applying the principle which (as I have just said) must be remembered in construing these provisions, viz., that a provision dealing with class rights is only one clause in the company's constitution, which must be construed as a whole. He found in the company's constitution an unqualified right to reduce the capital, and he negatived the suggestion that the class rights clause in the articles over-rode the power to reduce the capital.

Construing the provisions here, we must read the class rights as being confined to the express terms of the article, which alone can restrict the power of sub-division given by the Act and the articles … [T]he effect of this resolution is, of course, to alter the position of the 1941 2s. shareholders. Instead of Greenhalgh finding himself in a position of control, he finds himself in a position where the control has gone, and to that extent the rights of the 1941 2s. shareholders are affected, as a matter of business. As a matter of law, I am quite unable to hold that, as a result of the transaction, the rights are varied; they remain what they always were – a right to have one vote per share pari passu with the ordinary shares for the time being issued which include the new 2s. ordinary shares resulting from the subdivision.

In the result, the appeal must be dismissed with costs.

MORTON, LJ

I agree.

On the question as to whether there can be implied in the agreement of Mar. 27, 1941, the term which counsel for the appellant asked us to imply, I do not desire to add anything.

[Text omitted]

To my mind it is impossible to say that that voting right has been varied by the resolution of Mar. 12, 1943. All that has happened is that the company has exercised the power which it possesses under art. 37 of Table A of subdividing some of its other issued shares. The plaintiff, the present appellant, took his shares in 1941 on the footing of the company's memorandum and articles, i.e. he took them on the footing that the company had the power of subdivision. Thus the subdivision in 1943 took place under a provision which was part of the bargain under which Greenhalgh took his shares. He might, as my Lord has said, have preserved the balance of voting power by inserting some appropriate provision in the agreement of 1941, although I do not think it would have been a very easy provision to draft. No such provision, however, appears in the agreement. He is, therefore, unable to object, successfully to the resolution of Mar. 12, 1943. That being so, it is conceded by counsel for the appellant that no objection can be taken to the resolution of June 16, 1944, under which the capital of the company was increased. The only objection put forward to that resolution was that the voting rights were exercised on the footing that the earlier resolution of Mar. 12, 1943, was valid and effectual. As we have held that that earlier resolution was valid and effectual, the only objection to the second resolution falls to the ground.

I agree that the appeal must be dismissed with costs.

PART III

Governing the corporation

SUBPART A

The management

10

An introduction to the board and its governance

The benefits and risks of central management

I. Delegated authority and agency costs

In the first nine chapters of this text, we have looked closely at three of the essential characteristics of stock corporations. By incorporating, a stock corporation obtains *legal personality*. In this respect, certain requirements – in particular adequate capitalization – must be met in order that shareholders receive the benefit of *limited liability*. A company may structure its *freely transferable shares* in classes having characteristics that meet the needs of its shareholders and itself. In this part of the text, we will begin to look closely at the feature of the corporation that generates the bulk of litigation and scholarly investigation in corporate law: the delegation of power over the company's operations to a *central management*. This delegation of power to a central management is a characteristic of all large corporations. Power is delegated both because effective decisionmaking requires concentration of authority in a relatively agile group of persons and because shareholders either do not want to manage the company or do not have the necessary skills to do so. The result is that power passes from its residual owners (the shareholders) to persons who act on mandate from the shareholders to perform certain duties (the management).

The delegation of one's power and authority to another person – whether in the context of a simple principal/agent relationship, the somewhat more complex owner/manager relationship, or the citizen/minister relationship characteristic of representative democracies – creates the risk that the person receiving the delegated power will be disloyal or incompetent. To reduce the risks of incompetence and disloyalty, the person delegating the authority must incur certain costs to structure the rights and duties of the agent and also supervise the agent's performance. Economists refer to these expenses as *agency costs*. Professors Michael C. Jensen and William H. Meckling, in an important article on the subject, define such agency costs as the sum of:

1. the costs of creating and structuring contracts between the share-holder and the manager;
2. the costs of monitoring the manager to prevent both negligence and disloyalty;
3. the costs of the manager incurred in proving loyalty ("bonding expenditures"); and
4. the residual loss incurred because diligence and loyalty are never perfect.[1]

A central problem of corporate governance is to maximize the benefits of delegating authority to management while keeping *agency costs* as low as possible. Laws reduce the costs of contracting referred to in the first point by providing some ready-made terms of the appointment and relationship. The second point – monitoring – makes up the bulk of the legal work in corporate governance, and our three jurisdictions address monitoring with the standard techniques used in any situation to limit undesirable behavior.[2]

Managers are screened in advance. The law often requires that managers fulfill certain criteria (such as expertise or independence) in advance (*ex ante*). The law also gives shareholders the right to appoint managers, usually through election at a general meeting, which gives the shareholders an opportunity to review their qualifications in advance. Screening is not concerned with procedures or monitoring of actions, but rather seeks to select the right *types* of people, by their experience, qualities and character traits to bring about successful performance. For example, as discussed below, German company law seeks to protect labor interests in the corporation by requiring that a certain number of labor representatives sit on the supervisory board, but then specifies no further duties of procedure or substance to ensure they fulfill this goal. The background and orientation of the individual is considered guarantee enough. The *type* of person understood to have the "right stuff" may change as our understanding of human motivations and the needs of the moment change: when we believe that a sleepy economy or business should seize the moment, we seek hard-driving, dynamic managers with charisma, but, following scandals caused by excessive management freedom, we might well prefer independent, ethically minded managers.

---

[1] Jensen and Meckling (1976: 85).
[2] This schematic overview of the techniques used to address agency problems owes much to the landmark analysis presented in Armour, Hansmann and Kraakman (2009b: 35 *et seq.*).

Managers are regulated by rules and standards. While in office, regardless of how independent, qualified and ethical they are, managers must comply with certain *rules* (such as holding meetings in specified ways and disclosing specified information, refraining from insider trading) and also meet certain *standards* (such as acting in accordance with required duties of care and loyalty). Rules tend to be clear cut, and the "compliance officers" of corporations design formal procedures (e.g. any share sales of managers must be cleared by internal counsel) to ensure that management does not stray over the line. Standards, on the other hand, are broad and subject to definitional play: was, under *these circumstances*, the procedure used "adequate" and the result reached with "in the best interest of the company"? Standards allow management to act freely and flexibly, and also allow courts to catch new and unforeseen breaches of duty; cases decided on standards lend a certain level of predictability without the rigidity of rules. If managers break rules or standards, shareholders or their representatives can sue after-the-fact (*ex post*) to seek redress. The use of standard-based complaints *ex post* favors innovative business operations by leaving management free to act and disciplining it only when a complaint is actually made and a judge finds that the behavior under the circumstances violated the standard.

Lastly, managers are given incentives. In the best instances, remuneration can be structured as a guiding carrot to accompany the regulatory stick of rules and standards. Salaried management does not always have the same financial interest as the shareholders. Salary might be due and payable regardless of whether management guides the company to profitability. In order to better align the self-interest of management with the financial interest of the shareholders, executive compensation can be scaled on performance. This can be done by awarding management bonuses linked to the company's success or by granting them stock and stock options as a component of their pay.

The governance of a stock corporation uses these various techniques to harness the energy of the managers without unduly breaking their pace, and thus to guide management's activity toward the highest gain of the company. This part of the text will address the basic framework in which such techniques are employed. The remaining chapters in this subpart will examine specific techniques in more detail. Chapter 11 will explain how management is empowered to represent the company without binding it beyond the scope of the delegated discretion. Chapter 12 will then turn to the main standards used to reign in management's discretionary activity – the duties of care and loyalty. Chapter 13 will examine the delicate activity of monitoring management's judgment without second-guessing their business expertise: the business judgment rule. In Chapter 14, we will examine executive compensation to understand how the interests of management and shareholders can be aligned and the risks that certain remuneration schemes can entail. Chapter 15 will turn from standards to rules, and present many of the bright-line rules that apply to the management of a publicly listed company in our three jurisdictions. The following sections of this chapter offer an introductory sketch of the governance framework in each of our three jurisdictions.

II.   The general governance framework in the three jurisdictions

A.   Germany

1.   Screening and appointing management   The *Aktiengesetz* mandates a two-tier board structure in which certain directors fulfill a supervisory role and others perform a management role. Therefore, the attempt to predetermine "types" of managers who can be expected to act independently in a supervisory capacity is not as necessary as it is in one-tier board systems, for the supervisory activity is imposed on a group of managers by the very purpose of the legal body in which they sit. The *Aktiengesetz* does set out a few requirements for members of the supervisory board (*Aufsichtsrat*)[3] and the management board (*Vorstand*),[4] such as absence of criminal records and the maximum number of companies on whose boards they may sit. The German Code of Corporate Governance sets out additional recommendations regarding the practices of board members in publicly listed companies, such as recommending the creation of sub-committees within the *Aufsichtsrat*.[5] Section III of this chapter on co-determination of employees in Germany explains how shareholders appoint all or a portion of the *Aufsichtsrat* and the latter body then appoints the members of the *Vorstand*. Because the terms of office of the *Aufsichtsrat* and the *Vorstand* can be long (up to five years), the threat of facing re-election is weaker than it would be with a shorter term of office, but the shareholders must vote each year to "clear them of liability for their actions" (*Entlastung*) during the year,[6] and may remove the members of the *Aufsichtsrat* whom they elect.[7]

2.   Regulating management with rules and standards   The *Aktiengesetz* contains a number of rules for regulating the behavior of

---

[3] § 100 AktG.   [4] § 76(3) AktG.   [5] Para. 5.3 *Kodex*.
[6] § 120 AktG.   [7] § 103(1) AktG.

management. Many required procedures for meetings and decisionmaking are specified.[8] For example, the *Vorstand* is responsible for calling the general meeting[9] and assembling the financial statements to be presented in the context of the meeting.[10] Other rules address possible self-dealing by forbidding activity that competes with the company[11] and by requiring that one body represent the company when negotiating compensation contracts with the other,[12] and that any loans the company grants to a board member be approved by specified procedures.[13] Both the *Aktiengesetz* and the decisions of the High Federal Court set out specific standards of loyalty and care that directors are required to meet. These will be addressed in Chapters 11 and 12.

3. **Aligning management's interests to shareholders' interests** In 1998, German law was amended to facilitate the use of stock and stock options to create performance-linked compensation for members of the *Vorstand*.[14] In 2005, the law was again amended to ensure that executive compensation – both fixed and performance-linked – paid in listed companies be disclosed to the financial markets.[15]

B.   United Kingdom

1. **Screening and appointing management** Unlike German law, the Companies Act 2006 provides for a single-tier board of directors in which no director has specific, supervisory duties over any other. Unlike US law, the Companies Act does not, however, specify that the company will be managed "by or under" the board, although the model articles do state that "the directors are responsible for the management of the company's business."[16] Indeed, although the 2006 Act ascribes to the board a far more detailed set of fiduciary duties[17] than found in either the German or the US statutes, the exact powers of the board and the manner of its selection may be freely agreed upon in the company's articles, the only limit being rights of the shareholders and certain duties of directors expressly provided for in the law. Indeed, even where full management power is

---

[8] See e.g. §§ 90, 91, 107, 108–111 AktG.   [9] § 121(2) AktG.
[10] §§ 242, 264 HGB. The financial statements must also be submitted to the *Aufsichtsrat* for inspection and approval: see §§ 170–172 AktG.
[11] § 88 AktG.   [12] §§ 87, 107(3), 112 AktG.
[13] §§ 89, 115 AktG.
[14] See the KonTraG.   [15] See BGBl vol. I, p. 2267 (August 3, 2005).
[16] Reg. 3 SI 2008 No. 3229.
[17] See Chapter 12 for a detailed discussion of directors' duties under UK law.

vested in the board, if the board fails to act, the shareholders are generally considered to retain a residual power to take over the previously delegated power.[18] One of the few tasks of the board that is specifically stated in the statute is to prepare and issue the annual accounts and the directors' report.[19]

The Companies Act does not provide for the election of directors or their terms of office, and the shareholders are free to structure in the company's articles the manner in which directors are appointed.[20] Currently, the model articles provide for the election of directors by an ordinary resolution and retirement at the third annual general meeting.[21] Shareholders may remove a director at any time, regardless of any guarantees or terms of office specified in the articles, with an ordinary resolution.[22]

This situation changes when the company is listed and becomes subject to the Combined Code,[23] which requires that a board contain a "balance of executive and non-executive directors,"[24] appointed according to a "formal, rigorous and transparent procedure,"[25] and that a number of committees, particularly an audit committee,[26] be established. We shall examine these rules more closely in Chapter 15.

2. Regulating management with rules and standards The Companies Act 2006 contains a number of rules to guard against self-dealing by directors. It provides that directors must disclose any interest they might have in a transaction with the company,[27] obtain shareholder approval for substantial property transactions,[28] and obtain certain specified approvals before receiving a loan from the company.[29] When a company is listed, the number of rules increases through the addition of the Listing Rules and the FSA's Disclosure and Transparency Rules, both of which place further comportment and disclosure requirements on directors.[30] The 2006 Act also codifies the duties of care and the fiduciary duties of directors,[31] and these rules are supplemented where necessary

---

[18] See *Alexander Ward & Co.* v. *Samyang Navigation Co.* [1975] 1 WLR 673, 679 (HL Sc.); *Foster* v. *Foster* [1916] 1 Ch 532; Reg. 4 SI 2008 No. 3229 gives the members a residual right at any time to instruct the directors to act or refrain from acting .

[19] Secs. 394, 399 CA 2006.   [20] Davies (2008: 378–379).

[21] Regs. 20, 21 MAPC.   [22] Sec. 168 CA 2006.

[23] FSA Listing Rules, Rule 9.8.6(5), (6).   [24] Para. A.3 Combined Code.

[25] Para. A.4 Combined Code.   [26] Para. C.3 Combined Code.

[27] Secs. 177, 182 CA 2006.   [28] Sec. 190 CA 2006.

[29] Sec. 197 CA 2006.

[30] See e.g. FSA Listing Rules, Rule 11; and FSA Disclosure and Transparency Rules, Rule 3.

[31] Secs. 170–177 CA 2006.

by the decisions of UK courts.[32] These will be discussed in some detail in Chapter 12.

3. Aligning management's interests to shareholders' interests   The use of performance-linked remuneration is recommended by the UK Combined Code.[33] In a listed company, the shareholders must approve any share scheme or long-term incentive scheme for directors.[34] The Companies Act requires directors of listed companies to prepare a report on their remuneration annually and submit it to shareholders in connection with the AGM.[35] This will be addressed in more detail in Chapter 15.

C.   United States

1. Screening and appointing management   As mentioned above, US corporate statutes generally specify that the company will be managed "by or under" a board of directors,[36] which means that the directors either manage the company themselves or, as in larger corporations, monitor employee executives. Foremost among such employee executives is the "chief executive officer" (CEO) – who is often also the chairman of the board of directors. The DGCL and the Model Act provide for annual election of directors by a majority of the votes unless the constitutional documents specify otherwise.[37] As we have seen with regard to UK law, the amount of regulation increases also in the US as the company's equity becomes more widely distributed and eventually listed. We have seen that companies subject to SEC registration must comply with a layer of mandatory federal law and companies listed on a stock exchange must also comply with the listing requirements of the relevant exchange. Figure 10.1 shows how US law moves from maximum flexibility to a very uniform and restrictive set of rules.

Pursuant to the rules of the NYSE and the Nasdaq Stock Market, the board of directors of a listed company should contain audit, nominations and compensation committees to perform functions related to the accounts, the election of directors and officers, and the remuneration of the latter, respectively.[38] Exchange rules require that either all or a majority of the members of such committees be "independent." The criteria that make a director "independent" will be addressed in more detail

---

[32] Sec. 170(4) CA 2006.
[33] Para. B.1 Combined Code.   [34] FSA Listing Rules, Rule 9.4.
[35] Secs. 420–422 CA 2006.   [36] § 141(a) DGCL; § 8.01(b) Model Act.
[37] §§ 211(b), 216(3) DGCL; §§ 7.28, 8.03 Model Act.
[38] See para. 303A NYSE LCM; and Rule 5600 Nasdaq Marketplace Rules.

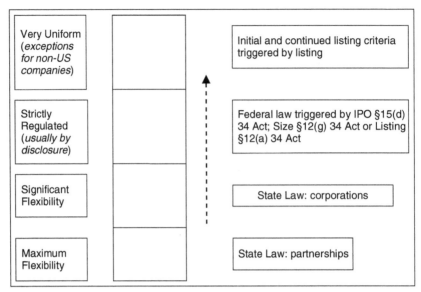

Figure 10.1 US law from the flexible to the rigid

in Chapter 15. Here it is sufficient to note that "independent" generally means having no financial or family connection to the company, its management or a major shareholder. Thus, the pre-screening of directors for listed companies uses the absence of such financial and family ties to qualify people as suited for acting in the best interests of the shareholders.[39] The aim of this pre-screening is to achieve a result quite similar to that of the German *Aufsichtsrat*, with the difference that, instead of being separated from management in a distinct body with functions provided for by law, different "types" of people are asked to perform different functions within the management body itself. It should also be noted that, where under German law the supervisory directors choose the managing directors, in the US framework, the managing directors may have significant power to choose their "supervisors."[40]

As noted, the term of directors in US companies will be one year unless provided otherwise. If the board is "staggered," the term will be longer. A

---

[39] Of course, this is based on the assumption that people are motivated primarily by economic drivers and family ties. If the best available science were to profess that people were more strongly motivated by other relationships, such as their nationality or ethnic background, then such criteria could potentially be used to choose directors with the "right" characteristics.

[40] See the discussion of the power held by the CEO in the *Disney* case in Chapter 13.

"staggered" board simply means that only a portion of the members come up for election each year. Thus, if a board were split into three classes with each class serving a term of three years, every year one class of the board would come up for re-election. Both Delaware law and the Model Act allow shareholders to remove directors with or without cause at a special meeting,[41] but this right is somewhat empty both because it can be eliminated in the articles of incorporation and because shareholders generally cannot call a special meeting.[42]

2.   Regulating management with rules and standards   State law contains some rules to regulate the behavior of management, such as rules on holding meetings and adopting resolutions, and rules on transactions between the company and directors,[43] but the rules on conflicted transactions are far less detailed than those found in the Companies Act 2006. Most rules applicable to the management of US companies are triggered only when the company is registered with the SEC, and primarily require disclosure and the certification of disclosure.[44] Standards are the primary tool that state law uses to regulate the behavior of management. The standards used are a duty of loyalty to punish self-dealing and the taking of corporate opportunities, and a duty of care to punish the grossly negligent behavior of directors. These standards will be explored in Chapter 12.

3.   Aligning management's interests to shareholders' interests   The use of performance-linked compensation is common in the US.[45] It is intended to align the interest of management in their own financial well-being with that of the shareholders in the market price of their shares. Unfortunately, it has also encouraged management to manipulate the price at which their stock options are issued as well as the price of the stock itself, in order make as much profit as possible on the options. This topic will be addressed in Chapter 14.

---

[41] § 141(k) DGCL; § 8.08 Model Act.
[42] § 7.02(a) Model Act does, like UK and German law, allow for shareholders (here, holding 10 percent of the votes to be cast) to call a special meeting, although the articles may increase the required percentage to 25 percent. Under the DGCL, this right would have to be created in the constitutional documents.
[43] § 144 DGCL; § 8.60 Model Act.   [44] See the materials for Chapter 12.
[45] For the 200 companies included in the 2009 *Wall Street Journal* Survey of Executive Compensation, incentives and grants of options and restricted stock make up the greatest portion of executive pay. See http://graphicsweb.wsj.com/php/CEOPAY09.html.

III.   German co-determination

A.   Brief history of German employee representation

Co-determination, or employee representation on the board of a company, is a way of protecting labor interests by inserting persons with
contacts and duties to the employees on the administrative organ of a
company. Here the composition of the board is itself seen as a protection.
The earliest attempts in Germany legally to provide for co-determination
date back to 1848.[46] A draft trade law introduced in a workers congress in
Berlin provided for labor participation in setting wages, deciding on termination and choosing supervisory personnel.[47] The draft trade legislation failed, as did most of the other legislation submitted during the 1848
attempt to unite Germany in a constitutional republic, as under Bismarck
Germany instead sought unity under Prussian hegemony.[48]

The first significant breakthrough for co-determination occurred in
1890, when an amendment to the Business Practice Act (*Gewerbeordnung*
or GewO) was passed to permit the voluntary formation of labor councils
at the factory level, and such councils became mandatory by 1916 in all
industries essential to Germany's war effort.[49] The next major advancement of co-determination was expressed in Article 165 of the Weimar
Constitution of 1919, which guaranteed employees the right to cooperate
with employers on an equal basis in the regulation of wages and working conditions, and in the economic development of production facilities. These objectives were implemented in 1920 through adoption of the
Works Council Act (*Betriebsrätegesetz*), which provided for representation of employees through workers' councils at the factory level and also
provided for some labor representatives to be seated directly on supervisory boards.[50]

Professor Thomas Raiser sees the birth of modern co-determination in
the post-war iron and steel industry. The shattered German industry in
its struggle to regroup offered labor equal representation on the boards
of corporations in the mining, iron and steel industries; however, as the
economy improved in the early 1950s, the industrialists and the government back-peddled. In 1950, the federal government submitted a draft
bill that provided for merely one-third co-determination in the supervisory boards of large corporations, and the labor unions demanded that

---

[46] Raiser and Veil (2009: Intro. mn. 1).   [47] Raiser and Veil (2009: Intro. mn. 1).
[48] See e.g. Gall (2001: 92–93).   [49] Raiser and Veil (2009: Intro. mn. 2).
[50] Raiser and Veil (2009: Intro. mn. 3).

the existing model of parity co-determination be retained. Only under the threat of a general strike did the German Parliament adopt the principle of parity representation on the supervisory boards and the institution of labor directors on the management boards of companies operating in the mining, iron and steel industries in the Law on Co-Determination of Employees in the Supervisory Boards and Management Boards of Enterprises Engaged in the Mining, Iron and Steel Industries of 21 May 1951 (*Montan-Mitbestimmungsgesetz*).[51] The structure of co-determination expressed in this law went far beyond previous forms of labor cooperation in productive enterprises, as it provided for equal representation of employees and shareholders on the supervisory board and for the appointment of a director responsible for social and personnel matters to the management board (labor director).

The next year, the Labor Management Relations Act of 1952 (*Betriebsverfassungsgesetz* 1952, or BetrVG 1952) introduced the principle of one-third employee representation on the supervisory board with no representation on the management board for all other industries.[52] This situation remained unaltered for almost twenty-five years until, in 1976, the Co-Determination Act (*Mitbestimmungsgesetz* or MitbestG) was enacted. The MitbestG has expanded co-determination of employees in the supervisory board of large corporations to near parity.

B.   The current co-determination rules in Germany

1. The three co-determination regimes   Under current German law, three co-determination regimes need to be distinguished.

First, there is co-determination pursuant to the Montan Co-Determination Act discussed above, which applies to corporations and corporate groups operating in the mining, iron and steel sectors. As a rule, corporations within the scope of these Acts have a supervisory board composed of eleven members, of whom five are appointed by the shareholders, five by the employees, and one (the eleventh member) by the representatives of both sides.[53]

Secondly, there is co-determination pursuant to the DrittelbG that, in 2004, replaced the co-determination provisions of the BetrVG 1952, leaving the substance of this co-determination regime unchanged. The DrittelbG applies, *inter alia*, to stock corporations and partnerships limited by shares (KGaA) in all other areas of industry, provided their

---

[51] Raiser and Veil (2009: Intro. mn. 4).   [52] Raiser and Veil (2009: Intro. mn. 5).
[53] § 8 Montan-MitbestG.

workforce exceeds 500[54] but remains under 2,000.[55] For AGs and KGaAs with less than 500 employees, the DrittelbG provides rather complicated rules for the application of co-determination.[56] If the relevant AG or KGaA was entered in the commercial register after August 10, 1994, it will not be subject to co-determination, but, if it was entered before that date, it will be subject to co-determination under the BetrVG 1952 unless all shares are owned by one natural person or a group of natural persons.[57]

Thirdly, there is co-determination under the Co-Determination Act 1976. This Act applies to AGs and KGaAs with more than 2,000 employees that are not engaged in the mining, coal or steel industries.[58] It requires that a supervisory board consist of an even number of members (twelve, sixteen or twenty, depending on the number of employees), equally divided between shareholder and employee representatives.[59] The supervisory board must have a chairman and (at least) one deputy chairman, who are elected by the vote of two-thirds of the entire supervisory board.[60] Therefore, any successful candidate for these positions will need some votes from the members of the other group on the first ballot. If the required two-thirds majority is not attained, a second ballot is held in which the board members representing the shareholders elect the chairman by a simple majority of votes cast and the board members representing the employees elect the deputy chairman by a simple majority of the votes cast.[61] Because the election often comes to a second ballot, the chairman of the supervisory board will usually be a shareholder representative, and the deputy chairman will usually be a labor representative.

This balance proves to be a decisive factor in appointing the members of the management board because the MitbestG gives the supervisory board chairman a tie-breaking vote.[62] The voting process for the management board members presents a multiple ballot structure similar to that used for supervisory board officers. On the first ballot, the election of the managing directors requires a two-thirds majority.[63] If this is not attained, a committee consisting of the chairman, deputy chairman and two further board members (one representing the shareholders, the other the employees) must be composed to submit a nomination slate to the entire supervisory board within one month after the first ballot, and

---

[54] § 1 DrittelbG.   [55] §§ 1(2) DrittelbG in conjunction with § 1(1) no. 2 MitbestG 1976.
[56] § 1(1) no. 1 second sentence DrittelbG.
[57] For the applicable definition of natural persons, see § 15(1) nos. 2–8 of the Tax Code.
[58] § 1(1), (2) MitbestG.   [59] See § 7 MitbestG.
[60] § 27(1) MitbestG.   [61] § 27(2) MitbestG.
[62] § 31 MitbestG.   [63] § 31(2) MitbestG.

election on this round requires only a simple majority of the members.[64] If the employee and the shareholder representatives reach a tied vote, a third ballot is triggered in which the chair of the supervisory board will have a tie-breaking vote.[65] Because, as explained above, the chair of the supervisory board will usually be a shareholder appointee, he or she will vote for the shareholders' candidates for the management board, thereby ensuring their election.

This slight predominance of shareholder influence on the appointment of the corporation's managing directors has held the Constitutional Court back from striking down the Co-Determination Act 1976 as an unjust taking of private property in violation of the protections set out in article 14 of the German Federal Constitution.[66]

---

[64] § 31(3) MitbestG.   [65] § 31(4) MitbestG.

[66] The Court's opinion is reported in German at BVerfGE 50, 290.

11

Directors' power to represent the company

Required reading

EU: First Company Law Directive, art. 9
D: AktG, §§ 37(3), 39(1), 78, 81, 82, 112, 246(2)
UK: CA 2006, secs. 39–41, 43–48, 270–271, 273, 275, 280
US: DGCL, §§ 122(3), 141(a), (c), 142

Capacity, authority and reliance in contracting

This chapter addresses one of the "topical" areas of law discussed in Chapter 1 that are not formally "company law," but are nevertheless integral to the operations of the company. All corporations enter into contracts with third parties, beginning with the purchase or lease of their means of production and ending with the sale of their goods or services. These relationships are governed by contract law, not corporate law, and whether the person purporting to act for the corporation can bind it when entering into such contracts is primarily a matter of the law of agency.[1]

Three concepts are central to this topic: capacity, authority and good faith reliance. If a five-year-old child were to appoint a neighbor to the position of chief negotiator with her parents regarding all future "disciplinary proceedings," the grant of authority may be formally valid, but it would nevertheless be without effect because the child does not have *capacity* to make it. Corporations have much in common with small children, as they can do nothing on their own. Companies depend fully on the agency of humans and have only the capacity that the law and their constitutional documents give them. Because of this, a company needs *agents*, and agents

---

[1] "Agency is the fiduciary relationship that arises when one person (a 'principal') manifests assent to another person (an 'agent') that the agent shall act on the principal's behalf and subject to the principal's control, and the agent manifests assent or otherwise consents so to act." Restatement (Third) of Agency, § 1.01 (2006).

need *authority* if they are to bind their principal in contract. The existence of *actual* authority is determined with reference to the relationship between the company as principal and the agent, and includes both the agent's expressly assigned rights and his customary activities. As will be discussed below, when entering into a large transaction with a corporation, the third party or his lawyers will always follow the chain of delegation backwards from the person actually holding the signature pen to the constitution of the company. In such circumstances, every link in the chain of authority from the valid existence of the company to the identity of the signing party will be checked for sufficient attribution of authority.

Actual authority is joined by another important issue of agency law. The very fact that a corporation's constitutional documents may limit its capacity and that the corporation can act only through agents, often leaves third parties uncertain as to whether the company has the capacity to enter into a transaction and whether the agent has the authority to bind it. One solution would be for agents always to carry up-to-date documentation proving capacity and authority, and present it to contracting parties for their examination before entering into even the smallest of transactions. Third parties could then bear all consequences of their error when actual capacity and authority were lacking, and in a large transaction the burden would be borne by the third party's lawyers and their liability insurer. This method, however, would be time-consuming and costly for corporations while acting as a disincentive for third parties to contract with legal entities. Another solution would be for courts to create fictive capacity or authority when necessary to achieve justice. Courts could look at the facts of a given case, and decide whether a person acting in good faith received the reasonable impression that the corporate agent had authority to act for a company within its range of capacity, and if the third party *relied* to her detriment on such impression. In such cases, the court could assume capacity and authority to exist even when they are actually absent. This will be discussed in section III of this chapter.

Thus, the main issues that arise when directors represent the company are summarily sketched in Figure 11.1. We will briefly discuss each of these issues below.

I.   The capacity of corporations and the ultra vires doctrine

Investors create corporations to pursue a specific range of activities, and thus one logical way to ensure that a company does not engage in activities other than those intended is to specify a "corporate purpose" or a

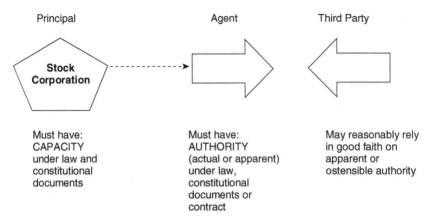

Principal   Agent   Third Party

Must have: Must have: May reasonably rely
CAPACITY   AUTHORITY   in good faith on
under law and   (actual or apparent)   apparent or
constitutional   under law,   ostensible authority
documents   constitutional
                           documents or
                           contract

Figure 11.1   Capacity, authority and reliance

"corporate object" in the constitutional documents and hold the company to such purpose or object.[2] In this way, the company has a restriction on its *capacity*. Actions beyond the delegated powers (in Latin, *ultra vires*) would be without capacity and therefore void. In the nineteenth century, this was a common way for investors to put a leash on company management.[3] As Ferran has observed, however, accounting rules and stock exchange disclosure requirements came to provide investors with more information about company operations, and, with "the investor demand for information met in other ways, the objects clause became, at least potentially, more of a hindrance than a help to investors because it could prevent companies from diversifying their business into more profitable lines of activity."[4] Investor monitoring and *ex post* action came to replace an *ex ante* contractual limitation as the most effective source of controlling management. Moreover, limiting the activities of a company through its objects can have an unfair impact on third parties. This could, for example, allow a company to enter into a risky agreement in an area beyond its power, and, if the deal turned out to be unprofitable, any shareholder could then sue to have the contract declared void as *ultra vires*.[5]

For reasons of both equity and commercial reality, in the early twentieth century, courts began reading objects clauses broadly and implying additional powers as necessary.[6] Later, legislatures eliminated the

---

[2] As we saw in Chapter 4, the corporation laws of each of our jurisdictions have at least in the past all required that a purpose or object be specified. See § 23(3) no. 2 AktG; sec. 2(1) (c) CA 1985; and § 102(a)(3) DGCL. The UK has been the first to move beyond this requirement in sec. 31(1) CA 2006.

[3] Friedman (2005: 395).   [4] Ferran (1999: 85–86).   [5] Friedman (2005: 395).

[6] Friedman (2005: 395–396).

use of *ultra vires* to void transactions with third parties,[7] while retaining the ability of shareholders to hold management to such restrictions as a matter of internal governance.[8] As a result, even if a company acts beyond its capacity as provided for in the constitutional documents, the laws of our jurisdictions will uphold the rights of the third party against the corporation arising out of the transaction. Complaints based on *ultra vires* remain available only for internal actions against directors that act beyond the powers granted to them.

II.   Actual or true authority

A.   Pursuant to company law

Each of our corporate law statutes expressly gives power to the board of directors to represent the company in dealings with third parties.[9] The only restrictions on this power arise in transactions with other directors, and such restrictions are designed to address conflicts of interest arising from self-dealing.[10] The statutes also expressly allow the board to delegate power to represent the company to committees, individual board members, and agents.[11] As a result, the link in the chain of authority directly following the valid and proper constitution of the company is the act delegating power to any such body or person.

The *Aktiengesetz* assigns the power to represent the company exclusively to the *Vorstand*, but gives the *Aufsichtsrat* the power to represent the company in dealings with the *Vorstand*.[12] The law assigns the *Vorstand* the power to represent the company collectively as a body,[13] so that any power of individual directors must be granted by the *Satzung* or a board resolution,[14] and any power of a director together with a statutory attorney-in-fact (*Prokurist*) to do the same must be included in the *Satzung*.[15] The Companies Act 2006 expressly gives each director acting alone the power to bind the company, provided a witness attests to the director's signature.[16] UK law assigns the company secretary a role comparable to a *Prokurist* for purposes of representing the company. Every public company must have a secretary,[17] and they are deemed "authorized signatories" able

---

[7] § 82(1) AktG; sec. 39(1) CA 2006; § 124(1) DGCL.
[8] § 82(2) AktG; sec. 40(4) CA 2006; § 124(1)–(2) DGCL.
[9] § 78(1) AktG; secs. 40(1), 44(2)–(3) CA 2006; § 141(a) DGCL.
[10] See Chapter 10.   [11] § 78(4) AktG; sec. 40(1) CA 2006; § 141(c) DGCL.
[12] §§ 78(1), 112 AktG.   [13] § 78(2) AktG.   [14] § 78(2), (4) AktG.
[15] § 78(2) AktG.   [16] Sec. 44(2)(b) CA 2006.
[17] Sec. 271 CA 2006.

to bind the company when signing together with one director.[18] Delaware law allows the board to assign most of its power, including the representation of the company, to committees and subcommittees that can be composed of an individual director.[19] In light of this, do you agree with the court's finding in *Hurley* v. *Ornsteen*? Both the DGCL and the Model Act expressly provide that officers may be appointed, but do not specify any powers for such officers.[20] The Delaware courts have for decades held that the office of "president" is the chief executive officer of the company and has all powers necessary for its ordinary operations.[21]

The laws also provide a means of proving that a given person has requisite authority. Our common law jurisdictions allow for the use of a company seal,[22] which is an engraved mould that allows the name and other distinguishing marks of the company to be stamped onto a document in lieu of a signature. Actually, this type of seal belongs to the company and not to the representative, so that the company itself contracts when the seal is applied, bypassing the chain of authority. The question then becomes whether the person applying the seal is authorized to do so, a question very close to the original query regarding the power to represent the company as signatory. It is therefore not surprising that courts treat the authorization to apply the seal much like the authorization to sign on behalf of the company. In *Northside Developments Pty Ltd* v. *Registrar-General*,[23] the High Court of Australia applied the rule from *Royal British Bank* v. *Turquand*, reprinted in part in this chapter, to protect a Barclays group company from the unauthorized use

---

[18]　Sec. 44(3)(b) CA 2006. The role of the secretary under UK law strengthened considerably during the twentieth century. In *Barnett, Hoares & Co.* v. *South London Tramways Co.* (1887) LR 18 QBD 815, 817, Lord Esher said: "A secretary is a mere servant; his position is that he is to do what he is told, and no person can assume that he has any authority to represent anything at all." About 100 years later, in *Panorama Developments (Guildford) Ltd* v. *Fidelis Furnishing Fabrics Ltd* [1971] 3 WLR 440, 443, Lord Denning MR stated that: "[T]imes have changed. A company secretary is a much more important person nowadays than he was in 1887. He is an officer of the company with extensive duties and responsibilities ... He regularly makes representations on behalf of the company and enters into contracts on its behalf which come within the day-to-day running of the company's business. So much so that he may be regarded as held out as having authority to do such things on behalf of the company."

[19]　§ 141(c) DGCL.　　[20]　§ 142 DGCL; § 8.41 Model Act.

[21]　See *Joseph Greenspon's Sons Iron & Steel Co.* v. *Pecos Valley Gas Co.*, 156 A 350 (1931); *Italo-Petroleum Corp. of America* v. *Hannigan*, 14 A 2d 401 (1940). For a recent discussion of the CEO and further cases, see Restatement (Third) of Agency, § 3.03, Comments, at e(3) (2006).

[22]　Sec. 43(1) CA 2006; § 122(3) DGCL; § 3.02(2) Model Act.

[23]　(1990) 170 CLR 146, 155.

of a seal by a company director and his son, who posed as the company secretary. The central problem in this type of case is to determine when the third party has been put on inquiry notice and when it may reasonably assume that the company's internal procedures have been fulfilled.

Germany solves this problem by using the type of central, public register (here the *Handelsregister* we have seen in connection with the incorporation process) for which it is so well known in connection with property transactions.[24] The authority of each director to bind the company and every change in the list of authorized persons, as well as a list of the company's *Prokurists*, must be entered in the commercial register together with information regarding the manner in which they are authorized.[25] The commercial register can be consulted electronically,[26] and allows offsite confirmation of the power of representation under guarantee of the state administration. The US states provide no such central register of signatories for stock corporations. Signatories would be named in a resolution or in the by-laws, neither of which are made public. The UK lies somewhere in between the US and Germany by having both a seal and a register of persons authorized to represent the company, given that the particulars of directors and secretaries must be recorded in a register held by the company and which may be consulted by any person.[27] The UK register of directors would, however, be held at the company's registered office and could be consulted only during business hours, making it much less accessible than Germany's electronic *Handelsregister*.

B.   Pursuant to contract law

Agency law is a branch of contract law, and allows agency relationships to be established in the same ways as contracts themselves: by written agreement, by oral agreement, or by tacit acceptance of conduct in practice.[28] Certain types of transaction have form requirements and may thus necessitate that authority be granted in a way having "equal dignity" with such requirement; for example, because a transaction to purchase land requires a written or notarized deed, the power of attorney must also be written or

---

[24] The institution of the German *Grundbuch* is considered a significant gift of Germanic law to other jurisdictions, which for centuries may have relied on the questionable proof offered by title documents. See Zweigert and Kötz (1996: 38).

[25] §§ 37(3), 39(1) and 81(1) AktG.

[26] See http://handelsregisterauszug-online.de.

[27] Secs. 162, 275–277 CA 2006.

[28] Restatement (Third) of Agency, §§ 1.03, 3.01 (2006); Schramm, in *MünchKommBGB* (2006: § 167 mn. 15, 37 *et seq.*).

notarized.[29] Generally, however, the principal – in our case the board, a committee or a director with statutory or constitutional power to delegate authority – may expressly or implicitly delegate authority to the agent to perform a given action or type of action. Implied authority can arise, for example, in connection with an act that is necessary or incidental to achieving the principal's objectives,[30] or from holding a position and performing certain tasks in a manner known to the principal without ever formally receiving an appointment or delegation of authority.[31] This is the type of authority that the president of a Delaware company developed over time that was later hardened into case law by the Delaware courts. Has the same been true for the office of treasurer? See *General Overseas Films Ltd* in this chapter.

III. Reliance on apparent or ostensible authority

As mentioned above, because of the complex, organizational nature of corporations, it is sometimes difficult for third parties to know whether (a) the corporation has capacity to engage in a given transaction and (b) the agent has actual authority to bind the corporation. By eliminating the use of *ultra vires* objections to challenge company obligations toward third parties, each of our jurisdictions has reduced a third party's concerns with respect to point (a). With respect to point (b), courts have developed various doctrines of agency law to protect third parties when the principal creates the impression that the "agent" has actual authority. These are in the UK and the US, "ostensible" and "apparent" authority, respectively, and in Germany *Duldungsvollmacht* (authority by forbearance) and *Anscheinsvollmacht* (apparent authority). As these doctrines are designed to achieve fairness where formal requirements are not met, their application depends heavily on the facts of each case, but does contain a number of common elements: first, the *principal* (not the agent) or someone with actual or apparent authority must create or allow the impression of authority,[32] and, secondly, the third party must "reasonably" rely in good

---

[29] See Restatement (Third) of Agency, § 3.02, Comment (b) (2006); Kanzleiter, in *MünchKommBGB* (2007: § 311b mn. 44 *et seq.*).

[30] Restatement (Third) of Agency, § 2.02(1) (2006).

[31] *Hely Hutchinson* v. *Brayhead Ltd* [1968] 1 QB 549, 583 (CA).

[32] This requirement can lead to two types of authority being discussed in the cases and in the texts on apparent authority: authority to *make representations* as to existing authority, and authority to bind the company.

faith on such impression, and must change his position (i.e. commit funds, value or relinquish an opportunity).

The action of the principal sufficient to create the impression of authority is not always unambiguous, as is shown in the case of a *Duldungsvollmacht*, which resembles ostensible authority derived from holding out under UK law.[33] Here, the principal does not create the impression of authority through words or actions, but rather by inaction. If the principal fails to stop the agent from acting in the name of the company or to notify the third party of the lack of actual authority, and the third party changes her position in reliance on the agent's actions in the reasonable belief that the agent has actual authority, the principal will be estopped (i.e. stopped by fairness) from denying that the agent was authorized. The case of an *Anscheinsvollmacht* is even more subtle. Here, the principal neither grants actual authority to the agent nor is aware of the agent's acting in the company's name, but could gain knowledge of such conduct through the exercise of due care. If the principal fails to stop the agent from so acting or to notify the third party of the lack of actual authority, and the third party changes position in reliance, the principal will again be estopped from denying authorization.[34]

Section 40 of the Companies Act 2006 is expressly designed to regulate such situations when the person acting with apparent authority is a director. The provision presents both the factual elements and rules of behavior that will determine whether a third party may rely on the declared or ostensible authority of a director. The third party must be "in good faith," which is presumed unless rebutted, and cannot be rebutted by mere knowledge that authority is lacking; moreover, the third party has no duty to inquire regarding limitations. For the laws of all our jurisdictions, if the agent and the third party were to plot together to the detriment of the principal, the third party obviously acts neither in good faith nor in reliance on the apparent authority. Thus, in such a case, the third party would be estopped from claiming apparent authority and the principal would not be bound. More difficult to assess are cases where the agent commits a breach of duty toward the principal without an agreement to that effect between the agent and the third party. This would be measured by the negligence standard discussed above in connection with

---

[33] Ferran (1999: 103–104).

[34] US law contains a similar doctrine, and expresses the standard used to measure the principal's behavior as "having notice of such belief [of actual authority] and that it might induce others to change their positions, the person did not take reasonable steps to notify them of the facts." Restatement (Third) of Agency, § 2.05(2) (2006).

Anscheinsvollmacht. While the third party is not under a duty to inquire into the internal relations between principal and agent, protection of the principal's interest may take priority over the interests of the third party where the facts that could give notice to the third party very clearly indicate a lack of authority. Compare section 40 of the Companies Act 2006 with *General Overseas Films Ltd* on this point. Each of the judicial and statutory rules in this chapter engages in balancing the equities and the reasonableness of the commercial behavior. What are the dangers of shifting the balance too far to one side or the other?

IV.   Documenting the chain of authority

A lawyer representing a client in a large transaction would never dream of resting on the doctrines of apparent or ostensible authority. Instead, they ascertain actual authority by following the chain of delegated authority from the constitution of the company to the identity of the person actually signing the contract. This is a very standardized process in most countries, and thus deserves a quick mention here.

In continental Europe, large companies will usually have a tool for this process that is referred to as a "signature book." Such books, which might look like a paperback with the company's name and logo on it, could contain all the elements necessary for tracing the chain of authority, for example:

1. a notarized excerpt from the corporate statute of the provision stating that the board has full power to represent the company, and a sworn translation of the excerpt;
2. a notarized excerpt from the board's minute books containing a resolution giving persons holding certain offices or one signatory from, for example, "list A" and one from "list B" the power to represent the company for transactions of a given value;
3. lists A and B, which should include the persons who will be at the closing to sign for the company, preferably containing a notarized excerpt of the board resolution appointing such people to the office that qualifies them to be on the list; and
4. lists of facsimile signatures for all persons on the lists in the "signature book," so they can be compared to the actual signatures applied to the contract.

In the case where a company seal will be used at the closing to sign the contract, the documentation offered will look somewhat different, and could contain the following:

1. a notarized excerpt from the relevant corporate statute provision stating that the affixing of the corporate seal is evidence that the company has executed the document, and a sworn translation of the excerpt;
2. notarized excerpts from (a) the company's articles of association stating that a director may apply the corporate seal and (b) the shareholders' resolution that appointed the signing person as a director; and
3. a witnessed attestation by the company secretary that the signing person is still a director and that the specimen signature provided belongs to such director.

How would you check the authority of a German director and a *prokurist* of a large bank who are about to sign jointly a €500 million guarantee that your client needs in order to enter a risky undertaking? Where does authority begin? What are the steps that evidence the chain of authority down to the director and the *prokurist*?

Questions for discussion

1. Why does a company need agents?
2. What is the difference between actual/true and apparent/ostensible authority?
3. What is the difference between express and implied authority and to which of the type(s) of authority in question 2 do these terms refer?
4. How can apparent authority by holding out be established and whose holding out must be shown by the third party?
5. How does the scope of the protection offered to third parties by section 40(2)(b) CA 2006 compare to the rule in the *Turquand* case?
6. Does the type of transaction affect whether a third party is put on inquiry notice under US and UK law?
7. § 82(1) AktG does not allow the *Vorstand*'s authority to represent the corporation to be restricted. Does that mean that there are no limits whatsoever on its authority under the AktG?
8. What is the difference between *Duldungsvollmacht* and *Anscheinsvollmacht* under German law?
9. Is an authorized algorithm constituting an electronic signature legally identical to a company seal?
10. In *General Overseas Films*, the district court cites the *Restatement of Agency* and Williston's treatise on contracts as support for crucial points. Is seeking the support of legal scholars thought of as a typical trait of Common Law or Civil Law courts?

Cases

Royal British Bank v. Turquand
Court of Exchequer Chamber
[1843–60] All ER Rep 435
Reproduced by permission of Reed Elsevier (UK) Limited, trading as LexisNexis
Butterworths
[*Text edited; headnotes and endnotes omitted*]

[*Editors' summary of facts*: The "deed of settlement" (previously the founding document of a joint stock company) of Cameron's Coalbrook Steam, Coal, and Swansea and London Rail Co, a company formed under the Joint Stock Companies Act, 1844, allowed the directors to borrow such sums of money as might from time to time be authorized by a resolution passed at a general meeting. The company borrowed (by a bond) £2,000 from the Royal British Bank with the bond under seal of the company signed by two directors. When the bank sought repayment, the company argued that there had been no resolution authorizing the borrowing and so it was not bound by the debt.

Turquand was the general manager of the company. The plaintiffs sued Turquand as official manager for the £2,000. The bank pointed to clauses of the company's constitutional document that authorized the directors to borrow, including one that the directors might borrow on bond such sums as should, from time to time, by a general resolution of the company, be authorized to be borrowed. The defendant argued that there had been no resolution authorizing the bond. Therefore the debt was incurred without the authority. The plaintiff alleged that an approving resolution did exist. The Court of Queen's Bench gave judgment for the plaintiffs. The defendant appealed to the Court of Exchequer Chamber.]

[*Text omitted*]

JERVIS CJ

I am of opinion that the judgment of the Court of Queen's Bench ought to be affirmed. I incline to think that the question which has been principally argued both here and in that court does not necessarily arise, and need not be determined. My impression is (though I will not state it as a fixed opinion) that the resolution set out in the replication goes far enough to satisfy the requisites of the deed of settlement. The deed allows the directors to borrow on bond such sum or sums of money as shall from time to time, by a resolution passed at a general meeting of the company, be authorised to be borrowed: and the replication shows a resolution, passed at a general meeting, authorising the directors to borrow on bond such sums for such periods and at such rates of interest as they might deem expedient, in accordance with the deed of settlement and the Act of Parliament; but the resolution does not otherwise define the amount to be borrowed.

That seems to me enough. If that be so, the other question does not arise. But whether it be so or not we need not decide; for it seems to us that the plea, whether we consider it as a confession and avoidance or a special non est factum, does not raise any objection to this advance as against the company. We may now take for granted that the dealings with these companies are not like dealings with other partnerships, and that the parties dealing with them are bound to read the statute and the deed of settlement. But they are not bound to do more. The party here, on reading the deed of settlement, would find, not a prohibition from borrowing, but a permission to do so on certain conditions. Finding that the authority might be made complete by a resolution, he would have a right to infer the fact of a resolution authorising that which on the face of the document appeared to be legitimately done.

POLLOCK, CB, ALDERSON, B, CRESSWELL, J, CROWDER, J, and BRAMWELL, B, concurred.
DISPOSITION: Appeal dismissed.
Hurley v. Ornsteen
Supreme Judicial Court of Massachusetts, Suffolk
42 NE 2d 273 (1942)

DOLAN, Justice

[*Editors' summary of facts*: Ornsteen was a customer of the brokerage house, Feldman & Company, Inc., and opened an account with the brokerage dealing only with Richard Feldman. Evidence showed that Richard Feldman gave Ornsteen a letter signed by Albert Feldman, president, secretary and director of the company, that forgave a debt that Ornsteen had to the brokerage. Later, when Feldman & Company went bankrupt, the brokerage's trustee in bankruptcy, Hurley, sued Ornsteen to collect the debt because he argued that Richard and Albert Feldman had no authority to forgive the debt acting alone. Ornsteen claimed that there was a binding contract that forgave the debt ("accord and satisfaction").]

[*Text omitted*]

We are of opinion, however, that it cannot be said properly that the evidence would support a finding in the present case of an accord satisfaction that was binding upon the corporation. It is true as argued by the defendant that the corporation through its board of directors had authority to compromise claims in its favor or against it under the terms of the agreement of association whereby 'the entire control and management of the corporation, its property and business' was confided to the directors. See G.L. (Ter. Ed.) c. 156, § 25. It is also true that where a majority of a board of directors of a corporation participate in the doing of a corporate act within their powers and the other directors have knowledge of and adopt it by acquiescence or otherwise the corporation is bound by their action, and this without a formal meeting and vote of the board ... but this does not mean that a majority may bind the corporation by an act required to be performed by the directors where the other members of the board have no knowledge of the transaction at the time it is entered into, and do not subsequently adopt it either expressly or impliedly, except in some rare and unusual circumstances not shown to have been present in the case at bar ...

In the present case there is nothing to show that the third director of the corporation had any knowledge of the alleged accord and satisfaction between Albert Feldman and Richard Feldman and the defendant. Although Albert Feldman was president and treasurer as well as a director of the corporation, and Richard Feldman was clerk and a director of the corporation, their respective offices as president and treasurer and as clerk, of themselves, did not confer upon them any power to bind the corporation outside of a 'comparatively narrow circle of functions specially pertaining to their offices.' ...

The evidence in the present case would warrant a finding that Richard Feldman had apparent or ostensible authority to deal with the defendant in the matter of the purchase and sale of securities and to determine whether he would have to furnish collateral security and, if so, the amount thereof, since an implied delegation of authority to an agent may arise from a course of conduct showing that a principal has repeatedly acquiesced therein and adopted acts of the same kind ... Am.Law Inst. *Restatement: Agency*, s. 43. The apparent scope of an agent's authority is limited, however, to that which falls within the general class of acts done by him over a considerable period of time ... And in the case before us there was no evidence that either Albert or Richard Feldman or both had at any time prior to the alleged accord and satisfaction entered into any compromise of claims in favor of or against the corporation, or of any course of conduct on their part tending to show any implied or ostensible authority from the board to compromise claims. 'It is settled that an agent or officer of a corporation has not ordinarily authority to cancel or release a contract of his principal which is in force.' ...

There is nothing, moreover, to show any knowledge of or ratification by acquiescence or otherwise of the alleged accord and satisfaction by the third member of the board of directors ... No book entries disclosing the transaction or the application of the collateral to its alleged consummation appear in the record, whatever would be the effect of such entries, in the light of the other evidence, had they been shown to have existed.

In these circumstances we cannot say rightly that a finding of an accord and satisfaction that was binding upon the corporation was supportable upon the evidence. It follows that there was no error in the denial of the defendant's second requested ruling.

Exceptions overruled.

General Overseas Films, Ltd v. Robin International, Inc.

US District Court, Southern District of New York

542 F Supp 684 (1982)

[*Text edited; some footnotes omitted*]

[*Editors' summary of the facts*: Nicholas Reisini owned and controlled Robin International, Inc. (Robin). Robin was building the Soviet Union's UN Mission in New York. Debts totaling $100,000 arose in connection with this construction project. In 1976, Reisini asked Robert Haggiag, (Haggiag) for a loan to pay off such debts. Haggiag was "solely empowered and responsible for the operations and transactions" of General Overseas Films, Ltd (GOF). Haggiag caused GOF to lend Robin and Reisini $500,000. When the debt fell due, Reisini could not pay, and he asked Haggiag for an extension on condition that the loan would be guaranteed by a public company. Charles H. Kraft (Kraft), the vice president and treasurer of The Anaconda Company (Anaconda) agreed that Anaconda would provide a guarantee for up to $1,000,000. Reisini gave Haggiag a note for $1,000,000 and Kraft gave Haggiag a guarantee, which specified September 1977 as the due date. Haggiag loaned Robin another $60,000. Before September, Reisini again told Haggiag that he could not repay at the moment. They exchanged the $1,000,000 note for a $800,000 note. Kraft gave Haggiag a letter confirming the guarantee. In 1978, after Reisini had repaid $500,000, Haggiag learned that Reisini and Kraft had been involved in fraudulent transactions and demanded payment. Robin was insolvent and could not repay. In this action, GOF seeks payment from Anaconda under the guarantee entered into by Kraft.]

SOFAER, District Judge

[*Text omitted*]

Anaconda asserts as its primary defense to the action that the guarantee extended by Kraft does not bind Anaconda, since Kraft lacked actual or apparent authority to engage in the transaction. Plaintiff concedes that Kraft had no actual authority to bind Anaconda to this undertaking; it relies solely on Kraft's apparent authority to do so ...

[*Text omitted*]

The general rule in New York is that "(o)ne who deals with an agent does so at his peril, and must make the necessary effort to discover the actual scope of authority." ... The doctrine of apparent authority delineates the grounds for imposing on the principal losses caused by its agent's unauthorized acts. The law recognizes that an agent, such as Kraft, may engage in a fraudulent transaction entirely without his principal's approval but nevertheless under circumstances that warrant holding his principal accountable. As the Court of Appeals for this Circuit explained:

> Apparent authority is based on the principle of estoppel. It arises when a principal places an agent in a position where it appears that the agent has certain powers which he may or may not possess. If a third person holds the reasonable belief that the agent was acting within the scope of his authority and changes his position in reliance on the agent's act, the principal is estopped to deny that the agent's act was not authorized.

... The doctrine rests not upon the agent's acts or statements but upon the acts or omissions of the principal. It is invoked when the principal's own misleading conduct is responsible for the agent's ability to mislead ... As defined in the *Restatement* a principal causes his agent to have apparent authority "by written or spoken words or any other conduct of the principal which, reasonably interpreted, causes the third person to believe that the principal consents to have the act done on his behalf ... " *Restatement, Agency 2d* s 27 (1958). Therefore, to determine whether Kraft had apparent authority to guarantee the loan on behalf of Anaconda requires a "factual inquiry (focusing upon) the principal's (Anaconda's) manifestations to the third person (Haggiag) ... " ... The Ninth Circuit has stated:

> The principal's manifestations giving rise to apparent authority may consist of direct statements to the third person, directions to the agent to tell something to the third person, or the granting of permission to the agent to perform acts and conduct negotiations under circumstances which create in him a reputation of authority in the area in which the agent acts and negotiates.

... The initial question, therefore, is whether Anaconda's conduct permitted Haggiag actually and reasonably to believe that Kraft was authorized to execute this guarantee. Under the law of New York, the circumstances of the transaction known to the plaintiff must also be scrutinized to determine whether it fulfilled its primary "duty of inquiry."

GOF relies on several aspects of Anaconda's conduct in arguing that Anaconda conferred apparent authority on Kraft for the transactions in which he engaged with GOF. Anaconda placed Kraft in a high and visible corporate position, with broad powers over financial affairs. It gave Kraft Anaconda stationery displaying his corporate titles, an office in the company's executive suite, business cards, access to the corporate seal, and put his picture in its annual report. Anaconda officers and publications announced to the financial community that Kraft was the individual at Anaconda with whom to discuss the company's "financial needs." Plaintiff argues that "Anaconda held Kraft out as having the full range of authority and responsibility for Anaconda's financial matters" ... and characterizes Kraft as Anaconda's "emissary to the financial community" ... Specifically, Anaconda adopted and made available to Kraft Article 9 of Anaconda's bylaws, conferring upon Kraft, as Treasurer, authority "to sign checks, notes, drafts, bills of exchange and other evidences of indebtedness ... " Kraft showed this bylaw, as well as his picture in Anaconda's annual report, to Haggiag at their initial meeting. By these actions, plaintiff contends, Anaconda gave such convincing evidence of Kraft's authority to sign guarantees that several sophisticated banks extended some $34 million in credit to Reisini's companies, at Kraft's request, through transactions similar to GOF's with Robin. GOF argues: "That six sophisticated banks had agreed to all of Kraft's proposals over a six-year period is vivid testimony to the widespread recognition among professionals of the authority inherent in the position of a corporate Treasurer." ...

Those transactions, moreover, constitute in plaintiff's view strong evidence of the reasonableness of GOF's conduct: "six sophisticated financial institutions and Kraft's own superiors did not question for more than six years the fact that Kraft's actions on behalf of Anaconda were proper, legitimate and fully authorized." ... Further, GOF cites as evidence of the reasonableness of its belief in Kraft's apparent authority the fact that Haggiag asked a distinguished member of the bar whether the papers Kraft presented Haggiag were in good order; the attorney allegedly told Haggiag that the papers appeared to be in proper form. Haggiag also inquired as to Anaconda's interest, and was told that the company had supplied or produced the walls of the Russian mission that Robin had built. Finally, GOF contends that, had Haggiag inquired further into Kraft's authority, he would not have discovered anything to cast doubt upon the transactions' propriety, since Kraft was the person at Anaconda authorized to produce evidence as to both the authority to transact business on behalf of Anaconda and any changes in that authority.

GOF's arguments would have force in a situation that fell within the range of transactions in which companies like Anaconda normally engage. But the transaction involved in this case is extraordinary, and should have alerted Haggiag to the danger of fraud. Because the circumstances surrounding the transaction were such as to put Haggiag on notice of the need to inquire further into Kraft's power and good faith, Anaconda cannot be bound ...

A corporate treasurer, it is true, must be regarded as having broad authority to commit his or her company in financial dealings. Large companies such as Anaconda generally establish ongoing relations with several banks. The banks are kept informed of the financial status of these companies through regular reports. They are also advised of exactly whom to deal with at such companies in all financial matters, and are provided with evidence of the individual officer's authority. In this case, Anaconda designated Kraft as its authorized contact in financial affairs, and it widely published Article 9 of its bylaws as evidencing the scope of Kraft's authority. Anaconda thereby placed Kraft in a position that enabled him to commit the company, when he was acting within the scope of Article 9, to any transaction that appeared reasonably related to Anaconda's business. See *Restatement 2d, Agency*, supra, s 39 ("Unless otherwise agreed, authority to act as agent includes only authority to act for the benefit of the principal.") Anaconda and companies like Anaconda often need on-the-spot, informal commitments from banks, and they operate in a manner that enables them to obtain such commitments. Banks, on the other hand, need and compete for customers such as Anaconda, and they reasonably attempt to meet the needs of such customers by dealing as swiftly and informally with authorized officers as the circumstances of a particular transaction reasonably permit.

The existence of apparent authority depends in part upon "who the contracting third party is." ... GOF is not a bank, or otherwise the type of company with whom Anaconda needed to deal swiftly and regularly in its financial affairs. It had no relationship with Anaconda before the transaction concerning Robin. It had neither the need nor the capacity to seek or compete for Anaconda's financial business by extending services or courtesies without the investigation normally made. GOF maintained no file on Anaconda; it had no idea of the company's financial condition beyond glancing at Anaconda's latest annual report. A bank with whom Anaconda (and Kraft) regularly dealt might more reasonably rely on Kraft's position as evidence of broad authority in most types of financial matters ... ("the largest class of cases of agency is that which relates to trade affairs, where the agency is proved by inference, from the habit and course of dealing between the parties"). But given GOF's lack of experience and knowledge in banking, GOF's lack of a prior relationship with Anaconda, and GOF's lack of any interest in creating an ongoing relationship with Anaconda, it cannot claim to have the same reasonable basis for such reliance. The messages Anaconda implicitly may have conveyed in its dealings with banks could not have been intended for a company in GOF's situation nor reasonably available to such a company as a basis for its reliance.

More important, the nature of the specific transaction – a guarantee by Anaconda of the debt of an unrelated corporation – was extraordinary and thus sufficient to require inquiry by GOF before it relied on Kraft's purported authority. Article 9 of Anaconda's bylaws is properly cited by plaintiff as conduct of the principal which could give rise to apparent authority. But GOF has no basis for arguing that Article 9 of Anaconda's bylaws conferred or reasonably appeared to confer authority on Kraft to sign a guarantee, let alone one to a third, unrelated company. The bylaw implicitly but clearly refutes the notion that Kraft had authority to sign guarantees. The language conferring power on him to sign evidences of indebtedness occurs in a context that pertains entirely to Anaconda's direct borrowing activities. It reads:

> The Treasurer or Assistant Treasurer shall have the custody of all the funds and securities of the Company, and shall have power on behalf of the Company to sign checks, notes, drafts, bills of exchange and other evidences of indebtedness, to borrow money for the current needs of the business of the Company and assign and deliver for money so borrowed stocks and securities and warehouse receipts or other documents representing metals in store or transit and to make short-term investments of surplus funds of the Company and shall perform such other duties as may be assigned to him from time to time by the Board of Directors, the Chairman of the Board, the Vice Chairman of the Board or the President.

... Plaintiff argues that the phrase "evidences of indebtedness" includes guarantees ... A guarantee is not, however, an "evidence of indebtedness"; it is an agreement collateral to the debt itself ... The general rule is that "(e)xpress authority to execute or indorse commercial paper in the principal's name ... does not include authority to draw or indorse negotiable paper for the benefit ... of any other person; authority to sign accommodation paper or as security for a third person must be specially given." ... In New York "the power of an agent to bind the principal in contracts of guaranty or suretyship can only be charged against the principal by necessary implication, where the duties to be performed cannot be discharged without the exercise of such a power, or where the power is a manifestly necessary and customary incident of the authority bestowed upon the agent, and where the power is practically indispensable to accomplish the object in view." ... No such necessity appears in Article 9, from Kraft's position, or from the circumstances of this transaction.

Plaintiff contends that, regardless of whether a guarantee is an evidence of indebtedness, the language of Article 9, when reasonably interpreted, gives the appearance of such authority. This argument proceeds on the theory that Kraft's actual "authority in other transactions gave him apparent authority in this transaction." ... But the nature of a guarantee is such that "(h)owever general the character of the agency may be, a contract of guaranty or suretyship is not normally to be inferred from such an agency." 2 S. Williston, *A Treatise on the Law of Contracts*, s 277A, at 230 (3d Ed. 1959); accord ... The guarantee of Robin's debt to GOF, standing alone, had no apparent connection with the financial interests of Anaconda. Unlike a loan or other debt undertaken by Anaconda for its own benefit, a guarantee results in a loan by the creditor of funds to a third party, or, as in this case, in the creditor's agreement to defer collecting on a loan previously extended to a third party. Unless the transaction has other elements connecting it to the guarantor, it is not the sort of arrangement in which the guarantor company's treasurer or other financial officer normally should be expected to engage:

> [S]uch a contract is unusual and extraordinary and so not normally within the powers accruing to an agent by implication, however general the character of the agency; ordinarily the power exists only if expressly given. Consequently a manager, superintendent, or the like, of business or property cannot ordinarily bind his principal as surety for third persons.

2A *CJS, Agency* s 181, at 849 (1979) (footnotes omitted). This widely recognized principle is accepted in New York, where, although the existence of authority to enter such contracts is a question of fact ... for example, "it is a thoroughly established rule of law that a partner has not implied authority to bind his partner or the partnership by contracts of guaranty or suretyship, either for himself individually or for third persons." ... Where an agent purports to bind his principal to such a commitment the third party is put on notice that the transaction is of questionable validity:

> If (the third person) knows that the agent is acting for the benefit of himself or a third person, the transaction is suspicious upon its face, and the principal is not bound unless the agent is authorized. Thus, where the agent signs the principal's

name as an accommodation endorser ... the other party obtains no rights against
the principal because of such transaction, unless authorized.

Restatement 2d, Agency, supra, s 165, comment c, at 390. Thus, "(g)enerally, contracts of guaranty and suretyship not in the regular line of corporate business cannot be made by corporate officers without express authority; ordinarily there is no
apparent authority in an officer to make such a contract." ...

   Had Kraft purported to borrow money for Anaconda, or in a credible manner
for Anaconda's benefit, he could have bound Anaconda even if he in fact intended
and managed to steal the money involved. Had Anaconda itself done anything to
suggest it had an interest in Robin or in the transactions at issue, a stronger case
for apparent authority would be presented. But in this case, Anaconda was neither
directly nor indirectly involved in the transaction between GOF and Robin, and
GOF has not pointed to any actions by Anaconda suggesting involvement. The
only connection between Anaconda and Robin suggested to Haggiag was a vague
statement by Reisini that Anaconda had provided "curtain walls" in the Russian
mission. These remarks are of minimal significance since they can in no way be
attributed to Anaconda, and therefore cannot give rise to apparent authority.
Moreover, Haggiag admits that the words curtain walls "sounded strange," and that
he had no real interest in the subject ... Kraft made no representation about any
connection between Robin and Anaconda, and even if he had, he could not thereby
have supplied any more of a basis for apparent authority than he did by his assertions to Haggiag that he had the power to execute the guarantee ... The situations in
which courts have bound principals on guarantees issued by their agents are those
in which authority to do so is express, or clearly implied from functions assigned to
and performed by the agent involved ... Otherwise, such a guaranty has no apparent relationship to the principal's business, and one who receives what appears to be
a guarantee is put on notice that he must inquire further before relying on it. Under
these circumstances, Kraft's authority to bind Anaconda to this transaction was far
from apparent.

   Plaintiff relies heavily on the fact that six banks were also taken in by Kraft
and Reisini in various ways. It argues that the banks' similar conduct shows that
GOF's belief in Kraft's authority, and its reliance on him, was commercially reasonable; GOF also argues that Haggiag properly relied on the existence of parallel
transactions as evidence of Kraft's authority. But the banks in fact treated Article
9 of Anaconda's bylaws as evidence that Kraft lacked authority to sign guarantees.
Not one of them accepted a simple guarantee arrangement. Instead they designed
alternative arrangements that they felt provided them security, but at the same time
avoided a guarantee as such. Thus, Marine Midland, Wells Fargo, Bank of America,
Paribas, and Bankers Trust, all accepted letters of credit, rather than guarantees;
Singer & Friedlander extended what was in form a loan to an Anaconda subsidiary, Anaconda International; and Bank of New York received a collateral agreement to repurchase Robin's debt, rather than an outright guarantee. The conduct of

these banks reflects the commercially reasonable view that Anaconda had not put Kraft in a position that made him appear authorized to execute guarantees ... More important, some of the banks also sought and obtained resolutions confirming Kraft's authority in more specific terms than contained in Article 9. Thus, Marine Midland at one point requested and obtained a corporate resolution stating that Kraft had authority to execute and deliver letters of credit ... and the Bank of New York sought at the outset and obtained an opinion of counsel from Anaconda that Kraft was authorized to execute a note purchase agreement ... None of these explanations or forged documents constituted strong proof of apparent authority, but they made the banks' reliance more reasonable than GOF's.

In any event, GOF cannot safely rely upon the conduct of the banks with whom Anaconda dealt as establishing Kraft's apparent authority or as reflecting reasonable reliance upon Kraft's position or representations.

[Text omitted]

A plaintiff "claiming reliance on (an) agent's apparent authority must not fail to heed warning or inconsistent circumstances." S. Williston, supra ... "The duty of diligence in ascertaining whether an agent is exceeding his authority devolves on those who deal with him, not on his principal." ... Moreover, the course of conduct pursued, with Haggiag's knowledge, by the Swiss Bank shows the weakness of plaintiff's assertion that further inquiry would have been futile because Kraft purportedly was the officer entrusted by Anaconda with producing evidence of its agents' authority. The documentation requested by the Swiss Bank required authorization Kraft could not easily provide. By requiring it, that bank avoided the fate that befell GOF.

Thus, the circumstances presented by the record not only demonstrate an absence of apparent authority, they also show that GOF failed to satisfy its obligation under New York law of making a reasonable attempt to discover the actual scope of Kraft's authority. "The unperformed duty of inquiry may, and often does, make it impossible to rely upon any so-called apparent authority of an agent." ... "(A) principal will not be bound by the act of his agent in excess of his actual authority where the facts and circumstances are such as to put the person dealing with the agent upon inquiry as to the power and good faith of the agent." ... Haggiag made no investigation of the circumstances of Anaconda's guarantee. He did not engage counsel. His purported "consultation" with an attorney consisted of showing the papers for a few moments to a lawyer he neither knew well nor retained ...

12

Directors' duties of loyalty, good faith and care

Required reading

D: AktG, §§ 82, 88, 93, 112, 116
UK: CA 2006, secs. 170–173, 175–180, 182, 187, 188, 190–192, 197–201, 217–219, 223; Insolvency Act 1986, sec. 214
US: Model Act, § 8.30 (including Comment) and §§ 8.60–8.63; DGCL, § 144

Directors' duty of loyalty

I. Rules, standards and fiduciary duties

The matters discussed in this chapter arise after shareholders have exercised their right to elect directors and the board is seated in office.[1] Each of our three jurisdictions uses a mixture of rules and standards to guard against management incompetence and disloyalty. Each of the jurisdictions requires that managers act in accordance with the standards of due care ("duty of care" or *Sorgfaltspflicht*) and loyally ("duty of loyalty" or *Treupflicht*). A "standard of conduct" prescribes how a person should act or fulfill a function or task, and it operates as an open-ended measure against which the quality of performance can be assessed *ex post*. A "rule," by contrast, names something specific that the management must do or not do. Standards flexibly adapt to acts and procedures that are not foreseen in their entirety when the standard is written, but standards can also create legal risks for directors because the scope of their requirements is often difficult to foresee. Rules, on the other hand, offer bright lines that are easy to apply, but for the same reason they can also be easy to evade – given that their parameters are clear and inflexible – unless

---

[1] We will discuss the powers of shareholders to appoint and remove directors, as well as those to approve or veto major structural changes to the company, in Chapter 16.

they are arranged with sufficiently contiguous density, and often fail to account for changing circumstances.[2]

In the context of directors' duties, standards are used to allow room for managerial discretion and innovation, but rules are also used where possible to reinforce standards if the probability of breach is high, or to reduce uncertainty. The SEC has coined the apt term "safe harbor" for the latter type of rules: if I comply with the bright line rule, I remain safely protected from a standard's possible application. For example, if an offering of securities to the "public" requires compliance with certain formalities, a "safe harbor" rule might specify that I may offer securities to a limited number of people (a "private" placement), or a certain kind of people (sophisticated, professional investors), without my offering considered to be "to the public."[3] If I stay on the safe side of the line, I need not worry that a relatively flexible word like "public" can be defined to apply to my sale of securities.

Directors are considered to be "fiduciaries" as they are appointed to manage assets (the company) that belong to the shareholders and not to themselves; they must therefore act in good faith with due regard to the interests of the company, and must subordinate their own interests to those of the company. Under the company laws of all our jurisdictions, a director will breach his duty of loyalty (a standard) if he causes the company to make a decision that damages it while benefiting himself. This standard leaves directors free to manage the company as they see fit until they do something disloyal. Such decisions can only arise when the director has some direct or indirect personal interest in the transaction. Therefore, if we know that directors might act disloyally when they have such an interest in a transaction, we can attempt to neutralize the interest through a *rule* requiring that such transactions be approved by directors that have no interest in the deal or by shareholders. Each of our jurisdictions provides more or less detailed rules for approving such transactions, particularly company loans to directors. While such a rule does intrude in the director's decisionmaking process and thereby reduces the flexibility of using a standard, it also reduces *both* the chance of disloyal action *and* the director's legal risk of being sued on the basis of the decision. Thus a rule may in one sense intrude on a director's freedom, but in another sense it can protect such

---

[2] This is obvious in a time of ever-changing technology like our own when the law specifies a particular technology, such as legally requiring that notice of a meeting be given "by first class mail" or "in the business newspapers." A standard requiring notice "in a commercially reasonable manner" would create more legal risk in its application, but would leave itself open to innovation such as use of the internet or whatever technology might replace it.

[3] See e.g. 17 CFR §§ 230.501 *et seq.* ("Regulation D"); 17 CFR § 230.144A.

freedom. Another example will make this point more clearly: if we know that shareholders want directors to make risky business decisions that can increase earnings or in some cases cause losses, we can impose a rule on courts to keep their "hands off" the substance of a director's decision if the director has no personal interest in the transaction, uses procedures that are generally accepted as adequate under the circumstances, and reaches a decision that is not plainly irrational. A rule that serves this purpose is often referred to as the "business judgment rule," and we will look at this rule in depth in Chapter 13. Thus, the use of rules can change the way that a court will review a director's behavior for compliance with the applicable standard of care or loyalty. In a loyalty situation, if disinterested directors approve a transaction, or, in a care situation, if the director acts on an informed basis, the court will switch from a close examination of the substance of the transaction to a deferential treatment of the decision.

In this chapter, we do not focus on the combination of standards of behavior and review that allow directors to take necessary risks while protecting shareholders from irrational business decisions (the duty of care under the business judgment rule), but on situations in which the director tends to serve personal interests rather than the good of the company. As noted, the standard used to prevent such activity is the directors' duty of loyalty (or "fiduciary duty"), and, in all of our jurisdictions, this standard derives from the fact that the director is managing property (whether we think of the company itself or its assets) that belongs to someone else (the company belongs to the shareholders and the assets belong to the company itself). This duty is a "fiduciary duty" or *treuhänderische Pflicht*. Fiduciary duties arise where "one party (the 'fiduciary') acts *on behalf of* another party (the 'beneficiary') while exercising *discretion* with respect to a *critical resource* belonging to the beneficiary."[4] Classic examples of fiduciary relationships are those between a trustee (*Treuhänder*) and a beneficiary, a managing partner and his co-partners, or an agent and a principal. In the Common Law, "[a]s the number of relations similar to existing fiduciary relations increased, the courts began to analogize the new relations to the established fiduciary prototypes, and to apply the rules of the prototypes to the new relations. Corporate law, for example, frequently analogizes directors to trustees, agents, and managing partners."[5] German law traces use of this fiduciary institution back to Roman law.[6] Irrespective of the different sources from which the duty

---

[4] Smith (2002: 1402).   [5] Frankel (1983: 805).
[6] Hopt, in *GroßKommAktG* (2005: § 116 mn. 176).

has developed in the Common and Civil Law traditions, corporate directors are now understood to be fiduciaries for either the company, the shareholders, or both: the shareholders elect the directors to act on their behalf by exercising expert discretion regarding the management of the company, which is an asset belonging in *pro rata* shares to each holder of the corporate stock. Two duties attributed to fiduciaries are those of care (competence or skill) and loyalty (acting in the best interest of the beneficiary rather than in one's own interest), and in this chapter we will focus primarily on the latter.

II.   To whom do directors owe duties?

In Germany, a director's duties of care and loyalty run directly to the company.[7] Directors must serve the interest of the company (*Unternehmensinteresse*) regardless of whether they are appointed by a person specified in the *Satzung*,[8] appointed by employees and labor unions,[9] or elected by shareholders. This concept of *Unternehmensinteresse* is meant to mediate the differing partial interests of various constituencies, and includes at a minimum the interests of the employees, the creditors and the shareholders.[10] It is interesting that, in Civil Law Germany, the express definition of *Unternehmensinteresse* to encompass the interests of these various constituencies was worked out by the courts.

In the Common Law UK, on the other hand, Parliament has codified directors' duties in the most detailed statutory statement on this topic of our three jurisdictions. A director's duty is owed "to the company,"[11] and courts traditionally found that the interest of the company was best understood as the aggregate of the shareholder's interests.[12] The codification, however, provides that a director "must act ... in good faith ... to promote the success of the company for the benefit of its members as a whole, and in doing so" must[13] "have regard ... (amongst other matters) to" (a) long-term consequences, (b) the employees' interests, (c) relationships

---

[7] Mertens and Cahn, in *KölnKommAktG* (2010: § 93 mn. 60, 88); Spindler, in *MünchKommAktG* (2008: § 93 mn. 92) for members of the management board; Habersack, in *MünchKommAktG* (2008: § 116 mn. 43) for members of the supervisory board.

[8] § 101(2) AktG.   [9] § 101(1) AktG.

[10] BGHZ 106, 54 at 65.   [11] Sec. 170(1) CA 2006.

[12] See e.g. *Heron International Ltd* v. *Lord Grade* [1983] BCLC 244, 5.11 (CA); *Brady* v. *Brady* [1988] BCLC 20, 40 (CA), reprinted in part in Chapter 26; Ferran (1999: 134); Davies (2003: 372).

[13] One should understand that grammatically the imperative "must" also applies to this second clause.

with suppliers, customers and others, (d) the impact on the community and the environment, (e) the company's ethical reputation, and (f) fair treatment of all members.[14] The codification also includes a monitoring mechanism. The directors of listed companies must in their annual report set out the company's policies to promote the interests of employees, the environment and the community, and state whether those policies were effective.[15] Although the 2006 Act does not address all the concerns that have been expressed by advocates of increased stakeholder rights in the corporation, it does seem to present a form of directors' duties representing what Professor Mathias M. Siems refers to as an "enlightened shareholder model."[16]

Under the DGCL, the duties of care and loyalty that directors owe to their corporation translate for practical purposes into a duty to serve the interests of the shareholders,[17] although a duty to creditors arises as the company approaches insolvency.[18] The express statement of the Model Act that directors act "in the best interests of the corporation" has been interpreted to "represent a fiduciary duty to a company and its shareholders,"[19] and to express a duty "to promote the interest of the shareholders."[20] However, it should be noted that, following the often destructive takeover battles of the 1980s, some US states with significant industrial interests and less interests in financial institutions enacted "constituency" statutes, which work like the provision of the Companies Act 2006 to allow directors to take into account the interests of employees, suppliers, customers and communities affected by the company's operations when making decisions.[21] Although these older laws do not generally contain an imperative requiring consideration of constituencies as found in the UK Act, they do allow directors to consider the impact of a transaction in all its facets without fearing suit for a breach of fiduciary duties to shareholders.

It seems, however, that the debate about the recipient of the directors' duties is often unnecessarily set in the context of ideological or political struggles between capital and labor or profit and the environment. It is argued that, if "shareholder primacy" (the theory that directors owe

---

[14] Sec. 172(1) CA 2006.   [15] Sec. 417(5)(b) CA 2006.

[16] Siems (2008: 179).   [17] *Aronson, et al.* v. *Lewis*, 473 A 2d 805 (Del. 1984).

[18] See e.g. *Credit Lyonnais Bank Nederland NV* v. *Pathe Communications Corp.*, 1991 WL 277613 (Del. Ch. 1991).

[19] *Central Iowa Power Co-op.* v. *Consumers Energy*, 741 NW 2d 822 (2007).

[20] *Storetrax.com, Inc.* v. *Gurland*, 915 A 2d 991, 1000 (2007).

[21] Pennsylvania Consolidated Statutes, Subpart B, Business Corporations, Article B, § 1716, which was enacted in 1990.

their duties primarily to shareholders) triumphs, then employees, the environment and the community will suffer. It should be remembered, however, that not all legal problems need be addressed with the same tools. I can prevent accidents at an intersection by posting a police officer at the crossing, installing a signal light, placing a stop sign, or even building a bridge so that the two roads do not intersect. In the corporate context, as explained above, different governance and monitoring techniques (such as rules and standards) are used to serve different ends. Pressure can also be placed on different actors in an overall context to achieve compliance or deterrence. For example, if a given company dominated its suppliers (such as the automotive industry tends to do for certain components like wheels or seats), directors could be ascribed a duty of care to the suppliers, which might allow suppliers to challenge the cancellation of a supply contract as a breach of such duty. However, this would not necessarily bring the best possible protection for suppliers. Indeed, any suit for breach of duty on this basis would be filed after the termination was made public, enforced by proceedings under corporate law that would either involve invocation of the business judgment rule to protect the decision or an evaluation of the process and the substance of the board's decision regarding the contract, and the evidence presented would have to go well beyond the merits of the contract. Mandatory clauses in major supply contracts protecting against termination without cause might serve the suppliers better. As noted, perhaps the main utility of broadening duties in this way is to prevent a director from being challenged for a breach of duty to one group for taking the interests of another into account.

III.   *The use of rules in situations where loyalty is often breached*

In order to function well, rules require that the problem to be contained appears in predictable situations. The situations in which directors have a high probability of acting disloyally determine the type of rules that can be set up in advance to reduce the risk that the duty will be violated. These situations always contain a conflict of interest and are nearly identical in each of our jurisdictions. Aside from the very easy cases like actually stealing, embezzling or appropriating money or the physical assets of the company (like "borrowing" the corporate jet for that special golf weekend), the situations in which conflicts of loyalty arise are the following:

1. A director has a personal interest in a transaction that the company enters into (self-dealing), which can take the form of:
   (a) a director actually being the contractual counterparty in the transaction, such as in the case of executive compensation, a loan or a sale of property; and
   (b) a director receiving compensation for the transaction's success or failure, such as a fee paid by a third party or being fired or promoted because of a merger.
2. A director competes with the company, which can take the form of:
   (a) a director owning or managing a competing business, or
   (b) a director taking a valuable opportunity from the company for personal use.

Each of these situations can arise in most companies in our jurisdictions. The first group entails the director making a decision, and thus implies that the judgment of the director may be biased in favor of personal gain when deciding the size of her compensation, the terms of a loan she will receive, the price the company will pay her for her property, or the attractiveness of a merger proposal that would increase her empire or leave her without a job. The second group of situations entails the use of inside information. Because a director has an intimate knowledge of the business operations of his company, he can use this knowledge to gain a competitive advantage against it, and, because the director may well be the first to know about an opportunity, he could potentially divert the chance to his own gain before the company can even evaluate it for acceptance. Each of these potential transactions come under the duty of loyalty, but can also be addressed with an outright ban or an *ex ante* rule that is meant to cleanse decisionmaking of personal interest. The choice of governance strategy, as discussed above, depends on the amount of flexibility and predictability desired.

IV.   *The duty of loyalty*

A.   Germany

1.   The source and nature of the duty   The main peculiarity about Germany is that it has two different boards and two different kinds of directors: supervisory directors and managing directors.[22] As the positions they hold differ, so does the actual application of their duty of loyalty. The

---

[22] We should remember, however, that our other two jurisdictions also divide their directors into "executive" directors and "non-executive," "outside" or "independent" directors

Aktiengesetz sets out the duty of care and one element of the duty of loyalty in §§ 93 and 116. The duty of care requires directors in both the *Vorstand* and the *Aufsichtsrat* to comport themselves as "proper and prudent managers" (*ordentliche und gewissenhafte Geschäftsleiter*).[23] As explained in the *ARAG* case reprinted in part in Chapter 13, German courts will allow management a certain amount of free discretion and not second-guess business decisions, although they do not apply the same standard of review to decisions regarding derivative suits. The element of the duty of loyalty is a requirement that all directors treat inside information as confidential.[24] The statute specifies a further duty of loyalty for members of the *Vorstand* only: they may not compete with the company.[25]

The general standard of the duty of loyalty is, however, not expressly provided for in the statute, but has been extrapolated by German courts and legal scholars from the nature of the position that directors hold and the tasks they are required to perform.[26]

2. Use of rules   The *Aktiengesetz* expressly regulates five conflict-laden situations through statutory rules:

1. As already noted, all directors are subject to a duty of *confidentiality*.[27]
2. Also as already noted, members of the *Vorstand may not compete* with the company.[28] No similar statutory rule is imposed for members of the *Aufsichtsrat* because they may well hold their board seats as a part-time position and serve as directors in a competing company.[29] Thus, courts are left to regulate any unreasonable competition of *Aufsichtsrat* members by applying the standard of loyalty.
3. The granting of *loans* to members of either board must be approved with a procedure specified in the statute. All terms of any loan that the company grants to a member of the *Vorstand*, a close relation thereof or any company the director represents must be individually approved by the *Aufsichtsrat* at most three months before the loan is granted.[30] The *Aufsichtsrat* must in a like manner approve any loans to members

---

when the company is publicly listed, even if they do not employ two completely separate boards governed by statute.

[23] For a detailed treatment of the duties of German directors, see Baums (1996).

[24] § 88 AktG.   [25] §§ 93(1), 116 AktG.

[26] §§ 93(1), 116 AktG; Mertens and Cahn, in *KölnKommAktG* (2010: § 93 mn. 88 *et seq.*); Habersack, in *MünchKommAktG* (2008: § 116 mn. 52 *et seq.*).

[27] §§ 93(1), 116 AktG.   [28] § 88 AktG.

[29] Hopt and Roth, in *GroßKommAktG* (2005: § 116 mn. 193).

[30] § 89(1), (3) AktG.

of the *Aufsichtsrat*, their close relations and companies they represent, with the conditions being similarly regulated.[31]

4. When *service contracts* are negotiated to compensate the members of the *Vorstand*, the *Aufsichtsrat* represents the company in its dealings with the board member to cleanse the negotiations of conflicts,[32] while the remuneration for the members of the *Aufsichtsrat* must be approved either by the general meeting or by the *Satzung*.[33]

5. If a member of the *Aufsichtsrat* enters into a consulting agreement or similar agreement with the company outside of his activities as a director, the entire *Aufsichtsrat* must approve the agreement.[34]

The rules structure used in German law is the same as that employed in both the United Kingdom and the United States. Disloyalty is checked by (1) requiring that directors avoid creating conflicts (here, for example, a prohibition on competition) and (2) where it is not practical to prohibit the creation of the conflict (such as in the case of executive compensation), having the decision made by a disinterested group of people.

3.   Use of the standard   There remain interstices between the rules – such as competition by an *Aufsichtsrat* member or ordinary commercial contracts between the company and a director – and these are covered by the normal governance procedures, including representation of the company by the *Aufsichtsrat* in dealings with members of the *Vorstand*, and the duty of loyalty (*Treupflicht*). The *Treupflicht* has been described as "the duty in all matters connected with the interest of the company to focus solely on the good of the company, to the exclusion of the interests of the director and any third parties."[35] If a director is found to have made a decision as director on the basis of an interest other than the good of the company, he will be liable to the company for damages.[36] Any transaction that a director enters into with the company must be at fair, "arm's length" conditions.[37] Members of the *Vorstand* may not take opportunities that could be exercised by the company,[38] and members of the *Aufsichtsrat* may not take opportunities that they learn of in their position as directors

---

[31] § 115(1), (3) AktG.   [32] § 112 AktG.

[33] § 113 AktG.   [34] § 114 AktG.

[35] Hopt, in *GroßKommAktG* (1999: § 93 mn. 145); see also Mertens and Cahn, in *KölnKommAktG* (2010: § 93 mn. 88).

[36] Mertens and Cahn, in *KölnKommAktG* (2010: § 93 mn. 50); and Habersack, in *MünchKommAktG* (2008: § 116 mn. 67).

[37] Hopt and Roth, in *GroßKommAktG* (2005: § 116 mn. 180 *et seq.*).

[38] Mertens and Cahn, in *KölnKommAktG* (2010: § 93 mn. 98).

with the company.[39] If a shareholder or the company challenges a director's decision, and proves that the company has suffered damage because of it, the director will then have the burden of proving that he acted with the requisite diligence in order to escape liability.[40] Unlike under Delaware law, the business judgment rule[41] does not create a presumption in favor of the director.[42] German courts have decided relatively few decisions on directors' duty of loyalty partly because the safeguards set up by the structural rules prevent much self-dealing, but mostly because the procedural hurdles for filing an action have historically been very high.[43] It is possible to provide directors with insurance coverage for a finding of liability in connection with a breach of duties (referred to as "directors & officers" or "D&O" insurance).

B.   United Kingdom

1.   The source and nature of the duty   As mentioned above, the United Kingdom has recently codified its body of directors' duties – which had been developed over the years in the Common Law and was partially codified in earlier versions of the statute – in Part 10 of the Companies Act 2006.[44] The most authoritative statement of the duty of loyalty under Common Law was that a director must act "in good faith" and in the "interests of the company."[45] This has been somewhat reformulated in section 172 of the Companies Act 2006 to require a director of an English company to "promote the *success* of the company," which appears to stress profit maximization more than the earlier rule, but is significantly limited by the express mandate to take constituencies other than shareholders into account. This basic standard is reinforced by express statutory standards creating duties to exercise independent judgment,[46] exercise reasonable care, skill and diligence,[47] and avoid conflicts of interest (except for transactions or arrangements with the company),[48] and statutory rules

---

[39] Habersack, in *MünchKommAktG* (2008: § 116 mn. 47); Hopt and Roth, in *GroßKommAktG* (2005: § 116 mn. 194).
[40] Baums (1996: 321); Mertens and Cahn, in *KölnKommAktG* (2010: § 93 mn. 131 *et seq.*).
[41] § 93(1) AktG.
[42] Mertens and Cahn, in *KölnKommAktG* (2010: § 93 mn. 36).
[43] Baums (1996: 322). The details of the procedure of direct and derivative actions against company management will be discussed in detail in Chapter 20.
[44] Sec. 170(3), (4) CA 2006.
[45] See e.g. *Re Smith and Fawcett Ltd* [1942] Ch 304, 306 (CA); and *Brady* v. *Brady* [1989] AC 755 (HL).
[46] Sec. 173(1) CA 2006.
[47] Sec. 174(1) CA 2006.   [48] Sec. 175 CA 2006.

requiring a director to refuse any benefits from third parties for acting as a director in the company,[49] and declare any interest in a proposed transaction or arrangement.[50] In this way, all standards creating directors' duties have been incorporated into the Companies Act 2006.

An interesting peculiarity of UK law not present in our other two jurisdictions is the concept of "shadow directors." A "shadow director" is a person other than a corporation or an advisor who gives "directions or instructions" to the directors of the company which the latter "are accustomed" to follow.[51] Many of the provisions applicable to directors are also equally applicable to "shadow directors," including directors' duties.[52]

2. Use of rules   Since rules either work to prevent *ex ante* acts that would violate the duty of loyalty, or serve as bright lines to determine whether a breach exists, it would seem that the extensive network of rules in sections 177–231 of the Companies Act 2006 will eliminate most of the uncertainty with regard to applying the duty of loyalty *ex post*. The rules cover all of the situations in which conflicts of interest normally arise:

1. The term of any *service contract* between a director and the company exceeding two years must be approved by the shareholders following full disclosure of the terms of the contract.[53]
2. A director may not accept any material *benefit* for acting as a director *from persons other than the company* or a person on whose behalf he acts as a director.[54]
3. A director must *avoid* all existing or potential, direct or indirect *interests that do or could conflict* with the interests of the company (such as using company property or taking its opportunities) – with the exception of matters with negligible value or transactions or arrangements with the company – unless the matter is approved by the disinterested directors where this is permitted in the articles.[55]
4. If a director has an interest that could reasonably give rise to a conflict of interest in deciding on a proposed "transaction or arrangement," he must *disclose* it to the other directors before the company enters into the transaction or arrangement.[56]

---

[49] Sec. 176(1) CA 2006.   [50] Sec. 177(1) CA 2006.
[51] Sec. 251 CA 2006.   [52] Sec. 170(5) CA 2006; and Ferran (1999: 155–156).
[53] Sec. 188 CA 2006.   [54] Sec. 176 CA 2006.
[55] Sec. 175 CA 2006.
[56] Sec. 177 CA 2006. A separate provision governs the case where the company has already entered into the relevant transaction or arrangement. See sec. 182 CA 2006.

5. Regardless of the above precautions, no purchase or sale of a *"substantial* non-cash asset"[57] may take place between a director and the company without the approval of the shareholders.[58]
6. With some minor exceptions covering business expenses, a company may not make *a loan* to a director without the approval of the shareholders following full disclosure of the terms of the loan.[59]
7. A public company may not provide a *guarantee or other credit support* ("quasi-loan") to a director without the approval of the shareholders following full disclosure of the terms of the loan;[60] similarly, it may not enter into a credit transaction with a director without full disclosure and approval by the shareholders.[61]
8. Arrangements that would achieve the ends of any of the foregoing transactions without the required approval are also forbidden.[62] The rules on substantial purchases or sales, loans, quasi-loans and credit arrangements also cover transactions with directors of a company's holding company and other persons connected with such holding company.
9. A company may also not make a payment to its own directors or those of its holding company for "loss of office" (*severance or retirement payments* or "golden handshakes") without the approval of the shareholders following full disclosure of the terms of the payment.[63]

The foregoing rules not only cover all foreseeable transactions involving conflicts of interest, but are also accompanied by definitions of terms that could be ambiguous (such as "substantial"[64] and "value"[65]) and an extensive list of exceptions that recreate the jagged border between the permissible and the impermissible that a flexible body of court decisions applying standards usually offers business planners.

3. Use of the standard   Before the codification of directors' duties through the 2006 Act, courts would apply the duty of loyalty standard to require that directors act "in good faith" and in the "interests of the company," and determine on the facts of each case whether that standard was met. Flexibility and its accompanying uncertainties are built into words like "good faith" and "interest." The provisions of the 2006 Act referred to above codify existing decisions, and use an extensive body of definitions

---

[57] A "substantial" asset is defined to mean having a value that exceeds 10 percent of the company's asset value and is more than £5,000, or exceeds £100,000. See sec. 191(2) CA 2006.
[58] Sec. 190(1) CA 2006.   [59] Sec. 197(1) CA 2006.
[60] Sec. 198(1), (2) CA 2006.   [61] Secs. 201, 202 CA 2006.
[62] Sec. 203 CA 2006.   [63] Sec. 217 CA 2006.
[64] Sec. 191 CA 2006.   [65] Sec. 211 CA 2006.

and exceptions to recreate the intricate patchwork of rules laid out by the existing case law. Moreover, the legal consequences of violation are also now provided in great detail in the 2006 Act for a breach of each of the existing duties.[66] For example, look at the *Regal (Hastings)* decision later in this chapter, and then consult section 175 of the 2006 Act. Do you think that the 2006 provisions fully codify the 1942 decision? What do you think would still be open for a court to decide in future cases? Take a look at section 203 of the 2006 Act.

Although, in contrast to US law, a company may not indemnify its directors against liability incurred in connection with a breach of their duties,[67] it may provide them with insurance against such liability.[68]

C.   United States

1.   The source and nature of the duty   In the United States, one finds two models for setting up the duty of loyalty. Delaware law has developed the duty in the courts as English law did over the decades preceding codification. The Model Act, on the other hand, codifies the duties of directors, although by no means as extensively as in the Companies Act 2006.[69] The duty of loyalty as formulated by Delaware courts looks very much like the UK Common Law formulation: a director must act "in the good faith belief that her actions are in the corporation's best interest."[70] This was fleshed out in the 1939 landmark case of *Guth* v. *Loft*,[71] which addressed a director of a candy company taking for himself an opportunity cheaply to purchase the recipe for Pepsi Cola. The court explained that:

> Corporate officers and directors are not permitted to use their position of trust and confidence to further their private interests ... A public policy ... has established a rule that demands of a corporate officer or director, peremptorily and inexorably, the most scrupulous observance of his duty, not only affirmatively to protect the interests of the corporation committed to his charge, but also to refrain from doing anything that would work injury to the corporation, or to deprive it of profit or advantage which his skill and ability might properly bring to it, or to enable it to make in the reasonable and lawful exercise of its powers. The rule that

---

[66] See e.g. secs. 178, 183, 185, 189, 195, 213, 222 CA 2006.   [67] Sec. 232 CA 2006.

[68] Sec. 233 CA 2006.

[69] § 8.30(a) Model Act ("Each member of the board of directors, when discharging the duties of a director, shall act: (1) in good faith, and (2) in a manner the director reasonably believes to be in the best interests of the corporation.").

[70] *Stone, ex rel. AmSouth Bancorporation* v. *Ritter*, 911 A 2d 362, 370 (2006), citing *Guttman* v. *Huang*, 823 A 2d 492, 506 note 34 (Del. Ch. 2003).

[71] *Guth* v. *Loft, Inc.*, 5 A 2d 503, 510 (Del. 1939).

requires an undivided and unselfish loyalty to the corporation demands
that there shall be no conflict between duty and self-interest.[72]

This duty has been found to be owed to both the corporation and the
shareholders, and does not view the interests of the shareholders taken as
a whole to be separate from the interests of the corporation.[73] A subsidiary
element of the duty of loyalty is that directors not act in bad faith, i.e. that
they not act "for some purpose *other than* a genuine attempt to advance
corporate welfare or [when the transaction] is *known to constitute* a violation of applicable positive law."[74]

2. Use of rules   Delaware law is indeed minimalist compared to the
company laws of Germany and the UK. It offers just one rule, which states
that a "contract or transaction between a corporation and one or more
of its directors or officers [or an entity in which they serve or that they
own]" is protected against challenge regarding the interest if "the material
facts" regarding the interest are disclosed, and the transaction is either (1)
approved by the majority of disinterested directors or the majority of the
shareholders in good faith, or (2) "fair to the corporation as of the time it
is authorized, approved or ratified."[75] The Model Act contains considerably more complex rules, but their effect is essentially the same: disclosure
of the interest and approval by disinterested directors sanitizes the conflict.[76] Neither US statute contains specific rules on negotiating compensation agreements, taking corporate opportunities, or otherwise competing
with the corporation, and the DGCL even expressly states that a "corporation may lend money to, or guarantee any obligations of … any officer or
employee who is a director of the corporation."[77] US law thus begins with
maximum flexibility, leaving directors relatively free in their dealings with
the corporation, bound primarily *ex post* by possible challenge under the
duty of loyalty. The type of review conducted on occasion of such a challenge is exemplified by the *Broz* decision, reprinted in part in this chapter.

The full picture of company law is, however, never found in the company law statute alone. If the company's shares are listed on a securities

---

[72] *Guth* v. *Loft, Inc.*, 5 A 2d 503, 510 (Del. 1939).

[73] *Cede & Co.* v. *Technicolor, Inc.*, 634 A 2d 345, 361 (Del. 1993) ("the best interest of the
corporation and its shareholders take … precedence over any interest possessed by a
director").

[74] *In Re the Walt Disney Company Derivative Litigation*, 907 A 2d 693, 753 (2005), citing *Gagliardi* v. *TriFoods International Inc.*, 683 A 2d 1049, 1051 note 2 (Del. Ch. 1996)
(emphasis in original).

[75] § 144(a) DGCL.   [76] §§ 8.60–8.62 Model Act.

[77] § 143 DGCL.

exchange, the picture comes to look much like that of a UK company. First, any transactions between the director and the company exceeding \$120,000 in value must be disclosed to the shareholders in connection with the annual meeting.[78] Secondly, except for banks that grant loans on a regular basis, a company may never grant a loan to a director or executive officer.[79] Thirdly, the compensation of directors must be disclosed in detail to shareholders.[80] Fourthly, unlike the European rule, which is restricted to listed companies, any use of inside information in connection with the purchase or sale of a security is punishable regardless of whether the company is listed or not.[81] Thus, when federal securities law is seen together with state corporate law, the rule-based regulation is comparable to that of a German or UK company.

3.   Use of the standard   US state courts applying both the DGCL and the Model Act have worked out detailed rules for the application of the duty of loyalty in a great number of cases applied to various factual situations. Given the great number of companies incorporated in Delaware and the quality of the Delaware courts, cases based on the DGCL are both more numerous and better known. The issues that normally attract judicial intervention of course arise in connection with flexible terminology like "fair," "reasonable," "adequate" and "disinterested." If, in the context of a challenged transaction in which one or more directors have an interest, the company fails to sanitize the decisionmaking process by full disclosure and the vote of disinterested directors, the court will then look to see whether the transaction is economically "fair" to the corporation.[82] This test of substantive fairness cannot be reduced to a rule, and must be argued and decided on the facts of each case. The uncertainty of this element thus encourages management to use disclosure and decision by disinterested directors to sanitize conflicts and avoid a judicial inquiry into disclosure. If the interest is sanitized, the decision will receive the protective presumptions of the business judgment rule, which we will discuss in the next chapter. Between an inquiry for substantive fairness and deferential treatment under the business judgment rule lies the rule on "intermediate scrutiny," which is used in reviewing the board's decision to use defensive measures against a hostile takeover.[83] Given the number of decisions on these matters in the Delaware courts, both the "business

---

[78]   17 CFR § 240.14a-101, Item 6, lit. (d), in connection with 17 CFR § 229.404.
[79]   Securities Exchange Act of 1934, § 13(k).
[80]   17 CFR § 240.14a-101, Item 8, in connection with 17 CFR § 229.402.
[81]   17 CFR § 240.10b5-1.   [82]   *Weinberger* v. *UOP, Inc.*, 457 A 2d 701, 711 (Del. 1983).
[83]   *Unocal Corp.* v. *Mesa Petroleum*, 493 A 2d 946 (Del. 1985).

judgment rule" and the "intermediate standard" between that rule and a fairness analysis are developed to an extent of detail that is lacking both in the UK and in Germany. A few of the more important cases on these topics may be found in Chapters 13 and 25. Unlike Germany and the UK, Delaware permits companies to indemnify their directors against breaches of the duty of care, but it does not allow them to offer like protection against a breach of the duty of loyalty.[84] Nevertheless, as in the other two jurisdictions, directors and officers (D&O) insurance is available to cover the costs incurred by directors when charged with a breach of fiduciary duty, unless the act is committed intentionally.

Questions for discussion

1. What is the difference between the duty of loyalty and the duty of care?
2. What standards of loyalty and care must directors meet?
3. Are there differences in the standards imposed in Germany, the UK and the US?
4. What problems and considerations make it difficult to define a standard of care?
5. What kinds of directors' transactions does the Companies Act 2006 indicate are "self-interested" or "self-dealing"?
6. How do the various jurisdictions deal with the problem of directors' self-dealing and their other self-interested transactions?
7. Do you agree that directors should act pursuant to the House of Lords decision in *Regal (Hastings)*?
8. How does the *Regal (Hastings)* decision compare to section 175(4) of the Companies Act 2006?
9. What standard does the Delaware Supreme Court apply in *Broz* to the taking of a corporate opportunity?
10. Are standards or rules more effective in checking breaches of fiduciary duty?

Cases

Regal (Hastings) Ltd v. Gulliver
House of Lords
[1967] 2 AC 134
Reproduced with permission of the Incorporated Council of Law Reporting for England and Wales
[Text edited; headnotes and footnotes omitted]

---

[84] § 102(b)(7) DGCL.

VISCOUNT SANKEY

My Lords, this is an appeal by Regal (Hastings) Ltd from an order of His Majesty's Court of Appeal dated February 15, 1941. That court dismissed the appeal of the appellants from a judgment of Wrottesley J, dated August 30, 1940. The appeal was brought by special leave granted by this House on April 2, 1941.

The appellants were the plaintiffs in the action and are referred to as Regal; the respondents were the defendants. The action was brought by Regal against the first five respondents, who were former directors of Regal, to recover from them sums of money amounting to £7,010 8s. 4d., being profits made by them upon the acquisition and sale by them of shares in the subsidiary company formed by Regal and known as Hastings Amalgamated Cinemas Ltd. This company is referred to as Amalgamated. The action was brought against the defendant, Garton, who was Regal's former solicitor, to recover the sum of £1,402 1s. 8d., being profits made by him in similar dealing in the said shares. There were alternative claims for damages and misfeasance and for negligence. The action was based on the allegation that the directors and the solicitor had used their position as such to acquire the shares in Amalgamated for themselves, with a view to enabling them at once to sell them at a very substantial profit, that they had obtained that profit by using their offices as directors and solicitor and were, therefore, accountable for it to Regal, and also that in so acting they had placed themselves in a position in which their private interests were likely to be in conflict with their duty to Regal. The facts were of a complicated and unusual character. I have had the advantage of reading and I agree with the statement as to them prepared by my noble and learned friend, Lord Russell of Killowen. [*Editors' note*: Lord Killowen's rendition of the facts is as follows: The appellant is a limited company called Regal (Hastings), Ltd, and may conveniently be referred to as Regal. Regal was incorporated in the year 1933 with an authorised capital of £20,000 divided into 17,500 preference shares of £1 each and 50,000 ordinary shares of one shilling each. Its issued capital consisted of 8,950 preference shares and 50,000 ordinary shares. It owned, and managed very successfully, a freehold cinema theater at Hastings called the Regal. In July, 1935, its board of directors consisted of one Walter Bentley and the respondents Gulliver, Bobby, Griffiths and Bassett. Its shareholders were twenty in number. The respondent Garton acted as its solicitor.

In or about that month, the board of Regal formed a scheme for acquiring a lease of two other cinemas ... which were owned and managed by a company called Elite Picture Theatres (Hastings & Bristol), Ltd. The scheme was to be carried out by obtaining the grant of a lease to a subsidiary limited Company, which was to be formed by Regal, with a capital of 5,000 £1 shares, of which Regal was to subscribe for 2,000 in cash, the remainder being allotted to Regal or its nominees as fully paid for services rendered. The whole beneficial interest in the lease would, if this scheme were carried out, enure solely to the benefit of Regal and its shareholders, through the share holding of Regal in the subsidiary company. The respondent Garton, on the instructions of Regal, negotiated for the acquisition of the lease, with the result that an offer to take a lease for 35 or 42 years at a rent of £4,600 for the first year, rising in the second and third years up to £5,000 in the fourth and subsequent years, was accepted on behalf of the owners on August 21, 1935, subject to mutual approval of the form of the lease. Subsequently, the owners of the two cinemas required the rent under the proposed lease to be guaranteed.

On September 11, 1935, Walter Bentley died; and on September 18, 1935, his son, the respondent Bentley, who was one of his executors, was appointed a director of Regal. It should now be stated that, concurrently with the negotiations for the acquisition of a lease of the two cinemas, Regal was contemplating a sale of its own cinema, together with the leasehold interest in the two cinemas which it was proposing to acquire. On September 18, 1935, at a board meeting of Regal, the respondent Garton was instructed that the directors were prepared to give a joint guarantee of the rent of the two cinemas, until the subscribed capital of the proposed subsidiary company amounted to £5,000. He was further instructed to deal with all offers received for the purchase of Regal's own assets. On September 26, 1935, the proposed subsidiary company was registered under the name Hastings Amalgamated Cinemas, Ltd, which may, for brevity, be referred to as Amalgamated. Its directors were the five directors of Regal, and in addition the respondent Garton.

Harry Bentley, who had been appointed a director of Regal only on September 18, at the end of the board meeting of that date, inquired from Garton the position as regards the new company, Amalgamated. In reply, he received a letter dated September 26, 1935, in which the position, as at that date, is set out by Garton. After stating that the capital of Amalgamated is £5,000, of which £2,000 is being subscribed by Regal, "which sum will form virtually the whole of the present paid up capital" of Amalgamated, and that the rent is to be guaranteed by the directors so long as the issued capital of Amalgamated is under £5,000, he concludes as follows:

> "In as much as it is the intention of all the parties that the Regal (Hastings), Ltd will not only control the Hastings (Amalgamated) Cinemas, Ltd, but will continue to hold virtually the whole of the capital, the position of a shareholder of Regal (Hastings), Ltd, is merely that he has the advantage of a possible asset of the two new cinemas on sale by the Regal (Hastings), Ltd, of its undertaking, so that the price realised to the shareholders of the Regal (Hastings), Ltd, will be the amount that he would normally have received for his interest in such company, plus his proportion of the sale price of such two new cinemas."

On October 2, 1935, an offer was received from would-be purchasers offering a net sum of £92,500 for the Regal cinema and the lease of the two cinemas. Of this sum £77,500 was allotted as the price of Regal's cinema, and £15,000 as the price of the two leasehold cinemas. This splitting of the price seems to have been done by the purchasers at the request of the respondent Garton; but it must be assumed in favour of the Regal directors that they were satisfied that £77,500 was not too low a price to be paid for their company's cinema, with the result that £15,000 cannot be taken to have been in excess of the value of the lease which Amalgamated was about to acquire. On the afternoon of October 2, the six respondents met at 62, Shaftesbury Avenue, London, the registered offices of Regal. Various matters were mentioned and discussed between them, and they came to certain decisions. Subsequently, minutes were prepared which record the different matters as having been transacted at two separate and distinct board meetings, viz., a meeting of the board of Regal, and a meeting of the board of Amalgamated. The respondent Gulliver stated in his evidence that two separate meetings were held, that of the Amalgamated board being held and concluded before that of the Regal board was begun. On the other hand, the respondent Bentley says: "It was more or less held in one lump, because we were talking about selling the three properties."

The respondent, Garton, states that, after it was decided that Regal could only afford to put up £2,000 in Amalgamated, which was purely a matter for the consideration of the Regal board, the next matter discussed was one which figures in the minutes of the Amalgamated board meeting. Moreover, both meetings are recorded in the minutes as having been held at 3 p.m.

Whatever may be the truth as to this, the matters discussed and decided included the following: (i) Regal was to apply for 2,000 shares in Amalgamated; (ii) the offer of £77,500 for the Regal cinema and £15,000 for the two leasehold cinemas was accepted; (iii) the solicitor reporting that completion of the lease was expected to take place on October 7, it was resolved that the seal of Amalgamated be affixed to the engrossment when available; and (iv) the respondent, Gulliver, having objected to guaranteeing the rent, it was resolved

> " ... that the directors be invited to subscribe for 500 shares each and that such shares be allotted accordingly."

On October 7, 1935, a lease of the two cinemas was executed in favour of Amalgamated, for the term of 35 years from September 29, 1935, in accordance with the agreement previously come to. The shares of Amalgamated were all issued, and were allotted as follows: 2,000 to Regal, 500 to each of the respondents, Bobby, Griffiths, Bassett, Bentley and Garton, and (by the direction of the respondent, Gulliver) 200 to a Swiss company called Seguliva AG, 200 to a company called South Downs Land Co. Ltd, and 100 to a Miss Geering.

In fact, the proposed sale and purchase of the Regal cinema and the two leasehold cinemas fell through. Another proposition, however, took its place, viz., a proposal for the purchase from the individual shareholders of their shares in Regal and Amalgamated. This proposal came to maturity by agreements dated October 24, 1935, as a result of which the 3,000 shares in Amalgamated held otherwise than by Regal were sold for a sum of £3 16s. 1d. per share, or in other words at a profit of £2 16s. 1d. per share over the issue price of par.

As a sequel to the sale of the shares in Regal, that company came under the management of a new board of directors, who caused to be issued the writ which initiated the present litigation. By this action Regal seek to recover from its five former directors and its former solicitor a sum of £8,142 10s. either as damages or as money had and received to the plaintiffs' use. The action was tried by Wrottesley J, who entered judgment for all the defendants with costs. An appeal by the plaintiffs to the Court of Appeal was dismissed with costs.]

[*Text omitted*]

The directors gave evidence and were severely cross-examined as to their good faith. The trial judge said:

> "All this subsequent history does not help me to decide whether the action of the directors of the plaintiff company and their solicitor on October 2 was bona fide in the interests of the company and not mala fide and in breach of their duty to the company … I must take it that, in the realisation of those facts, it means that I cannot accept what has to be established by the plaintiff, and that is that the defendants here acted in ill faith … Finally, I have to remind myself, were it necessary, that the burden of proof, as in a criminal case, is the plaintiffs', who must establish the fraud they allege. On the whole, I do not think the plaintiff company succeeds in doing that and, therefore, there must be judgment for the defendants."

This latter statement was criticised in the Court of Appeal by du Parcq LJ, who said:

> "To anyone who has read the pleadings, but not followed the course of the trial, that would seem a remarkable statement, because it is common ground that there is no allegation of fraud in the pleadings whatever … but the course which the case has taken makes the learned judge's statement quite apprehensible, because it does appear to have been put before him as, in the main at any rate, a case of fraud. It must be taken, therefore, that the respondents acted bona fide and without fraud."

In the Court of Appeal, Lord Greene MR said:

> "If the directors in coming to the conclusion that they could not put up more than £2,000 of the company's money had been acting in bad faith, and if that restriction of the company's investment had been done for the dishonest purpose of securing for themselves profit which not only could but which ought to have been procured for their company, I apprehend that not only could they not hold that profit for themselves if the contemplated transaction had been carried out, but they could not have held that profit for themselves even if that transaction was abandoned and another profitable transaction was carried through in which they did in fact realise a profit through the shares … but once they have admittedly bona fide come to the decision to which they came in this case, it seems to me that their obligation to refrain from acquiring these shares came to an end. In fact, looking at it as a matter of business, if that was the conclusion they came to, a conclusion which, in my judgment, was amply justified by the evidence from a business point of view, then there was only one way left of raising the money, and that was putting it up themselves … That being so, the only way in which these directors could secure that benefit for the company was by putting up the money themselves. Once that decision is held to be a bona fide one and fraud drops out of the case, it seems to me there is only one conclusion, namely, that the appeal must be dismissed with costs."

It seems therefore that the absence of fraud was the reason of the decision. In the result, the Court of Appeal dismissed the appeal and from their decision the present appeal is brought.

The appellants say they are entitled to succeed: (i) because the respondents secured for themselves the profits upon the acquisition and sale of the shares in Amalgamated by using the knowledge acquired as directors and solicitors respectively of Regal and by using their said respective positions and without the knowledge or consent of Regal; (ii) because the doctrine laid down with regard to trustees is equally applicable to directors and solicitors. Although both in the court of first instance and the Court of Appeal the question of fraud was the prominent feature, the appellants' counsel in this House at once stated that it was no part of his case and quite irrelevant to his arguments. His contention was that the respondents were in a fiduciary capacity in relation to the appellants and, as such, accountable in the circumstances for the profit which they made on the sale of the shares.

As to the duties and liabilities of those occupying such a fiduciary position, a number of cases were cited to us which were not brought to the attention of the trial judge. In my view, the respondents were in a fiduciary position and their liability to account does not depend upon proof of mala fides. The general rule of equity is that no one who has duties of a fiduciary nature to perform is allowed to enter into engagements in which he has or can have a personal interest conflicting with the interests of those whom he is bound to protect. If he holds any property so acquired as trustee, he is bound to account for it to his cestui que trust. The earlier cases are concerned with trusts of specific property … The rule, however, applies to agents, as, for example, solicitors and directors, when acting in a fiduciary capacity.

[*Text omitted*]

Lord Cranworth LC said:

> "A corporate body can only act by agents, and it is of course the duty of those agents so to act as best to promote the interests of the corporation whose affairs they are conducting. Such agents have duties to discharge of a fiduciary nature towards their principal, and it is a rule of universal application that no one having such duties to discharge shall be allowed to enter into engagements in which he has, or can have, a personal interest conflicting, or which possibly may conflict, with the interests of those whom he is bound to protect."

It is not, however, necessary to discuss all the cases cited, because the respondents admitted the generality of the rule as contended for by the appellants, but were concerned rather to confess and avoid it. Their contention was that, in this case, upon a true perspective of the facts, they were under no equity to account for the profits which they made. I will deal first with the respondents, other than Gulliver and Garton … No doubt there may be exceptions to the general rule, as, for example, where a purchase is entered into after the trustee has divested himself of his trust sufficiently long before the purchase to avoid the possibility of his making use of special information acquired by him as trustee …

It was then argued that it would have been a breach of trust for the respondents as directors of Regal, to have invested more than £2,000 of Rogues money in Amalgamated, and that the transaction would never have been carried through if they had not themselves put up the other £3,000. Be it so, but it is impossible to maintain that, because it would have been a breach of trust to advance more than £2,000 from Regal and that the only way to finance the matter was for the directors to advance the balance themselves, a situation arose which brought the respondents outside the general rule and permitted them to retain the profits which accrued to them from the action they took. At all material times they were directors and in a fiduciary position, and they used and acted upon their exclusive knowledge acquired as such directors. They framed resolutions by which they made a profit for themselves. They sought no authority from the company to do so, and, by reason of their position and actions, they made large profits for which, in my view, they are liable to account to the company.

I now pass to the cases of Gulliver and Garton. Their liability depends upon a careful examination of the evidence. Gulliver's case is that he did not take any shares and did not make any profit by selling them. His evidence, which is substantiated by the documents, is as follows. At the board meeting of October 2 he was not anxious to put any money of his own into Amalgamated. He thought he could find subscribers for £500 but was not anxious to do so. He did, however, find subscribers by South Down Land Company, £100 by a Miss Geering and £200 by Seguliva AG, a Swiss company. The purchase price was paid by these three, either by cheque or in account, and the shares were duly allotted to them. The shares were held by them on their own account. When the shares were sold, the moneys went to them, and no part of the moneys went into Gulliver's pocket or into his account. In these circumstances, and bearing in mind that Gulliver's evidence was accepted, it is clear that he made no profits for which he is liable to account. The case made against him rightly fails, and the appeal against the decision in his favour should be dismissed.

Garton's case is that in taking the shares he acted with the knowledge and consent of Regal, and that consequently he comes within the exception to the general rule as to the liability of the person acting in a fiduciary position to account for profits. At the meeting of October 2, Gulliver, the chairman of Regal, and his co-directors were present. He was asked in cross-examination about what happened as to the purchase of the shares by the directors. The question was:

> "Did you say to Mr. Garton, 'Well, Garton, you have been connected with Bentley's for a long time, will you not put up £500?'"

His answer was:

> "I think I can put it higher. I invited Mr. Garton to put the £500 and to make up the £3,000."

This was confirmed by Garton in examination in chief. In these circumstances, and bearing in mind that this evidence was accepted, it is clear that he took the shares with the full knowledge and consent of Regal and that he is not liable to account for profits made on their sale. The appeal against the decision in his favour should be dismissed.

The appeal against the decision in favour of the respondents other than Gulliver and Garton should be allowed, and I agree with the order to be proposed by my noble and learned friend Lord Russell of Killowen as to amounts and costs. The appeal against the decision in favour of Gulliver and Garton should be dismissed with costs.

LORD RUSSELL OF KILLOWEN

My Lords, the very special facts which have led up to this litigation require to be stated in some detail ...
[Omission of facts inserted above]
... If a case of wilful misconduct or fraud on the part of the respondents had been made out, liability to make good to Regal any damage which it had thereby suffered could, no doubt, have been established; and efforts were apparently made at the trial, by cross-examination and otherwise, to found such a case. It is, however, due to the respondents to make it clear at the outset that this attempt failed. The case was not so presented to us here. We have to consider the question of the respendants' [*sic*] liability on the footing that, in taking up these shares in Amalgamated, they acted with bona fides, intending to act in the interest of Regal.

Nevertheless, they may be liable to account for the profits which they have made, if, while standing in a fiduciary relationship to Regal, they have by reason and in course of that fiduciary relationship made a profit ...
[Text omitted]
Other passages in [the trial court] judgment indicate that, in addition to this "corrupt" action by the directors, or, perhaps, alternatively, the plaintiffs in order to succeed must prove that the defendants acted mala fide, and not bona fide in the interests of the company, or that there was a plot or arrangement between them to divert from the company to themselves a valuable investment. However relevant such considerations may be in regard to a claim for damages resulting from misconduct, they are irrelevant to a claim against a person occupying a fiduciary relationship towards the plaintiff for an account of the profits made by that person by reason and in course of that relationship.
[Text omitted]
... The rule of equity which insists on those, who by use of a fiduciary position make a profit, being liable to account for that profit, in no way depends on fraud, or absence of bona fides; or upon such questions or considerations as whether the profit would or should otherwise have gone to the plaintiff, or whether the profiteer was under a duty to obtain the source of the profit for the plaintiff, or whether he took a risk or acted as he did for the benefit of the plaintiff, or whether the plaintiff has in fact been damaged or benefited by his action. The liability arises from the mere fact of a profit having, in the stated circumstances, been made. The profiteer, however honest and well-intentioned, cannot escape the risk of being called upon to account.

[Text omitted]

Let me now consider whether the essential matters, which the plaintiff must prove, have been established in the present case. As to the profit being in fact made there can be no doubt. The shares were acquired at par and were sold three weeks later at a profit of £2 16s. 1d. per share. Did such of the first five respondents as acquired these very profitable shares acquire them by reason and in course of their office of directors of Regal? In my opinion, when the facts are examined and appreciated, the answer can only be that they did. The actual allotment no doubt had to be made by themselves and Garton (or some of them) in their capacity as directors of Amalgamated: but this was merely an executive act, necessitated by the alteration of the scheme for the acquisition of the lease of the two cinemas for the sole benefit of Regal and its shareholders through Regal's share-holding in Amalgamated. That scheme could only be altered by or with the consent of the Regal board. Consider what in fact took place on October 2, 1935. The position immediately before that day is stated in Garton's letter of September 26, 1935. The directors were willing to guarantee the rent until the subscribed capital of Amalgamated reached £5,000. Regal was to control Amalgamated and own the whole of its share capital, with the consequence that the Regal shareholders would receive their proportion of the sale price of the two new cinemas. The respondents then meet on October 2, 1935. They have before them an offer to purchase the Regal cinema for £77,500, and the lease of the two cinemas for £15,000. The offer is accepted. The draft lease is approved and a resolution for its sealing is passed in anticipation of completion in five days. Some of those present, however, shy at giving guarantees, and accordingly the scheme is changed by the Regal directors in a vital respect. It is agreed that a guarantee shall be avoided by the six respondents bringing the subscribed capital up to £5,100. I will consider the evidence and the minute in a moment. The result of this change of scheme which only the Regal directors could bring about may not have been appreciated by them at the time; but its effect upon their company and its shareholders was striking. In the first place, Regal would no longer control Amalgamated, or own the whole of its share capital. The action of its directors had deprived it (acting through its shareholders in general meeting) of the power to acquire the shares. In the second place, the Regal shareholders would only receive a large reduced proportion of the sale price of the two cinemas. The Regal directors and Garton would receive the moneys of which the Regal shareholders were thus deprived. This vital alteration was brought about in the following circumstances – I refer to the evidence of the respondent Garton. He was asked what was suggested when the guarantees were refused, and this is his answer:

> "Mr. Gulliver said 'We must find it somehow. I am willing to find £500. Are you willing,' turning to the other four directors of Regal, 'to do the same?' They expressed themselves as willing. He said, 'That makes £2,500,' and he turned to me and said 'Garton, you have been interested in Mr. Bentley's companies; will you come in to take £500?' I agreed to do so."

Although this matter is recorded in the Amalgamated minutes, this was in fact a decision come to by the directors of Regal, and the subsequent allotment by the directors of Amalgamated was a mere carrying into effect of this decision of the Regal board. The resolution recorded in the Amalgamated minute runs thus:

> "After discussion it was resolved that the directors be invited to subscribe for 500 shares each, and that such shares be allotted accordingly."

As I read that resolution, and my reading agrees with Garton's evidence, the invitation is to the directors of Regal, and is made for the purpose of effectuating the decision which the five directors of Regal had made, that each should take up 500 shares in the Amalgamated. The directors of Amalgamated were not conveying an "invitation" to themselves. That would be ridiculous. They were merely giving effect to the Regal directors' decision to provide £2,500 cash capital themselves, a decision which had been followed by a successful appeal by Gulliver to Garton to provide the balance.

My Lords, I have no hesitation in coming to the conclusion, upon the facts of this case, that these shares, when acquired by the directors, were acquired by reason, and only by reason of the fact that they were directors of Regal, and in the course of their execution of that office.

It now remains to consider whether in acting as directors of Regal they stood in a fiduciary relationship to that company. Directors of a limited company are the creatures of statute and occupy a position peculiar to themselves ...

[Text omitted]

In the result, I am of opinion that the directors standing in a fiduciary relationship to Regal in regard to the exercise of their powers as directors, and having obtained these shares by reason and only by reason of the fact that they were directors of Regal and in the course of the execution of that office, are accountable for the profits which they have made out of them ... It was contended that these cases were distinguishable by reason of the fact that it was impossible for Regal to get the shares owing to lack of funds, and that the directors in taking the shares were really acting as members of the public. I cannot accept this argument. It was impossible for the *cestui que* trust [i.e. the beneficiary of the trust – *editors' note*] in *Keech* v. *Sandford* to obtain the lease. Nevertheless the trustee was accountable. The suggestion that the directors were applying simply as members of the public is a travesty of the facts. They could, had they wished, have protected themselves by a resolution (either antecedent or subsequent) of the Regal shareholders in general meeting. In default of such approval, the liability to account must remain. The result is that, in my opinion, each of the respondents Bobby, Griffiths, Bassett and Bentley is liable to account for the profit which he made on the sale of his 500 shares in Amalgamated.

The case of the respondent Gulliver, however, requires some further consideration, for he has raised a separate and distinct answer to the claim. He says: "I never promised to subscribe for shares in Amalgamated. I never did so subscribe. I only promised to find others who would be willing to subscribe. I only found others who did subscribe. The shares were theirs. They were never mine. They received the profit. I received none of it." If these are the true facts, his answer seems complete. The evidence in my opinion establishes his contention.

[*Text omitted*]

It is of the first importance on this part of the case to bear in mind that these directors have been acquitted of all suggestion of mala fides in regard to the acquisition of these shares. They had no reason to believe that they could be called to account. Why then should Gulliver go to the elaborate pains of having the shares put into the names of South Downs Land Co. and Miss Geering, and of having the proceeds of sale paid into the respective accounts before mentioned, if the shares and proceeds really belonged to him? Ex hypothesi he had no reason for concealment; and no question was raised against the transaction until months after the proceeds of sale had been paid into the banking accounts of those whom Gulliver asserts to have been the owners of the shares. I can see no reason for doubting that the shares never belonged to Gulliver, and that he made no profit on the sale thereof.

[*Text omitted*]

It was further said that Gulliver must account for whatever profits he may have made indirectly through his share holding in the two companies, and that an inquiry should be directed for this purpose. As to this, it is sufficient to say that there is no evidence upon which to ground such an inquiry. Indeed, the evidence so far as it goes, shows that neither company has distributed any part of the profit. Finally, it was said that Gulliver must account for the profit on the 200 shares as to which the certificate was in his name. If in fact the shares belonged beneficially to the Swiss company (and that is the assumption for this purpose), the proceeds of sale did not belong to Gulliver, and were rightly paid into the Swiss company's banking account. Gulliver accordingly made no profit for which he is accountable. As regards Gulliver, this appeal should, in my opinion, be dismissed.

There remains to consider the case of Garton. He stands on a different footing from the other respondents in that he was not a director of Regal. He was Regal's legal adviser; but, in my opinion, he has a short but effective answer to the plaintiffs' claim. He was requested by the Regal directors to apply for 500 shares. They arranged that they themselves should each be responsible for £500 of the Amalgamated capital, and they appealed, by their chairman, to Garton to subscribe the balance of £500 which was required to make up the £3,000. In law his action, which has resulted in a profit, was taken at the request of Regal, and I know of no principle or authority which would justify a decision that a solicitor must account for profit resulting from a transaction which he has entered into on his own behalf, not merely with the consent, but at the request of his client.

My Lords, in my opinion the right way in which to deal with this appeal is (i) to dismiss the appeal as against the respondents Gulliver and Garton with costs, (ii) to allow it with costs as against the other four respondents, and (iii) to enter judgment as against each of these four respondents for a sum of £1,402 1s. 8d. with interest at

4 per cent from October 25, 1935, as to £1,300 part thereof and from December 5, 1935, as to the balance ...

One final observation I desire to make. In his judgment Lord Greene MR, stated that a decision adverse to the directors in the present case involved the proposition that, if directors bona fide decide not to invest their company's funds in some proposed investment, a director who thereafter embarks his own money therein is accountable for any profits which he may derive therefrom. As to this, I can only say that to my mind the facts of this hypothetical case bear but little resemblance to the story with which we have had to deal.

LORD MACMILLAN

... The issue, as it was formulated before your Lordships, was not whether the directors of Regal (Hastings), Ltd, had acted in bad faith ... The sole ground on which it was sought to render them accountable was that, being directors of the plaintiff company and therefore in a fiduciary relation to it, they entered in the course of their management into a transaction in which they utilised the position and knowledge possessed by them in virtue of their office as directors, and that the transaction resulted in a profit to themselves ...

The equitable doctrine invoked is one of the most deeply rooted in our law. It is amply illustrated in the authoritative decisions which my noble and learned friend Lord Russell of Killowen has cited. I should like only to add a passage from Principles of Equity by Lord Kames, 3rd ed. (1778) vol. 2, p. 87, which puts the whole matter in a sentence: "Equity," he says, "prohibits a trustee tram making any profit by his management, directly or indirectly."

[*Text omitted*]

... The conditions are, therefore, in my opinion, present which preclude the four directors who made a personal profit by the transaction from retaining such profit.

[*Text omitted*]

LORD WRIGHT

... That question can be briefly stated to be whether an agent, a director, a trustee or other person in an analogous fiduciary position, when a demand is made upon him by the person to whom he stands in the fiduciary relationship to account for profits acquired by him by reason of his fiduciary position, and by reason of the opportunity and the knowledge, or either, resulting from it, is entitled to defeat the claim upon any ground save that he made profits with the knowledge and assent of the other person.

[*Text omitted*]

... I think the answer to this reasoning is that, both in law and equity, it has been held that, if a person in a fiduciary relationship makes a secret profit out of the relationship, the court will not inquire whether the other person is damnified or has lost a profit which otherwise he would have got. The fact is in itself a fundamental breach of the fiduciary relationship ...

[*Text omitted*]

It is suggested that it would have been mere quixotic folly for the four respondents to let such an occasion pass when the appellant company could not avail itself of it; Lord King LC faced that very position when he accepted that the person in the fiduciary position might be the only person in the world who could not avail himself of the opportunity. It is, however, not true that such a person is absolutely barred, because he could by obtaining the assent of the shareholders have secured his freedom to make the profit for himself. Failing that, the only course open is to let the opportunity pass ...

In the case of the other two respondents, I agree with Lord Russell of Killowen that the appeal should be dismissed for the several reasons which he has given in regard to each of them. These appeals turn on issues of evidence and fact, and I do not desire to add to what has fallen from my noble and learned friend.

LORD PORTER

[*Text omitted*]

My Lords, I am conscious of certain possibilities which are involved in the conclusion which all your Lordships have reached. The action is brought by the Regal company. Technically, of course, the fact that an unlooked for advantage may be gained by the shareholders of that company is immaterial to the question at issue. The company and its shareholders are separate entities. One cannot help remembering, however, that in fact the shares have been purchased by a financial group who were willing to acquire those of the Regal and the Amalgamated at a certain price. As a result of your Lordships' decision that group will, I think, receive in one hand part of the sum which has been paid by the other. For the shares in Amalgamated they paid £3 16s. 1d. per share, yet part of that sum may be returned to the group, though not necessarily to the individual shareholders by reason of the enhancement in value of the shares in Regal – an enhancement brought about as a result of the receipt by the company of the profit made by some of its former directors on the sale of Amalgamated shares. This, it seems, may be an unexpected windfall, but whether it be so or not, the principle that a person occupying a fiduciary relationship shall not make a profit by reason thereof is of such vital importance that the possible consequence in the present case is in fact as it is in law an immaterial consideration.

[*Text omitted*]

Robert F. Broz and RFB Cellular, Inc. v. Cellular Information Systems, Inc.
Delaware Supreme Court
673 A 2d 148 (1996)

VEASEY, Chief Justice

In this appeal, we consider the application of the doctrine of corporate opportunity. The Court of Chancery decided that the defendant, a corporate director, breached his fiduciary duty by not formally presenting to the corporation an opportunity which had come to the director individually and independent of the director's relationship with the corporation. Here the opportunity was not one in which the corporation in its current mode had an interest or which it had the financial ability to acquire, but, under the unique circumstances here, that mode was subject to change by virtue of the impending acquisition of the corporation by another entity.

We conclude that, although a corporate director may be shielded from liability by offering to the corporation an opportunity which has come to the director independently and individually, the failure of the director to present the opportunity does not necessarily result in the improper usurpation of a corporate opportunity. We further conclude that, if the corporation is a target or potential target of an acquisition by another company which has an interest and ability to entertain the opportunity, the director of the target company does not have a fiduciary duty to present the opportunity to the target company. Accordingly, the judgment of the Court of Chancery is REVERSED.

I.   *The contentions of the parties and the decision below*

Robert F. Broz ("Broz") is the President and sole stockholder of RFB Cellular, Inc. ("RFBC"), a Delaware corporation engaged in ... cellular telephone service in the Midwestern United States. At the time of the conduct at issue in this appeal, Broz was also a member of the board of directors of plaintiff below-appellee, Cellular Information Systems, Inc. ("CIS"). CIS is a publicly held Delaware corporation and a competitor of RFBC.

The conduct before the Court involves the purchase by Broz of a cellular telephone service license [the Michigan-2 Rural Service Area Cellular License (Michigan-2)] for the benefit of RFBC ... CIS brought an action against Broz and RFBC for equitable relief, contending that the purchase of this license by Broz constituted a usurpation of a corporate opportunity properly belonging to CIS, irrespective of whether or not CIS was interested in the Michigan-2 opportunity at the time it was offered to Broz.

The principal basis for the contention of CIS is that PriCellular, Inc. ("PriCellular"), another cellular communications company which was contemporaneously engaged in an acquisition of CIS, was interested in the Michigan-2 opportunity. CIS contends that, in determining whether the Michigan-2 opportunity rightfully belonged to CIS, Broz was required to consider the interests of PriCellular insofar as those interests would come into alignment with those of CIS as a result of PriCellular's acquisition plans.

After trial, the Court of Chancery agreed with the contentions of CIS and entered judgment against Broz and RFBC ...

Broz contends that the Court of Chancery erred in holding that he breached his fiduciary duties to CIS and its stockholders ...

II.   Facts

Broz has been the President and sole stockholder of RFBC since 1992. RFBC owns and operates an FCC license area, known as the Michigan-4 Rural Service Area Cellular License ("Michigan-4"). The license entitles RFBC to provide cellular telephone service to a portion of rural Michigan. Although Broz' efforts have been devoted primarily to the business operations of RFBC, he also served as an outside director of CIS at the time of the events at issue in this case. CIS was at all times fully aware of Broz' relationship with RFBC and the obligations incumbent upon him by virtue of that relationship.

In April of 1994, Mackinac Cellular Corp. ("Mackinac") sought to divest itself of Michigan-2 the license area immediately adjacent to Michigan-4. To this end, Mackinac contacted Daniels & Associates ("Daniels") and arranged for the brokerage firm to seek potential purchasers for Michigan-2. In compiling a list of prospects, Daniels included RFBC as a likely candidate. In May of 1994, David Rhodes, a representative of Daniels, contacted Broz and broached the subject of RFBC's possible acquisition of Michigan-2. Broz later signed a confidentiality agreement at the request of Mackinac, and received the offering materials pertaining to Michigan-2.

Michigan-2 was not, however, offered to CIS. Apparently, Daniels did not consider CIS to be a viable purchaser for Michigan-2 in light of CIS' recent financial difficulties. The record shows that, at the time Michigan-2 was offered to Broz, CIS had recently emerged from lengthy and contentious Chapter 11 proceedings. Pursuant to the Chapter 11 Plan of Reorganization, CIS entered into a loan agreement that substantially impaired the company's ability to undertake new acquisitions or to incur new debt. In fact, CIS would have been unable to purchase Michigan-2 without the approval of its creditors.

The CIS reorganization resulted from the failure of CIS' rather ambitious plans for expansion. From 1989 onward, CIS had embarked on a series of cellular license acquisitions. In 1992, however, CIS' financing failed, necessitating the liquidation of the company's holdings and reduction of the company's total indebtedness. During the period from early 1992 until the time of CIS' emergence from bankruptcy in 1994, CIS divested itself of some fifteen separate cellular license systems. CIS contracted to sell four additional license areas on May 27, 1994, leaving CIS with only five remaining license areas, all of which were outside of the Midwest.

On June 13, 1994, following a meeting of the CIS board, Broz spoke with CIS' Chief Executive Officer, Richard Treibick ("Treibick"), concerning his interest in acquiring Michigan-2. Treibick communicated to Broz that CIS was not interested in

Michigan-2. Treibick further stated that he had been made aware of the Michigan-2 opportunity prior to the conversation with Broz, and that any offer to acquire Michigan-2 was rejected. After the commencement of the PriCellular tender offer, in August of 1994, Broz contacted another CIS director, Peter Schiff ("Schiff"), to discuss the possible acquisition of Michigan-2 by RFBC. Schiff, like Treibick, indicated that CIS had neither the wherewithal nor the inclination to purchase Michigan-2. In late September of 1994, Broz also contacted Stanley Bloch ("Bloch"), a director and counsel for CIS, to request that Bloch represent RFBC in its dealings with Mackinac. Bloch agreed to represent RFBC, and, like Schiff and Treibick, expressed his belief that CIS was not at all interested in the transaction. Ultimately, all the CIS directors testified at trial that, had Broz inquired at that time, they each would have expressed the opinion that CIS was not interested in Michigan-2.

On June 28, 1994, following various overtures from PriCellular concerning an acquisition of CIS six CIS directors entered into agreements with PriCellular to sell their shares in CIS at a price of $2.00 per share. These agreements were contingent upon, inter alia, the consummation of a PriCellular tender offer for all CIS shares at the same price. Pursuant to their agreements with PriCellular, the CIS directors also entered into a "standstill" agreement which prevented the directors from engaging in any transaction outside the regular course of CIS' business or incurring any new liabilities until the close of the PriCellular tender offer. On August 2, 1994, PriCellular commenced a tender offer for all outstanding shares of CIS at $2.00 per share. The PriCellular tender offer mirrored the standstill agreements entered into by the CIS directors.

PriCellular's tender offer was originally scheduled to close on September 16, 1994. At the time the tender offer was launched, however, the source of the $106,000,000 in financing required to consummate the transaction was still in doubt. PriCellular originally planned to structure the transaction around bank loans. When this financing fell through, PriCellular resorted to a junk bond offering. PriCellular's financing difficulties generated a great deal of concern among the CIS insiders whether the tender offer was, in fact, viable. Financing difficulties ultimately caused PriCellular to delay the closing date of the tender offer from September 16, 1994 until October 14, 1994 and then again until November 9, 1994.

On August 6, September 6 and September 21, 1994, Broz submitted written offers to Mackinac for the purchase of Michigan-2. During this time period, PriCellular also began negotiations with Mackinac to arrange an option for the purchase of Michigan-2. PriCellular's interest in Michigan-2 was fully disclosed to CIS' chief executive, Treibick, who did not express any interest in Michigan-2, and was actually incredulous that PriCellular would want to acquire the license. Nevertheless, CIS was fully aware that PriCellular and Broz were bidding for Michigan-2 and did not interpose CIS in this bidding war.

In late September of 1994, PriCellular reached agreement with Mackinac on an option to purchase Michigan-2. The exercise price of the option agreement was set at $6.7 million, with the option remaining in force until December 15, 1994. Pursuant to the agreement, the right to exercise the option was not transferable to any party other than a subsidiary of PriCellular. Therefore, it could not have been transferred to CIS. The agreement further provided that Mackinac was free to sell Michigan-2 to any party who was willing to exceed the exercise price of the Mackinac-PriCellular option contract by at least $500,000. On November 14, 1994, Broz agreed to pay Mackinac $7.2 million for the Michigan-2 license, thereby meeting the terms of the option agreement. An asset purchase agreement was thereafter executed by Mackinac and RFBC.

Nine days later, on November 23, 1994, PriCellular completed its financing and closed its tender offer for CIS. Prior to that point, PriCellular owned no equity interest in CIS. Subsequent to the consummation of the PriCellular tender offer for CIS, members of the CIS board of directors, including Broz, were discharged and replaced with a slate of PriCellular nominees. On March 2, 1995, this action was commenced by CIS in the Court of Chancery.

At trial in the Court of Chancery, CIS contended that the purchase of Michigan-2 by Broz constituted the impermissible usurpation of a corporate opportunity properly belonging to CIS. Thus, CIS asserted that Broz breached his fiduciary duty to CIS and its stockholders. CIS admits that, at the time the opportunity was offered to Broz, the board of CIS would not have been interested in Michigan-2, but CIS asserts that Broz usurped the opportunity nevertheless. CIS claims that Broz was required to look not just to CIS, but to the articulated business plans of PriCellular, to determine whether PriCellular would be interested in acquiring Michigan-2. Since Broz failed to do this and acquired Michigan-2 without first considering the interests of PriCellular in its capacity as a potential acquiror of CIS, CIS contends that Broz must be held to account for breach of fiduciary duty.

In assessing the contentions of the parties in light of the facts of record, the Court of Chancery concluded:

> (1) that [CIS] ... could have legitimately required its director [Broz] to abstain from the Mackinac transaction out of deference to its own interests in extending an offer, despite the fact that it came to such director in a wholly independent way, (that is the transaction is one that falls quite close to the core transactions that the corporation was formed to engage in); (2) that by no later than the time by which Price had extended the public tender offer, the circumstances of the company had changed so that it was quite plausibly in the corporation's interest and financially feasible for it to pursue the Mackinac transaction; (3) that in such circumstances as existed at the latest after October 14, 1994 (date of PriCellular's option contract on Michigan 2 RSA) it was the obligation of Mr. Broz as a director of CIS to take the transaction to the CIS board for its formal action; and (4) the after the fact testimony of directors to the effect that they would not have been interested in pursuing this transaction had it been brought to the board, is not helpful to defendant, in my opinion, because most of them did not know at that time of PriCellular's interest in the property and how it related to PriCellular's plan for CIS.

... Based on these conclusions, the court held that:

even though knowledge of the availability of the Michigan 2 RSA license and its associated assets came to Mr. Broz wholly independently of his role on the CIS board, that opportunity was within the core business interests of CIS at the relevant times; that at such time CIS would have had access to the financing necessary to compete for the assets that were for sale; and that the CIS board of directors were not asked to and thus did not consider whether such action would have been in the best interests of the corporation. In these circumstances I conclude that Mr. Broz as a director of CIS violated his duty of loyalty to CIS by seizing this opportunity without formally informing the CIS board fully about the opportunity and facts surrounding it and by proceeding to acquire rights for his benefit without the consent of the corporation ...

[Text omitted]

IV. Application of the corporate opportunity doctrine

The doctrine of corporate opportunity represents but one species of the broad fiduciary duties assumed by a corporate director or officer. A corporate fiduciary agrees to place the interests of the corporation before his or her own in appropriate circumstances. In light of the diverse and often competing obligations faced by directors and officers, however, the corporate opportunity doctrine arose as a means of defining the parameters of fiduciary duty in instances of potential conflict. The classic statement of the doctrine is derived from the venerable case of *Guth* v. *Loft, Inc.* In *Guth*, this Court held that:

> if there is presented to a corporate officer or director a business opportunity which the corporation is financially able to undertake, is, from its nature, in the line of the corporation's business and is of practical advantage to it, is one in which the corporation has an interest or a reasonable expectancy, and, by embracing the opportunity, the self-interest of the officer or director will be brought into conflict with that of the corporation, the law will not permit him to seize the opportunity for himself ...

The corporate opportunity doctrine, as delineated by *Guth* and its progeny, holds that a corporate officer or director may not take a business opportunity for his own if: (1) the corporation is financially able to exploit the opportunity; (2) the opportunity is within the corporation's line of business; (3) the corporation has an interest or expectancy in the opportunity; and (4) by taking the opportunity for his own, the corporate fiduciary will thereby be placed in a position inimicable to his duties to the corporation. The Court in *Guth* also derived a corollary which states that a director or officer may take a corporate opportunity if: (1) the opportunity is presented to the director or officer in his individual and not his corporate capacity; (2) the opportunity is not essential to the corporation; (3) the corporation holds no interest or expectancy in the opportunity; and (4) the director or officer has not wrongfully employed the resources of the corporation in pursuing or exploiting the opportunity. *Guth*, 5 A 2d at 509.

Thus, the contours of this doctrine are well established. It is important to note, however, that the tests enunciated in *Guth* and subsequent cases provide guidelines to be considered by a reviewing court in balancing the equities of an individual case. No one factor is dispositive and all factors must be taken into account insofar as they are applicable. Cases involving a claim of usurpation of a corporate opportunity range over a multitude of factual settings … In the instant case, we find that the facts do not support the conclusion that Broz misappropriated a corporate opportunity.

We note at the outset that Broz became aware of the Michigan-2 opportunity in his individual and not his corporate capacity. As the Court of Chancery found, "Broz did not misuse proprietary information that came to him in a corporate capacity nor did he otherwise use any power he might have over the governance of the corporation to advance his own interests." … This fact is not the subject of serious dispute. In fact, it is clear from the record that Mackinac did not consider CIS a viable candidate for the acquisition of Michigan-2. Accordingly, Mackinac did not offer the property to CIS. In this factual posture, many of the fundamental concerns undergirding the law of corporate opportunity are not present (e.g. misappropriation of the corporation's proprietary information). The burden imposed upon Broz to show adherence to his fiduciary duties to CIS is thus lessened to some extent … Nevertheless, this fact is not dispositive. The determination of whether a particular fiduciary has usurped a corporate opportunity necessitates a careful examination of the circumstances, giving due credence to the factors enunciated in *Guth* and subsequent cases.

We turn now to an analysis of the factors relied on by the trial court. First, we find that CIS was not financially capable of exploiting the Michigan-2 opportunity … The record shows that CIS was in a precarious financial position at the time Mackinac presented the Michigan-2 opportunity to Broz. Having recently emerged from lengthy and contentious bankruptcy proceedings, CIS was not in a position to commit capital to the acquisition of new assets. Further, the loan agreement entered into by CIS and its creditors severely limited the discretion of CIS as to the acquisition of new assets and substantially restricted the ability of CIS to incur new debt.

The Court of Chancery based its contrary finding on the fact that PriCellular had purchased an option to acquire CIS' bank debt. Thus, the court reasoned, PriCellular was in a position to exercise that option and then waive any unfavorable restrictions that would stand in the way of a CIS acquisition of Michigan-2. The trial court, however, disregarded the fact that PriCellular's own financial situation was not particularly stable. PriCellular was unable to finance the acquisition of CIS through conventional bank loans and was forced to use the more risky mechanism of a junk bond offering to raise the required capital. Thus, the court's statement that "PriCellular had other sources of financing to permit the funding of that purchase" is clearly not free from dispute. Moreover, as discussed infra, the fact that PriCellular had available sources of financing is immaterial to the analysis. At the time that Broz was required to decide whether to accept the Michigan-2 opportunity, PriCellular had not yet acquired CIS, and any plans to do so were wholly speculative. Thus, contrary to the Court of Chancery's finding, Broz was not obligated to consider the contingency of a PriCellular acquisition of CIS and the related contingency of PriCellular thereafter waiving restrictions on the CIS bank debt. Broz was required to consider the facts only as they existed at the time he determined to accept the Mackinac offer and embark on his efforts to bring the transaction to fruition ...

Second, while it may be said with some certainty that the Michigan-2 opportunity was within CIS' line of business, it is not equally clear that CIS had a cognizable interest or expectancy in the license. Under the third factor laid down by this Court in *Guth*, for an opportunity to be deemed to belong to the fiduciary's corporation, the corporation must have an interest or expectancy in that opportunity ... ["T]here must be some tie between that property and the nature of the corporate business." Despite the fact that the nature of the Michigan-2 opportunity was historically close to the core operations of CIS, changes were in process. At the time the opportunity was presented, CIS was actively engaged in the process of divesting its cellular license holdings. CIS' articulated business plan did not involve any new acquisitions. Further, as indicated by the testimony of the entire CIS board, the Michigan-2 license would not have been of interest to CIS even absent CIS' financial difficulties and CIS' then current desire to liquidate its cellular license holdings. Thus, CIS had no interest or expectancy in the Michigan-2 opportunity ...

Finally, the corporate opportunity doctrine is implicated only in cases where the fiduciary's seizure of an opportunity results in a conflict between the fiduciary's duties to the corporation and the self-interest of the director as actualized by the exploitation of the opportunity. In the instant case, Broz' interest in acquiring and profiting from Michigan-2 created no duties that were inimicable to his obligations to CIS. Broz, at all times relevant to the instant appeal, was the sole party in interest in RFBC, a competitor of CIS. CIS was fully aware of Broz' potentially conflicting duties. Broz, however, comported himself in a manner that was wholly in accord with his obligations to CIS. Broz took care not to usurp any opportunity which CIS was willing and able to pursue. Broz sought only to compete with an outside entity, PriCellular, for acquisition of an opportunity which both sought to possess. Broz was not obligated to refrain from competition with PriCellular. Therefore, the totality of the circumstances indicates that Broz did not usurp an opportunity that properly belonged to CIS.

A.   Presentation to the board

In concluding that Broz had usurped a corporate opportunity, the Court of Chancery placed great emphasis on the fact that Broz had not formally presented the matter to the CIS board. The court held that "in such circumstances as existed at the latest after October 14, 1994 (date of PriCellular's option contract on Michigan 2 RSA) it was the obligation of Mr. Broz as a director of CIS to take the transaction to the CIS board for its formal action ... " ... In so holding, the trial court erroneously grafted a new requirement onto the law of corporate opportunity, viz., the requirement of formal presentation under circumstances where the corporation does not have an interest, expectancy or financial ability.

The teaching of *Guth* and its progeny is that the director or officer must analyze the situation ex ante to determine whether the opportunity is one rightfully belonging to the corporation. If the director or officer believes, based on one of the factors articulated above, that the corporation is not entitled to the opportunity, then he may take it for himself. Of course, presenting the opportunity to the board creates a kind of "safe harbor" for the director, which removes the specter of a post hoc judicial determination that the director or officer has improperly usurped a corporate opportunity. Thus, presentation avoids the possibility that an error in the fiduciary's assessment of the situation will create future liability for breach of fiduciary duty. It is not the law of Delaware that presentation to the board is a necessary prerequisite to a finding that a corporate opportunity has not been usurped.

The numerous cases decided since *Guth* are in full accord with this view of the doctrine. For instance, in *Field* v. *Allyn* ... the Court of Chancery held that a director or officer is free to take a business opportunity for himself once the corporation has rejected it or if it can be shown that the corporation is not in a position to take the opportunity. The *Field* court held this to be true even if the fiduciary became aware of the opportunity by virtue of the fiduciary's position in the corporation. Id. at 1099. Notably, this Court affirmed the *Field* holding on the basis of the well reasoned opinion of the court below ... The view that presentation to the board is not required where the opportunity is one that the corporation is incapable of exercising is also expressed in other cases ...

Other cases, such as *Kaplan* v. *Fenton* ... have found no violation of the corporate opportunity doctrine where the director determined that the corporation was not interested in the opportunity, but never made formal presentation to the board. The director in *Kaplan* asked the CEO and another board member if the corporation would be interested in the opportunity and whether he should present the opportunity to the board. These questions were answered in the negative and the director then acquired the opportunity for himself. The *Kaplan* Court found no breach of the doctrine, despite the absence of formal presentation.

[Text omitted]

Thus, we hold that Broz was not required to make formal presentation of the Michigan-2 opportunity to the CIS board prior to taking the opportunity for his own. In so holding, we necessarily conclude that the Court of Chancery erred in grafting the additional requirement of formal presentation onto Delaware's corporate opportunity jurisprudence.

B.   Alignment of interests between CIS and PriCellular

In concluding that Broz usurped an opportunity properly belonging to CIS, the Court of Chancery held that "for practical business reasons CIS' interests with respect to the Mackinac transaction came to merge with those of PriCellular, even before the closing of its tender offer for CIS stock." Based on this fact, the trial court concluded that Broz was required to consider PriCellular's prospective, post-acquisition plans for CIS in determining whether to forego the opportunity or seize it for himself ...

We disagree. Broz was under no duty to consider the interests of PriCellular when he chose to purchase Michigan-2. As stated in *Guth*, a director's right to "appropriate [an] ... opportunity depends on the circumstances existing at the time it presented itself to him without regard to subsequent events." ... At the time Broz purchased Michigan-2, PriCellular had not yet acquired CIS. Any plans to do so would still have been wholly speculative ...

Whether or not the CIS board would, at some time, have chosen to acquire Michigan-2 in order to make CIS a more attractive acquisition target for PriCellular or to enhance the synergy of any combined enterprise, is speculative ... This speculative finding cuts against the statements made by CIS' Chief Executive and the entire CIS board of directors and ignores the fact that CIS still lacked the wherewithal to acquire Michigan-2, even if one takes into account the possible availability of PriCellular's financing. Thus, the fact of PriCellular's plans to acquire CIS is immaterial and does not change the analysis.

In reaching our conclusion on this point, we note that certainty and predictability are values to be promoted in our corporation law ... Broz, as an active participant in the cellular telephone industry, was entitled to proceed in his own economic interest in the absence of any countervailing duty. The right of a director or officer to engage in business affairs outside of his or her fiduciary capacity would be illusory if these individuals were required to consider every potential, future occurrence in determining whether a particular business strategy would implicate fiduciary duty concerns. In order for a director to engage meaningfully in business unrelated to his or her corporate role, the director must be allowed to make decisions based on the situation as it exists at the time a given opportunity is presented. Absent such a rule, the corporate fiduciary would be constrained to refrain from exploiting any opportunity for fear of liability based on the occurrence of subsequent events. This state of affairs would unduly restrict officers and directors and would be antithetical to certainty in corporation law.

VI. Conclusion

The corporate opportunity doctrine represents a judicially crafted effort to harmonize the competing demands placed on corporate fiduciaries in a modern business environment. The doctrine seeks to reduce the possibility of conflict between a director's duties to the corporation and interests unrelated to that role. In the instant case, Broz adhered to his obligations to CIS. We hold that the Court of Chancery erred as a matter of law in concluding that Broz had a duty formally to present the Michigan-2 opportunity to the CIS board. We also hold that the trial court erred in its application of the corporate opportunity doctrine under the unusual facts of this case, where CIS had no interest or financial ability to acquire the opportunity, but the impending acquisition of CIS by PriCellular would or could have caused a change in those circumstances.

Therefore, we hold that Broz did not breach his fiduciary duties to CIS ...

13

Judicial review of management decisions (the business judgment rule)

Required reading

D: AktG, §§ 93, 116
UK: CA 2006, secs. 170, 172, 173–174
US: DGCL, §§ 143, 144; Model Act, §§ 8.30–8.31

Judging business judgment

Operation under central management is a core characteristic of the corporation. Management authority is delegated to a board of directors and other executive officers who control the aggregated assets of the corporation because it is expected that full-time, professional managers can operate the company more successfully than can the shareholders.[1] In the course of managing the company, these expert directors make decisions to determine the course of the company's business operations. As discussed in Chapter 12, under the company laws of the UK, Germany and the US, directors must fulfill duties of care, skill and diligence, which, while not identical to those imposed on other fiduciaries like agents and trustees, are quite similar. Take, for example, the Companies Act 2006, which formulates the duty of care as follows:

> A director of a company must exercise ... the care, skill and diligence that would be exercised by a reasonably diligent person with ... the general knowledge, skill and experience that may reasonably be expected of a person carrying out [such] functions ... and ... the general knowledge, skill and experience that the director has.[2]

---

[1] See e.g. Clark (1986: 21–24) with respect to how corporate law is designed to allow efficient, centralized management; and Chandler (1990: 82–83) with respect to the appearance of specialized education for corporate management.
[2] Sec. 174 CA 2006.

In an ordinary negligence action under a standard of this type outside of the corporate context, a court could be expected to hear evidence from an expert witness as to whether the defendant in fact showed the "knowledge, skill and experience" required to meet the objective standard of care plus any special (subjective) skills held. In such an analysis, the standard of care to be met by the defendant and the standard of review that the court would apply would be substantially indistinguishable.[3] When it comes to assessing a corporate director's exercise of due care and skill, however, courts do something different. In each of our jurisdictions, whether by statutory rule (as in the *Aktiengesetz* or the Model Act),[4] by express rule formulated in the case law (as in Delaware)[5] or by undeclared practice (as in the UK),[6] courts presume that disinterested directors making business decisions in good faith have met their duty of care absent egregious mismanagement.

In his seminal article on the divergence between the standard of care and the standard of review for alleged breaches of the duty of care, Professor Melvin A. Eisenberg explained that the free room for discretion granted by courts to business judgment does not result merely from the fact that managers are experts in an activity for which judges are not trained. Expert decisions in most fields can be assessed by verifying correct application of the proper procedures and protocols.[7] By contrast, a business decision cannot be similarly verified as it must consciously assume a risk of uncertain outcome:

> A decision maker faced with uncertainty must make a judgment concerning the relevant probability distribution and must act on that judgment. If the decision maker makes a reasonable assessment of the probability distribution, and the outcome falls on the unlucky tail, the decision maker has not made a bad decision, because in any normal probability distribution some outcomes will inevitably fall on the unlucky tail ... For example, suppose that Corporation C has $100 million in assets. C's board must choose between Decision X and Decision Y. Each decision requires an investment of $1 million. Decision X has a 75 percent likelihood of succeeding. If the decision succeeds, C will gain $2 million. If it fails, C will lose its $1 million investment. Decision Y has a 90 percent chance of succeeding. If the decision succeeds, C will gain $1 million. If it fails,

---

[3] Eisenberg (1993: 437).   [4] § 93(1) AktG; § 8.31 Model Act.

[5] In this text, see *Aronson v. Lewis*, *Sinclair Oil Corp. v. Levien* and *In Re the Walt Disney Company Derivative Litigation*.

[6] See e.g. *Re Brazilian Rubber Plantations and Estates Ltd* [1911] 1 Ch 425, 437; *In Re Sam Weller & Sons Ltd* [1990] Ch 682, 694; *Re Elgindata Ltd* [1991] BCLC 959.

[7] Eisenberg (1993: 444).

C will recover its investment. It is in the interest of C's shareholders that the board make Decision X, even though it is riskier, because the expected value of Decision X is $1.25 million (75 percent of $2 million, minus 25 percent of $1 million) while the expected value of Decision Y is only $900,000 (90 percent of $1 million). If, however, the board was concerned about liability for breaching the duty of care, it might choose Decision Y, because as a practical matter it is almost impossible for a plaintiff to win a duty-of-care action on the theory that a board should have taken greater risks than it did.[8]

Although the type and quality of the information management obtains and the procedure it uses to make the decision can be tested against accepted practices and procedures for which a court may hear expert testimony, the business decision itself cannot be found to trigger liability just because a possible negative outcome indeed materializes. Uncertainty is built into the heart of the activity and management should be encouraged to seek it, as high-yielding risky projects benefit the company and its constituents. This is different from the idea that directors are specialists in an area foreign to judges (the performance of a neurosurgeon in a malpractice suit would also be quite foreign to the education of most judges). It is likewise different from the flexible "forbearance" that Professor Oliver E. Williamson describes as the "implicit contract law of internal organization" that allows avoidance of "disputes [that] would sorely test the competence of courts and would undermine the efficacy of hierarchy."[9] Neither specialized information nor organizational hierarchy exhaust the particular nature of a choice to abstain from retrospectively condemning a decision made in conscious acceptance of uncertainty. This distinction between that which can be certain (the professional procedure leading up to a decision) and that which is always uncertain (the identity of the right decision) brings a divergence of the standard of care and the standard of review. It shows that our limited knowledge of how a risk will unfold in a given factual circumstance (bounded rationality) necessitates a distinction between the two standards for review of unconflicted business decisions.[10] Judging business decisions *de novo* from hindsight would both be unfair and discourage management from taking on entrepreneurial risk.

This problem is recognized in the formulation of the "business judgment rule" in the US and in § 93(1) of the *Aktiengesetz*. Although the

---

[8] Eisenberg (1993: 445–446).   [9] Williamson (1991: 274–275).
[10] Eisenberg (1993: 466).

UK does not articulate the distinction conceptually,[11] courts do see a legal difference between a director's decision that fails to achieve success (which is not actionable) and "serious mismanagement" (which may be actionable).[12] In Delaware, the distinction is accounted for by a "business judgment rule," which is formulated as "a presumption that in making a business decision the directors of a corporation acted on an informed basis, in good faith and in the honest belief that the action taken was in the best interests of the company" (quoted from *Aronson* v. *Lewis*, reprinted in part in this chapter). If a plaintiff challenging a business decision can rebut any of the presumed elements, then the director must respond by showing that the decision was a good one, i.e. that it was in substance fair to the company. If the presumption stands, the decision will not be actionable unless grossly negligent. See the *Disney Company Derivative Litigation* opinion, in this chapter. As *Disney* makes clear, under the business judgment rule, a director's action does not trigger liability simply because it does not meet best practices. While § 93(1) AktG is supposed to serve the same end, i.e. the protection of managers from the risk of personal liability for taking business decisions involving risk, unlike its US counterpart it does not create a presumption in favor of the directors. Before they can enjoy the protection of the business judgment rule, they will have to show that they were disinterested and took their decision based on reasonably thorough information. Thus, while the elements of the business judgment rule under US and German law are essentially the same, the level of protection afforded to management under German law is substantially lower.[13]

Of course, as already generally referred to above, company directors perform tasks other than making business decisions. In particular, they must keep themselves properly informed about the company's activity and, in particular, monitor management.[14] Supervisory activities clearly fail to include the calculus of risk and chance inherent to entrepreneurial choices. Supervisory activities can include deciding whether a shareholder's desire to bring a claim against one or more directors for a breach of duty should go forward. This last issue is the decision disputed in *ARAG* v. *Garmenbeck*, reprinted in part in this chapter, and in *Aronson*. Each of

---

[11] In 1999, the Law Commissions advised against the adoption of a business judgment rule in the UK as they thought it could lead courts to over-emphasize compliance with accepted procedures as a test for meeting the duty of care. See Davies (2008: 493).

[12] Gore-Browne (2004: Enforcement of Duties [12]); Morse (2003: 8.2810).

[13] See Mertens and Cahn, in *KölnKommAktG* (2010: § 93 mn. 14).

[14] Eisenberg (1993: 448).

these cases discusses a decision by directors not to pursue a shareholder challenge against the management. How do the Delaware and the German courts proceed on this similar issue? Is the reasoning in each case consistent with the rationale for the business judgment rule?

Questions for discussion

1. What distinguishes the decisionmaking process of corporate directors when addressing business opportunities from that of other professionals?
2. What activities of directors are like those of other professionals?
3. What is the business judgment rule?
4. Should the rule be formulated in a statute as in Germany or left to the courts as in Delaware?
5. Do you agree with the UK position that company law should not have a business judgment rule, or do you agree with the Delaware position on the rule?
6. How does the business judgment rule relate to breaches of fiduciary duty?
7. Do you agree with the position of the German court in *ARAG* or that of the Delaware court in *Aronson*? For a greater understanding of the procedure discussed in *Aronson*, you can consult *Zapata Corp.* v. *Maldonado* in Chapter 20.

Cases

ARAG v. Garmenbeck
High Federal Court, Second Civil Division
April 21, 1997 / BGHZ 135, 244
[*Partial, unofficial translation of official opinion text*]

Official head note

a) Members of a supervisory board hold positions in a management body, which means that they have a common responsibility to ensure that the resolutions they adopt are adopted duly and legally, and they therefore have standing in a judicial challenge of such resolutions for a determination of nullity.

   b) Because it must monitor and supervise the activity of the management board, the supervisory board has a duty to examine whether the corporation has any claim for damages against members of the management board.

   When it carries out such duty, the supervisory board must allow the management board a broad area in which to exercise its business judgment in managing the corporation's business without which commercial activity would be impossible.

The ability of the shareholders' meeting under to § 147(1) AktG to adopt a resolution to seek legal enforcement of a claim does not affect the above duty.

c) If the supervisory board reaches the conclusion that the management board has acted so as to incur liability, it must determine on the basis of a thorough and appropriate risk assessment whether, and to what extent, a judicial action would lead to sufficient compensation for the damages. It need not be conclusively established that the claim for compensation of damages will be successful.

d) If this examination leads to a finding that the corporation has an enforceable claim for damages, the supervisory board must generally prosecute such claim. The only exceptional case in which the claim need not be prosecuted is when the good of the corporation presents material reasons against it and such circumstances outweigh or at least equal the reasons for prosecuting the claim.

The supervisory board may only in exceptional cases take into account reasons unrelated to the good of the corporation and personally affecting the management board members.

Holding

On the appeal of the plaintiff, the June 22, 1995 judgement of the sixth civil division of the Düsseldorf State Court of Appeals is hereby reversed to the extent that the claim was dismissed and the plaintiff was ordered to pay costs.

The matter is to such extent remanded to the Court of Appeals for rehearing and judgment, including with regard to the payment of the costs for the appeal.

Facts

The Plaintiffs, members of the supervisory board of the Defendant, a liability insurer having the legal form of a stock corporation (*Aktiengesellschaft*), challenge the supervisory board resolutions regarding Point 8 b) of the Agenda of June 25, 1992 and Point 9 of the Agenda of June 25, 1993, with which a proposal to enforce a claim for damages against the Chairman of the management board of the Defendant, Dr. Ludwig F., was rejected.

The Defendant, its 100% owned subsidiaries, A[RAG] GmbH and A[RAG] Finanz BV, which were incorporated in 1984 and 1989, respectively, and which were legally represented in dealings with third parties by each of their executive managers severally, including Dr. Ludwig F., entered into commercial dealings with G[armenbeck] Ltd. G[armenbeck] was incorporated in London, but only maintained a post office box in that city; its managing director was a Mr. W, an electrician who had a record of previous violations of law, and whose primary activity was to effect brokerage transactions through the company for investors from Switzerland. G[armenbeck] Ltd borrowed funds at interest rates substantially exceeding market levels and then lent them at sub-market interest rates. The losses generated by this business activity could be supported only for a limited period of time by spreading out a "pyramid scheme" type of business structure. At the beginning of 1990, the G[armenbeck] Group collapsed.

As a result of such collapse, the Defendant and its subsidiaries suffered damages of approximately DM 421,000 in lost interest payments from loan transactions. In addition, the Defendant suffered losses from related credit transactions with A[RAG] Finanz BV that the Plaintiffs estimate at more than DM 80 million. Because of its bankrupt condition, G[armenbeck] Ltd was unable to perform on its obligation to A[RAG] Finanz BV (consisting of a loan of funds that A[RAG] Finanz BV obtained from a bank and granted to G[armenbeck] Ltd) when due in 1990 by directly repaying the bank that provided the funds. A[RAG] Finanz BV was also unable to make such repayment to the bank. As a result, the Defendant was forced to provide such repayment. The Defendant had provided letters of patronage signed by, *inter alia*, the Chairman of its management board, to secure certain guarantees that were provided to the banks that loaned the credit. At the time that G[armenbeck] Ltd received payment of the loan amount to its managing director, A., a letter of guarantee from the S. Reinsurance company, which had been contemplated as security for the transaction, was in fact not available.

The Plaintiffs argue that the Chairman of the Defendant's management board violated the duty of care that he owed his company by entering into the transactions with G[armenbeck] Ltd, and must therefore reimburse the company for the resulting damages. In its meetings of June 25, 1992 and June 15, 1993, the supervisory board adopted resolutions to reject the Plaintiff's proposal 1 that an appropriate resolution for such prosecution be adopted.

The Plaintiffs argue that such resolutions are in violation of law and pray that the court declare them null and void.

The State Regional Court ... found merit in the complaint, but the Court of Appeals ... found that the complaint should be dismissed. We vacate the decision of the Court of Appeals and remand for further proceedings.

Discussion

I. Contrary to the respondent's argument, the Court of Appeals correctly found that the request for declaratory judgment was admissible.

1. The Court of Appeals interpreted the decisions of the Civil Division to mean that declaratory judgments on the legality of supervisory board resolutions are not subject to the restrictions set out in §§ 241 *et seq.* AktG. Rather, supervisory board resolutions that violate mandatory provisions of law or the articles of association in substance or in their adoption are null, and the procedure for confirming such nullity is a declaratory judgment pursuant to § 256(1) of the Code of Civil Procedure (BGHZ 122, 342, 347 *et seq.*; 124, 111, 125). The respondent's pleading did not dispute this finding.

However, the Court of Appeals found that a supervisory board member had a legal right to seek a declaratory judgment on the nullity of a supervisory board resolution because of its contents only if the rights of such supervisory board *qua* member were violated or limited, or if the supervisory board refused to comply with a shareholders' resolution adopted pursuant to § 147(1) AktG to take recourse against a member of the management board. Since the facts here do not present a like situation, the Court of Appeals found that the Plaintiffs did not have standing to seek a declaratory judgment. We disagree with that holding.

a) We need not address at this time whether a supervisory board member may obtain standing on the basis of his personal interest to distance himself from a supervisory board resolution so as to avoid being sued in possible challenges under § 116 AktG for aiding and abetting the illegal actions of a management body (see Bork, ZIP 1991, 137, 146; Stodolkowitz, ZHR 154 (1990), 1, 18). This position may also be disputed by the fact that the minutes recording the member votes could be used as a defense against any such challenge (Noack, DZWiR 1994, 341, 343). In any case, the interest of a supervisory board member to seek such a judgment flows from his or her position on the board and the related common responsibility for the legality of the resolutions that body adopts (BGHZ 122, 342, 350). A supervisory board member has not only the right and duty to fulfill his assigned tasks as a board member in compliance with law and the articles of association, but rather his board position also gives him at least the right to act so that the board to which he belongs makes its decisions in a way that does not violate the law or the articles of association. If a board member cannot achieve this through discussions and decision-making in the board, he then has the right to seek clarity through judicial action. The Civil Division has already made this point in an earlier decision – which did not limit or violate the rights of board members to influence the board: the legal interest to seek a declaration regarding the nullity of a supervisory board resolution flows from the plaintiff's position as a member of the supervisory board (BGHZ 83, 144, 146; also see BGHZ 124, 111, 115).

The great majority of the legal literature has agreed with this holding (Kölner Kommentar/Mertens, 2nd ed., § 108 no. 89; Lutter/Krieger, *Rechte und Pflichten des Aufsichtsrates*, 3rd ed. no. 289; Hoffmann/Becking, *Münchner Handbuch des Gesellschaftsrechts*, Vol. 4, Aktiengesellschaft, § 33 no. 49 with more citations in footnote 59; Thomas Raiser, ZGR 1989, 44, 67 *et seq.*).

b) The above holding is not contradicted by § 245(5) AktG, which allows a member of the supervisory or management board to challenge a shareholders' resolution only if the carrying out of the resolution would violate law or administrative regulations, or create liability for damages. The law has placed the examination of shareholders' resolutions for conformity to law and the articles solely in the hands of the shareholders, as the body adopting the resolution, and the entire management board, as the management body; it has not placed such authority with members of the management and supervisory boards who take no part in adopting the resolution. The law has correcly given such persons a right to raise challenges only when they would be particularly affected in their position on the board by the carrying out of the shareholders' resolution.

c) Contrary to the holding of the Court of Appeals, standing to seek judicial remedy may not in cases like that before us be restricted to situations where the majority of the supervisory board has refused to carry out a shareholders' resolution adopted pursuant to § 147(1) AktG to exercise a claim for damages against a member of the management board. The function of the supervisory board to monitor the entire management activity of the management board – including measures already taken – creates a duty to examine existing damages claims against the management board and to act on them if they have merit (§ 111(1) AktG), as well as to represent the corporation in and out of court *vis-à-vis* the management board pursuant to § 112 AktG (see Kölner Kommentar/Mertens, *supra*, § 111 no. 37; Geßler, in Geßler/Hefermehl/Eckardt/Kropff, AktG, § 112 no. 12; Wiesner, in *Münchner Handbuch des Gesellschaftsrechts*, *supra*, § 26 no. 24). The supervisory board is not released from this duty of examination and prosecution by the mere possibility that the shareholders' meeting may reach a decision pursuant to § 147(1) AktG with regard to exercising a damages claim against a management board member as long as the shareholders' meeting has neither exercised such right with a resolution to prosecute or waived its right to prosecute in a binding manner (§ 93(4), sentence 3, AktG). As a consequence, the right of each member of the supervisory board to submit the decision of the supervisory board for judicial examination of its legality is not prejudiced by the possibility that the shareholders' meeting could adopt a resolution pursuant to § 147(1) AktG.

2. The lawful interest of the Plaintiff in receiving a judicial declaration regarding the legality of the supervisory board resolution is not eliminated by the fact that the Defendant, represented by a special representative within the meaning of § 147(3) AktG, sued for compensation of damages at the close of 1994 against the members of its management board (Düsseldorf State Regional Court – 4 O 226/94). In such continuing proceedings, the defendant managing directors have raised the defense that the shareholders' resolutions adopted pursuant to § 147(1) and (3) AktG on October 26, 1994 and January 10, 1995 and serving as the basis of the claim are null. To this end, the management board members have filed a claim for a judicial declaration of the nullity of such resolutions. If either the defence of nullity or the declaratory judgment action for nullity is successful, neither the resolution pursuant to § 147(1) AktG nor the appointment of the special representative pursuant to § 147(3) AktG would be effective. In this case, the supervisory board would again be the Defendant's legal representative (§ 112 AktG) for the prosecution of the disputed damages claim. The supervisory board would be able to pick up the action for damages and consent to the special representative as *procurator litis*. If the action were to be dismissed, which is advisable on procedural grounds, the supervisory board could file a new action against the members

of the management board seeking compensation for damages. The objection of an expired statute of limitations could not be raised as a bar to such claim because the defendant managing directors have signed declarations waiving such objection. Under these circumstances, the question whether the resolutions of June 25, 1992 and June 15, 1993 are null remains of decisive importance for the prosecution of the damages claims against the Defendant's managing directors. The right to standing for the desired declaratory judgment thus continues to exist.

II. The Court of Appeals nevertheless incorrectly dismissed the claim.

In light of the conclusions reached above, we cannot rule out that the supervisory board of the Defendant may have an obligation to seek damages from the Chairman of the management board, and that the supervisory board resolutions of June 25, 1992 and June 15, 1993, with which such an action was rejected, would therefore be null and void.

1. The Court of Appeals initially grants the supervisory board a certain "decisionmaking prerogative" in evaluating whether the damages action against the managing directors has a chance of success in court, and in so doing partially eliminates the court's ability to review the decision because of the prognostic element that any such decision contains. In addition, the supervisory board is supposed to receive additional discretionary freedom when performing its duties, thereby restraining the scope of judicial review – in a similar way as the restraint that must be exercised pursuant to § 114 of the Rules of Administrative Courts in administrative proceedings – in connection with the board's decisions made to fulfil tasks solely in the interest of the corporation. This includes a decision whether to prosecute a claim against a member of the management board for damages inflicted on the corporation. Such restraints on judicial review are advisable in order to avoid an overly legalistic encasing of the work of the supervisory board, which includes supervision of not only the legality, but also the meaningfulness and commercial wisdom, of the management board's direction, and to leave the corporate management bodies a certain free space in which to exercise independent, business judgment. Such free discretion may be completely eliminated, thereby triggering a duty to take a specific action, only in exceptional cases, such as where the supervisory board's refusal to undertake a certain requested action is clearly illegal or where it would create substantial prejudice for the corporation, such as impairing corporate assets. In the case at hand, even without performing a detailed balancing test of the pros and cons of prosecuting the action against the management board Chairman, such a complete elimination of free discretion must be rejected. Neither an overreaching of discretion nor an abuse of discretion has been claimed by the Plaintiffs or is evident on the record.

2. These reasons presented by the Court of Appeals may only be partially upheld on appeal.

a) The Court of Appeals is correct in finding that the supervisory board has the duty to take responsibility for discerning the existence of a damage claim of the corporation against its managing directors and as a body to examine the merits of the claim and prosecute it in accordance with law and the articles of association if the legal requirements for the prosecution of such claim exist. This duty arises both from the responsibility of the supervisory board to monitor the management activity of the management board (§ 111(1) AktG), which includes transactions that have already been concluded (BGHZ 114, 127, 129), and from the fact that the supervisory board represents the corporation in dealings with the management board both in and out of court (§ 112 AktG). Contrary to the opinion of the Court of Appeals, this duty exists regardless of whether the law gives the shareholders' meeting the possibility of resolving to prosecute a claim itself. This right of the shareholders' meeting serves solely to protect the shareholders. It does not free the supervisory board from its duty appropriately to protect the interests of the corporation on its own within the scope of its legal functions, evaluating the existence and merits of damages claims, and making an independent decision on whether such claims should be prosecuted. Pursuant to the unambiguous provisions of § 147(1) AktG, only after the shareholders resolve to prosecute a claim for damages must the supervisory board implement such resolution by taking the necessary measures for enforcement of the claim.

b) However, according to the decision of the Court of Appeals, the standards that should guide the supervisory board's examination and decision are either ambiguous or inapplicable.

aa) A supervisory board decision on whether a managing director should be sued for damages for violating his management duties first of all requires a determination of whether facts exist that create a liability for damages pursuant to law and an analysis of the procedural risks and merits of the claim. When deciding whether a given fact pattern justifies a claim that the management board has acted culpably and violated its duties, the supervisory board must take into account that, in directing the corporation's business, the management board must be given the wide range of free discretion that is essential for the operation of a business. In addition to consciously running business risks, this generally also includes the danger of bad decisions and incorrect evaluations, to which every businessman – regardless of how responsible – is subject. If the supervisory board receives the impression that the management board lacks the necessary good sense for the successful management of the company, that is, it just does not have the "right touch" in performing its management functions, this may lead the supervisory board to seek the removal of the relevant managing directors. This does not lead to a claim for compensation of damages. Such a claim may be raised only when a manager goes significantly beyond the limits of a business judgment characterized by responsible management oriented solely towards the good of the corporation and based on a careful evaluation of the relevant facts, i.e. where the readiness to engage in business risks is irresponsibly breached, or the comportment of the management board is otherwise in breach of duty.

bb) Contrary to the opinion of the Court of Appeals, the supervisory board may not invoke a "decisionmaking prerogative" to restrict the scope of the court's review with regard to this part of its decisionmaking. In examining whether a claim for damages exists and the merits thereof, the supervisory board does nothing other than anyone else who evaluates – for himself or for another – whether a claim exists and whether it may be successfully prosecuted in court. The substance and correctness of such an evaluation of the merits of judicial prosecution of a claim may, in cases of a dispute, generally be fully tested in a court, given that such an evaluation does not regard business dealings but rather solely regards an area of knowledge for which we may always consider positing a limited freedom for discretion. Questions entail business judgment only if the decision concerns a choice between various business alternatives.

cc) If the supervisory board performs such a thorough and appropriate procedural risk assessment and concludes that the corporation probably – in these circumstances, certainty cannot be required – has a claim for damages against one of its managing directors, the question may be asked at the next step (the Court of Appeals correctly followed this in principle) whether the supervisory board may in any case refrain from prosecuting the claim and with it the compensation of the corporation for damages suffered.

Contrary to the opinion of the Court of Appeals, in making this decision the supervisory board has no free space for autonomous discretion. Freedom of business judgment is a part and a necessary complement given to the management duties of the management board, but not to those of the supervisory board. The supervisory board shares in such freedom only where the law gives it business-related tasks, such as in appointing and removing the members of the management board, or in connection with § 111(4), sentence 2 AktG, i.e. above all in all those areas where the supervisory board must accompany the management board's business activities with prospective examination. Decisions regarding prosecuting damages claims against a managing director's breach of duty are, rather, a part of its retrospective supervisory activity, which is designed to ensure that the management board fulfils its duties and to avoid damage to the corporation (see Raiser, NJW 1996, 552, 554 for a particularly correct analysis). It should be noted that the supervisory board does receive the same freedom of business judgment as the management board when it exercises such supervisory activity (see aa) *supra*) in connection with its examination of whether the management board has breached its duties. However, the breadth of freedom for business judgment that the Court of Appeals gave to the supervisory board in connection with its own decision was incorrect. Since this decision must be guided solely by the good of the corporation, which generally requires that any damage to the assets of the corporation be compensated, the supervisory board may refrain from prosecuting an apparently well-grounded claim for damages against a management board that has breached its duties only in those exceptional cases in which important interests and needs of the corporation argue that the damage should be suffered without compensation. Such requirement will as a rule only be met if the interests and needs of the corporation that seem to argue against compensating the corporation for the damage caused by the management board outweigh, or at least roughly equal, the considerations that argue for prosecution. In this regard, the considerations raised by the Court of Appeals, such as a negative impact on the business activity, the public reputation of the corporation, impairment of the management board's productivity, and damage to the business climate may certainly be meaningful. On the other hand, the supervisory board may give weight to considerations other than the good of the corporation, such as protecting a deserving management board member or the potential social consequences of the prosecution for the board member and his family, only in exceptional cases. Such an exceptional case could be, for example, where the breach of duty is insubstantial and the damage suffered by the corporation is relatively slight, but the foreseeable consequences for the board member who would be liable for compensation are quite threatening.

c) The analysis set out above leads to the conclusion that damages claims against managing directors must, as a rule, be prosecuted. Only very important countervailing reasons and a special justification will support not prosecuting a claim that has a probability of success – which would closely resemble the corporation itself waiving the claim – and thus must be an exceptional case (Jaeger, WiB 1997, 10, 15; Thomas Raiser, NJW 1996, 552, 554). In this regard, the State Regional Court (ZIP 1994, 628, 630) correctly made reference to the limitations applicable by law to the waiver of a damages claim (§ 93(4), sentence 3 AktG).

Only within these narrow limits may, following the approach of the Court of Appeals, the supervisory board be granted discretionary freedom in deciding whether, in exceptional cases, to refrain from prosecuting a damages claim, in spite of its chances of success, because of very important considerations regarding the good of the corporation. However, such discretionary freedom of the supervisory board may only apply after the counterbalancing circumstances have been established.

III. Because its legal approach deviated from our own, the Court of Appeals failed to make any findings as to whether the Chairman of the Defendant's management board is in fact subject to a claim for damages that has a likelihood of success on the merits. There also have been no findings as to whether there are important considerations regarding the good of the corporation that allow the supervisory board, as an exceptional case, to exercise its discretion in deciding whether to refrain from prosecuting the claim. The Court of Appeals also failed to perform a detailed evaluation and balancing of the considerations for and against prosecuting the claim against the Chairman of the management board. The appealed decision is hereby overruled and the matter is therefore remanded back to the Court of Appeals for a re-examination and decision.

Aronson, et al. v. Lewis
Supreme Court of Delaware
473 A 2d 805 (1984)
[*Text edited. Most footnotes omitted*]

MOORE, Justice

[*Text omitted*]

A cardinal precept of the General Corporation Law of the State of Delaware is that directors, rather than shareholders, manage the business and affairs of the corporation. 8 Del. C. § 141(a). Section 141(a) states in pertinent part:

> The *business and affairs* of a corporation organized under this chapter *shall be managed by or under the direction* of a board of directors except as may be otherwise provided in this chapter or in its certificate of incorporation.

8 Del. C. § 141(a) (Emphasis added). The existence and exercise of this power carries with it certain fundamental fiduciary obligations to the corporation and its shareholders. [Note 4] ... Moreover, a stockholder is not powerless to challenge director action which results in harm to the corporation. The machinery of corporate democracy and the derivative suit are potent tools to redress the conduct of a torpid or unfaithful management ...

[Note 4] The broad question of structuring the modern corporation in order to satisfy the twin objectives of managerial freedom of action and responsibility to shareholders has been extensively debated by commentators. See, e.g. Fischel, *The Corporate Governance Movement*, 35 VanderbiltLaw Review 1259 (1982) ...

[*Text omitted*]

... The business judgment rule is an acknowledgment of the managerial prerogatives of Delaware directors under Section 141(a). See *Zapata Corp.* v. *Maldonado* ... It is a presumption that in making a business decision the directors of a corporation acted on an informed basis, in good faith and in the honest belief that the action taken was in the best interests of the company ... Absent an abuse of discretion, that judgment will be respected by the courts. The burden is on the party challenging the decision to establish facts rebutting the presumption ...

[*Text omitted*]

First, its protections can only be claimed by disinterested directors whose conduct otherwise meets the tests of business judgment. From the standpoint of interest, this means that directors can neither appear on both sides of a transaction nor expect to derive any personal financial benefit from it in the sense of self-dealing, as opposed to a benefit which devolves upon the corporation or all stockholders generally ... See also 8 Del. C. § 144. Thus, if such director interest is present, and the transaction is not approved by a majority consisting of the disinterested directors, then the business judgment rule has no application whatever in determining demand futility. See 8 Del. C. § 144(a)(1).

Second, to invoke the rule's protection directors have a duty to inform themselves, prior to making a business decision, of all material information reasonably available to them. Having become so informed, they must then act with requisite care in the discharge of their duties. While the Delaware cases use a variety of terms to describe the applicable standard of care, our analysis satisfies us that under the business judgment rule director liability is predicated upon concepts of gross negligence. [Note 6] See Veasey & Manning, *Codified Standard – Safe Harbor or Uncharted Reef?* 35 Bus. Law. 919, 928 (1980).

[Note 6] While the Delaware cases have not been precise in articulating the standard by which the exercise of business judgment is governed, a long line of Delaware cases holds that director liability is predicated on a standard which is less exacting than simple negligence. *Sinclair Oil Corp.* v. *Levien* ... ("fraud or gross overreaching"); *Getty Oil Co.* v. *Skelly Oil Co.* ... ("gross and palpable overreaching"); *Warshaw* v. *Calhoun* ... ("bad faith ... or a gross abuse of discretion"); *Moskowitz* v. *Bantrell* ... ("fraud or gross abuse of discretion"); *Penn Mart Realty Co.* v. *Becker* ... ("directors may breach their fiduciary duty ... by being grossly negligent"); *Kors* v. *Carey* ... ("fraud, misconduct or abuse of discretion"); *Allaun* v. *Consolidated Oil Co.* ... ("reckless indifference to or a deliberate disregard of the stockholders").

However, it should be noted that the business judgment rule operates only in the context of director action. Technically speaking, it has no role where directors have either abdicated their functions, or absent a conscious decision, failed to act. [Note 7] But it also follows that under applicable principles, a conscious decision to refrain from acting may nonetheless be a valid exercise of business judgment and enjoy the protections of the rule.

[Note 7] Although questions of director liability in such cases have been adjudicated upon concepts of business judgment, they do not in actuality present issues of business judgment ...

[Text omitted]

... the Court of Chancery in the proper exercise of its discretion must decide whether, under the particularized facts alleged, a reasonable doubt is created that: (1) the directors are disinterested and independent and (2) the challenged transaction was otherwise the product of a valid exercise of business judgment. Hence, the Court of Chancery must make two inquiries, one into the independence and disinterestedness of the directors and the other into the substantive nature of the challenged transaction and the board's approval thereof.

[Text omitted]

In Re the Walt Disney Company Derivative Litigation
Court of Chancery of Delaware
907 A 2d 693 (2005)
Affirmed by Delaware Supreme Court, 906 A 2d 27 (2006)
[Text edited; many footnotes omitted; facts summarized in brackets]

CHANDLER, J

INTRODUCTION

This is the Court's decision after trial in this long running dispute over an executive compensation and severance package. The stockholder plaintiffs have alleged that the director defendants breached their fiduciary duties in connection with the 1995 hiring and 1996 termination of Michael Ovitz as President of The Walt Disney Company ... After carefully considering all of the evidence and arguments ... I conclude that the director defendants did not breach their fiduciary duties or commit waste ...

[T]here are many aspects of defendants' conduct that fell significantly short of the best practices of ideal corporate governance. Recognizing the protean nature of ideal corporate governance practices, particularly over an era that has included the Enron and WorldCom debacles, and the resulting legislative focus on corporate governance, it is perhaps worth pointing out that the actions (and the failures to act) of the Disney board that gave rise to this lawsuit took place ten years ago, and that applying 21st century notions of best practices in analyzing whether those decisions were actionable would be misplaced.

Unlike ideals of corporate governance, a fiduciary's duties do not change over time. How we understand those duties may evolve and become refined, but the duties themselves have not changed, except to the extent that fulfilling a fiduciary duty requires obedience to other positive law. This Court strongly encourages directors and officers to employ best practices, as those practices are understood at the time a corporate decision is taken. But Delaware law does not – indeed, the common law cannot – hold fiduciaries liable for a failure to comply with the aspirational ideal of best practices, any more than a common-law court deciding a medical malpractice dispute can impose a standard of liability based on ideal – rather than competent or standard – medical treatment practices, lest the average medical practitioner be found inevitably derelict.

Fiduciaries are held by the common law to a high standard in fulfilling their stewardship over the assets of others, a standard that (depending on the circumstances) may not be the same as that contemplated by ideal corporate governance. Yet therein lies perhaps the greatest strength of Delaware's corporation law. Fiduciaries who act faithfully and honestly on behalf of those whose interests they represent are indeed granted wide latitude in their efforts to maximize shareholders' investment. Times may change, but fiduciary duties do not ... [T]he common law of fiduciary duties [should not] become a prisoner of narrow definitions or formulaic expressions. It is thus both the province and special duty of this Court to measure, in light of all the facts and circumstances of a particular case, whether an individual who has accepted a position of responsibility over the assets of another has been unremittingly faithful to his or her charge ...

[Text omitted]

Even where decisionmakers act as faithful servants, however, their ability and the wisdom of their judgments will vary. The redress for failures that arise from faithful management must come from the markets, through the action of shareholders and the free flow of capital, and not from this Court. Should the Court apportion liability based on the ultimate outcome of decisions taken in good faith by faithful directors or officers, those decisionmakers would necessarily take decisions that minimize risk, not maximize value. The entire advantage of the risk-taking, innovative, wealth-creating engine that is the Delaware corporation would cease to exist, with disastrous results for shareholders and society alike. That is why, under our corporate law, corporate decisionmakers are held strictly to their fiduciary duties, but within the boundaries of those duties are free to act as their judgment and abilities dictate, free of *post hoc* penalties from a reviewing court using perfect hindsight. Corporate decisions are made, risks are taken, the results become apparent, capital flows accordingly, and shareholder value is increased.

[Text omitted]

I. FACTS

A.   *Michael Ovitz joins the Walt Disney Company*

1.   Background

[*Editors' summary*: Michael Ovitz revolutionized the Hollywood agent industry by using a "packaging" concept of grouping actors and writers together. The firm he built with some friends, Creative Artist Agency ("CAA"), came to lead the industry. When Ovitz's close friend and co-founder of CAA, Ron Meyer, announced after failed negotiations to merge CAA and MCA, that he was leaving for MCA, Ovitz felt it was also time to leave CAA. In the mean time, Disney's President and Chief Operating Officer died and Michael Eisner, Disney's Chairman and CEO, could not continue to hold both jobs because of heart problems.]

[Text omitted]

3.   Ovitz seriously considers joining the Walt Disney Company

[*Editors' summary*: Eisner testified that he decided to hire Ovitz before a competitor could, and these efforts to recruit Ovitz received support from Sid Bass and Roy Disney, two of the company's largest individual shareholders (Roy Disney was also a director of the Company). Eisner and Irwin Russell (the chairman of Disney's compensation committee) reached out to Ovitz on terms that did not exceed another offer Ovitz received from MCA. Ovitz did not accept. Renewed efforts to hire Ovitz became more important when Disney decided to acquire CapCities/ABC, which would double the size of Disney. Russell, in his negotiations with Bob Goldman, Ovitz's attorney, learned that Ovitz was making approximately $20 to $25 million a year from CAA and owned fifty-five percent of the company. Ovitz made it clear that he would not give up his fifty-five percent interest in CAA without protection. Ovitz understood that it was his skills and experience in talent relationships and foreign growth that were sought and he wanted assurances from Eisner that Eisner really wanted to "reinvent" Disney. Ovitz came to the understanding that he and Eisner would run Disney as partners. Ovitz was mistaken, for Eisner had a much different perception of their respective roles at Disney.]

4.   Ovitz's contract with disney begins to take form

[*Editors' summary*: In August 1995 Ovitz's employment agreement (the "OEA") was drafted to include $1 million in annual salary and a performance-based, discretionary bonus, a five-year contract with two tranches of options. The first tranche consisted of three million options vesting in equal parts in the third, fourth and fifth years, and if the value of those options at the end of the five years had not appreciated to $50 million, Disney would make up the difference. The second tranche consisted of two million options that would vest immediately if Disney and Ovitz opted to renew the contract. The OEA was designed to protect both parties in the event that Ovitz's employment ended prematurely and provided that absent defined causes, neither party could terminate the agreement without penalty, a so-called No Fault Termination payment (NFT payment).]

5.   Crystal is retained to assist Russell and Watson in evaluating the OEA

[*Editors' summary*: Irwin Russell provided Eisner and Ovitz with a "Case Study" of the OEA. The study said that Ovitz was an "exceptional corporate executive" who was a "highly successful and unique entrepreneur," but cautioned that Ovitz's salary under the OEA was at the top level for any corporate officer and significantly above that of the CEO and that the number of stock options granted under the OEA was far beyond the standards applied within Disney and corporate America "and will raise very strong criticism." A second opinion was sought from Graef Crystal, an executive compensation consultant, who is a well known critic of extravagant compensation. Crystal prepared a memorandum concluding that the OEA, during the first five years, was worth $23.6 million annually, and the value of the OEA's two-year renewal option would increase the value of the entire OEA to $24.1 million per year. The memorandum also expressed doubts about the manner in which Ovitz could exercise the two tranches of options (3 million in the first 5 years and 2 million if the contract was renewed). Crystal's letter was never circulated to any board member other than Eisner. Up until this point, only three members of Disney's board of directors were in the know concerning the status of the negotiations with Ovitz or the particulars of the OEA – Eisner, Russell and Watson.]

6.   Ovitz accepts Eisner's offer

[*Editors' summary*: Eisner gave Ovitz a take-it-or-leave-it offer: If Ovitz joined Disney as its new President, he would not assume the duties or title of COO or co-CEO. Ovitz accepted. Eisner called a meeting of Ovitz, Russell, Sanford Litvack (Disney's General Counsel) and Stephen Bollenbach (Disney's Chief Financial Officer). Litvack and Bollenbach were not happy with the decision to hire Ovitz and they both made it clear that they would not agree to report to Ovitz but would continue to report to Eisner. Eisner was able to assuage Ovitz's concern about his shrinking authority in the Company, and Ovitz acceded to Litvack and Bollenbach's terms.

The next day, August 14, Ovitz and Eisner signed the letter agreement ("OLA") that outlined the basic terms of Ovitz's employment. Eisner contacted each of the other board members by phone to inform them of the impending deal. During these calls, Eisner described his friendship with Ovitz, and Ovitz's background and qualifications. When news of Ovitz's hiring was made public, Disney was applauded for the decision, and Disney's stock price increased 4.4 percent in a single day – increasing Disney's market capitalization by more than $1 billion.]

7.   Disney's board of directors hires Michael Ovitz

[*Editors' summary*: Disney's legal department concluded that a $50 million guarantee of options granted to Ovitz in the OLA must be eliminated.] On September 26, 1995, the compensation committee met *for one hour* to consider (1) the proposed terms of the OEA, (2) the compensation packages for various Disney employees, (3) 121 stock option grants, (4) Iger's CapCities/ABC employment agreement and (5) Russell's compensation for negotiating the Ovitz deal. The discussion concerning the OEA focused on a term sheet (the actual draft of the OEA was not distributed) … the Committee unanimously voted to approve the terms of the OEA subject to "reasonable further negotiations within the framework of the terms and conditions" described in the OEA. [The committee did not discuss purchasing Ovitz's private jet for $187,000 over the appraised value, his BMW at acquisition cost rather than market value, his computers at replacement value instead of lower book value, or any specific list of perquisites, despite Eisner already agreeing to provide Ovitz with numerous such benefits. The committee voted to award director Russell $250,000 for the time and energy he put into the negotiations. An executive meeting of Disney's board immediately followed the compensation committee's meeting and voted unanimously to elect Ovitz as President.]

8.   The October 16, 1995 Compensation Committee meeting

[*Editors' summary*: This meeting approved Ovitz stock options and priced them as of the date of the meeting.]

B.   *Ovitz's performance as President of The Walt Disney Company*

1.   Ovitz's early performance

[*Editors' summary*: Ovitz began as President of The Walt Disney Company October 1, 1995. Initial evaluations by Eisner were "Our partnership is born in corporate heaven … " and at the end of 1995, Eisner wrote, "1996 is going to be a great year – We are going to be a great team – We every day are working better together – Time will be on our side – We will be strong, smart, and unstoppable!!!"]

2.   A mismatch of cultures and styles

[*Editors' summary*: In 1996, however, it came to be seen that] Ovitz "was a little elitist for the egalitarian Walt Disney World cast members [employees]," and a poor fit with his fellow executives [when at a firm outing he failed to mix with the others and demanded a private limousine when Eisner and the others took a bus. Ovitz failed to adapt to the Company's culture].

3. Approaching the endgame

By the fall of 1996, directors began discussing that the disconnect between Ovitz and the Company was likely irreparable, and that Ovitz would have to be terminated. Additionally, the industry and popular press were beginning to publish an increasing number of articles describing dissension within The Walt Disney Company's executive suite.

4. Specific examples of Ovitz's performance as President of the Walt Disney Company

Throughout this litigation, plaintiffs have argued that Ovitz acted improperly while in office. The specific examples discussed below demonstrate that the record created at trial does not support those allegations ...

Although the general consensus on Ovitz's tenure is largely negative, Ovitz did make some valuable contributions while President of the Company ...

There are three competing theories as to why Ovitz was not successful. First, plaintiffs argue that Ovitz failed to follow Eisner's directives, especially in regard to acquisitions, and that generally, Ovitz did very little. Second, Ovitz contends that Eisner's micromanaging prevented Ovitz from having the authority necessary to make the changes that Ovitz thought were appropriate. In addition, Ovitz believes he was not given enough time for his efforts to bear fruit. Third, the remaining defendants simply posit that Ovitz failed to transition from a private to public company, from the "sell side to the buy side," and otherwise did not adapt to the Company culture or fit in with other executives. In the end, however, it makes no difference why Ovitz was not as successful as his reputation would have led many to expect, so long as he was not grossly negligent or malfeasant.

[*Text omitted*]

5. Veracity and "agenting"

[*Editors' summary*: Plaintiffs attempted to persuade the Court that Ovitz was a habitual liar, but the evidence did not support the allegation.]

6. Gifts and expenses

[*Editors' summary*: Plaintiffs criticized Ovitz's gift giving as self-serving and not in accordance with Company policies, but the record failed to support these assertions.]

C. *Ovitz's termination*

1. The beginning of the end

Ovitz's relationship with Eisner, and with other Disney executives and directors, continued to deteriorate through September 1996. In mid-September ... Eisner, hoping to make Ovitz realize that there was no future for him at Disney, sent Litvack back to Ovitz and asked Litvack to make it clear that Eisner no longer wanted Ovitz at Disney and that Ovitz should seriously consider other employment opportunities, including the opportunity at Sony … At trial, Ovitz testified that he felt that "as far as [he] was concerned, [he] was chained to that desk and that company. [That he] wasn't going to leave there a loser," that the guy that hired him or the full board would have to fire him, and that he hoped he could still make it work and make all these problems just disappear …

On November 1, Ovitz wrote a letter to Eisner notifying Eisner that things had failed to work out with Sony and that Ovitz had instead decided to recommit himself to Disney with "an even greater commitment of [his] own energies" than he had before and an "increased appreciation" of the Disney organization …

2. The September 30, 1996 board meeting

… [T]he Disney board convened a meeting on September 30, 1996 … and it is undisputed that neither Ovitz's future with Disney nor his conversations to date with Eisner and Litvack were discussed at the general board meeting … Although Eisner never sat down at a full board meeting to discuss the persistent and growing Ovitz problem, it is clear that he made an effort to notify and talk with a large majority, if not all of the directors … On the night of September 30, Eisner and Ovitz made their now-famous appearance on *The Larry King Live Show* in which Eisner refuted the then current Hollywood gossip that there was a growing rift between himself and Ovitz and emphatically stated that if given the chance, he would hire Ovitz again … Eisner was informed on November 1 that Ovitz's negotiations with Sony had failed to result in Ovitz leaving Disney. Once Eisner discovered that the Sony negotiations had failed to produce the desired result, Eisner decided that Ovitz must be gone by the end of the year …

3. Options for Ovitz's termination

… Eisner hoped to obtain a termination for cause because he believed that although Ovitz "had not done the job that would warrant [the NFT] payment" Disney was obliged to honor the OEA. Honoring the OEA meant that if Ovitz was terminated without cause, he would receive the NFT payment that the OEA called for, which consisted of the balance of Ovitz's salary, an imputed amount of bonuses, a $10 million termination fee and the immediate vesting of his three million stock options at the time. Litvack advised Eisner from the very beginning that he did not believe that there was cause to terminate Ovitz under the OEA … Despite the paucity of evidence, it is clear to the Court that both Eisner and Litvack wanted to fire Ovitz for cause to avoid the costly NFT payment, and perhaps out of personal motivations. The Court is convinced, based upon these two factors, that Eisner and Litvack did in fact make a concerted effort to determine if Ovitz could be terminated for cause, and that despite these efforts, they were unable to manufacture the desired result …

4.   The November 25, 1996 board meeting

The Disney board held its next meeting on November 25, and Ovitz was present. The minutes of this meeting contain no record that the board engaged in any discussion concerning Ovitz's termination, or that they were informed of the actions that Eisner and Litvack had taken to this point concerning Ovitz. The only action recorded in the minutes concerning Ovitz is his unanimous renomination to a new three-year term to the board ... [but] it is apparent, despite the lack of a written record, that directly following the board meeting, there was some discussion concerning Ovitz at the executive session which was held at Disney Imagineering in a glass-walled room ... One of the more striking images of this trial is that apparently Ovitz was directly outside the glass walls – looking in at this meeting – while his fate at Disney was being discussed ... It is also clear that Eisner notified the directors in attendance at the executive session that it was his intention to fire Ovitz by year's end ...

5.   The illusion dispelled

[*Editors' summary*: At Eisner's request, Wilson, who jointly owned a yacht called "The Illusion" with Ovitz, scheduled a Thanksgiving trip to the British Virgin Islands with Ovitz and their two families and made it clear to Ovitz that Eisner wanted Ovitz out of the company.] At some point during the trip, Eisner contacted Wilson by phone and ... [according to] notes, dated December 1, taken by Eisner following the conversation ... Wilson recalled describing Ovitz as a "wounded animal ... in a corner," and stated that by this he meant that Ovitz could become dangerous to the organization if the relationship with Disney continued ... On December 3, having returned from his Thanksgiving trip, Ovitz, armed with his newfound understanding that his time at Disney was rapidly coming to an end, met with Eisner to discuss the terms of his departure ... Ovitz ... asked for several concessions from Disney, including keeping his seat on the board, obtaining a consulting/advising arrangement with Disney, the continued use of an office and staff (but not on the Disney lot), continued health insurance and home security, continued use of the company car and the repurchase of his plane ... Over the next week, Disney, and more accurately, Eisner, rejected every request that Ovitz had made, informing him that all he would receive is what he had contracted for in the OEA and nothing more ...

6.   Ovitz's bonus and his termination

On December 10, the Executive Performance Plan Committee ("EPPC") met to consider annual bonuses for Disney's most highly compensated executive officers ... At this meeting, Russell recommended that Ovitz, despite his poor performance and imminent termination, should receive a $7.5 million bonus for his services during the 1996 fiscal year because Disney had done so well during the fiscal year and because Disney had a large bonus pool. The EPPC approved this recommendation and it appears that Russell may have even advised the EPPC (despite the *clear* language in the OEA stating that the *bonus was discretionary*) that Disney was contractually obligated to pay Ovitz his bonus. Despite the fact that all of those in attendance should have known better, nobody spoke up to correct the mistaken perception that Ovitz had to receive a bonus, let alone a $7.5 million bonus ...

Ovitz's termination was memorialized ... in a letter signed by Litvack and dated December 12 ... The board was not shown the December 12 letter, nor did it meet to approve its terms ...

Thus, as of December 12, Ovitz was officially terminated without cause. Up to this point, however, the Disney board had never met in order to vote on, or even discuss, the termination at a full session, and few if any directors did an independent investigation of whether Ovitz could be terminated for cause. As a result, the Disney directors had been taken for a wild ride, and most of it was in the dark ... Although there was no meeting called to vote on or even discuss Ovitz's termination, it is clear that most, if not all, directors trusted Eisner's and Litvack's conclusion that there was no cause and that Ovitz should still be terminated without cause even though this entailed making the costly NFT payment ... [Stories started appearing in the newspapers implying that Ovitz left because of Disney's fault and that Disney gave him a $90 million severance package.] On December 16, Eisner reacted to these stories by sending an e-mail to John Dreyer, Disney's communications chief, which among other things stated that Ovitz was a "psychopath" and "totally incompetent." ...

Following the official termination, the EPPC met on December 20 with the sole purpose of rescinding Ovitz's $7.5 million bonus ... Gold testified that within a week of the December 10 meeting, Litvack and Russell came to him "sheepishly, and said 'we've made a mistake'" [because the bonus was not required by the OEA] ... Russell's self-prepared agenda for the meeting outlines what was discussed before revoking Ovitz's bonus, including that it would be "illogical and impossible to justify any bonus one day and fire him the next, [and that] Committee members [could not] be asked to try to justify it based on good performance." The EPPC then revoked Ovitz's bonus ...

The full board next met on January 27, 1997. By this time, the board was aware of the negative publicity that the Ovitz termination and NFT payment had received. There was an extensive discussion of Ovitz's termination at this meeting and the pending lawsuit. Litvack, addressing the full board for the first time concerning the cause issue, notified the board that in his opinion there had been no gross negligence or malfeasance and, thus, Ovitz could not be terminated for cause. Litvack stood by his decision at trial, stating he had learned nothing since 1996 that made him reconsider his original advice to the board that Disney could not fire Ovitz for cause.

[Text omitted]

II. LEGAL STANDARDS

The outcome of this case is determined by whether the defendants complied with their fiduciary duties in connection with the hiring and termination of Michael Ovitz. At the outset, the Court emphasizes that the best practices of corporate governance include compliance with fiduciary duties. Compliance with fiduciary duties, however, is not always enough to meet or to satisfy what is expected by the best practices of corporate governance.

The fiduciary duties owed by directors of a Delaware corporation are the duties of due care and loyalty. Of late, much discussion among the bench, bar, and academics alike, has surrounded a so-called third fiduciary duty, that of good faith. Of primary importance in this case are the fiduciary duty of due care and the duty of a director to act in good faith. Other than to the extent that the duty of loyalty is implicated by a lack of good faith, the only remaining issues to be decided herein with respect to the duty of loyalty are those relating to Ovitz's actions in connection with his own termination ...

A. The business judgment rule

A comprehensive review of the history of the business judgment rule is not necessary here, but a brief discussion of its boundaries and proper use is appropriate. Delaware law is clear that the business and affairs of a corporation are managed by or under the direction of its board of directors. The business judgment rule serves to protect and promote the role of the board as the ultimate manager of the corporation. Because courts are ill equipped to engage in *post hoc* substantive review of business decisions, the business judgment rule "operates to preclude a court from imposing itself unreasonably on the business and affairs of a corporation."

The business judgment rule is not actually a substantive rule of law, but instead it is a presumption that "in making a business decision the directors of a corporation acted on an informed basis, and in the honest belief that the action taken was in the best interests of the company [and its shareholders]." [Note 407] This presumption applies when there is no evidence of "fraud, bad faith, or self-dealing in the usual sense of personal profit or betterment" on the part of the directors. [Note 408] In the absence of this evidence, the board's decision will be upheld unless it cannot be "attributed to any rational business purpose." [Note 409] When a plaintiff fails to rebut the presumption of the business judgment rule, she is not entitled to any remedy, be it legal or equitable, unless the transaction constitutes waste.

[Note 407] *Aronson* v. *Lewis* ...

[Note 408] *Grobow* v. *Perot* ... *Cede III* ... In *Gagliardi*, Chancellor Allen described the policy rationale for the business judgment rule in the paragraph quoted below. Although this statement, made in 1996, may at first appear to be undercut by the increased incentive compensation of the dot-com era, the rationale still applies because of the relatively small percentages of stock held by officers and directors of public companies.

Corporate directors of public companies typically have a very small proportionate ownership interest in their corporations and little or no incentive compensation. Thus, they enjoy (as residual owners) only a very small proportion of any "upside" gains earned by the corporation on risky investment projects. If, however, corporate directors were to be found liable for a corporate loss from a risky project on the ground that the investment was too risky (foolisly risky! stupidly risky! egregiously risky – you supply the adverb), their liability would be joint and several for the whole loss (with I suppose a right of contribution). Given the scale of operation of modern public corporations, this stupefying disjunction between risk and reward for corporate directors threatens undesirable effects. Given this disjunction, only a very small probability of director liability based on "negligence," "inattention," "waste," etc. could induce a board to avoid authorizing risky investment projects to any extent! Obviously, it is in the shareholders' economic interest to offer sufficient protection to directors from liability for negligence, etc., to allow directors to conclude that, as a practical matter, there is no risk that, if they act in good faith and meet minimalist proceduralist standards of attention, they can face liability as a result of a business loss. *Gagliardi* v. *TriFoods Int'l Inc.* ...

[Note 409] *Sinclair Oil Corp.* v. *Levien* ... see also *Unocal Corp.* v. *Mesa Petroleum Co.* ...

This presumption can be rebutted by a showing that the board violated one of its fiduciary duties in connection with the challenged transaction. In that event, the burden shifts to the director defendants to demonstrate that the challenged transaction was "entirely fair" to the corporation and its shareholders.

In *Van Gorkom*, the Delaware Supreme Court analyzed the Trans Union board of directors *as a whole* in determining whether the protections of the business judgment rule applied. More recent cases understand that liability determinations must be on a director-by-director basis. In *Emerging Communications*, Justice Jacobs wrote (while sitting as a Vice Chancellor) that the "liability of the directors must be determined on an individual basis because the nature of their breach of duty (if any), and whether they are exculpated from liability for that breach, can vary for each director." There is a not significant degree of tension between these two positions, notwithstanding the procedural differences between the two cases.

Even if the directors have exercised their business judgment, the protections of the business judgment rule will not apply if the directors have made an "unintelligent or unadvised judgment." Furthermore, in instances where directors have not exercised business judgment, that is, in the event of director inaction, the protections of the business judgment rule do not apply. Under those circumstances, the appropriate standard for determining liability is widely believed to be gross negligence, but a single Delaware case has held that ordinary negligence would be the appropriate standard.

B.   Waste

Corporate waste is very rarely found in Delaware courts because the applicable test imposes such an onerous burden upon a plaintiff – proving "an exchange that is so one sided that no business person of ordinary, sound judgment could conclude that the corporation has received adequate consideration." In other words, waste is a rare, "unconscionable case where directors irrationally squander or give away corporate assets."

The Delaware Supreme Court has implicitly held that committing waste is an act of bad faith. It is not necessarily true, however, that every act of bad faith by a director constitutes waste. For example, if a director acts in bad faith (for whatever reason), but the transaction is one in which a businessperson of ordinary, sound judgment concludes that the corporation received adequate consideration, the transaction would not constitute waste.

C.   The fiduciary duty of due care

The fiduciary duty of due care requires that directors of a Delaware corporation "use that amount of care which ordinarily careful and prudent men would use in similar circumstances," and "consider all material information reasonably available" in making business decisions, and that deficiencies in the directors' process are actionable only if the directors' actions are grossly negligent. Chancellor Allen described the two contexts in which liability for a breach of the duty of care can arise:

> First, such liability may be said to follow *from a board decision* that results in a loss because that decision was ill advised or "negligent." Second, liability to the corporation for a loss may be said to arise from an *unconsidered failure of the board to act* in circumstances in which due attention would, arguably, have prevented the loss.

Chancellor Allen then explained with respect to board decisions:

> ... [These] cases will typically be subject to review under the director-protective business judgment rule, assuming the decision made was the product of *a process* that was *either* deliberately considered in good faith or was otherwise rational. What should be understood, but may not widely be understood by courts or commentators who are not often required to face such questions, is that compliance with a director's duty of care can never appropriately be judicially determined by reference to *the content of the board decision* that leads to a corporate loss, apart from consideration of the good faith or rationality of the process employed. That is, whether a judge or jury considering the matter after the fact, believes a decision substantively wrong, or degrees of wrong extending through "stupid" to "egregious" or "irrational," provides no ground for director liability, so long as the court determines that the process employed was either rational or employed in a

good faith effort to advance corporate interests. To employ a different rule – one that permitted an "objective" evaluation of the decision – would expose directors to substantive second guessing by ill-equipped judges or juries, which would, in the long-run, be injurious to investor interests. Thus, the business judgment rule is process oriented and informed by a deep respect for all *good faith* board decisions.

Indeed, one wonders on what moral basis might shareholders attack a *good faith* business decision of a director as "unreasonable" or "irrational." Where a director *in fact exercises a good faith effort to be informed and to exercise appropriate judgment*, he or she should be deemed to satisfy fully the duty of attention. [Note 426]

[Note 426] *Caremark* ...

With respect to liability for director inaction, Chancellor Allen wrote that in order for the inaction to be so great as to constitute a breach of the director's duty of care, a plaintiff must show a "lack of good faith as evidenced by sustained or systematic failure of a director to exercise reasonable oversight." The Chancellor rationalized this extremely high standard of liability for violations of the duty of care through inaction by concluding that:

> [A] demanding test of liability in the oversight context is probably beneficial to corporate shareholders as a class, as it is in the board decision context, since it makes board service by qualified persons more likely, while continuing to act as a stimulus to *good faith performance of duty* by such directors [emphasis in original].

In the duty of care context with respect to corporate fiduciaries, gross negligence has been defined as a "'reckless indifference to or a deliberate disregard of the whole body of stockholders' or actions which are 'without the bounds of reason.'" Because duty of care violations are actionable only if the directors acted with gross negligence, and because in most instances money damages are unavailable to a plaintiff who could theoretically prove a duty of care violation, duty of care violations are rarely found.

D.   The fiduciary duty of loyalty

The fiduciary duty of loyalty was described in the seminal case of *Guth* v. *Loft, Inc.,* in these strict and unyielding terms:

> "Corporate officers and directors are not permitted to use their position of trust and confidence to further their private interests ... A public policy, existing through the years, and derived from a profound knowledge of human characteristics and motives, has established a rule that demands of a corporate officer or director, peremptorily and inexorably, the most scrupulous observance of his duty, not only affirmatively to protect the interests of the corporation

committed to his charge, but also to refrain from doing anything that would work injury to the corporation, or to deprive it of profit or advantage which his skill and ability might properly bring to it, or to enable it to make in the reasonable and lawful exercise of its powers. The rule that requires an undivided and unselfish loyalty to the corporation demands that there be no conflict between duty and self-interest."

More recently, the Delaware Supreme Court stated that there is no safe-harbor for divided loyalties in Delaware, and that the duty of loyalty, in essence, "mandates that the best interest of the corporation and its shareholders take precedence over any interest possessed by a director, officer or controlling shareholder and not shared by the stockholders generally." The classic example that implicates the duty of loyalty is when a fiduciary either appears on both sides of a transaction or receives a personal benefit not shared by all shareholders.

In the specific context at issue here with respect to a classic duty of loyalty claim, Ovitz, as a fiduciary of Disney, was required to act in an "adversarial and arms-length manner" when negotiating his termination and not abuse or manipulate the corporate process by which that termination was granted. He was obligated to act in good faith and "not advantage himself at the expense of the Disney shareholders."

E.   Section 102(b)(7)

Following the Delaware Supreme Court's landmark decision in *Van Gorkom*, the Delaware General Assembly acted swiftly to enact 8 Del. C. § 102(b)(7). Section 102(b)(7) states that a corporation may include in its certificate of incorporation:

> (7) A provision eliminating or limiting the personal liability of a director to the corporation or its stockholders for monetary damages for breach of fiduciary duty as a director, provided that such provision shall not eliminate or limit the liability of a director: (i) For any breach of the director's duty of loyalty to the corporation or its stockholders; (ii) for acts or omissions not in good faith or which involve intentional misconduct or a knowing violation of law; (iii) under § 174 of this title; or (iv) for any transaction from which the director derived an improper personal benefit. No such provision shall eliminate or limit the liability of a director for any act or omission occurring prior to the date when such provision becomes effective. All references in this paragraph to a director shall also be deemed to refer (x) to a member of the governing body of a corporation which is not authorized to issue capital stock, and (y) to such other person or persons, if any, who, pursuant to a provision of the certificate of incorporation in accordance with § 141(a) of this title, exercise or perform any of the powers or duties otherwise conferred or imposed upon the board of directors by this title.

The purpose of Section 102(b)(7) was explained by the Delaware Supreme Court in this manner:

> "The purpose of Section 102(b)(7) was to *permit shareholders* – who are entitled to rely upon directors to discharge their fiduciary duties at all times – to adopt a provision in the certificate of incorporation to exculpate directors from any personal liability for the payment of monetary damages for breaches of their duty of care, but not for duty of loyalty violations, good faith violations and certain other conduct."

Recently, Vice Chancellor Strine wrote that, "[o]ne of the primary purposes of § 102(b)(7) is to encourage directors to undertake risky, but potentially value-maximizing, business strategies, so long as they do so in good faith." … Or in other words, § 102(b)(7) is most useful "when, despite the directors' good intentions, [the challenged transaction] did not generate financial success and … the possibility of hindsight bias about the directors' prior ability to foresee that their business plans would not pan out" could improperly influence a *post hoc* judicial evaluation of the directors' actions …

The vast majority of Delaware corporations have a provision in their certificate of incorporation that permits exculpation to the extent provided for by § 102(b)(7). This provision prohibits recovery of monetary damages from directors for a successful shareholder claim, either direct or derivative, that is exclusively based upon establishing a violation of the duty of due care. The existence of an exculpation provision authorized by § 102(b)(7) does not, however, eliminate a director's fiduciary duty of care, because a court may still grant injunctive relief for violations of that duty.

An exculpation provision such as that authorized by § 102(b)(7) is in the nature of an affirmative defense. As a result, it is the burden of the director defendants to demonstrate that they are entitled to the protections of the relevant charter provision.

F.   Acting in good faith

Decisions from the Delaware Supreme Court and the Court of Chancery are far from clear with respect to whether there is a separate fiduciary duty of good faith. Good faith has been said to require an "honesty of purpose," and a genuine care for the fiduciary's constituents, but, at least in the corporate fiduciary context, it is probably easier to define bad faith rather than good faith. This may be so because Delaware law presumes that directors act in good faith when making business judgments. Bad faith has been defined as authorizing a transaction "for some purpose *other than* a genuine attempt to advance corporate welfare or [when the transaction] is *known to constitute* a violation of applicable positive law." … In other words, an action taken with the intent to harm the corporation is a disloyal act in bad faith. A similar definition was used seven years earlier, when Chancellor Allen wrote that bad faith (or lack of good faith) is when a director acts in a manner "unrelated to a pursuit of the corporation's best interests." It makes no difference the reason why the director intentionally fails to pursue the best interests of the corporation.

Bad faith can be the result of "any emotion [that] may cause a director to [intentionally] place his own interests, preferences or appetites before the welfare of the corporation," including greed, "hatred, lust, envy, revenge … shame or pride." … Sloth could certainly be an appropriate addition to that incomplete list if it constitutes a systematic or sustained shirking of duty. Ignorance, in and of itself, probably does not belong on the list, but ignorance attributable to any of the moral failings previously listed could constitute bad faith. It is unclear, based upon existing jurisprudence, whether motive is a necessary element for a successful claim that a director has acted in bad faith, and, if so, whether that motive must be shown explicitly or whether it can be inferred from the directors' conduct.

Shrouded in the fog of this hazy jurisprudence, the defendants' motion to dismiss this action was denied because I concluded that the complaint, together with all reasonable inferences drawn from the well-plead allegations contained therein, could be held to state a non-exculpated breach of fiduciary duty claim, insofar as it alleged that Disney's directors *consciously and intentionally disregarded their responsibilities*, adopting a 'we don't care about the risks' attitude concerning a material corporate decision."

Upon long and careful consideration, I am of the opinion that the concept of *intentional dereliction of duty*, a *conscious disregard for one's responsibilities*, is an appropriate (although not the only) standard for determining whether fiduciaries have acted in good faith. Deliberate indifference and inaction *in the face of a duty to act* is, in my mind, conduct that is clearly disloyal to the corporation. It is the epitome of faithless conduct.

To act in good faith, a director must act at all times with an honesty of purpose and in the best interests and welfare of the corporation. The presumption of the business judgment rule creates a presumption that a director acted in good faith. In order to overcome that presumption, a plaintiff must prove an act of bad faith by a preponderance of the evidence. To create a definitive and categorical definition of the universe of acts that would constitute bad faith would be difficult, if not impossible. And it would misconceive how, in my judgment, the concept of good faith operates in our common law of corporations. Fundamentally, the duties traditionally analyzed as belonging to corporate fiduciaries, loyalty and care, are but constituent elements of the overarching concepts of allegiance, devotion and faithfulness that must guide the conduct of every fiduciary. The good faith required of a corporate fiduciary includes not simply the duties of care and loyalty, in the narrow sense that I have discussed them above, but all actions required by a true faithfulness and devotion to the interests of the corporation and its shareholders. A failure to act in good faith may be shown, for instance, where the fiduciary intentionally acts with a purpose other than that of advancing the best interests of the corporation, where the fiduciary acts with the intent to violate applicable positive law, or where the fiduciary intentionally fails to act in the face of a known duty to act, demonstrating a conscious disregard for his duties. There may be other examples of bad faith yet to be proven or alleged, but these three are the most salient. As evidenced by previous rulings in this case both from this Court and the Delaware Supreme Court, issues of the Disney directors' good faith (or lack thereof) are central to the outcome of this action. With this background, I now turn to applying the appropriate standards to defendants' conduct.

III. ANALYSIS

Stripped of the presumptions in their favor that have carried them to trial, plaintiffs must now rely on the evidence presented at trial to demonstrate by a preponderance of the evidence that the defendants violated their fiduciary duties and/or committed waste. More specifically, in the area of director action, plaintiffs must prove by a preponderance of the evidence that the presumption of the business judgment rule does not apply either because the directors breached their fiduciary duties, acted in bad faith or that the directors made an "unintelligent or unadvised judgment," by failing to inform themselves of all material information reasonably available to them before making a business decision.

If plaintiffs cannot rebut the presumption of the business judgment rule, the defendants will prevail. If plaintiffs succeed in rebutting the presumption of the business judgment rule, the burden then shifts to the defendants to prove by a preponderance of the evidence that the challenged transactions were entirely fair to the corporation ...

A. Ovitz did not breach his duty of loyalty

As previously mentioned, the only issue remaining in this case with respect to the traditional duty of loyalty (aside from whether there is an overlap between loyalty and good faith) is whether Ovitz breached his fiduciary duty of loyalty in the course of his termination ...

Ovitz did not breach his fiduciary duty of loyalty by receiving the NFT payment because he played no part in the decisions: (1) to be terminated and (2) that the termination would not be for cause under the OEA. Ovitz did possess fiduciary duties as a director and officer while these decisions were made, but by not improperly interjecting himself into the corporation's decisionmaking process nor manipulating that process, he did not breach the fiduciary duties he possessed in that unique circumstance. Furthermore, Ovitz did not "engage" in a transaction with the corporation – rather, the corporation imposed an unwanted transaction upon him. ...

[Text omitted]

B. Defendants did not commit waste

Plaintiffs pursued a claim for waste at trial and argued in their briefs that they have proven this claim. As stated above, the standard for waste is a very high one that is difficult to meet. Plaintiffs [argue on the basis of expert testimony] that the OEA improperly incentivized Ovitz to leave the Company and receive an NFT, rather than complete the term of the OEA, to support their argument for waste ... The record does not support these assertions in any conceivable way ... As it relates to job performance, I find it patently unreasonable to assume that Ovitz intended to perform just poorly enough to be fired quickly, but not so poorly that he could be terminated for cause ... More importantly, however, I conclude that given his performance, Ovitz could not have been fired for cause under the OEA. Any early termination of his employment, therefore, had to be in the form of an NFT ...

As a result, terminating Ovitz and paying the NFT did not constitute waste because he could not be terminated for cause and because many of the defendants gave credible testimony that the Company would be better off without Ovitz, meaning that it would be impossible for me to conclude that the termination and receipt of NFT benefits resulted in "an exchange that is so one sided that no business person of ordinary, sound judgment could conclude that the corporation has received adequate consideration," or a situation where the defendants have "irrationally squander[ed] or give[n] away corporate assets." In other words, defendants did not commit waste.

C. The Old Board's decision to hire Ovitz and the Compensation Committee's approval of the OEA was not grossly negligent and not in bad faith

The members of the "Old Board" (Eisner, Bollenbach, Litvack, Russell, Roy Disney, Gold, Nunis, Poitier, Stern, Walker, Watson, Wilson, Bowers, Lozano and Mitchell) were required to comply with their fiduciary duties on behalf of the Company's shareholders while taking the actions that brought Ovitz to the Company. For the future, many lessons of what not to do can be learned from defendants' conduct here. Nevertheless, I conclude that the only reasonable application of the law to the facts as I have found them, is that the defendants did not act in bad faith, and were at most ordinarily negligent, in connection with the hiring of Ovitz and the approval of the OEA. In accordance with the business judgment rule (because, as it turns out, business judgment *was* exercised), ordinary negligence is insufficient to constitute a violation of the fiduciary duty of care. I shall elaborate upon this conclusion as to each defendant.

1. Eisner

Eisner was clearly the person most heavily involved in bringing Ovitz to the Company and negotiating the OEA. He was a long-time friend of Ovitz and the instigator and mastermind behind the machinations that resulted in Ovitz's hiring and the concomitant approval of the OEA ...

... By virtue of his Machiavellian (and imperial) nature as CEO, and his control over Ovitz's hiring in particular, Eisner to a large extent is responsible for the failings in process that infected and handicapped the board's decisionmaking abilities. [Note 487] Eisner stacked his (and I intentionally write "his" as opposed to "the Company's") board of directors with friends and other acquaintances who, though not necessarily beholden to him in a legal sense, were certainly more willing to accede to his wishes and support him unconditionally than truly independent directors. On the other hand, I do not believe that the evidence, considered fairly, demonstrates that Eisner actively took steps to defeat or short-circuit a decisionmaking process that would otherwise have occurred ...

[Note 487] It is precisely in this context – an imperial CEO or controlling shareholder with a supine or passive board – that the concept of good faith may prove highly meaningful. The fiduciary duties of care and loyalty, as traditionally defined, may not be aggressive enough to protect shareholder interests when the board is well advised, is not legally beholden to the management or a controlling shareholder and when the board does not suffer from other disabling conflicts of interest, such as a patently self-dealing transaction. Good faith may serve to fill this gap and ensure that the persons entrusted *by shareholders* to govern Delaware corporations do so with an honesty of purpose and with an understanding of whose interests they are there to protect ...

... Eisner obtained no consent or authorization from the board before agreeing to hire Ovitz, before agreeing to the substantive terms of the OLA, or before issuing the press release ... As a general rule, a CEO has no obligation to continuously inform the board of his actions as CEO, or to receive prior authorization for those actions. [Note 490] Nevertheless, a reasonably prudent CEO (that is to say, a reasonably prudent CEO with a board willing to think for itself and assert itself against the CEO when necessary) would not have acted in as unilateral a manner as did Eisner when essentially committing the corporation to hire a second-in-command, appoint that person to the board, and provide him with one of the largest and richest employment contracts ever enjoyed by a non-CEO ...

[Note 490] In a corporation of the Company's size and scope, the only logical way for the corporation to operate is that the everyday governance should be "under the direction" of the board of directors rather than "by" the board. More than twenty years ago, this Court wrote (and it is even more true today):

> "A fundamental precept of Delaware corporation law is that it is the board of directors, and neither shareholders nor managers, that has ultimate responsibility for the management of the enterprise. Of course, given the large, complex organizations though which modern multi-function business corporations often operate, the law recognizes that corporate boards, comprised as they traditionally have been of persons dedicating less than all of their attention to that role, cannot themselves manage the operations of the firm, but may satisfy their obligations by

thoughtfully appointing officers, establishing or approving goals and plans and monitoring performance. Thus Section 141(a) of DGCL expressly permits a board of directors to delegate managerial duties to officers of the corporation, except to the extent that the corporation's certificate of incorporation or bylaws may limit or prohibit such a delegation." *Grimes* v. *Donald* ...

Because considerations of improper motive are no longer present in this case, the decision to hire Ovitz and enter into the OEA is one of business judgment, to which the presumptions of the business judgment rule apply. In order to prevail, therefore, plaintiffs must demonstrate by a preponderance of the evidence that Eisner was either grossly negligent or acted in bad faith in connection with Ovitz's hiring and the approval of the OEA.

As I mentioned earlier, Eisner was very much aware of what was going on as the situation developed ... In light of this knowledge, I cannot find that plaintiffs have demonstrated by a preponderance of the evidence that Eisner failed to inform himself of all material information reasonably available or that he acted in a grossly negligent manner.

[Text omitted]

Despite all of the legitimate criticisms that may be leveled at Eisner, especially at having enthroned himself as the omnipotent and infallible monarch of his personal Magic Kingdom, I nonetheless conclude, after carefully considering and weighing all the evidence, that Eisner's actions were taken in good faith. That is, Eisner's actions were taken with the subjective belief that those actions were in the best interests of the Company ... In conclusion, Eisner acted in good faith and did not breach his fiduciary duty of care because he was not grossly negligent.

2. Russell

Apart from Eisner, Russell, who was familiar with the Company's compensation policies and practices from his service as chairman of the Company's compensation committee, was the next most heavily involved director in hiring Ovitz, as he was the main negotiator on behalf of the Company ... Russell did not independently and objectively verify the representations made by Ovitz's negotiators that his income from CAA was $20 to $25 million annually because Russell, based upon his pre-existing knowledge, believed that representation to be accurate ...

Would the better course of action have been for Russell to have objectively verified Ovitz's income from CAA? Undoubtedly, yes. Would it have been better if Russell had more rigorously investigated Ovitz's background in order to uncover his past troubles with the Department of Labor? Yes. Would the better course of action have been for someone other than Eisner's personal attorney to represent the Company in the negotiations with Ovitz? Again, yes. Have plaintiffs shown by a preponderance of the evidence that Russell's actions on behalf of the Company were *grossly* negligent (in that he failed to inform himself of all material information *reasonably* available in making decisions) or that he acted in bad faith? No ...

3. Watson

Watson's main role in Ovitz's hiring and his election as President of the Company was helping Russell evaluate the financial ramifications of the OEA ... Watson conducted extensive analyses of Ovitz's proposed compensation package, sharing those analyses with Crystal and Russell at their meeting on August 10, and in their later discussions stemming from that meeting ... Nothing in his conduct leads me to believe that he took an "ostrich-like" approach to considering and approving the OEA. Nothing in his conduct leads me to believe that Watson consciously and intentionally disregarded his duties to the Company. Nothing in his conduct leads me to believe that Watson had anything in mind other than the best interests of the Company when evaluating and consenting to Ovitz's compensation package. Finally, nothing in his conduct leads me to believe that Watson failed to inform himself of all material information reasonably available before making these decisions.

4. Poitier and Lozano

Poitier and Lozano were the remaining members of the compensation committee that considered the economic terms of the OEA ... The question in dispute is whether their level of involvement in the OEA was so low as to constitute gross negligence and, therefore, a breach of their fiduciary duty of care, or whether their actions evidence a lack of good faith ... At [the compensation committee] meeting, both Poitier and Lozano received the term sheet that explained the key terms of Ovitz's contract, and they were present for and participated in the discussion that occurred. Both then voted to approve the terms of the OEA, and both credibly testified that they believed they possessed sufficient information at that time to make an informed decision ... The board meeting was not called on short notice, and the directors were well aware that Ovitz's hiring would be discussed at the meeting as a result of the August 14 press release more than a month before ... Russell testified that the discussion of the OEA took about 25–30 minutes, significantly more time than the brief discussion reflected in the minutes would seem to indicate. Lozano believed that the committee spent "perhaps four times as much time on Mr. Ovitz's contract than we did on Mr. Russell's compensation."

I am persuaded by Russell and Lozano's recollection that the OEA was discussed for a not insignificant length of time ... In sum, although Poitier and Lozano did very little in connection with Ovitz's hiring and the compensation committee's approval of the OEA, they did not breach their fiduciary duties. I conclude that they were informed by Russell and Watson of all *material* information reasonably available, even though they were not privy to every conversation or document exchanged amongst Russell, Watson, Crystal and Ovitz's representatives ... Without [actual] knowledge [of incorrect calculations in the OEA], I conclude that the compensation committee acted in good faith and relied on Crystal in good faith, and that the fault for errors or omissions in Crystal's analysis must be laid at his feet, and not upon the compensation committee.

[Text omitted]

Poitier and Lozano did not intentionally disregard a duty to act, nor did they bury their heads in the sand knowing a decision had to be made. They acted in a manner that they believed was in the best interests of the corporation. Delaware law does not require (nor does it prohibit) directors to take as active a role as Russell and Watson took in connection with Ovitz's hiring. There is no question that in comparison to those two, the actions of Poitier and Lozano may appear casual or uninformed, but I conclude that they did not breach their fiduciary duties and that they acted in good faith in connection with Ovitz's hiring.

5.   The remaining members of the Old Board

In accordance with the compensation committee's charter, it was that committee's responsibility to establish and approve Ovitz's compensation arrangements. In accordance with the OLA and the Company's certificate of incorporation, it was the full board's responsibility to elect (or reject) Ovitz as President of the Company ...

The record gives adequate support to my conclusion that the directors, before voting, were informed of who Ovitz was, the reporting structure that Ovitz had agreed to and the key terms of the OEA. Again, plaintiffs have failed to meet their burden to demonstrate that the directors acted in a grossly negligent manner or that they failed to inform themselves of all material information reasonably available when making a decision. They did not intentionally shirk or ignore their duty, but acted in good faith, believing they were acting in the best interests of the Company.

[Text omitted]

D.   Eisner and Litvack did not act in bad faith in connection with Ovitz's termination, and the remainder of the new board had no duties in connection therewith

The New Board was likewise charged with complying with their fiduciary duties in connection with any actions taken, or required to be taken, in connection with Ovitz's termination. The key question here becomes whether the board was under a duty to act in connection with Ovitz's termination ...

1.   The New Board was not under a duty to act

Determining whether the New Board was required to discuss and approve Ovitz's termination requires careful consideration of the Company's governing instruments ...

Having considered these documents, I come to the following conclusions: 1) the board of directors has the sole power to elect the officers of the Company; 2) the board of directors has the sole power to determine the "duties" of the officers of the Company (either through board resolutions or bylaws); 3) the Chairman/ CEO has "general and active management, direction, and supervision over the business of the Corporation and over its officers," and that such management, direction and supervision is subject to the control of the board of directors; 4) the Chairman/CEO has the power to manage, direct and supervise the lesser officers and employees of the Company; 5) the board has the *right*, but not the *duty* to remove the officers of the Company with or without cause, and that right is non-exclusive; and 6) because that right is non-exclusive, and because the Chairman/ CEO is affirmatively charged with the management, direction and supervision of the officers of the Company, together with the powers and duties incident to the office of chief executive, the Chairman/CEO, subject to the control of the board of directors, also possesses the *right* to remove the inferior officers and employees of the corporation.

The New Board unanimously believed that Eisner, as Chairman and CEO, possessed the power to terminate Ovitz without board approval or intervention. Nonetheless, the board was informed of and supported Eisner's decision ... Because Eisner unilaterally terminated Ovitz, as was his right, the New Board was not required to act in connection with Ovitz's termination ... This is true regardless of the fact that Ovitz received a large cash payment and the vesting of three million options in connection with his termination ... Because the board was under no duty to act, they did not violate their fiduciary duty of care, and they also individually acted in good faith. For these reasons, the members of the New Board (other than Eisner and Litvack, who will be discussed individually below) did not breach their fiduciary duties and did not act in bad faith in connection with Ovitz's termination and his receipt of the NFT benefits included in the OEA.

2. Litvack

Litvack, as an officer of the corporation and as its general counsel, consulted with, and gave advice to, Eisner, on two questions relevant to Ovitz's termination ... whether Ovitz could or should have been terminated for cause and, second, whether a board meeting was required to ratify or effectuate Ovitz's termination or the payment of his NFT benefits ... Litvack properly concluded that the Company did not have good cause under the OEA to terminate Ovitz. He also properly concluded that no board action was necessary in connection with the termination. Litvack was familiar with the relevant factual information and legal standards regarding these decisions. Litvack made a determination in good faith that a formal opinion from outside counsel would not be helpful and that involving more people in the termination process increased the potential for news of the impending termination to leak out.

I do not intend to imply by these conclusions that Litvack was an infallible source of legal knowledge ... Litvack's silence at the December 10, 1996 EPPC meeting, when Russell informed the committee that Ovitz's bonus was contractually required, was unquestionably curious, and some might even call it irresponsible. His excuse that he did not want to embarrass Russell in front of the committee is, in a word, pathetic ... Luckily for Litvack, no harm was done because in the end Ovitz's bonus was rescinded ...

In conclusion, Litvack gave the proper advice and came to the proper conclusions when it was necessary. He was adequately informed in his decisions, and he acted in good faith for what he believed were the best interests of the Company.

3.   Eisner

Having concluded that Eisner alone possessed the authority to terminate Ovitz and grant him the NFT, I turn to whether Eisner acted in accordance with his fiduciary duties and in good faith when he terminated Ovitz ... When Eisner hired Ovitz in 1995, he did so with an eye to preparing the Company for the challenges that lay ahead, especially in light of the CapCities/ABC acquisition and the need for a legitimate potential successor to Eisner. To everyone's regret, including Ovitz ... Eisner was unable to work well with Ovitz, and Eisner refused to let Ovitz work without close and constant supervision. Faced with that situation, Eisner essentially had three options: 1) keep Ovitz as President and continue trying to make things work; 2) keep Ovitz at Disney, but in a role other than President; or 3) terminate Ovitz ...

Eisner unexpectedly found himself confronted with a situation that did not have an easy solution. He weighed the alternatives, received advice from counsel and then exercised his business judgment in the manner he thought best for the corporation. Eisner knew all the material information reasonably available when making the decision, he did not neglect an affirmative duty to act (or fail to cause the board to act) and he acted in what he believed were the best interests of the Company, taking into account the cost to the Company of the decision and the potential alternatives. Eisner was not personally interested in the transaction in any way that would make him incapable of exercising business judgment, and I conclude that plaintiffs have not demonstrated by a preponderance of the evidence that Eisner breached his fiduciary duties or acted in bad faith in connection with Ovitz's termination and receipt of the NFT.

IV.   CONCLUSION

Based on the findings of fact and conclusions of law made herein, judgment is hereby entered in favor of the defendants on all counts.

Unocal Corp. v. Mesa Petroleum Co.
Supreme Court of Delaware
493 A 2d 946 (1985).
[*Text edited; some footnotes omitted*]

MOORE, Justice

We confront an issue of first impression in Delaware – the validity of a corporation's self-tender for its own shares which excludes from participation a stockholder making a hostile tender offer for the company's stock.

[*Text omitted*]

On April 8, 1985, Mesa, the owner of approximately 13% of Unocal's stock, commenced a two-tier "front loaded" cash tender offer for 64 million shares, or approximately 37%, of Unocal's outstanding stock at a price of $54 per share. The "back-end" was designed to eliminate the remaining publicly held shares by an exchange of securities purportedly worth $54 per share. However, pursuant to [a court] order ... Mesa issued a supplemental proxy statement to Unocal's stockholders disclosing that the securities offered in the second-step merger would be highly subordinated, and that Unocal's capitalization would differ significantly from its present structure. Unocal has rather aptly termed such securities "junk bonds."

Unocal's board consists of eight independent outside directors and six insiders. It met on April 13, 1985, to consider the Mesa tender offer. Thirteen directors were present, and the meeting lasted nine and one-half hours. The directors were given no agenda or written materials prior to the session. However, detailed presentations were made by legal counsel regarding the board's obligations under both Delaware corporate law and the federal securities laws. The board then received a presentation from Peter Sachs on behalf of Goldman Sachs & Co. (Goldman Sachs) and Dillon, Read & Co. (Dillon Read) discussing the bases for their opinions that the Mesa proposal was wholly inadequate. Mr. Sachs opined that the minimum cash value that could be expected from a sale or orderly liquidation for 100% of Unocal's stock was in excess of $60 per share. In making his presentation, Mr. Sachs showed slides outlining the valuation techniques used by the financial advisors, and others, depicting recent business combinations in the oil and gas industry. The Court of Chancery found that the Sachs presentation was designed to apprise the directors of the scope of the analyses performed rather than the facts and numbers used in reaching the conclusion that Mesa's tender offer price was inadequate.

Mr. Sachs also presented various defensive strategies available to the board if it concluded that Mesa's two-step tender offer was inadequate and should be opposed. One of the devices outlined was a self-tender by Unocal for its own stock with a reasonable price range of $70 to $75 per share. The cost of such a proposal would cause the company to incur $6.1–6.5 billion of additional debt, and a presentation was made informing the board of Unocal's ability to handle it. The directors were told that the primary effect of this obligation would be to reduce exploratory drilling, but that the company would nonetheless remain a viable entity.

The eight outside directors, comprising a clear majority of the thirteen members present, then met separately with Unocal's financial advisors and attorneys. Thereafter, they unanimously agreed to advise the board that it should reject Mesa's tender offer as inadequate, and that Unocal should pursue a self-tender to provide the stockholders with a fairly priced alternative to the Mesa proposal. The board then reconvened and unanimously adopted a resolution rejecting as grossly inadequate Mesa's tender offer. Despite the nine and one-half hour length of the meeting, no formal decision was made on the proposed defensive self-tender.

On April 15, the board met again with four of the directors present by telephone and one member still absent. This session lasted two hours. Unocal's Vice President of Finance and its Assistant General Counsel made a detailed presentation of the proposed terms of the exchange offer. A price range between $70 and $80 per share was considered, and ultimately the directors agreed upon $72. The board was also advised about the debt securities that would be issued, and the necessity of placing restrictive covenants upon certain corporate activities until the obligations were paid. The board's decisions were made in reliance on the advice of its investment bankers, including the terms and conditions upon which the securities were to be issued. Based upon this advice, and the board's own deliberations, the directors unanimously approved the exchange offer. Their resolution provided that if Mesa acquired 64 million shares of Unocal stock through its own offer (the Mesa Purchase Condition), Unocal would buy the remaining 49% outstanding for an exchange of debt securities having an aggregate par value of $72 per share. The board resolution also stated that the offer would be subject to other conditions that had been described to the board at the meeting, or which were deemed necessary by Unocal's officers, including the exclusion of Mesa from the proposal (the Mesa exclusion). Any such conditions were required to be in accordance with the "purport and intent" of the offer.

Unocal's exchange offer was commenced on April 17, 1985, and Mesa promptly challenged it by filing this suit in the Court of Chancery. On April 22, the Unocal board met again and was advised by Goldman Sachs and Dillon Read to waive the Mesa Purchase Condition as to 50 million shares. This recommendation was in response to a perceived concern of the shareholders that, if shares were tendered to Unocal, no shares would be purchased by either offeror. The directors were also advised that they should tender their own Unocal stock into the exchange offer as a mark of their confidence in it.

Another focus of the board was the Mesa exclusion. Legal counsel advised that under Delaware law Mesa could only be excluded for what the directors reasonably believed to be a valid corporate purpose. The directors' discussion centered on the objective of adequately compensating shareholders at the "back-end" of Mesa's proposal, which the latter would finance with "junk bonds." To include Mesa would defeat that goal, because under the proration aspect of the exchange offer (49%)

every Mesa share accepted by Unocal would displace one held by another stockholder. Further, if Mesa were permitted to tender to Unocal, the latter would in effect be financing Mesa's own inadequate proposal.

On April 24, 1985 Unocal issued a supplement to the exchange offer describing the partial waiver of the Mesa Purchase Condition. On May 1, 1985, in another supplement, Unocal extended the withdrawal, proration and expiration dates of its exchange offer to May 17, 1985.

Meanwhile, on April 22, 1985, Mesa amended its complaint in this action to challenge the Mesa exclusion ...

On April 29, 1985, the Vice Chancellor temporarily restrained Unocal from proceeding with the exchange offer unless it included Mesa ... [T]he Vice Chancellor decided that in a selective purchase of the company's stock, the corporation bears the burden of showing: (1) a valid corporate purpose, and (2) that the transaction was fair to all of the stockholders, including those excluded.

Unocal immediately sought certification of an interlocutory appeal to this Court ...

[*Text omitted*]

II.

The issues we address involve these fundamental questions: Did the Unocal board have the power and duty to oppose a takeover threat it reasonably perceived to be harmful to the corporate enterprise, and if so, is its action here entitled to the protection of the business judgment rule?

Mesa contends that the discriminatory exchange offer violates the fiduciary duties Unocal owes it. Mesa argues that because of the Mesa exclusion the business judgment rule is inapplicable, because the directors by tendering their own shares will derive a financial benefit that is not available to *all* Unocal stockholders. Thus, it is Mesa's ultimate contention that Unocal cannot establish that the exchange offer is fair to *all* shareholders, and argues that the Court of Chancery was correct in concluding that Unocal was unable to meet this burden.

Unocal answers that it does not owe a duty of "fairness" to Mesa, given the facts here. Specifically, Unocal contends that its board of directors reasonably and in good faith concluded that Mesa's $54 two-tier tender offer was coercive and inadequate, and that Mesa sought selective treatment for itself. Furthermore, Unocal argues that the board's approval of the exchange offer was made in good faith, on an informed basis, and in the exercise of due care. Under these circumstances, Unocal contends that its directors properly employed this device to protect the company and its stockholders from Mesa's harmful tactics.

III.

We begin with the basic issue of the power of a board of directors of a Delaware corporation to adopt a defensive measure of this type. Absent such authority, all other questions are moot. Neither issues of fairness nor business judgment are pertinent without the basic underpinning of a board's legal power to act.

The board has a large reservoir of authority upon which to draw. Its duties and responsibilities proceed from the inherent powers conferred by Del. C. § 141(a), respecting management of the corporation's "business and affairs." Additionally, the powers here being exercised derive from Del. C. § 160(a), conferring broad authority upon a corporation to deal in its own stock. From this it is now well established that in the acquisition of its shares a Delaware corporation may deal selectively with its stockholders, provided the directors have not acted out of a sole or primary purpose to entrench themselves in office ...

Finally, the board's power to act derives from its fundamental duty and obligation to protect the corporate enterprise, which includes stockholders, from harm reasonably perceived, irrespective of its source ... Thus, we are satisfied that in the broad context of corporate governance, including issues of fundamental corporate change, a board of directors is not a passive instrumentality. [Note 8]

[Note 8] Even in the traditional areas of fundamental corporate change, i.e. charter, amendments [§ 242(b)], mergers [§§ 251(b), 252(c), and 254(d)], sale of assets [8 Del. C. § 271(a)], and dissolution [8 Del. C. § 275(a)], director action is a prerequisite to the ultimate disposition of such matters ...

Given the foregoing principles, we turn to the standards by which director action is to be measured. In *Pogostin* v. *Rice* ... we held that the business judgment rule, including the standards by which director conduct is judged, is applicable in the context of a takeover ... The business judgment rule is a "presumption that in making a business decision the directors of a corporation acted on an informed basis, in good faith and in the honest belief that the action taken was in the best interests of the company." *Aronson* v. *Lewis* ... A hallmark of the business judgment rule is that a court will not substitute its judgment for that of the board if the latter's decision can be "attributed to any rational business purpose." *Sinclair Oil Corp.* v. *Levien* ...

When a board addresses a pending takeover bid it has an obligation to determine whether the offer is in the best interests of the corporation and its shareholders. In that respect a board's duty is no different from any other responsibility it shoulders, and its decisions should be no less entitled to the respect they otherwise would be accorded in the realm of business judgment ... There are, however, certain caveats to a proper exercise of this function. Because of the omnipresent specter that a board may be acting primarily in its own interests, rather than those of the corporation and its shareholders, there is an enhanced duty which calls for judicial examination at the threshold before the protections of the business judgment rule may be conferred.

This Court has long recognized that: "We must bear in mind the inherent danger in the purchase of shares with corporate funds to remove a threat to corporate policy when a threat to control is involved. The directors are of necessity confronted with a conflict of interest, and an objective decision is difficult." ... In the face of this inherent conflict directors must show that they had reasonable grounds for believing that a danger to corporate policy and effectiveness existed because of another person's stock ownership … However, they satisfy that burden "by showing good faith and reasonable investigation … " … Furthermore, such proof is materially enhanced, as here, by the approval of a board comprised of a majority of outside independent directors who have acted in accordance with the foregoing standards …

IV.

A.

In the board's exercise of corporate power to forestall a takeover bid our analysis begins with the basic principle that corporate directors have a fiduciary duty to act in the best interests of the corporation's stockholders. *Guth* v. *Loft, Inc.* … As we have noted, their duty of care extends to protecting the corporation and its owners from perceived harm whether a threat originates from third parties or other shareholders. But such powers are not absolute. A corporation does not have unbridled discretion to defeat any perceived threat by any Draconian means available.

The restriction placed upon a selective stock repurchase is that the directors may not have acted solely or primarily out of a desire to perpetuate themselves in office … Of course, to this is added the further caveat that inequitable action may not be taken under the guise of law. *Schnell* v. *Chris-Craft Industries, Inc.* … The standard of proof … is designed to ensure that a defensive measure to thwart or impede a takeover is indeed motivated by a good faith concern for the welfare of the corporation and its stockholders, which in all circumstances must be free of any fraud or other misconduct … However, this does not end the inquiry.

B.

A further aspect is the element of balance. If a defensive measure is to come within the ambit of the business judgment rule, it must be reasonable in relation to the threat posed. This entails an analysis by the directors of the nature of the takeover bid and its effect on the corporate enterprise. Examples of such concerns may include: inadequacy of the price offered, nature and timing of the offer, questions of illegality, the impact on "constituencies" other than shareholders (i.e. creditors, customers, employees, and perhaps even the community generally), the risk of nonconsummation, and the quality of securities being offered in the exchange. See Lipton and Brownstein, *Takeover Responses and Directors' Responsibilities: An Update*, p. 7, ABA National Institute on the Dynamics of Corporate Control (December 8, 1983). While not a controlling factor, it also seems to us that a board may reasonably consider the basic stockholder interests at stake, including those of short term speculators, whose actions may have fueled the coercive aspect of the offer at the expense of the long term investor. Here, the threat posed was viewed by the Unocal board as a grossly inadequate two-tier coercive tender offer coupled with the threat of greenmail.

Specifically, the Unocal directors had concluded that the value of Unocal was substantially above the $54 per share offered in cash at the front end. Furthermore, they determined that the subordinated securities to be exchanged in Mesa's announced squeeze out of the remaining shareholders in the "back-end" merger were "junk bonds" worth far less than $54. It is now well recognized that such offers are a classic coercive measure designed to stampede shareholders into tendering at the first tier, even if the price is inadequate, out of fear of what they will receive at the back end of the transaction. Wholly beyond the coercive aspect of an inadequate two-tier tender offer, the threat was posed by a corporate raider with a national reputation as a "greenmailer." [Note 13]

[Note 13] The term "greenmail" refers to the practice of buying out a takeover bidder's stock at a premium that is not available to other shareholders in order to prevent the takeover. The Chancery Court noted that "Mesa has made tremendous profits from its takeover activities although in the past few years it has not been successful in acquiring any of the target companies on an unfriendly basis." Moreover, the trial court specifically found that the actions of the Unocal board were taken in good faith to eliminate both the inadequacies of the tender offer and to forestall the payment of "greenmail."

In adopting the selective exchange offer, the board stated that its objective was either to defeat the inadequate Mesa offer or, should the offer still succeed, provide the 49% of its stockholders, who would otherwise be forced to accept "junk bonds," with $72 worth of senior debt. We find that both purposes are valid.

However, such efforts would have been thwarted by Mesa's participation in the exchange offer. First, if Mesa could tender its shares, Unocal would effectively be subsidizing the former's continuing effort to buy Unocal stock at $54 per share. Second, Mesa could not, by definition, fit within the class of shareholders being protected from its own coercive and inadequate tender offer.

Thus, we are satisfied that the selective exchange offer is reasonably related to the threats posed. It is consistent with the principle that "the minority stockholder shall receive the substantial equivalent in value of what he had before." ... This concept of fairness, while stated in the merger context, is also relevant in the area of tender offer law. Thus, the board's decision to offer what it determined to be the fair value of the corporation to the 49% of its shareholders, who would otherwise be forced to accept highly subordinated "junk bonds," is reasonable and consistent with the directors' duty to ensure that the minority stockholders receive equal value for their shares.

V.

Mesa contends that it is unlawful, and the trial court agreed, for a corporation to discriminate in this fashion against one shareholder. It argues correctly that no case has ever sanctioned a device that precludes a raider from sharing in a benefit available to all other stockholders. However, as we have noted earlier, the principle of selective stock repurchases by a Delaware corporation is neither unknown nor unauthorized. The only difference is that heretofore the approved transaction was the payment of "greenmail" to a raider or dissident posing a threat to the corporate enterprise. All other stockholders were denied such favored treatment, and given Mesa's past history of greenmail, its claims here are rather ironic.

However, our corporate law is not static. It must grow and develop in response to, indeed in anticipation of, evolving concepts and needs. Merely because the General Corporation Law is silent as to a specific matter does not mean that it is prohibited … In the days when *Cheff, Bennett, Martin* and *Kors* were decided, the tender offer, while not an unknown device, was virtually unused, and little was known of such methods as two-tier "front-end" loaded offers with their coercive effects. Then, the favored attack of a raider was stock acquisition followed by a proxy contest. Various defensive tactics, which provided no benefit whatever to the raider, evolved. Thus, the use of corporate funds by management to counter a proxy battle was approved. *Hall* v. *Trans-Lux Daylight Picture Screen Corp.* … Litigation, supported by corporate funds, aimed at the raider has long been a popular device.

More recently, as the sophistication of both raiders and targets has developed, a host of other defensive measures to counter such ever mounting threats has evolved and received judicial sanction. These include defensive charter amendments and other devices bearing some rather exotic, but apt, names: Crown Jewel, White Knight, Pac Man, and Golden Parachute. Each has highly selective features, the object of which is to deter or defeat the raider.

Thus, while the exchange offer is a form of selective treatment, given the nature of the threat posed here the response is neither unlawful nor unreasonable. If the board of directors is disinterested, has acted in good faith and with due care, its decision in the absence of an abuse of discretion will be upheld as a proper exercise of business judgment.

To this Mesa responds that the board is not disinterested, because the directors are receiving a benefit from the tender of their own shares, which because of the Mesa exclusion, does not devolve upon *all* stockholders equally. See *Aronson* v. *Lewis* … However, Mesa concedes that if the exclusion is valid, then the directors and all other stockholders share the same benefit. The answer of course is that the exclusion is valid, and the directors' participation in the exchange offer does not rise to the level of a disqualifying interest. The excellent discussion in *Johnson* v. *Trueblood*, 629 F 2d at 292–293, of the use of the business judgment rule in takeover contests also seems pertinent here.

Nor does this become an "interested" director transaction merely because certain board members are large stockholders. As this Court has previously noted, that fact alone does not create a disqualifying "personal pecuniary interest" to defeat the operation of the business judgment rule.

Mesa also argues that the exclusion permits the directors to abdicate the fiduciary duties they owe it. However, that is not so. The board continues to owe Mesa the duties of due care and loyalty. But in the face of the destructive threat Mesa's tender offer was perceived to pose, the board had a supervening duty to protect the corporate enterprise, which includes the other shareholders, from threatened harm.

Mesa contends that the basis of this action is punitive, and solely in response to the exercise of its rights of corporate democracy. Nothing precludes Mesa, as a stockholder, from acting in its own self-interest ... (majority shareholder owes a fiduciary duty to the minority shareholders). However, Mesa, while pursuing its own interests, has acted in a manner which a board consisting of a majority of independent directors has reasonably determined to be contrary to the best interests of Unocal and its other shareholders. In this situation, there is no support in Delaware law for the proposition that, when responding to a perceived harm, a corporation must guarantee a benefit to a stockholder who is deliberately provoking the danger being addressed. There is no obligation of self-sacrifice by a corporation and its shareholders in the face of such a challenge.

Here, the Court of Chancery specifically found that the "directors' decision [to oppose the Mesa tender offer] was made in the good faith belief that the Mesa tender offer is inadequate." ... [W]e are satisfied that Unocal's board has met its burden of proof. *Cheff* v. *Mathes*, 199 A 2d at 555.

VI.

In conclusion, there was directorial power to oppose the Mesa tender offer, and to undertake a selective stock exchange made in good faith and upon a reasonable investigation pursuant to a clear duty to protect the corporate enterprise. Further, the selective stock repurchase plan chosen by Unocal is reasonable in relation to the threat that the board rationally and reasonably believed was posed by Mesa's inadequate and coercive two-tier tender offer. Under those circumstances the board's action is entitled to be measured by the standards of the business judgment rule. Thus, unless it is shown by a preponderance of the evidence that the directors' decisions were primarily based on perpetuating themselves in office, or some other breach of fiduciary duty such as fraud, overreaching, lack of good faith, or being uninformed, a Court will not substitute its judgment for that of the board.

In this case that protection is not lost merely because Unocal's directors have tendered their shares in the exchange offer. Given the validity of the Mesa exclusion, they are receiving a benefit shared generally by all other stockholders except Mesa. In this circumstance the test of *Aronson* v. *Lewis* ... is satisfied ... If the stockholders are displeased with the action of their elected representatives, the powers of corporate democracy are at their disposal to turn the board out. *Aronson* v. *Lewis* ...

With the Court of Chancery's findings that the exchange offer was based on the board's good faith belief that the Mesa offer was inadequate, that the board's action was informed and taken with due care, that Mesa's prior activities justify a reasonable inference that its principle objective was greenmail, and implicitly, that the substance of the offer itself was reasonable and fair to the corporation and its stockholders if Mesa were included, we cannot say that the Unocal directors have acted in such a manner as to have passed an "unintelligent and unadvised judgment" ... The decision of the Court of Chancery is therefore REVERSED, and the preliminary injunction is VACATED.

14

Executive compensation

Required reading

D: AktG, §§ 78, 87, 112, 186(3), 192, 193; HGB, § 285
UK: CA 2006, secs. 188, 420–422, 439, 566, 1166; SI 2008 No. 410; FSA
Listing Rules, Rules 9.4, 9.86, 9.8.8
US: DGCL, §§ 122(15), 141(h); 17 CFR §§ 229.402, 240.14a-101, Items 8
and 10; NYSE, *Listed Company Manual*, para. 303A.05

Incentives and risks of executive compensation

I. *Performance-linked pay and moral hazard*

Executive compensation can be used to create desirable incentives for management, and thus is an instrument of corporate governance, but, because management often controls the machinery used to grant itself compensation and also because of the nature of certain forms of compensation, it can equally present moral hazard – an incentive for directors to breach their fiduciary duties. Performance-linked compensation can align the interests of management with those of shareholders because a manager whose pay increases in relation to a company's success has an economic incentive to increase such success by her own performance. A manager who holds the company's shares or options to buy them can be expected to share the interests of the shareholders. On the other hand, giving directors shares and options can set the stage for governance risks that do not arise with a straight salary.

Compensation contracts entail the same risks as any contract between the directors and the company: directors stand on both sides of the transaction in setting their own pay, and, when setting officers' pay, their decisions may be influenced by such officers. Stock and options carry other dangers because they can give management incentives to commit fraud or undertake excessive business risks to maximize the value of their stock and options. Compensating executives is also connected to cultural concepts, such as how humans are motivated and what leadership deserves. In the US, a CEO has been seen as a dominant factor in his firm's success, and it is thought that the output of this CEO can be increased through high pay. This has led to a culture of what most commentators find to be excessive executive compensation. In Germany, the board is understood as a collegial body, and traditionally the compensation of directors is informally capped by a shared understanding of a proper ratio to the compensation of ordinary employees.

Granting stock and options as executive compensation also brings with it certain corporate finance and accounting questions. The awarded stock and options must be available for distribution, which means that sufficient shares must be available or capital increased, and any existing preemption rights waived. This is procedurally more complex in Germany and the UK because of the requirements of the Second Company Law Directive, as discussed in Chapters 6 to 8. Moreover, the award of securities to management must also be entered on the company's books, and the accounting treatment may determine how freely a distribution can be made.

II.   Compensation as a governance tool

Although many good managers interested in challenging work and with a desire for a good reputation will be motivated by factors aside from their compensation, such compensation will undoubtedly influence their behavior. A straight cash salary can make management over-cautious because the manager's ultimate goal would be to avoid the company's bankruptcy – which would destroy the source of her salary – rather than to maximize the value of the firm. For example, when, in the US in the 1970s, executive management was paid a cash salary that tended to increase in relation to the overall revenues of the firm, managers were inclined to build large, diversified conglomerates that, although not efficient, did increase the overall revenue of assets managed (and thus salary) and also diversified against the risk of bankruptcy.[1] When opportunities for such empire-building were not present, management carefully accumulated large cash reserves, which then led perceptive investors to launch hostile takeovers to break up the conglomerates (for increased efficiency)

---

[1] Jensen, Murphy and Wruck (2004: 26–27).

and distribute the accumulated excess cash to the shareholders (i.e. to themselves).[2]

Compensation that gives management incentives to pursue the best course for the company helps to obviate such exterior controls as the market for corporate control. Professors Michael Jensen, Kevin Murphy and Eric Wruck have noted that:

> A well-designed remuneration package for executives (or for employees at all levels of the organization), will accomplish three things: attract the right executives at the lowest cost; retain the right executives at the lowest cost (and encourage the right executives to leave the firm at the appropriate time); and motivate executives to take actions that create long-run shareholder value and avoid actions that destroy value.[3]

The elements of a compensation package that one might use to achieve this end include cash salary, cash bonuses, loans,[4] stock, stock options and retirement plans, in any mixture of short, medium and long terms, as well as a number of other "perquisites."[5] Stock granted as compensation is usually "restricted" in the sense that it cannot be traded for a certain period of time,[6] and options are usually restricted by the price at which they may be exercised and as to the time of exercise. Retirement plans are likely to vest (i.e. become enforceable against the company) only after a certain period of service with the company. The mix of these elements in a given compensation package will be used to attract, motivate and retain the specific executive in the specific

---

[2] Jensen, Murphy and Wruck (2004: 27).   [3] Jensen, Murphy and Wruck (2004: 19).

[4] Where permitted by law. As discussed in Chapter 12, § 13(k) of the US Exchange Act prohibits loans to the management of listed companies. An example of the abuses this section sought to address was WorldCom lending its CEO, Bernard Ebbers, over $400 million at only 2.15 percent per annum interest. As discussed in Chapter 12, UK law requires member approval for a public company to grant credit to a director; Germany is less strict, as loans to supervisory or managing directors must be approved by the supervisory board.

[5] The "extras" such as a company plane, car, club membership and an expense account, referred to as "perquisites", are also often called "perks" in English. The peculiar sounding word "perquisite" comes from the Middle English *perquisites*, which is "property acquired otherwise than by inheritance"; the latter is in turn derived from the medieval Latin *perquisītum*, meaning "acquisition," and *perquisītum* itself comes from the Latin, neuter past participle of *perquīrere*, meaning "to search diligently for." *American Heritage Dictionary* (2004: 1038), so, at least linguistically, diligence is at the root of executive perks.

[6] Even if the compensation plan does not restrict resale of stock received from the company, under US law, stock that is not sold through a registered offering cannot be resold without the seller being deemed an underwriter subject to registration unless a number of conditions are met, including the expiration of a waiting period. See 17 CFR § 230.144.

context. For example, it has been argued that the growth of equity compensation in California's "Silicon Valley" was caused at least in part by California law failing to recognize covenants not to compete, so the best way for a technology company to prevent executives from jumping ship to competitors was through stock, options and long-term compensation plans.[7]

Equity compensation finds its limits, however, in the very nature of stock, the value of which reflects much more than the performance of an individual. First, the value of a share of stock will rise or fall based on the prospects of the issuer, not a particular division of an issuer.[8] Thus, if an executive of Daimler AG were in charge of developing the "Smart" division, but the larger Mercedes division had a greater impact on the Daimler share price, compensation in the form of Daimler shares would not be tied to the executive's performance. In such circumstances, either "tracking stock," which tracks the performance of a single company division, or cash bonuses might be a more suitable form of remuneration. Secondly, the share price of a company tends to rise or fall with the sector of the economy in which it is located. For example, even though management at the UK bank HSBC acted quickly in mid-2007 to limit exposure to US mortgages and was financially sound in 2008, its share price still plummeted with the rest of the banking sector as the financial crisis panic took hold. The best efforts of management were drowned in market trend. Thirdly, the value of shares and options are closely linked to information about the company and the terms of their issue. Management has significant control over both.

The design of an equity compensation plan is therefore crucial to its effectiveness as a tool for motivation and reward.

III.   The risks of executive compensation

A.   Self-dealing: the moral hazard of inflating pay

Like all contracts between management and the company, the negotiation and signing of a compensation contract raises the question of self-dealing. We have already examined this issue and the applicable rules and standards for conflicted transactions in Chapter 12 on directors' duties, and will look at further rules for listed companies in Chapter 15. Executive remuneration contracts, however, have a number of characteristics that

---

[7] Gilson (1999: 602–613); Booth (2006).   [8] See the discussion in Booth (2006: 7–10).

set them apart from other contracts that might arise between the management and the company:

- These contracts predictably recur, and do so in very similar form, as management does not work for free and compensation structures are set by market forces.
- The fairness to the company of a performance-linked contract is difficult to evaluate, as the perfect mix of substantive elements and vesting terms may well be impossible to determine.
- Compensation in the form of shares or options to buy shares presents management with a moral hazard, as they have the power to manipulate such compensation's value.

With respect to the substantive fairness of a given contract, although expert compensation consultants have the necessary skills to tackle these questions, such consultants are usually retained by the company's human resources department, which answers to top management, and thus tend to favor management's interests rather than those of the company.[9] For example, studies have shown that, even when a company is underperforming the market, consultants will use the pay of companies in the same sector as a benchmark, and "argue that CEO compensation should be higher to reflect prevailing industry levels."[10] Jensen and Murphy explain that "[v]irtually all these agreements now provide compensation for executives terminated for reasons other than moral turpitude, gross negligence, or felony convictions. Notably compensation cannot be denied for termination due to incompetence."[11] Bebchuk and Fried explain the details of one egregious severance arrangement:

> "[W]hen Mattel CEO Jill Barad resigned under fire, the board forgave a $4.2 million loan, gave her an additional $3.3 million in cash to cover the taxes for forgiveness of another loan, and allowed her unvested options to vest automatically. These gratuitous benefits were in addition to the considerable benefits that she received under her employment agreement, which included a termination payment of $26.4 million and a stream of retirement benefits exceeding $700,000 per year."[12]

As Bebchuk and Fried note, "[i]t is not easy to reconcile such gratuitous payments with the arm's length, optimal contracting model. The board has

---

[9] Jensen, Murphy and Wruck (2004: 55).
[10] Bebchuk and Fried (2003: 79), with further references; also see Bebchuk and Fried (2004: 39).
[11] Jensen, Murphy and Wruck (2004: 29).
[12] Bebchuk and Fried (2003: 81); also see Bebchuk and Fried (2004: 88).

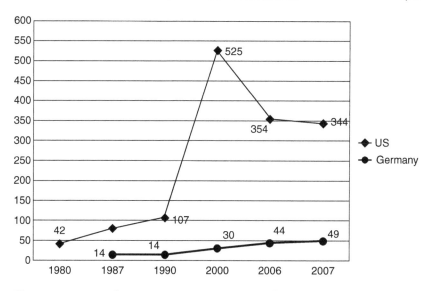

Figure 14.1   Ratio of average executive to average employee pay

the authority to fire the CEO and pay the CEO her contractual severance benefits. Thus, there is no need to 'bribe' a poorly performing CEO to step down."[13] Abusively high executive compensation, while not completely restricted to the US, has been much more prominent in the US during the last decade. In 2006, the average compensation of the twenty highest paid executives in European firms was estimated at $12.5 million, while that of their US counterparts was at $36.4 million, nearly three times as much.[14] Figure 14.1 shows the multiple by which CEO pay exceeds the average pay of a company employee in the US and Germany.

In the wake of the 2008 financial crisis, the US and Germany both introduced a number of limitations on directors' pay, with particular focus on companies receiving government assistance, to counter the incongruity of executives being awarded extravagant bonuses while share prices plummeted and thousands of workers were being laid off. A further worry was that performance-linked bonuses and equity compensation gave directors of financial institutions an incentive to take excessive risks with their companies, confident in the knowledge that the governments of the respective countries in which their institutions were based would insure downside risk to protect depositors and other retail participants

---

[13] Bebchuk and Fried (2003: 12); also see Bebchuk and Fried (2004: 88).
[14] Anderson, Cavanagh, Collins, Pizzigati and Lapham (2007: 17).

in the financial system. Each of our jurisdictions has taken action in this respect. To the extent that these actions apply to companies generally, they are discussed briefly together with the other applicable rules of the respective jurisdiction in section IV of this chapter.

B.   Earnings management

The award of stock or options can tempt directors to use their power and knowledge to manipulate the price of the company's shares. Executive managers are hired exactly because they are clever, bargain hard and use every advantage they can. Regrettably, this tendency is nowhere more apparent than in the way some directors use their intelligence and ingenuity to protect themselves and augment their own remuneration at the expense of the company's other shareholders. Although we may hope that self-restraint, a strong character and fiduciary duties help prevent management from abusing their power, even where a director has a strong sense of duty and sound ethics, self-restraint will be of no avail if an abuse of power is not recognized as such. As we will see in the next chapter, insider trading was not outlawed in Germany until 1995 and a number of US scholars still argue it is salutary for price formation. Whilst the first hurdle is thus knowing of a questionable practice, the second is to assess its merits; the third – if so decided – is to eliminate it.

If directors hold a quantity of company shares N with an acquisition price of P, or N options at an exercise price of P, by somehow inflating the company's net earnings they can at least temporarily inflate the company's share price to $P + I$, so that an immediate sale of shares (or exercise of options and sale of shares) at this price will net them a gain of $I \times N$. Thus, a form of compensation designed to align management and shareholder interests can incite the former to act as a predator of the latter.[15] As Professor John C. Coffee Jr. explains, a major abuse of the 1990s dot.com bubble was for management to improperly recognize future earnings and report them at an earlier time.[16] However, the types of earnings-management available to directors are as broad as the imagination of a creative accountant. Some popular techniques include: (i) improperly classifying accounting items, such as classifying an asset or liability as current when it is not; (ii) improperly excluding liabilities from the company's balance sheet; (iii) failing to account for assets in a merger or acquisition, or doing so improperly; and (iv) improperly recognizing costs or expenses, and improperly capitalizing

---

[15] Coffee (2004b: 275–279).   [16] Coffee (2004b: 285).

expenditures.[17] As discussed in the next chapter, the US Sarbanes–Oxley Act included a number of measures against such accounting manipulation, including restructuring the supervision of the accounting profession, preventing auditors from providing consulting services, requiring auditor rotation, requiring listed companies to have an audit committee, requiring executive officers to certify accounting statements, and imposing stricter rules on the reporting of off-balance sheet transactions and *pro forma* accounting.[18] Similar requirements were introduced in Europe through the Transparency Directive, the IFRS Regulation, and the governance codes of the UK and Germany.

C.   Manipulating the value of options

The stock options[19] used to compensate executives typically set the "exercise" or "strike" price of the options *at-the-money*, which means that the price of the stock underlying the option on the day of the grant will be the price at which the option can be exercised when it vests.[20] The difference between the strike price of the option and the market price of the stock on the day the option is exercised represents the value of the option. Options become more valuable if the stock price increases rapidly after the date of issue. This can occur if negative information is released immediately before the grant date so as to drive stock price down, the stock is otherwise at a low price on the grant date, or positive information is disclosed after the grant to increase the share price.

Whilst the grant of options is intended to spur management to drive up the value of the *company and its shares*, many managers choose instead simply to drive up the value of *their own options* through fraudulent techniques. Since the board controls the release of market sensitive information, they found they could release negative information just before the grant date to drive the share price down (referred to as "bullet-dodging") or grant the options just before the release of positive information so the share price then jumps up (referred to as

---

[17]   The US Government Accounting Office (GAO) has prepared a number of reports on accounting restatements resulting from errors or intentional irregularities in financial statements. See the GAO Financial Restatement Database (GAO-06-1079sp), available at www.gao.gov; and the GAO reports numbered GAO-03-138, GAO-03-395R and GAO-06-1053R.

[18]   §§ 10A and 13 Exchange Act; and Title I, Sarbanes–Oxley Act.

[19]   I.e. call options, options to purchase the security at a pre-agreed price.

[20]   Bebchuk and Fried (2003: 84–85); also see Bebchuk and Fried (2004: 159–162); and Bebchuk, Grinstein and Peyer (2006).

"spring-loading").[21] In the case of spring-loaded options, the Delaware court has found that, where "a board of directors later concealed the true nature of a grant of stock options, [the court] may further conclude that those options were not granted consistent with a fiduciary's duty of utmost loyalty."[22] When reading the section on insider trading (dealing) in the next chapter, consider whether the grant of an option to oneself before the disclosure of known, price sensitive information (spring-loading) would also constitute insider trading (dealing).

Rather than leaving the price change to the whim of the market, however, some management decided simply to back-date the options to a date on which the price of the company's shares was at an historical low. They would grant options on day T, but the corporate records would be falsified to indicate a grant on, say, T – 14, the day on which the company's stock was at an historical low. Widespread back-dating of options in the US was first exposed by the *Wall Street Journal* in early 2006.[23] One of the cases involved Mr. Jacob "Kobi" Alexander, chairman and CEO of Comverse Technologies Inc., against whom the SEC filed a civil suit for reaping millions of dollars by securities fraud (under, *inter alia*, Rule 10b-5), explaining: "At some point in the grant process, Alexander 'cherry-picked' the grant date. He looked back at CTI's historical stock prices and, with the benefit of hindsight, chose a grant date that corresponded to a date on which CTI's common stock was trading at a relative low."[24] Even though the SEC's case may have been strong, the trial was not brought to its regular conclusion, for Mr. Alexander, with a flash of that creative energy characteristic of good management, took his millions and escaped to Namibia, which has no formal extradition treaty with the US.[25]

D. Hedging with zero-cost collars and equity swaps: a breach of fiduciary duty?

Equity compensation is designed to place managers under the same risk as shareholders – an economic fate tied to the value of the stock. As employees, executive managers also invest significant human capital in their companies. Between the investment of human capital and the effects of

---

[21] Simmons (2009: 317).

[22] *In Re Tyson Foods, Inc.*, 2007 WL 2351071, at 5 (Del. Ch. 2007) (No. CIV.A. 1106-CC).

[23] Forelle and Banler (2006).

[24] Complaint of the Securities and Exchange Commission against Jacob "Kobi" Alexander, David Kreinberg, and William F. Sorin, before the US District Court for the Eastern District of New York, August 8, 2006, available at www.sec.gov, under litigation releases.

[25] Stecklow (2008).

equity compensation, a director's finances can become highly vulnerable to a drop in their company's share price. It is therefore not surprising that some managers seek to hedge against such a drop with derivative instruments like "zero-cost collars" and "equity swaps." If a manager sells a call option on the company's stock and uses the sale proceeds to simultaneously purchase a put option at the same price, he has created a zero-cost collar.[26] Thus, for example, if a manager holds shares of a company at a time when the market price is P, he might be able to sell a call option with a strike price of $P + 10$ and purchase a put option with a price of $P - 5$, which trades his potential upside gain for limiting in his potential loss on the stock to 5.[27] If a director exchanges the returns on her stock for the cash flows on another asset, such as an index fund or risk-free security, she has made an equity swap, which will also hedge against the risk that some event (including her own performance) will negatively affect the value of the company's shares.[28] Both devices protect the manager from a falling share price, and thus reduce the negative side of performance-based compensation. They limit the degree to which director interests are aligned with those of the shareholders, leaving the risks of equity compensation discussed above whilst removing many of its advantages.

Do you think that the law should allow managers to use these devices to insulate themselves from risk in the company they manage? Could an equity swap for the return on a competing company's shares or a high number of put options constitute a conflict of interest breaching a director's fiduciary duties?

IV. Compensation in our jurisdictions: approval, accounting, disclosure

A.   United States

As is evident from Figure 14.1, US executive compensation grew rapidly from 1980 to 2000. In fact, during the thirty years between 1970 and 2000, average executive compensation grew by a factor of sixteen, from approximately $850,000 annually in 1970 to over $14 million in 2000.[29] During the ten years from 1992 to 2002, the equity component of US compensation nearly doubled, from 24% to 47% (down from a high of 54% in 2001).[30] The absolute size of this compensation and the moral

---

[26] Bettis, Bizjak, and Lemmon (1999: 345).   [27] See e.g. Hu and Black (2008: 706–207).
[28] Bettis, Bizjak and Lemmon (1999: 345).   [29] Jensen, Murphy and Wruck (2004: 24).
[30] Jensen, Murphy and Wruck (2004: 31, Figure 3).

hazard it presents for directors has led to considerable concern in the US and to three primary types of solutions: disclosure, recourse to supervisory directors in compensation committees, and increase in shareholder decision rights. Changes in the law and SEC rules were introduced following the bursting of the dot.com bubble and again in the wake of the global financial crisis. The following subsections outline the current US rules.

1. Required disclosure of executive compensation   Neither Delaware law nor the Model Act contains any disclosure requirements for executive compensation. Companies required to file reports with the SEC, however, must render extensive disclosure regarding their policies on executive compensation, and the compensation itself, in their proxy statements. The rules on compensation have been amended a number of times to address concerns that the disclosure was ineffective or incomplete, and the most recent major amendments were in 2006[31] and in 2009.[32] The current US rules require not only a detailed disclosure of the compensation of the CEO, the CFO and the three other officers who are most highly paid, but also a general discussion of the company's compensation policies and practices, including an analysis of any risks the compensation policies or practices may create for the company. The bulk of the numerical disclosure is tabular, preceded by the narrative "Compensation Discussion and Analysis" that presents the policies behind and the purposes of the compensation program, and a list of specific circumstances in which compensation practices may pose risks for the company. The discussion will include an explanation of the behavior the compensation is designed to reward, each element of compensation and its purpose, how such elements are determined and approved, and each element's role in the overall program.[33] The tables are divided into three main categories: (i) compensation over the last three years; (ii) holdings of equity interests received as compensation; and (iii) retirement plans, deferred compensation and other

---

[31] The requirements are found in Item 402 of Regulation S-K, 17 CFR § 229.402, and are cross-referenced by the requirements in connection with proxies found at 17 CFR § 240.14a-101, Items 8 and 10.

[32] The 2009 amendments also feed into Regulation S-K and Regulation 14A. They were issued in Final Rule: Proxy Disclosure Enhancements, SEC Release Nos. 33-9089 and 34-61175, 74 *Federal Register* 68334 (December 23, 2009).

[33] 17 CFR §229.402(b)(1).

post-employment payments and benefits. The information must be provided for each of the included executive officers and must include:

- salary and bonuses;
- the value of stock and stock options awarded;
- all value given under non-equity compensation plans;
- annual change in the present value of accumulated pension benefits;
- perquisites exceeding $10,000;
- agreed severance payments and golden parachutes; and
- the total value of compensation.[34]

The disclosure of equity interests must show, for each executive, the grant date, the estimated future payout, the number of shares or options to be paid out upon satisfaction of plan conditions, the strike prices, expiration dates and the fair value of all options.[35] The disclosure of pension benefits must show, for each executive, the number of years of service attributed to the plan and present value of accumulated benefits under the plan, as well as details of any arrangement that provides other payments or benefits at or following termination, a change in responsibilities, or a change in control of the company.[36]

2. Introduction of supervisory directors As discussed in earlier chapters, a major technique used to reduce self-dealing by corporate directors is to introduce supervisory directors into the board structure. Germany has always used this as a basic governance tool in the *Aktiengesetz* through its bifurcated management/supervisory board. US and UK securities exchanges began by recommending the presence of non-executive directors and then solidified this supervisory tool by introducing audit committees of directors who would both be independent and have financial expertise, which the US made mandatory for listed companies after the accounting scandals of the late 1990s.[37] The NYSE requires the creation of similarly composed "compensation" committees also,[38] as does the Nasdaq Stock Market.[39] Following the 2008 global financial crisis, new legislation was adopted to mandate such

---

[34] 17 CFR § 229.402(c).
[35] 17 CFR § 229.402(d), (f), (g).   [36] 17 CFR § 229.402(h), (j).
[37] See 15 USC 78j-1(m), 17 CFR § 240.10A-3.   [38] Para. 303A.05 NYSE LCM.
[39] CEO compensation must be approved *either* by a compensation committee *or* by a board, the majority of which is composed of independent directors. Rule 5605(d) Nasdaq Marketplace Rules.

compensation committees in financial institutions receiving aid just as Congress had done seven years earlier for audit committees.[40]

3. Shareholder say on compensation   The DGCL expressly gives directors broad power to set their own compensation unless otherwise provided in the certificate of incorporation.[41] Moreover, because pre-emption rights are the exception rather than the rule under US corporate law, and because the DGCL and the Model Act allow the certificate of incorporation to delegate authority to issue securities to the board of directors,[42] company law presents no shareholder approval requirement for the creation of an equity compensation plan. However, following the problems with earnings management in the 1990s, discussed above, US securities exchanges tightened their shareholder approval requirements for any arrangement that provides for the delivery of equity securities (whether stocks or options) to employees or directors. Currently, both the NYSE and the Nasdaq Stock Market require shareholder approval for either the creation or the material alteration of an equity compensation plan for management.[43]

Unlike UK law, neither the DGCL nor the Model Act requires shareholder approval of executive compensation packages. SEC regulations and securities exchange rules are no stricter. However, following the 2008 global financial crisis, legislation was adopted to give shareholders of companies receiving aid a non-binding vote on the compensation packages of the executives, subject to disclosure in the proxy statement, as discussed above.[44] This "say-on-pay" rule was expressly modeled on the UK rule adopted in 2002 and discussed below.

4. Accounting treatment of options   Another important brake on excessive equity compensation is the cost of such compensation to the company. Until 2004, US listed companies issuing options to employees could treat them for accounting purposes as issued at their "intrinsic

---

[40] See The American Recovery and Reinvestment Act of 2009, sec. 111(e), Pub. Law 111–5 (ARRA).

[41] See § 122(15), in connection with § 141(h).

[42] See e.g. § 151(a) DGCL.

[43] NYSE LCM, para. 303A.08, Shareholder Approval of Equity Compensation Plans, and para. 5635(c), Nasdaq Marketplace Rules.

[44] See ARRA sec. 111(e) and Final Rule: Shareholder Approval of Executive Compensation of TARP Recipients, SEC Release No. 34-61335, 75 Federal Register 2789 (Jan. 19, 2010).

value" (the difference between the strike price and the market price), which resulted in the options having a value of zero if issued at-the-money. Thus, a company would incur no expense at the time of issue, and, when the option was exercised, it would again incur no cash expense when issuing the new share, but would receive a tax deduction for the difference between the strike price and the current market value of the share. In addition, because an employee's shareholdings received from the company would not be diversified, she would apply a risk discount to the options (as opposed to cash compensation) received. Jensen, Murphy and Wruck remark that "[t]hese factors [made] the 'perceived cost' of an option to the company much lower than the economic cost, and often even lower than the value of the option to the employee. As a result, too many options [were] granted to too many people, and options with favourable accounting treatment [were] preferred to better incentive plans with less favourable accounting treatment."[45]

In 2002, the International Accounting Standards Board (IASB) proposed a single, fair-value-based method to account for all equity plans issuing options. In 2004, the Financial Accounting Standards Board (FASB) issued Statement 123(R), which required that options be accounted under a fair value method that takes into account: the strike price, the expected term of the option, the current market price of the stock, expected dividends on the underlying stock, its expected volatility, and the expected risk-free rate of return.[46] Reporting companies are thus now required to expense all options issued to employees at the fair value of the option, calculated in accordance with the guidance provided in FASB Statement 123(R).

B. Germany

1. Required disclosure of executive compensation German disclosure rules cover both listed and unlisted companies. Unlisted companies must disclose in their annual accounts the total compensation received by all members of their *Vorstand* and the *Aufsichtsrat*.[47] Unlike the US and UK rules, German law does not require disclosure of the policy and purposes of company compensation practices.[48] Like the other two legal systems, however, the HGB does require disclosure of the total of all elements of compensation, including cash salary, participation in the profits, all equity-based compensation, reimbursement of expenses,

---

[45] Jensen, Murphy and Wruck (2004: 39).   [46] Neuhausen, Kesner and Maffei (2006).
[47] § 285(9) HGB, as amended by the VorstOG.   [48] Langenbucher (2008: 31).

severance payments, insurances, fees, and perquisites of all kinds, as well as deferred compensation that has not yet been paid.[49] The exact number and grant date value of options must likewise be disclosed.[50] Listed companies must break down the compensation figures into straight salary and performance-linked elements, as well as any agreed severance payments and any payments rendered by third parties, for each member of the *Vorstand*.[51]

The German disclosure rules could perhaps have extra bite, given the statutory requirement that compensation be "appropriate" in relation to the tasks of the given board member and the condition of the company,[52] as well as the readiness of German prosecutors to initiate actions against management granting themselves what appear to be unearned or unreasonable sums, as shown in the *Mannesmann* case. The availability of a statutory measure and the presence of a will to take action lends the disclosure a utility not found in the US or the UK, where action is usually limited to venting frustration or at the most refusing to support a given director in the next corporate election.

2. Use of supervisory directors The basic structure of the *Aktiengesetz* employs supervisory directors as a key governance tool. The *Aufsichtsrat* represents the company for the negotiation of the *Vorstand* members' compensation agreements,[53] and the compensation of the *Aufsichtsrat* is set by the *Satzung* or by a shareholder resolution.[54] The *Aktiengesetz* expressly provides that the salaries of the *Vorstand* and the *Aufsichtsrat* must be "in appropriate proportion" to the board member's tasks and "the situation of the company," and the compensation of the *Vorstand* members of a listed company must create "long-term incentives for lasting business improvement."[55] The supervisory directors are required to reduce executive pay if a deterioration of the company's condition so advises.[56] The use of supervisory directors as already required by the basic statute has not been adjusted by the creation of smaller groups of supervisory directors, but has been strengthened by giving the *Aufsichtsrat* additional duties and power. In fact, recent legislation took decisions on management pay out of *Aufsichtsrat* committees and returned it to the entire board.[57]

---

[49] § 285 no. 9 lit. a HGB.   [50] § 285 no. 9 lit. a HGB.   [51] § 285 no. 9 lit. a HGB.
[52] § 87(1) AktG.   [53] § 112 AktG.   [54] § 113 AktG.
[55] § 87(1) AktG; with respect to the pay of supervisory directors, see § 113(1) AktG.
[56] § 87(2) AktG.   [57] § 107(3) AktG.

3. Shareholder say on compensation Like US law, the *Aktiengesetz* gives shareholders a vote only on equity compensation plans, and not on setting other forms of executive pay. A new § 120(4) AktG introduced by the VorstAG of 2009 gives shareholders a non-binding, advisory vote on the compensation of managing directors; since the resolution is not binding, the primary power of shareholders remains in connection with the approvals necessary for increasing capital and waiving preemption rights.

The shares used to service the equity compensation plan must be either created or repurchased, and, unlike the DGCL, the *Aktiengesetz* requires shareholder approval for both actions. As discussed in Chapter 9, every member of an AG has preemption rights to acquire new shares.[58] Preemption rights may be excluded in the resolution approving a capital increase or share repurchase.[59] As discussed in Chapter 6, an increase in conditional capital must be approved by three-quarters of the shares represented at the relevant meeting.[60] When conditional capital is used to stock an equity compensation plan, the resolution must also set out the agreed equity allocation and the holding period, for which the law sets a minimum of four years.[61] The increase in conditional capital for an option plan may not exceed one-tenth of the corporate capital.[62] Any repurchase of shares for an option plan must have the approval of a majority of the shareholders voting at a meeting, although such approval may be given up to five years before the actual repurchase.[63]

The two-tiered board structure brings with it different tasks and incentives for each set of directors. Members of the *Aufsichtsrat* are involved primarily in supervision rather than in the management of the company and its business operations. It is therefore understandable that the *Bundesgerichtshof* has held that recourse may be had neither to the creation of conditional capital nor to the repurchase of shares for the purpose of awarding members of the *Aufsichtsrat* stock options.[64]

4. Accounting treatment of options Pursuant to the IFRS Regulation, all listed companies incorporated under the law of a member state were required after January 2005 to prepare their consolidated financial statements according to International Accounting Standards (IAS).[65] In 2002, the IASB issued International Financial Reporting

---

[58] § 186(1) AktG.   [59] §§ 186(3), 71 no. 8 AktG.   [60] § 193 AktG.
[61] § 193(2) no. 4 AktG.   [62] § 192(3) AktG.   [63] § 71(1) no. 8 AktG.
[64] BGHZ 158, 122 (*Mobilcom*).   [65] Art. 4 IFRS Regulation.

Standard 2 on share-based payment, which requires a fair-value-based method – measured at the date of the grant or that of the services received – to account for all equity plans issuing options. For individual accounts, and for the accounts of unlisted companies, the instruction of § 285 no. 9, lit (a) HGB that companies should report stock options in the required management report discussed above at "their current value at the time of their grant" (*Zeitwert zum Zeitpunkt ihrer Gewährung*) has been interpreted to mean that German accounting principles require recording the option at the difference between the strike price and the market price on the day of the grant (as under the former US rule).[66] As discussed above, this would result in the options having no cost if they are issued at-the-money.

C.   United Kingdom

1.   Required disclosure of executive compensation   Both the Companies Act 2006 and the Listing Rules require listed companies to disclose executive remuneration. Since 2002, the boards of UK quoted companies have had to prepare a Directors' Remuneration Report (DRR) for each of the company's financial years.[67] Like the US rules that are to a certain extent modeled on it, the DRR is bifurcated, with one part presenting policy and purposes and the other stating the figures. One part of the DRR must give details on the composition of the remuneration committee, the performance criteria used, and how the granted remuneration relates to the conditions offered to employees and returns to shareholders.[68] In another, audited part, the DRR must set out figures for salary, bonuses, share options, severance payment and pension benefits.[69] The Listing Rules themselves contain a corresponding, somewhat more limited, set of disclosure requirements for executive compensation, which requires the annual report to shareholders to explain the company's remuneration policy and all components and time frames of remuneration.[70] These rules do not incorporate the Companies Act DRR requirements by reference, creating a certain amount of guesswork as to possible differences arising from divergences in phrasing. Given the skill with which the FSA carries EU norms into its own regulations with nearly verbatim phrasing – thereby eliminating uncertainty of meaning and scope – this duplication

---

[66] Lange, in *MünchKommHGB* (2001: § 285 mn. 157).

[67] Sec. 420 CA 2006; and Davies (2008: 385–389). The requirements for approving loans to directors, discussed in Chapter 12, are also of course relevant in this context.

[68] SI 2008 No. 410, Schedule 8, paras. 2–6.   [69] SI 2008 No. 410, Schedule 8, paras. 7–16.

[70] See FSA Listing Rules, Rule 9.8.8.

of rules is of questionable value, especially as both sets apply only to listed companies incorporated in the UK.[71]

Unlike the US rules, the information in the DRR and the annual report under the Listing Rules extends to every director on the board, rather than just to the five highest paid executives.[72] Like the US rules, the UK disclosure attempts to reveal the information members need about straight salary, equity compensation and pension benefits so as to evaluate whether executive remuneration is fair and honest. Both reports must provide details for each director of any long-term incentive schemes and of any entitlements or commitments made under such schemes during the year, with an indication of when they vest.[73] The specific terms of share options granted and the monetary value and number of shares, cash payments or other benefits also have to be provided, together with an explanation and justification of any element of a director's remuneration, other than basic salary, which is pensionable.[74] Details of payments made during the year or agreed to be made in the future upon a director's loss of office must also be disclosed.[75] Lastly, the DRR must contain a detailed breakdown of the value of pension schemes for each individual director.[76] As the DRR contains all of the information required by the annual report described in the Listing Rules and both must be made available in connection with notice to the annual meeting, the company may use one report for both purposes.

2. Introduction of supervisory directors UK law relies more on shareholder decision rights than on the use of supervisory directors. The Combined Code requires listed companies to create a remuneration committee composed of independent, non-executive directors.[77] As discussed at more length in the next chapter, however, compliance with the Code is on a "comply or explain" basis enforced by market reputation rather than strictly by law. If a remuneration committee is created, the Code instructs that it should be in charge of formulating executive remuneration.[78]

---

[71] FSA Listing Rules, Rule 9.8.8 together with Rule 9.8.6.
[72] SI 2008 No. 410, Schedule 8, para. 7(1); FSA Listing Rules, Rule 9.8.8(2)(a).
[73] SI 2008 No. 410, Schedule 8, para. 11; FSA Listing Rules, Rule 9.8.8(3)–(4).
[74] SI 2008 No. 410, Schedule 8, paras. 9–10; FSA Listing Rules, Rule 9.8.8(5)–(7).
[75] SI 2008 No. 410, Schedule 8, paras. 7(1)(d), 11(5)(b); FSA Listing Rules, Rule 9.8.8(2), (8) (if the payment exceeds one year's salary).
[76] SI 2008 No. 410, Schedule 8, paras. 13–14; FSA Listing Rules, Rule 9.8.8(11)–(12).
[77] Para. B.2.1 Combined Code.   [78] Para. B.2.2 Combined Code.

3. Shareholder say on compensation   Like the *Aktiengesetz*, the Companies Act 2006 incorporates the Second Company Law Directive, and thus the shareholders have preemption rights, which must usually be expressly waived before new shares may be freely distributed. However, unlike the *Aktiengesetz*, the Companies Act 2006 expressly strips preemption rights from shares used for "employees' share schemes."[79] The Act does not state that all employees be eligible for such schemes or expressly prevent such schemes from applying to executive employees.[80] Nevertheless, once this hurdle has been overcome, the capital maintenance requirements of the Second Directive as incorporated into UK law still apply, and this necessitates that any increase in capital or repurchase of shares be approved by the shareholders.[81] Further, the Act also expressly requires shareholder approval for terms of directors' service contracts that are or may be longer than two years.[82]

For listed companies, the FSA Listing Rules require shareholder approval of employees' share schemes and long-term incentive schemes that are not open to all company employees.[83] The shareholders of quoted companies also have an opportunity to approve or disapprove of the DRR by ordinary resolution,[84] although this vote merely expresses the position of the shareholders and does not have any effect on the company's payment obligations to the directors in question.[85]

4. Accounting treatment of options   As in Germany, UK listed companies are subject to the EU IFRS Regulation,[86] and thus IASB Standard 2 will apply to the consolidated accounts of such companies. Companies may prepare their individual accounts according to either IAS or the Companies Act.

Questions for discussion

1. What kinds of compensation are common?
2. How can executive compensation be a tool of corporate governance?

---

[79] Sec. 566 CA 2006.   [80] Sec. 1166 CA 2006.

[81] See secs. 551, 693 CA 2006. It should be remembered that share repurchases are also regulated as a possible source of market manipulation by the Market Abuse Directive and FSA Listing Rules, Rule 12.2.1.

[82] See sec. 188 CA 2006.   [83] See FSA Listing Rules, Rule 9.4.

[84] Sec. 439 CA 2006.   [85] Sec. 439(5) CA 2006.

[86] Sec. 395(1) CA 2006. Sec. 403 CA 2006 provides that "certain" (i.e. listed) companies must prepare group accounts pursuant to IAS.

3. Who sets the compensation of directors and officers under UK, US and German law?

4. Which country's rules best ameliorate the moral hazards connected with executive compensation?

5. What are the risks of using equity compensation and how can these risks be countered?

6. The controlling shareholders of X-Co, a Delaware corporation, would like to have a stock option compensation scheme adopted by X-Co as well as by X-Co's UK and German subsidiaries, Y-Co and Z-Co. Provide them with advice on:

   (a) how the scheme should be fashioned to create the appropriate incentives;

   (b) the disclosure rules regarding the plan; and

   (c) how the plan must be approved.

7. How do you reconcile a finding that, in the US, a pay package the size of Michael Ovitz is considered a good faith exercise of business judgment in the *Disney* case and, in Germany, a bonus to Klaus Esser provoked criminal charges for abuse of trust in the *Mannesmann* case?

Cases

In Re the Walt Disney Company Derivative Litigation
Court of Chancery of Delaware
907 A 2d 693 (2005)
[*Reprinted in part in Chapter 13*]

Mannesmann Criminal Litigation
High Federal Court, Third Criminal Division
December 21, 2005; Doc. No. 3 StR 470/04 / BGHSt 50, 331
[*Unofficial, partial translation of official text*]

I.

[Text omitted]

The Mannesmann AG against which Vodafone plc launched a hostile takeover in 2000 had traditionally been active in the heavy machinery, machine tool, and steel tubing sectors.[87] In 1990, Mannesmann acquired a license to operate Germany's first private mobile communications network. Subsequently, in partnership with the US company, AirTouch Inc., and accompanied by substantial capital investments, Mannesmann developed and built up the "D2" mobile communications network.

---

[87] This summary of facts is taken from a 2004 paper that Professor Theodor Baums delivered at Harvard University, entitled "The Mannesmann Case: A Study of Corporate Governance Practice in Germany." A copy of this paper is on file with the authors.

In the period between 1994 and 1998, during which the later defendant Joachim A. Funk served as chairman of the management board and the later defendant Klaus Esser served as CFO on the managing board of Mannesmann, the Company extended its geographical telecommunications markets both in Germany and in France, Italy, Austria and Great Britain on the basis of a Value Increase Process (VIP), which Esser had developed … During this period, the revenues of [Mannesmann's telecommunications subsidiary,] Mannesmann Mobilfunk GmbH were climbing at significant annual jumps from approximately €0.9 billion in 1994 to approximate figures of €1.4 billion (1995), €2.1 billion (1996), €2.9 billion (1997), and €3.7 billion (1998). Annual profits similarly skyrocketed from about €104 million in 1994 to approximate figures of €218 million (1995), €330 million (1996), €515 million (1997) and €719 million (1998). In 1995, Mannesmann Mobilfunk GmbH employed a total of 3,438 persons; this climbed to 4,213 (1996), 5,401 (1997), and 6,711 (1997).

The annual profits of Mannesmann AG were also climbing. They rose from about €174 million in 1994 to approximate figures of €358 million (1995), €308 million (1996), €312 million (1997), and €620 million (1998). The financial statements for fiscal 1998 showed revenues of approximately €19 billion and profits from ordinary operations of about €1.3 billion. EBITDA for the same year was about €3.1 billion, and Mannesmann AG employed a total of 16,247 persons.

2.   The governance structure of Mannesmann AG

The Mannesmann supervisory board had established a special committee, referred to as the "*Präsidium*." One of the committee's tasks was to set the compensation of the management board members. During the period of time that is relevant for our discussion, the Präsidium was composed of the following persons:

- Joachim A. Funk, chairman of the supervisory board and former CEO of Mannesmann AG;
- Josef Ackermann, shareholder representative in the supervisory board and member of the management board (today, the CEO) of Deutsche Bank AG;
- Jürgen Ladberg, employee representative in the supervisory board of Mannesmann AG and chairman of the shop council for the Mannesmann Group;
- Klaus Zwickel, representative of the labor union, Industriegewerkschaft IG Metall (of which he was the chairman), in the supervisory board of Mannesmann AG.

3.   Business developments in 1999; acquisition of the
mobile communications company, Orange plc

Mannesmann continued to expand its telecommunications activities in 1999 under the leadership of later defendant Klaus Esser, who was appointed chairman of the management board on May 28 of that year. The Company's holdings in Omnitel and

Mannesmann Arcor were increased, the Italian fixed network company Infrostrada [in which Mannesmann previously acquired a holding], was completely taken over, and the fixed network companies o.tel.o and ISIS were acquired ...

4. The exchange capitalization of Mannesmann AG between 1994 and February 2000

The development of Mannesmann AG's stock exchange value was to play an important role in the defense's argument. In 1994 and 1995, the exchange capitalization of Mannesmann AG stayed in the range of about €7.5 billion. When Esser replaced Funk as chairman of the management board on May 28, 1999, the exchange capitalization was about €50 billion. In November 1999, it was at €75 billion, and in February 2000 it had nearly doubled to €146 billion.

In total, the price of Mannesmann stock increased from the beginning of 1998 until the end of February 2000 by 600%. During the same period, the European stock index EuroStoxx 50 increased by 100% and the German stock index DAX 30 climbed by 80%. Those of Mannesmann's competitors which also expanded into telecommunications activity in the mid-1990s ... experienced only a 30–40% increase in share price during the same period. In comparison to the four, leading telecommunications companies on the Continent, Mannesmann AG achieved significantly better share price performance between September 1999 and the end of February 2000.

II.   Vodafone plc's takeover of Mannesmann AG

1.   The tender offer and first phase of defense until February 1st, 2000

On November 14, 1999, Vodafone CEO Sir Christopher Gent met with Mannesmann CEO Klaus Esser. At that meeting, Gent gave Esser a written exchange offer for merging Mannesmann AG into Vodafone plc, with each Mannesmann share being exchanged for 43.7 shares of Vodafone. On the basis of the then current stock exchange quotations, this offer gave each Mannesmann share a value of about €203. The Mannesmann stockholders would own about 42% of the resulting company. Gent also offered Esser the position of CEO or Co-CEO in the resulting company. Esser rejected both the job offer and the exchange offer.

Next, on November 19, 1999, Vodafone formulated an exchange offer directly to the stockholders of Mannesmann AG, with an exchange ratio of 53.7 Vodafone shares for each Mannesmann share, thus valuing each Mannesmann share at €240 on the basis of the then current market quotations ...

The management board of Mannesmann AG concluded that this offer was also too low and thus unattractive for the stockholders. It advised that, given the market value of Mannesmann shares, an offer would have to be around €260–300 per share to be seriously considered. The supervisory board, in which the future defendants Joachim A. Funk, Klaus Zwickel, Jürgen Ladberg and Josef Ackermann sat, supported this position.

Thus the Mannesmann management board then began a media-oriented defensive battle under the leadership of CEO Klaus Esser ...

Esser kept the supervisory board regularly updated on the Company's defense concept and on the specific defensive measures being taken, as well as on the institutional investors' opinions regarding the offer. The management board's position, which the supervisory board condoned, was also supported by a valuation of Mannesmann shares prepared by Merrill Lynch and Morgan Stanley. This valuation, which was reported to the supervisory board, advised rejecting the offer by arriving at a per share value of between €220 and 260 for each Mannesmann share, and thus an appropriate exchange ratio of 1:63.

At the close of January 2000, the majority of Mannesmann's shareholders still declined to tender into the Vodafone exchange offer. At that point in time, shares constituting only about 4.6% of the share capital of Mannesmann AG had been tendered; the vast majority of the investors contacted had voiced support for Mannesmann AG's strategic concept. Since publication of the offer, the price of Vodafone shares had experienced a marked drop, and those of Mannesmann a significant gain ...

... Esser telephoned Gent in the afternoon of February 2 and attempted to get an improvement in the exchange ratio and the position of Mannesmann stockholders in a merged enterprise. Gent ... explained that the negotiating authority delegated to him by the Vodafone Board only allowed him to go up to a maximum holding of 49.5% for the Mannesmann stockholders ... An exchange ratio of 58.96 Vodafone shares for each Mannesmann share was agreed upon and a holding structure of 50.5% for Vodafone stockholders and 49.5% for Mannesmann stockholders became the goal. In addition, Esser insisted that Gent's concessions of the day before should still be considered binding. He asked Gent to come to Düsseldorf, to which Gent agreed after receiving assurances that he would not be wasting his time on pointless negotiations. Esser was confident that he could convince the management board to accept the agreements the two had reached.

On the evening of February 2, Klaus Esser met with Mr. Fok, the representative of Hutchinson Whampoa Ltd [a major shareholder of Mannesmann]; Fok assumed that Esser would lose his position on the board. Fok thought that Esser had done a great job for Mannesmann AG and that he really should be compensated for it with stock options, but lacking that, Fok recommended that as compensation Esser be granted a £10 million bonus, which Hutchinson Whampoa Ltd would pay. In suggesting this figure, he oriented himself on the payments that had been made in the takeover of Orange plc ...

Following this conversation, Fok spoke with Gent. Fok asked whether it was true that nothing more could be done for the Mannesmann stockholders than that which Esser had reported. Gent assured him that what Esser had been told was absolutely the limit. Fok then conveyed his suggestion regarding the bonus and sought Vodafone's approval. Gent explained that Vodafone would like to heal the wounds caused by the takeover battle. He said that he would submit Fok's recommendation to the Vodafone board of directors and that if Mannesmann AG approved a resolution granting bonuses, he would support it by seeking the consent of the Vodafone board. Vodafone itself saw no reason to award such bonuses ...

3. February 3rd and 4th, 2000: Mannesmann AG's supervisory board approves a friendly takeover

On February 3rd, Mr. Fok met with the chairman of the supervisory board, Joachim Funk, to explain his suggestion regarding bonuses. He recommended paying the bonuses he had discussed with Esser to CEO Esser and his team in recognition of their services to the shareholders. He mentioned a figure of £10 million for each bonus. He asked Joachim Funk to arrange for approval of his suggestion by the competent bodies within Mannesmann AG. At the same time, Sir Christopher Gent and Klaus Esser signed an "agreement" dated February 3, 2000, in which Mannesmann AG agreed to recommend to its stockholders that they accept Vodafone plc's tender offer. This was immediately communicated to the media.

On February 4th, Mannesmann AG's supervisory board held a meeting at which the chairman informed the other members of the agreement concluded with Vodafone the day before and the contents thereof. The Term Sheet was submitted to the supervisory board. The supervisory board resolved to approve the merger with Vodafone on the basis of the terms contained therein and expressed its agreement with the recommendations of the management board. Mr. Fok's suggestion that bonuses be paid was not discussed in the meeting. However, the structural changes to the Mannesmann management board were discussed: its chairman, Klaus Esser, explained that he would resign from the management board with effect as from July 31, 2000 ...

When Vodafone's offer expired on March 27 after having been once extended, Mannesmann's stockholders had exchanged 97.96% of the Company's share capital for Vodafone shares. This included the Mannesmann stock previously held by Hutchison Whampoa Ltd, a large block of which had been sold earlier in March. The high point of 98.66% was reached on March 29. The remaining Mannesmann stockholders chose not to tender, and were bought out with appraisal right payments of €228 per share in 2002. Vodafone had become the sole shareholder of Mannesmann AG, which then became Vodafone AG. The stock corporation was later reorganized into a limited liability company (Gesellschaft mit beschränkter Haftung) and its name was changed to "Vodafone Holding GmbH." The sole shareholder became Vodafone.

Vodafone bore transaction costs of €180 billion for the takeover of Mannesmann AG. The last agreed exchange ratio of 1:58.96 valued each Mannesmann share at about €360 on the basis of the closing quotation of February 3. This was €125 per share higher than the previous offer and in total about €63 billion higher than the offer made in November of 1999 …

On February 4th, only Joachim Funk and Josef Ackermann attended the Präsidium meeting in person. At the outset, Funk informed Ackermann that Fok had recommended giving a £10 million appreciation award to Esser in recognition of the enormous increase in the Company's value that his efforts had brought about, and that Esser had explained to Fok that he could only accept such an award if it came from his employer. Funk recounted that Vodafone thought an appreciation award for Esser would be a good idea.

Within a few minutes, Funk and Ackermann agreed upon awarding the recommended bonus. Funk supported granting the appreciation award in light of what he considered to be the outstanding success story of Mannesmann AG, the Company's market capitalization, its financial condition, and the value of Mannesmann shares, as well as the performance of Esser in the takeover battle …

In the minutes of the resolution of February 4th, 2000 that Esser prepared at the request of Funk, Point 4 stated: "Dr. Esser shall, at the request of the major shareholder, Hutchison Whampoa, and following an agreement reached between Hutchison and Vodafone, be paid an appreciation award of GB£10 million. The committee for management board affairs consents. The appreciation award shall be paid when Vodafone acquires a majority of the shares." …

On March 7th, 2000 the Düsseldorf federal attorney's office informed Mannesmann AG that a criminal complaint had been filed against Klaus Esser and others. The complaint was filed by an attorney located in southern Germany whose practice focused on small and medium-sized companies. In such "Mittelstand" companies there had been a considerable amount of bitterness about the high severance payments that officers granted to the managers of listed companies …

On March 28th, Mannesmann AG transferred a Deutsche Mark countervalue of £10 million to Klaus Esser.

Esser left the Company earlier than planned … Esser was paid (in addition to the appreciation award) a severance payment of DM 29,151,933.17 for the premature termination of his contract … The components of his compensation were his annual salary of DM 1.4 million for "all activities performed for the Mannesmann Group," an annual performance bonus TOPP-200, a Medium Term Performance Bonus, and the Mannesmann shares transferred to him on January 15, 1999, which had a market value of 25% of his annual salary. The annual bonus TOPP-200 was calculated according to the contract on the basis of the target components of budget (yield and earnings per share), growth (yield and earnings per share) and VIP-Milestones …

[In 2001, in exchange for a lump sum payment of €2 million, Esser renounced his claim against Vodafone to receive lifetime use of a secretary, office, and chauffeured company car.]

Official head note from the criminal proceedings

1) It constitutes damage to entrusted corporate assets, which violates the duty of loyalty for the supervisory board of a stock corporation, to approve, after-the-fact, payment to a management board member of a sum not previously foreseen in the relevant service contract for an act that in any case had to be performed under such contract and had already been performed, when the payment has exclusively the character of a reward and brings the corporation no future benefit (uncompensated appreciation awards – *kompensationslose Anerkennungsprämie*).

2) For a failure to manage entrusted assets to constitute a breach of the duty of loyalty it shall not also be necessary, including in the case of a management body's business judgment, that the act be "aggravating" (clarification of decision BGHSt 47, 148 und 187).

[Text omitted]

33. The opinion of the [lower] criminal court cannot be followed to the extent that it states that, in the context of business judgments involving risk, a finding of breach of trust requires the additional element of an "aggravated" breach of duty, which here must be evaluated taking into account the overall picture, particularly the healthy state of the profits and assets of Mannesmann AG, the preservation of transparency within the company, and that the members of the executive committee (*Präsidium*) were duly informed of the facts necessary for their decision, as well as the absence of impermissible motives.

[Text omitted]

38. Defendants Prof. Dr. Funk, Dr. Ackermann and Mr. Zwickel were not presented with a business judgment involving risk as described by the lower court when they resolved to grant appreciation awards for the Defendant Dr. Esser and the four other members of the management board. The granting of the awards had – as explained above – an exclusively negative impact on the assets of Mannesmann AG that had been given into their trust. No foreseeable advantage, even if unintended, could have been hoped for the company under the circumstances presented in this case. The executive committee (*Präsidium*) thus had no room for free judgment. For a case of this type, it is certain – even in light of the decision of the First Criminal Division [cited by the lower court to support its holding] – that a manager can violate his duty to care for entrusted assets pursuant to § 266(1) of the Criminal Code without an "aggravating" violation of duty having the slightest significance (see also BGH, decision of November 22, 2005, 1 StR 571/04).

15

Directors' duties in listed companies

Required reading

1. Directors' transactions with the company

D: *Kodex*, paras. 4, 5
UK: FSA Listing Rules, Rule 11
US: Securities Exchange Act of 1934, § 13(k); Regulation S-K, Items 402–404

2. Composition of the board: audit committees and independent directors

D: *Kodex*, para. 5.3.2
UK: Combined Code, A.3, D.2–D.3
US: Exchange Act, §§ 3(a)(58) and 10A(m); SEC Release on "Standards Relating to Listed Company Audit Committees," pp. 18790–18796

3. Directors' dealings in the company's securities

D: WpHG, § 15a
UK: FSA Listing Rules, Rule 9, Annex, 4–11
US: Exchange Act, § 16

4. Prohibiting insider dealing

EU: Market Abuse Directive
D: WpHG, §§ 12–14, 21–29
UK: FSA Disclosure and Transparency Rules, Rule 2; Criminal Justice Act 1993, secs. 52–64
US: Exchange Act, §§ 10(b), 14(e); Rules 10b-5, 10b5-1, 14e-3

Why regulation changes for listed companies

I.   What it means to "list" on a securities exchange

When a company places its securities for sale on an organized market, this is often referred to as an "initial public *offering*" (IPO), but the term is incomplete. An IPO is a public offering of the company's stock, but a listing on a securities exchange is a separate matter. The two go together because a *primary* offering of shares to the public is made much more attractive by the availability of a *secondary* market for those shares. One purpose of a securities exchange is to provide such a secondary market. In German, the distinction is clearer, as one speaks of a *Börseneinführung* ("insertion into the stock exchange") when the stock will be listed, and an *öffentliches Angebot* (literally, "public offering") when the stock will just be sold publicly because it will not be listed or is already listed. Thus, a company can list without offering (where a security is already sufficiently widely held) and offer without listing (such as might be done for bonds offered to institutional investors). Although, in each of our jurisdictions, offering entails preparation and publication of a disclosure document, it is in the vast majority of cases listing that forces a company to adopt governance standards that exceed those required for an unlisted public company. Here we will look at those standards. Before doing so, however, a brief look at how a securities exchange facilitates a market in stock will explain why listing requires a company to introduce stricter (or at least more rule-based) governance.

Imagine that you are walking through a parking lot near the train station one evening and a cloaked figure approaches you with an offer to sell you a piece of cheese – or rather a certificate that will give you a claim to 500 grams of this victual at another time and place – for only €5.27. Not only is the quality of the product unknown, but the connection between the certificate and the actual product is uncertain. Would it be reasonable to accept the offer? Now imagine that the next morning you are shopping in your local market, which is divided into individual stalls (for meat, cheese, fruit, etc.), each owned by a different entrepreneur, but all operating within a single market building that has been called the "Never Yucky or Spoiled Emporium" (or "NYSE") for the last 200 years. At a sales counter that – like all the others – is clean, well-lit and offers a good view of the wares, you see some cheese for €10.54 per kilogram placed behind a neatly printed card providing its name, origin and ingredients as well as briefly describing how it is made. Upon your inquiry, the vendor says the displayed piece is already sold, but she can offer you a "rain check" (a certificate) giving you a guaranteed claim on 500 grams from tomorrow's shipment from Provence for only €5.27. How does this differ from your parking lot encounter of the previous evening?

Aside from a better frame of expectation (you entered the market to shop), the main differences are *transparency* (information makes your decision less uncertain), *reputation* (which lends the information reliability and gives a positive spin to your assembly of the details) and *legal recourse* (you know where to find the originator of the certificate) in the case of non-delivery. Indeed, your neighborhood market hall, the "NYSE," offers the same advantages as a securities exchange. In addition to the crucial concentration of buyers and sellers in a market, which creates liquidity, listing on a securities exchange takes a company's stock from being an unknown commodity sold by an opaque neighborhood local to being a transparent product among other products of good reputation and reliability, with performance enforceable by law.[1] This is the transition that a company must make when embarking on an IPO. The process divides functionally into three parts:

- *Issuing the stock*. Because the existing shareholders will either not own enough stock for the offering or not want to sell all their stock, the company must increase its capital and issue the new shares.
- *The offering triggers investor protection rules*. As for other public sales of merchandise, the law requires that investors be given certain information about the shares and that the information be correct and complete, which means drafting a prospectus and conducting a due diligence investigation of the issuer.
- *The market has its rules*. Securities exchanges and regulatory authorities require listed companies to conform to specific standards of governance, transparency, and use of inside information designed to protect investors and uphold the market's reputation.

In Chapter 6, we saw the rules for increasing capital and issuing new shares. For this text, an analysis of the *primary market* rules connected with the one-time event of writing an offering prospectus and regulating disclosure during the offering period would take us too far afield from our topic. Here we will concentrate on the regularly applicable corporate governance duties with which directors must comply as soon as the shares of the company are listed. Many of the duties found in these rules

---

[1] On the roles played by a securities exchange, see Schwartz and Francioni (2004: 1–29).

could be derived from standards already applicable under the corporate statutes. The rules have the advantage of offering more concrete, definite and predictable supplements to the standards applied to all company directors. These rules greatly increase the amount of available information, reduce the costs of monitoring directors' behavior, advertise to investors the rights they enjoy and facilitate enforcement of such rights.

II.   Listing triggers application of the market's rules

A.   Securities law

For the UK and Germany, listing securities on a regulated market will trigger application of separate rules focusing on disclosure and prevention of related-party transactions. We have discussed these rules in various contexts in earlier chapters. This section summarizes them to make clear the changes that listing brings. The Transparency Directive, the Market Abuse Directive and the Takeover Directive all apply only to companies whose securities are listed on a regulated market. In the UK, the bulk of these regulations are found in the FSA's Disclosure and Transparency Rules (DTRs) and the Takeover Code, although some are found in the Companies Act 2006 and the Criminal Justice Act 1993. In Germany, similar rules are found in the Securities Trading Act (WpHG), the Exchange Act (BörsenG) and the Takeover Act (WpÜG). The *Aktiengesetz* also contains a number of provisions applicable only to listed companies.

The application of the US securities laws is not tied to listing on an exchange, but rather to the company and the mass of its free float of shares reaching a particular dimension. Companies with total assets of at least $10 million and at least 500 shareholders must register with the SEC and become subject to the securities laws,[2] particularly the Exchange Act and the rules issued under that Act. Rules against insider trading and other forms of security fraud, however, apply to all companies, regardless of size and listing.

B.   Exchange rules

Exchange rules are contractual in nature and apply by virtue of the company entering into a listing agreement. They only apply to those companies listed on the relevant exchange. In the UK, the rules also bring with them two codes of best practices, the Combined Code and the Model Code, with which a company should comply.

---

[2] § 12(g) Exchange Act, in connection with Exchange Act Rule 12g-1, 17 CFR § 240.12g-1.

C.   Corporate governance codes

Germany has followed the UK in supplementing its exchange rules with a corporate governance code. As mentioned above, the FSA Listing Rules require companies to comply with the Combined Code or explain in their annual financial report why it chose not to so comply,[3] and to regulate any dealings of their directors in the company's securities with rules at least as strict as those in the Model Code.[4] Like the Combined Code, the German Corporate Governance Code (*Kodex*) is not mandatory *per se*. The *Aktiengesetz* requires the *Vorstand* and the *Aufsichtsrat* of listed companies to declare on an annual basis whether they comply with the Code, and, if they do not, to state the extent of and reasons for such non-compliance.[5] Both the Combined Code and the *Kodex* change the composition of the board of directors, something which the US has done primarily through exchange rules, recently enforced by the Sarbanes–Oxley Act and SEC rules.

In the following sections of this chapter we will examine specific areas in which the duties of directors become subject to more detailed rules when the company's shares are listed or, in the US, registered with the SEC. As Chapters 24 and 25 are specifically dedicated to takeovers, this chapter will not address the takeover rules, even though they do create duties for directors and are triggered by a listing or regulatory registration.

III.   Rules on directors' transactions with the company

In Chapter 12, we saw how transactions between directors and their companies entail conflicts of interest and create opportunities for breaches of fiduciary duty, as the director might well place her own interest before that of the company. We saw that Delaware regulates these transactions quite generally, relying on disinterested directors to approve any conflicted transaction, that Germany is somewhat more formal, requiring specific supervisory board approval for transactions such as compensation and loans, and that the UK is by far the most formal, as the 2006 Act provides an extensive body of rules, each specifically dedicated to a certain type of conflicted transaction. The German framework remains substantially unchanged even after the company is listed. In the listed context, as explained in Chapter 14, the US federal rules begin to approach the UK model, but still remain significantly more general.

---

[3] FSA Listing Rules, Rule 9.8.6.   [4] FSA Listing Rules, Rule 9.2.7.
[5] § 161 AktG.

A. United States

When a company is listed, it may not make loans or provide any other form of credit to its directors or executive officers unless such loans are in the ordinary course of business (i.e. the corporation is a bank or finance company).[6] The remaining federal rules rely on disclosure. A company registered with the SEC must disclose in its annual report any transaction between the director or executive officer and the company exceeding $120,000 in value, and also disclose its policy and procedures for approving the consummation of such transactions.[7] As was discussed in detail in Chapter 14, the company's annual report must also contain a report on the compensation and share ownership of its directors and executive officers.[8] Further, the creation or significant change of any stock or stock option plan used to compensate directors or other employees must be approved by the shareholders.[9]

B. United Kingdom

The FSA Listing Rules build on the extensive body of rules in the Companies Act regarding transactions between directors and the company, and apply only to companies with their primary listing in the UK,[10] which would usually be UK-incorporated companies.

The level of codification found in these UK rules is remarkable, and would leave very little discretion in their application. The rules extend the definition of related party to include persons who were directors (shadow directors) during the twelve months preceding the transaction and include subsidiaries of the director's company in the rule.[11] They do not apply to transactions "of a revenue nature in the ordinary course of business,"[12] to "small transactions" or to transactions that do not have "any unusual features."[13] The latter two concepts are defined in an Annex entitled "Transactions to which related-party transaction rules do not apply," and this document provides exact numerical ratios to define "small" transactions and a detailed list of transactions that are not "unusual."[14] If the rules do apply, the company must notify the public of the transaction, provide shareholders with a circular with all necessary

---

[6] 15 USC § 78m(k) (2000).   [7] 17 CFR § 229.404.   [8] 17 CFR § 229.402–403.
[9] Para. 303A.08 NYSE LCM; para. 5635(c) Nasdaq Marketplace Rules.
[10] FSA Listing Rules, Rule 11.1.1.   [11] FSA Listing Rules, Rules 11.1.3–11.1.4.
[12] FSA Listing Rules, Rule 11.1.5.   [13] FSA Listing Rules, Rule 11.1.5A.
[14] FSA Listing Rules, Rule 11, Annex 1R.

information on it, and obtain shareholder approval.[15] The rules also provide an approval process for what is referred to as "small*er*" (as opposed to exempted "small") transactions, with "percentage ratios" less than 5 percent, but where "one or more of the percentage ratios exceeds 0.25%."[16] For such "smaller" transactions a company need only inform the FSA, obtain the opinion of an independent adviser on the terms, and provide information on the transaction in the next annual report.[17] The detail provided in these UK rules would seem to offer one of the clearest possible examples of "Civil Law" codification when compared to the general Common Law imperative that a director act in "good faith" in the "best interest of the company."

C.   Germany

As discussed in Chapter 3, the rules of the Frankfurt Stock Exchange do not contain extensive governance provisions, but the *Aktiengesetz* does require that listed companies either apply the governance *Kodex* or explain in their accounts why they do not. This Code, however, contains nothing like the codification of governance procedures found in the FSA rules. It merely repeats that managing directors must not compete with the company and that supervisory directors must act in the best interests of the company[18] – two fiduciary duties already found in the statute. The *Kodex* does require that the *Vorstand* disclose conflict transactions to the supervisory board and that members of the latter disclose conflicts to that body and to the general meeting.[19] "Important" conflicted transactions in the *Vorstand* must be approved by the *Aufsichtsrat*, but "important" is not defined, and the only other guidance on procedure is that approval of conflicted transactions in the *Vorstand* "must comply with standards customary in the sector."[20] The reason for this flexibility is not wholly clear. It may come from the German law's dependence on the two-tier board structure coupled with the fact that neither management nor the members may alter the structure set out in the *Aktiengesetz*. However, it is also possible that it reacts to the (incorrect) rumor spread in the market by relatively inexact comparative scholarship in the early 2000s that the UK and US markets owe their strength to flexible, judge-made standards and an absence of rigid rules.[21]

---

[15] FSA Listing Rules, Rule 11.1.7.   [16] FSA Listing Rules, Rule 11.1.10.
[17] FSA Listing Rules, Rule 11.1.10(2).   [18] Paras. 4.3.1 and 5.5.1 *Kodex*, respectively.
[19] Paras. 4.3.4, 5.5.2, 5.5.3 *Kodex*, respectively.   [20] Para. 4.3.4 *Kodex*.
[21] See Roe (2006: 462–466).

IV.   Inserting committees in the board

As the preceding section makes clear, a standard tool for sanitizing transactions in which a director has an interest conflicting with that of the company is to have a neutral, disinterested person make, or at least approve, the decision. If these neutral persons are other directors, there is the chance that they could be influenced or intimidated by the interested director, thus reducing the effectiveness of their supervisory function. Germany recognized and addressed this very early by inserting a two-tiered board in the *Aktiengesetz*. The UK and the US began in the 1970s to require a certain number of "independent" supervisory members on the board, later found it useful to group these people into separate commit-tees (audit, compensation and nomination or governance committees), and have progressed to insulating the committees from influence still more by requiring them to have separate charters and providing them with funds for separate legal counsel. This evolution looks like it is mov-ing in the direction of the German *Aufsichtsrat*, although the authors of the *Kodex* apparently disagree, as they recommend that the *Aufsichtsrat* of a listed company follow the US and UK model to contain an audit com-mittee, essentially placing a supervisory committee within a supervisory board. Currently, the rules on committees for listed companies in the three jurisdictions can be summarized as follows.

A.   United States

The Exchange Act requires every listed company to have an audit com-mittee composed entirely of independent directors.[22] "Independence" means, generally, an absence of significant employment, financial, shareholding and family relationships.[23] To this, the NYSE adds a nomination/corporate governance committee and a compensation com-mittee to deal with appointing directors and management as well as compensating them.[24] The Nasdaq Stock Market requires only an audit and, as discussed in Chapter 14, perhaps a compensation committee.[25] As the committees are composed of independent directors, have their own rules of procedure, meet without the managing directors and have access to separate advisors, the main power that separates them from the German *Aufsichtsrat* is the ability to appoint the managing directors, but

---

[22] 15 USC § 78j-1(m); 17 CFR § 240.10A-3.   [23] 17 CFR § 240.10A-3(b)(ii), (e).
[24] Paras. 303A.4, 303A.5 NYSE LCM.
[25] Para. 5605(c), (d)(1)(B) Nasdaq Marketplace Rules.

in the US they would (very much only in theory) influence such appointment through membership in the nominating committee.

B.   United Kingdom

The UK rules also take a significant step toward creating a supervisory
board. As mentioned above, the FSA Listing Rules, together with the
Combined Code,[26] require that a board contain a "balance of executive and non-executive directors,"[27] appointed according to a "formal,
rigorous and transparent procedure."[28] Each board should have an audit
committee composed of independent directors,[29] a remuneration committee, also composed entirely of independent directors,[30] and a nomination committee, a majority of whose members are independent and
non-executive.[31]

C.   Germany

Even for a small AG with one shareholder, a supervisory board will be
mandatory. As we have seen, pursuant to the *Aktiengesetz*, the supervisory board acts to reduce the danger of conflicts of interest between the
company and the *Vorstand* by representing the company in dealings with
the latter, reviewing decisions with the latter (such as in the formulation
of the accounts), and making the ultimate decision for the latter, such as
with respect to *Vorstand* remuneration. Of course, the *Aufsichtsrat* also
selects candidates for the *Vorstand* and appoints them. The *Aufsichtsrat* is
therefore an audit, nomination and compensation committee in itself. It
serves as the primary international model for a separate body of independent directors acting in a supervisory capacity over managing directors.

Nevertheless, the Code requires the *Aufsichtsrat* to set up an audit
committee within it to focus on accounting and risk management, and
to manage the appointment of the auditor.[32] The committee's chairman
should have specialized accounting knowledge and experience, and
should not be a former member of the *Vorstand*. The *Aufsichtsrat* should
also set up a nomination committee to propose candidates for supervisory directors; this could be an attempt to weaken co-determination, as,
instead of independence, it requires that the members are all shareholder

---

[26] See FSA Listing Rules, Rule 9.2.8.   [27] Para. A.3 Combined Code.
[28] Para. A.4 Combined Code.   [29] Para. C.3.1 Combined Code.
[30] Para. B.2.1 Combined Code.   [31] Para. A.4.1 Combined Code.
[32] Para. 5.3.2 *Kodex*. This is done despite the fact that shareholders, not managing directors,
have the right to appoint the company's auditor pursuant to § 119(1) no. 4 AktG.

appointees.[33] As observed above, it is too early to tell whether this recommended partition of the supervisory board indicates a defect in the original German structure or is a gesture to appease institutional investors steeped in US and UK rules and convinced of their necessity in all circumstances. Perhaps, if it becomes apparent that audit, nomination or compensation committees need to be further divided into sub-committees, this will indicate a defect in the partitioning technique itself, and a rational basis in the *Kodex*.

V. Prophylactic rules on directors' dealings

A. United States

We have often observed in this text that *ex ante* rules regulating a given transaction are introduced when it becomes clear that the transaction in question presents a high probability of resulting in a violation of standards, such as the fiduciary duties of directors. This process was evidenced in the legislative history of an early rule on directors' dealings. At the close of hearings that the US Congress held in the early 1930s to investigate the causes of the market crash of 1929, it was concluded that:

> Among the most vicious practices unearthed … was the flagrant betrayal of their fiduciary duties by directors and officers of corporations who used their positions of trust and the confidential information which came to them in such positions, to aid them in their market activities. Closely allied to this type of abuse was the unscrupulous employment of inside information by large stockholders who, while not directors and officers, exercised sufficient control over the destinies of their companies to enable them to acquire and profit by information not available to others.[34]

As a direct result, in 1934 the Congress enacted § 16 of the Exchange Act to regulate the dealings in a company's securities by every person "who is a director or an officer of the issuer of such security," and "every person who is directly or indirectly the beneficial owner of more than 10 percent of any class of any equity security." Section 16 applies only to companies that must be registered with the SEC, and requires insiders both to report their securities transactions to the SEC and to disgorge to the company any profits from purchases or sales of the company's securities made within a six-month period. Details on the manner of reporting ownership and paying profits over to the company are specified in Rules 16a and

---

[33] Para. 5.3.3 *Kodex*.   [34] Senate Report 1455, 73rd Congress, 2nd Session, p. 55 (1934).

16b issued under the Exchange Act.[35] Thus, § 16 combats possible insider trading with rules that *always* apply, regardless of whether the trade is abusive, and no specific inside information is necessary because it is based on the insider's *status*, not on the specific facts of a given case.

Under § 16(a), insiders must report their transactions in the company's shares to the SEC when they first acquire them or become an insider, when material changes take place in the holdings, and at the end of each year.[36] Under § 16(b), insiders must pay back to the company any profits (referred to as "short-swing profits") they earn on short-term, speculative dealings in the company's securities. Short term means a purchase and sale (or a sale and purchase) within any six-month period. Factual uncertainty can arise in connection with the definitions of purchase, sale and the six-month period. In cases presenting facts of a type that are clearly not what § 16 was designed to combat, such as the purchase of options in connection with a takeover battle and the sale of shares as a result of a merger following the takeover transaction, § 16(b) has been found not to apply.[37] For purposes of measuring the six-month period, the purchase or sale of an option (to purchase or sell a security) is equivalent to the purchase or sale of the security itself.[38] Also, Rule 16b-3 specifies certain acquisitions and dispositions of securities and options, occurring in connection with employee stock option plans, that are exempted from § 16.

For shareholder insiders, reaching the 10 percent threshold specified in § 16 triggers an obligation to report holdings in all types of the issuer's securities held, not just the class in which the 10 percent threshold was reached. Further, a concept of a shareholder "group" that can aggregate the holdings of any shareholders who actively work in a coordinated way toward changing the company's management could bring even small shareholders under the duties applicable to "insider," 10 percent holders, and thus burden them with insider restrictions simply for actively participating in the company's management. In addition, the court-made concept of "deputization" can result in a shareholder being deemed a director

---

[35] See 17 CFR §§ 240.16a-1–16b-8.

[36] See 17 CFR § 240.16a-3. For shareholders, these rules can overlap with requirements that a holder of more than 5 percent of a class of shares report such fact to the SEC. The latter requirement is found in § 13(d) Exchange Act and is part of legislation for the regulation of takeovers. Thus, requirements enacted for different purposes at different times (1934 and 1968) can create a dense net of regulatory requirements for the shareholders of a registered company.

[37] *Kern County Land Co.* v. *Occidental Petroleum Corp.*, 411 US 582 (1973).

[38] 17 CFR § 240.16b-6.

of the issuer if it elects a director to the board and has contact indicating the exercise of sufficient control over such person.

B. United Kingdom

The UK initially introduced restrictions on directors' dealings in the company's securities following recommendations of the 1945 Cohen Committee.[39] These requirements were most recently incorporated in sections 323 and 234 of the Companies Act 1985. In light of the EU Insider Dealing and Market Abuse Directive's requirements on the reporting of directors' dealings for listed companies,[40] Companies Act 2006 has repealed the former requirements,[41] and the FSA issued rules to monitor directors' dealings in connection with listed companies,[42] and requires compliance with the Model Code.[43]

The UK has very strong restrictions on directors' dealings. Instead of using the technique of forced disgorgement, the UK combines requirements for approval, straight bans on trading, and disclosure to dampen directors' appetites for insider dealing. The Model Code requires directors and executive officers to obtain approval for any dealing in the company's securities,[44] and the company must keep a record of all such dealings.[45] During the sixty days preceding release of the financial statements and at any other time at which the management is in possession of inside information, no manager or closely connected person may trade in the company's securities.[46] Beyond these requirements, managers must notify the company within four days after trading in the company's securities or derivatives based on them,[47] and the company must notify an authorized information service.[48]

C. Germany

Germany introduced its first rules on directors' dealings to implement the Market Abuse Directive. The relevant provision, § 15a WpHG, requires executive managers of listed companies to notify the company and BaFin within five days of their transactions in the company's shares or related derivatives exceeding in aggregate €5,000 (including if effected

---

[39] Davies (2008: 1085).   [40] Art. 6(4) Market Abuse Directive.
[41] Sec. 1177 CA 2006.   [42] FSA Disclosure and Transparency Rules, Rule 3.
[43] FSA Listing Rules, Rule 9.2.7.   [44] FSA Listing Rules, Rule 9; Model Code, 4(a)–(d).
[45] FSA Listing Rules, Rule 9; Model Code, 6.
[46] FSA Listing Rules, Rule 9; Model Code, 6 nos. 21, 22.
[47] FSA Disclosure and Transparency Rules, Rule 3.1.2.
[48] FSA Disclosure and Transparency Rules, Rule 3.1.4.

by a spouse or children). Companies must also compile and continuously update a list of persons who have access to inside information and file this list with BaFin.[49] As with directors' conflicted transactions, German law again offers the lightest regulation of our three jurisdictions. While the US forces disgorgements of short-swing profits and the UK sets up a strict combination of blackout periods and approvals, Germany has implemented the minimum requirement of the Market Abuse Directive, a simple disclosure to the regulator: "Persons discharging managerial responsibilities within an issuer of financial instruments ... shall, at least, notify to the competent authority."[50]

VI.   *The regulation of insider trading: from breach of fiduciary duties to market abuse*

When someone who has privileged access to confidential information regarding a company uses such information to her own advantage to buy or sell the company's securities, we speak of insider "trading" (US) or "dealing" (UK). This apparently clear-cut activity has generated a surprising amount of discussion and varieties of regulation. First of all, when considering those "insiders" who are company directors, the use of company information for personal gain would be a question of company law to be regulated by fiduciary duties or rules crafted to enforce such duties. However, if we consider that "trading" takes place in the public market for the company's securities, then the presence of certain traders with secret, unfair advantages presents a threat of market abuse that should be addressed through market regulation. Moreover, the basic components of the activity – insiders, non-public information, and trading – do not have precise and exclusive meanings. If we consider that the person who actually buys or sells the company's securities may not be the "insider" herself, but another person who may be anyone from a willing co-conspirator to a trader who has virtually no connection with the insider, we see that the group of persons we are trying to regulate becomes increasingly large. Also, we will remember that a great deal of the investment services industry is based on the hope that, through their skill and hard work, professionals can obtain better information than others regarding the value of market securities, and that these people do not always publicly announce their information. Should we condemn the activity of securities analysts as unfair insider trading? Beyond the localization of

---

[49] § 15b WpHG.   [50] Art. 6(4) Market Abuse Directive.

the problem in company law or in market regulation, a number of questions thus remain: Who are "insiders"? What is "inside" information? How should inside information be disclosed to the market? When should passing such information on be permitted, and when should trading on the basis of it be punishable? Further, the same issues arise that we have already discussed in Chapter 12: should we regulate the activity with a standard or a rule, and should any rule be primarily operative *ex ante* or *ex post*?

We saw in Chapter 12 that all of our jurisdictions ascribe fiduciary duties to directors to prevent them from acting to the detriment of the corporation. Under German law, both managing and supervisory directors have a duty of confidentiality and a duty to act in the company's interest rather than their own.[51] This would seem sufficient to prevent a director from both trading in the company's securities in such a way as to damage the corporation and tipping off a third party about confidential information that had not yet been made public (such as a decision to reduce or increase dividends). Although Delaware and UK law do not contain an express, statutory duty of confidentiality, they do require directors to act in the best interests of the company, which would prohibit them from both divulging confidential information in such a way as to damage the company and using their positions of trust to extract personal profits.[52] Indeed, the new Companies Act 2006 expressly prohibits directors from exploiting information belonging to the company.[53] Why do we need anything more than these duties to regulate insider trading?

One objection against understanding insider trading as a breach of duty is the argument that insider trading does not damage the company, but is a legitimate form of executive compensation that also helps introduce information into market prices in an extremely efficient manner.[54] This argument has generally been found to be without merit, and most scholars, regulators and judges are of the opinion that insider trading not only damages the reputation of the company and the integrity of the market, but is also a breach of fiduciary duties.[55] Another good reason

---

[51] §§ 93, 116 AktG; and the discussion in Chapter 12.

[52] See *Diamond* v. *Oreamuno*, 248 NE 2d 910 (NY App. 1969); *Regal (Hastings) Ltd* v. *Gulliver* [1967] 2 AC 134; [1942] 1 All ER 378, reprinted in part in Chapter 4.

[53] Sec. 175(2) CA 2006.   [54] See, in particular, Manne (1966).

[55] Loss, Seligman and Parades (2004: 923 *et seq.*). The EU Insider Dealing and Market Abuse Directive declares in its 15th Recital: "Insider dealing and market manipulation prevent full and proper market transparency, which is a prerequisite for trading for all economic actors in integrated financial markets." Market Abuse Directive, OJ 2003 L96/16, at 17.

for special capital market rules is that the procedural and informational hurdles in a derivative action or other available judicial procedure under company law to proving that a director used inside information in a way that breached a duty of loyalty are simply too high to make the remedy a practical deterrent against insider trading.[56] Thus, when the United States introduced securities legislation in the early 1930s, it adopted the first prophylactic rules against insider trading. The United Kingdom followed suit in the 1940s, and, after the adoption of the first EC Insider Trading Directive in 1989,[57] Germany enacted rules against insider trading in 1994. Rules against insider trading generally take two forms, prophylactic rules regulating all dealing by insiders in the company's securities and rapid disclosure of significant information, and rules specifically targeted toward prohibiting the use of inside information as a basis for trading in the company's securities.

A.   Required, rapid disclosure of material events

The other side of the coin for regulating transactions by insiders on the basis of unpublished information is to require that material information be published as soon as possible. If information is not allowed to accumulate "inside" the company, the informational asymmetry between insiders and outsiders, which can give insiders an advantage when trading in the company's shares, is eliminated. All of our jurisdictions require listed companies promptly to publish most information that could affect the market value of their shares unless the interests of the company require otherwise. The US requires that current reports be filed with the SEC on Form 8-K within four business days of the occurrence of any of the material events listed on that form, but does not require all such information to be disclosed.[58] Germany requires that inside information as defined in the Securities Trading Act – which includes all matters a reasonable shareholder would take into account when making an investment decision – be published promptly (*unverzüglich*).[59] The FSA's Listing Rules require that a company notify the FSA or other regulatory body as soon as possible upon

---

[56] Loss, Seligman and Paredes (2004: 927 *et seq.*); Davies (2008: 1088–1092).

[57] Council Directive 89/592/EEC of 13 November 1989 coordinating regulations on insider dealing, OJ 1989 L334/30.

[58] 17 CFR § 240.13a-11 and § 249.308. Events include such matters as entry into bankruptcy, acquisitions or disposals of assets, changes in financial condition, and the conclusion or termination of major contracts, among others. Stock exchange rules, however, require disclosure of all material information. See e.g. NYSE LCM, para. 202.05.

[59] § 15(1) WpHG.

the occurrence of a number of specified events that could affect the company's share price,[60] and disclose any inside information.[61] These rules all ensure that, unless a good reason for keeping information confidential exists – such as ongoing negotiations regarding a merger or planned takeover – inside information is eliminated promptly through disclosure to the market. Further rules, such as those in the US Regulation FD and in article 6 of the Insider Dealing and Market Abuse Directive, then work to ensure that disclosure is not selectively made to favored market professionals, but to the market as a whole.[62]

B. Regulating the use of inside information

Because insider trading or dealing is an economic phenomenon that presents the same characteristics regardless of the jurisdiction in which it occurs, the regulatory frameworks of each of our jurisdictions face a nearly identical problem. As discussed above, the problem begins in the sphere of company law and ends in the market for the company's securities. The path that the act takes from the inside to the market can pass through any number of persons.

One major difference in the rules of our three jurisdictions is that about fifty years of market development separate the creation of rules in the US (1942) and the EC (1989, 2003). The first US rule was adopted almost casually to address a single complaint of fraud from the SEC's Boston office,[63] and then a large body of judicial doctrine grew out of it as courts interpreted its application over the decades. The EU rules were enacted as part of a systematic harmonization program following both the US experience and an extensive academic debate on the market impact of insider trading; they focus less on fraud and more on preserving the integrity of the market. This makes the rational basis of the EU rules in theories of efficient markets much clearer, and the capillary network of the US judicial rules rather opaque but very sensitive to certain practical nuances of information flows in the market.

1. The United States The basic US rule against insider trading, Rule 10b-5 under the Exchange Act, was adopted in 1942 under the statutory prohibition of fraudulent behavior in § 10(b) of the Exchange Act, and was followed in 2000 by Rules 10b5-1 and 10b5-2, which greatly codify the case law that developed on the basis of the original rule. Rule 10b-5

---

[60] FSA Listing Rules, Chapter 9.6. [61] FSA Disclosure and Transparency Rule 2.2.1.
[62] See 17 CFR Part 243; and Insider Dealing and Market Abuse Directive, art. 6(3).
[63] Loss, Seligman and Parades (2004: 937 *et seq.*).

makes it illegal to engage in fraud, deceit or misrepresentation in connection with the purchase or sale of any security, even if unlisted and sold "face-to-face" in personal dealings between two persons, and thus does not focus specifically on insider trading, but covers all forms of securities fraud.

Rule 10b5-1 incorporates the insider trading doctrine under Rule 10b-5 and prohibits "the purchase or sale of a security of any issuer, on the basis of material nonpublic information about that security or issuer, in breach of a duty of trust or confidence that is owed directly, indirectly, or derivatively, to the issuer of that security or the shareholders of that issuer, or to any other person who is the source of the material nonpublic information."[64] The "duty of trust or confidence" language is a key point in the rule, and follows court decisions that attempted to distinguish between desirable and undesirable flows of information between the inside of a company and the market.[65] In addition to directors and officers, who are subject to fiduciary duties of loyalty under company law, and to those persons who have specifically been named in decisions like *Dirks* v. *SEC* – such as attorneys, accountants and underwriters – because they have a position of confidence *vis-à-vis* the corporation, Rule 10b5-2 defines the relationships that create a "duty of trust or confidence" to include:

- persons who agree to maintain information in confidence;
- relationships between persons having a history, pattern or practice of sharing confidences, such that the recipient reasonably should know that the person communicating the information expects that it will remain confidential; or

---

[64] 17 CFR § 240.10b5-1(a). Mere awareness of the relevant information at the time of the purchase or sale is considered to be an act "on the basis of" such information unless the defendant had entered into a binding agreement to sell prior to gaining such knowledge. See 17 CFR § 240.10b5-1(c).

[65] For example, in *Dirks* v. *SEC*, 463 US 646 (1983), a securities analyst named Dirks investigated allegations of fraud at a company and discussed his investigation with others as it progressed. Before he had concluded and published his results, persons with whom he had discussed his results sold shares of the company. The SEC charged Dirks with insider trading and a lower court agreed. The Supreme Court reversed, finding that such prosecutions would inhibit the desirable work of securities analysts, and decided that only persons who improperly violate a position of trust to the company by divulging inside information to others who then trade (referred to as "tipping") can be prosecuted under Rule 10b-5. Such persons include not only directors, but also persons such as attorneys, accountants and underwriters who occupy a position of trust. See *Dirks* v. *SEC*, 463 US 646, 655 note 14 (1983).

- the receipt of material non-public information from a spouse, parent, child or sibling.

This test for deciding whether an outsider who uses inside information to trade in the company's securities has broken the law is referred to as the "misappropriation theory."[66] Applying this test, should directors expect a securities analyst conducting an interview to keep information regarding a board decision not to pay dividends confidential? What if a director were to disclose the information to someone in a position of relative confidence, but not protected by professional privilege, like a golf, yoga or tai chi instructor? Should such an instructor know that disclosure would breach the director's duty to the company? Would the case indeed be clearer if the director told a psychoanalyst about the dividend decision?

A further element that must be proven in order to find a violation of Rule 10b-5 is an intent to act (referred to as "scienter") in a manner that violates the law, that is, mere negligent action is not enough to charge someone with insider trading. However, the standard of scienter can be met where the person charged has recklessly disregarded facts that any ordinary person should have known.[67] Because Rule 10b-5 is so broad, there is also the problem of discerning whether the fraud has taken place "in connection with a purchase or sale of any security." This requires that the plaintiff must be a buyer or a seller (i.e. deciding *not* to sell or buy is not enough),[68] and that the defendant's misrepresentation or non-disclosure have "some nexus but not necessarily a close relationship" with the purchase or sale.[69] If a private plaintiff (as opposed to the SEC) sues for damages suffered from the act of the insider, he must also prove both "transaction causation" (i.e. the violation caused the trading decision) and "loss causation" (i.e. the violation caused the loss).[70]

When investors who trade in the market at the time that an insider violates Rule 10b-5 sue for damages, the measure typically used is for the insider to disgorge unjust profits,[71] and, if the SEC were to prosecute the

---

[66] "The 'misappropriation theory' holds that a person commits fraud 'in connection with' a securities transaction, and thereby violates § 10(b) and Rule 10b-5, when he misappropriates confidential information for securities trading purposes, in breach of a duty owed to the source of the information … [T]he misappropriation theory premises liability on a fiduciary-turned-trader's deception of those who entrusted him with access to confidential information." *United States* v. *O'Hagan*, 521 US 642, 651 (1997).

[67] *Sanders* v. *John Nuveen & Co., Inc.*, 554 F 2d 790, 793 (7th Cir. 1977).

[68] *Blue Chip Stamps* v. *Manor Drug Stores*, 421 US 723 (1975).

[69] *Abrams* v. *Oppenheimer Government Securities, Inc.*, 737 F 2d 582 (7th Cir. 1984).

[70] *Dura Pharmaceuticals, Inc., et al.* v. *Broudo*, 544 US 336, 342 (2005).

[71] Hazen (2006: § 12.12[2]).

same insider, a civil penalty of up to three times the illegal gain and a criminal fine of up to $100,000 could be added to this.[72]

2. United Kingdom The UK rules for insider trading were enacted to implement the first EC Insider Dealing Directive, and are found in the Criminal Justice Act 1993. Unlike Rule 10b-5, the UK rules apply only to transactions on a regulated market or effected through a securities intermediary,[73] but like Rule 10b-5 an intent to commit the violation is necessary for a conviction.[74] However, only individuals are covered by the prohibition, and thus legal persons cannot be prosecuted for insider trading under UK law.[75]

The rule under the Criminal Justice Act 1993 prohibits an insider with inside information from trading in the affected securities, encouraging another to do so, or disclosing the information to another person otherwise than in the proper performance of the functions of his employment, office or profession.[76] An "insider" is someone who has information through:

- being a director, employee or shareholder of an issuer of securities; or
- having access to the information by virtue of his employment, office or profession; or
- the direct or indirect source of his information is a person as specified above.[77]

Thus, UK law makes professionals who are not directors and persons who are "tipped off" to inside information through directors and such professionals, insiders themselves, and removes much of the complexity found in the US "misappropriation theory." The definition of "inside information" also clarifies the rule by building in a connection with the purchase or sale of securities. Such information not only must be non-public, but must also be specific or precise information that relates to particular

---

[72] Hazen (2006: § 12.17[7][A]).   [73] Sec. 52(3) Criminal Justice Act 1993.
[74] Sec. 57(1) Criminal Justice Act 1993; and Davies (2008: 1104).
[75] Davies (2008: 1095–1096). This distinction avoids much of the complex debate in US law regarding corporate entities with more than one function, such as an investment bank with analyst and brokerage units where one unit will trade in stock for customers and on its own account and another may well have damaging or positive information about the issuer of the securities traded. This leads to labyrinthine confidentiality barriers (referred to as "Chinese Walls") between units and to complex questions of compliance. See Loss, Seligman and Parades (2004: 1008 *et seq.*).
[76] Sec. 52(1), (2) Criminal Justice Act 1993.   [77] Sec. 57(2) Criminal Justice Act 1993.

securities or to particular issuers and not to the market generally, and is likely to have a significant effect on the price of any securities if made public.[78] Information is considered to have been made public if it "can be readily acquired by those likely to deal in any securities to which the information relates."[79] Thus, the intentional disclosure of information that is not generally available yet which would be likely to affect the price of listed securities will constitute a violation of the UK law even if no trading takes place as a result of the violation. How would the disclosure of information to a securities analyst, as discussed above, be treated under UK law?

3. Germany The German rules on insider trading were also originally enacted in response to the 1989 EC Insider Dealing Directive, and have been recently amended to implement the 2003 Directive. Two leading commentators remark that, prior to the enactment of the WpHG in 1994, it might have been considered a premium service of a custodian bank to warn select customers holding securities with them to sell the securities of a credit customer that the bank had discovered in, say, rescheduling negotiations to be experiencing financial problems.[80] This gives us some insight into the massive transformation that the German securities markets underwent in the 1990s.

As both are based on EU Directives, the German rules have the same tight organization and rational design as found in the UK Criminal Justice Act 1993. Unlike the latter, however, the German rules are not restricted to natural persons, apply not only to the officially regulated markets but also to the over-the-counter markets (*Freiverkehr*),[81] and allow prosecution not only for intentional but also for negligent acts.[82] It therefore appears that what German companies lose in the regulation of directors' dealings they gain in the breadth to which insider trading can be prosecuted.

The prohibition is otherwise substantially the same as that found in UK law with certain minor differences that derive from the newer EU Directive. First, "insiders" are no longer defined as a group, so that any person engaging in prohibited activity with inside information comes under the restrictions, the rules expressly apply to derivative instruments

---

[78] Sec. 56(1) Criminal Justice Act 1993.

[79] Sec. 58(2)(c) Criminal Justice Act 1993. This provision also includes other, specific examples of when information may be considered to have been made public.

[80] Kübler and Assmann (2006: 478).   [81] § 12(1) WpHG.   [82] § 39 WpHG.

based on both securities and commodities,[83] and orders to sell securities are specifically included under the definition of "inside information" to combat front-running.[84]

As a result, the German rules prohibit any person in possession of concrete, non-public information that could affect a reasonable investor's investment decision from disclosing it, trading on it for himself or another, or recommending that another person so trade. This prohibition may well allow a person with inside information to recommend that a third party *not enter into transactions* in a specific security, which would resemble permission to give a "hold" recommendation.[85] Share repurchase plans and stabilization activities as provided for in EU law[86] are expressly excluded from the prohibition.[87] The rules also expressly exclude influential valuations derived on the basis of public information.[88]

Questions for discussion

1. Why do companies list on an exchange in connection with an IPO?
2. Why do governance rules change when a company is listed?
3. What special requirements do the directors of listed companies have to fulfill?
4(a) A is a member of the management board of X-AG, a German stock corporation. In 2003, A buys a house in one of the more exclusive suburbs of Frankfurt. He wants to finance part of the purchase price for his house with a €250,000 loan from X-AG. A's income as a board member of X-AG consists of a fixed salary of €1,800,000. In addition, as part of a stock option scheme, he has been granted 25,000 options for the purchase of X-AG shares in 2002. The options can be exercised in 2005 if at that time the price for X-AG stock has increased by 30 percent as compared to the price in July 2002. A is also a member of the supervisory boards of five other stock corporations. The total remuneration for these activities amounts to €100,000–150,000 per year, depending on the number of board meetings. Advise A on the procedure he must follow for obtaining the loan by X-AG
4(b) What procedural requirements apply to credit extended by:
    (aa) X-AG to the managing director of its subsidiary Y-GmbH?
    (bb) X-GmbH to a member of the management board of its subsidiary Y-AG?

---

[83] § 13(1) no. 2 WpHG.   [84] § 12(1) no. 1 WpHG.   [85] Kübler and Assmann (2006: 484).
[86] See the EU Buy-back Regulation.   [87] § 14(2) WpHG.   [88] § 13(2) WpHG.

    (cc) X-GmbH to a member of the management board of its controlling shareholder Y-AG?

    (dd) Y-AG to the managing director of its controlling shareholder X-GmbH?

    (ee) X-AG to a partnership consisting of A, a member of X-AG's management board, B, C and D?

    (ff) X-AG to Y-GmbH if A, a member of X-AG's management board, owns 25 percent of Y-GmbH's shares?

    (gg) X-AG to Y-GmbH if A, a member of X-AG's management board is a director of Y-GmbH but does not own any shares of that corporation?

5.   Compare the German and UK rules on conflicted transactions and directors' dealings. Which type of regulation best suits the needs of the listed company?

6.   The US has developed its insider trading rules for well over half a century, while the European jurisdictions have enacted specific regulations on this question only relatively recently. What are the advantages and disadvantages of the two frameworks?

SUBPART B

The members

16

Shareholder voting rights

Required reading

EU: Directive 2007/36/EC, arts. 2(a), (c) and 4
D: AktG, §§ 53a, 101(1), 103(1), 119, 120(1), 122, 133, 134, 179(1), 182(1), 186(3), 262(1), 293(1)
UK: CA 2006, secs. 21, 22, 160, 168, 188, 190(1), 282, 283, 303, 314, 338, 339, 416(3), 439(1), 467(1), 489(4), 527, 551, 907(1), 922(1)
US: DGCL, §§ 211(b), 212, 214, 221, 228(a), 242(b), 251(c), 271(a), 275(c)

Why and on what do shareholders vote?

I. A shareholder's options: exit or voice?[1]

Regardless of the law applicable to a corporation, a shareholder who has concerns about a company's management has two choices: sell the shares or voice the concerns. The concept pair "voice" and "exit" come from Professor Albert O. Hirschman's 1970 volume, *Exit, Voice and Loyalty,*[2] and are standard categories for discussing the options of shareholders confronted with poorly managed companies. Exit is an "economics" solution, like switching bakeries when the bread is stale, while voice is a "political" solution, like voting for a more responsive government official.[3] The action one tends to take is greatly determined by the nature of the relationship, and voice and exit tend to be inversely related. Where high barriers to exit are combined with free use of voice, such as (often is the case) in a family, the use of voice increases and that of exit decreases.[4] Where free exit is combined with high barriers to the successful use of voice, such as in a relationship between a consumer and the mass producer of

---

[1] Material in this section is adapted from "Shareholder Voice and Its Opponents," *Journal of Corporate Law Studies* (2005) 5: 305–361. We are grateful to Hart Publishing for permission to use this material.

[2] Hirschman (1970).   [3] Hirschman (1970: 15–17).

[4] Hirschman (1970: 33).

a commonly available product, the use of exit increases.[5] Loyalty, such as family ties, patriotism or brand loyalty can countervail the tendency to exit.[6] Voice is generally more expensive than exit, and thus may be used less when multiple interests are present, such as when an investor holds shares in a number of companies, which would require him to exercise voice on a number of different fronts. Unlike exit, voice is a public good, for, if it improves the management or the political leadership to which it is directed, everyone – not just the person exercising voice – will benefit from the improvement.[7] In the case of a shareholder, voice may improve not only her corporation, but the entire market in which the corporation is active, and, while it is possible to exit from a deteriorating corporation, it may not be possible to exit from the market that suffers from the corporation's failure.[8]

In the corporate setting, a shareholder can react to deteriorating performance by using voting rights or litigation to try to change the course of the management (voice) or by selling out (exit). As exit corresponds to sale, exit disciplines management by driving down the company's share price and increasing its cost of raising capital. The message sent by exit is, however, semantically generic; it communicates to the market either that the seller needs liquidity or that something could be amiss with the issuer, and even in the latter case does not specify what.[9] Exit also provides absolutely no guarantee that the new owner of the shares will take measures to correct the original problem, which can augment if no steps are taken to correct it. This means, from the perspective of a market regulator and the economy as a whole, that use of exit as an exclusive remedy could increase the number of avoidable corporate failures and reduce market efficiency.[10] Voice is thus beneficial, but why should shareholders have it?

II.   Why do shares have voting rights?

A.   The rights-based theory of voting rights

In each of our jurisdictions, at least one class of shares must have the right to vote, and this right is assumed to be equally distributed among the shares of that class. Why is it considered essential that shares have voting rights? Three major theories have arisen over time to explain voting

---

[5] Hirschman (1970: 21).   [6] Hirschman (1970: 77–78).   [7] Hirschman (1970: 101).
[8] Hirschman (1970: 102).   [9] See Thel (1994: 242), with further citations.
[10] See Remarks of Lawrence E. Harris, SEC Chief Economist, in "Unofficial Transcript of SEC Roundtable on Proposed Security Holder Director Nominations Rules" (March 10, 2004), available at www.sec.gov, under "Webcasts," "Roundtable Discussion Re: Proposed Rules Relating to Security Holder Director Nominations," "Additional Materials."

rights: a rights-based, or "doctrinal," theory that is the most traditional; an instrumentalist, "economic" theory that is currently the most influential; and a systemic, "political" theory that mixes the other two in an analogy to political democracy and is often expressed by US courts.

As we saw in Chapter 9, shareholders own their companies, and the ownership interest is structured in a way that allows a large group of owners acting together to control and operate the commonly owned enterprise while delegating management to experts. As owners, shareholders have the right to appoint managers for the company and make any decision to change, sell or dissolve it. To protect the rights of each co-owner, the influence of any shareholder is limited to certain decisions (e.g. mergers) that can be made only in specific ways (e.g. in a general meeting) and with a specified weight (e.g. one vote) for each share. The ownership rights of a shareholder are designed to maximize the value of the property (i.e. the corporation), for if each shareholder had a right to sole dominion over the company and its assets the corporate structure would not work. The right to vote is thus an essential element of the rights attaching to a share of stock.

According to the rights-based or "doctrinal" reasoning that is much more prevalent in Germany than in our other two jurisdictions, the right to vote can also be seen as a logically inherent characteristic of membership.[11] In this way, the right to vote is a "constituent element" of the share.[12] All shareholders are members of the company. Membership creates an "entitlement" to vote,[13] because the right to exercise influence in an association is an "essential component of membership."[14] This right entitles members "to influential participation in the affairs of the company."[15] From the proposition that the voting right is an essential component of membership, it follows that the voting right may not be transferred to another person without the transfer of the share itself – i.e. it may not be separated from the share.[16] Pursuant to German law, any such transfer is void,[17] and may even be criminally punished.[18] Delaware law currently

---

[11] See e.g. Brändel, in *GroßKommAktG* (1992: § 12 mn. 4); Heider, in *MünchKommAktG* (2008: § 12 mn. 6); Schmidt (2002: § 19 III).

[12] Brändel, in *GroßKommAktG* (1992: § 12 mn. 4).

[13] Brändel, in *GroßKommAktG* (1992: § 12 mn. 4).

[14] Heider, in *MünchKommAktG* (2008: § 12 mn. 6).

[15] Brändel, in *GroßKommAktG* (1992: § 12 mn. 4).

[16] Heider, in *MünchKommAktG* (2008: § 8 mn. 89); Brändel, in *GroßKommAktG* (1992: § 12 mn. 12).

[17] § 134 BGB; Heider, in *MünchKommAktG* (2008: § 8 mn. 98); Brändel, in *GroßKommAktG* (2008: § 8 mn. 57).

[18] Vote selling and vote buying are misdemeanors. See § 405 III nos. 2, 3, 6, 7 AktG.

allows the "sale of votes" if it is done without deception and in conformance with fiduciary duties.[19] Just as a farmer can sell only the right to passage through his fields, a shareholder can sell only the right to vote her shares. This freedom to separate a voting right from the other rights in a share can, depending on the requirements for disclosing shareholdings, lead to the use of share lending and other available techniques to mask the true holder of voting rights.[20] Thus, the sale and lending of votes will likely lead to adjustments in the disclosure rules discussed in Chapter 19.

All of our jurisdictions require that similarly situated shareholders be treated equally,[21] although some rights are proportional to shareholding and others are absolute. A single share will give a shareholder the right to demand information from the company, and this right will not increase as a matter of law with the shareholding. On the other hand, rights such as the right to receive dividends and to vote in general meetings do increase in proportion to the holding, except in the case of voting by a show of hands under UK law.[22] The reason usually given to explain why voting power increases with investment is that influence should increase as risk increases. This coupling of risk and influence that serves as an *explanation* of the proportional accumulation of voting rights in the rights-based theory becomes the very *ground* for voting rights in the economic theory discussed in the next subsection. Note that, while economic theory provides a much more convincing *explanation* for voting rights, the reverse side of the coin is that it provides a much less stable grounding for the rights. The disadvantage of reasoning "instrumentally," as one does using economic theory, is that if the "result" disappears so does the right that was granted to achieve that result (e.g. if free speech is an instrument to discuss possible governments, once the "perfect" government is found, free speech is no longer necessary).

[19] *Hewlett* v. *Hewlett-Packard*, 2002 WL 549137, at 4 (Del. Ch.) ("Shareholders are free to do whatever they want with their votes, including selling them to the highest bidder.").

[20] Hu and Black (2006: 1014 *et seq.*). Under US law, the sale of a controlling majority can under certain circumstances trigger a fiduciary duty for the seller. See *Perlman* v. *Feldmann*, 219 F 2d 173 (D. Conn. 1957). Under German law, although sales of votes are strictly prohibited, it may still be possible to use derivative instruments to exercise voting rights without ownership. See Cahn and Ostler (2008).

[21] The DGCL expresses this principle with regard to voting rights in § 212 ("each stockholder shall be entitled"), with regard to information rights in § 220 ("any stockholder ... shall ... have the right"), and with regard to judicial recourse in § 327 ("in any derivative suit ... it shall be averred ... that the plaintiff was a stockholder"). The *Aktiengesetz* expresses the general norm in § 53a ("shareholders shall be treated equally in similar circumstances").

[22] Secs. 282(3), 283(4) CA 2006.

B. The economic theory of voting rights

The key to the economic theory of voting rights is the link between the risks and interests of each shareholder and the proper operation of the company. The voting right acts as a channel that connects the shareholder, who bears the risk of the company's success or failure (referred to as the "residual claimant") and the managers, who have the power to steer the company on the desired course.[23] Shareholders are called "residual claimants" because – in contrast to employees and creditors – their compensation is not specified by contract and if the company were to be liquidated they would receive their investment back only after all the other claimants are paid. As Judge Frank Easterbrook and Professor Daniel Fischel, the principal exponents of this theory, explain:

> [S]hareholders are the residual claimants to the firm's income. Creditors have fixed claims, and employees generally negotiate compensation schedules in advance of performance. The gains and losses from abnormally good or bad performance are the lot of shareholders, whose claims stand last in line. As the residual claimants, shareholders have the appropriate incentives (collective choice problems notwithstanding) to make discretionary decisions … [M]anagers' knowledge that they are being monitored by those who have the right incentives … leads managers to act in shareholders' interests in order to advance their own careers and to avoid being ousted.[24]

The shareholder is well situated to exercise control because the fate of his investment exactly reflects the economic fate of the company. He benefits from its success and suffers from its failure without the cushioning effect of contractual guarantees. Thus, the attribution of a voting right has nothing to do with legal position (as an owner or a member) or with his skill and aptitude, but with his spontaneous interests as deriving from his legal and economic position. For the economic theory of voting rights, the key is not a shareholder's ability to freely make decisions – such as to force a company to eliminate profitable but unethical labor or adopt environmental practices – but rather to react automatically to maximize economic well-being. Like a nerve running from a burned hand to the brain, the vote channels signals of pain or pleasure to the company's management. As long as the management of the company truly reflects the collective wills of the shareholders' drive toward economic well-being, the company will be efficiently guided toward profit maximization, just as if it were an owner-managed company.[25]

---

[23] Easterbrook and Fischel (1996: 67).   [24] Easterbrook and Fischel (1996: 67).
[25] Easterbrook and Fischel (1996: 67).

A second reason provided by the economic literature for voting rights appears to derive from system theory: the vote allows the system to incorporate the unforeseen future.[26] Voting rights allow the company's owners to adapt it to changing circumstances.[27] This corrects a flaw in the understanding of a company as a nexus of contracts forming a system of negotiated interests and rights. Such a closed system would not be able to address a task that was not envisioned at the time of its creation. Through the exercise of decision rights, shareholders can alter and adapt the terms of a contract over time,[28] and through appointment rights they can monitor, ratify or correct the course of management.[29]

Obviously, there is a significant difference between the rights-based understanding and the economic justification of voting rights. From an economic point of view, voting rights organically channel the right kind of impulses and reactions into the company, which drives it to maximize profits. If voting rights did not do this, because, say, the shareholders were to become altruists and seek to sell products as cheaply as possible, which left less funding for research and top talent in management, voting rights would be undesirable. By the same token, if the purpose of the company were to change – as it does when entering insolvency – from a going concern to an aggregate of assets to be liquidated, shareholder voting rights would also be undesirable. From a purely rights-based point of view, the owners can do whatever they want to with the company as long as they do not violate the law or a duty they owe to others (whether that be minority shareholders or creditors). Thus, the economic theory of voting rights gives systemically plausible *reasons* for the rights (it is descriptive), but in so doing it subjects the rights to serving those reasons (it becomes normative). An understanding of voting rights from the point of view of political legitimacy does much to unify the rights-based and the economic theories.

C. The shareholder democracy theory of voting rights

Robert Monks and Nell Minow see the governance structure of stock corporations in analogy to representative democracy, and argue that US legislators sought to strengthen this form in the 1930s when they enacted the securities laws that required disclosure of information to the market:

> [Lawmakers] tried to set up a process of corporate accountability –
> an impartial set of rules preserving the widest possible latitude for

---

[26] See e.g. Luhmann (1968: 218).   [27] Easterbrook and Fischel (1996: 66).
[28] Easterbrook and Fischel (1996: 66).   [29] Jensen and Smith (1985: 142).

shareholders to protect their financial interests. In searching for a reliable and familiar model, they turned to America's own traditions of political accountability.

Shareholders were seen as voters, boards of directors as elected representatives, proxy solicitations as election campaigns, corporate charters and by-laws as constitutions and amendments. Just as political democracy acted to guarantee the legitimacy of governmental or public power, the theory went, so corporate democracy would control – and therefore legitimate – the otherwise uncontrollable growth of power in the hands of private individuals. Underpinning that corporate democracy, as universal franchise underpinned its political counterpart, was the principle of one share, one vote.[30]

From this perspective, shareholders have individual rights comparable to citizens in a democracy and voting rights serve as a channel of control to keep management *accountable* to those rights. As in economic theory, voting rights are instrumental, not essential, but they serve not to attain a preconceived goal (e.g. maximizing profits), but rather to reign in the power of management, to make it accountable to the shareholders who – as in the rights-based theory – have inherent rights as owners and members. Voting legitimizes management power by making management accountable to the will of the shareholders.

The Delaware Chancery Court understands voting rights in this vein. *Blasius Industries* v. *Atlas Corporation*, reprinted in part in this chapter, is perhaps the most famous in a line of cases that see voting rights as the key to legitimate management power.[31] As the court explains, voting rights are "critical to the theory that legitimates the exercise of power by some (directors and officers) over vast aggregations of property that they do not own."[32]

How does the Court's position in *Blasius* differ from the economic understanding of voting rights? Was the proposal that the new shareholders were seeking to adopt a good business decision? What did the management do in response to the shareholder initiative? What should management have done? What is the difference between methods that the court would have apparently approved and those that it disapproved?

Professor John Pound argues that the "political" method of governing a corporation is superior to the "economic" method through

---

[30] Monks and Minow (2004: 126).

[31] Also see e.g. *MM Companies, Inc.* v. *Liquid Audio, Inc.*, 813 A 2d 1118, 1126 (Del. Supr. 2003).

[32] *Blasius Industries, Inc.* v. *Atlas Corp.*, 564 A 2d 651, 659 (Del. Ch. 1988).

which raiders take over underperforming companies and replace their management.[33] He sees the anti-takeover devices that governments tend to adopt as proof that takeovers are inferior to controlling management through voting.[34] You may want to keep this thought in mind as we move through the procedures for exercising voting rights and then look at takeovers in Chapters 24 and 25.

III.　Collective action problems

In a certain sense, the strength of voting rights as a governance technique is also its basic weakness: they must be exercised by an aggregate of individuals, each of whom makes an independent decision (even if only a decision to imitate the other shareholders). In the best of cases, this can lead to mass collaboration that brings creative energy from a number of sources to bear on a single problem,[35] but in the worst of cases it can lead to apathetic non-participation.[36] Moreover, a number of behaviors documented by psychology and economics, such as "rational apathy" and "free riding" work against successful collective action. This section will review some of the collective action problems that are generally considered to hinder effective shareholder action and their traditional solutions.

"Rational apathy" describes behavior that is deemed rational when the cost of a shareholder becoming informed significantly exceeds the expected return from making a good decision (sit down after work some evening and read a 150-page proxy statement!). The relationship can be graphically depicted as shown in Figure 16.1.

In a company that is 100 percent owned, when a shareholder invests time to make a decision, she receives 100 percent of the benefits of a good decision. When the shareholder owns only 10 percent of the stock, she must still invest enough time to make a complete decision – as opposed to, say, reading only 10 percent of the annual report – but receives no more than 10 percent of the benefits from a good decision. If the shareholders

---

[33] Pound (1993: 1007).　　[34] Pound (1993: 1024).

[35] Since the early 1990s, the internet has been steadily facilitating the creation of this kind of model. See the descriptions in Friedman (2005: 81 *et seq.*) of "self-organizing collaborative communities" that take place when otherwise unrelated people "patch" open source software or build the "Wikipedia." In recent years, governments shy of press coverage have found spontaneous action through "YouTube" more threatening than the criticism of professional journalists.

[36] This state of affairs was observed by the authors in a landmark study of the US economy in the 1920s. See Berle and Means (1968: 8). Notably, growth at the time was fast, communication technology was relatively primitive, and disclosure requirements were scarce.

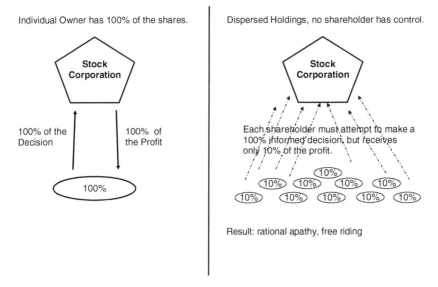

Figure 16.1   Dispersed holdings hinder collective action

holding the other 90 percent of the stock were to simply vote in favor of a good proposal formulated and advocated by our 10 percent shareholder, they would receive the benefits of her research, analysis and decision without incurring any of the costs. Thus, they are said to "free ride" on the efforts of the other shareholders. This can be particularly troublesome when the various shareholders are fund managers competing with each other for clients on the basis of portfolio performance. Thus, when the cost of voice is disproportionate to the possible benefits, and even those benefits will be shared by competitors, shareholders may rationally decide not to take an active part in corporate affairs.

A number of instruments have developed over time to ease the collective action problems of shareholders. These include the right to grant proxies, which is a way of allowing voting power to be concentrated in a single agent and exercised in the absence of the principals. Access to information is also a key to exercising voting rights. We will discuss how shareholders obtain information about the company in Chapter 17. Voting rights function together with the transferability of shares to make takeover offers possible: in a takeover, dispersed, unrelated shareholders transfer their shares to a single bidder who then eliminates the rational apathy problem by concentrating the voting power of the purchased shares. We will look closely at takeovers in Chapters 24 and 25.

IV. Matters on which shareholders vote

Company law usually gives shareholders the right to appoint directors and – in circumstances that affect the structure of the company – the right to at least veto a management proposal. The voting rights of shareholders are not identical in Germany, the United Kingdom and the United States. Moreover, to understand the practical impact of voting rights in each jurisdiction, it is necessary to know not only the *matters* subject to a vote, but also *how* these matters come up for a vote. If a matter is not proposed for a vote, the right to vote on it has little impact. In addition, the majority required for the relevant approval can also separate meaningful votes from "rubber stamp" votes. Our analysis of voting rights must therefore be presented on three levels for each jurisdiction. In this section, Section IV, we will present the first and most commonly studied level: the matters that require a shareholder vote under the applicable law. This is the black-letter law one normally studies. The next section, Section V, will address a second level by discussing how matters can come up for a vote – i.e. at the initiative of the management or of the shareholders. Section VI will then briefly illustrate how the majority necessary for a given decision can sometimes determine a vote's outcome. In each section, some differences will arise between privately held and listed companies, as law and exchange rules often impose specific requirements with respect to shareholder voting in publicly held companies.

A. Germany

1. Appointment rights As we have seen in previous chapters, an AG has a two-tier board that is divided into a supervisory board (*Aufsichtsrat*) and a management board (*Vorstand*). In the absence of co-determination and special appointment rights,[37] shareholders elect the entire *Aufsichtsrat*.[38] *Aufsichtsrat* members can be elected for a maximum term of roughly five years (measured from the annual meeting that elects them until the annual meeting that reviews their performance for the fourth, full year following that of their election)[39] and they can be re-elected, but either the *Satzung* or the shareholder resolution electing a given member may specify a shorter period.[40] As a result, it

---

[37] Pursuant to § 101(2) AktG, the *Satzung* may give specific shares or shareholders the right to appoint up to one-third of the members of the *Aufsichtsrat* that shareholders have the right to elect.

[38] § 101(1) AktG.   [39] § 102(1) AktG.

[40] Habersack, in *MünchKommAktG* (2008: § 102 mn. 8).

is possible to stagger board terms so members do not all come up for election in the same year.[41] Although the terms of office are quite long in comparison to Delaware, shareholders do have an opportunity each year at the annual meeting to approve or disapprove of the actions that the *Aufsichtsrat* members have taken during the financial year with a resolution on "exculpation" (referred to as *Entlastung*).[42] A disapproval of a director's actions during the year amounts to a vote of no confidence against such director, and, although it does not automatically remove the director from office or create liability, it does focus significant media attention on the relevant director and often raises a number of issues that can later serve as the basis for a lawsuit.[43] See the discussion of *Entlastung* in the *Macrotron* decision, reprinted in part in this chapter. Shareholders may also remove the shareholder-appointed supervisory board members with or without cause,[44] although the high, required majority of three-quarters of the votes prevents such board members from being removed frequently,[45] unless a takeover has occurred. Beyond these appointment rights, shareholders also appoint the AG's auditors,[46] and may appoint a special auditor to investigate the board's handling of contributions to capital or management.[47]

As explained in Chapter 10, shareholder appointment of supervisory directors is subject to significant qualification through a peculiar German institution: the *Mitbestimmungsgesetz* requires that an AG with more than 2,000 employees fill half of its *Aufsichtsrat* seats with labor representatives,[48] part of which is directly elected by the employees and part of which is appointed by the labor unions that are active in the company.[49] The purpose of co-determination is of course to give a particular group of stakeholders – the company's employees – significant influence over the company's policy and management,[50] and its effectiveness is periodically debated in Germany.

---

[41] Habersack, in *MünchKommAktG* (2008: § 102 mn. 17).   [42] § 120(1) AktG.

[43] Kubis, in *MünchKommAktG* (2004: § 120, mn. 2, 24, 33–36).

[44] § 103(1) AktG. Removal requires three-quarters of the votes cast pursuant to § 103(1) AktG.

[45] See Baums (1993: 155–56).   [46] § 318(1) HGB.   [47] § 142 AktG.

[48] It should be recalled that this also applies to a GmbH with more than 2,000 employees. See § 1 MitbestG. The *Drittelbeteiligungsgesetz* requires that any company with more than 500 employees have a supervisory board and that one-third of its members be appointed by employees.

[49] § 7(2) MitbestG.

[50] It is often discussed, and some authors have called it "the most remarkable experiment in corporate governance of the twentieth century." Enriques, Hansmann and Kraakman (2009b: 100).

The *Aufsichtsrat* in turn then appoints the managing directors seated on the *Vorstand*.[51] The statutory maximum term of *Vorstand* members is the same as that for the *Aufsichtsrat*, and, as in the case of the latter, they may be reappointed.[52] The actions of each managing director are subject to review and approval at each annual meeting.[53] The *Aufsichtsrat* may also remove individual members of the *Vorstand* from office for good cause (*wichtiger Grund*), such as gross breach of duty, incompetence or disloyalty.[54] Because such a removal will be effective until a court determines whether good cause for dismissal in fact exists, the current length of legal proceedings on such matters usually means that the director will not be reinstated before his term has expired even if the removal was groundless.

2. Decision rights Shareholders usually have a right to approve or veto decisions that will have a significant and lasting impact on their company. German law requires shareholder approval for decisions that affect the constitutional documents, the assets or the structural integrity of the company.

Amendment of the Satzung. Any amendment of an AG's *Satzung* must be approved by the shareholders.[55]

Decisions regarding assets. The shareholders of an AG make their own decision whether they will receive dividends out of the profits that are distributable pursuant to law.[56] The capital of an AG may be increased or decreased including by way of an issue of convertible debt securities,[57] only with shareholder approval,[58] and shareholders must also approve "ordinary" repurchases of company shares.[59] Given that the shareholders of an AG have statutory preemptive rights, they must vote to waive such rights before any new shares may be issued to third parties free of rights.[60] What about a decision to delist a company from a securities exchange, would that affect the property of the shareholders in the company? See *Macrotron*, reprinted in part later in this chapter.

Decisions regarding structural integrity. Any merger of an AG with another company must be approved by the shareholders of the AG,[61] as must any sale of all or substantially all of an AG's corporate assets.[62] Shareholders of an AG must also vote on spin-offs of business units

---

[51] § 84(1) AktG.   [52] § 84(1) AktG.   [53] § 120(1) AktG.   [54] § 84(3) AktG.

[55] § 179 AktG.   [56] § 174(1) AktG.   [57] § 221 AktG.

[58] §§ 182, 192, 202 207, 222, 229, 237 AktG.   [59] § 71(1) no. 8 AktG.

[60] § 186 AktG.   [61] §§ 319, 320 AktG; §§ 13, 65, 73 UmwG.   [62] § 179a AktG.

or split-ups of the company,[63] and in corporate alliance contracts that create relationships of control or diversions of profits.[64] In addition, the management board may place management decisions before the shareholders for decision,[65] and, as will be discussed in more detail in Chapter 23, it must do so under the doctrine formulated by the High Federal Court in its *Holzmüller* and *Gelatine* decisions, if the decision would effect a fundamental change that would reasonably require an amendment of the *Satzung*.

B. United Kingdom

1. Appointment rights In contrast to the *Aktiengesetz* and the DGCL, the Companies Act 2006 does not specifically provide that directors be appointed by shareholders. The only statutory provision on the matter is that, in the case of a public company, a proposal to elect more than one director on a single slate may not be put to the shareholders unless unanimously approved.[66] Likewise, the Act specifies no maximum term for directors, but does give shareholders the right to remove directors at any time regardless of provisions to the contrary in their employment contracts.[67] Rules for the appointment of directors to the board of an unlisted company and any maximum terms of office would be provided for in that company's articles of association.[68] The Companies (Model Articles) Regulations 2008 provide for appointment of directors of public companies by ordinary resolution or by the directors themselves.[69] For listed companies, the Listing Rules require that the company comply with the Combined Code or explain any deviation.[70] The Code states that "[a]ll directors should be subject to election by shareholders at the first annual general meeting after their appointment, and to re-election thereafter at intervals of no more than three years."[71] The Act gives shareholders a right to both appoint[72] and remove[73] the company's auditors, as well as the right to demand that disagreements on important accounting issues be posted on the company's website.[74]

2. Decision rights The decision rights of shareholders under the Companies Act are somewhat more extensive than those under the

---

[63] §§ 65, 125 UmwG.   [64] §§ 293, 295 AktG.   [65] § 119(2) AktG.
[66] Sec. 160(1) CA 2006.   [67] Sec. 168(1) CA 2006.   [68] See Davies (2008: 378–381).
[69] See Reg. 19 SI 2008 No. 3229.   [70] See FSA Listing Rules, Rule 9.8.6(5), (6).
[71] See Combined Code, Principle A.7.1.   [72] Secs. 486, 489 CA 2006.
[73] Sec. 510(1) CA 2006.   [74] Sec. 527(1) CA 2006.

Aktiengesetz. Shareholders must approve decisions that affect the constitutional documents, the assets or the structural integrity of the company.

Amendment of the articles. Neither the company's articles, nor its memorandum (the provisions of which, beyond the intent to form a company, are now deemed one with the articles),[75] may be amended without the shareholders' approval.[76]

Decisions regarding assets. The shareholders must approve or provide authorization for any allotment of the company's shares.[77] The capital of a limited company may be decreased only with shareholder approval,[78] and detailed rules for approving share repurchases ensure that shareholders control this process as well.[79] Although the full procedure for determining and declaring dividends is not set out in the Act, authority over the process is generally shared by the directors and the shareholders. First, the directors recommend that a specific portion of distributable profits be distributed as dividends,[80] and then – pursuant to a provision of the articles – the shareholders vote on the distribution in the annual meeting within the limits of the law.[81] As the shareholders of a limited company have statutory preemptive rights, shares free of such rights may not be issued to third parties until the shareholders have voted to waive their right of preemptive subscription.[82]

Directors' service contracts. Shareholder approval is also required for directors' service contracts that are or may be longer than two years,[83] and, in the case of listed companies, an annual report on executive compensation,[84] employees' share schemes, and long-term incentive schemes that are not open to all employees must be submitted to the shareholders for approval.[85] Most material transactions

---

[75] Sec. 28 CA 2006.   [76] Sec. 21 CA 2006.   [77] Sec. 551(1) CA 2006.

[78] Sec. 641(1) CA 2006. In the case of a public company, this provision requires that the court confirms the decision.

[79] See sec. 658 (general prohibition), sec. 690 (general exception), sec. 694(2) (approval of off-market transactions) and sec. 701 (approval of open market transactions) CA 2006.

[80] Sec. 416(3) CA 2006.   [81] See Ferran (1999: 413); Reg. 70(2) MAPC.

[82] Secs. 567(1), 571(1), 573(4) CA 2006.   [83] Sec. 188 CA 2006.   [84] Sec. 439(1) CA 2006.

[85] See FSA Listing Rules, Rule 9.4. Long-term incentive schemes are exempted from shareholder approval if the only participant is a director "or an individual whose appointment as a director of the listed company is being contemplated and the arrangement is established specifically to facilitate, in unusual circumstances, the recruitment or retention of the relevant individual." FSA Listing Rules, Rule 9.4.2(2).

between a director and the company are also subject to shareholder approval.[86]

Decisions regarding structural integrity. Shareholder approval is necessary for any merger[87] or division[88] of a limited company. The FSA's Listing Rules also require that shareholders be informed and approve trans-actions having an impact equal to or exceeding 25 percent of gross assets (such as when assets sold have that value), gross profits (such as a contract with comparable value), or gross capital (such as when con-sideration paid or the value of a company acquired have that value).[89] In addition, if a company is to opt in to the takeover regime in which defensive measures are not permitted, the decision to opt in is one for the shareholders.[90]

C. United States

1. Appointment rights As in the UK, many shareholder rights under US law are provided for in the certificate of incorporation. Most provi-sions of the Delaware General Corporation Law are fallback rules that apply only if not otherwise provided in the certificate. Indeed, although the statute provides that a corporation is managed "by or under the dir-ection of the board of directors," it also gives the shareholders a residual right to remove some or all of this power from the board in the corpor-ate charter.[91] This occurs very rarely.[92] In almost all cases, directors man-age the company and elections must be held annually to elect (at least some of) them.[93] Board members usually have a term of one year, unless

---

[86] See sec. 190(1) (substantial transactions), secs. 197(1), 200 (loans, quasi-loans), sec. 203 (other qualifying transactions) and sec. 218 (golden parachutes) CA 2006.

[87] Sec. 907(1) CA 2006. [88] Sec. 922(1) CA 2006.

[89] See FSA Listing Rules, Rule 10.5. [90] Sec. 966(1) CA 2006.

[91] The second sentence of § 141(a) allows the certificate of incorporation to specify that "*the powers* and duties *conferred* or imposed *upon the board of directors* by this chapter" shall be exercised "to such extent and *by such person or persons* as shall be *provided in the cer-tificate of incorporation.*" DGCL § 141(a) (emphasis added). See Balotti and Finkelstein (2008: § 4.1).

[92] That probably is the result of various causes, including efficiency considerations and that most shareholders buy into corporations already established, that statutes normally give the board an exclusive right to propose charter amendments in the annual meeting. See DGCL § 242(b)(1). Boards have no interest in making proposals to reduce their own power. If a number of possible amendments could be proposed, the proposal actually selected "will be very much influenced by which change would best serve management's interests." Bebchuk (2005: 862). For a detailed discussion of the power dynamics in mak-ing charter amendments and the board's reluctance to enact amendments that decrease its own power, see Bebchuk (1989: 1820–1825).

[93] DGCL § 211(b).

the terms are staggered, but this is not provided for in the law. As will be discussed in Section V, elections for directors can take place either in a general meeting or by informal, direct consents that shareholders give to each other. Shareholders have no right under law or listing rules to appoint the company's auditor.

2. Decision rights

Amendment of the certificate of incorporation. Shareholder approval is necessary for any amendment of the certificate of incorporation.[94] However, the certificate may give the board sole power to amend the by-laws,[95] which usually provide the more detailed rules regarding the operation of the company. We will examine by-law amendments in more detail in the context of the *Hollinger International* case in Chapter 23.

Decisions regarding assets. In comparison to Germany and the United Kingdom, the decision rights of US shareholders *vis-à-vis* the company's assets are very limited. The board controls dividends.[96] The certificate of incorporation can, and often does, give the board power to issue new classes of shares.[97] Because preemption rights are not mandatory under Delaware law,[98] the shareholders do not have the leverage that a waiver requirement in connection with the issue of new shares would give them. However, both the NYSE and the Nasdaq Stock Market require shareholder approval for either the creation or the material alteration of an equity compensation plan.[99]

Decisions regarding structural integrity. Shareholder power mainly resides in approving major transactions that change the company's structure. This very much resembles our two other jurisdictions, in that shareholders must approve or veto any merger of the company,[100] any sale of substantially all of the company's assets,[101] and any proposal to dissolve the company.[102] Beyond that, neither the law of Delaware nor the Model Act gives shareholders any power unless an action affects the rights of a particular class of shares, as discussed in Chapter 9.

---

[94] DGCL § 242(b)(2).   [95] DGCL § 109(a).   [96] DGCL § 170(a).
[97] DGCL § 161.   [98] DGCL § 102(b)(3).
[99] See NYSE LCM, para. 303A.08, Shareholder Approval of Equity Compensation Plans, and Nasdaq Marketplace Rules, para. 4350(i)(1)(A).
[100] DGCL § 251(c).   [101] DGCL § 271(a).   [102] DGCL § 275.

V. *How matters come up for a vote*

The right to vote on a decision or an appointment is limited to a right to *veto* the decision or appointment unless the person with the voting right also has a right to bring the matter up for a vote. For example, if the board had the sole right to propose an amendment to the constitutional documents, even if the shareholders had a right to vote on and approve such amendments, the board could simply refrain from making a proposal, and in this way render the voting right useless until the shareholders appointed new directors willing to propose the matter.

A. Germany

German shareholders exercise their voting rights only in a general meeting of shareholders, and thus the key to initiative lies in the right to call a meeting. As a rule, the *Vorstand* calls the general meeting.[103] The members of the *Aufsichtsrat* that are elected by the shareholders are elected at that meeting, and the *Aufsichtsrat* is required to draft a slate of candidates for the *Vorstand* to distribute with the call to meeting.[104] Thus, in most cases, management controls the timing and content of the annual meeting's agenda. However, German law gives shareholders a number of tools for bringing matters to the annual meeting on their own initiative.

First, shareholders representing 5 percent of an AG's capital may demand that the *Vorstand* call a meeting.[105] There is no duration requirement on the 5 percent holding: it must merely exist at the time the demand is made,[106] and need not be made personally by the shareholder, but may be exercised by anyone holding a power to represent the shareholder.[107] Either together with a demand for a shareholders' meeting or in the context of an existing call to meeting, shareholders may also have one or more items placed on the meeting agenda if they either represent 5 percent of the AG's corporate capital or have a holding with a par value of at least €500,000,[108] which sum would represent significantly less than 5 percent of the capital of a large, publicly traded company.[109] Shareholders may

---

[103] § 121(2) AktG.   [104] § 124(2), (3) AktG.

[105] § 122(1) AktG. The *Satzung* may specify a lower percentage of capital to trigger this right.

[106] Kubis, in *MünchKommAktG* (2004: § 122 mn. 7).

[107] Kubis, in *MünchKommAktG* (2004: § 122 mn. 5).   [108] § 122(2) AktG.

[109] In Germany, such proposals are by no means limited to environmental or ethical initiatives or procedural modifications to the balance of shareholder/management power, as shareholder proposals would be in the United States. For example, during the 2008 proxy season, Professors Ekkehard Wenger and Leonhard Knoll used their positions

make proposals with regard to the agenda items they demand.[110] Again, there is no minimum holding period to be eligible for this right.[111] All costs for the meeting and the preparation and distribution of the call to meeting, agenda and proposals are paid by the company.[112]

All shareholders may also submit counter-proposals to proposals made by management.[113] Such counter-proposals may either oppose[114] or supplement management proposals, but the management need not distribute a counter-proposal if:

- it could subject the management board to prosecution for making it known;[115]
- it violates the law or the charter;[116]
- it is materially false, misleading or defamatory;[117]
- it has already been submitted to a general meeting in the past;[118]
- it has been repeatedly rejected in the past;[119]
- it is proposed by a shareholder who does not plan to be present or represented at the relevant meeting;[120] or
- it is proposed by a shareholder who failed to support one of her proposals at the last, two meetings.[121]

All shareholders also have a right to propose candidates for election to the supervisory board.[122] The shareholder may nominate either a full or a short slate of candidates.[123] The management board is not required to publish or dispatch such a proposal with the call to meeting, but it must "make the proposal available" to the shareholders, which is satisfied by placing the proposed nomination and any supporting statement of up to

---

as modest shareholders of Deutsche Bank AG to propose that the company spins off its investment banking activities and trims back its operations in the United States. Deutsche Bank's management incorporated these items into a supplemental meeting agenda and distributed them to the shareholders for their consideration and vote.

[110] Werner, in *GroßKommAktG* (1993: § 122 mn. 70).

[111] Kubis, in *MünchKommAktG* (2004: § 122 mn. 29).

[112] See § 122(4) AktG; and Kubis, in *MünchKommAktG* (2004: § 122 mn. 65); Werner, in *GroßKommAktG* (1993: § 122 mn. 77 *et seq.*).

[113] § 126 AktG.

[114] This offers an interesting opportunity for comparison to the US Rule 14a-8, which allows a proposal to be excluded if it *does conflict with* a management proposal. See 17 CFR § 240.14a-8(i)(9). If a shareholder wants to disagree with management, she must arrange and pay for her own contesting proxy statement against that of the management.

[115] § 126(2) no. 1 AktG.   [116] § 126(2) no. 2 AktG.   [117] § 126(2) no. 3 AktG.

[118] § 126(2) no. 4 AktG.   [119] § 126(2) no. 5 AktG.   [120] § 126(2) no. 6 AktG.

[121] § 126(2) no. 7 AktG.   [122] § 127 AktG.

[123] Kubis, in *MünchKommAktG* (2004: § 127 mn. 4).

5,000 words on the company's website.[124] Shareholder nominations take place through analogical application of a shareholder proposal rule, § 127 AktG,[125] and can be excluded for the same reasons as a § 126 proposal.

B. United Kingdom

The Companies Act 2006 is somewhat less generous than the *Aktiengesetz* in giving shareholders opportunities to take the initiative on decision-making. As in Germany, shareholders of a UK company have a statutory right to demand that the board call a general meeting,[126] although the required percentage of capital is 10 percent rather than 5 percent of the capital with voting rights.[127] The shareholders also have a right to specify the resolutions that will be put to a vote in such meeting.[128] The board may refuse to have the resolution considered at the meeting only in the relatively extreme cases that it would be:

- ineffective if passed (whether by reason of inconsistency with any enactment of law or the company's constitution or otherwise);
- defamatory of any person; or
- frivolous or vexatious.[129]

In the case of a public company, members also have a right to have a proposed resolution distributed even when the meeting is called at the initiative of the board.[130] This right can be exercised by one or more members who hold at least 5 percent of the total voting rights or at least 100 members acting together, provided the *average* paid-up sum on their shareholdings is at least £100.[131] The board must distribute the resolution in the same manner as the notice of the meeting and at the same time as, or promptly after, it gives notice of the meeting,[132] but may refuse to distribute the resolution for the same reasons listed above (because it is ineffective, defamatory or frivolous or vexatious).[133]

---

[124] Kubis, in *MünchKommAktG* (2004: § 127 mn. 1, and Comment to § 126 mn. 21). This resembles the use of "increased communications capabilities" that the ABA Task Force on Shareholder Proposals recommends as Alternative II in its Report. See Task Force on Shareholder Proposals (2003: 122).

[125] See generally, Noack (2003).   [126] Sec. 303(1) CA 2006.

[127] Sec. 303(3) CA 2006. This provision also states that, in the case of a private company, if more than twelve months have elapsed since the last general meeting, the percentage is lowered to 5 percent. When comparing the German and UK thresholds, it should be noted that, since the denominator in Germany is capital and that in the UK is shares with voting rights, the actual amount to be compared for the exercise of the right will depend on the percentage of the capital consisting of non-voting shares.

[128] Sec. 303(4) CA 2006.   [129] Sec. 303(5) CA 2006.   [130] Sec. 338(1) CA 2006.

[131] Sec. 338(3) CA 2006.   [132] Sec. 339(1) CA 2006.   [133] Sec. 338(2) CA 2006.

In addition, the members of all UK companies have the right to demand that the company distribute written statements regarding proposed resolutions.[134] This right can be exercised by the same percentage of members required to propose a resolution,[135] and the board may refuse to distribute it if it can convince a court that the members are abusing the right to demand distribution.[136] In each of the above cases, the company bears the costs of the meeting or distribution of the resolution or written statement.[137] The Companies Act does not give members a right to nominate candidates for the board, but, as with other aspects of appointing directors, such right could be specified in the company's articles.

In the case of a private company, members holding at least 5 percent of the voting rights may circumvent the general meeting altogether by requiring the company to circulate a written resolution for the vote of all members, and thus take action directly.[138] The resolution can be accompanied by a written statement of up to 1,000 words.[139] The Act imposes severe penalties against any members of the board who hinder the exercise of this right.[140]

C.   United States

Under the US corporate law statutes, shareholders occupy a very passive position in the shareholders' meeting unless they are given a right of initiative in the constitutional documents. Any amendments to the certificate of incorporation – such as to give the shareholders a right of initiative – must, however, be proposed by the board.[141] General meetings are called by the board under Delaware law.[142] Delaware law was amended in 2009 to allow by-law provisions that would give shareholders the right to nominate candidates for election to the board in the company's proxy materials.[143] This nomination practice was previously permitted by

---

[134] Sec. 314(1) CA 2006.   [135] Sec. 314(2) CA 2006.   [136] Sec. 317(1) CA 2006.

[137] Sec. 305(6) (expenses for calling meeting), sec. 316(1) (circulate written statement) and sec. 340 (circulate resolutions for public company) CA 2006.

[138] Sec. 292(1) CA 2006.   [139] Sec. 292(3) CA 2006.

[140] Sec. 293(5), (6) CA 2006.   [141] DGCL § 242(b).

[142] See DGCL § 211 (meeting requirements), § 213 (preparation of lists) and § 222 (rules on notice). The Model Act, similar to UK law, allows shareholders with 10 percent of the votes entitled to be cast at a meeting to call a special meeting of shareholders. See § 7.02(a) Model Act.

[143] DGCL § 112.

Delaware case law,[144] but, because federal law prohibited it for companies registered with the SEC,[145] it was a right that was seldom used.

Historically, the SEC rules have conceived proposing board candidates as an act that is hostile to the management and thus better placed in a proxy contest, for which the shareholder would have to pay unless victorious. This led to candidates for the board being nominated by the board itself. Major transactions such as mergers and asset sales must also be proposed by the board.[146] If a company does not provide for shareholder initiative in its constitutional documents, two avenues for shareholder initiative remain. First, shareholders may act without a meeting by seeking written consents from other shareholders. Secondly, shareholders of companies registered with the SEC may make proposals using Rule 14a-8 under the Exchange Act.[147]

Delaware law allows shareholders to act in complete independence of the board by soliciting "written consents" from each other to approve any resolution that could be adopted at a shareholders' meeting.[148] Use of this technique is discussed in the *Blasius* case, in this chapter. With steadily improving communications, and the possibility of cost-effective email consents,[149] this type of spontaneous, "wikinomics" coordination among shareholders could become increasingly practical. Currently, there are a number of statutory disadvantages to action by consents. First, the power to act by consents can be eliminated in the certificate of incorporation.[150] Secondly, unless the action by consent fills "all of the directorships to which directors could be elected at an annual meeting" in one vote, an impossibly high standard of a unanimous vote must be met to elect directors.[151] Thirdly, the denominator used to calculate whether a required majority has been reached is "all shares entitled to vote" on the particular issue,[152] which will generally be higher than the normal denominator of shares present in person or by proxy at the meeting and entitled to vote on the relevant matter.[153] Fourthly, under SEC rules, the solicitation of written

---

[144] See *Stroud* v. *Grace*, 606 A 2d 75, 96 (Del. 1992); *Millenco LP* v. *meVC Draper Fischer Jurvetson Fund I, Inc.*, 824 A 2d 11, 19 (Del. Ch. 2002) ("the 'right of shareholders to participate in the voting process includes the right to nominate an opposing slate'"); *Hubbard* v. *Hollywood Park Realty Enterprises, Inc.*, 1991 WL 3151, at 11–13 (Del. Ch.).

[145] Regulation 14A, Schedule 14A, at 17 CFR § 240.101.   [146] §§ 251(b), 271 DGCL.

[147] 17 CFR § 240.14a-8.   [148] DGCL § 228.

[149] Consents may be delivered by "electronic transmission." See DGCL § 228(d)(1).

[150] DGCL § 228(a).   [151] DGCL § 211(b).

[152] DGCL § 228(a). This is comparable to the majority required at a meeting to approve mergers and asset sales, so it will not make a difference for such transactions. See §§ 251(c), 271(a) DGCL.

[153] § 216 DGCL.

consents is treated the same as the solicitation of proxies and triggers extensive and expensive regulatory requirements.

The second avenue for shareholder initiative is Exchange Act Rule 14a-8, which in theory allows shareholders to make proposals, which the management must distribute together with the invitation to the meeting. Under this Rule, shareholders may request distribution of a proposal if they have held at least $2,000 in market value, or 1 percent, of the company's shares entitled to be voted on the proposal for at least one year before submitting their proposal.[154] These requirements are not very high, but the main problem with the Rule is that management can refuse to distribute most proposals that offer anything challenging their control. There are no less than thirteen grounds that management may use to reject a proposal, including that the proposal "conflicts" with their own position.[155]

One of the grounds for exclusion that has particularly frustrated shareholder action is if the proposal concerns "ordinary business operations." Historically, the SEC has found a matter "ordinary" until it causes enough damage to gain a prominent place in the media. For example, the SEC allowed proposals challenging executive compensation to be excluded as affecting "ordinary business operations" until the problem became bad enough to cause controversy in the media, at which point the matter was no longer "ordinary" and such proposals could then be

---

[154]   17 CFR § 240.14a-8(b).

[155]   See 17 CFR § 240.14a-8. In addition to eligibility requirements and procedural requirements to qualify for submission, a proposal may be excluded if (1) it is not a proper subject for action by shareholders under the laws of the jurisdiction of the company's organization; (2) if implemented, it would cause the company to violate any state, federal, or foreign law to which it is subject; (3) it or its supporting statement is contrary to an SEC proxy rules, including Rule 14a-9, prohibiting materially false or misleading statements in proxy soliciting materials; (4) it relates to the redress of a personal claim or grievance against the company or any other person, or seeks a personal benefit; (5) it relates to operations which account for less than 5 percent of the company's total assets and for less than 5 percent of its net earnings and gross sales for its most recent fiscal year, and is not otherwise significantly related to the company's business; (6) the company would lack the power or authority to implement it; (7) it deals with a matter relating to the company's ordinary business operations; (8) it relates to an election for membership on the company's board of directors or analogous governing body; (9) it directly conflicts with one of the company's own proposals to be submitted to shareholders at the same meeting; (10) the company has already substantially implemented the proposal; (11) it substantially duplicates another proposal previously submitted that will be included in the proxy materials; (12) it deals with substantially the same subject matter as another proposal that has been previously included in the proxy materials in the past five years and has received little support; or (13) it relates to specific amounts of cash or stock dividends. 17 CFR § 240.14a-8(i).

distributed.[156] The same thing happened when shareholders sought to ensure auditor independence,[157] or attempted to impose the expensing of stock options.[158] Under this Rule, shareholders may propose to correct an activity only after it creates damage or scandal worthy of widespread public notice, and is thus no longer "ordinary business."

The SEC has recommended that shareholders avoid encroaching on the board's powers to run the business by making mere recommendations, referred to as "precatory" proposals.[159] The problem with this solution is that boards routinely ignore such proposals, even when they are repeatedly adopted by a majority of shareholders and address such extraordinary and sensitive matters as dismantling staggered boards so shareholders have a right to elect the entire board at an annual meeting.[160]

Prior to 2009, Rule 14a-8 was of no use for nominating board candidates. Federal rules require management to prepare a proxy statement for the general meeting containing information on the company and the candidates for the board.[161] Even if state law generally allowed the shareholders to nominate a candidate for the board – as Delaware did – Rule 14a-8 expressly prevents shareholders from making a proposal relating to "election for membership on the company's board of directors or analogous governing body."[162] In this way, the state law right to nominate a candidate for the board was frustrated by a federal law requirement that excludes such a nomination from the primary document through which it realistically could be made. In 2003, the SEC considered a rule that would have allowed shareholders some power to nominate candidates for the board,[163]

---

[156] Fisch (1993: 1158–1159).   [157] See Quinn and Jarmel (2006: 29).

[158] See Quinn and Jarmel (2006: 30).

[159] In a note to this section, the SEC has explained: "Depending on the subject matter, some proposals are not considered proper under state law if they would be binding on the company if approved by shareholders. In our experience, most proposals that are cast as recommendations or requests that the board of directors take specified action are proper under state law. Accordingly, we will assume that a proposal drafted as a recommendation or suggestion is proper unless the company demonstrates otherwise." 17 CFR § 240.14a-8(i)(1).

[160] Professor Bebchuk provides empirical evidence gathered by the Investor Responsibility Research Center (IRRC) showing that, although resolutions to eliminate staggered boards were repeatedly adopted during the period between 1997 and 2003, boards refused to implement more than two-thirds of the resolutions adopted. Bebchuk (2005: 852).

[161] 17 CFR § 240.14a-3(a).   [162] 17 CFR 240.14a-8(i)(8).

[163] See Proposed Rule: Security Holder Director Nominations, SEC Release No. 34–48626, 68 *Federal Register* 60784 (October 14, 2003). This rule was considered again in 2007 and then dropped. See Manne (2007).

but the right would have been so limited and could have been exercised under such limited conditions that US companies would not even begin to approach the power given to shareholders under German and UK law. In any case, management lobby defeated the rule. Perhaps embarrassed by the Delaware Assembly's initiative in 2009 and perhaps riding a wave of public anti-management sentiment following the 2008 financial crisis, the SEC once again proposed a rule on shareholder nominations in June 2009.[164] Although the SEC did not adopt the rule upon expiration of the comment period, it has expressly stated it is still considering the matter.[165]

VI. Required majorities

The number of votes required to take a given action will of course determine how difficult it is to take that action. The actual figure will be determined by both its numerator and its denominator, and the denominator can consist of either voting power or capital. For example, the denominator "votes present and cast" will usually be smaller than "votes of all outstanding shares of the class," and the denominator "votes" or "voting power" may be different from the denominator "capital," depending on the number of non-voting shares the company has issued. Thus, it is important to know both the percentage that must be reached and the components of the fraction constituting that percentage in order to understand the difficulty of adopting a given resolution.

A. Germany

Unless otherwise specified in the *Satzung* or the law, shareholder resolutions require a simple majority of the votes cast.[166] This applies, for example, to the election of the *Aufsichtsrat* members whom shareholders elect, and to the appointment of a special auditor.[167] The law specifies a three-quarters majority of the votes cast for a resolution to remove members of the *Aufsichtsrat* from office,[168] as well as for other, basic resolutions, such as to amend the *Satzung*,[169] transfer all of the company's assets,[170] increase its capital,[171] or waive preemption rights.[172] For all such

164 See Proposed Rule: Facilitating Shareholder Director Nominations, SEC Release No. 34-60089, 74 *Federal Register* 29024 (June 18, 2009).
165 Final Rule: Proxy Disclosure Enhancements, SEC Release Nos. 33-9089; 34-61175, 74 Federal Register 68334, 68335 (Dec. 23, 2009).
166 § 133(1) AktG.   167 § 142(1) AktG.   168 § 103(1) AktG.   169 § 179(2) AktG.
170 § 179a(2) AktG.   171 §§ 182(1), 193(1), 202(2) AktG.   172 § 186(3) AktG.

supermajority decisions, it is important to note the strategic importance of a blocking minority, which can stymie the course the majority has chosen to pursue. As will be discussed in the *Girmes* case in Chapter 19, such power can also trigger fiduciary duties for minority shareholders.

B.   United Kingdom

The Companies Act 2006 classifies resolutions as "ordinary" and "special." An ordinary resolution requires a majority of either:

- the total *voting rights present*, eligible and used, if the vote is taken on a poll;[173]
- a majority of the *persons* who are present, eligible and vote on a matter, if the vote is taken by a show of hands;[174] or
- a majority of the *total voting rights* of eligible members if the vote is taken by written resolution.[175]

Likewise, parallel to the requirements for an ordinary resolution, a special resolution requires the higher percentage of 75 percent of the (i) voting rights present, (ii) of the persons present, or (iii) of the total voting rights in the case of a vote taken (i) on a poll, (ii) by a show of hands, or (iii) by written resolution.[176]

Ordinary resolutions are necessary for matters that include the removal of a director,[177] approval of the directors' remuneration report,[178] removal of the company's auditor,[179] and approval of the transfer of non-cash assets as consideration for shares.[180] Special resolutions are necessary for such matters as the approval of a scheme of merger,[181] the waiver of preemption rights[182] and the approval of a division of the company.[183]

C.   United States

Delaware law allows the certificate of incorporation to specify the majority required for a given action. If no majority is specified and the law does not provide otherwise, shareholder resolutions require a simple majority of the votes present at a meeting and entitled to vote on a matter.[184] For

---

[173] Sec. 282(4) CA 2006.   [174] Sec. 282(3) CA 2006.   [175] Sec. 282(2) CA 2006.

[176] Sec. 283 CA 2006.   [177] Sec. 168(1) CA 2006.   [178] Sec. 439(1) CA 2006.

[179] Sec. 510(2) CA 2006.   [180] Sec. 601(1) CA 2006.   [181] Sec. 907(1) CA 2006.

[182] Sec. 571(1) CA 2006.   [183] Sec. 922(1) CA 2006.

[184] DGCL § 216. The same section specifies that a meeting will not be duly constituted unless at least one-third of the shares entitled to vote on an issue are present at the meeting (referred to as the "quorum"), and that the certificate of incorporation may provide a higher quorum.

approving a merger,[185] a sale of assets[186] or the dissolution of the company, the law sets the higher figure of a majority of the outstanding shares entitled to vote.[187]

Among our three jurisdictions, approving action by "plurality" is unique to the US. Unless the company's certificate of incorporation provides otherwise, directors are elected by a "plurality" of the votes present at the meeting.[188] A "plurality" of the votes means the largest portion of votes cast.[189] Thus, if the votes were to be fragmented among twenty different candidates, the candidate who receives the highest portion of the votes would win the election even if that portion was only 6 percent of the total.

Current SEC regulations do not provide for alternative candidates to be listed for a given board position and the voting card allows shareholders to either vote for management's candidate or "withhold" their vote for such candidate.[190] It is not possible to vote *against* a candidate, and so votes "withheld" disappear for legal purposes of the election. This means that, when no alternative candidate is available, which is usually the case absent a "proxy contest,"[191] any vote at all for the listed candidate constitutes a winning plurality. Professor Joseph Grundfest provides a graphic illustration of the point: under a plurality rule, if "a million shares count as a quorum, and if 999,999 ballots strike your name out and say no, you, as the director, owning only one share, and you vote for yourself, congratulations, you win. You have the plurality."[192] In this way, the shareholder vote is rendered useless and the act of nominating candidates in fact serves as the act of appointing them. Institutional shareholders have sought to introduce majority voting in US companies. In an attempt to meet this problem half way, Delaware amended the General Corporation Law in 2006 to provide that, if the shareholders amend the by-laws to insert a majority vote rule for the election of directors, the board may not use its power to rescind the by-laws amendment.[193]

---

[185] DGCL § 251(c).   [186] DGCL § 271(a).   [187] DGCL § 275(b).

[188] DGCL § 216; and Model Act § 7.28(a).

[189] "Plurality. A large number or quantity that does not constitute a majority; a number greater than another, regardless of the margin." *Black's Law Dictionary* (1999: 1176).

[190] 17 CFR § 240.14a-4(b)(2).

[191] Proxies and proxy contests will be discussed in Chapter 17.

[192] Remarks of Professor Joseph Grundfest, in L. A. Bebchuk (ed.), "Symposium on Corporate Elections," (2003), p. 95, available at http://ssrn.com/abstract=471640.

[193] DGCL § 216.

Cases

Blasius Industries, Inc. v. Atlas Corporation
Delaware Court of Chancery
564 A 2d 651 (1988)
[*Text edited; some footnotes omitted*]

ALLEN, Chancellor

[*Text omitted*]

I.

Blasius acquires a 9% stake in Atlas

Blasius is a new stockholder of Atlas. It began to accumulate Atlas shares for the first time in July, 1987. On October 29, it filed a Schedule 13D with the Securities Exchange Commission disclosing that, with affiliates, it then owed 9.1% of Atlas' common stock. It stated in that filing that it intended to encourage management of Atlas to consider a restructuring of the Company or other transaction to enhance shareholder values. It also disclosed that Blasius was exploring the feasibility of obtaining control of Atlas, including instituting a tender offer or seeking "appropriate" representation on the Atlas board of directors.

Blasius has recently come under the control of two individuals, Michael Lubin and Warren Delano, who after experience in the commercial banking industry, had, for a short time, run a venture capital operation for a small investment banking firm. Now on their own, they apparently came to control Blasius with the assistance of Drexel Burnham's well noted junk bond mechanism. Since then, they have made several attempts to effect leveraged buyouts, but without success.

... According to its public filings with the SEC, Blasius' debt service obligations arising out of the sale of the junk bonds are such that it is unable to service those obligations from its income from operations.

... Atlas had a new CEO, defendant Weaver, who had, over the course of the past year or so, overseen a business restructuring of a sort ... The goal was to focus the Company on its gold mining business. By October, 1987, the structural changes to do this had been largely accomplished. Mr. Weaver ... wrote in his diary on October 30, 1987:

> 13D by Delano & Lubin came in today. Had long conversation w/MAH & Mark Golden [of Goldman, Sachs] on issue. All agree we must dilute these people down by the acquisition of another Co. w/stock, or merger or something else.

The Blasius proposal of a leverage recapitalization or sale

Immediately after filing its 13D on October 29, Blasius' representatives sought a meeting with the Atlas management. Atlas dragged its feet. A meeting was arranged for

December 2 ... Attending that meeting were Messrs. Lubin and Delano for Blasius, and, for Atlas, Messrs. Weaver, Devaney (Atlas' CFO), Masinter (legal counsel and director) and Czajkowski (a representative of Atlas' investment banker, Goldman Sachs) ...

Immediately following the meeting, the Atlas representatives expressed among themselves an initial reaction that the proposal was infeasible. On December 7, Mr. Lubin sent a letter detailing the proposal. In general, it proposed the following: (1) an initial special cash dividend to Atlas' stockholders in an aggregate amount equal to (a) $35 million, (b) the aggregate proceeds to Atlas from the exercise of option warrants and stock options, and (c) the proceeds from the sale or disposal of all of Atlas' operations that are not related to its continuing minerals operations; and (2) a special non-cash dividend to Atlas' stockholders of an aggregate $125 million principal amount of 7% Secured Subordinated Gold-Indexed Debentures. The funds necessary to pay the initial cash dividend were to principally come from (i) a "gold loan" in the amount of $35,625,000, repayable over a three to five year period and secured by 75,000 ounces of gold at a price of $475 per ounce, (ii) the proceeds from the sale of the discontinued Brockton Sole and Plastics and Ready-Mix Concrete businesses, and (iii) a then expected January, 1988 sale of uranium to the Public Service Electric & Gas Company. (DX H.)

... On December 9, Mr. Weaver issued a press release expressing surprise that Blasius would suggest using debt to accomplish what he characterized as a substantial liquidation of Atlas at a time when Atlas' future prospects were promising. He noted that the Blasius proposal recommended that Atlas incur a high debt burden in order to pay a substantial one time dividend consisting of $35 million in cash and $125 million in subordinated debentures. Mr. Weaver also questioned the wisdom of incurring an enormous debt burden amidst the uncertainty in the financial markets that existed in the aftermath of the October crash ...

The delivery of Blasius' consent statement

On December 30, 1987, Blasius caused Cede & Co. (the registered owner of its Atlas stock) to deliver to Atlas a signed written consent (1) adopting a precatory resolution recommending that the board develop and implement a restructuring proposal, (2) amending the Atlas bylaws to, among other things, expand the size of the board from seven to fifteen members – the maximum number under Atlas' charter, and (3) electing eight named persons to fill the new directorships. Blasius also filed suit that day in this court seeking a declaration that certain bylaws adopted by the board on September 1, 1987 acted as an unlawful restraint on the shareholders' right, created by Section 228 of our corporation statute, to act through consent without undergoing a meeting.

The reaction was immediate. Mr. Weaver conferred with Mr. Masinter, the Company's outside counsel and a director, who viewed the consent as an attempt to take control of the Company. They decided to call an emergency meeting of the board ... The point of the emergency meeting was to act on their conclusion (or to seek to have the board act on their conclusion) "that we should add at least one and probably two directors to the board … " … A quorum of directors, however, could not be arranged for a telephone meeting that day. A telephone meeting was held the next day. At that meeting, the board voted to amend the bylaws to increase the size of the board from seven to nine and appointed John M. Devaney and Harry J. Winters, Jr. to fill those newly created positions. Atlas' Certificate of Incorporation creates staggered terms for directors; the terms to which Messrs. Devaney and Winters were appointed would expire in 1988 and 1990, respectively.

The motivation of the incumbent board in expanding the board and appointing new members

In increasing the size of Atlas' board by two and filling the newly created positions, the members of the board realized that they were thereby precluding the holders of a majority of the Company's shares from placing a majority of new directors on the board through Blasius' consent solicitation, should they want to do so. Indeed the evidence establishes that that was the principal motivation in so acting …

There is testimony in the record to support the proposition that, in acting on December 31, the board was principally motivated simply to implement a plan to expand the Atlas board that preexisted the September, 1987 emergence of Blasius as an active shareholder. I have no doubt that the addition of Mr. Winters, an expert in mining economics, and Mr. Devaney, a financial expert employed by the Company, strengthened the Atlas board and, should anyone ever have reason to review the wisdom of those choices, they would be found to be sensible and prudent. I cannot conclude, however, that the strengthening of the board by the addition of these men was the principal motive for the December 31 action …

[Text omitted]

The January 6 rejection of the Blasius proposal

On January 6, the board convened for its scheduled meeting. At that time, it heard a full report from its financial advisor concerning the feasibility of the Blasius restructuring proposal. The Goldman Sachs presentation included a summary of five year cumulative cash flows measured against a base case and the Blasius proposal, an analysis of Atlas' debt repayment capacity under the Blasius proposal, and pro forma income and cash flow statements for a base case and the Blasius proposal, assuming prices of $375, $475 and $575 per ounce of gold.

After completing that presentation, Goldman Sachs concluded with its view that if Atlas implemented the Blasius restructuring proposal (i) a severe drain on operating cash flow would result, (ii) Atlas would be unable to service its long-term debt and could end up in bankruptcy, (iii) the common stock of Atlas would have little or no value, and (iv) since Atlas would be unable to generate sufficient cash to service its debt, the debentures contemplated to be issued in the proposed restructuring could have a value of only 20% to 30% of their face amount. Goldman Sachs also said that it knew of no financial restructuring that had been undertaken by a company where the company had no chance of repaying its debt, which, in its judgment, would be Atlas' situation if it implemented the Blasius restructuring proposal. Finally, Goldman Sachs noted that if Atlas made a meaningful commercial discovery of gold after implementation of the Blasius restructuring proposal, Atlas would not have the resources to develop the discovery.

The board then voted to reject the Blasius proposal. Blasius was informed of that action. The next day, Blasius caused a second, modified consent to be delivered to Atlas. A contest then ensued between the Company and Blasius for the votes of Atlas' shareholders ...

[*Text omitted*]

III.

One of the principal thrusts of plaintiffs' argument is that, in acting to appoint two additional persons of their own selection, including an officer of the Company, to the board, defendants were motivated not by any view that Atlas' interest (or those of its shareholders) required that action, but rather they were motivated improperly, by selfish concern to maintain their collective control over the Company. That is, plaintiffs say that the evidence shows there was no policy dispute or issue that really motivated this action, but that asserted policy differences were pretexts for entrenchment for selfish reasons. If this were found to be factually true, one would not need to inquire further. The action taken would constitute a breach of duty. *Schnell* v. *Chris Craft Industries* ...

[*Text omitted*]

On balance, I cannot conclude that the board was acting out of a self-interested motive in any important respect on December 31. I conclude rather that the board saw the "threat" of the Blasius recapitalization proposal as posing vital policy differences between itself and Blasius ...

The real question the case presents, to my mind, is whether, in these circumstances, the board, even if it is acting with subjective good faith (which will typically, if not always, be a contestable or debatable judicial conclusion), may validly act for the principal purpose of preventing the shareholders from electing a majority of new directors. The question thus posed is not one of intentional wrong (or even negligence), but one of authority as between the fiduciary and the beneficiary (not simply legal authority, i.e. as between the fiduciary and the world at large).

IV.

It is established in our law that a board may take certain steps ... that have the effect of defeating a threatened change in corporate control, when those steps are taken advisedly, in good faith pursuit of a corporate interest, and are reasonable in relation to a threat to legitimate corporate interests posed by the proposed change in control ...

1. Why the deferential business judgment rule does not apply to board acts taken for the primary purpose of interfering with a stockholder's vote, even if taken advisedly and in good faith.

A.   The question of legitimacy

The shareholder franchise is the ideological underpinning upon which the legitimacy of directorial power rests. Generally, shareholders have only two protections against perceived inadequate business performance. They may sell their stock (which, if done in sufficient numbers, may so affect security prices as to create an incentive for altered managerial performance), or they may vote to replace incumbent board members.

It has, for a long time, been conventional to dismiss the stockholder vote as a vestige or ritual of little practical importance. [Note 1] It may be that we are now witnessing the emergence of new institutional voices and arrangements that will make the stockholder vote a less predictable affair than it has been. Be that as it may, however, whether the vote is seen functionally as an unimportant formalism, or as an important tool of discipline, it is clear that it is critical to the theory that legitimates the exercise of power by some (directors and officers) over vast aggregations of property that they do not own. Thus, when viewed from a broad, institutional perspective, it can be seen that matters involving the integrity of the shareholder voting process involve consideration [*sic*] not present in any other context in which directors exercise delegated power.

[Note 1] See, e.g. E. Rostow, To Whom and For What Ends Is Corporate Management Responsible, in *The Corporation in Modern Society* (E. S. Mason ed. 1959). The late Professor A. A. Berle once dismissed the shareholders' meeting as a "kind of ancient, meaningless ritual like some of the ceremonies that go with the mace in the House of Lords." Berle, *Economic Power and the Free Society* (1957), quoted in Balotti, Finkelstein, Williams, *Meetings of Shareholders* (1987) at 2.

B.   Questions of this type raise issues of the allocation of authority as between the board and the shareholders

The distinctive nature of the shareholder franchise context also appears when the matter is viewed from a less generalized, doctrinal point of view. From this point of view ... the ordinary considerations to which the business judgment rule originally responded are simply not present in the shareholder voting context. That is, a decision by the board to act for the primary purpose of preventing the effectiveness of a shareholder vote inevitably involves the question who, as between the principal and the agent, has authority with respect to a matter of internal corporate governance ... A board's decision to act to prevent the shareholders from creating a majority of new board positions and filling them does not involve the exercise of the corporation's power over its property, or with respect to its rights or obligations; rather, it involves allocation, between shareholders as a class and the board, of effective power with respect to governance of the corporation. This need not be the case with respect to other forms of corporate action that may have an entrenchment effect – such as the stock buy-backs present in *Unocal*, *Cheff* or *Kors* v. *Carey*. Action designed principally to interfere with the effectiveness of a vote inevitably involves a conflict between the board and a shareholder majority. Judicial review of such action involves a determination of the legal and equitable obligations of an agent towards his principal. This is not, in my opinion, a question that a court may leave to the agent finally to decide so long as he does so honestly and competently; that is, it may not be left to the agent's business judgment.

A similar concern, for credible corporate democracy, underlies those cases that strike down board action that sets or moves an annual meeting date upon a finding that such action was intended to thwart a shareholder group from effectively mounting an election campaign ... The cases invalidating stock issued for the primary purpose of diluting the voting power of a control block also reflect the law's concern that a credible form of corporate democracy be maintained ...

Similarly, a concern for corporate democracy is reflected (1) in our statutory requirement of annual meetings ... and in the cases that aggressively and summarily enforce that right ...

2. What rule does apply: per se invalidity of corporate acts intended primarily to thwart effective exercise of the franchise or is there an intermediate standard?

Plaintiff argues for a rule of per se invalidity once a plaintiff has established that a board has acted for the primary purpose of thwarting the exercise of a shareholder vote. Our opinions ... could be read as support for such a rule of per se invalidity. *Condec* [*Corporation* v. *Lunkenheimer Company*] is informative.

There, plaintiff had recently closed a tender offer for 51% of defendants' stock. It had announced no intention to do a follow-up merger. The incumbent board had earlier refused plaintiffs' offer to merge and, in response to its tender offer, sought alternative deals. It found and negotiated a proposed sale of all of defendants' assets for stock in the buyer, to be followed up by an exchange offer to the seller's shareholders. The stock of the buyer was publicly traded in the New York Stock Exchange, so that the deal, in effect, offered cash to the target's shareholders. As a condition precedent to the sale of assets, an exchange of authorized but unissued shares of the seller (constituting about 15% of the total issued and outstanding shares after issuance) was to occur. Such issuance would, of course, negate the effective veto that plaintiffs' 51% stockholding would give it over a transaction that would require shareholder approval. Plaintiff sued to invalidate the stock issuance.

The court concluded, as a factual matter, that: "... the primary purpose of the issuance of such shares was to prevent control of Lunkenheimer from passing to Condec ..." ... The court then implied that not even a good faith dispute over corporate policy could justify a board in acting for the primary purpose of reducing the voting power of a control shareholder ...

... A per se rule that would strike down, in equity, any board action taken for the primary purpose of interfering with the effectiveness of a corporate vote would have the advantage of relative clarity and predictability. It also has the advantage of most vigorously enforcing the concept of corporate democracy. The disadvantage it brings along is, of course, the disadvantage a per se rule always has: it may sweep too broadly.

In two recent cases dealing with shareholder votes, this court struck down board acts done for the primary purpose of impeding the exercise of stockholder voting power. In doing so, a per se rule was not applied. Rather, it was said that, in such a case, the board bears the heavy burden of demonstrating a compelling justification for such action.

In *Aprahamian* v. *HBO & Company* ... the incumbent board had moved the date of the annual meeting on the eve of that meeting when it learned that a dissident stockholder group had or appeared to have in hand proxies representing a majority of the outstanding shares. The court restrained that action and compelled the meeting to occur as noticed, even though the board stated that it had good business reasons to move the meeting date forward, and that that action was recommended by a special committee. The court concluded as follows:

> The corporate election process, if it is to have any validity, must be conducted with scrupulous fairness and without any advantage being conferred or denied to any candidate or slate of candidates. In the interests of corporate democracy, those in charge of the election machinery of a corporation must be held to the highest standards of providing for and conducting corporate elections. The business judgment rule therefore does not confer any presumption of propriety on the acts of directors in postponing the annual meeting. Quite to the contrary. When the election machinery appears, at least facially, to have been manipulated those in charge of the election have the burden of persuasion to justify their actions. *Aprahamian* ... at 1206–07.

In *Phillips* v. *Insituform of North America, Inc.* ... the court enjoined the voting of certain stock issued for the primary purpose of diluting the voting power of certain control shares. The facts were complex. After discussing *Canada Southern* and *Condec* in light of the more recent, important Supreme Court opinion in *Unocal Corp.* v. *Mesa Petroleum Company*, it was there concluded as follows:

> One may read *Canada Southern* as creating a black-letter rule prohibiting the issuance of shares for the purpose of diluting a large stockholder's voting power, but one need not do so. It may, as well, be read as a case in which no compelling corporate purpose was presented that might otherwise justify such an unusual course. Such a reading is, in my opinion, somewhat more consistent with the recent *Unocal* case.
>
> ...
>
> In my view, our inability to foresee now all of the future settings in which a board might, in good faith, paternalistically seek to thwart a shareholder vote, counsels against the adoption of a per se rule invalidating, in equity, every board action taken for the sole or primary purpose of thwarting a shareholder vote, even though I recognize the transcending significance of the franchise to the claims to legitimacy of our scheme of corporate governance. It may be that some set of facts would justify such extreme action. This, however, is not such a case.

3. Defendants have demonstrated no sufficient justification for the action of December 31 which was intended to prevent an unaffiliated majority of shareholders from effectively exercising their right to elect eight new directors.

The board was not faced with a coercive action taken by a powerful shareholder against the interests of a distinct shareholder constituency (such as a public minority). It was presented with a consent solicitation by a 9% shareholder. Moreover, here it had time (and understood that it had time) to inform the shareholders of its views on the merits of the proposal subject to stockholder vote. The only justification that can, in such a situation, be offered for the action taken is that the board knows better than do the shareholders what is in the corporation's best interest. While that premise is no doubt true for any number of matters, it is irrelevant (except insofar as the shareholders wish to be guided by the board's recommendation) when the question is who should comprise the board of directors. The theory of our corporation law confers power upon directors as the agents of the shareholders; it does not create Platonic masters. It may be that the Blasius restructuring proposal was or is unrealistic and would lead to injury to the corporation and its shareholders if pursued. Having heard the evidence, I am inclined to think it was not a sound proposal. The board certainly viewed it that way, and that view, held in good faith, entitled the board to take certain steps to evade the risk it perceived. It could, for example, expend corporate funds to inform shareholders and seek to bring them to a similar point of view … But there is a vast difference between expending corporate funds to inform the electorate and exercising power for the primary purpose of foreclosing effective shareholder action. A majority of the shareholders, who were not dominated in any respect, could view the matter differently than did the board. If they do, or did, they are entitled to employ the mechanisms provided by the corporation law and the Atlas certificate of incorporation to advance that view. They are also entitled, in my opinion, to restrain their agents, the board, from acting for the principal purpose of thwarting that action.

I therefore conclude that, even finding the action taken was taken in good faith, it constituted an unintended violation of the duty of loyalty that the board owed to the shareholders … That action will, therefore, be set aside by order of this court.

[*Text omitted*]

Macrotron Shareholder Litigation
High Federal Court
November 25, 2002, BGHZ 153, 47
[*Partial, unofficial translation of official opinion text*]

Official head note

a) A shareholder resolution exculpating the actions of a board member (*Entlastungsbeschluss*) may be challenged in cases where the activity exculpated is action by the *Vorstand* or *Aufsichtsrat* that clearly constitutes a grave violation of the law or the articles of incorporation (*Satzung*) ...

If the *Aufsichtsrat* breaches its duty to provide a report pursuant to § 314(2) AktG, the resolution exculpating its action may be challenged.

b) Voluntary delisting has a negative impact on share property by drastically reducing the liquidity of shares. Its approval must be by shareholders' resolution and it requires a mandatory bid by the company or the majority shareholder to purchase the shares of the minority shareholders.

The resolution does not require a material justification. The *Vorstand* need not write a report to such effect.

c) In the case of voluntary delisting, sufficient protection for the minority can only be guaranteed if the mandatory bid compensates for the full value of the share property and the minority shareholders can have this value audited in judicial proceedings.

The examination must take place pursuant to the rules of a statutory appraisal proceeding (*Spruchverfahren*) freely entered into.

[*Text omitted*]

Facts

The Defendant [Macrotron], a listed corporation, has a corporate capital of €11 million, which consists equally of common stock and nonvoting preferred shares. The owner of the majority of the shares is a foreign company; 1.07% of the common stock and 8.5% of the preferred shares are widely held.

Plaintiffs generally continue to challenge on appeal the shareholders' resolution adopted in the general meeting of May 21, 1999 under Item 9 (Delisting), Plaintiffs 1 and 2 further challenge the resolutions on Items 5 through 8 (Exculpating (*Entlastung*) the *Vorstand* and the *Aufsichtsrat*). The underlying facts are as follows:

The shares of the Defendant were admitted to the official lists of the Frankfurt Stock Exchange and the Bavarian Exchange. According to the Defendant's pleadings, because of the low number of shares that were widely held, there was very little trading in its stock and so it found the costs connected with listing no longer justified. Defendant also alleges that the low trading volume led to drastic price swings that did not reflect the Defendant's business fundamentals and thus damaged the company. In addition, it feared price manipulation. Its general meeting thus approved management's proposal (Item 9) and authorized the *Vorstand* to apply to both exchanges for the revocation of its listing. The Defendant further states that its majority shareholder intends to make an offer to the minority shareholders holding DM 50 nominal value stock of DM 1,057 (for common stock) and DM 820 (for preferred stock).

Plaintiffs allege the authorizing resolution to be defective because it has an unlimited duration, lacks material justification and is an overly drastic measure (*unverhältnismäßig*), as well as because it lacks an accompanying management report.

Plaintiffs 1 and 2 further allege that the resolutions exculpating the performance of the *Vorstand* and the *Aufsichtsrat* (Items 5–6 for the *Vorstand*; Items 7–8 for the *Aufsichtsrat*) to be illegitimate because the dependent company reports that the *Vorstand* prepared for the financial year 1997/1988 and the partial year 1998 did not meet the requirements of law. To the extent that one could at all conclude the *Aufsichtsrat* discussed its examination of the *Vorstand's* dependent company report in its own report prepared pursuant to § 171(2) AktG, its reporting does not meet the requirements of law.

The regional court dismissed the complaint. The court of appeals rejected the Plaintiffs' appeal as well as the motion of Plaintiffs 3 and 4 requesting transfer of the proceedings ...

On appeal, Plaintiffs pursue their complaint to the extent described above. This Division did not accept the appeal with regard to the dismissed challenge to the resolution exculpating the *Vorstand's* actions.

Reasons

The appeal of Plaintiffs 1 and 2 has been successful to the extent that the appeals court dismissed the challenge to the resolution exculpating the *Aufsichtsrat's* actions.

The appeal of Plaintiffs 3 and 4 has been successful to the extent that the appeals court dismissed their motion requesting transfer of the proceedings on the sufficiency of the majority shareholder's offer to the competent commercial court.

The remaining appeals of Plaintiffs 1 and 2 and Plaintiffs 3 and 4 find no success.

I.

The appeal of Plaintiffs 1 and 2 correctly asserts that the appeals court approved the legality of the shareholders' resolutions exculpating the action of the *Aufsichtsrat* members on the grounds that the *Aufsichtsrat* met its reporting obligations to the general meeting on the results of its examination of the *Vorstand's* dependent company report. These Plaintiffs also correctly point out that the appeals court failed to notice that the *Aufsichtsrat's* report contains no auditor's certification. The exculpating resolutions demarcated Items 7 and 8 rest on violations of law, and must therefore be declared null (§ 243(1) AktG) by revoking the trial court's decision and amending the decision of the court of appeals.

1. Both courts and the legal scholarship debate the conditions under which an exculpating resolution may be challenged. With reference to §§ 120(2) and 93(4) AktG, one opinion is that exculpation may be given even to management that has

neglected its duties and committed grave violations of law or the *Satzung* ... The exculpation need only state that the management has followed business goals and still has the trust of the shareholders. A challenge may then be raised only in cases of procedural errors, in particular defects in information, or very specific substantive defects ...

The opposing opinion is that exculpation is primarily a declaration of the general meeting that approves the management as – on the whole – in compliance with the law and the *Satzung*; only indirectly does it evidence trust for the future ...

The decisions of this Division on the matter appear somewhat ambiguous. One judgment states that the general meeting may dispense exculpation even when facts are present that would justify refusing exculpation, for one shareholder may not impose his opinion on the other shareholders through a judicial challenge (Decision of March 30, 1967 ... WM 1967, 503, 507). In a later judgment, this Division explained that it is illegal for the general meeting to dispense exculpation on the *Aufsichtsrat* members despite their having failed to render a report pursuant to § 314(2) AktG, or done so improperly (BGHZ 62, 193, 194 *et seq.*). A judgment regarding a GmbH states that through an exculpation the general meeting finds, *inter alia*, that the management has made purposeful decisions within the parameters of its freedom of discretion as drawn by the law, the *Satzung*, or individual instructions (BGHZ 94, 324, 326 *et seq.*).

Clarifying the meaning of these decisions, the Division here holds that an exculpation resolution may be challenged in court if it exculpates an action that presents a clear and grave violation of the law or the *Satzung*. It has been correctly observed that the provisions of § 120(2) AktG do not contradict this (Hüffer, AktG, § 120, mn 12). The rule of law stated in § 243(1) AktG, that every shareholders' resolution violating law or the *Satzung* may be challenged, is not eliminated by the waiver of a compensation claim expressed in an exculpation resolution ... If an exculpation resolution were to replace such rule of law, a majority voting to approve illegal actions could always exculpate the management against the will of a minority seeking to uphold the law or the *Satzung* ... That would contradict not only the provisions of § 243(1) AktG, but would also be irreconcilable with the majority's duty of loyalty to the minority (see Linotype, BGHZ 103, 184, 193 *et seq.*).

Nor does the rule in § 93(4) AktG contradict our holding. In contrast to § 243(1) AktG, which grants an unrestricted right to challenge the general meeting's violations of the law or the *Satzung*, § 93(4) AktG refers to agreements waiving damage claims only with a limited effect.

This understanding of the nature of exculpation by no means dictates that the resolution on exculpation cannot be drafted so as to be safe from challenge ... If the general meeting's judgment is passed merely on behavior that remains within the boundaries set by law and the *Satzung*, it regards management's business dealings and the trust placed in them for the future. If a judgment must be made on actions that violate the law or the *Satzung*, an overall refusal of exculpation expresses no trust in the director, including for the future. It does not necessarily follow from this that the general meeting cannot leave a director in office despite a loss of trust, if it is possible to conclude that this is nonetheless in the best interests of the company and that the board will respect the law and the *Satzung* in the future.

2. The court of appeals also correctly understood as a general rule that a resolution dispensing exculpation on board members despite a clear and serious violation of law is itself illegal, and may be challenged under § 243(1) AktG. In the case at hand, however, that court incorrectly failed to perceive that the members of the *Aufsichtsrat* had violated § 314(2) AktG.

It first failed to see that the report drafted by the *Aufsichtsrat* pursuant to § 171(2) AktG and presented to the general meeting does not state, as required by § 314(2) AktG, that the *Aufsichtsrat* had examined the *Vorstand's* dependent company report. Rather, the report only states that Auditors P examined the annual accounts and the management reports for the companies and the group, including the accounting records for the relevant financial year, and gave an unqualified auditor's certification. The *Aufsichtsrat* was informed of this fact and itself approved the annual accounts. Its further remarks concerned the group accounts, the auditors' report on the latter, and the use of the profits. There is no mention of a dependent company report. An examination of the latter was also not discussed in a passage in which all matters that require *Aufsichtsrat* approval under the law or the *Satzung* were examined and, where necessary, approved by the *Aufsichtsrat*. This apparently concerned only transactions requiring approval, such as those encompassed by § 111(4) or § 204(1) AktG. However, the law does not require that the *Aufsichtsrat* approve the dependent company report.

The *Aufsichtsrat's* report does mention that Auditors P gave an "unqualified auditor's certification" to the "reports of the management." This can also include the *Vorstand's* dependent company report. However, this reference is not enough, as the appellant correctly observes. The law (§ 314(2) AktG) rather requires that "a certification given by the auditors be included in the report." The Regional Court of Munich also understands this requirement to require an exact reproduction of the certification …

II.

The appeal is, however, unsuccessful to the extent that the Plaintiffs challenge the shareholders' resolution authorizing the *Vorstand* voluntarily to delist the Defendant's shares from the Exchanges in Frankfurt and Munich (Item 9).

1. Contrary to the view of the appellant, the appeals court correctly takes the position that voluntary delisting – i.e. the withdrawal of the company out of official trading and the regulated market on all exchanges – requires a resolution adopted with a simple majority of the general meeting.

However, the competence of the general meeting to decide on voluntary delisting cannot be deduced from the fact that delisting would affect the internal structure of the stock corporation or the rights of shareholders to participate in governance. The internal structure of the company will not be changed by withdrawing from the exchange ... Similarly, neither the body of shareholders' rights – such as rules on "squeeze outs" under §§ 327a *et seq.* AktG – nor membership as a proportional participation right (rights to dividends, claims to a share at liquidation) will be affected, nor will the asset value of the holding be watered ... or the position of the shareholder be weakened by mediating his governance rights (see *Holzmüller*, BGHZ 83, 129, 136 *et seq.*).

It may nevertheless not be overlooked that by withdrawing the company from official trading (§ 38(4) BörsG) or from the regulated market (§ 52(2) BörsG), shareholders lose the market in which they may at any time liquidate their shares by sale. For a majority shareholder or a blockholder who uses her holding to pursue a governance agenda and not just as an investment, this is not important. Yet for a minority shareholder or a small shareholder, whose engagement in the company's affairs is solely to protect his rights as a shareholder, loss of the market does entail serious economic disadvantages that cannot be compensated for by inserting the shares in the over-the-counter market.

This liquidity (*Verkehrsfähigkeit*) of the shares of a corporation admitted to a securities exchange has special significance in the decisions of the Federal Constitutional Court on the valuation of equity holdings: if a shareholder has appraisal rights following the conclusion of an enterprise agreement pursuant to § 291 AktG or subsequent to a merger by absorption within the meaning of §§ 319 *et seq.* AktG, the amount of compensation must be determined in a way that a minority shareholder receives no less for her shares than she would by a free decision to sell at the same time ... The market price and the possibility to receive it at any time are characteristics of share property (see DAT/Altana, BVerfGE 100, 289, 305 *et seq.*), which, like share ownership itself, are constitutionally protected. They have a direct impact on the range of property rights protected as part of the membership of a shareholder. It is true that pursuant to the statutory rules, the protected property rights of members directly extend only to a guarantee of dividend payments, a share of any liquidation proceeds and the relative asset value of the holding. If, however, the market price, including the liquidity of the shareholding, is included in the guarantee of property rights set out in art. 14(1) GG, its protection must also be guaranteed in the relationship between a corporation and its shareholders. Under these circumstances it certainly does not regard only the legal relationship between a shareholder and a third party, occurring in a realm beyond that of membership; rather, in listed companies it constitutes an indispensible element of the legal relationship between the corporation and its shareholders ... Since the role of protecting the asset value of membership has been entrusted to the general meeting rather than to the management, it is the general meeting which is competent to make decisions affecting such value. The general meeting, not the management, must make the decision whether delisting – as a measure that reduces the liquidity of the shares and thus the market value of shareholdings – should be carried out in light of the duty to protect the minority …

2. Reserving the decision over delisting to the general meeting is however in itself not enough to protect the minority shareholders. Such protection is only secured when the minority shareholders are compensated for the value of their shares, and they are given a chance to have such value audited in judicial proceedings (see BVerfGE 100, 289, 303 …).

a) The applicable provisions of the Exchange Act do not guarantee an effective protection of the minority under company law. However, the previous version of § 43(4) BörsG (§ 38(4) as amended by the Fourth Financial Market Promotion Act of July 1, 2002, BGBl. vol. I, p. 2010) provides that a withdrawal of listing may not prejudice the protection of investors. In the newer formulation of this protection, the law leaves the details to the securities exchanges (§ 43(4) BörsG, previous version; § 38(4) BörsG, as amended). The exchange regulation does provide rules designed to protect investors. They do not, however, meet the standards of minority protection required under corporate law.

On the one hand, the applicable provisions of the exchange regulation could be changed at any time by the competent committee of the securities exchange. This is well exemplified by the case of the Frankfurt Stock Exchange: The version of § 54a(1) BörsO FWB that was in force until March, 26, 2002 required that an application for voluntary delisting could only be approved if a public tender offer were made at a price adequately related to the highest market price on the Exchange during the last six months preceding the application; however, under the new rules, a withdrawal from listing can be announced as long as investors have sufficient time (i.e. six months, see § 54a(1) No. 2 BörsO FWB) after publication of the decision to delist to sell the shares affected by the delisting … This rule does not provide sufficient investor protection if only because immediately after the announcement of the delisting the market price of the shares usually drops steeply, which makes it impossible for the shareholder to realize the value of his investment …

On the other hand, the exchange regulations do not require that compensation be paid for the value of the shares, but rather normally ask – as the Frankfurt Stock Exchange used to – reimbursement of an amount adequately related to the highest market price on the Exchange during the last six months preceding the announcement of the delisting. Since this amount could also be lower than the value of the shares, full indemnification of the minority shareholders – as is required by the cases of the Constitutional Court – is not guaranteed.

Consequently, capital markets law does not exclude the possibility that delisting will damage the property rights of the minority shareholders. This possibility must be foreclosed through granting a corporate law protection for the minority.

b) The minority shareholders can only be adequately protected by having the corporation (within the limits of §§ 71 *et seq.* AktG) or the majority shareholder make a mandatory bid for their shares at the time that the application for the resolution is made. As the minority shareholders have a right to full compensation, the offer price must equal the value of their shares.

c) Pursuant to the cases of the Constitutional Court, shareholders must be guaranteed the right to have the adequacy of the sum given them for their shares examined by a court. The Court left it open whether this examination should be carried out through an action challenging the resolution or through analogical application of the provisions on appraisal proceedings (§ 306 AktG, §§ 305 *et seq.* UmwG) ...

This Division does not find that an action challenging the resolution is the best method to examine whether the tender offer equals the market price of the shares. It fully meets the needs of neither party. The shareholders would only be able to achieve a declaration that the resolution was null and thus prevent its execution. In this way they would only indirectly be able to have the company or the majority shareholder raise the bid price. The need to call another general meeting would create disproportionate costs for the company. Furthermore, a delay of the delisting could create significant disadvantages for the company.

As shown by the rules applicable to enterprise agreements (§ 304(3), § 305(5) AktG) and in the Reorganization Act (§§ 15, 34, 196, 212 UmwG), the needs of the interested parties can be better met if the adequacy of the amount offered is tested in a procedure created for this purpose (appraisal proceeding – *Spruchverfahren*). These considerations, which led to the introduction of an appraisal proceeding in the law applicable to enterprise agreements and reorganizations, also apply to the process of delisting. It is therefore meaningful that, just as in the case of a squeeze out, the conflict between the parties not be solved by a challenge to the resolution but by an appraisal proceeding.

The analogical application of these procedural rules is unproblematic from the perspective of constitutional law (see BVerfG ZIP 2000, 1670, 1673). Such application can also be approved from the perspective of procedural law ... By applying the provisions on appraisal proceedings to cases of delisting, it will be guaranteed that a court will determine the value of the shares simultaneously for all shareholders.

3. Contrary to the view of the appellant, the shareholders' resolution does not require a material justification, as this Division has found necessary for an exclusion of pre-emptive rights ... The decision regarding delisting made on recommendation of the *Vorstand* has the character of a business decision. As the general meeting is competent to decide, it rests in the discretion of the majority of shareholders

whether the measure is in the interest of the company and appears advisable. The property rights of the minority shareholders are protected by the requirement of a mandatory bid to buy their shares at their full value, as well as by the possibility of having the price examined in an appraisal proceeding.

There is no need for a *Vorstand* report pursuant to § 186(4) AktG in the case of delisting. In the general meeting, the Defendant coherently presented the reasons for the delisting. It discussed the reduction of costs, the threatened price volatility and the threatened dangers for the company, as well as the danger of market manipulation. These reasons are understandable in themselves and carry the general meeting's decision.

As the appeals court explained, the information needs of the minority shareholders were adequately met. Pursuant to the legal standard of § 124(2) AktG, which should be consulted here mutatis mutandis, it is sufficient that the details of the delisting application and of the majority shareholder's buyout offer be disclosed to them. According to the determinations of the appeals court, the Defendant met these requirements.

4. The objection of the appellant that the authorizing resolution was not sufficiently definite as to time is also unfounded. This would be true in those cases in which the law permits the general meeting to authorize the *Vorstand* to undertake specific measures, for which the duration of the authorization is limited by law (see § 71(1) No. 8 AktG) or the general meeting is given a maximum time limit beyond which the authorization may not extend (§ 202(2) AktG). If the law makes no rule on the duration of the authorization, the general meeting is free to specify a time limit. If the meeting does not set a term for the authorization, the *Vorstand* must decide on the basis of its legal duties according to its free business judgment if and when to undertake the measure for which it has been authorized. It would have to report on the status of the matter in the next, annual general meeting (§ 175(1) AktG). If at this time the measure has not yet been carried out, the general meeting would be able to resolve whether to leave the authorization standing or revoke it. In this way, the authorization is subjected to adequate, concrete, periodic checks by the general meeting. Further temporal restrictions are unnecessary.

The appeal of Plaintiffs 1 and 2 further complains that the appeals court incorrectly rejected their argument that the measure of delisting was abusive because it was used to force the minority shareholders out of the Defendant company with arbitrary means. The arbitrariness was evidenced because the dividend for common and preferred shares was significantly reduced as compared to previous years, although the earnings of the Defendant had not fallen. This Division disagrees with this argument as well. The appellees have made reference to a presentation of the Defendant according to which the profit margins greatly decreased because of a significant increase in materials costs in relation to turnover, which forced the

Defendant to lower its costs through current investments. This increased investment cost reduced the distributable profits. The appellate record shows no statement with which Plaintiffs 1 and 2 confront this coherent explanation of the Defendant with plausible arguments. The appeals court found correctly on the basis of these facts that there was no case of abusive delisting.

[Text omitted]

17

Shareholder information rights

Required reading

EU: Transparency Directive, arts. 1–7

D: AktG, §§ 124, 125, 131, 132, 142(1), 145, 243(4), 258(1) and (2), 259(1)

UK: CA 2006, secs. 238(1), 355, 423(1), 430(1), 431, 441, 444–447, 463, 1112, 1136; FSA Disclosure and Transparency Rules, Rules 1.1.1, 1.3.4, 2.2.1, 2.3.2, 2.5, 3.1, 4.1.1, 4.1.5, 4.2.1, 4.2.2, 4.3.1, 4.3.2, 4.3.6, 6.1.2, 6.1.9; FSA Listing Rules, Rule 9.2.6, 9.6, 9.7A.1, 9.8.4, 9.8.6, 9.8.8, 10.3.1, 11.1.7

US: DGCL, §§ 219, 220; Exchange Act Rules 14a-3(a) and 14a-7(a); scan each item of Schedule 14A

The information rights of shareholders

In the previous chapter, we looked at the voting rights of shareholders. Before a shareholder can exercise a voting right, he must be able to make a decision about the matter up for vote, and this presupposes access to information. The information rights of shareholders come in three basic forms: (i) inspection upon request; (ii) routine, regular disclosure; and (iii) *ad hoc* disclosure of significant events. When a company is small and the shareholders are in close contact with the management, inspection upon request is a good way to obtain information because it is flexible and provides only what the shareholder needs. This type of inspection is provided for in different forms in the company law statutes of our three jurisdictions. When a company lists its securities on the capital market, however, the number of shareholders can dramatically increase and the geographical proximity of shareholders to management usually decreases. Such companies also assume a certain responsibility to potential investors, their potential future shareholders. For existing shareholders, routine, regular disclosure of certain information across the market allows them both to decide on matters coming up for a vote and to compare their investments with those in other companies when making decisions on whether to buy, hold or sell the company's securities. For potential investors, market disclosure facilitates price formation and guides investment decisions.

At least for listed companies, each of our jurisdictions provides detailed rules for annual and (what is in effect) quarterly disclosure of information regarding the issuer and its financial condition.[1] Current or *ad hoc* disclosure is also required by the laws of each of our jurisdictions. It both fills the gaps between regular reports and promptly transforms *inside* information into *market* information, which reduces opportunities for inside abuse and increases the information content of market prices. Information is of little use unless it discloses the true state of the company for present and future shareholders. That is why each of the jurisdictions we examine prohibits the release of false and misleading information in ways ranging from the general principles against fraud in legal dealings to specially drafted rules focused on specific types of disclosure documents. The enforcement of such rules and principles is primarily a subject for a course on "Securities Regulation" or "Capital Markets Law"; but, by including the *ComROAD* case and an excerpt from *Basic Inc.* v. *Levinson* in this chapter, this text offers a passing reference to the important problem of distinguishing between disclosure on the primary and secondary markets (this latter being our focus here) and the degree of causal connection that must be proven between an incorrect disclosure and an investor's decision to buy, sell or hold a security, in order to support a successful claim for damages.

The remainder of this introductory note examines the various types of information rights in turn.

I.   *Information upon request*

A.   Germany

German law gives shareholders a comparatively limited right to seek information from the company. All rights to request information revolve around the general meeting and are limited to the items on the agenda. The primary information right is a right to request information *during*

---

[1] Since at the beginning of the twenty-first century few principles are as universally accepted as transparency, it may surprise the reader to learn that the desirability of mandatory disclosure has been hotly debated. The crux of this argument is that, if disclosure was good, issuers would do it voluntarily and regulation would distort market forces. See Easterbrook and Fischel (1996: 276 *et seq.*) and a response in Coffee (1984), as well as Romano (2002: 16 *et seq.*).

the general meeting, and includes information "regarding the company's affairs."[2] This right can be used in the general meeting to obtain information about a matter that is not already fully disclosed, but lies within the proper interest of a shareholder in the company, such as permissible additional details regarding executive compensation or the background and activities of directors, explanations of items on the financial statements, relationships with affiliated companies, or the intended use of funds from a proposed capital increase.[3] Shareholders may request information for the sole reason of seeking to further their own interests as shareholders. The *Vorstand* may deny requested information only for one of the reasons expressly listed in the statute,[4] and an unjustified denial of information triggers a right to seek relief from a court, which can then order the release of information on the matter in question.[5] Moreover, if a request for relevant information is unduly denied, this may furnish the basis for a challenge of a related shareholder resolution.[6]

Another set of rights allows shareholders to request information *before* the meeting. These rights resemble routine, regular disclosure *à la carte*, in that, for specific transactions such as sales of assets,[7] the contracting of corporate alliances,[8] mergers,[9] and changes in corporate form,[10] the shareholder can request that copies of the relevant documents – which must in any case be presented to the general meeting – be delivered to them before the meeting.

B.   United Kingdom

The types of information that shareholders can request from a UK company are closely tied to the registers, reports and contracts that a company must keep on various matters, and access to these documents and registers is not always limited to shareholders. The registers that may be inspected and copied include the register of members,[11] including any register of overseas branch members,[12] general meeting minutes and resolutions for the last ten years,[13] the register of debenture holders,[14] the register of disclosed interests in the company's shares,[15] and the register of charges on the company's assets.[16] The reports that must be kept available for inspection include the directors' statement and the auditor's report,[17] and any report

---

[2] § 131(1) AktG.   [3] See Butzke (2001: 248 *et seq.*).   [4] § 131(3) AktG.
[5] § 132 AktG.   [6] § 243(4) AktG.   [7] § 179a(2) AktG.   [8] § 293f(2) AktG.
[9] § 63(3) UmwG.   [10] § 230(2) UmwG.   [11] Sec. 116 CA 2006.
[12] Sec. 132 CA 2006.   [13] Secs. 358(3), 355 CA 2006.   [14] Sec. 744(1) CA 2006.
[15] Sec. 809(1) CA 2006.   [16] Sec. 877 CA 2006.   [17] Sec. 720 CA 2006.

prepared on an investigation of undisclosed holders of the company's shares.[18] A number of contracts and conveyance documents must also be kept for inspection. These include directors' service contracts,[19] provisions indemnifying a director against liability to a person other than the company,[20] contracts to repurchase the company's shares,[21] *instruments* creating charges on the company's assets (as opposed to the mere existence of the charge),[22] and all required documents in connection with a merger (draft terms, directors' report, expert's report and supplementary accounting statement) for at least one month before the general meeting voting on the transaction.[23]

C.   United States

Compared to the European jurisdictions, the right to request information that Delaware law gives shareholders is quite open-ended. It allows any stockholder, upon written demand, to inspect and copy for any "proper purpose" the stock ledger, a list of stockholders, and "other books and records."[24] This right also extends to the records of a corporation's subsidiaries.[25] The statute states that "[a] proper purpose shall mean a purpose reasonably related to such person's interest as a stockholder." The courts have generally found "proper purposes" to be attempts to exercise or protect other shareholder rights, such as to investigate the value of a company to sell one's shares, contact other shareholders to exercise one's votes, or protect one's investment when there is evidence that management has breached or is breaching a fiduciary duty. Read *Melzer* v. *CNET Networks, Inc.* According to the court, what is a "proper purpose" for requesting inspection? What are the "books and records" to which access is granted? Why can the right of inspection go back before the plaintiff's share ownership?

II.   *Routine, regular disclosure*

Three questions arise in connection with a scheme of regular disclosure: Which companies must comply with the disclosure rules? What must be disclosed? How often must disclosure occur? The basic answers to these questions are as simple as real answers in practice are complicated: Rules requiring detailed disclosure normally apply to listed companies. Among

---

[18] Sec. 807(1) CA 2006.   [19] Sec. 228(1) CA 2006.   [20] Sec. 238(1) CA 2006.
[21] Sec. 702(2) CA 2006.   [22] Sec. 892(4) CA 2006.   [23] Sec. 911 CA 2006.
[24] DGCL § 220(b)(1).   [25] DGCL § 220(b)(2).

the main items our jurisdictions require disclosed are accounting and financial information, significant company policies, actions and events, as well as potential conflicts of interest. Disclosure must in all cases be made annually and, for listed companies, quarterly.

Exceptions to the general rule that only listed companies must make disclosure are found in each of our jurisdictions. Germany and the United Kingdom, pursuant to the First Company Law Directive, require all companies to publish annual accounts that include a director's report on the state of the company. The *Aktiengesetz* requires the *Vorstand* of an AG to present the annual balance sheet and management report to the general meeting,[26] and the HGB requires that these annual accounts then be published in the national *Official Gazette* (referred to in Germany as the *Bundesanzeiger*[27]) unless the corporation qualifies for the relaxed regime applicable to small and medium-sized enterprises.[28] The Companies Act 2006 also requires every company to send a copy of its annual accounts and reports for each financial year to every member, every holder, and every person who is entitled to receive notice of general meetings,[29] as well as to file them with the Companies Registrar.[30] Delaware law contains no such requirements regarding annual accounts, although the Model Act does contain a requirement that an annual report be made to the Secretary of State, which keeps a publicly accessible file on the company.[31] As discussed in Section D, US federal law requires disclosure from many large, unlisted companies.

The remainder of this subsection will focus on rules applicable to listed companies, and in particular the "secondary market" disclosures of such companies. Disclosure can be categorized as aimed at the "primary" or the "secondary" market. Disclosure to the primary market occurs in the context of a public offering of securities; securities come on the market in this way for the first time, and hence the word "primary." Primary market disclosure is regulated in the EU by legislation implementing the Prospectus Directive[32] and in the US by the Securities Act of 1933.[33] Primary market disclosure is transaction oriented – focusing on the publication of a prospectus when securities are offered and sold to the public – whilst regular

---

[26] § 175 AktG.

[27] §§ 325–329 HGB. The *Bundesanzeiger* is now an online database that is referred to as the *elektronischer Bundesanzeiger*.

[28] See §§ 326, 267(1) HGB (for small corporations); §§ 327, 267(2) HGB (for medium-sized corporations).

[29] Sec. 423(1) CA 2006.   [30] Sec. 441 CA 2006.   [31] § 16.21 Model Act.

[32] The Prospectus Directive has been further implemented by the Commission Prospectus Regulation.

[33] Securities Act of 1933, 15 USCA §§ 77a–77aa (2000).

disclosure to the secondary market is a continuing obligation that attaches to a company because it is listed or is in any case a large company with dispersed shareholdings.[34] In Europe, disclosure rules for both the primary and secondary markets originate at the European level or are found in the rules of individual securities exchanges. In the US, these rules are found either in federal law or in the relevant exchange rules. State "blue sky" laws on disclosure are preempted by federal law when a company's securities are registered with the SEC.[35]

A.   Transparency Directive disclosure requirements

The EU Transparency Directive, adopted in 2004, consolidates a number of listed company disclosure obligations that were originally contained in older directives, and also adds some important new rules. However, as discussed in Chapter 3, the most significant innovation of the Transparency Directive is its modified passport structure for the disclosure rules applicable to issuers. Under the Transparency Directive, the home member state of an issuer – i.e. where it has its registered office – not a host state where its securities are listed, regulates the issuer's disclosure,[36] unless the issuer does not list its shares in its home state.[37] The EU home state of an issuer that is incorporated outside of the EU, such as a US company, will be the state in the EU in which it is required to file disclosures under the Prospectus Directive, i.e. the state where it lists its shares.[38] The home member state may impose rules stricter than the Directive on its own issuers, but the disclosure rules of a host state for a secondary listing may not exceed those of the Directive, which means that the Directive not only establishes an EU-wide floor for disclosure requirements, but ties corporate and securities law together for purposes of "regulatory competition." From the perspective of a country like the United Kingdom with a large and active capital market, the Directive ties the hands of the market's host state to push disclosure standards higher by linking the ceiling

---

[34] It should be noted, however, that, especially for companies that have been listed for a certain period of time, are quite large and have frequent recourse to the markets (in the US referred to as "well-known" or "seasoned" issuers), the prospectuses used for primary markets can incorporate by reference information contained in the various reports and disclosures filed with a supervisory authority or securities exchange pursuant to the rules for secondary market disclosure. This model has long been used for "shelf" or "programme" offerings of debt instruments.

[35] 15 USC § 77r(a)(2)(B) (2000).

[36] Art. 3 Transparency Directive. The discussion here is restricted to the listing of shares. Other rules apply for debt securities, in particular for debt securities in denominations larger than €1,000.

[37] Art. 21(3) Transparency Directive.   [38] Art. 2(1)(i) Transparency Directive.

for applicable standards to the various laws of the home countries where the listed companies originate. Indeed, this technique removes a primary incentive for a secondary listing, which usually comes from the bonding effects of complying with the stricter regulatory requirements of the second state.[39]

The disclosure rules in the Transparency Directive are straightforward. A listed issuer must publish an "annual financial report" within four months after the close of each financial year, and this report must contain:

- audited financial statements;
- a management report (describing significant related-party transactions, the development of the company's business, its position, important events, likely future developments, research and development, and information concerning acquisitions of own shares);
- statements by the issuer's officers responsible for the annual report that, to the best of their knowledge, the financial statements and the management report give true and fair views of the issuer; and
- the audit report, signed by the issuer's auditors.[40]

As discussed earlier in this text, the EU has harmonized the consolidated group accounting of all listed member state companies on International Financial Reporting Standards through the IFRS Regulation. Moreover, the European Union has published a mechanism for accepting third country accounting standards on EU exchanges, work that was achieved primarily through negotiations with the SEC on the mutual acceptance of accounting standards.[41] The statement that those responsible for the annual report must make is a technique first used by the US in the wake of the accounting scandals (in companies like Enron) that arose at the turn of the century, and differs from the US rule primarily by requiring a collegial declaration, rather than by pinning responsibility and liability on the CEO and the CFO.[42]

The Directive also expressly requires the publication of a half-yearly report containing condensed financial statements, an interim management report and a statement pledging that these documents present a

---

[39] See Coffee (2002: 1780 *et seq.*); Doidge, Karolyi and Stulz (2004: 205–238).

[40] Art. 4 Transparency Directive.

[41] Commission Regulation (EC) No 1569/2007 of 21 December 2007 establishing a mechanism for the determination of equivalence of accounting standards applied by third country issuers of securities pursuant to Directives 2003/71/EC and 2004/109/EC of the European Parliament and of the Council, OJ 2007 L340/66.

[42] See Subsection II.C.

true and fair view.[43] The level 2 Directive implementing the Transparency Directive provides that companies not required to prepare accounts according to IFRS must include in their half-yearly financial statements a condensed balance sheet and profit and loss accounts with the headings and subtotals in the most recent annual statements, plus any additional line items needed to avoid the statements being misleading, and a year-to-year comparison of the six months reported.[44] The interim management report must also disclose new related-party transactions and changes in such transactions since the publication of the annual report.[45]

The Transparency Directive's "interim management statements" are in substance quarterly reports. The Directive gives issuers the option of publishing such statements in the quarters when neither an annual nor a semi-annual report is published or simply publishing quarterly reports at those times.[46] An interim management statement would have to contain explanations of the "material events and transactions" in the period and a "general description" of the issuer's financial position,[47] and thus be quarterly reports in all but name. The level 2 Directive does not provide more detailed guidance, as such disclosure is likely to be covered by member state rules on quarterly reports. The remainder of the Directive focuses on the disclosure obligations of shareholders, and will be discussed in Chapter 19.

The information that must be disclosed pursuant to the Transparency Directive must be either communicated to the media in full or given to the officially appointed mechanism for the central storage of regulated information and posted on a website, with a notice to the media that the information has been posted and the web address.[48]

B. Germany

German law has for many years contained annual and semi-annual disclosure requirements for companies listed on exchanges in its national territory. In addition to the requirements of the *Aktiengesetz* and the HGB referred to above, these were found in the *Börsengesetz* and the Exchange Admission Regulation (*Börsenzulassungsverordung*).[49] The passport structure of the Transparency Directive has, however, added a cross-border twist to German regulation. As home member states must regulate the

---

[43] Art. 5 Transparency Directive.   [44] Art. 3 Level 2 Transparency Directive.
[45] Art. 4 Level 2 Transparency Directive.   [46] Art. 6(2) Transparency Directive.
[47] Art. 6(1) Transparency Directive.   [48] Art. 12(3) Directive 2007/14/EC.
[49] *Börsenzulassungs-Verordnung* of 9 September 1998, BGBl I: 2832.

disclosure obligations of their national companies listed on the exchanges of *another* member state, and in their role as host states may regulate the disclosure of issuers from other EU member states only at the level of the Directive, differences between national laws could violate the Transparency Directive. In response to this new state of affairs, the German Parliament adopted the Transparency Directive Implementing Act in January 2007 (usually referred to by its German acronym, TUG), which pulled a number of provisions out of the *Börsenzulassungsverordung* and concentrated all disclosure requirements in the WpHG.

The provisions of the WpHG as amended by TUG closely track the Directive, and require domestic issuers[50] to file annual reports in Germany and to publish the documents provided for in the Directive. Although Germany is expected to adopt legislation that would impose the incorporation theory by statute, under previous principles of international private law, Germany would be the home state not for companies *incorporated* under German law, but for companies with their *Sitz*, i.e. their actual seat of administration, in Germany. This could well raise interpretive questions and freedom of establishment problems of the type we discussed in Chapter 3, which is no doubt why Germany is expected to change its law. For example, German disclosure requirements might apply to the company, Überseering BV (discussed in the ECJ case of the same name) if it were listed in Frankfurt and Amsterdam. This requirement would almost certainly run afoul of *Inspire Art*.

The TUG also amended the WpPG to require that companies listed on a German securities exchange make an annual disclosure, the contents of which are drawn from the disclosure requirements included in the WpHG which implements the Transparency Directive.[51] Thus, Germany has taken the course of ensuring that disclosure requirements for listed companies are uniform regardless of an issuer's national origin by closely tracking the requirements set out in the 2004 Transparency Directive.

The required publications for a listed company are an annual report,[52] a semi-annual report,[53] and either interim management statements or quarterly reports,[54] the contents of which all closely follow the requirements of the Transparency Directive, as discussed above. The persons responsible for the disclosure must, in a manner substantially identical

---

[50] For a definition, see § 2(7), (6) WpHG.   [51] § 10 WpPG.   [52] § 37v WpHG.
[53] § 37w WpHG.   [54] § 37x WpHG.

to that required by the Directive, provide a certification that annual and semi-annual reports provide a true and fair view of the company.[55]

The Frankfurt Stock Exchange requires companies in the "Prime Standard" market segment to publish quarterly reports,[56] which – since the Transparency Directive equates such reports to interim management statements – should be considered to fullfil the requirements of that Directive even for dual-listed companies incorporated in another member state.

All officially disclosed information regarding German companies is available through an electronic companies register (*Unternehmensregister*) at www.unternehmensregister.de. German issuers must also make their accounts available on a generally accessible website.[57]

C. United Kingdom

The London Stock Exchange has long required its listed companies to meet a number of regular disclosure requirements, and continues to do so.[58] In order to implement the Transparency Directive, however, the FSA adopted Disclosure and Transparency Rules (DTRs) separate from the Listing Rules, and these DTRs apply both to issuers incorporated in the UK and to other issuers listed in the UK.[59] We looked at some of these DTRs in Chapter 15. Unlike the German rules, however, the United Kingdom has retained distinctions between rules applicable to its own listed companies and rules that apply only to EU "guest" companies with a secondary listing in the UK. Although the FSA rules on inside information apply uniformly to all listed companies, those on regular reporting repeat the requirements of the Directive (annual, semi-annual and interim reports) but are applicable only to listed companies incorporated in the UK.[60] The Listing Rules, however, incorporate the rules for which

---

[55] §§ 37v, 37w WpHG, referring to §§ 264, 289 HGB. Taking, for example, the declaration on the annual accounts, § 37v(2) no. 3 WpHG refers to § 264(2) HGB. § 264(2) HGB requires the *"gesetzlichen Vertreter"* of the corporation to state that the accounts provide a true and fair view. The *"gesetzlicher Vertreter"* of an AG would be the *Vorstand*, which is required to draw up the accounts within the first three months of the fiscal year (see § 264(1) HGB) and then to submit them to the *Aufsichtsrat* (§ 170(1) AktG) for their review pursuant to § 171 AktG.

[56] § 65 of the Rules of the Frankfurt Stock Exchange (*Börsenordnung für die Frankfurter Wertpapierbörse*) (April 15, 2009).

[57] § 37v(1) WpHG. [58] FSA Listing Rules, Rule 9.

[59] FSA Disclosure and Transparency Rules, Rule 1.1.

[60] FSA Disclosure and Transparency Rules, Rules 4.1, 4.2, 4.3.

the DTRs provide an exemption to foreign companies, and reapply them as a continued obligation of listing:

> A listed company that is not already required to comply with the trans-parency rules (or with corresponding requirements imposed by another 9.2.6B EEA Member State) must comply with DTR 4 [Periodic Financial Reporting], DTR 5 [Vote Holder and Issuer Notification Rules] and DTR 6 [Continuing Obligations and Access to Information] as if it were an issuer for the purposes of the transparency rules.[61]

This recognizes the distinction between hosted and home companies even though the current content of the DTRs does not deviate from the Directive. Pursuant to the relevant DTRs, an annual report must be pub-lished during the first four months after the close of the financial year, and contain information that exactly follows the Transparency Directive.[62] A half-yearly report must be published within the first two months after the close of the six-month period, and must contain items drawn specif-ically from the Transparency Directive and the level 2 Directive.[63] The FSA Rules on interim management statements also closely follow the Transparency Directive.[64] Like the German rules, the UK rules will be popular with large issuers active in a number of EU member states, as they will allow a high degree of standardization and consequent reduc-tion of costs.

D.   United States

US secondary market disclosure rules are found in the Securities Exchange Act of 1934[65] and the rules issued under that Act, some of which – most notably Regulation S-K[66] – also apply to primary market disclosure under the Securities Act of 1933. Unlike the European rules, the Exchange Act and rules apply both to listed companies and to large, unlisted compan-ies with a relatively large body of shareholders.[67] These rules are not sup-plemented in any significant way by the rules of securities exchanges.

---

[61] FSA Listing Rules, Rule 9.2.6B.
[62] FSA Disclosure and Transparency Rules, Rule 4.1.
[63] FSA Disclosure and Transparency Rules, Rule 4.2.
[64] FSA Disclosure and Transparency Rules, Rule 4.3.
[65] Securities Exchange Act of 1934, 15 USCA § 78m(a) (2000).
[66] 17 CFR Part 229.
[67] Securities must be registered with the SEC under § 12 of the Exchange Act if either (i) they are listed on a national securities exchange (§ 12(a) Exchange Act) or (ii) the issuer of the securities has more than 500 shareholders and total assets exceeding $10 million (§ 12(g) Exchange Act, in connection with 17 CFR § 240.12g-1). In addition to securities

Pursuant to § 13(a) of the Exchange Act, every registered issuer must file documents and annual reports with the SEC as specified in the rules that the SEC issues under the Exchange Act. The SEC has created itemized "forms" to structure the reports that must be given, as well as three detailed sets of instructions that specify in minute detail exactly what must be disclosed. The multiplication of instruments under US law can be confusing, so it is useful to remember that the legal hierarchy is first the Exchange Act, followed by rules and regulations (the latter being rules bundled in the form of a "regulation") and then the forms. The rules of stock exchanges are purely contractual in nature.

Under the Exchange Act, two regular reports are due from US-registered issuers, annual and quarterly reports. Exchange Act Rule 13a-1 requires that annual reports be filed with the SEC on Form 10-K, which must be filed either sixty (large accelerated filers), seventy-five (accelerated filers) or ninety (other issuers) days after the end of the financial year.[68] Annual reports must also be distributed to shareholders at the time that a proxy statement or an information statement is distributed in connection with a shareholders' meeting. Exchange Act Rule 13a-13 requires that quarterly reports be filed with the SEC on Form 10-Q, which must be filed either forty or forty-five days after the last quarter, depending on whether the issuer qualifies as "accelerated" or not.[69] The contents of these reports are specified in the relevant form and in three regulations that the SEC issued to provide more specific information on the required disclosure. Often, the instructions on the forms merely cross-reference these regulations. Much of the content of the annual and quarterly reports is governed by the instructions in Regulation S-K.[70] Together, Form 10-K and Regulation

registered under § 12 Exchange Act, Rule 13d-1 also applies to "any equity security of any insurance company which would have been required to be so registered except for the exemption contained in section 12(g)(2)(G) of the Act, or any equity security issued by a closed-end investment company registered under the Investment Company Act of 1940." 17 CFR § 240.13d-1(i).

[68] 17 CFR § 249.310(b). These categories depend upon the company's size and its experience with the capital markets. An "accelerated filer" is an issuer that has been registered with the SEC for over one year and has issued common equity that is held by unrelated parties with a value between $75 million and $700 million. See 17 CFR § 240.12b-2(1).

[69] 17 CFR § 249.308a(a).

[70] 17 CFR Part 229, Standard Instructions for Filing Forms under Securities Act of 1933, Securities Exchange Act of 1934 and Energy Policy and Conservation Act of 1975. As the title of this Regulation makes clear, there is significant overlap in the information that must be disclosed under the Securities Act and the Exchange Act – which allows the cross-referencing referred to above.

S-K specify that an annual report must contain information on matters including:

- the nature of the issuer's business, its property and its financial condition (including both audited financial statements and a narrative analysis by management of financial developments, the so-called MD&A);[71]
- factors that create risks for the value of the issuer's securities, any disagreements with the company's accountants and any concerns the SEC has about the issuer's disclosure that have not been completely settled;
- any pending or threatened legal proceedings against the company;
- information on management, corporate governance, executive compensation, and major transactions between management and the company, and similar information on major shareholders;
- accounting fees and services.[72]

The report must contain a certificate signed by the CEO and the CFO that each such person has reviewed the report and that it contains no material untrue statement or omission, the financial statements fairly present the company's financial condition, and make similar declarations regarding internal controls for accounting and information disclosed.[73] The major differences between this declaration and that required by the Transparency Directive are that the US declaration must be given by the CEO and the CFO, which is designed to make these specific officers accountable, and that knowingly false statements trigger criminal liability.[74]

Like the European Union, the United States both coordinates the development of accounting standards and imposes certain types of information that must be included in the accounts of listed companies. Financial statements for companies registered with the SEC must be prepared pursuant to the rules for the presentation of accounting data provided in Regulation S-X.[75] Regulation S-X requires that annual reports

---

[71] MD&A is an acronym for "Management's discussion and analysis of financial condition and results of operations." See Regulation S-K, Item 303 (17 CFR § 229.303).

[72] See Form 10-K, generally.

[73] Form 10-K, Item 15(b), which refers to Regulation S-K, Item 601 (17 CFR § 229.601(31)), which refers to 17 CFR § 240.13a-14(a).

[74] The maximum penalty for knowing violation is a fine of $1 million and a prison term of ten years. See 18 USC § 1350(c)(1). As with many EU directives, member states are free to issue rules stricter than the floor set out in the directive, and, under German law, § 331 no. 3a HGB imposes criminal liability on directors who make a false declaration pursuant to § 264(2) sentence 3 HGB that the accounts provide a true and fair view.

[75] 17 CFR Part 210, Form and Content of Financial Statements.

contain audited financial statements for the previous two financial years and audited statements of income and cash flows for each of the previous three financial years.[76] This Regulation also provides specific rules on the use of *pro forma* data and consolidation, together with numerous rules on the accounting treatment of many items. Filings with the SEC are made primarily in electronic form over its Electronic Data Gathering and Retrieval (EDGAR) system.[77]

Issuers incorporated outside the US are subject to US annual reporting requirements if their securities are listed on a US exchange or if they have at least 300 holders of their securities resident in the US.[78] These issuers are referred to as "foreign private issuers."[79] Foreign private issuers are exempt[80] from reporting under the proxy rules and the rules requiring management and 10 percent shareholders to make disclosures and avoid speculative trading. Foreign private issuers file annual reports on Form 20-F, which – like the annual report for listed companies under the applicable EU Prospectus Directive[81] – is closely modeled on the 1998 IOSCO International Disclosure Standards for Cross-Border Offerings and Initial Listings by Foreign Issuers. In addition, the SEC in 2008 began to accept financial statements compiled pursuant to IFRS without reconciliation to

---

[76] 17 CFR §§ 210.3-01 and 3-02.

[77] EDGAR is available at www.sec.gov. Detailed instructions for electronic filings are provided in "Regulation S-T." 17 CFR Part 232, General Rules and Regulations for Electronic Filers.

[78] 17 CFR § 240.12g3-2. Such issuers that have complied with US disclosure requirements for over twelve months may terminate their registration if either (i) they have less than 300 worldwide record shareholders, (ii) less than 300 US resident record shareholders, or (iii) the average daily trading volume of the securities in the US constitutes no more than 5 percent of the worldwide trading volume for the twelve months preceding a filing of the necessary request (Form 15F). See 17 CFR § 240.12h-6. Obviously, the numerical trigger for the listing requirement, particularly in an age when issuers rarely know the identity of their shareholders, is seen as a trap and has been much lamented by such issuers. It appears a practice of the SEC to allow good faith errors in this respect to pass with a notice to comply.

[79] This term is defined in 17 CFR § 230.405 as any foreign issuer other than a foreign government unless it (1) has more than 50 percent of its outstanding voting securities directly or indirectly owned of record by residents of the United States, and (2) either (i) the majority of its executive officers or directors are US citizens or residents, (ii) more than 50 percent of its assets are located in the United States, or (iii) its business is administered principally in the United States.

[80] 17 CFR § 240.3a12-3(b).

[81] Directive 2003/71/EC of the European Parliament and of the Council of 4 November 2003 on the prospectus to be published when securities are offered to the public or admitted to trading and amending Directive 2001/34/EC, OJ 2003 L345/64 (December 31, 2003).

US GAAP.[82] The reporting requirements of a European company listed in the US are thus very similar to those it fulfils in its European home market. The disappearance of regulatory differences between the US and EU markets is a primary reason why fewer European issuers choose to incur the expense of a second listing in the US.[83]

III.   Current disclosures of significant events

Current, or as they are referred to in Germany, "*ad hoc*" disclosure rules require that material information regarding the issuer, its management and its securities be published as soon as possible. This serves two main purposes. First, if information is not allowed to accumulate "inside" the company, the informational asymmetry between insiders and outsiders regarding the value of a company's shares is eliminated. Secondly, a smooth and regular flow of information to the market facilitates efficient and complete pricing of the issuer's securities. All of our jurisdictions require that listed companies promptly publish information that could affect the market value of their shares unless the interests of the company require otherwise. These rules all ensure that, unless a good reason for keeping information confidential exists – such as ongoing negotiations regarding a merger – inside information is eliminated promptly by being disclosed to the market. The decision on when to hold and when to disclose is delicate, and can trigger a liability suit for spoiling a transaction on the one hand, or a claim of securities fraud for keeping the information secret, on the other. Read *Basic* v. *Levinson*. Do you agree with the test the US Supreme Court formulates? Would it work under the Transparency Directive?

A.   Germany

We have already discussed the German regulation of insider trading in Chapter 15. The WpHG makes a distinction between the companies to which the prohibition of insider trading applies and those to which the related *ad hoc* disclosure requirements apply. Taking the definition provided in article 1 of the Market Abuse Directive, "inside information"

---

[82] See e.g. Final Rule: Acceptance from Foreign Private Issuers of Financial Statements Prepared in Accordance with International Financial Reporting Standards Without Reconciliation to US GAAP, SEC Release Nos. 33-8879 and 34-57026, 73 *Federal Register* 986 (January 4, 2008).

[83] On the convergence of regulations and trading infrastructure, see Jackson and Pan (2008: 269).

under German law is non-public information regarding an issuer of securities that are traded on a regulated market or on the OTC market, if such information could have a significant influence on the exchange or market prices of such securities.[84] Domestic issuers must publish inside information promptly (*unverzüglich*).[85] Since domestic issuers by definition have securities admitted to trading on a regulated exchange, whilst the prohibition of insider trading extends to unlisted securities traded in *Freiverkehr* as well, the scope of the insider trading prohibition is broader than that of the *ad hoc* disclosure requirements. The general effects test for inside information used in the Market Abuse Directive has been fleshed out by guidance from CESR.[86] CESR provides an extensive, "non-exhaustive and purely indicative" list of events that may constitute inside information, including:

- changes in control and control agreements;
- changes in management and supervisory boards;
- changes in auditors or any other information related to the auditors' activity;
- operations involving capital increases or the issue of debt securities or warrants to buy or subscribe securities;
- mergers, splits and spin-offs;
- restructurings or reorganizations affecting assets;
- changes in the class rights of the issuer's own listed shares;
- major legal disputes, such as for product liability or environmental damage;
- changes in the value of assets;
- new licenses, patents and registered trademarks;
- receiving acquisition bids for relevant assets;
- innovative products or processes; and
- orders received from customers, their cancellation or important changes.[87]

The requirement of § 15 WpHG does not give issuers *carte blanche* to release any and all information to the market. As the German High Court of Justice explains in *ComROAD*, although current reports are not prospectuses, rules of tort liability derived from the German Civil Code do

---

[84] §§ 12, 13(1) WpHG.   [85] § 15(1) WpHG.
[86] Committee of European Securities Regulators, "Market Abuse Directive: Level 3 – Second Set of CESR Guidance and Information on the Common Operation of the Directive to the Market," CESR/06-562b (July 2007).
[87] Level 3 Market Abuse Directive at 1.15.

apply. In terms of impact on investment decisions, how does the court distinguish current reports from prospectuses? Do you agree with this argument?

B.   United Kingdom

The FSA's Disclosure and Transparency Rules also contain new rules for *ad hoc* disclosure of inside information,[88] although these requirements come not from the Transparency Directive but from the Insider Dealing and Market Abuse Directive discussed in Chapter 15. These rules apply to all issuers with securities listed in the UK, not just to issuers whose home country is the UK.[89]

The basic rule is that an issuer must notify a "regulated information service" (RIS) as soon as possible of any inside information[90] that directly concerns the issuer.[91] The exception to this rule is drawn directly from the Market Abuse Directive, i.e. disclosure may be omitted to serve a legitimate business interest provided that the omission would not be likely to mislead the public, any person receiving the information is under a duty of confidentiality, and the issuer can ensure the confidentiality of the information.[92] The notion of a "regulated information service" is based on the criteria for the distribution of regulated information set out in article 12 of the level 2 Directive for the Transparency Directive, and generally means a service approved by the FSA as meeting those criteria.[93] Within one day after the information is given to an RIS, the issuer must post it on its own website,[94] and issuers must attempt to synchronize the publication of the information in all countries where their securities are listed, so as to reduce possible uneven market effects.[95]

As discussed in Chapter 15, the FSA Listing Rules also require that a company notify an RIS as soon as possible upon the occurrence of one of a number of specified events that could affect the company's share price.[96] This requirement resembles current reports as required by US SEC rules,

---

[88] FSA Disclosure and Transparency Rules, Rule 2.2.
[89] FSA Disclosure and Transparency Rules, Rule 1.1.1.
[90] The definition of the exact nature of inside information is very important and varies between the EU and the US. See Chapter 12 of this text.
[91] FSA Disclosure and Transparency Rules, Rule 2.2.1.
[92] FSA Disclosure and Transparency Rules, Rule 2.5.1.
[93] See Glossary, entry for "Regulated Information Service." Such services include companies like Reuters, Bloomberg and Dow Jones.
[94] FSA Disclosure and Transparency Rules, Rule 2.3.2.
[95] FSA Disclosure and Transparency Rules, Rule 2.4.1.
[96] FSA Listing Rules, Chapter 9.6.

and are not specifically tied to insider trading requirements, but are meant to feed a steady stream of price relevant information to the market. Events to be disclosed under the UK DTRs include:

- proposed change in capital structure or redemption of listed securities;[97]
- changes in the board, such as appointment or resignation of directors;[98]
- details regarding new directors, including other posts held, outstanding offenses and ongoing receiverships;[99] and
- the creation or change of a lock-up arrangement regarding the company's shares.[100]

C. United States

Exchange Act Rule 13a-11[101] requires that current reports be filed with the SEC on Form 8-K[102] within four business days of the occurrence of any one of the "material" events listed on that form. "Materiality" is a concept very similar to that of "price relevance" under the EU Market Abuse Directive. This concept is important not only for disclosure, but also for determining whether the failure to disclose or misrepresentation of information can trigger a claim for damages. Take a look at the brief discussion of the concept of "materiality" in *Basic* v. *Levinson*. As mentioned, US current reports are unlike the European disclosure rule in that the requirement is not tied to the insider trading prohibition. Because these "current reports" are considered an element of regular disclosure, Form 8-K provides a list of the events that must be promptly reported without linking the events to inside information.[103] The events include:

- events affecting business operations (entry into or termination of a material agreement, bankruptcy or receivership);
- financial information (acquisition or disposition of a significant amount of assets, results of operations, triggering events for financial obligations);
- securities and the market (delisting, unregistered sales of securities, changes in the rights of security holders);

---

[97] FSA Listing Rules, Rule 9.6.4.   [98] FSA Listing Rules, Rule 9.6.11.
[99] FSA Listing Rules, Rule 9.6.13.   [100] FSA Listing Rules, Rule 9.6.16.
[101] 17 CFR § 240.13a-11 and § 249.308. "Material" events include such matters as entry into bankruptcy, acquisitions or disposals of assets, changes in financial condition, and conclusion or termination of major contracts, among others.
[102] Form 8-K, Current Report Pursuant to Section 13 or 15(d) of the Securities Exchange Act of 1934, General Instructions, B.1.
[103] NYSE rules, however, do require continuous disclosure of inside information. See NYSE LCM, para. 202.05.

- accountants and financial statements (a change of auditors, revision of issued financial statements); and
- corporate governance and management (a change in control, departure of a director or principal officer, amendment of articles).

A rule issued in 2000, entitled "Regulation FD" (standing for "fair disclosure") works together with the current reports requirement to ensure that disclosure is not selectively made to favored market professionals, but to the market as a whole.[104] Foreign private issuers must also make current reports, and these are submitted to the SEC on Form 6-K,[105] which primarily requires that a foreign private issuer publish the same information in the US as required by its home law or its securities exchange, or that it in fact voluntarily discloses, in the foreign market.[106] Disclosure on Form 6-K thus follows e.g. disclosure pursuant to § 15 WpHG, FSA Disclosure and Transparency Rules, Rule 2 and FSA Listing Rules, Rule 9.6.

IV.   Policing disclosed information

In Chapter 20, we will briefly look at the types of judicial remedies available for shareholders. Remedies is a subject that involves a great number of elements, which range from specifying the eligible plaintiffs to determining the measure of damages. In the context of our discussion of shareholder information rights, it is fitting to discuss whether and how a shareholder can seek redress from an issuer that releases false or misleading information to the market or omits information that is important for an investment decision. In a traditional tort action for misrepresentation, the steps are quite clear: one party provides the other with false or incomplete information, the second party relies on this information to make a decision as a result of which she is damaged, so the deception causes damage to the deceived. Most retail investors, however, are unlikely to study the prospectuses published by issuers, let alone read the issuer's quarterly or current reports. We have an entire industry whose sole purpose is to process such information and turn it into conveniently formulated advice. Analysts and journalists read primary sources and write reports and articles. Brokers read the reports and articles and contact clients with advice. A client may speak with friends or other advisers before deciding to buy

---

[104] 17 CFR Part 243.
[105] Form 6-K Report of Foreign Private Issuer Pursuant to Rule 13a-16 or 15d-16 under the Securities Exchange Act of 1934.
[106] Form 6-K, General Instructions, B.

or sell. However, in a society with open markets, it would be a rare case if A were to be punished for saying something to B, who remained undamaged but conveyed it to C, who remained undamaged but gave advice to D, who was then damaged. Especially with respect to information, holding someone liable for the indirect, belated and tertiary impact of disclosure is a very difficult and even dangerous activity. It can inhibit free speech. Look at *ComROAD* and *Basic*. With which court do you agree? What are the effects of sticking to traditional tort principles or shaping tort to meet the current understanding of the market?

Questions for discussion

1. When, where and from whom are shareholders entitled to request information?
2. On what issues are shareholders entitled to request or receive information?
3. May shareholders request information from a corporation for any purpose?
4. What are the differences in the right to information in Germany, the UK and the US?
5. Do all companies have obligations under corporate law to provide regular reports?
6. What is the "fraud-on-the-market" theory?
7. When does a mistake or omission in information justify damages?

Cases

Melzer v. CNET Networks, Inc.
Delaware Court of Chancery
934 A 2d 912 (2007)
[*Text edited; footnotes omitted*]

OPINION: CHANDLER, Chancellor

[*Text omitted*]

CNET's options issues first came to light in May 2006, when the Center for Financial Research and Accountability ("CFRA") published an analysis of option-granting practices of one hundred publicly traded companies. The CFRA report specifically identified CNET as a company whose pattern of granting options indicated backdating [to a recent, historical low of the company's share price]. On June 27, 2006, CNET disclosed that its option granting practices were under investigation by the US Attorney for the Northern District of California and by the Securities and Exchange Commission. The next month, CNET announced that an internal investigation conducted by a special committee confirmed the CFRA report and announced that the company would need to restate its financial statements from 2003–05. In mid-October 2006, CNET released further, more specific findings from the special committee, which concluded backdating had been a problem for the company from the time of its IPO in 1996.

On June 19, 2006, plaintiffs filed their initial complaint in the District Court for the Northern District of California alleging federal securities and state law claims against CNET and its directors relating to backdated stock options ... and the defendants moved to dismiss for failure to make a demand on the CNET board. Applying the *Aronson* test for demand futility, the district court granted the motion to dismiss.

Plaintiffs had alleged several theories to support their contention that demand on the CNET board would have been futile. First, to the extent a director materially benefited from a backdated option, he or she would not be disinterested under the first prong of the *Aronson* test. Thus, to the extent that plaintiffs could plead with particularity facts demonstrating that a majority of the directors received backdated options, demand would be excused. Second, to the extent a director knowingly backdated a stock option in violation of the company's charter, that director's action is *ultra vires* and is not the product of valid business judgment. If a majority of the current board engaged in backdating, demand would be excused.

Thus, key to establishing demand futility was particularized facts demonstrating that backdating occurred and either that (1) a majority of the current board received backdated options or (2) a majority of the current board engaged in backdating itself. The district court analyzed individually the eight option grants that plaintiffs alleged were backdated and concluded that plaintiffs successfully pleaded particularized facts with respect to only the grants on June 3, 1998, April 17, 2000, and October 8, 2001. Consequently, plaintiffs had demonstrated that only *one* member of the then-current board received backdated options. Judge Alsup also found unpersuasive plaintiffs' attempts to show demand futility under the second prong of *Aronson*, concluding that plaintiffs failed to allege the particularized facts necessary to demonstrate that board members actually engaged in the process of backdating.

After dismissing plaintiffs' amended complaint, however, Judge Alsup granted further leave to amend, and issued a stay pending a books and records demand in Delaware. The stay specifically requested that CNET cooperate and expedite the inspection because "CNET itself raised the availability of such an inspection in its recent memoranda." Judge Alsup listed four categories of books and records that would be helpful in the California action:

1. All books and records showing the extent to which the CNET compensation committee delegated (or did not delegate) to management, either expressly or by custom and practice, the authority to select the exercise price or grant date of stock options under the 1997 plan and, if such delegation occurred, the extent to which the compensation committee was made aware of the exercise prices and dates selected.

2. All books and records establishing the specific chronology and events leading to the stock-option grants alleged in the complaint and exercise prices and grant dates associated therewith.
3. All books and records needed to determine whether Messrs. Colligan and Robison received stock options that were backdated.
4. All books and records necessary to show the extent to which any minutes or unanimous written consents for the compensation committee (while Colligan and Robison were members) were backdated, at least as to those minutes involving stock-option grants.

Judge Alsup also noted that those categories were without prejudice to other possible requests, and ordered plaintiffs to make their books and records demand by May 14, 2007.

Indeed, on May 14, 2007, plaintiffs sent their demand to inspect books and records to CNET via certified mail. In this demand letter, plaintiffs made six requests:

1. All books and records created by, distributed to, or reviewed by CNET's Board of Directors (the "Board"), or any member or committee thereof, showing the extent to which the CNET Compensation Committee delegated (or did not delegate) to management, either stock options under CNET's 1997 Stock option Plan ("1997 Plan") and, if such delegation occurred, the extent to which the Compensation Committee was made aware of the exercise prices and dates selected.
2. All books and records establishing the specific chronology and events leading to the stock option grants alleged in the Amended Consolidated Verified Shareholder Derivative Complaint and exercise prices and grant dates associated therewith.
3. All books and records needed to determine whether John C. Colligan and/or Eric Robison received stock options that were backdated, misdated, mispriced or incorrectly dated.
4. All books and records necessary to show the extent to which any minutes or unanimous written consents for the Compensation Committee (while Colligan and Robison were members) were backdated, at least as to those minutes involving or relating to stock option grants.
5. The written report and findings of the Special Committee of the CNET Board on the Company's option granting practices and procedures.
6. All documents that CNET provided to the Securities and Exchange Commission ("SEC") in connection with the SEC's investigation into the stock option granting practices and procedures at CNET.

In this demand letter, the plaintiffs identified their purpose as "investigating possible violations of law … in connection with the Company's granting practices" and "determining whether the Company's officers and directors are independent and/or disinterested and whether they have acted in good faith."

CNET ... did not comply, and plaintiffs initiated the present action in this Court on June 14, 2007 ... Specifically, the parties disagree about whether plaintiffs may properly inspect books and records predating plaintiffs' ownership of stock. It is that question this opinion now resolves.

II.   Legal analysis

A.   Investigation of admitted stock option backdating constitutes a proper purpose under Section 220

Section 220 provides shareholders of Delaware corporations with a qualified right to inspect corporate books and records ...

The statute is an expansion of the common law right of shareholders to protect themselves by keeping abreast of how their agents were conducting corporate affairs, but it does not permit unfettered access. Before shareholders may inspect books and records, they must (1) comply with the technical requirements of section 220 and (2) demonstrate a proper purpose for seeking inspection. There is no shortage of proper purposes under Delaware law, but perhaps the most common "proper purpose" is the desire to investigate potential corporate mismanagement, wrongdoing, or waste. Merely stating that one has a proper purpose, however, is necessarily insufficient. For example, a shareholder seeking a books and records inspection under section 220 in order to investigate mismanagement or wrongdoing "must present 'some evidence' to suggest a 'credible basis' from which a court can infer that mismanagement, waste or wrongdoing may have occurred."

Here, as noted above, the plaintiffs have identified two purposes, but both really relate to plaintiffs' desire to bring derivatively in California a suit alleging a breach of fiduciary duty in connection with backdated options granted by CNET. Defendant does not dispute this characterization. In fact, defendant relies on this characterization to support its chief argument: plaintiffs are not entitled to books and records from the time period before plaintiffs owned stock in CNET, because plaintiffs lack standing under 8 Del. C. § 327 to bring a derivative suit for any claims that accrued before they owned such stock. Thus, all parties agree that plaintiffs have a proper purpose. At issue, however, is the scope of the investigation that plaintiffs' proper purpose will permit.

B.   A stockholder must be given sufficient access to books and records to effectively address the problem of backdating through derivative litigation

Section 220 does not sanction a "broad fishing expedition," but "where a § 220 claim is based on alleged corporate wrongdoing ... the stockholder should be given enough information to effectively address the problem ... " Generally, this Court has "wide latitude in determining the proper scope of inspection," and this Court must "tailor the inspection to the stockholder's stated purpose."

Defendant argues that plaintiffs should be barred from inspecting any books and records that predate plaintiffs' ownership of CNET stock. Because plaintiffs are only seeking to bring a derivative claim, defendant argues, and because plaintiffs can only bring claims for wrongs that occurred after plaintiffs purchased stock, there is no reason for plaintiffs to inspect documents before the purchase date. In so arguing, defendant relies heavily on *Polygon Global Opportunities Master Fund* v. *West Corp.* and *West Coast Management & Capital, LLC* v. *Carrier Access Corp.* In *Polygon*, Vice Chancellor Lamb refused to grant an investigation under section 220 where the shareholder, an arbitrage fund, purchased shares in the West Corporation *after* an announced reorganization and then sought a books and records inspection to look into potential derivative claims in connection with the proposed reorganization plan. Because the fund could not possibly have standing to challenge any breach it purportedly wanted to investigate, allowing an inspection of books and records under section 220 was improper. In *West Coast*, shareholders attempted to conduct a section 220 inspection after their federal derivative claim was dismissed for failure to adequately plead demand futility. There, however, the federal judge "specifically denied the plaintiffs' request for leave to replead." With this explicit ruling in hand, Vice Chancellor Lamb concluded that the shareholders were estopped from relitigating demand futility and, therefore, lacked a proper purpose under section 220. Finally, defendant also cites language from the Supreme Court's opinion in *Saito* that indicates "if the stockholder's only purpose [in pursuing a section 220 books and records inspection] was to institute derivative litigation," one might reasonably question "whether the stockholder's purpose was reasonably related to his or her interest as a stockholder."

However, *Polygon* and *West Coast* are distinguishable, and *Saito*, while instructive, mandates a different result than what defendant proposes. Plaintiffs here do not seek the pre-2000 books and records in order to investigate potential *new* causes of action – claims plaintiffs would admittedly have no standing to assert. Rather, plaintiffs seek access to those documents in order to plead demand futility with respect to the causes of action plaintiffs *do* have standing to bring.

Judge Alsup told plaintiffs to go to Delaware to find the particularized facts they needed to properly plead demand futility. There are several ways plaintiffs can attempt to accomplish this, one of which is the second prong of *Aronson* v. *Lewis*. To plead demand futility under the second prong of *Aronson*, a shareholder must allege particularized facts that create a reasonable doubt that the "challenged transaction was ... the product of a valid exercise of business judgment." This invites an inquiry "into the substantive nature of the challenged transaction and the board's approval thereof." One potential way to show that the board was not exercising valid business judgment is to show that there was a "sustained or systematic failure of the board to exercise oversight" – a violation of the board's duty of loyalty by way of bad faith. To show a "sustained or systematic failure of the board to exercise oversight," the plaintiffs might reasonably need to consult documents that predate their ownership of CNET stock.

In *Polygon*, the shareholder's articulated purpose was solely to investigate potential claims – claims that the shareholder would be barred from bringing. Here, plaintiffs are seeking particularized facts to replead demand futility; they are not fishing for new claims. In *West Coast*, the federal judge overseeing the derivative action explicitly barred the shareholder from repleading demand futility. Here, Judge Alsup explicitly asked plaintiffs to do just that. Indeed, *Saito* is ultimately controlling. There, Justice Berger defined the appropriate scope of a books and records investigation as "enough information to *effectively address the problem ...*" Here, plaintiffs cannot effectively address the alleged problem through a derivative suit unless they can properly plead demand futility. Because *Stone* v. *Ritter* held that a violation of the duty of loyalty/good faith described in *Caremark* can, in theory, excuse demand, and because plaintiffs might need older documents to establish a "sustained or systematic failure" of oversight, I must conclude that plaintiffs' request for the documents here is reasonably related to their proper purpose as shareholders of CNET.

III.   Conclusion

Plaintiffs should have access to books and records that predate their purchase of stock in order to allow them to explore a potential lapse in the good faith of the CNET board that would excuse demand in the California derivative suit. The outer bounds of this disclosure are defined by plaintiffs' demand letter itself; not by plaintiffs' interrogatories. It is about time defendant takes Judge Alsup's advice, provides the requested documents, and gets "going, going / back, back / to Cali, Cali." [Note 40]

[Note 40] THE NOTORIOUS B.I.G., *Going Back to Cali*, on LIFE AFTER DEATH (Bad Boy Records 1997).

ComROAD Securities Litigation No. IV
High Federal Court, Second Civil Division
June 4, 2007, Doc. No. II ZR 147/05, NZG 2007, 708
[*Partial, unofficial translation of official opinion text*]

Official head note

a) In the context of liability for false information under § 826 BGB for releasing erroneous current reports (*Ad-hoc-Publizität*) to the secondary market, proof of concrete causality for the investor's decision cannot be waived even in cases of extremely irresponsible capital market information. Therefore, a disappointed general trust of the investor in the integrity of the market's pricing mechanism is insufficient to constitute causality.

b) Also in the primary market, pursuant to § 47(2) BörsG, the special provision on liability for listing particulars (§§ 44 *et seq.* BörsG) and unwaived tort liability under § 826 BGB, a plaintiff/investor must prove concrete (as a basis for liability) causality of false prospectus information for his decision. To this end, a disappointed general trust of the investor in the integrity of the foregoing exchange admission procedure, including the presence of a bank accompanying the initial listing on the exchange, is not enough.

Facts

The Plaintiff seeks compensation for damages on the theory of civil liability for false capital market information from the Defendant, ComROAD AG, in connection with the purchase of ComROAD stock.

The Defendant's shares were admitted to trading in November 1999 to the regulated market with trading on the Neuer Markt and were listed on November 26, 1999 at an initial price of €20.50 (corresponding to €5.17 following the later 1 to 4 share split). The stock's market price climbed within a short time to reach a high point at the end of February 2000 of €64 (not considering the split), which – following lower prices of around €25.00 in the interim period – was again reached in September 2000. The Plaintiff acquired a total of 410 ComROAD shares through purchases on October 9, 2000 at a price of €49.98, on January 9, 2001 at €30.00, on February 16, 2001 at €43.00, on February 21, 2001 at €33.00, and on April 12, 2001 at €20.00, totaling €12,869.90 for the purchases. In the subsequent period, the price of the shares sunk further. On April 11, 2002 the Plaintiff sold 150 of his ComROAD shares for a total of €35.10 (Price per share of €0.30).

Following its initial listing, and until the end of January 2001, the Defendant made more than 40 current reports to the market through its then Chairman (*Vorstandsvorsitzenden*) and majority shareholder B[odo] S[chnabel]. These current reports essentially disclosed new customers and updated performance figures; the figures for each quarter showed a significant increase in revenue over the foregoing quarter. After the Defendant's auditor terminated its relationship on February 20, 2002, it was discovered that S[chnabel] – who because of these actions has in the mean time been sentenced to a number of years in prison – invented a substantial part of the Defendant's alleged revenue with the help of imaginary companies. A special audit revealed, *inter alia*, that only 1.4% of the €93.6 million in revenues for 2001 reported most recently in current reports was realized. Since this fact was disclosed, the market price of the Defendant's shares has for the most part been significantly lower than €1.00.

In his complaint, the Plaintiff seeks recovery from the Defendant of damages in a sum equal to the purchase price of the shares minus the proceeds from sale at the bottom out price. He bases this claim on the argument that the ComROAD Chairman's disclosure of largely fictitious revenue and earnings figures conditioned the market positively toward the shares and led to his own purchases; the Defendant must pay for the wrongful actions of its Chairman. The Defendant disputes that the incorrect current reports caused the Plaintiff's decisions to purchase the shares, and denies any responsibility for the behavior of its chairman, referring to §§ 57, 71 *et seq.* AktG.

The regional court dismissed the complaint and the court of appeals approved it after hearing the Plaintiff's testimony, but only against transfer of the shares that the Plaintiff still owns. With the permission of the trial court, the Defendant pursued its motion to dismiss further.

Discussion

The Defendant's appeal is well-founded and leads to reversal of the challenged judgment and remand of the matter back to the trial court.

I. Findings of the court of appeals:

The Plaintiff's claim for compensation of damages based on the theory of intentional and wrongful infliction of damages (§ 826 BGB) is justified. The mainly fictional revenue figures that B[odo] S[chnabel] published as an organ of the Defendant for the purpose of deceiving the investing public were a cause of the Plaintiff's purchases. Through his false current reports, S[chnabel] was able to deceive the entire, interested public, and lead the Defendant's shares to be vastly inflated in value, which aside from all price swings, lasted from 1999 until the beginning of 2002. As the Plaintiff confirmed in testimony with material credibility and in a personally convincing manner, he "apparently followed the general line." The Defendant is responsible for the behavior of its Chairman pursuant to § 31 BGB and may raise neither the prohibition of the return of contributions (§ 57(1) AktG) nor the prohibition on purchase of own shares (§§ 71 *et seq.* AktG) against the Plaintiff.

II. This judgment does not stand up to scrutiny on appeal with respect to the decisive point of the causality of the incorrect current reports for the Plaintiff's decision to buy.

1. The court of appeals begins with the correct, basic approach that the direct, intentional, unfair manipulation of the secondary market through grossly incorrect current reports – as is without doubt occurred in the present case – violates the minimum requirements of fair commercial behavior on the capital markets and, in the case of causation for the buy decisions of potential investors would establish for the latter a claim for restitution as compensation for damages pursuant to § 826 BGB (see BGHZ 160, 134 – *Infomatec I*; 160, 149 – *Infomatec II*).

The court of appeals also correctly assumed that by analogical application of § 31 BGB the Defendant company would be jointly liable for the actions of its *Vorstand's* duly appointed representative for wrongful, intentional damage inflicted through false current reports. In such cases, as this Division in the mean time decided in its judgment of May 9, 2005 (see *EM.TV*, ZIP 2005, 1270, 1272 *et seq.*), restitution as a form of compensation for damages is not limited or excluded by the special corporate law rules on creditor protection that prohibit repayment of capital contributions (§ 57 AktG) or by the prohibition of repurchasing own shares (§ 71 AktG); the arguments of the appellant on the point give this Division no reason to change its newer decisions …

2. On the other hand, drastic legal considerations confront the court of appeal's arguments for affirming causality between the Defendant's false current reports and the Plaintiff's decision to purchase its shares.

a) The court of appeals correctly takes the initial approach of referring to the decisions of this Division on the requirements of proving causality, explaining that the investment decision of a potential share purchaser is an individual choice whose composition is not open to observation, but that is influenced by a multiplicity of rational and irrational factors, in particular also by speculative elements, so that as a rule, for such individual choices there can be no circumstantial evidence (*Anscheinsbeweis*) which creates a specific presumption that people will have a certain type of comportment in certain situations (see *Infomatec I*, BGHZ 160, 134, 144 *et seq.*). In light of this, the principles on evidence presumed from circumstances within the context of an investment mood, as developed by the court decisions on prospectus liability under the old version of the Exchange Act cannot be directly applied to tort liability under § 826 BGB for incorrect current reports within the meaning of § 15(1) to (3) WpHG. This is because the informational content of a current report is generally limited to snippets of essential, current, new facts from the business area. They usually can be relevant for an individual, immediate decision to buy or sell the shares, but as a rule are not well suited to create a so-called investment mood. It is certainly conceivable that in individual cases – depending upon the importance of the information – the positive signals of a current report could create a real investment mood for the purchase of shares; however, even then, one may not use a mode of observation that rests on a schematic, fixed period to form a judgment on its nature and duration (see *Infomatec I*, BGHZ 160, 146 *et seq.*).

b) The court of appeals did not – at not least sufficiently to satisfy review on appeal – determine that prerequisites for such an investment mood, which only exceptionally is ascertained and justifies the application of the principles of circumstantial evidence, had been met. It restricted itself to concluding – without making the legal meaning of the conclusion clear – that "in this way S[chnabel] was able to deceive the entire, interested public with his false reports about the Defendant, and lead the Defendant's shares to be vastly inflated in value, which aside from all price swings, lasted from 1999 until the beginning of 2002."

If it was the intention of the appeals court that the particular type and dimension of market deception effected by B[odo] S[chnabel]'s false reports, as well as the duration of the market's misjudgments until S[chnabel]'s machinations were discovered, constituted a permanent, concrete investment mood, the hypothesis lacks sufficient foundation. The determination of the regional court of appeals in this way creates a curt, superficial description of the situation; it lacks any sign of market analysis supported by concrete facts and placement of the movements of the ComROAD shares, from which an investment mood is supposed to have sprung for the case at hand in a manner legally sufficient to withstand review on appeal, and does so without procuring an expert opinion and without presenting the elements of the court's own reasoning. This applies in particular for the appeals court's unlikely assumption that an investment mood lasted uninterrupted from the commencement of listing to the discovery of the manipulation, i.e. during a period of at least two years, despite the extreme volatility of the shares, including sharp drops in price shortly after first reaching its high point in February 2000 (see the discussion of the many factors influencing prices on the capital market in Infomatec I, BGHZ 160, 134, 146 with further references).

In any case, it is clear that the impact of the appeals court's determination is restricted to asserting that the extremely irresponsible financial information of the Defendant's *Vorstand* generally deceived the investing public for a long period of time in respect of its estimations and valuations of the company and its securities, and that in spite of the volatility it brought investors to buy and sell the shares, and that the Plaintiff also "followed this general line." If the court of appeals intends to allow the general market condition to serve as concrete proof of causality, its argumentation is just as unconvincing as that of another division of the same court, which was of the opinion that in cases of extremely irresponsible financial information, a potential investor's trust in the correctness of general information about the Defendant and the consequent belief in the economic substance and long-term success of the company are sufficient to affirm the existence of causality on which liability may be predicated. Such points of view would eliminate the requirement for a concrete, causal connection between the deception and the decision of the investor in the context of § 826 BGB, and instead – borrowing the so-called fraud-on-the-market theory of US securities law – look to the disappointment of an investor's general trust in the integrity of the market pricing mechanism. In earlier securities law decisions on incorrect current reports, this Division has chosen not to follow this line of thought regarding the causality on which liability may be predicated, for in this area it would lead to a boundless expansion of an already wide-open set of circumstances under which liability can be incurred for wrongful, intentional inflicting of damage; here we retain this position. As a result, to establish liability for deceptive information pursuant to § 826 BGB, proof of a concrete causal connection between the incorrect current report and the individual investment decision must be presented, even when the information that was released on the capital market was repeated and extremely irresponsible.

3. The lack of sufficient evidence on the causal connection between the false information released to the capital market and the Plaintiff's investment decision will also not be eliminated by the court of appeals' receipt of testimony from the Plaintiff stating, as the court assumes without going further into the matter, "with material credibility and in a personally convincing manner" that when making his investment decision he "followed the general line" and would not have purchased his shares if he had known the degree of the ComROAD *Vorstand's* deceptions. This evidentiary hearing clearly did not go beyond the – insufficient – general information on which the court of appeals based its decision regarding causality.

4. We need not discuss the extent to which the Defendant's current reports could at least partially be capable of justifying a claim from the Plaintiff for damages also pursuant to § 823(2) BGB in connection with § 400(1)(1) AktG. Also here, the findings of the appeals court are insufficient to allow assumption of concrete causality between any improper behavior of the Defendant under such sections and the Plaintiff's share purchases. The error of law discussed earlier with respect to § 826 BGB also applies to any claims from alleged violations of the protections of § 400(1) No. 1 AktG.

[Text omitted]

III. For cause of the error of law discussed in II.2 supra, the appealed decision is rescinded (§ 562 ZPO). For lacking ripeness the matter is remanded back to the court of appeals (§ 563(1) ZPO).

1. It is true that the determinations of the court of appeals currently do not establish that the false current reports caused the Plaintiff's share purchases. Nevertheless, pursuant to the Plaintiff's testimony, which the court of appeals found convincing without examining its basis, at least in this stage of the proceedings it does not appear completely improbable that proof of a concrete, causal nexus between the deceptive behavior of the Defendant and the Plaintiff's share purchases could be established.

a) In his pleading of April 10, 2005, the Plaintiff states that he always "checked the consistently false current reports close to the time of making a decision not only to purchase, but also to hold the securities," and on this basis applied for admission as party to give evidence. In the context of evidence given to the court of appeals, the Plaintiff also declared that he "continuously studied the current reports, mornings in the newspaper and then over the internet at the office, and also evenings." In addition, the Plaintiff even purchased at least part of the shares on the day that the Defendant's current reports were released or shortly thereafter, and these current reports were generally suitable to bring a potential investor to a buy decision. If one further considers that the court of appeals found other decision-relevant information provided by the Plaintiff in his testimony to have "material credibility and be in a personally convincing manner," then at least at this stage of the proceedings one cannot fully exclude a certain probability of correctness in the statements of his pleadings that he read specific, concrete current reports from the Defendant and that they influenced his investment decision.

b) However, on the basis of the clearly incorrect understanding of the law that the court of appeals held until now, it restricted its evidentiary investigation to whether and to what extent the Plaintiff followed "the general line" of the investing public on ComROAD shares in his decisions, and thus did not hear evidence on further, relevant details regarding his decisionmaking process or did not include such details in its evaluation of the evidence.

c) Consequently, this Division can make no final determination on the merits of the matter.

2. In its new appellate proceedings, the court of appeals shall therefore examine for probity the concrete pleadings of the Plaintiff – supplemented by new evidence if necessary – on the causal connection ...

[Text omitted]

Basic Inc. v. Levinson et al.
US Supreme Court
485 US 224 (1988)
[Text edited; some footnotes omitted]

OPINION BY: BLACKMUN

... This case requires us to apply the materiality requirement of § 10(b) of the Securities Exchange Act of 1934 ... and the Securities and Exchange Commissions Rule 10b-5 ... in the content of preliminary corporate merger discussions. We must also determine whether a person who traded a corporation's shares on a securities exchange after the issuance of a materially misleading statement by the corporation may invoke a rebuttable presumption that, in trading, he relied on the integrity of the price set by the market.

I.

Prior to December 20, 1978, Basic Incorporated was a publicly traded company primarily engaged in the business of manufacturing chemical refractories for the steel industry. As early as 1965 or 1966, Combustion Engineering, Inc., a company producing mostly alumina-based refractories, expressed some interest in acquiring Basic, but was deterred from pursuing this inclination seriously because of antitrust concerns it then entertained ...

Beginning in September 1976, Combustion representatives had meetings and telephone conversations with Basic officers and directors, including petitioners here, concerning the possibility of a merger. During 1977 and 1978, Basic made three public statements denying that it was engaged in merger negotiations. On December 18, 1978, Basic asked the New York Stock Exchange to suspend trading in its shares and issued a release stating that it had been "approached" by another company concerning a merger. On December 19, Basic's board endorsed Combustion's offer of $46 per share for its common stock ... and on the following day publicly announced its approval of Combustion's tender offer for all outstanding shares.

Respondents are former Basic shareholders who sold their stock after Basic's first public statement of October 21, 1977, and before the suspension of trading in December 1978. Respondents brought a class action against Basic and its directors, asserting that the defendants issued three false or misleading public statements and thereby were in violation of § 10(b) of the 1934 Act and of Rule 10b-5. Respondents alleged that they were injured by selling Basic shares at artificially depressed prices in a market affected by petitioners' misleading statements and in reliance thereon.

The District Court adopted a presumption of reliance by members of the plaintiff class upon petitioners' public statements ... On the merits, however, the District Court ... held that, as a matter of law, any misstatements were immaterial: there were no negotiations ongoing at the time of the first statement, and although negotiations were taking place when the second and third statements were issued, those negotiations were not "destined, with reasonable certainty, to become a merger agreement in principle."

The US Court of Appeals for the Sixth Circuit ... reasoned that while petitioners were under no general duty to disclose their discussions with Combustion, any statement the company voluntarily released could not be "'so incomplete as to mislead.'" ... In the Court of Appeals' view, Basic's statements that no negotiations were taking place, and that it knew of no corporate developments to account for the heavy trading activity, were misleading ...

The Court of Appeals joined a number of other circuits in accepting the "fraud-on-the-market theory" to create a rebuttable presumption that respondents relied on petitioners' material misrepresentations, noting that without the presumption it would be impractical to certify a class under Fed. Rule Civ. Proc. 23(b)(3) ...

II.

The 1934 Act was designed to protect investors against manipulation of stock prices ... Underlying the adoption of extensive disclosure requirements was a legislative philosophy: "There cannot be honest markets without honest publicity. Manipulation and dishonest practices of the market place thrive upon mystery and secrecy." HR Rep. No. 1383, 73d Cong., 2d Sess., 11 (1934) ...

The Court previously has addressed various positive and common-law requirements for a violation of § 10(b) or of Rule 10b-5 ... The Court also explicitly has defined a standard of materiality under the securities laws, see *TSC Industries, Inc. v. Northway, Inc.* ... concluding in the proxy-solicitation context that "an omitted fact is material if there is a substantial likelihood that a reasonable shareholder would consider it important in deciding how to vote." ... Acknowledging that certain information concerning corporate developments could well be of "dubious significance" ... the Court was careful not to set too low a standard of materiality; it was concerned that a minimal standard might bring an overabundance of information within its reach, and lead management "simply to bury the shareholders in an avalanche of trivial information – a result that is hardly conducive to informed decisionmaking." ... It further explained that to fulfill the materiality requirement "there must be a substantial likelihood that the disclosure of the omitted fact would have been viewed by the reasonable investor as having significantly altered the 'total mix' of information made available." ... We now expressly adopt the *TSC Industries* standard of materiality for the § 10(b) and Rule 10b-5 context.

[*Text omitted*]

C.

Even before this Court's decision in *TSC Industries*, the Second Circuit had explained the role of the materiality requirement of Rule 10b-5, with respect to contingent or speculative information or events, in a manner that gave that term meaning that is independent of the other provisions of the Rule. Under such circumstances, materiality "will depend at any given time upon a balancing of both the indicated probability that the event will occur and the anticipated magnitude of the event in light of the totality of the company activity." *SEC* v. *Texas Gulf Sulphur Co.* ...

In a subsequent decision, the late Judge Friendly, writing for a Second Circuit panel, applied the *Texas Gulf Sulphur* probability/magnitude approach in the specific context of preliminary merger negotiations. After acknowledging that materiality is something to be determined on the basis of the particular facts of each case, he stated:

> Since a merger in which it is bought out is the most important event that can occur in a small corporation's life, to wit, its death, we think that inside information, as regards a merger of this sort, can become material at an earlier stage than would be the case as regards lesser transactions – and this even though the mortality rate of mergers in such formative stages is doubtless high. *SEC* v. *Geon Industries, Inc.* ...

We agree with that analysis.

Whether merger discussions in any particular case are material therefore depends on the facts. Generally, in order to assess the probability that the event will occur, a factfinder will need to look to indicia of interest in the transaction at the highest corporate levels. Without attempting to catalog all such possible factors, we note by way of example that board resolutions, instructions to investment bankers, and actual negotiations between principals or their intermediaries may serve as indicia of interest. To assess the magnitude of the transaction to the issuer of the securities allegedly manipulated, a factfinder will need to consider such facts as the size of the two corporate entities and of the potential premiums over market value. No particular event or factor short of closing the transaction need be either necessary or sufficient by itself to render merger discussions material.

As we clarify today, materiality depends on the significance the reasonable investor would place on the withheld or misrepresented information. The fact-specific inquiry we endorse here is consistent with the approach a number of courts have taken in assessing the materiality of merger negotiations. Because the standard of materiality we have adopted differs from that used by both courts below, we remand the case for reconsideration of the question whether a grant of summary judgment is appropriate on this record.

IV.

A.

We turn to the question of reliance and the fraud-on-the-market theory. Succinctly put:

> "The fraud on the market theory is based on the hypothesis that, in an open and developed securities market, the price of a company's stock is determined by the available material information regarding the company and its business ... Misleading statements will therefore defraud purchasers of stock even if the purchasers do not directly rely on the misstatements ... The causal connection between the defendants' fraud and the plaintiffs' purchase of stock in such a case is no less significant than in a case of direct reliance on misrepresentations."
> *Peil* v. *Speiser* ...

... This case required resolution of several common questions of law and fact concerning the falsity or misleading nature of the three public statements made by Basic, the presence or absence of scienter, and the materiality of the misrepresentations, if any. In their amended complaint, the named plaintiffs alleged that in reliance on Basic's statements they sold their shares of Basic stock in the depressed market created by petitioners ... Requiring proof of individualized reliance from each member of the proposed plaintiff class effectively would have prevented respondents from proceeding with a class action, since individual issues then would have overwhelmed the common ones. The District Court found that the presumption of reliance created by the fraud-on-the-market theory provided "a practical resolution to the problem of balancing the substantive requirement of proof of reliance in securities cases against the procedural requisites of [Fed. Rule Civ. Proc.] 23." The District Court thus concluded that with reference to each public statement and its impact upon the open market for Basic shares, common questions predominated over individual questions, as required by Fed. Rule Civ. Proc. 23(a)(2) and (b)(3).

Petitioners and their amici complain that the fraud-on-the-market theory effectively eliminates the requirement that a plaintiff asserting a claim under Rule 10b-5 prove reliance. They note that reliance is and long has been an element of common-law fraud, see e.g. *Restatement (Second) of Torts* § 525 (1977); *Prosser and Keeton on The Law of Torts* § 108 (5th ed. 1984), and argue that because the analogous express right of action includes a reliance requirement, see, e.g. § 18(a) of the 1934 Act, as amended, 15 USC § 78r(a), so too must an action implied under § 10(b).

We agree that reliance is an element of a Rule 10b-5 cause of action. See *Ernst & Ernst* v. *Hochfelder* ... (quoting Senate Report). Reliance provides the requisite causal connection between a defendant's misrepresentation and a plaintiff's injury ... There is, however, more than one way to demonstrate the causal connection ...

The modern securities markets, literally involving millions of shares changing hands daily, differ from the face-to-face transactions contemplated by early fraud cases, and our understanding of Rule 10b-5's reliance requirement must encompass these differences.

"In face-to-face transactions, the inquiry into an investor's reliance upon information is into the subjective pricing of that information by that investor. With the presence of a market, the market is interposed between seller and buyer and, ideally, transmits information to the investor in the processed form of a market price. Thus the market is performing a substantial part of the valuation process performed by the investor in a face-to-face transaction. The market is acting as the unpaid agent of the investor, informing him that given all the information available to it, the value of the stock is worth the market price." In Re *LTV Securities Litigation* ...

B.

Presumptions typically serve to assist courts in managing circumstances in which direct proof, for one reason or another, is rendered difficult ... The courts below accepted a presumption, created by the fraud-on-the-market theory and subject to rebuttal by petitioners, that persons who had traded Basic shares had done so in reliance on the integrity of the price set by the market, but because of petitioners' material misrepresentations that price had been fraudulently depressed. Requiring a plaintiff to show a speculative state of facts, i.e. how he would have acted if omitted material information had been disclosed ... would place an unnecessarily unrealistic evidentiary burden on the Rule 10b-5 plaintiff who has traded on an impersonal market ...

[Text omitted]

... The presumption is also supported by common sense and probability. Recent empirical studies have tended to confirm Congress' premise that the market price of shares traded on well-developed markets reflects all publicly available information, and, hence, any material misrepresentations ... Indeed, nearly every court that has considered the proposition has concluded that where materially misleading statements have been disseminated into an impersonal, well-developed market for securities, the reliance of individual plaintiffs on the integrity of the market price may be presumed. Commentators generally have applauded the adoption of one variation or another of the fraud-on-the-market theory. An investor who buys or sells stock at the price set by the market does so in reliance on the integrity of that price. Because most publicly available information is reflected in market price, an investor's reliance on any public material misrepresentations, therefore, may be presumed for purposes of a Rule 10b-5 action.

C.

The Court of Appeals found that petitioners "made public material misrepresentations and [respondents] sold Basic stock in an impersonal, efficient market. Thus the class, as defined by the district court, has established the threshold facts for proving their loss." ... The court acknowledged that petitioners may rebut proof of the elements giving rise to the presumption, or show that the misrepresentation in fact did not lead to a distortion of price or that an individual plaintiff traded or would have traded despite his knowing the statement was false ...

Any showing that severs the link between the alleged misrepresentation and either the price received (or paid) by the plaintiff, or his decision to trade at a fair market price, will be sufficient to rebut the presumption of reliance. For example, if petitioners could show that the "market makers" were privy to the truth about the merger discussions here with Combustion, and thus that the market price would not have been affected by their misrepresentations, the causal connection could be broken: the basis for finding that the fraud had been transmitted through market price would be gone. Similarly, if, despite petitioners' allegedly fraudulent attempt to manipulate market price, news of the merger discussions credibly entered the market and dissipated the effects of the misstatements, those who traded Basic shares after the corrective statements would have no direct or indirect connection with the fraud. Petitioners also could rebut the presumption of reliance as to plaintiffs who would have divested themselves of their Basic shares without relying on the integrity of the market. For example, a plaintiff who believed that Basic's statements were false and that Basic was indeed engaged in merger discussions, and who consequently believed that Basic stock was artificially underpriced, but sold his shares nevertheless because of other unrelated concerns, e.g. potential antitrust problems, or political pressures to divest from shares of certain businesses, could not be said to have relied on the integrity of a price he knew had been manipulated.

[Text omitted]

18

Shareholder meetings

Required reading

EU: Shareholder Rights Directive, arts. 5–14
D: AktG, §§ 121–138
UK: CA 2006, secs. 290–333, 336–342; FSA Listing Rules, Rule 13.3
US: DGCL, §§ 211–217, 219, 222, 225, 231, 232; Securities Exchange Act,
Schedule 14A

The general meetings of shareholders

I.   *The general meeting is a medium for collective action*

The general meeting is the primary decisionmaking body for shareholders. The form of the meeting allows a large number of people to share information and make comments on the statements of others in real time. It also allows shareholders to cast votes personally on the matters discussed in Chapter 16. The need for shareholders to physically gather together has been determined mostly by technology. The technique of having all vote carrying persons gather in one place to discuss the issues pertinent to such persons and cast their votes has existed at least since the fifth century BC, when Athenian citizens gathered in the Pynx for such purpose. This technique has changed very little during the last 2,500 years.

The first major innovation in holding meetings came from law, in the form of a "proxy" or *Stimmrechtsvollmacht*. A "proxy" is a special-purpose agency relationship in which one person engages another to perform a specific task on her behalf during a specified period. This relationship should not be confused with the general representation performed by persons like senators (in politics) or managers (in business), who act with broad authority over a longer period. The granting of a proxy to a third party for the exercise of one's personal membership rights in a company was forbidden at common law,[1] but, as investors became more numerous and less connected with the direct management of their companies, it became more difficult for them to attend all of the shareholders' meetings of the companies in which they owned shares, especially when the meeting was geographically distant. As will be discussed in the following sections of this chapter, all of our jurisdictions allow proxies. Granting a proxy to the management (as is often done in the US) or a bank (as is often done in Germany) became a convenient way of exercising voting rights without incurring the expense of visiting meetings. Thus, all of the shareholders no longer had to gather together to cast their votes. A proxy could potentially concentrate the votes of all the shareholders in the hands of one proxy holder, as can happen in the US when the company solicits proxies for a general meeting.

Hundreds of years passed before the arrival of the next really significant development for general meetings: networked electronic data transfer. Because the goal of a general meeting is to allow multiple participants simultaneously to share the information presented to the meeting and comment thereon, it is obvious that controlled "shareholder forums" and "webcasts," with the ability to submit questions by email, can offer real-time, multilateral participation with significantly increased convenience, given that even great distances between shareholders are rendered irrelevant. As a result, each of our jurisdictions has adopted legislation to allow meetings to be held by electronic means. Germany and the US have also created "chat sites," usually called "shareholder forums," to facilitate the exchange of ideas among shareholders. These rules and the technology with which they combine are still relatively new, and it is difficult to predict the range of their future impact.

As we saw in Chapter 16, shareholders have rather limited rights, even if they do have access to extensive information about the company and its operations. Will the ease and capacity of electronic communications increase shareholder activity? Will shareholders, like the unrelated mass of individuals who write the Wikipedia without compensation in about 250 languages, use electronic communication to make their small contributions to the company? Can – like philanthropic authors of software – remotely located shareholders offer "patches" for the company's problems that they see from their unique perspectives? Is there anything about the

---

[1] See *Harben* v. *Philips*, (1883) 23 ChD 14 (CA). For a discussion of the history of proxies and their rise as shareholders became more dispersed and companies became more geographically dispersed, see Thomas and Dixon (1998: § 1.01); and Loss, Seligman and Parades (2004: 529 *et seq.*).

role of being a "shareholder" and the nature of voting rights that would prevent shareholder activism from being as successful as the "wikinomic" participation of unrelated individuals in other online projects? Just as the journalistic image of "democracy" appears for many to be stuck on the image of a mass of people marching down a street with chants and banners (in which most people really only see the heads or shoulders of their neighbor) rather than calmly sitting at home communicating over the internet, are we stuck on the idea of physical presence (even with intellectual distraction) in shareholder gatherings?

Regardless of your answers to the above questions, and whether a meeting is held in a field at the foot of the Parthenon or in cyberspace, it remains an event that is organized by someone for the discussion of specific issues and the casting of votes. As a result, aside from possible media of communication, the issues that concern the law in connection with a general meeting remain quite simple:

- Who can call a meeting?
- When must a general meeting be called?
- Who must be invited to participate?
- How are they invited?
- What information does the invitation have to contain?
- Is the truthfulness of the information policed?
- Who can participate in the meeting?
- Who can present proposals, ask questions and make comments?
- Who can vote?
- How are votes cast?
- How are they counted?

The answers to these questions tend to be dry and factual, and the following section will present brief answers for each of our three jurisdictions. In order to benefit most from these schematic summaries, you should read them together with the relevant provisions of law and try to imagine the course of an actual meeting. One need not remember the content of each provision, but it is important to know where to look for the details. Indeed, a practicing lawyer must know all the details (Are twenty or thirty days' notice required? Do holidays count as "days"?) at least when she has the law in front of her.

Our comparative review of these three frameworks will pursue a more general evaluation of the functions of the meeting and question whether the legal structures currently at hand provide the best tools to serve those functions. Aside from calling and holding the meeting, there is another set of important legal issues. Where there is power, there is usually abuse. In the context of general meetings, since management usually has the power to call the meeting and formulate its agenda, it also has ample opportunity for abuse. Proxy holders have the power to cast the votes for the grantors of proxies, and thus negligence and fraud can follow such exercise. Since power in the meeting derives from voting rights, any majority shareholder will be able to dominate the meeting to the detriment of the minority. To keep these abuses in check, our jurisdictions have developed rules to ensure that management communicates the nature of the meeting fully and truthfully, that persons soliciting proxies behave as good agents, and that majority shareholders do not unfairly prejudice the interests of the minority.

II. The mechanics of the general meeting

Shareholders meet annually either to approve the accounts, elect directors, or both, and they also meet for special purposes, such as to approve a significant transaction like a merger. Thus, descriptively enough, there are "annual"[2] meetings (UK: "annual general meeting" or "AGM";[3] Germany: *ordentliche Hauptversammlung*[4]) and "special"[5] meetings (UK: simply "general meeting";[6] Germany: referred to in the scholarship as *außerordentliche Hauptversammlung*[7]). As noted, an annual meeting is called each year to perform annually repeating tasks, like approving the financial statements, approving dividends and electing directors, but could be specially called at any time shareholder approval becomes necessary. These two different types of meetings are not to be confused with the different types of resolutions (such as "ordinary" and "special") required to approve specific acts, as discussed in Chapter 16. There, we discussed the power of shareholders to call a general meeting. Here, we will focus on the mechanics of calling and holding meetings.

A. United States

1. When should an annual general meeting be called? The board of a Delaware corporation must call a general meeting as specified in the by-laws, but may do so no later than thirteen months after the last annual meeting or the formation of the corporation.[8] SEC rules apply to general

---

[2] DGCL § 211(b). [3] Sec. 336(1) CA 2006. [4] § 175(1) AktG.
[5] DGCL § 211(d). [6] Secs. 302, 303 CA 2006.
[7] Such special purpose meetings are provided for in §§ 92(1), 121(1), 122(1) AktG.
[8] DGCL § 211(b), (c).

meetings of registered companies once a meeting is called,[9] but do not in themselves require such meetings.

2. Who should be invited to participate? All shareholders who are on the stockholder list on the "record date" must receive notice of the meeting.[10] The record date must be no more than sixty and no less than ten days before the meeting.[11] Because the securities settlement system and arrangements with brokers usually require that an intermediary rather than a shareholder is entered on the stockholder lists, SEC rules instruct issuers to look beyond that list. Issuers must ask each intermediary (broker, dealer, voting trustee, bank or association) on the stockholder list if it holds the company's shares for beneficial owner-customers and provide the intermediary with as many copies of the meeting materials as it needs for such persons.[12] Broker-dealers[13] and banks[14] have a duty to distribute the materials to their customers. This distribution process is complicated, time-consuming and can lead to errors in passing along the materials and exercising voting rights. Proxy services have sprung up to address this market inefficiency.

3. How should they be invited? Under Delaware law, shareholders must be given written notice of the meeting not less than ten nor more than sixty days before the date of the meeting either by mail[15] or, if the stockholder consents, by electronic communication.[16] SEC Rules provide that the required meeting materials may be distributed to shareholders by a posting on the internet and a direct notice of the posting sent to each shareholder at least forty days before the meeting.[17] This can reduce the bulk of materials that have to be handled through the chains of brokers and banks to the shareholders. The NYSE's *Listed Company Manual* requires the company to notify the NYSE of a general meeting at least ten days before the meeting.[18]

4. What information regarding the issues should shareholders be given? The Delaware statute requires that shareholders be informed of the place, date and hour of the meeting or the means of remote communications for participating in the meeting, as well as the purpose for which any special meeting is being called.[19] Delaware case law sets out a broad

---

[9] 17 CFR § 240.14c-2.   [10] DGCL § 213(a).   [11] DGCL § 213(a).

[12] 17 CFR § 240.14a-13.   [13] 17 CFR § 240.14b-1.   [14] 17 CFR § 240.14b-2.

[15] DGCL § 222(b).   [16] DGCL § 232.   [17] 17 CFR § 240.14a-16.

[18] NYSE LCM, para. 401.02.   [19] DGCL § 222(a).

standard, requiring that shareholders be given the information necessary to make a reasonable decision regarding the exercise of their rights.[20] If the company's shares are registered with the SEC, the situation shifts from a general standard to detailed rules. If the company solicits proxies from the shareholders it must provide a "proxy statement" according to Regulation 14A,[21] and, if the company will merely be holding a meeting without soliciting proxies, it must provide shareholders with an "information statement" pursuant to Regulation 14C.[22] Issuers must also provide shareholders with annual reports.[23] The information that an issuer must provide under Regulation 14A is gathered together in an instruction form referred to as "Schedule 14A."[24] The most important information required by Schedule 14A is:

- Item 1: the date, time and place of the general meeting.
- Item 2: whether or not the person giving the proxy has the power to revoke it.
- Item 3: whether, if a shareholder votes against a given transaction, she will have the right to be bought out at a fair price if the transaction is approved (appraisal rights).
- Item 4: the names of the persons soliciting the proxies, any employment relationship between the soliciting persons and the issuer, whether any director intends to oppose the action up for vote, the monies expended on the solicitation, and the names of the persons – including lenders – paying for the solicitation.
- Item 5: any substantial direct or indirect interest – through security holdings or otherwise – with each director of the issuer, other soliciting person, nominee for office of director, or associate of any of these persons.
- Item 6: information regarding the securities, including the record date for voting at the meeting, the number of securities outstanding, and significant shareholders filing a Schedule 13D.
- Item 7: names of directors and officers and persons nominated for election as directors, as well as their significant transactions and indebtedness with the issuer, the presence of audit, nominating and compensation committees on the board, and how nominees are selected for the board.

---

[20] See *Stroud* v. *Grace*, 606 A 2d 75, 86–87 (Del. 1992), with further references.
[21] 17 CFR § 240.14a-1 *et seq.*   [22] 17 CFR § 240.14c-1 *et seq.*
[23] 17 CFR § 240.14a-3(b).
[24] 17 CFR § 240.14a–101, Schedule 14A, Information required in proxy statement.

- Item 8: detailed information regarding the compensation of directors.
- Item 9: the name of the issuer's registered accountant and the fees paid thereto.
- Item 10: detailed information regarding stock or stock-option plans.

The "proxy statement" that contains this information must be filed with the SEC before, or in some cases at the same time as, it is given to the shareholders.[25] If the general meeting has been called to approve a merger or other significant transaction, Item 14 of Schedule 14A requires detailed disclosure regarding the proposed transaction.[26] A similar "Schedule 14C"[27] must be prepared and distributed if proxies are not solicited in connection with the annual meeting.

5. May the shareholders also present items for the meeting to consider? In 2009, the DGCL introduced rules to facilitate shareholder participation in the general meeting.[28] Traditionally, the Delaware courts have held that shareholders may ask questions, make comments and proposals, and also nominate candidates for the board both at and before the meeting.[29] As discussed in Chapter 16, the SEC rules have historically prohibited such shareholder involvement for registered companies, as shareholders' proposals may be made before the meeting exclusively under Exchange Act Rule 14a-8 and management may exclude shareholder proposals from proxy materials if they regard the nomination of directors or conflict with a management proposal.[30] The DGCL now allows a company's by-laws to provide for shareholder nomination of candidates for the board in the company's proxy materials as well as to provide for reimbursement of shareholders who seek to have their own candidates elected through a proxy contest.[31] In past SEC rulemaking processes, such rights were seen as dangerous and disruptive to company management, although some gestures toward shareholder nomination have been made on occasion since 2003.[32] As substantive corporate law rests squarely in the jurisdiction of each state, it can be expected that the federal rules will gradually give ground to these shareholder rights if advocated by bodies such as the Delaware Assembly. The Assembly overrode the state's own Court of Chancery, which just months earlier had invalidated a proposed

---

[25] 17 CFR § 240.14a-6.
[26] Further SEC Rules also apply to the specific circumstance of a merger transaction.
[27] 17 CFR § 240.14c-101, Schedule 14C, Information required in information statement.
[28] DGCL §§ 112, 113.   [29] Balotti and Finkelstein (2008: §§ 7.63–7.64).
[30] 17 CFR § 240.14a-8(i).   [31] DGCL §§ 112, 113.   [32] Donald (2005: 358–361).

by-law amendment that would provide reimbursement of shareholder expenses.[33]

6. Is the truthfulness of the information policed? To police the truthfulness and completeness of proxy statements and information statements, SEC Rule 14a-9 makes it illegal for such communications to contain:

> any statement which, at the time and in the light of the circumstances under which it is made, is false or misleading with respect to any material fact, or which omits to state any material fact necessary in order to make the statements therein not false or misleading or necessary to correct any statement in any earlier communication with respect to the solicitation of a proxy for the same meeting or subject matter which has become false or misleading.[34]

This rule may be enforced either by a shareholder suing the issuer directly or by an SEC enforcement action.[35] An analysis of "materiality" like that found in *Basic* v. *Levinson* in Chapter 20 would be part of an action under Rule 14a-9.

7. What is the necessary quorum for a meeting and who may attend? Although the certificate of incorporation may specify a higher percentage, the DGCL provides that a meeting may only be validly held if one-third of the members of the corporation are present in person or by proxy at the meeting (referred to as a "quorum").[36] Where the law requires approval by a majority of all outstanding shares entitled to vote, as in the case of a merger, the presence requirement would actually be higher even though no higher quorum is specified. Neither US nor Delaware statutory law contains detailed rules on the formalities of a general meeting. The DGCL requires that at least one officer record the minutes of the meeting,[37] and that, for companies that are listed or have more than 2,000 shareholders, inspectors be appointed to monitor the meeting and count the votes.[38] Delaware cases generally hold that shareholders have the rights necessary to exercise their voting rights, which would include reasonable

---

[33] *CA, Inc.* v. *AFSCME Employees Pension Plan*, 953 A 2d 227 (2008). As the court noted in *CA*, a challenger could in the past be reimbursed for a contest run for "policy" questions as opposed to one merely seeking to oust the board. The controlling case is *Hall* v. *Trans-Lux Daylight Picture Screen Corp.*, 171 A 226, 227 (Del. Ch. 1934).

[34] 17 CFR § 240.14a-9(a).   [35] *J. I. Case Co.* v. *Borak*, 377 US 426 (1964).

[36] DGCL § 216.   [37] DGCL § 142(a).

[38] DGCL § 231(e). The role of inspectors is discussed in subsection 11.

participation at the general meeting.[39] Beyond this, any detailed rules on participation at the meeting would be provided in the company's certificate of incorporation or by-laws.

8. Who may present proposals, ask questions and make comments at the meeting? As noted above, Delaware courts generally leave companies free to arrange the proceedings of their meetings themselves, and allow by-law provisions specifying rules on the shareholder nomination of directors. If challenged as in conflict with Rule 14a-8, this state rule will quite likely stand up to the federal objection.

9. Who can vote? Shareholders recorded on the list of stockholders prepared for calling the meeting are entitled to vote at the meeting.[40] The cut-off date may be a "record date" if so declared by the directors, a date ten days before the meeting is held, or even one day before the meeting is held if notice of the meeting is waived.[41] As discussed above, SEC Rules 14b-1 and 14b-2 require broker-dealers and banks holding shares for their clients to give them an opportunity to vote the shares. However, under the Rules of the NYSE, if at least fifteen days before the meeting a broker asks its client to provide voting instructions, and then does not receive such instructions by the tenth day before the meeting, the broker may vote on "uncontested matters," which includes the election of directors, at its own discretion.[42] This is referred to as a "broker vote," and is hotly contested by shareholder groups. In January 2010, the NYSE changed the instructions to its Rule 451, so that brokers must now inform beneficial owners that no broker will vote on an election of directors without express instruction; however, Rule 252 itself was not amended at the time this manuscript went to press.

As discussed in Chapter 9, resolutions that concern a particular class of shares will be open for the votes only of the shareholders of the relevant class. This would be the case for decisions that either exclude or specifically include the votes of preferred shareholders.

10. How are votes cast? Election for directors must be by written ballot.[43] No specific provision exists on the form of vote for other matters. All votes may be given by electronic means if the directors so decide.[44]

---

[39] This would include the right to nominate candidates for director positions on the floor of the meeting. See Balotti and Finkelstein (2008: §§ 7.63).

[40] §§ 213(a), 219(a) DGCL.   [41] §§ 213(a), 219(a) DGCL.   [42] Rule 452 NYSE Rules.

[43] § 211(e) DGCL.   [44] § 211(e) DGCL.

All stockholders have the right to cast their votes by written proxy,[45] which also may be given by electronic means.[46] Like a power of attorney or other agency relationship, a proxy relationship may be "specific," by being restricted to specified behavior (e.g. "vote 'NO' on proposal No. 5"), or "general" by giving the proxy holder free reign to exercise discretion (e.g. "vote wisely"). As an agent, a proxy holder is a fiduciary and thus has a duty to act in the best interests of the proxy-giving principal (the shareholder).[47] In the case of a company registered with the SEC, specific rules apply to the form to be used for the proxy.[48] No rules or requirements exist at the state or federal level on the casting of votes electronically. So-called proxy service companies like Broadridge Financial Solutions and Georgeson Shareholder provide platforms for electronic voting.

Delaware law expressly allows shareholders to enter into agreements on how their voting rights will be exercised.[49]

11. How are votes counted? If a Delaware company is listed or has more than 2,000 shareholders, the management must appoint at least one "inspector" before each meeting.[50] The inspectors must sign an "oath faithfully to execute the duties of inspector with strict impartiality" to the best of their abilities, and, in connection with the meeting, they must:

- ascertain the number of shares outstanding and the voting power of each;
- determine the shares represented at a meeting and the validity of proxies and ballots;
- count all votes and ballots and certify their findings; and
- decide and record any challenges made to any determination on the votes.[51]

B. Germany

1. When should an annual general meeting be called? The *Aktiengesetz* requires the annual general meeting to be called during the first eight months of the financial year.[52] The Rules of the Frankfurt Stock Exchange, however, require that companies listed on the "prime standard" market segment present their annual accounts to the public within four months after the close of the financial year.[53] Because pursuant to

---

[45] § 212(b) DGCL.   [46] § 212(c)(2) DGCL.   [47] Frankel (1983: 795).
[48] 17 CFR § 240.14a-4.   [49] § 218(c) DGCL.   [50] § 231(e) DGCL.
[51] § 231(b) DGCL.   [52] § 175(1) AktG.
[53] § 65(2) of the Rules of the Frankfurt Stock Exchange.

the *Aktiengesetz* the annual accounts must be submitted to the general meeting,[54] this would mean that German companies listed in the prime standard segment would have to hold their annual meeting during the first four months of the financial year (i.e., in the vast majority of cases, by April). Special meetings should be called when it is necessary for the "good of the company" (*Wohl der Gesellschaft*).[55]

2. Who should be invited to participate?   Because AGs issue both bearer and registered shares, there are two different procedures for calling the meeting. The primary notice to bearer shares is given in a way that is not directed toward any addressee, so there is no need to determine the set of eligible shareholders at the invitation stage. A second form of notice to the holders of bearer shares does not rely on a strict criterion of eligibility, but a rough rule of probability: the company must send an invitation to the custodian banks and shareholder associations that represented shareholders at the annual general meeting held the previous year.[56] For the holders of registered shares, the invitation is sent to the shareholders entered in the share register no later than two weeks before the meeting.[57] Thus, the share register lists who should be invited.

3. How should they be invited?   As mentioned in the previous subsection, there are three ways of notifying the shareholders. For the holders of bearer shares, the call to meeting must first be published (electronically) in the *Bundesanzeiger*[58] at least thirty days before the date of the meeting,[59] and sent at least twenty-one days prior to the meeting to custodian banks and shareholder associations that represented shareholders at the previous meeting.[60] The notice to the holders of registered shares is mailed directly to the addresses of the shareholders as entered in the share register.[61] Banks[62] in Germany often hold shares in custodian accounts for their customers, and, if such banks are entered in the share register on the twenty-first day before the meeting date or hold bearer shares in custody on behalf

---

[54] § 175(1) AktG. In addition, the general meeting may also be requested to review and finalize the annual accounts, which would make it not only difficult, but also impossible to release them to the public before the meeting. See § 173 I AktG.

[55] § 121(1) AktG.   [56] § 125(1) AktG.   [57] § 125(2) AktG.   [58] §§ 121(4), 25 AktG.

[59] § 123(1) AktG.   [60] § 125(1) AktG.   [61] §§ 121(4), 125(2) AktG.

[62] The reason why "banks" are found in this role in Germany and "brokers" perform the same function in the US is the separation of investment and brokerage activities from savings and credit banking activities introduced by US banking legislation between 1933 and 1999. German "universal" banks also perform brokerage services.

of customers, they must promptly distribute the call to meeting to their shareholder-customers.[63] This function of banks resembles that of brokers in the US, although the possibility that banks might abuse the voting process is taken more seriously and is more regulated than in the US.

4. What information regarding the issues should they be given? The call to meeting must indicate the company's name, its registered address, the time, date and place of the meeting and contain the meeting agenda (*Tagesordnung*).[64] For listed companies, the call to the meeting also has to include information on:

- conditions for participation in the meeting and the exercise of voting rights;
- the record date and its relevance;
- the procedure of voting by proxy, by letter or by electronic communication;
- shareholder rights to include items, counter-proposals and shareholder nominations on the agenda and to ask questions in the general meeting; this information can be limited to a notice of the relevant deadlines for exercising these rights if it is accompanied by a direction to further explanations on the company's website; and
- the company's website on which the additional information prescribed by § 124a AktG is available.[65]

In order to give shareholders easy access to information required for the exercise of their rights, § 124a AktG requires listed companies to post the following information on their website immediately after the call to the meeting:

- the meeting notice;
- an explanation of agenda items on which no resolution is to be taken;
- the texts of the resolutions and the other documents submitted to the meeting;
- the total number of shares and voting rights; and
- the forms for voting by correspondence and by proxy.

If the agenda includes a proposed amendment of the *Satzung* or the approval of a proposed contract, the text or the amendment, in the first case, or a summary of the contract, in the second, must be published together with the agenda.[66] Both the *Vorstand* and the *Aufsichtsrat* must

---

[63] § 128(1) AktG.   [64] § 121(3) AktG.   [65] § 121(3) AktG.   [66] § 124(2) AktG.

provide recommendations for the various items on the agenda, with the restriction that only the *Aufsichtsrat* may make recommendations regarding candidates for board and auditor positions.[67] The *Vorstand* must send any shareholder who so requests a copy of the annual accounts, management report and recommendation on dividends.[68] If shareholders have requested that items be placed on the agenda, their proposals must be distributed either together with the call to the meeting or immediately after receipt of the shareholder request.[69]

5. May the shareholders also present items for the meeting to consider? As discussed in detail in Chapter 16, the holders of shares constituting 5 percent of the capital or having a value of €500,000 may place items on the meeting's agenda.[70] Otherwise, any shareholder, regardless of the size or duration of his shareholding, may make counterproposals to proposals submitted by management that, together with a supporting statement of up to 5,000 words, the management must "make available."[71] All shareholders may also propose candidates for election to the *Aufsichtsrat* in the same manner and receive the same manner of distribution.[72] At the meeting itself, shareholders have a right to speak, but the chair of the meeting may place reasonable restrictions on such right.

6. Is the truthfulness of the information policed? If due notice of a proposed resolution is not given, it may not be adopted at the meeting.[73] A resolution adopted on the basis of false information can be challenged and voided,[74] and providing false information to the shareholders in the general meeting may trigger criminal liability.[75] See Chapter 20 for a discussion of judicial actions challenging shareholders' resolutions under German law.

7. What is the necessary quorum for a meeting and who may attend? The *Aktiengesetz* does not provide a minimum quorum for the constitution of a meeting, although as discussed in Chapter 16, it

---

[67] § 124(3) AktG.   [68] § 175(2) AktG.   [69] § 124(1) AktG.   [70] § 122(2) AktG.

[71] § 126(1) AktG. Note that the *Vorstand* need not distribute such proposals or nominations with the meeting agenda, but only "make them available," which is satisfied by the relevant proposal or nomination, together with any supporting statement, on the company's website. Kubis, in *MünchKommAktG* (2004: § 126 mn. 21).

[72] § 127 AktG.   [73] § 124(4) AktG.

[74] § 124(4), in connection with § 243(1) AktG.   [75] § 400(1) no. 1 AktG.

provides specific majorities for various types of decisions, and some of these are based on outstanding capital rather than capital present at the meeting.

The *Satzung* of an AG may require that shareholders specially register with the company before each meeting.[76] In the case of bearer shares, such "registration" (*Anmeldung*) has traditionally meant depositing the shares before the meeting with a notary public or a custodian bank.[77] In the case of registered shares, the proof of shareholder status is provided by entry in the share register.[78] The *Satzung* may specify the manner of proof to be used for bearer shares, but, in the case of a listed company, the statute requires companies to accept an account statement from the shareholder's custodian bank as of the twenty-first day before the meeting, the record date, as sufficient proof of shareholder status.[79] Thus, German law is compliance with the Shareholders' Rights Directive, which requires that "[t]he right to participate and to vote in a general meeting shall not be subject to any condition requiring the shareholder to block the relevant shares by deposit or other means with a credit institution or another entity ahead of the general meeting, even if the blocking has no effect on the possibility of trading the shares."[80]

8.   Who may present proposals, ask questions and make comments at the meeting?   As in US law, the *Aktiengesetz* generally leaves detailed provisions on the conduct of the meeting to any procedural rules (*Geschäftsordnung*) that the company and its shareholders decide to draw up.[81] One difference, as discussed in the last chapter, is that the right to request information under German law may be exercised only during the meeting. Otherwise, the law merely provides that a list of the shareholders attending the meeting be prepared and made available to the shareholders,[82] and that the proceedings of the meeting be recorded in minutes, which for listed companies must be notarized, and submitted in copy to the commercial register.[83] Because a number of important resolutions adopted at a meeting do not take effect until filed in the commercial register, individual shareholders have been able to obtain very significant leverage against the company by filing a "strike suit" that, although perhaps groundless, would

---

[76] § 123(2) AktG.   [77] See Baums (1999: 116).   [78] § 67(2) AktG.
[79] § 123(3) AktG.   [80] Art. 7(1) Directive 2007/36/EC.   [81] § 129(1) AktG.
[82] § 129 AktG.
[83] § 130 AktG. Unlisted companies must also have the minutes notarized if a resolution requiring a three-quarters majority is adopted at the meeting.

block the entry in the commercial register[84] and the effectiveness of the resolution until the court was able to address the issues on the merits.[85] Such suits are discussed in more detail in Chapter 20.

Although the statute does not permit a completely virtual general meeting, it does allow the company's *Satzung* to provide that general meeting may be transmitted in an audio and visual medium.[86]

9. Who can vote? The procedures on registering for the meeting, discussed above, and the entry in the share register determine in general who can vote at a general meeting. Classes of shares are another determining factor, in that preferred shares may not carry voting rights except when dividends are not paid for a certain period of time, and classes are given a separate vote on matters specifically affecting the class (see Chapter 9). As in Delaware and UK law, a corporation may not vote its own shares.[87] Like UK law, the *Aktiengesetz* prohibits persons who have certain specified conflicts of interest with respect to a decision – such as in connection with the ratification of a director's acts or release of an obligation to the company – from exercising their voting rights on such decisions.[88]

As discussed in the next subsection, custodian banks may vote their clients' shares under certain conditions that are somewhat stricter than the US rules.

10. How are votes cast? Votes are cast personally, through a representative, through an appointed proxy (*Bevollmächtigte*), which may include proxies nominated by the issuer,[89] or through a custodian bank empowered (*ermächtigt*) to exercise voting rights.[90] Unless the *Satzung* provides otherwise, proxies must be in writing or comparably memorialized, for example by email.[91]

---

[84] While a suit challenging a shareholder resolution does not constitute a prohibition to file the resolution, judges are reluctant to enter challenged resolutions into the register because of potential liability if the suit were to prove ultimately successful.

[85] For example, a resolution amending the *Satzung*, such as to increase the capital, only becomes effective upon entry in the commercial register. See § 181(3) AktG. As will be discussed in greater detail in Chapter 19, the law was recently amended to allow the court in charge of the commercial register to allow the resolution to enter into effect pending resolution of the suit (see § 246a AktG), but the effectiveness of this rule has not yet been established.

[86] § 118(1) AktG.   [87] § 71b AktG.   [88] § 136(1) AktG; sec. 239(4) CA 2006.

[89] § 135(9) AktG. I.e. a stockholding corporation would cast votes through its legal representative, the *Vorstand*.

[90] § 135 AktG.   [91] § 134(3) AktG.

In Germany, it has been the practice since the late nineteenth century for shareholders to keep their shares with custodian banks. Because these banks were usually major creditors of and often held sizeable equity stakes in the same companies, they were notorious for dipping into the shares of their custody account customers to supplement their own voting power and reinforce their influence at the general meeting. Even after the requirement for written proxies was introduced with the *Aktiengesetz* of 1937, banks still exercised a significant amount of power over their customers' shares.[92] Following a reform initiative of Professor Theodor Baums to replace bank voting with independent, competing proxy agents,[93] the German legislature in 1997 took steps to reduce the influence that banks could exercise over the shares of beneficial owners held in their custody accounts.[94] As a result, current law strictly regulates the participation of custodian banks in the general meeting on behalf of their account holders.

In contrast to US law, even if a bank is the registered shareholder for shares it holds for a customer, it must be authorized (*ermächtigt*) by the customer to exercise the voting rights of such shares.[95] If a bank holds bearer shares for a customer or registered shares for which the customer is entered in the share register, it must have an express power of attorney granted separately from its custody account with the customer.[96] Banks may hold an enduring proxy for their customers, but must inform customers on an annual basis that the proxy can be revoked and that other proxy agents (such as shareholder associations) are available to act for them at the general meeting.[97]

If a bank intends to represent its account holders in the general meeting, it must vote according to the account holders' instructions. If an account holder does not give specific instructions, the bank may exercise the voting rights on the basis of a general proxy provided it votes either according to its own proposal as communicated to the account holder or in favor of the proposals of the company's management sent out with the invitation to the meeting.[98] In the latter case, the bank has to forward the management proposals to the customer unless they have been otherwise made available.[99] If a bank offers to vote according to its own proposals, it

---

[92] Hommelhoff (1987: 92); Schröer, in *MünchKommAktG* (2004: § 135 mn. 8).
[93] Baums and von Randow (1995: 435).
[94] See *Gesetz zur Kontrolle und Transparenz im Unternehmensbereich* (Law for Monitoring and Transparency in Business Undertakings), November 6, 1997 (BGBl I: 786).
[95] §§ 129(3), 135(6) AktG.   [96] § 135(1) AktG.   [97] § 135(1) AktG.
[98] § 135(1) AktG.   [99] § 135(4) AktG.

must formulate these proposals in the best interests of the account holders, and must take "organizational steps to ensure that interests arising in other business areas" of the bank do not influence voting.[100] Together with the proposals, the bank must request voting instructions from the account holders and inform them that the bank will vote according to its own proposals if it receives no instructions.[101] Each bank must disclose conflicts of interest by listing in its financial statements those companies either in which it has a holding exceeding 5 percent or to which it has elected a supervisory board member,[102] and must notify customers holding stock custody accounts if:

- any of its managing directors or employees are members of the supervisory board of the company whose shares are to be voted, or if any employee or managing director of such company holds a seat in its own supervisory board;
- it has a holding in the company exceeding the threshold of 3 percent; and
- it has been a member of an underwriting syndicate for a securities issue of such company during the last five years.[103]

Substantial lending positions or a *Hausbank* relationship do not, oddly enough, trigger similar duties.

A bank may deviate from a customer's instructions if it "may reasonably assume that had the customer been aware of the circumstances she would have approved such different vote," and it subsequently informs the customer of such different vote.[104] A bank may vote customer shares in its own general meeting or in the general meeting of a company in which it has a 20 percent equity holding only on the basis of express instructions for each agenda point.[105]

The *Aktiengesetz* allows shareholders to make agreements on how their votes will be exercised provided that neither the company nor a director is party to the agreement,[106] and the agreement does not rise to the level of an outright sale of shares.[107]

11. How are votes counted? Votes are calculated on the basis of the voted shares' nominal value, or, for no-par shares, the number of

---

[100] § 135(2) AktG.   [101] § 135(2) AktG.   [102] § 340a(4) HGB.
[103] § 135(2) AktG.   [104] § 135(3) AktG.   [105] § 135(3) AktG.
[106] This is prohibited by § 136 AktG.
[107] It is a general principle of German corporate law that shares may not be split up (see § 8(5) AktG), which is considered to be the case when certain rights are sold to third parties for use and divorced from the rest of the share.

shares.[108] The *Aktiengesetz* requires that the chairperson of the meeting ascertain the results of each vote, and that all resolutions adopted be recorded by a notary public (in the case of listed companies) or the chairperson of the supervisory board (for unlisted companies), and that this record be filed with the commercial register.[109] Any resolution adopted in violation of the majority requirements, such as through an incorrect vote count, can be challenged in court.

C. United Kingdom

1. When should an annual general meeting be called? A public company must hold an annual general meeting during the first six months after its "accounting reference date" for its financial year.[110] No similar requirement applies to private companies. Otherwise, a general meeting must also be called when any action requiring shareholder approval, as discussed in Chapters 16 and 22, are to be taken.

2. Who should be invited to participate? Notice of a meeting must be given to every member and every director.[111] No provision is made for the further distribution of notices through financial intermediaries acting as shareholders for their clients. A report prepared by Paul Myners in 2004 showed that the structure of share ownership and the presence of multiple intermediaries in the United Kingdom can lead to delays in the distribution of communications to the ultimate shareholders.[112] Thus, as in the US and Germany, holding shares through intermediaries such as brokers and banks can negatively affect the exercise of voting rights.

3. How should they be invited? Unless the company's articles provide a longer period, a public company must provide at least twenty-one days' notice for an annual general meeting, fourteen days' notice for other general meetings,[113] or twenty-eight days' notice if a resolution requiring special notice (such as a proposal to remove a director) is to be adopted.[114] Notice may be provided in hard copy mailed to the addressee, by electronic communication, or by posting the invitation on a website and notifying the addressee of such posting.[115]

---

[108] § 134(1) AktG. [109] § 130 AktG. [110] Sec. 336(1) CA 2006.
[111] Sec. 310(1) CA 2006.
[112] See Myners (2004), "Review of the Impediments to Voting UK Shares."
[113] Sec. 307 CA 2006. [114] Sec. 312(1) CA 2006. [115] Secs. 308, 309 CA 2006.

4. What information regarding the issues should they be given? Much like under US law, there are three layers of general requirements for the contents of notices to the meeting. All companies must provide the time, date and place of the meeting, and state the general nature of the business to be dealt with at the meeting,[116] as well as a reminder that members may appoint proxies to exercise their rights.[117] Public companies must "lay before the company in general meeting copies of its annual accounts and reports,"[118] which include the "directors' report" and the "directors' remuneration report."[119] In addition, meetings called to resolve on certain matters will trigger requirements that additional elements of information – such as a report on a transaction or a summary of a contract – also be distributed. A further set of requirements applies to listed companies.[120] For the annual general meeting of a listed company that is called to resolve on matters of ordinary business, a circular containing at least the following information must be provided with the notice of meeting:

- a clear and adequate explanation of the meeting's subject matter, appropriately emphasizing its essential characteristics, benefits and risks;
- why the member is being asked to vote or, if not so requested, the reason for the circular;
- all information necessary for a properly informed decision;
- the board's reasoned recommendation on how to vote;
- instructions for passing the materials on to any transferee if the shares have been sold; and
- if new securities are replacing existing securities, an explanation of what will happen to the latter.[121]

5. May the shareholders also present items for the meeting to consider? As discussed in Chapter 16, members of a public company who hold at least 5 percent of the total voting rights or act in a group of 100 members holding an average paid-up sum of at least £100,[122] may have the board distribute a proposed resolution.[123] The board must distribute the resolution in the same manner as the notice of the meeting and at the same time, or promptly thereafter.[124] Members of the same number and

---

[116] Sec. 311 CA 2006.   [117] Sec. 325 CA 2006.   [118] Sec. 437(1) CA 2006.
[119] Secs. 415, 420 CA 2006.   [120] FSA Listing Rules, Rule 13 (2007).
[121] FSA Listing Rules, Rule 13.3.1, in connection with Rule 13.8.8(3) (2007).
[122] Sec. 338(3) CA 2006.   [123] Sec. 338(1) CA 2006.   [124] Sec. 339(1) CA 2006.

with the same holdings may demand that the board distribute written statements regarding proposed resolutions.[125]

6. Is the truthfulness of the information policed? If false information is included in the directors' report, the directors' remuneration report or the financial statements, every director of the company that knew of the falsity, or was reckless in ignoring it, is liable to the company for damages suffered.[126] For listed companies, the Listing Rules require companies to provide the FSA with a copy of each circular to be voted on,[127] and subject issuers to penalty and liability for failing to take reasonable care to ensure that the information it notifies to the media or makes available through the FSA is not "misleading, false or deceptive and does not omit anything likely to affect the import of the information."[128]

As discussed in Chapter 16, the directors may refuse to distribute resolutions or statements proposed by members for a number of reasons that go to the content of the proposed resolution or statement.

7. What is the necessary quorum for a meeting and who may attend? Unless the company has only one member, the presence of two members in person or through representatives or proxy constitutes a quorum for a valid meeting.[129] As members are evidenced by the entry of their names in the share register and they are on this basis invited to the meeting, the statute does not contain a procedure for determining who may attend the meeting, other than specifying that representatives and proxies of members may participate in the proceedings. It does allow companies to require in their articles that proxy holders submit their proxies to the company up to forty-eight hours before the meeting.[130]

Aside from stating that a chairman may make determinations on the adoption of resolutions by show of hands,[131] the statute resembles the *Aktiengesetz* and the DGCL in leaving the governance of the meeting to the articles. However, one particularly British institution, voting by show of hands, requires special rules. As discussed in Chapter 16, in a vote by show of hands, each person has the same vote regardless of the number of shares held. Because this may well be unappealing to large shareholders,

---

[125] Sec. 314(1) CA 2006.   [126] Sec. 463 CA 2006.   [127] FSA Listing Rules, Rule 13.2.5.
[128] FSA Listing Rules, Rule 1.3.3.   [129] Sec. 318 CA 2006.
[130] Sec. 327(2) CA 2006.   [131] Sec. 320 CA 2006.

the law also allows voting by "poll," which means that votes are tallied per share and not per holder. A poll must be "demanded," and the model articles provide that a poll may be demanded by:

- the chairman of the meeting;
- the directors;
- two or more persons having the right to vote on the resolution; or
- one or more persons representing at least 10 percent of the total voting rights of the members eligible to vote on the resolution.[132]

It is important to note that the Act expressly allows a proxy holder to demand a poll.[133] The articles may not remove this right except for housekeeping matters such as electing the chairman of the meeting.[134]

8. Who may present proposals, ask questions and make comments at the meeting?   As discussed in Chapter 16 and referred to in subsection 5 above, members may have resolutions or statements distributed *before* the meeting. However, the Companies Act does not give members a right to ask questions or make comments or proposals *during* a general meeting. For listed companies, the Combined Code does provide that "[t]he chairman of the board should arrange for the chairmen of the audit, remuneration and nomination committees to be available to answer questions at the AGM."[135] It is, however, not completely clear whether the person asking the questions will be a director or a member. The model articles state that a member may exercise the right to speak "when that person is in a position to communicate to all those attending the meeting, during the meeting," which does not create an unambiguous right to pose questions.[136] Clearer provisions may well be introduced into UK law in the near future, because the EU Shareholders' Rights Directive requires that the shareholders of listed companies be given a right to:

- ask questions during or before the meeting;
- receive answers directly or in the form of answers to "frequently asked questions" on the company's website; and
- have the answer to an individual shareholder's question posted on the company's website for access by all shareholders.[137]

---

[132] Reg. 36 MAPC.   [133] Sec. 329(1) CA 2006.   [134] Sec. 321 CA 2006.
[135] FSA Listing Rules; Combined Code, Principle C.2.3.
[136] Reg. 29(1) MAPC.   [137] Art. 9 Directive 2007/36/EC.

9. Who can vote? Leaving aside any special rules for the voting rights of various classes of shares, generally all members may vote on a resolution at a meeting. Moreover, corporate members may send representatives to exercise their votes,[138] and all members may appoint proxies to exercise their vote.[139] If a company sends the call to meeting electronically, a member may grant a proxy by electronic communication.[140] In listed companies a person who is party to a "related-party transaction" may not vote on the approval of such transaction.[141]

10. How are votes cast? In voting by a show of hands, votes are cast in an informal manner. A proxy holder has the same right to vote by a show of hands as the member himself would have.[142] In voting on a poll, votes are cast in writing or electronically. The operator of the securities settlement system of the London Stock Exchange, CRESTCo, has installed a system for electronically casting votes in the meetings of listed companies. What do *Puddephatt* v. *Leith* and *Greenwell* v. *Porter* tell you about the enforceability of agreements on the casting of voting rights under UK law?

11. How are votes counted? In a vote on a resolution by show of hands at a meeting, every member present in person or by proxy has one vote.[143] In a vote on a poll at a meeting, unless provided otherwise in the articles, every member has one vote for each share or each £10 of stock held.[144] The model articles do not address this question further. Public companies must post detailed information on each resolution adopted by a poll vote on their website.[145] Listed companies must appoint an independent assessor to inspect the results of a vote by poll and to prepare a report thereon if members constituting either 5 percent of eligible voting rights or a group of 100 holders with average £100 holdings, as discussed in subsection 5, so demand.[146] The Act provides detailed rules for the appointment and the report of the assessor in sections 342 *et seq.*

---

[138] Sec. 323 CA 2006.   [139] Sec. 324 CA 2006.   [140] Sec. 333 CA 2006.
[141] See FSA Listing Rules, Rule 11.1.7(4). A "related-party transaction" in this case would be a substantial transaction outside the ordinary course of business in which the company was on one side and a "substantial" shareholder was on the other. See Rules 11.1.4 and 11.1.5.
[142] Sec. 285(1) CA 2006.   [143] Sec. 284(2) CA 2006.   [144] Sec. 284(3) CA 2006.
[145] Sec. 341 CA 2006.   [146] Sec. 342 CA 2006.

Questions for discussion

Be prepared to walk through the calling and the holding (i.e. voting procedure) of a general meeting under UK, German and US law with reference to the statutory sections.

Cases

Schnell v. Chris-Craft Industries, Inc.
Supreme Court of Delaware
285 A 2d 437 (1971)
[*Text edited; footnotes omitted*]

HERRMANN, Justice

This is an appeal from the denial by the Court of Chancery of the petition of dissident stockholders for injunctive relief to prevent management from advancing the date of the annual stockholders' meeting from January 11, 1972, as previously set by the by-laws, to December 8, 1971 ...

It will be seen that the Chancery Court considered all of the reasons stated by management as business reasons for changing the date of the [shareholders'] meeting [from January 11, 1972 forward to December 8, 1971]; but that those reasons were rejected by the Court below in making the following findings:

> I am satisfied, however, in a situation in which present management has disingenuously resisted the production of a list of its stockholders to plaintiffs or their confederates and has otherwise turned a deaf ear to plaintiffs' demands about a change in management designed to lift defendant from its present business doldrums, management has seized on a relatively new section of the Delaware Corporation Law [see § 211(a)] for the purpose of cutting down on the amount of time which would otherwise have been available to plaintiffs and others for the waging of a proxy battle. Management thus enlarged the scope of its scheduled October 18 directors' meeting to include the by-law amendment in controversy after the stockholders committee had filed with the SEC its intention to wage a proxy fight on October 16.
> "Thus plaintiffs reasonably contend that because of the tactics employed by management (which involve the hiring of two established proxy solicitors as well as a refusal to produce a list of its stockholders, coupled with its use of an amendment to the Delaware Corporation Law to limit the time for contest), they are given little chance, because of the exigencies of time, including that required to clear material at the SEC, to wage a successful proxy fight between now and December 8 ..."

In our view, those conclusions amount to a finding that management has attempted to utilize the corporate machinery and the Delaware Law for the purpose of perpetuating itself in office; and, to that end, for the purpose of obstructing the legitimate efforts of dissident stockholders in the exercise of their rights to undertake a proxy contest against management. These are inequitable purposes, contrary to established principles of corporate democracy. The advancement by directors of the by-law date of a stockholders' meeting, for such purposes, may not be permitted to stand …

When the by-laws of a corporation designate the date of the annual meeting of stockholders, it is to be expected that those who intend to contest the reelection of incumbent management will gear their campaign to the by-law date. It is not to be expected that management will attempt to advance the date in order to obtain an inequitable advantage in the contest.

Management contends that it has complied strictly with the provisions of the new Delaware Corporation Law in changing the by-law date. The answer to that contention, of course, is that inequitable action does not become permissible simply because it is legally possible.

Management relies upon *American Hardware Corp.* v. *Savage Arms Corp.* … The case is inapposite for two reasons: It involved an effort by stockholders, engaged in a proxy contest, to have the stockholders' meeting adjourned and the period for the proxy contest enlarged; and there was no finding there of inequitable action on the part of management. We agree with the rule of *American Hardware* that, in the absence of fraud or inequitable conduct, the date for a stockholders' meeting and notice thereof, duly established under the by-laws, will not be enlarged by judicial interference at the request of dissident stockholders solely because of the circumstance of a proxy contest. That, of course, is not the case before us.

[Text omitted]

Accordingly, the judgment below must be reversed and the cause remanded, with instruction to nullify the December 8 date as a meeting date for stockholders; to reinstate January 11, 1972 as the sole date of the next annual meeting of the stockholders of the corporation; and to take such other proceedings and action as may be consistent herewith regarding the stock record closing date and any other related matters.

Puddephatt v. Leith

Chancery Division

[1916] 1 Ch 200

Reproduced with permission of the Incorporated Council of Law Reporting for England and Wales

[Text edited; footnotes omitted]

The plaintiff was the owner of 2500 fully paid shares in the London and Cosmopolitan Mining Company, Limited, which she had mortgaged to the defendant, the shares being transferred into his name. The terms of the loan were contained in an agreement dated February 14, 1913, but the Court in these proceedings held that there was a collateral agreement binding on the defendant relating to the voting power in respect of the shares, the terms of which were contained in a letter dated January 20, 1913, sent by the defendant to the plaintiff, as follows:

> I should have mentioned to you to-day that your voting rights in virtue of the shares held in mortgage by me during the period of the loan will be untouched. Though the shares will be in my name and my voice may give the vote, I shall give no such vote without first consulting you. I shall vote in all cases, when a vote is necessary, in respect of these shares as you wish me to do. This proviso will not be mentioned in the agreement, but you can preserve this note if you like.

Differences had arisen in connection with the management of the company's business, and at the last general meeting of the company the defendant, who was himself a director of the company, had voted in respect of the mortgaged shares against the wishes of the plaintiff, and was insisting on his right to do so at the approaching general meeting to be held on December 21, 1915.

The plaintiff then brought this action, in which she now moved (1.) for an injunction to restrain the defendant from voting in respect of the shares otherwise than in accordance with the plaintiff's direction, and (2.) that the defendant might be ordered to vote in respect of the shares at any poll to be taken at the approaching general meeting of the company to be held on December 21, 1915, or at any adjournment thereof, against a certain proposed resolution and to vote in favour of certain other resolutions. By consent the motion was treated as the trial of the action. The only part of the case which calls for a report relates to the claim for a mandatory injunction.

[*Text omitted*]

SARGANT J

After stating the facts and holding that the undertaking to vote in accordance with the plaintiff's wishes contained in the letter constituted a collateral agreement binding on the defendant, continued: In my opinion, therefore, the right of the plaintiff is clear, and the only remaining question is whether she is entitled to a mandatory injunction to enforce her right. It is not disputed that she is entitled to a prohibitive injunction, and in my opinion she is also entitled to a mandatory injunction. Prima facie this Court is bound, as Cotton LJ said in *Hermann Loog* v. *Bean*, to give effect to a clear right by way of a mandatory injunction. There are no doubt certain exceptions from this rule, as in the case of a contract of service, because in such cases it is impossible for the Court to make its order effective, but in *Wolverhampton Corporation* v. *Emmons* a mandatory injunction was granted to compel the defendant to build in accordance with certain plans; and in the present case, inasmuch as there is one definite thing to be done about the mode of doing which there can be no possible doubt, I am of opinion that I ought to grant not only the prohibitive but also the mandatory injunction claimed by the plaintiff, and I make an order accordingly.

Greenwell v. Porter

Chancery Division

[1902] 1 Ch 530

Reproduced with permission of the Incorporated Council of Law Reporting for England and Wales

[*Text edited; footnotes omitted*]

JANE PORTER, John Herbert Porter, Gerald Stanley Porter, and William Allan Miller, as executors and trustees of the will of James Porter, deceased, held a large number of preference and ordinary shares in a company called Robinson's Brewery, Limited. The shares formed part of the residuary estate of the testator which the trustees held upon trust for sale, with power to postpone the sale.

In 1898 the trustees were in want of money for the purposes of the estate, and they agreed to sell 5500 preference and 1000 ordinary shares in the company to Walpole Greenwell. As part of the consideration for the sale he stipulated for the agreement below mentioned.

The agreement was dated July 26, 1898, and was made between the four executors and trustees, thereinafter called "the executors" of the one part and Greenwell of the other part, and after recitals that the executors were the executors and trustees of James Porter's will, and as such the owners of or otherwise well entitled to certain large numbers of ordinary and preference shares in Robinson's Brewery, Limited, and that Greenwell was "also largely interested in that company," it contained the following clauses:

> (1.) The executors shall take all steps and do all things within their power which may be required for obtaining the election, as directors of Robinson's Brewery, Limited, of Aynsley Greenwell and Thomas Trevor White, and shall at all times hereinafter vote for and not against the re-election as directors of the said Aynsley Greenwell and Thomas Trevor White upon their retirement by rotation, so long as they shall be willing to remain directors of the company, unless in case of either of them, the said Aynsley Greenwell and Thomas Trevor White, the other four directors shall concur in his not being re-elected. The executors shall not at any time, except with such concurrence as aforesaid, vote for the removal of either of the said Aynsley Greenwell and Thomas Trevor White, and shall not, except with such concurrence as aforesaid, take any steps or do any acts to induce or compel them or either of them to relinquish their or his office of director, but shall at all times to the best of their ability, by their votes and otherwise, support them and each of them in their office. Each of them, the parties hereto of the first part, agrees that the provisions of this clause shall apply to him or her and to any shares now or at any time hereafter held by him or her in his or her own personal capacity, and not only as such executor and trustee as aforesaid.
>
> (2.) The executors shall sell to the said Thomas Trevor White, for his qualification as director, one hundred ordinary shares of the company at the price of 10l. per share, and shall sell to the said Walpole Greenwell (who shall purchase the same and shall qualify the said Aynsley Greenwell as a director) one thousand ordinary shares also at the price of 10l. per share.

Aynsley Greenwell and Trevor White were appointed directors, and the other directors were J. H. Porter, G. S. Porter, and W. A. Miller.

At the ordinary meeting of the company on December 20, 1901, it became the turn of Trevor White to retire from the directorate by rotation. His re-election was, however, moved and seconded, and on a show of hands there was a majority in favour of the motion. A great number of shares stood in the joint names of the executors, and, Jane Porter's name being the first on the register of shareholders, she was entitled to exercise the power of voting. They were also entitled in respect of shares which they held in their own separate names beneficially.

A poll was demanded by the number of shareholders required by the articles, the demand being signed by G. S. Porter, J. H. Porter, Jane Porter, and another shareholder.

It was not disputed that the three members of the Porter family intended on the poll to oppose the re-election of Trevor White as a director.

Aynsley Greenwell was absent abroad with the leave of the directors.

On December 24, 1901, Walpole Greenwell commenced an action against Jane Porter, J. H. Porter, G. S. Porter, and W. A. Miller, for (1.) "an injunction to restrain the defendants and each of them, their proxies and agents, from voting at the poll to be taken on January 28, 1902, or on any other date on which the same may be fixed pursuant to the demand for a poll made at the ordinary general meeting of Robinson's Brewery, Limited, held on December 20, 1901, against the resolution for the re-election of Thomas Trevor White as a director of Robinson's Brewery, Limited, or from otherwise voting contrary to the provisions of an agreement dated July 26, 1898, and made between the defendants of the one part and the plaintiff of the other part; (2.) in the alternative, and in any event, damages."

The four defendants were sued in their capacity as executors of James Porter, deceased, and the first three defendants were also sued in their individual capacity.

On January 6, 1902, the plaintiff served notice of motion for an interlocutory injunction in the terms of the indorsement of his writ of summons, and the motion was heard on January 21.

[Text omitted]

[SWINFEN EADY J asked whether Trevor White would give an undertaking to retire from the directorate, and he, by the plaintiff's counsel, consented to give an undertaking that, if the Court at the trial should so direct, he would resign his seat on the board at the annual meeting next following the date of the trial, and then offer himself for re-election.]

SWINFEN EADY, J

(After referring to the notice of motion). The plaintiff does not claim to compel the defendants to vote pursuant to the agreement, but he asks for an injunction restraining them from voting contrary to the provisions of the agreement. [His Lordship read the material parts of the agreement, and continued:]

The plaintiff has brought this action to enforce the agreement so far as regards the provision as to voting. The agreement was entered into as part of a transaction under which the defendant executors sold to the plaintiff for a large price a considerable block of shares, and it appears from the evidence that it was at the time considered by all parties, and certainly by the executors, that it was to the interest of their testator's estate that the block of shares should be sold, that the terms were advantageous, and that at that time it was to the interest of the estate that the money should be obtained by a sale of shares in the way the transaction was carried into effect. The plaintiff stipulated as part of the transaction that he should have the benefit of the agreement.

Three of the defendant executors seek now to escape from performing the agreement. They say, in the first place, that the agreement was ultra vires – that as executors they had no power to, what they term, delegate their discretion as executors. At the present moment I am not satisfied that that point has any validity whatever. It will be observed that the sale of the shares retained by the executors is not tied up. It is only in consideration of the plaintiff purchasing a certain block of shares that the executors agree with him that so long as they hold certain shares they will vote in a particular way, and will not vote in a particular other way. The realization of the estate vested in them as executors is not agreed to be postponed with regard to these shares, and the executors do not bind themselves not to part with the whole of the shares next day. On the facts as they are at present before me, I am of opinion that the arrangement embodied in the agreement was for the benefit of the executors and their estate, and that it was not beyond the powers of the executors to enter into it.

The next point made was that, so far as regards shares held by any of the defendants in their individual capacity, because they were directors they could not enter into an agreement with regard to their voting in respect of these shares; and that, although an ordinary shareholder might do so, still, if the shareholder happened to be a director, that fact precluded him from entering into such an agreement. No authority was produced for such a proposition, and I do not consider it well founded.

Then it was said – and upon this I was pressed by Mr. Eve [counsel for first three defendants] – that the effect of granting an injunction to restrain the defendants from voting against the reappointment would be that Mr. Trevor White would be in the position of a director of the company for three years, even although it should turn out that the plaintiff should fail at the trial. It was to prevent that, which apparently might create or give rise to some injustice, that I endeavoured to see whether any undertaking could be given to meet the point. That point is now covered by the undertaking which Mr. Vernon Smith was instructed to give on behalf of Mr. Trevor White, who is not a party to the action, but is in court. Therefore the undertaking will be entered in the registrar's book, and Mr. Trevor White will sign the book.

That undertaking being given, I grant an injunction until the trial of the action restraining the first three defendants from voting against the resolution for the re-election of Mr. Trevor White as a director.

19

Shareholder duties

Required reading

EU: Transparency Directive, arts. 9–13
D: WpHG, §§ 21, 22; AktG, §§ 20, 21
UK: CA 2006, secs. 791–797; FSA Disclosure and Transparency Rules, Rule 5
US: Exchange Act, §§ 13(d), 16(a); Exchange Act Rule 13d-1, 13d-3, 16a-2, 3, 6

The fiduciary and reporting duties of shareholders

In the preceding three chapters, we discussed shareholder rights and how they are exercised. Shareholders have the right to vote on important decisions affecting the company and to receive information on which to base their voting decisions. Voting takes place primarily in general meetings, which must be called and held in certain ways to ensure transparency and fairness. In this chapter, we examine shareholder duties. Here, we will look at the duty to disclose large shareholdings and to exercise voting power with a certain degree of loyalty *vis-à-vis* the shareholders affected by this power. In the next chapter, we will discuss how minority shareholders can have recourse to court to defend rights that they are not able to protect in the general meeting because of the insufficiency of their voting power.

The duties discussed in this chapter fall into two quite different categories. On the one hand, courts have developed duties that apply to limit the power which shareholders have under the law. These duties resemble the duty of loyalty that applies to corporate directors. On the other hand, legislatures and regulatory authorities have imposed transparency rules, which have become increasingly detailed and fine-tuned (see DTR 5, for example) to create transparency in shareholding structures. In the US, these rules were designed to combat insider trading and unfair takeover techniques. Generally, they also counteract a tendency of the capital markets to make shareholdings anonymous by burying holdings in layers of financial intermediaries. The two types of duties are very different, as is evidenced by the contents of this chapter – which contains both cases discussing general principles of fairness and detailed rules defining percentages of holdings and degrees of control over holdings that must be disclosed.

I. Shareholder fiduciary duties

Fiduciary duties arise in a relationship in which "one party (the 'fiduciary') acts *on behalf of* another party (the 'beneficiary') while exercising *discretion* with respect to a *critical resource* belonging to the beneficiary."[1] "What distinguishes a fiduciary from many other contracting parties ... is that a fiduciary exercises discretion with respect to a critical resource belonging to the beneficiary, whereas most contracting parties exercise discretion only with respect to their own performance under the contract."[2] Classic examples of fiduciary relationships are those between a trustee and a beneficiary, a managing partner and his co-partners, and an agent and a principal. Another is the relationship between a corporate director and the company's shareholders: the shareholders elect the director to exercise expert discretion in the management of the corporation on their behalf, and the corporation is an asset belonging in *pro rata* shares to each shareholder. As we saw in Chapter 16, the corporate statutes in each of our jurisdictions also give shareholders the power to exercise discretion over the fate of the company in certain situations, but only if they act as an aggregate of individuals constituting at least a majority of the total voting rights. The shareholders who do not join the majority decision remain *pro rata* owners of the company, but they have through their purchase of shares and acceptance of the statutory framework and articles or by-laws delegated decisionmaking power to those shareholders who from time to time constitute the statutory majority. Thus, the only difference between this relationship and the fiduciary duty of a director is that the obligor of the duty is an *ad hoc* group and the "beneficiary" of the duty is a different *ad hoc* group, whose members might on another day constitute part of the group on the other side of the duty.

Courts have recognized at least since the late nineteenth century that majority shareholders may not use their statutory power to the unfair

---

[1] Smith (2002: 1402) (emphasis in original). [2] Smith (2002: 1403).

detriment of minority shareholders. One of the earliest cases, *Menier v. Hooper's Telegraph Works*, which is reprinted in part in this chapter, reaches this conclusion without expressly stating that majority shareholders have a fiduciary duty. UK courts have dealt with such cases primarily under the rubric of "unfair prejudice," now provided for in section 994 of the Companies Act 2006. The type of action by a majority shareholder constituting unfair prejudice against the minority and the court's analysis of such action closely resembles the judicial treatment given to a breach of fiduciary duty,[3] and thus majority shareholders under UK law are policed by case law in a manner comparable to that achieved by such duty. "Fraud against the minority" is clearly not permitted.

Delaware courts, by contrast, explicitly and repeatedly recognize that controlling shareholders (even if not majority shareholders) have a duty of loyalty to the minority. See *Lynch Communications*, reprinted in part in this chapter. In another major case, *Sinclair Oil Corp. v. Levien*, which we will read in Chapter 23, a majority shareholder's decision to force the company to pay dividends is found not to violate the shareholders' fiduciary duty, but a decision causing the subsidiary not to enforce a contract between the subsidiary and the parent is found to do so. What is the difference between these two actions? What group of persons does each affect?

A shareholder owes a fiduciary duty to the corporation and the minority shareholders if it either "owns a majority in or exercises control over the business affairs of the corporation."[4] What about minority shareholders? Should they owe such a fiduciary duty? Under what circumstances? Take a look at the *Girmes* decision. Does the imposition of a fiduciary duty on the exercise of voting rights from corporate stock violate the shareholder's property right?

If you agree with the BGH's decision in *Girmes* that a minority shareholder under some circumstances must comply with a fiduciary duty in the exercise of voting rights, what do you think about the following scenario? Hedge Fund has put options to sell 250,000 shares of blue chip P1 Co. at the current market price. P1 Co. has made much in public of its plan to merge Target Co. into itself once Target Co. shareholders approve the merger. Hedge Fund also has call options at the current market price for

---

[3] See Lower (2000: 232).

[4] *Ivanhoe Partners v. Newmont Mining Corp.*, 535 A 2d 1334, 1344 (Del. 1987). Also see the ALI Principles of Corporate Governance, § 5.10. Such duties are particularly evident for the shareholders of closed corporations, who are often attributed fiduciary duties resembling those of a partner. See *Donahue v. Rodd Electrotype Co.*, 328 NE 2d 505 (Mass. 1975); and Thompson (1993).

250,000 shares of heavily indebted and poorly managed P2 Co., which has been stalking the cash-rich Target and plans to launch a bid. Hedge Fund borrows 7 percent of the shares of Target Co., including voting rights, and votes against the merger with P1 Co. for the *sole purpose* of damaging P1 Co. (to increase the value of its put options) and benefit P2 Co. (to increase the value of its call options). P1 Co. is humiliated, and its share price drops 10 percent (at which point Hedge Fund sells its options). P2 Co. steps into the broken merger transaction, launches a successful tender offer for Target, and uses the latter's assets to pay off its debts. Although P2 Co.'s shares briefly rise by 10 percent (at which point Hedge Fund sells its options), P2 and its subsidiary Target enter insolvency proceedings eighteen months later. Hedge Fund earned a 10 percent return on its 500,000 options and only paid 3 percent interest per annum for the share loan. By voting its 7 percent stake in Target Co. for the sole purpose of causing the improbable transaction and profiting from its options in P1 and P2, has the hedge fund violated its fiduciary duties as a shareholder in Target?

II. Shareholders' duty to report significant holdings

In theory, companies that issue registered shares – as do all stock corporations in the US and the UK and nearly half of those in Germany – would know who their shareholders are and be aware of any person building up a significant holding in their capital. Although it is possible to legally transfer ownership in registered shares without registering the new owner in the stockholder list, only the registered owners have rights (such as rights to vote or collect dividends) as shareholders.[5] This encourages registration of share transfers. However, stock exchanges often require that shareholders register a financial intermediary or another agent in their stead in the share register to allow book-entry transfers on the intermediary's books, which facilitates settlement of share transfers. UK and German law allow a company to demand that the real owner of its registered shares reveal herself, and thus allows it to uncover a "beneficial" owner standing behind a "registered" owner.[6] US law does not provide for such an inquiry, although it also does not forbid it. Moreover, many German companies issue bearer shares, which provide the company with no way of ascertaining who owns its shares or how the overall shareholding is structured. As a result, it would be possible for a hostile bidder to "creep up" on a company, slowly building up a block shareholding, and then launching a

---

[5] See e.g. § 219 DGCL; § 67(2) AktG.   [6] Sec. 793 CA 2006; § 67(4) AktG.

surprise takeover from a position of strength. This allows a purchaser to acquire shares at a lower, pre-bid price, and the larger the holding she can amass before disclosing her intentions, the greater the pressure she can place on shareholders and management to accept her offer.[7]

As part of the Williams Act, which introduced express takeover legislation into the Securities Exchange Act in 1968, a legal duty was established in § 13(d) of the Exchange Act to disclose significant holdings in the equity of registered companies. Similar requirements were introduced into EU law twenty years later in the predecessors to the Transparency Directive,[8] and are now found in articles 9–13 of that Directive. The basic application of these rules is very straightforward and involves five main issues:

- the fractional threshold(s) at which disclosure must be made;
- the shares that must be included in the numerator of the fraction (attribution);
- the content of the denominator of the fraction (e.g. percentage of capital, percentage of voting power, or percentage of a class);
- the dimension of a change in the holding that triggers a new reporting duty; and
- the details of the disclosure (content and timing).

What are the fractional thresholds in our jurisdictions? Consult article 9(1) of the Transparency Directive, § 21(1) WpHG, FSA DTR 5.1.2 and Exchange Act Rule 13d-1(a). How are voting rights attributed? For example, if Shareholder X has 2 percent of the voting rights of a listed company and 49 percent of the voting rights of another company that owns 3.1 percent of the voting rights in the same listed company, will all of the votes be attributed to Shareholder X? See the attribution rules discussed in § 22 WpHG and DTR 5.2.1. What are the denominators in our jurisdictions, and what shares are counted in the overall figure? What types of changes will trigger a duty to disclose again? See Rule 13d-2(a). What are the content and the timing of the disclosure?

A different type of problem lies at the level of policy, and is connected with the attribution rules: this is the negative effect that such rules can have on shareholder participation in governance. In the original design of companies issuing registered shares, each shareholder's name, address and holding would be recorded in the share register, and the company

---

[7] How is the problem of price difference addressed in takeover legislation? See the materials for Chapter 24.
[8] Council Directive 88/627/EEC of 12 December 1988 on the information to be published when a major holding in a listed company is acquired or disposed of, OJ 1988 L348/62.

and the other shareholders would have access to this information in the manner and for the reasons discussed in Chapter 17. When a shareholder bought or sold shares, the entries in the share register would change. Because, for various reasons connected with the settlement of securities transactions and the ambitions of financial intermediaries, share registers no longer provide the necessary information, the shareholder disclosure rules were introduced to prevent oppressive, surprise takeovers. However, they tend to affect a much broader area of shareholder activity, and can present a significant obstacle to the coordinated exercise of shareholder voice in normal governance.

For example, under Exchange Act Rule 13d, any person who acquires directly or indirectly more than 5 percent of either the "voting power"[9] or the "investment power"[10] of any class of equity security registered under § 12 of the Exchange Act, must file a Schedule 13D with the SEC within ten days after the acquisition.[11] In a Schedule 13D, aside from specifying the securities purchased, the shareholder and each member of a group, must file:

- name(s), citizenship(s), place(s) of incorporation and taxpayer identification number(s);
- details regarding any judgments against the shareholder(s) under state or federal securities laws or convictions under criminal laws during the last five years;
- the source of funds or other consideration used or to be used in making the purchases as required (with a copy of any lending agreements to be attached as exhibits);
- the purpose or purposes of the acquisition of securities, in particular any plans to purchase or sell additional securities, effect an extraordinary corporate transaction, such as a merger, reorganization, liquidation or sale of assets, plans to change the composition of the current board or management, or amend the company's charter or by-laws, or plans to delist or de-register any class of the company's securities;
- the aggregate amount of shares beneficially owned (with a breakdown within the group);
- a description of any transactions in the class of securities reported on that were effected during the past sixty days; and

---

[9] "Voting power" includes "the power to vote, or to direct the voting of, such security." 17 CFR § 240.13d-3(a)(1).

[10] "Investment power" includes "the power to dispose, or to direct the disposition of, such security." 17 CFR § 240.13d-3(2).

[11] 17 CFR § 240.13d-1(a).

- a description of all contracts and understandings – such as for the purchase, sale, pledge, call, put or voting of the securities – among the reporting persons and the company (with a copy of any written agreements to be attached as an exhibit).[12]

It is understandable that many shareholders – absent an actual intent to take the company over – would prefer to exit by selling their shares or accept the risks of bad management rather than to run the risk of having to pay for the preparation of a Schedule 13D in which they are forced to make the above disclosures, immediately update the disclosure with each one percent change in the (group's) aggregate holding, and subject themselves to significant potential liability on the basis of these filings.[13] Moreover, in order to prevent collusive activity to avoid the disclosure rules, the "person" to whom the shares belong is deemed to include "two or more persons" who agree "to act together for the purpose of acquiring, holding, voting or disposing of equity securities."[14] The threat of aggregation into a group, which would result in a duty to file a Schedule 13D,[15] can thus prevent shareholders with small holdings from coordinating action with their fellow shareholders in connection with an annual meeting, lest they be found to "act together for … voting" their shares and trigger the requirements of § 13. Although mere informal discussions among shareholders regarding management's performance has been found not to constitute a "group" for the purposes of § 13(d) of the Exchange Act,[16] the type of more formal coordination that is actually necessary to have an impact on governance could well trigger the requirement.[17]

---

[12] 17 CFR § 240.13d-101, Items 1–7.

[13] Declarations and documents "filed" with the SEC are subject to civil liability for misstatements and omissions pursuant to § 18 Exchange Act, as well as the penalties of a fine and imprisonment pursuant to § 32 Exchange Act.

[14] 17 CFR § 240.13d-5(b).

[15] An alternative, less intrusive Schedule 13G that must normally be updated only annually was made available in 1978 for certain institutional investors who have "acquired such securities in the ordinary course of … business and not with the purpose nor with the effect of changing or influencing the control of the issuer." The adopting release was Final Rules: Filing and Disclosure Requirements Relating to Beneficial Ownership, SEC Release Nos. 33-5925 and 34-14692, 1978 WL 170898 (April 21, 1978). The current requirements are found in 17 CFR § 240.13d-1(b)(1)(i).

[16] See *Bath Industries, Inc.* v. *Blot*, 427 F 2d 97, 110 (7th Cir. 1970).

[17] Evidence of a group for these purposes has been found where there is a common plan and goal, a coordination of activities and communications, public expression of a position among the shareholders, and parallel and continued purchases of the company's shares during a specific time period. *Champion Parts Rebuilders, Inc.* v. *Cormier*, 661 F Supp 825, 850 (ND Ill. 1987).

Questions for discussion

1. Compare the contents of Schedule 13D with the contents required in article 12(1) of the Transparency Directive and DTR 5.8.1. What are the advantages and disadvantages of each type of disclosure scheme?
2. Do you think it is useful to declare shareholdings to the *public* or should they be disclosed by means of entering data in the share register (i.e. disclosed to the company and to shareholders for specified purposes)?
3. If you think disclosure to the public is advisable, what are the positive aspects of such disclosure?

Cases

Menier v. Hooper's Telegraph Works
Court of Appeal in Chancery
(1873–74) LR 9 Ch App 350
Reproduced with permission of the Incorporated Council of Law Reporting for England and Wales
[*Text edited; some footnotes omitted*]

Sir W. M. JAMES and Sir G. MELLISH, LJJ

THE bill in this case was filed by E. J. Menier, on behalf of himself and all other shareholders of the European and South American Telegraph Company (except such of them as were Defendants), against a company called Hooper's Telegraph Works, W. Hooper, H. W. Crace, and the European and South American Telegraph Company, and stated (amongst other things) as follows:

> That the European Company was incorporated in 1871 with the object of carrying out an agreement between the Plaintiff, Menier, and one Bradford, and others, for constructing a submarine telegraph from Europe to South America ... the only shares allotted were 3000 to Hooper's Company, 2000 to the Plaintiff, and 325 to thirteen persons, ten of whom were the directors ... That on the 12th of February, 1873, an extraordinary meeting of the European Company was held, at which a resolution was passed that the company be wound up voluntarily, and that the Defendant Crace be the liquidator. That the resolution was proposed by one Kennedy, a director of Hooper's Company, and that Crace was secretary of Hooper's Company. That this resolution was confirmed at another extraordinary meeting, at which five persons only were present, of whom three were directors nominated by Hooper's Company, and one was Crace, the secretary. That the Plaintiff protested against these proceedings. That the Plaintiff was then ignorant, but had since discovered, that these proceedings took place through the influence of Hooper's Company. The bill then stated the circumstances of an arrangement ... under which it would be to the advantage of Hooper's Company that the agreement between them and the European Company should be put an end ...

and in order that Hooper's Company might sell to another company the cable
they were making for the European Company. That these arrangements were concealed from the Plaintiff and the other shareholders in the European Company.
That Hooper's Company procured the ... winding-up of the European Company,
through the influence which they had as holders of 3000 shares in the European
Company, and through the influence of the directors nominated by them ...

The Vice-Chancellor Bacon [held for the Plaintiffs] ... and the Defendants
appealed.

Mr. Fry QC and Mr. Millar, for Hooper's Company [argued]:

A shareholder has a right to vote as he pleases, and to suit his own interests. If
not, the Court in every case might have to interfere wherever there was a small
majority, and consider what were the motives of each shareholder. If there was a
suit by the company against any individual shareholder, he would not be disabled
from voting. He is not a trustee for any one, and he may vote against the interests
of the company or of any of the other shareholders. No constructive trust can be
raised: *Gray* v. *Lewis* [Law Rep. 8 Ch. 1035]. In *Atwool* v. *Merryweather* [Law Rep. 5
Eq. 464] the vote was impeached. If such a suit can be maintained, one shareholder
may file a bill to have a certain contract set aside, and another to have it carried on.
Such a suit can only be maintained by the company against the directors. At all
events, the proceedings ought to be in the liquidation, and not by bill ...

Sir W. M. JAMES, LJ

I am of opinion that the order of the Vice-Chancellor in this case is quite right.

The case made by the bill is very shortly this: The Defendants, who have a majority
of shares in the company, have made an arrangement by which they have dealt with
matters affecting the whole company, the interest in which belongs to the minority
as well as to the majority. They have dealt with them in consideration of their obtaining for themselves certain advantages. Hooper's Company have obtained certain
advantages by dealing with something which was the property of the whole company. The minority of the shareholders say in effect that the majority has divided
the assets of the company, more or less, between themselves, to the exclusion of the
minority. I think it would be a shocking thing if that could be done, because if so the
majority might divide the whole assets of the company, and pass a resolution that
everything must be given to them, and that the minority should have nothing to do
with it. Assuming the case to be as alleged by the bill, then the majority have put
something into their pockets at the expense of the minority. If so, it appears to me
that the minority have a right to have their share of the benefits ascertained for them
in the best way in which the Court can do it, and given to them.

It is said, however, that this is not the right form of suit, because, according to
the principles laid down in *Foss* v. *Harbottle* [2 Hare 461], and other similar cases,
the Court ought to be very slow indeed in allowing a shareholder to file a bill, where
the company is the proper Plaintiff. This particular case seems to me precisely one
of the exceptions referred to by Vice-Chancellor Wood in *Atwool* v. *Merryweather*, a

case in which the majority were the Defendants, the wrong-doers, who were alleged to have put the minority's property into their pockets. In this case it is right and proper for a bill to be filed by one shareholder on behalf of himself and all the other shareholders.

Therefore the demurrer ought to be overruled [holding for Plaintiff].

Sir G. MELLISH, LJ

I am entirely of the same opinion.

It so happens that Hooper's Company are the majority in this company, and a suit by this company was pending which might or might not turn out advantageous to this company. The Plaintiff says that Hooper's Company being the majority, have procured that suit to be settled upon terms favourable to themselves, they getting a consideration for settling it in the shape of a profitable bargain for the laying of a cable. I am of opinion that although it may be quite true that the shareholders of a company may vote as they please, and for the purpose of their own interests, yet that the majority of shareholders cannot sell the assets of the company and keep the consideration, but must allow the minority to have their share of any consideration which may come to them. I also entirely agree that, under the circumstances, the suit is properly brought in the name of the Plaintiff on behalf of himself and all the other shareholders.

The appeal will be dismissed with costs.

In Re Linotype

High Federal Court, Second Civil Division
February 1, 1988, Doc. No. II ZR 75/87, BGHZ 103, 184
[*Partial, unofficial translation of official opinion text*]

Facts

The Plaintiff is a minority shareholder of the Defendant, with four votes. The majority shareholder is L[inotype] GmbH. According to the annual report covering the period between October 1, 1983 and September 30, 1984, over 80% of the Defendant's turnover is generated by the "print technologies" manufacturing division, which is primarily engaged in business dealings with companies of the L[inotype] Group ...

The Defendant's annual meeting took place on April 24, 1985. Pursuant to a proposal to dissolve the corporation with effect from April 30, 1985, which the management and supervisory boards made in Point 4 of the Meeting Agenda, the meeting adopted a resolution with the votes of the majority shareholder, which owns 96% of the share capital, an amount exceeding the 80% majority required by the *Satzung* for the dissolution of the company. The Defendant's majority shareholder voted for this resolution because it wanted to absorb the print technologies manufacturing division into its production activities, thereby acquiring the facilities and employees of the division for its use. However, the majority shareholder was unable to achieve this goal through a reorganization that would change its legal form or effect a merger because it could not meet the legal requirement of unanimous shareholder approval, as it explained in January 1985 in an offering to acquire the shares of the minority shareholders.

The Plaintiff ... seeks to have the resolution to dissolve the corporation declared null and void ...

Discussion

[Text omitted]

[Following a discussion explaining that the resolution could not be challenged for incomplete disclosure or for evading the requirements of the reorganization rules, the Civil Division addressed the question of fiduciary duties of shareholders.]

3 ... (a) The court may not subject the resolution to dissolve the corporation to a test for correctness in substance ... such a resolution requires only that the majority required by law be achieved, unless the *Satzung* sets out a higher majority ... Whether the exercise of this right can constitute an abuse of power, and the circumstances under which this may occur, requires examination in each individual case, but does not mean that all resolutions to dissolve a corporation must be subjected to examination.

(b) Moreover, a declared (and later realized) intention to acquire essential assets of the Defendant through a resolution to dissolve the Defendant corporation that is pushed through solely with the voting power of the majority shareholders, against the votes of the minority shareholders, does not allow the resolution to be challenged as an abuse of voting power ...

4. However, the resolution may be challenged pursuant to § 243(2) AktG to the extent that L[inotype] GmbH as majority shareholder conducted negotiations and reached agreement with the Defendant's management board regarding the acquisition of the Defendant's essential assets before the resolution was adopted on April 24, 1988. Under such circumstances, the majority shareholders would have used their voting rights to violate their fiduciary duties to the Plaintiff as minority shareholder by attempting to obtain special advantages to the detriment of the minority shareholders. The resolution was well suited to achieve such purpose.

(a) The trial court held that any violation of the Plaintiff's rights would hinge on whether, before the adoption of the dissolution resolution, more than negotiations existed between the management board of the Defendant and L[inotype] GmbH, such as a firmly agreed upon price, a right of first refusal for L[inotype], or a concluded purchase agreement. In this way, the majority shareholder would have preemptively removed the minority shareholder's right to acquire the undertaking – whether alone or together with others – and continue its operations.

The trial court's holding is correct ... Moreover, this position could also be held even if no contractually binding obligation had been created – on which a cause of action could be based – but other circumstances created commitments resembling contractual obligations that were sufficient to, as a practical matter, guarantee a sale solely to the majority shareholder and exclude third parties. This would constitute a breach of the majority shareholder's fiduciary duties to the minority shareholder because, following adoption of the resolution to dissolve the Defendant, it would allow the majority shareholder to complete its premeditated plan of acquiring essential assets and assuming the necessary employees from the Defendant.

There is also a corporate law fiduciary duty between shareholders. In the context of limited liability companies (*Gesellschaft mit beschränkter Haftung* – GmbH), the Civil Division of this Court has recognized that a corporate law fiduciary duty may determine not only the legal relationships between shareholders and the corporation, but also such relationships among shareholders. The grounds for this assumption lie not only in the fact that a GmbH's shareholders often exercise a strong, direct influence on the formation, organization and business operations of the corporation, and that its structure may thus be seen as closely resembling that of a partnership. Rather, it is because the majority shareholders are able to influence the company's management to the prejudice of the interests of their fellow shareholders in the company, thus requiring introduction of the counter-balancing duty to take such interests into consideration (BGHZ 65, 15, 18/19; see also BGHZ 14, 25, 38). For stock corporations (*Aktiengesellschaften*), the Civil Division has held that there is a fiduciary duty between shareholders and the corporation (see BGHZ 14, 25, 38). On the other hand, the Civil Division had denied the existence of any fiduciary duty between stock corporation shareholders that would extend beyond the general principles found in §§ 226, 242 and 826 BGB (see BGHZ 18, 350, 365; decision of February 16, 1976 – 2nd Civ. Div. 61/74, reported in JZ 1976, 561, 562). This denial rests on an over-emphasis given to the "corporate body" (*Körperschaft*) nature of the stock corporation, which leads to the idea that legal relationships exist only between the corporation and its shareholders (for an evaluation of the "corporate body" structure, see Immenga, *Die personalistische Kapitalgesellschaft*, 1970, 270/271; and the contribution of Meyer/Landrut to the *GroßKomm zum AktG* 3rd ed. § 1 Note 35). By contrast, newer scholarship recognizes that the relationships among the members of a corporate body may also have the character of special relationships (see in particular, Lutter, *Zur Treupflicht des Großaktionärs*, JZ 1976, 225; Lutter, Note to Civil Division decision of February 16, 1976, JZ 1976, 362; Wiedemann, *Gesellschaftsrecht*, vol. I, § 2(1)(1b), § 8(2)(3); Wiedemann, *Die Bedeutung der ITT-Entscheidung*, JZ 1976, 392, 394; Karsten Schmidt, *Gesellschaftsrecht*, p. 437 et seq., 610 et seq.; Zöllner in KölnKommAktG, 1985 § 243, mn 195). In stock corporations as well, the majority shareholders are able to influence management to the prejudice of the minority shareholders' interests in the corporation. Thus, also in this case, a corporate law duty should be recognized to take such interests into account …

[The Civil Division then remanded the case for determination whether the negotiations and agreements regarding the printing technology division sufficiently locked up the sale to the majority shareholder so as to remove this opportunity from the minority shareholder.]

Kahn v. Lynch Communication Systems, Inc.
Supreme Court of Delaware
638 A 2d 1110 (1994)
[*Text edited; some footnotes omitted*]

HOLLAND, Justice

This is an appeal by the plaintiff-appellant, Alan R. Kahn ("Kahn"), from a final judgment of the Court of Chancery which was entered after a trial ...

... Kahn alleged that Alcatel was a controlling shareholder of Lynch and breached its fiduciary duties to Lynch and its shareholders. According to Kahn, Alcatel dictated the terms of the merger; made false, misleading, and inadequate disclosures; and paid an unfair price.

The Court of Chancery concluded that Alcatel was, in fact, a controlling shareholder that owed fiduciary duties to Lynch and its shareholders. It also concluded that Alcatel had not breached those fiduciary duties. Accordingly, the Court of Chancery entered judgment in favor of the defendants.

Kahn has raised three contentions in this appeal. Kahn's first contention is that the Court of Chancery erred by finding that "the tender offer and merger were negotiated by an independent committee," and then placing the burden of persuasion on the plaintiff, Kahn. Kahn asserts the uncontradicted testimony in the record demonstrated that the committee could not and did not bargain at arm's length with Alcatel. Kahn's second contention is that Alcatel's Offer to Purchase was false and misleading because it failed to disclose threats made by Alcatel to the effect that if Lynch did not accept its proposed price, Alcatel would institute a hostile tender offer at a lower price. Third, Kahn contends that the merger price was unfair. Alcatel contends that the Court of Chancery was correct in its findings, with the exception of concluding that Alcatel was a controlling shareholder ...

Facts

Lynch, a Delaware corporation, designed and manufactured electronic telecommunications equipment ... Alcatel, a holding company, is a subsidiary of Alcatel (SA), a French company involved in public telecommunications, business communications, electronics, and optronics. Alcatel (SA), in turn, is a subsidiary of Compagnie Generale d'Electricite ("CGE"), a French corporation with operations in energy, transportation, telecommunications and business systems.

In 1981, Alcatel acquired 30.6% of Lynch's common stock pursuant to a stock purchase agreement. As part of that agreement, Lynch amended its certificate of incorporation to require an 80% affirmative vote of its shareholders for approval of any business combination. In addition, Alcatel obtained proportional representation on the Lynch board of directors and the right to purchase 40% of any equity securities offered by Lynch to third parties. The agreement also precluded Alcatel from holding more than 45% of Lynch's stock prior to October 1, 1986. By the time of the merger which is contested in this action, Alcatel owned 43.3% of Lynch's outstanding stock; designated five of the eleven members of Lynch's board of directors; two of three members of the executive committee; and two of four members of the compensation committee.

In the spring of 1986, Lynch determined that in order to remain competitive in the rapidly changing telecommunications field, it would need to obtain fiber optics technology to complement its existing digital electronic capabilities. Lynch's management identified a target company, Telco Systems, Inc. ("Telco"), which possessed both fiber optics and other valuable technological assets ... Telco expressed interest in being acquired by Lynch. Because of the supermajority voting provision ... in order to proceed with the Telco combination Lynch needed Alcatel's consent. In June 1986, Ellsworth F. Dertinger ("Dertinger"), Lynch's CEO and chairman of its board of directors, contacted Pierre Suard ("Suard"), the chairman of Alcatel's parent company, CGE, regarding the acquisition of Telco by Lynch. Suard expressed Alcatel's opposition to Lynch's acquisition of Telco. Instead, Alcatel proposed a combination of Lynch and Celwave Systems, Inc. ("Celwave"), an indirect subsidiary of CGE ...

Alcatel's proposed combination with Celwave was presented to the Lynch board at a regular meeting held on August 1, 1986. Although several directors expressed interest in the original combination which had been proposed with Telco, the Alcatel representatives on Lynch's board made it clear that such a combination would not be considered before a Lynch/Celwave combination. According to the minutes of the August 1 meeting, Dertinger expressed his opinion that Celwave would not be of interest to Lynch if Celwave was not owned by Alcatel.

At the conclusion of the meeting, the Lynch board unanimously adopted a resolution establishing an Independent Committee, consisting of Hubert L. Kertz ("Kertz"), Paul B. Wineman ("Wineman"), and Stuart M. Beringer ("Beringer"), to negotiate with Celwave and to make recommendations concerning the appropriate terms and conditions of a combination with Celwave. On October 24, 1986, Alcatel's investment banking firm, Dillon, Read & Co., Inc. ("Dillon Read") made a presentation to the Independent Committee. Dillon Read expressed its views concerning the benefits of a Celwave/Lynch combination and submitted a written proposal of an exchange ratio of 0.95 shares of Celwave per Lynch share in a stock-for-stock merger.

However, the Independent Committee's investment advisors, Thomson McKinnon Securities Inc. ("Thomson McKinnon") and Kidder, Peabody & Co. Inc. ("Kidder Peabody"), reviewed the Dillon Read proposal and concluded that the 0.95 ratio was predicated on Dillon Read's overvaluation of Celwave. Based upon this advice, the Independent Committee determined that the exchange ratio proposed by Dillon Read was unattractive to Lynch. The Independent Committee expressed its unanimous opposition to the Celwave/Lynch merger on October 31, 1986.

Alcatel responded to the Independent Committee's action on November 4, 1986, by withdrawing the Celwave proposal. Alcatel made a simultaneous offer to acquire the entire equity interest in Lynch, constituting the approximately 57% of Lynch shares not owned by Alcatel. The offering price was $14 cash per share.

On November 7, 1986, the Lynch board of directors revised the mandate of the Independent Committee. It authorized Kertz, Wineman, and Beringer to negotiate the cash merger offer with Alcatel. At a meeting held that same day, the Independent Committee determined that the $14 per share offer was inadequate. The Independent's Committee's own legal counsel, Skadden, Arps, Slate, Meagher & Flom ("Skadden Arps"), suggested that the Independent Committee should review alternatives to a cash-out merger with Alcatel, including a "white knight" third party acquiror, a repurchase of Alcatel's shares, or the adoption of a shareholder rights plan.

On November 12, 1986, Beringer, as chairman of the Independent Committee, contacted Michiel C. McCarty ("McCarty") of Dillon Read, Alcatel's representative in the negotiations, with a counteroffer at a price of $17 per share. McCarty responded on behalf of Alcatel with an offer of $15 per share. When Beringer informed McCarty of the Independent Committee's view that $15 was also insufficient, Alcatel raised its offer to $15.25 per share. The Independent Committee also rejected this offer. Alcatel then made its final offer of $15.50 per share.

At the November 24, 1986 meeting of the Independent Committee, Beringer advised its other two members that Alcatel was "ready to proceed with an unfriendly tender at a lower price" if the $15.50 per share price was not recommended by the Independent Committee and approved by the Lynch board of directors. Beringer also told the other members of the Independent Committee that the alternatives to a cash-out merger had been investigated but were impracticable. [Note 3] After meeting with its financial and legal advisors, the Independent Committee voted unanimously to recommend that the Lynch board of directors approve Alcatel's $15.50 cash per share price for a merger with Alcatel. The Lynch board met later that day. With Alcatel's nominees abstaining, it approved the merger.

[Note 3] The minutes reflect that Beringer told the Committee the "white knight" alternative "appeared impractical with the 80% approval requirement"; the repurchase of Alcatel's shares would produce a "highly leveraged company with a lower book value" and was an alternative "not in the least encouraged by Alcatel"; and a shareholder rights plan was not viable because of the increased debt it would entail.

Alcatel dominated Lynch

Controlling shareholder status

This Court has held that "a shareholder owes a fiduciary duty only if it owns a majority interest in or *exercises control* over the business affairs of the corporation." *Ivanhoe Partners* v. *Newmont Mining Corp.* ... (emphasis added). With regard to the exercise of control, this Court has stated:

> [A] shareholder who owns less than 50% of a corporation's outstanding stocks does not, without more, become a controlling shareholder of that corporation,

with a concomitant fiduciary status. For a dominating relationship to exist in the absence of controlling stock ownership, a plaintiff must allege domination by a minority shareholder through actual control of corporation conduct.

Citron v. Fairchild Camera & Instrument Corp. ...

Alcatel held a 43.3% minority share of stock in Lynch. Therefore, the threshold question to be answered by the Court of Chancery was whether, despite its minority ownership, Alcatel exercised control over Lynch's business affairs. Based upon the testimony and the minutes of the August 1, 1986 Lynch board meeting, the Court of Chancery concluded that Alcatel did exercise control over Lynch's business decisions.

... The record supports the Court of Chancery's factual finding that Alcatel dominated Lynch.

At the August 1 meeting, Alcatel opposed the renewal of compensation contracts for Lynch's top five managers. According to Dertinger, Christian Fayard ("Fayard"), an Alcatel director, told the board members, "[y]ou must listen to us. We are 43% owner. You have to do what we tell you." The minutes confirm Dertinger's testimony. They recite that Fayard declared, "you are pushing us very much to take control of the company. Our opinion is not taken into consideration."

Although Beringer and Kertz, two of the independent directors, favored renewal of the contracts, according to the minutes, the third independent director, Wineman, admonished the board as follows:

> Mr. Wineman pointed out that the vote on the contracts is a "watershed vote" and the motion, due to Alcatel's "strong feelings," might not carry if taken now. Mr. Wineman clarified that "you [management] might win the battle and lose the war." With Alcatel's opinion so clear, Mr. Wineman questioned "if management wants the contracts renewed under these circumstances." He recommended that management "think twice." Mr. Wineman declared: "I want to keep the management. I can't think of a better management." Mr. Kertz agreed, again advising consideration of the "critical" period the company is entering.

The minutes reflect that the management directors left the room after this statement. The remaining board members then voted not to renew the contracts.

At the same meeting, Alcatel vetoed Lynch's acquisition of the target company, which, according to the minutes, Beringer considered "an immediate fit" for Lynch. Dertinger agreed with Beringer, stating that the "target company is extremely important as they have the products that Lynch needs now." Nonetheless, Alcatel prevailed. The minutes reflect that Fayard advised the board: "Alcatel, with its 44% equity position, would not approve such an acquisition as ... it does not wish to be diluted from being the main shareholder in Lynch." From the foregoing evidence, the Vice Chancellor concluded:

> Alcatel did control the Lynch board, at least with respect to the matters under consideration at its August 1, 1986 board meeting. The interplay between the directors was more than vigorous discussion, as suggested by defendants. The management and independent directors disagreed with Alcatel on several important issues.

> However, when Alcatel made its position clear, and reminded the other directors of its significant stockholdings, Alcatel prevailed. Dertinger testified that Fayard "scared [the non-Alcatel directors] to death." While this statement undoubtedly is an exaggeration, it does represent a first-hand view of how the board operated. I conclude that the non-Alcatel directors deferred to Alcatel because of its position as a significant stockholder and not because they decided in the exercise of their own business judgment that Alcatel's position was correct ...

The record supports the Court of Chancery's underlying factual finding that "the non-Alcatel [independent] directors deferred to Alcatel because of its position as a significant stockholder and not because they decided in the exercise of their own business judgment that Alcatel's position was correct." ... notwithstanding its 43.3% minority shareholder interest, Alcatel did exercise actual control over Lynch by dominating its corporate affairs. The Court of Chancery's legal conclusion that Alcatel owed the fiduciary duties of a controlling shareholder to the other Lynch shareholders followed syllogistically as the logical result of its cogent analysis of the record.

Entire fairness requirement

Dominating interested shareholder

A controlling or dominant shareholder standing on both sides of a transaction, as in a parent–subsidiary context, bears the burden of proving its entire fairness. *Weinberger v. UOP, Inc.* ... The demonstration of fairness that is required was set out by this Court in *Weinberger*:

> The concept of fairness has two basic aspects: fair dealing and fair price. The former embraces questions of when the transaction was timed, how it was initiated, structured, negotiated, disclosed to the directors, and how the approvals of the directors and the stockholders were obtained. The latter aspect of fairness relates to the economic and financial considerations of the proposed merger, including all relevant factors: assets, market value, earnings, future prospects, and any other elements that affect the intrinsic or inherent value of a company's stock. However, the test for fairness is not a bifurcated one as between fair dealing and price. All aspects of the issue must be examined as a whole since the question is one of entire fairness.

[Text omitted]

Once again, this Court holds that the exclusive standard of judicial review in examining the propriety of an interested cash-out merger transaction by a controlling or dominant shareholder is entire fairness ... The initial burden of establishing entire fairness rests upon the party who stands on both sides of the transaction ... However, an approval of the transaction by an independent committee of directors or an informed majority of minority shareholders shifts the burden of proof on the issue of fairness from the controlling or dominant shareholder to the challenging shareholder-plaintiff ... Nevertheless, even when an interested cash-out merger transaction receives the informed approval of a majority of minority stockholders or an independent committee of disinterested directors, an entire fairness analysis is the only proper standard of judicial review ...

Independent committees, interested merger transactions

[Text omitted]

The same policy rationale which requires judicial review of interested cash-out mergers exclusively for entire fairness also mandates careful judicial scrutiny of a special committee's real bargaining power before shifting the burden of proof on the issue of entire fairness. A recent decision from the Court of Chancery articulated a two-part test for determining whether burden shifting is appropriate in an interested merger transaction ... In [*Rabkin v. Olin Corp.*], the Court of Chancery stated:

> The mere existence of an independent special committee ... does not itself shift the burden. At least two factors are required. First, the majority shareholder must not dictate the terms of the merger ... Second, the special committee must have real bargaining power that it can exercise with the majority shareholder on an arm's length basis.
>   ... [Note 6] ...

[Note 6] In *Olin*, the Court of Chancery concluded that because the special committee had been given "the narrow mandate of determining the monetary fairness of a non-negotiable offer," and because the majority shareholder "dictated the terms" and "there were no arm's-length negotiations," the burden of proof on the issue of entire fairness remained with the defendants ... In making that determination, the Court of Chancery pointed out that the majority shareholder "could obviously have used its majority stake to effectuate the merger" regardless of the committee's or the board's disapproval, and that the record demonstrated that the directors of both corporations were "acutely aware of this fact." ...

Lynch's Independent Committee

In the case *sub judice*, the Court of Chancery observed that although "Alcatel did exercise control over Lynch with respect to the decisions made at the August 1, 1986 board meeting, it does not necessarily follow that Alcatel also controlled the terms of the merger and its approval." This observation is theoretically accurate, as this opinion has already stated ... However, the performance of the Independent Committee merits careful judicial scrutiny to determine whether Alcatel's demonstrated pattern of domination was effectively neutralized so that "each of the contending parties had in fact exerted its bargaining power against the other at arm's length." *Id.* The fact that the same independent directors had submitted to Alcatel's demands on August 1, 1986 was part of the basis for the Court of Chancery's finding of Alcatel's domination of Lynch. Therefore, the Independent Committee's ability to bargain at arm's length with Alcatel was suspect from the outset.

The Independent Committee's original assignment was to examine the merger with Celwave which had been proposed by Alcatel. The record reflects that the

Independent Committee effectively discharged that assignment and, in fact, recommended that the Lynch board reject the merger on Alcatel's terms. Alcatel's response to the Independent Committee's adverse recommendation was not the pursuit of further negotiations regarding its Celwave proposal, but rather its response was an offer to buy Lynch. That offer was consistent with Alcatel's August 1, 1986 expressions of an intention to dominate Lynch, since an acquisition would effectively eliminate once and for all Lynch's remaining vestiges of independence.

The Independent Committee's second assignment was to consider Alcatel's proposal to purchase Lynch. The Independent Committee proceeded on that task with full knowledge of Alcatel's demonstrated pattern of domination. The Independent Committee was also obviously aware of Alcatel's refusal to negotiate with it on the Celwave matter.

[Text omitted]

The power to say no, the parties' contentions, arm's length bargaining

The Court of Chancery properly noted that limitations on the alternatives to Alcatel's offer did not mean that the Independent Committee should have agreed to a price that was unfair:

> The power to say no is a significant power. It is the duty of directors serving on [an independent] committee to approve only a transaction that is in the best interests of the public shareholders, to say no to any transaction that is not fair to those shareholders and is not the best transaction available. It is not sufficient for such directors to achieve the best price that a fiduciary will pay if that price is not a fair price ...

The Alcatel defendants argue that the Independent Committee exercised its "power to say no" in rejecting the three initial offers from Alcatel, and that it therefore cannot be said that Alcatel dictated the terms of the merger or precluded the Independent Committee from exercising real bargaining power ... [Note 9] The Alcatel defendants contend, alternatively, that "even assuming that such a threat [of a hostile takeover] could have had a coercive effect on the [Independent] Committee," the willingness of the Independent Committee to reject Alcatel's initial three offers suggests that "the alleged threat was either nonexistent or ineffective." ...

[Note 9] Alcatel also points to the fairness opinions of two investment banking firms employed by the Committee, Kidder Peabody and Thomson McKinnon, and the involvement of independent legal counsel, Skadden Arps, in considering and rejecting alternatives to the Alcatel cash offers.

Kahn contends the record reflects that the conduct of Alcatel deprived the Independent Committee of an effective "power to say no." Kahn argues that Alcatel not only threatened the Committee with a hostile tender offer in the event its $15.50 offer was not recommended and approved, but also directed the affairs of Lynch for Alcatel's benefit in such a way as to make it impossible for Lynch to continue as a public company under Alcatel's control without injury to itself and its minority shareholders. In support of this argument, Kahn relies upon another proceeding wherein the Court of Chancery has been previously presented with factual circumstances comparable to those of the case *sub judice*, albeit in a different procedural posture ...

In *American General*, in the context of an application for injunctive relief, the Court of Chancery found that the members of the Special Committee were "truly independent and ... performed their tasks in a proper manner," but it also found that "at the end of their negotiations with [the majority shareholder] the Committee members were issued an ultimatum and told that they must accept the $16.50 per share price or [the majority shareholder] would proceed with the transaction without their input." ... The Court of Chancery concluded based upon this evidence that the Special Committee had thereby lost "its ability to negotiate in an arms-length manner" and that there was a reasonable probability that the burden of proving entire fairness would remain on the defendants if the litigation proceeded to trial ...

[*Text omitted*]

Alcatel's entire fairness burden did not shift to Kahn

A condition precedent to finding that the burden of proving entire fairness has shifted in an interested merger transaction is a careful judicial analysis of the factual circumstances of each case. Particular consideration must be given to evidence of whether the special committee was truly independent, fully informed, and had the freedom to negotiate at arm's length ... "Although perfection is not possible," unless the controlling or dominant shareholder can demonstrate that it has not only formed an independent committee but also replicated a process "as though each of the contending parties had in fact exerted its bargaining power at arm's length," the burden of proving entire fairness will not shift ...

Subsequent to *Rosenblatt*, this Court pointed out that "the use of an independent negotiating committee of outside directors may have significant advantages to the majority stockholder in defending suits of this type," but it does not *ipso facto* establish the procedural fairness of an interested merger transaction. *Rabkin* v. *Philip A. Hunt Chem. Corp.* ... In reversing the granting of the defendants' motion to dismiss in *Rabkin*, this Court implied that the burden on entire fairness would not be shifted by the use of an independent committee which concluded its processes with "what could be considered a quick surrender" to the dictated terms of the controlling shareholder ... This Court concluded in *Rabkin* that the majority stockholder's "attitude toward the minority," coupled with the "apparent absence of any meaningful negotiations as to price," did not manifest the exercise of arm's length bargaining by the independent committee ...

The Court of Chancery's determination that the Independent Committee "appropriately simulated a third-party transaction, where negotiations are conducted at arm's-length and there is no compulsion to reach an agreement," is not supported by the record. Under the circumstances present in the case *sub judice*, the Court of Chancery erred in shifting the burden of proof with regard to entire fairness to the contesting Lynch shareholder-plaintiff, Kahn. The record reflects that the ability of the Committee effectively to negotiate at arm's length was compromised by Alcatel's threats to proceed with a hostile tender offer if the $15.50 price was not approved by the Committee and the Lynch board. The fact that the Independent Committee rejected three initial offers, which were well below the Independent Committee's estimated valuation for Lynch and were not combined with an explicit threat that Alcatel was "ready to proceed" with a hostile bid, cannot alter the conclusion that any semblance of arm's length bargaining ended when the Independent Committee surrendered to the ultimatum that accompanied Alcatel's final offer ...

Conclusion

Accordingly, the judgment of the Court of Chancery is reversed. This matter is remanded for further proceedings consistent herewith, including a redetermination of the entire fairness of the cash-out merger to Kahn and the other Lynch minority shareholders with the burden of proof remaining on Alcatel, the dominant and interested shareholder.

In Re Girmes
High Federal Court, Second Civil Division
March 20, 1995, Doc. No. II ZR 205/95, BGHZ 129, 136
[*Partial, unofficial translation of official opinion text*]

Facts

The Plaintiff seeks DM 30,450 in damages from the Defendant. This claim is based on the following facts:

The Plaintiff held 350 shares of G[irmes] AG, which had its registered office in G. This corporation entered into financial difficulties due to operational losses and pension fund commitments. It had not paid dividends since 1982. In the years 1987 and 1988, the corporation recorded losses of DM 14.3 million and DM 13 million. At the end of 1987, the corporation's liabilities to the social security fund totaled DM 54.8 million. In spite of having closed its pension account as from December 31, 1986, the corporation still had pension liabilities of DM 75 million in 1993.

At the general meeting held on February 3, 1989, the management board made it known that, according to the draft financial statements as at December 31, 1988, the corporation's share capital of more than DM 49.9165 million had decreased by more than half. The board then presented the meeting with a reorganization plan to which the corporation's creditors had agreed. Under the plan, creditors would forgive claims of approximately DM 78 million (Pension Insurance Association: DM 44 million; Labor Administration: DM 16 million; Employees: DM 5.3 million;

Banks: DM 10 million plus 5% interest for the years 1989 and 1990; Suppliers: DM 2 million). To further compensate for the balance sheet as at December 31, 1988, the share capital was to be decreased by DM 29.9499 million to DM 19.9666 million. In addition, an authorized capital of DM 9.9833 million was to be created.

The capital decrease could not be undertaken because the number of votes required by law for its approval could not be mustered. There were 228 abstaining and 226,939 votes (42.39%) against the proposal, leaving only 308,207 votes (57.61%) to approve it. [The corporation entered bankruptcy on February 28, 1989. Its shares dropped from a high of DM 87 in 1989 to eventually become worthless.]

The Defendant is the editor and owns a substantial holding in the operating company of the periodical, *Securities Spiegel*. He reported on, among other things, the condition of the G[irmes] AG in this publication. He presented the opinion that the reorganization plan proposed by the management served to disadvantage solely the minority shareholders. If the creditor banks would forgive more of their claims, he stated that it would only be necessary to decrease the share capital by a ratio of 10: 9. He solicited proxies from the shareholders to vote at the general meeting on February 3, 1989 against the planned capital decrease by a ratio of 5: 2. Immediately before the general meeting, he announced that 150,000 votes had been delegated to him, which allowed him to create a blocking minority ... [The Defendant in fact succeeded in blocking the planned reorganization].

The Plaintiff, who did not grant any proxy to the Defendant, alleges that the reorganization of G[irmes] AG failed because of the Defendant ...

[*Text omitted*]

Discussion

I.

... Because the Defendant is not a shareholder, he has no fiduciary duty *qua share-holder* under corporate law. He can therefore incur no liability arising from a breach of such fiduciary duty.

1. In a stock corporation, not only the majority shareholder has a fiduciary duty to the minority shareholder or shareholders with small holdings, but conversely the minority or small shareholder also has a fiduciary duty to the majority shareholder and to other minority and small shareholders.

According to the more recent decisions of the Civil Division, not only the relationships between the shareholders and the stock corporation, but also the relationships among the shareholders are subject to a fiduciary duty under corporate law. This arises from the fact that also in a stock corporation, shareholders are able to influence the company's management to the prejudice of the interests of their fellow shareholders in the company, thus requiring introduction of the counter-balancing duty to take such interests into consideration ([*Linotype*] BGHZ 103, 184, 194 *et seq.*; for the GmbH form, see BGHZ 65, 15, 18 *et seq.*). This principle referred to the fact pattern presented in that case, which was a majority shareholder's comportment toward a minority shareholder. With regard to the duties of minority shareholders, the Civil Division stated that, *as a rule*, minority shareholders would not be affected by a fiduciary duty (*[Linotype]* BGHZ 103, 184, 195). In this way the question was left open, as the Civil Division also noted in a later decision (Decision of June 22, 1992 – 2nd Civil Division 178/90, published in ZIP 1992, 1464, 1470), whether a fiduciary duty extended beyond the status of majority shareholder to limit shareholders generally in the exercise of their membership rights, particularly their rights to affect the corporation's management and control. This question should be answered in the affirmative, which accords with a nearly unanimous consensus of the legal scholarship in this area (*citations omitted*).

2. Regardless of whether the core idea of a fiduciary duty – to the extent that it can be generally applied in corporate law – consists in the quantum of a shareholder's power determining the quantum of such shareholder's duty to give consideration to the interests of the corporation and of the other shareholders in connection with the corporation (*citations omitted*), or, as expressed in the precedent decisions, the ability of a shareholder to exercise influence to the prejudice of the interests of his or her fellow shareholders requires a counter-balancing duty to take such interests into consideration (BGHZ 65; 15, 19; 103, 184, 195), this idea is pertinent not only for majority shareholders, but also for minority shareholders. Because influence is usually seen in the exercise of dominant control and a majority holding is a prerequisite to such control, the responsibilities and duties of shareholders to give consideration to the interests of their fellow shareholders in a stock corporation – in particular in a publicly held stock corporation – often arise only for majority shareholders or a majority of shareholders (*citations omitted*). The ability of the minority shareholders to exercise influence is by comparison rather slight. However, minority shareholders also have rights that, when exercised under certain circumstances, are capable of prejudicing the interests of fellow shareholders in the corporation and the exercise of which should therefore be subject to a counter-balancing duty to take such interests into consideration. For example, the right to participate in the general meeting can create opportunities for abuses through disrupting the meeting or misuse of the right to speak through filibustering (regarding the meaning of these rights, see BGHZ 44, 245, 252, as well as BGHZ 119, 305, 317 *et seq.*). In such cases, the limitations set by fiduciary duty become meaningful (see Brändel in GroßKommAktG, 4th ed., § 1 mn 87; Zöllner in KölnKommAktG § 119 mn 88) ... In most cases, shareholders with small holdings are unable to exercise influence through their voting rights, so that their fiduciary duty to consider the interests of others sees little application. However, this situation changes when the holding of a minority shareholder is large enough to force the implementation of certain rights (see § 122(1) and (3), § 142(2), § 147(1) AktG) or to veto the adoption of binding resolutions (see *inter alia* § 179(2), § 182(1), § 186(3), § 222(1) AktG; regarding minority rights under law in stock corporations, see the compilation by Lehmann AG 1983,

1983, 113, 117 *et seq.*, also printed in Semler in MünchHdbGesR, vol. 4, AktG, 1988
§ 242 Introduction, p. 484 *et seq.*). If a shareholder can exercise such influence with
his or her minority holding, thereby necessitating a check on this power to prejudice the interests of the other shareholders, such minority shareholder may only
exercise rights derived from such holding in accordance with the applicable fiduciary duty (citations omitted) ... [The Civil Division then considered application of
this fiduciary duty to voting agreements and proxy holders.]

5. The Civil Division is of the opinion that a breach of shareholder's fiduciary
duty may not be applied to a proxy holder who has accumulated a number of voting
rights to achieve a particular purpose, as in the present case, if such proxy holder
does not own shares in the company (such application is also rejected by Hammen
ZBB 1993, 239, 242 *et seq.*; Heermann ZIP 1994, 1243, 1244). There is a very good reason for refusing to stretch corporate law fiduciary duties to cover proxy holders: the
fiduciary duty derives from having membership in the corporation. Without transfer of the shares, this duty may no more be severed from the membership rights and
transferred than may other rights connected with membership ... In contrast to the
shareholders who transferred proxies to him, the Defendant has not violated any
fiduciary duty that applies to him *qua shareholder* under corporate law. No liability
may therefore be applied on the basis of this theory.

II.

However, a claim may be made against the Defendant for liability under § 179(1)
BGB.

1. It is recognized both in precedent decisions and in legal scholarship that a
person who enters into a transaction for another without disclosing the principal or
reserving the right to make such disclosure is liable through appropriate application
of § 179 BGB if the transaction collapses and the agent refuses to disclose the name
of the principal (*citations omitted*) ... This general principle is also applicable to a
case in which a proxy holder at a general meeting votes for a number of shareholders, the voting violates shareholder fiduciary duties, and the proxy holder refuses
to name the shareholders for whom he votes. Since under these circumstances the
individual shareholders cannot be held liable for violations of fiduciary duty committed through the voting of their shares, only the proxy holder – as in the case of
a transaction entered into by an agent – remains as a person to be held accountable
for the violation ...

2. The rejection through the Defendant of the reorganization plan proposed by
the management of G[irmes] AG was a violation of the fiduciary duty that the represented shareholders owed to the Plaintiff ... However, no fiduciary duty to the corporation requires that shareholders of G[irmes] AG take part in a reorganization of
the company ... [Rather,] the prohibition of a self-interested blocking of a reorganization sought by the majority must rightly be conditioned upon the certainty that

[i] upon failure of the plan the corporation would collapse and that in the case of a collapse the position of the shareholders would be less favorable than in the case of exiting a going concern … and that [ii] if the reorganization were to be completed a reasonable, objective observer could find that the operations of the corporation could be continued on a permanent basis and that no more favorable reorganization plan was possible …

[Text omitted]

[The Civil Division remanded the case to the trial court to determine whether on the basis of the facts as supplemented and clarified in further proceedings, the comportment of the proxy holder violated § 179(1) and § 826 (regarding violation of standards of reasonable and due comportment) BGB.]

20

Judicial enforcement of shareholder rights

Required reading

D: AktG, §§ 147, 148, 241–248
UK: CA 2006, Part 11
US: DGCL, §§ 325–327; New York Business Corporations Law, § 627; ALI
  Principles §§ 7.01–7.12

Judicial remedies and the stock corporation

I. *The goals and the difficulties of shareholder suits*

Many of the preceding chapters have discussed various types of shareholder rights. We have examined the rights of shareholders to receive a
portion of the company's income in the form of dividends, the manner in
which shares can be separated into various classes with attendant rights,
and the right of all shareholders to have their management act loyally and
manage the company with due care. Minority shareholders also have a
right that majority shareholders act loyally and not use their voting power
to damage the company or unfairly prejudice the minority. Chapters 16
and 18 explained the types of matters on which shareholders can vote and
the way voting rights are exercised. Chapter 17 briefly delved into the rights
to information that allow shareholders to make informed decisions in
exercising their other rights. As these rights all coexist in the hybrid property interest constituted by a share of stock, they are designed to work in a
complementary fashion that is tailored to the needs of a shareholder as co-
owner of the company. For example, if through a legally required regular
disclosure shareholders were to receive information indicating that management could have acted improperly, and they confirmed this through
a specific request for more information, the shareholders could then use
their voting rights to remove the director from office. What recourse do the
shareholders have, however, when, as in *Blasius*, the board takes action to

weaken or eliminate the shareholder vote? Or if, as in *Linotype*, the minority's voting rights are simply not sufficient to prevent abusive action by the majority? Exactly in these situations where collective use of voting rights no longer provides effective protection because the "political" process is being abused, or the injured party has insufficient power in this process, courts can be called in with the power of the state to protect a minority.

This counter-majoritarian strength of litigation is, however, also its main weakness. From a plaintiff's point of view the costs and rewards of judicial action greatly affect the decision to sue, and from a policy perspective the fairness of a judicial action's impact determines whether such remedy should be available in such form. Unlike the voting rights attached to common stock, the power a plaintiff can wield in court is not apportioned in the same ratio as her economic interest in the company. This imbalance can both cause difficulties for a potential plaintiff and lead to unfair results. For example, if, in the context of a "derivative" action – the nature of which will be discussed in more detail below – a diversified, 1 percent shareholder were to sue to stop a 99 percent shareholder from damaging the company, any award would go to the company, with 99 percent of any benefit indirectly accruing to the party in the wrong. This does not give the 1 percent shareholder a strong incentive to incur the costs of the lawsuit. The manner in which compensation is awarded shapes the incentive to take recourse to the courts. Seen from another perspective, if the company were about to complete an important, time-sensitive merger, the interest of a 99 percent shareholder in consummating the transaction would be substantially greater than that of a diversified, 1 percent shareholder. From a strategic point of view, if the 1 percent holder were to hold the transaction hostage by filing suit, the majority shareholder would have a strong incentive to pay the minority a ransom to give up her claim.

Factors affecting judicial relief also come from the broader system of law in which a company finds itself. In the US legal system, the incentive problem discussed above has been addressed by allowing lawyers to be compensated for representation in civil suits on a performance-linked basis. This is referred to as a "contingent fee," which is "[a] fee charged for a lawyer's services only if the lawsuit is successful or is favorably settled out of court ... usually calculated as a percentage of the client's net recovery (such as 25% of the recovery if the case is settled, and 33% if the case is won at trial)."[1] Such fees allow lawyers to profit from the overall value of a legal action rather than receiving payment from the plaintiff, which

---

[1] Entry for "Contingent fees" in *Black's Law Dictionary* (1999: 315).

corrects some of the incentive problems when damages will be awarded to the corporation rather than the plaintiff. As discussed below, the disadvantage of this incentive structure is that not shareholders, but rather lawyers, have the primary economic incentive to bring lawsuits, and their approach to litigation is determined by the business needs of their legal practice (maximizing revenue, reducing expenses, limiting risk) rather than by the corporate governance interests of the plaintiff. The procedural possibility of using "contingent fees" thus greatly affects the landscape of shareholder litigation in the US.

German law, too, contains peculiarities that tend to shape the nature of shareholder litigation. For example, as we have seen throughout this text, many major company decisions – such as amending the *Satzung* or increasing or decreasing the capital – cannot take effect until they are entered into the commercial register.[2] Although such registration requirement is not designed to create a level of state supervision over corporate decisions, it does in fact create a convenient, strategic bottleneck where a plaintiff can apply pressure to the majority and the management. If a shareholder can block the registration of a shareholders' resolution, she can block the effectiveness of the decision itself, thus creating a strong position for negotiating with the majority or the management.

As will be discussed in more detail below, contingent fees in the US and the possibility of blocking registration in Germany have shaped the way in which shareholder litigation is pursued in those countries. Other, less prominent aspects of law and procedure also always have an impact on the operations of corporations in every country, which again shows that a corporate lawyer must be careful to anticipate pitfalls coming from any point in the entire legal system of which a given corporate law forms part. For the purposes of this brief discussion of the very important area of shareholder judicial remedies, we will divide the topic into sections that answer a few basic questions: Does the shareholder sue for himself or on behalf of the company? How does a shareholder's judicial remedy relate to a shareholder's voting rights? If the board has the legal duty to manage and represent the company, why can a shareholder sometimes act for the company in court?

II.   Direct, derivative and class actions

When someone is injured by the acts of another and asks a court to stop the wrongdoer from continuing the injurious action or to force the wrongdoer

---

[2] See e.g. §§ 181(3), 189, 211, 224 AktG.

to compensate for damages suffered, we speak of a *direct* or a *personal* action. The plaintiff directly defends his own rights under, say, contract or tort law. When someone commences such a suit on the basis of a claim derived from the injury suffered by another person who cannot or is not defending himself, we speak of a *derivative* action. The plaintiff defends rights derived from another person, such as a corporation whose management has not acted to right the wrong. When a person suffers an injury that is also suffered in a substantially identical manner by an entire class of persons – such as thousands of investors who all purchased shares on the basis of a misleading prospectus – and asks a court to order the wrongdoer to compensate him *and the entire class he represents* for such wrong, we speak of a *class* action. The plaintiff suffered the same wrong as the others in the class and acts in court to represent that class of injured persons. Like the contingent fee, the class action is a procedural tool that can make prosecuting small claims less burdensome on the injured parties. If, for example, Microsoft Word were to contain a defect that destroyed documents on the 200th time they were saved, think of the difference in terms of ultimate damage and possible court award between you suing the company if your Master's Thesis disappeared in its semi-final draft and all users of the software worldwide seeking compensation for their aggregate damages from the company together in a single lawsuit. Each of our jurisdictions provides for some form of direct, derivative and representative actions.

Because a derivative claim essentially intrudes on the actions of another and asks a court to defend that person's rights even though they themselves do not, derivative suits are inevitably subjected to more procedural safeguards than are direct actions, where a person speaks personally for himself. While distinguishing a personal from a derivative claim might seem straightforward, when the person from whom a claim is supposed to derive is a legal person owned in part by the person prosecuting the claim, the distinction is not always clear. Is there any damage a corporation can suffer that will not reduce the value of its shares and thus negatively affect each shareholder *personally*? Seen the other way around, can an injury affect all shares equally and yet be "individual" to a given shareholder? Read *Tooley* v. *Donaldson, Lufkin & Jenrette, Inc.* How does a Delaware court distinguish between a direct and a derivative claim? How does the court's distinction compare to § 117(1) AktG, pursuant to which anyone who, by virtue of his influence on the corporation, intentionally induces its management to harm the corporation or its shareholders is liable to the shareholders for damages insofar as their damage does not merely reflect a damage suffered by the corporation?

While the derivative action may well be an "ingenious accountability mechanism," when combined with contingent fees, as in the US, it shifts the incentive to bring corporate wrongs to court from the persons who are injured (to which the damages will not be paid) to the lawyer prosecuting the case (who will receive a percentage of any damages paid to the corporation). Class actions lead to a similar result for different reasons. In such actions, an individual plaintiff may recover very little (e.g. a difference of €2 per share on 50 shares owned, equals €100), but the lawyer's fee could be a percentage of the total sum awarded to tens of thousands of individual plaintiffs in the class (e.g. €100 times 10,000 shareholders equals €1 million), thus becoming very substantial. Both of these procedural mechanisms lead to a situation in which, as Professors Jonathan Macey and Geoffrey Miller have shown, the lawyer essentially uses damaged shareholders as a source from which litigation fees can be harvested:

> The traditional image of the lawyer is of an independent professional providing advice and advocacy on behalf of a client. The attorney, in this view, is an agent of the client and subject to the client's control in all important matters. Plaintiffs' class action and derivative attorneys do not fit this mold. They are subject to only minimal monitoring by their ostensible "clients," who are either dispersed and disorganized (in the case of class action litigation) or under the control of hostile forces (in the case of derivative litigation). Accordingly, plaintiffs' class and derivative attorneys function essentially as entrepreneurs who bear a substantial amount of the litigation risk and exercise nearly plenary control over all important decisions in the lawsuit.[3]

This reversal of roles changes the strategic calculus of the parties when contemplating and conducting litigation. In the traditional scenario, a shareholder experiences an injury or detects the corporation being injured, calculates the costs and the probabilities of success for various avenues of relief (visiting the board, starting a shareholders' initiative, filing a lawsuit), and then takes action. According to Macey and Miller, we should view the process from a different angle. In a scenario driven by contingent fees, a lawyer behaving as a rational economic agent will see each lawsuit as part of ongoing business operations. She will first need a source of information on possible corporate wrongs, which could be the existence of a government investigation,[4] and when prosecuting the case she will not focus on the need to correct the company's governance in the case at hand, but on how the suit fits into her overall portfolio of

---

[3] Macey and Miller (1991: 3).   [4] Coffee (1983: 252).

shareholder actions, particularly the liabilities they generate and the risks associated with the contingency of payoffs.[5] When it comes time to decide whether the case should be settled or go forward to court, these differences in incentives between the entrepreneurial lawyer prosecuting the action and the "real" plaintiff whose claim is being prosecuted can lead to significant distortions in the decisionmaking on how to proceed with the lawsuit.[6]

III.   How do judicial actions and general meeting decisions relate?

As we have seen, through the exercise of voting rights, shareholders can achieve anything from appointing directors to liquidating the company. Under German and UK law, minority shareholders are able to call general meetings, and, under Delaware law, a shareholder is able to launch an action for written consents. Can a shareholder simply circumvent this internal, "democratic" governance mechanism and ask a court to impose her will on the company and the remaining shareholders? How do the two mechanisms for voicing shareholder rights relate to each other? Although the answer to this question is generally that judicial action intervenes when the voting mechanism has been frustrated, the details of the relationship vary in the three jurisdictions.

A.   Germany

German law contains provisions for direct actions for securities fraud,[7] derivative actions for corporate wrongs,[8] a form of class action,[9] and a special appraisal proceeding in cases of forced shareholder cash-outs.[10] Individual topical laws such as the Reorganization Act (UmwG)[11] and the Takeover Act (WpÜG)[12] also contain their own special provisions for shareholder remedies. Under the *Aktiengesetz*, the general meeting

---

[5] Coffee (1983: 230–232).

[6] See the very instructive discussion by Gevurtz (2000: 423–425).

[7] See the *ComROAD* decision, reprinted in part in Chapter 16.

[8] §§ 147 *et seq.* AktG.

[9] Securities Investor Class Action Act (*Kapitalanleger-Musterverfahrensgesetz*) of August 16, 2005 (BGBl I: 2437), most recently amended on January 5, 2007 (BGBl I: 10).

[10] The Appraisal Act (*Spruchverfahrensgesetz*) of June 12, 2003 (BGBl I: 838), most recently amended on December 12, 2004 (BGBl I: 3675).

[11] See §§ 14, 15, 32, 195, 210 UmwG.

[12] The procedure for squeeze-outs, particularly the compensation for cashing out minority shareholders, is provided for in §§ 39a *et seq.* WpÜG.

can appoint a special representative to pursue a derivative action against the management,[13] as we saw in *ARAG* v. *Garmenbeck* (Chapter 13). Primarily due to a strong US push in the corporate law scholarship for strengthening "private" enforcement techniques, the principle of shareholder action has been extended downwards to smaller groups of shareholders, and currently allows one or more persons holding shares constituting at least 1 percent of the company's capital or having a nominal value of at least €100,000 also to file a derivative action.[14] Because German law does not recognize contingent fees, however, the incentives they create for derivative suits are not available, and the most common type of shareholder action in Germany is to challenge a shareholders' resolution.[15]

The nature of a challenge to a shareholders' resolution depends on the type of resolution being challenged. It can try to stop a positive act, such as the suit in the *Linotype* case which tried to block a resolution to dissolve the company, or reverse a shareholder decision not to act, such as the challenge to the shareholder exculpation of the *Aufsichtsrat* in the *Macrotron* case. Obviously, where a shareholder's judicial action is structured as a right to challenge shareholders' resolutions, the matters that can be resolved by judicial action is limited to those matters requiring approval by a resolution. A challenge may be raised if a shareholders' resolution violates the law or the *Satzung*, conveys special advantages on certain shareholders, or the exercise of voting rights through a custodian bank was not conducted pursuant to law.[16] The challenge can be brought by any shareholder who obtained his shares before the notice of the meeting was sent, attended the relevant meeting and lodged a dissent, or was unjustly excluded from the meeting by the *Vorstand* or by any member of the *Aufsichtsrat*.[17] This requirement, a similar version of which is called the "contemporaneous ownership rule" in the US, serves, among other things, to prevent a buyer who obtains shares cheaply because the company is mismanaged from receiving a "windfall" damages payment exactly because of the same mismanagement.[18] Unlike German and US law, the Companies Act 2006 expressly allows a shareholder to raise a claim about a wrong that occurred before she purchased her shares.[19] What policy do you think might convince the UK to have such a rule?

---

[13] § 147(1) AktG.   [14] § 148(1) AktG.

[15] §§ 241 *et seq.* AktG.   [16] § 243 AktG.

[17] § 245 AktG.

[18] *Bangor Punta Operations, Inc.* v. *Bangor & Aroostook*, 417 US 703 (1974).

[19] Sec. 260(4) CA 2006.

Like US derivative actions, most challenges under § 243 AktG tend to be brought where there is an economic incentive to do so rather than as a last resort by damaged shareholders seeking justice from the court.[20] There are no contingent fees in Germany, but professional litigants have organized their litigation in such a way and adopted strategies that allow them to yield significant profits from shareholder suits. A study led by Professor Theodor Baums examining 97 shareholder proceedings containing 619 individual challenges to resolutions showed that 72 percent of these challenges were filed by professional litigation groups holding a token number of shares, with more than half of these being filed by a mere eleven plaintiffs.[21] In this group, litigants held effectively diversified portfolios of up to twenty-nine lawsuits each.[22] The business model for such litigation is, as in the US, to catch the company in a position where its costs for continuing the lawsuit would be high, thus creating leverage for a sizeable settlement payment, which both accelerates receipt of the litigant's cash inflow and reduces its operating costs. In Germany, a company is weakest when the entry – and thus the effectiveness – of a shareholders' resolution in the commercial register can be blocked. Take, for example, a company undertaking an initial public offering of its shares. In such case, if the shares for the offering were created by means of a capital increase shortly before the planned offering, a litigant could attempt to block the entire transaction by blocking the effectiveness of the capital increase resolution until the company met the shareholder-litigant's demands. It is not surprising, therefore, that each of the professional litigants examined in the Baums study focused with very few exceptions on blocking the registration of a resolution while negotiating a settlement with management.[23]

This strategy has been known, even if not transparently documented, in Germany for some time. The *Aktiengesetz* was amended in 2005 to allow companies to sue for immediate registration of a resolution despite a challenge where the challenge is impermissible or clearly unfounded, or if a delay in registration would damage the company to a degree that would

---

[20] It should be noted, however, that simply because litigation professionals file most claims of this type in the United States and Germany, this does not exclude the possibility that passive, truly injured shareholders may well benefit from this industry's activities. In many cases, legitimately injured shareholders may ride free on the actions of litigation professionals rather than filing their own actions. The fact that such passive shareholders do not show up on the statistical radar screen does not prove their non-existence.

[21] See Baums, Keinath and Gajek (2007: 1650), as well as the discussion in Baums and Drinhausen (2008: 145).

[22] Baums, Keinath and Gajek (2007: 1644, Table 13).

[23] Baums, Keinath and Gajek (2007: 1644, column 2 of Table 13).

outweigh the alleged damage to the plaintiff.[24] In light of the nature of the litigants and their proven strategy, however, Baums has argued that the company's position should be strengthened. The ability to raise a challenge should be subjected to a minimum shareholding requirement and registration should never be blocked without the kind of balancing test which is now used only for an action to *unblock* registration.[25] The latter would in effect reverse a presumption in favor of blocking registration as expressed in current law.

B. United Kingdom

The United Kingdom offers shareholders direct suits for both violations of corporate law and securities fraud under common law and statute,[26] class actions (referred to as "group litigation"),[27] and derivative actions.[28] Like Germany, the United Kingdom has also linked shareholder suits closely to the ability to act in the general meeting. The current common law on derivative suits finds its origin in the 1843 rule of *Foss* v. *Harbottle*,[29] which is understood to mean that "an individual shareholder cannot bring an action in the courts to complain of an irregularity (as distinct from an illegality) in the conduct of the company's internal affairs if the irregularity is one which can be cured by a vote of the company in general meeting."[30] The company, not the shareholder, would be the proper plaintiff, and, if the company decides to ratify the act, a shareholder has no place to raise the action.[31] This rule was replaced without being in substance fully eliminated in the Companies Act 2006, which gives the court express authority to allow an action to proceed.[32] Thus, consideration of the elements of *Foss* v. *Harbottle* can arise later in the proceedings.[33]

Under the new rules, an individual shareholder may bring a derivative action "in respect of a cause of action vested in the company, and seeking relief on behalf of the company" against a director for "an actual or proposed act or omission involving negligence, default, breach of duty or

---

[24] § 246a AktG. [25] Baums and Drinhausen (2008: 156).

[26] See e.g. sec. 90 FSMA 2000.

[27] See UK Ministry of Justice, Practice Direction, Part 19B; and *Menier* v. *Hooper's Telegraph Works* (1873–74) LR 9 Ch App 350, reprinted in part in Chapter 18.

[28] See Part 11 CA 2006. [29] *Foss* v. *Harbottle* (1843) 2 Hare 461.

[30] *Prudential Assurance Co. Ltd* v. *Newman Industries (No. 2)* [1982] Ch 204, 210. Although there has been debate on what sort of breaches of duties may be ratified, it is well settled that fraud and illegal acts could not be cured by a shareholder vote and thus fall outside the competence of the general meeting. See Reisberg (2007: 88–90).

[31] Reisberg (2007: 84–85). [32] Sec. 261(1) CA 2006; and Reisberg (2007: 134–135).

[33] Reisberg (2007: 135–138).

breach of trust."[34] The possibility of suing for a "proposed act" that could constitute negligence indeed seems much more permissive than *Foss* v. *Harbottle*. However, the plaintiff may continue the suit only with the court's permission, and the court must refuse such permission if either a duty to promote the success of the company advises dismissing it or the act or omission complained of has been authorized or ratified by the company.[35] Thus, as under *Foss* v. *Harbottle*, action by the general meeting still acts significantly to determine whether a derivative suit may go forward. The result is of course that authorization or ratification by the general meeting will preempt any derivative action.

C.   United States

In the US, direct actions can be filed individually or in a class under either state corporate law or federal securities law, and derivative suits can be filed to defend the corporation from a director's violation of law. As discussed above, contingent fees make each of these suits economically feasible for the plaintiff. Unlike German law, a US derivative suit is a remedy having no relation to action in the general meeting. Some states, such as Massachusetts, do allow disinterested shareholders to vote in order to have a derivative suit dismissed,[36] but, in the US, collective shareholder participation in derivative actions is not common.

IV.   How do judicial actions relate to the board's duty to manage the company?

In each of our jurisdictions, directors have a duty not only to make business decisions but also to monitor and supervise the management. A core characteristic of the stock corporation is that owners/shareholders delegate control over the company to a centralized management, except for those decisions reserved to the general meeting pursuant to law. If an individual shareholder could circumvent this governance structure at will, the company's operations would be subject to the will of any person holding one share and who files a lawsuit. Since the board is charged with protecting the company's interests, it must also act to prevent unwarranted interference. As we have seen, both German and UK law address this danger by either allowing the general meeting to override the individual shareholder's recourse to court or by restricting the filing of a

---

[34] Sec. 260(3) CA 2006.   [35] Sec. 263(2) CA 2006.
[36] See Massachusetts General Laws, Title 22, Chapter 156D, § 7.44(b)(3).

derivative suit to the meeting itself or a shareholder with a substantial interest in the company.

US law addresses the danger of excessive or disruptive shareholder derivative litigation differently, by vesting the power to sue primarily in the board and requiring a litigant to make a demand on the board to act before having recourse to the court. If the directors were to vote to hold meetings six times a year in five-star resorts and buy each other corporate jets to attend such meetings, and a shareholder were to demand that the board sue itself, how would the demand rule work? What if the board appointed the managers of these resorts as independent directors to decide on the merits of the lawsuit? Would a shareholder be able to skip demand and ask the court to begin proceedings in the name of the company against the directors? Read *Zapata Corp.* v. *Maldonado* and §§ 7.03–7.08 of the American Law Institute's Principles of Corporate Governance. How would you answer the above questions? Would the result be different in Delaware and under the ALI Principles?

Cases

Tooley v. Donaldson, Lufkin & Jenrette, Inc.
Supreme Court of Delaware
845 A 2d 1031 (2004)
[*Text edited; some footnotes omitted*]

OPINION BY: VEASEY

[*Text omitted*]

Patrick Tooley and Kevin Lewis are former minority stockholders of Donaldson, Lufkin & Jenrette, Inc. (DLJ), a Delaware corporation engaged in investment banking. DLJ was acquired by Credit Suisse Group (Credit Suisse) in the Fall of 2000. Before that acquisition, AXA Financial, Inc. (AXA), which owned 71% of DLJ stock, controlled DLJ. Pursuant to a stockholder agreement between AXA and Credit Suisse, AXA agreed to exchange with Credit Suisse its DLJ stockholdings for a mix of stock and cash. The consideration received by AXA consisted primarily of stock. Cash made up one-third of the purchase price. Credit Suisse intended to acquire the remaining minority interests of publicly held DLJ stock through a cash tender offer, followed by a merger of DLJ into a Credit Suisse subsidiary.

The tender offer price was set at $90 per share in cash. The tender offer was to expire 20 days after its commencement. The merger agreement, however, authorized two types of extensions. First, Credit Suisse could unilaterally extend the tender offer if certain conditions were not met, such as SEC regulatory approvals or certain payment obligations. Alternatively, DLJ and Credit Suisse could agree to postpone acceptance by Credit Suisse of DLJ stock tendered by the minority stockholders.

Credit Suisse availed itself of both types of extensions to postpone the closing of the tender offer. The tender offer was initially set to expire on October 5, 2000, but Credit Suisse invoked the five-day unilateral extension provided in the agreement. Later, by agreement between DLJ and Credit Suisse, it postponed the merger a second time so that it was then set to close on November 2, 2000.

Plaintiffs challenge the second extension that resulted in a 22-day delay. They contend that this delay was not properly authorized and harmed minority stockholders while improperly benefitting AXA. They claim damages representing the time-value of money lost through the delay.

[Text omitted]

The Court of Chancery correctly noted that "the Court will independently examine the nature of the wrong alleged and any potential relief to make its own determination of the suit's classification ... Plaintiffs' classification of the suit is not binding." The trial court's analysis was hindered, however, because it focused on the confusing concept of "special injury" as the test for determining whether a claim is derivative or direct. The trial court's premise was as follows: "In order to bring a direct claim, a plaintiff must have experienced some 'special injury.'" A special injury is a wrong that "is separate and distinct from that suffered by other shareholders ... or a wrong involving a contractual right of a shareholder, such as the right to vote, or to assert majority control, which exists independently of any right of the corporation." In our view, the concept of "special injury" that appears in some Supreme Court and Court of Chancery cases is not helpful to a proper analytical distinction between direct and derivative actions. We now disapprove the use of the concept of "special injury" as a tool in that analysis.

The proper analysis to distinguish between direct and derivative actions

The analysis must be based solely on the following questions: Who suffered the alleged harm – the corporation or the suing stockholder individually – and who would receive the benefit of the recovery or other remedy? This simple analysis is well imbedded in our jurisprudence, but some cases have complicated it by injection of the amorphous and confusing concept of "special injury."

The Chancellor, in the very recent *Agostino* [v. *Hicks*] correctly points this out and strongly suggests that we should disavow the concept of "special injury." In a scholarly analysis of this area of the law, he also suggests that the inquiry should be whether the stockholder has demonstrated that he or she has suffered an injury that is not dependent on an injury to the corporation. In the context of a claim for breach of fiduciary duty, the Chancellor articulated the inquiry as follows: "Looking at the body of the complaint and considering the nature of the wrong alleged and the relief requested, has the plaintiff demonstrated that he or she can prevail without showing an injury to the corporation?" [Note 9] We believe that this approach is helpful in analyzing the first prong of the analysis: what person or entity has suffered the alleged harm? The second prong of the analysis should logically follow.

[Note 9] *Agostino* ... The Chancellor further explains that the focus should be on the person or entity to whom the relevant duty is owed ... As noted in *Agostino*, this test is similar to that articulated by the American Law Institute (ALI), a test that we cited with approval in *Grimes* v. *Donald* ... The ALI test is as follows: A direct action may be brought in the name and right of a holder to redress an injury sustained by, or enforce a duty owed to, the holder. An action in which the holder can prevail without showing an injury or breach of duty to the corporation should be treated as a direct action that may be maintained by the holder in an individual capacity. 2 American Law Institute, PRINCIPLES OF CORPORATE GOVERNANCE: ANALYSIS AND RECOMMENDATIONS § 7.01(b) at 17.

... The derivative suit has been generally described as "one of the most interesting and ingenious of accountability mechanisms for large formal organizations." It enables a stockholder to bring suit on behalf of the corporation for harm done to the corporation ...

... if an action is derivative, the plaintiffs are then required to comply with the requirements of Court of Chancery Rule 23.1, that the stockholder: (a) retain ownership of the shares throughout the litigation; (b) make presuit demand on the board; and (c) obtain court approval of any settlement. Further, the recovery, if any, flows only to the corporation. The decision whether a suit is direct or derivative may be outcome-determinative. Therefore, it is necessary that a standard to distinguish such actions be clear, simple and consistently articulated and applied by our courts ...

In *Bokat* v. *Getty Oil Co.*, a stockholder of a subsidiary brought suit against the director of the parent corporation for causing the subsidiary to invest its resources wastefully, resulting in a loss to the subsidiary. The claim in *Bokat* was essentially for mismanagement of corporate assets. Therefore, the Court held that any recovery must be sought on behalf of the corporation, and the claim was, thus, found to be derivative.

In describing how a court may distinguish direct and derivative actions, the *Bokat* Court stated that a suit must be maintained derivatively if the injury falls equally upon all stockholders. Experience has shown this concept to be confusing and inaccurate. It is confusing because it appears to have been intended to address the fact that an injury to the corporation tends to diminish each share of stock equally because corporate assets or their value are diminished. In that sense, the indirect injury to the stockholders arising out of the harm to the corporation comes about solely by virtue of their stockholdings. It does not arise out of any independent or direct harm to the stockholders, individually. That concept is also inaccurate because a direct, individual claim of stockholders that does not depend on harm to the corporation can also fall on all stockholders equally, without the claim thereby becoming a derivative claim.

[Text omitted]

Thus, two confusing propositions have encumbered our caselaw governing the direct/derivative distinction. The "special injury" concept ... can be confusing in identifying the nature of the action. The same is true of the proposition that ... an action cannot be direct if all stockholders are equally affected or unless the stockholder's injury is separate and distinct from that suffered by other stockholders. The proper analysis has been and should remain that ... a court should look to the nature of the wrong and to whom the relief should go. The stockholder's claimed direct injury must be independent of any alleged injury to the corporation. The stockholder must demonstrate that the duty breached was owed to the stockholder and that he or she can prevail without showing an injury to the corporation.

Standard to be applied in this case

In this case it cannot be concluded that the complaint alleges a derivative claim. There is no derivative claim asserting injury to the corporate entity. There is no relief that would go the corporation. Accordingly, there is no basis to hold that the complaint states a derivative claim.

But, it does not necessarily follow that the complaint states a direct, individual claim. While the complaint purports to set out a direct claim, in reality, it states no claim at all ... The contractual claim is nonexistent until it is ripe, and that claim will not be ripe until the terms of the merger are fulfilled, including the extensions of the closing at issue here. Therefore, there is no direct claim stated in the complaint before us.

[Text omitted]

Zapata Corp. v. Maldonado
Supreme Court of Delaware
430 A 2d 779 (1981)
[Text edited; most footnotes omitted]

OPINION BY: QUILLEN

[Text omitted]

In June, 1975, William Maldonado, a stockholder of Zapata, instituted a derivative action in the Court of Chancery on behalf of Zapata against ten officers and/or directors of Zapata, alleging, essentially, breaches of fiduciary duty. Maldonado did not first demand that the board bring this action, stating instead such demand's futility because all directors were named as defendants and allegedly participated in the acts specified. [Note 1] In June, 1977, Maldonado commenced an action in the US District Court for the Southern District of New York against the same defendants, save one, alleging federal security law violations as well as the same common law claims made previously in the Court of Chancery.

[Note 1] Court of Chancery Rule 23.1 states in part: "The complaint shall also allege with particularity the efforts, if any, made by the plaintiff to obtain the action he desires from the directors or comparable authority and the reasons for his failure to obtain the action or for not making the effort."

By June, 1979, four of the defendant-directors were no longer on the board, and the remaining directors appointed two new outside directors to the board. The board then created an "Independent Investigation Committee" (Committee), composed solely of the two new directors, to investigate Maldonado's actions, as well as a similar derivative action then pending in Texas, and to determine whether the corporation should continue any or all of the litigation. The Committee's determination was stated to be "final … not … subject to review by the Board of Directors and … in all respects … binding upon the Corporation."

Following an investigation, the Committee concluded, in September, 1979, that each action should "be dismissed forthwith as their continued maintenance is inimical to the Company's best interests … " Consequently, Zapata moved for dismissal or summary judgment in the three derivative actions. On January 24, 1980, the District Court for the Southern District of New York granted Zapata's motion for summary judgment, *Maldonado* v. *Flynn*, SDNY, 485 F Supp 274 (1980), holding, under its interpretation of Delaware law, that the Committee had the authority, under the "business judgment" rule, to require the termination of the derivative action. Maldonado appealed that decision to the Second Circuit Court of Appeals.

On March 18, 1980, the Court of Chancery, in a reported opinion, the basis for the order of April 9, 1980, denied Zapata's motions, holding that Delaware law does not sanction this means of dismissal. More specifically, it held that the "business judgment" rule is not a grant of authority to dismiss derivative actions and that a stockholder has an individual right to maintain derivative actions in certain instances. *Maldonado* v. *Flynn*, Del. Ch., 413 A 2d 1251 (1980) (herein *Maldonado*) … Zapata filed an interlocutory appeal with this Court shortly thereafter …

… As the Vice Chancellor noted, 413 A 2d at 1257, "it is the law of the State of incorporation which determines whether the directors have this power of dismissal …"

[Text omitted]

… Corporations, existing because of legislative grace, possess authority as granted by the legislature. Directors of Delaware corporations derive their managerial decision making power, which encompasses decisions whether to initiate, or refrain from entering, litigation, from 8 Del. C. § 141 (a). This statute is the fount of directorial powers. The "business judgment" rule is a judicial creation that presumes propriety, under certain circumstances, in a board's decision. Viewed defensively, it does not create authority. In this sense the "business judgment" rule is not relevant in corporate decision making until after a decision is made. It is generally used as a defense to an attack on the decision's soundness. The board's managerial decision making power, however, comes from § 141(a). The judicial creation and legislative grant are related because the "business judgment" rule evolved to give recognition and deference to directors' business expertise when exercising their managerial power under § 141(a) ...

... the focus in this case is on the power to speak for the corporation as to whether the lawsuit should be continued or terminated. As we see it, this issue in the current appellate posture of this case has three aspects: the conclusions of the Court below concerning the continuing right of a stockholder to maintain a derivative action; the corporate power under Delaware law of an authorized board committee to cause dismissal of litigation instituted for the benefit of the corporation; and the role of the Court of Chancery in resolving conflicts between the stockholder and the committee.

Accordingly, we turn first to the Court of Chancery's conclusions concerning the right of a plaintiff stockholder in a derivative action. We find that its determination that a stockholder, once demand is made and refused, possesses an independent, individual right to continue a derivative suit for breaches of fiduciary duty over objection by the corporation ... as an absolute rule, is erroneous ...

... the question before us relates to the power of the corporation by motion to terminate a lawsuit properly commenced by a stockholder without prior demand. No Delaware statute or case cited to us directly determines this new question ...

[*Text omitted*]

... *McKee* v. *Rogers* ... stated "as a general rule" that "a stockholder cannot be permitted ... to invade the discretionary field committed to the judgment of the directors and sue in the corporation's behalf when the managing body refuses. This rule is a well settled one." ...

The *McKee* rule, of course, should not be read so broadly that the board's refusal will be determinative in every instance. Board members, owing a well-established fiduciary duty to the corporation, will not be allowed to cause a derivative suit to be dismissed when it would be a breach of their fiduciary duty. Generally disputes pertaining to control of the suit arise in two contexts.

Consistent with the purpose of requiring a demand, a board decision to cause a derivative suit to be dismissed as detrimental to the company, after demand has been made and refused, will be respected unless it was wrongful ... A claim of a wrongful decision not to sue is thus the first exception and the first context of dispute. Absent a wrongful refusal, the stockholder in such a situation simply lacks legal managerial power ...

But it cannot be implied that, absent a wrongful board refusal, a stockholder can never have an individual right to initiate an action. For, as is stated in *McKee*, a "well settled" exception exists to the general rule. "(A) stockholder may sue in equity in his derivative right to assert a cause of action in behalf of the corporation, *without prior demand* upon the directors to sue, when it is apparent that a demand would be futile, that the officers are under an influence that sterilizes discretion and could not be proper persons to conduct the litigation." ... (emphasis added). This exception, the second context for dispute, is consistent with the Court of Chancery's statement below, that "the stockholders' individual right to bring the action does not ripen, however ... unless he can show a demand to be futile." *Maldonado*, 413 A 2d at 1262.

These comments in *McKee* and in the opinion below make obvious sense. A demand, when required and refused (if not wrongful), terminates a stockholder's legal ability to initiate a derivative action. But where demand is properly excused, the stockholder does possess the ability to initiate the action on his corporation's behalf.

These conclusions, however, do not determine the question before us. Rather, they merely bring us to the question to be decided ...

The question to be decided becomes: When, if at all, should an authorized board committee be permitted to cause litigation, properly initiated by a derivative stockholder in his own right, to be dismissed? ... Even when demand is excusable, circumstances may arise when continuation of the litigation would not be in the corporation's best interests. Our inquiry is whether, under such circumstances, there is a permissible procedure under § 141(a) by which a corporation can rid itself of detrimental litigation. If there is not, a single stockholder in an extreme case might control the destiny of the entire corporation ...

Before we pass to equitable considerations as to the mechanism at issue here, it must be clear that an independent committee possesses the corporate power to seek the termination of a derivative suit. Section 141(c) allows a board to delegate all of its authority to a committee. Accordingly, a committee with properly delegated authority would have the power to move for dismissal or summary judgment if the entire board did ...

The corporate power inquiry then focuses on whether the board, tainted by the self-interest of a majority of its members, can legally delegate its authority to a committee of two disinterested directors. We find our statute clearly requires an affirmative answer to this question ...

[Text omitted]

At the risk of stating the obvious, the problem is relatively simple. If, on the one hand, corporations can consistently wrest bona fide derivative actions away from well-meaning derivative plaintiffs through the use of the committee mechanism, the derivative suit will lose much, if not all, of its generally recognized effectiveness as an intra-corporate means of policing boards of directors ... It thus appears desirable to us to find a balancing point where bona fide stockholder power to bring corporate causes of action cannot be unfairly trampled on by the board of directors, but the corporation can rid itself of detrimental litigation ...

We are not satisfied, however, that acceptance of the "business judgment" rationale at this stage of derivative litigation is a proper balancing point. While we admit an analogy with a normal case respecting board judgment, it seems to us that there is sufficient risk in the realities of a situation like the one presented in this case to justify caution beyond adherence to the theory of business judgment.

The context here is a suit against directors where demand on the board is excused. We think some tribute must be paid to the fact that the lawsuit was properly initiated. It is not a board refusal case. Moreover, this complaint was filed in June of 1975 and, while the parties undoubtedly would take differing views on the degree of litigation activity, we have to be concerned about the creation of an "Independent Investigation Committee" four years later, after the election of two new outside directors. Situations could develop where such motions could be filed after years of vigorous litigation for reasons unconnected with the merits of the lawsuit.

Moreover, notwithstanding our conviction that Delaware law entrusts the corporate power to a properly authorized committee, we must be mindful that directors are passing judgment on fellow directors in the same corporation and fellow directors, in this instance, who designated them to serve both as directors and committee members. The question naturally arises whether a "there but for the grace of God go I" empathy might not play a role. And the further question arises whether inquiry as to independence, good faith and reasonable investigation is sufficient safeguard against abuse, perhaps subconscious abuse.

[*Text omitted*]

The Court should apply a two-step test to the motion.

First, the Court should inquire into the independence and good faith of the committee and the bases supporting its conclusions ... The corporation should have the burden of proving independence, good faith and a reasonable investigation, rather than presuming independence, good faith and reasonableness. If the Court determines either that the committee is not independent or has not shown reasonable bases for its conclusions, or, if the Court is not satisfied for other reasons relating to the process, including but not limited to the good faith of the committee, the Court shall deny the corporation's motion. If, however, the Court is satisfied ... that the committee was independent and showed reasonable bases for good faith findings and recommendations, the Court may proceed, in its discretion, to the next step.

The second step provides, we believe, the essential key in striking the balance between legitimate corporate claims as expressed in a derivative stockholder suit and a corporation's best interests as expressed by an independent investigating committee. The Court should determine, applying its own independent business judgment, whether the motion should be granted. This means, of course, that instances could arise where a committee can establish its independence and sound bases for its good faith decisions and still have the corporation's motion denied. The second step is intended to thwart instances where corporate actions meet the criteria of step one, but the result does not appear to satisfy its spirit, or where corporate actions would simply prematurely terminate a stockholder grievance deserving of further consideration in the corporation's interest. The Court of Chancery of course must carefully consider and weigh how compelling the corporate interest in dismissal is when faced with a non-frivolous lawsuit. The Court of Chancery should, when appropriate, give special consideration to matters of law and public policy in addition to the corporation's best interests.

If the Court's independent business judgment is satisfied, the Court may proceed to grant the motion, subject, of course, to any equitable terms or conditions the Court finds necessary or desirable.

The interlocutory order of the Court of Chancery is reversed and the cause is remanded for further proceedings consistent with this opinion.

PART IV

Corporate combinations, groups and takeovers

SUBPART A

Mergers and acquisitions

21

Techniques for business combinations

Required reading

EU: Cross Border Merger Directive, art. 2(2)
D: UmwG, § 2
UK: CA 2006, sec. 904
US: DGCL, §§ 251(a), (d), 103(d)

Tools and structures for corporate acquisitions

I.   Transaction structures and protective tools

The essential characteristics of all stock corporations in each of our jurisdictions – a separate legal person owned by shareholders and managed by a central management – lead to like structures for transferring all or part of a company to a new owner. Because the legal person itself owns the corporate assets, and is in turn controlled by votes attaching to its shares, one can gain control of its assets by (a) directly purchasing those assets or (b) purchasing enough stock to control their owner, the company. A third way is also made possible by the laws of each of our three jurisdictions: have one entity "merge" (disappear, be absorbed) into the other or have both entities "merge" into a third entity, in each case by operation of law through a filing with the state, not unlike the way a new corporation is established. This is why we speak of "mergers" and "acquisitions" in the same context – because they are different roads to transferring assets to new control.

Mergers and acquisitions have rightly been described as "among the most complex of business transactions."[1] When working on the legal or business side of a merger or acquisition, the facts of the transaction will loom large and individual details will tend to eclipse an overall understanding (particularly for someone at a junior level of a legal team, who may see only parts of a deal). It is therefore useful first to understand the

---

[1]   Allen and Kraakman (2003: 423).

transaction as a matrix of simple, legal components. Each simple structure and tool has a specific function and can be applied alone or in combination with others to address specific needs. A solid understanding
of these basic components and how they work together should help to
untangle some of the complexity behind these transactions.

The structures and tools actually used in an acquisition will be determined by what is legally possible, by the desire to limit various forms of
risk, and by cost – which can take the form of taxes, professional fees or
opportunity costs, among other things. This chapter will divide such
mechanisms into two groups: structures for transactions and deal protection tools. The basic transaction structures are purchases of assets, purchases of shares, and statutory mergers. The basic deal protection tools
are confidentiality agreements and various types of contracts that require
the party in breach to compensate the innocent party for breaking exclusivity or walking away from the deal.

Although, as mentioned above, the uniform nature of the corporation
leads to substantial uniformity in transaction structures employed, divergence in law can change not only the details of a given arrangement, but
also the possibility of having a cross-border transaction recognized by foreign law. This problem has been addressed on a number of fronts in the EU,
as will be readily apparent from the decision in *SEVIC Systems*, reprinted
in part in this chapter, and in the Cross Border Mergers Directive.

II.   Basic structures for transferring control of corporate assets

The best route for an acquisition will depend on a number of economic and
legal variables. The foremost determinant will be the goal of the acquisition. If a buyer wants to acquire only one valuable asset from a failing corporation, it would probably make no sense to purchase the entire company,
unless the asset in question could only be acquired in this way, such as
taking over a significant loss for tax purposes. Other business factors will
also be very important, such as whether the purchaser intends to acquire
a new technology, create synergies, integrate vertically or horizontally, or
increase the scale of its production.[2] On the other hand, a purchaser may
be "deal-driven": he may simply want to acquire an undervalued target,
improve it, and resell it for a profit.[3] The boundaries of the law will then

---

[2] For a general discussion of the business motives for a merger or acquisition, see Brealey,
Myers and Allen (2006: 871 *et seq.*).
[3] Reed, Lajoux and Nesvold (2007: 9 *et seq.*).

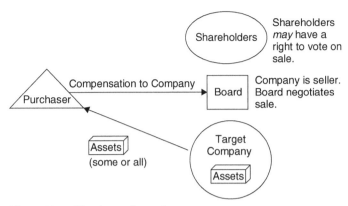

Figure 21.1   Simple purchase of assets

determine what is possible in designing an acquisition structure. This law may be the corporate statute, which may permit only certain structural options. In this regard, the state of incorporation or territorial location of the management of the acquiring and acquired companies' centers of administration will also be decisive: the laws of the relevant jurisdictions may conflict or may even prohibit "mixed" mergers, and the diversity of jurisdictions may trigger the applicability of a supranational law, such as that of the EU. All the other laws that could apply to a business can also play a role, such as environmental law or tort law (products liability), but among these tax law and, for larger companies, antitrust (or competition) law stand out as of particular importance in planning a merger. Because an acquisition involves a transfer of assets or stock, tax law will inevitably play a very important role. Because a merger combines business entities, most jurisdictions monitor the antitrust (or competition) law aspects of such transactions.

A.   Purchase of assets

One essential characteristic of a corporation is separate legal personality. Although shareholders own the corporation, the corporation itself owns its assets. As a result, the corporation may sell any or all of those assets, subject to any shareholder rights to approve or veto the transaction and subject to any applicable capital maintenance rules. A schematic of a simple purchase of assets is shown in Figure 21.1.

A purchase of assets allows selected items – such as a piece of land, a technology or a business division – to be carved out of the overall going concern and sold separately. The consideration for the purchase need not be cash, but may be anything of value that the parties agree to exchange and is permitted by law, principle among which are shares of the acquirer's stock. Asset deals have advantages for tax treatment, the ability to select items purchased, and the ability to exclude liability.

Under most accounting principles, an asset purchase will raise the book value of the asset from the price at which the seller held it to the purchase price, and will thus give the buyer a higher tax basis – which could lower tax liability in the future. In this way, however, it would also be likely to create an immediate tax liability for the seller (which may be at a rate higher than that applicable to capital gains on a sale of stock).

A purchase of assets allows a buyer to obtain specific, valuable assets while avoiding other, less attractive parts of the company (such as purchasing a profitable oil facility from a multinational company while avoiding dry oil fields). This makes it useful for extracting that part of a conglomerate's business which has the best future outlook. It also allows the buyer to leave the liabilities of the company itself (e.g. environmental liability from an oil spill) with the seller. As discussed below, a merger results in the purchaser acquiring both the assets and the liabilities of the target.

The principal disadvantage of an asset purchase is the probability of high transaction costs. Asset sales require enforceable sales contracts for each asset or an enforceable sale of a collection of assets that can be allocated to a specific branch of the concern, as well as the fulfillment of any applicable rules for conveying title to the particular assets. Drafting individual contracts for each of numerous individual assets is expensive and both the risk of error in meeting the individual conveyance rules and meeting special form requirements (i.e. notarized deeds) and taxes add further expense. Moreover, the transfer of ownership in contractual assets, such as a favorable credit, lease or supply contract, may well require the consent of the obligated counterparty, which could well open the door to a renegotiation of its terms upon transfer.

Moreover, many of the advantages mentioned above can be negated by special statutory rules. For example, asset sales can help a selling company in financial difficulty raise funds for operations. However, if such a sale were made at a favorable price for the buyer, it could also risk being voided as a fraudulent conveyance if the company later enters bankruptcy. An asset purchase is used to avoid taking on unwanted liabilities, but in some jurisdictions liability will follow the assets by operation of special legislation designed to protect consumers, tort victims and employees. Although purchasers can limit such exposure to liability by conducting

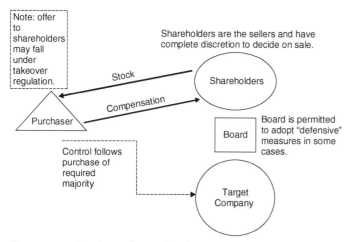

Figure 21.2 Simple purchase of stock

the purchase through a subsidiary, the asset purchase would then have few (non-tax) advantages over the other structural options, as discussed below, which use a subsidiary to shield against liability.

B. Purchase of stock

Whilst corporations own their assets, the corporation itself is owned by the stockholders. As a result, another way to acquire control of a corporation's assets is to acquire control of the corporation itself through a purchase of stock. A schematic of a simple purchase of stock is shown in Figure 21.2.

Compared to the purchase of each individual asset of a corporation, a purchase of stock is very simple. The more numerous and complex the assets to be purchased and the fewer the shareholders controlling the company's stock, the greater are the transactional savings achieved through a share deal. A large number of dispersed shareholders could force the buyer to make a public offer for the shares, which would increase legal costs, and create notice and disclosure requirements connected with making a public offering under the applicable takeover legislation (these rules are discussed in Chapter 24). Moreover, if securities of the purchaser rather than cash are used as the consideration for the purchase, the transaction might well be regulated not only as a takeover offer, but also as a public offering of stock.

The tax effect of a share deal, depending on the rules in a given jurisdiction, could well be to postpone the taxable event in relation to the assets because the basis in the assets as held by the seller would be carried forward in the company as owned by the buyer. The seller might well be taxed on capital gains (the difference between the historical cost of the stock and the sale price) rather than on ordinary income derived from the sale of the assets.

The primary disadvantage of a stock purchase can be that the buyer receives the entire company, with all of its actual and contingent liabilities and unfavorable contracts. Although the liabilities of the company will remain limited to the company except in the extraordinary case of a veil piercing, it can still result in unattractive components of the company off-setting the value of those components the purchaser seeks to acquire. Of course, such "unattractive" parts of the target, as well as its known liabilities, would be factored into the purchase price. The buyer can then seek protection against undisclosed liabilities through warranties in the stock purchase agreement, which would shift the costs of any such liabilities back to the seller.

Another problem could arise from contractual clauses triggering termination or renegotiation of valuable contacts upon a change of control of the company. This would bring back a disadvantage of an asset deal, namely, having to revisit and perhaps lose contractual arrangements that are currently favorable to the target.

In an asset purchase, the assets would be pooled with those already owned by the purchaser. In a stock purchase, the purchaser would own a company as a subsidiary. Although retaining the separate company could reduce the risks of hidden liabilities, the additional management costs of owning a separate subsidiary, such as a second set of managers and their compliance with all corporate formalities, could be substantial. A follow-up merger would be one way to eliminate such administration costs.

C.   Statutory merger

Each of our jurisdictions provide for what in American English is called a "statutory merger." These transactions are referred to as "statutory" because their consequences are expressly provided for in the statute, and take effect upon a filing with the official register – analogous to the incorporation process. An act is said to occur "by operation of law" rather than by a privately drafted contract or other action of the parties when certain events trigger the results provided for in the law. For example, German law provides that, upon registration of the merger in the commercial register, "the assets of the transferring entity, including its liabilities, are transferred to the acquiring entity," and "the transferring entity

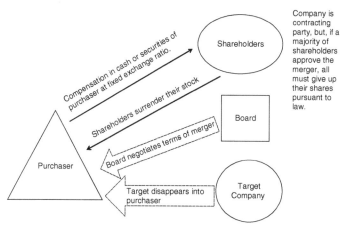

Figure 21.3 Simple statutory merger

is extinguished" without any further action.[4] From this it may be seen that a merger is a creature of law designed to achieve desired economic and legal results. A schematic of a simple statutory merger is shown in Figure 21.3.

The type of merger shown in Figure 21.3 is referred to in UK law as a "merger by absorption." In this transaction (generally speaking, without referring to a specific national law), the purchaser and the target would each agree in their general meetings to merge, upon an exchange of cash or securities at an agreed exchange ratio, with any of the target's shareholders dissenting to the merger being bought out at a legally monitored appraisal price. Such a merger would also be referred to as "forward" because the acquired company disappears (or is absorbed) into the acquiring company. The transaction can also be structured as a "reverse" merger, in which the target company survives and the purchasing company is absorbed.

Like a stock purchase, a merger allows the transfer of all the target's assets without contracting for the transfer of each one, and thus brings the entire company to the purchaser. Like both stock and asset deals, a merger can also be placed on either a lower or a higher level by establishing a subsidiary or a holding company as the merger vehicle. When a merger is carried out through a subsidiary, the transaction is referred to as a "triangular" merger. In a "forward" triangular merger, the target company would disappear (or be absorbed) into the subsidiary, and

[4] See § 20(1) UmwG.

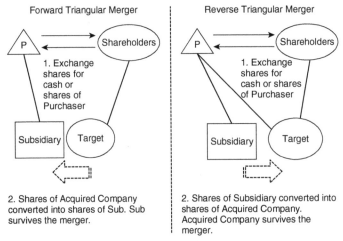

Figure 21.4   Triangular mergers

in a "reverse" triangular merger, the subsidiary would disappear into the acquired company. As the merger vehicle might well be a special purpose company without any operating assets and the parent would not want the target's shareholders coming to control it through a share exchange, the compensation for the shares of the target would ultimately come from the parent company. This could be cash or shares, perhaps contributed to the vehicle at its formation, or the result of an exchange of the vehicle's shares for the parent's following the share exchange between the vehicle and the target. A schematic of simple forward and reverse triangular mergers is shown in Figure 21.4.

The purchaser's creditors are likely to prefer this merger form because the assets of the target become assets of the surviving company and are thus available to cover their credit. From a different angle, because mergers pool the liabilities of the disappearing and surviving companies, the assets of a cash-rich target can be used to finance its own buyout, provided that the transaction does not violate the rules against either financial assistance or fraudulent conveyances discussed in Chapter 26. In the opposite scenario of a failing target, a company with high profits in a given year may decide to acquire a company with heavy losses to offset such profits and, where permitted by law, reduce its tax liability. As many of the cases included in this text demonstrate, it is typical for a merger to constitute the "back end" of a stock purchase (i.e. a bidder acquires a majority of the shares of the target and then, as its majority shareholder, merges the target into itself or a subsidiary). For this reason, it is difficult to separate the discussion in this chapter from the problems grouped under the heading "takeovers" in Chapter 24, as a stock purchase is very often a takeover, and a merger is often the second step of a takeover transaction.

III.   The transaction forms permitted by local law

A.   United States

Each of the transaction structures discussed above is available in the US. An asset sale would require a sale and purchase contract, taking the necessary steps to eliminate the transfer of liability for past actions (such as products previously produced by a transferred business division) to the purchaser or providing indemnity for any liability arising after the sale. In some US jurisdictions (but not Delaware), courts may well decide that a sale of assets followed by dissolution of the selling company should be treated as a "*de facto* merger," which would mean that the liabilities of the seller would transfer to the buyer, and the seller's stockholders would have the protections of appraisal rights.[5]

A sale of stock would merely require endorsement and delivery of the stock itself, and the registration of the buyer on the stockholder list. However, if the target company is registered with the SEC and the offer to purchase the stock were to rise to the level of a public offer (see *Hanson Trust*, reprinted in part in Chapter 24), it would be necessary for the purchaser to comply with the extensive filing, publication and substantive requirements of the Exchange Act.[6] These requirements will be discussed in some detail in Chapter 24.

Delaware corporate law expressly regulates mergers and consolidations, and provides that "any two or more entities … may merge into a single corporation, which may be any one of the constituent entities or may consolidate into a new corporation,"[7] which means that both the number of corporations involved and the role of the company that eventually survives to operate the disappearing corporations is unrestricted. This openness permits both straight and triangular transactions and

---

[5] See e.g. *Farris* v. *Glen Alden Corp.*, 143 A 2d 25 (Pa. 1958); *Hariton* v. *Arco Electronics, Inc.*, 188 A 2d 123 (1963). Individual actions (such as a purchase of assets, an assumption of liabilities and a dissolution) will be seen in Delaware as having independent legal significance rather than as "*de facto*" mergers.

[6] 15 USC § 78n(d) (2000); 17 CFR § 240.14d-1 *et seq.*

[7] DGCL § 251(a). The terminology used in the provision includes a "merger," in which one or more "constituent" corporations disappear into the "surviving" corporation, and a "consolidation," in which all the constituent corporations disappear into a newly formed, "resulting" corporation.

allows any of the entities involved – the purchaser, the target, a subsidiary or otherwise – to be the surviving entity. The type of transaction and whether the companies are registered with the SEC will determine the type of procedure and approvals necessary to complete a merger. These procedures will be discussed together with applicable fiduciary duties in the next chapter of this text.

Like incorporation itself, a statutory merger enters into effect when the approved merger agreement or a certificate of merger is filed with the secretary of state.[8]

B.   Germany

Asset sales are common under German law, and present only a couple of unique features. First, all sales transactions under German law have a bi-level property and contract law structure somewhat similar to what persons from a Common Law background see in transfers of real property (contract plus conveyance). A sale of assets under German law would require a "contractual" agreement governed by contract law (*Verpflichtungsgeschäft*) and a "property transfer" agreement governed by property law (*Verfügungsgeschäft*), which means that each sales transaction must meet legal requirements on both of these levels. Secondly, the strong labor law of Germany means that usually labor contracts will stay in place when assets constituting the means of production that employs the relevant laborers are transferred.[9] The laborers have a right to stay with their factory. Thirdly, German law contains additional, special rules for the transfer of all or part of a company's assets to particular types of entities, such as the state or a municipality.[10] This can significantly reduce transaction costs.

Share purchases are also common in Germany, although, if the target is listed, they run the same risk as under US law that they will be characterized as "public purchase or exchange offers" and trigger the disclosure, publication and pricing rules under the WpÜG.[11] Given the frequency of large blockholders in the German economy, however, private negotiations with a limited number of sellers would be possible more often than in the US.

As in Delaware, German law expressly provides for both mergers (*Verschmelzung durch Aufnahme*) and consolidations (*Verschmelzung durch Neugründung*), but does so by means of a specially designed statute,

---

[8] § 251(c) DGCL.   [9] § 613a BGB.
[10] §§ 174 *et seq.* UmwG.   [11] § 2(1) WpÜG.

the Transformation (or Reorganization) Act (*Umwandlungsgesetz* or UmwG).[12] As we have seen in other contexts and now also for mergers, German law is not quite as flexible as the law of Delaware. The types of mergers and consolidations provided for in the UmwG constitute an exclusive *numerus clausus*, although it is argued by scholars that the provisions should allow closely similar, analogical transactions.[13] Also, the consideration provided for in a merger or consolidation under German law is generally limited to an exchange of shares,[14] rather than being opened up to any property, which means that mergers cannot be used in Germany to cash out minority shareholders of the target against their will.

A statutory merger enters into effect – transferring all assets and liabilities to the surviving or new company and dissolving the disappearing company or companies – with the entry of the merger resolution in the commercial register.[15]

C.   United Kingdom

Asset purchases and stock sales are available under UK law, and present generally the same advantages and disadvantages discussed above for US and German law.

The Companies Act 2006 provides for both mergers (referred to as "mergers by absorption") and consolidations (referred to as "mergers by formation of a new company").[16] This Act presents many rules that were set out in Schedule 15B to its predecessor, the Companies Act 1985. The current rules – particularly the procedure and approvals required, which will be discussed in the following chapter – closely track the Third Company Law Directive and thus also resemble German law to a significant extent. In this way, UK law has shifted from its traditionally open-ended "scheme of arrangement" process that could not be achieved without close judicial supervision to a menu of statutory options for mergers, and thus from court monitoring to an enabling statute with increased party autonomy. As in the other jurisdictions, merger resolutions must be filed with the companies registrar.[17]

---

[12] § 2 UmwG.   [13] Kübler and Assmann (2006: 402).
[14] §§ 5(1) no. 3, 20(1) no. 3 UmwG; for exceptions, see § 29(1) UmwG.
[15] § 20 UmwG. Pursuant to § 19(1) UmwG, the disappearing companies must file their resolutions with the registrars at the location of their headquarters before the surviving company may do so.
[16] Sec. 904(1) CA 2006.   [17] Secs. 907(1), 30(1) CA 2006.

IV.   Cross-border merger structures

A.   United States

Delaware law permits a Delaware corporation to merge or consolidate with a non-US corporation if the law of such other jurisdiction permits such a merger.[18] However, in addition to the expected filing requirements with the Delaware secretary of state, the law also sets out an extensive list of requirements as to the merger or consolidation that will require any foreign corporation participating in the transaction to effectively comply both with its home law and with Delaware law in undertaking the merger or consolidation. This situation sheds light on why the EU has adopted specific sets of norms for similar types of transactions.

If a merger involves a foreign company listed on a US exchange, or a public use of foreign shares as a currency in the offering, the relevant SEC rules will also apply. If a foreign purchaser were interested in acquiring a Delaware company, it would be common practice for it to use a domestic acquisition or holding vehicle. For example, in the facts of *Kahn* v. *Lynch Communication Systems*, reprinted in part in Chapter 19, we see that the French company, Alcatel SA, uses Alcatel USA Corporation to conduct its US operations, including an attempted acquisition of Lynch.

B.   European Union

Given the limited size of individual European markets, cross-border transactions in the EU, far from being exotic, are economically vital to European competitiveness and a prime reason for the EU's internal market program, which it launched in 1987. Even decades later, however, significant obstacles continued to hamper cross-border transactions, as we saw in the *Überseering* case, where the purchase of a Dutch company's shares by German citizens turned a legitimate Dutch NV into an illegitimate German corporation under German law. A similar problem arose in *SEVIC Systems AG*, reprinted in part below. What aspect(s) of the UmwG led to the problems discussed in that case?

To date, the European Union has offered three, not necessarily coordinated, techniques to facilitate cross-border mergers. In 2001, the European Council offered a supranational, statutory form that can be employed by any EU national who follows the procedures dictated for establishing a *Societas Europaea*. In October 2005, the Parliament and the Council enacted the Cross Border Mergers Directive, which is essentially a set of

---

[18]   DGCL § 252(a).

procedures for such transactions, essentially repeating the Third Company Law Directive on an international basis. Then, in December 2005, the ECJ declared that national restrictions on mergers between companies of different member states burden the right of establishment and are invalid unless justified. In this way, Europeans have been given an EU statutory form, an approved procedure to merge national forms, and a simple permission to use national law across borders. Which structure/tool do you prefer for your clients? Do the three options complement each other?

The Cross Border Merger Directive applies to mergers between companies "formed in accordance with the law of a Member State and having their registered office, central administration or principal place of business within the Community, provided at least two of them are governed by the laws of different Member States."[19] It is designed to facilitate such cross-border mergers "if the national law of the relevant Member States permits mergers between such types of company."[20] The governance rules of the Directive will be discussed in the next chapter, and here it is useful to note that the Directive contains some flexibility on the consideration that may be paid: it provides that the compensation paid for the target's shares may include a cash payment exceeding 10 percent of the surviving company's share capital if one of the national laws so provides.[21] It also makes the full effectiveness of a cross-border merger very clear by providing a list of specific consequences that result from such a merger duly executed, including:

- all the assets and liabilities of each company being acquired or merging shall be transferred to the acquiring or new company;
- the members of each company being acquired or merging shall become members of the acquiring or new company;
- the members of the merging companies shall become members of the new company; and
- each company being acquired or merging shall cease to exist.[22]

The SE Regulation goes beyond procedure by providing a substantive corporate form. Article 2 of the Regulation states that a supranational SE may be created by merging two or more EU companies, provided that at least two are governed by the law of different member states.[23] The regime for employee participation in the entity, which given the great differences between the United Kingdom (no representation) and Germany (great representation) is always a difficult issue in EU company law, is governed

---

[19] Art. 1 Cross Border Merger Directive.   [20] Recital 2 Cross Border Merger Directive.
[21] Art. 3(1) Cross Border Merger Directive.   [22] Art. 14 Cross Border Merger Directive.
[23] Art. 2(1) SE Regulation.

by the related SE Directive. According to the latter, if a special negotiating body for the participating companies fails to agree on an employee participation scheme, the default scheme is the highest level of employee participation found in any of the merging companies,[24] so that, if a German company is one of the merging corporations, the resulting SE will have full co-determination unless the negotiations produce a different result. As the Regulation makes no reference to the type of consideration (shares or cash) used, this will be governed by national law under the Third Company Law Directive. The SE has proved to be a popular vehicle in conducting cross-border mergers in the EU.[25]

The SE comes into existence and the merger takes effect upon registration in the companies register of the country where the SE will have its registered office.[26] The effects of the merger are expressly provided for, including the transfer of all assets and liabilities to the acquiring or new SE, the existing shareholders becoming shareholders of the acquiring or new SE, and the participating national companies ceasing to exist.[27] If you were going to undertake a cross-border consolidation in Europe, would you prefer to create an SE, use the procedural rules under the Cross Border Directive, or simply rely on national law under protection of *SEVIC*?

V. Tools to protect the deal

Merging two large companies is a very difficult and very complex undertaking, which can entail enormous risk. The process is made even more difficult by the presence of competitive pressures to find a better partner and the desires of competitors to break into and perhaps usurp the transaction. The expression "stalking horse" is often used to refer to a company that investigates a transaction opportunity only to lose it to a more aggressive competitor. This term goes back to a hunting technique by which hunters would stalk their prey walking next to a horse in order to approach the prey more closely before shooting because the prey was not frightened of the horse. In a merger transaction, a "stalking horse" incurs the transaction costs entailed in investigating the target's value and negotiating with its board, including the costs of bringing such board

---

[24] Art. 7(1)(b), in connection with Annex, Part 3(b), SE Directive.

[25] Eidenmüller, Engert and Hornuf (2009: 18) point out that, in each of the years 2005, 2006 and 2007, the number of SEs incorporated rose from twenty-one to forty and again to eighty-five, and predicted that incorporations would continue to grow at a similar rate in 2008. Bachmann, Baums, Habersack *et al.* (2009: 885) point out that large, German AGs are reorganizing as SEs in a bid to reduce the level of co-determination.

[26] Arts. 27 and 12(1) SE Regulation.   [27] Art. 29 SE Regulation.

to consider a deal in the first place. Once the terrain has been so prepared, a competitor can simply step in, riding free on these initial costs, and use its savings to offer a slightly higher acquisition price, thus both seizing the prize and mauling the stalking horse.

To avoid losing a transaction in this way, clients ask their lawyers to protect inchoate deals with the tools of their trade: structuring enforceable rights and duties, preferably connected to effective penalties, in order to increase the probability of favorable comportment and reduce the risk of losing the transaction. A few of these techniques are discussed in *Paramount* v. *QVC* and *John Crowther Group*, both reprinted in part in this chapter. Another way to protect a deal is simply through speed. The less time a transaction takes, the less that can intervene to disrupt it, including market changes and the appearance of competitors. This can explain why M&A lawyers often miss holidays with family!

The following paragraphs set out a general list of deal protection tools that might be used in a letter of intent or merger agreement.

A. Confidentiality agreement

For many reasons, confidentiality will be demanded regarding both the negotiated deal until it is publicly announced, and on a permanent basis regarding information disclosed in the process of negotiations and any due diligence investigation. As we saw in *Basic* v. *Levinson* (see Chapter 20), the disclosure of merger negotiations can have a material effect on the participant companies' share prices; such negotiations should, therefore, be kept confidential until management can be sure that the deal is likely to be consummated. Moreover, the "stalking horse" price-creation function is effective only when the market is aware of what is taking place. If a deal between unlisted companies is kept completely confidential among insiders, there is very little chance of a competitor breaking it up.

A different level of confidentiality regards the information learned in a due diligence investigation. Such investigations delve into the value of every asset and liability the company has, including historical aspects that even public companies need not disclose annually or currently pursuant to law. Its results must be kept confidential. If a law firm were to use or release the information found in a major due diligence investigation, the impact on its reputation would be significant.

For these reasons, deal participants will include a confidentiality clause in any letter of intent, prohibiting discussion of the negotiations and would certainly sign a wide-ranging confidentiality agreement before allowing any due diligence investigation to begin.

B.   Duty of good faith negotiations

A letter of intent is meant only to set a framework for negotiations leading to a definitive merger agreement. Because it is not designed to be binding as to the substantive terms of the deal, some parties may decide simply to walk away from the deal after signing the letter and refuse to look seriously at entering into a definitive agreement. To avoid this possibility, unless the duty of good faith negotiations exists in the jurisdiction's contract law, a binding obligation to conduct good faith negotiations for the purpose of concluding a definitive merger agreement can give the parties both the freedom and the security they need.

C.   No-talk and no-shop agreements

An agreement not to conduct negotiations with a competitor can prohibit all contact with competitors (no-talk) or only actively sought contact (no-shop). We see clauses of this type in both *Paramount* and *John Crowther*. Sample no-shop wording from a leading text on mergers and acquisitions runs as follows:

> After executing this letter and until _____ , the [Target] agrees, and shall use its best efforts to cause its officers, directors, employees, agents and stockholders, not to solicit or encourage, directly or indirectly, in any manner any discussion with, or furnish or cause to be furnished any information to, any person other than Purchaser in connection with, or negotiate for or otherwise pursue, the sale of the Stock of the [Target] or the capital stock of its subsidiaries, all or substantially all of the assets of the [Target] or its subsidiaries or any portion or all of its business or that of its subsidiaries, or any business combination or merger of the [Target] or its subsidiaries with any other party. You shall promptly inform Purchaser of any inquiries or proposals with respect to the foregoing.[28]

D.   Termination fee

In *Paramount*, the merger agreement contained termination fees. As discussed above, because negotiations moving toward a merger are very expensive in terms not only of professional fees and the time and attention of management, but also the participants' reputations, and because good faith compliance with confidentiality and no-shop commitments could cause a party to the agreement to lose other opportunities, a termination fee can be used to compensate a party for the other's bad faith exit from the deal. The type of termination fee provision used in *Paramount* was

---

[28]   Reed, Lajoux and Nesvold (2007: 515).

triggered by: (a) a party terminating the agreement because of a competing transaction, (b) a party's stockholders not approving the merger, or (c) a party's board recommending a competing transaction to its stockholders. Some termination fee provisions are legal and others are not. What aspects did the Delaware court examine as important? What other aspects could make a fee reasonable or unreasonable?

E. Fiduciary out clause

The contract laws of most jurisdictions allow contracts to be terminated without penalty in certain circumstances. Examples are when a contract becomes illegal between its conclusion and its performance or performance becomes impossible. As circumstances change in the environment of a planned merger, such as with the entrance of an uninvited, higher-bidding buyer, management may be required by its fiduciary duties to recommend such buyer to its shareholders. Yet, if a no-shop agreement expressly forbids recommending a different party, and attaches a termination fee to such recommendation, a director can find himself caught between breaching a fiduciary duty, on the one hand, and breaching a contract that triggers a termination fee, on the other.

The *John Crowther Group* decision discusses the relationship of contractual and fiduciary duties when management enters into a merger. Should contracts that boards enter into expressly provide that they will not be enforceable in the event that they breach the board's fiduciary duty? Should this be tacitly assumed by all parties? A "fiduciary out" clause is designed to allow management to escape its obligation under a no-shop or other exclusivity agreement when fiduciary duties so demand. This is not a "deal protection device" in that it protects the deal from competitors, but it does protect deals from creating situations that force management to violate corporate fiduciary duties. Should simply submitting a deal to a shareholder vote after the board has withdrawn its recommendation be considered a breach of fiduciary duty?

Questions for discussion

1. What are the different techniques of acquiring a corporation?
2. Who are the parties to a share deal? How do the shareholders of the acquiring corporation participate in the transaction?
3. What are the features of a statutory merger?
4. What is the difference between a forward and a reverse merger?
5. What is a (forward or reverse) triangular merger?

6. Name some advantages and disadvantages of a statutory merger, a purchase of shares and an acquisition of assets as means to effect a corporate combination.
7. How does the Cross Border Merger Directive facilitate mergers in the EU?
8. How would you characterize the type of merger required to form an SE?

Cases

SEVIC Systems AG
European Court of Justice
Case C-411/03
[*Text edited; footnotes omitted*]

Judgment

1. The reference for a preliminary ruling concerns the interpretation of Articles 43 EC and 48 EC.

2. The reference is made in the context of an action brought by SEVIC Systems AG ('SEVIC'), a company established in Neuwied (Germany), against a decision of the Amtsgericht Neuwied rejecting its application for registration in the national commercial register of the merger between itself and Security Vision Concept SA ('Security Vision'), a company established in Luxembourg, on the ground that the German law on company transformations provides only for mergers between companies established in Germany.

Legal context

3. Paragraph 1 of the German Law on transforming companies (*Umwandlungsgesetz*), of 28 October 1994 (BGBl. 1994 I, p. 3210), as amended in 1995 and subsequently ('the UmwG'), headed 'Types of transformation, statutory restrictions', provides:

> 1. (1) Legal entities established in Germany may be transformed
>
> 1. by merger;
> 2. by demerger ...;
> 3. by transfer of assets;
> 4. by change of legal form.
>
> (2) Apart from the cases governed by this law, transformation within the meaning of subparagraph (1) is possible only if express provision is made for it by another federal law, or by a law of a Land.
>
> (3) Derogations from the provisions of this law are possible only if expressly authorised. Supplementary provisions appearing in contracts, memoranda and articles of association or statements of intention are permitted, save where this law makes exhaustive provision.'

4. Paragraph 2 of the UmwG, headed 'Types of merger', provides:

Legal entities may merge by dissolution without liquidation

1. by way of absorption through the transfer of all the assets of one or more legal entities (the absorbed entities) to another existing legal entity (the absorbing entity) or

2. ... by the allocation of shares ... in the absorbing entity or the new entity to the shareholders ... of the absorbed entity.

[*Text omitted*]

The dispute in the main proceedings and the question referred for a preliminary ruling

6. The merger contract concluded in 2002 between SEVIC and Security Vision provided for the dissolution without liquidation of the latter company and the transfer of the whole of its assets to SEVIC, without any change in the latter's company name.

[*Text omitted*]

11. SEVIC has applied for registration in the commercial register, in accordance with the UmwG, of the merger with Security Vision, the relevant contract providing for the absorption of the latter company and its dissolution without liquidation.

12. That application was rejected by the Amtsgericht Neuwied on the ground that, in Paragraph 1(1)(1), the UmwG provides that only legal entities established in national territory may be the subject of transformation by merger ('internal mergers') and that, therefore, that law does not apply to transformations resulting from cross-border mergers.

13. In Germany, there are no general rules, analogous to those laid down by that law, which apply to cross-border mergers.

14. There is therefore a difference in treatment in Germany between internal and cross-border mergers.

15. In those circumstances, the question referred by the national court should be understood as asking essentially whether Articles 43 EC and 48 EC preclude registration in the national commercial register of the merger by dissolution without liquidation of one company and transfer of the whole of its assets to another company from being refused in general in a Member State where one of the two companies is established in another Member State, whereas such registration is possible, on compliance with certain conditions, where the two companies participating in the merger are both established in the territory of the first Member State.

Applicability of Articles 43 EC and 48 EC

16. Contrary to the arguments of the German and Netherlands Governments, Articles 43 EC and 48 EC apply to a merger situation such as that at issue in the main proceedings.

17. In accordance with the second paragraph of Article 43 EC, read in conjunction with Article 48 EC, the freedom of establishment for companies referred to in that latter article includes in particular the formation and management of those companies under the conditions defined by the legislation of the State of establishment for its own companies.

18. As the Advocate General points out in point 30 of his Opinion, the right of establishment covers all measures which permit or even merely facilitate access to another Member State and the pursuit of an economic activity in that State by allowing the persons concerned to participate in the economic life of the country effectively and under the same conditions as national operators.

19. Cross-border merger operations, like other company transformation operations, respond to the needs for cooperation and consolidation between companies established in different Member States. They constitute particular methods of exercise of the freedom of establishment, important for the proper functioning of the internal market, and are therefore amongst those economic activities in respect of which Member States are required to comply with the freedom of establishment laid down by Article 43 EC

The existence of a restriction on the freedom of establishment

20. In this regard, it is sufficient to note that in German law, unlike what exists for internal mergers, there is no provision for registration in the commercial register of cross-border mergers, and that, therefore, applications for the registration of such mergers are generally refused.

21. As the Advocate General has pointed out in point 47 of his Opinion, a merger such as that at issue in the main proceedings constitutes an effective means of transforming companies in that it makes it possible, within the framework of a single operation, to pursue a particular activity in new forms and without interruption, thereby reducing the complications, times and costs associated with other forms of company consolidation such as those which entail, for example, the dissolution of a company with liquidation of assets and the subsequent formation of a new company with the transfer of assets to the latter.

22. In so far as, under national rules, recourse to such a means of company transformation is not possible where one of the companies is established in a Member State other than the Federal Republic of Germany, German law establishes a difference in treatment between companies according to the internal or cross-border nature of the merger, which is likely to deter the exercise of the freedom of establishment laid down by the Treaty.

23. Such a difference in treatment constitutes a restriction within the meaning of Articles 43 EC and 48 EC, which is contrary to the right of establishment and can be permitted only if it pursues a legitimate objective compatible with the Treaty and is justified by imperative reasons in the public interest. It is further necessary, in such

a case, that its application must be appropriate to ensuring the attainment of the objective thus pursued and must not go beyond what is necessary to attain it ...

Possible justification for the restriction

24. The German and Netherlands Governments argue that internal mergers are subject to conditions more particularly designed to protect the interests of creditors, minority shareholders and employees, and to preserve the effectiveness of fiscal supervision and the fairness of commercial transactions ...

25. In that context, the Netherlands Government points out that the Commission of the European Communities submitted to the Community legislature on 18 November 2003 the Proposal for a Directive of the European Parliament and of the Council on cross-border mergers ...

[Text omitted]

26. It should be noted in that respect that, whilst Community harmonisation rules are useful for facilitating cross-border mergers, the existence of such harmonisation rules cannot be made a precondition for the implementation of the freedom of establishment ...

28. ... it is not possible to exclude the possibility that imperative reasons in the public interest such as protection of the interests of creditors, minority shareholders and employees ... and the preservation of the effectiveness of fiscal supervision and the fairness of commercial transactions ... may, in certain circumstances and under certain conditions, justify a measure restricting the freedom of establishment.

29. But such a restrictive measure would also have to be appropriate for ensuring the attainment of the objectives pursued and not go beyond what is necessary to attain them.

30. To refuse generally, in a Member State, to register in the commercial register a merger between a company established in that State and one established in another Member State has the result of preventing the realisation of cross-border mergers even if the interests mentioned in paragraph 28 of this judgment are not threatened. In any event, such a rule goes beyond what is necessary to protect those interests.

[Text omitted]

Paramount Communications Inc. v. QVC Networks Inc.
Supreme Court of Delaware
637 A 2d 34 (1994)
[Text edited; some footnotes omitted]

OPINION BY: VEASEY, Chief Justice

[Text omitted]
I.   Facts

... Paramount is a Delaware corporation with its principal offices in New York City. Approximately 118 million shares of Paramount's common stock are outstanding and traded on the New York Stock Exchange ...

Viacom is a Delaware corporation with its headquarters in Massachusetts. Viacom is controlled by Sumner M. Redstone ("Redstone"), its Chairman and Chief Executive Officer, who owns indirectly approximately 85.2% of Viacom's voting Class A stock and approximately 69.2% of Viacom's nonvoting Class B stock through National Amusements, Inc. ("NAI"), an entity 91.7% owned by Redstone. Viacom has a wide range of entertainment operations, including a number of well-known cable television channels such as MTV, Nickelodeon, Showtime, and The Movie Channel. Viacom's equity co-investors in the Paramount-Viacom transaction include NYNEX Corporation and Blockbuster Entertainment Corporation.

QVC is a Delaware corporation with its headquarters in West Chester, Pennsylvania. QVC has several large stockholders, including Liberty Media Corporation, Comcast Corporation, Advance Publications, Inc., and Cox Enterprises Inc. Barry Diller ("Diller"), the Chairman and Chief Executive Officer of QVC, is also a substantial stockholder. QVC sells a variety of merchandise through a televised shopping channel. QVC has several equity co-investors in its proposed combination with Paramount including BellSouth Corporation and Comcast Corporation.

Beginning in the late 1980s, Paramount investigated the possibility of acquiring or merging with other companies in the entertainment, media, or communications industry. Paramount considered such transactions to be desirable, and perhaps necessary, in order to keep pace with competitors in the rapidly evolving field of entertainment and communications ...

Although Paramount had considered a possible combination of Paramount and Viacom as early as 1990, recent efforts to explore such a transaction began at a dinner meeting between Redstone and [Martin S.] Davis [Paramount's Chairman and CEO] on April 20, 1993. Robert Greenhill ("Greenhill"), Chairman of Smith Barney Shearson Inc. ("Smith Barney"), attended and helped facilitate this meeting. After several more meetings between Redstone and Davis, serious negotiations began taking place in early July.

It was tentatively agreed that Davis would be the chief executive officer and Redstone would be the controlling stockholder of the combined company, but the parties could not reach agreement on the merger price and the terms of a stock option to be granted to Viacom. With respect to price, Viacom offered a package of cash and stock (primarily Viacom Class B nonvoting stock) with a market value of approximately $61 per share, but Paramount wanted at least $70 per share.

... On August 20, 1993, discussions between Paramount and Viacom resumed when Greenhill arranged another meeting between Davis and Redstone. After a short hiatus, the parties negotiated in earnest in early September, and performed due diligence with the assistance of their financial advisors, Lazard Freres & Co. ("Lazard") for Paramount and Smith Barney for Viacom. On September 9, 1993, the Paramount Board was informed about the status of the negotiations and was provided information by Lazard, including an analysis of the proposed transaction.

On September 12, 1993, the Paramount Board met again and unanimously approved the Original Merger Agreement whereby Paramount would merge with and into Viacom. The terms of the merger provided that each share of Paramount common stock would be converted into 0.10 shares of Viacom Class A voting stock, 0.90 shares of Viacom Class B nonvoting stock, and $9.10 in cash ... The Original Merger Agreement also contained several provisions designed to make it more difficult for a potential competing bid to succeed. We focus, as did the Court of Chancery, on three of these defensive provisions: a "no-shop" provision (the "No-Shop Provision"), the Termination Fee, and the Stock Option Agreement.

First, under the No-Shop Provision, the Paramount Board agreed that Paramount would not solicit, encourage, discuss, negotiate, or endorse any competing transaction unless: (a) a third party "makes an unsolicited written, bona fide proposal, which is not subject to any material contingencies relating to financing"; and (b) the Paramount Board determines that discussions or negotiations with the third party are necessary for the Paramount Board to comply with its fiduciary duties.

Second, under the Termination Fee provision, Viacom would receive a $100 million termination fee if: (a) Paramount terminated the Original Merger Agreement because of a competing transaction; (b) Paramount's stockholders did not approve the merger; or (c) the Paramount Board recommended a competing transaction.

The third and most significant deterrent device was the Stock Option Agreement, which granted to Viacom an option to purchase approximately 19.9% (23,699,000 shares) of Paramount's outstanding common stock at $69.14 per share if any of the triggering events for the Termination Fee occurred. In addition to the customary terms that are normally associated with a stock option, the Stock Option Agreement contained two provisions that were both unusual and highly beneficial to Viacom: (a) Viacom was permitted to pay for the shares with a senior subordinated note of questionable marketability instead of cash, thereby avoiding the need to raise the $1.6 billion purchase price (the "Note Feature"); and (b) Viacom could elect to require Paramount to pay Viacom in cash a sum equal to the difference between the purchase price and the market price of Paramount's stock (the "Put Feature"). Because the Stock Option Agreement was not "capped" to limit its maximum dollar value, it had the potential to reach (and in this case did reach) unreasonable levels.

After the execution of the Original Merger Agreement and the Stock Option Agreement on September 12, 1993, Paramount and Viacom announced their proposed merger. In a number of public statements, the parties indicated that the pending transaction was a virtual certainty. Redstone described it as a "marriage" that would "never be torn asunder" and stated that only a "nuclear attack" could break the deal. Redstone also called Diller and John Malone of Tele-Communications Inc., a major stockholder of QVC, to dissuade them from making a competing bid.

Despite these attempts to discourage a competing bid, Diller sent a letter to Davis on September 20, 1993, proposing a merger in which QVC would acquire

Paramount for approximately $80 per share, consisting of 0.893 shares of QVC common stock and $30 in cash. QVC also expressed its eagerness to meet with Paramount to negotiate the details of a transaction. When the Paramount Board met on September 27, it was advised by Davis that the Original Merger Agreement prohibited Paramount from having discussions with QVC (or anyone else) unless certain conditions were satisfied. In particular, QVC had to supply evidence that its proposal was not subject to financing contingencies. The Paramount Board was also provided information from Lazard describing QVC and its proposal.

On October 5, 1993, QVC provided Paramount with evidence of QVC's financing. The Paramount Board then held another meeting on October 11, and decided to authorize management to meet with QVC. Davis also informed the Paramount Board that Booz-Allen & Hamilton ("Booz-Allen"), a management consulting firm, had been retained to assess, *inter alia*, the incremental earnings potential from a Paramount-Viacom merger and a Paramount-QVC merger. Discussions proceeded slowly, however, due to a delay in Paramount signing a confidentiality agreement. In response to Paramount's request for information, QVC provided two binders of documents to Paramount on October 20.

On October 21, 1993, QVC filed this action and publicly announced an $80 cash tender offer for 51% of Paramount's outstanding shares (the "QVC tender offer") ...

... Within hours after QVC's tender offer was announced, Viacom entered into discussions with Paramount concerning a revised transaction. These discussions led to serious negotiations concerning a comprehensive amendment to the original Paramount-Viacom transaction ...

At a special meeting on October 24, 1993, the Paramount Board approved the Amended Merger Agreement and an amendment to the Stock Option Agreement. The Amended Merger Agreement was, however, essentially the same as the Original Merger Agreement, except that it included a few new provisions. One provision related to an $80 per share cash tender offer by Viacom for 51% of Paramount's stock, and another changed the merger consideration so that each share of Paramount would be converted into 0.20408 shares of Viacom Class A voting stock, 1.08317 shares of Viacom Class B nonvoting stock, and 0.20408 shares of a new series of Viacom convertible preferred stock. The Amended Merger Agreement also added a provision giving Paramount the right not to amend its Rights Agreement [which acted as a "poison pill" to defend against acquisition of Paramount, in order] to exempt Viacom if the Paramount Board determined that such an amendment would be inconsistent with its fiduciary duties because another offer constituted a "better alternative." Finally, the Paramount Board was given the power to terminate the Amended Merger Agreement if it withdrew its recommendation of the Viacom transaction or recommended a competing transaction.

Although the Amended Merger Agreement offered more consideration to the Paramount stockholders and somewhat more flexibility to the Paramount Board than did the Original Merger Agreement, the defensive measures designed to make a competing bid more difficult were not removed or modified. In particular, there is no evidence in the record that Paramount sought to use its newly acquired leverage to eliminate or modify the No-Shop Provision, the Termination Fee, or the Stock Option Agreement when the subject of amending the Original Merger Agreement was on the table.

Viacom's tender offer commenced on October 25, 1993, and QVC's tender offer was formally launched on October 27, 1993 ...

[Text omitted]

III. Breach of fiduciary duties by Paramount board

We now turn to duties of the Paramount Board under the facts of this case and our conclusions as to the breaches of those duties which warrant injunctive relief.

A. The Specific Obligations of the Paramount Board

Under the facts of this case, the Paramount directors had the obligation: (a) to be diligent and vigilant in examining critically the Paramount-Viacom transaction and the QVC tender offers; (b) to act in good faith; (c) to obtain, and act with due care on, all material information reasonably available, including information necessary to compare the two offers to determine which of these transactions, or an alternative course of action, would provide the best value reasonably available to the stockholders; and (d) to negotiate actively and in good faith with both Viacom and QVC to that end.

Having decided to sell control of the corporation, the Paramount directors were required to evaluate critically whether or not all material aspects of the Paramount-Viacom transaction (separately and in the aggregate) were reasonable and in the best interests of the Paramount stockholders in light of current circumstances, including: the change of control premium, the Stock Option Agreement, the Termination Fee, the coercive nature of both the Viacom and QVC tender offers, the No-Shop Provision, and the proposed disparate use of the Rights Agreement as to the Viacom and QVC tender offers, respectively.

These obligations necessarily implicated various issues, including the questions of whether or not those provisions and other aspects of the Paramount-Viacom transaction (separately and in the aggregate): (a) adversely affected the value provided to the Paramount stockholders; (b) inhibited or encouraged alternative bids; (c) were enforceable contractual obligations in light of the directors' fiduciary duties; and (d) in the end would advance or retard the Paramount directors' obligation to secure for the Paramount stockholders the best value reasonably available under the circumstances.

The Paramount defendants contend that they were precluded by certain contractual provisions including the No-Shop Provision, from negotiating with QVC or seeking alternatives. Such provisions, whether or not they are presumptively valid in the abstract, may not validly define or limit the directors' fiduciary duties under

Delaware law or prevent the Paramount directors from carrying out their fiduciary duties under Delaware law. To the extent such provisions are inconsistent with those duties, they are invalid and unenforceable. See *Revlon, Inc.* v. *MacAndrews & Forbes Holdings, Inc.* …

[Text omitted]

When entering into the Original Merger Agreement, and thereafter, the Paramount Board clearly gave insufficient attention to the potential consequences of the defensive measures demanded by Viacom. The Stock Option Agreement had a number of unusual and potentially "draconian" provisions, including the Note Feature and the Put Feature. Furthermore, the Termination Fee, whether or not unreasonable by itself, clearly made Paramount less attractive to other bidders, when coupled with the Stock Option Agreement. Finally, the No-Shop Provision inhibited the Paramount Board's ability to negotiate with other potential bidders, particularly QVC which had already expressed an interest in Paramount.

[Text omitted]

John Crowther Group plc v. Carpets International plc
Chancery Division
[1990] BCLC 460
[Text edited; footnotes omitted]
Reproduced by permission of Reed Elsevier (UK) Limited, trading as LexisNexis Butterworths

VINELOTT J

The applications which are now before me relate to a dispute which has arisen concerning the acquisition by the plaintiff, John Crowther Group plc (Crowther) from the first defendant, Carpets International plc, (International) of the shares of a subsidiary in that company called Carpets International (UK) Ltd (UK).

Under the terms of an agreement dated 12 September, but in fact executed in the early hours of 13 September, between International and Crowther, Crowther agreed to buy the shares of UK for £1 and also to pay to International £5m and to procure the issue to International of a further one and a quarter million fully paid ordinary shares of Crowther of 25p each in consideration of, in effect, the acquisition by Crowther of very considerable debts owed by UK to International, amounting to some £40m.

The transaction affected a substantial part of the business of International and, under Stock Exchange requirements, it had to be made conditional on approval of the shareholders of International. Accordingly one of the conditions which had to be satisfied was the passing at a general meeting of International of a resolution approving the transaction before 14 October 1985. Clause 2(3) of the agreement reads as follows:

'The parties hereto shall use all reasonable endeavours to procure the satisfaction of the conditions set out in Schedule 4, which apply to them by the dates therein mentioned, in particular without prejudice to the generality of the foregoing the vendors hereby irrevocably undertake (a) to use all reasonable endeavours to post and to do nothing to prevent the posting of the circular to the shareholders of the vendors by 11 am on Friday 13 September containing a recommendation to such shareholders to vote in favour of the ordinary resolution to approve the transaction; (b) to procure that the aforesaid resolutions are properly proposed and put to the aforesaid meeting whatever circumstances may exist at that time in relation to any offers as made for the share capital of the company or its business or any part thereof by any third party; (c) not to adjourn the said meeting, save as may be required either by law or pursuant to the articles of association of the vendors.' ...

It is said on behalf of Crowther in these proceedings that it is implicit in the undertakings or covenants in cl 2(3) that International would not entertain any rival offer until the resolution had been put before International shareholders. Whether that is so or not is not, I think, a point which I need to consider further because in the course of the negotiations it was known that there was a rival bidder in the field, namely the seventh defendant, PMA Textiles Ltd, (PMA) and some few days before the agreement was executed International, through Kleinwort Benson, its merchant bankers, agreed that it would cease to negotiate with rival bidders. That was something insisted on by the chairman of Crowthers. He also sought and obtained a formal undertaking by a United States shareholder, holding 41.3% of the shares of International, that it would vote in favour of the resolution.

I have already mentioned the circular which had to be sent round to shareholders. In its original form it contained a statement that the directors of International and its merchant bankers considered the term of the sale were fair and reasonable and continued:

> 'In the absence of a materially better offer being received (in which event, shareholders will be informed forthwith) your directors recommend you to vote in favour of the resolution.'

That somewhat lukewarm recommendation did not appeal to Crowthers, who through their merchant bankers, required the first part, 'In the absence of a materially better offer being received (in which event shareholders will be informed forthwith)' to be deleted. The circular went out in that amended form.

The circular went out on 13 September and on the same day PMA made a press announcement. It announced that it was considering an offer if it could arrange the necessary finance and that discussions for the provision of finance were at an advanced stage. The circular went on to say that it was expected that an announcement would be made before the 7 October, the date on which an extraordinary general meeting to approve the sale to Crowther had been fixed ...

Mr Eugster [a director of Kleinwort Benson] says that on 10 September, after the undertaking had been given by International, he told Mr Shrager [a director of Morgan Grenfell] that he could no longer negotiate with him, while adding a rider that 'if he and his clients made an offer, that was their privilege but that negotiations were at an end'.

During the week commencing on 16 September Coopers & Lybrand on behalf of PMA were given information by International concerning the business of UK. On 23 September the deputy chairman of International was telephoned by the chairman of PMA and told that PMA was serious in its intention to make an offer and confident that it would secure the necessary financial backing. Mr Eugster in his affidavit continues by saying that following that conversation:

> 'it became increasingly apparent that PMA were going to make an offer at a price in excess of Crowthers. It also became apparent that time would be critical. It became evident that in the time likely to be available all the Board would be able to do would be to compare whatever price was offered by PMA against that already referred to in the Crowther Agreement.'

So, following the telephone conversation, there were discussions between the solicitors for International and PMA with regard to the form a written agreement would take if PMA wanted to make an offer. On 26 September Mr Shrager told Mr Eugster that PMA wanted to make an offer of £7m, some one and a quarter million more than the offer made by Crowther, but the whole in cash instead of £5m cash and the balance in shares. Thereafter, Mr Shrager says, meetings took place between representatives of PMA and International, in the course of which the offer was incorporated in a formal agreement which was signed on 1 October. Moreover, on 1 October a circular was sent out by International in terms approved by PMA's advisers, though Mr Shrager says the recommendation in that circular was prepared entirely by International and that it was not part of any agreement or understanding between International and PMA that any recommendation would be made.

The agreement with PMA is a perfectly straightforward agreement similar to the agreement with Crowther, except of course that it is conditional on the first agreement not becoming unconditional and is itself in turn conditional upon shareholder approval.

In the circular to the shareholders of International the board, having referred to the offer said to have been received 'today', that is, 1 October, with assurances that PMA had the necessary financial resources, go on to say that the consideration is materially higher than that payable under the Crowther agreement, and they continue in these terms:

> 'In these circumstances your board consider that it would be appropriate to secure this offer by entering into a conditional agreement with PMA which would only become effective if the Crowther agreement did not proceed. In view of the materially higher consideration which would be received from PMA and the substantial identity of the other terms, your board is now recommending that the proposed disposal to Crowther should not proceed. Your board has been informed by Crowther that it considers that under the terms of the agreement with Crowther your board is obliged to continue to recommend the disposal to Crowther. Your board has, however, been advised that, notwithstanding the terms of the agreement, if it considers it would be in the interests of International to dispose of UK to PMA and if there is a prospect that the agreement with Crowther will not proceed,

then it is obliged to recommend that course, which would not constitute a breach
of the agreement with Crowther.'

And then they refer to the undertaking by the United States shareholder, the size
of whose shareholding is such that a very large proportion of the other shareholders
will have to vote against the Crowther resolution if it is to be defeated. I need say
no more about that circular or any more, indeed, about the evidence or the facts of
this case.

The case for Crowther, as I understand it, is that the undertaking in cl 2(3) of the
agreement is not only to take steps to procure the passing of the resolution if the
board think it reasonable that it should be passed but to take all steps reasonably
available to procure the passing of the resolution whether the board think it in the
interests of the company that the resolution approving the sale be passed or not.

I think I should say (and this is, of course, an interlocutory hearing) that I am
not persuaded that is a possible view. The terms of the agreement must clearly be
read in the light of the fact known to all parties that directors owe a fiduciary duty
to act in the interests of their company and to make full and honest disclosure to
shareholders before they vote on such a resolution. It seems to me that it must have
been understood by all that if the undertaking was to use reasonable endeavours to
procure the passing of the resolution it was necessarily subject to anything which
the directors had to do in pursuance of that fiduciary duty. Indeed, as counsel for
International and the second to fourth defendants (Mr Sykes QC) pointed out, this
is underlined by the fact that it is made clear in sub-para (b) of cl 2(3) that the resolutions must be put whatever other offers may have been made at the time they
are put, whereas there is no similar qualification of the covenant to use reasonable
endeavours. That contrast is some indication that any obligation to use reasonable
endeavours to procure the passing of the resolution ceases if an offer plainly more in
the interests of the company is made before that resolution is passed.

The point is, it seems to me, very well illustrated by the unhappily unreported
decision of Templeman J in Rackham and Vavasseur v. Peek Foods Ltd (6 April
1977, unreported). That was a case where the resolution required was one approving
the purchase of the shares of a property company which, because of the collapse of
the property market, had become virtually worthless when the resolution fell to be
passed. It could equally be illustrated by an example I gave in argument where the
contract is for sale of land or the shares of a property holding company if the land is
found to contain valuable reserves of oil between the date of the conditional agreement and the date when the resolution comes to be passed.

It seems to me plain beyond question that directors are under a duty to disclose
the facts to the shareholders. Indeed a resolution passed in ignorance of them would
be worthless. If directors must disclose the facts, then it seems to me they must
equally express their honest opinion as to what is in the interests of the company.

Counsel for Crowther (Mr Heslop QC) says that it is quite different if the change
in circumstances comes about as a result of a breach of duty in entertaining a further

offer or doing something to induce a further offer. I shall assume in his favour that there is here an arguable claim that there has been some such breach of duty, though I should stress that I do not find that to be the case. Assuming in his favour that that is the case, the conclusion that the directors are in some way no longer under any duty to inform the shareholders of that change of circumstances, that is, the existence of a higher offer, does not in my judgment follow. The fact, however it may come about, that a higher offer is there must be disclosed.

What is said (and I think this has, in the course of argument, emerged as the nub of the argument of counsel for Crowther) is that if, in allowing a state of affairs to come about or in assisting bringing about a state of affairs (a higher offer from a rival bidder) which when disclosed to the shareholders may induce them to vote against a resolution to approve a conditional contract of sale, the directors acted in breach of an undertaking to use their best endeavours to procure the passing of a resolution approving the conditional contract the company is prima facie liable for damages for breach of the undertaking. Then, it is said, the claim for damages must be equal to or greater than any benefit to be derived from accepting the higher offer with the result that it cannot be in the interests of the company that a resolution approving the conditional contract should not be passed and I suppose it becomes the duty of sufficiently subtle and far sighted directors not to disclose the existence of the potentially damaging higher offer. Alternatively, it is said the existence of that claim for damages is a matter which the directors are as much obliged to disclose as the existence of the higher offer.

At this point the argument becomes, to my mind, somewhat fanciful. It is for the directors to decide for themselves what they consider to be in the interests of the company and to take whatever steps they think appropriate to advance the interests of the company. It is also for the directors to decide what steps they should take to discharge their duty to ensure that proper disclosure is made to the shareholders. If they act honestly in the belief and on advice that acceptance of a higher offer would not give rise to any claim for damages, then I do not see it would be right for the court to compel them to put out some circular or press release explaining that such a claim has been made. There is, as I see it, nothing to prevent Crowther from issuing a press release or, if time permits, an appropriate circular containing a proper and fair statement of the claim which it contends will arise if the resolution is not approved.

The point that has troubled me to some extent is whether the directors are entitled to go further than informing shareholders of the existence of the higher offer and giving honest and fair advice, in particular whether they are entitled to go further and take positive steps to communicate directly with shareholders and, by themselves or with their merchant bankers, to endeavour to persuade them to vote against the resolution.

As I have said, I felt some anxiety about the point, but on the facts of this case I do not think I need pursue further the question how far it is the duty of the directors, having formed a view that a particular course is in the interests of the company, to ensure that that cause is taken, even if it means persuading shareholders to vote against a resolution which they, on behalf of the company, have agreed the company will use its best endeavours to advance. I think the answer to that question may well lie, as counsel for International and the second to fourth respondents has suggested, in the fact that the covenant itself is, in effect, to be read as subject to anything which the directors properly consider they should do in the interests of the company. Be that as it may, I do not think this is a case where I need consider the matter further. The circular, to my mind, is clearly unexceptionable. It has gone out. The meeting is on Tuesday. The matter has attracted some publicity. It seems to me that in this situation where the court must now leave it to the shareholders to make up their own minds whether the resolution should be passed or not and refrain from making any orders which might affect the information and advice available to the shareholders in making up their minds on this point.

I have not dealt separately with the situation of PMA, against which relief is sought, on the footing, as I understand it, that has entered into an agreement in circumstances where it knew that by entering into the agreement of 1 October or into the negotiations which necessarily preceded it International were acting in a manner inconsistent with prior contractual obligations owed to Crowther. For the reasons I have given, I do not think a case has been made out against International justifying interlocutory relief and that must apply a fortiori to PMA ...

[*Editors' Note*: On the reach of the holding in *John Crowther*, note that the Court of Appeals, in *Fulham Football Club Ltd and others* v. *Cabra Estates plc*, [1994] 1 BCLC 363, CA, stated: "We were referred to two English cases at first instance where in each the court held that an undertaking by directors to use their best endeavours to ensure that their shareholders should approve a particular deal by the company (in one case a purchase, in the other a sale) was unenforceable. The cases are *Rackham* v. *Peck Foods Ltd* and *John Crowther Group* v. *Carpets International* ... It may be that these decisions can be justified on their particular facts, but they should not be read as laying down a general proposition that directors can never bind themselves as to the future exercise of their fiduciary powers. If they could be so read then they would be wrong."]

22

Governance rules for business combinations

Required reading

EU: Cross Border Merger Directive; SE Regulation, arts. 2(1), 17–29
D: AktG, § 179a; UmwG, §§ 2, 16, 20, 22, 29; HGB, § 25; BGB, § 613a
UK: CA 2006, secs. 904–918
US: DGCL, §§ 251–253, 259–262(a) and (d), 271

Governance of mergers and acquisitions

I.   *Three governance techniques*

In the last chapter, we looked at the types of structures used in acquisitions and the legal tools that can be used to protect a deal. Here, we will examine the manner in which UK, German and US law govern merger and acquisitions transactions. Many mergers and major sales of assets significantly change the company's economic makeup and the degree of control current shareholders exercise. For this reason, early corporate statutes either prohibited such transactions altogether or required unanimous shareholder approval before allowing management radically to change the nature of the investment into which shareholders entered when purchasing their shares.[1] As economic development demanded increased scale and scope of industries,[2] mergers and acquisitions became more common and the law became more flexible, and lawmakers have developed three types of interrelated governance techniques to protect the interests of shareholders. Shareholders have been given a right to know and decide, a right not to be unfairly oppressed by those in power, and a right to fair compensation for their investment. In their present form, these rights take clear shape in the governance rules for corporate combinations: first, the transaction must be disclosed to and approved by

---

[1] Manning (1962: 246–248).   [2] Chandler (1990: 78–82).

a majority (or a supermajority) of shareholders unless its impact on the company is small; secondly, the management (and the controlling shareholders) must not discriminate against the (other) shareholders when effecting the transaction; and, thirdly, shareholders who unsuccessfully vote against the transaction must be given a right to be bought out at a fair price rather than being locked into a new or substantially altered company that was not part of their investment bargain. The following sections will discuss each of these governance techniques in our three jurisdictions.

II.   Shareholder approval

A.   United States

Shareholder approval is required before a company can sell "all or substantially all of its property and assets."[3] The word "all" is very clear: it means 100 percent. How about "substantially all"? Take a look at *Katz* v. *Bregman*. Note, however, that *Katz* should be read with an understanding that it represents the outside boundary of the term "substantially all," not the norm. If shareholders must vote on a transaction constituting a sale of assets in the range of value discussed in *Katz*, should they also be allowed to vote if the company were to *purchase* assets having a very high value in comparison to the purchaser's total assets?

Under Delaware law, unless a merger is between a parent and a subsidiary or has a small impact on the purchaser, as described below, the board of each corporation participating in the transaction must independently reach its own decision that the transaction is "advisable" for its own company and draft a resolution to be offered to the shareholders for approval, setting out:

- the terms and conditions of the merger or consolidation agreement;
- the way the transaction will be carried out;
- if a merger, the planned amendments to the certificate of incorporation of the surviving corporation;
- if a consolidation, the certificate of incorporation of the resulting corporation; and
- the ratio for converting the shares of each of the constituent corporations into securities of the surviving or resulting corporation, or the cash, property, rights or securities which the holders of such shares are to receive.[4]

---

[3] § 271 DGCL.   [4] § 251(b) DGCL.

The resolution and the agreement must be presented to the shareholders at a general meeting for approval (by an absolute majority of the shareholders entitled to vote on the transaction).[5] Registered US companies will likely also have to comply with one or more additional layers of disclosure under SEC rules. First, when companies registered with the SEC call the meeting to vote on the transaction, they must, pursuant to Rule 14a, disclose detailed information on the nature of the transaction in the proxy materials they send to shareholders.[6] Secondly, both a registered and an unregistered company will in most cases have to provide notice of the merger or acquisition to the SEC on a form specially designed for mergers and acquisitions (Form S-4), providing detailed information not only about the company and the securities, but also regarding the form and substance of the transaction.[7] Unregistered companies are pulled into the federal regulatory system because a Rule 145 under the Securities Act of 1933 deems the exchange of shares in the context of a statutory merger to be an "offer" within § 2(3) of that Act, triggering a duty to register with the SEC.[8]

For dealings with controlled companies, Delaware law provides for an abbreviated approval process commonly referred to as a "short form merger." A corporation that owns at least 90 percent of a subsidiary may decide unilaterally to merge the latter into itself solely on the basis of a resolution of the parent's board of directors without a shareholder vote in either the purchaser or the target subsidiary.[9] If the parent owns less than 100 percent of the subsidiary's stock, the board resolution to undertake the merger must describe in detail the compensation paid for the subsidiary's shares.[10] Any minority shareholders will have a right to receive a "fair" cash compensation for their shares (see Section III below).

A comparable shortcut is available for mergers that have low economic impact. Think of Microsoft buying a startup software company by exchanging shares with the startup's two founding shareholders. Specifically, for the board to undertake a merger without shareholder participation, the merger agreement must not amend the company's charter, no new shares must be issued as compensation, any authorized shares or securities convertible into shares used as compensation must not exceed 20 percent of the common stock currently outstanding, and the existing shares of the purchaser must not be transformed (such as through a reverse merger) in any way.[11] The smaller company would still have to receive shareholder approval for the merger.

[5] § 251(c) DGCL.   [6] 17 CFR § 240.14a-101, Item 14.
[7] 17 CFR § 230.145; Form S-4.   [8] 17 CFR § 230.145(a).
[9] § 253(a) DGCL.   [10] § 253(a), first sentence, second clause DGCL.
[11] § 251(f) DGCL.

B. Germany

Perhaps the economic logic of mergers and major asset sales is clear and universal, and the Delaware rules accurately reflect that logic. In any case, without any obvious influence (as in the case of the German business judgment rule) or international coordination (as in the case of IOSCO and securities regulation), German governance rules on approving mergers look quite like those used in Delaware (except for some labor aspects, an audit requirement and better creditor protection). Like Delaware, German law contains approval requirements for asset sales and mergers, with exceptions for smaller transactions and transactions with controlled companies.

Under the *Aktiengesetz*, any transfer of a company's entire assets must be approved by a three-quarters majority of the shareholders present and voting at the meeting, and shareholders must be given an opportunity to inspect the sale contract at the meeting before casting their vote.[12] As in Delaware law, however, "entire assets" does not necessarily mean *entire* assets, and the test to determine whether shareholder approval is necessary is likely to be whether the asset transfer would prevent the company from pursuing its corporate object unhindered,[13] which in any case would entail at least an implied amendment to the *Satzung*, and could thus very well trigger a shareholder vote under the rule on such amendments.[14] Also, somewhat analogously to US regulation under Rule 145, the use of shares to purchase assets runs the same risk of being characterized as "public purchase or exchange offers," triggering the disclosure, publication and pricing rules of the WpÜG,[15] although the application of these provisions would not reach as far as Rule 145.

As explained in the last chapter, the German procedure for approving a statutory merger is found in the UmwG. This procedure closely tracks the Third Company Law Directive. The management boards of the merging companies must draft a merger agreement, which must expressly set forth, among other things:

- the contracted agreements on the transfer of assets and shares;
- the share exchange ratio and the amount of any cash payment;
- details regarding the transfer of shares in the acquiring company;
- the date from which the shares entitle the holders to participate in profits and any special conditions affecting that entitlement;
- the date from which the merger will take effect;

---

[12] § 179a AktG.   [13] Stein, in *MünchKommAktG* (2005: § 179a mn. 18 *et seq.*).
[14] § 179 AktG; and Stein, in *MünchKommAktG* (2005: § 179a mn. 18).
[15] § 2(1) WpÜG.

- rights conferred by the acquiring company on the holders of preferred shares and debt instruments;
- any special advantage granted to board members or auditors; and
- the consequences of the merger for employees and their representatives, as well as the measures planned to address them.[16]

In addition to the contract, the *Vorstand* must prepare a "detailed, written" merger report describing the transaction and the contents of the merger contract – particularly the exchange ratio and any cash payments – and provide it to the shareholders.[17] The cumulative effect of the detailed agreement and report look much like the requirements of US Form S-4, again evidencing the similarity of the German and US regulatory scheme. Mergers and consolidations of AGs must also be audited by an independent examiner who in turn will prepare a report on the transaction, and in particular on whether the exchange ratio used is adequate.[18] As in Delaware, in the case of a consolidation, the constitutional documents (*Satzung*) of the new company, rather than amendments to the surviving company's documents, must be disclosed.[19] The resolution to approve the transaction requires a three-quarters majority of the capital represented at the meeting.[20]

A "short form" merger is available where the acquiring company owns at least 90 percent of the capital of the disappearing company. In the case of at least a 90 percent holding, the *Vorstand* of the surviving company may make the decision to merge without a shareholder resolution,[21] and, if the holding reaches 100 percent, neither a report on nor an audit of the merger would be necessary.[22] In the case of an EU cross-border merger, a 100 percent holding would also eliminate the requirement for shareholder approval from the subsidiary.[23]

Another aspect of the process deriving from European law is provision for creditor protection; under the UmwG, creditors may demand that the surviving or new company provide security for any debts reasonably demonstrated to be insufficiently backed.[24] Shareholders accidentally receive considerable advantage from the fact that the merger resolution

---

[16] § 5 UmwG.   [17] § 8 UmwG.

[18] §§ 9–12, 60 UmwG.   [19] §§ 36, 37, 17(1) UmwG.

[20] § 65 UmwG.

[21] § 62(1) UmwG. It should be noted, however, that, unlike under Delaware law, shareholders constituting 5 percent of the capital of the parent company may still demand that a general meeting be called to resolve on the transaction.

[22] §§ 8(3), 9(2) UmwG.   [23] § 122g(2) UmwG.

[24] § 22 UmwG.

must be filed with the commercial register. In addition to a claim for cash compensation, a shareholder may, as discussed in Chapter 20, challenge an approving resolution in court. Without meeting the high standard of probable success or imminent harm that would be required for an injunction or restraining order, such action can block the entry of the resolution in the commercial register, and thus its entry into force, which stops the transaction in its tracks. The law was recently amended expressly to provide that such a challenge could not go to the adequacy of the exchange ratio.[25] This could somewhat alleviate the problem of shareholder strike suits.

C.   United Kingdom

Neither the Companies Act 2006 nor UK case law directly provides a procedure to approve a sale of all or substantially all of a company's assets. Inclusion of such a provision was specifically recommended by a committee of experts as far back as 1962, but has not been followed.[26] In cases where such transactions arose, it was common in the past that UK companies had from the outset provided for a sale of "the whole of the company's undertaking" in the memorandum and made such sale contingent upon a special resolution of shareholders.[27] The model articles do not provide for such sales or their approval, except to allow the directors to make provision for employees in the circumstance of such a sale.[28] As under German law, it would appear that a sale of substantially all the company's assets would likely change its corporate object, which would well trigger a requirement for shareholder approval, given the implied change to the memorandum.[29] However, because the 2006 Act no longer requires that registering companies specify a corporate object,[30] this possibility of introducing shareholder control will diminish as new companies are formed and old ones are liquidated. Another possible hook on which to hang shareholder approval could well be an equation of a sale of "substantially the whole undertaking" with a decision to liquidate the company, given that, unless a company altered its activity to holding the cash or

---

[25] § 14(2) UmwG.

[26] A recommendation was made by the Jenkins Committee in 1962 that any proposal to sell the whole or substantially the whole of a company's undertaking and assets be made subject to shareholder approval. See Ferran (1999: 254).

[27] See e.g. *Manners* v. *St. David's Gold and Copper Mines, Ltd* [1904] 2 Ch 593; *Cotton* v. *Imperial and Foreign Agency and Investment Corporation* [1892] 3 Ch 454; *Doughty* v. *Lomagunda Reefs Ltd* [1902] 2 Ch 837.

[28] Reg. 84 MAPC.   [29] Sec. 21 CA 2006.

[30] Sec. 31(1) CA 2006.

stock it receives for its assets, it could not continue to function without its operating assets. Cases disputing this question do not arise, probably because the FSA Listing Rules contain highly detailed regulations specifying transactions that require shareholder approval based on the percentage of gross assets, profits, the capital they entail or the consideration paid, and such transactions include major asset sales.[31]

The Companies Act 2006 regulation of mergers involving public companies, which has been carried over in great part from Schedule 15B to the 1985 Act, also closely tracks the Third Company Law Directive, and thus resembles the procedure under German law.[32] The board must prepare draft terms of merger[33] and publish them[34] before the general meeting that is asked to approve the transaction with a three-quarters (in value) majority of each class of shares represented at the meeting.[35] For each company participating in the transaction, the relevant directors[36] and an independent expert (statutory auditor)[37] must prepare a report, focusing particularly on the share exchange ratio, and this report must be made available to the shareholders for one month preceding the general meeting that is asked to approve the transaction.[38] As in the other jurisdictions, in the case of a consolidation (merger by formation of a new company), the articles of this new company must also be approved at the meeting.[39]

As in Germany, because German law on this point derives from the Third Directive,[40] two types of short-form mergers are available. If the acquiring/surviving company owns at least 90 percent, of the disappearing company, then approval by the general meeting of the surviving company is not required,[41] and, if the company on one side of the transaction is wholly owned by the company on the other, then neither draft terms on share allocation, nor reports, nor a general meeting in either company is required.[42] Court review and approval of short-form merger transactions are unique to UK law, and, in the case of less than a 100 percent holding, a meeting may be omitted only if the court is satisfied that the disclosure and

---

[31] FSA Listing Rules, Rules 10.2.2(3), 10.5.1(2), 10.8.1, Annex 1, 2R(6).

[32] It should be noted that, for listed companies, the UK City Code on Takeovers and Mergers also regulates statutory mergers. The work of the Takeover Panel and the provisions of the Code will be discussed in more detail in Chapter 24.

[33] Sec. 905 CA 2006.

[34] Sec. 906 CA 2006. The company delivers the draft terms to the registrar and the latter publishes them in the Gazette.

[35] Sec. 907(1) CA 2006.   [36] Sec. 908 CA 2006.

[37] Sec. 909 CA 2006.   [38] Sec. 911 CA 2006.

[39] Sec. 912 CA 2006.   [40] Arts. 24 *et seq.* Third Company Law Directive.

[41] Sec. 916 CA 2006.   [42] Sec. 915 CA 2006.

document access requirements have been met.[43] The court's close watch on mergers in the United Kingdom probably comes from the traditional understanding of mergers (amalgamations) as a type of reorganization transaction in which management and shareholders submit the company to the supervision of a trustee or judge.[44] Court protection also extends to creditors, who may individually apply to the court for protection.[45]

D.   European Union

The approval procedure set out in the Cross Border Mergers Directive basically repeats the structure already provided for in the Third Directive with certain adjustments to reduce time and costs, such as allowing the participating companies to prepare common draft terms of merger[46] and allowing expert audits of the merger to be prepared by a common examiner.[47] The Cross Border Mergers Directive does, however, add a level of formality to the transactions by requiring advance, "pre-merger" review of each transaction by a court – something previously required in the UK but not in many other jurisdictions.[48]

In a cross-border transaction, draft terms of merger must be published,[49] the management of each company must prepare a report,[50] and – as mentioned above – an independent audit must be performed. Although the Directive provides for shareholder approval[51] in cases other than those where the "short-form" rules apply (wholly or 90 percent owned disappearing companies),[52] it also specifies that the national laws applicable to each participating company will determine the nature of the formalities to be fulfilled.[53] The United Kingdom provided for cross-border mergers with a statutory instrument that entered into effect in December 2007,[54] and Germany implemented the Directive by adding a new part to the UmwG.[55]

The approval procedure set out in the SE Regulation mixes its own provisions with those of national law and the Third Directive, basically repeating the requirements of a merger plan, an audit, and finally a vote. The really *sui generis* aspect of the SE schema is the elaborate negotiation procedure for deciding the level of employee participation to be provided for in the

---

[43] Sec. 916(2), 917(2) CA 2006.   [44] Secs. 427, 427A CA 1985.
[45] Sec. 899(2) CA 2006.   [46] Art. 5 Cross Border Merger Directive.
[47] Art. 8(2) Cross Border Merger Directive.   [48] Art. 10 Cross Border Merger Directive.
[49] Art. 6 Cross Border Merger Directive.   [50] Art. 7 Cross Border Merger Directive.
[51] Art. 9 Cross Border Merger Directive.   [52] Art. 15 Cross Border Merger Directive.
[53] Art. 4(1)(b) Cross Border Merger Directive.
[54] See Companies (Cross-Border Mergers) Regulations 2007, SI 2007 No. 2974.
[55] See §§ 122a *et seq.* UmwG.

new SE.[56] It requires the creation of a special negotiating committee of the employees of the companies involved,[57] the negotiation of an agreement on employee participation[58] during a period that may last up to six months (but may be extended up to an additional year),[59] and, if no agreement is reached in this period, the imposition of the highest level of employee participation existing in any of the companies involved in the transaction.[60]

III.   A right to be bought out

It was mentioned above that the right of a dissenting minority to be bought out was historically seen as a right to exit an arrangement when the agreed-upon structure was changed. The right of shareholders who dissent to a merger to be bought out at a fair price, however, also has a liquidity function that generally encourages investment in an economy's private firms. If legislation provides minority shareholders with a right to exit a transaction on fair terms where there is no market in which the shares may be readily sold, such law supplements the organized equity markets by extending (judicially enforced) liquidity into these very desirable, yet somewhat sporadic and opaque types of investments, and increases their value *ex ante*.[61] Thus, appraisal rights, by encouraging outside investors to enter private companies, provide *ad hoc* liquidity as is the function of a capital market. By the same token, do appraisal rights encourage majority shareholders to avoid outside investors and turn elsewhere – such as to banks – for funds? Why or why not?

A.   United States

The Delaware statute expressly provides for "appraisal rights" of shareholders who unsuccessfully vote against a merger, and allows them to sue the court to enforce such rights if they continue to hold their shares until filing suit.[62] Appraisal rights were originally conceived as compensation to minority shareholders in exchange for reducing the unanimity requirement for approving a merger to a majority requirement.[63] In order to claim this right, a shareholder must hold his shares when making the demand, continuously hold them through the effective date of the transaction, and not vote in favor of the merger or consolidation.[64] The valuation technique

---

[56] Arts. 3–7 SE Directive.   [57] Art. 3 SE Directive.
[58] Art. 4 SE Directive.   [59] Art. 5 SE Directive.
[60] Art. 7(1)(b) SE Directive, in connection with Annex, Part 3(b).
[61] Easterbrook and Fischel (1996: 145–149).   [62] § 262 DGCL.
[63] *Hariton* v. *Arco Electronics, Inc.*, 182 A 2d 22, 25 (Del. Ch. 1962).
[64] § 262(a) DGCL.

to achieve a "fair" buyout right is discussed in *Weinberger* v. *UOP, Inc.*, reprinted in part in this chapter. How does a shareholder action against directors for a breach of fiduciary duty in a merger compare to an action seeking appraisal rights? How is the value of an appraisal right determined? How are damages for a breach of fiduciary duty determined?

B.   Germany

If the surviving entity has a different legal form than the target or if a listed company is merged or consolidated into an unlisted company, the UmwG provides an appraisal right proceeding for those shareholders who find the payment they receive too low.[65] To retain such right, a shareholder must vote against the transaction and then file an appraisal suit (*Spruchverfahren*) with the court within three months after the resolution on the transaction.[66] German states may create special commercial courts for such appraisal proceedings, but only a few have done so.[67] The right to a payment as determined in appraisal proceedings must be distinguished from the separate, statutory rights to compensation which are provided for in connection with a squeeze-out following a takeover.[68]

C.   United Kingdom

Appraisal rights are not required by EU law, and thus, notwithstanding their presence in the UmwG, UK law does not expressly provide for appraisal rights. The Companies Act 2006 does, however, give the court power in the context of a merger or other arrangement to make "provision … for any persons who … dissent from the compromise or arrangement."[69] This has been understood to include an order to the company to make payment of a fair price for the dissenting shareholders' investment.

IV.   *Fiduciary duties in a merger context*

Both the company law statutes and numerous cases reprinted in this text show that the laws of Germany, the United Kingdom and Delaware

---

[65] See §§ 29 *et seq.*, 36 UmwG. If the surviving or new company has a different legal form than the disappearing company, every member of the latter who objects to the adequacy of the exchange payment has a right to an additional "appraisal right" payment. See § 29(1) UmwG.

[66] § 4 of the *Gesetz über das gesellschaftsrechtliche Spruchverfahren* (*Spruchverfahrensgesetz* or SpruchG).

[67] Baums and Drinhausen (2008: 153).

[68] § 327b AktG.   [69] Sec. 900(2)(e) CA 2006.

impose fiduciary duties on directors and majority shareholders in their dealings with the company. Would mergers form an exception to this rule? Look at *Menier* v. *Hooper's Telegraph Works* and *Linotype*, reprinted in part in Chapter 19. What do these cases offer to support an argument against abusive dealing by management or a controlling shareholder in the context of a merger or an acquisition?

Cases

Katz v. Bregman
Court of Chancery of Delaware
431 A 2d 1274 (1981)
[*Text edited; some footnotes omitted*]

MARVEL, Chancellor

The complaint herein seeks the entry of an order preliminarily enjoining the proposed sale of the Canadian assets of Plant Industries, Inc. to Vulcan Industrial Packaging, Ltd, the plaintiff Hyman Katz allegedly being the owner of approximately 170,000 shares of common stock of the defendant Plant Industries, Inc. ... Significantly, at common law, a sale of all or substantially all of the assets of a corporation required the unanimous vote of the stockholders, Folk, *The Delaware General Corporation Law*, p. 400.

The complaint alleges that during the last six months of 1980, the board of directors of Plant Industries, Inc., under the guidance of the individual defendant Robert B. Bregman, the present chief executive officer of such corporation, embarked on a course of action which resulted in the disposal of several unprofitable subsidiaries ...

According to the complaint, Mr. Bregman thereupon proceeded on a course of action designed to dispose of a subsidiary of the corporate defendant known as Plant National (Quebec) Ltd, a business which constitutes Plant Industries, Inc.'s entire business operation in Canada and has allegedly constituted Plant's only income producing facility during the past four years. The professed principal purpose of such proposed sale is to raise needed cash and thus improve Plant's balance sheets. And while interest in purchasing the corporate defendant's Canadian plant was thereafter evinced not only by Vulcan Industrial Packaging, Ltd but also by Universal Drum Reconditioning Co. ... One reason advanced by Plant's management for declining to negotiate with Universal is that a firm undertaking having been entered into with Vulcan that the board of directors of Plant may not legally or ethically negotiate with Universal ...

In seeking injunctive relief, as prayed for, plaintiff relies on two principles, one that found in 8 Del. C. § 271 to the effect that a decision of a Delaware corporation to sell "... all or substantially all of its property and assets ..." requires not only the approval of such corporation's board of directors but also a resolution adopted by a majority of the outstanding stockholders of the corporation entitled to vote thereon at a meeting duly called upon at least twenty days' notice ...

Turning to the possible application of 8 Del. C. s 271 to the proposed sale of substantial corporate assets of National to Vulcan, it is stated in *Gimbel* v. *Signal Companies, Inc.*, Del. Ch., 316 A 2d 599 (1974) as follows: "If the sale is of assets quantitatively vital to the operation of the corporation and is out of the ordinary and substantially affects the existence and purpose of the corporation then it is beyond the power of the Board of Directors."

According to Plant's 1980 10K form, it appears that at the end of 1980, Plant's Canadian operations represented 51% of Plant's remaining assets. Defendants also concede that National represents 44.9% of Plant's sales' revenues and 52.4% of its pre-tax net operating income. Furthermore, such report by Plant discloses, in rough figures that while National made a profit in 1978 of $2,900,000, the profit from the US businesses in that year was only $770,000. In 1979, the Canadian business profit was $3,500,000 while the loss of the US businesses was $344,000. Furthermore, in 1980, while the Canadian business profit was $5,300,000, the corporate loss in the US was $4,500,000. And while these figures may be somewhat distorted by the allocation of overhead expenses and taxes, they are significant. In any event, defendants concede that "... National accounted for 34.9% of Plant's pre-tax income in 1976, 36.9% in 1977, 42% in 1978, 51% in 1979 and 52.4% in 1980."

While in the case of *Philadelphia National Bank* v. *BSF Co.* ... the question ... was tested by provisions of an indenture agreement covering subordinated debentures, the result was the same as if the provisions of 8 Del. C. s 271 had been applicable, the trial Court stating: "While no pertinent Pennsylvania case is cited, the critical factor in determining the character of a sale of assets is generally considered not the amount of property sold but whether the sale is in fact an unusual transaction or one made in the regular course of business of the seller ..."

[Text omitted]

In the case at bar, I am first of all satisfied that historically the principal business of Plant Industries, Inc. has not been to buy and sell industrial facilities but rather to manufacture steel drums for use in bulk shipping as well as for the storage of petroleum products, chemicals, food, paint, adhesives and cleaning agents, a business which has been profitably performed by National of Quebec. Furthermore, the proposal, after the sale of National, to embark on the manufacture of plastic drums represents a radical departure from Plant's historically successful line of business, namely steel drums. I therefore conclude that the proposed sale of Plant's Canadian operations, which constitute over 51% of Plant's total assets and in which are generated approximately 45% of Plant's 1980 net sales, would, if consummated, constitute a sale of substantially all of Plant's assets. By way of contrast, the proposed sale of Signal Oil in *Gimbel* v. *Signal Companies, Inc., supra,* represented only about 26%

of the total assets of Signal Companies, Inc. And while Signal Oil represented 41% of Signal Companies, Inc. total net worth, it generated only about 15% of Signal Companies, Inc. revenue and earnings.

[Text omitted]

Weinberger v. UOP, Inc.
Supreme Court of Delaware
457 A 2d 701 (1983)
[Text edited; some footnotes omitted]

MOORE, Justice

[Text omitted]

Signal is a diversified, technically based company operating through various subsidiaries. Its stock is publicly traded on the New York, Philadelphia and Pacific Stock Exchanges. UOP, formerly known as Universal Oil Products Company, was a diversified industrial company engaged in various lines of business ... Its stock was publicly held and listed on the New York Stock Exchange.

In 1974 Signal sold one of its wholly owned subsidiaries for $420,000,000 in cash ... While looking to invest this cash surplus, Signal became interested in UOP as a possible acquisition. Friendly negotiations ensued, and [a combination of direct purchase and public tender offer] ...

... permitted Signal to acquire 5,800,000 shares of stock, representing 50.5% of UOP's outstanding shares ...

[Text omitted]

Although UOP's board consisted of thirteen directors, Signal nominated and elected only six. Of these, five were either directors or employees of Signal. The sixth, a partner in the banking firm of Lazard Freres & Co., had been one of Signal's representatives in the negotiations and bargaining with UOP concerning the tender offer and purchase price of the UOP shares.

However, the president and chief executive officer of UOP retired during 1975, and Signal caused him to be replaced by James V. Crawford, a long-time employee and senior executive vice president of one of Signal's wholly owned subsidiaries. Crawford succeeded his predecessor on UOP's board of directors and also was made a director of Signal.

By the end of 1977 Signal basically was unsuccessful in finding other suitable investment candidates for its excess cash, and by February 1978 considered that it had no other realistic acquisitions available to it on a friendly basis. Once again its attention turned to UOP.

The trial court found that at the instigation of certain Signal management personnel, including William W. Walkup, its board chairman, and Forrest N. Shumway, its president, a feasibility study was made concerning the possible acquisition of the balance of UOP's outstanding shares. This study was performed by two Signal officers, Charles S. Arledge, vice president (director of planning), and Andrew J. Chitiea, senior vice president (chief financial officer). Messrs. Walkup, Shumway, Arledge and Chitiea were all directors of UOP in addition to their membership on the Signal board.

Arledge and Chitiea concluded that it would be a good investment for Signal to acquire the remaining 49.5% of UOP shares at any price up to $24 each. Their report was discussed between Walkup and Shumway who, along with Arledge, Chitiea and Brewster L. Arms, internal counsel for Signal, constituted Signal's senior management. In particular, they talked about the proper price to be paid if the acquisition was pursued, purportedly keeping in mind that as UOP's majority shareholder, Signal owed a fiduciary responsibility to both its own stockholders as well as to UOP's minority. It was ultimately agreed that a meeting of Signal's executive committee would be called to propose that Signal acquire the remaining outstanding stock of UOP through a cash-out merger in the range of $20 to $21 per share.

The executive committee meeting was set for February 28, 1978. As a courtesy, UOP's president, Crawford, was invited to attend, although he was not a member of Signal's executive committee. On his arrival, and prior to the meeting, Crawford was asked to meet privately with Walkup and Shumway. He was then told of Signal's plan to acquire full ownership of UOP and was asked for his reaction to the proposed price range of $20 to $21 per share. Crawford said he thought such a price would be "generous," and that it was certainly one which should be submitted to UOP's minority shareholders for their ultimate consideration. He stated, however, that Signal's 100% ownership could cause internal problems at UOP. He believed that employees would have to be given some assurance of their future place in a fully owned Signal subsidiary. Otherwise, he feared the departure of essential personnel. Also, many of UOP's key employees had stock option incentive programs which would be wiped out by a merger. Crawford therefore urged that some adjustment would have to be made, such as providing a comparable incentive in Signal's shares, if after the merger he was to maintain his quality of personnel and efficiency at UOP.

Thus, Crawford voiced no objection to the $20 to $21 price range, nor did he suggest that Signal should consider paying more than $21 per share for the minority interests. Later, at the executive committee meeting the same factors were discussed, with Crawford repeating the position he earlier took with Walkup and Shumway. Also considered was the 1975 tender offer and the fact that it had been greatly oversubscribed at $21 per share. For many reasons, Signal's management concluded that the acquisition of UOP's minority shares provided the solution to a number of its business problems.

Thus, it was the consensus that a price of $20 to $21 per share would be fair to both Signal and the minority shareholders of UOP ...

[*Text omitted*]

Between Tuesday, February 28, 1978 and Monday, March 6, 1978, a total of four business days, Crawford spoke by telephone with all of UOP's non-Signal, i.e.

outside, directors. Also during that period, Crawford retained Lehman Brothers to render a fairness opinion as to the price offered the minority for its stock ...

Crawford telephoned [James W. Glanville, a long-time director of UOP and a partner in Lehman Brothers], who gave his assurance that Lehman Brothers had no conflicts that would prevent it from accepting the task. Glanville's immediate personal reaction was that a price of $20 to $21 would certainly be fair, since it represented almost a 50% premium over UOP's market price. Glanville sought a $250,000 fee for Lehman Brothers' services, but Crawford thought this too much. After further discussions Glanville finally agreed that Lehman Brothers would render its fairness opinion for $150,000 ...

Glanville assembled a three-man Lehman Brothers team to do the work on the fairness opinion. These persons examined relevant documents and information concerning UOP, including its annual reports and its Securities and Exchange Commission filings from 1973 through 1976, as well as its audited financial statements for 1977, its interim reports to shareholders, and its recent and historical market prices and trading volumes. In addition, on Friday, March 3, 1978, two members of the Lehman Brothers team flew to UOP's headquarters in Des Plaines, Illinois, to perform a "due diligence" visit, during the course of which they interviewed Crawford as well as UOP's general counsel, its chief financial officer, and other key executives and personnel.

As a result, the Lehman Brothers team concluded that "the price of either $20 or $21 would be a fair price for the remaining shares of UOP." They telephoned this impression to Glanville, who was spending the weekend in Vermont.

On Monday morning, March 6, 1978, Glanville and the senior member of the Lehman Brothers team flew to Des Plaines to attend the scheduled UOP directors meeting. Glanville looked over the assembled information during the flight. The two had with them the draft of a "fairness opinion letter" in which the price had been left blank. Either during or immediately prior to the directors' meeting, the two-page "fairness opinion letter" was typed in final form and the price of $21 per share was inserted.

On March 6, 1978, both the Signal and UOP boards were convened to consider the proposed merger. Telephone communications were maintained between the two meetings. Walkup, Signal's board chairman, and also a UOP director, attended UOP's meeting with Crawford in order to present Signal's position and answer any questions that UOP's non-Signal directors might have. Arledge and Chitiea, along with Signal's other designees on UOP's board, participated by conference telephone. All of UOP's outside directors attended the meeting either in person or by conference telephone.

First, Signal's board unanimously adopted a resolution authorizing Signal to propose to UOP a cash merger of $21 per share as outlined in a certain merger agreement and other supporting documents. This proposal required that the merger be approved by a majority of UOP's outstanding minority shares voting at the stockholders meeting at which the merger would be considered, and that the minority shares voting in favor of the merger, when coupled with Signal's 50.5% interest would have to comprise at least two-thirds of all UOP shares. Otherwise the proposed merger would be deemed disapproved.

UOP's board then considered the proposal. Copies of the agreement were delivered to the directors in attendance, and other copies had been forwarded earlier to the directors participating by telephone. They also had before them UOP financial data for 1974–1977, UOP's most recent financial statements, market price information, and budget projections for 1978. In addition they had Lehman Brothers' hurriedly prepared fairness opinion letter finding the price of $21 to be fair. Glanville, the Lehman Brothers partner, and UOP director, commented on the information that had gone into preparation of the letter.

Signal also suggests that the Arledge-Chitiea feasibility study, indicating that a price of up to $24 per share would be a "good investment" for Signal, was discussed at the UOP directors' meeting. The Chancellor made no such finding, and our independent review of the record, detailed *infra*, satisfies us by a preponderance of the evidence that there was no discussion of this document at UOP's board meeting. Furthermore, it is clear beyond peradventure that nothing in that report was ever disclosed to UOP's minority shareholders prior to their approval of the merger.

After consideration of Signal's proposal, Walkup and Crawford left the meeting to permit a free and uninhibited exchange between UOP's non-Signal directors. Upon their return a resolution to accept Signal's offer was then proposed and adopted. While Signal's men on UOP's board participated in various aspects of the meeting, they abstained from voting ...

... In the notice of that meeting and proxy statement sent to shareholders in May, UOP's management and board urged that the merger be approved. The proxy statement also advised: "The price was determined after *discussions* between James V. Crawford, a director of Signal and Chief Executive Officer of UOP, and officers of Signal which took place during meetings on February 28, 1978, and in the course of several subsequent telephone conversations." (Emphasis added.)

In the original draft of the proxy statement the word "negotiations" had been used rather than "discussions." However, when the Securities and Exchange Commission sought details of the "negotiations" as part of its review of these materials, the term was deleted and the word "discussions" was substituted ...

As of the record date of UOP's annual meeting, there were 11,488,302 shares of UOP common stock outstanding, 5,688,302 of which were owned by the minority. At the meeting only 56%, or 3,208,652, of the minority shares were voted. Of these, 2,953,812, or 51.9% of the total minority, voted for the merger, and 254,840 voted against it. When Signal's stock was added to the minority shares voting in favor, a total of 76.2% of UOP's outstanding shares approved the merger while only 2.2% opposed it.

By its terms the merger became effective on May 26, 1978, and each share of UOP's stock held by the minority was automatically converted into a right to receive $21 cash.

II.

A.

A primary issue mandating reversal is the preparation by two UOP directors, Arledge and Chitiea, of their feasibility study for the exclusive use and benefit of Signal. This document was of obvious significance to both Signal and UOP. Using UOP data, it described the advantages to Signal of ousting the minority at a price range of $21-$24 per share ...

Having written those words, solely for the use of Signal, it is clear from the record that neither Arledge nor Chitiea shared this report with their fellow directors of UOP. We are satisfied that no one else did either. This conduct hardly meets the fiduciary standards applicable to such a transaction ...

[Text omitted]

The Arledge-Chitiea report speaks for itself in supporting the Chancellor's finding that a price of up to $24 was a "good investment" for Signal. It shows that a return on the investment at $21 would be 15.7% versus 15.5% at $24 per share. This was a difference of only two-tenths of one percent, while it meant over $17,000,000 to the minority. Under such circumstances, paying UOP's minority shareholders $24 would have had relatively little long-term effect on Signal, and the Chancellor's findings concerning the benefit to Signal, even at a price of $24, were obviously correct ...

Certainly, this was a matter of material significance to UOP and its shareholders. Since the study was prepared by two UOP directors, using UOP information for the exclusive benefit of Signal, and nothing whatever was done to disclose it to the outside UOP directors or the minority shareholders, a question of breach of fiduciary duty arises. This problem occurs because there were common Signal-UOP directors participating, at least to some extent, in the UOP board's decisionmaking processes without full disclosure of the conflicts they faced.

[Text omitted]

... When directors of a Delaware corporation are on both sides of a transaction, they are required to demonstrate their utmost good faith and the most scrupulous inherent fairness of the bargain ... The requirement of fairness is unflinching in its demand that where one stands on both sides of a transaction, he has the burden of establishing its entire fairness, sufficient to pass the test of careful scrutiny by the courts ...

There is no dilution of this obligation where one holds dual or multiple directorships, as in a parent–subsidiary context. *Levien* v. *Sinclair Oil Corp.*, Del. Ch., 261 A 2d 911, 915 (1969). Thus, individuals who act in a dual capacity as directors of two corporations, one of whom is parent and the other subsidiary, owe the same duty of good management to both corporations, and in the absence of an independent negotiating structure ... or the directors' total abstention from any participation in the matter, this duty is to be exercised in light of what is best for both companies ... The record demonstrates that Signal has not met this obligation.

C.

The concept of fairness has two basic aspects: fair dealing and fair price. The former embraces questions of when the transaction was timed, how it was initiated, structured, negotiated, disclosed to the directors, and how the approvals of the directors and the stockholders were obtained. The latter aspect of fairness relates to the economic and financial considerations of the proposed merger, including all relevant factors: assets, market value, earnings, future prospects, and any other elements that affect the intrinsic or inherent value of a company's stock. Moore, *The "Interested" Director or Officer Transaction*, 4 Del. J. Corp. L. 674, 676 (1979); Nathan & Shapiro, *Legal Standard of Fairness of Merger Terms Under Delaware Law*, 2 Del. J. Corp. L. 44, 46–47 (1977). See *Tri-Continental Corp. v. Battye*, Del.Supr., 74 A 2d 71, 72 (1950); 8 Del. C. § 262(h). However, the test for fairness is not a bifurcated one as between fair dealing and price. All aspects of the issue must be examined as a whole since the question is one of entire fairness. However, in a non-fraudulent transaction we recognize that price may be the preponderant consideration outweighing other features of the merger. Here, we address the two basic aspects of fairness separately because we find reversible error as to both.

D.

Part of fair dealing is the obvious duty of candor … Moreover, one possessing superior knowledge may not mislead any stockholder by use of corporate information to which the latter is not privy … it is inevitable that the obvious conflicts posed by Arledge and Chitiea's preparation of their "feasibility study," derived from UOP information, for the sole use and benefit of Signal, cannot pass muster.

The Arledge-Chitiea report is but one aspect of the element of fair dealing. How did this merger evolve? It is clear that it was entirely initiated by Signal. The serious time constraints under which the principals acted were all set by Signal. It had not found a suitable outlet for its excess cash and considered UOP a desirable investment, particularly since it was now in a position to acquire the whole company for itself. For whatever reasons, and they were only Signal's, the entire transaction was presented to and approved by UOP's board within four business days …

The structure of the transaction, again, was Signal's doing. So far as negotiations were concerned, it is clear that they were modest at best. Crawford, Signal's man at UOP, never really talked price with Signal …

This cannot but undermine a conclusion that this merger meets any reasonable test of fairness. The outside UOP directors lacked one material piece of information generated by two of their colleagues, but shared only with Signal. True, the UOP board had the Lehman Brothers' fairness opinion, but that firm has been blamed by the plaintiff for the hurried task it performed, when more properly the responsibility for this lies with Signal. There was no disclosure of the circumstances surrounding the rather cursory preparation of the Lehman Brothers' fairness opinion. Instead, the impression was given UOP's minority that a careful study had been made, when in fact speed was the hallmark, and Mr. Glanville, Lehman's partner in charge of the matter, and also a UOP director, having spent the weekend in Vermont, brought a draft of the "fairness opinion letter" to the UOP directors' meeting on March 6, 1978 with the price left blank. We can only conclude from the record that the rush imposed on Lehman Brothers by Signal's timetable contributed to the difficulties under which this investment banking firm attempted to perform its responsibilities. Yet, none of this was disclosed to UOP's minority.

Finally, the minority stockholders were denied the critical information that Signal considered a price of $24 to be a good investment. Since this would have meant over $17,000,000 more to the minority, we cannot conclude that the shareholder vote was an informed one. Under the circumstances, an approval by a majority of the minority was meaningless ...

Given these particulars and the Delaware law on the subject, the record does not establish that this transaction satisfies any reasonable concept of fair dealing, and the Chancellor's findings in that regard must be reversed.

E.

Turning to the matter of price, plaintiff also challenges its fairness. His evidence was that on the date the merger was approved the stock was worth at least $26 per share. In support, he offered the testimony of a chartered investment analyst who used two basic approaches to valuation: a comparative analysis of the premium paid over market in ten other tender offer-merger combinations, and a discounted cash flow analysis.

In this breach of fiduciary duty case, the Chancellor perceived that the approach to valuation was the same as that in an appraisal proceeding. Consistent with precedent, he rejected plaintiff's method of proof and accepted defendants' evidence of value as being in accord with practice under prior case law. This means that the so-called "Delaware block" or weighted average method was employed wherein the elements of value, i.e. assets, market price, earnings, etc., were assigned a particular weight and the resulting amounts added to determine the value per share. This procedure has been in use for decades ... However, to the extent it excludes other generally accepted techniques used in the financial community and the courts, it is now clearly outmoded. It is time we recognize this in appraisal and other stock valuation proceedings and bring our law current on the subject.

While the Chancellor rejected plaintiff's discounted cash flow method of valuing UOP's stock, as not corresponding with "either logic or the existing law" ... it is significant that this was essentially the focus, i.e. earnings potential of UOP, of Messrs. Arledge and Chitiea in their evaluation of the merger. Accordingly, the standard "Delaware block" or weighted average method of valuation, formerly employed in appraisal and other stock valuation cases, shall no longer exclusively control such proceedings. We believe that a more liberal approach must include proof of value by any techniques or methods which are generally considered acceptable in the financial community and otherwise admissible in court, subject only to our interpretation of 8 Del. C. § 262(h) ...

Fair price obviously requires consideration of all relevant factors involving the value of a company. This has long been the law of Delaware as stated in *Tri-Continental Corp.*, 74 A 2d at 72:

> The basic concept of value under the appraisal statute is that the stockholder is entitled to be paid for that which has been taken from him, viz., his proportionate interest in a going concern. By value of the stockholder's proportionate interest in the corporate enterprise is meant the true or intrinsic value of his stock which has been taken by the merger. In determining what figure represents this true or intrinsic value, the appraiser and the courts must take into consideration all factors and elements which reasonably might enter into the fixing of value. Thus, market value, asset value, dividends, earning prospects, the nature of the enterprise and any other facts which were known or which could be ascertained as of the date of merger and which throw any light on *future prospects* of the merged corporation are not only pertinent to an inquiry as to the value of the dissenting stockholders' interest, but *must be considered* by the agency fixing the value. (Emphasis added.)

This is not only in accord with the realities of present day affairs, but it is thoroughly consonant with the purpose and intent of our statutory law. Under 8 Del. C. § 262(h), the Court of Chancery:

> shall appraise the shares, determining their *fair* value exclusive of any element of value arising from the accomplishment or expectation of the merger, together with a fair rate of interest, if any, to be paid upon the amount determined to be the *fair* value. In determining such *fair* value, the Court shall take into account *all relevant factors* ... (Emphasis added)

[*Text omitted*]

It was not until the 1981 amendment to section 262 that the reference to "fair value" was repeatedly emphasized and the statutory mandate that the Court "take into account all relevant factors" appeared [section 262(h)]. Clearly, there is a legislative intent to fully compensate shareholders for whatever their loss may be, subject only to the narrow limitation that one can not take speculative effects of the merger into account.

Although the Chancellor received the plaintiff's evidence, his opinion indicates that the use of it was precluded because of past Delaware practice. While we do not suggest a monetary result one way or the other, we do think the plaintiff's evidence should be part of the factual mix and weighed as such. Until the $21 price is measured on remand by the valuation standards mandated by Delaware law, there can be no finding at the present stage of these proceedings that the price is fair. Given the lack of any candid disclosure of the material facts surrounding establishment of the $21 price, the majority of the minority vote, approving the merger, is meaningless.

The plaintiff has not sought an appraisal, but rescissory damages ... In view of the approach to valuation that we announce today, we see no basis in our law for [limitation to an] … exclusive monetary formula for relief. On remand the plaintiff will be permitted to test the fairness of the $21 price by the standards we herein establish, in conformity with the principle applicable to an appraisal – that fair value be determined by taking "into account all relevant factors" [see 8 Del. C. § 262(h), *supra*] …

While a plaintiff's monetary remedy ordinarily should be confined to the more liberalized appraisal proceeding herein established, we do not intend any limitation on the historic powers of the Chancellor to grant such other relief as the facts of a particular case may dictate. The appraisal remedy we approve may not be adequate in certain cases, particularly where fraud, misrepresentation, self-dealing, deliberate waste of corporate assets, or gross and palpable overreaching are involved … Under such circumstances, the Chancellor's powers are complete to fashion any form of equitable and monetary relief as may be appropriate, including rescissory damages. Since it is apparent that this long completed transaction is too involved to undo, and in view of the Chancellor's discretion, the award, if any, should be in the form of monetary damages based upon entire fairness standards, i.e. fair dealing and fair price.

[Text omitted]

SUBPART B

Companies in groups

23

Corporate groups

Required reading

D: AktG, §§ 15–19, 291–293, 302–318; HGB, §§ 266, 290, 291
UK: CA 2006, secs. 1159, 1162, Schedules 6 and 7
US: DGCL, § 220(b)(2); Exchange Act, § 20; Securities Act, § 15

Corporate groups: governance by statutory rules and judicial standards

I. What are "corporate groups" and why are they formed?

A. The corporate group

We all know the names of some corporate groups. They produce everything from common consumer items like coffee and chocolate (e.g. Nestlé) to sophisticated products like pharmaceuticals (e.g. Bayer) and aircraft (e.g. Boeing). Aside from producing and selling products under a common name, what are corporate groups? Dean Phillip Blumberg, who has written as much as anyone about corporate groups, describes them as "enterprises organized in the form of a dominant parent corporation with scores or hundreds of subservient sub-holding, subsidiary, and affiliated companies. These typically conduct a single integrated enterprise under common control and often under a common public persona."[1] The words "dominant" and "subservient" in Dean Blumberg's description reveal what is unusual, problematic and interesting about corporate groups. When a corporation's central management gives instructions to its branch management and the latter transfers its profits at the close of an accounting period to the central account, we do not think of the central office as "dominating" a "subservient" branch office.

---

[1] Blumberg (2005: 606).

However, as we have seen throughout this text, each corporate entity has its own legal personality, and the management of a corporation owes specific duties to their company and its shareholders, who themselves stand completely separate from the entity's own liability and incur no risk beyond the amount of their investment. Misusing the words of the English poet, John Donne, one might say that "each corporation is an island entire of itself." When, however, each separate island is strapped into "a single integrated enterprise under common control and often under a common public persona," by equity participation or contractual obligations, various tensions between independence and interdependence arise, and most of these tensions make themselves felt as particular problems in the law of corporate groups: Directors must pursue the good of their corporation, so how may they sacrifice this good for the well-being of the entire group? Directors must exercise independent judgment, so how may they be forced to follow instructions from the management of their holding company? A company's debts are its own, so how may a parent company be held liable for the debts of an undercapitalized subsidiary that it has used as a mere instrumentality? The source of these tensions is visible even in the name which is often applied to corporate groups – "concern" – which is the primary term used in German (*Konzern*). "Concern" derives from the Latin *concernere*, meaning to mingle separate things together.[2] In this chapter, we will examine the regulation of group governance. We will also look at how the existence of a group can strain the law's understanding of a corporation's core characteristics.

B.   Why are corporate groups formed?

Professor Alfred Chandler has written the history of how industrial corporate groups arose in the US, Britain and Germany at the end of the nineteenth century, showing how enterprises expanded dramatically in their pursuit of economies of scale and scope.[3] In the US, companies such as General Electric and E. I. du Pont de Nemours formed groups through acquisitions that were part of a shift from "a strategy of achieving market control through contractual cooperation to one of achieving market dominance" through taking control of competitors.[4] In Germany, growth was pursued less through M&A than organically; this was exemplified by Siemens AG, then Europe's primary producer of telegraphic equipment,

---

[2] *American Heritage College Dictionary* (2004: 296).
[3] An economy of "scope" is "the use of processes within a single operating unit to produce or distribute more than one product." Chandler (1990: 17).
[4] Chandler (1990: 77).

which fanned out by establishing subsidiaries for projects such as electro-chemicals, telephone equipment, and the production of fertilizers electrolytically, while also entering joint ventures for projects such as wireless telegraphy (Telefunken, which was Europe's pioneer in radio technology) and manufacturing batteries (AFA, which became Europe's largest battery manufacturer).[5] Chandler sums up the various techniques that firms used to expand outward from an entrepreneurial nucleus to a corporate group with the economies of scale and scope necessary to achieve market dominance:

> Once the necessary managerial hierarchy was in place, the industrial enterprise grew – it added new units – in four ways. One was by acquiring or merging with enterprises using much the same processes to make much the same products for much the same markets; that is, it grew by horizontal combination. Another was by taking on units involved in the earlier or later stages of making a product, from the mining or processing of raw materials to the final assembling or packaging; that is, it grew by vertical integration. The third way of growth was to expand geographically to distant areas. The fourth was to make new products that were related to the firm's existing technologies or markets.[6]

Besides the aspiration for fast growth by acquisition of existing corporations, a number of other reasons may determine the organization of an enterprise in the form of a corporate group rather than as a single corporate entity with multiple divisions. One of the most important advantages is limited liability. In a single corporation, liabilities incurred on behalf of an unprofitable division may wipe out the profits of the entire business and, indeed, drive the corporation into insolvency. By segregating parts of the enterprise into separate legal entities, the risk of failure of a particular activity is shifted to the entity's creditors while the rest of the enterprise may remain unaffected. Thus, limited liability, which was originally designed as a means to encourage capital investments by individuals has become a force driving the organization of large multi-company enterprises. Group-building also allows for control of large enterprises with comparatively little capital. If parent company A acquires 50.1 percent of the shares of corporation B, A can determine all shareholder decisions that require only a simple majority of the votes and thus effectively exercise control over B, including the investment of the other shareholders in that company. If, in turn, B acquires 50.1 percent of corporation C, A's control extends to that corporation even though its total

---

[5] Chandler (1990: 467).   [6] Chandler (1990: 37).

investment amounts to little more than 25 percent of C's equity. Other potential advantages of corporate groups over single corporate entities include shallow hierarchies that facilitate faster decisionmaking, the opportunity for the management of the holding company to focus on long-term strategy and monitoring operations rather than on day-to-day business, greater incentives for managers, who can be employed as senior officers of a subsidiary rather than as mid-level managers of the parent, easier integration of acquired companies and use of the value embodied in their firm names, as well as access to foreign markets where it might be more difficult to establish and to operate through a mere branch office. However, not all of these advantages come without cost. Viewing Chandler's work from the perspective of economic analysis, Williamson argues that a danger of using a holding company with separate subsidiaries for each activity is that "subsidiaries ... have preemptive claims against their own earnings [and thus] are unlikely to return those resources to the center but will 're-invest' to excess."[7]

II.   Interests affected by corporate groups

The same factors that make a group structure attractive for a parent company can cause concern to other stakeholders. While activities of subsidiaries are conducted in the interest of the whole group, liability arising from these activities is limited to the assets of the individual subsidiary. For the creditors of a subsidiary this is particularly dangerous if the company is engaged in hazardous activities or is thinly capitalized and sustained by intra-group loans. Transfers of value from the subsidiary to its parent or other related corporations by way of pricing arrangements for goods or services, or the taking of the subsidiary's corporate opportunities, may be harder to detect than in a single corporation where conveyances to a dominant shareholder will usually be more obvious. For these reasons, corporate groups can present significant dangers for the minority shareholders of a subsidiary.

Less obviously, group structures may also affect the interests of minority shareholders of a parent corporation. As first explained by Eisenberg,[8] veto rights that such shareholders have with respect to corporate actions requiring supermajority approval can effectively be undermined by setting up a holding structure where the assets are owned and the business

---

[7] Williamson (1985: 283).

[8] Eisenberg (1976); the book is based on a series of four articles published between 1969 and 1975.

activities are conducted by subsidiaries while the parent corporation merely acts as a holding company. The parent's voting rights in the subsidiaries are exercised by, or under the direction of, the parent's management. Since directors are usually elected by no more than a simple majority of the votes, a majority shareholder will usually control the board. Thus, by virtue of its influence over the parent's management, a dominant shareholder of the parent company can control decisions on matters in subsidiary corporations that could have been vetoed by the parent's minority had the assets remained at the parent level. Where, as under German law, shareholders decide on the distribution of profits,[9] this right is in effect exercised by the parent's management if the business is conducted and the profits earned by a subsidiary, rather than by the parent itself. Retention of profits in the subsidiary can be used to starve out the parent's minority shareholders; absent a dominant shareholder, the parent's management could also use it to control the group's internal financing. Therefore, the decision to structure an enterprise as a corporate group rather than as a single corporation not only is a matter of expediency, but can have major effects on the governance of a shareholder's investment.

III.   How are corporate groups regulated?

Groups of companies are regulated by a number of special laws focused on particular areas such as accounting (preparation of consolidated group accounts), taxation (concept of worldwide unitary taxation), antitrust (concept of conglomerate mergers) and insolvency law (worldwide assets in liquidations), and particular types of companies, such as financial institutions (bank holding companies) and public utilities are specially regulated. Each of these laws addresses the fact that, although the units are legally separate entities, they operate in a unified group that is guided by central management. In this chapter, rather than recounting the rules in these specialized topics, we will examine the real heart of the problem. We look at how the existence of a group can affect the basic characteristics of a corporation, such as independent legal personality, the duties of management to the company, the integrity of corporate capital, and the protection of shareholders against liability for corporate debts.

Of our three jurisdictions, Germany is the only one with a statutory body of "group law." This is in part a function of the mandatory nature of German law. That is, Delaware law would allow the certificate of

---

[9] § 174(1) AktG.

incorporation of a company to place all management powers in the hands of a body other than the board, which would include the board of a holding company, and regulate the relationship between the two companies relying on the dominant shareholder's fiduciary duty to protect the minority shareholders. Rather than delegation to private ordering, German *Konzernrecht* overrides other mandatory provisions of the *Aktiengesetz* and allows fundamental characteristics of the corporation to be altered, so as to achieve in practice what Williamson describes as the benefits of the M-form, such as creating an "internal capital market" to allocate resources among the group members.

A.   The regulation of groups by specific statute: German Konzernrecht

German *Konzernrecht* is found in §§ 15–19 and 291–328 of the *Aktiengesetz*. These rules are designed for the protection of the subsidiary's minority shareholders and creditors. They are based on the notion that the general rules on minority and shareholder protection are insufficient if a controlling shareholder has substantial business interests besides the stake in the controlled corporation because the controlling shareholder may have an incentive to damage the corporation for the sake of promoting these other business interests, and because it may be difficult to detect whether the controlled corporation has in fact been damaged if it is engaged in business with other companies dominated by the controlling shareholder.

These basic concerns are reflected in the statutory rules and their interpretation. The definition sections[10] apply to "enterprises" (*Unternehmen*) irrespective of their legal form. An "enterprise" as referred to in these provisions is any entity engaged in commercial activities of a dimension making it reasonable to suspect that the entity might promote these other activities at the expense of the controlled corporation. This definition of "enterprise" can apply both to individuals and to public entities such as states. The substantive rules of §§ 291 *et seq.* of the *Aktiengesetz* deal only with situations where a stock corporation is the subsidiary of an enterprise. The practical effect of these provisions is to allow an independent corporate entity and its management to be turned into a unit of a larger whole and serve within it, as well as to provide specific safeguards to protect the most vulnerable constituencies in this arrangement. There are two ways in which a concern may be formed: expressly, by contracts

---

[10] §§ 15–19 AktG.

referred to as "enterprise agreements" (*Unternehmensverträge*), or in fact (*de facto*) by actual influence (*faktischer Konzern*). With regard to groups formed by contract, the law provides the types of enterprise contracts available, certain mandatory conditions they must contain, and the manner in which they must be approved. With regard to *de facto* concerns, the law specifies the conditions constituting such concerns and the protections that are triggered by its existence.

1. Enterprise agreements Only stock corporations (AGs), partnerships limited by shares (KGaAs)[11] and limited liability companies (GmbHs)[12] may take part as a subsidiary in an enterprise agreement. Because such agreements allow the parent to offset its profits against losses of the subsidiary and *vice versa*, they are frequently entered into as a prerequisite for taxation of the parties on a consolidated basis. Enterprise agreements may subject a subsidiary company to the instructions of its parent (*Beherrschungsvertrag*) or divert all or part of the profit of the subsidiary into the coffers of the parent (*Gewinnabführungsvertrag*).[13] Enterprise agreements must be approved by a 75 percent majority of the votes cast by the dominated or profit-transferring company's shareholders[14] and, if the parent corporation is an AG, by 75 percent of the votes cast by its own shareholders.[15] Prior to the shareholder vote, the *Vorstand* must prepare a report on the contents of the agreement, focusing particularly, in the case of a profit transfer agreement, on the amount of compensation to be given for profits diverted.[16] Unless the subsidiary is wholly owned, enterprise agreements must be examined by auditors.[17] Like charter documents and shareholder resolutions, an enterprise agreement does not take effect until it is entered into the commercial register for the seat of the subsidiary.[18]

A domination agreement (*Beherrschungsvertrag*) directly overrides § 76 of the *Aktiengesetz* by subjecting the *Vorstand* of the subsidiary to the instructions of the parent.[19] The range of such instructions is quite open-ended, and could include orders to relinquish corporate opportunities, make discount deliveries, transfer proprietary information, and perform services without compensation.[20] Another possible effect of a domination agreement is that, when the parent is not subject to co-determination and the subsidiary is, the effects of co-determination on the subsidiary

---

[11] § 291(1) AktG.   [12] See § 30(1) GmbHG).   [13] § 291(1) AktG.   [14] § 293(1) AktG.
[15] § 293(2) AktG.   [16] § 293a AktG.   [17] § 293b AktG.   [18] § 294(2) AktG.
[19] § 308(1) AktG.   [20] Kübler and Assmann (2006: 428).

are essentially side-stepped.[21] Would a valid domination agreement have changed the way the Delaware court decided *Sinclair* v. *Levien*?

The *Aktiengesetz* both opens up the possibility of making a corporation a unit of an overall group and sets boundaries on the domination relationship. For example, both the legal representative of the parent and the *Vorstand* of the subsidiary must meet the standard of care of a "prudent and reasonable manager" when performing their duties in connection with the domination agreement.[22]

A profit transfer agreement (*Gewinnabführungsvertrag*) requires the transferring corporation to divert all or a part of its profits to the recipient corporation. Although such agreements do not give the recipient company the right to demand the transfer of funds at any time, they do directly override the capital maintenance rules that are otherwise applicable to the transferring AG.[23] However, the *Aktiengesetz* sets a maximum amount that can be diverted; in particular, profits that have been retained prior to the profit transfer agreement may not be transferred to the parent[24] and legal reserves may not be reduced by profit transfers.[25]

In order to allow effective integration of the subsidiary in the corporate group, neither the capital maintenance rules nor the financial assistance rules apply to it after conclusion of the enterprise agreement.[26] The *Aktiengesetz* does, however, contain a number of protections for the subsidiary's minority shareholders and creditors in the case of enterprise agreements. First, the parent must compensate the subsidiary for all losses incurred during the duration of the agreement, regardless of their cause.[27] Secondly, the minority shareholders of the subsidiary may demand to either receive a guaranteed dividend[28] or to be bought out by the parent at a fair price.[29] Finally, the creditors of the subsidiary can demand the posting of security for outstanding debts upon termination of the agreement.[30]

2. The *de facto* concern   Because of the extensive procedures and requirements for entering into and operating under enterprise contracts, many companies operate groups that are in fact dominated by a holding or lead company without ever signing a formal enterprise agreement.

---

[21] Kübler and Assmann (2006: 427).   [22] §§ 309–310 AktG.   [23] § 291(3) AktG.
[24] § 301 AktG.   [25] § 300 AktG.   [26] §§ 291(3), 57(1), 71a(1) AktG.   [27] § 302 AktG.
[28] § 304 AktG.   [29] § 305 AktG.   [30] § 303 AktG.

This type of relationship would not need to be based solely on influence from a shareholding, although the primary element should derive from corporate law (i.e. voting rights), and when a "dominating undertaking" is present without an enterprise agreement between the parties, it is referred to as a "*de facto*" concern.[31] The statutory key to whether two or more companies have formed a *de facto* concern is the existence of domination/dependence relationships as defined in § 17 of the *Aktiengesetz*. This provision specifies that the primary evidence of such a relationship is the ability to exercise dominant influence,[32] but, beyond stating that a majority holding creates a presumption of such influence,[33] does not provide guidance on the other circumstances that would create the triggering influence. One such circumstance would certainly be the ability of the management of one company to appoint or remove the management of another – which can exist even absent a majority holding. The policy behind the regulation of *de facto* concerns is that, where any person (legal, physical or governmental) through her dominant influence has the capacity to cause conflicts between the duty of the subsidiary's management to serve the subsidiary's best interests and the influence of the dominating person, legal safeguards should be available. It is important to remember that the *possibility* of influence and not its *actual exercise* is determinative under § 17 of the *Aktiengesetz*. On the other hand, if a majority holding does not in fact give its owner the possibility of exercising a dominant influence on the issuer – such as when a voting cap applies to the shares of an unlisted company or an agreement guaranteeing independence is in place – the presumption set out in § 17 can be rebutted.

If a dominant influence is present the provisions of §§ 311–318 of the *Aktiengesetz* apply to this *de facto* group. First, the *Vorstand* of the subservient company must draw up a "dependence report" (*Abhängigkeitsbericht*) detailing the relationship with the dominant company.[34] Although the report need not be disclosed to the shareholders, it must be examined by the company's accountants[35] and its *Aufsichtsrat*,[36] and, if irregularities are present, the shareholders may demand a special audit of the report,[37]

---

[31] §§ 311 *et seq.* AktG.   [32] § 17(1) AktG.

[33] § 17(2) AktG. The calculation of whether a company in fact has a majority holding, like the calculation of holdings for reporting requirements under § 21 WpHG and for the making of a mandatory bid under § 30 WpÜG, includes voting rights counted as belonging to the company pursuant to the attribution rules of § 16 AktG.

[34] § 312 AktG.   [35] § 313 AktG.   [36] § 314 AktG.   [37] § 315 AktG.

which they may inspect under their information rights,[38] and on which they can base a derivative suit against the *Vorstand*.[39] The basic rules for *de facto* groups are that any actions adverse to the interests of the subsidiary are presumed to have been caused by the parent, and, if the parent causes the subservient company to act to its own prejudice, the former must compensate for such damage by the close of the financial year.[40] If this compensation is not paid or promised, the dominating company and its *Vorstand* are liable for the damages the subservient company has suffered.[41] Pursuant to § 311(2) of the *Aktiengesetz*, the parent may postpone this compensation for damages until the end of the financial year, and even a binding agreement to compensate the subsidiary at some later date is sufficient. While the law of *de facto* groups does not expressly provide for an exemption from the capital maintenance rules, the High Federal Court[42] and a majority of scholars interpret the privilege granted by § 311(2) as such exemption. However, the scope of this exemption has lately become uncertain because, according to a recent judgment by the High Federal Court,[43] the management of a subsidiary AG in a *de facto* group may comply with a parent's requests only if it can reasonably expect compensation.

3.   Extension of Konzernrecht by the courts   The statutory rules of German *Konzernrecht* were designed to protect minority shareholders and creditors of subsidiary corporations from what the German legislator perceived as the specific dangers of corporate groups. The potential of group structures for undermining the rights of the shareholders of the parent corporation was recognized only later. The German courts addressed this problem in a series of cases culminating in the *Holzmüller* and *Gelatine* decisions, both reprinted in part in this chapter. In these cases, the courts extended the statutory law to new matters through judicial precedent (*Rechtsfortbildung*) in a process that is quite common in Germany but often unrecognized by Common Law observers of the Civil Law.

The problem later addressed by the courts was actually raised first by Eisenberg, who of course is an American scholar, in the mid-1970s.[44] His work was adopted and expanded by German scholars in numerous

---

[38] § 145(4) AktG.
[39] §§ 317(4), 318(4) AktG, in connection with § 309(4) AktG.   [40] § 311 AktG.
[41] §§ 317–318 AktG.   [42] BGH, *Der Konzern* 2009, 49, 50 (MPS).
[43] BGH, *Der Konzern*, 2009, 49, 51 (MPS).   [44] See Eisenberg (1976: 255–315).

articles and books, some of which are cited in the *Holzmüller* decision. After the issue had been discussed by the legal community for almost eight years, the *Holzmüller* case came up for decision in the High Federal Court. The Court was careful not to expound a general doctrine of unwritten shareholder rights, but limited its decision to the particular issue of the case. In the wake of *Holzmüller*, a substantial body of lower court "case law" dealing with the judicially expounded rights of shareholders of a parent company developed, accompanied by a large body of legal commentary. The doctrine arising from *Holzmüller* still presented a number of ambiguities and uncertainties, as most judicial doctrines do, which the High Federal Court attempted to clarify in the *Gelatine* decision in 2004.

B.   The regulation of groups through constitutional documents

While the UK does not provide a statutory law of groups like that found in the *Aktiengesetz*, the Companies Act 2006 nevertheless includes provisions on parent–subsidiary "control contracts" that function like a German *Beherrschungsvertrag*. Under UK law, a "control contract" is "a contract in writing conferring such a right which (a) is of a kind authorised by the articles of the undertaking in relation to which the right is exercisable, and (b) is permitted by the law under which that undertaking is established."[45] From this, one understands that the articles of a subsidiary may be drafted to convey control powers to a parent company unless the rights sought to be conveyed are not of a type that are "permitted by law" to be so conveyed, such as excessive distributions to shareholders or violation of the rights of minority shareholders. Because the Companies Act incorporates a number of mandatory rules – not least the capital maintenance rules – from the Second Directive, the freedom to custom tailor governance and finance is restricted by the same type of rules that operate in Germany. As a result, UK companies are free to set up interlocking concerns to the extent that the operation of the concern does not infringe on rights otherwise guaranteed. In practice, the principal difference may be transaction costs, because, for a UK company, the rules would have to be drafted for the articles of the subservient company, whereas German law provides them in the statute.

---

[45]   Schedule 7, para. 4(2) CA 2006.

In comparison to the EU rules (particularly on such matters as capital maintenance), Delaware law allows significantly more play for freedom of contract in parent–subsidiary dealings. It is true that Delaware law contains no rules on the regulation of corporate groups, but this is largely because the flexibility of the law allows the parties to adapt their constitutional documents to the desired framework of governance. For example, a corporation is to be "managed by or under the direction of a board ... except as may be otherwise provided in ... its certificate of incorporation,"[46] which would allow a parent to place management in the hands of itself, as majority shareholder, if that would be expedient. Such free structuring is, however, held in check by the fiduciary duties of the dominant company, as we discussed in *Kahn* v. *Lynch Communication* (see Chapter 19) and the fiduciary duties of the subservient company's board of directors, as discussed in *Weinberger* v. *UOP, Inc.* (see Chapter 22). How the behavior of the parent will be evaluated will depend on whether it engages in self-dealing when exercising its influence over the subsidiary, as the Delaware Supreme Court explained in the *Sinclair* decision reprinted in part immediately below.

Legal form versus economic function

Some groups can be quite large. Major oil companies, for example, may have an entire group of companies in their home and principal markets and at least one subsidiary in every other country in the world. Other companies, though by no means as global or well-established, can also make extensive use of compartmentalization through subsidiaries. For example, the infamous Enron Corporation listed about 2,500 subsidiaries on its annual 10-K filing for the year 2000.[47]

Even if a corporate group has 2,500 subsidiaries, if these companies are corporations, each one has the five core characteristics we have discussed throughout this text: (1) legal personality; (2) limited liability; (3) transferable shares; (4) centralized management; and (5) shared ownership by investors. Each of these characteristics can lead to tensions when the company is a mere unit within the structure of a larger corporate

---

[46] § 141(a) DGCL.
[47] See Enron's corporate filings on the SEC's electronic data gathering and retrieval system (EDGAR) at www.sec.gov.

group. The insertion of a company into a group can call into question the very characteristics that make it a corporation. When facing these situations, judges are often confronted with a choice between "legal form" and "economic reality."

If a corporate statute authorizes the board of directors to make a disposition of assets or to change the holding structure in a way that does not trigger a shareholder vote (see Chapter 22), can a shareholder complain that the change – albeit following the order of governance foreseen in the statute – has an effect on his rights that requires a shareholder vote? Should judges change the balance of competencies set out in corporate statutes? Read the German High Federal Court's decisions in *Holzmüller* and *Gelatine*. What is the difference between the two cases? Has the court changed its position on judicial intervention for shareholder rights or do the transactions addressed have significantly different impacts on the shareholders?

Looking at the group from the other side of the holding structure, what if a majority shareholder decides to sell his shares? What if he decides to replace management or undertake legal changes in the corporate documents to regulate the structure and procedures of the board in the company he controls? Should a court prevent a shareholder from exercising power expressly provided for in the statute if it disapproves of the shareholder's behavior? When should it so intervene? Read *Hollinger International Inc. v. Conrad M. Black*.

If a group presents a seamless economic entity, should the liability of its separate entities be compartmentalized and separate or collapsed to match economic reality? Read *Re Polly Peck International plc*, *In Re Rave Communications, Inc. v. Entertainment Equities, Inc.* and *In Re Oil Spill by the "Amoco Cadiz."* When will a court consider disregarding the separate legal existence of a legal entity ("piercing its veil") and attributing liability to the parent company? Are the tests used in *Polly Peck* and *Rave Communications* different? Do you agree with the decision in *Amoco Cadiz*? If all courts agreed with that holding – which they do not, as the *Amoco Cadiz* is an isolated, minority position that might have been taken solely because of political pressure resulting from damage to a foreign country's shores – would the use of corporate groups decrease? Which position is on the whole more just? Is limited liability in a corporate group unnecessary? How does the *Polly Peck* decision relate to § 15 of the Securities Act?

Questions for discussion

1. Name some reasons for structuring an enterprise as a corporate group rather than as a single corporation.
2. How does the law allow groups to enjoy the benefits of what Williamson calls an "internal capital market" while also retaining compartmentalized, limited liability?
3. Section 1162(2)(c) of and paragraph 4 of Schedule 7 to the Companies Act 2006 deal with the right to exercise a dominant influence: Could covenants in loan agreements between a company and a bank, requiring the bank's approval of any major transaction, bring the bank within the ambit of these provisions?
4. Pursuant to German doctrine fleshing out §§ 15 *et seq.* and §§ 291 *et seq.* AktG, an "enterprise" within the meaning of these provisions is any person (even an individual shareholder or the state) with an economic interest beyond his investment in the corporation, provided such outside interest is substantial enough to give rise to an expectation that the shareholder might abuse his influence to the detriment of the corporation in order to promote his outside interest. Compare this approach to that taken by UK and US law. Are there valid reasons to design special rules for dominant "enterprises" (defined as referred to above), or is it preferable to apply the same set of rules to all dominant shareholders regardless of their economic interests outside of the corporation?
5. What are the major differences in regulation under German law between groups based on enterprise contracts and groups based on de facto domination?
6. § 17 AktG establishes the presumption that an AG is dominated by its majority shareholder. What is this presumption based on in view of the fact that shareholders of a German AG are not allowed to manage the corporation and do not even elect and dismiss the management board? How can the presumption be rebutted?
7. What is the purpose of a control report pursuant to § 312 AktG? Who has access to that report (see §§ 314, 315 AktG)?
8. How are the rights of minority shareholders of subsidiaries protected in our jurisdictions?
9. §§ 291(3), 57(1), 71a(1) AktG exempt payments made by a subsidiary to the parent company pursuant to an enterprise contract from the capital maintenance rules of §§ 57, 58 AktG and the prohibition of financial assistance. Are these exemptions compatible with the capital maintenance framework imposed by the Second Company Law Directive?

Cases

Protection of the subsidiary's minority shareholders

Sinclair Oil Corporation v. Francis S. Levien
Supreme Court of Delaware
280 A 2d 717 (1971)
[*Text edited; citations and footnotes omitted*]

WOLCOTT, Chief Justice

This is an appeal by the defendant, Sinclair Oil Corporation (hereafter Sinclair) ... in a derivative action requiring Sinclair to account for damages sustained by its subsidiary, Sinclair Venezuelan Oil Company (hereafter Sinven), organized by Sinclair for the purpose of operating in Venezuela, as a result of dividends paid by Sinven, the denial to Sinven of industrial development, and a breach of contract between Sinclair's wholly owned subsidiary, Sinclair International Oil Company, and Sinven.

Sinclair, operating primarily as a holding company, is in the business of exploring for oil and of producing and marketing crude oil and oil products. At all times relevant to this litigation, it owned about 97% of Sinven's stock. The plaintiff owns about 3000 of 120,000 publicly held shares of Sinven. Sinven, incorporated in 1922, has been engaged in petroleum operations primarily in Venezuela and since 1959 has operated exclusively in Venezuela.

Sinclair nominates all members of Sinven's board of directors. The Chancellor found as a fact that the directors were not independent of Sinclair. Almost without exception, they were officers, directors, or employees of corporations in the Sinclair complex. By reason of Sinclair's domination, it is clear that Sinclair owed Sinven a fiduciary duty ...

The Chancellor held that because of Sinclair's fiduciary duty and its control over Sinven, its relationship with Sinven must meet the test of intrinsic fairness. The standard of intrinsic fairness involves both a high degree of fairness and a shift in the burden of proof. Under this standard the burden is on Sinclair to prove, subject to careful judicial scrutiny, that its transactions with Sinven were objectively fair ...

Sinclair argues that the transactions between it and Sinven should be tested, not by the test of intrinsic fairness with the accompanying shift of the burden of proof, but by the business judgment rule under which a court will not interfere with the judgment of a board of directors unless there is a showing of gross and palpable overreaching ...

We think, however, that Sinclair's argument in this respect is misconceived. When the situation involves a parent and a subsidiary, with the parent controlling the transaction and fixing the terms, the test of intrinsic fairness, with its resulting shifting of the burden of proof, is applied ... The basic situation for the application of the rule is the one in which the parent has received a benefit to the exclusion and at the expense of the subsidiary.

Recently, this court dealt with the question of fairness in parent–subsidiary dealings in *Getty Oil Co.* v. *Skelly Oil Co., supra*. In that case, both parent and subsidiary were in the business of refining and marketing crude oil and crude oil products. The Oil Import Board ruled that the subsidiary, because it was controlled by the parent, was no longer entitled to a separate allocation of imported crude oil. The subsidiary then contended that it had a right to share the quota of crude oil allotted to the parent. We ruled that the business judgment standard should be applied to determine this contention. Although the subsidiary suffered a loss through the administration of the oil import quotas, the parent gained nothing. The parent's quota was derived solely from its own past use. The past use of the subsidiary did not cause an increase in the parent's quota. Nor did the parent usurp a quota of the subsidiary. Since the parent received nothing from the subsidiary to the exclusion of the minority stockholders of the subsidiary, there was no self-dealing. Therefore, the business judgment standard was properly applied.

A parent does indeed owe a fiduciary duty to its subsidiary when there are parent–subsidiary dealings. However, this alone will not evoke the intrinsic fairness standard. This standard will be applied only when the fiduciary duty is accompanied by self-dealing – the situation when a parent is on both sides of a transaction with its subsidiary. Self-dealing occurs when the parent, by virtue of its domination of the subsidiary, causes the subsidiary to act in such a way that the parent receives something from the subsidiary to the exclusion of, and detriment to, the minority stockholders of the subsidiary.

We turn now to the facts. The plaintiff argues that, from 1960 through 1966, Sinclair caused Sinven to pay out such excessive dividends that the industrial development of Sinven was effectively prevented, and it became in reality a corporation in dissolution.

From 1960 through 1966, Sinven paid out $108,000,000 in dividends ($38,000,000 in excess of Sinven's earnings during the same period). The Chancellor held that Sinclair caused these dividends to be paid during a period when it had a need for large amounts of cash. Although the dividends paid exceeded earnings, the plaintiff concedes that the payments were made in compliance with 8 Del. C. s 170, authorizing payment of dividends out of surplus or net profits. However, the plaintiff attacks these dividends on the ground that they resulted from an improper motive – Sinclair's need for cash. The Chancellor, applying the intrinsic fairness standard, held that Sinclair did not sustain its burden of proving that these dividends were intrinsically fair to the minority stockholders of Sinven.

Since it is admitted that the dividends were paid in strict compliance with 8 Del. C. § 170, the alleged excessiveness of the payments alone would not state a cause of action. Nevertheless, compliance with the applicable statute may not, under all circumstances, justify all dividend payments. If a plaintiff can meet his burden of proving that a dividend cannot be grounded on any reasonable business objective, then the courts can and will interfere with the board's decision to pay the dividend.

Sinclair contends that it is improper to apply the intrinsic fairness standard to dividend payments even when the board which voted for the dividends is completely dominated. In support of this contention, Sinclair relies heavily on *American District Telegraph Co. (ADT)* v. *Grinnell Corp.* ... Plaintiffs were minority stockholders of ADT, a subsidiary of Grinnell. The plaintiffs alleged that Grinnell, realizing that it would soon have to sell its ADT stock because of a pending anti-trust action, caused ADT to pay excessive dividends. Because the dividend payments conformed with applicable statutory law, and the plaintiffs could not prove an abuse of discretion, the court ruled that the complaint did not state a cause of action ...

We do not accept the argument that the intrinsic fairness test can never be applied to a dividend declaration by a dominated board ... If such a dividend is in essence self-dealing by the parent, then the intrinsic fairness standard is the proper standard. For example, suppose a parent dominates a subsidiary and its board of directors. The subsidiary has outstanding two classes of stock, X and Y. Class X is owned by the parent and Class Y is owned by minority stockholders of the subsidiary. If the subsidiary, at the direction of the parent, declares a dividend on its Class X stock only, this might well be self-dealing by the parent. It would be receiving something from the subsidiary to the exclusion of and detrimental to its minority stockholders. This self-dealing, coupled with the parent's fiduciary duty, would make intrinsic fairness the proper standard by which to evaluate the dividend payments.

Consequently it must be determined whether the dividend payments by Sinven were, in essence, self-dealing by Sinclair. The dividends resulted in great sums of money being transferred from Sinven to Sinclair. However, a proportionate share of this money was received by the minority shareholders of Sinven. Sinclair received nothing from Sinven to the exclusion of its minority stockholders. As such, these dividends were not self-dealing. We hold therefore that the Chancellor erred in applying the intrinsic fairness test as to these dividend payments. The business judgment standard should have been applied.

We conclude that the facts demonstrate that the dividend payments complied with the business judgment standard and with 8 Del. C. § 170. The motives for causing the declaration of dividends are immaterial unless the plaintiff can show that the dividend payments resulted from improper motives and amounted to waste ...

The plaintiff proved no business opportunities which came to Sinven independently and which Sinclair either took to itself or denied to Sinven. As a matter of fact, with two minor exceptions which resulted in losses, all of Sinven's operations have been conducted in Venezuela, and Sinclair had a policy of exploiting its oil properties located in different countries by subsidiaries located in the particular countries.

From 1960 to 1966 Sinclair purchased or developed oil fields in Alaska, Canada, Paraguay, and other places around the world. The plaintiff contends that these were all opportunities which could have been taken by Sinven. The Chancellor concluded that Sinclair had not proved that its denial of expansion opportunities to Sinven was intrinsically fair. He based this conclusion on the following findings of fact. Sinclair made no real effort to expand Sinven. The excessive dividends paid by Sinven resulted in so great a cash drain as to effectively deny to Sinven any ability to expand. During this same period Sinclair actively pursued a company-wide policy of developing through its subsidiaries new sources of revenue, but Sinven was not permitted to participate and was confined in its activities to Venezuela.

However, the plaintiff could point to no opportunities which came to Sinven. Therefore, Sinclair usurped no business opportunity belonging to Sinven. Since Sinclair received nothing from Sinven to the exclusion of and detriment to Sinven's minority stockholders, there was no self-dealing. Therefore, business judgment is the proper standard by which to evaluate Sinclair's expansion policies.

[Text omitted]

Next, Sinclair argues that the Chancellor committed error when he held it liable to Sinven for breach of contract.

In 1961 Sinclair created Sinclair International Oil Company (hereafter International), a wholly owned subsidiary used for the purpose of coordinating all of Sinclair's foreign operations. All crude purchases by Sinclair were made thereafter through International.

On September 28, 1961, Sinclair caused Sinven to contract with International whereby Sinven agreed to sell all of its crude oil and refined products to International at specified prices. The contract provided for minimum and maximum quantities and prices. The plaintiff contends that Sinclair caused this contract to be breached in two respects. Although the contract called for payment on receipt, International's payments lagged as much as 30 days after receipt. Also, the contract required International to purchase at least a fixed minimum amount of crude and refined products from Sinven. International did not comply with this requirement.

Clearly, Sinclair's act of contracting with its dominated subsidiary was self-dealing. Under the contract Sinclair received the products produced by Sinven, and of course the minority shareholders of Sinven were not able to share in the receipt of these products. If the contract was breached, then Sinclair received these products to the detriment of Sinven's minority shareholders. We agree with the Chancellor's finding that the contract was breached by Sinclair, both as to the time of payments and the amounts purchased.

Although a parent need not bind itself by a contract with its dominated subsidiary, Sinclair chose to operate in this manner. As Sinclair has received the benefits of this contract, so must it comply with the contractual duties.

Under the intrinsic fairness standard, Sinclair must prove that its causing Sinven not to enforce the contract was intrinsically fair to the minority shareholders of Sinven. Sinclair has failed to meet this burden. Late payments were clearly breaches for which Sinven should have sought and received adequate damages. As to the quantities purchased, Sinclair argues that it purchased all the products produced by Sinven. This, however, does not satisfy the standard of intrinsic fairness. Sinclair has failed to prove that Sinven could not possibly have produced or someway have obtained the contract minimums. As such, Sinclair must account on this claim.

[*Text omitted*]

Protection of the parent's minority shareholders

In Re Holzmüller
High Federal Court, Second Civil Division
February 25, 1982, BGHZ 83, 122
[*Partial, unofficial translation of official opinion text*]

Official head note

1. In the case of a serious encroachment on the rights and interests of the shareholders, for example, in the case of a spin-off of operations constituting the most valuable part of the corporate assets into a subsidiary specially established for this purpose, the *Vorstand* can exceptionally not only be authorized, but also obligated pursuant to § 119(2) AktG to obtain a decision from the shareholders' meeting.

2. If a shareholder proves that the *Vorstand* failed to obtain the necessary approval of the shareholders' meeting for the spin-off of a corporate division, the shareholder may file a complaint to have the measure declared null or illegal.

3. The court addresses the question if and at what point in time a shareholder in such a case may also seek an injunction to desist from action or to unwind a transaction.

4. No transfer of assets within the meaning of § 361 AktG[48] shall exist, in spite of a spin-off of the most valuable part of the business, if the company itself still remains sufficiently able to pursue, even to a limited extent, its corporate purpose pursuant to the *Satzung* with the remaining corporate assets.

---

[48] *Editors' note*: now § 179a AktG.

5. If the *Vorstand* has transferred the most valuable part of the corporate assets to a subsidiary especially established for this purpose, the parent company is obligated to each of its shareholders to obtain the approval of its shareholders' meeting for an increase in capital of the subsidiary with the same majority as would be required for an equivalent measure in the parent company itself. This does not address whether the same would apply if the shareholders' meeting had approved or ratified the spin-off with the majority necessary to amend the *Satzung*.

Facts

The deceased businessman/merchant, Mr. R, the executor of whose estate filed the underlying complaint in this action (hereinafter referred to as "the Plaintiff"), was a shareholder of the Defendant Corporation, and held DM 250,000 of its DM 3.2 million corporate capital. The corporate purpose of the Defendant Corporation included and still includes, pursuant to § 2 of its *Satzung*, the operation of a handling and warehousing facility for lumber and other goods, as well as the broking, execution and financing of transactions in lumber. The original version of § 2(1) No. 3 of the articles also contained the purpose of "taking holdings in other companies engaged in the lumber business or in similar industries and/or types of commerce, including the takeover or purchase of such companies." In a shareholders' meeting of July 14, 1972, this provision was amended – with the affirmative vote of the Plaintiff – to read as following (§ 2(2)):

> "The corporation is further authorized to establish and purchase other companies, as well as to take holdings in other companies. The corporation may cede [*überlassen*] its operations in whole or in part to such companies."

A member of the *Vorstand* explained the purpose of this amendment in the shareholders' meeting. It is intended to:

> "establish the precondition for a spin-off of the corporation's port operations into a planned partnership limited by shares, in the course of which the corporation would become a holding of the investment capital of the port operations in exchange for a block of the partnership's shares."

The director justified this by stating that the port operations, following the granting of complete handling rights that the corporation obtained for it in 1967, had developed into a corporate division that was now mostly separate from the originally dominant lumber dealing and brokerage activities, and had an independent organization.

Following the establishment of the H Seaport-Holding GmbH on June 22, 1972, the latter company, the Defendant Corporation and three other incorporators set up the H Partnership Limited by Shares (hereinafter Holzmüller KGaA) on November

13, 1972, with the Seaport-Holding GmbH as the general partner and a capital of DM 4.8 million. Pursuant to the *Satzung*, the Defendant Corporation contributed the port operations, including all of its assets and liabilities, to the partnership in exchange for 95,997 shares with a nominal value of DM 50 each. Holzmüller KGaA was entered into the commercial register on December 27, 1972. Today, the Defendant Corporation alone holds all of the shares and the entire corporate capital of the Holding GmbH that acts as general partner.

The Plaintiff complains that the spin-off of the port operations without the approval of the shareholders' meeting is without effect because it violates § 361 AktG, as a disallowed amendment of the corporate purpose, and also violates § 138 BGB. The Plaintiff alleges that these operations were the core activities of the corporation, and significantly outweighed the activity that remained in the Defendant corporation, particularly the lumber business, in terms of absolute value and income generated. It is alleged that the spin-off made it possible to increase the capital of the growing port operations without allowing the minority shareholders to participate, and thus to eliminate their pre-emptive rights. In particular, the Plaintiff seeks:

1. A determination that the contribution of the port operations to the assets of the Holzmüller KGaA and all related legal actions are void;
2. As relief, to order the Defendant Corporation in its capacity as sole member of the Holzmüller KGaA to re-transfer the port operations;
3. As relief, to determine that the Defendant Corporation in the aforesaid capacity must,
   a) obtain the approval of the Defendant Corporation's shareholders with the required majority for all measures that the law requires to be approved with a shareholders' resolution carried by at least three-quarters of the corporate capital;
   b) particularly for increases in the capital of Holzmüller KGaA, even if already provided for in the *Satzung*, obtain the approval of the Defendant Corporation's shareholders' meeting with the majority the law requires for the relevant measure, and disallow the measure if such approval is not obtained;
4. As relief, to order the Defendant Corporation to make a binding declaration that it will give the Plaintiff, in the case of an increase in capital of Holzmüller KGaA, the right to acquire shares with the same economic effect as if the port operations were still an asset of the Defendant corporation.

In its response to the complaint, the Defendant Corporation denied the legal claims of the Plaintiff, expressed doubt regarding the active and passive standing of the parties for this action, and disagreed with the factual allegation that the spun-off port operations were the core activity of its business, whose central focus was the traditional lumber business that has suffered only in recent years because of the depressed building industry. The legal division of the two corporate divisions was advisable from both an economic and organizational point of view because of their actual development. No increase in capital is currently necessary and thus none is planned.

The trial court and the court of appeals both dismissed the claim. The Plaintiff continues to seek relief with its appeal to this Court.

Discussion

I.

The Court of Appeals was correct in finding that the Plaintiff's first plea for a determination that the spin-off of the port operations from the assets of the Defendant Corporation and all related legal actions are void, is permissible but not supported on the merits (see the printed text of the decision in ZIP 1980, 1000, and JZ 1981, 231, with a comment from Großfeld; Regional Ct. Decision: AG 1980, 199).

1. The complaint does not address a legal relationship between the parties. A request pursuant to § 256 Code of Civil Procedure can, however, also seek a determination that a legal relationship exists between the defendants and a third party, provided that this is also meaningful for the legal relationships between the parties, the plaintiff has a legal interest in a prompt clarification of this question, and – what is necessary in this case – corporate law does not provide a sufficient mechanism for the resolution of this type of dispute. None of these points cast doubt upon the admissibility of the complaint.

The complaint that is to be understood as correctly falling under § 256 Code of Civil Procedure is primarily that the obligation of the Defendant to transfer all of the assets and liabilities of the port operations into Holzmüller KGaA and the consequent, actual conveyance of such assets should never have become effective without the permission of the shareholders' meeting pursuant to § 361 AktG. The Plaintiff sees the spin-off that nevertheless took place as an illegal encroachment upon the competence of the shareholders' meeting and upon the governance rights of the individual shareholders intended to eliminate the pre-emptive rights to which they are entitled in the case of an increase in capital. The Plaintiff's questioning of the legality of the spin-off therefore is related to his status as a shareholder and his legal relationship to the Defendant Corporation. If the spin-off were to be found null and void, the Plaintiff would have good reason to demand that the management bodies take the appropriate, consequent actions. If, rather, the Defendant Corporation in the face of such a judgment still sought to retain the actual state of affairs to the detriment of the Plaintiff, and use it to take further actions that affected, for example, the corporate capital or the allocation of profits, this could serve the Plaintiff as a basis for concrete remedial requests or damage claims. It could also at the least prompt the appropriate proposals in the shareholders' meeting to refuse approval of the management of the corporation's affairs by the *Vorstand* and *Aufsichtsrat*. Here lies the Plaintiff's legal interest in the desired judicial determination.

No specific provision of corporate law preempts the Plaintiff's action on the basis of § 256 Code of Civil Procedure. The provisions in §§ 241 *et seq.* AktG that allow claims of nullity and other challenges do not exclude ordinary requests for judicial determination, even from shareholders, when a legal interest exists (see BGHZ 76, 191, 198 *et seq.*), particularly when there is no resolution that can be challenged under such provisions. In particular, one may not argue that a shareholder's right to be heard in the affairs of the corporation is limited to the casting of voting rights at the general meeting (RG JW 1927, 1677 *et seq.*), in a case like that before us in which a transaction is alleged to be void, precisely because of an impermissible circumvention of the shareholders' meeting. We may also not force an individual shareholder who is threatened by personal, financial damage from such state of affairs to wait until the disadvantages have crystallized into concretely measurable property damages. It is completely uncertain whether a proceeding against the responsible persons pursuant to § 117 or § 147 AktG would achieve the desired end, given the strict prerequisites stated in these provisions. It is currently possible under § 122 AktG to demand that a shareholders' meeting be called, but this would require the support of a minimum number of shareholders and could simply boil down to a request that the general meeting approve transfers of assets (see § 83 AktG). This, however, is not what the Plaintiff seeks. It would rather be up to management or to a shareholder with an interest in this matter to seek adoption of such a resolution. A well-founded claim for relief cannot be thwarted simply because the relief measures offered in the Stock Corporation Act fail with respect to a particular set of facts. A shareholder whose rights have been violated must rather be given access to the relief available under the provisions of the general laws unless a provision of corporate law has the purpose of preventing such access for specific reasons; the Act does not, and in particular § 118(1) AktG does not, express any such purpose.

2. The facts do not, however, support the Plaintiff's request for a declaration of nullity.

a) In this case, the transfer of assets without the approval of the shareholders' meeting cannot be declared contractually ineffective pursuant to § 361 AktG as undertaken by a *Vorstand* that lacked power to represent the corporation because the Defendant Corporation did not, as this provision requires, transfer *all* of its assets to Holzmüller KGaA. It would be a different situation if the Defendant Corporation had retained only assets that were unimportant fragments in relation to the whole (RGZ 124, 279, 294 *et seq.*; Schilling in Großkomm. AktG 3rd ed. § 361 note 4). However, this is not the case.

... Unlike § 419 BGB, it is not the purpose of § 361 AktG to protect the creditors of a corporation from unforeseeable changes in attachable collateral, but rather the provision is designed to protect the shareholders against the corporation giving away, without their approval, all the assets that are necessary for its activities as specified in its *Satzung* (Division decision of Nov. 16 1981 – II ZR 150/80, WM 1982, 86). If, as in the case at hand, the object of the asset transfer is a going concern, § 361 AktG would according to its literal meaning cease to apply only when the company itself, with the assets that remain, is still able to pursue its corporate purpose as specified in its *Satzung*, albeit in a limited scope.

The Defendant Corporation retained this capability. The findings of the Court of Appeals, which are supported by the financial statements in the court records and an opinion given by an accounting firm, state that the remaining lumber business, which constituted an independently viable corporate division, was, at the time that the port operations were transferred, a separate corporate division intended to exist and capable of acting independently. It is true that the income from this business has significantly decreased and it has even begun to record losses since that time, so that the financial statements now show the only profits as being derived from the subsidiaries. However, at least until the time of the asset transfer that concerns us here, at the end of 1972, the lumber business had generated profits of its own (Defendant's Briefs of June 21, 1976, p. 3 *et seq.* and of December 20, 1976, p. 9 *et seq.*, Plaintiff's Brief of July 5, 1976, p. 14 *et seq.*). If a business division that remains with the parent company is able and intended to be further operated independently, the examination whether the "company's entire assets" have been transferred may not exclude from consideration the value of a retained shareholding and the income it generates, as the Defendant Corporation has on the basis of its agreement to assume the income of the foreign trading company J. F. M. & Sohn GmbH (see RG JW 1929, 1371). Such shareholders have doubtless been a part of the Defendant Corporation's activities according to its articles (§ 2 in the old and new versions) for a significant period of time.

The Court of Appeals correctly refused to apply § 361 AktG *analogically* to a case in which a significant or even core segment of the previous business activity, but not an independent component that completely depletes the business, is transferred (accord in Timm, *Die Aktiengesellschaft als Konzernspitze*, 1980, 114 *et seq.* and AG 1980, 172, 176 *et seq.*). Such an application would be in conflict with the wording of the Act, which is to be understood to mean a complete sale, and is clearly different from the wording of § 23(2) No. 1 Unfair Competition Act ("all or a significant part"). In addition, this would create difficulties of boundary drawing that would spawn legal uncertainty incompatible with the limitation on powers of representation provided for in § 361 AktG.

b) The argument that there has been a "de facto amendment of the *Satzung*," i.e. a violation of the articles by changing or expanding the corporate purpose described therein without a formal resolution pursuant to § 179 AktG, also – without even considering the purely internal effect of such a violation (§ 82(1) AktG) – fails to support the declaration of nullity that the Plaintiff seeks.

As the Court of Appeals correctly assumed, the 1972 version of the Defendant Corporation's *Satzung* covers the establishment of dependent companies having the same corporate purpose as Holzmüller KGaA with its general partner GmbH, so that there is no need for this court to decide whether an express provision in this regard was necessary. The new corporate relationships established in this way did not therefore change the corporate purpose as it had developed in the course of the corporation's history (Mertens, AG 1978, 309, 311), given that the Defendant Corporation already constituted a corporate group with the foreign trading company J. F. M. & Sohn GmbH, which itself had significant holdings in two foreign subsidiaries. It could, however, be questioned whether the spin-off of a corporate division as important as the port operations remained within the scope of the articles. An affirmative answer is however already given by the new version of § 2(2), in which the Defendant corporation is expressly permitted to "cede" its "operations in whole or in part" to other companies that it has established or acquired, or in which it has a holding. The broad formulation of this clause and its connection to the clause regulating the acquisition of shareholdings clearly indicate in the context of an objective interpretation – which is here appropriate – that the concept "to cede" could be intended to include not only the today relatively rare "contract to cede operations" ("*Betriebsüberlassungsverträge*") provided for in § 292(1) No. 3 AktG (see on this point Biedenkopf/Koppensteiner in KölnKommAktG § 292 mn 23), but also precisely the transfer of company assets to a subsidiary.

c) This would only mean that a formal amendment of the *Satzung* was unnecessary. This does not yet answer whether the *Vorstand* may decide to spin-off the port operations without asking the shareholders. If the competence of the shareholders' meeting is provided for by law, such as in § 293 or § 361 AktG, these provisions themselves establish their own mandatory character, by which the articles are bound (§ 23(5) AktG). However, even where the prerequisites of such provisions are not met, but a factual circumstance is very close to them or is not covered by the articles, the *Vorstand* can exceptionally be committed to submit a matter to the shareholders' meeting. Indeed, unless the law provides otherwise, it generally remains within the discretion of the *Vorstand* whether to submit a decision to the shareholders' meeting pursuant to § 119(2) AktG in order to alleviate its own responsibility (§ 93(4) AktG). There are, however, fundamental decisions that, while covered by the power of the *Vorstand* to represent the corporation *vis-à-vis* third parties, its limited management authority pursuant to § 82(2) AktG and the express provisions of the articles, yet so deeply affect the membership rights of the shareholders and the property interests contained in their equity ownership that the *Vorstand* may not reasonably assume it can make them exclusively under its own supervision without consulting the shareholders' meeting. In such cases, the *Vorstand* breaches its duty of care if it does not take recourse to § 119(2) AktG (see

Barz in GroßkommAktG, 3rd ed. § 119 mn 7; but see Timm, *Die Aktiengesellschaft als Konzernspitze*, 175 *et seq.*).

The spin-off of the W port operations and its transfer to a newly established subsidiary was a measure of such importance for the company and the shareholders that the *Vorstand* should not have circumvented the shareholders' meeting. This included the core of the companies business activities, affected according to the findings of the Court of Appeals the most valuable branch of operations, and fundamentally changed the structure of the company. In this way, it greatly exceeded the ordinary context of management activities, which would commonly include the establishment or acquisition of a subsidiary and its endowment with the necessary capital. This "spin-off" made a decisive difference for the legal status of the shareholders, as will be explained in detail below. The *Vorstand* should thus not have carried this out without the approval of the Defendant Corporation's general meeting.

d) The breach of this (internal) duty of collaboration does not however prejudice the external effect of the measure the Plaintiff challenges. Pursuant to § 82(1) AktG, the *Vorstand*'s power of representation may be limited by law only.

The idea expressed by the Court of Appeals that this principle is waived where the counter-party knows of the abuse of the power of representation (BGHZ 50, 112) or in transactions with wholly owned subsidiaries, because the transactional protection is not an issue in such cases (Uwe H. Schneider in FS Bärmann, 1975, p. 873, 891), is here irrelevant. The challenged promise of the Defendant Corporation to make a contribution in kind is a component of the contract for the establishment of the Holzmüller KGaA. After this incorporation agreement has been carried out and the company commences to exist with its stated capital as provided for in its articles, it can no longer be asserted that the commitment to make the contribution to capital affects solely the internal relationship with the subsidiary and not also commerce in general and the public as well. It would be prohibited pursuant to § 57(1) in connection with § 278(3) AktG to retransfer the port operations to the Defendant Corporation without a decrease in the stated capital (§ 222 *et seq.* AktG) or to dissolve the company. The Defendant Corporation is thus not able legally to challenge the transfer merely because its *Vorstand* made the promise to contribute impermissibly without the approval of the shareholders' meeting and thus abused its unlimited power of representation in external dealings (see Lutter, *Die Rechte der Gesellschafter beim Abschluß fusionsähnlicher Unternehmensverbindungen*, 1974, p. 30 at Fn. 73 with further references).

As a result, it is not possible to approve the central plea of the Plaintiff and declare either the contribution of the port operations into Holzmüller KGaA or even the obligation to do so null and void, on the theory that the Defendant Corporation's *Vorstand* breached its duty in the way it used its power to represent the company, or – as the Court of Appeals states – violated good commercial practice (*gute Sitten*) (see BGHZ 21, 378, 382 *et seq.*; RGZ 124, 279, 287 *et seq.*).

[Text omitted]

II.

The Court of Appeals also correctly denied the Plaintiff's first request for relief, to order the Defendant Corporation in its capacity as (commercially) sole member of the Holzmüller KGaA to re-transfer the port operations to itself.

1. However, under corporate law, such a complaint cannot generally be excluded.

a) Like all shareholders, the Plaintiff has a claim under company law principles that the company respects his rights as a member and avoids all actions beyond limits provided for by law and the articles that could infringe on such rights. This claim is violated if the *Vorstand* excludes the general meeting, and thus the individual shareholders, from participating in a decision whose subject matter requires such participation. If a shareholder wants to protect himself against such action, he is not limited to filing an action against the *Vorstand*, which does not stand in a direct legal relationship to the shareholders, and thus – aside from the special case provided for in § 117(1) AktG – may only be prosecuted for torts (see Mertens, AG 1978, 309 *et seq.* and in FS Robert Fischer, 1979, p. 460, 470). If a *Vorstand* acts alone in dealings with third parties on the basis of its power to represent, without the general meeting, which it has an obligation to involve as a matter of internal affairs, it does this as a company body. Therefore, the company acting through the company bodies must give relief to the shareholders, compensate the damaged shareholders, and take measures so that their membership rights will not be violated in the future.

b) It is not a valid argument against a shareholder action that seeks an injunction to desist from action or to unwind a transaction, to argue that a non-managing shareholder is generally prohibited personally to interfere in management affairs through directions or prohibitions, even if designed to ensure dutiful action (regarding limited partnerships, see BGHZ 76, 160, 167 f). The case at hand does not concern an ordinary measure falling into the sole responsibility of the body authorized to represent, but rather regards a complaint that the *Vorstand* has circumvented shareholder approval in a matter in which they had an internal right of co-decision. It is also implausible to speak of a disturbance of authority delegated under corporate law where a shareholder complaint seeks exactly to obtain or restore such order of authority that has been allegedly violated by the *Vorstand*, and thus also to protect shareholder rights. The protection of a company's internal order is thus not a goal that may be excluded from an action seeking goal-oriented injunctions to desist from or to unwind an action. Rather, shareholders must – unless they are to be rendered bereft of rights – be able to make such claims where corporate law mechanisms are not available adequately to protect their rights, or can only achieve such end following difficult detours (reaching the same result, Knobbe-Keuk in FS Ballerstedt, 1975, p. 239, 251 *et seq.*; Großfeld, JZ 1981, 234 *et seq.*; see also regarding GmbH: BGHZ 65, 15, 21; but see RGZ 115, 246, 251; expressing doubt also Wiedemann, *Gesellschaftsrecht*, Vol. I, 1980, § 8 IV 1 c dd p. 463 *et seq.*;

Hommelhoff, ZHR 1979, 288, 310 *et seq.*; further citations cited in decision of the Court of Appeals, cited *supra*).

We are not suggesting to give individual shareholders a "substitute supervisory right," i.e. to approve a right to act on behalf of the company against the management bodies that overstep their boundaries and thus disturb the order of the organization, a right to file a judicial action when the first line of supervisory organs breaks down (argument of Lutter AcP Bd. 180 p. 84, 142; Timm, AG 1980, 172, 185). The right of the shareholders to file an action rests, rather, as in the case at hand, on an impermissible exclusion of the shareholders' meeting that affects the shareholder's membership rights.

There should be no concern that this technique would ignore the will of the majority of shareholders. The company retains the power to eliminate the ground for the claim by ratifying the relevant action in the general meeting. If this is not done, the shareholders cannot complain if an individual shareholder prosecutes his claim and is forced to seek relief for the damage his rights have suffered. The danger that a company may have to defend itself against an abusive claim seeking an injunction to act or desist from acting can hardly be more troublesome than the possibility of being drawn into a suit seeking to avoid or challenge a shareholders' resolution.

2. Like every other claim, the Plaintiff's request to re-transfer the port operations must be conditioned upon it not being misused in a way that violates the careful consideration that the shareholders owe to the corporation. This includes the necessity that the claim be acted upon without undue delay. If the general meeting has approved a *Vorstand* action, and the resolution violates the law or the articles, or aims to bestow impermissible special advantages (§ 243 AktG), a shareholder can only challenge it within the one month period provided for in § 246 AktG. Thus a shareholder may not allow an unreasonable amount of time pass before filing an action if he, as here, suffers damage or threat to his membership rights through *Vorstand* action that was not approved by a shareholders' resolution. Under the circumstances here, a Plaintiff may no longer demand that a Defendant return a state of affairs to its earlier condition …

[*Text omitted*]

III.

The Plaintiff's second plea for relief is without merit to the extent that it requests specification of a duty of the Defendant Corporation to obtain the approval in its own shareholders' meeting for *all* measures taken in the Holzmüller KGaA requiring approval with a shareholders' resolution carried by at least three-quarters of the corporate capital.

1. With his complaint, the Plaintiff raises issues that the newer legal scholarship have raised and attempted to solve as a problem in the law of corporate groups not addressed by the Stock Corporation Act.

If a stock corporation places a significant part of its operating assets in a subsidiary, this structural change weakens the legal position of the shareholders even if the parent company owns all of the shares of the subsidiary. Through such measure the shareholders lose their power reserved to the general meeting pursuant to § 119 AktG to directly influence the use of the spun-off operating capital, the risk of its losses, and the employment of its income. In the case of a wholly owned subsidiary, the *Vorstand* of the parent company exercises all of the shareholder's rights in the subsidiary and the merely formal requirements – without prejudice to its responsibilities under § 93 AktG – such as the subsidiary's *Satzung* or super-majority requirements, present no insurmountable hurdle to, for example, the free employment of annual earnings without almost any constraints. In this way, through the transfer of the corporate capital, important decisions are shifted from the parent to the subsidiary. In addition, there is the danger that the *Vorstand*, through enterprise agreements with a third party or by taking on unrelated shareholders, such as through an increase in capital, may hollow out the membership rights of the shareholders in the parent company; this can at the same time entail (such as, e.g. through a depressed issue price for the new shares) concrete losses of assets (see on this question the decision of the Division dated November 16, 1981 cited *supra*; Report on the Proceedings of the Company Law Commission, 1980, Tz 1258 *et seq.*, 1282 *et seq.*, 1290; Lutter in FS Harry Westermann, 1974, p. 347, 351 *et seq.*).

The express provisions of the Stock Corporation Act offer the shareholders of the parent company insufficient protection against such encroachments. Its protective provisions are aimed primarily at the outside shareholders of subsidiaries. Indeed, it does contain some protection for shareholders of parent companies against the legal and economic disadvantages created by ties within a corporate group, such as § 293(2) AktG. According to this provision, the shareholders' meeting of a stock corporation parent company must also approve a domination or profit transfer agreement. However, this protection is not present in a merely de facto corporate group, as exists here between the Defendant Corporation and the Holzmüller KGaA.

As this is justly found to be an unsatisfactory state of affairs, a portion of the legal scholarship has advocated giving the shareholders' meeting of the parent company "unwritten rights to participate in decisionmaking" ("*ungeschriebene Mitwirkungsbefugnisse*") (Ulmer, AG 1975, 15). Such rights would exist when the consequences of structural measures in a subsidiary also affect the legal position of the parent company shareholders. Just as in a partnership, where certain rights of the non-managing partners to participate in decisionmaking can have effects on an external, legally separate part of the undertaking (see BGHZ 25, 115, 118; Division decision of May 8, 1972 – II ZR 108/70, LM § 116(2) HGB), this would allow the right of the shareholders to participate in decisionmaking to "reach" subsidiary companies in a similar manner, despite the strict separation of governance powers among corporate entities like the stock corporation. This would allow the parent's

shareholders internally to take part – in the same manner and with the same majorities as is specified for similar decisions in the parent company – in those important,
basic decisions of the subsidiary that could have a lasting impact on their own legal
rights, before the subsidiary can carry them out (this result is reached – with a few
differences – by: Lutter in FS Westermann, p. 364 *et seq.*; Uwe H. Schneider in "Der
GmbH-Konzern," 1976, p. 78, 95 *et seq.*, and in FS Bärmann, p. 881 *et seq.* and ZHR
1979, 485, 498 *et seq.* regarding the GmbH and partnerships as parent undertakings; Timm, AG 1980, 172, 182 *et seq.* and *Die Aktiengesellschaft als Konzernspitze*,
135 *et seq.*, 165 *et seq.*).

2. The case at hand does not require the Division to expound at length on
whether this model offers a practically feasible, "internal order specifically for corporate groups" on the basis of existing law that is consistent with economic reality.
Thus we need not offer an opinion with respect to the treatment of a subsidiary
created with operating assets rather than through a spin-off, or on how the competent bodies of a subsidiary would fulfill their required duty of care to shareholders
where a right of the parent's shareholders to participate in decisionmaking exists,
external shareholders have holdings in the subsidiary, and there is no enterprise
agreement (see §§ 311 *et seq.* AktG). The Division need only decide the case at hand,
in which management transferred a part of the operating assets – that at the time
was unquestionably the most valuable unit in terms of absolute value and income –
to a wholly owned subsidiary set up especially for this purpose, and in which it may
be feared that the legal actions of the subsidiary could prejudice the membership
and property rights of the parent's shareholders.

At least in this case, it is certainly necessary to protect these shareholders from
the danger that, by making fundamental decisions in the subsidiary, the *Vorstand*
will exploit the structure it has created through its power of representation to further diminish those shareholder rights that have already been weakened by the
spin-off. Otherwise the spin-off of a business unit would be a very simple method
for the management to eliminate the right that the law provides shareholders to
participate in decisionmaking. This is a real gap in the Stock Corporation Act that
should be closed in accordance with the Act's systematic design and policy aims. It
would unduly restrict a necessary extension of the law through judicial precedent
(*Rechtsfortbildung*) to ask the damaged shareholders to wait for a future legislative amendment or further clarification in the legal scholarship, as the Court of
Appeals in effect found proper. This would above all contradict a tendency found in
existing corporate law to protect minority shareholders in manifold ways against a
debasement of their membership status through direct or indirect encroachments
of the majority and against a management under their influence, particularly in
corporate groups. De facto changes in the nature of rights regarding control and
assets, brought about through the creation of corporate groups, as is the case here,
have a stronger impact on the minority than on the majority, which can much more

easily influence the management in the general meeting by, for example, refusing to approve of their management (*Entlastung*) or votes of no confidence.

3. These aspects of current law designed to protect shareholders can be made meaningful and effective in the case at hand by, as recommended in the legal scholarship, giving the shareholders of the parent company a claim to make decisions in their shareholders' meeting with respect to fundamental decisions in the subsidiary that have an impact on their rights, just as if the matters were being decided in the parent company. For the reasons set out in Part II.1, above, every shareholder would have such a right against her company. We need not here address whether such right would be dispensed with if the shareholders' meeting approved or ratified the spin-off with the majority necessary to amend the *Satzung* or subjected its legal affects to further conditions, as here the Plaintiffs did not benefit from such a resolution.

4. The case at hand also does not require us to explain in detail which decision would have to be subjected internally to the approval of the shareholders' meeting. As the Court of Appeals correctly concluded, the Plaintiff's complaint is overbroad by abstractly seeking to subject all measures to such approval if, in the subsidiary itself, they should be approved by a super-majority. It is true that such resolutions regularly concern matters of particular importance for shareholders, and their structuring will have numerous effects at the level of the parent company; such measures would include, in addition to enterprise agreements and increases in capital, as mentioned above, certainly the further transfer of corporate assets pursuant to § 361 AktG or a resolution to dissolve the company (§ 262(1) No. 2, § 289(4) AktG). However, this is not always the case. For example, some amendments of the *Satzung* are unimportant or have absolutely no effect on the legal and economic relationships of the parent company and its shareholders, as, for example a transfer of the corporation's registered office, a change of the company name, or perhaps, subjecting the representative body to the approval of the *Aufsichtsrat* as is done in certain companies (§ 111(4) AktG; regarding partnerships limited by shares, see Kraft in KölnKommAktG § 278 mn 84, § 287 mn 9), which at least when the parent company owns 100% of the subsidiary's capital, barely change the control relationship. In such cases, it would not be justified to encroach upon the *Vorstand*'s power to manage the company under its own authority (§ 76(1) AktG).

This defeats the Plaintiff's general request in Point 3.a, which given the numerous possible applications of such a rule cannot take the limited form of judicial relief. On this point, the decision to deny the Plaintiff relief must stand.

IV.

The second half of the request for relief (Point 3.b), which restricts itself to increases in the capital of Holzmüller KGaA, can be treated more favorably.

1. Contrary to the opinion of the Court of Appeals, the Plaintiff does not seek to bind the *Vorstand* of the Defendant Corporation in advance by subjecting its management power to general rules of comportment for future, undetermined situations. Rather, the complaint regards the nature of a specific legal claim that is disputed by the Defendant Corporation, and is neither tied to a specific situation nor subject to the free, untrammeled discretion of the *Vorstand*. The question is whether the Plaintiff and the other shareholders have the right through the Defendant Corporation's general meeting to take part in decisions on capital increases in Holzmüller KGaA.

Contrary to the opinion of the Court of Appeals, this determination does not suppose that an increase in capital has already been resolved or is imminent. As the Defendant Corporation itself has stated, at the time that the port operations were spun off, it was a leading idea that the spin-off would make it easier to find outside investors for these operations if it became necessary to increase the limited partnership's corporate capital (Brief of July 10, 1975, p. 4, 5). To this end, § 6 of the articles of Holzmüller KGaA already contains an authorization for the general partner acting with the approval of the *Aufsichtsrat* to raise the corporate capital by DM 2,400,000 and to decide upon an exclusion of preemptive rights in the process. This authorization was valid until November 30, 1977. However, the Defendant Corporation's *Vorstand* could renew it at any time, given that the latter is both the only limited partner, and also the sole shareholder of the managing general partner GmbH, able to adopt resolutions pursuant to § 285(2) AktG, by an amendment of the *Satzung*, if this had not already been done. In addition, § 6(4) of the articles authorized the general partner in the case of an increase in capital to determine the manner in which the profit attributable to the newly issued shares would be allocated, in derogation from § 60 AktG; this authorization is particularly dangerous for the shareholders of the Defendant Corporation.

It is true that the Defendant Corporation gave assurances that it currently did not intend to undertake an increase in capital because it was not commercially necessary. However, that situation could change unexpectedly. In such case, it may be too late for the Plaintiff to file another action (see Part I.2.d). He therefore has an interest worthy of protection in requesting that, at this time, an answer be given on whether a capital increase in the Holzmüller KGaA requires approval, which answer could be of value to the other shareholders and the Defendant Corporation as well.

2. Capital increases in a subsidiary created by spinning off a significant corporate unit always contain special dangers for the shareholders of the parent company. Even when the parent company retains control of management through a general partner that the parent fully controls, such subsidiaries can indirectly lead to an impairment of the membership of the shareholders, a watering down of their

holdings, and an emptying of their pre-emptive rights. The scholarship referred to in Part III.1 for good reason refers to increases in capital as a primary case in which a company can be required to obtain the approval of its shareholders' meeting before it effects a change in the capital structure of its subsidiary.

It is important for the protection of shareholders that the highest decisionmaking body of the parent company takes part in making such decisions. This is true even if the management intends to fully exercise the pre-emptive rights of the parent company as the sole shareholder of the subsidiary (but see Timm, AG 1980, 183 *et seq.*, also in *Die Aktiengesellschaft als Konzernspitze*, 174 f., as well as Lutter in FS Westermann p. 359, 365 *et seq.*). Thus in this case as well, if a spin-off takes place without the approval of the shareholders, the shareholders lose the opportunity to improve their holding in absolute terms and in value by investing further capital in "their" undertaking. Instead, operating funds that they have invested in the parent company are pulled out of it and placed in another legal entity with the result that the weight and the risks of the capital investment, as well as the corresponding governance powers of the management, are buried even deeper in the subsidiary. Aside from the specific norms on pre-emptive rights in § 186(3) AktG, a resolution on an increase in capital does not offer an unconditional guarantee that the *Vorstand* will not wholly or partially waive the parent company's pre-emptive rights in favor of an outside investor. The possibility at least quantitatively increases with each increase in capital that outside investors will later be brought in through share sales.

Therefore, the shareholders' meeting of the Defendant Corporation – which has hitherto not taken part in decisions – should be given the opportunity to decide if an increase in Holzmüller KGaA's capital should take place under these conditions or whether, perhaps, the Defendant Corporation's pre-emptive rights should be excluded and passed through to its shareholders via analogical application of § 186(1), (2) and (5) AktG. If this is not desired because, for example, a contribution in kind is preferred, the shareholders' meeting can approve this as well; it is noted that such a resolution requires specific, expert support (BGHZ 71, 40, 44 *et seq.*). The resolutions adopted to approve such measures must be adopted pursuant to the same rules and with the same majorities as would be required if a like capital measure were to be taken in the Defendant Corporation, i.e. pursuant to §§ 182 *et seq.* AktG.

3. Thus the Plaintiff's complaint has merit. Contrary to the opinions of the lower courts, the complaint is approved, although the Division finds it important to clarify in its decision that the requirements for adopting resolutions in the general meeting are neither lower nor higher than those that would be applicable to an increase in capital in the Defendant Corporation itself, and that this duty to obtain a resolution does not affect the power of the *Vorstand* to represent the company. In all other respects, the Plaintiff's pleas are denied.

In Re Gelatine
High Federal Court, Second Civil Division
April 26, 2004, Doc. No. II ZR 154/02, *Der Konzern* 2004, 421
[*Partial, unofficial translation of official opinion text*]

Official head note

1. Only in exceptional cases and within narrow limits shall an implied power of the shareholders' meeting to participate in making a decision regarding an act that the law ascribes as an administrative task to the *Vorstand* be recognized. Such powers shall be considered to exist only if the *Vorstand* plans to undertake a reorganization of the company and such act will impinge on the core competence of the shareholders' meeting to determine the constitution of the stock corporation, as it brings with it changes that at least approach the type that may only be achieved through an amendment of the *Satzung*.

2. Aside from cases of spin-offs, such exceptional competence can also arise in cases when a subsidiary is restructured to become a second-tier subsidiary, given the additional mediation effect that is connected with such measures. However, a significant impairment of the shareholders' power to participate in decision-making will exist in such cases only if the economic importance of the measure reaches a dimension similar to that addressed in this Division's decision in BGHZ 83, 122.

3. If the shareholders' meeting is exceptionally called in this way to participate in decisionmaking, its consent shall require, given the importance of the matter for the shareholders, a three-quarters majority.

Facts

The €25 million capital stock of the Defendant stock corporation is held as follows: approximately 10% is held by a series of minority shareholders, a total of 29.7589% (270,805 no-par shares) is held by four Plaintiffs, and approximately 60% is held by the step-mother of Plaintiff 1, her daughters and a nephew of Plaintiff 1.

The *Satzung* of the Defendant provide in § 2 that:

> Purpose
> (1) The purpose of the company is the manufacture and sale of gelatin and gelatin products, including special products as well as other chemical products.
> (2) The company is authorized to enter into all transactions that can serve to promote the company purpose. The company may open domestic and foreign branches, take holdings in other domestic and foreign companies, acquire or establish such companies, and join such companies wholly or partially together under unified management.

With regard to voting rights and adopting resolutions in the shareholders' meeting, § 19 provides as follows:

(1) In the shareholders' meeting, each no par share shall carry one vote.
(2) The shareholders' meeting shall adopt resolutions with a simple majority of the votes cast unless a majority of the capital is required, and in such case with a simple majority of the capital represented, unless the articles of incorporation or the law state that something different is mandatory ...

The principal business activity of the Defendant is the production and sale of gelatin and products related to it. The Defendant itself directly operates in this area, but it also pursues its company purpose through various other entities in which it has holdings. These include, among others, the R. S. GmbH & Co. KG and its *Komplementärin* [i.e. its "general partner" without limitation of liability], R. S. Verwaltungs GmbH, in which the Defendant has a 49% holding, with the other shareholder being a US company. The limited partnership [R. S. GmbH & Co. KG] produces and sells gelatin capsules for the pharmaceuticals industry; from this activity it generated earnings of €18.6 million in the 1998 fiscal year and €27 million in the 1999 fiscal year. The Defendant and the limited partnership, which purchases in large quantities of the raw products that are necessary for its business from the Defendant, have a number of relationships with each other. The Defendant's *Vorstand* referred to such relationships in its management report of March 2000 as follows:

	RS GmbH & Co. KG	Defendant	Entire Group
Turnover and other income*	155,584	167,935	357,091
Balance sheet total*	121,384	333,904	391,086
Employees (Dec. 31, 1999)	1,009	893	1,826

*In thousands of euro.

2. Importance of holdings in overall corporate group
   There is an equity holding between ... (the Defendant) and R. S. GmbH & Co. KG. The operations of both companies are on the same area of land. (The Defendant) alone owns the land and the building. The space that R. S. GmbH & Co. KG uses is leased from (the Defendant) on a long-term basis. The operations of both companies share a single facility for providing fresh water and one for the recycling and disposing of water, as well as a common source of energy.

The current economic importance of the holding in R. S. GmbH & Co. KG is shown by the following comparison of figures:

In the shareholders' meeting held on May 5, 2000, the Defendant's *Vorstand* proposed a plan to restructure the Defendant into a holding company, which the shareholders did not approve, and proposed for vote under "Point 11" that the *Vorstand* be authorized, with the approval of the *Aufsichtsrat*, to transfer the Defendant's holding in the limited partnership and its general partner, as referred to above – plus any lots of land used by the companies – into a 100% owned subsidiary of the Defendant. The *Vorstand* based this proposal on tax considerations connected with the Government Draft Legislation on Business Tax Reform 2001, which was being discussed at the time; the *Vorstand* wanted to give the Defendant's shareholders' meeting the opportunity to sell the company's equity stakes in the future tax free or with reduced tax, if such a sale at the time in question would be in the best interests of the company. A total of 66.4% voted to approve the proposal, and the votes against the proposal, totaling 30.02% of the capital present, came only from the Plaintiffs, except for those from some minority shareholders. The latter filed a complaint on the record of the meeting's notary public, as they were of the opinion that the resolution was ineffective because it required approval by three-quarters of the capital present, a position that the chair of the meeting did not share. The Plaintiffs argue that a measure like the transfer of the Defendant's holdings in R. S. GmbH & Co. KG and its general partner is of such importance for the shareholders of the parent company – not least, on the basis of the presentation of the Defendant's *Vorstand* regarding the economic importance of the holdings – that the principles of this Court's *Holzmüller* decision (BGHZ 83, 122) must be observed.

The Regional Court agreed with the Plaintiffs, but the Regional Court of Appeals reversed. The Appellants/Plaintiffs ask this Court to reinstate the holding of the trial court.

Discussion

The appeal is without merit … The resolution of the Defendant's May 5, 2000 shareholders' meeting on Point 11 was effective. It did not require, as the Plaintiffs assert, a three-quarters majority of the capital stock present.

[*Text omitted*]

II.

The Court of Appeals found that the planned transfer of the Defendant's holdings in R. S. GmbH & Co. KG and its general partner were covered by the company purpose set out in § 2(2) of the *Satzung*, so that the resolution that the Plaintiffs challenge did not require a super-majority under § 179(2) AktG because necessitating an amendment of the *Satzung*. A shareholders' resolution adopted with three-quarters is also not necessary under an implied power of the shareholders' meeting to participate in making a decision pursuant to our *Holzmüller* principles (BGHZ 83, 122 ff.). No circumstances were present that would have required the Defendant's *Vorstand* to obtain the approval of the shareholders' meeting for the planned actions, as the transfer of the Defendant's holdings to a wholly owned subsidiary does not cut into the core activities of the company, the structure of the undertaking is not fundamentally affected, and neither the membership rights nor the economic rights of the shareholders are affected. Aside from such considerations, any resolution that did in fact require shareholder approval, as it concerns a management measure, would have required only a simple majority, which in the case at hand would have doubtless been achieved.

III.

The material aspects of this point withstand the criticism of the appeal.

1. The resolution granting authority pursuant to Point 11 did not require a supermajority pursuant to § 179(2) AktG because it was included within the company purpose specified in § 2 of the Defendant's *Satzung*, and not – as we have before us for review – a de facto change of the *Satzung*. Section 2(2) of the articles expressly allows the company purpose specified § 2(1) to be pursued through holdings in or establishment of other companies, rather than only through the company's own operational activity, and permits these undertakings to be directed wholly or partially together under unified management. In 1989, when the company that had existed as a limited liability company (GmbH) for decades was reorganized into the present stock corporation, the author of the *Satzung* found that a large body of equity holdings already existed, and thus – taking into account the existing double function of the Defendant as both an operative and a holding company – demarcated the boundaries within which the *Vorstand*, in exercising its received authority to manage under its own responsibility (§ 76 AktG), can conduct relevant transactions (see Röhricht in GroßkommAktG, 4th ed., § 23 mn 83; Pentz in MünchKommAktG, 2nd ed., § 23 mn 78). The articles therefore give the *Vorstand* alone authority to determine, pursuant to prudent discretion, whether equity participations should be held by the Defendant itself, thereby placing the direction of subsidiaries more in the hands of the parent's *Vorstand*, or at a lower hierarchical level within the corporate group. This also applies in particular when the *Vorstand* – as it explained in this case – uses the planned rearrangement of the equity holdings in the two entities to create the legal prerequisites for the shareholders' meeting to be able to decide at a later point in time whether the company should take advantage of a tax-free or reduced tax sale of the holdings.

2. The complaint is also otherwise unfounded. The meeting chair correctly assumed that the challenged resolution did not require a supermajority of the

capital present – which the Plaintiffs making reference to the *Holzmüller* principles believe to be necessary – and thus correctly concluded that the resolution had been duly adopted with an actual majority of 66.4% of the votes.

a) This Court has held (BGHZ 83, 122) that certain decisions of a stock corporation for which – in contrast to what is expressly provided in § 119(1) AktG or, for example, for obligations to transfer the entire assets of a company (§ 179a AktG), for enterprise contracts (§§ 293, 295 AktG), for the adoption of a resolution to continue operations (§ 274 AktG) or for resolutions to absorb a company (§§ 319, 320 AktG) – the law does not require a shareholder vote, in exceptional cases trigger an internally effective obligation of the *Vorstand* to seek a shareholder vote. We recognized this "implied" right of the shareholders' meeting in a case in which a stock corporation did not transfer its entire assets, but a business area that constituted the most valuable part of its company assets, to a subsidiary established for this purpose (BGHZ 83, 122). This Division's decision did not restrict the required consultation of the shareholders' meeting to the spin-off itself (BGHZ 83, 122, 131 *et seq.*), but extended it also to the later decision regarding a capital increase in the subsidiary (BGHZ 83, 122, 141 *et seq.*). The Division did not derive the duty of the *Vorstand* to allow the shareholders of the parent company to participate in decisionmaking in these two circumstances from those circumstances specified by law as requiring the approval of the shareholders' meeting. Rather, considering that this duty to involve the shareholders exclusively regards the internal relationship of the *Vorstand* to the company and does not affect the company's ability to transact with third parties, the Division specified § 119(2) AktG as the controlling provision of law from which the internally effective restriction on the *Vorstand*'s transactional authority derives (BGHZ 83, 122, 131).

Our recognition of an implied competence of the shareholders' meeting that only affects the internal relationship between the *Vorstand* and the company is today approved in the majority of the academic literature ... There is no uniform understanding of how these principles are to be applied to individual cases (see BGHZ 83, 122, 140; a summary from Mülbert in GroßkommAktG, cited *supra*, § 119 mn 20; Habersack cited *supra*, vor § 311 mn 33; Reichert in *Beck'sches Handb. der AG* § 5 mn 27 *et seq.*), because the purpose of the protection (see aa, *infra*) and the legal basis (see bb, *infra*) are both debated, just as are the requirement of determining the borders of "significant" or "trivial" transactions (see cc, *infra*) and the majority vote (see b, *infra*) with which the shareholders' meeting must adopt resolutions pursuant to its implied power.

aa) A part of the academic literature immediately welcomed the *Holzmüller* decision because – well beyond the concrete case of a spin-off that changes company structure – it was thought to confirm the opinion that there are many fundamental management decisions both in the stock corporation and in the group that it leads in which the shareholders should participate through the shareholders' meeting of the lead company (see for this line of thinking above all Lutter, FS Stimpel, p. 825, 833 *et seq.*; similarly Timm, *Die Aktiengesellschaft als Konzernspitze*, p. 135 *et seq.*, 165 *et seq.*; U. H. Schneider, FS Bärmann, p. 873, 881 *et seq.*; rejecting this position, Mertens in KölnKommAktG, 2nd ed., § 76 mn 51; Hüffer, *AktG*, 6th ed., § 119 mn 18; *Id.*, FS Ulmer, 2003, 279, 286 *et seq.*).

Our *Holzmüller* decision does not support any such principle. This is already evident from our extremely cautious observation that this Court cannot be expected extensively to explain "the extent to which this model of an 'internal order for the corporate group' can be founded on currently applicable law, is compatible with economic necessities and is workable in practice" (BGHZ 83, 122, 138). It is indeed unmistakable that requiring the participation of the shareholders' meeting in certain cases not provided for by law to participate in decisions whose effect may be to strengthen its influence on the building and management of a corporate group. This effect nevertheless is merely a collateral consequence of what this Court considers to be the necessary participation of the shareholders. In light of the well-balanced division of competence in the stock corporation (on developments, see for example Assmann in GroßkommAktG, cited *supra*, Intro. mn 133, 156 *et seq.*, 164; "1st Report of the Chairman of the Committee for Corporate Law," Schubert, *Protokolle des Ausschusses für Aktienrecht der Akademie für Deutsches Recht*, p. 485 *et seq.*; 2nd Report, *id.* p. 503 *et seq.*; *Official Legislative Report to AktG 1937*, in *Deutscher Reichsanzeiger und Preußischer Staatsanzeiger* 1937, No. 28, p. 3; Kropff, AktG 1965, p. 95 *et seq.* and 165 on § 119; Mertens in KölnKommAktG, cited *supra*, § 76 mn 9; Hefermehl/Spindler in MünchKommAktG, 2nd ed., § 76 mn 21 *et seq.*) the exceptional involvement of the shareholders' meeting should remain restricted to those types of administrative decisions of the *Vorstand* that were unknown when the law was enacted (Geßler, FS Stimpel, 771, 780; Hüffer cited *supra*, § 119 mn 18a "*Anschauungslücke*") and account only for the exceptional case where, even though the actions of the *Vorstand* might fall formally under its power of representation, the literal wording of the *Satzung*, and the management power that is limited internally by § 82(2) AktG, yet the measures "so deeply affect the membership rights of the shareholders and the property interests contained in their equity ownership" (see BGHZ 83, 122, 131) that these consequences come close to the necessity of amending the *Satzung*. The required participation of the shareholders' meeting is designed to counter the mediating effect on the shareholders' influence that is caused by spinning off a significant part of the company's business to subsidiary companies (see BGHZ 153, 47, 54; accepting this principle, e.g. Habersack cited *supra*, vor § 311 mn 34, and Wiedemann, *Die Unternehmensgruppe im Privatrecht*, p. 53 *et seq.*; rejecting, solely with regard to protection of property interests Mülbert, *Aktiengesellschaft, Unternehmensgruppe und Kapitalmarkt*, p. 416 *et seq.*; *Id.* in GroßkommAktG, cited *supra*, § 119 mn 33), given that the shareholders, as the authors of the *Satzung*, determine the company purpose and the limits of its commercial activity for the management bodies (BGHZ 83, 122, 136, 139). At the same time, we must be sure that shareholders have the ability to protect themselves against a lasting decrease in the value of their shareholdings caused by a fundamental decision of the *Vorstand* (BGHZ 83, 122, 142 *et seq.*; see Kubis in MünchKommAktG, 2nd ed., § 119 mn 44 *et seq.*; Zimmermann/Pentz, FS Welf Müller, 151, 163). This addresses the rightful interests of shareholders in a preventative way – rather than restricting them only to filing lawsuits for damages against the management for the wrongful exercise of their managerial authority, a right which remains unfettered in view of the *Vorstand*'s broad discretion to shape the company's affairs.

The case at hand does not require this Court to give a comprehensive list of all management decisions that would internally obligate the *Vorstand*, although not required by the letter of the law, to seek the approval of the shareholders' meeting because the action seriously affects the powers of the shareholders arising from their membership. However, a mediating effect on the influence of the shareholders (see Liebscher, *Konzernbildungskontrolle*, p. 65 *et seq.*, 74 *et seq.*; Wiedemann, *Unternehmensgruppe*, p. 53 *et seq.*; Kubis cited *supra*, § 119 mn 74; Habersack cited *supra*, vor § 311 mn 35; see generally BGHZ 153, 47, 54) whose capital the *Vorstand* is charged with administering through its management activity (see "1st Report of the Chairman of the Committee for Corporate Law," Schubert, *Protokolle*, cited *supra*, p. 485), and which it may, therefore, not bring about without the consent of the shareholders can not only result from spinning-off an important business division and placing it in a specially incorporated subsidiary, as in the *Holzmüller* decision (BGHZ 83, 122). Because of the (additional) displacement of power that can disadvantage the shareholders of the parent company the *Vorstand* can become obligated to seek the consent of the shareholders' meeting also in cases of a restructuring of the equity holdings, as in the facts occasioning this legal dispute.

bb) In the *Holzmüller* decision, this Division found that a legal basis for the involvement of the shareholders' meeting in the decisionmaking was derived from § 119(2) AktG (BGHZ 83, 122, 131): The discretion of the *Vorstand* pursuant to this norm whether to ask, in exceptional cases, for the shareholders' meeting to vote on a management measure, turns into the duty of a prudent *Vorstand* to seek the participation of the shareholders in cases of actions that significantly affect the membership and economic rights of shareholders, such as the spin-off of a business division constituting a significant part of the company assets.

The majority of legal scholarship has criticized this derivation of an unwritten competence for the shareholders' meeting (see Habersack, cited *supra* § 311 mn 36; Mülbert in GroßkommAktG, cited *supra* § 119 mn 21, both with further references; but see Hüffer, cited *supra* § 119 mn 18; agreement is expressed also by Reichert, Supp. 68 of ZHR p. 45). Although it should be recognized that the legislature, in enacting § 119(2) AktG, did not intend to give the *Vorstand* even an indirect duty to allow the shareholders' meeting to participate in management beyond those cases specified by law (see regarding the legislative history Geßler, FS Stimpel, 771, 773 *et seq.*), the critical scholarship does not always adequately note that the Division focused primarily on § 119(2) AktG because it wanted to make clear that the duty the Division found only affected the internal relationship with the shareholders' meeting, and had no effect on the *Vorstand*'s unlimited capacity of representation *vis-à-vis* third parties (on the majority position, see Habersack, cited *supra* § 311 mn 48; Koppensteiner in KölnKommAktG, cited *supra* § 291 mn 22; for a dissenting view see Hübner, FS Stimpel, 791, 798). Although the analogy to some or all of the corporate law provisions requiring shareholders' approval for specific acts that scholars recommend (see with further citations, Habersack, cited *supra* § 311 mn 36, Fn. 154; Mülbert in GroßkommAktG, cited *supra* § 119 mn 23) may be well suited for singling out those cases in which unwritten competence of the shareholders' meeting is supposed to exist, it begs the argument that the legal consequences of such cases render the extension inappropriate because it not only robs the *Vorstand* of its management authority but also would make the acts it takes null and void due to a lack of representative capacity.

It would thus appear preferable – as the legislature in spite of its awareness of the longstanding discussion has taken no initiative to settle the matter (see Hüffer, FS Ulmer, 279, 301 *et seq.*) – to base an unwritten right of the shareholders to participate in management actions neither on § 119(2) AktG nor on an analogy to other principles of law. Rather, the relevant characteristics of both bases, i.e. the limitation to purely internal effectiveness on the one hand and the relationship of the cases in question to the powers of participation set by law on the other, should be included and this special competence of the shareholders' meeting should be understood as the product of freely developing case law (see Geßler, FS Stimpel, 771, 780, already advocating such treatment).

cc) Even that part of the academic scholarship that advocates the broadest extension of the implied competence of the shareholders' meeting recognizes that not every *Vorstand* measure that negatively affects the legal rights of the shareholders triggers a right of shareholders' meeting participation. It is consistent with this view to seek only those minimal boundaries within which the *Vorstand* is always free to act.

However, such an approach is not compatible with the protective purpose of the shareholders' competence as developed by this Court. The Stock Corporation Act gives the *Vorstand* alone the right and the duty to manage the company on its own authority, following objective standards of due care and with its actions subject to the monitoring of the *Aufsichtsrat* elected by the shareholders' meeting; the shareholders' meeting is, on the other hand, except for those cases provided for by law, denied any participation in or influence on management actions. In evaluating the experience gained up to the end of the Weimar Republic, the legislature consciously decided to cancel the previously central position of the shareholders' meeting as the primary body for determining the powers of the stock corporation, as the body from which the *Aufsichtsrat* and the *Vorstand* derived their powers. This was done because the meeting's overall structure did not allow it adequately to fulfill the tasks previously attributed to it. Following years of discussion in academic circles and in practice (see Schubert, *Quellen zur Aktienrechtsreform der Weimarer Republik 1926 – 1931 und Protokolle des Ausschusses für Aktienrecht der Akademie für Deutsches Recht*; Assmann in GroßkommAktG, cited *supra*, Introduction mn 133, 156 *et seq.*, 164) the idea gained dominance that the shareholders' meeting, given its heterogeneous, contingent composition and its distance from the relevant management decisions to be made, was structurally inappropriate to participate in the management of a stock corporation, but that it must retain its primary power over the company's "constitution," i.e. the formulation and amendment of the *Satzung*, including decisions on capital increases, as well as for the appointment and removal of the *Aufsichtsrat* and the release (*Entlastung*) of management for the year's activity (see "1st and 2nd Report of the Chairman of the Committee for Corporate Law," in Schubert, *Protokolle*, cited *supra*, p. 486, 503 ff.; Legislative Report to AktG 1937, cited *supra*, p. 3). With the norm contained in § 70 AktG 1937, the legislature expressly carried this idea into the Stock Corporation Act without differentiating between the concrete structures of actual corporations (see *contra*, Liebscher, *Konzernbildungskontrolle*, p. 100 *et seq.*), and extended the powers of the shareholders' meeting only on specific matters where it could be assumed – like the conclusion of enterprise agreements – of such importance for the continued operation of the corporation, that they could not be left to the *Vorstand* alone (Kropff, *AktG* vor § 76 p. 95 *et seq.*). In a globally connected economy, in which it is important promptly to take advantage of opportunities or to take immediate action against approaching dangers, it would be completely impractical and in fact lame the company if too restrictive a requirement were imposed to obtain the approval of a shareholders' meeting that is not continuously present, and that can be convened only with significant expenditure of time and money.

Therefore, a right of the shareholders' meeting to participate in the *Vorstand*'s administrative actions, when not expressly provided for by law, can only be considered to exist within narrow boundaries, in particular, if such actions affect the core competences of the shareholders' meeting to determine the constitution of the company, and have consequences that approach a state of affairs that can only be reached by an amendment of the *Satzung*. Consequently, the exceeding of one of the various thresholds specified in the academic literature – they are based on various parameters and range from 10% to 50% (see Habersack cited *supra*, vor § 311 mn 41; Kubis cited *supra*, § 119 mn 55; Krieger in *Münch. Handb.d.Gesellschaftsrechts*, Vol. 2, 2nd edn., § 69 mn 7 *et seq.*) – cannot be sufficient; the described prerequisite of breaking through the division of powers and tasks set by law will usually only be reached when the spun-off business division affected by the measure is as important for the company as the one that this Court addressed in its *Holzmüller* decision.

b) If pursuant to the above – in an exceptional case – the approval of the shareholders' meeting must be sought for a management action, it shall require a three-quarters majority of the capital present, just as most of the academic literature has also come to believe (see e.g. Hübner, FS Stimpel, 791, 795 *et seq.*; Priester, ZHR 163 [1999], 187, 199 *et seq.*; Joost, ZHR 162 [1999], 164, 172; Altmeppen, DB 1998, 49, 51; Raiser, *Recht der Kapitalgesellschaften*, 3rd ed. § 16 mn 15; Habersack cited *supra*, vor § 311 mn 45 with further citations; different view in Hüffer, FS Ulmer, 279, 297 *et seq.*; Semler in MünchHdbGesR, vol. 2, 2nd edn., § 34 mn 42). This is not contradicted by the fact that the measures demanding in exceptional cases the consent of the shareholders' meeting – the Court of Appeals based its auxiliary ground on this point (see Liebscher cited *supra*, p. 92 *et seq.* for a similar position) – are management actions rather than amendments of the articles. Rather, it is crucial that the object of the decision is a measure that technically does not require an amendment of the *Satzung*, but comes so close to requiring one because of its significant effect on the membership position of the shareholders that the technically valid power of the *Vorstand* to act must take second place to the participation rights of the shareholders' meeting. Along these lines, the legislature has not only ordered the participation of the shareholders' meeting, but also that the decision be by a three-quarters majority for actions that do not amend the articles but are technically management measures, such as the conclusion of enterprise agreements (see Kropff cited *supra*, p. 96, who points out this case) or substance changing reorganizations pursuant to the Transformation Act of 1994.

This requirement cannot be avoided – contrary to the opinion of the Defendant – even if the articles contain a so-called group clause (*accord* Habersack cited *supra*, vor § 311 mn 45; for a different position, see Lutter, FS Stimpel, 825, 847 *et seq.*; Wiedemann, *Unternehmensgruppe*, cited *supra*, p. 57) or it is specified – as in the case at hand in § 19(2) of the articles – that all resolutions of the shareholders' meeting may be adopted with a simple majority unless the law or the articles provides otherwise in a mandatory provision. By placing a general corporate group clause in the *Satzung*, the shareholders merely increase the transactional freedom of the *Vorstand*, which accordingly is not required to pursue the company purpose exclusively through the activity of the corporation itself, but is allowed to do so also by establishing or acquiring other companies, as well as by taking equity holdings. The shareholders do not thereby relinquish the right protected by recognizing an implied competence of the shareholders' meeting; as this Court has recognized in the *Holzmüller* decision (BGHZ 83, 122, 141 *et seq.*), there may be a participation right for the shareholders' meeting of the parent company even in the case of fundamental measures in a subsidiary following a spin-off that required the consent of the shareholders.

Given the grave, potential prejudice to the membership rights of the share-holders, the *Satzung* may not, to the disadvantage of the shareholders, lower the majority required to approve such planned measures. Rather, the supermajority requirement is here no different than, for example, in the mandatory cases named in §§ 179a(1), 293(1), or 319(2) AktG.

3. Pursuant to the criteria described above, the authorizing resolution named in Point 11 and carried with a vote of 66.4% of the capital present is effective. The resolution did not affect the membership rights of the Defendant's shareholders so deeply that the shareholders' meeting had to resolve on the matter and give its con-sent with a supermajority vote.

The Plaintiff's point of departure is, however, correct that the planned transfer of the Defendant's holdings in R. S. GmbH & Co. KG and its general partner to a subsidiary wholly owned by the parent company is a measure that will create a mediation effect (see on this point BGHZ 153, 47, 54) to the detriment of the share-holders. This result follows – otherwise than in the case where equity holdings are transferred from one 100% held subsidiary to another (see on this point Kubis cited *supra*, § 119 mn 74) – simply from the fact that the planned transfer will create an additional layer of hierarchy and thus decrease the influence of the controlling par-ent company and its shareholders' meeting on the management of operations, and also on decisions regarding the use of profits and other actions of this company which has become a second-tier subsidiary. This is so because the management bodies of such company will no longer have to act within boundaries set by the *Vorstand* of the parent company controlled by the shareholders' meeting, but rather within directives of the legal representative of the newly inserted subsidiary, which in turn will follow the directives of the parent company's *Vorstand*, which makes its decisions under its own authority pursuant to § 76 AktG.

This structural measure for which the *Vorstand* – apparently not with the inten-tion of restricting itself, but motivated by the uncertainty, much discussed in prac-tice, regarding the reasons and the boundaries for the implied right of participation of the shareholders' meeting extending beyond that required by the letter of the law – sought shareholder approval, does not however affect the legal position of the shareholders' with an intensity like that described above.

According to the Plaintiff's written complaint, which depicts significantly lower requirements for the "threshold of significance," and thus highlights the character of the spin-off as a "structural measure," the holding of the Defendant in the sub-sidiary companies was not unimportant. However, pursuant to the parameters that the *Vorstand* specified in its report for the shareholders' meeting, and on which the Court of Appeals primarily based its decision, the economic importance is signifi-cantly below the levels that must be surpassed to justify an implied competence of the shareholders' meeting. According to such report, the subsidiary holding, in particular, contributed no more than a quarter of group income before taxes;

the Court of Appeals does not show that these companies had some key value for the controlling company – e.g. because of the ownership of intellectual property, real estate or machines that the Defendant needed for the pursuit of its business activity – beyond that reported. Even if the special lease and purchase relationships between the Defendant and these held companies – as the Plaintiffs affirm – should be included in the test for "significance," no different result is reached. These legal relationships between the Defendant and the subsidiary companies are not affected by the restructuring that the Plaintiffs contest, and they do not affect the membership of the subsidiary companies within the Defendant's corporate group.

Interest of company versus interest of group

Hollinger International Inc. v. Conrad M. Black, Hollinger Inc.
Delaware Court of Chancery
844 A 2d 1022 (2004)

STRINE, Vice Chancellor
[Text omitted]

Factual background

The "Hollinger" corporate structure

An understanding of the relationship among three corporate entities and [Lord] Conrad M. Black [of Crossharbour] is critical to the resolution of this dispute. I begin by emphasizing that Black was the creator of this group of companies, has personally dominated their affairs …

[Text omitted]

At the bottom of this now-unhappy corporate family is the plaintiff Hollinger International, Inc., a Delaware corporation whose shares trade on the NYSE ["International"] … International owns, through wholly owned subsidiaries, *The Chicago Sun-Times* and several community papers in the Chicago area, *The Daily Telegraph* and certain other assets in the United Kingdom, and *The Jerusalem Post* in Israel.

Since it became a public company, International has had a controlling stockholder, Hollinger, Inc., an Ontario corporation whose shares trade on the Toronto Stock Exchange ["Inc."] … Since the mid-1990s … Inc. has solely been a holding company, the principal – but not sole – asset of which is the ownership of 30.3% of the equity of International … The bulk – some 14,990,000 shares – of Inc.'s International stock consists of shares of Class B Common Stock which have a 10-to-1 voting preference over shares of International's Class A Common Stock, which is largely held by the public … Inc.'s stockholdings in International give it control of 72.8% of International's voting power.

When International went public in the early 1990s, public investors were ...

... informed that International's certificate of incorporation provided that "If a share of Class B Common Stock held ... by Hollinger Inc. ... is to be sold, transferred or disposed of to a third party ... other than in a Permitted Transaction ... each such share of Class B Common Stock shall be automatically converted into one ... share of Class A Common Stock immediately prior to ... the time of transfer to such third party."

The public disclosures create the impression that this was a substantial tag-along right, because the certificate provision (the "Tag-Along Provision") seems designed to make sure that Inc. would share any control premium ratably with the other International shareholders ... A Permitted Transaction is ... an offer for the Class B Common Stock that includes a simultaneous offer for all Class A Common Stock at the same price.

As the defendants in this action have noted, however, the Tag-Along Provision has a rather gigantic loophole. By its explicit terms, the Tag-Along Provision is not triggered by a sale of Inc. itself ... Indeed, under the defendants' interpretation, Inc. could, at any time, have dropped its International shares into a subsidiary and simply sold that subsidiary. In their view, that type of transaction would not trigger the Tag-Along Provision and the purchaser of the subsidiary would continue to control Class B shares with super-voting power.

[*Text omitted*]

At all relevant times to this dispute, Inc. has been controlled by the last entity through which Black ultimately controls International: The Ravelston Corporation Limited ("Ravelston"), which owns approximately 78% of Inc.'s common stock and is a private company Black personally dominates and controls. Black, through another personal holding company, owns over 65% of Ravelston. Inc. ...

The evidence reveals that Black ... has held himself out to the world as able to control Ravelston, Inc., and International ... The Inc. and Ravelston boards, as now composed, have comported themselves in a supine manner that confirmed Black's confidence in his power. As to International, the picture is more complex but one thing is clear: Black believed himself to be the initial arbiter of what should be done with International and its assets, to the exclusion of the rest of the company's directors ...

What is also obvious is that there is a disparity between Black's voting power over ... International ... and his actual economic stake in the equity ... there is a great discrepancy between the voting control Black practically wielded (which was nearly absolute) and his personal economic stake, which, when filtered through Inc. and Ravelston, was around 15%.

The International Board of directors

Immediately before the events relevant to this case, the International Board was composed of a close balance between inside and outside directors ...

[*Text omitted*]

The management structure at International

As of the beginning of 1993, International's top management was employed through a contract with an affiliate of Ravelston. That is, most of the executives, including Black and his top subordinates, were directly employed by and owned stock in Ravelston, which received payments from International for its management of International. Put simply, International's top executives not only worked for Black in his capacity as CEO of International and understood the practical voting control he exercised over that company, they were also subordinate to and drew benefits from Black in their roles at Inc. and Ravelston.

International adds new independent directors to begin an internal investigation

In May 2003, Tweedy Browne Company, LLC ("Tweedy Browne"), one of International's largest stockholders ... demanded that the board investigate the payment of over $70 million in non-competition payments made to Black, Radler, Atkinson, and another International executive, J. A. Boultbee ...

At a June board meeting, the International Board resolved to form a "Special Committee" with the mandate and power to investigate and, if it believed warranted, prosecute litigation on behalf of International ...

[*Text omitted*]

... As advisors, the Special Committee hired O'Melveny & Myers and Richard Breeden ... Breeden had served for many years in high-level positions in the federal government under Presidents Reagan, Bush, and Clinton, culminating in his service as Chairman of the Securities and Exchange Commission.

The Barclays approach Black about the Daily Telegraph

Tweedy Browne filed a copy of its demand letters on Schedule 13-D with the SEC ... Newspaper reports suggested that Inc. was under some financial pressure.

These reports followed on stories in the press in May 2003. At that time, David Barclay had written to Black and "register[ed]" an interest in Black's "UK interests" – i.e. in *The Daily Telegraph* and other related British assets owned by International. Along with his brother Frederick, David Barclay controls an array of businesses, which own media assets in the UK and Europe such as the newspapers *The Scotsman, Edinburgh Evenings News*, and *The Business* ... In June, David Barclay wrote Black again about the Telegraph. Black rebuffed the Barclays.

[*Text omitted*]

... After a news story came out indicating that Inc.'s credit rating might be downgraded, Barclay again wrote to Black, stating [he would be primarily interested in the *Telegraph* but would consider any part of the business. Black replied by asking him not to raise the topic again] ...

Despite the fact that International owned the *Telegraph*, Black did not inform the International Board of any of these communications. On his own, Black decided to reject the opportunity.

The Special Committee concludes that it must take urgent action regarding the non-competition payments

By late October 2003, the Special Committee had come to a troubling conclusion; namely, that $15.6 million in so-called "non-competition" payments had been made by International to Black, Radler, Atkinson, and Boultbee – i.e. the International management team – without proper authorization. Furthermore, another $16.55 million in "non-competition" payments had been made by International to Inc. – even though Inc. had no operational capacity to compete with anyone. Of these amounts, Black had received $7.2 million personally, as had Radler.

[Text omitted]

Furthermore, the Special Committee was unable to find any evidence in the corporate minute book, or through other sources, that any of the non-competition payments had been the subject of specific approval by either International's audit committee or its board of directors ...

... The Special Committee brought all of its preliminary findings to the attention of International's audit committee ... What was done jointly was the transmittal of a letter to each of the executives who had received non-competition payments ...

[Text omitted]

[Black, who had already investigated the payments with his own management team, responded with a letter justifying them on the basis of Delaware law, and then stating that given International's liquidity problems]

In the circumstances, *it is Lord Black's tentative conclusion that the best course of action is to seek the approval of the Hollinger International directors for a public announcement that the company will seek and will evaluate proposals for a range of financing alternatives at the Hollinger International level,* **including the sale of some or all assets, and including the solicitation of an offer for all Hollinger International shares, including those owned by [Inc.] itself** ... [emphasis added by Court of Chancery] ...

[Text omitted]

Black and the independent directors forge a restructuring agreement

Black was invited to a meeting in International's offices in New York ... Black bargained hard.

[Text omitted]

By November 15, 2003, the parties reached accord on a specific written agreement, the "Restructuring Proposal." ...

[Text omitted]

[A] key aspect of the Restructuring Proposal was that the Strategic Process would be conducted with "overall control" by a newly reconstituted board including a solid majority of independent directors. *That is, by its terms, the Restructuring Proposal had removed two inside directors from the board, leaving a firm independent majority.*

On November 17, 2003, International publicly announced the key features of the Restructuring Proposal. Black reviewed and participated in crafting the release. The release stated that, among other things:

> Hollinger International Inc. ... today announced that its board of directors has retained Lazard LLC ("Lazard") to review and evaluate its strategic alternatives, including a possible sale of the company, a sale of one or more of its major properties or other possible transactions (the "Strategic Process") ...

As Black had desired, neither the Restructuring Proposal nor the press release indicated that he had engaged in any wrong-doing in connection with the non-compete payments ...

The Inc. independent directors revolt – then resign

The events at the International level soon drew interest from Inc.'s four independent directors – who formed that company's audit committee – and its auditors, KPMG. After performing its own inquiry into the non-compete payments ... Among other things, the Inc. audit committee recommended that Black, Radler, and Boultbee immediately resign from their management positions at Inc., and that Atkinson, Boultbee, and Radler resign from Inc.'s board of directors ... [The inside directors voted down this suggestion.] The independent directors promptly resigned from the Inc. board.

Black immediately begins to violate the Restructuring Proposal
[Text omitted]

... Black provided a report to the Inc. board regarding the Restructuring Proposal. In that report, he focused the Inc. board on June 1, 2004 as the target date that Inc. needed to weather in terms of cash flow because that was the date about which the Strategic Process was expected to end ...

Knowing [this] ... and knowing that the International Board was relying upon the contractual commitments he had made ... Black used this breathing room to pursue transactions in violation of the Restructuring Proposal. Most notably, on November 17, 2003, Black began to turn the Barclays away from their interest in a direct purchase of *The Daily Telegraph* and towards a purchase of Inc. ...

Stated bluntly, Black steered the Barclays toward doing an end-run around the Strategic Process, knowing that his contractual assurances … gave the International Board a false sense that they had the time for adequate deliberation …

On November 20, 2003, Black took further steps to direct the Barclays towards a purchase of Inc. as a method of acquiring control of International. That day, he specifically proposed that the Barclays purchase Inc. and indicated what value he would be looking to receive for the equity of Inc. and that he wanted a $10 million "redundancy" (i.e. managerial severance) package for himself. In this communication, Black expressly based his proposal on a range "of value of Hollinger International, (HII) according to Lazard's opening document, [which] is $18 to $24 per share." Stated simply, Black used confidential advice given to him in his official capacity at International to negotiate behind International's back with the Barclays …

[Text omitted]

… when the Barclays got wind of the Restructuring Proposal, they harbored grave concerns that Black was violating that Proposal and could not deliver the deal he had proposed. Again, Black devoted his efforts to convincing the Barclays that they could get around the Proposal.

[Text omitted]

Black assures the International Board that he was not violating the Restructuring Proposal

During the post-Restructuring Proposal period, Black … also engaged in discussions with Hicks, Muse, Tate & Furst. Daniel Colson, an International director and its COO, gave Hicks, Muse a tour of International's Chicago operations without informing [International's board] … Black shared information about his dealings with the Barclays with Colson, but Colson did not tell the other International directors. Black also discussed deals with Triarc Corp. and later sent them confidential materials from a presentation made to the International Board. At all times, Black felt free to share confidential information from International with whomever he wished …

[Text omitted]

In late December, Black was questioned by the SEC about matters within the scope of the Special Committee's investigation, including the non-competes. He invoked the Federal Constitution's privilege against self-incrimination and refused to cooperate …

Black also began steps to repudiate his commitment to repay the monies due back to International under the Restructuring Proposal … When his obligation to repay International 10% of the total sum owed came due on December 31, 2003, Black did not pay and thereby breached the literal words of the Restructuring Proposal. All of the other individuals who had promised to make payments (i.e. Radler, Atkinson, and Boultbee) did so.

[Text omitted]

When Black did not make his contractually required payment and when rumors of his violations of ... the Restructuring Proposal persisted, the International Board members began to consider ... the adoption of a shareholder rights plan that would enable the board to protect the company's plan of completing the Strategic Process and the Special Committee process ...

In early January, Black and the other International directors received a briefing about a shareholder rights plan. Black responded in two ways. First, he communicated the confidential advice provided to the International Board to both the Barclays and to Triarc – without permission from the International Board. Second, he called director Kissinger and threatened to remove the International Board if it adopted a rights plan.

[Text omitted]

By early January, Black's negotiations with the Barclays were well along and they had settled on a sale of Inc. – Black having dissuaded the Barclays from pursuing any deal with International directly or from purchasing Inc.'s International shares ...

Even so, Black and the Barclays continued to conceal their dealings from International ...

[Text omitted]

Meanwhile, International's ... Special Committee had concluded that a lawsuit ought to be brought against Black and others for self-dealing. They filed that suit on January 16, 2004 ...

The SEC had also threatened suit against the company for securities law violations in connection with the non-competes and other matters. The SEC gave the company an imminent take-it-or-leave it choice of being sued by the federal government for securities fraud or cooperating by entering a stipulated consent order ("the Consent Order"). Paris, as company CEO, agreed to sign the Consent Order ...

[Text omitted]

On January 17, 2004, the International Executive Committee met. The Committee voted to remove Black as Chairman ... because he had refused to cooperate with the SEC (a failure that helped motivate the SEC's legal action), had violated the Restructuring Proposal in several respects, and had, in the Special Committee's view, engaged in additional breaches of fiduciary duty ... During the meetings in the preceding days, Black continued to conceal his dealings with the Barclays ...

On the evening of Saturday, January 17 – i.e. after the Executive Committee meeting that day – Black faxed the following letter to International's empty offices:

> I am writing to inform Hollinger International Inc. that The Ravelston Corporation Limited and the undersigned intend tomorrow to enter into an agreement with Press Holdings International Limited, an English company, that will provide for Press Holdings to make an offer in Canada to purchase any and all of the outstanding common

shares and preference shares of Hollinger Inc. and for Ravelston and the undersigned to tender all such common and preference shares held directly or indirectly by us into the Offer, all on the terms and conditions to be set out in the agreement.

Sincerely yours,
Conrad M. Black

...

The Barclays announce their deal with Black and Black repudiates the Restructuring Proposal

The transaction that Black struck with the Barclays ("the Barclays Transaction") involves an offer by the Barclays to purchase all of the equity of Inc. and to redeem certain of its preference shares, as well as an agreement by Black and Ravelston to support the offer. The implied value of International under the Barclays Transactions is below the bottom end of the Lazard ranges Black gave the Barclays. The Inc. board played no role in crafting the agreement.

[Text omitted]

The same day, the Barclays sent a letter to the International Board offering to meet with it and promising their support of the Strategic Process and the possible benefits to International of having the Barclays as controlling stockholders. The letter also suggested that they might cause Inc. to repay the non-competes once they were convinced that repayment was due.

Also on that day Black sent a letter to the International Board repudiating the Restructuring Proposal ...

The International Board responds

The International Board met on January 20, 2004 to address these events. It formed a Corporate Review Committee ("CRC"), which was comprised of all directors other than Black, Mrs. Black, and Colson. The CRC was given broad authority to act for the company and to adopt such measures as a shareholder rights plan ...

[Text omitted]

... Black caused Inc. to file a written consent [under § 228 DGCL] profoundly affecting the operation of the International Board [by abolishing the CRC, stripping the Special Committee of authority it was given in the January 20th resolution, and amending the Bylaws to force the board to act slower and with higher majority requirements so he could veto its decisions].

[Text omitted]

The independent directors were not cowed by the Bylaw Amendments. They believed them to be invalid. The CRC therefore continued to meet. On January 25, 2004, the CRC adopted the "Rights Plan." ...

[Text omitted]

Legal analysis

[*Text omitted*]

Did Black breach his fiduciary duties in the process leading to the Barclays transaction?

The *Telegraph* was an asset that belonged to International. It constitutes far less than half of International's assets. The International Board is empowered by Delaware law to dispose of that asset without seeking stockholder assent ... The opportunity to sell the *Telegraph* belonged to International.

[*Text omitted*]

Thus, Black violated his fiduciary duty of loyalty by, among other acts, (1) purposely denying the International Board the right to consider fairly and responsibly a strategic opportunity within the scope of its Strategic Process and diverting that opportunity to himself; (2) misleading his fellow directors about his conduct and failing to disclose his dealings with the Barclays, under circumstances in which full disclosure was obviously expected; (3) improperly using confidential information belonging to International to advance his own personal interests and not those of International, without authorization from his fellow directors; and (4) urging the Barclays to pressure Lazard with improper inducements to get it to betray its client, International, in order to secure the board's assent to the Barclays Transaction. In sum, Black intentionally subverted the International Strategic Process he had pledged to support through a course of conduct involving misleading and deceptive conduct toward his fellow directors, all designed with the goal of presenting them with a "*fait accompli.*" Most critically, the Restructuring Proposal did exist and constricted Black's, and therefore Inc.'s, range of action. It is difficult to conceive of a meaningful definition of the duty of loyalty that tolerates conduct of this kind.

... Inc. is, regrettably, not an innocent bystander to Black's breaches of fiduciary duty. As International's controlling stockholder, Inc. was well aware of the Restructuring Proposal and Black's obligations to International under it. Inc. was also aware of Black's obligations as Chairman of International. To the extent Inc. is claiming independent rights in the Barclays Transaction, it is compromised by its imputed knowledge of its agent, Black, who took the leadership role for Inc. in negotiating the Barclays Transaction. Indeed, from the evidence, it is patently clear that Black dominated Inc. in the relevant period and felt free to and did act for Inc. – as in function both its principal and agent – in a manner that was obviously inconsistent with the duties Black owed International.

[*Text omitted*]

Were the Bylaw Amendments properly adopted?

... [T]he Bylaw Amendments prevent the International Board from acting on any matter of significance except by unanimous vote; set the board's quorum requirement at 80%; require that seven-days' notice be given for special meetings; and provide that the stockholders, and not the directors, shall fill board vacancies.

International argues quite plausibly that the Bylaw Amendments were designed to ensure that Black, and thereafter the Barclays, can veto any action at the International Board level that they oppose ...

... In essence, the Bylaw Amendments permit Black to proceed with the Barclay Transaction even though that Transaction was the product of improper and inequitable conduct ...

By contrast to International, the defendants contend that the Bylaw Amendments simply are a proper attempt by Inc. as a majority stockholder to prevent itself from being wrongly excluded from exercising the power that legitimately flows from voting control ...

... In general, there are two types of corporate law claims. The first is a legal claim, grounded in the argument that corporate action is improper because it violates a statute, the certificate of incorporation, a bylaw or other governing instrument, such as a contract. The second is an equitable claim, founded on the premise that the directors or officers have breached an equitable duty that they owe to the corporation and its stockholders. *Schnell* v. *Chris-Craft Industries, Inc.* is the classic recent statement of the principle that "inequitable action does not become permissible simply because it is legally possible."

... The DGCL is intentionally designed to provide directors and stockholders with flexible authority, permitting great discretion for private ordering and adaptation. That capacious grant of power is policed in large part by the common law of equity, in the form of fiduciary duty principles. The judiciary deploys its equitable powers cautiously to avoid intruding on the legitimate scope of action the DGCL leaves to directors and officers acting in good faith. The business judgment rule embodies that commitment to proper judicial restraint. At the same time, Delaware's public policy interest in vindicating the legitimate expectations stockholders have of their corporate fiduciaries requires its courts to act when statutory flexibility is exploited for inequitable ends.

The Bylaw Amendments are not inconsistent
with the DGCL

With those principles in mind, I now determine whether the Bylaw Amendments are effective. I begin by rejecting International's claim that the aspect of the Bylaw Amendments that abolishes the CRC is statutorily invalid. International bases that argument on § 141(c)(2), which [allows the board to create committees] ...

International contends that § 141(c)(2) empowers only directors to eliminate a committee established by a board resolution and not stockholders acting through a bylaw.

I agree with the defendants that this argument is not convincing. Stockholders are invested by § 109 with a statutory right to adopt bylaws. By its plain terms, § 109 provides stockholders with a broad right to adopt bylaws "relating to the business of the corporation, the conduct of its affairs, and its rights or powers or the rights or powers of its stockholders, directors, officers or employees." This grant of authority is subject to the limitation that the bylaws may not conflict with law or the certificate of incorporation.

[Text omitted]

In *Frantz Manufacturing Co.* v. *EAC Industries*, the Delaware Supreme Court made clear that bylaws could impose severe requirements on the conduct of a board without running afoul of the DGCL. In *Frantz*, a majority stockholder implemented bylaw amendments when it feared that the incumbent board would divest it of its voting power. The amendments required, among other things, that there be unanimous attendance and board approval for any board action, and unanimous ratification of any committee action. The Supreme Court found that the bylaws were consistent with the terms of the DGCL. In so ruling, the Court noted that the "bylaws of a corporation are presumed to be valid, and the courts will construe the bylaws in a manner consistent with the law rather than strike down the bylaws."

... § 141(c)(2) permits a board committee to exercise the power of the board only to the extent "provided in the resolution of the board ... or in the bylaws of the corporation." As the defendants note, the statute therefore expressly contemplates that the bylaws may restrict the powers that a board committee may exercise ...

[Text omitted]

For these reasons, I agree with the defendants that the provision in the Bylaw Amendments eliminating the CRC does not contravene § 141(c)(2). The question therefore becomes whether that and the other Bylaw Amendments are impermissible because they were adopted for an inequitable purpose.

The Bylaw Amendments are inequitable

In *Frantz*, the Supreme Court also made clear that the rule of *Schnell* – that inequitable action does not become permissible simply because it is legally possible – applies to bylaw amendments. In *Frantz*, the Supreme Court ... found the very restrictive bylaws at issue proper because the majority stockholder – which had committed no acts of wrongdoing – was acting to protect itself from being diluted.

In this case, the Bylaw Amendments were clearly adopted for an inequitable purpose and have an inequitable effect ...

[Text omitted]

As recounted, Black (acting for himself and as Inc.'s agent) violated the Restructuring Proposal and his fiduciary duties and undermined the Strategic Process. Once the independent directors of International acted to try to alleviate the harm caused by Black and to ensure the proper procession of the Strategic Process in accordance with Black's prior agreement (which was understood by Inc. and Ravelston), Black caused Inc. – with support from the Barclays – to adopt the Bylaw Amendments. The plain purpose of these Bylaw Amendments was to disable the International Board and prevent it from completing the Strategic Process and utilizing the tools available to the board under the DGCL.

Although it is no small thing to strike down bylaw amendments adopted by a controlling stockholder, that action is required here because those amendments complete a course of contractual and fiduciary improprieties ...

[*Text omitted*]

... This situation is importantly distinct from the usual situation when a controlling stockholder closes down a subsidiary's exploration of ... alternatives [to auction itself]. In the typical case, the parent owes no contractual or fiduciary obligation to permit the subsidiary to proceed. Here, by contrast, International secured a binding commitment from its ultimate controlling stockholder, Black, who dominated Inc., to lead its Strategic Process and to seek an International Level transaction that would benefit its stockholders. Black even told the board that he sought a deal for the "equal and ratable" benefit of all International stockholders. Critically, Black promised to eschew an Inc.-level transaction that would negatively affect the Process except in narrow circumstances that do not exist.

[*Text omitted*]

... American corporation law has recognized that there are circumstances when a subsidiary has a legitimate right to contest a parent's sale of its control position. The classic example is if the controlling stockholder is going to sell to a known looter ... [or] when a "controlling shareholder ... was in the process or threatening to violate his fiduciary duties to the corporation."

[*Text omitted*]

LIMITED LIABILITY OR ECONOMIC UNITY?

In Re Rave Communications, Inc. v. Entertainment Equities, Inc.
United States Bankruptcy Court, Southern District of New York
138 BR 390 (1992)

CORNELIUS BLACKSHEAR, Bankruptcy Judge

I.   Facts

On October 9, 1990, the Trustee for Rave Communications, Inc. ("Rave" or "Debtor") filed the original complaint in this action naming four corporate defendants, and four individual defendants. The corporate defendants, all firms closely related to the Debtor, are Entertainment Equities, Inc. ("EE"), a Delaware corporation; Entertainment Media Group, Ltd ("EMG"), a Delaware corporation; Media Partners, Ltd ("MP"), a Canadian corporation; and Rockbill Inc. ("Rockbill"), a New York corporation (collectively, "Corporate Defendants"). The individual defendants, all officers or board members of the Debtor, are Joshua C. Simons

("Simons"), Jay Coleman ("Coleman"), William Kosovitch ("Kosovitch"), and Steven Grossman ("Grossman") (collectively, "Individual Defendants").

The Corporate Defendants and the Individual Defendants, separately and jointly, moved to dismiss the original complaint. Rather than respond to these motions prior to the return date, the Trustee filed an amended complaint on March 8, 1991, asserting essentially the same causes of action against the same defendants as asserted in the original complaint.

The Amended Complaint contains ten claims for relief pursuant to the Bankruptcy Code, the New York Debtor & Creditor Law ("DCL"), the New York Business Corporations Law ("BCL"), and the common law; seeking, in summary: (1) to pierce the corporate veil, and reach the Individual Defendants, to hold them jointly and severally liable with the Corporate Defendants for all debts of Rave; (2) to avoid asset transfers as fraudulent conveyances pursuant to § 548(a) (1) & (a)(2) and the Alter Ego Doctrine; (3) to disallow any claims asserted by the Individual Defendants in the bankruptcy proceeding; (4) to impose punitive damages upon all Defendants; (5) to impose joint and several liability upon the Individual Defendants for breach of their fiduciary duties to the Debtor pursuant to § 544(b) of the Bankruptcy Code and §§ 717, 719, and 720 of the New York BCL.

[*Text omitted*]

II. Background

The Trustee alleges that the Debtor, essentially a captive company, was stripped and rendered inoperable by its corporate parent and affiliates (the Corporate Defendants), and by the individuals who controlled these corporate entities (the Individual Defendants) ... The facts, pled primarily upon information and belief, that allegedly gave rise to the claims of fraudulent transfer, are as follows:

Rave and EMG, are wholly owned by Rockbill. The parent company of Rockbill is EE, a holding company. Rockbill's primary business is providing corporate marketing and promotional services to music industry clients. The Debtor's primary purpose was to publish, and to bear the costs of publishing, programs for rock concerts, for Rockbill. The Debtor did not have facilities for printing the publications, so they subcontracted the work out to various printers. This resulted in the accumulation of accounts payable that, allegedly, perpetually exceeded Debtor's receivables.

The accumulation of unpaid printing costs caused the Debtor to become insolvent on or before July 1, 1986. Allegedly, both Simons and Coleman were aware of the Debtor's cash flow deficiencies prior to 1988, but used the Debtor to insulate its parent, Rockbill, from publishing costs ...

Prior to 1988, the Debtor applied for and obtained a loan of $500,000 from Chemical Bank. The loan was collateralized by the assets of the Debtor, the guaranty of Rockbill, the hypothecation of Rockbill's assets, and the personal guarantees of both Coleman and Simons. In May 1988, Chemical extended the maturity date of the loan, and provided an additional line of credit of $400,000, which was collateralized by a $200,000 certificate of deposit from Rockbill and a $200,000 certificate of deposit from Entertainment Marketing Communications International Ltd, an affiliated company ... Despite the loans and extensions, the Debtor's financial condition continued to deteriorate. Further, despite the deterioration, the Debtor and Rockbill allegedly continued their practice of executing intercompany loans and paying one another's bills.

Coleman and Simons, allegedly aware of the financial weakness of the Debtor and Rockbill, solicited Grossman and Kosovitch for a capital infusion through investment in Debtor and Rockbill, among others. The investment caused a restructuring of both the management and the ownership of the enterprise.

First, Coleman was no longer the sole shareholder of Rockbill. Instead, Kosovitch formed Entertainment Equities ("EE") as a holding company to wholly own Rockbill ... Coleman, Media Partners and Simons were the owners of EE. Kosovitch was Chief Financial Officer ("CFO") of EE and served as Secretary/ Treasurer. Rockbill was managed by Coleman (President), Simons (Vice President), and Grossman (Executive Vice President).

Rockbill remained sole owner of the Debtor, Rave, which was now managed by Simons (President and Director), Kosovitch (Secretary/Treasurer and Director), and Coleman (Chairman of the Board) ... Kosovitch was CFO of Rockbill in addition to being CFO of EE, the holding company. "In effect, Coleman and Simons exchanged direct ownership of Rockbill and the Debtor for a combined 65% ownership interest in EE, the sole owner of Rockbill and, in turn, the Debtor's ultimate corporate parent." ...

The Trustee alleges the Defendants planned to rid the EE enterprise of its major liability, Rave, while preserving the other subsidiaries. EE, controlled by Coleman, Simons, Media Partners and Kosovitch, formed a wholly owned subsidiary, EMG, on August 26, 1988, allegedly for the primary purpose of acquiring the assets of the Debtor ... The Debtor, pursuant to an asset purchase agreement dated August 30, 1988, transferred its assets to EMG, while leaving its liabilities in its corporate shell ... This transfer allegedly rendered the Debtor inoperable, depriving its creditors of the opportunity to become whole, while allowing EE and its individual owners to continue in business free of the Debtor's liabilities ...

Therefore, the principal claim concerns the allegedly fraudulent conveyance of assets from the Debtor to EMG; and the liability of the transferee of the assets to restore the transferred assets or their value.

III.   Law
[Text omitted]

B.   Requirements for pleading piercing of corporate veil
This motion does not require us to decide whether to pierce the corporate veil, but merely to decide whether the pleadings are sufficient to begin litigation of the veil

piercing issue. The leading case on this issue is *Walkovszky* v. *Carlton* ... [Note 3] There, the court held that pleadings were insufficient to maintain an action to pierce the corporate veil because the pleadings alleged only that the assets of the defendant corporation, together with the statutorily mandated minimum amount of liability insurance coverage, were insufficient to fully compensate the plaintiff, a tort victim ... Merely pleading that a corporation has insufficient assets to pay a claim is not enough to state a cause of action for fraud, and is not enough to state a cause of action to pierce the corporate veil.

[Note 3] In *Walkovszky*, the plaintiff, a tort victim, was injured by a taxicab owned by one of defendant's corporations. The plaintiff sought to hold the defendant personally liable for damages exceeding the amount paid by the insurer, on the theory that "the multiple corporate structure was an unlawful attempt to defraud members of the general public who might be injured by the cabs." ...

The defendant was a stockholder in ten such corporations, each of which owned two cabs. Furthermore, each cab carried the statutorily mandated minimum amount of liability insurance. The defendant, by properly incorporating and insuring each taxicab, had complied with the state law in all respects ... According to the court, the case involved "a rather common practice in the taxicab industry of vesting the ownership of a taxi fleet in many corporations, each owning only one or two cabs." ... In finding the complaint insufficient, the court noted that the multiple ownership practice was clearly legal, as the multiple corporations were formed pursuant to statutory authorization ... [*Editors' note*: when the Plaintiff filed an amended complaint, the Appellate Division found sufficient facts to disregard the corporate entity and hold Carlton and other defendants personally liable for the claim. See *Walkovsky* v. *Carlton*, 29 AD 2d 763 (1968) and 244 NE 2d 55 (1968).]

The court in *Walkovszky* recognized that, "[b]roadly speaking, the courts will disregard the corporate form ... whenever necessary 'to prevent fraud or to achieve equity.'" ... The *Walkovszky* court instructed the plaintiff on what additions would be necessary to make plaintiff's pleadings sufficient. Plaintiff could plead that none of a group of affiliated corporations had their own separate existence, naming all the affiliates as defendants. Under such a fact pattern it might be appropriate to pierce the corporate veil and hold the *larger corporate* entity financially responsible ... The corporate veil may also be pierced when a corporation is a "dummy" for its stockholders, who are "in reality carrying on the business in their personal capacities for purely personal rather than corporate ends" ... This type of veil piercing seeks to hold the individual stockholders personally liable. [Note 4]

[Note 4] A cause of action seeking to impose corporate liability on a shareholder will lie when there are sufficiently particular allegations to the effect that the shareholder was merely using the corporate name to conduct personal business, was commingling funds or assets, perverting the privilege of doing business in a corporate form, or disregarding corporate formalities ...

C.   Requirements for pleading fraud in
bankruptcy cases

Two types of fraud can be charged in a Bankruptcy case. Claims of actual fraud fall under § 548(a)(1), where the scienter requirement is "actual intent to hinder, delay, or defraud." In contrast, claims of constructive fraud fall under § 548(a)(2) where intent is not a factor. The relevant factors in [constructive fraud] are the transferor's financial condition and the sufficiency of the value provided by the transferee. The Amended Complaint alleges fraudulent conveyance under both [types of fraud].

[Text omitted]

IV.   Analysis

The Amended Complaint charges actual fraud ... [and] constructive fraud ... actual fraud and actual control on behalf of the Individual Defendants sufficient to pierce the corporate veil ... The Amended Complaint further alleges either a nonfunctional or a nonexistent board of directors, although a board of directors existed "on paper" ... interlocking directorates and financing, a transfer of assets for less than reasonably equivalent value ... and, knowledge of the Debtor's insolvency at the time of the transfer ...

[Text omitted]

The Amended Complaint has sufficiently stated a claim to litigate the propriety of piercing the corporate veil. Particular allegations with respect to holding the larger corporate entity financially responsible include the lack of a separate corporate existence. Particular allegations with respect to holding the Individual Defendants personally responsible include allegations of commingling funds or assets, perverting the privilege of doing business in corporate form and the disregard of corporate formalities. The Amended Complaint clearly fulfills the pleading requirements set out in *Walkovszky*.

Conclusion

Plaintiff has sufficiently pled the elements ... to satisfy the purposes of Rule 9(b), and to allow the Defendants to begin preparations to litigate on the merits. Accordingly, the Dismissal Motion is denied with respect to Counts 1, 2, 3, 4, 5, 6, and 7 of the Complaint.

Further, count 8 (for disallowance of any claims asserted by defendants), count 9 (for punitive damages), and count 10 (for breach of fiduciary duty) have been pled with sufficient specificity for Defendants to begin preparations for litigation on the merits. Any additional information necessary to the litigation may be obtained through use of the discovery process.

The Dismissal Motions are denied in all respects.

[Text omitted]

In Re Oil Spill by the "Amoco Cadiz" off the Coast of France on March 16, 1978
US District Court, Northern District of Illinois Eastern Division
1984 US Dist. LEXIS 17480; 20 ERC (BNA) 2041
[*Text edited; footnotes omitted*]

Judge McGarr, Memorandum Opinion and Final Judgment
Order of the issue of liability

I.   Findings of fact

A.   *Parties, nature of the proceedings, and jurisdictional facts*

1. This complex, multidistrict litigation arises from the grounding of the oil tanker Amoco Cadiz off the coast of France on March 16, 1978, and the subsequent spill of its cargo of crude oil. The Amoco Cadiz lost steering when its hydraulic steering gear failed, and the vessel grounded 12 hours later.

2. The registered owner of the Amoco Cadiz was Amoco Transport Company ("Transport"), a Liberian corporation with its principal place of business in Hamilton, Bermuda. The Amoco Cadiz was designed and constructed in Cadiz, Spain by Astilleros Espanoles, SA ("Astilleros"), a Spanish Corporation with its principal place of business in Madrid, Spain. The Amoco Cadiz was of Liberian registry, official number 4773, having its home port at Monrovia, Liberia.

3. On the day of the casualty, the West German salvage tug Pacific attempted to assist the Amoco Cadiz. The tug Pacific is owned and operated by Bugsier Reederei and Bergungs, AG ("Bugsier"), which is a corporation organized under the laws of the Federal Republic of Germany with its principal place of business in Hamburg, West Germany.

4. The Amoco Cadiz went aground in the territorial waters of the Republic of France ("France"), a sovereign nation. In addition to lawsuits filed by France, actions for oil pollution damages also have been brought by the French administrative departments of Finistere and Conseil General des Cotes du Nord ("Cotes du Nord"), numerous municipalities ("communes") and a number of French individuals, businesses and associations. (These parties are referred to herein as "the French claimants" or "the claimants.")

5. The cargo on board the Amoco Cadiz was owned by affiliates of the Royal Dutch/Shell group. Another affiliate of that group, Petroleum Insurance Limited ("PIL"), provided the insurance covering this cargo and by virtue of its payment pursuant to this coverage, became subrogated to the cargo loss claims. (PIL is also referred to as one of "the claimants" unless the context requires otherwise.)

6. At all times material to these actions, Standard Oil Company (Indiana) ("Standard"), was an Indiana corporation having its principal office and place of business in Chicago, Illinois.

7. At all times material to these actions, Amoco International Oil Company ("AIOC") was a Delaware corporation wholly owned by Standard and having its principal office and place of business in Chicago, Illinois.

8. At all times material to these actions, Amoco Transport Company ("Transport") was a Liberian corporation all of whose stock was indirectly owned by Standard through a chain of wholly owned subsidiaries.

9. From the time of its formation in August 1970, and at all times thereafter material to these actions, Amoco Tankers Company ("Tankers") was a Liberian corporation all of whose stock was indirectly owned by Standard through a chain of wholly owned subsidiaries.

10. At all times material to these actions, Standard and consolidated subsidiaries, including AIOC, Transport and Tankers (collectively "the Amoco parties"), formed a large integrated petroleum and chemical company conducting operations on a worldwide basis. Standard, as the parent company, concerned itself with overall policy guidance, financing, coordination of operations, staff services, performance evaluation and planning.

[*Text omitted*]

2.   The tort claims

15. Most of the claims before the court are maritime negligence tort claims. France, Cotes du Nord and various other French claimants have filed actions against the Amoco parties in which they claim that the Amoco Cadiz casualty was caused by the negligence of the Amoco parties in the course of constructing, maintaining and operating the tanker.

E.   *The Roles Of Standard, AIOC and Transport with respect to the Amoco Cadiz*

1.   Design, acquisition, ownership and control

282. The AIOC Marine Transportation Department was responsible for developing, planning and implementing measures necessary to meet the transportation requirements for the consolidated subsidiary companies of Standard. Its Marine Operations Department was responsible for all of the day-to-day planning and operating functions of vessels owned by Standard subsidiaries ...

297. The decision to purchase the Amoco Cadiz was made by Standard on the recommendation of AIOC and with no significant participation in that decision on the part of Transport. AIOC was not authorized to make such a decision without Standard's approval ...

300. In conjunction with the signing of the contract with Astilleros, a letter from Amoco International Limited ("Limited") was delivered to Astilleros by which Limited undertook to form Tankers as a wholly owned subsidiary and to cause it

to ratify the purchase contract. Limited was a Bermuda corporation wholly owned by Amoco International Finance Corporation ("AIFC"), a Delaware corporation, which in turn was wholly owned, directly or indirectly, by Standard …

2. Standard controlled its subsidiaries

344. Standard is the controlling parent corporation of a large and intricate corporate structure, the companies, of which, including International and Transport, exist and complement one another for the financial benefit of and to carry out the corporate will of Standard.

345. Standard had a consolidated balance sheet so that the reportings to the Securities and Exchange Commission ("SEC") for Standard included the profit and losses of AIOC and Transport.

346. In its Form 10K filed with the SEC for 1978, Standard described its relationship with its subsidiaries as follows: "Standard and its consolidated subsidiaries (herein sometimes collectively also called 'Standard') form a large integrated petroleum and chemical company that conducts operations on a worldwide basis."

347. Standard described itself as "a parent company concerned with overall policy guidance, financing, coordination of operations, staff services, performance evaluation, and planning for its subsidiaries."

348. None of the stock of AIOC was publicly held. Standard owned 100% of the voting stock of AIOC …

355. Standard, AIOC, Transport and other Standard subsidiaries were managed by a network of interlocking directors and officers …

365. Within the Standard family of corporations, key personnel continuously moved among corporate officess in the parent and its subsidiaries.

366. Standard treated its subsidiaries' operations as its own; its officers and directors had little or no perception of separateness with respect to the various Standard companies.

[Text omitted]

II. Conclusions of law

[Text omitted]

11. Whether AIOC and Standard may be sued is determined by United States law.

12. The CLC is the law of France and not the law of the United States; it thus does not apply to a determination of whether AIOC and Standard may be sued in this country …

[Text omitted]

F. The liability of Standard

43. As an integrated multinational corporation which is engaged through a system of subsidiaries in the exploration, production, refining, transportation and

sale of petroleum products throughout the world, Standard is responsible for the tortious acts of its wholly owned subsidiaries and instrumentalities AIOC and Transport.

44. Standard exercised such control over its subsidiaries AIOC and Transport, that those entities would be considered to be mere instrumentalities of Standard. Furthermore, Standard itself was initially involved in and controlled the design, construction, operation and management of the Amoco Cadiz and treated that vessel as if it were its own.

45. Standard therefore is liable for its own negligence and the negligence of AIOC and Transport with respect to the design, operation, maintenance, repair and crew training of the Amoco Cadiz.

46. Standard therefore is liable to the French claimants for damages resulting from the grounding of the Amoco Cadiz.

[Text omitted]

Re Polly Peck International plc (in administration)
Chancery Division (Companies Court)
[1996] 2 All ER 433; [1996] 1 BCLC 428; [1996] BCC 486
[Text edited; some footnotes omitted]
Reproduced by permission of Reed Elsevier (UK) Limited, trading as LexisNexis Butterworths

ROBERT WALKER J

Polly Peck: the scheme of arrangement

In the late 1980s Polly Peck International plc (PPI) was the holding company of a fast-growing group with a diversified range of interests. The group's core activities were agriculture and food production but they extended to electrical consumer goods, textiles, pharmaceuticals, cosmetics and tourism. PPI had subsidiaries in many countries including England, north Cyprus, Turkey, Hong Kong, the United States, Switzerland and Liberia.

PPI ran into severe financial difficulties in 1990 and on 25 October 1990 it went into administration ... The purposes of the administration have been extended to seeking approval of a scheme of arrangement ... [which] took effect on 18 May.

The scheme provides (para 2) for the usual moratorium and (para 3) for the collection and realisation of PPI's assets ... Paragraph 7(i) provides that the supervisors are not to admit any claim which would not be admissible in a liquidation if PPI had gone into compulsory liquidation on the date when the scheme took effect.

Paragraph 9 of the scheme provides for the distribution of the scheme assets (after provision for costs and preferential claims and subject to some special provisions as to the so-called club banks) rateably between scheme creditors whose claims have been admitted. Paragraph 9.9 is in these terms: "No scheme creditor shall be entitled to receive an amount in the scheme which exceeds the amount of his scheme claim nor to prove more than once in respect of any scheme claim, and for the avoidance of doubt the rule against double proof shall apply in respect of all distributions and reserves made in the scheme."

... The issue is as to the application of the rule against double proof. The circumstances in which the issue arises are connected with a subsidiary of PPI, Polly Peck International Finance Ltd (PPIF), which was incorporated in the Cayman Islands on 20 May 1987.

The bond issues

Between June 1987 and February 1990 there were no fewer than eight bond issues which raised a total of SwF 665m and DM 100m – a total of over £400m at current exchange rates – for the PPI group. Except for some points of difference summarised below, all eight issues were arranged on the same general lines: they comprised unsecured, unsubordinated fixed-rate bearer bonds issued by PPIF and guaranteed by PPI. The lead manager for the Swiss franc issues was SG Warburg Soditic SA (Warburg SA) and for the single DM issue, Arab Banking Corporation-Daus & Co. GmbH (ABC-Daus). ABC-Daus assumed the position of trustee for the bondholders under the DM issue. Each of these lead managers also acted as principal paying agent.

The eight bond issues were as follows.

Amount	Payment date	Rate	Redemption
1 SwF 65m	7 July 1987	3%	1997
2 SwF 75m	13 Aug 1987	6%	1992
3 SwF 50m	19 Nov 1987	6 1/4%	1990
4 SwF 100m	7 April 1988	5 3/4%	1993
5 DM 100m	20 April 1988	6%	1993
6 SwF 125m	20 Sept 1989	5 5/8%	1994
7 SwF 100m	1 March 1989	6 1/4%	1996
8 SwF 200m	1 March 1990	8 3/4%	1997

[Text omitted]

There were two main differences between the issues. The first issue was convertible into ordinary shares of PPI (a right reflected in the interest rate) and the whole issue was in fact converted into PPI ordinary shares, or (as to a small balance) redeemed, before PPI crashed. The first issue is nevertheless significant because in other respects it set the pattern for later issues. The DM issue was established with

ABC-Daus as a trustee – a feature not found in the SwF issues – and it did not in terms provide for PPI to be liable as a principal obligor (although PPI's obligations as guarantor were stated in cl 3 of the guarantee agreement to be 'autonomous and independent'). It is however common ground that nothing turns on any difference between PPI's obligations under the SwF issues (which were governed by Swiss law) and its obligations under the DM issue (which was governed by German law).

The first issue was discussed at a meeting at 42 Berkeley Square, London W1 (then PPI's head office) on 5 May 1987. It was chaired by Mr David Fawcus, then PPI's finance director, and attended by representatives of Warburg SA, two firms of London solicitors, and Stoy Hayward (PPI's auditors) as well as by PPI personnel. It considered a board paper (prepared by Mr Wood, the group treasurer) which proposed 'that the bonds be issued in the name of a new Cayman Islands subsidiary under the guarantee of [PPI]' in order to avoid onerous listing requirements in London, and achieve certain tax advantages. The board paper estimated the costs of the issue: "In simple terms, front end costs are likely to be about £1.6m or just under 4% of total raised. Annual costs will be about 373% or 670%, inclusive of hedging expenses, for tranche A and B respectively."

(The two tranches had different coupons and conversion terms.) The board paper assumes, but does not refer to the proceeds of the issue being lent on to PPI.

PPI, through its London solicitors, then took advice from Cayman attorneys as to the formation and use of a Cayman financial vehicle. The Cayman attorneys gave full written advice in a faxed letter dated 11 May 1987. Their advice included the following advice as to the on-loan from PPIF (as it was named on its incorporation) to PPI:

> It is usually the case that commercial paper issues and traditional forms of Eurocurrency financing can be structured so as not to constitute "banking business." However, some care needs to be paid to the manner in which funds are raised and are then on-lent to the parent or other companies within the relevant group. Thus, the on-lending arrangements should be evidenced by appropriate documentation (which can of course be relatively brief given the in-house nature of the transactions). In particular those on-lending arrangements should be structured so that the repayment of the loans is not simply on a demand basis ... Cayman Islands' Companies Law follows English legal principles. Thus a company should only enter into transactions intended for its benefit and the directors must act in good faith in the interests of the company. As a result, the financing arrangements should be structured so as to produce a profit (albeit small) for the Cayman Islands' company. Generally speaking this is achieved by the company charging a rate of interest when on-lending these funds which is higher than the rate it pays on the borrowed funds or by the company charging a fee.

On 13 May 1987 there was a board meeting of PPI at 42 Berkeley Square attended by Mr Asil Nadir (the chairman and chief executive of PPI), Mr Ellis (a senior executive), Mr Fawcus (the finance director) and others. The board considered the paper on the convertible SwF issue and approved it, subject to approval by certain other interests. PPIF was then incorporated with Mr Moon (a Cayman attorney), Mr Nadir, Mr Ellis and Mr Fawcus as its directors. It had an authorised capital of SwF 1m, divided into shares of SwF 1; 25,000 of them were issued and credited as fully paid. PPIF has always been a wholly owned subsidiary of PPI. Mr Moon resigned as a director at the first board meeting of PPIF held on 28 May 1987. Thereafter the board of PPIF consisted solely of individuals who were also PPI directors, meeting at 42 Berkeley Square. There was never any attempt to argue that PPIF's directing mind was outside the United Kingdom or that the company was non-resident for United Kingdom tax purposes (indeed, its residence in the United Kingdom was necessary for purposes of group relief).

There are some features common to all the bond issues which call for mention, because they were relied on by counsel in their submissions. Each of the bond issues stated in its prospectus that the proceeds of the issue were to be used for refinancing and development of the Polly Peck group's business activities. The form of words used varied to some extent ... but the general effect did not vary much.

Each of the Swiss bond issues also included in its conditions a provision for PPI or another non-Swiss subsidiary of PPI to be substituted for PPIF as the principal obligor, with the consent of Warburg SA, such consent not to be unreasonably withheld so long as the bondholders' interests were adequately protected (especially as regards tax). The DM bond issue contained a similar provision for substitution in a manner satisfactory to ABC-Daus.

The on-loan from PPIF to PPI

The Cayman attorneys' advice that the on-lending arrangements should be evidenced by appropriate (if brief) documentation was not carried through, so far as the administrators' scrutiny of PPI's papers has revealed. In October 1987 London solicitors sent instructions to tax counsel to settle a draft loan agreement for the on-loan from PPIF to PPI ... [T]ax counsel settled the draft agreement on 29 February 1988 in a form which recited an on-loan from PPIF to PPI of approximately SwF 135715m, the balance of SwF 4785m (representing the costs of the first two SwF issues totalling SwF 140m) being treated as an arrangement fee payable by PPI to PPIF ... The draft loan agreement provided for the on-loan to carry interest:

> 'payable half-yearly at the rate of per cent above the rate of interest payable by PPIF in respect of the corresponding tranche of the Bonds [viz the first two issues] or at such other rate or rates as shall from time to time be agreed between the parties.'

As I have said, no executed loan agreement between PPIF and PPI (either in the above or in any other form) has been found and there is no evidence (either in the form of board minutes or in any other form) that any such loan agreement ever existed. The draft settled by tax counsel provides some evidence at least as to the transaction having had the character of a loan.

In practice, once PPIF had formally joined in a bond issue, its involvement in the subsequent management of the issue seems to have been minimal. It had no current account at a bank (though the proceeds of each issue do seem to have been held briefly to an account in PPIF's name at the lead manager's bank.) In practice all payments of interest, fees and costs in connection with the bonds seem to have been made by PPI, and the state of account between PPI and PPIF can be determined only by internal accounting records kept at PPI's offices and from PPIF's financial statements. There are financial statements of PPIF for the accounting period to 31 December 1988, signed by Mr Nadir and Mr Fawcus and audited by Stoy Hayward, which show PPIF as having a revenue reserve of SwF 696,000 at 31 December 1988. This appears to reflect the% turn (provided for in the draft loan agreement) on outstanding bonds to the amount of about SwF 435m; this was on the basis that PPI had borne initial costs of bond issues which by then amounted to SwF 10m. PPI's practical responsibility for servicing the bonds was also reflected in communications from the principal paying agents: Warburgs SA sent demands for interest direct to PPI, and ABC-Daus sent them to PPIF 'care of' PPI.

Another scrap of evidence is a letter that Mr Spencer of Stoy Hayward wrote to Mr Fawcus on 29 September 1987. Mr Spencer referred to an election under the Income and Corporation Taxes Act 1970, s 256 (group relief) which was outstanding and advised that:

> 'if you are funding the interest payment from PPI it is important initially that this will be in the form of an interest-free advance which can be set off against the interest payment due and payable once we have formally received clearance from the Inland Revenue.'

Mr Fawcus wrote on the letter a manuscript note to Mr Wood:

> 'A lot of garbage. Just note that PPI should not pay interest to PPIF until tax status of PPI is cleared. Until then payments should take the form of an advance.'

So despite his initial comment Mr Fawcus seems to have understood and accepted the essential point of the advice.

Apart from its involvement in the bond issues PPIF was a party to two other group transactions. On 4 November 1987 it provided security to Banque Paribas (Suisse) SA for an advance of SwF 15m. On or about 19 October 1987 it joined with PPI in a joint and several guarantee to a Hong Kong group creditor, BSR International plc. Both these seem to have been short-term transactions which give rise to no continuing liability.

I have gone into these factual matters at what would be, in other circumstances, excessive detail because of the submission made to me by Mr Leslie Kosmin QC (who appears with Mr David Chivers for the supervisors) that PPIF was, in relation to the bond issues, a cipher, agent or nominee. That submission is controverted by Mr Gabriel Moss QC, who appears for both the respondents, PPIF and ABC-Daus. They have a common interest in resisting the conclusion that this is a case of double proof (if they fail in that their interests will diverge as to which claim should be rejected; but the order for a preliminary issue recognises that that second stage may not be reached).

Before making any finding on the secondary issues of fact (that is whether PPIF was a cipher, agent or nominee) I must summarise the claims that have been put in, and then turn to the questions of law that have been argued before me.

The notices of claim

PPIF was placed in creditors' voluntary liquidation in the Cayman Islands on 23 March 1995 ... On 24 May 1995 the London-based liquidator, Mr Beirne, submitted to the scheme supervisors a notice of claim (as at 15 May 1995) approximately as follows:

	SwF	DM	Total (£)
Principal	600m	100m	361m
Interest	209m	32m	124m
Total	809m	123m	485m

The claim for interest was based on the bond rates, plus%, for periods starting in late 1989 or in 1990.

On 9 June 1995 ABC-Daus gave notice of a claim (as at 15 May 1995) for about £64,765m, about £44m of which represented principal (the rest was for interest, including £7m default interest under the German civil code, and £170,000 legal costs). It has been agreed that Warburg SA should act as agent for the Swiss bondholders, who have claims against both PPIF and PPI. The total claims against PPI so far notified by Warburg SA amount to about £421m.

When Mr Kidd swore his affidavit on 27 September 1995 the position was that the bulk of the ABC-Daus claim had been admitted by the scheme supervisors, apart from the default interest, and the Warburg SA claim had been admitted almost in its entirety. Mr Moss tells me, no doubt correctly, that the default interest has since been admitted. Bondholders' admitted claims against PPI as guarantor are therefore of the order of £485m. PPIF's unadmitted claim is approximately the same size. Apart from these claims and the 'club bank' claims, there are other scheme claims against PPI amounting to a sum of the order of £1bn. The double proof point does therefore have a significant effect on the distribution of assets.

A dividend of 171p in the pound has already been paid under compromise arrangements approved by Mr Registrar Buckley on 19 October 1995. The scale of further dividends will, I understand, depend on the outcome of pending litigation.

The issue which I have to decide is put this way in para 44 of Mr Kidd's affidavit.

> 'Having investigated PPIF's claim in the Scheme, the Supervisors have become concerned that, due to what appeared to them to be the lack of separate corporate personality on the part of PPIF, the Court might hold that the corporate veil should be lifted so preventing PPIF from maintaining a claim separate from the bondholders' claims against PPI. Alternatively, even if PPIF is entitled to a separate claim, such a claim might be held to arise out of what is, in substance, the same debt (being the debt to the bondholders), so that PPIF would be barred from receiving a dividend in addition to that payable to the bondholders by the rule against double proof. In these circumstances the Supervisors have decided, on the basis of legal advice that they should seek directions from the Court before paying any dividends to both the bondholders and PPIF.'

The rule against double proof

The rule against double proof is a long-standing principle of the law of bankruptcy, and has applied in the winding up of companies since the Companies Act 1862 ... It has often been described in terms of straightforward and obvious fairness, depending on substance, not form. Thus in that case Mellish LJ said (at 103–104):

> 'But the principle itself – that an insolvent estate, whether wound up in Chancery or in Bankruptcy, ought not to pay two dividends in respect of the same debt – appears to me to be a perfectly sound principle. If it were not so, a creditor could always manage, by getting his debtor to enter into several distinct contracts with different people for the same debt, to obtain higher dividends than the other creditors, and perhaps get his debt paid in full. I apprehend that is what the law does not allow; the true principle is, that there is only to be one dividend in respect of what is in substance the same debt, although there may be two separate contracts.'

[Text omitted]

In *Barclays Bank Ltd* v. *TOSG Trust Fund Ltd* ... Oliver LJ said in a passage which I have referred to but not yet set out ... that it was a fallacy to argue:

> 'that, because overlapping liabilities result from separate and independent contracts with the debtor, that, by itself, is determinative of whether the rule can apply. The test is in my judgment a much broader one which transcends a close jurisprudential analysis of the persons by and to whom the duties are owed. It is simply whether the two competing claims are, in substance, claims for payment of the same debt twice over.' ...

'Substance', corporate personality and the corporate veil

Mr Kosmin relied strongly on this passage in contending that the bond issues by PPIF (guaranteed by PPI) and PPIF's on-lending to PPI were so closely connected as to result in the bondholders' claim against PPI as guarantor and PPIF's claim against PPI as principal creditor being 'in substance, claims for payment of the same debt twice over'. Mr Kosmin developed his argument in various ways which naturally involved some overlap; but I hope I can fairly summarise the way he put his case as follows: (1) that on a correct view of the facts, PPIF was in effecting the bond issues (a) an agent or nominee for PPI or alternatively (b) a cipher or facade for PPI; (2) that even if PPIF acted as an independent principal, the on-lending within the Polly Peck group was still so much a part of the same composite transaction as not to rank, in substance, as a separate debt ...

Mr Moss for his part says, rightly, that this sort of transaction of guaranteed borrowing and on-lending by a special-purpose financial vehicle is a common-place occurrence in capital markets (this point is borne out by the letter from the Cayman attorneys, which seems to be giving fairly standard advice in a fairly standard situation). Mr Moss goes on to submit that the double proof point, if sound, would introduce a new and alarming element of uncertainty into capital markets. I think this argument in terrorem may be a bit overstated, since investors in unsecured bonds issued in this way must be relying on the credit rating of the guarantor, and not on some calculation of the chances of a 'double-dip' against the guarantor and the financial subsidiary in the event of default. Nevertheless the point raised is a novel point of some commercial importance.

... In *Welsh Development Agency* v. *Export Finance Co. Ltd* ... Staughton LJ said (in the context of deciding whether a commercial document effected a sale or a charge):

> 'The problem is not made any easier by the variety of language that has been used: substance, truth, reality, genuine are good words; disguise, cloak, mask, colourable device, label, form, artificial, sham, stratagem and pretence are "bad names" ... It is necessary to discover, if one can, the ideas which these words are intended to convey. One can start from the position that statute law in this country, when it enacts rules to be applied to particular transactions, is in general referring to the legal nature of a transaction and not to its economic effect. The leading authority on this point, albeit in a case from Malaya, is the advice of Lord Devlin in *Chow Yoong Hong* v. *Choong Fah Rubber Manufactory Ltd* ... : "There are many ways of raising cash besides borrowing ... If in form it is not a loan, it is not to the point to say that its object was to raise money for one of them or that the parties could have produced the same result more conveniently by borrowing and lending money."'

Those were statutory contexts (registration of charges and regulation of moneylending) but I think they also support the general proposition that when the law is looking for the substance of a matter, it is normally looking for its legal substance, not its economic substance (if different). As Robert Goff LJ put it in *Bank of Tokyo Ltd* v. *Karoon* ...

Second, the House of Lords affirmation in ... *Salomon & Co. Ltd* v. *Salomon* ... of the separate legal personality of even a 'one-man' company does not of course mean that registered companies have all the characteristics of, and no characteristics not shared by, natural persons ... Another aspect is that whereas natural persons do not (since the abolition of slavery and the passing of the Married Women's Property Acts) own the persons or property of other human beings, commercial companies do have owners. Their shareholders have an economic interest in their commercial success. Although the shareholders do not own their company's assets, a wrong to the company (if uncompensated) may cause them economic loss. But in general the shareholders will have no direct right of action in respect of such loss (see *Prudential Assurance Co. Ltd* v. *Newman Industries Ltd (No. 2)*) ... This point was not mentioned in argument, being neither controversial nor directly relevant; but I think it worth mentioning both in order to identify and distinguish another corporate 'double recovery' problem which does not arise here, and because it leads on to the topic of intra-group indebtedness, which is directly relevant in this case.

The third point is that where there is a group of companies and they are all solvent, a claim by one group company against another, even though sound in law, is likely to have only marginal economic effects (it may have some, for instance in connection with taxation). But as soon as both companies go into insolvent liquidation, any claim between them assumes much greater importance (unless by an extraordinary coincidence both have identical creditors with identical claims, which is certainly not the case here). That is, I think, the point that Lord Wilberforce must have had in mind when he said in *Ford & Carter Ltd* v. *Midland Bank Ltd* (1979) ...:

> 'When creditors become involved, as they do in the present case, the separate legal existence of the constituent companies of the group has to be respected.'

...

Issue 1(a): was PPIF an agent or nominee?

In *Salomon* v. *Salomon & Co.* the House of Lords roundly rejected the conclusion of the lower courts that Salomon & Co. was a 'mere nominee or agent' of Mr Aron Salomon, or his 'alias', or that his fellow shareholders were 'dummies' ... There are of course many cases in which it has been held, on the facts, that a company has acted as an agent or nominee, either for its principal shareholder or for some other party, and several of them were cited to me ... But neither agency nor nomineeship – nor, still less, sham or something akin to sham – is to be inferred simply because a subsidiary company has a small paid-up capital and has a board of directors all or most of whom are also directors or senior executives of its holding company.

Mr Kosmin does not, as I understand his submissions, contend that the arrangements between PPI, PPIF and the lead mangers were a sham (I will return below to 'cipher' and 'facade'). He does contend that a variety of factors lead to an inference of agency or nomineeship. The most important of these factors (which are all set out in the detailed skeleton argument prepared by Mr Kosmin and Mr Chivers) are the following: (i) PPIF was incorporated solely for the purpose of the bond issues; (ii) it had no separate, independent management; (iii) it had a very small paid-up capital; (iv) it did not pay the costs of the transactions and could not have done so; (v) it had no normal bank account and no separate financial records (in practice PPI saw to everything and acted as PPIF's banker and bookkeeper); (vi) the terms of the on-loan were not independently negotiated, did not serve any commercial purpose and in any case were never finally agreed, nor was the% turn paid otherwise than as a paper transaction; and (vii) no lender could or would have relied on PPIF's covenant, as opposed to PPI's (which could substitute itself as principal debtor if it got the approval of the principal paying agents).

In short, Mr Kosmin submits that PPIF had only a nominal role in the arrangements, and that as a matter of substance PPI should be recognised as having borrowed direct from the original bondholders, so depriving the on-loan of any legal significance (or indeed existence). To come to that conclusion I would have to find that that was the effect, not merely of what was informally arranged in the boardroom at 42 Berkeley Square, but also of the formal legal documents which were entered into on the occasion of each bond issue. On the second SwF issue (which is typical since it was the first issue of non-convertible bonds) the formal documents consisted of (i) a public bond issue agreement between PFIF, PPI and Warburg SA as lead managers on behalf of a consortium including 26 other banks (the agreement annexed the form of the bearer bonds and the terms of their issue); (ii) a guarantee agreement between PPI, Warburg SA and the consortium; and (iii) a 42-page prospectus. All these documents made clear that the bond issue was to be made by PPIF and that PPIF's obligations were to be guaranteed by PPI subject to the provision for substitution which I have already mentioned. The documentation on the later loans was essentially similar, subject to small variations (already mentioned) on the DM issue.

[Text omitted]

Some of the factors on which Mr Kosmin relies do tend to show that the Polly Peck personnel who were concerned with the matter at 42 Berkeley Square were (to say the least) less than meticulous in their administrative procedures. I make no specific finding about that. But even blatant and reprehensible 'cutting of corners' (if it occurred) could not, it seems to me, retroactively alter the character of the transactions embodied in the formal documents by which the bond issues were effected. The factors which Mr Kosmin relies on cannot and do not in my judgment establish PPIF's role as that of agency or nomineeship, and so they do not eliminate the on-loan as a significant part of the composite transaction.

Issue 1(b): sham, pretence, cipher, facade

My conclusion that there was no conventional relationship of agency or nominee-ship is not conclusive of the case, because Mr Kosmin had further submissions. On what I have called his point (1)(b) and his point (2) I was referred to quite a lot of authority touching on what is sometimes called lifting (or piercing) the corporate veil. That is a vivid but imprecise metaphor which has possible application in several different contexts, some far removed from this case. The most relevant, it seems to me, is where corporate personality is (in the words of Lord Keith in *Woolfson* v. *Strathclyde Regional Council* ...) used as 'a mere facade concealing the true facts'.

Sham, pretence, cipher and facade are all ... 'bad names' implying a value judg-ment of disapprobation. 'Sham' was at least half way to becoming a term of art (re-quiring an intention common to all parties) but has now, it seems, been supplanted (at least in the context of licence or tenancy) by 'pretence' ... Mr Kosmin did not rely on sham or pretence. He did submit (orally) that PPIF was a 'cipher' and (in his skel-eton argument) that it was a 'facade'. I think that his use of 'cipher' was to add colour and force to his submission on agency or nomineeship (which I have already consid-ered). 'Facade' (or 'cloak' or 'mask') is perhaps most aptly used where one person (in-dividual or corporate) uses a company either in an unconscionable attempt to evade existing obligations ... or to practise some other deception (a sort of unilateral sham, since the corporate facade has no independent mind). In *Adams* v. *Cape Industries plc* ... the establishment and interposition of the Liechtenstein corporation referred to as AMC was a facade in this sense, and 'no more than a corporate name', though the new Illinois corporation, CPC, was not. But the notion that regular sales of large volumes of South African asbestos to an United States purchaser were being effected through a lawyer's office in Vaduz is to my mind of a quite different order of artifici-ality from the function of PPIF as a single-purpose financial vehicle (I am not over-looking the two other isolated transactions entered into by PPIF; but they add little to its independent reality). In my judgment PPIF was more than a mere facade.

Issue (2): single economic unit

It is on this part of the case that I have found Mr Kosmin's submissions most per-suasive, though I am not ultimately persuaded by them. The arguments for consid-ering a closely integrated group of companies as a single economic unit were fully considered (principally in the context of corporate presence as founding jurisdic-tion) in *Adams* v. *Cape Industries plc* ... both by Scott J and, with a full citation of authority, in the judgment of the Court of Appeal ... Both passages merit careful study. The Court of Appeal concluded that:

save in cases which turn on the wording of particular statutes or contracts, the court is not free to disregard the principle of *Salomon* v. *Salomon & Co. Ltd* ... merely because it considers that justice so requires.' ...

Mr Kosmin seeks to add to these exceptions (turning on particular statutes or contracts) a further exception where a rule of law founded in public policy (the rule against double proof) would be frustrated by ignoring the economic reality of the single group. In that submission Mr Kosmin can and does call in aid the words of Oliver LJ in *Barclays Bank Ltd* v. *TOSG Trust Fund Ltd* ... that the test is 'a much broader one which transcends a close jurisprudential analysis of the persons by and to whom the duties are owed'.

Nevertheless I am not persuaded by the argument. I can accept that as a matter of economic reality the bondholders (whose presumed intentions may be material) must have intended to rely on the credit-rating and covenant of PPI, whether as guarantor or (after substitution) as principal obligor. It is doubtful whether even the most far-sighted of them can have calculated that in the event of a crash, PPIF might have fewer unsecured creditors than PPI, and a claim against PPI under an on-loan. It was perfectly possible, consistently with each prospectus, that the proceeds of some or all of the bond issues would be loaned on, not to PPI, but to other group subsidiaries. It is also possible, though less likely, to imagine a situation in which PPIF lent on to another subsidiary, with PPI guaranteeing that borrowing also, and the second subsidiary then lending on to PPI. Each of those sequences of events would be likely to produce a different result in the event of a crash of the whole group, whether or not the rule against double proof has any application. The possibility of there being subsidiaries which were not wholly owned subsidiaries adds to the range of imaginable variations.

Were I to accede to Mr Kosmin's submission it would create a new exception unrecognised by the Court of Appeal in *Adams* v. *Cape Industries plc* and that is not open to me. Moreover I think that Mr Kosmin is in one sense assuming what he seeks to prove, since the unjust or inequitable result which he asserts does not occur unless the group is recognised as being in substance a single economic entity, whose constituent members' internal rights and obligations are to be disregarded. But the authorities to which I have already referred show that substance means legal substance, not economic substance (if different), and that ... the separate legal existence of group companies is particularly important when creditors become involved. Injustice may be in the eye of the beholder, but I do not perceive any obvious injustice – certainly not such as the court can remedy – in the unpredictable consequences that may follow from the unforeseen insolvency of a large international group of companies such as the Polly Peck group.

[*Text omitted*]

SUBPART C

The market for corporate control

24

The regulation of takeover bids and prices

Required reading

EU: Takeover Directive, arts. 1–8 and 13–16

D: Securities Acquisitions and Takeovers Act (WpÜG), §§ 1–3, 10–26, 29–32, 34–39c

UK: CA 2006, secs. 942–943, 974–991; City Code, General Principles 1–6, Rules 9, 19, 20

US: Exchange Act, §§ 14(d)–(f); Rules 14d-2, 14d-3(a), 14d-5(a)–(c), 14d-6(d) (scan Regulation M-A, Items 1–10)

Regulating disclosure, timing and price of bids

I.   Introduction

A.   What is a "takeover"?

In Chapter 21, we discussed various techniques for acquiring a company. One of those is a purchase of the company's stock from its shareholders. Because the ownership interests of shareholders in the corporation are represented by transferable securities, a company can be acquired through transfer of these securities directly from the current owner to a new owner. Not all stock purchases are takeovers (or, in US terminology, "tender offers"). If a buyer were to approach an entrepreneur and ask whether she was interested in selling five of the 10 million shares of her wholly owned company, this offer would not be considered a "takeover bid" (or "tender offer") in our jurisdictions. In US law, the term "tender offer" is not specifically defined, as you can see by how much time the court spends discerning the boundaries of this term in *Hanson Trust*, reprinted in part in this chapter. What, then, are the characteristics the court decides are determinative for a tender offer?

Under the EU Takeover Directive, a "takeover bid" is a "public offer" (other than by the issuer itself) made to the shareholders of a company "to acquire all or some of those securities ... which ... has as its objective the acquisition of control of the offeree company,"[1] and the Directive itself applies only to bids for securities listed on a "regulated market."[2] Thus, regardless of what jurisdiction we are in, when we talk about a "takeover" or "tender" offer, we discuss an offer made publicly to a number of shareholders for the purpose of acquiring a significant portion of a listed (or, in the US, registered) company's capital.

B.   Why are takeover bids specially regulated?

For a number of years, takeover offers were not specially regulated in any of our jurisdictions. The UK and the US introduced mandatory rules on takeovers in 1968, and Germany first made its rules on takeovers mandatory thirty years later. An alternative transaction type, a purchase of assets, is regulated by nothing more than a required shareholder vote. Why did developed economies choose to specially regulate this particular type of transaction? Certainly, one characteristic is something it shares with consumer protection legislation: takeover bids are made to a large number of people, who have limited information about the bidder and the offer, and who may have little bargaining power. It is also possible for a bidder to provide the shareholders with false, misleading or incomplete information about the bid, its financing, or any securities used as consideration. Thus, both disclosure requirements and rules to police disclosure are essential. A second aspect is the way in which the acquisition of a controlling block of shares interacts with corporate law. Because, under corporate law, holding less than 100 percent of the shares still allows control of the company, the first problem is one of collective action. If a sub-optimal offer is made to a group of people, the best option may well be that no one accepts the offer. However, if members holding a majority of the voting rights were to accept the sub-optimal offer, the state of affairs facing those who did not accept might well become worse than if they had accepted the offer. In this way, members of a group can be herded into accepting a sub-optimal offer against their own best interest. Some form of regulation to reduce such collective action problems is therefore necessary. Further problems arise because an offer

---

[1] Art. 2(1)(a) Takeover Directive.

[2] Art. 1(1) Takeover Directive. Art. 4(14) of the Markets in Financial Instruments Directive (MiFID) defines a "regulated market" as "a multilateral system operated and/or managed by a market operator, which brings together or facilitates the bringing together of multiple third party buying and selling interests in financial instruments ... admitted to trading under its rules ... which is authorized" by a member state.

for the shares of a company may be paid for with the shares of the bidder company. If this occurs, a takeover can entail the complexity of a public offering of shares in addition to what has been discussed above. The shareholders of the target would need to understand the values of both the bidder's and the target's going concerns to decide if the share-for-share exchange ratio constitutes a fair price. This necessitates still further disclosure.

The first regulatory measure is thus to ensure that the bidder provide complete and correct *information* about the offer and the company, so that each shareholder can make a reasoned decision. Such information is reinforced by having the target company obtain the opinion of an independent expert on the value of the company. Secondly, measures should be taken to reduce the herding of a group into accepting a sub-optimal bid. One simple technique is to give the shareholders enough *time* to inform themselves and make a careful decision on whether or not to sell. A third way by which the pressure can be reduced significantly is by forcing the bidder to pay the same *price* to all sellers in and around the offer. The collective action problems associated with a bid can thus be reduced by requiring full information, a minimum period for acceptance, and uniform pricing.

The manner in which the acquisition interacts with corporate law creates a related, but different set of problems. If you were to pay 75 percent of the purchase price of a new suit, would you obtain full and irrevocable control of the item? Even if you were to receive control of the item subject to making financing payments (expensive suit!), your control would not be full and irrevocable because a default on the remaining payments could lead to repossession of the suit. In all of our jurisdictions, the design of corporate governance provides that a purchase of 75 percent of the voting common stock of a company will give the buyer complete control over the company and its assets, so that the holders of the other 25 percent of the stock, especially if dispersed among a number of people who do not coordinate their actions, would be powerless to affect the fate of the company. Thus, unlike a sale of most other items, owners of a company who find themselves in the minority can lose control of their property without even selling it. This can be addressed by forcing the bidder to *buy 100 percent* of the company's stock (either during or after the offer) at a price either paid to all the other shareholders or determined as fair by a court. In Section II below, we will review how these general types of protections have been incorporated in the laws of our three jurisdictions.

II.   *The regulatory structures of our jurisdictions*

A.   United Kingdom

1.   The rules and the regulator   The Companies Act 2006 gives the Panel on Takeovers and Mergers express statutory power to issue rules implementing the EU Takeover Directive and to administer the enforcement of such rules.[3] The Panel is composed of thirty-four members, the core of which are appointed by the representative associations of the UK financial industries, with the others being appointed by those first appointees.[4] This statutory anchoring is the latest stage of a long march that began in 1959 with the Bank of England's release of informal "Notes on Amalgamation of British Businesses," which in 1968 were transformed into a "Takeover Code" administered by a panel of representatives from City of London financial firms (thus often called the "City Code") and enforced by sanctions of the London Stock Exchange and the Board of Trade without any legislative provision.[5] The Panel is now the official UK "supervisory authority" as referred to in article 4 of the Takeover Directive.

Unlike its predecessor, the Companies Act 2006 contains provisions for the regulation of takeovers, such as the necessary delegation of power and duties to the Panel as official supervisory authority,[6] rules implementing articles 9–12 of the Takeover Directive (on impediments to takeovers)[7] and rules on "squeeze-outs" and "sell-outs."[8] Otherwise, all UK rules on takeovers are found in the Takeover Code alone. The Panel also issues interpretive statements and decisions on specific cases, which are available on its website (www.thetakeoverpanel.org. uk). The Code was amended in response to the Takeover Directive and the endowment of the Panel with an express statutory role as national authority. The Panel's succinct statement of the Code's purpose well describes the function of takeover legislation in each of our jurisdictions:

> The Code is designed principally to ensure that shareholders are treated fairly and are not denied an opportunity to decide on the merits of a takeover and that shareholders of the same class are afforded equivalent treatment by an offeror. The Code also provides an orderly framework within

---

[3] Part 28, Chapter 1 CA 2006.   [4] Introduction, 4(a) Takeover Code.
[5] Armour and Skeel (2007: 1744–1745).   [6] Secs. 942–965 CA 2006.
[7] Secs. 966–973 CA 2006.   [8] Secs. 974–991 CA 2006.

which takeovers are conducted. In addition, it is designed to promote ...
the integrity of the financial markets.[9]

The Code applies to UK companies listed on a UK regulated market or
(with selective application) listed on a regulated market anywhere in the
European Economic Area,[10] and faithfully reproduces from the Takeover
Directive[11] its definition of the offers to which it applies. The Code is
divided into six general principles – taken verbatim from the Takeover
Directive – and thirty-eight Rules. The following subsections sketch the
Code's general framework and discuss a part of its detailed content.

2.   **Required disclosure**   A general purpose of the Code is to ensure
that shareholders are "given sufficient information and advice to enable
them to reach a properly informed decision as to the merits or demerits
of an offer."[12] Unlike the US tender offer rules, the Code requires that disclosure be made "in the first instance to the board of the offeree company or to its advisers."[13] The board of the target must then announce
the offer as soon as it is "firm" and not subject to any pre-condition.[14] The
target's board must also obtain independent advice on the offer (from,
for example, an unaffiliated investment bank) and make the substance of
such advice known to its shareholders.[15]

A purchaser itself need not announce an offer unless it reaches the
threshold of 30 percent of a class of the target's securities,[16] which is
deemed to constitute "control" of the target,[17] but, if the purchaser does
choose to announce a "firm intention" to make an offer, it must disclose
its identity, the terms of the offer (including conditions), and its holdings
of the target's securities (including any options on the securities or contracts to borrow shares).[18] Determinations that a person has reached the
30 percent threshold, and, like determinations regarding other thresholds such as a holding of 50 percent,[19] trigger the application of duties

---

[9]   Introduction, 2(a) Takeover Code. On the last point of financial market integrity,
an interesting example that lies outside the boundaries of this chapter is the US prohibition on "short tendering" shares that one does not own into an offer. See 17 CFR
§ 240.14e-4.

[10] Introduction, 3(a) Takeover Code.   [11] Introduction, 3(b) Takeover Code.

[12] Rule 23 Takeover Code.   [13] Rule 1(a) Takeover Code.

[14] Rule 2.2(a) Takeover Code.   [15] Rule 3.1 Takeover Code.

[16] Rule 9.1(a) Takeover Code. However, the share disclosure rules would require disclosure
at 3 percent of the target's voting rights. See FSA Disclosure and Transparency Rules,
Rule 5.1.2, discussed in Chapter 18.

[17] Definitions, "Control," Takeover Code.   [18] Rule 2.5(b) Takeover Code.

[19] Rule 9.1(b) Takeover Code.

under the Code. As the facts of the *British Telecommunications plc Offer for PlusNet plc* illustrate, in the context of active securities trading, it can be a delicate art to approach a threshold without triggering the duties of the Code. Moreover, the determination whether a bidder has reached a threshold is not based just on that bidder's holdings, but includes the holdings of all persons "acting in concert" with the bidder. The Code provides a detailed definition of "acting in concert," the core of which is as follows:

> Persons acting in concert comprise persons who, pursuant to an agreement or understanding (whether formal or informal), co-operate to obtain or consolidate control ... of a company or to frustrate the successful outcome of an offer for a company. A person and each of its affiliated persons [present when a 20 percent holding exists] will be deemed to be acting in concert all with each other.[20]

Compare this codified definition to § 30 WpÜG as applied in *Württembergische Metallfabrik*. Do you think that under the UK Code voting rights would be attributed similarly to the manner in which the German court shaped its judgment? How do these sets of rules compare to the US notion of "group" under § 13(d) of the Exchange Act (discussed in Chapter 19)?

The announcement of a firm intention to make an offer triggers the obligation to make a bid and starts the clock running on the offer period.[21] In addition to the timetable and procedure for acceptance,[22] the offer document must contain financial statements for a three-year period prior to the offer and detailed information regarding the bidder and its management.[23] Reflecting the European social policy that addresses concerns broader than the US focus on investor protection, share price and a level playing field, each bid document must also spell out the bidder's plans for the future business of the target, including any redeployment of the target's fixed assets, changes to its locations, and the continued employment of the employees and management.[24] The requirement that any bid document contain this information derives from the Takeover Directive, which mandates information on the bidder's intentions regarding "safeguarding ... the jobs of ... employees ... any material change in

---

[20] Definitions, "Acting in Concert," Takeover Code.
[21] Rules 2.6 and 2.7 Takeover Code.   [22] Rule 24.6 Takeover Code.
[23] Rule 24.2 Takeover Code. This rule contains a very detailed list of items that must be disclosed, of which only a highlighting summary is presented in this text.
[24] Rule 24.1 Takeover Code.

the conditions of employment, and in particular … likely repercussions on employment."[25] The Directive also instructs the target board, in its opinion on the offer, to address this same issue.[26]

Information must of course also be provided with respect to the financing and financial impact of the offer. If a merger is planned and the bidder makes any statements about an increase in value due to synergy, this must in some cases be supported by a "merger benefits statement."[27] Key to any offer is the prospect that payment will actually be made as promised, and thus the offer document must also contain:

> a description of how the offer is to be financed and the source of the finance. The principal lenders or arrangers of such finance must be named. Where the offeror intends that the payment of interest on, repayment of or security for any liability (contingent or otherwise) will depend to any significant extent on the business of the offeree company, a description of the arrangements contemplated will be required. Where this is not the case, a negative statement to this effect must be made.[28]

The last point of information is in effect a requirement that any arrangement approaching a leveraged buyout or "financial assistance" be disclosed. We will discuss the legally permissible limits of such arrangements in Chapter 26. Any arrangements between the bidder, any person acting in concert with it, and any of the directors, recent directors, shareholders or recent shareholders of the target must also be set out in the offer document.[29] As the facts of *ex parte Guinness plc* make clear, the type of agreements constituting concerted action go well beyond those that are disclosed. The target's board must circulate an opinion on the offer to the shareholders, specifically opining on the bidder's strategic plan for the company and its effect on employment and the locations of the company's facilities.[30] Both the bidder and the target must make an extensive number of documents – including constitutional documents, management service contracts and the company's other material contracts – available for inspection during the offer term.[31]

Before the offer document is made public, a copy must be given to the Panel.[32] Any information distributed to the target company's shareholders "must be made equally available to all offeree company shareholders

---

[25] Art. 6(3)(i) Takeover Directive.   [26] Art. 9(5) Takeover Directive.
[27] Rule 19.1, Note 8, Takeover Code.   [28] Rule 24.2(f) Takeover Code.
[29] Rule 24.5 Takeover Code.   [30] Rule 25.1 Takeover Code.
[31] Rule 26 Takeover Code.   [32] Rule 19.7 Takeover Code.

as nearly as possible at the same time and in the same manner."[33] The content and accuracy of the disclosure documents and advertisements issued and statements made during the course of the offer must meet the "highest standards of care and accuracy and the information given must be adequately and fairly presented."[34] Moreover, just as for the disclosure documents of listed companies under the Transparency Directive, the directors of the bidder must issue a declaration that they accept "responsibility for the information contained in the document or advertisement and that, to the best of their knowledge and belief (having taken all reasonable care to ensure that such is the case), the information contained in the document or advertisement is in accordance with the facts and, where appropriate, that it does not omit anything likely to affect the import of such information."[35]

Immediately after the expiration of an offer or upon its revision, the bidder must announce the number of acceptances it has received, including subscription rights, share loans and letters of intent.[36]

3.   Timing   A target company may announce a "possible offer" if the purchaser has approached it but not yet made a "firm" offer, and it may then ask the Panel to impose a time limit for the bidder to "clarify its intentions with regard to the offeree company."[37] The offer document should be sent to the target's shareholders within twenty-eight days after the firm intention to make an offer is announced.[38] Within fourteen days after the offer document is sent out, the target's board must send the circular containing its opinion on the offer and its understanding of the offer's effects on the company and its employees to shareholders and also make it available to employees.[39]

An offer must remain open for a minimum of twenty-one days,[40] and does not require a maximum term ("until further notice" is sufficient), although, if no term is given or the term is more than seventy days, the bidder must provide fourteen days' notice before closing the offer.[41] If the offer is revised, it must remain open for at least fourteen days after the day the revised offer document is sent out.[42] If within twenty-one days after a closing date the offer cannot be unconditionally accepted ("unconditional

---

[33] Rule 20.1 Takeover Code.   [34] Rule 19.1 Takeover Code.
[35] Rule 19.2 Takeover Code.   [36] Rule 17.1 Takeover Code.
[37] Rule 2.4(b) Takeover Code.   [38] Rule 30.1(a) Takeover Code.
[39] Rule 30.2 Takeover Code.   [40] Rule 31.1 Takeover Code.
[41] Rule 31.2 Takeover Code.   [42] Rule 32.1(b) Takeover Code.

as to acceptances"), a shareholder who has accepted the offer may with-draw.[43] If an offer fails to become unconditional, lapses or is withdrawn, the bidder may not make another offer for the target during the following twelve-month period.[44]

4. **Equal treatment of shareholders during the bid**   Before launching a bid for less than 30 percent of the target's voting rights, a purchaser must obtain the Panel's permission,[45] and shareholders must be able to accept the bid on a *pro rata* basis.[46] At this point, the UK regulation resembles the fair treatment rules used in the US. However, UK rules go significantly fur-ther. If a purchaser acquires an interest in the target's shares, which (taken together with similar shares of persons acting in concert with him) carry 30 percent or more of the voting rights of the target, it must launch a bid for all outstanding classes of equity and voting securities of the target, unless the Panel consents to other action.[47] The bidder must condition such offer on acquiring a holding exceeding 50 percent of the target's voting rights,[48] and this is the only condition that may be imposed.[49] If the target has more than one class of equity share capital, the bidder must make a "comparable offer" for each class, whether they carry voting rights or not.[50]

Fairness protections in the UK extend beyond the time period of the offer itself. The offer must be at a price in cash or a cash alternative no less than the highest price the bidder paid for *any* interest in shares of the same class during the twelve months prior to the announcement of the offer.[51] This is the strictest rule specified in the Takeover Directive, which requires a price matching prior purchases between six (as done in Germany) and twelve months preceding the offer.[52] The Panel may, how-ever, at the bidder's request, grant a dispensation from the highest price rule.[53] If the bidder acquires any shares at a price higher than the offer, she must increase the offer price accordingly.[54] If the bidder has used cash to purchase shares carrying at least 10 percent of the target's voting rights during the twelve months prior to the offer, the offer itself must be in cash

---

[43] Rule 34 Takeover Code.
[44] Rule 35.1 Takeover Code.   [45] Rule 36.1 Takeover Code.
[46] Rule 36.7 Takeover Code.   [47] Rule 9.1(a) Takeover Code.
[48] Rule 10 Takeover Code.   [49] Rule 9.3(b) Takeover Code.
[50] Rule 14.1 Takeover Code. When the target has convertible securities outstanding, the bidder must make an "offer or proposal to the stockholders to ensure that their interests are safeguarded." Rule 15.
[51] Rule 9.5(a) Takeover Code.   [52] Art. 5(4) Takeover Directive.
[53] Rule 11.3 Takeover Code.   [54] Rule 9.5(b) Takeover Code.

or "accompanied by a cash alternative at not less than the highest price paid" for such shares.[55] The reciprocal rule applies if during the three months prior to the offer the bidder used securities to purchase at least 10 percent of the target's shares.[56]

5.   Treatment of remaining shareholders   If a small minority of shareholders does not sell out to a successful purchaser, they will have lost their chance to influence the company's policy and management without having received anything in return. Their presence can also be troublesome for the new parent company, in that as shareholders the minority will have the right to receive information and at least participate in corporate decisionmaking, which could be expensive and inconvenient for the majority shareholder. For these reasons, both the purchaser and the minority shareholders are given a right to cause all of the company's shares to be transferred to the purchaser ("squeeze out" and "sell out").

If a bidder acquires through the offer at least 90 percent (in value) of the shares to which the offer relates and (if they are voting shares) this is at least 90 percent of the votes, the bidder may notify those holders of the respective classes who have not yet accepted the bid that it intends to purchase their shares.[57] This applies *mutatis mutandis* to each class included in the offer.[58] If the purchaser intends to "squeeze out" the minority in this way, he must give them notice by the earlier of three months after the close of the offer or six months after its beginning.[59] He may then purchase this remainder on the same terms as the offer.[60] Within three months after the close of the offer, those shareholders who do not tender into the offer also have a right to sell their shares at the offer price to a bidder who reaches one of these 90 percent thresholds.[61]

Under the UK rules, the highest price thus reaches back to twelve months before the beginning of the offer and forward to three months after the close of the offer, ensuring equal treatment of all shareholders, regardless of when they make their decision to sell.

B.   Germany

1.   The rules and the regulator   The historical development of the German takeover rules took a path similar to the UK rules, albeit at a significant interval. First, a subcommittee of the stock exchange drew up

---

[55] Rule 11.1 Takeover Code.   [56] Rule 11.2 Takeover Code.   [57] Sec. 979(2) CA 2006.
[58] Sec. 979(4) CA 2006.   [59] Sec. 980(2) CA 2006.   [60] Sec. 981(2) CA 2006.
[61] Secs. 983, 984(2) CA 2006.

precatory guidelines for takeovers in 1979, which were converted into a code, adherence to which was made a requirement for listing on the premium segments of the Frankfurt Stock Exchange in 1998.[62] Then, in connection with Germany's negotiation of the draft EU Takeover Directive and the recalcitrance of some countries (particularly France) to remove what Germany saw as hidden barriers to takeovers launched by purchasers in other EU member states, Germany enacted the Securities Acquisitions and Takeovers Act (*Wertpapiererwerbs- und Übernahmegesetz* or WpÜG) in 2001. BaFin is the supervisory authority that administers and enforces the WpÜG; it has issued a number of implementing regulations, particularly the WpÜG Bid Regulation, which provide detailed treatment of technical issues in the WpÜG.

The WpÜG is broader than the Takeover Directive in that it also regulates partial bids, or acquisitions of shares that do not aim to, or in fact, achieve control of a target company; however, the rules are still limited to companies listed on a regulated market.[63] As a result of its inclusion of partial bids, the Act distinguishes three types of regulated transactions: partial "bids to purchase securities" (§§ 10–28); takeover bids, which from the outset have the declared intention to acquire control of the company (§§ 29–34); and "mandatory bids" to acquire the entire company when the bidder acquires control (i.e. 30 percent of the voting rights)[64] of the company (§§ 35–39).[65] The WpÜG gives the board of a target company somewhat more flexibility to take measures against a takeover bid than does the UK Takeover Code. Thus, as will be discussed in more detail in Chapter 25, German law forms somewhat of a conceptual bridge between the UK stance of "non-frustration" and the US stance that sees the board as a fiduciary defender of the company's integrity.

2. **Required disclosure**   Unlike the UK Takeover Code, the WpÜG does not impose a preferred course of transaction by requiring a bidder to first approach the target's board with its intention to make an offer. Rather, as soon as the bidder has decided to launch an offer, it must first publish this intention on the internet and in an electronic information service,[66] send a copy of the publication to BaFin and the relevant stock exchange, and then inform the target's *Vorstand* of the bid.[67] Both the

---

[62] See Baums and Rieder, in Baums and Thoma (2008: §§ 1.1–1.3).
[63] § 1(1) WpÜG.   [64] § 29(2) WpÜG.
[65] Note that the provisions listed do not apply solely to one kind of bid. Those addressing bids generally also apply to the more specific takeover and mandatory bids.
[66] § 10(1), (3) WpÜG.   [67] § 10(4), (5) WpÜG.

bidder and the target's *Vorstand* must inform their company's employees of the potential bid.[68]

Beginning from the date of publishing the intention to make an offer, the bidder has four weeks to submit the bid document to BaFin, which will either make comments or approve the document either expressly or tacitly by not objecting to it within ten business days.[69] The bidder must then publish the document electronically.[70] Similar to the UK bid document, the German document must contain:

- complete details of the identity of the bidder and the target;
- a description of the securities to be purchased and the amount of the offer;
- the type and amount of consideration offered, as well as details on the bidder's financing and an opinion from an independent securities firm on its sufficiency;
- any conditions for the offer;
- the bidder's plans for the target's future business, assets and finances, location, and employment;
- details of any payments or benefits to the target's *Aufsichtsrat* or *Vorstand*; and
- the timetable for the acceptance period and the procedures for acceptance.[71]

If securities are used as consideration, the bidder must include the information required for an approved prospectus for the securities pursuant to the Securities Prospectus Act.[72] The bidder and persons who have prepared or taken responsibility for the content of the offer materials are jointly and severally liable for misstatements or omissions of material facts if this results from gross negligence, unless the shareholder did not reach a decision to accept the offer on the basis of the materials or was aware of the misstatement or omission.[73] The bidder must regularly publish status reports on the number of securities that it has acquired through the offer and outside of it, and must also publish a tally immediately after the term for acceptance has expired.[74]

Promptly after receiving the offer document, the *Vorstand* and *Aufsichtsrat* of the target company must publish an opinion on the bid, specifically addressing the adequacy of the consideration, the impact of a successful bid on the company, its employees and its physical locations, and whether the management itself intends to support the bid.[75]

---

[68] § 10(5) WpÜG.   [69] § 14(1), (2) WpÜG.   [70] § 14(1), (2) WpÜG.   [71] § 11 WpÜG.
[72] § 2(2) WpÜG Bid Regulation.   [73] § 12 WpÜG.   [74] § 23 WpÜG.   [75] § 27 WpÜG.

3. **Timing**   The clock for an offer under the WpÜG begins when the bidder announces its intention to make an offer. As mentioned above, from that point the bidder has four weeks to submit its offer document to BaFin. If BaFin does not contact the bidder with comments within ten business days, the bidder may publish the document.[76] An offer must stay open for an acceptance term of at least four weeks from the date the offer document is published, and, subject to revision or the introduction of competing bids, may not stay open longer than ten weeks.[77] If a bid is changed, the term for acceptance is extended by two weeks,[78] and if, a competing bid is introduced, the term for the preexisting bid is lengthened to match that for the newly introduced bid.[79]

If a bidder that is not making a takeover bid nevertheless obtains control (defined as 30 percent of the voting rights)[80] of the target company, it has seven calendar days to inform BaFin of this fact, and four weeks from giving this notice to submit an offer document for a mandatory bid to BaFin and also publish it.[81] In a takeover bid, a "second" term for acceptance of two weeks begins to run upon the expiration of the "first" term for acceptance;[82] this is intended to reduce collective action pressures by allowing the shareholders to wait and see how the bid develops without the fear of being penalized by selling their shares on different terms than the shareholders who accepted early. If the target company calls a general meeting during a bid, the term for acceptance is automatically extended to ten weeks.[83]

If a bidder fails to reach a majority upon which the bid was conditioned, the bidder is blocked from launching another takeover offer for a period of one year.[84]

4. **Equal treatment of shareholders during the bid**   If the bidder offers to purchase a specific, non-controlling block of the target's shares and more than the specified amount of shares are tendered for acceptance, the bidder must accept the tendered shares *pro rata* the number that each selling shareholder tenders into the bid.[85] If the bidder gains control of the target and does not notify BaFin of an intention to reduce its holding, it must make an offer for the entire outstanding capital of the company.[86]

---

[76] § 14(2) WpÜG.   [77] § 16(1) WpÜG.   [78] § 21(5) WpÜG.   [79] § 22(2) WpÜG.
[80] § 29(2) WpÜG.   [81] § 35 WpÜG.
[82] § 16(2) WpÜG; this provision does not apply to mandatory bids, § 39 WpÜG.
[83] § 16(3) WpÜG.   [84] § 26(1) WpÜG.   [85] § 19 WpÜG.   [86] § 35 WpÜG.

The persons whose voting rights are attributed to the bidder for this purpose include:

- subsidiaries of the bidder;
- persons acting on the bidder's account;
- collateral takers of the bidder unless the bidder has retained voting rights;
- persons over whose shares the bidder may exercise rights;
- persons who have sold a call option to the bidder; and
- persons who have given the bidder a general proxy to exercise voting rights with free discretion.[87]

Beyond these clearly defined relationships, the voting rights of any person who generally acts in concert with the bidder or one of its subsidiaries on a contractual basis or otherwise will be attributed to the bidder's holdings.[88] As discussed in the *Württembergische Metallwarenfabrik* decision, an *ad hoc* agreement to vote together in a single meeting will not create action in concert for a German court.[89] If a bidder – together with the aforementioned persons – crosses the control threshold without launching a takeover bid, it owes the shareholders interest on the unpaid purchase amount for the length of the non-compliance.[90]

The offer itself must be at a price no less than the highest price the bidder paid for any interests in shares of the same class during the six months prior to the announcement of the offer.[91] As mentioned above, shareholders who do not accept a takeover offer during the first term for acceptance have an additional two weeks for acceptance so that they can act on the basis of the success or failure of the bid as reported by the bidder in its mandatory publication of shares held.

5. Treatment of remaining shareholders   Shareholders who do not accept a takeover offer or a mandatory bid offer may be forcibly squeezed out if the bidder obtains control of 95 percent of the voting rights of the target.[92] To do this, the bidder applies to the court for an order approving

---

[87] § 30(1) WpÜG.
[88] § 30(2) WpÜG. This does not include agreements to vote in a coordinated fashion on specific matters.
[89] While the range of the acting-in-concert provision has been expanded by the amendment to § 30(2) WpÜG by the Risk Limitation Act (*Risikobegrenzungsgesetz*) of August 12, 2008 (BGBl I: 1666) to include coordination by shareholder action outside the general meeting if such action is intended to substantially and permanently influence the target's business, the exception for *ad hoc* shareholder agreements is still valid.
[90] § 38 WpÜG.   [91] § 4 Bid Regulation.   [92] § 39a(1) WpÜG.

the squeeze-out and the consideration paid to the minority must be comparable to the offer price or its equivalent in cash.[93] If the bidder obtains 95 percent of the overall corporate capital (which may be higher if the target has issued non-voting preference shares), it may under the *Aktiengesetz* convene a general meeting and resolve to buy the minority out for "a suitable cash compensation."[94] The potential advantage of the procedure pursuant to § 39a WpÜG is that, if the bidder succeeded in acquiring at least 90 percent of the shares to which the bid pertained, the price offered in the bid is presumed to be fair for the squeeze-out.

If the bidder obtains control of at least 95 percent of the ordinary shares of the target, the remaining shareholders may within three months after expiration of the offer period demand to be bought out.[95] If the bidder were to merge the target into itself, it would have to offer the minority shareholders a cash buyout payment as discussed in Chapter 22.[96]

C.   United States

1. **The rules and the regulator**   The US takeover rules were introduced into §§ 13 and 14 of the Exchange Act by the Williams Act of 1968. The SEC has periodically issued and amended rules designed to implement these provisions.[97] The rules created the disclosure duties of shareholders on Schedule 13D (as discussed in Chapter 19), a prospectus-like disclosure document for tender offers, Schedule TO,[98] and some minimal substantive rules enforcing equal treatment of equally situated shareholders in a tender offer. The rules apply to offers for securities registered with the SEC, which is in turn, as we have often had occasion to mention, required under §§ 12 and 15 Exchange Act.[99]

The US states have also enacted laws that regulate tender offers. Because state law is constitutionally supplanted by duly adopted federal law where the two conflict, state laws on tender offers must not conflict with or frustrate the purposes of the Williams Act, which rests on the power of Congress to regulate interstate commerce, and must not discriminate against interstate commerce or subject such activity to inconsistent regulation in different states.[100] This results in state regulation of tender offers

---

[93] § 39a(3) WpÜG.   [94] § 327a AktG.   [95] § 39c WpÜG.

[96] See § 29 UmwG. A similar cash buyout offer is available under German law if the target were to enter into a domination or transfer of profit agreement with the bidder pursuant to § 305 AktG.

[97] 17 CFR §§ 240.14d-1 *et seq.*   [98] 17 CFR § 240.14d-100.

[99] See principally, 15 USC § 78l(g); 17 CFR §§ 240.12g-1 *et seq.*

[100] *CTS Corp. v. Dynamics Corp. of America*, 481 US 69 (1987).

clinging quite closely to the provisions of state company law. Section 203 of the DGCL, which we will examine in the next chapter, is an example of the kind of tender offer rule that most US states have adopted.

When moving from the European to the US rules on tender offers, two characteristics immediately become apparent. The first is the just mentioned division of the rules on takeovers between state and federal legislation. The matters addressed in this chapter, such as timing, disclosure and price, are governed primarily by federal rules, and the standards for judging the behavior of the target's board when confronted with a hostile offer, which are found in § 33 WpÜG and Rule 21 of the Takeover Code, are governed primarily by state case law. The second characteristic is that, although the federal rules on takeovers are voluminous and detailed, they offer less guidance for a preferred course of the transaction and less control of bidder opportunism than either the Takeover Code or the WpÜG. The latter framework – particularly the Takeover Code – prescribes a specific approach to a takeover, from mandating initial contact with the target's board to requiring strict price parity even for non-tendering shareholders post-bid. The US rules specify that, however the bidder chooses to proceed, certain disclosures must be made and certain minimum rules of substantive fairness must be met. Because the US rules proscribe very little but attempt to cover most permutations of possible offers, they appear both intricate and sketchy, whereas the UK rules set out a path for the transaction and thus appear both more complete and focused. This could well be the result of a small, culturally and professionally homogeneous group of people – primarily bankers and investors active in the City of London – shaping the UK rules among themselves, while the US rules are created by three diverse groups of people in check and balance against each other: the finance and corporate professionals who guide the takeover culture and its techniques; federal regulators who respond primarily to persons with complaints against such techniques; and state lawmakers who respond primarily to corporate managers who have the power to incorporate in a given jurisdiction.[101] However, this does not yet explain

---

[101] Professors Armour and Skeel highlight the influence of institutional shareholders in framing the UK rules and that of management in framing the US (state law) rules. See Armour and Skeel (2007: 1771–1776, 1780–1784). Professors Davies and Hopt highlight the systematic nature of the division of rules – where management power expands, formal rules on the bidding process proportionately contract, and *vice versa*: "[I]t is probably no accident that those systems which, historically, most clearly favor shareholder decision-

the larger political and cultural dynamics at work between EU member states with different economic policies and philosophies, which has significantly shaped the European takeover rules.

2. Required disclosure   If a bidder makes a tender offer for more than 5 percent of a class of registered securities, it must file a Schedule TO disclosure statement with the SEC and deliver a copy to the target, any other bidder, and the exchanges on which the target is listed.[102] If a purchaser were to obtain control of this amount of securities without intending to make a tender offer, it would file a Schedule 13D and explain the purpose for the purchase, as discussed in Chapter 19. On the same day that the bidder notifies the SEC of its offer, it must also make the offer to the target shareholders by either publishing the full document ("long form") in a national newspaper, or publishing a summary of the offer and sending the document to the shareholders who request a copy, or sending out the document to each shareholder with the assistance of the target itself.[103] Through various cross-references, the required contents of Schedule TO are actually found in Regulation M-A, and include:

- a "summary term sheet," briefly describing in "plain English" the most material terms of the proposed transaction;
- information on the target and its securities;
- information on the bidder, including any judicial or criminal sanctions suffered during the last five years, and its financial statements for the last two years;
- information on the offer and any offers made for the target or dealings in the target's securities during the past two years;
- the purpose of the transaction, including any plans to merge the target, sell its assets, change its dividend policy, capitalization, indebtedness or the composition of its board, and any plans to delist the company;
- the amount of funds necessary for the offer and their source, including any conditions attached to the financing and summaries of each agreement used to borrow funds for the offer; and
- the number of target securities held by bidder, its subsidiaries and its associates.[104]

---

making in bid contexts (France, UK) also have the most developed rules against acquirer opportunism." Davies and Hopt (2009a: 189).

[102] 17 CFR § 240.14d-3.   [103] 17 CFR § 240.14d-4.

[104] 17 CFR § 240.14d-6(d), referring to § 240.14d-100, referring to § 229.1000.

When comparing the US disclosure to the European rules, it is interesting to note that the bid document need not discuss effects on employment or potential plant closings, but rather stresses clarity of the offer terms and transparency with respect to the bidder's background. For the US lawmaker, securities law disclosure comes very close to consumer protection legislation – the investor is a consumer and has a right to understand what she is being offered. For the European lawmaker, takeovers have traditionally represented somewhat violent, private incursions into public industrial policy – and the collateral effects of such incursions on the normal goals of such policy, such as employment, are thus important. As will be discussed in Chapter 24, it remains to be seen whether the decisions of the ECJ will bring Europe into the US camp on this topic.

Within ten days after the offer is published, the target board must notify the target shareholders whether it supports, opposes or takes no position on the bid.[105] Depending on the circumstances, fiduciary duties under state law might require faster action or a certain quality of procedure in making the determination. The board must also file a Schedule 14D-9, which primarily discloses any relationships between the board and the bidder that might create conflicts of interest affecting its opinion on the offer.[106] Any such interests would trigger state law requirements to introduce independence into the decisionmaking process, as discussed in *Weinberger* v. *UOP* and *Kahn* v. *Lynch Communications*.

The information in the offer document and the board's opinion must be updated if any material change of circumstances takes place. If the information contained in any filing made during the offer contains material misstatements or omissions, the persons making and those responsible for the statements are open to civil liability actions by investors and by the SEC.[107]

3.   **Timing**   Unlike its European counterparts, the US offer process does not start with the intention to make an offer, but rather with the offer itself. Similarly to the prospectus rules in connection with a public offering of securities, at the moment that the bidder makes a public tender offer that would result in its holding more than 5 percent of a class of registered securities, the bidder must send out the Schedule TO.[108] From this point, the offer must stay open for at least twenty business days.[109] This period may be extended for an additional period of between three and twenty days,[110] and must be extended by ten days if the bidder increases or decreases the

---

[105] 17 CFR § 240.14e-2.   [106] 17 CFR § 240.14d-101, Schedule 14D-9.   [107] 15 USC § 78n(e).
[108] 15 USC § 78n(d)(1); 17 CFR § 240.14d-2.   [109] 17 CFR § 240.14e-1.
[110] 17 CFR § 240.14d-11.

percentage of securities in or the price of the offer.[111] The Exchange Act gives accepting shareholders the right to withdraw their acceptances for up to sixty days after the bid commences or up to seven days after the close of the bid.[112]

4. Equal treatment of shareholders during the bid   With the exception of some states of minor importance for the takeover market, such as Pennsylvania and Maine, US law does not contain a mandatory bid rule. The principle that shareholders should be treated equally in a tender offer is addressed by requiring equality as to the terms and the effects of the offer. First, an offer for a class of securities must be open to all holders of that class.[113] Secondly, the price paid to any shareholder of the class must be the highest price paid to any other shareholder in the class.[114] Thirdly, if more shares are tendered than the bidder has offered to buy, the bidder must accept the tenders *pro rata* the number of shares tendered by each selling shareholder.[115] Thus, if a bidder were to offer to buy 33.3 percent of the company's shares, and the shareholders holding 100 percent of the company equally with 90 shares each all tendered their entire holdings, each would have a right to sell only 30 of his shares to the bidder, regardless of who tendered first. Fourthly, with some exceptions – such as the exercise of convertible securities already held and proprietary purchases of an intermediary working for the bidder – persons participating in the bid may not purchase securities outside of the offer itself during the course of the offer.[116] This operates as a form of the European "highest price" rule, and shows that – contrary to what one might expect – the US laws do not always lead to a freer market, but are often somewhat draconian, such as here by forbidding purchases altogether rather than introducing a highest price requirement.

The second protection that the US federal rules offer on "highest price" contains a significant flaw which has led to much litigation of takeovers at the *state* level. The Exchange Act itself provides that, if the offer price is *increased* during the offer, those persons who have already tendered into the offer before the increase must also receive the higher price.[117] The Act says nothing about a price *decrease*. The highest price rule that implements this section also provides that, if more than one form of consideration is

---

[111] 17 CFR § 240.14e-1(b).   [112] 15 USC § 78n(d)(5).

[113] 17 CFR § 240.14d-10(a)(1). On this point, see *Unocal Corp.* v. *Mesa Petroleum Co.*, reprinted in part in Chapter 13, where the Delaware court permitted an offer to repurchase shares that excluded a hostile bidder. The *Unocal* decision was handed down before the SEC adopted Rule 14d-10. If a similar decision were made today, it would be in direct conflict with this Rule.

[114] 17 CFR § 240.14d-10(a)(2).   [115] 17 CFR § 240.14d-8.   [116] 17 CFR § 240.14e-5.

[117] 15 USC § 78n(d)(7).

given, it is sufficiently fair if "the highest consideration *of each type* paid to any security holder is paid to any other security holder *receiving that type of consideration*."[118] As a result, it is possible under US law to construct the infamous "two-tier" tender offers in which one block of shareholders is offered cash and the second block is offered some consideration that is less desirable than cash. As will be discussed in more detail in the next chapter, this technique pressures shareholders into accepting the first tier of the offer, in which they receive a specified amount of cash, so as to escape being herded into the second tier of the offer, in which high-yield securities of questionable value ("junk bonds") might well be the consideration.[119] Within each tier of the offer, the shareholders receiving their respective consideration are considered to have received equal treatment. Further, when it comes in the context of merging the target into the purchaser to squeezing out any residual shareholders who hang on beyond the second tier, an argument can be made that they have a right to consideration equal to that in the second tier, but not in the first.

How do the rules on equal treatment of shareholders in the US compare to those in Europe? Is the absence of a mandatory bid rule in the US compensated for by (i) the increased likelihood that an offer will be made or (ii) the protection that the board could offer the shareholders against unfair offers? We will return to focus on this question in the next chapter.

5. Treatment of remaining shareholders   US law does not create any right under the Exchange Act for a majority shareholder to squeeze a minority shareholder out of the company. Nor does it provide the minority with a right to be bought out, as the Companies Act 2006 does. The elimination of a dissenting minority would be accomplished under US law through a cash-out merger of the type discussed in *Weinberger* v. *UOP*. You will remember that the protections offered minority shareholders in that context are appraisal rights and the fiduciary duties of dominant shareholders. This is why states like Delaware have placed the hook of their anti-takeover legislation exactly on the cash-out merger following a tender offer.[120]

Like Delaware, the SEC understands that offers to a captive minority or mergers forced through by a dominant majority place the minority in a weak position, especially because they can result in the target company losing its listing or registration with the SEC, and thus the SEC rules require that special disclosure be made in these "going private" transactions.[121]

---

[118] 17 CFR § 240.14d-10(c)(2) (emphasis added).
[119] Loss, Seligman and Parades (2004: 643).   [120] § 203 DGCL.   [121] 17 CFR § 240.13e-3.

Questions for discussion

1. What is a takeover according to the laws of the jurisdictions we study?
2. What is the difference between a takeover and other forms of acquiring a business?
3. Are takeovers salutary or damaging to business?
4. What positive/negative effects do takeovers have?
5. Should takeovers be regulated?
6. What should takeover regulation seek to achieve? Whose interests require protection and why?
7. What is the purpose of disclosing significant shareholdings (pre-takeover disclosure)?
8. Why do all of the jurisdictions we study require the publication of a bid document?
9. What information does a bid document provide?

Cases

Hanson Trust plc v. SCM Corp.
US Court of Appeals, Second Circuit
774 F 2d 47 (1985)
[Text edited; footnotes omitted]

MANSFIELD, Circuit Judge

Hanson Trust PLC, HSCM Industries, Inc., and Hanson Holdings Netherlands BV (hereinafter sometimes referred to collectively as "Hanson") appeal from an order of the Southern District of New York ... granting SCM Corporation's motion for a preliminary injunction restraining them ... from acquiring any shares of SCM and from exercising any voting rights with respect to 3.1 million SCM shares acquired by them on September 11, 1985. The injunction was granted on the ground that Hanson's September 11 acquisition of the SCM stock through five private and one open market purchases amounted to a "tender offer" for more than 5% of SCM's outstanding shares, which violated §§ 14(d)(1) and (6) of the Williams Act ... and rules promulgated by the Securities and Exchange Commission (SEC) thereunder ... We reverse.

The setting is the familiar one of a fast-moving bidding contest for control of a large public corporation: first, a cash tender offer of $60 per share by Hanson, an outsider, addressed to SCM stockholders; next, a counter-proposal by an "insider" group consisting of certain SCM managers and their "White Knight," Merrill Lynch Capital Markets (Merrill), for a "leveraged buyout" at a higher price ($70 per share); then an increase by Hanson of its cash offer to $72 per share, followed by a revised SCM-Merrill leveraged buyout offer of $74 per share with a "crown jewel" irrevocable lock-up option to Merrill designed to discourage Hanson from seeking control by providing that if any other party (in this case Hanson) should acquire more than one-third of SCM's outstanding shares (66 2/3% being needed under NY Bus. L. § 903(a)(2) to effectuate a merger) Merrill would have the right to buy SCM's two most profitable businesses (consumer foods and pigments) at prices character-ized by some as "bargain basement." The final act in this scenario was the decision of Hanson, having been deterred by the SCM-Merrill option ... to terminate its cash tender offer and then to make private purchases, amounting to 25% of SCM's outstanding shares, leading SCM to seek and obtain the preliminary injunction from which this appeal is taken ...

[Text omitted]

Hanson ... concluded that even if it increased its cash tender offer to $74 per share it would end up with control of a substantially depleted and damaged com-pany. Accordingly, it announced on the Dow Jones Broad Tape at 12:38 P.M. on September 11 that it was terminating its cash tender offer ...

At some time in the late forenoon or early afternoon of September 11 Hanson decided to make cash purchases of a substantial percentage of SCM stock in the open market or through privately negotiated transactions ... If Hanson could ac-quire slightly less than one-third of SCM's outstanding shares it would be able to block the $74 per share SCM-Merrill offer of a leveraged buyout ...

Within a period of two hours on the afternoon of September 11 Hanson made five privately negotiated cash purchases of SCM stock and one open-market pur-chase, acquiring 3.1 million shares or 25% of SCM's outstanding stock. The price of SCM stock on the NYSE on September 11 ranged from a high of $73.50 per share to a low of $72.50 per share. Hanson's initial private purchase, 387,700 shares from Mutual Shares, was not solicited by Hanson but by a Mutual Shares official, Michael Price, who, in a conversation with Robert Pirie of Rothschild, Inc., Hanson's finan-cial advisor, on the morning of September 11 (before Hanson had decided to make any private cash purchases), had stated that he was interested in selling Mutual's Shares' SCM stock to Hanson ...

Pirie then telephoned Ivan Boesky, an arbitrageur who had a few weeks earlier disclosed in a Schedule 13D statement filed with the SEC that he owned approxi-mately 12.7% of SCM's outstanding shares. Pirie negotiated a Hanson purchase of these shares at $73.50 per share after rejecting Boesky's initial demand of $74 per share. At the same time Rothschild purchased for Hanson's account 600,000 SCM shares in the open market at $73.50 per share. An attempt by Pirie next to negotiate the cash purchase of another large block of SCM stock (some 780,000 shares) from

Slifka & Company fell through because of the latter's inability to make delivery of the shares on September 12.

Following the NYSE ticker and Broad Tape reports of the first two large anonymous transactions in SCM stock, some professional investors surmised that the buyer might be Hanson. Rothschild then received telephone calls from (1) Mr. Mulhearn of Jamie & Co. offering to sell between 200,000 and 350,000 shares at $73.50 per share, (2) David Gottesman, an arbitrageur at Oppenheimer & Co. offering 89,000 shares at $73.50, and (3) Boyd Jeffries of Jeffries & Co., offering approximately 700,000 to 800,000 shares at $74.00. Pirie purchased the three blocks for Hanson at $73.50 per share. The last of Hanson's cash purchases was completed by 4:35 P.M. on September 11, 1985.

In the early evening of September 11 SCM successfully applied to Judge Kram in the present lawsuit for a restraining order barring Hanson from acquiring more SCM stock for 24 hours ...

... Judge Kram ... concluded that "[w]ithout deciding what test should ultimately be applied to determine whether Hanson's conduct constitutes a 'tender offer' within the meaning of the Williams Act ... SCM has demonstrated a likelihood of success on the merits of its contention that Hanson has engaged in a tender offer which violates Section 14(d) of the Williams Act." ...

[Text omitted]

... this appeal turns on whether the district court erred as a matter of law in holding that when Hanson terminated its offer and immediately thereafter made private purchases of a substantial share of the target company's outstanding stock, the purchases became a "tender offer" within the meaning of § 14(d) of the Williams Act. Absent any express definition of "tender offer" in the Act, the answer requires a brief review of the background and purposes of § 14(d).

Congress adopted § 14(d) in 1968 "in response to the growing use of cash tender offers as a means of achieving corporate takeovers ... which ... removed a substantial number of corporate control contests from the reach of existing disclosure requirements of the federal securities laws." *Piper* v. *Chris-Craft Industries* ...

Prior to the Williams Act a tender offeror had no obligation to disclose any information to shareholders when making a bid. The Report of the Senate Committee on Banking and Currency aptly described the situation: "by using a cash tender offer the person seeking control can operate in almost complete secrecy. At present, the law does not even require that he disclose his identity, the source of his funds, who his associates are, or what he intends to do if he gains control of the corporation." ... The average shareholder, pressured by the fact that the tender offer would be available for only a short time and restricted to a limited number of shares, was forced "with severely limited information, [to] decide what course of action he should take." ... "Without knowledge of who the bidder is and what he plans to do, the shareholder cannot reach an informed decision. He is forced to take a chance.

For no matter what he does, he does it without adequate information to enable him to decide rationally what is the best possible course of action." ...

The purpose of the Williams Act was, accordingly, to protect the shareholders from that dilemma by insuring "that public shareholders who are confronted by a cash tender offer for their stock will not be required to respond without adequate information." *Piper* v. *Chris-Craft Industries* ...

[Text omitted]

... The borderline between public solicitations and privately negotiated stock purchases is not bright and it is frequently difficult to determine whether transactions falling close to the line or in a type of "no man's land" are "tender offers" or private deals. This has led some to advocate a broader interpretation of the term "tender offer" ... and to adopt the eight-factor "test" of what is a tender offer, which was recommended by the SEC and applied by the district court in *Wellman* v. *Dickinson* ... The eight factors are:

(1) active and widespread solicitation of public shareholders for the shares of an issuer;
(2) solicitation made for a substantial percentage of the issuer's stock;
(3) offer to purchase made at a premium over the prevailing market price;
(4) terms of the offer are firm rather than negotiable;
(5) offer contingent on the tender of a fixed number of shares, often subject to a fixed maximum number to be purchased;
(6) offer open only for a limited period of time;
(7) offeree subjected to pressure to sell his stock;

      ...

[(8)] public announcements of a purchasing program concerning the target company precede or accompany rapid accumulation of large amounts of the target company's securities." (475 F Supp at 823–24).

Although many of the above-listed factors are relevant ...

We prefer to be guided by the principle followed by the Supreme Court in deciding what transactions fall within the private offering exemption provided by § 4(1) of the Securities Act of 1933, and by ourselves in *Kennecott Copper* in determining whether the Williams Act applies to private transactions. That principle is simply to look to the statutory purpose. In *SEC* v. *Ralston Purina Co.* ... the Court stated, "the applicability of § 4(1) should turn on whether the particular class of persons affected need the protection of the Act. An offering to those who are shown to be able to fend for themselves is a transaction 'not involving any public offering.'" ... Similarly, since the purpose of § 14(d) is to protect the ill-informed solicitee, the question of whether a solicitation constitutes a "tender offer" within the meaning of § 14(d) turns on whether, viewing the transaction in the light of the totality of circumstances, there appears to be a likelihood that unless the pre-acquisition filing strictures of that statute are followed there will be a substantial risk that solicitees will lack information needed to make a carefully considered appraisal of the proposal put before them.

Applying this standard, we are persuaded on the undisputed facts that Hanson's September 11 negotiation of five private purchases and one open market purchase of SCM shares, totalling 25% of SCM's outstanding stock, did not under the circumstances constitute a "tender offer" within the meaning of the Williams Act. Putting aside for the moment the events preceding the purchases, there can be little doubt that the privately negotiated purchases would not, standing alone, qualify as a tender offer, for the following reasons:

(1) In a market of 22,800 SCM shareholders the number of SCM sellers here involved, six in all, was miniscule compared with the numbers involved in public solicitations of the type against which the Act was directed.

(2) At least five of the sellers were highly sophisticated professionals, knowledgeable in the market place and well aware of the essential facts …

(3) The sellers were not "pressured" to sell their shares by any conduct that the Williams Act was designed to alleviate, but by the forces of the market place. Indeed, in the case of Mutual Shares there was no initial solicitation by Hanson; the offer to sell was initiated by Mr. Price …

(4) There was no active or widespread advance publicity or public solicitation, which is one of the earmarks of a conventional tender offer …

(5) The price received by the six sellers, $73.50 per share, unlike that appearing in most tender offers, can scarcely be dignified with the label "premium." The stock market price on September 11 ranged from $72.50 to $73.50 per share …

(6) Unlike most tender offers, the purchases were not made contingent upon Hanson's acquiring a fixed minimum number or percentage of SCM's outstanding shares. Once an agreement with each individual seller was reached, Hanson was obligated to buy …

(7) Unlike most tender offers, there was no general time limit within which Hanson would make purchases of SCM stock …

In short, the totality of circumstances that existed on September 11 did not evidence any likelihood that unless Hanson was required to comply with § 14(d)(1)'s pre-acquisition filing and waiting-period requirements there would be a substantial risk of ill-considered sales of SCM stock by ill-informed shareholders.

[*Text omitted*]

SCM further contends, and in this respect it is supported by the SEC as an amicus, that upon termination of a tender offer the solicitor should be subject to a waiting or cooling-off period (10 days is suggested) before it may purchase any of the target company's outstanding shares. However, neither the Act nor any SEC rule promulgated thereunder prohibits a former tender offeror from purchasing stock of a target through privately negotiated transactions immediately after a tender offer has been terminated ...

[Text omitted]

British Telecommunications plc ("BT") Offer for PlusNet plc ("PlusNet")
Panel on Takeovers and Mergers
Statement 2007/6 – February 12, 2007
Reproduced with permission of the Panel on Takeovers and Mergers
[Text edited; references omitted]

Introduction

This is a statement of criticism by the Panel Executive of N M Rothschild & Sons Limited ("Rothschild"), financial advisers to BT, for failing to prevent breaches of Rules 9.1 and 7.1 of the Takeover Code (the "Code") in connection with the purchase of shares in PlusNet on behalf of BT on 21 November 2006.

Background

On 16 November 2006 BT announced a firm intention to make a recommended cash offer for PlusNet under Rule 2.5 of the Code at 210p per share. BT was advised by Rothschild.

BT's offer document was posted to PlusNet shareholders on 17 November.

On 20 November BT requested JPMorgan Cazenove Limited ("JPM Cazenove"), which had not previously been involved in this transaction, to purchase shares in PlusNet on behalf of BT. A telephone call took place between BT, Rothschild and JPM Cazenove to discuss and agree the proposed share buying. Following that call a total of 5,093,104 PlusNet shares were acquired during the course of that day, all at a price of 210p per share. The shares acquired represented approximately 17.1% of the existing issued share capital of PlusNet.

Following those purchases, on the evening of 20 November BT, Rothschild and JPM Cazenove participated in a further telephone call to discuss the possibility of making additional purchases of PlusNet shares the following day. On that call, BT gave instructions to JPM Cazenove to purchase up to a further 28% of PlusNet shares (which, taken together with shares it already held and shares in respect of which it had secured irrevocable commitments from the PlusNet directors to accept its offer, would represent over 50% of the existing issued share capital of PlusNet). Consequently, during the morning of 21 November a further 4,531,413 PlusNet shares were acquired, all at a price of 210p per share. The additional shares acquired represented approximately 15.2% of the existing issued share capital of PlusNet. Following these further acquisitions BT had acquired, in aggregate, 9,624,517 PlusNet shares representing approximately 32.4% of the issued share capital of PlusNet and carrying 32.4% of the votes in PlusNet.

As described in more detail below, the acquisition of an interest in shares carrying 30% or more of the voting rights of a company triggers a requirement under Rule 9.1 of the Code to make an offer for the rest of the equity share capital of the company or alternatively to alter the terms and conditions of any existing offer to conform with the requirements of Rule 9. However, at no stage prior to 20 November had Rothschild explained to BT these provisions of the Code. Furthermore, on 20 November neither Rothschild nor JPM Cazenove raised concerns about the Rule 9 consequences of the share buying exercise that was discussed and agreed with BT.

As a result BT was not aware of the requirements of Rule 9 at the time it gave instructions in relation to the share purchases. It was not the intention of BT to trigger a Rule 9 obligation; indeed, BT was keen to retain the benefit of the regulatory conditions to its offer and these conditions would have had to have been waived were the offer to conform with Rule 9.

It was only on the afternoon of 21 November that the potential Rule 9 consequences of the share purchasing instruction that had been given the previous afternoon were raised, the issue having been identified by BT's legal advisers who had not been on the previous afternoon's call. Rothschild then contacted JPM Cazenove to see how much of the order had been filled and JPM Cazenove confirmed that, as described above, share purchases had been made giving BT an aggregate interest in shares carrying more than 30% of the votes in PlusNet. The requirements of Rule 9 had therefore been triggered. Rothschild subsequently contacted the [Takeover Panel] Executive to explain what had happened and to request a dispensation from Rule 9.1 on the grounds that an inadvertent mistake had been made.

Following representations from Rothschild and discussions with the financial adviser to PlusNet, the Executive agreed not to require BT to conform its offer with Rule 9.1 on the condition that BT disposed of such number of PlusNet shares as would result in BT's holding of PlusNet shares falling below the 30% threshold in Rule 9.1 (as permitted under Note 4 of the Notes on Dispensations from Rule 9). This disposal took place early on the morning of 22 November. The acquisition of PlusNet shares on 21 November and the subsequent sale on 22 November were announced to the market by BT early on the morning of 22 November.

[Text omitted]

Rules 9.3 and 9.5 provide, in general terms, that any mandatory offer made under Rule 9.1 must be in cash at not less than the highest price paid by the offeror (or any person acting in concert with it) during the 12 months prior to the announcement of that offer and the offer must be conditional only upon the offeror having received acceptances in respect of shares which, together with shares already acquired, will result in the offeror (and persons acting in concert with it) holding shares carrying more than 50% of the voting rights of the offeree company.

Rule 7.1 provides that immediately following any acquisition of shares which triggers the mandatory offer obligation under Rule 9.1 an appropriate announcement must be made by the offeror.

[Text omitted]

Application of Rule 9 in this case

The acquisition of PlusNet shares on 21 November took BT's aggregate interest in shares carrying voting rights of PlusNet through the 30% threshold. By virtue of Note 9 on Rule 9.1 the Panel should have been consulted in advance of these purchases.

Further, by virtue of Rule 9.1 and Rule 7.1 BT should, on making the purchases, immediately have conformed its offer with Rule 9.1 and immediately have made an announcement of that fact.

The Executive accepted that the failure to identify the consequences of the acquisitions under Rule 9.1 was an inadvertent mistake and, in accordance with Note 4 of the Notes on the Dispensations from Rule 9, the Executive permitted BT to dispose of sufficient shares so that the percentage of PlusNet shares held by BT was reduced to below 30%.

[Text omitted]

Rothschild

Primary responsibility for ensuring that BT was aware of, and would comply with, the provisions of the Code rested with Rothschild as financial adviser to BT. The Executive is of the opinion that Rothschild failed adequately to fulfil its responsibilities under the Code and thereby failed to prevent the breaches of the Code described in this statement.

In considering the appropriate sanction in respect of Rothschild the Executive has taken into account all relevant factors and in particular (i) the seriousness of the error, which led to a breach of a fundamental rule; and (ii) the compliance history of Rothschild, in which regard the Executive notes that on two previous occasions in recent years offerors for whom Rothschild was acting as financial adviser breached an important provision of the Code in the context of share purchasing operations.

Rothschild is hereby criticised for its conduct in relation to this case. Rothschild has accepted this criticism.

[Text omitted]

Württembergische Metallwarenfabrik AG
High Federal Court, Second Civil Division
September 18, 2006, Doc. No. II ZR 137/05; BGHZ 169, 98
[Partial, unofficial translation of official opinion text]

Official head note

a) The attribution rule of § 30(2) WpÜG encompasses only those agreements governing the exercise of voting rights deriving from shares in the target company, i.e. only the exercise of voting rights at its general meeting.

b) Unlike the election of *Aufsichtsrat* members by the general meeting, the election of the *Aufsichtsrat* Chair from among such members (§ 107(1)AktG; § 27 MitbestG) is not a case for attribution pursuant to § 30(2) WpÜG. A broad application of this provision to internal voting within the *Aufsichtsrat* beyond the clear statutory meaning is contrary to the legally defined independence of the *Aufsichtsrat* members, who are obligated to pursue only the best interests of the company, and are not obligated to take instructions from anyone in the fulfilling the personal duties of their offices (§ 111(5)AktG).

c) A target shareholder who participates in the coordinated action of a bidder pursuant to § 30(2) WpÜG, in such a way that he also would have a duty to report and make a bid (§ 35 WpÜG) has no standing to make an (independent) claim to interest pursuant to § 38 WpÜG.

Judgment

Facts

The Plaintiff, the Defendant and the Co-Parties who have joined the proceedings (1st W. and W. AG – W & W; 2nd D. Bank AG) are – in part through various subsidiaries – large shareholders of W[ürttembergischer] [Metallwarenfabrik] AG (hereinafter "WMF"), which is subject to the Co-Determination Act. The Plaintiff [Dr. S Group] holds 33.36%, the Defendant and W. & W. each hold 17%, and D. Bank holds 17.56% of the shares carrying voting rights; the remainder of the voting shares are widely held. The Defendant and its two Co-Parties (hereinafter the "Financial Investors") purchased their shares in 1993 from the Dr. S Corporate Group – which also controls the Plaintiff – and then concluded a contract with the Plaintiff in December 1993 not only granting rights of first refusal to the other large shareholders with respect to their blocks of WM shares, but also coordinated voting for the members of the *Aufsichtsrat*. Pursuant to the agreement, the Plaintiff was to appoint two members and each of the Financial Investors one member of the 12 person *Aufsichtsrat* of WMF; these directors were to elect the Chair and Vice Chair of the *Aufsichtsrat*, the former nominated by the Financial Investors and the latter nominated by the Plaintiff.

During the second half of 2002, both the Co-Parties and the Plaintiff attempted – in vain – discretely to sell their holdings in WMF. For this reason and in regard to the election of *Aufsichtsrat* members scheduled for June 26, 2003, differences arose between the large shareholders at the beginning of 2003. In the context of informal, preliminary discussions, the other Financial Investors reacted skeptically for "corporate governance reasons" to a proposal of the sitting *Aufsichtsrat* Chair, K. (of D. Bank) to appoint the then sitting *Vorstand* Chair of WMF, A., as the new *Aufsichtsrat* Chair. In a meeting of the four, large shareholders on February 10, 2003, the Financial Investors explained to Dr. S. that because of the unfavorable market conditions they did not want to part with their holdings of WMF stock at least at that point in time; by contrast, the Dr. S. Group wanted to continue to seek a buyer for its holding, but not at a price lower than the 1993 acquisition price. At the same time agreement was reached to propose K. – again as Chair – Dr. H. (of W & W), Dr. Ha. (of the Defendant), A. and two other persons to be designated from the Dr. S Group for election to the *Aufsichtsrat*.

By written agreement in March 2003, the large shareholders of WMF arranged to rescind the contract of December 1993 as from March 31, 2003 and did not replace it. At the same time they agreed to vote for [persons representing each of them] ... as shareholder representatives in the *Aufsichtsrat* of WMF at the general meeting of June 26, 2003. In spite of this agreement, significant differences of opinion arose regarding who should serve as the future Chair of the *Aufsichtsrat*. Because Dr. S. sought to block the reelection of K. as Chair and instead advocated S.'s confidant M., the [Financial] Investor Group – who did not want to see an increase in the power of the S. Group – agreed on A. Shortly before the general meeting, the Financial Investors informed the S. Group that they found it important for the shareholders' side to vote "with a single voice" for A. and for this reason – even when the agreement of the employees' side had already been secured – would not accept that the Plaintiff withhold its vote; if such abstention were to occur, they would see to it that the position of the second Vice Chair would not be filled by M., as previously agreed, and would not be filled at all. The S. Group agreed grudgingly to comply. In the general meeting of June 26, 2003, the *Aufsichtsrat* members of the shareholders were elected according to the agreement of March 2003. Thereafter the *Aufsichtsrat* in its first meeting elected – with the votes of Mrs. S. and M. – A. as Chair of the *Aufsichtsrat* and M. as second Vice Chair.

Plaintiff ... alleging that, in particular regarding the agreed-upon election of A. as *Aufsichtsrat* Chair, the Defendant acted in concert with both Financial Investors to take over control of WMF, and did so without publishing notice or launching a mandatory bid. The regional court ... dismissed the complaint; the court of appeals ... admitted the complaint. In this appeal – which the court of appeals allowed – the Defendant and Co-Party 1 again seek to have the complaint dismissed.

Reasons

The appeal has merit, which leads to the reversal of the challenged decision of the court of appeals and reinstatement of the regional court's dismissal of the complaint ...

I. The court of appeals found that the Defendant ... together with the shares of the other Financial Investors which should rightly be attributed to it, held altogether more than 51% of the voting shares and gained control over WMF, without complying with the duties under § 35 WpÜG to publish disclosure and make a mandatory bid. Such attribution recommends itself above all because the election of A as *Aufsichtsrat* Chair by the three Financial Investors in an agreed-upon manner was coordinated behavior to influence the target company within the meaning of § 30(2) WpÜG that went beyond a single occurrence.

II. This judgment does not stand up to scrutiny on appeal.

[*Text omitted*]

According to the facts determined by the lower courts, representatives of the Financial Investors told the Plaintiff on the evening before the general meeting that its candidate M. would be elected as second Vice Chair only if the Plaintiff's representatives in the *Aufsichtsrat* voted to elect A. as Chair, i.e. refrain from withholding their votes. All parties concerned voted as agreed. That the Plaintiff did not support the election of the *Aufsichtsrat* Chair in complete freedom, but rather acted under pressure from the Financial Investors does not contradict a mutual attribution of voting rights that consequentially gives all large shareholders the duty to launch a bid. For concerted action within the meaning of § 30(2) WpÜG the motives for voting are essentially irrelevant. It is sufficient that comportment is mutually coordinated on the basis of intentional contact – which also includes the possibility that voting takes place under duress ...

Such was the case here as the Plaintiff's candidate M. was elected in exchange for election of the Financial Investors' candidate A. As to the Plaintiff's argument that mutual attribution of voting rights is not possible when cooperation is obtained through threats ... on the facts of this case the merit of such argument is irrelevant. This is because the position of the three Financial Investors on the eve of the general meeting contained no illegal threat with a (perceived) evil within the meaning of § 123 BGB; rather, their behavior was merely a part of the – in practice quite common – struggle for power between various interest groups of large shareholders trying to push through the respective candidates favored by each side. These struggles are often fought with "hardball tactics" and usually – as in this case – end in a compromise on the lowest common denominator. This was especially clear in the present case as neither side was able to push through their favorite candidate for *Aufsichtsrat* Chair and they finally had to bring in A. as the agreed compromise candidate. The fact that the Financial Investors did not want to accept a withholding of votes in connection with A's election – because in their opinion the shareholders should vote for members of the *Aufsichtsrat* in a codetermined corporation "with one voice" – and strengthened this hardly inappropriate demand by linking it to a withholding of their votes for the other side's candidate, M., for Vice Chair of the *Aufsichtsrat*, obviously does not contain the inequity of an impermissible threat within the meaning of § 123 BGB.

In this type of power struggle between the various, large shareholders, in which an "amicable" election is arranged, the Plaintiff has no right ... to claim interest from its "co-conspirators" because the law's sanction for a violation of the duty to disclose and launch a mandatory bid should not benefit the person who equally breaches that duty. The person who has the duty to launch a bid cannot be the person the duty is designed to protect.

b) Aside from the above and contrary to the opinion of the court of appeals, an arranged election of an *Aufsichtsrat* Chair is in any case not the a situation for attribution of votes under § 30(2) WpÜG. The unambiguous wording of the provision states it includes only those agreements governing the exercise of voting rights deriving from the target company's shares, that is, only the exercise of votes in the general meeting ... If one were to join the court of appeals by including meetings of the *Aufsichtsrat* and votes taken purely within such meetings within the ambit of this provision, the plain text of § 30(1) WpÜG would be deprived of its meaning; such votes would also no longer come within the purpose of the norm, which aims only at attributing directly exercised voting rights of shares following agreements between shareholders and does not regard the indirect influence of shareholders on members of the *Aufsichtsrat*, which is an independent governance body ...

A broad application of § 30(2) WpÜG to votes taken within the *Aufsichtsrat* – as here the election of the Chair and second Vice Chair of the *Aufsichtsrat* – essentially contradicts the independent legal standing of the *Aufsichtsrat*. The members of the *Aufsichtsrat* have a duty to pursue solely the best interests of the company and may not follow the instructions of others in carrying out their personal duties of office ... This applies equally to elected and appointed members, whether representing shareholders or employees. Contrary to what the Plaintiff deems appropriate, it is therefore erroneous to see those persons as "representatives" of the shareholders in whose employment they earlier served or do now serve, or on whose proposal they were elected. The corporate voting right deriving from a shareholding does not somehow continue to live in the *Aufsichtsrat* in the body of that member who is or was employed by one shareholder or other, or who was proposed for election by this or that shareholder (see BGHZ vol. 36, pp. 296, 306 regarding directly appointed members of the *Aufsichtsrat*).

c) Even on the basis of its assumed, erroneous position that the attribution rules of § 30(2) WpÜG generally apply to the election of the *Aufsichtsrat* Chair, the court of appeals further misunderstood the exception for "individual cases" of concerted behavior under § 30(2) WpÜG.

aa) This is obvious if one joins the majority opinion among appellate courts and legal scholars in defining the presence of an "individual case" – at least in the first analysis – formally, that is, with respect to the frequency of the voting behavior ... It is beyond doubt that after the expiration of the original agreement on March 31, 2003, the Financial Investors agreed among themselves in only one ("selected") case, i.e. for voting on the election of the *Aufsichtsrat* Chair.

A formal understanding of "individual cases" is supported not only by the wording of the statute, but also by the concern of legal certainty; if one were to join the court of appeals in finding even agreement on a single vote sufficient, provided the vote created a material, lasting impact in the future, the type of matter with adequate significance to trigger such treatment would be uncertain.

bb) Even if one were to follow this substance oriented legal approach advocated by the court of appeals ... and deny application of the exception for individual cases even where there was only a single occurrence of agreement, provided such agreement was also connected with a longer range agreed-upon goal, the simple understanding to elect A as *Aufsichtsrat* Chair must constitute an individual case.

As the court of appeals also admits, such rule would be restricted by the condition that it apply only when the agreed-upon goal be more specific than generally held goals, and pursue more detailed, concretely formulated business plans. Otherwise the situation – which the court of appeals correctly seeks to avoid – would arise in which the quite common practice of coordinated action to elect the *Aufsichtsrat* and the subsequent "agreed" election of the Chair of this body would trigger a mutual attribution of voting rights.

The court of appeals found that a concrete business concept, more specific than generally held goals, was not entailed in the investors group coordinated voting. Obviously the latter test would not be met by the general goal to represent the interests of the Financial Investors and of the company, like the desire in this case to present a unified front of the shareholders in the *Aufsichtsrat* or the *Aufsichtsrat's* closely following its new Chair. A more detailed, concrete agreement on a goal would be conceivable if the election of a certain person as *Aufsichtsrat* Chair were inexorably linked to a specific management concept.

No such case is supported either by the determinations of the court of appeals or by evidence presented in the pleadings of the parties. Rather, after termination of the original 1993 agreement between the four large shareholders, to the extent there was a uniform interest among the Financial Investors, it was not directed toward shaping the business, but rather in just the opposite direction. They were interested in the – rather challenging – task of unloading their holdings and when they were not able to do so, in this regard they wanted to prevent the influence of the Dr. S. Group from increasing. This obviously does not represent a common concept for a lasting and wide-ranging influence ... as the intended consequence of A.'s election as *Aufsichtsrat* Chair.

III. There are no other grounds on which the decision of the court of appeals can rest ... On the basis of that court's record there are no other arrangements constituting "acting in concert" between the Financial Investors that could in themselves support an attribution under § 30(2) WpÜG. In particular, the so called standstill agreement between the Financial Investors does not support such attribution ...

According to the record, this agreement had the purpose in the case at hand of ensuring uniform comportment among the three Financial Investors in order to sell their holdings with as little loss as possible, not to influence the business policy of the target company in any (lasting) way.

Contrary to the Plaintiff's position, viewing the standstill agreement and the arranged election of the *Aufsichtsrat* Chair as a unified course of action does not lead to a different conclusion.

Upon appeal of the Defendant and Co-Party 1, the April 29, 2005 judgment of the seventh division of the Munich Court of Appeals is hereby reversed.

Guinness plc The Distillers Company plc
Panel on Takeovers and Mergers
Statement 1989/13 – Decision of September 1987
[*Text edited; references omitted*]
Reproduced with permission of the Panel on Takeovers and Mergers

The substantive issue

1. The issue before the Panel, which came before it on a reference by the Executive, is of considerable importance. It arises out of the successful offer in 1986 by Guinness, in competition with Argyll, for all the shares in Distillers. The issue is whether at a critical stage of the bid, Pipetec AG, a subsidiary of Bank Leu, in purchasing approximately 10.6mn Distillers shares which were subsequently assented to the Guinness offer, was acting in concert with Guinness. The purchase ... was made ... at which time Guinness, and persons declared to be acting in concert with Guinness, already held 14.99% of Distillers shares acquired during the offer and within twelve months prior to its commencement. Accordingly, if the purchase by Pipetec was made in concert, such purchase should not have been made and serious consequences would have arisen under the Code.

Relevant aspects of the Code

2. One of the cardinal requirements of the Code stated in General Principle 1 is as follows:

> All shareholders of the same class of an offeree company must be treated similarly by an offeror [*Editors' note*: see the current version for slight differences].

It is in order to give effect to this principle that Rule 11.1 provides:

> Except with the consent of the Panel in cases falling under (a), where:- (a) the shares of any class under offer in the offeree company purchased for cash by the offeror and any person acting in concert with it during the offer period and within 12 months prior to its commencement carry 15% [*Editors' note*: in current version, threshold is 10%] or more of the voting rights currently exercisable at a class meeting of that class; or (b) in the view of the Panel there are circumstances which render such a course necessary in order to give effect to General Principle 1, then the offer for that class shall be in cash or accompanied by a cash alternative at not less than the highest price paid by the offeror or any person acting in concert with it for shares of that class during the offer period and within 12 months prior to its commencement.

[*Text omitted*]

On 20 February 1986 Guinness announced a new offer for Distillers, also recommended by the board of Distillers, which is the offer from which the present issue arises. Its essential terms were that, for every three Distillers Ordinary Shares Guinness offered five new Guinness Ordinary Stock Units and 516p in cash. There was a right for shareholders to elect to take Convertible Preference Shares in Guinness or further Ordinary Stock Units in place of the cash element. A full cash underwritten alternative at 630.3p per Distillers share was available. The offer document was posted on 3 March 1986.

8. On 21 March 1986 Argyll announced a final increased offer. The terms were that, for every 100 Distillers shares, 125 new Argyll Ordinary Shares, 100 new B Convertible Preferences shares and £162.75 in cash would be offered. A full underwritten cash alternative of 660p per Distillers share was included.

9. On 3 April 1986 Guinness announced that its offer was final and would not be increased. On 17 April 1986, the day of the purchase which falls to be considered by the Panel, an announcement on behalf of Guinness showed that the level of purchases made by Guinness and persons acting in concert with it totalled just under 15% of Distillers shares: thus Guinness and persons acting in concert with it could purchase no more Distillers shares.

10. On 17 April 1986, Samuel Montagu & Co. Ltd, as advisers to Argyll, informed the Executive that they understood that Cazenove & Co, as brokers to Guinness, had purchased some 10 million Distillers shares at £7 a share in the stock market that morning. They asked the Executive to investigate this purchase. The Executive spoke to Mr Mayhew of Cazenove. Mr Mayhew said that the order had been received from Bank Leu in Switzerland, but he thought that they were acting as agents rather than principals in the deal. The Executive accordingly telephoned Bank Leu in Zurich, and were informed that Pipetec, an investment company and a client of Bank Leu, had agreed to buy the shares. The Executive sought to speak to a representative of Pipetec, and was informed in the morning of the following day (ie 18 April 1986) by telephone by Dr Frey, speaking on behalf of Pipetec, that Pipetec had no connection with Guinness, Distillers or Argyll. Dr Frey expressed the view that the shares were a good investment as a potential way into Guinness. As the Guinness shares on 17 April stood at about 330p, and the terms of the Guinness offer translated a Distillers price of 700p to a Guinness price of approximately 317p, such an investment decision could not be regarded by the Executive as impossible. The Executive, however, sought from Guinness, through its merchant bankers Morgan Grenfell, formal assurances that there were no arrangements which might give rise to any form of acting in concert between Guinness and Pipetec. Such an assurance was given to the Executive in a letter of 17 April 1986, signed by Mr Roux on behalf of Guinness in the following terms:

> Dear Sir
> Distillers
> You have asked us to write to you with respect to the reported purchase today of approximately 10 million shares in Distillers through Cazenove & Co. We have

spoken to Cazenoves and can confirm that the purchaser is not a subsidiary or associated company of Guinness, that such shares were not bought for our account and that we have made no financial arrangements with the purchaser with respect to such shares (including any arrangement linked to the sale of Distillers' listed investments).

Yours faithfully,
Olivier Roux
For and on behalf of Guinness PLC

[Text omitted]

13. It is public knowledge that on 1 December 1986, Inspectors were appointed under Sections 432 and 442 of the Companies Act 1985 to report on Guinness. The Panel issued a statement on 30 January 1987, indicating that it considered it appropriate to await the outcome of the enquiries of the Inspectors before publishing any findings or judgments of its own ...

[Text omitted]

Analysis of evidence

23. We turn to the facts relied upon by the Executive in support of the submission that there was action in concert. We have already commented that the very essence of acting in concert makes it necessary in most cases to draw inferences from circumstantial evidence. In the present case, however, there was a considerable body of evidence put before the Executive, all of which was considered, and a number of elements are dealt with in detail below. We will outline first the general circumstances of the transaction.

24. The block of shares in Distillers was offered for sale by Mercury Warburg Investment Management Limited through the stock market to the highest bidder. The block amounted to some 3% of Distillers shares in issue. It was important to Guinness and its advisers that a purchaser of the shares should be found who would assent them to the Guinness bid. There was potential competition from Argyll to secure the shares. Argyll could have paid up to 660p per share. There was extremely little scope left for the purchase by institutional investors of a very large block of shares involving an outlay of some £76 million. It is normally the function of the broker to seek out a purchaser of shares, and Mr Mayhew of Cazenoves considered it would be impossible for his firm to find a purchaser. Mr Seelig, of Morgan Grenfell, also thought that it would be very difficult to find a purchaser for a block of shares of this size on investment grounds. The availability of the shares was reported to Guinness, and Mr Mayhew was very shortly thereafter informed that Guinness had found a purchaser. He was informed later that day, by Mr Roux of Guinness, that it was Mr Ward of Guinness who had actually found the purchaser. Guinness was therefore able to find a purchaser of this very large block of shares at short notice in a way which experienced stockbrokers themselves felt quite unable to do. This

suggests the unlikelihood that such an investor should buy a large block of shares on purely investment grounds and without some form of comfort or reassurance from Guinness, as the offeror which had a vital interest in the shares being purchased by a favourable party.

25. The approach to Bank Leu, the Panel considered, reflected the close relationships that existed between certain personalities in the two companies. Dr Furer, then Chairman of Bank Leu, was apparently well known to both Mr Saunders, then Chief Executive of Guinness, and Mr Ward, then a director of Guinness, from previous business dealings. Dr Furer had relatively recently been brought onto the board of Guinness. In the course of its submission Guinness indicated that Bank Leu had disclosed letters suggesting that a subsidiary of Bank Leu, other than Pipetec, had already invested in shares in Guinness, on a basis which would suggest it was acting in close association with Guinness. During the hearing, however, Guinness indicated it did not accept that the documents evidencing these transactions were genuine. The Panel has made no investigation of these transactions and, accordingly places no reliance upon them as evidence of a close relationship between Bank Leu and Guinness. It is, however, clear that by 7 January 1987 Bank Leu held 41,080,599 shares in Guinness. The Panel considered this would be an investment far beyond the size which would normally be held by a commercial bank for its own account as an investment. This, coupled with the close relationship between the individuals to whom we have referred, tends to suggest that Guinness turned to Bank Leu because, in the absence of other investors, it felt that the nature of the relationship was such that it could obtain help from Bank Leu at the critical time in April 1986.

26. The Panel further considered that the willingness of Guinness to provide some £76 million to Cazenove to cover the purchase on 17 April 1986 was consistent with the existence of a special approach on the part of Guinness to this purchase …

27. We have not, as Guinness observed, heard evidence from Mr Ward. He may or may not give evidence to the Inspectors, but there is no reason for assuming that he would ever be willing to give evidence to the Panel. He declined to do so on this occasion though he was asked. The Panel has, however, been provided with a photocopy of a letter from Pipetec to Mr Ward, as a Director of Guinness, and countersigned by Mr Ward. This letter, of which the present management of Guinness have known since January 1987, only became known to the Executive on 7 August 1987. By a Statutory Instrument made in May 1987 it was ordered, in summary, that the DTI should be able to disclose to the Panel, for the purposes of the Panel's functions, information obtained by Inspectors, which disclosure would otherwise be prohibited. Pursuant to this power, the DTI have made available to the Panel, subject to certain undertakings, a copy of the Pipetec letter. The DTI have also informed the Panel in a letter dated 7 August 1987 that no evidence had been given to the Inspectors which contradicts the Pipetec letter.

28. The terms of the Pipetec letter are of such importance that we set out a photocopy of the letter on the following page ...

Dear Mr. Ward,

We are pleased to confirm our yesterday's telephone conversation with Mr. W. Frey as follows: We, Pipetec AG, Luzern/Switzerland, have upon respective instructions received from yourself bought Distillers Shares on the London Stock Exchange in an aggregate value of 75,612,149.38 pound sterling. Guinness Plc, London, on the other hand undertakes to

a) To pay to us an up front arrangement fee of 47,250. – pound sterling
b) Repurchase from us the shares bought as per above (or the respective securities issued by Guinness Plc upon conversion, as the case may be) within 60 days at a price determined by adding (I) the original purchase price, (II) commissions, fees and other costs charged in London in connections with such purchase, (III) the taxes levied in Switzerland for securities transactions of 0,33% flat (i.e. 0,165% each for purchase and sale of the shares), (IV) our commission of 0,1% flat calculated on the purchase price and (V) our refinancing cost for the period from the purchase of the shares to their sale on the basis of our actual funding cost plus a margin of 1/8% p.a.

We ask you to kindly confirm your agreement with the above by returning to us the enclosed duplicate of this letter duly signed on behalf of Guinness Plc.

Yours faithfully,
PIPETEC AG [Signed]
Dr. F. Burger

29. Guinness, no doubt after seeing this letter, made a statement to shareholders on 16 January 1987. Insofar as relevant, it reads as follows:

"In particular, it has been established that substantial purchases of both Guinness and Distillers shares were made by wholly owned subsidiaries of Bank Leu AG on the strength of Guinness' agreement, signed on its behalf by Mr Ward or Mr Roux, to repurchase the shares at cost plus carrying charges – an agreement which, at least as regards its own shares, Guinness could not lawfully have fulfilled."

[Text omitted]

Bank Leu made a separate written statement to the Panel which is set out on the following page ...

The question of Bank Leu buying Distillers shares was first raised on the morning of 17th April 1986 when Tom Ward, a Guinness director, telephoned Dr. Werner Frey (a senior vice president of the Bank and deputy head of its trading division) at the Bank's offices in Zurich. Mr. Ward explained that approximately £75m worth of Distillers shares was being offered for sale and asked whether the Bank would be in a position to make an immediate purchase of these shares for cash settlement that same day. After Dr. Frey had first consulted with members of the Bank's board of management and reverted to Mr. Ward, he spoke (at the suggestion of Mr. Ward) to David Mayhew of Cazenove, Guinness' brokers, and confirmed the purchase of a total of 10,598,826 shares for the account of Pipetec AG, an investment company which was a sub-subsidiary of the Bank. The price was £7.0544 per share (exclusive of commission and stamp duty). The Bank's efforts to secure the necessary funds at short notice were successful and Cazenove duly received payment of the inclusive purchase price of £75,612,149.38 during the afternoon of 17th April. (The Bank has no knowledge whatever of any funds being advanced, temporarily or otherwise, by Guinness in connection with the transaction).

Following the purchase, on 17/18th April, both Mr. Kurt Baumann (in charge of the foreign stock exchange department within the Bank's trading division and responsible to Dr. Frey for processing the transaction) and Dr. Frey himself received telephone calls from Mr. Hinton of the Take-over Panel. Mr. Hinton was primarily concerned to know whether Pipetec had any connection with either Guinness, Distillers or Argyll. There being no shareholding relationship between Pipetec and any of those companies, Mr. Baumann and Dr. Frey confirmed in separate conversations that Pipetec had no such connection.

The arrangements agreed between Mr. Ward and Dr. Frey for the purchase of the Distillers shares were subsequently confirmed in a letter from Pipetec to Mr. Ward dated 18th April 1986, of which the Panel apparently has a copy, supplied (it is understood) by the DTI. This letter sets out the arrangements for an up-front fee and the repurchase of the shares (or the Guinness shares representing them) within a 60 day period. The fee was not in fact paid nor were the shares repurchased.

The Distillers shares were purchased by Pipetec in non-assented form and registered in the name of Cazenove Nominees. They were subsequently accepted to the Guinness offer for a mix of Guinness ordinary and convertible preference shares.

The £50m was not deposited by Guinness with the Bank until some weeks after the Distillers share purchase: no such security was in contemplation at the time of the purchase. To the best of the Bank's knowledge, no other Distillers shares were bought for the account of the Bank or any of its subsidiaries in connection with the Guinness bid, either before or after 17th April 1986.

This statement by Bank Leu is, of course, a clear admission by Bank Leu of its acting in concert with Guinness in respect of the purchase.

31. We consider that further support is derived from the subsequent payment by G & C Moore, a subsidiary of Guinness, of £50 million on deposit to Bank Leu. At that time Bank Leu had made no loans to Guinness and, accordingly, such a deposit could not be explained by such a pre-existing loan. The Panel considers that it was probably arranged in a manner to ensure maximum confidentiality within Guinness. As the Guinness submission discloses, the apparent reason that it was made by G and C Moore was to preserve confidentiality. Guinness did not have a previous history of placing funds on deposit with Bank Leu ...

[Text omitted]

33. The Panel had regard to the suggestion that it may be established, as a result of the Inspectors' report in due course, that the Guinness director responsible for the arrangement with Pipetec, perhaps Mr Ward, was acting totally alone, quite

apart from the rest of the Guinness side involved in the offer. The Panel considered that nevertheless Pipetec would have to be regarded as having acted in concert with Guinness: the arrangement was made by a person with charge of the conduct of the offer for Guinness in material ways; the purchase was very significant in enabling Guinness to succeed in the offer; such success would be to the detriment of Distillers shareholders with disregard for the equality of treatment principle.

34. Guinness also relied on the fact that the transaction as now described by Bank Leu differed from the terms in which it was put to the Panel Executive in April 1986. In particular, at that time it was suggested to the Executive that Pipetec was a client of Bank Leu, and it was denied that there was any connection between Pipetec and Guinness. As to the latter point, Bank Leu said in their statement of 27 August 1987: "There being no shareholding relationship between Pipetec and any of those companies, Mr Baumann and Dr Frey confirmed in separate conversations with the Executive that Pipetec had no such connection."

Whether this explains a misunderstanding at the time or not, there was obvious reason for Bank Leu, Pipetec and Guinness to gloss the true nature of the transaction in their dealings with the Executive on 17 and 18 April 1986. This does not, in our view, cast doubt on the true nature of the transaction.

[*Text omitted*]

Summary of conclusions

37. Whatever the nuances of dealings between Mr Ward, or any other representative of Guinness, and Bank Leu, the Panel was in no doubt that the material demonstrated that there was clearly an understanding leading to co-operation between Bank Leu/Pipetec and Guinness in the terms of acting in concert for the purposes of the Code ...

[*Editors' note*: In a later Statement delivered in 1989 after a decision of the Court of Appeal – R. v. *Panel on Take-overs and Mergers, ex parte Guinness plc* [1990] QB 146, [1989] 1 All ER 509 – the Panel ordered Guinness to pay investors the difference between the price at which they sold Distillers shares and the highest cash price during the twelve months preceding the offer.]

25

Management interference with takeovers bids

Required reading

EU: Takeover Directive, arts. 9–12
D: WpÜG, §§ 33–33c
UK: CA 2006, secs. 966–971; City Code, Rules 20.2, 21, 24.4, 25, 31.9
US: DGCL, §§ 146, 203

Do shareholders need protection from offers to buy their shares?

I. *The basis for evaluating hostile takeovers as a governance tool*

Policy discussions evaluating takeovers build on numerous principles and theories taken from both law and economics, primary among which are the theory of collective action problems and an understanding of the efficiency of markets in pricing assets. A parallel consideration is the proper allocation of duties and powers between management and shareholders. The classic argument for takeovers as a necessary tool of corporate governance runs along the following lines:[1]

1. *Ordinary governance is not effective.* A company's management may be unable or unwilling to cause a company to perform up to the level of its true potential. Shareholders, as we discussed in Chapter 16, may well be rationally apathetic when it comes to spending the money necessary to influence or replace management. The way that directors are nominated and elected and the fact that others will ride free on any efforts shareholders make to exercise their voting rights can dissuade shareholders from actively pursuing "political voice" in the general meeting as a way to change the management. Launching an

---

[1] Clark (1986: 533–535); Easterbrook and Fischel (1996: 171–174).

all-out proxy contest against incumbent management can be both expensive and inefficient in terms of potential gain because it does not entail increasing the active shareholder's stake in and return from the company.

2. *The stock price reflects the true value of the firm under the relevant management.* If, as is generally accepted, the stock price of a company reflects the value of its assets under current management, a low stock price *vis-à-vis* the market value of comparable companies in a given industry may well indicate bad management. A competing management team can therefore estimate the value they expect to add to the company in the expectation that the share price would reflect such value if they were to assume control of the company. The competing team can then offer existing shareholders part of that value by way of a bid premium over market price so that they transfer their shares to the bidder and exit the firm. In the same way, if the target's management wants to avoid being replaced by a takeover, the best way is to keep the company's share price high through quality management.

3. *Concentrated holdings bring strong incentives.* The new owner, who will hold a controlling percentage of the company's stock, will receive a majority of the gains from appointing the right managers or making the right management decisions, thus ensuring active and diligent decisionmaking. The new owner has both the incentive to run the company well and the power to do so.

4. *Gains to selling shareholders demonstrate the value of takeovers.* Because all of the extremely numerous studies done on takeovers show that they significantly increase the price of a target company's shares, paying a handsome premium to target shareholders, policymakers can conclude that takeovers add value to companies.

In addition to these mainstay arguments in favor of takeovers, two additional positions are particularly relevant for deciding whether management should have the power to interfere with tender offers made to the company's shareholders. These positions are:

1. *Auctions increase bid premiums.* A single purchaser making a bid for a company's shares will offer a premium somewhere between the current market price for the target's shares and the share price the new team hopes to achieve through superior management skills. It is fair to assume that the premium offered will be no higher than the purchaser thinks is necessary to encourage the shareholders to give up their shares. If the target's management can discourage shareholders

from accepting the first bid and meanwhile encourage other bidders to enter the fray, a bidding contest will ensue. This will force the first bidder to increase its takeover premium, thus increasing the value of the takeover for the shareholders.

2. *Greater deterrence is more valuable than occasional increases from auctions.* The counter-argument is that this *ex post* increase occurs at the expense of reducing *ex ante* benefits.[2] It is true that, if the target's management has the power to fight a hostile offer with the techniques discussed in *Unocal, Hanson Trust, Carmody* and *Revlon*, the price the shareholders finally receive for their stock will likely increase. However, this increase will reduce the benefit the bidder expects to reap from taking over the company and increasing its value. Therefore, if potential bidders know that target's management has the power to hold up bids and auction the company, this will reduce their incentive to launch a takeover. With a lower number of people who are prepared actively to seek control of mismanaged targets, the *deterrence* effect of *potential* takeovers against management abuse is also reduced. This in turn reduces management incentive to keep the share price high through good performance, and reduces benefits to investors. Succinctly put, isolated *ex post* gains to shareholders from protracted auctions reduce systematic *ex ante* gains to shareholders that derive from quick, easy and cheap takeovers.

II.   Arguments against takeovers

In 1986, at a time when US institutional investors had not yet begun to exercise influence and the US proxy rules still strongly discouraged shareholder action, one of the most astute US corporate law experts, Professor Robert Clark, could observe that a voting system, which was ineffective given that "shareholders [were] generally apathetic about voting," was "justified primarily by the relatively rare transfers of corporate power it makes possible."[3] That is, because shareholders could do little with their voting rights, the best use of voting stock was to transfer it *to someone else* who would gather a large enough interest to exercise voting rights effectively. Takeovers were seen as a market tool for supplementing a nonfunctioning governance system. This theory of the market for corporate control is generally accepted today, although it may well be losing its power to convince. One problem is that not all takeover offers are good for

---

[2] Easterbrook and Fischel (1996: 187–190).   [3] Clark (1986: 398).

the company – a position that Delaware courts have explained repeatedly in their decisions on takeovers. Take, for example, the factual scenario discussed in the *Blasius* case reprinted in part in Chapter 16 (which was a written consent proceeding but could well have been a takeover): two heavily indebted financiers attempt to acquire control of a gold mining company for the sole purpose of having it use gold to collateralize a massive loan and pay out the proceeds to them, which would push the target toward bankruptcy. At the point the proposal is made, the target is healthy and happy and the proposing investors are indebted and looking for a way to pay their debt. Proposals that would impoverish the target while enriching the takeover bidder are good neither for investors seeking a stable stream of income nor for the economy as a whole.

Another aspect of takeovers that requires clarification is that, contrary to the traditional justification of the market for corporate control as a cure for ineffective shareholder rights and influence under corporate law, takeovers do not at all solve the collective action problems of shareholders. The argument goes that, because shareholders with small holdings do not have sufficient economic incentives to spend time on monitoring and voting, they become rationally apathetic and the board comes to exercise a control over the company exceeding its statutory boundaries. When shares are transferred to a single owner, this person has a good economic motive to exercise the voting rights actively, and will replace a board if necessary. Voting rights are inherently defective unless transferred to a large blockholder.

This argument has a number of defects. First, the solution is only temporary. The rescuing purchaser will either merge the company into the acquiring company, retain it as a controlled subsidiary, or resell it after shaking up the management. Absent the intention of employing the target as a unit in the corporate group, if the purchaser were to continue to hold a large majority of the target's stock – rather than diversify its holdings – this would create an unsustainable investment risk. As a result, a takeover only temporarily concentrates voting rights for efficient use before releasing them once again to safely diversified (for investment risk purposes) but inefficient (for governance purposes) dispersed holdings. The result is the circle shown in Figure 25.1, with heavy transaction costs at the points where shares are accumulated or dispersed. The necessary transactions (takeover offers and IPOs) require the special services of at least an investment bank and a law firm for the issuer. Takeovers transfer value from shareholders to investment banks and law firms as a way of temporarily correcting collective action problems. Although the threat

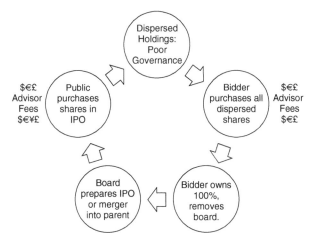

Figure 25.1   The effects of takeovers on governance

of such takeovers may make them unnecessary (deterrence), its fundamental assumption is that the governance system cannot be made to work
properly on a permanent basis.

In an economy where the possibility of collective action by shareholders is permanently disabled, takeovers offer at least a temporary solution to bad management. However, events increasingly demonstrate
that the collective action situation on which takeover theory is based
may well have been a phenomenon limited to late-twentieth-century
America. The way in which pension, private equity and hedge funds
have used ordinary governance mechanisms to change management
beginning in the early 2000s supports this possibility. First, the holdings of small shareholders are decreasing while those of sophisticated
funds are increasing. Most retail investors now hold equity investments
through mutual funds in order to diversify risk and benefit from expert
management. Moreover, the increasing importance of private pension
schemes has funneled enormous sums of money into employee pension
funds. Secondly, information can now be distributed at only a fraction
of the time and cost previously known. Although photocopiers and fax
machines came into regular use in highly developed countries only in
the 1970s and 1980s, respectively, today we can instantaneously send
complex text and graphic files as well as videos to unlimited numbers of
people at extremely low cost. Thirdly, a convergence of securities regulation and accounting principles now allows the information presented in
annual reports and proxy statements to be understood and compared

with ease. Fourthly, information services – ranging from proxy services like Institutional Shareholder Services (ISS), which offers neutral voting recommendations on complex transactions, to financial newspapers like the *Wall Street Journal*, which gather most of the significant market and legal data about companies on internet portals for a small, annual fee – have dramatically reduced the costs of making informed decisions. Increasingly, it seems that the purpose of voting rights is *not* simply to give them to someone else who can use them better, but rather to exercise them oneself.

III.   The role of management in shareholders' decisions on whether to accept offers

A "takeover" is a public offer to the shareholders of a listed company to purchase their stock. If Honda Motor Co. were to decide that their vehicles were comparable to those of BMW AG at a price 30 percent lower, and target BMW owners with a special trade-in offer, it would be impossible that BMW AG could "defend" BMW against the offer by attaching additional conditions to the existing financing of their automobiles, making them less attractive to Honda. The automobile owners have purchased their vehicles and have a right to use or dispose of them freely. If we switch from the product market to the equity market, we see a different result. Why? Certainly, a company's products are not the same as its shares. As we have seen throughout this text, shares represent a special form of ownership in a corporation imparting both rights and duties. Thus, management power to intervene in the equity market is understandably different from its power to intervene in the product market.

However, management's power to act is not identical in all of our jurisdictions. Takeovers is an area where different jurisdictions have chosen to protect the target's shareholders in different ways. Company directors in their capacities as managers or employees of the company are not stockholders. They are, moreover, very interested in the outcome of a takeover offer because their jobs usually depend on defeating it. Given this strong conflict of interest, it is understandable that UK law strictly shuts management out of the picture except for allowing them to present information to the shareholders. Delaware and other US states take a different approach, entrusting management with the duty of protecting the company from threatening takeover offers. In this way, US law delegates protective functions to management in their fiduciary capacity. Other jurisdictions, particularly the UK, build protection into their bid rules rather than placing it in the hands of management.[4]

A US board of directors would be responsible for evaluating the type of consideration offered for the target's shares, while Rule 11 of the UK Takeover Code provides detailed rules on permitted consideration. The result of delegating a judgment on the adequacy of consideration to US directors is the need for the Delaware Chancery and Supreme Courts to develop a body of decisions on directors' duties of care and loyalty in a takeover situation. One sees significantly fewer German and UK decisions because European rules provide *ex ante* for many points that US directors must regulate *ex post*. Which approach do you prefer? Does one approach advantage or disadvantage one side or the other in a takeover contest?

IV.   Takeovers across borders

Industry and commerce are highly political matters. Since the beginning of recorded history, empires and kingdoms have been built on their ability to generate wealth. Should foreign countries be permitted to purchase the productive industries of their allies? Of their neighbors? Of their enemies? This policy question is very broad. When an international legal framework is present, such as in the *Volkswagen Law* case, the decision on international takeovers has a much narrower basis. Is the duty to leave a company open to unrestricted investment based on a governance theory? What is the basis of the ECJ's decision in the *Volkswagen Law* case? Does that have any relationship to the governance argument for takeovers discussed above?

How would you recommend addressing international takeovers when no framework is involved? For example, if Iran – which is not yet a member of the World Trade Organization and thus no issue of "Trade Related Investment Measures" would arise – were to launch a tender offer with a 60 percent premium for the shares of Lockheed, a major US contractor for high-tech weapons, should the shareholders be free to tender?

Questions for discussion

1. Compared to neutrality as required by Rule 21 of the Takeover Code, what are the advantages and disadvantages of defensive measures?

---

[4] Davies and Hopt (2009: 233–245).

2. As a matter of policy, should the implementation of such defenses be allowed, and, if yes, under which circumstances and upon whose decision?

3. If management can usefully exercise a fiduciary duty to protect corporate constituencies, should a state be allowed to do so as well?

4. How do the information, bidding and pricing requirements under securities law fit together with the duties of directors under corporate law?

5. Compare *Carmody* and *Revlon* with §§ 33 and 60 of the German Securities Acquisitions and Takeovers Act and to the EC Takeover Directive.

6. Explain the mechanics of article 9(3) of the Takeover Directive. Does the reciprocity provision make sense with a view to establishing a level playing field for takeovers in Europe? Can this provision be (ab)used as a defensive measure against takeovers?

Cases

Commission of the European Communities v. Federal Republic of Germany
European Court of Justice
Case C–112/05, October 23, 2007
© The European Community

Judgment

1. By its application, the Commission of the European Communities asks the Court for a declaration that Paragraphs 2(1) and 4(1) and (3) of the Law of 21 July 1960 on the privatisation of equity in the Volkswagenwerk limited company (*Gesetz über die Überführung der Anteilsrechte an der Volkswagenwerk Gesellschaft mit beschränkter Haftung in private Hand*, BGBl. 1960 I, p. 585, and BGBl. 1960 III, p. 641-1-1), in the version applicable to the present proceedings ('the VW Law'), infringe Articles 43 EC and 56 EC.

Legal context

The law on public limited companies

2. Paragraph 134(1) of the Law on public limited companies (*Aktiengesetz*) of 6 September 1965 (BGBl. 1965 I, p. 1089; 'the Law on public limited companies'), as amended by the *Law on the monitoring and transparency of companies (Gesetz zur Kontrolle und Transparenz im Unternehmensbereich)* of 27 April 1998 (BGBl. 1998 I, p. 786), provides:

> Voting rights shall be exercised by reference to the par value of shares or, in the case of no par value shares ('*Stückaktien*'), the number of shares held. In the case of unquoted companies, where one shareholder holds a large number of shares, the

articles of association may restrict its voting rights by an absolute or progressive ceiling.

3. Paragraph 101(2) of the Law on public limited companies provides:

> The right to appoint representatives to the supervisory board shall be laid down in the articles of association and such rights may be granted only to specified shareholders or to the holders of specified shares. In the case of the latter, the right of representation is granted only where the shares are par value and where their transfer is subject to approval by the company. The shares of the shareholders having this right shall not belong to a specific category. In aggregate, the rights of representation granted shall not exceed one third of the number of members of the supervisory board appointed by the shareholders in accordance with the law or the articles of association. Paragraph 4(1) of the [VW Law] shall remain unchanged.

The VW Law

4. Paragraph 1(1) of the VW Law states that the limited liability company, Volkswagenwerk, is to be converted into a public limited company ('Volkswagen').

5. Paragraph 2(1) of the VW Law, concerning the exercise of voting rights and the limitations on that right, provides:

> The voting rights of a shareholder whose par value shares represent more than one fifth of the share capital shall be limited to the number of votes granted by the par value of shares equivalent to one fifth of the share capital.

6. Paragraph 3(5) of the VW Law, concerning representation for the exercise of voting rights, provides: "At the general meeting, no person may exercise a voting right which corresponds to more than one fifth of the share capital."

7. Paragraph 4 of the VW Law, headed 'The company's articles of association', is worded as follows:

> 1. The Federal Republic of Germany and the Land of Lower Saxony may each appoint two members to the supervisory board on condition that they hold shares in the company.
>
> ...
>
> 3. Resolutions of the general meeting which, under the Law on public limited companies, require the favourable vote of at least three quarters of the share capital represented at the time of their adoption, shall require the favourable vote of more than four fifths of the share capital represented at the time of that adoption.'

[Text omitted]

The action

9. The Commission asserts, in essence, that, first, by limiting, in derogation from the general law, the voting rights of every shareholder to 20% of Volkswagen's share capital, secondly, by requiring a majority of over 80% of the shares represented for resolutions of the general assembly, which, according to the general law, require

only a majority of 75%, and thirdly, by allowing, in derogation from the general law, the Federal State and the Land of Lower Saxony each to appoint two representatives to the company's supervisory board, the disputed provisions of the VW Law are liable to deter direct investment and for that reason constitute restrictions on the free movement of capital within the meaning of Article 56 EC.

[Text omitted]

Findings of the Court

38. As the Federal Republic of Germany has observed, the capping of voting rights is a recognised instrument of company law.

39. It is common ground, moreover, that, while the first sentence of Paragraph 134(1) of the Law on public limited companies lays down the principle that voting rights must be proportionate to the share of capital, the second sentence thereof allows a limitation on the voting rights in certain cases.

40. However, as the Commission has correctly noted, there is a difference between a power made available to shareholders, who are free to decide whether or not they wish to use it, and a specific obligation imposed on shareholders by way of legislation, without giving them the possibility to derogate from it.

41. In addition, the parties are in agreement that the first sentence of Paragraph 134(1) of the Law on public limited companies, as amended by the Law on the control and transparency of companies, removed the possibility of inserting a limitation on voting rights in the articles of association of listed companies. As the Commission has submitted, without being contradicted on this point by the German Government, since Volkswagen is a listed company, a ceiling on the voting rights cannot for that reason normally be inserted into its articles of association.

42. The Federal Republic of Germany submits that the limitation laid down in Paragraph 2(1) of the VW Law, since it applies without distinction to all shareholders, may be seen both as an advantage and as a disadvantage. While on the one hand there is the restriction on voting rights to which a shareholder holding more than 20% of the share capital is subject, on the other there is a corresponding protection against the influence of other possible shareholders having significant holdings, and thus, the guarantee of effective participation in the company's management.

43. Prior to assessing this argument, it is appropriate to examine the effects of the cap on voting rights alongside the requirement contained in Paragraph 4(3) of the VW Law of a majority of over 80% of the share capital in order to pass certain resolutions of the general assembly of Volkswagen's shareholders.

44. As the Commission has argued, without being contradicted by the Federal Republic of Germany, such resolutions include amendment of the company's articles of association, capital or financial structures, for which the Law on public limited companies fixes the required majority at a minimum of 75% of the share capital.

45. As the Federal Republic of Germany has observed, the percentage of 75% of the share capital provided for in the Law on public limited companies may be increased and fixed at a higher level by the particular company's articles of association. However, as the Commission has correctly noted, it is open to shareholders to decide whether or not to make use of that power. Conversely, the fact that the threshold of the required majority has been fixed by Paragraph 4(3) of the VW Law at more than 80% of the capital results, not from the will of the shareholders, but, as was held in Paragraph 29 of the present judgment, from a national measure.

46. This requirement, derogating from general law, and imposed by way of specific legislation, thus affords any shareholder holding 20% of the share capital a blocking minority.

47. Admittedly, as the Federal Republic of Germany has stated, this power applies without distinction. In the same way as the cap on voting rights, it may operate both to the benefit and to the detriment of any shareholder in the company.

48. However, it is apparent from the file that, when the VW Law was adopted in 1960, the Federal State and the Land of Lower Saxony were the two main shareholders in Volkswagen, a recently privatised company, and each held 20% of its capital.

49. According to the information provided to the Court, while the Federal State has chosen to part with its interest in the capital of Volkswagen, the Land of Lower Saxony, for its part, still retains an interest in the region of 20%.

50. Paragraph 4(3) of the VW Law thus creates an instrument enabling the Federal and State authorities to procure for themselves a blocking minority allowing them to oppose important resolutions, on the basis of a lower level of investment than would be required under general company law.

51. By capping voting rights at the same level of 20%, Paragraph 2(1) of the VW Law supplements a legal framework which enables the Federal and State authorities to exercise considerable influence on the basis of such a reduced investment.

52. By limiting the possibility for other shareholders to participate in the company with a view to establishing or maintaining lasting and direct economic links with it which would make possible effective participation in the management of that company or in its control, this situation is liable to deter direct investors from other Member States.

53. This finding cannot be undermined by the argument advanced by the Federal Republic of Germany to the effect that Volkswagen's shares are among the most highly traded in Europe and that a large number of them are in the hands of investors from other Member States.

54. As the Commission has argued, the restrictions on the free movement of capital which form the subject-matter of these proceedings relate to direct investments in the capital of Volkswagen, rather than portfolio investments made solely with the intention of making a financial investment (see *Commission* v. *Netherlands*, paragraph 19) and which are not relevant to the present action. As regards direct investors, it must be pointed out that, by creating an instrument liable to limit the

ability of such investors to participate in a company with a view to establishing or maintaining lasting and direct economic links with it which would make possible effective participation in the management of that company or in its control, Paragraphs 2(1) and 4(3) of the VW Law diminish the interest in acquiring a stake in the capital of Volkswagen.

55. This finding is not affected by the presence, among Volkswagen's shareholders, of a number of direct investors, which, according to the Federal Republic of Germany, is similar to such a presence among the shareholders of other large undertakings. This circumstance is not such as to cast doubt on the fact that, because of the disputed provisions of the VW Law, direct investors from other Member States, whether actual or potential, may have been deterred from acquiring a stake in the capital of that company in order to participate in it with a view to establishing or maintaining lasting and direct economic links with it which would make possible effective participation in the management of that company or in its control, even though they were entitled to benefit from the principle of the free movement of capital and the protection which that principle affords them.

56. It must therefore be held that the combination of Paragraphs 2(1) and 4(3) of the VW Law constitutes a restriction on the movement of capital within the meaning of Article 56(1) EC.

The third complaint, based on the right to appoint two representatives to Volkswagen's supervisory board

[Text omitted]

Findings of the Court

59. Under Paragraph 4(1) of the VW Law, the Federal State and the Land of Lower Saxony are each entitled, on condition that they are shareholders in the company, to appoint two representatives as members of the supervisory board of Volkswagen, that is, a total of four persons.

60. Such an entitlement constitutes a derogation from general company law, which restricts the rights of representation conferred on certain shareholders to one third of the number of the shareholders' representatives on the supervisory board. As the Commission has argued without being contradicted on this point, in the case of Volkswagen, the supervisory board of which comprises 20 members, 10 of whom are appointed by the shareholders, the number of representatives who may be appointed by the Federal State and the Land of Lower Saxony may not exceed a maximum of three according to general company law.

61. This right of appointment is therefore a specific right, which derogates from general company law and is laid down by a national legislative measure for the sole benefit of the Federal and State authorities.

62. The right of appointment conferred on the Federal State and the Land of Lower Saxony thus enables them to participate in a more significant manner in the activity of the supervisory board than their status as shareholders would normally allow.

63. Even if, as the Federal Republic of Germany has observed, the right of representation of that Land is not disproportionate to the interest which it currently holds in the share capital of Volkswagen, the fact remains that both that Land and the Federal State have the right to appoint two representatives to the supervisory board of Volkswagen on condition that they hold shares in that company, irrespective of the extent of their holdings.

64. Paragraph 4(1) of the VW Law thus establishes an instrument which gives the Federal and State authorities the possibility of exercising influence which exceeds their levels of investment. As a corollary, the influence of the other shareholders may be reduced below a level commensurate with their own levels of investment.

65. The fact that the supervisory board, as the Federal Republic of Germany submits, is not a decisionmaking body, but a simple monitoring body, is not such as to undermine the position and influence of the Federal and State authorities concerned. While German company law assigns to the supervisory board the task of monitoring the company's management and of providing reports on that management to the shareholders, it confers significant powers on that body, such as the appointment and dismissal of the members of the executive board, for the purpose of performing that task. Furthermore, as the Commission has pointed out, approval by the supervisory board is necessary for a number of transactions, including, in addition to the setting-up and transfer of production facilities, the establishment of branches, the sale and purchase of land, investments and the acquisition of other undertakings.

66. By restricting the possibility for other shareholders to participate in the company with a view to establishing or maintaining lasting and direct economic links with it such as to enable them to participate effectively in the management of that company or in its control, Paragraph 4(1) of the VW Law is liable to deter direct investors from other Member States from investing in the company's capital.

67. For the same reasons as those set out in paragraphs 53 to 55 of this judgment, this finding cannot be undermined by the Federal Republic of Germany's argument that there is a keen investment interest in Volkswagen shares on the international financial markets.

68. In the light of the foregoing, it must be held that Paragraph 4(1) of the VW Law constitutes a restriction on the movement of capital within the meaning of Article 56(1) EC.

69. The question of whether or not the Federal State and the Land of Lower Saxony make use of their right under Paragraph 4(1) is entirely irrelevant. It need merely be stated in this regard that the specific right, which derogates from the general law, conferred on those Federal and State authorities, to appoint representatives to the supervisory board of Volkswagen continues to exist in the German legal system.

Possible justification for the restrictions

[*Text omitted*]

Findings of the Court

72. The free movement of capital may be restricted by national measures justified on the grounds set out in Article 58 EC or by overriding reasons in the general interest to the extent that there are no Community harmonising measures providing for measures necessary to ensure the protection of those interests ...

73. In the absence of such Community harmonisation, it is in principle for the Member States to decide on the degree of protection which they wish to afford to such legitimate interests and on the way in which that protection is to be achieved. They may do so, however, only within the limits set by the Treaty and must, in particular, observe the principle of proportionality, which requires that the measures adopted be appropriate to secure the attainment of the objective which they pursue and not go beyond what is necessary in order to attain it ...

74. As regards the protection of workers' interests, invoked by the Federal Republic of Germany to justify the disputed provisions of the VW Law, it must be held that that Member State has been unable to explain, beyond setting out general considerations as to the need for protection against a large shareholder which might by itself dominate the company, why, in order to meet the objective of protecting Volkswagen's workers, it is appropriate and necessary for the Federal and State authorities to maintain a strengthened and irremovable position in the capital of that company.

75. In addition, as regards the right to appoint representatives to the supervisory board, it must be stated that, under German legislation, workers are themselves represented within that body.

76. Consequently, the Member State's justification based on the protection of workers cannot be upheld.

77. The same applies to the justification which the Federal Republic of Germany seeks to base on the protection of minority shareholders. While the desire to provide protection for such shareholders may also constitute a legitimate interest and justify legislative intervention, in accordance with the principles referred to in paragraphs 72 and 73 above, even if it were also liable to constitute a restriction on the free movement of capital, it must be held that, in the present case, such a desire cannot justify the disputed provisions of the VW Law.

78. It should be recalled, in this regard, that those provisions form part of a legal framework giving the Federal State and the Land of Lower Saxony the ability to exercise a greater level of influence than would normally be linked to their investment. However, the Federal Republic of Germany has not shown why, in order to protect the general interests of minority shareholders, it is appropriate or necessary to maintain such a position for the benefit of the Federal and State authorities.

79. It cannot be ruled out that, in certain special circumstances, the Federal and State authorities in question may use their position in order to defend general interests which might be contrary to the economic interests of the company concerned, and therefore, contrary to the interests of its other shareholders.

80. Finally, to the extent to which the Federal Republic of Germany contends that the activity of an undertaking as large as Volkswagen may have such an impact on the general interest that it justifies the existence of statutory guarantees which go beyond the control measures provided for under general company law, it must be pointed out that, even if this argument were well founded, that Member State has failed to explain, beyond setting out general considerations as to the risk that shareholders may put their personal interests before those of the workers, why the provisions of the VW Law criticised by the Commission are appropriate and necessary to preserve the jobs generated by Volkswagen's activity.

81. In the light of all the foregoing, the complaints relied on by the Commission alleging breach of Article 56(1) EC must be upheld.

82. Consequently, it must be held that, by maintaining in force Paragraph 4(1), as well as Paragraph 2(1) in conjunction with Paragraph 4(3), of the VW Law, the Federal Republic of Germany has failed to fulfil its obligations under Article 56(1) EC.

[Text omitted]

BAT Industries plc
Panel on Takeovers and Mergers
Statement 1989/20 – September 15, 1989
[Text of opinion edited]
Reproduced with permission of the Panel on Takeovers and Mergers

The issue

Hoylake Investments Limited ("Hoylake") announced an offer for the entire issued share capital of BAT Industries plc ("BAT") on 11 July 1989. The offer contained a standard condition relating to the obtaining of all necessary regulatory approvals.

BAT indirectly owns Farmers Group, Inc. ("Farmers"), a US insurance company. So the necessary regulatory approvals included approval by the insurance commissioners in the states in which Farmers is authorised to carry on business. There are nine such states.

Since the announcement of the offer by Hoylake, BAT and Farmers have taken various actions in the United States which Hoylake submitted have frustrated its offer.

Hoylake invited the Panel to rule that the directors of BAT are in breach of General Principle 7 of the Code, which requires the approval of shareholders prior to the taking of frustrating action. The Executive ruled that the action of BAT did not constitute frustrating action within General Principle 7, and Hoylake appealed that decision.

Hoylake also suggested that the position has now been reached in which it is effectively impossible to achieve the relevant United States regulatory approvals within the Code timetable. It therefore requested the Panel to rule that, if Hoylake were to lapse its offer immediately, it should be permitted to make a new offer for BAT once the United States regulatory position is resolved in its favour. It thus submitted that the Panel should give its consent under Rule 35.1(a) to a relaxation of the usual one year moratorium. The Executive did not itself rule on this issue but referred it to the full Panel.

Rulings

The Panel met on 13 September 1989 and ruled as follows:

(1) That the actions to date of BAT, either directly or through Farmers, in lobbying politicians and others who they considered might influence the outcome of the offer in the United States did not constitute frustrating action. Nor did the participation by Farmers in the regulatory processes in the nine states, nor its intervention in legal proceedings brought by Hoylake to restrain the insurance commissioners from conducting regulatory proceedings.

(2) The regulatory proceedings are most unlikely to be concluded within the timetable prescribed by the Code. This will have the effect that shareholders will not have a real opportunity to consider an offer for BAT on its merits. In these circumstances, the Panel considers that it should grant its consent pursuant to Rule 35.1 (a) so that, if and when it becomes lawful as a matter of US law for Hoylake to complete its offer for BAT, Hoylake will be entitled within 21 days to announce a fresh offer, subject to the conditions set out below.

By this ruling, we attempt to apply the principles of the Code to a situation in which a foreign regulatory process, as distinct from a reference to the Monopolies and Mergers Commission ("MMC"), may operate so as to prevent shareholders considering an offer for their company. In essence, BAT and Farmers will continue to be able to participate in the regulatory processes in the United States but, should Hoylake obtain the necessary regulatory clearances, it will be entitled to offer again within a 21 day period in the same way as if an offer had been referred to, and cleared by, the MMC. During the period between now and the expiry of the 21 day period, BAT will be bound by General Principle 7 and Rule 21 to the same extent as it would have been bound had the Hoylake offer been referred to the MMC.

The consent granted to Hoylake is conditional, however, on three things. First, that it lapses its current offer as soon as is reasonably practicable following this decision and the completion of any appeal against it. Secondly, it continues to use its best efforts to conclude the regulatory processes within as short a timescale as practicable and thirdly, neither it nor any concert party purchases any BAT shares between now and the announcement of any new offer within the 12 month period. This third condition is important to ensure that the status quo is preserved.

The principle of our ruling is that Hoylake should be entitled to make a new offer at any time within 21 days after it has become lawful as a matter of US law for it to complete its offer for BAT. The exact definition of this date, to remove any residual uncertainties as to precisely when Hoylake might be free to offer again, will be determined shortly by the Executive (subject, of course, to the right of appeal to the full Panel) after hearing the suggestions of Hoylake and the comments of BAT.

Hoylake is required to make an announcement as soon as this date is reached. We emphasise subsequently in this ruling that we are applying the existing Principles of the Code to a situation which is novel. But situations of this kind, where the interaction of the Code and foreign regulatory processes falls to be considered, are likely to recur. Whilst, inevitably, decisions must be made on a basis which takes account of the facts of individual cases, and which may be refined and developed in the light of further experience, the Panel will seek to prepare an additional note to Rule 35.1 which gives an indication of the general approach which we think should be adopted in cases of this kind.

[*Text omitted*]

Background

BAT acquired Farmers in 1988. Before doing so, it had to satisfy the insurance commissioners in those states of the United States in which Farmers carried on business as to the propriety of such acquisition. Farmers carried on insurance business, directly or indirectly, in nine states of the United States where, subject to certain limited exceptions, state insurance holding company legislation requires regulatory approval of any direct or indirect acquisition of control of a domestic insurer. These states are Arizona, California, Idaho, Illinois, Kansas, Ohio, Oregon, Texas and Washington. Farmers is an important company within the United States insurance markets, and within each of the individual states. This has regulatory consequences.

The regulation of the business of insurance in the United States is conducted by the individual states. The object of such regulation is to protect the financial security of policyholders within that state. The state regulators, in discharging this function, are entitled to review both the plans and financial condition of a party who proposes to acquire an insurance company.

The procedure for securing regulatory approval is as follows. The proposed acquirer is required to submit an application for approval of the transfer by filing a statement on Form A. This Form calls for detailed information. The commissioners not infrequently request supplementary information. In some states there is a timetable of 60 days for completion of the regulatory processes, but this may be extended. In some cases the timetable does not start to run until the insurance department decides that the submission by the applicant is substantially complete.

The insurance commissioners invariably seek the views of the target company on the application. The target company, however, will often go well beyond responding to requests for information. It is common ground that it has a fiduciary duty to policyholders to lay before the commissioners information which is relevant to the protection of such policyholders. The form of the proceedings reflects the constitutional requirement of due process, and there are provisions for documentary and oral discovery. In practice, the submissions of the target company may affect the extent to which the insurance commissioners require further assistance and information from the potential bidder. If the target company contests the acquisition, the process may inevitably go less smoothly and more slowly than if the target company is cooperating with the acquirer. Whilst the proceedings are technically administrative in concept, they have a very substantial quasi-judicial element. The procedures, in a contested case, were said to be nearly as onerous as those in litigation. They are, however, ultimately in the control of the insurance commissioner.

They are, moreover, initiated by the proposed acquirer and never by the target company.

The facts

It is in this context that Hoylake made its offer for BAT. Hoylake will become a subsidiary of Anglo Group plc ("Anglo"). At the time of the announcement of its offer, on 11 July, the other investors in Hoylake included General Oriental Investments Ltd, the Chairman of which is Sir James Goldsmith, J Rothschild Holdings plc and its associate company RIT Capital Partners plc, and also CP Investments (Singapore) Pte. Limited, a company indirectly controlled by Mr Kerry Packer. Anglo was, and is, controlled jointly by General Oriental Investments, J Rothschild Holdings and RIT Capital Partners, since together they hold 75% of its existing share capital.

Under the Hoylake offer, each BAT shareholder who accepts will, if that offer goes wholly unconditional, receive £4,250 nominal of Hoylake's senior secured notes, $4,182 nominal of Hoylake's subordinated notes and 387 Anglo Ordinary shares for every 1,000 BAT shares held. Thus, if all BAT shareholders were to accept the Hoylake offer and it were to be declared wholly unconditional, BAT shareholders would hold 92% of the issued ordinary share capital of Anglo. Anglo would in turn hold approximately 75% of the issued ordinary share capital of Hoylake which would then own 100% of BAT.

It has been disclosed since the offer was announced that various new investors will subscribe for shares in Hoylake. These new shareholders will, in essence, hold shares which would otherwise have been held by the original investors in Hoylake, other than Anglo. So they do not materially affect the nature and effect of the offer as we have described it. They do, however, affect the position of shareholders in Hoylake other than Anglo. In particular, Axa Midi Assurances ("Axa Midi") has conditionally agreed to invest £600mn in Hoylake subject to Hoylake announcing a revised offer for BAT or Hoylake's offer for BAT lapsing. In the light of this, Axa Midi may become the second largest shareholder in Hoylake, after Anglo, holding 15% of its Class A shares.

As is now well known, at the time of announcing its offer Hoylake had, and now has, no intention of retaining Farmers should it acquire control of BAT. It therefore proposed to the insurance commissioners a "standstill" agreement and an agreement whereby the shareholding in Farmers would be put into a voting trust with independent US trustees. In due course, the new ultimate owner would have to be approved by the commissioners. The use of such voting trusts is apparently not new in the United States. It is said on behalf of Hoylake that there is some limited precedent in the context of takeovers in the insurance business, although BAT cast doubt on whether any such voting trust would be approved unless the commissioners were also able to approve Hoylake as acquirer.

On 9 August Hoylake announced that three independent trustees had been chosen. Hoylake followed this by entering into an agreement on 23 August for the sale of Farmers to Axa Midi for $4.5bn, subject to certain conditions. It was this agreement which committed Axa Midi to its investment in Hoylake in the event of a revised offer.

We turn to the entry of Farmers into the regulatory process. Hoylake, as required by statute, sent copies of its Form A submissions to Farmers at the same time as they were submitted to the local insurance regulatory authorities. Farmers thereafter participated in the state regulatory proceedings. This participation has undoubtedly been diligent and thorough.

Hoylake has made a number of submissions to the United States regulators. Hoylake submits, in a number of the states, that there is a statutory exemption from the need for approval because, as it is suggested, the target company is engaged primarily in business other than insurance. It has also argued that the effect of the voting trust would be to cause the regulators to minimise their review of Hoylake since they could rely on the protection which the trust provides. Hoylake has also suggested that there would be no change of control since, if the offer were successful, BAT's shareholders would own approximately 92% of Anglo, with Anglo being the ultimate parent of Hoylake.

At the time it made its offer, Hoylake held the view that the commissioners would be inclined to give prompt attention to an offer outside the US by a UK group for another UK group. Hoylake, in the light of legal advice, apparently concluded that there was a reasonable prospect of resolving the United States regulatory process by day 81 of its offer (ie the last day for fulfilment of all conditions of its offer pursuant to the Code). This advice appears to have been based on the belief that the creation of the voting trust would have the effect of lessening the extent to which the full regulatory process would have to be conducted. BAT make the point that Hoylake should instead have concentrated on satisfying the regulators that it met on the merits the criteria for control of an insurance company.

In addition to the submissions which Hoylake has made to the insurance commissioners, Hoylake has commenced Federal legal proceedings against commissioners in all nine states alleging that the relevant state laws constituted an unconstitutional interference in inter-state commerce to the extent that they applied to Hoylake's offer for BAT. It only commenced these proceedings at the end of July after, as it suggested, BAT had sought to "poison the well" with the insurance regulators. Hoylake has claimed interim relief by way of preliminary injunction in all these proceedings. So far the only courts which have ruled on this claim, the District Courts in California, Texas, and Washington, have denied it. Hoylake says it will appeal these decisions. Whilst the proceedings were brought against the commissioners alone, Farmers has in each of the states filed a motion to intervene as a defendant opposing Hoylake's claim. This has apparently been welcomed by several insurance commissioners, since it is said that additional resources will be brought to the assistance of the regulators. The regulators inevitably consider that they would otherwise be hard pressed effectively to defend a major constitutional case. There is no prospect whatsoever of this litigation being completed in a short period of time. It might be thought at first sight that any preliminary injunction granted to Hoylake in these proceedings would inevitably have the effect of preventing Hoylake's offer being considered by the commissioners during the Code timetable.

However, according to Hoylake and its advisers, (and not, we understand, disputed by BAT), if Hoylake had obtained the preliminary injunction preventing the regulators temporarily from ruling on the proposed acquisition, Hoylake would then have had a "window of opportunity" to complete its offer while the regulators were in baulk. If the preliminary injunction were subsequently discharged, the regulators' powers would include the ability to order divestment of the insurance company, but the offer would not be unscrambled. This consideration in part explains why Hoylake pursued litigation which might otherwise be thought to give rise to self-induced frustration of its offer.

In addition to participating in the regulatory process, and intervening in the constitutional proceedings, BAT and Farmers also engaged in intensive lobbying in the United States. Hoylake suggested that it is the influence of BAT which led two Senators from Kentucky, the state where the headquarters for BAT's United States operations is located and a state with a large tobacco industry, to obtain signatures of 200 members of Congress to a letter to the US Secretary of State, James Baker, urging him to "communicate our concern to the British Government" about Hoylake's bid and about how "foreign financiers are seeking to buy up America." Hoylake also claimed that one of the Kentucky Senators has asked the United States General Accounting Office to conduct within sixty days an investigation of the

Hoylake offer, including the implications of the offer for investors in markets, and that in making this request he was prompted by BAT. Hoylake points to lobbying which it suggests has taken effect at the state level.

We would emphasise that these are but illustrations of the conduct of which Hoylake complains. The scale of operations on both sides in the United States has been massive and intense. Hoylake has deployed in excess of 110 individual lawyers, lobbyists and public relations personnel on a full time basis. BAT's battalions are said to include 21 law firms, 15 lobbying firms and 12 public relations companies. It is against this background that Hoylake submitted that BAT have breached General Principle 7 of the Code by acting in such a way as to frustrate the offer, whereas BAT submitted that Hoylake have failed to act effectively so as to secure the appropriate regulatory decisions within the Code timetable.

General Principle 7

General Principle 7 of the Code provides as follows:

> At no time after a bona fide offer has been communicated to the board of the offeree company, or after the board of the offeree company has reason to believe that a bona fide offer might be imminent, may any action be taken by the board of the offeree company in relation to the affairs of the company, without the approval of the shareholders in general meeting, which could effectively result in any bona fide offer being frustrated or in the shareholders being denied an opportunity to decide on its merits." [*Editors' note*: see a somewhat softened Principle 3 in the new version of the Code and Rule 21.1, where a conditional form of the original language is now found.]

This principle is fundamental to the Code. It cannot always be easy for the management of a target company to distinguish its own interests from those of its shareholders; this is potentially damaging in circumstances where the two do not necessarily correspond. One of the principal objects of the Code is to enable the shareholders in the target company to have an opportunity to consider an offer for their company on its merits on an informed basis in an orderly and limited timescale. There are no corresponding provisions in United States law or practice. In general the primary limitation in the United States is that the directors must act in accordance with their fiduciary duty, and the courts allow considerable latitude to the directors to exercise their business judgment in deciding what action to take in response to a takeover offer. Thus in the BAT offer for Farmers, Farmers vigorously participated in the regulatory process which took substantially longer than the timescale provided by the Code. This was, however, irrelevant since the offer for Farmers, as a US company, by BAT was not subject to the Code and, accordingly, no issue arose in the UK as to whether Farmers had engaged in frustrating action.

The issue which we now have to consider arises in an increasingly important context. Where multi- national companies, based in this country and subject to the

Code, have interests in the United States or other countries, the possibility of foreign regulatory scrutiny on public interest grounds may often be present.

Hoylake submitted that the board of BAT has sought to frustrate the offer in three ways:

i) by lobbying of Congressmen and others;
ii) by encouraging and persuading the various US commissioners to block Hoylake's offer and by taking every opportunity to delay the regulatory proceedings by seeking extensive discovery, depositions and adjournments; and
iii) by intervening in Hoylake's legal actions against the US insurance commissioners.

Hoylake submitted that the words of General Principle 7 of the Code are wide enough to cover each of these situations. However, paragraph 3(a) of the Introduction to the Code states that the General Principles are "expressed in broad general terms and the Code does not define the precise extent of, or limitations on, their application." The Code is to be interpreted in accordance with its spirit and purpose, and with regard both to common sense and the precedent which has developed over the twenty-one years of the Panel's existence. In this context we turn to the specific allegations.

Lobbying

Historically, it has been common in this country for target companies to lobby both the Department of Trade and Industry ("DTI") and the Office of Fair Trading ("OFT") in order to seek to secure a reference of an offer to the MMC. In such event, the offer would automatically lapse (pursuant to Rule 12(a) of the Code). The target company would hope that the effect of such a reference would be that the MMC would be persuaded that the offer was contrary to the public interest, or that the bidding company would simply lose interest in the light of the reference or, at very least, that the target company would gain time which might, in the event of clearance and a renewed offer, give it a better prospect of a successful defense.

Hoylake does not challenge the view which has historically been taken that such lobbying is unobjectionable. It submitted, however, that the position is not analogous to an investigation by the OFT. In particular, it suggested that the OFT procedure is designed to fit in with the Code timetable, and so does not offer the opportunity for frustration which is offered by the US procedure.

This misses, however, what we consider to be the essential point. We do not consider that lobbying generally of politicians and others is capable of contravening General Principle 7. It is not a very direct way of obstructing an offer, and since it is possible for the bidder to engage in counter lobbying, the effect of the process is simply to enable one of the public interest decision takers to have presented to them both sides of the argument. Irrespective of its effectiveness the lobbying of politicians is a democratic right which it would be inappropriate for the Panel to inhibit. Nor could the Panel properly draw a line between permissible and impermissible lobbying. If it is accepted by Hoylake that an offeror is entitled to engage in lobbying on the public interest issue, it would be one-sided if the target company was not permitted to do so. The scale of the publicity or the lobbying must inevitably depend upon the efforts which the parties consider sensible in the light of the issues involved. Illustrations of extensive lobbying in this country can be found in the offer by BTR for Pilkington and by Nestle for Rowntree. The nature of Hoylake's offer for BAT was, bearing in mind the presence of Farmers in the United States, perhaps bound to attract intense public interest and give scope for considerable lobbying. In the event, the Panel does not consider that lobbying constitutes frustrating action. The proceedings before the insurance commissioners Hoylake submitted that the proceedings before the insurance commissioners were tantamount to adversarial proceedings between parties, and, accordingly, that BAT and Farmers should not be able to participate without the consent of shareholders, since the effect of such action will be to prevent Hoylake obtaining appropriate consents within the bid timetable.

Whilst there is some conflict of evidence as to the exact effect of what has been done by BAT and Farmers in regard to the US regulatory proceedings, there is no doubt that such involvement has been substantial. We are concerned about the opportunities which may be created by the nature of the United States regulatory proceedings for a party to delay the regulatory process. We do not exclude the possibility that, in an appropriate case, it may be established that the target company had acted in such a way as constitutes frustrating action. Indeed, in the present case, we note with approval that BAT/Farmers were specifically advised by their English lawyers that, in discharging their fiduciary duty to policyholders to place information before the insurance commissioners, they should have regard to the obligations of BAT under General Principle 7. We do, however, consider that in general the nature of litigation and administrative proceedings are different. The administrative proceedings are initiated by the regulators, and the target company may have as in the present case an obligation to cooperate, whilst its legal duties to shareholders or policyholders may extend the ambit of that formal obligation.

We would, therefore, be very slow to characterise conduct in regulatory proceedings which are controlled by the regulator as being frustrating action. We emphasise, however, that we cannot be too dogmatic on this issue, since in each case something must depend upon the nature of the foreign regulatory process and the action taken by the target company. It is the responsibility of the target company at all times to keep General Principle 7 well in mind. In the present case, we do not consider we would be justified in reaching the conclusion that the actions of BAT, through Farmers, can be regarded as frustrating conduct. They are certainly wide-ranging, and thorough, and in another jurisdiction might be regarded as overdiligent. But those foreign regulators who have been contacted by the Executive have not suggested that Farmers have in any way behaved inappropriately or been other than prompt in the actions they have taken.

[*Text omitted*]

Federal Court proceedings

The decision of the Panel in regard to Minorco's offer for Consgold clearly established that the taking of legal proceedings, whether in the jurisdiction of the UK Courts or elsewhere, might fall within General Principle 7. In that case, Consgold were acting as plaintiffs. In the present case, however, Farmers are not plaintiffs. The proceedings were initially brought against the insurance commissioners as defendants. Farmers took the initiative in seeking to join in those suits, and have succeeded in doing so in eight of the nine relevant states. They thus were not joined in the proceedings as defendants, but the effect of their voluntary intervention is that they have at their own initiative been added as defendants. It is accepted by BAT that Farmers has done so with the intention of seeking to assist the commissioners to succeed in resisting those actions. In the litigation, BAT has confined itself to supporting the commissioners in their unsuccessful motions for summary dismissal and in their successful resistance of the applications for a preliminary injunction. Both these actions are designed to uphold the jurisdiction of the regulators, so that they can fulfil their statutory function of deciding whether an acquisition should be permitted. Whilst this may deprive Hoylake of the benefits which a preliminary injunction might give, we consider it is essentially linked to the participation by the target company in the regulatory process.

We consider that it is not frustrating action for the target company, having regard to its fiduciary duty to policyholders, to uphold the jurisdiction of the regulators to seek to protect those policyholders. If this litigation continues, however, BAT should consider its future involvement very carefully with regard to General Principle 7.

Finally, in coming to the conclusion that the Panel should be slow to hold that actions such as taken by BAT/Farmers in this case are a breach of General Principle 7, we had regard to the fact that any disadvantage to shareholders would be mitigated if, as discussed in the next section, the Panel were to exercise its discretion under Rule 35.1(a) to permit an early new offer.

Rule 35.1(a)

It should be emphasised that Hoylake does not seek an extension of the Code timetable in regard to the present offer. Hoylake submits that, by analogy with the procedure where an offer is referred to the MMC in this country, it should be permitted to renew its offer as soon as the US regulatory position is completely resolved in Hoylake's favour.

Rule 35.1(a) provides as follows:

> Except with the consent of the Panel, where an offer has been announced or posted but has not become or been declared wholly unconditional and has been withdrawn or has lapsed, neither the offeror, nor any person who acted in concert with the offeror in the course of the original offer, nor any person who is subsequently acting in concert with any of them, may within 12 months from the date on which such offer is withdrawn or lapses either:
>
> i) make an offer for the offeree company; or
> ii) acquire any shares of the offeree company if the offeror or any such person would thereby become obliged under Rule 9 to make an offer.

The principal purpose of the Code is to uphold the interests of shareholders in the target company, as well as seeing fair play between the respective parties. In order to secure the interests of shareholders, the Panel is frequently required to ensure that shareholders are given the opportunity of considering an offer which someone wishes to make for their shares. This is, for example, the central philosophy underlying General Principle 7. The Code recognises, however, that it is not in the interests of shareholders for their company to be continually under siege. This may result in the management devoting considerable time and resources to defending offers, rather than managing the company for the benefit of shareholders ... the main consideration which the Panel has to apply in considering whether to grant consent to a renewed offer within the 12- month period is the interests of shareholders.

[Text omitted]

... We recognise that, even if all regulatory consents had been obtained, the offer might fail. We consider, however, that a significant number of shareholders might be influenced towards inaction by the uncertainty surrounding the regulatory process. To this extent the offer could not be properly considered on its merits ... Hoylake submitted that, in the light of the inability to complete the regulatory process within the Code timetable, fairness to shareholders in BAT makes it appropriate that consent should be given to Hoylake to re-bid within 12 months of the lapsing of its current offer. It pointed to the fact that, without flexibility in the application of Rule 35.1, the ability of the Code to provide a sensible framework for offers, particularly for multi-national companies, could be called into question and certain companies rendered bid proof by the interaction of the Code and foreign regulatory systems.

[Text omitted]

... The Panel considers that, with hindsight, the view that all the consents could be obtained within the Code timescale even if vigorously opposed by BAT was perhaps too hopeful. So the Panel does not consider that Hoylake's application should fail because of the way in which it has conducted its application for regulatory consents.

[Text omitted]

In our view, the central consideration must be that the effect of the US regulatory process means that shareholders will not have an opportunity of considering an offer from Hoylake free from regulatory consents and within the Code timescale. Whatever controversy there may be over Hoylake's offer, and whatever public interest considerations it may raise, our principal function is to ensure that shareholders are dealt with fairly. We do not regard it as desirable that the management of BAT should be subject to uncertainty during the 12 month period after the offer lapses. We understand their concern that such uncertainty, particularly having regard to the nature of Hoylake's offer, may inhibit their raising of finance, and their acquisition policy, as well as being of anxiety to employees. But we consider that, even if the twelve month moratorium applied, many of the same features would be present if Hoylake continued to seek to discharge the requirement of the United States regulatory commissioners. Hoylake would be entitled to do this without an actual offer being in existence, irrespective of any refusal on our part to grant an exception to the twelve month moratorium period. We regard it as undesirable that, should Hoylake complete the United States regulatory processes, they should be inhibited from putting an offer to shareholders during the remainder of the twelve month period. We think there is much to be said for requiring Hoylake to use its best efforts to conclude the regulatory processes as speedily as possible, and then to decide whether or not to bid again for BAT, so that the uncertainty may at least be resolved as speedily as possible. We think the bid might well hang over the head of BAT in any event. We consider, however, that Hoylake should proceed as fast as it is reasonably able, so that shareholders may know whether they are going to receive an offer for their company and its future should be resolved. We therefore consider that the balance is in favour of granting consent that, on the condition that it lapses its current bid as soon as reasonably practicable following this decision and the completion of any appeal against it, Hoylake should, if and when during the subsequent 12 months it becomes lawful as a matter of US law for Hoylake to complete its offer for BAT, be permitted within 21 days after the final clearance to announce a new offer for BAT.

The principle of our ruling is that Hoylake should be entitled to make a new offer at any time within 21 days after it has become lawful as a matter of US law for it to complete its offer for BAT. The exact definition of this date, to remove any residual uncertainties as to precisely when Hoylake might be free to offer again, will be determined by the Executive (subject, of course, to the right of appeal to the full Panel) after hearing the suggestions of Hoylake and the comments of BAT. Hoylake will be required to make an announcement as soon as this date is reached. Whilst BAT will be entitled to raise before the Panel any suggestion that Hoylake has not used its best efforts to obtain regulatory consents as speedily as possible during the ensuing period, we should expect such an application only to be made if there was real evidence of serious dilatoriness or incompetence. In particular, we would not entertain any objection from BAT on this score unless Hoylake's efforts were materially less than they have been to date.

Finally, we should make it clear that nothing in this decision should be taken to restrict the Panel's ability to give Hoylake permission under Rule 35 to rebid within 12 months on other grounds, in particular those listed in the Note on Rules 35.1 and 35.2.

We think it desirable in the interests of the market that the nature of this decision should be announced immediately even though BAT has the right to appeal.

Carmody v. Toll Brothers, Inc.
Court of Chancery of Delaware
723 A 2d 1180 (1998)
[*Text edited; some footnotes omitted*]

OPINION: JACOBS, Vice Chancellor

At issue on this Rule 12(b)(6) motion to dismiss is whether a most recent innovation in corporate antitakeover measures – the so-called "dead hand" poison pill rights plan – is subject to legal challenge on the basis that it violates the Delaware General Corporation Law and/or the fiduciary duties of the board of directors who adopted the plan. As explained more fully below, a "dead hand" rights plan is one that cannot be redeemed except by the incumbent directors who adopted the plan or their designated successors. As discussed below, the Court finds that the "dead hand" feature of the rights plan as described in the complaint (the "Rights Plan") is subject to legal challenge on both statutory and fiduciary grounds, and that because the complaint states legally cognizable claims for relief, the pending motion to dismiss must be denied.

I.   Facts

A.   *Background Leading to Adoption of the Plan*

The firm whose rights plan is being challenged is Toll Brothers (sometimes referred to as "the company"), a Pennsylvania-based Delaware corporation that designs, builds, and markets single family luxury homes in thirteen states and five regions in the United States. The company was founded in 1967 by brothers Bruce and Robert Toll, who are its Chief Executive and Chief Operating Officers, respectively, and who own approximately 37.5% of Toll Brothers' common stock. The company's board of directors has nine members, four of whom (including Bruce and Robert Toll) are senior executive officers. The remaining five members of the board are "outside" independent directors.

From its inception in 1967, Toll Brothers has performed very successfully, and "went public" in 1986. As of June 3, 1997, the company had issued and outstanding 34,196,473 common shares that are traded on the New York Stock Exchange. After going public, Toll Brothers continued to enjoy increasing revenue growth, and it expects that trend to continue into 1998, based on the company's ongoing expansion, its backlog of home contracts, and a continuing strong industry demand for luxury housing in the regions it serves.

The home building industry of which the company is a part is highly competitive. For some time that industry has been undergoing consolidation through the acquisition process, and over the last ten years it has evolved from one where companies served purely local and regional markets to one where regional companies have expanded to serve markets throughout the country. That was accomplished by home builders in one region acquiring firms located in other regions. Inherent in any such expansion-through-acquisition environment is the risk of a hostile takeover. To protect against that risk, the company's board of directors adopted the Rights Plan.

B.   The Rights Plan

The Rights Plan was adopted on June 12, 1997, at which point Toll Brothers' stock was trading at approximately $18 per share – near the low end of its established price range of $16 3/8 to $25 3/16 per share. After considering the industry economic and financial environment and other factors, the Toll Brothers board concluded that other companies engaged in its lines of business might perceive the company as a potential target for an acquisition. The Rights Plan was adopted with that problem in mind, but not in response to any specific takeover proposal or threat. The company announced that it had done that to protect its stockholders from "coercive or unfair tactics to gain control of the Company" by placing the stockholders in a position of having to accept or reject an unsolicited offer without adequate time.

1.   The Rights Plan's "flip in" and "flip over" features

The Rights Plan would operate as follows: there would be a dividend distribution of one preferred stock purchase right (a "Right") for each outstanding share of common stock as of July 11, 1997. Initially the Rights would attach to the company's outstanding common shares, and each Right would initially entitle the holder to purchase one thousandth of a share of a newly registered series Junior A Preferred Stock for $100. The Rights would become exercisable, and would trade separately from the common shares, after the "Distribution Date," which is defined as the earlier of (a) ten business days following a public announcement that an acquiror has acquired, or obtained the right to acquire, beneficial ownership of 15% or more of the company's outstanding common shares (the "Stock Acquisition Date"), or (b) ten business days after the commencement of a tender offer or exchange offer that would result in a person or group beneficially owning 15% or more of the company's outstanding common shares. Once exercisable, the Rights remain exercisable until their Final Expiration Date (June 12, 2007, ten years after the adoption of the Plan), unless the Rights are earlier redeemed by the company.

The dilutive mechanism of the Rights is "triggered" by certain defined events. One such event is the acquisition of 15% or more of Toll Brothers' stock by any person or group of affiliated or associated persons. Should that occur, each Rights holder (except the acquiror and its affiliates and associates) becomes entitled to buy two shares of Toll Brothers common stock or other securities at half price. That is, the value of the stock received when the Right is exercised is equal to two times the exercise price of the Right. In that manner, this so-called "flip in" feature of the Rights Plan would massively dilute the value of the holdings of the unwanted acquiror. [Note 5]

[Note 5] The "flip-in" feature of a rights plan is triggered when the acquiror crosses the specified ownership threshold, regardless of the acquiror's intentions with respect to the use of the shares. At that point, rights vest in all shareholders other than the acquiror, and as a result, those holders become entitled to acquire additional shares of voting stock at a substantially discounted price, usually 50% of the market price. Commonly, rights plans also contain a "flip-over" feature entitling target company shareholders (again, other than the acquiror) to purchase shares of the acquiring company at a reduced price. That feature is activated when, after a "flip-in" triggering event, the acquiror initiates a triggering event, such as a merger, self-dealing transaction, or sale of assets. See Shawn C. Lese, *Note, Preventing Control From the Grave: A Proposal for Judicial Treatment of Dead Hand Provisions in Poison Pills*, 96 Colum. Law Review 2175, 2180–81 (1996).

The Rights also have a standard "flip over" feature, which is triggered if after the Stock Acquisition Date, the company is made a party to a merger in which Toll Brothers is not the surviving corporation, or in which it is the surviving corporation and its common stock is changed or exchanged. In either event, each Rights holder becomes entitled to purchase common stock of the acquiring company, again at half-price, thereby impairing the acquiror's capital structure and drastically diluting the interest of the acquiror's other stockholders.

The complaint alleges that the purpose and effect of the company's Rights Plan, as with most poison pills, is to make any hostile acquisition of Toll Brothers prohibitively expensive, and thereby to deter such acquisitions unless the target company's board first approves the acquisition proposal. The target board's "leverage" derives from another critical feature found in most rights plans: the directors' power to redeem the Rights at any time before they expire, on such conditions as the directors "in their sole discretion" may establish. To this extent there is little to distinguish the company's Rights Plan from the "standard model." What is distinctive about the Rights Plan is that it authorizes only a specific, defined category of directors – the "Continuing Directors" – to redeem the Rights. The dispute over the legality of this "Continuing Director" or "dead hand" feature of the Rights Plan is what drives this lawsuit.

2.   *The "dead hand" feature of the Rights Plan*

In substance, the "dead hand" provision operates to prevent any directors of Toll Brothers, except those who were in office as of the date of the Rights Plan's adoption

(June 12, 1997) or their designated successors, from redeeming the Rights until they expire on June 12, 2007. That consequence flows directly from the Rights Agreement's definition of a "Continuing Director," which is:

> (i) any member of the Board of Directors of the Company, while such person is a member of the Board, who is not an Acquiring Person, or an Affiliate [as defined] or Associate [as defined] of an Acquiring Person, or a representative or nominee of an Acquiring Person or of any such Affiliate or Associate, *and was a member of the Board prior to the date of this agreement,* or (ii) any Person who subsequently becomes a member of the Board, while such Person is a member of the Board, who is not an Acquiring Person, or an Affiliate [as defined] or Associate [as defined] of an Acquiring Person, or a representative or nominee of an Acquiring Person or of any such Affiliate or Associate, if such Person's *nomination for election or election to the Board is recommended or approved by a majority of the Continuing Directors* ... (emphasis added).

According to the complaint, this "dead hand" provision has a twofold practical effect. First, it makes an unsolicited offer for the company more unlikely by eliminating a proxy contest as a useful way for a hostile acquiror to gain control, because even if the acquiror wins the contest, its newly elected director representatives could not redeem the Rights. Second, the "dead hand" provision disenfranchises, in a proxy contest, all shareholders that wish the company to be managed by a board empowered to redeem the Rights, by depriving those shareholders of any practical choice except to vote for the incumbent directors. Given these effects, the plaintiff claims that the only purpose that the "dead hand" provision could serve is to discourage future acquisition activity by making any proxy contest to replace incumbent board members an exercise in futility.

II. Overview of the problem and the parties' contentions

[Text omitted]

A. Overview

The critical issue on this motion is whether a "dead hand" provision in a "poison pill" rights plan is subject to legal challenge on the basis that it is invalid as *ultra vires*, or as a breach of fiduciary duty, or both. Although that issue has been the subject of scholarly comment, it has yet to be decided under Delaware law, and to date it has been addressed by only two courts applying the law of other jurisdictions.

Some history may elucidate the issue by locating its relevance within the dynamic of state corporate takeover jurisprudence. Since the 1980s, that body of law, largely judge-made, has been racing to keep abreast of the ever-evolving and novel tactical and strategic developments so characteristic of this important area of economic endeavor that is swiftly becoming a permanent part of our national (and international) economic landscape.

For our purposes, the relevant history begins in the early 1980s with the advent of the "poison pill" as an antitakeover measure. That innovation generated litigation focused upon the issue of whether any poison pill rights plan could validly be adopted under state corporation law. The seminal case, *Moran v. Household International, Inc.*, answered that question in the affirmative ...

In *Moran*, this Court and the Supreme Court upheld the "flip over" rights plan in issue there based on three distinct factual findings. The first was that the poison pill would not erode fundamental shareholder rights, because the target board would not have unfettered discretion arbitrarily to reject a hostile offer or to refuse to redeem the pill. Rather, the board's judgment not to redeem the pill would be subject to judicially enforceable fiduciary standards. The second finding was that even if the board refused to redeem the pill (thereby preventing the shareholders from receiving the unsolicited offer), that would not preclude the acquiror from gaining control of the target company, because the offeror could "form a group of up to 19.9% and solicit proxies for consents to remove the Board and redeem the Rights." Third, even if the hostile offer was precluded, the target company's stockholders could always exercise their ultimate prerogative – wage a proxy contest to remove the board. On this basis, the Supreme Court concluded that "the Rights Plan will not have a severe impact upon proxy contests and it will not preclude all hostile acquisitions of Household."

It being settled that a corporate board could permissibly adopt a poison pill, the next litigated question became: under what circumstances would the directors' fiduciary duties require the board to redeem the rights in the face of a hostile takeover proposal? That issue was litigated, in Delaware and elsewhere, during the second half of the 1980s. The lesson taught by that experience was that courts were extremely reluctant to order the redemption of poison pills on fiduciary grounds. The reason was the prudent deployment of the pill proved to be largely beneficial to shareholder interests: it often resulted in a bidding contest that culminated in an acquisition on terms superior to the initial hostile offer.

Once it became clear that the prospects were unlikely for obtaining judicial relief mandating a redemption of the poison pill, a different response to the pill was needed. That response, which echoed the Supreme Court's suggestion in *Moran*, was the foreseeable next step in the evolution of takeover strategy: a tender offer coupled with a solicitation for shareholder proxies to remove and replace the incumbent board with the acquiror's nominees who, upon assuming office, would redeem the pill. Because that strategy, if unopposed, would enable hostile offerors to effect an "end run" around the poison pill, it again was predictable and only a matter of time that target company boards would develop counter-strategies. With one exception – the "dead hand" pill – these counterstrategies proved "successful" only in cases where the purpose was to delay the process to enable the board to develop alternatives to the hostile offer. The counterstrategies were largely unsuccessful, however, where the goal was to stop the proxy contest (and as a consequence, the hostile offer) altogether.

For example, in cases where the target board's response was either to (i) amend the by-laws to delay a shareholders meeting to elect directors, or (ii) delay an annual meeting to a later date permitted under the bylaws, so that the board and management would be able to explore alternatives to the hostile offer (but not entrench themselves), those responses were upheld. On the other hand, where the target board's response to a proxy contest (coupled with a hostile offer) was (i) to move the shareholders meeting to a later date to enable the incumbent board to solicit revocations of proxies to defeat the apparently victorious dissident group, or (ii) to expand the size of the board, and then fill the newly created positions so the incumbents would retain control of the board irrespective of the outcome of the proxy contest, those responses were declared invalid.

Another statutorily permissible defensive device – the "staggered" or classified board – was useful, but still of limited effectiveness. Because only one third of a classified board would stand for election each year, a classified board would delay – but not prevent – a hostile acquiror from obtaining control of the board, since a determined acquiror could wage a proxy contest and obtain control of two thirds of the target board over a two year period, as opposed to seizing control in a single election.

This litigation experience taught that a target board, facing a proxy contest joined with a hostile tender offer, could, in good faith, employ non-preclusive defensive measures to give the board time to explore transactional alternatives. The target board could not, however, erect defenses that would either preclude a proxy contest altogether or improperly bend the rules to favor the board's continued incumbency.

In this environment, the only defensive measure that promised to be a "show stopper" (i.e. had the potential to deter a proxy contest altogether) was a poison pill with a "dead hand" feature. The reason is that if only the incumbent directors or their designated successors could redeem the pill, it would make little sense for shareholders or the hostile bidder to wage a proxy contest to replace the incumbent board. Doing that would eliminate from the scene the only group of persons having the power to give the hostile bidder and target company shareholders what they desired: control of the target company (in the case of the hostile bidder) and the opportunity to obtain an attractive price for their shares (in the case of the target company stockholders). It is against that backdrop that the legal issues presented here, which concern the validity of the "dead hand" feature, attain significance.

B.   The contentions

[Text omitted]

III.   Analysis

A.   The "ripeness" and "derivative claim" defenses

1.   The ripeness argument

Because they are easily disposed of, the Court considers first the defendants' threshold arguments that (a) the plaintiff's claims are not ripe [i.e. an event or act causing damage has not yet occurred], but (b) even if ripe, the claims must be dismissed because they are derivative and, therefore, subject to the demand requirement of Court of Chancery Rule 23.1 [i.e. the shareholder must ask the corporation to take action, and if it does not, then go to court], which the plaintiff has not satisfied. Neither defense, in my view, has merit.

[Text omitted]

Stripped of its bells and whistles, this argument boils down to the proposition that the adoption of a facially invalid rights plan, on a "clear day" where there is no specific hostile takeover proposal, can never be the subject of a legal challenge. Not surprisingly, the defendants cite no authority which supports that proposition, nor could they, since the case law holds to the contrary.

In *Moran*, the defendants made, and this Court rejected, the same ripeness argument being advanced here ...

[Text omitted]

Here, as in *Moran*, the plaintiff complains of the Rights Plan's (specifically, its "dead hand" feature's) *present* depressing and deterrent effect upon the shareholders' interests, in particular, the shareholders' *present* entitlement to receive and consider takeover proposals and to vote for a board of directors capable of exercising the full array of powers provided by statute, including the power to redeem the poison pill. Because of their alleged *current* adverse impact, the plaintiff's claims of statutory and equitable invalidity are ripe for adjudication, for the reasons articulated by the Supreme Court in *Moran*.

2.   The "derivative claim" defense

Also misguided is the argument that the invalidity claims are derivative and must be dismissed under Rule 23.1 for failure to make a pre-suit demand or plead facts establishing that a demand would be futile. That argument lacks merit because the plaintiff's claims are individual, not derivative, and even if the claims were derivative, the complaint satisfies the requirements for demand excusal.

[Text omitted]

Even if the claims were regarded as derivative, the complaint's entrenchment allegations are sufficient to excuse compliance with the demand requirement. A demand is deemed excused if the complaint's particularized factual allegations create a reason to doubt that the board would consider the demand in a disinterested, impartial manner. The complaint in this case alleges in a particularized way that the Toll Brothers directors acted for entrenchment purposes. Under our case law, that is sufficient to excuse the requirement of a demand.

Having considered and rejected the threshold defenses, the Court turns to the crux of this case – the validity under Delaware law of the "dead hand" feature of the Toll Brothers Rights Plan.

B.   *The validity of the "dead hand" provision*

[Text omitted]

2.   The statutory invalidity claims

Having carefully considered the arguments and authorities marshaled by both sides, the Court concludes that the complaint states legally sufficient claims that the "dead hand" provision of the Toll Brothers Rights Plan violates 8 Del. C. §§ 141(a) and (d). There are three reasons.

First, it cannot be disputed that the Rights Plan confers the power to redeem the pill only upon some, but not all, of the directors. But under § 141(d), the power to create voting power distinctions among directors exists only where there is a classified board, and where those voting power distinctions are expressed in the certificate of incorporation. Section 141(d) pertinently provides:

> ... The certificate of incorporation may confer upon holders of any class or series of stock the right to elect 1 or more directors who shall serve for such term, and have such voting powers as shall be stated in the certificate of incorporation. The terms of office and voting powers of the directors elected in the manner so provided in the certificate of incorporation may be greater than or less than those of any other director or class of directors ...

The plain, unambiguous meaning of the quoted language is that if one category or group of directors is given distinctive voting rights not shared by the other directors, those distinctive voting rights must be set out in the certificate of incorporation. In the case of Toll Brothers (the complaint alleges), they are not.

Second, § 141(d) mandates that the "right to elect 1 or more directors who shall ... have such [greater] voting powers" is reserved to the stockholders, not to the directors or a subset thereof. Absent express language in the charter, nothing in Delaware law suggests that some directors of a public corporation may be created less equal than other directors, and certainly not by unilateral board action ... For that reason, and because it is claimed that the Rights Plan's allocation of voting power to redeem the Rights is nowhere found in the Toll Brothers certificate of incorporation, the complaint states a claim that the "dead hand" feature of the Rights Plan is *ultra vires*, and hence, statutorily invalid under Delaware law.

Third, the complaint states a claim that the "dead hand" provision would impermissibly interfere with the directors' statutory power to manage the business and affairs of the corporation. That power is conferred by 8 Del. C. § 141(a), which mandates:

> The business and affairs of every corporation organized under this chapter shall be managed by or under the direction of a board of directors, *except as may be otherwise provided in this chapter or in its certificate of incorporation* ... (emphasis added)

The "dead hand" poison pill is intended to thwart hostile bids by vesting shareholders with preclusive rights that cannot be redeemed except by the Continuing Directors. Thus, the one action that could make it practically possible to redeem the pill – replacing the entire board – could make that pill redemption legally impossible to achieve. The "dead hand" provision would jeopardize a newly elected future board's ability to achieve a business combination by depriving that board of the power to redeem the pill without obtaining the consent of the "Continuing Directors," who (it may be assumed) would constitute a minority of the board. In this manner, it is claimed, the "dead hand" provision would interfere with the board's power to protect fully the corporation's (and its shareholders') interests in a transaction that is one of the most fundamental and important in the life of a business enterprise.

The statutory analysis employed, and the result reached here, are consistent with and supported by *Bank of New York Co. v. Irving Bank Corp.* There, the New York Supreme Court invalidated a "continuing director" provision that the target company board had adopted as an amendment to a preexisting rights plan, as a defense against a tender offer/proxy contest initiated by a hostile bidder. The New York court observed that the continuing director provision at issue there created several different classes of directors having different powers, and that it also effectively limits the powers of the future board which is not a continuation of the present board or which is not approved by it, while still leaving those powers to a board which is approved. For example, the present board, or one approved by it, may redeem the rights. A future board, properly elected by a fifty-one percent majority, but not approved by the present board, may not redeem the shares.

Those observations apply equally here.

In *Bank of New York*, the court found that the continuing director provision violated the New York Business Corporation Law requirement that restrictions upon the board's powers are invalid, unless all the incorporators or all shareholders of record authorize the inclusion of the limitations or restrictions in the certificate of incorporation. Although the relevant language of the Delaware and New York statutes is not identical, their underlying intent is the same: both statutes require that limitations upon the directors' power be expressed in the corporation's charter. In *Bank of New York*, the rights plan was determined to be invalid because the target company's certificate of incorporation contained no such limitation. Neither (it is alleged) does the Toll Brothers certificate.

The defendants offer two arguments in response. First, they contend that the Rights Plan does not facially preclude or interfere with proxy contests as a means to gain control, or coerce shareholders to vote for or against any particular director slate. The second argument is that the "dead hand" provision is tantamount to a delegation to a special committee, consisting of the Continuing Directors, of the power to redeem the pill.

Neither contention has merit. The first is basically an argument that the Rights Plan does not violate any fiduciary duty of the board. That is unresponsive to the statutory invalidity claim. The second argument rests upon an analogy that has no basis in fact. In adopting the Rights Plan, the board did not, nor did it purport to, create a special committee having the exclusive power to redeem the pill. The analogy also ignores fundamental structural differences between the creation of a special board committee and the operation of the "dead hand" provision of the Rights Plan. The creation of a special committee would not impose long term structural power-related distinctions between different groups of directors of the same board. The board that creates a special committee may abolish it at any time, as could any successor board. On the other hand, the Toll Brothers "dead hand" provision, if legally valid, would embed structural power-related distinctions between groups of directors that no successor board could abolish until after the Rights expire in 2007.

For these reasons, the statutory invalidity claims survive the motion to dismiss.

3.   The fiduciary duty invalidity claims

Because the plaintiff's statutory invalidity claims have been found legally cognizable, the analysis arguably could end at this point. But the plaintiff also alleges that the board's adoption of the "dead hand" feature violated its fiduciary duty of loyalty. For the sake of completeness, that claim is addressed as well.

The duty of loyalty claim, to reiterate, has two prongs. The first is that the "dead hand" provision purposefully interferes with the shareholder voting franchise without any compelling justification, and is therefore unlawful under *Blasius*. The second is that the "dead hand" provision is a "disproportionate" defensive measure, because it either precludes or materially abridges the shareholders' rights to receive tender offers and to wage a proxy contest to replace the board. Under *Unocal/ Unitrin*, in such circumstances the board's approval of the "dead hand" provision would not enjoy the presumption of validity conferred by the business judgment review standard, and therefore would be found to constitute a breach of fiduciary duty.

I conclude, for the reasons next discussed, that both fiduciary duty claims are cognizable under Delaware law.

a) The Blasius fiduciary duty claim

The validity of antitakeover measures is normally evaluated under the *Unocal/ Unitrin* standard. But where the defensive measures purposefully disenfranchise shareholders, the board will be required to satisfy the more exacting *Blasius* standard, which our Supreme Court has articulated as follows:

> A board's unilateral decision to adopt a defensive measure touching "upon issues of control" that purposefully disenfranchises its shareholders is strongly suspect under *Unocal*, and cannot be sustained without a "compelling justification."

The complaint alleges that the "dead hand" provision purposefully disenfranchises the company's shareholders without any compelling justification. The disenfranchisement would occur because even in an election contest fought over the issue of the hostile bid, the shareholders will be powerless to elect a board that is both willing and able to accept the bid, and they "may be forced to vote for [incumbent] directors whose policies they reject because only those directors have the power to change them." [Note 40]

[Note 40] Jeffrey N. Gordon, *"Just Say Never" Poison Pills, Deadhand Pills and Shareholder Adopted By-Laws: An Essay for Warren Buffett*, 19 Cardozo Law Review 511, 540 (1997) (cited herein as "Gordon").

A claim that the directors have unilaterally "create[d] a structure in which shareholder voting is either impotent or self defeating" is necessarily a claim of purposeful disenfranchisement ... Those observations reflect the fundamental value that the shareholder vote has primacy in our system of corporate governance because it is the "ideological underpinning upon which the legitimacy of directorial power rests."

As former Chancellor Allen stated in *Sutton Holding Corp. v. DeSoto, Inc.*:

> Provisions in corporate instruments that are intended principally to restrain or coerce the free exercise of the stockholder franchise are deeply suspect. The shareholder vote is the basis upon which an individual serving as a corporate director must rest his or her claim to legitimacy. Absent quite extraordinary circumstances, in my opinion, it constitutes a fundamental offense to the dignity of this corporate office for a director to use corporate power to seek to coerce shareholders in the exercise of the vote.

The defendants contend that the complaint fails to allege a valid stockholder disenfranchisement claim, because the Rights Plan does not on its face limit a dissident's ability to propose a slate or the shareholders' ability to cast a vote. The defendants also urge that even if the Plan might arguably have that effect, it could occur only in a very specific and unlikely context, namely, where (i) the hostile bidder makes a fair offer that it is willing to keep open for more than one year, (ii) the current board refuses to redeem the Rights, and (iii) the offeror wages two successful proxy fights and is committed to wage a third.

This argument, in my opinion, begs the issue and is specious. It begs the issue because the complaint does not claim that the Rights Plan facially restricts the shareholders' voting rights. What the complaint alleges is that the "dead hand" provision will either preclude a hostile bidder from waging a proxy contest altogether, or, if there should be a contest, it will coerce those shareholders who desire the hostile offer to succeed to vote for those directors who oppose it – the incumbent (and "Continuing") directors. Besides missing the point, the argument is also specious, because the hypothetical case the defendants argue must exist for any disenfranchisement to occur, rests upon the unlikely assumption that the hostile bidder will keep its offer open for more than one year. Given the market risks inherent in financed hostile bids for public corporations, it is unrealistic to assume that many bidders would be willing to do that.

For these reasons, the plaintiff's *Blasius*-based breach of fiduciary duty claim is cognizable under Delaware law.

b) The Unocal/Unitrin fiduciary duty claim

The final issue is whether the complaint states a legally cognizable claim that the inclusion of the "dead hand" provision in the Rights Plan was an unreasonable defensive measure within the meaning of *Unocal*. I conclude that it does.

As a procedural matter, it merits emphasis that a claim under *Unocal* requires enhanced judicial scrutiny. In that context, the board has the burden to satisfy the Court that the board (1) "had reasonable grounds for believing that a danger to corporate policy and effectiveness existed," and (2) that its "defensive response was reasonable in relation to the threat posed." Such scrutiny is, by its nature, fact-driven and requires a factual record. For that reason, as the Supreme Court recently observed, enhanced scrutiny "will usually not be satisfied by resting on a defense motion merely attacking the pleadings." Only "conclusory complaints without well-pleaded facts [may] be dismissed early under Chancery Rule 12."

The complaint at issue here is far from conclusory. Under *Unitrin*, a defensive measure is disproportionate (i.e. unreasonable) if it is either coercive or preclusive. The complaint alleges that the "dead hand" provision "disenfranchises shareholders by forcing them to vote for incumbent directors or their designees if shareholders want to be represented by a board entitled to exercise its full statutory prerogatives." That is sufficient to claim that the "dead hand" provision is coercive. The complaint also alleges that that provision "makes an offer for the Company much more unlikely since it eliminates use of a proxy contest as a possible means to gain control ... [because] ... any directors elected in such a contest would still be unable to vote to redeem the pill;" and the provision "renders future contests for corporate control of Toll Brothers prohibitively expensive and effectively impossible." A defensive measure is preclusive if it makes a bidder's ability to wage a successful proxy contest and gain control either "mathematically impossible" or "realistically unattainable." These allegations are sufficient to state a claim that the "dead hand" provision makes a proxy contest "realistically unattainable," and therefore, disproportionate and unreasonable under *Unocal*.

IV.   Conclusion

The Court concludes that for the reasons discussed above, the complaint states claims under Delaware law upon which relief can be granted. Accordingly, the defendants' motion to dismiss is denied. IT IS SO ORDERED.

Revlon, Inc. v. MacAndrews & Forbes Holdings, Inc.
Supreme Court of Delaware
506 A 2d 173 (1986)
[*Text edited; some footnotes omitted*]

MOORE, Justice

In this battle for corporate control of Revlon, Inc. (Revlon), the Court of Chancery enjoined certain transactions designed to thwart the efforts of Pantry Pride, Inc. (Pantry Pride) to acquire Revlon. The defendants are Revlon, its board of directors, and Forstmann Little & Co. and the latter's affiliated limited partnership (collectively, Forstmann). The injunction barred consummation of an option granted Forstmann to purchase certain Revlon assets (the lock-up option), a promise by Revlon to deal exclusively with Forstmann in the face of a takeover (the no-shop provision), and the payment of a $25 million cancellation fee to Forstmann if the transaction was aborted. The Court of Chancery found that the Revlon directors had breached their duty of care by entering into the foregoing transactions and effectively ending an active auction for the company. The trial court ruled that such arrangements are not illegal *per se* under Delaware law, but that their use under the circumstances here was impermissible. We agree ... Thus, we granted this expedited interlocutory appeal to consider for the first time the validity of such defensive measures in the face of an active bidding contest for corporate control. Additionally, we address for the first time the extent to which a corporation may consider the impact of a takeover threat on constituencies other than shareholders ...

In our view, lock-ups and related agreements are permitted under Delaware law where their adoption is untainted by director interest or other breaches of fiduciary duty. The actions taken by the Revlon directors, however, did not meet this standard. Moreover, while concern for various corporate constituencies is proper when addressing a takeover threat, that principle is limited by the requirement that there be some rationally related benefit accruing to the stockholders. We find no such benefit here.

Thus, under all the circumstances we must agree with the Court of Chancery that the enjoined Revlon defensive measures were inconsistent with the directors' duties to the stockholders. Accordingly, we affirm.

I.

The somewhat complex maneuvers of the parties necessitate a rather detailed examination of the facts. The prelude to this controversy began in June 1985, when Ronald O. Perelman, chairman of the board and chief executive officer of Pantry Pride, met with his counterpart at Revlon, Michel C. Bergerac, to discuss a friendly acquisition of Revlon by Pantry Pride. Perelman suggested a price in the range of

$40–50 per share, but the meeting ended with Bergerac dismissing those figures as considerably below Revlon's intrinsic value. All subsequent Pantry Pride overtures were rebuffed, perhaps in part based on Mr. Bergerac's strong personal antipathy to Mr. Perelman.

Thus, on August 14, Pantry Pride's board authorized Perelman to acquire Revlon, either through negotiation in the $42-$43 per share range, or by making a hostile tender offer at $45. Perelman then met with Bergerac and outlined Pantry Pride's alternate approaches. Bergerac remained adamantly opposed to such schemes and conditioned any further discussions of the matter on Pantry Pride executing a standstill agreement prohibiting it from acquiring Revlon without the latter's prior approval.

On August 19, the Revlon board met specially to consider the impending threat of a hostile bid by Pantry Pride. [Note 3] At the meeting, Lazard Freres, Revlon's investment banker, advised the directors that $45 per share was a grossly inadequate price for the company. Felix Rohatyn and William Loomis of Lazard Freres explained to the board that Pantry Pride's financial strategy for acquiring Revlon would be through "junk bond" financing followed by a break-up of Revlon and the disposition of its assets. With proper timing, according to the experts, such transactions could produce a return to Pantry Pride of $60 to $70 per share, while a sale of the company as a whole would be in the "mid 50" dollar range. Martin Lipton, special counsel for Revlon, recommended two defensive measures: first, that the company repurchase up to 5 million of its nearly 30 million outstanding shares; and second, that it adopt a Note Purchase Rights Plan. Under this plan, each Revlon shareholder would receive as a dividend one Note Purchase Right (the Rights) for each share of common stock, with the Rights entitling the holder to exchange one common share for a $65 principal Revlon note at 12% interest with a one-year maturity. The Rights would become effective whenever anyone acquired beneficial ownership of 20% or more of Revlon's shares, unless the purchaser acquired all the company's stock for cash at $65 or more per share. In addition, the Rights would not be available to the acquiror, and prior to the 20% triggering event the Revlon board could redeem the rights for 10 cents each. Both proposals were unanimously adopted.

[Note 3] There were 14 directors on the Revlon board. Six of them held senior management positions with the company, and two others held significant blocks of its stock. Four of the remaining six directors were associated at some point with entities that had various business relationships with Revlon. On the basis of this limited record, however, we cannot conclude that this board is entitled to certain presumptions that generally attach to the decisions of a board whose majority consists of truly outside independent directors ...

Pantry Pride made its first hostile move on August 23 with a cash tender offer for any and all shares of Revlon at $47.50 per common share and $26.67 per preferred share, subject to (1) Pantry Pride's obtaining financing for the purchase, and (2) the Rights being redeemed, rescinded or voided.

The Revlon board met again on August 26. The directors advised the stockholders to reject the offer. Further defensive measures also were planned. On August 29, Revlon commenced its own offer for up to 10 million shares, exchanging for each share of common stock tendered one Senior Subordinated Note (the Notes) of $47.50 principal at 11.75% interest, due 1995, and one-tenth of a share of $9.00 Cumulative Convertible Exchangeable Preferred Stock valued at $100 per share. Lazard Freres opined that the notes would trade at their face value on a fully distributed basis. Revlon stockholders tendered 87% of the outstanding shares (approximately 33 million), and the company accepted the full 10 million shares on a *pro rata* basis. The new Notes contained covenants which limited Revlon's ability to incur additional debt, sell assets, or pay dividends unless otherwise approved by the "independent" (non-management) members of the board.

At this point, both the Rights and the Note covenants stymied Pantry Pride's attempted takeover. The next move came on September 16, when Pantry Pride announced a new tender offer at $42 per share, conditioned upon receiving at least 90% of the outstanding stock. Pantry Pride also indicated that it would consider buying less than 90%, and at an increased price, if Revlon removed the impeding Rights. While this offer was lower on its face than the earlier $47.50 proposal, Revlon's investment banker, Lazard Freres, described the two bids as essentially equal in view of the completed exchange offer.

The Revlon board held a regularly scheduled meeting on September 24. The directors rejected the latest Pantry Pride offer and authorized management to negotiate with other parties interested in acquiring Revlon. Pantry Pride remained determined in its efforts and continued to make cash bids for the company, offering $50 per share on September 27, and raising its bid to $53 on October 1, and then to $56.25 on October 7.

In the meantime, Revlon's negotiations with Forstmann and the investment group Adler & Shaykin had produced results. The Revlon directors met on October 3 to consider Pantry Pride's $53 bid and to examine possible alternatives to the offer. Both Forstmann and Adler & Shaykin made certain proposals to the board. As a result, the directors unanimously agreed to a leveraged buyout by Forstmann. The terms of this accord were as follows: each stockholder would get $56 cash per share; management would purchase stock in the new company by the exercise of their Revlon "golden parachutes"; [Note 5] Forstmann would assume Revlon's $475 million debt incurred by the issuance of the Notes; and Revlon would redeem the Rights and waive the Notes covenants for Forstmann or in connection with any other offer superior to Forstmann's. The board did not actually remove the covenants at the October 3 meeting, because Forstmann then lacked a firm commitment on its financing, but accepted the Forstmann capital structure, and indicated that the outside directors would waive the covenants in due course. Part of Forstmann's plan was to sell Revlon's Norcliff Thayer and Reheis divisions to American Home Products for $335 million. Before the merger, Revlon was to sell its cosmetics and fragrance division to Adler & Shaykin for $905 million. These transactions would facilitate the purchase by Forstmann or any other acquiror of Revlon.

[Note 5] In the takeover context "golden parachutes" generally are understood to be termination agreements providing substantial bonuses and other benefits for managers and certain directors upon a change in control of a company.

When the merger, and thus the waiver of the Notes covenants, was announced, the market value of these securities began to fall. The Notes, which originally traded near par, around 100, dropped to 87.50 by October 8. One director later reported (at the October 12 meeting) a "deluge" of telephone calls from irate noteholders, and on October 10 the Wall Street Journal reported threats of litigation by these creditors.

Pantry Pride countered with a new proposal on October 7, raising its $53 offer to $56.25, subject to nullification of the Rights, a waiver of the Notes covenants, and the election of three Pantry Pride directors to the Revlon board. On October 9, representatives of Pantry Pride, Forstmann and Revlon conferred in an attempt to negotiate the fate of Revlon, but could not reach agreement. At this meeting Pantry Pride announced that it would engage in fractional bidding and top any Forstmann offer by a slightly higher one. It is also significant that Forstmann, to Pantry Pride's exclusion, had been made privy to certain Revlon financial data. Thus, the parties were not negotiating on equal terms.

Again privately armed with Revlon data, Forstmann met on October 11 with Revlon's special counsel and investment banker. On October 12, Forstmann made a new $57.25 per share offer, based on several conditions. [Note 6] The principal demand was a lock-up option to purchase Revlon's Vision Care and National Health Laboratories divisions for $525 million, some $100-$175 million below the value ascribed to them by Lazard Freres, if another acquiror got 40% of Revlon's shares. Revlon also was required to accept a no-shop provision. The Rights and Notes covenants had to be removed as in the October 3 agreement. There would be a $25 million cancellation fee to be placed in escrow, and released to Forstmann if the new agreement terminated or if another acquiror got more than 19.9% of Revlon's stock. Finally, there would be no participation by Revlon management in the merger. In return, Forstmann agreed to support the par value of the Notes, which had faltered in the market, by an exchange of new notes. Forstmann also demanded immediate acceptance of its offer, or it would be withdrawn. The board unanimously approved Forstmann's proposal because: (1) it was for a higher price than the Pantry Pride bid, (2) it protected the noteholders, and (3) Forstmann's financing was firmly in place. [Note 7] The board further agreed to redeem the rights and waive the covenants on the preferred stock in response to any offer above $57 cash per share. The covenants were waived, contingent upon receipt of an investment banking opinion that the Notes would trade near par value once the offer was consummated.

[Note 6] Forstmann's $57.25 offer ostensibly is worth $1 more than Pantry Pride's $56.25 bid. However, the Pantry Pride offer was immediate, while the Forstmann proposal must be discounted for the time value of money because of the delay in approving the merger and consummating the transaction. The exact difference between the two bids was an unsettled point of contention even at oral argument.

[Note 7] Actually, at this time about $400 million of Forstmann's funding was still subject to two investment banks using their "best efforts" to organize a syndicate to provide the balance. Pantry Pride's entire financing was not firmly committed at this point either, although Pantry Pride represented in an October 11 letter to Lazard Freres that its investment banker, Drexel Burnham Lambert, was highly confident of its ability to raise the balance of $350 million. Drexel Burnham had a firm commitment for this sum by October 18.

Pantry Pride, which had initially sought injunctive relief from the Rights plan on August 22, filed an amended complaint on October 14 challenging the lock-up, the cancellation fee, and the exercise of the Rights and the Notes covenants. Pantry Pride also sought a temporary restraining order to prevent Revlon from placing any assets in escrow or transferring them to Forstmann. Moreover, on October 22, Pantry Pride again raised its bid, with a cash offer of $58 per share conditioned upon nullification of the Rights, waiver of the covenants, and an injunction of the Forstmann lock-up.

On October 15, the Court of Chancery prohibited the further transfer of assets, and eight days later enjoined the lock-up, no-shop, and cancellation fee provisions of the agreement. The trial court concluded that the Revlon directors had breached their duty of loyalty by making concessions to Forstmann, out of concern for their liability to the noteholders, rather than maximizing the sale price of the company for the stockholders' benefit ...

II.

To obtain a preliminary injunction, a plaintiff must demonstrate both a reasonable probability of success on the merits and some irreparable harm which will occur absent the injunction ... Additionally, the Court shall balance the conveniences of and possible injuries to the parties ...

A.

We turn first to Pantry Pride's probability of success on the merits. The ultimate responsibility for managing the business and affairs of a corporation falls on its board of directors ... In discharging this function the directors owe fiduciary duties of care and loyalty to the corporation and its shareholders. *Guth* v. *Loft, Inc.* ... These principles apply with equal force when a board approves a corporate merger ... and of course they are the bedrock of our law regarding corporate takeover issues ... While the business judgment rule may be applicable to the actions of corporate directors responding to takeover threats, the principles upon which it is founded – care, loyalty and independence – must first be satisfied ...

If the business judgment rule applies, there is a "presumption that in making a business decision the directors of a corporation acted on an informed basis, in good faith and in the honest belief that the action taken was in the best interests of the company." *Aronson* v. *Lewis* ... However, when a board implements anti-takeover measures there arises "the omnipresent specter that a board may be acting primarily in its own interests, rather than those of the corporation and its shareholders ..." *Unocal Corp.* v. *Mesa Petroleum Co.* ... This potential for conflict places upon the directors the burden of proving that they had reasonable grounds for believing there was a danger to corporate policy and effectiveness, a burden satisfied by a showing of good faith and reasonable investigation ... In addition, the directors must analyze the nature of the takeover and its effect on the corporation in order to ensure balance – that the responsive action taken is reasonable in relation to the threat posed ...

B.

The first relevant defensive measure adopted by the Revlon board was the Rights Plan, which would be considered a "poison pill" in the current language of corporate takeovers – a plan by which shareholders receive the right to be bought out by the corporation at a substantial premium on the occurrence of a stated triggering event. See generally *Moran* v. *Household International, Inc.* ... By 8 Del. C. §§ 141 and 122(13), the board clearly had the power to adopt the measure ... Thus, the focus becomes one of reasonableness and purpose.

The Revlon board approved the Rights Plan in the face of an impending hostile takeover bid by Pantry Pride at $45 per share, a price which Revlon reasonably concluded was grossly inadequate. Lazard Freres had so advised the directors, and had also informed them that Pantry Pride was a small, highly leveraged company bent on a "bust-up" takeover by using "junk bond" financing to buy Revlon cheaply, sell the acquired assets to pay the debts incurred, and retain the profit for itself. [Note 12] In adopting the Plan, the board protected the shareholders from a hostile takeover at a price below the company's intrinsic value, while retaining sufficient flexibility to address any proposal deemed to be in the stockholders' best interests.

[Note 12] As we noted in *Moran*, a "bust-up" takeover generally refers to a situation in which one seeks to finance an acquisition by selling off pieces of the acquired company, presumably at a substantial profit ...

To that extent the board acted in good faith and upon reasonable investigation. Under the circumstances it cannot be said that the Rights Plan as employed was unreasonable, considering the threat posed. Indeed, the Plan was a factor in causing Pantry Pride to raise its bids from a low of $42 to an eventual high of $58. At the time of its adoption the Rights Plan afforded a measure of protection consistent with the directors' fiduciary duty in facing a takeover threat perceived as detrimental to corporate interests. *Unocal* ... Far from being a "show-stopper," as the plaintiffs had contended in *Moran*, the measure spurred the bidding to new heights, a proper result of its implementation ...

Although we consider adoption of the Plan to have been valid under the circumstances, its continued usefulness was rendered moot by the directors' actions on October 3 and October 12. At the October 3 meeting the board redeemed the Rights conditioned upon consummation of a merger with Forstmann, but further acknowledged that they would also be redeemed to facilitate any more favorable offer. On October 12, the board unanimously passed a resolution redeeming the Rights in connection with any cash proposal of $57.25 or more per share. Because all the pertinent offers eventually equalled or surpassed that amount, the Rights clearly were no longer any impediment in the contest for Revlon. This mooted any question of their propriety under *Moran* or *Unocal*.

C.

The second defensive measure adopted by Revlon to thwart a Pantry Pride takeover was the company's own exchange offer for 10 million of its shares. The directors' general broad powers to manage the business and affairs of the corporation are augmented by the specific authority conferred under 8 Del. C. § 160(a), permitting the company to deal in its own stock ... However, when exercising that power in an effort to forestall a hostile takeover, the board's actions are strictly held to the fiduciary standards outlined in *Unocal*. These standards require the directors to determine the best interests of the corporation and its stockholders, and impose an enhanced duty to abjure any action that is motivated by considerations other than a good faith concern for such interests ...

The Revlon directors concluded that Pantry Pride's $47.50 offer was grossly inadequate. In that regard the board acted in good faith, and on an informed basis, with reasonable grounds to believe that there existed a harmful threat to the corporate enterprise. The adoption of a defensive measure, reasonable in relation to the threat posed, was proper and fully accorded with the powers, duties, and responsibilities conferred upon directors under our law ...

D.

However, when Pantry Pride increased its offer to $50 per share, and then to $53, it became apparent to all that the break-up of the company was inevitable. The Revlon board's authorization permitting management to negotiate a merger or buyout with a third party was a recognition that the company was for sale. The duty of the board had thus changed from the preservation of Revlon as a corporate entity to the maximization of the company's value at a sale for the stockholders' benefit. This significantly altered the board's responsibilities under the *Unocal* standards. It no longer faced threats to corporate policy and effectiveness, or to the stockholders' interests, from a grossly inadequate bid. The whole question of defensive measures became moot. The directors' role changed from defenders of the corporate bastion to auctioneers charged with getting the best price for the stockholders at a sale of the company.

III.

This brings us to the lock-up with Forstmann and its emphasis on shoring up the sagging market value of the Notes in the face of threatened litigation by their holders. Such a focus was inconsistent with the changed concept of the directors' responsibilities at this stage of the developments. The impending waiver of the Notes covenants had caused the value of the Notes to fall, and the board was aware of the noteholders' ire as well as their subsequent threats of suit. The directors thus made support of the Notes an integral part of the company's dealings with Forstmann, even though their primary responsibility at this stage was to the equity owners.

The original threat posed by Pantry Pride – the break-up of the company – had become a reality which even the directors embraced. Selective dealing to fend off a hostile but determined bidder was no longer a proper objective. Instead, obtaining the highest price for the benefit of the stockholders should have been the central theme guiding director action. Thus, the Revlon board could not make the requisite showing of good faith by preferring the noteholders and ignoring its duty of loyalty to the shareholders. The rights of the former already were fixed by contract ... The noteholders required no further protection, and when the Revlon board entered into an auction-ending lock-up agreement with Forstmann on the basis of impermissible considerations at the expense of the shareholders, the directors breached their primary duty of loyalty.

The Revlon board argued that it acted in good faith in protecting the noteholders because *Unocal* permits consideration of other corporate constituencies. Although such considerations may be permissible, there are fundamental limitations upon that prerogative. A board may have regard for various constituencies in discharging its responsibilities, provided there are rationally related benefits accruing to the stockholders ... However, such concern for non-stockholder interests is inappropriate when an auction among active bidders is in progress, and the object no longer is to protect or maintain the corporate enterprise but to sell it to the highest bidder.

Revlon also contended that by *Gilbert* v. *El Paso Co.* ... it had contractual and good faith obligations to consider the noteholders. However, any such duties are limited to the principle that one may not interfere with contractual relationships by improper actions. Here, the rights of the noteholders were fixed by agreement, and there is nothing of substance to suggest that any of those terms were violated. The Notes covenants specifically contemplated a waiver to permit sale of the company at a fair price. The Notes were accepted by the holders on that basis, including the risk of an adverse market effect stemming from a waiver. Thus, nothing remained for Revlon to legitimately protect, and no rationally related benefit thereby accrued to the stockholders. Under such circumstances we must conclude that the merger agreement with Forstmann was unreasonable in relation to the threat posed.

A lock-up is not *per se* illegal under Delaware law. Its use has been approved in an earlier case. *Thompson* v. *Enstar Corp.* ... Such options can entice other bidders to enter a contest for control of the corporation, creating an auction for the company and maximizing shareholder profit. Current economic conditions in the takeover market are such that a "white knight" like Forstmann might only enter the bidding for the target company if it receives some form of compensation to cover the risks and costs involved ... However, while those lock-ups which draw bidders into the battle benefit shareholders, similar measures which end an active auction and foreclose further bidding operate to the shareholders' detriment ...

Recently, the United States Court of Appeals for the Second Circuit invalidated a lock-up on fiduciary duty grounds similar to those here. *Hanson Trust* ... the court stated:

> In this regard, we are especially mindful that some lock-up options may be beneficial to the shareholders, such as those that induce a bidder to compete for control of a corporation, while others may be harmful, such as those that effectively preclude bidders from competing with the optionee bidder ...

In *Hanson Trust*, the bidder, Hanson, sought control of SCM by a hostile cash tender offer. SCM management joined with Merrill Lynch to propose a leveraged buy-out of the company at a higher price, and Hanson in turn increased its offer. Then, despite very little improvement in its subsequent bid, the management group sought a lock-up option to purchase SCM's two main assets at a substantial discount. The SCM directors granted the lock-up without adequate information as to the size of the discount or the effect the transaction would have on the company. Their action effectively ended a competitive bidding situation. The Hanson Court invalidated the lock-up because the directors failed to fully inform themselves about the value of a transaction in which management had a strong self-interest. "In short, the Board appears to have failed to ensure that negotiations for alternative bids were conducted by those whose only loyalty was to the shareholders." ...

The Forstmann option had a similar destructive effect on the auction process. Forstmann had already been drawn into the contest on a preferred basis, so the result of the lock-up was not to foster bidding, but to destroy it. The board's stated reasons for approving the transactions were: (1) better financing, (2) noteholder protection, and (3) higher price. As the Court of Chancery found, and we agree, any distinctions between the rival bidders' methods of financing the proposal were nominal at best, and such a consideration has little or no significance in a cash offer for any and all shares. The principal object, contrary to the board's duty of care, appears to have been protection of the noteholders over the shareholders' interests.

While Forstmann's $57.25 offer was objectively higher than Pantry Pride's $56.25 bid, the margin of superiority is less when the Forstmann price is adjusted for the time value of money. In reality, the Revlon board ended the auction in return for very little actual improvement in the final bid. The principal benefit went to the directors, who avoided personal liability to a class of creditors to whom the board owed no further duty under the circumstances. Thus, when a board ends an intense bidding contest on an insubstantial basis, and where a significant by-product of that action is to protect the directors against a perceived threat of personal liability for consequences stemming from the adoption of previous defensive measures, the action cannot withstand the enhanced scrutiny which *Unocal* requires of director conduct ...

In addition to the lock-up option, the Court of Chancery enjoined the no-shop provision as part of the attempt to foreclose further bidding by Pantry Pride ... The no-shop provision, like the lock-up option, while not *per se* illegal, is impermissible under the *Unocal* standards when a board's primary duty becomes that of an auctioneer responsible for selling the company to the highest bidder. The agreement to negotiate only with Forstmann ended rather than intensified the board's involvement in the bidding contest.

It is ironic that the parties even considered a no-shop agreement when Revlon had dealt preferentially, and almost exclusively, with Forstmann throughout the contest. After the directors authorized management to negotiate with other parties, Forstmann was given every negotiating advantage that Pantry Pride had been denied: cooperation from management, access to financial data, and the exclusive opportunity to present merger proposals directly to the board of directors. Favoritism for a white knight to the total exclusion of a hostile bidder might be justifiable when the latter's offer adversely affects shareholder interests, but when bidders make relatively similar offers, or dissolution of the company becomes inevitable, the directors cannot fulfill their enhanced *Unocal* duties by playing favorites with the contending factions. Market forces must be allowed to operate freely to bring the target's shareholders the best price available for their equity. Thus, as the trial court ruled, the shareholders' interests necessitated that the board remain free to negotiate in the fulfillment of that duty.

The court below similarly enjoined the payment of the cancellation fee, pending a resolution of the merits, because the fee was part of the overall plan to thwart Pantry Pride's efforts. We find no abuse of discretion in that ruling.

IV.

Having concluded that Pantry Pride has shown a reasonable probability of success on the merits, we address the issue of irreparable harm. The Court of Chancery ruled that unless the lock-up and other aspects of the agreement were enjoined, Pantry Pride's opportunity to bid for Revlon was lost. The court also held that the need for both bidders to compete in the marketplace outweighed any injury to Forstmann. Given the complexity of the proposed transaction between Revlon and Forstmann, the obstacles to Pantry Pride obtaining a meaningful legal remedy are immense. We are satisfied that the plaintiff has shown the need for an injunction to protect it from irreparable harm, which need outweighs any harm to the defendants.

V.

In conclusion, the Revlon board was confronted with a situation not uncommon in the current wave of corporate takeovers. A hostile and determined bidder sought the company at a price the board was convinced was inadequate. The initial defensive tactics worked to the benefit of the shareholders, and thus the board was able to sustain its *Unocal* burdens in justifying those measures. However, in granting an asset option lock-up to Forstmann, we must conclude that under all the circumstances the directors allowed considerations other than the maximization of shareholder profit to affect their judgment, and followed a course that ended the auction for Revlon, absent court intervention, to the ultimate detriment of its shareholders. No such defensive measure can be sustained when it represents a breach of the directors' fundamental duty of care ... In that context the board's action is not entitled to the deference accorded it by the business judgment rule. The measures were properly enjoined. The decision of the Court of Chancery, therefore, is AFFIRMED.

26

Special problems of leveraged buyouts

Required reading

EU: Second Company Law Directive, art. 23
D: AktG, §§ 56, 57, 71a, 71d, 291 III, 308, 311
UK: CA 2006, secs. 677–683
US: Uniform Fraudulent Transfer Act, §§ 1–8

Using the target's assets to pay for the purchaser's plans

I. Introduction

A. What is a leveraged acquisition?

In Chapters 24 and 25, we looked at the regulation of takeover offers, focusing on required disclosure and the timing and scope of bids, as well as the actions that boards may take to block such offers. This chapter turns to the special problems connected with bids that are financed with debt, particularly debt secured by the assets of the target corporation or assumed by the target when it is merged into a successful bidder. Such a leveraged acquisition is usually referred to as a "leveraged buyout" or LBO, and has been defined as "a shorthand expression describing a business practice wherein a company is sold to a small number of investors, typically including members of the company's management, under financial arrangements in which there is a minimum amount of equity and a maximum amount of debt."[1] The debt is usually incurred, secured or assumed by the target company itself. As we have discussed at length in Chapter 6, the word "leverage" refers to an increase in the proportion of fixed obligations (here, debt) in the capital structure to maximize the stream of earnings per share of the equity interests.[2] As explained in Chapter 16, when only a small number of investors

---

[1] *US* v. *Tabor Court Realty Corp.*, 803 F 2d 1288, 1304 (3rd Cir. 1986).
[2] Brealey, Myers and Allen (2006: 457–459).

participate in a company's profits, this maximizes the equity share held by each investor, which in turn increases the potential return for each investor from participating in governance to improve the management and thus the company's performance. Beyond this basic "participation/return ratio," if debt financing is used to decrease the number of outstanding shares, and the focused energies of few shareholders successfully improve the target's performance, the gains to those few will be increased at a "leveraged" or "geared" rate that is higher than 1:1 because equity fully participates in the profits once debt is serviced. Leveraging plays the characteristics of these two forms of corporate finance against each other to increase upside returns.[3] This makes leveraged buyouts doubly attractive.

The players in a leveraged acquisition would include at least the purchaser, its lender(s) and the target. Professors Douglas Baird and Thomas Jackson give a good example of the main problem of an LBO in the context of a transaction in which the target's own management buys out the company's public shareholders (this type of transaction is referred to as a "management buyout" or MBO):

> Assume that Firm owes its general creditors 4 million dollars and has no secured debt. Firm's managers decide to acquire it, and the old shareholders agree to sell their shares for 1 million dollars. The managers put up 200,000 dollars of their own money and borrow 800,000 dollars from Bank. They agree to give Bank, a security interest in all of Firm's assets to support the loan. The managers then proceed to use that money to buy the stock in the hands of all the shareholders. When the transaction is over, the managers own all the stock, the old shareholders are cashed out, and Firm has 4.8 million dollars in debt. The general creditors take a second priority position to Bank. As a result, the pool of assets available to satisfy their loans is 800,000 dollars smaller.[4]

B. Why do leveraged acquisitions concern regulators?

As Eilís Ferran pointed out in 2007: "From a company law perspective (which provides only a partial glimpse of the risks posed by the phenomenal growth of private equity-funded LBOs), classic agency problems are inherent in LBOs: managers who are liable to promote their own interests over those of the general body of shareholders; majority shareholders who are poised to exploit minorities; and controllers who may load their

---

[3] On the other hand, leverage also increases the negative effects of a decrease in earnings, and thus presents a real risk in the case that a buyout group is not successful in improving performance. Brealey, Myers and Allen (2006: 455–456).

[4] Baird and Jackson (1985: 850).

company with a heavy additional debt burden that could threaten the interests of the existing creditors and of employees."[5] In a 2006 discussion paper on private equity, the FSA added to this list risks of unclear ownership of economic risk, market manipulation, market access constraints and market opacity.[6] In the fallout of the 2008 financial crisis, we saw many of these risks materialize.

The incentives to engage in excessive "gearing" increase with the availability of cheap credit. It was therefore no surprise that, in the period between 2002 and 2006, when a combination of central bank policies, rising real estate values, accelerating distribution of debt through securitization and a revolution in credit support derivative instruments created an abundance of cheap credit, that the number and size of leveraged buyouts correspondingly increased.[7] Indeed, between 2004 and 2007, leveraged transactions in which a US company was acquired totaled approximately $535 billion, or over ten times the volume of comparable transactions between 1996 and 2003.[8] While these leveraged transactions created upside benefits for shareholders, they often threatened the soundness of the company to the disadvantage of unsecured creditors. In its 2006 paper, the FSA explained that "holders of public company debt without adequate covenant protection may find that the value of their debt falls significantly in the event of a private equity acquisition of the relevant company ... Private equity transactions that inject new debt into a capital structure can, in certain circumstances, lead to the subordination of existing debt."[9] Moreover, because a buyout often takes a company from being publicly listed to being privately held, it can pull the company under the "radar screen" of disclosure obligations and other safeguards covering public companies, thus introducing risks otherwise covered by the regulatory umbrella.

The exit from a purchased target also presents risks. Firms offered to the public after a buyout (referred to as a "reverse leveraged buyout" or RLBO) have a mean debt to asset ratio of 32.41 percent, some 16 percent higher than their industry median.[10] At the Davos World Economic Forum in 2007, UNI Global Union's General Secretary Philip Jennings "accused the

---

[5] Ferran (2007: 29–30).
[6] See the list in the FSA Discussion Paper, 06/06 (November 2006), pp. 6–9.
[7] See e.g. Committee on the Global Financial System of the Bank for International Settlements (2008: 20); and a very readable and well-documented account in Ferguson (2008: 259–274).
[8] Shivdasani and Wang (2009: 1).
[9] FSA Discussion Paper, 06/06 (November 2006), p. 36.
[10] Cao and Lerner (2009: 145, Table 4).

equity funds of crippling the businesses they buy with too much debt, fees and dividends and driving down working conditions to help pay for it all." He asserted, "It's like a slasher movie – you slash jobs, health, pensions and working conditions … Your philosophy is buy it, strip it and flip it."[11] Indeed, based on an analysis of nearly 500 public offerings of former LBOs on the US market between 1981 and 2003, Professors Jerry Cao and Josh Lerner made two significant findings in this respect. First, the operating income of RLBO firms held privately for more than one year is 5.27 percent higher than the industry-adjusted average of other IPOs, which confirms the improved governance expected with a reduction of shareholders.[12] Secondly, whilst those firms sold to the public within one year of the LBO do worse, Cao and Lerner point out that the differences are not statistically significant.[13] From this it would seem that arguments against LBOs with "quick flips" must primarily focus on the effects on labor and other corporate stakeholders rather than on the company's overall performance. In this respect, it is understandable why German law, in particular, requires significant disclosures on a transaction's effect on employees before a merger can take place. Beyond such routine regulation of mergers, however, each of our jurisdictions shows an awareness of the potential dangers of leveraged acquisitions, but the US and Europe display significant differences in their regulatory approaches.

When, in 2007, the actual value of the various instruments used to off-load and repackage debt was called into question and scores of the loans made to "sub-prime" borrowers with cheap credit became worthless, the rise of private equity halted and dramatically reversed. In a predictable over-reaction to the lending euphoria, credit tightened as the market fell, and governments worldwide stepped in to provide liquidity to the markets. The buyout market, which was relatively strong during the first three-quarters of 2008, virtually disappeared for a quarter after the collapse of the US investment bank Lehman Brothers in September 2008. For example, in the UK, the transaction value of the buyout market fell from a record of £46.5 billion in 2007 to £19.7 billion in 2008, with only £1.3 billion of the 2008 total attributable to the fourth quarter.[14]

---

[11] "Union Spotlight at Davos on Private Equity Raiders, 26/01/2007," available at www.uni-globalunion.org, under "UNI & Private Equity," "News."
[12] Cao and Lerner (2009: 145, Table 4).
[13] Cao and Lerner (2009: 149).
[14] Source: Centre for Management Buy-out and Private Equity (CMBOR) at Nottingham University Business School: www.nottingham.ac.uk/business/cmbor/Privateequity.html.

The 2008 financial crisis was addressed primarily through banking regulation and increased oversight of derivative instruments.[15] Company law must address the "excessive leverage" that arises when a company takes on burdensome debt in connection with a purchase of its own shares, regardless of the cause. Company law can address such purchases through capital maintenance rules to regulate the flow of company funds or checks on management actions through the fiduciary duties of management and controlling shareholders.

II.   EU and US regulation of leveraged acquisitions

A.   European Union

The EU rules are broad and prophylactic. They go to the funding source of leveraged acquisitions. The version of the Second Company Law Directive in force between 1977 and 2006 laid down a blanket rule that forbade the target from giving any form of loan or collateral for the purchase of its shares; following the 2006 amendment to the Directive, such "financial assistance" is now permitted, subject to a number of conditions.[16] Article 23 of the Directive, as amended, provides that a member state may flatly prohibit a public company from rendering financial assistance or may permit it to advance funds, make loans or provide security "with a view to the acquisition of its shares by a third party," on condition that:

- the general meeting approves each such transaction in advance by at least two-thirds of the outstanding capital;
- the board provides a report to such general meeting, stating the company's interest in the transaction, the conditions for the transaction, the risks for the company's liquidity and solvency, and the price at which the company's shares are to be acquired;
- the transaction takes place at fair market conditions;
- the amount advanced, loaned or provided as collateral may not reduce the target's net assets by more than the amount of distributable profits; and
- a reserve, unavailable for distribution, in the amount of the aggregate financial assistance, must be constituted as a liability on the company's balance sheet.[17]

---

[15] See e.g. the summary of necessary initiatives in International Monetary Fund (2009: 8–24).

[16] On the 2006 amendments to the Second Company Law Directive, see Wymeersch (2006).

[17] Art. 23 Second Company Law Directive.

The concerns regarding management conflicts of interest and potential damage to shareholders are addressed by the requirement that an informed supermajority of shareholders approve the transaction. The concern that minority shareholders could be damaged by a controlling shareholder is addressed by the fairness requirement, and the danger of damage to the target's creditors is addressed by the capital maintenance requirement and the constitution of a reserve. Although these rules are significantly more flexible than the earlier prophylactic prohibition, commentators still view them as overbroad.[18] As Wymeersch explains, "[o]ne can understand that board [sic] should not grant loans imprudently, but that is a general principle, and bears no relationship with the acquisition of shares in that company."[19] Along the same lines, Ferran points out that: "In the case … of financial assistance in the form of a loan to a counterparty with a strong credit rating, since the loan merely had the effect of substituting one asset for another, it had no implications with regard to distributable reserves. However, under the Directive, the condition appears to have the effect of requiring an increase in undistributable reserves by the amount of the loan, even where there is minimal risk of default."[20] This approach adopted by the Directive may not seem unreasonable given the fact that in most LBOs the buyer is a thinly capitalized special-purpose vehicle whose post-acquisition assets will consist only of the acquired shares in the target. However, while blanket rules significantly reduce the risk that the undesired transactions they are designed to control will occur, they can also reduce the benefits of desired transactions closely related to the latter. This effect is captured in the English expression "throwing the baby out with the bathwater."

B. United States

Rather than turning immediately to the implementation of the Second Directive in Germany and the UK, it well serves the comparative aims of this text to jump directly from article 23 to the US (non)regulation of leveraged acquisitions. Article 23 follows the money to the source of the leveraged transaction: once the transfer of funds (whether as advance, loan or security) from the target is prohibited or tightly regulated, no financial assistance can occur without safeguards, and thus the regulation

---

[18] Ferran (2007: 26) finds the amended art. 23 to be "onerous" and "excessively cautious." Wymeersch (2006: 22) concludes that art. 23 in its current form is "burdened by considerable restrictions and raises a number of serious questions."

[19] Wymeersch (2006: 10).

[20] Ferran (2007: 26).

has caught and contained potential abuses. Every drop of the bathwater is cleaned out, even that clinging to the baby; using a different metaphor, Ferran calls financial assistance "too blunt an instrument."[21]

The alternative to an *ex ante* blanket rule is a network of *ex post* remedial rules addressing undesired effects. The US regulation of leveraged acquisitions takes this latter route. By shifting regulation to the *ex post* stage, US federal and state law can leave companies free to engage in the forms of financing they find most beneficial, while eliminating only those effects that turn out to be damaging. The disadvantage of this strategy is that relief often only follows damage and sometimes damage is not remedied at all.

As we saw, a principal concern of leveraged acquisitions is their potential impact on unsecured creditors. This concern could be addressed by imposing a fiduciary duty of the board to such creditors when contemplating a transaction. Indeed, as we read in the last chapter in *Revlon v. MacAndrews & Forbes Holdings*, under Delaware law "concern for various corporate constituencies is proper when addressing a takeover."[22] However, when the board of Revlon favored one bid over another because of the differing effects of the two bids on creditors, the court found that because the rights of creditors were protected by contract the board should not take action to protect creditors if it has no benefit for the shareholders.[23] This shows that protection of creditors against leveraged transactions through the fiduciary duties of the board is not a perfect solution, particularly when there are various constituencies competing for the board's protection.

If the main concern is that a company will take on debt in a leveraged transaction and be unable to pay its creditors, a possibility would be to allow bankruptcy trustees to unwind such transactions in the liquidation proceedings. This is the process discussed in *Moody v. Security Pacific Credit Business, Inc.* What, according to the court in *Moody*, is the rule under the Uniform Fraudulent Conveyance Act (now the Uniform Fraudulent Transfer Act)? How does this relate to the rules under the US Bankruptcy Code? Do you agree with the court's finding?

Moody repeatedly refers to the *Tabor Court Realty* case. In that case, a leveraged transaction was invalidated as a fraudulent conveyance. The transaction was essentially an MBO conducted through an acquisition vehicle, in which loans secured by mortgages were made by the target's

---

[21] Ferran (2007: 27).   [22] *Revlon*, 506 A 2d 173, 176 (1986).
[23] *Revlon*, 506 A 2d 173, 182 (1986).

subsidiaries. That transaction structure did not essentially differ from the transaction analyzed in *Moody*, yet the court struck it down while upholding that in *Moody*. This is because, unlike the analysis of financial assistance under UK law as performed in *Brady* v. *Brady*, neither the transaction structure nor the intent to provide financing for a share purchase is determinative. Rather, under this US analysis, the actual and foreseeable financial condition of the lender at the time of the transaction decides the case. As the court remarks in *Tabor Court Realty*, at the instant the transaction was entered into, "the cash that could be generated by the operation of the [target's] business was grossly insufficient to meet its obligations."[24] The US approach does not screen out dangerous transactions, but attempts through *ex post* analysis to determine whether the damage that the creditors of a failed company suffer is caused by the leveraged transaction, which would then render it "fraudulent" and therefore voidable.

Since leveraged acquisitions are often complex and create an opportunity for insiders to mislead outside participants with respect to the transaction, another approach is to focus on disclosure. In fact, article 23 of the Second Directive requires directors to prepare a report on the details of a proposed transaction. A similar approach is taken under US law when the nature of the transaction and the companies involved trigger disclosure obligations under the federal securities laws. In *Dasho* v. *Susquehanna Corporation*,[25] managing shareholders of Susquehanna arranged to cash out their holdings by causing a purchase vehicle to buy their shares at an inflated price with the proceeds of a loan, and then merged the vehicle into Susquehanna, whereby the latter assumed the obligations under the loan contract, in effect paying for the share purchase. Outside shareholders filed a derivative suit claiming that Susquehanna as a purchaser of the securities had been the victim of a scheme to defraud prohibited by § 10 of the Exchange Act and § 17 of the Securities Act because the true nature of the transaction was hidden; the court affirmed that the plaintiffs had a cause of action to go forward with their claim.[26] Because the anti-fraud provisions apply to companies regardless of whether they are registered with the SEC, US law thus also offers an *ex post* avenue of relief for minority shareholders who received information disguising the leveraged nature of a transaction.

In sum, although US law has no rules on financial assistance, it does offer the possibility of challenging leveraged transactions as a breach of

---

[24] *US* v. *Tabor Court Realty*, 803 F 2d 1288, 1304 (1986).
[25] 380 F 2d 262 (7th Cir. 1967).   [26] 380 F 2d 262, 270 (1967).

fiduciary duty, a fraudulent transfer or a scheme to defraud, depending upon the facts of the case. As always when deciding whether a given activity should be addressed *ex ante* or *ex post*, one must balance the value of the activity and the degree to which it is inhibited by *ex ante* regulation against the costs to society of allowing damaging transactions to go forward unchecked. The policy decision will always depend on the available facts, and a position taken in 2006 (at the height of the LBO boom) would differ significantly from one taken in 2007 (at the height of the sub-prime crisis) and from one taken in 2010 (when the dust has somewhat settled on that particular phase of history). The following discussion of the law and practice in our two European jurisdictions offers more details to flesh out our balancing of these concerns.

III.   Law and practice in Germany and the UK

A.   Germany

The *Aktiengesetz* incorporates the pre-2006 version of article 23 as a prohibition of transactions aimed at circumventing restrictions on share repurchases. Section 71a of the *Aktiengesetz* provides that: "A transaction through which a company advances funds, makes a loan, or provides security to a third party for the purpose of acquiring the issuer's shares is void." This straightforward prophylactic rule contains no exceptions other than loans made by banks in the ordinary course of business. As with any rule of law, the scope of the rule's applicability depends upon the meaning of its terms in the context of individual cases. For example, if an AG were to provide security for a purchase of convertible bonds, this could lead to the purchaser acquiring the AG's shares, but would it be "for the purpose of acquiring" such shares? Unless there is a clear intention to acquire shares through the convertibles, such a transaction would not be covered by § 71a.[27]

A more interesting example, which we have already seen in our discussion of corporate groups, is the applicability of § 71a to transactions within a corporate group, which in Germany are regulated by specific sections (§§ 291–328) of the *Aktiengesetz*. For example, § 291 of the *Aktiengesetz* provides for domination arrangements within a corporate group in which one company may completely control another or the entire profits of the second company are transferred to the dominating company. This section expressly overrides the capital maintenance rules in § 57 of the

---

[27] Cahn, in Spindler and Stilz (2010: § 71a mn. 32).

Aktiengesetz.[28] Because the purpose of the financial assistance rules, like that of § 57, is to protect the integrity of the company's capital, the express allowances of § 291 also escape the prohibition of § 71a.[29] In a *de facto* corporate group where no express domination agreement has been signed, a similar situation arises. Do you think the specialized rules on corporate groups should replace the more general provisions of § 71a? On the other hand, where there is no express statutory statement that the rules on groups supersede those on capital maintenance, do you think that the protection afforded by the financial assistance rule – especially as it is meant to catch transactions designed to evade the capital maintenance rules – should be displaced?[30]

A report on leveraged acquisitions prepared for the European Private Equity and Venture Capital Association explains that, because the rules on financial assistance do not apply to the GmbH form, it is possible to circumvent them by transforming a target AG into a GmbH before using its assets to pay off the debt incurred for the takeover. As § 71a is designed to catch such circumventing transactions, do you think it should be interpreted to catch financial assistance provided within a certain amount of time after such transformations? What arguments speak against such an interpretation?

B.   United Kingdom

The UK has been home to the prohibition of financial assistance since 1928, and it was from UK law that the Second Directive took financial assistance in 1977.[31] Thus, the prohibition in section 678(1) of the Companies Act 2006 looks very much like the pre-2006 Second Directive:

> Where a person is acquiring or proposing to acquire shares in a public company, it is not lawful for that company, or a company that is a subsidiary of that company, to give financial assistance directly or indirectly for the purpose of the acquisition before or at the same time as the acquisition takes place.

As the wording indicates, the prohibition applies to *public* companies only. Beyond its inapplicability to private companies, perhaps the most important exceptions are when the "principal purpose" of the transaction is not that of acquiring shares or the acquisition of shares "is only an incidental

---

[28] § 291(3) AktG.   [29] §§ 71a(1), 291(3) AktG.
[30] See Cahn, in Spindler and Stilz (2010: § 71a mn. 22).
[31] Ferran (2008: 267–269).

part of some larger purpose."[32] Although the current Companies Act was not in force when the House of Lords decided *Brady* v. *Brady*, the "principal purpose" exception addressed by the court is essentially the same as that in the current Act. On what evidence does the court rely in making its assessment? Does the court interpret the exception broadly or narrowly?

As in Germany, a leveraged acquisition may avoid the rules on financial assistance by transforming a public into a private company before tapping its assets. Another technique would be to have the target provide assistance for a purchase of its *assets* rather than its stock. As a violation of the rule against financial assistance can subject a director to a fine and imprisonment of up to two years, do you agree that the weight of the prohibition matches the dangers that such transactions present for creditors, shareholders and employees?

Questions for discussion

1. Article 23 of the Second Directive is situated amidst the provisions on share repurchases; the official heading of § 71a is "Avoidance Transactions" (*Umgehungsgeschäfte*). Do you agree that the rules on financial assistance really prevent illegal share repurchases?
2. Would a takeover structured to employ financial assistance (a typical LBO) make the bid less attractive for the shareholders of a target company? What group of stakeholders are most negatively affected?
3. How do the previous UK rules on financial assistance discussed in *Brady* compare to those now found in the Companies Act 2006? Do the rules of the Companies Act go as far as permitted by article 23 of the revised Second Directive?
4. Does use of a fraudulent conveyance statute discussed in *Moody* achieve the same ends as a prohibition of financial assistance? What are the costs and benefits of the two techniques?
5. Do you agree with the decision reached in *Moody* regarding the relationship between the debts assumed by the Jeanette Corp. and its eventual bankruptcy? Would the EU rules have addressed this transaction more effectively?
6. When using a fraudulent conveyance rule, do you think that a loan should be invalidated if funds are used indirectly by a person other than the lender to purchase the company's shares?

---

[32] Sec. 678(2) CA 2006. Further "exceptions" are for transactions other than leveraged acquisitions, such as dividends or purchases for an employee share plan: sec. 682(2) CA 2006.

7. A "leveraged buyout" concentrates voting power in the hands of knowledgeable, active and often managing owners. Given this benefit, should LBOs be exempted from rules against financial assistance or fraudulent conveyances?

8. Are the following transactions caught by the ban on financial assistance?

   (a) T buys an asset at market value from P, who then uses the proceeds to acquire T's shares.

   (b) T sells part of its business to a third party to lower the price P must pay for T's shares.

   (c) T loans P the purchase price of bonds convertible into T's shares.

   (d) T loans P the purchase price of options to buy T's shares.

   (e) T loans P the purchase price for a majority holding in T's parent corporation.

   (f) P sets up a shell corporation, which issues high-yield bonds, and uses the issue proceeds to buy T's shares; P then transfers the acquired shares to the shell as collateral for the bonds.

   (g) P sets up a shell corporation, which obtains a bank loan to purchase 90 percent of T's shares. Upon completion of the purchase, P causes shell to merge into T.

Cases

Brady v. Brady
House of Lords
[1989] AC 755
Reproduced with permission of the Incorporated Council of Law Reporting for England and Wales
[*Text edited; references omitted*]

LORD OLIVER OF AYLMERTON

[*Editors' summary of facts*: The parties were shareholders of a family business consisting of a parent company, T. Brady & Sons Ltd (Brady), and several subsidiaries, operating in both the hauling and the soft-drink business. Because of irreconcilable personal differences between the shareholders, the appellants Jack and Robert on the one hand and the respondents Bob and John on the other hand, a management deadlock occurred. To save the business, the parties resolved to divide it up so that two of the shareholders would own the hauling business and the other two would own the soft drink business. To achieve this result, they worked out a complicated scheme of reorganisation and implemented it in part. They first created a new company (Ovalshield) and transferred all their holdings in the existing companies to it in return for Ovalshield shares. Next they created two holding companies: Motoreal (for the hauling business) and Activista (for the soft-drink business). Motoreal purchased from Ovalshield all the shares in the former principal hauling company (Brady) in exchange for, *inter alia*, over £600,000 of unsecured debentures (redeemable loan stock). Activista then issued shares to Ovalshield in return for, *inter alia*, the Motoreal debentures. Thus, after this, Motoreal owed Activista more than £600,000. This debt was to be discharged by transfering assets from Brady, Motoreal's new subsidiary, to Activista. The transfer would be reflected in a £600,000 indebtedness of Motoreal to Brady. After rebutting the respondents' argument that the reorganisation was *ultra vires* and amounted to waste, Lord Aylmerton set out his opinion as follows:]

My Lords, it follows from what I have said [that the transaction was not a mere waste and thus *ultra vires*] that if the appellants' claim is to be successfully resisted at all, it can only be on the ground that the transaction proposed infringes the provisions of section 151 of the Act of 1985. Subsections (1) and (2) of section 151[33] provide:

> (1) Subject to the following provisions of this chapter, where a person is acquiring or is proposing to acquire shares in a company, it is not lawful for the company or any of its subsidiaries to give financial assistance directly or indirectly for the purpose of that acquisition before or at the same time as the acquisition takes place.
> (2) Subject to those provisions, where a person has acquired shares in a company and any liability has been incurred (by that or any other person), for the purpose of that acquisition, it is not lawful for the company or any of its subsidiaries to give financial assistance directly or indirectly for the purpose of reducing or discharging the liability so incurred.

The acquisition of the Brady shares by Motoreal has already taken place and has given rise to the issue of the loan stock to Activista. The proposed transfer therefore falls within the provisions of subsection (2) and it is not in dispute that it does indeed constitute the provision of assistance by Brady to reduce Motoreal's liability incurred in the course of that acquisition. The appellants, however, rely upon the provisions of section 153(2)[34] which is in the following terms:

> Section 151(2) does not prohibit a company from giving financial assistance if:
>
> (a) the company's principal purpose in giving the assistance is not to reduce or discharge any liability incurred by a person for the purpose of the acquisition of shares in the company or its holding company, or the reduction or discharge of any such liability is but an incidental part of some larger purpose of the company, and
> (b) the assistance is given in good faith in the interests of the company.

[Text omitted]

Where I part company both from the trial judge and from the Court of Appeal is on the question of whether paragraph (a) can, on any reasonable construction

---

[33] See sec. 678(1), (3) CA 2006.   [34] See sec. 678(2) CA 2006.

of the subsection, be said to have been satisfied. As O'Connor LJ observed [1988] BCLC 20, 25, the section is not altogether easy to construe. It first appeared as part of section 42 of the Companies Act 1981 and it seems likely that it was introduced for the purpose of dispelling any doubts resulting from the query raised in *Belmont Finance Corporation Ltd* v. *Williams Furniture Ltd* (No. 2) [1980] 1 All ER 393 whether a transaction entered into partly with a genuine view to the commercial interests of the company and partly with a view to putting a purchaser of shares in the company in funds to complete his purchase was in breach of section 54 of the Companies Act 1948. The ambit of the operation of the section is, however, far from easy to discern, for the word "purpose" is capable of several different shades of meaning. This much is clear, that paragraph (a) is contemplating two alternative situations. The first envisages a principal and, by implication, a subsidiary purpose. The inquiry here is whether the assistance given was principally in order to relieve the purchaser of shares in the company of his indebtedness resulting from the acquisition or whether it was principally for some other purpose – for instance, the acquisition from the purchaser of some asset which the company requires for its business. That is the situation envisaged by Buckley LJ in the course of his judgment in the *Belmont Finance* case as giving rise to doubts. That is not this case, for the purpose of the assistance here was simply and solely to reduce the indebtedness incurred by Motoreal on issuing the loan stock. The alternative situation is where it is not suggested that the financial assistance was intended to achieve any other object than the reduction or discharge of the indebtedness but where that result (i.e. the reduction or discharge) is merely incidental to some larger purpose of the company. Those last three words are important. What has to be sought is some larger overall corporate purpose in which the resultant reduction or discharge is merely incidental. The trial judge found Brady's larger purpose to be that of freeing itself from the deadlock and enabling it to function independently and this was echoed in the judgment of O'Connor LJ [1988] BCLC 20, 26 where he observed that the answer "embraces avoiding liquidation, preserving its goodwill and the advantages of an established business." Croom-Johnson LJ found the larger purpose in the reorganisation of the whole group. My Lords, I confess that I have not found the concept of a "larger purpose" easy to grasp, but if the paragraph is to be given any meaning that does not in effect provide a blank cheque for avoiding the effective application of section 151 in every case, the concept must be narrower than that for which the appellants contend.

The matter can, perhaps, most easily be tested by reference to section 153(1)(a) where the same formula is used. Here the words are "or the giving of the assistance for that purpose" (i.e. the acquisition of shares) "is but an incidental part of some larger purpose of the company." The words "larger purpose" must here have the same meaning as the same words in subsection (2)(a). In applying subsection (1) (a) one has, therefore, to look for some larger purpose in the giving of financial assistance than the mere purpose of the acquisition of the shares and to ask whether the giving of assistance is a mere incident of that purpose. My Lords, "purpose" is, in some contexts, a word of wide content but in construing it in the context of the fasciculus of sections regulating the provision of finance by a company in connection with the purchase of its own shares there has always to be borne in mind the mischief against which section 151 is aimed. In particular, if the section is not, effectively, to be deprived of any useful application, it is important to distinguish between a purpose and the reason why a purpose is formed. The ultimate reason for forming the purpose of financing an acquisition may, and in most cases probably will, be more important to those making the decision than the immediate transaction itself. But "larger" is not the same thing as "more important" nor is "reason" the same as "purpose." If one postulates the case of a bidder for control of a public company financing his bid from the company's own funds – the obvious mischief at which the section is aimed – the immediate purpose which it is sought to achieve is that of completing the purchase and vesting control of the company in the bidder. The reasons why that course is considered desirable may be many and varied. The company may have fallen on hard times so that a change of management is considered necessary to avert disaster. It may merely be thought, and no doubt would be thought by the purchaser and the directors whom he nominates once he has control, that the business of the company will be more profitable under his management than it was heretofore. These may be excellent reasons but they cannot, in my judgment, constitute a "larger purpose" of which the provision of assistance is merely an incident. The purpose and the only purpose of the financial assistance is and remains that of enabling the shares to be acquired and the financial or commercial advantages flowing from the acquisition, whilst they may form the reason for forming the purpose of providing assistance, are a by-product of it rather than an independent purpose of which the assistance can properly be considered to be an incident.

Now of course in the instant case the reason why the reorganisation was conceived in the first place was the damage being occasioned to the company and its shareholders by reason of the management deadlock, and the deadlock was the reason for the decision that the business should be split in two, so that the two branches could be conducted independently. What prompted the particular method adopted for carrying out the split was the commercial desirability of keeping Brady in being as a corporate entity. That involved, in effect, Jack buying out Bob's interest in Brady and it was, presumably, the fact that he did not have free funds to do this from his own resources that dictated that Brady's own assets should be used for the purpose. No doubt the acquisition of control by Jack was considered, at any rate by Jack and Robert, who were and are Brady's directors, to be beneficial to Brady. Indeed your Lordships have been told that the business has thriven under independent management. But this is merely the result, and no doubt the intended result, of Jack's assumption of control and however one analyses the transaction the only purpose that can be discerned in the redemption of loan stock is the payment in tangible form of the price payable to enable the Brady shares to be acquired and ultimately vested in Jack or a company controlled by him. The scheme of reorganisation was framed and designed to give Jack and Robert control of Brady for the best of reasons, but to say that the "larger purpose" of Brady's financial assistance is to be found in the scheme of reorganisation itself is to say only that the larger purpose was the acquisition of the Brady shares on their behalf. For my part, I do not think that a larger purpose can be found in the benefits considered to be likely to flow or the disadvantages considered to be likely to be avoided by the acquisition which it was the purpose of the assistance to facilitate. The acquisition was not a mere incident of the scheme devised to break the deadlock. It was the essence of the scheme itself and the object which the scheme set out to achieve. In my judgment therefore, subsection (2)(a) of section 153 is not satisfied and if the matter rested there the appeal ought to fail on that ground.

That is a conclusion which I reach with a measure of regret, for the bargain between the appellants and the respondents was freely negotiated and the respondents' attempt to resile from it is not immediately attractive. It is, however, a conclusion which makes it necessary to consider two additional points which the appellants have sought leave to raise in their written case, neither of which was raised either at the trial or in the Court of Appeal but each of which, it is claimed, would be sufficient to dispose of any objection to specific performance based upon section 151.

[Text omitted]

... where an agreement can be performed in alternative ways, one lawful and one unlawful, it is to be presumed that the parties intend to carry it out in the lawful and not the unlawful manner. In the instant case, when clause 15 of the letter of 2 December speaks of the parties taking "all steps necessary to complete the remaining stages of the reorganisation," this must be construed as obliging them, assuming this to be possible within the framework of what has been agreed, to complete those steps in a lawful manner. I emphasise the words "within the framework of what has been agreed" because they dispose, in my judgment, of Mr. Sykes's first point. It has not been contended that the reorganisation agreed upon was upon any other basis than that of the creation of the Motoreal indebtedness nor is it in contest that it was for the implementation of that scheme and that scheme alone that the necessary revenue clearances were to be obtained. Mr. Sykes's first contention involves a departure from the scheme. It is, he submits, clear that both Brady and Athersmith [*Editors' note*: A subsidiary of Brady] had undistributed profits from which a dividend in specie could lawfully be declared of the assets specified in the letter of 2 December. Motoreal could then apply the dividend in discharging the loan stock held by Activista and the transaction would not infringe section 151 because section 153(3) specifically provides that section 151 does not prohibit a distribution of a company's assets by way of dividend lawfully made. Thus the transfer contemplated could, at the time of the agreement, be perfectly lawfully made in this way. This is incontestible but the short answer to it is that it was not what was agreed between the parties and that it involves the consequence that, in the absence of a fresh revenue clearance which, it is common ground, has not been obtained, the individual shareholders in Ovalshield will suffer tax on the dividends. It is unnecessary, therefore, to consider this point further.

The second point, however, is a much more formidable one and, for my part, I can see no answer to it nor has Mr. Price suggested any. It is simply this, that since all the companies concerned are private companies the transaction can be perfectly lawfully carried out in the manner contemplated without any departure from the agreed terms. The accounts for the years 1983 and 1984 demonstrate that both Brady and Athersmith were fully solvent at all material times. Your Lordships have not seen accounts for any year subsequent to 1984 but have been told (and this has not been controverted) that the business of the haulage group has shown consistent improvement since it came under Jack's and Robert's management. There is no reason to believe that sufficient distributable profits to cover the proposed transfers either have been since 1984 or are now unavailable in Brady. In that situation, the directors of Brady (who, of course, are individually parties to the agreement of which specific performance is sought) are and have at all material times been able to ensure that the scheme of reorganisation can be lawfully carried out precisely in the manner agreed without any infringement of the provisions of section 151. This can quite simply be done by operating the provisions of section 155, 156 and 158 of the Act of 1985, which have the effect of disapplying the provisions of section 151. This is a matter which lies entirely in their hands and which does not involve the respondents in doing or concurring in the doing of anything which they have not agreed to do.

It is unnecessary, for present purposes, to set out the statutory provisions in full. In summary they provide that, where financial assistance is provided by a private company in connection with the acquisition of its shares or the shares of its parent company (being also a private company) the prohibitions in section 151 can be disapplied in certain circumstances by the adoption of the statutory procedure prescribed in sections 156, 157 and 158. These provisions apply only if either the assets of the company providing the assistance are not reduced by the provision of assistance or if the assistance is provided out of distributable profits: section 155(2). Provision is made for the rendering of assistance to be approved by special resolution (which may be cancelled by the court on application by a dissentient minority) but this does not apply where the company giving the assistance is (as each of Brady and Athersmith is) the wholly owned subsidiary of the company to which assistance is given. All that is required to avoid the prohibitions contained in section 151 is that the directors of the company giving the assistance (in this case the directors both of Brady and Athersmith) shall make a statutory declaration in a prescribed form to the effect that there is no ground upon which, immediately following the giving of the assistance, it could be found to be unable to pay its debts and that it will be able to pay its debts as they fall due during the year immediately following that date: section 156(2). There has also to be annexed to the statutory declaration a report by the auditors stating that, after due inquiry, they are not aware of anything to indicate that the opinion expressed by the directors in the declaration is unreasonable: section 156(4). These documents have to be delivered to the Registrar of Companies within 15 days after the making of the declaration and the assistance must be given, if given at all, within eight weeks from the date on which the declaration is made: section 158.

There can, in my judgment, be no doubt that in the absence of some startling change in the financial position of either Brady or Athersmith since the date of the last accounts, the conditions specified in section 155(2) are fulfilled. Whilst the proposed transfer will have the effect of reducing the net worth of Motoreal, since although the amount of its liabilities will remain unchanged, the underlying assets will be reduced by the value of the assets transferred out of the Motoreal group, the net assets of Brady and Athersmith as opposed to those of the Motoreal group, remain unchanged. I have already pointed out that there is, for instance, no reason to doubt the ability of Motoreal to pay its prospective indebtedness to Athersmith, if required, which would justify treating the debt as not worth its face value. The same applies to Brady, but even if it did not and even if the debt fell to be treated as worth less than its face value or should prove to be irrecoverable in toto, the amount of Brady's distributable accumulated profits is ample to cover the value of the Brady assets to be transferred. Compliance with the remaining provisions of sections 155, 156 and 158 rests, therefore, entirely in the hands of Jack and Robert and assuming that the company's auditors are able to make the report required by section 156(4) there can be no impediment to reliance upon these provisions. The evidence before the judge of Mr. Lewis of Binder Hamlyn, who were then Brady's auditors clearly indicates that such a report could properly have been given both at the date of the agreement and at the date of the trial and there is no reason to doubt that it can still be given. If this is right, then there appears to be – and indeed, always to have been – a complete answer to the suggestion that the agreement is rendered unlawful by section 151 of the Act of 1985 and therefore incapable of specific performance, though clearly any decree of specific performance would have to contain appropriate conditions or undertakings to ensure that the provisions of sections 156 and 158 are complied with. Subject to this, therefore, I would allow the appeal but only upon the terms previously indicated.

As regards the mechanics of the order, the matter is necessarily complicated by the necessity for the imposition, in any decree of specific performance, of the condition to which I have referred and by the opportunity which must be afforded to the respondents to reinstate their abandoned defences, if they desire to do so and are prepared for the further delay and costs which that will entail. That is a matter upon which they will, no doubt, require to obtain further professional advice and adequate time must be allowed for that purpose. What I would propose, therefore, is that the order of your Lordships' House should contain, initially, a declaration that, subject to compliance with the provisions of sections 156 and 158 of the Act of 1985, the agreement pleaded in the statement of claim is not rendered illegal by virtue of the provisions of section 151 of the Act or otherwise and a decree of specific performance which will take effect unless within a period of 28 days the respondents signify, by serving an amended defence and counterclaim, that they elect to reinstate all or any of their abandoned defences. The action will have to be remitted to the High Court in any event, either for the working out of the order or for the abandoned issues to be tried. I have included an appropriate form of order in a schedule to this speech ... [discussion of costs omitted]

Moody v. Security Pacific Business Credit, Inc.
US Court of Appeals for the Third Circuit
971 F 2d 1056 (1992)
[*Text edited; some footnotes omitted*]

OPINION BY: SCIRICA, Circuit Judge

This bankruptcy case requires us to address, once again, the application of the fraudulent conveyance laws to a failed leveraged buyout. In *United States* v. *Tabor Court Realty Corp.* ... we established that the Pennsylvania Uniform Fraudulent Conveyance Act (UFCA) extends to leveraged buyouts. This case raises several questions about the application of this Act to the failed leveraged buyout of Jeannette Corporation.

On July 31, 1981, a group of investors acquired Jeannette in a leveraged buyout. Less than a year and a half later, Jeannette, which had been profitable for many years, was forced into bankruptcy. The bankruptcy trustee brought this action to set aside the advances made and obligations incurred in connection with the acquisition. The trustee alleges that the leveraged buyout constitutes a fraudulent conveyance under the UFCA and is voidable under the Bankruptcy Code. After a bench trial, the district court entered judgment for defendants. *Moody* v. *Security Pac. Business Credit, Inc.*, 127 Bankr. 958 (WD Pa. 1991). We will affirm.

I.A

Founded in 1898, Jeannette Corporation manufactured and sold glass, ceramic, china, plastic, and candle houseware products in the United States and Canada. For many years, Jeannette was a profitable enterprise ...

In 1978, the Coca-Cola Bottling Company of New York, Inc. acquired Jeannette for $39.6 million. Shortly thereafter, Coca-Cola increased the total net book value of Jeannette's property, plant, and equipment (PP & E) by $5.7 million after a manufacturer's appraisal valued these assets at $29 million. From 1978 to 1981, Coca-Cola invested $6 million in Jeannette for capital expenditures, and $5 million for maintenance and repair of its physical plant.

At first, Jeannette was not as profitable under Coca-Cola's ownership ... However, Jeannette's performance rebounded in 1980 ... Jeannette projected that this trend would continue into 1981. Although Jeannette had an operating loss of $1.1 million in the first half of 1981, because its business cycle produced stronger cash flows in the latter half of the year, the company projected a pre-tax profit of $500,000 before interest expenses.

I.B

In late 1979, Coca-Cola decided to sell Jeannette and focus attention on its core bottling business. In June 1981, John P. Brogan expressed an interest in acquiring Jeannette. Brogan was affiliated with a small group of investors in the business of acquiring companies through leveraged buyouts, the hallmark feature of which is the exchange of equity for debt. [Note 2] On July 22, 1981, Coca-Cola agreed to sell Jeannette for $12.1 million on condition that Brogan complete the transaction by the end of the month.

[Note 2] As this court recently explained: A leveraged buyout refers to the acquisition of a company ("target corporation") in which a substantial portion of the purchase price paid for the stock of the target corporation is borrowed and where the loan is secured by the target corporation's assets. Commonly, the acquirer invests little or no equity. Thus, a fundamental feature of leveraged buyouts is that equity is exchanged for debt. *Mellon Bank, NA* v. *Metro Communications, Inc.* ...

Brogan contacted Security Pacific Business Credit Inc., a lending group that had financed one of his prior acquisitions, about obtaining financing. He submitted one year of monthly projections, based in large part on Jeannette's 80-page business plan for 1981, which showed that Jeannette would have sufficient working capital under the proposed financing arrangement in the year following the acquisition. Before agreeing to finance the transaction, however, Security Pacific undertook its own investigation of Jeannette.

Security Pacific assigned this task to credit analyst Stephen Ngan. Based on his discussions with Jeannette personnel and a review of the company's financial records, Ngan made his own set of projections. He concluded that Jeannette would

earn a pre-tax profit of $800,000 after interest expenses in its first year of oper-
ation, and recommended that Security Pacific finance the acquisition. He thought
Jeannette was a "well-established" company with "a good track record for growth
and earnings."

After reviewing Ngan's recommendation, together with an inventory report, the
1978 appraisal of Jeannette's PP & E, Brogan's projections, and a 55-page report on
Jeannette prepared by another bank, Security Pacific decided to finance the acquisition. At that point, Coca-Cola formally approved the sale of Jeannette to J. Corp.,
which had been incorporated for the purpose of acquiring Jeannette.

I.C

The acquisition of Jeannette was consummated on July 31, 1981. J. Corp. purchased
Jeannette with funds from a $15.5 million line of credit Security Pacific extended
Jeannette secured by first lien security interests on all Jeannette's assets. J. Corp.
never repaid Jeannette any portion of, or executed a promissory note for, the amount
($11.7 million) Security Pacific initially forwarded to J. Corp. on behalf of Jeannette
to finance the acquisition. Other than new management, the only benefit Jeannette
received was access to credit from Security Pacific. [Note 3]

[Note 3] The transaction comprised the following steps, which were deemed by the parties to have taken place at once: (1) J. Corp. entered into an agreement with Coca-Cola
and KNY Development Corporation, a wholly owned subsidiary of Coca-Cola, to purchase all outstanding stock of Jeannette; (2) J. Corp. obtained a $12.1 million unsecured
loan from Security Pacific and executed a demand note therefor; (3) these funds were
transferred from Security Pacific to Coca-Cola to fund the purchase of Jeannette stock,
which was transferred from KNY Development to J. Corp.; (4) upon acquisition of the
stock, J. Corp. appointed a new board of directors for Jeannette and named Brogan
chairman; (5) Jeannette entered into a $15.5 million revolving credit arrangement with
Security Pacific, in exchange for which it granted Security Pacific first lien security
interests in all its assets; (5) on behalf of Jeannette, Brogan directed Security Pacific to
remit $11.7 million from the revolving credit facility to J. Corp., which was used to repay
all but $400,000 of the demand note to Security Pacific; and (6) Jeannette and Security
Pacific entered into a "lock box" agreement, whereby Jeannette's accounts receivable
would be forwarded to the Mellon Bank and credited against the outstanding balance on
Jeannette's line of credit.

As with most leveraged buyouts, the acquisition left Jeannette's assets fully
encumbered by the security interests held by Security Pacific. Jeannette could not
dispose of its assets, except in the ordinary course of business, without the consent
of Security Pacific, and was prohibited from granting security interests to anyone
else. As a result, Jeannette's sole source of working capital after the transaction was
its line of credit with Security Pacific.

Although Jeannette's total outstanding balance never exceeded the amount of
the initial advance ($11.7 million), the total credit advanced Jeannette was many
times this amount because of the "revolving" nature of its line of credit with Security

Pacific. Jeannette's accounts receivable were forwarded to Security Pacific by way of the Mellon Bank, and were credited against its outstanding loan balance. As this balance was paid down, more credit was made available, which Jeannette drew on to finance operations and generate sales.

Although the initial advance was payable on demand, Jeannette carried this obligation as long-term debt. This reflected the parties' understanding that the transaction would give rise to a long-term lending relationship in which the balance on the revolving credit facility would be paid down over several years. Security Pacific obtained no up-front fees and stood to profit by earning interest on the line of credit at 3 1/4% above prime (at that time about 20%).

I.D

Jeannette operated as a going concern from the latter half of 1981 into 1982. From August through December 1981, its net sales exceeded $31 million and the company realized a $6 million gross profit. During the same period, Jeannette had a positive cash flow of $3 million. Part of Jeannette's success during this period is attributable to its business cycle, which produced stronger cash flows in the latter half of the year.

By the end of 1981, Jeannette had received over $43 million in credit advances from Security Pacific, and had $4 million of available credit. A year after the leveraged buyout Jeannette had received $77 million in advances, and had $2.3 million in available credit. Jeannette never exhausted its credit and Security Pacific never refused a request for funds, although on several occasions it suggested that Jeannette withdraw smaller amounts.

Although Jeannette's performance initially tracked expectations, its financial condition deteriorated steadily in 1982. Jeannette experienced a shrinking domestic glassware market, a marked increase in foreign competition, dramatic price slashing and inventory dumping by its domestic competitors, and a continued nationwide recession. In January 1982, orders for Jeannette products fell to 86% of projected levels and in February orders fell to 70%. This decline in sales constricted cash flow and contributed to an inventory build-up.

Jeannette responded by reducing production and lengthening its accounts payable schedule. From late 1981 to early 1982, the company extended its payment period from 30 days to 45 days and then to 60 days. In late February (or early March) 1982, it invoked an 88-day period. However, it remained unable to pay its creditors in a timely fashion. In March 1982, Jeannette was forced to shut down one of the three glass tanks at its Jeannette Glass division, and, in late July, it shut down another. Shortly thereafter, Jeannette sold the inventory and fixed assets of its Old Harbor subsidiary for $2 million. In August 1982, the last tank was shut down at the Jeannette Glass division, bringing operations there to a halt.

Still, Jeannette's financial condition deteriorated. By August 1982, sales had fallen to 69% of traditional levels, and by October sales were 44% of 1981 levels. On October 4, 1982, an involuntary bankruptcy petition was filed under Chapter 7 of the Bankruptcy Code ...

I.E

On September 22, 1983, plaintiff James Moody, the trustee of the bankruptcy estate of Jeannette, filed this action in federal district court against defendants Security Pacific, Coca-Cola, KNY Development, J. Corp., M-K Candle, Brogan, and other individuals. He alleges that the leveraged buyout constitutes a fraudulent conveyance under the UFCA, 39 Pa. Cons. Stat. Ann. §§ 354–57, and is voidable under § 544(b) of the Bankruptcy Code, 11 USC § 544(b). [Note 5] After a bench trial, the district court made findings of fact and conclusions of law and entered judgment for defendants.

[Note 5] Section 544(b) of the Bankruptcy Code provides that "the trustee may avoid any transfer of an interest of the debtor in property or any obligation incurred by the debtor that is voidable under *applicable law* by a creditor holding an unsecured claim ... " 11 USC § 544(b) (emphasis added). The "applicable law" here is the UFCA, and it is clear that there is an unsecured creditor into whose shoes plaintiff trustee may step. See *Moody*, 127 Bankr. at 989 n. 6.

Plaintiff also alleges that the leveraged buyout is voidable under the fraudulent conveyance provisions of the Bankruptcy Code, 11 USC §§ 548–549, and that certain defendants engaged in an unlawful dividend and/or distribution of Jeannette's assets under the Pennsylvania Business Corporations Law, 15 Pa. Cons. Stat. Ann. §§ 1701–02, superseded by 15 Pa. Cons. Stat. Ann. § 1552–53. After concluding that the transaction did not constitute a fraudulent conveyance under the UFCA, however, the district court summarily rejected these claims. It reasoned that, because the fraudulent conveyance provisions of the Bankruptcy Code are modeled after and typically interpreted in conjunction with those of the UFCA, it follows that if the leveraged buyout is not fraudulent under the UFCA, it is not fraudulent under § 548 of the Bankruptcy Code. And if the transaction does not constitute a fraudulent conveyance under § 548, it is not voidable as an "unauthorized" transfer under § 549. Likewise, if Jeannette was not rendered insolvent by the leveraged buyout, no unlawful dividend and/or distribution of assets could have occurred under §§ 1701 and 1702 of the Pennsylvania Business Corporations Law because those provisions proscribe transfers of shares and dividends made by insolvents ...

We agree with the district court's analysis of plaintiff's federal bankruptcy and unlawful dividend and/or distribution of assets claims. Accordingly, because we conclude that the leveraged buyout does not constitute a fraudulent conveyance under the UFCA, we do not address these claims.

According to the district court, the leveraged buyout was not intentionally fraudulent because it was "abundantly clear" that defendants expected the transaction to succeed and hoped to profit from it. *Moody* ... Likewise, although the leveraged buyout was made for less than fair consideration to Jeannette, the district court held that it was not constructively fraudulent.

... Jeannette was not rendered insolvent in the "bankruptcy sense" because the "present fair salable value" of Jeannette's assets immediately after the leveraged buyout exceeded total liabilities by at least $1–2 million. *Id.* at 995. In making this determination, the district court valued assets on a going concern basis ...

Nor was Jeannette rendered insolvent in the "equity sense" or left with an unreasonably small capital ... Based on the parties' projections, which it found "reasonable and prudent when made," and the availability on Jeannette's line of credit with Security Pacific, the district court found that Jeannette was not left with an unreasonably small capital after the acquisition ... Rather than a lack of capital, the district court attributed Jeannette's demise to intense foreign and domestic competition, a continued recession, and, to a lesser degree, mismanagement, which led to a drastic decline in sales beginning in early 1982 ...

After entry of judgment, plaintiff moved for final judgment under Fed. R. Civ. P. 54(b), which the district court granted. This appeal followed.

II.

[*Text omitted*]

III.A

The UFCA proscribes both intentional and constructive fraud. Under the Act's intentional fraud provisions, any conveyance made or obligation incurred either without fair consideration by one who "intends or believes that he will incur debts beyond his ability to pay as they mature" ... or with an "actual intent ... to hinder, delay, or defraud ... creditors" is fraudulent ... Actual intent to defraud may be inferred from the circumstances surrounding a transfer. *Tabor Court Realty Corp.* ...

The UFCA's constructive fraud provisions operate without regard to intent. Under § 4, any conveyance made or obligation incurred "by a person who is or will be thereby rendered insolvent" is fraudulent if it is made or incurred for less than fair consideration ... Insolvency has two components under Pennsylvania law: insolvency in the "bankruptcy sense" (a deficit net worth immediately after the conveyance), and insolvency in the "equity sense" (an inability to pay debts as they mature) ... Fair consideration requires a "good faith" exchange of "a fair equivalent." ...

Under § 5, any conveyance made or obligation incurred by a person engaged in "a business or transaction" is fraudulent if it is made or incurred without fair consideration and leaves that person with an "unreasonably small capital." ... The relationship between "insolvency" under § 4 of the UFCA and "unreasonably small capital" under § 5 is not clear. However, as we discuss below, the better view would seem to be that "unreasonably small capital" denotes a financial condition short of equitable insolvency. The UFCA's constructive fraud provisions furnish a standard of causation that attempts to link the challenged conveyance with the debtor's bankruptcy.

At first, the applicability of the UFCA's fraudulent conveyance provisions to leveraged buyouts was a matter of some dispute ... However, we think it settled, as a general matter at least, that the fraudulent conveyance provisions of the UFCA extend to leveraged buyouts, [Note 10] and defendants do not contest their applicability here.

[Note 10] In *Tabor Court Realty Corp.* we upheld the district court's determination that certain mortgages executed in connection with a leveraged buyout constituted fraudulent conveyances under the UFCA. We noted that "the Act's broad language ... extends to any 'conveyance' which is defined as 'every payment of money ... and also the creation of any lien or incumbrance,'" and declined to exempt from the fraudulent conveyance laws the leveraged buyout challenged there simply because it was "innovative" or "complicated." "If the UFCA is not to be applied to leveraged buyouts," we said, "it should be for the state legislatures, not the courts, to decide." ... *Mellon Bank, NA* v. *Metro Communications, Inc.* ... (holding that the fraudulent conveyance provisions of the Bankruptcy Code are applicable to leveraged buyouts).

This conclusion is consistent with that reached by the other courts that have considered the applicability of the fraudulent conveyance provisions of the UFCA to leveraged buyouts ...

Because of the difficulty in proving intentional fraud, challenges to leveraged buyouts tend to be predicated on the constructive fraud provisions of the UFCA ... Accordingly, the question whether a leveraged buyout constitutes a fraudulent conveyance will typically turn on application of the UFCA's constructive fraud provisions.

With these general principles in mind, we turn now to an analysis of the leveraged buyout of Jeannette under the constructive and then intentional fraud provisions of the UFCA.

III.B.1

According to the district court, the leveraged buyout was without fair consideration to Jeannette because, in exchange for granting Security Pacific security interests in all its assets and undertaking an $11.7 million demand obligation at 3 1/4% above prime, all Jeannette received was new management and access to credit. Moody, 127 Bankr. at 992. Defendants do not challenge this finding, and we accept it for purposes of our analysis here. Cf. *Mellon Bank, NA* v. *Metro Communications, Inc.* ... ("The target corporation ... receives no direct benefit to offset the greater risk of now operating as a highly leveraged corporation.").

The district court's allocation of the burden of proving solvency is a different matter ...

Because leveraged buyouts are consummated between distinct corporate entities at arm's length, defendants assert that the potential for collusion and concealment is less than in intrafamilial transfers and, therefore, judicial scrutiny should be less searching. However, the stakes are higher in the typical leveraged buyout, and, at least from the perspective of unsecured creditors, the potential for abuse is great. As we noted in *Mellon Bank, NA*:

> The effect of an LBO is that a corporation's shareholders are replaced by secured creditors. Put simply, stockholders' equity is supplanted by debt. The level of risk facing the newly structured corporation rises significantly due to the increased debt to equity ratio. This added risk is borne primarily by the unsecured creditors, those who will most likely not be paid in the event of insolvency.

945 F 2d at 646 ... Accordingly, we do not believe the Pennsylvania Supreme Court would scrutinize leveraged buyouts less closely than intrafamilial transfers.

Although we are inclined to hold that the Pennsylvania Supreme Court would impose the same burden on defendants in leveraged buyouts as that imposed in intrafamilial transfers, we need not decide the issue here because we conclude that defendants have met even the clear and convincing evidence standard. Similarly, because we conclude that defendants have proven adequacy of capital by clear and convincing evidence, we need not decide the standard applicable to defendants' burden of proving adequacy of capital.

III.B.2

We turn now to the thrust of plaintiff's attack, the district court's solvency and adequacy of capital analyses. As we have discussed, under § 4 of the UFCA a conveyance is fraudulent if it is made without fair consideration and renders the transferor insolvent ... "A person is insolvent when the *present, fair, salable value* of his assets is less than the amount that will be required to pay his probable liability on his existing debts *as they become absolute and matured." Id.* § 352(1) (emphasis added). The Pennsylvania Supreme Court has interpreted this provision as requiring solvency in both the "bankruptcy" and "equity" sense ... Insolvency is determined "as of the time of the conveyance." ...

The district court valued Jeannette's assets on a going concern basis and found that immediately after the leveraged buyout the present fair salable value of Jeannette's total assets was at least $26.2-$27.2 million (of which $5–6 million comprised PP & E). It then found that the company's total liabilities were $25.2 million ... Thus, the district court concluded that Jeannette was solvent in the bankruptcy sense "by at least $1–2 million and most probably by more, given the conservative value ... assigned Jeannette's PP & E." ...

At trial, plaintiff argued that Jeannette was rendered insolvent in the bankruptcy sense because the present fair salable value of Jeannette's total assets could not have exceeded the $12.1 million J. Corp. paid for Jeannette's stock ... The district court rejected this argument and undertook its own valuation of Jeannette's assets. We find no error here. Although purchase price may be highly probative of a company's value immediately after a leveraged buyout, it is not the only evidence ... The parties here viewed the $12.1 million purchase price as a "significant bargain," made possible by Coca-Cola's decision to focus attention on its bottling business and Brogan's ability to close the deal quickly ...

On appeal, plaintiff focuses on the district court's valuation of Jeannette's PP & E. He argues that the district court erred in valuing Jeannette's PP & E on a going concern basis because these assets were not "presently salable" at the time of the leveraged buyout. In addition, he asserts that the $5–6 million the district court assigned Jeannette's PP & E is unsupported by the record. If the district court overstated Jeannette's PP & E by more than $1 million, the company is left with a deficit net worth and we must find that Jeannette was rendered insolvent in the bankruptcy sense.

To be "salable" an asset must have "an existing and not theoretical market." ... Jeannette's PP & E, which comprised real estate and machinery used in the production of glass and pottery, was not highly liquid. Therefore, in determining the present fair salable value of Jeannette's PP & E, the time frame in which these assets must be valued is critical.

Plaintiff argues that valuation on a going concern basis fails to give effect to "present" in the UFCA's "present fair salable value" language ... and the district court should have calculated the amount the company would have received had it attempted to liquidate its PP & E on the date of the acquisition or immediately thereafter. We disagree. Where bankruptcy is not "clearly imminent" on the date of the challenged conveyance, the weight of authority holds that assets should be valued on a going concern basis ...

Although most of these cases involve application of the Bankruptcy Code, we have previously looked to the federal bankruptcy laws in interpreting the UFCA. As we noted in *Tabor Court Realty Corp.*, "the fraudulent conveyance provisions of the [Bankruptcy] Code are modeled on the UFCA, and uniform interpretation of the two statutes [is] essential to promote commerce nationally." ... Thus, although the UFCA's "present fair salable value" language differs from the Bankruptcy Code's "fair valuation" requirement, see 11 USC § 101(31)(A), we find the bankruptcy cases instructive on the proper valuation standard here ...

[*Text omitted*]

To determine whether the district court properly valued Jeannette's PP & E on a going concern basis, then, we must ascertain whether Jeannette was either insolvent or on the brink of insolvency on the date of the leveraged buyout. The district court found that "Jeannette was not a company whose failure was clearly imminent on July 31, 1981." ... This conclusion is supported by the record. Prior to the transaction, Jeannette had a net worth of over $40 million ... Moreover, at the time of the transaction Jeannette had a positive cash flow and was coming off a break-even year before acquisition costs. Accordingly, we think the district court properly valued Jeannette's assets, and, in particular, its PP & E, on a going concern basis.

Plaintiff also maintains that the district court erred in finding that the present fair salable value of Jeannette's PP & E on the date of the acquisition was $5–6 million. At trial, plaintiff presented no evidence on the going concern value of Jeannette's PP & E, or any other assets, because he argued that the company could not be worth more than the amount J. Corp. paid for Jeannette's stock. Plaintiff now asserts that the district court used a "hodgepodge of irrelevant numbers" to arrive at the $5–6 million figure it set for Jeannette's PP & E. We disagree. The record supports the district court's finding that the present fair salable value of Jeannette's PP & E on the date of the acquisition was at least $5–6 million and probably more.

We find the $5.65 million Jeannette received for PP & E in liquidating its divisions and subsidiaries particularly probative of the going concern value of Jeannette's PP & E on July 31, 1981 because these components were sold as going concerns on something approaching a liquidation basis. Therefore, although these assets were sold long after the leveraged buyout, the conditions under which they were sold approximated, and may have been more immediate than, that required by the UFCA's "present fair salable value" language. Accordingly, we conclude that the district court did not err in finding that Jeannette was solvent in the bankruptcy sense after the leveraged buyout.

III.B.3

Next, we look at whether the leveraged buyout either rendered Jeannette insolvent in the equity sense or left it with an unreasonably small capital. Although it recognized that these issues were "conceptually distinct," the district court considered them together ... Plaintiff contends this was improper because "unreasonably small capital" denotes a financial condition short of equitable insolvency.

As we have discussed, under § 5 of the UFCA any conveyance made or obligation incurred by a person engaged in "a business or transaction" is fraudulent if it is made or incurred without fair consideration and leaves that person with an "unreasonably small capital." 39 Pa. Cons. Stat. Ann. § 355. Unlike "insolvency," "unreasonably small capital" is not defined by the UFCA. This has engendered confusion over the relationship between these concepts: some courts have equated a finding of equitable insolvency with that of unreasonably small capital, whereas others have said that unreasonably small capital encompasses financial difficulties short of equitable insolvency.

We believe the better view is that unreasonably small capital denotes a financial condition short of equitable insolvency. As plaintiff points out, there is some support for this position in *Fidelity Trust Co.* v. *Union National Bank* ... where the Pennsylvania Supreme Court said that "insolvency at the time" of the challenged conveyance is "of no moment" under § 5 ...

Moreover, we think it telling that having adopted § 4 of the UFCA, which proscribes conveyances made without fair consideration that render the debtor "insolvent," the drafters saw fit to add § 5, which proscribes conveyances made without fair consideration that leave the debtor with an "unreasonably small capital." If the drafters viewed these concepts interchangeably, one would expect them to have employed the same language ...

Finally, whereas § 4 covers conveyances by persons generally, § 5 covers conveyances by "persons in business." ... In the business setting, "capital" is a term of art. As a general matter, it refers to "accumulated goods, possessions, and assets, used for the production of profits and wealth." *Black's Law Dictionary* 189 (5th ed. 1979). Viewed in this light, an "unreasonably small capital" would refer to the inability to generate sufficient profits to sustain operations. Because an inability to generate enough cash flow to sustain operations must precede an inability to pay obligations as they become due, unreasonably small capital would seem to encompass financial difficulties short of equitable insolvency.

In any event, we do not think the district court erred in considering whether the leveraged buyout left Jeannette with an unreasonably small capital in conjunction with whether it rendered the company equitably insolvent. These distinct but related concepts furnish a standard of causation which looks for a link between the challenged conveyance and the debtor's insolvency. Moreover, where the debtor is a corporation, adequacy of capital is typically a major component of any solvency analysis. This is true of the district court's analysis here.

III.B.4

In undertaking its adequacy of capital analysis, the district court focused on the reasonableness of the parties' projections, but also considered the availability of Jeannette's line of credit with Security Pacific. It found the parties' projections reasonable and, based on the availability of credit as well as the company's historical cash flow needs, determined that Jeannette was not left with an unreasonably small capital under the circumstances ... Rather than a lack of capital, the district court attributed Jeannette's demise to the "substantial drop in orders and sales that began in 1982," which it attributed in turn to increased foreign and domestic competition and the continued recession ...

Because creditors cannot execute on a debtor's ability to borrow, plaintiff maintains that the district court erred in considering Jeannette's line of credit with Security Pacific in undertaking its adequacy of capital analysis. He relies on

Larrimer v. *Feeney* ... where the Pennsylvania Supreme Court said that the ability to survive on borrowed funds does not render an individual debtor solvent for purposes of § 4 of the UFCA. The district court found these cases inapposite. We agree.

Larrimer and *Fidelity Trust Co.* involved individual debtors who had engaged in speculative stock trading schemes and borrowed funds to stay afloat. In *Larrimer* the Pennsylvania Supreme Court observed that the debtor's "sanguine expectations that the stock market would fluctuate sufficiently [to cover his losses] were in vain," 192 A 2d at 354; and in *Fidelity Trust Co.* the court referred to the debtor's stock manipulation efforts as "highly speculative" and "unlawful," 169 A at 212. By contrast, defendants' decision to enter into the lending arrangement challenged here was predicated on their projections that the acquisition would succeed, and, as we discuss below, these projections were reasonable.

Moreover, unlike the debtors in *Larrimer* and *Fidelity Trust Co.*, at least initially, Jeannette did not borrow funds to stay afloat. As we have noted, the company was solvent by $1–2 million immediately after the leveraged buyout. Finally, we think the lending relationship here is different in important respects from those in *Larrimer* and *Fidelity Trust Co.* Jeannette granted Security Pacific first priority security interests in all its assets, which the district court valued at $26 million, to secure a $15.5 million line of credit to provide Jeannette with working capital in the year following the transaction.

In the absence of controlling Pennsylvania caselaw, it was proper for the district court to look to caselaw in other jurisdictions, and, in particular, *Credit Managers Ass'n* v. *Federal Co.* ... In that case the district court held that the focus of the adequacy of capital inquiry in a leveraged buyout should be the reasonableness of the parties' cash flow projections. In finding that the target corporation was not left with an unreasonably small capital after the leveraged buyout, the court also considered availability of credit ... [Note 25]

[Note 25] *Credit Managers Ass'n* involved a challenge to the failed leveraged buyout of the Crescent Food Company under § 5 of the California UFCA. Despite a $10 million line of credit, less than a year and a half after the acquisition, Crescent had accounts payable of $3 million and insufficient cash flow to continue operations. Although it recognized that the acquisition placed Crescent "heavily in debt," the district court found it "was not undercapitalized and had sufficient *expected* cash flow to stay in business." *Id.* at 184 (emphasis added). In reaching this conclusion, the district court focused on the reasonableness of the lender's cash flow projections entering into the acquisition, and, to a degree, the resulting availability on Crescent's line of credit. *Id.* at 186. Rather than a lack of capital, the district court attributed Crescent's demise to a series of unexpected setbacks – in particular, a two-month strike. *Id.* at 178.

Plaintiff urges us to follow *Murphy* v. *Meritor Savings Bank (In Re O'Day Corp.)* ... in which the bankruptcy court said that availability of credit alone does not establish adequate capitalization after a leveraged buyout ... However, this statement is not necessarily at odds with *Creditor Managers Ass'n*, which the *In Re O'Day Corp.* court explicitly embraced. The *Credit Managers Ass'n* analysis turns on the reasonableness of projections, not availability of credit *per se*. If projections are unreasonable, as was the case in *In Re O'Day Corp.* ... it will follow that the debtor was left with an unreasonably small capital even though it may not have exhausted its credit.

The bankruptcy court held that the leveraged buyout left O'Day with an unreasonably small capital under § 5 of the UFCA. In reaching this conclusion, it observed: "In perhaps the leading case on the issue of unreasonably small capital, the court concluded that its task in determining whether a company had sufficient working capital as evidenced by cash flow projections was not to examine what happened to the company but whether the projections employed prior to the LBO were prudent." *Credit Managers* ...

We cannot say that Jeannette was left with an unreasonably small capital merely because after the leveraged buyout its sole source of operating capital was its line of credit with Security Pacific. As we noted in *Mellon Bank, NA* ... "the ability to borrow money has considerable value in the commercial world." This is particularly true in the case of leveraged buyouts, which are predicated on the exchange of equity for debt and the ability to borrow ...

Because a leveraged buyout may fail for reasons other than the structure of the transaction itself, we think the determination whether a leveraged buyout leaves a target corporation with an unreasonably small capital requires a more careful inquiry. At least from the viewpoint of the unsecured creditor, leveraged buyouts present great potential for abuse. As we noted in *Mellon Bank, NA*, "an LBO may be attractive to the buyer, seller, and lender because the structure of the transaction ... allows all parties to shift most of the risk of loss to other creditors ... " ...

The *Credit Managers Ass'n* analysis appears to strike a proper balance. It holds participants in leveraged buyout responsible under § 5 of the UFCA when it is reasonably foreseeable that an acquisition will fail, but at the same time takes into account that "businesses fail for all sorts of reasons, and that fraudulent [conveyance] laws are not a panacea for all such failures." ... Therefore, we hold the test for unreasonably small capital is reasonable foreseeability. Under this analysis, it was proper for the district court to consider availability of credit in determining whether Jeannette was left with an unreasonably small capital. The critical question is whether the parties' projections were reasonable.

III.B.5

[Text omitted]

Defendants here relied on two sets of one-year projections, one prepared by Brogan and the other by Ngan. Brogan's projections were based on a month-by-month analysis of Jeannette's balance sheet, income statement, and resulting credit availability. Ngan's projections were grounded in his interviews with Jeannette personnel and examination of the company's financial records for the year and a half preceding the acquisition. The district court found these projections reasonable and prudent when made ... We agree.

[Text omitted]

The district court properly found that Jeannette's failure was caused by a dramatic drop in sales due to increased foreign and domestic competition, rather than a lack of capital. Plaintiff plausibly contends that defendants should have anticipated some of these problems and incorporated a margin for error. But we cannot say the district court erred in finding that the drastic decline in sales was unforeseeable as of the date of the leveraged buyout. Therefore, we conclude that the district court properly determined that the leveraged buyout did not leave Jeannette with an unreasonably small capital.

[Text omitted]

III.C

All that remains to be decided is whether the district court properly determined that the leveraged buyout did not violate the UFCA's intentional fraud provisions. As we have discussed, a conveyance is intentionally fraudulent if it is made either without fair consideration by one who "intends or believes that he will incur debts beyond his ability to pay as they mature," 39 Pa. Cons. Stat. Ann. § 356, or with an "actual intent ... to hinder, delay, or defraud either present or future creditors," *id.* § 357. Actual intent to defraud need not be shown by direct evidence, but rather may be inferred from the circumstances surrounding a conveyance. *United States* v. *Tabor Court Realty Corp.* ...

The district court found that "defendants did not know or believe that Jeannette's creditors could not be paid, and did not intend to hinder, defraud, or delay creditors." ... This conclusion followed from the absence of any direct evidence of fraud, as well as defendants' profit motives, the parties' awareness of the transaction's leveraged nature, and Jeannette's operation as a going concern for at least five months following the acquisition ...

Plaintiff apparently concedes that there is no direct evidence that defendants intended to defraud Jeannette's creditors. However, he asserts that the district court erred in failing to consider the "well-established principle" that "parties are held to have intended the natural consequences of their acts." Applying this principle, plaintiff reasons that because the leveraged buyout had the foreseeable "effect" of hindering and delaying creditors of Jeannette, it follows that defendants intended to defraud them. We cannot agree.

In *Tabor Court Realty Corp.* we relied in part on the principle that "a party is deemed to have intended the natural consequences of his acts" in upholding the district court's finding of intentional fraud ... The facts of that case, however, are more egregious than those here. The target corporation in *Tabor* was "clearly on the brink of insolvency" at the time of the challenged leveraged buyout ... Thus, the leveraged buyout was not only voidable under the intentional fraud provisions of the UFCA, but also under the Act's constructive fraud provisions.

By contrast, Jeannette was not on the brink of insolvency at the time of the leveraged buyout, and the acquisition was not constructively fraudulent. Therefore, even assuming participants in leveraged buyouts may be held accountable under the intentional fraud provisions of the UFCA for the natural consequences of their actions, we do not believe Jeannette's insolvency was a natural consequence of the leveraged buyout. We conclude, then, that the district court properly held that the leveraged buyout was not intentionally fraudulent.

IV.

In sum, we will affirm the district court's conclusions that the leveraged buyout does not constitute a fraudulent conveyance under either the constructive or intentional fraud provisions of the UFCA ...

[Text omitted]

REFERENCES

Allen, William T., and Kraakman, Reinier, 2003. *Commentaries and Cases on the Law of Business Organizations*. New York: Aspen Publishers

American Bar Association, Committee on Corporate Laws, Section of Business Law, 2008. *Model Business Corporation Act Annotated*, 4th edn., Chicago: American Bar Association

American Heritage Dictionary of the English Language, 2002. 4th edn., Boston: Houghton Mifflin

Anderson, Sarah, Cavanagh, John, Collins, Chuck, Pizzigati, Sam, and Lapham, Mike, 2007. *Executive Excess 2007: The Staggering Social Cost of US Business Leadership, Institute for Policy Studies, 14th Annual CEO Compensation Survey*, available at www.ips-dc.org/reports/

Armour, John, 2005. "Who Should Make Corporate Law? EU Legislation versus Regulatory Competition," *Current Legal Problems* **58**: 369

2006. "Legal Capital: An Outdated Concept?," *European Business Organization Law Review* **7**: 5

Armour, John, Hansmann, Henry, and Kraakman, Reinier, 2009a. "What Is Corporate Law?," in Kraakman, Davies, Hansmann, Hertig, Hopt, Kanda and Rock (eds.), *The Anatomy of Corporate Law: A Comparative and Functional Approach*, 2nd edn., Oxford: Oxford University Press, p. 1

2009b. "Agency Problems and Legal Strategies," in *The Anatomy of Corporate Law: A Comparative and Functional Approach*, 2nd edn., Oxford: Oxford University Press, p. 35

Armour, John, Hertig, Gerard, and Kanda, Hideki, 2009. "Transactions with Creditors," in Kraakman, Davies, Hansmann, Hertig, Hopt, Kanda and Rock (eds.), *The Anatomy of Corporate Law: A Comparative and Functional Approach*, 2nd edn., Oxford: Oxford University Press, p. 115

Armour, John, and Skeel, David A. Jr., 2007. "Who Writes the Rules for Hostile Takeovers, and Why?: The Peculiar Divergence of US and UK Takeover Regulation," *Georgetown Law Journal* **95**: 1727

Armour, John, and Whincop, Michael J., 2007. "Proprietary Foundations of Corporate Law," *Oxford Journal of Legal Studies* **27**: 429

Bachmann, Gregor, Baums, Theodor, Habersack, Mathias, Henssler, Martin, Lutter, Marcus, Oetker, Hartmut, and Ulmer, Peter, 2009. "Entwurf einer

Regelung zur Mitbestimmungsvereinbarung sowie zur Größe des mitbes-timmten Aufsichtsrats," *ZIP* **19**: 885

Baird, Douglas G., 2006. "Legal Approaches to Restricting Distributions to Shareholders: The Role of Fraudulent Transfer Law," *European Business Organization Law Review* 7: 199

Baird, Douglas G. and Jackson, Thomas H., 1985. "Fraudulent Conveyance and Its Proper Domain," *Vanderbilt Law Review* 38: 829

Ballantine, Henry Winthrop, 1946. *Ballantine on Corporations*. Chicago: West Publishing

Balotti, R. Franklin, and Finkelstein, Jesse A., 2008. *Delaware Law of Corporation and Business Organizations*. 3rd edn., Englewood Cliffs, NJ: Prentice-Hall

Banks, R. C. l'Anson, 2000. *Lindley and Banks on Partnership*, 18th edn., London: Sweet & Maxwell

Barca, Fabrizio and Becht, Marco, 2001. *The Control of Corporate Europe*. Oxford: Oxford University Press

Barclay, Michael J., Holderness, Clifford G., and Sheehan, Dennis P., 2003. *Dividends and Dominant Corporate Shareholders*, AFA 2004 San Diego Meetings, available at SSRN: http://ssrn.com/abstract=472201/

Baums, Theodor, 1993. "Takeovers versus Institutions in Corporate Governance in Germany," in Prentice and Holland (eds.), *Contemporary Issues in Corporate Governance*. Oxford: Clarendon Press, p. 151

1996. "Personal Liabilities of Company Directors in German Law," *ICCLR* **9**: 318

1999. "Germany," in Baums and Wymeersch (eds.), *Shareholder Voting Rights and Practices in Europe and the United States*. London: Wolters Kluwer, p. 109

2002. *Company Law Reform in Germany, Johann Wolfgang Goethe-Universität, Institute for Banking Law*, Working Paper No. 100, available at www.jura.uni-frankfurt.de/baums/

2005. "Zur Offenlegung von Vorstandsvergütungen," *ZHR* **169**: 299, also in Johann Wolfgang Goethe-Universität, Institute for Banking Law, Working Paper No. 122, available at www.jura.uni-frankfurt.de/ifawz1/baums/Arbeitspapiere.html

2007. *European Company Law Beyond the Action Plan*, European Corporate Governance Institute, Law Working Paper No. 81/2007

Baums, Theodor, and Andersen, Paul Krüger, 2008. *The European Model Company Law Act Project*, ILF Working Paper No. 78, available from SSRN at http://ssrn.com/abstract=1115737/

Baums, Theodor, and Drinhausen, Florian, 2008. "Weitere Reform des Rechts der Anfechtung von Hauptversammlungsbeschlüssen," *ZIP* 145, also available as ILF Working Paper No. 70, www.ilf-frankfurt.de/uploads/media/ILF_WP_070.pdf

Baums, Theodor, Keinath, Astrid, and Gajek, Daniel, 2007. "Fortschritte bei Klagen gegen Hauptversammlungsbeschlüsse? Eine empirische Studie," *ZIP* 1629, also available as ILF Working Paper No. 65, www.ilf-frankfurt.de/uploads/media/ILF_WP_065.pdf

Baums, Theodor, and von Randow, 1995. "Shareholder Voting and Corporate Governance: The German Experience and a New Approach," in Aoki and Kim (eds.), *Corporate Governance in Transitional Economies: Insider Control and the Role of Banks*, Washington DC: World Bank, p. 435

Baums, Theodor, and Thoma, Georg F., 2008. *Kommentar zum Wertpapiererwerbs- und Übernahmegesetz*. Cologne: RWS

Bebchuk, Lucien Arye, 1989. "Limiting Contractual Freedom in Corporate Law: The Desirable Constraints on Charter Amendments," *Harvard Law Review* **102**: 1820

1992. "Federalism and the Corporation: The Desirable Limits on State Competition in Corporate Law," *Harvard Law Review* **105**: 1435

2005. "The Case for Increasing Shareholder Power," *Harvard Law Review* **118**: 833

Bebchuk, Lucian Arye, and Fried, Jesse M., 2003. "Executive Compensation as an Agency Problem," *Journal of Economic Perspectives* **17**: 71

2004. *Pay without Performance*. Cambridge: Harvard University Press

Bebchuk, Lucian Arye, Grinstein, Yaniv, and Peyer, Urs, 2006. *Lucky Directors*, Harvard Law and Economics Discussion Paper No. 573, available from SSRN at http://ssrn.com/abstract=952239/

Bebchuk, Lucian Arye, and Roe, Mark J., 1999. "A Theory of Path Dependence in Corporate Ownership and Governance," *Stanford Law Review* **52**: 127, also published in Gordon and Roe (eds.), 2004. *Convergence and Persistence in Corporate Governance*. Cambridge: Cambridge University Press, p. 69

Bell, Abraham, and Parchomovsky, Gideon, 2005a. "What Property Is," *Cornell Law Review* **90**: 3

2005b. "A Theory of Property," *Cornell Law Review, Virginia Law Review* **90**: 531, also available from SSRN at http://ssrn.com/abstract=509862

Berle, Adolf A., and Means, Gardiner C., 1968. *The Modern Corporation and Private Property*. 8th edn., New York: Harcourt Brace

Bettis, J. Carr, Bizjak, John M., and Lemmon, Michael L. 1999. "Insider Trading in Derivative Securities: An Empirical Examination of the Use of Zero-Cost Collars and Equity Swaps by Corporate Insiders," available at SSRN: http://ssrn.com/abstract=167189 or doi:10.2139/ssrn.167189/

Black's Law Dictionary, 1999. Bryan A. Garner (ed.), *Black's Law Dictionary*, 7th edn., St. Paul, MN: West Publishing

Blair, Margaret M., and Stout, Lynn A., 1999. "A Team Production Theory of Corporate Law," *Virginia Law Review* **85**: 247

2001. "Director Accountability and the Mediating Role of the Corporate Board," *Washington University Law Quarterly* **79**: 403

Blumberg, Phillip I., 2005. "The Transformation of Modern Corporation Law: The Law of Corporate Groups," *Connecticut Law Review* **37**: 605

Bratton, William W., and McCahery, Joseph A., 2006. "The Equilibrium Content of Corporate Federalism," *Wake Forest Law Review* **41**: 619

Brealey, Richard A., Myers, Stewart C., and Allen, Franklin, 2006. *Principles of Corporate Finance*. 8th edn., Homewood, IL: Richard D. Irwin, Inc.

Booth, Richard A., 2000. "A Chronology of the Evolution of the MBCA," *Business Law* 56: 63

    2002. *Financing the Corporation*. St. Paul, MN: Clark Boardman Callaghan/West Publishing

    2006. *Give Me Equity or Give Me Death – The Role of Competition and Compensation in Building Silicon Valley*, University of Maryland Legal Studies Research Paper No. 2006–44, available from SSRN at http://ssrn.com/abstract=940022/

Butzke, Volker, 2001. *Die Hauptversammlung der Aktiengesellschaft*, Obermüller, Werner, Winden (eds.), 4th edn., Stuttgart: Schäffer-Poeschel

Buxbaum, Richard M., 1987. "The Threatened Constitutionalization of the Internal Affairs Doctrine in Corporation Law," *California Law Review* 75: 29

Cahn, Andreas, 2007a. "Eigene Aktien und gegenseitige Beteiligungen," in Bayer and Habersack (eds.), *Aktienrecht im Wandel*, vol. II, p. 763, also available as ILF Working Paper No. 50: www.ilf-frankfurt.de/uploads/media/ILF_WP_050.pdf

    2007b. "Die Auswirkungen der Kapitaländerungsrichtlinie auf den Erwerb eigener Aktien," *Der Konzern* 385

    2009a. "Das Zahlungsverbot nach § 92 Abs. 2 Satz 3 AktG – aktien- und konzernrechtliche Aspekte des neuen Liquiditätsschutzes," *Der Konzern*: 7

    2009b. "Kredite an Gesellschafter – zugleich Anmerkung zur MPS-Entscheidung des BGH," *Der Konzern*: 67

Cahn, Andreas, and Ostler, Nicolas, 2008. "Eigene Aktien und Wertpapierleihe," *Die AG* 221

Calamari, John D., and Perillo, Joseph M., 1998. *The Law of Contracts*. 4th edn., St. Paul, MN: West Publishing

Cao, Jerry, and Lerner, Josh, 2009. "The Performance of Reverse Leveraged Buyouts," *Journal of Financial Economics* 91: 139

Cary, William L., 1974. "Federalism and Corporate Law: Reflections on Delaware," *Yale Law Journal* 83: 663

Chandler, Alfred D., 1990. *Scale and Scope: The Dynamics of Industrial Capitalism*. Cambridge, MA: Belknap Press

Cheffins, Brian R., 2009. *Corporate Ownership and Control: British Business Transformed*. Oxford and New York: Oxford University Press

Clark, Robert Charles, 1986. *Corporate Law*. Boston and Toronto: Little, Brown and Co.

Coffee Jr., John C., 1983. "Rescuing the Private Attorney General: Why the Model of the Lawyer as Bounty Hunter Is Not Working," *Maryland Law Review* 42: 215

    1984. "Market Failure and the Economic Case for a Mandatory Disclosure System," *Virginia Law Review* 70: 717

1999a. "The Direction of Corporate Law: The Scholar's Perspective," *Delaware Journal of Corporate Law* **25**: 79

1999b. "The Future as History: The Prospects for Global Convergence in Corporate Governance and Its Implications," *Northwestern University Law Review* **93**: 641

2001. "The Rise of Dispersed Ownership: The Roles of Law and the State in the Separation of Ownership and Control," *Yale Law Journal* **111**: 1

2002. "Racing Towards the Top?: The Impact of Cross-Listing and Stock Market Competition on International Corporate Governance," *Columbia Law Review* **102**: 1757

2004a. "Gatekeeper Failure and Reform: The Challenge of Fashioning Relevant Reforms," *Boston University Law Review* **84**: 301

2004b. "What Caused Enron? A Capsule Social and Economic History of the 1990s," *Cornell Law Review* **89**: 269

Committee on the Global Financial System of the Bank for International Settlements, 2008. *Private Equity and Leveraged Finance Markets.* CGFS Papers No. 30

Cools, Sofie, 2005. "The Real Difference in Corporate Law Between the United States and Continental Europe: Distribution of Powers," *Delaware Journal of Corporate Law* **30**: 697

Cox, James D., and Hazen, Thomas Lee, 2002. *Cox and Hazen on Corporations.* 2nd edn., New York: Aspen

Craig, Paul, and de Búrca, Gráinne, 2008. *EU Law: Text, Cases and Materials.* 4th edn., New York: Oxford University Press

Davies, Paul L., 2003. *Gower and Davies' Principles of Modern Company Law.* 7th edn., London: Sweet & Maxwell

2008. *Gower and Davies' Principles of Modern Company Law.* 8th edn., London: Sweet & Maxwell

Davies, Paul, Enriques, Luca, Hertig, Gerard, Hopt, Klaus, and Kraakman, Reinier, 2009. "Beyond the Anatomy," in Kraakman, Davies, Hansmann, Hertig, Hopt, Kanda and Rock (eds.), *The Anatomy of Corporate Law: A Comparative and Functional Approach*, 2nd edn., Oxford: Oxford University Press, p. 305

Davies, Paul, and Hopt, Klaus, 2009. "Control Transactions," in Kraakman, Davies, Hansmann, Hertig, Hopt, Kanda and Rock (eds.), *The Anatomy of Corporate Law: A Comparative and Functional Approach.* 2nd edn., Oxford: Oxford University Press, p. 225

Department for Business, Innovation and Skills (BIS), 2008. "Reform of Limited Partnership Law: Legislative Reform Order to repeal and replace the Limited Partnerships Act 1907, A Consultation Document"

2009. "The Legislative Reform (Limited Partnerships) Order 2009, Explanatory Document"

Doidge, Craig, Karolyi, G. Andrew, and Stulz, René M., 2004. "Why Are Foreign Firms That Are Listed in the US Worth More?," *Journal of Financial Economics* **71**: 205

Donahue, Charles, 2006. "Comparative Law Before the Code Napoléon," in Reimann and Zimmermann (eds.), *The Oxford Handbook of Comparative Law*. Oxford: Oxford University Press

Donald, David C., 2005. "Shareholder Voice and Its Opponents," *Journal of Corporate Law Studies* **5**: 305

2008. "Approaching Comparative Company Law," *Fordham Journal of Corporate and Financial Law* **14**: 83

Drury, R. R., 1985. "Nullity of Companies in English Law," *Modern Law Review* **48**: 644

Easterbrook, Frank H., and Fischel, Daniel R., 1985. "Limited Liability and the Corporation," *University of Chicago Law Review* **52**: 89

1996. *The Economic Structure of Corporate Law*. Cambridge, MA: Harvard University Press

Edwards, Vanessa, 1999. *EC Company Law*. New York: Oxford University Press

Eidenmüller, Horst, Engert, Andreas, and Hornuf, Lars, 2009. "Incorporating under European Law: The Societas Europaea as a Vehicle for Legal Arbitrage," *European Business Organization Law Review* **10**: 1

Eisenberg, Melvin Aron, 1976. *The Structure of the Corporation*. Boston and Toronto: Little, Brown and Co.

1993. "The Divergence of Standards of Conduct and Standards of Review in Corporate Law," *Fordham Law Review* **62**: 437

2005. *Corporations and Other Business Organizations: Cases and Materials*. Concise 9th edn., New York: Foundation Press

Enriques, Luca, and Gatti, Matteo, 2007. "Is There a Uniform EU Securities Law After the Financial Services Action Plan?," *Stanford Journal of Law, Business and Finance* **14**:43

Enriques, Luca, Hansmann, Henry, and Kraakman, Reinier, 2009a. "The Basic Governance Structure: The Interests of Shareholders as a Class," in Kraakman, Davies, Hansmann, Hertig, Hopt, Kanda and Rock (eds.), *The Anatomy of Corporate Law: A Comparative and Functional Approach*, 2nd edn., Oxford: Oxford University Press, p. 55

2009b. "The Basic Governance Structure: Minority Shareholders and Non-Shareholder Constituencies," in Kraakman, Davies, Hansmann, Hertig, Hopt, Kanda and Rock (eds.), *The Anatomy of Corporate Law: A Comparative and Functional Approach*, 2nd edn., Oxford: Oxford University Press, p. 89

Enriques, Luca, Hertig, Gerard, and Kanda, Hideki, 2009. "Related-Party Transactions," in Kraakman, Davies, Hansmann, Hertig, Hopt, Kanda and Rock (eds.), *The Anatomy of Corporate Law: A Comparative and Functional Approach*, 2nd edn., Oxford: Oxford University Press, p. 153

Enriques, Luca, and Macey, Jonathan R., 2001. "Creditors v. Capital Formation: The Case Against the European Legal Capital Rules," *Cornell Law Review* **86**: 1165

Enriques, Luca, and Tröger, Tobias H., 2007. "Issuer Choice in Europe," *European Business Organization Law Review* **8**: 58

Ferguson, Niall, 2008. *The Ascent of Money: A Financial History of the World.* Penguin Press

Ferran, Eilís, 1999. *Company Law and Corporate Finance.* New York: Oxford University Press

2004. *Building an EU Securities Market.* Cambridge: Cambridge University Press

2007. *Regulation of Private Equity-Backed Leveraged Buyout Activity in Europe,* European Corporate Governance Institute, Law Working Paper No. 84/2007, available at http://ssrn.com/abstract=989748/

2008. *Principles of Corporate Finance Law.* New York: Oxford University Press

Fisch, Jill E., 1993. "From Legitimacy to Logic: Reconstructing Proxy Regulation," *Vanderbilt Law Review* **46**: 1129

Fischer, Robert, 1969. "Zur Methode revisionsrechtlicher Rechtsprechung auf dem Gebiet des Gesellschaftsrechts – dargestellt an Hand der Rechtsprechung zu den Stimmrechtsbindungsverträgen," in Ballerstedt (ed.), *Festgabe für Otto Kunze.* Berlin: Duncker und Humblot, p. 95

Fletcher, William Meade, 2005. *Fletcher Cyclopedia of the Law of Private Corporations.* St. Paul, MN: West Publishing

Foelsch, Martin E., 2007. "Grundzüge des Börsenwesens", in Hellner and Steuer (eds.), *Bankrecht und Bankpraxis,* vol. 4, Cologne: Bank Verlag

Forelle, Charles, 2007. "Executives Get Bonuses As Firms Reprice Options," *Wall Street Journal,* January 20, 2007, p. A1

Forelle, Charles, and Banler, James, 2006. "The Perfect Payday," *Wall Street Journal,* March 18, 2006, p. A1

Fox, Meritt B., 1998. "The Political Economy of Statutory Reach: US Disclosure Rules in a Globalizing Market for Securities," *Michigan Law Review* **97**: 696

Frankel, Tamar, 1983. "Fiduciary Law," *California Law Review* **71**: 795

Frésard, Laurent, and Salva, Carolina, 2007. *Does Cross-listing in the US Really Improve Corporate Governance? Evidence from the Value of Corporate Liquidity,* EFA 2007 Ljubljana Meetings Paper, available from SSRN at http://ssrn.com/abstract=958506/

Friedman, Lawrence M., 2002. *American Law in the 20th Century.* New Haven, CT: Yale University Press

2005. *A History of American Law.* 3rd edn., New York: Touchstone

Friedman, Thomas, 2005. *The World Is Flat.* New York: Farrar, Straus and Giroux

Gall, Lothar, 2001. *Bismarck: Der weiße Revolutionär.* Berlin: Propyläen Verlag

Gelter, Martin, 2005. "The Structure of Regulatory Competition in European Corporate Law," *Journal of Corporate Law Studies* **5**: 247

Gevurtz, Franklin A., 2000. *Corporation Law*. St. Paul, MN: West Publishing

    2004. "The Historical and Political Origins of the Corporate Board of Directors," *Hofstra Law Review* **33**: 89

Gilson, Ronald J., 1999. "The Legal Infrastructure of High Technology Industrial Districts: Silicon Valley, Route 128, and Covenants Not to Compete," *New York University Law Review* **74**: 575

    2001. "Globalizing Corporate Governance, Convergence of Form or Function," *American Journal of Comparative Law* **49**: 329

Gilson, Ronald J., and Gordon, Jeffrey N., 2005. "Controlling Controlling Shareholders," *University of Pennsylvania Law Review* **152**: 785

Glenn, H. Patrick, 2005. *On Common Laws*. Oxford and New York: Oxford University Press

Goode, Roy, 2004. *Commercial Law*. 3rd edn., Toronto: Penguin

Gordon, Jeffrey N., 1989. "The Mandatory Structure of Corporate Law," *Columbia Law Review* **89**: 1549

Gore-Browne, Sir Francis, 2004. *Gore-Browne on Companies*. 45th edn., Bristol: Jordans

Groeben, Hans von der, and Schwarze, Jürgen, 2003–. *Kommentar zum Vertrag über die Europäische Union und zur Gründung der Europäischen Gemeinschaft*. 6th edn., Baden-Baden: Nomos

Großkommentar zum Aktiengesetz. Hopt, Klaus J., and Wiedemann, Herbert (eds.), 1992–. 4th edn., Berlin: de Gruyter (cited as *GroßkommAktG*)

Großkommentar zum GmbH-Gesetz. Ulmer, Peter, Habersack, Mathias, and Winter, Martin (eds.), 2005–. Tübingen: Mohr Siebeck (cited as *GroßkommGmbHG*)

Grundfest, Joseph, 2003. *Legal Problems in Designing a Shareholder Access Rule*, Harvard Law and Economics Discussion Paper No. 448, available from SSRN at http://ssrn.com/abstract=471640/

Grundmann, Stefan, 2004. "The Structure of European Company Law: From Crisis to Boom," *European Business Organization Law Review* **5**: 601

Grundmann, Stefan, and Möslein, Florian, 2007. *European Company Law: Organization, Finance, and Capital Markets*. Antwerp: Intersentia

Gruson, Michael, Jánszky, Andrew B., and Weld, Jonathan M., 2005. "Issuance and Listing of Securities by Foreign Banks and the US Securities Laws," in Gruson and Reisner (eds.), *Regulation of Foreign Banks*, 4th edn., Newark, NJ: LexisNexis, vol. 1, p. 353, Ch. 7

Gunlicks, Arthur B., 2005. "German Federalism and Recent Reform Efforts," *German Law Journal* **6**: 1283

Guttman, Egon, 2007. *Modern Securities Transfers*. 3rd edn., looseleaf volume, St. Paul, MN: West Publishing

Habersack, Mathias, Mülbert, Peter O., and Schlitt, Michael, 2008. *Unternehmensfinanzierung am Kapitalmarkt*. 2nd edn., Munich: C. H. Beck

Hansmann, Henry, and Kraakman, Reinier, 1991. "Toward Unlimited Shareholder Liability for Corporate Torts," *Yale Law Journal* **100**: 1879

2000. "The Essential Role of Organizational Law," *Yale Law Journal* **110**: 387

2001. "The End of History for Corporate Law," *Georgetown Law Journal* **89**: 439

2002. "Property, Contract and Verification: The Numerus Clausus Problem and the Divisibility of Rights," *Journal of Legal Studies* **31**: 373

2004. "What Is Corporate Law?," in Kraakman, Davies, Hansmann, Hertig, Hopt, Kanda and Rock (eds.), *The Anatomy of Corporate Law: A Comparative and Functional Approach*. Oxford: Oxford University Press, p. 1

Hansmann, Henry, Kraakman, Reinier, and Squire, Richard, 2006. "Law and the Rise of the Firm," *Harvard Law Review* **119**: 1333

Harris, Lawrence E., 2004. *Unofficial Transcript of SEC Roundtable on Proposed Security Holder Director Nominations Rule*, available at www.s.gov/spotlight/dir-nominations/transcript03102004.txt

Harris, Ron, 2004. *The Formation of the East India Company as a Deal Between Entrepreneurs and Outside*, Working Paper, Boalt Hall School of Law, UC Berkeley, available from SSRN at http://ssrn.com/abstract=567941/ or DOI: 10.2139/ssrn.567941

2005. *The Formation of the East India Company as a Cooperation-Enhancing Institution*, Working Paper Series, Buchmann Faculty of Law, Tel Aviv University, available from SSRN at http://ssrn.com/abstract=874406/

2008. *The Institutional Dynamics of Early Modern Eurasian Trade: The Commenda and the Corporation*, available from SSRN at http://ssrn.com/abstract=1294095/

Hass, Jeffrey J., 1996. "Directorial Fiduciary Duties in a Tracking Stock Equity Structure: The Need for a Duty of Fairness," *Michigan Law Review* **94**: 2089

Hazen, Thomas Lee, 2006. *Treatise on the Law of Securities Regulation*. 6th edn., St. Paul, MN: West. Publishing

Henn, Günter, 2002. *Handbuch des Aktienrechts*. 7th edn., Heidelberg: C. F. Müller

Hirschman, Albert O., 1970. *Exit, Voice and Loyalty: Responses to Decline in Firms, Organizations, and States*. Cambridge, MA, and London: Harvard University Press

Hommelhoff, P., 1987. "Machtbalancen im Aktienrecht," in Schubert, W., and Hommelhoff, P. (eds.), *Die Aktienrechtsreform am Ende der Weimarer Republik*, Berlin and New York: de Gruyter, p. 71

Honoré, A. M., 1961. "Ownership," in A. G. Guest (ed.), *Oxford Essays in Jurisprudence*. London: Oxford University Press, p. 107

Hopt, Klaus, 1997. "The German Two-Tier Board (Aufsichtsrat): A German View on Corporate Governance," in Hopt and Wymeersch (eds.), *Comparative Corporate Governance*, Berlin and New York: de Gruyter, p. 3

2006. "Comparative Company Law," in Reimann and Zimmermann (eds.), *The Oxford Handbook of Comparative Law*. Oxford: Oxford University Press, p. 1161

Horn, Norbert, 1995. *Heymann, Handelsgesetzbuch, Kommentar*, 2nd edn., Berlin and New York: Walter de Gruyter

Hu, Henry T. C., and Black, Bernard, 2006, "Empty Voting and Hidden Ownership: Taxonomy, Implications and Reform," 61 *Business Lawyer* **61**: 1011

2008. "Equity and Debt Decoupling and Empty Voting II: Importance and Extensions," *University of Pennsylvania Law Review* **156**: 625

Hueck, Alfred, and Canaris, Claus-Wilhelm, 1986. *Recht der Wertpapiere*. 12th edn., Munich: C. H. Beck

Hüffer, Uwe, 2008. *Aktiengesetz*. 8th edn., Munich: C. H. Beck

International Monetary Fund, 2009. *Lessons of the Financial Crisis for Future Regulation of Financial Institutions and Markets and for Liquidity Management*, February 4, 2009

Jackson, Howell, and Pan, Eric J., 2008. "Regulatory Competition in International Securities Markets: Evidence from Europe – Part II," *Virginia Law and Business Review* **3**: 207

Jennings, Philip, 2007. *Speech on behalf of UNI Global Union at the Davos World Economic Forum*, January 27, 2007, available at www.unionnetwork.org/UNIFlashes.nsf/0/F8B280D736E74DB3C125-727A00524BD3/

Jensen, Michael C., and Meckling, William H., 1976. "Theory of the Firm: Managerial Behavior, Agency Costs, and Ownership Structure," *Journal of Financial Economics* **3**: 305, also reprinted in Jensen, Michael C. (ed.), 2000. *A Theory of the Firm: Governance, Residual Claims, and Organizational Forms*. Cambridge, MA: Harvard University Press

Jensen, Michael C., Murphy, Kevin J., and Wruck, Eric G., 2004. *Remuneration: Where We've Been, How We Got to Here, What Are the Problems, and How to Fix Them*, European Corporate Governance Institute, Finance Working Paper No. 44/2004, also in Harvard NOM Working Paper No. 04-28, available from SSRN at http://ssrn.com/abstract=561305 or DOI: 10.2139/ssrn.561305/

Judt, Tony, 2005. *Postwar*. London: Random House

Kahan, Marcel, and Rock, Edward, 2004. *Our Corporate Federalism and the Shape of Corporate Law*, University of Pennsylvania Law School, Institute for Law and Economics, Research Paper No. 04–12

Karmel, Roberta S., 2003. "Reconciling Federal and State Interests in Securities Regulation in the United States and Europe," *Brooklyn Journal of International Law* **28**: 495

2004. "Should a Duty to the Corporation Be Imposed on Institutional Shareholders?," *Business Lawyer* **60**: 1

Karolyi, G. Andrew, 1998. "Why Do Companies List Shares Abroad? A Survey of the Evidence and Its Managerial Implications," *Financial Markets, Institutions and Instruments* 7: 1

Kirchner, Christian, Painter, Richard, and Kaal, Wulf, 2004. "Regulatory Competition in EU Corporate Law after Inspire Art: Unbundling Delaware's Product for Europe," *European Company and Financial Law* 2: 159

Klein, Stefan, 2004. *Die Rechtsstellung auswärtiger Gesellschaften im deutschen und US-amerikanischen Recht.* Frankfurt: Peter Lang

Klein, William A., and Coffee Jr., John C., 2007. *Business Organization and Finance: Legal and Economic Principles.* 9th edn., Westbury, NY: Foundation Press

Kölner Kommentar zum Aktiengesetz. 2004–. Zöllner, Wolfgang, and Noack, Ulrich (eds.), 3rd edn., Cologne: Carl Heymanns (cited as *KölnKommAktG*)

Kraakman, Reinier, Davies, Paul L., Hansmann, Henry, Hertig, Gérard, Hopt, Klaus J., Kanda, Hideki, and Rock, Edward (eds.), *The Anatomy of Corporate Law: A Comparative and Functional Approach*, 2nd edn., Oxford: Oxford University Press

Kübler, Friedrich, and Assmann, Heinz-Dieter, 2006. *Gesellschaftsrecht.* 6th edn., Heidelberg: C. F. Müller

Kümpel, Siegfried, 2005. "Kapitalmarktrecht – Eine Einführung," in Kümpel, Hammen and Ekkenga (eds.), *Kapitalmarktrecht Handbuch für die Praxis.* Berlin: Erich Schmidt

La Porta, Rafael, Lopez-De-Silanes, Florencio, and Shleifer, Andrei, 2006. "What Works in Securities Laws?," *Journal of Finance* 61: 1

Langenbucher, Katja, 2008. *Aktien- und Kapitalmarktrecht.* Munich: C. H. Beck

Langevoort, Donald C., 1987. "The Supreme Court and the Politics of Corporate Takeovers: A Comment on CTS Corp. v. Dynamics Corp. of America," *Harvard Law Review* 101: 96

2001. "Seeking Sunlight in Santa Fe's Shadow: The SEC's Pursuit of Managerial Accountability," *Washington University Law Quarterly* 79: 449

Lipton, Martin, and Rosenblum, Steven A., 2003. "Election Contests in the Company's Proxy: An Idea Whose Time Has Not Come," *Business Lawyer* 59: 67.

Loss, Louis, Seligman, Joel, and Paredes, Troy, 2004. *Fundamentals of Securities Regulation.* 5th edn., New York: Aspen

Lower, Michael, 2000. "Good Faith and the Partly Owned Subsidiary," *Journal of Business Law* 232

Luhmann, Niklas, 1968. *Zweckbegriff und Systemrationalität.* Frankfurt: Suhrkamp

2004. *Law as a Social System*, K. A. Zeigert (trans.), Oxford: Oxford University Press

Macey, Jonathan R., 2002. *Macey on Corporation Law.* New York: Aspen

Macey, Jonathan R., and Miller, Geoffrey P., 1987. "Toward an Interest-Group Theory of Delaware Corporate Law," *Texas Law Review* 65: 469

1991. "The Plaintiffs' Attorney's Role in Class Action and Derivative Litigation: Economic Analysis and Recommendations for Reform," *University of Chicago Law Review* **58**: 1

Mahoney, Paul G., 2000. "Contract or Concession? An Essay on the History of Corporate Law," *Georgia Law Review* **34**: 873

Manne, Henry, 1966. *Insider Trading and the Stock Markets*. New York: Free Press

2007. "The 'Corporate Democracy' Oxymoron" *Wall Street Journal*, January 2, 2007, p. A23

Manning, Bayless, 1958. "Book Review of J. A. Livingstone, The American Stockholder," *Yale Law Journal* **67**: 1475

1962. "The Shareholder's Appraisal Remedy: An Essay for Frank Coker," *Yale Law Journal* **72**: 223

1981. *A Concise Textbook on Legal Capital*. 2nd edn., Mineola, NY: Foundation Press

1990. *Legal Capital*, 3rd edn., St. Paul, MN: West Publishing

Martin, Jill E., 2008. *Hanbury and Martin: Modern Equity*. 18th edn., London: Sweet & Maxwell

McConnell, Michael W., 1987. "Federalism: Evaluating the Founders' Design," *University of Chicago Law Review* **54**: 1484

Merrill, Thomas W., 2000. "The Landscape of Constitutional Property," *Virginia Law Review* **86**: 885

Merryman, John Henry, and Pérez-Perdomo, R., 2007. *The Civil Law Tradition: An Introduction to the Legal Systems of Europe and Latin America*. Stanford, CA: Stanford University Press

Mertens, Hans-Joachim, 1994. "Satzungs- und Organisationsautonomie im Aktien- und Konzernrecht," *ZGR* 426

Michaels, Ralf, 2006. "The Functional Method of Comparative Law," in Reimann and Zimmermann (eds.), *The Oxford Handbook of Comparative Law*. Oxford: Oxford University Press, p. 339

Milhaupt, Curtis J., 1998. "Property Rights in Firms," *Virginia Law Review* **84**: 6

Modigliani, Franco, and Miller, Merton H., 1958. "The Cost of Capital, Corporation Finance and the Theory of Investment," *American Economic Review* **48**: 461

Monks, Robert A. G., and Minow, Nell, 2004. *Corporate Governance*. 3rd edn., Malden, MA: Blackwell

Morse, Geoffrey (ed.), 2003. *Palmer's Company Law*. London: Sweet & Maxwell

2006. *Partnership Law*. 6th edn., Oxford: Oxford University Press

Mossoff, Adam, 2003. "What Is Property, Putting the Pieces Back Together," *Arizona Law Review* **45**: 371

Mülbert, Peter O., 2006. "A Synthetic View of Different Concepts of Creditor Protection, or: A High-Level Framework for Corporate Creditor Protection," *European Business Organization Law Review* **7**: 357

Münchener Kommentar zum Aktiengesetz, 2000–. Kropff, Bruno and Semler, Johannes (eds.), 2nd edn., Munich: C. H. Beck (cited as *MünchKommAktG*)

Münchener Kommentar zum Aktiengesetz, 2008–. Goette, Wulf and Habersack, Mathias (eds.), 3rd edn., Munich: C. H. Beck (cited as *MünchKommAktG*)

Münchener Kommentar zum Bürgerlichen Gesetzbuch, 2006–. Säcker, Franz Jürgen and Rixecker, Roland (eds.), Munich: C. H. Beck (cited as *MünchKommBGB*)

Münchener Kommentar zum Handelsgesetzbuch, 1996–. Schmidt, Karsten (ed.), 1st edn., Munich: C. H. Beck (cited as *MünchKommHGB*)

Myers, Stewart C., 1984. "The Capital Structure Puzzle," *Journal of Finance* **39**: 575

Myners, Paul, 2004. *Review of the Impediments to Voting UK Shares*, available at www.investmentuk.org/common/search.asp?s=paul/

Neuhausen, Benjamin S., and Kesner, Michael S., 2006. "Accounting for Stock-Based Compensation," in Goodman and Olson (eds.), *A Practical Guide to SEC Proxy and Compensation Rules*. 3rd edn., New York: Aspen, p. 8–1

Noack, U., 2003. "Das neue Recht der Gegenanträge nach § 126 AktG," *Betriebs-Berater* 1393

Panel on Takeovers and Mergers, 2009. *The Takeover Code*. 9th edn., available at www.thetakeoverpanel.org.uk/wp-content/uploads/2008/11/code/

Pennington, Robert R., 2001. *Pennington's Company Law*. 8th edn., London: Butterworths

Pistor, Katharina, 2005. "Legal Ground Rules in Coordinated and Liberal Market Economies," European Corporate Governance Inst., Law Working Paper No. 30, 2005, available at http://ssrn.com/abstract=695763

2006. "Legal Ground Rules in Coordinated and Liberal Market Economies," in Hopt, Wymeersch, Kanda and Baum (eds.), *Corporate Governance in Context: Corporations, States, and Markets in Europe, Japan, and the US*. New York: Oxford University Press, p. 249, also as European Corporate Governance Institute, Law Working Paper No. 30/2005

Poser, Norman S., 2003. *Broker-Dealer Law and Regulation*. 3rd edn., New York: Aspen

Pound, John, 1993. "The Rise of the Political Model of Corporate Governance and Corporate Control," *New York University Law Review* **68**: 1003

Quinn, Linda C., and Jarmel, Ottilie L., 2006. "The Shareholder Proposal Process," in Goodman and Olson (eds.), *A Practical Guide to SEC Proxy and Compensation Rules*. 3rd edn., New York: Aspen, p. 15-1

Raiser, Thomas, and Veil, Rüdiger, 2009. *Mitbestimmungsgesetz und Drittelbeteiligungsgesetz*. 5th edn., Berlin: Walter de Gruyter

Reed, Stanley Foster, Lajoux, Alexandra Reed, and Nesvold, H. Peter, 2007. *The Art of M&A: A Merger Acquisition Buyout Guide*. 4th edn., New York: McGraw-Hill

Reese, Willis L. M., and Kaufman, Edmund M., 1958. "The Law Governing Corporate Affairs: Choice of Law and the Impact of Full Faith and Credit," *Columbia Law Review* **58**: 1118

Reimann, Mathias, and Zimmermann, Reinhard (eds.), 2006. *The Oxford Handbook of Comparative Law*. Oxford: Oxford University Press

Reisberg, Arad, 2007. *Derivative Actions and Corporate Governance*. Oxford: Oxford University Press

Ribstein, Larry E., 2003. "Making Sense of Entity Rationalization," *Business Lawyer* **58**: 1023

Rock, Edward, Davies, Paul, Kanda, Hideki, and Kraakman, Reinier, 2009. "Fundamental Changes," in Kraakman, Davies, Hansmann, Hertig, Hopt, Kanda and Rock (eds.), *The Anatomy of Corporate Law: A Comparative and Functional Approach*, 2nd edn., Oxford: Oxford University Press, p. 183.

Roe, Mark J., 1996a. *Strong Managers, Weak Owners: The Political Roots of American Corporate Finance*. 2nd edn., Princeton, NJ: Princeton University Press

1996b. "Chaos and Evolution in Law and Economics," *Harvard Law Review* **109**: 641

2003. "Delaware's Competition," *Harvard Law Review* **117**: 588

2006. "Legal Origins, Politics, and Modern Stock Markets," *Harvard Law Review* **120**: 460

Romano, Roberta, 1993. *The Genius of American Corporate Law*. Washington DC: AEI Press

2002. *The Advantage of Competitive Federalism for Securities Regulation*, Washington DC: AEI Press

2004. "The Sarbanes–Oxley Act and the Making of Quack Corporate Governance," *Yale Law Journal* **114**: 1521

2005. *The States as a Laboratory: Legal Innovation and State Competition for Corporate Charters*, Yale University International Center for Finance (ICF) Working Paper No. 05–08, also as European Corporate Governance Institute, Law Working Paper No. 34/2005, available from SSRN at http://ssrn.com/abstract=706522/

2006. "The States as a Laboratory: Legal Innovation and State Competition for Corporate Charters," *Yale Journal on Regulation* **23**: 209

Roth, Wulf-Henning, 2003. "From Centros to Ueberseering: Free Movement of Companies, Private International Law, and Community Law," *ICLQ* **52**: 175

Santella, Paolo, and Turrini, Riccardo, 2008. "Capital Maintenance in the EU: Is the Second Company Law Directive Really That Restrictive?," *European Business Organization Law Review* **9**: 427

Schanz, Kay-Michael, 2002. *Börseneinführung*. 2nd edn., Munich: C. H. Beck

Schmidt, Karsten, 2002. *Gesellschaftsrecht*. 4th edn., Cologne: Heymanns

Schmidt, Karsten, and Lutter, Marcus, 2008. *Aktiengesetz, Kommentar*. 1st edn., Cologne: Dr. Otto Schmidt

Schmidt, Reinhard H., and Spindler, Gerald, 2004. "Path Dependence and Complementarity in Corporate Governance," in Gordon and Roe (eds.), *Convergence and Persistence in Corporate Governance.* Cambridge: Cambridge University Press, p. 114

Schwalbach, Joachim, 2009. *Vergütungsstudie 2009 Vorstandsvergütung und Personalkosten DAX30-Unternehmen* 1987–2008, available at http://lehre. wiwi.hu-berlin.de/Professuren/bwl/management/

Schwartz, Robert A., and Francioni, Reto, 2004. *Equity Markets in Action.* Hoboken, NJ: Wiley & Sons

Scoles, Eugene F., Hay, Peter, Borchers, Patrick J., and Symeonides, Symeon C., 2000. *Conflicts of Laws.* 3rd edn., St. Paul, MN: West Publishing

Seifert, Bruce, and Gonenc, Halit, 2008. "The International Evidence on the Pecking Order Hypothesis," *Journal of Multinational Financial Management* **18**: 244

Seligman, Joel, 2003. *The Transformation of Wall Street.* 3rd edn., New York: Aspen 2005. "A Modest Revolution in Corporate Governance," *Notre Dame Law Review* **80**: 1159

Shivdasani, Anil, and Wang, Yihui, 2009. "Did Structured Credit Fuel the LBO Boom?" (April 24, 2009). AFA 2010 Atlanta Meetings Paper, available at SSRN: http://ssrn.com/abstract=1285058/

Siems, Mathias M., 2008. *Convergence in Shareholder Law.* Cambridge: Cambridge University Press

Simmons, Omari Scott, 2009. "Taking the Blue Pill: The Imponderable Impact of Executive Compensation Reform," *Southern Methodist University Law Review* **62**: 299

Skeel, David A., and Krause-Wilmar, Georg, 2006. "Recharacterization and the Nonhindrance of Creditors," *European Business Organization Law Review* **7**: 259

Slater, Jr., John, 1984. "Publicly Traded Limited Partnership: An Emerging Financial Alternative to the Public Corporation," *Business Lawyer* **39**: 709

Smith, D. Gordon, 2002. "The Critical Resource Theory of Fiduciary Duty," *Vanderbilt Law Review* **55**: 1399

Spindler, Gerald, and Stilz, Eberhard, 2010. *Aktiengesetz, Kommentar.* 2nd edn., Munich: C. H. Beck

Staub, H., 1998. *Handelsgesetzbuch, Großkommentar,* Canaris, Schilling and Ulmer (eds.). 4th edn., Berlin: de Gruyter

Stecklow, Steve, 2008. "On the Lam and Living Large: Comverse Ex-CEO Parties in Namibia," *Wall Street Journal,* June 12, 2008, p. A1

Stout, Lynn A., 2002. "Lecture and Commentary on the Social Responsibility of Corporate Entities: Bad and Not-So-Bad Arguments for Shareholder Primacy," *Southern California Law Review* **75**: 1189

"Symposium on Entity Rationalization," 2003. *Business Lawyer* **58**: Nos. 3 and 4

Task Force on Shareholder Proposals of the Committee on Federal Regulation of Securities, Section of Business Law of the American Bar Association, 2003. "Report on Proposed Changes in Proxy Rules and Regulations Regarding Procedures for the Election of Corporate Directors," *Business Lawyer* **59**: 109

Thel, Steve, 1994. "$850,000 in Six Minutes – The Mechanics of Securities Manipulation," *Cornell Law Review* **79**: 219

Thomas, Randall S., and Dixon, Catherine T., 1998. *Aranow and Einhorn on Proxy Contests for Corporate Control.* 3rd edn., New York: Aspen

Thompson, Robert B., 1993. "The Shareholder's Cause of Action for Oppression," *Business Lawyer* **48**: 699

2003. "Collaborative Corporate Governance: Listing Standards, State Law and Federal Regulation," *Wake Forest Law Review* **38**: 961

2004. "Delaware, the Feds, and the Stock Exchange: Challenges to the First State as First in Corporate Law," *Delaware Journal of Corporate Law* **29**: 779

Thompson, Robert B., and Thomas, Randall S., 2004. "The New Look of Shareholder Litigation: Acquisition-Oriented Class Actions," *Vanderbilt Law Review* **57**: 133

Timmermans, Christiaan, 2003. "Harmonization in the Future Company Law in Europe," in Hopt and Wymeersch (eds.), *Capital Markets and Company Law.* Oxford: Oxford University Press, p. 623

Tröger, Tobias H., 2005. "Choice of Jurisdiction in European Corporate Law – Perspectives of European Corporate Governance," *European Business Organization Law Review* **6**: 3

Tushnet, Mark V., 2000. "Globalization and Federalism in a Post-Printz World," *Tulsa Law Journal* **36**: 11

Vahtera, Veikko 2008. "Capital Structure and Corporate Governance," in Andersen and Sørensen (eds.), *Company Law and Finance*, 1st edn., Copenhagen: Thomson, p. 63

Vaines, J. Crossley, 1962. *Personal Property.* 3rd edn., London: Butterworths

Weber, Hansjörg, 1997. *Kreditsicherheiten. Recht der Sicherungsgeschäfte.* 4th edn., Munich: C. H. Beck

Williamson, Oliver E., 1985. *The Economic Institutions of Capitalism.* New York: Free Press

1991. "Comparative Economic Organization: The Analysis of Discrete Structural Alternatives," *Administrative Science Quarterly* **36**: 269

Wolf, Manfred, 2001. "Der Ausschluß vom Neuen Markt und die Aufnahme von Ausschlußgründen in das Regelwerk Neuer Markt," *WM* **38**: 1785

Wood, Philip R., 1995. *Comparative Financial Law.* London: Sweet & Maxwell

2007. *Regulation of International Finance.* London: Sweet & Maxwell

Wymeersch, Eddy, 2006. *Reforming the Second Company Law Directive*, available from SSRN at http://ssrn.com/abstract=957981/

Zuleeg, Manfred, 2003. "Grundsätze," in Groeben and Schwarze (eds.), *Kommentar zum Vertrag über die Europäische Union und zur Gründung der Europäischen Gemeinschaft*. 6th edn., Baden-Baden: Nomos, vol. 1, p. 574

Zweigert, Konrad, and Kötz, Hein, 1996. *Einführung in die Rechtsvergleichung*. 3rd edn., Tübingen: Mohr Siebeck

1998. *An Introduction to Comparative Law* (trans. T. Weir). Oxford: Clarendon Press

INDEX

Lightning Source UK Ltd.
Milton Keynes UK
UKHW04f2023150718
325754UK00001B/32/P

9 780521 143790